The Adventures
in Literature Program

Adventures for Readers: Book One

Test Booklet
Steps to Better Reading: Book 1 *
Teacher's Manual
Many Voices 7, a longplay record

Adventures for Readers: Book Two

Test Booklet
Steps to Better Reading: Book 2 *
Teacher's Manual
Many Voices 8, a longplay record

Adventures in Reading

Test Booklet
Steps to Better Reading: Book 3 *
Teacher's Manual
Many Voices 9, a two-record
(longplay) album

Adventures in Appreciation

Test Booklet
Steps to Reading Literature: Book 1 *
Teacher's Manual
Many Voices 10A, a longplay record
Many Voices 10B, a longplay record
of *Julius Caesar*

Adventures in American Literature

Test Booklet
Steps to Reading Literature: Book 2 *
Teacher's Manual
Many Voices 11, a two-record
(longplay) album

Adventures in English Literature

Test Booklet
Steps to Reading Literature: Book 3 *
Teacher's Manual
Many Voices 12A, a longplay record
Many Voices 12B, a longplay record
of *Macbeth*

* Programed Instruction

ADVENTURES

IN

APPRECIATION

WALTER LOBAN
ROSALIND A. OLMSTED

Series Editor: MARY RIVES BOWMAN
Reading Consultant: HERBERT POTELL

Harcourt, Brace & World, Inc.
New York Chicago Atlanta Dallas Burlingame

WALTER LOBAN was born in Brookings, South Dakota, and was educated at the University of Chicago and the University of Minnesota. Except for service as an officer in the Navy during World War II, he has taught English in various Midwestern public schools and universities. Now at the University of California in Berkeley, Dr. Loban is Supervisor of the Teaching of English and Associate Professor of Education. He is a co-author of *Teaching Language Through Literature* and has been a co-editor of five earlier editions of *Adventures in Appreciation*.

ROSALIND A. OLMSTED is a member of the English Department at the Kent School in Kent, Connecticut. Born in Detroit, Michigan, she received her A.B. degree in English from Siena Heights College and her M.A. from the University of Detroit. Miss Olmsted was a teacher of English in Detroit high schools for eight years. From 1957–1959 she was the "on camera" television teacher of literature for the Detroit Public School System.

The Series Editor, MARY RIVES BOWMAN, holds degrees in English from the University of Texas (B.A.) and the University of Chicago (M.A.) and has also done graduate work in English at the University of Colorado and at East Texas State College. She has been active in various professional organizations and has devoted much of her time to the training and supervision of high school English teachers. She was co-editor of the last three editions of *Adventures in American Literature* and of two editions of *Adventures for Readers, Books 1* and *2*.

The Reading Consultant, HERBERT POTELL, is reading co-ordinator and teacher of English at New Utrecht High School, Brooklyn, New York. A graduate of Brooklyn College, he has done graduate work in English at Columbia University and the College of the City of New York. He is a member of the International Reading Association and has served as reading consultant on two other editions of the Adventures in Literature Series. In addition, he is co-author of the ninth and tenth grade books in the Adventures in Literature Companion Series — *Adventures for Today* and *Adventures in Living*.

FRONTISPIECE: *Detail from the "Battle of San Romano" by Paolo Uccello, painted in Italy in the mid-fifteenth century, now in the Louvre in Paris.*

Artists who have contributed illustrations to this book are: Lawrence Bjorklund, Donald Bolognese, Harvey Dinnerstein, William Hofmann, Raymond Houlihan, Eugene Karlin, Jack Ezra Keats, Howard Koslow, Marilyn Miller, Isadore Seltzer, and Robert Shore.

"Contents of the Dead Man's Pocket," p. 2, from The Third Level *by Jack Finney. Copyright 1956 by Jack Finney. Reprinted by permission of Holt, Rinehart and Winston, Inc.*

CONTENTS

Short Stories

Nonfiction

WORDS AND WISDOM

BIOGRAPHIES

Poetry

Drama

The King Arthur Legend

The Novel

ADVENTURES IN APPRECIATION

Short Stories

The world of literature offers many rewards — pleasure, insight, and wisdom, to mention just a few. To gain such rewards, however, requires more than an ability to read. You must be able to read with understanding, relating your own experiences to the material at hand and recognizing the author's true purpose in writing. You must also appreciate the meaning (what is said) and structure (how it is said) of a literary work — and the way in which these function together.

One pleasant and effective way to begin the study of literature is with the short story. Stories concern people, and all of us are curious about our fellow men, wanting to understand how they think, act, and feel. We like the feeling of suspense that a story provides, the promise of a rapid succession of new events and experiences. There are also practical reasons for beginning with short stories. Since they have only a few characters and limited action, the whole picture can be grasped quickly and then the details can be examined closely.

Every short story combines the structural elements of plot, tone, setting, character, and theme. In this book, the stories have been grouped together so that you can identify and focus upon one of these elements at a time. The first three stories, for instance, feature plot. Other clusters of stories follow, putting the spotlight on tone, setting, character, and theme — always, though, seeing each element in relation to the whole story.

The eighteen stories that you are about to read include representatives from China, Sweden, Russia, Ireland, France, and England, as well as the United States. Among them are mystery stories, human interest stories, and stories with serious messages. Each offers you its own special brand of entertainment and an opportunity to expand your world.

◀ Detail from "Return of the Hunters" by the Flemish artist Pieter Brueghel the Elder (1525–1569). Brueghel is famous for his paintings of robust peasant life and for the skill with which he ordered the many colorful details of that life into grand compositions.

Plot

Plot is the sequence of events in a story, the plan of what happens. Of course, these things happen to people, somewhere, and at some time, so that every story also has characters and a setting. Though plot never does exist by itself, we can still focus on it and thereby come to a better understanding of how stories are constructed. While doing this, we can observe *plot patterns* and *conflict*, the struggle between opposing forces that creates plot. In the three stories that follow we will take a close look at plot, noting its relation to the story's impact and total meaning.

(An Untitled Story)

JACK FINNEY

In the dark, on a skyscraper's narrow ledge, a young man tests his will to live. Suspense — "What will happen next?" — figures prominently in this story. Yet, even though it dominates this story, the plot points toward something beyond the actual events. When you have finished this untitled story, try to think of an effective title for it.

At the little living-room desk Tom Benecke rolled two sheets of flimsy and a heavier top sheet, carbon paper sandwiched between them, into his portable.

Inter-office Memo, the top sheet was headed, and he typed tomorrow's date just below this; then he glanced at a creased yellow sheet, covered with his own handwriting, beside the typewriter. "Hot in here," he muttered to himself. Then, from the short hallway at his back, he heard the muffled clang of wire coat hangers in the bedroom closet, and at this reminder of what his wife was doing he thought: Hot, no — guilty conscience.

He got up, shoving his hands into the back pockets of his gray wash slacks,

This story is from *The Third Level* by Jack Finney. Copyright 1956 by Jack Finney. Reprinted by permission of Holt, Rinehart and Winston, Inc.

stepped to the living-room window beside the desk and stood breathing on the glass, watching the expanding circlet of mist, staring down through the autumn night at Lexington Avenue, eleven stories below. He was a tall, lean, dark-haired young man in a pullover sweater, who looked as though he had played not football, probably, but basketball in college. Now he placed the heels of his hands against the top edge of the lower window frame and shoved upward. But as usual the window didn't budge, and he had to lower his hands and then shoot them hard upward to jolt the window open a few inches. He dusted his hands, muttering.

But still he didn't begin his work. He crossed the room to the hallway entrance and, leaning against the door-jamb, hands shoved into his back pockets again, he called, "Clare?" When his wife answered, he said, "Sure you don't mind going alone?"

"No." Her voice was muffled, and he knew her head and shoulders were in the bedroom closet. Then the tap of her high heels sounded on the wood floor and she appeared at the end of the little hallway, wearing a slip, both hands raised to one ear, clipping on an earring. She smiled at him — a slender, very pretty girl with light brown, almost blonde, hair — her prettiness emphasized by the pleasant nature that showed in her face. "It's just that I hate you to miss this movie; you wanted to see it too."

"Yeah, I know." He ran his fingers through his hair. "Got to get this done though."

She nodded, accepting this. Then, glancing at the desk across the living room, she said, "You work too much, though, Tom — and too hard."

He smiled. "You won't mind though, will you, when the money comes roll-ing in and I'm known as the Boy Wizard of Wholesale Groceries?"

"I guess not." She smiled and turned back toward the bedroom.

At his desk again, Tom lighted a cigarette; then a few moments later as Clare appeared, dressed and ready to leave, he set it on the rim of the ash tray. "Just after seven," she said. "I can make the beginning of the first feature."

He walked to the front-door closet to help her on with her coat. He kissed her then and, for an instant, holding her close, smelling the perfume she had used, he was tempted to go with her; it was not actually true that he had to work tonight, though he very much wanted to. This was his own project, unannounced as yet in his office, and it could be postponed. But then they won't see it till Monday, he thought once again, and if I give it to the boss tomorrow he might read it over the weekend. . . . "Have a good time," he said aloud. He gave his wife a little swat and opened the door for her, feeling the air from the building hallway, smelling faintly of floor wax, stream past his face.

He watched her walk down the hall, flicked a hand in response as she waved, and then he started to close the door, but it resisted for a moment. As the door opening narrowed, the current of warm air from the hallway, channeled through this smaller opening now, suddenly rushed past him with accelerated force. Behind him he heard the slap of the window curtains against the wall and the sound of paper fluttering from his desk, and he had to push to close the door.

Turning, he saw a sheet of white paper drifting to the floor in a series of arcs, and another sheet, yellow, moving toward the window, caught in the dying current flowing through the narrow opening. As he watched, the paper struck the bottom edge of the window and hung there for an instant, plastered against the glass and wood. Then as the moving air stilled completely the curtains swinging back from the wall to hang free again, he saw the yellow sheet drop to the window ledge and slide over out of sight.

He ran across the room, grasped the bottom edge of the window and tugged, staring through the glass. He saw the yellow sheet, dimly now in the darkness outside, lying on the ornamental ledge a yard below the window. Even as he watched, it was moving, scraping slowly along the ledge, pushed by the breeze that pressed steadily against the building wall. He heaved on the window with all his strength and it shot open with a bang, the window weight rattling in the casing. But the paper was past his reach and, leaning out into the night, he watched it scud steadily along the ledge to the south, half plastered against the building wall. Above the muffled sound of the street traffic far below, he could hear the dry scrape of its movement, like a leaf on the pavement.

The living room of the next apartment to the south projected a yard or more farther out toward the street than this one; because of this the Beneckes paid seven and a half dollars less rent than their neighbors. And now the yellow sheet, sliding along the stone ledge, nearly invisible in the night, was stopped by the projecting blank wall of the next apartment. It lay motionless, then, in the corner formed by the two walls — a good five yards away, pressed firmly against the ornate corner ornament of the ledge, by the breeze that moved past Tom Benecke's face.

He knelt at the window and stared at the yellow paper for a full minute

or more, waiting for it to move, to slide off the ledge and fall, hoping he could follow its course to the street, and then hurry down in the elevator and retrieve it. But it didn't move, and then he saw that the paper was caught firmly between a projection of the convoluted [1] corner ornament and the ledge. He thought about the poker from the fireplace, then the broom, then the mop — discarding each thought as it occurred to him. There was nothing in the apartment long enough to reach that paper.

It was hard for him to understand that he actually had to abandon it — it was ridiculous — and he began to curse. Of all the papers on his desk, why did it have to be this one in particular! On four long Saturday afternoons he had stood in supermarkets counting the people who passed certain displays, and the results were scribbled on that yellow sheet. From stacks of trade publications, gone over page by page in snatched half hours at work and during evenings at home, he had copied facts, quotations and figures onto that sheet. And he had carried it with him to the Public Library on Fifth Avenue, where he'd spent a dozen lunch hours and early evenings adding more. All were needed to support and lend authority to his idea for a new grocery-store display method; without them his idea was a mere opinion. And there they all lay in his own improvised shorthand — countless hours of work — out there on the **ledge**.

For many seconds he believed he was going to abandon the yellow sheet, that there was nothing else to do. The work could be duplicated. But it would take two months, and the time to present this idea was *now*, for use in the spring displays. He struck his fist on the win-

[1] **convoluted** (kŏn′vô·lūt′ĕd): coiled or twisted.

dow ledge. Then he shrugged. Even though his plan were adopted, he told himself, it wouldn't bring him a raise in pay — not immediately, anyway, or as a direct result. It won't bring me a promotion either, he argued — not of itself.

But just the same, and he couldn't escape the thought, this and other independent projects, some already done and others planned for the future, would gradually mark him out from the score of other young men in his company. They were the way to change from a name on the payroll to a name in the minds of the company officials. They were the beginning of the long, long climb to where he was determined to be, at the very top. And he knew he was going out there in the darkness, after the yellow sheet fifteen feet beyond his reach.

By a kind of instinct, he instantly began making his intention acceptable to himself by laughing at it. The mental picture of himself sidling [1] along the ledge outside was absurd — it was actually comical — and he smiled. He imagined himself describing it; it would make a good story at the office and, it occurred to him, would add a special interest and importance to his memorandum, which would do it no harm at all.

To simply go out and get his paper was an easy task — he could be back here with it in less than two minutes — and he knew he wasn't deceiving himself. The ledge, he saw, measuring it with his eye, was about as wide as the length of his shoe, and perfectly flat. And every fifth row of brick in the face of the building, he remembered — leaning out, he verified this — was indented half an inch, enough for the tips of his

[1] **sidling** (sī'dlĭng): moving sideways.

fingers, enough to maintain balance easily. It occurred to him that if this ledge and wall were only a yard above ground — as he knelt at the window staring out, this thought was the final confirmation of his intention — he could move along the ledge indefinitely.

On a sudden impulse, he got to his feet, walked to the front closet and took out an old tweed jacket; it would be cold outside. He put it on and buttoned it as he crossed the room rapidly toward the open window. In the back of his mind he knew he'd better hurry and get this over with before he thought too much, and at the window he didn't allow himself to hesitate.

He swung a leg over the sill, then felt for and found the ledge a yard below the window with his foot. Gripping the bottom of the window frame very tightly and carefully, he slowly ducked his head under it, feeling on his face the sudden change from the warm air of the room to the chill outside. With infinite care he brought out his other leg, his mind concentrating on what he was doing. Then he slowly stood erect. Most of the putty, dried out and brittle, had dropped off the bottom edging of the window frame, he found, and the flat wooden edging provided a good gripping surface, a half inch or more deep, for the tips of his fingers.

Now, balanced easily and firmly, he stood on the ledge outside in the slight, chill breeze, eleven stories above the street, staring into his own lighted apartment, odd and different-seeming now.

First his right hand, then his left, he carefully shifted his finger-tip grip from the puttyless window edging to an indented row of bricks directly to his right. It was hard to take the first shuffling sideways step then — to make him-

tugging a little, at each mortared crack. He simply did not permit himself to look down, though the compulsion to do so never left him; nor did he allow himself actually to think. Mechanically — right foot, left foot, over and again — he shuffled along crabwise, watching the projecting wall ahead loom steadily closer. . . .

Then he reached it and, at the corner — he'd decided how he was going to pick up the paper — he lifted his right foot and placed it carefully on the ledge that ran along the projecting wall at a right angle to the ledge on which his other foot rested. And now, facing the building, he stood in the corner formed by the two walls, one foot on the ledging of each, a hand on the shoulder-high indentation of each wall. His forehead was pressed directly into the corner against the cold bricks, and now he carefully lowered first one hand, then the other, perhaps a foot farther down, to the next indentation in the rows of bricks.

Very slowly, sliding his forehead down the trough of the brick corner and bending his knees, he lowered his body toward the paper lying between his outstretched feet. Again he lowered his fingerholds another foot and bent his knees still more, thigh muscles taut, his forehead sliding and bumping down the brick V. Half squatting now, he dropped his left hand to the next indentation and then slowly reached with his right hand toward the paper between his feet.

He couldn't quite touch it, and his knees now were pressed against the wall; he could bend them no farther. But by ducking his head another inch lower, the top of his head now pressed against the bricks, he lowered his right shoulder and his fingers had the paper by a corner, pulling it loose. At the

self move — and the fear stirred in his stomach, but he did it, again by not allowing himself time to think. And now — with his chest, stomach, and the left side of his face pressed against the rough cold brick — his lighted apartment was suddenly gone, and it was much darker out here than he had thought.

Without pause he continued — right foot, left foot, right foot, left — his shoe soles shuffling and scraping along the rough stone, never lifting from it, fingers sliding along the exposed edging of brick. He moved on the balls of his feet, heels lifted slightly; the ledge was not quite as wide as he'd expected. But leaning slightly inward toward the face of the building and pressed against it, he could feel his balance firm and secure, and moving along the ledge was quite as easy as he had thought it would be. He could hear the buttons of his jacket scraping steadily along the rough bricks and feel them catch momentarily, same instant he saw, between his legs and far below, Lexington Avenue stretched out for miles ahead.

He saw, in that instant, the Loew's theater sign, blocks ahead past Fiftieth Street; the miles of traffic signals, all green now; the lights of cars and street lamps; countless neon signs; and the moving black dots of people. And a violent instantaneous explosion of absolute terror roared through him. For a motionless instant he saw himself externally — bent practically double, balanced on this narrow ledge, nearly half his body projecting out above the street far below — and he began to tremble violently, panic flaring through his mind and muscles, and he felt the blood rush from the surface of his skin.

In the fractional moment before horror paralyzed him, as he stared between his legs at that terrible length of street far beneath him, a fragment of his mind raised his body in a spasmodic jerk to an upright position again, but so violently that his head scraped hard against the wall, bouncing off it, and his body swayed outward to the knife edge of balance, and he very nearly plunged backward and fell. Then he was leaning far into the corner again, squeezing and pushing into it, not only his face but his chest and stomach, his back arching; and his finger tips clung with all the pressure of his pulling arms to the shoulder-high half-inch indentation in the bricks.

He was more than trembling now; his whole body was racked with a violent shuddering beyond control, his eyes squeezed so tightly shut it was painful, though he was past awareness of that. His teeth were exposed in a frozen grimace, the strength draining like water from his knees and calves. It was extremely likely, he knew, that he would faint, slump down along the wall, his face scraping, and then drop backward, a limp weight, out into nothing. And to save his life he concentrated on holding on to consciousness, drawing deliberate deep breaths of cold air into his lungs, fighting to keep his senses aware.

Then he knew that he would not faint, but he could not stop shaking nor open his eyes. He stood where he was, breathing deeply, trying to hold back the terror of the glimpse he had had of what lay below him; and he knew he had made a mistake in not making himself stare down at the street, getting used to it and accepting it, when he had first stepped out onto the ledge.

It was impossible to walk back. He simply could not do it. He couldn't bring himself to make the slightest movement. The strength was gone from his legs; his shivering hands — numb, cold and desperately rigid — had lost all deftness; his easy ability to move and balance was gone. Within a step or two, if he tried to move, he knew that he would stumble and fall.

Seconds passed, with the chill faint wind pressing the side of his face, and he could hear the toned-down volume of the street traffic far beneath him. Again and again it slowed and then stopped, almost to silence; then presently, even this high, he would hear the click of the traffic signals and the subdued roar of the cars starting up again. During a lull in the street sounds, he called out. Then he was shouting *"Help!"* so loudly it rasped his throat. But he felt the steady pressure of the wind, moving between his face and the blank wall, snatch up his cries as he uttered them, and he knew they must sound directionless and distant. And he remembered how habitually, here in New York, he himself heard and ignored shouts in the night. If anyone heard him, there was no sign of it, and presently Tom Benecke knew he had to try moving; there was nothing else he could do.

Eyes squeezed shut, he watched scenes in his mind like scraps of motion-picture film — he could not stop them. He saw himself stumbling suddenly sideways as he crept along the ledge and saw his upper body arc outward, arms flailing. He saw a dangling shoestring caught between the ledge and the sole of his other shoe, saw a foot start to move, to be stopped with a jerk, and felt his balance leaving him. He saw himself falling with a terrible speed as his body revolved in the air, knees clutched tight to his chest, eyes squeezed shut, moaning softly.

Out of utter necessity, knowing that any of these thoughts might be reality in the very next seconds, he was slowly able to shut his mind against every thought but what he now began to do. With fear-soaked slowness, he slid his left foot an inch or two toward his own impossibly distant window. Then he slid the fingers of his shivering left hand a corresponding distance. For a moment he could not bring himself to lift his right foot from one ledge to the other; then he did it, and became aware of the harsh exhalation of air from his throat and realized that he was panting. As his right hand, then, began to slide along the brick edging, he was astonished to feel the yellow paper pressed to the bricks underneath his stiff fingers, and he uttered a terrible, abrupt bark that might have been a laugh or a moan. He opened his mouth and took the paper in his teeth, pulling it out from under his fingers.

By a kind of trick — by concentrating his entire mind on first his left foot, then his left hand, then the other foot, then the other hand — he was able to

move, almost imperceptibly, trembling steadily, very nearly without thought. But he could feel the terrible strength of the pent-up horror on just the other side of the flimsy barrier he had erected in his mind; and he knew that if it broke through he would lose this thin artificial control of his body.

During one slow step he tried keeping his eyes closed; it made him feel safer, shutting him off a little from the fearful reality of where he was. Then a sudden rush of giddiness swept over him and he had to open his eyes wide, staring sideways at the cold rough brick and angled lines of mortar, his cheek tight against the building. He kept his eyes open then, knowing that if he once let them flick outward, to stare for an instant at the lighted windows across the street, he would be past help.

He didn't know how many dozens of tiny sidling steps he had taken, his chest, belly and face pressed to the wall; but he knew the slender hold he was keeping on his mind and body was going to break. He had a sudden mental picture of his apartment on just the other side of this wall — warm, cheerful, incredibly spacious. And he saw himself striding through it, lying down on the floor on his back, arms spread wide, reveling in its unbelievable security. The impossible remoteness of this utter safety, the contrast between it and where he now stood, was more than he could bear. And the barrier broke then, and the fear of the awful height he stood on coursed through his nerves and muscles.

A fraction of his mind knew he was going to fall, and he began taking rapid blind steps with no feeling of what he was doing, sidling with a clumsy desperate swiftness, fingers scrabbling along the brick, almost hopelessly resigned to the sudden backward pull and swift motion outward and down. Then his moving left hand slid onto not brick but sheer emptiness, an impossible gap in the face of the wall, and he stumbled.

His right foot smashed into his left anklebone; he staggered sideways, began falling, and the claw of his hand cracked against glass and wood, slid down it, and his finger tips were pressed hard on the puttyless edging of his window. His right hand smacked gropingly beside it as he fell to his knees; and, under the full weight and direct downward pull of his sagging body, the open window dropped shudderingly in its frame till it closed and his wrists struck the sill and were jarred off.

For a single moment he knelt, knee bones against stone on the very edge of the ledge, body swaying and touching nowhere else, fighting for balance. Then he lost it, his shoulders plunging backward, and he flung his arms forward, his hands smashing against the window casing on either side; and — his body moving backward — his fingers clutched the narrow wood stripping of the upper pane.

For an instant he hung suspended between balance and falling, his finger tips pressed onto the quarter-inch wood strips. Then, with utmost delicacy, with a focused concentration of all his senses, he increased even further the strain on his finger tips hooked to these slim edgings of wood. Elbows slowly bending, he began to draw the full weight of his upper body forward, knowing that the instant his fingers slipped off these quarter-inch strips he'd plunge backward and be falling. Elbows imperceptibly bending, body shaking with the strain, the sweat starting from his forehead in great sudden drops, he pulled, his entire being and thought concentrated in his finger tips. Then

suddenly, the strain slackened and ended, his chest touching the window sill, and he was kneeling on the ledge, his forehead pressed to the glass of the closed window.

Dropping his palms to the sill, he stared into his living room — at the red-brown davenport across the room, and a magazine he had left there; at the pictures on the walls and the gray rug; the entrance to the hallway; and at his papers, typewriter and desk, not two feet from his nose. A movement from his desk caught his eye and he saw that it was a thin curl of blue smoke; his cigarette, the ash long, was still burning in the ash tray where he'd left it — this was past all belief — only a few minutes before.

His head moved, and in faint reflection from the glass before him he saw the yellow paper clenched in his front teeth. Lifting a hand from the sill he took it from his mouth; the moistened corner parted from the paper, and he spat it out.

For a moment, in the light from the living room, he stared wonderingly at the yellow sheet in his hand and then crushed it into the side pocket of his jacket.

He couldn't open the window. It had been pulled not completely closed, but its lower edge was below the level of the outside sill; there was no room to get his fingers underneath it. Between the upper sash and the lower was a gap not wide enough — reaching up, he tried — to get his fingers into; he couldn't push it open. The upper window panel, he knew from long experience, was impossible to move, frozen tight with dried paint.

Very carefully observing his balance, the finger tips of his left hand again hooked to the narrow stripping of the window casing, he drew back his right hand, palm facing the glass, and then struck the glass with the heel of his hand.

His arm rebounded from the pane, his body tottering. He knew he didn't dare strike a harder blow.

But in the security and relief of his new position, he simply smiled; with only a sheet of glass between him and the room just before him, it was not possible that there wasn't a way past it. Eyes narrowing, he thought for a few moments about what to do. Then his eyes widened, for nothing occurred to him. But still he felt calm: the trembling, he realized, had stopped. At the back of his mind there still lay the thought that once he was again in his home, he could give release to his feelings. He actually *would* lie on the floor, rolling, clenching tufts of the rug in his hands. He would literally run across the room, free to move as he liked, jumping on the floor, testing and reveling in its absolute security, letting the relief flood through him, draining the fear from his mind and body. His yearning for this was astonishingly intense, and somehow he understood that he had better keep this feeling at bay.

He took a half dollar from his pocket and struck it against the pane, but without any hope that the glass would break and with very little disappointment when it did not. After a few moments of thought he drew his leg onto the ledge and picked loose the knot of his shoelace. He slipped off the shoe and, holding it across the instep, drew back his arm as far as he dared and struck the leather heel against the glass. The pane rattled, but he knew he'd been a long way from breaking it. His foot was cold and he slipped the shoe back on. He shouted again, experimentally, and then once more, but there was no answer.

The realization suddenly struck him that he might have to wait here till Clare came home, and for a moment the thought was funny. He could see Clare opening the front door, withdrawing her key from the lock, closing the door behind her and then glancing up to see him crouched on the other side of the window. He could see her rush across the room, face astounded and frightened, and hear himself shouting instructions: "Never mind how I got here! Just open the wind — " She couldn't open it, he remembered, she'd never been able to; she'd always had to call him. She'd have to get the building superintendent or a neighbor, and he pictured himself smiling, and answering their questions as he climbed in. "I just wanted to get a breath of fresh air, so — "

He couldn't possibly wait here till Clare came home. It was the second feature she'd wanted to see, and she'd left in time to see the first. She'd be another three hours or — He glanced at his watch; Clare had been gone eight minutes. It wasn't possible, but only eight minutes ago he had kissed his wife good-by. She wasn't even at the theater yet!

It would be four hours before she could possibly be home, and he tried to picture himself kneeling out here, finger tips hooked to these narrow strippings, while first one movie, preceded by a slow listing of credits, began, developed, reached its climax and then finally ended. There'd be a newsreel next, maybe, and then an animated cartoon, and then interminable scenes from coming pictures. And then, once more, the beginning of a full-length picture — while all the time he hung out here in the night.

He might possibly get to his feet, but he was afraid to try. Already his legs were cramped, his thigh muscles tired; his knees hurt, his feet felt numb and his hands were stiff. He couldn't possibly stay out here for four hours, or anywhere near it. Long before that his legs and arms would give out; he would be forced to try changing his position often — stiffly, clumsily, his co-ordination and strength gone — and he would fall. Quite realistically, he knew that he would fall; no one could stay out here on this ledge for four hours.

A dozen windows in the apartment building across the street were lighted. Looking over his shoulder, he could see the top of a man's head behind the newspaper he was reading; in another window he saw the blue-gray flicker of a television screen. No more than twenty-odd yards from his back were scores of people, and if just one of them would walk idly to his window and glance out. . . . For some moments he stared over his shoulder at the lighted rectangles, waiting. But no one appeared. The man reading his paper turned a page and then continued his reading. A figure passed another of the windows and was immediately gone.

In the inside pocket of his jacket he found a little sheaf of papers, and he pulled one out and looked at it in the light from the living room. It was an old letter, an advertisement of some sort; his name and address, in purple ink, were on a label pasted to the envelope. Gripping one end of the envelope in his teeth, he twisted it into a tight curl. From his shirt pocket he brought out a book of matches. He didn't dare let go the casing with both hands but, with the twist of paper in his teeth, he opened the matchbook with his free hand; then he bent one of the matches in two without tearing it from the folder, its red-tipped end now touching the striking surface. With

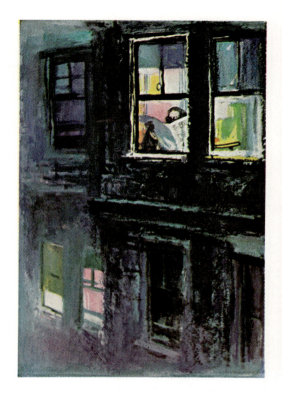

his thumb, he rubbed the red tip across the striking area.

He did it again, then again, and still again, pressing harder each time, and the match suddenly flared, burning his thumb. But he kept it alight, cupping the matchbook in his hand and shielding it with his body. He held the flame to the paper in his mouth till it caught. Then he snuffed out the match flame with his thumb and forefinger, careless of the burn, and replaced the book in his pocket. Taking the paper twist in his hand, he held it flame down, watching the flame crawl up the paper, till it flared bright. Then he held it behind him over the street, moving it from side to side, watching it over his shoulder, the flame flickering and guttering in the wind.

There were three letters in his pocket and he lighted each of them, holding each till the flame touched his hand and then dropping it to the street below. At one point, watching over his shoulder while the last of the letters burned, he saw the man across the street put down his paper and stand — even seeming to glance toward Tom's window. But when he moved, it was only to walk across the room and disappear from sight.

There were a dozen coins in Tom Benecke's pocket and he dropped them, three or four at a time. But if they struck anyone, or if anyone noticed their falling, no one connected them with their source.

His arms had begun to tremble from the steady strain of clinging to this narrow perch, and he did not know what to do now and was terribly frightened. Clinging to the window stripping with one hand, he again searched his pockets. But now — he had left his wallet on his dresser when he'd changed clothes — there was nothing left but the yellow sheet. It occurred to him irrelevantly that his death on the sidewalk below would be an eternal mystery; the window closed — why, how, and from where could he have fallen? No one would be able to identify his body for a time, either — the thought was somehow unbearable and increased his fear. All they'd find in his pockets would be the yellow sheet. *Contents of the dead man's pockets,* he thought, *one sheet of paper bearing penciled notations — incomprehensible.*

He understood fully that he might actually be going to die; his arms, maintaining his balance on the ledge, were trembling steadily now. And it occurred to him then with all the force of a revelation that, if he fell, all he was ever going to have out of life he would then, abruptly, have had. Nothing, then, could ever be changed; and nothing more — no least experience or pleasure — could ever be added to his life. He wished, then, that he had not allowed his wife to go off by herself tonight — and on similar nights. He thought of all the evenings he had spent away from her, working; and he regretted them. He thought wonderingly of his fierce ambition and of the direction his life had taken; he thought of the hours he'd spent by himself, filling the yellow sheet that had brought him out here. *Contents of the dead man's pockets,* he thought with sudden fierce anger, *a wasted life.*

He was simply not going to cling here till he slipped and fell; he told himself that now. There was one last thing he could try; he had been aware of it for some moments, refusing to think about it, but now he faced it. Kneeling here on the ledge, the finger tips of one hand pressed to the narrow strip of wood, he could, he knew, draw his other hand back a yard perhaps, fist clenched tight, doing it very slowly till he sensed the outer limit of balance, then, as hard as he was able from the distance, he could drive his fist forward against the glass. If it broke, his fist smashing through, he was safe; he might cut himself badly, and probably would, but with his arm inside the room, he would be secure. But if the glass did not break, the rebound, flinging his arm back, would topple him off the ledge. He was certain of that.

He tested his plan. The fingers of his left hand clawlike on the little stripping, he drew back his other fist until his body began teetering backward. But he had no leverage now — he could feel that there would be no force to his swing — and he moved his fist slowly forward till he rocked forward on his knees again and could sense that his swing would carry its greatest force. Glancing down, however, measuring the distance from his fist to the glass, he saw it was less than two feet.

It occurred to him that he could raise his arm over his head, to bring it down against the glass. But, experimenting in slow motion, he knew it would be an awkward girl-like blow without the force of a driving punch, and not nearly enough to break the glass.

Facing the window, he had to drive a blow from the shoulder, he knew now, at a distance of less than two feet; and he did not know whether it would break through the heavy glass. It might; he could picture it happening, he could feel it in the nerves of his arm. And it might not; he could feel that too — feel his fist striking this glass and being instantaneously flung back by the unbreaking pane, feel the fingers of his other hand breaking loose, nails scraping along the casing as he fell.

He waited, arm drawn back, fist balled, but in no hurry to strike; this pause, he knew, might be an extension of his life. And to live even a few seconds longer, he felt, even out here on this ledge in the night, was infinitely better than to die a moment earlier than he had to. His arm grew tired, and he brought it down.

Then he knew that it was time to make the attempt. He could not kneel here hesitating indefinitely till he lost all courage to act, waiting till he slipped off the ledge. Again he drew back his arm, knowing this time that he would not bring it down till he struck. His elbow protruding over Lexington Avenue far below, the fingers of his other hand pressed down bloodlessly tight against the narrow stripping, he waited, feeling the sick tenseness and terrible excitement building. It grew and swelled toward the moment of action, his nerves tautening. He thought of Clare — just a wordless, yearning thought — and then drew his arm back just a bit more, fist so tight his fingers pained him, and knowing he was going to do it. Then with full power, with every last scrap of strength he could bring to bear, he shot his arm forward toward the glass, and he said, "Clare!"

He heard the sound, felt the blow, felt himself falling forward, and his hand closed on the living-room curtains, the shards [1] and fragments of glass showering onto the floor. And then, kneeling there on the ledge, an arm thrust into the room up to the shoulder, he began picking away the protruding slivers and great wedges of glass from the window frame, tossing them in onto the rug. And, as he grasped the edges of the empty window frame and climbed into his home, he was grinning in triumph.

He did not lie down on the floor or run through the apartment, as he had promised himself; even in the first few moments it seemed to him natural and normal that he should be where he was. He simply turned to his desk, pulled the crumpled yellow sheet from his pocket and laid it down where it had been, smoothing it out; then he absently laid a pencil across it to weight it down. He shook his head wonderingly, and turned to walk toward the closet.

There he got out his topcoat and hat and, without waiting to put them on, opened the front door and stepped out, to go find his wife. He turned to pull the door closed and the warm air from the hall rushed through the narrow opening again. As he saw the yellow paper, the pencil flying, scooped off the desk and, unimpeded by the glassless window, sail out into the night and out of his life, Tom Benecke burst into laughter and then closed the door behind him.

[1] **shards** (shärds): sharp pieces.

THINKING IT OVER

1. How is suspense created in this story? Describe the crises, or critical moments, that occur while Tom Benecke is on the ledge. What makes each new crisis seem more critical than the one before it?

2. There are two aspects to the setting in this story: (a) the Beneckes' apartment — familiar, warm, and safe; and (b) the ledge — strange, frightening, and dangerous. Why are both parts of the setting essential to the plot? What do they add to the story?

3. What did you learn about Tom Benecke and his wife? Did you find out anything about them that was not directly related to the plot? What do you think was the purpose of having Tom's wife in the story?

4. What comments on work and on ambition does the story make? In answering, refer to Tom Benecke's thoughts and to incidents in the story. Explain why you either agree or disagree with the story's attitude toward ambition.

SELECTING A TITLE FOR THIS STORY

When Jack Finney wrote this story, he, of course, gave it a title. However, he agreed to let the story appear in this anthology without a title so that you might have a chance to select one for yourself.

There is no single, perfect title for this story. What you want to strive for is a title that in some way captures the essence of the story and has an imaginative appeal. Answering the questions under "Thinking It Over" should help to bring the story into focus and may help you to think of a title that reflects an essential aspect of the story. Perhaps you will be able to find an effective title in a brief quotation from the story itself. Stories often contain meaningful phrases or particularly descriptive words that make good titles when quoted directly.

After you have considered the various possibilities, decide upon a title for Jack Finney's story and be prepared to defend your selection in a class discussion.

WHERE DO YOU STAND?

Where do you stand when you read a story? Some readers enter into a story; they share in the characters' experiences, feelings, and attitudes; they step into the shoes of one or more characters in the story. Other readers remain at a distance, watching the characters, knowing what happens but not becoming deeply involved themselves. Which way did you read this story? What might be said for both ways of reading literature?

ABOUT THE AUTHOR

Jack Finney (1911–   ) graduated from Knox College in Galesburg, Illinois. While he was getting his start as a writer, he worked in an advertising agency in New York. Finney has written novels, short stories, and novelettes. These have appeared in several magazines including *Cosmopolitan*, *McCall's*, and the *Saturday Evening Post*. Readers also find reprints of his stories in science-fiction magazines. Two of his novels, *Five Against the House* (1954) and *The Body Snatchers* (1955), have been made into movies. His most recent novel, *Assault on a Queen*, was published in 1959. With his family, Finney now makes his home in Mill Valley, California, and works in San Francisco.

As the Camera Saw It ➤

The photograph on the opposite page shows a view similar to the one Tom Benecke saw in this story. Like Tom Benecke, photographer Susan McCartney was looking down on Lexington Avenue, one of New York's busiest streets.

Study the view in this photograph for a moment or two. Try to put yourself in Tom Benecke's place — to hear and feel, as well as see, as he did. Then turn back to the story itself and reread the parts in which the author describes what Tom Benecke saw and heard and felt as he stood on the ledge. Is the story more successful than the photograph in making you feel as if you were actually sharing in Tom's experience?

What is it that words can do that the camera cannot? The answer to this question lies in the magic of imagination, awakened in you by the words of a creative writer.

Four and Twenty Blackbirds

AGATHA CHRISTIE

Stories consist of events, events which must happen in some kind of a time sequence. Thus no story ends exactly as it began; always some change, some progress, occurs. In this detective story, the opening events seem innocent enough — on the surface — yet an order of blackberry pie is the first clue to a complicated crime. The brilliant detective is Hercule Poirot (ĕr′kül′ pwä·rō′). To readers of detective and mystery stories this Belgian master of deduction is as famous as Sherlock Holmes.

Hercule Poirot was dining with his friend, Henry Bonnington, at the Gallant Endeavor in the King's Road, Chelsea.

Mr. Bonnington was fond of the Gallant Endeavor. He liked the leisurely atmosphere, he liked the food which was "plain" and "English" and "not a lot of made-up messes."

Molly, the sympathetic waitress, greeted him as an old friend. She prided herself on remembering her customers' likes and dislikes in the way of food.

"Good evening, sir," she said, as the two men took their seats at a corner table. "You're in luck today — turkey stuffed with chestnuts — that's your favorite, isn't it? And ever such a nice Stilton we've got! Will you have soup first or fish?"

The question of food and wine settled, Mr. Bonnington leaned back with a sigh and unfolded his napkin as Molly sped away.

"Good girl, that!" he said approvingly. "Was quite a beauty once — artists used to paint her. She knows about food, too — and that's a great deal more

Noting the Purpose of Details. Unless it contributes to the author's purpose, no detail, no event can claim a place in a short story. Every incident, every conversation, every character must serve this purpose.

This economy of materials is well illustrated in "Four and Twenty Blackbirds." As you read, be alert to every detail. You will find that all of them fall into place as indispensable parts of an intriguing story.

important. Women are very unsound on food as a rule. There's many a woman, if she goes out with a fellow she fancies, won't even notice what she eats. She'll just order the first thing she sees."

Hercule Poirot shook his head.

"C'est terrible."

"Men aren't like that, thank goodness!" said Mr. Bonnington complacently.

"Never?" There was a twinkle in Hercule Poirot's eye.

"Well, perhaps when they're very young," conceded Mr. Bonnington. "Young puppies! Young fellows nowadays are all the same — no guts — no stamina. I've no use for the young — and they," he added with strict impartiality, "have no use for me. Perhaps they're right! But to hear some of these young fellows talk you'd think no man had a right to be *alive* after sixty! From the way they go on, you'd wonder more of them didn't help their elderly relations out of the world."

"It is possible," said Hercule Poirot, "that they do."

"Nice mind you've got, Poirot, I must say. All this police work saps your ideals."

Hercule Poirot smiled.

"Nevertheless," he said, "it would be interesting to make a table of accidental deaths over the age of sixty. I assure you it would raise some curious speculations in your mind. . . . But tell me, my friend, of your own affairs. How does the world go with you?"

"Mess!" said Mr. Bonnington. "That's what's the matter with the world nowadays. Too much mess. And too much fine language. The fine language helps to conceal the mess. Like a highly flavored sauce concealing the fact that the fish underneath it is none of the best! Give me an honest filet of sole and no messy sauce over it."

It was given him at that moment by Molly and he grunted approval.

"You know just what I like, my girl," he said.

"Well, you come here pretty regular, don't you, sir? So I ought to know."

Hercule Poirot said: "Do people then always like the same things? Do not they like a change sometimes?"

"Not gentlemen, sir. Ladies like variety — gentlemen always like the same thing."

"What did I tell you?" grunted Bonnington. "Women are fundamentally unsound where food is concerned!"

He looked around the restaurant.

"The world's a funny place. See that odd-looking old fellow with a beard in the corner? Molly'll tell you he's always here Tuesday and Thursday nights. He has come here for close on ten years now — he's a kind of landmark in the place. Yet nobody here knows his name or where he lives or what his business is. It's odd when you come to think of it."

When the waitress brought the portions of turkey he said: "I see you've still got Old Father Time over there?"

"That's right, sir. Tuesdays and Thursdays, his days are. Not but what he came in here on a *Monday* last week! It quite upset me! I felt I'd got my dates wrong and that it must be Tuesday without my knowing it! But he came in the next night as well — so the Monday was just a kind of extra, so to speak."

"An interesting deviation from habit," murmured Poirot. "I wonder what the reason was."

"Well, sir, if you ask me, I think he'd had some kind of upset or worry."

"Why did you think that? His manner?"

"No, sir — not his manner exactly. He was very quiet as he always is. Never

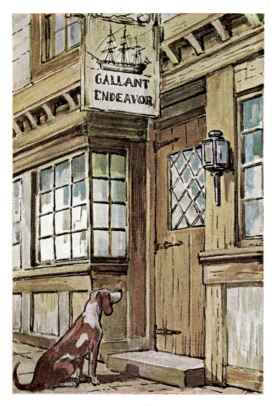

says much except 'Good evening' when he comes and goes. No, it was his *order*."

"His order?"

"I dare say you gentlemen will laugh at me." Molly flushed. "But when a gentleman has been here for ten years, you get to know his likes and dislikes. He never could bear suet pudding or blackberries and I've never known him to take thick soup — but on that Monday night he ordered thick tomato soup, beefsteak and kidney pudding and blackberry tart! Seemed as though he just didn't notice *what* he ordered!"

"Do you know," said Hercule Poirot, "I find that extraordinarily interesting."

Molly looked gratified and departed.

"Well, Poirot," said Henry Bonnington with a chuckle. "Let's have a few deductions from you. All in your best manner."

"I would prefer to hear yours first."

"Want me to be Watson,[1] eh? Well, old fellow went to a doctor and the doctor changed his diet."

"To thick tomato soup, steak and kidney pudding and blackberry tart? I cannot imagine any doctor doing that."

"Don't you believe it, old boy. Doctors will put you onto anything."

"That is the only solution that occurs to you?"

Henry Bonnington said: "Well, seriously, I suppose there's only one explanation possible. Our unknown friend was in the grip of some powerful mental emotion. He was so perturbed by it that he literally did not notice what he was ordering or eating."

He paused a minute, and then said: "You'll be telling me next that you know just *what* was on his mind. You'll say perhaps that he was making up his mind to commit a murder."

He laughed at his own suggestion.

Hercule Poirot did not laugh.

He has admitted that at that moment he was seriously worried. He claims that he ought then to have had some inkling of what was likely to occur.

His friends assure him that such an idea is quite fantastic.

It was some three weeks later that Hercule Poirot and Bonnington met again — this time their meeting was in the subway.

They nodded to each other, swaying about, hanging onto adjacent straps. Then at Piccadilly Circus[2] there was a general exodus and they found seats right at the forward end of the car — a peaceful spot since nobody passed in or out that way.

[1] **Watson:** the confidant and foil of Sherlock Holmes and fictional narrator of most of the Sherlock Holmes stories by Sir Arthur Conan Doyle.

[2] **Piccadilly Circus:** a London shopping area where there is a subway entrance.

"By the way," said Mr. Bonnington. "Do you remember that old boy we noticed at the Gallant Endeavor? I shouldn't wonder if he'd hopped it to a better world. He's not been there for a whole week. Molly's quite upset about it."

Hercule Poirot sat up. His eyes flashed.

"Indeed?" he said. "Indeed?"

Bonnington said: "D'you remember I suggested he'd been to a doctor and been put on a diet? Diet's nonsense of course — but I shouldn't wonder if he had consulted a doctor about his health and what the doctor said gave him a bit of a jolt. That would account for him ordering things off the menu without noticing what he was doing. Quite likely the jolt he got hurried him out of the world sooner than he would have gone otherwise. Doctors ought to be careful what they tell a chap."

"They usually are," said Hercule Poirot.

"This is my station," said Mr. Bonnington. "Bye-bye. Don't suppose we shall ever know now who the old boy was — not even his name. Funny world!"

He hurried out of the carriage.

Hercule Poirot, sitting frowning, looked as though he did not think it was such a funny world.

He went home and gave certain instructions to his faithful valet, George.

Hercule Poirot ran his finger down a list of names. It was a record of deaths within a certain area.

Poirot's finger stopped.

"Henry Gascoigne.[1] 69. I might try him first."

Later in the day, Hercule Poirot was

[1] **Gascoigne:** The English pronunciation for this French name would probably be gàs'-koin'.

sitting in Dr. MacAndrew's surgery just off the King's Road. MacAndrew was a tall, red-haired Scotsman with an intelligent face.

"Gascoigne?" he said. "Yes, that's right. Eccentric old bird. Lived alone in one of those derelict old houses that are being cleared away in order to build a block of modern flats. I hadn't attended him before, but I'd seen him about and I knew who he was. It was the dairy people got the wind up first. The milk bottles began to pile up outside. In the end the people next door sent word to the police and they broke the door in and found him. He'd pitched down the stairs and broken his neck. Had on an old dressing gown with a ragged cord — might easily have tripped himself up with it."

"I see," said Hercule Poirot. "It was quite simple — an accident."

"That's right."

"Had he any relations?"

"There's a nephew. Used to come along and see his uncle about once a month. Ramsey, his name is, George Ramsey. He's a medico himself. Lives at Wimbledon."

"How long had Mr. Gascoigne been dead when you saw him?"

"Ah!" said Dr. MacAndrew. "This is where we get official. Not less than forty-eight hours and not more than seventy-two hours. He was found on the morning of the 6th. Actually, we got closer than that. He had a letter in the pocket of his dressing gown — written on the 3rd — posted in Wimbledon that afternoon — would have been delivered somewhere around 9:20 P.M. That puts the time of death at after 9:20 on the evening of the 3rd. That agrees with the contents of the stomach and the processes of digestion. He had had a meal about two hours before death. I examined him on the morning of the 6th and his condition was quite consistent with death having occurred about sixty hours previously — around about 10 P.M. on the 3rd."

"It all seems very consistent. Tell me, when was he last seen alive?"

"He was seen in the King's Road about seven o'clock that same evening, Thursday the 3rd, and he dined at the Gallant Endeavor restaurant at 7:30. It seems he always dined there on Thursdays."

"He had no other relations? Only this nephew?"

"There was a twin brother. The whole story is rather curious. They hadn't seen each other for years. As a young man Henry was by way of being an artist, you know. An extremely bad one. It seems the other brother, Anthony Gascoigne, married a very rich woman and gave up art — and the brothers quarreled over it. Hadn't seen each other since, I believe. But oddly enough, *they died on the same day.* The elder twin passed away at one o'clock on the afternoon of the 3rd. Once before I've known a case of twins dying on the same day — in different parts of the world! Probably just a coincidence — but there it is."

"Is the other brother's wife alive?"

"No, she died some years ago."

"Where did Anthony Gascoigne live?"

"He had a house on Kingston Hill. He was, I believe, from what Dr. Ramsey tells me, very much of a recluse."

Hercule Poirot nodded thoughtfully.

The Scotsman looked at him keenly.

"What exactly have you got in your mind, M. Poirot?" he asked bluntly. "I've answered your questions — as was my duty seeing the credentials you brought. But I'm in the dark as to what it's all about."

Poirot said slowly: "A simple case of accidental death, that's what you said. What I have in mind is equally simple — a simple push."

Dr. MacAndrew looked startled.

"In other words, murder! Have you any grounds for that belief?"

"No," said Poirot. "It is a mere supposition."

"There must be something —" persisted the other.

Poirot did not speak.

MacAndrew said, "If it's the nephew, Ramsey, you suspect, I don't mind telling you here and now that you are barking up the wrong tree. Ramsey was playing bridge in Wimbledon from 8:30 till midnight. That came out at the inquest."

Poirot murmured: "And presumably it was verified. The police are careful."

The doctor said: "Perhaps you know something against him?"

"I didn't know that there was such a person until you mentioned him."

"Then you suspect somebody else?"

"No, no. It is not that at all. It's a case of the routine habits of the human animal. That is very important. And the dead M. Gascoigne does not fit in. It is all wrong, you see."

"I really don't understand."

Hercule Poirot smiled. He rose and the doctor rose also.

"You know," said MacAndrew, "honestly, I can't see anything the least bit suspicious about the death of Henry Gascoigne."

The little man spread out his hands.

"I'm an obstinate man — a man with a little idea — and nothing to support it! By the way, did Henry Gascoigne have false teeth?"

"No, his own teeth were in excellent preservation. Very creditable indeed at his age."

"He looked after them well — they were white and well brushed?"

"Yes, I noticed them particularly."

"Not discolored in any way?"

"No. I don't think he was a smoker if that is what you mean."

"I did not mean that precisely — it was just a long shot — which probably will not come off! Good-by, Dr. Mac-Andrew, and thank you for your kindness."

He shook the doctor's hand and departed.

"And now," he said, "for the long shot."

At the Gallant Endeavor, he sat down at the same table that he had shared with Bonnington. The girl who served him was not Molly. Molly, the girl told him, was away on a holiday.

It was just seven and Hercule Poirot found no difficulty in entering into conversation with the girl on the subject of old Mr. Gascoigne.

"Yes," she said. "He'd been here for years and years. But none of us girls ever knew his name. We saw about the inquest in the paper, and there was a picture of him. 'There,' I said to Molly, 'if that isn't our Old Father Time —' as we used to call him."

"He dined here on the evening of his death, did he not?"

"That's right. Thursday, the 3rd. He was always here on a Thursday. Tuesdays and Thursdays — punctual as a clock."

"You don't remember, I suppose, what he had for dinner?"

"Now let me see, it was mulligatawny soup,[1] that's right, and beefsteak pudding or was it the mutton? — no pudding, that's right, and blackberry-and-apple pie and cheese. And then to think

[1] mulligatawny (mŭl'ĭ·gȧ·tô'nĭ) soup: a soup made of chicken or other meat and flavored with curry, a spice made from the leaves of a tree in India.

of him going home and falling down those stairs that very same evening. A frayed dressing-gown cord they said it was as caused it. Of course, his clothes were always something awful — old-fashioned and put on anyhow, and all tattered, and yet he *had* a kind of air, all the same, as though he was *somebody!* Oh, we get all sorts of interesting customers here."

She moved off.

Hercule Poirot ate his sole.

Armed with introductions from a certain influential quarter, Hercule Poirot found no difficulty at all in dealing with the coroner for the district.

"A curious figure, the deceased man Gascoigne," he observed. "A lonely, eccentric old fellow. But his decease seems to arouse an unusual amount of attention."

He looked with some curiosity at his visitor as he spoke.

Hercule Poirot chose his words carefully: "There are circumstances connected with it, Monsieur, which make investigation desirable."

"Well, how can I help you?"

"It is, I believe, within your province to order documents produced in your court to be destroyed, or to be impounded — as you think fit. A certain letter was found in the pocket of Henry Gascoigne's dressing gown, was it not?"

"That is so."

"A letter from his nephew, Dr. George Ramsey?"

"Quite correct. The letter was produced at the inquest as helping to fix the time of death."

"Is that letter still available?"

Hercule Poirot waited rather anxiously for the reply.

When he heard that the letter was still available for examination he drew a sigh of relief.

When it was finally produced he

studied it with some care. It was written in a slightly cramped handwriting with a stylographic pen.[1] It ran as follows:

"Dear Uncle Henry:

I am sorry to tell you that I have had no success as regards Uncle Anthony. He showed no enthusiasm for a visit from you and would give me no reply to your request that he would let bygones be bygones. He is, of course, extremely ill, and his mind is inclined to wander. I should fancy that the end is very near. He seemed hardly to remember who you were.

I am sorry to have failed you, but I can assure you that I did my best.

Your affectionate nephew,
George Ramsey."

The letter itself was dated 3rd November. Poirot glanced at the envelope's postmark — 4:30 P.M.

He murmured: "It is beautifully in order, is it not?" . . .

Kingston Hill was his next objective. After a little trouble, with the exercise of good-humored pertinacity, he obtained an interview with Amelia Hill, cook-housekeeper to the late Anthony Gascoigne.

Mrs. Hill was inclined to be stiff and suspicious at first, but the charming geniality of this strange-looking foreigner soon had its effect. Mrs. Amelia Hill began to unbend.

She found herself, as had so many other women before her, pouring out her troubles to a really sympathetic listener.

For fourteen years she had had charge of Mr. Gascoigne's household — *not* an easy job! No, indeed! Many a woman would have quailed under the

burdens *she* had had to bear! Eccentric the poor gentleman was and no denying it. Remarkably close with his money — a kind of mania with him it was — and he as rich a gentleman as might be! But Mrs. Hill had served him faithfully, and put up with his ways, and naturally she'd expected at any rate a *remembrance*. But no — nothing at all! Just an old will that left all his money to his wife and if she predeceased him then everything to his brother, Henry. A will made years ago. It didn't seem fair!

Gradually Hercule Poirot detached her from her main theme of unsatisfied cupidity.[2] It was indeed a heartless injustice! Mrs. Hill could not be blamed for feeling hurt and surprised. It was well known that Mr. Gascoigne was tight-fisted about money. It had even been said that the dead man had refused his only brother assistance. Mrs. Hill probably knew all about that.

"Was it that that Dr. Ramsey came to see him about?" asked Mrs. Hill. "I knew it was something about his brother, but I thought it was just that his brother wanted to be reconciled. They'd quarreled years ago."

"I understand," said Poirot, "that Mr. Gascoigne refused absolutely?"

"That's right enough," said Mrs. Hill with a nod. "'Henry?' he says, rather weak-like. 'What's this about Henry? Haven't seen him for years and don't want to. Quarrelsome fellow, Henry.' Just that."

The conversation then reverted to Mrs. Hill's own special grievances, and the unfeeling attitude of the late Mr. Gascoigne's solicitor.

With some difficulty Hercule Poirot took his leave without breaking off the conversation too abruptly.

And so, just after the dinner hour, he came to Elmcrest, Dorset Road, Wimbledon, the residence of Dr. George Ramsey.

The doctor was in. Hercule Poirot was shown into the surgery and there presently Dr. George Ramsey came to him, obviously just risen from the dinner table.

"I'm not a patient, doctor," said Hercule Poirot. "And my coming here is, perhaps, somewhat of an impertinence — but I believe in plain and direct dealing. I do not care for lawyers and their long-winded roundabout methods."

He had certainly aroused Ramsey's interest. The doctor was a clean-shaven man of middle height. His hair was brown but his eyelashes were almost white, which gave his eyes a pale, boiled appearance. His manner was brisk and not without humor.

"Lawyers?" he said, raising his eyebrows. "Hate the fellows! You rouse my curiosity, my dear sir. Pray sit down."

Poirot did so and then produced one of his professional cards which he handed to the doctor.

George Ramsey's white eyelashes blinked.

Poirot leaned forward confidentially. "A good many of my clients are women," he said.

"Naturally," said Dr. George Ramsey, with a slight twinkle.

"As you say, naturally," agreed Poirot. "Women distrust the official police. They prefer private investigations. They do not want to have their troubles made public. An elderly woman came to consult me a few days ago. She was unhappy about a husband she'd quarreled with many years before. This husband of hers was your uncle, the late Mr. Gascoigne."

George Ramsey's face went purple.

"My uncle? Nonsense! His wife died many years' ago."

"Not your uncle, Mr. *Anthony* Gas-

coigne. Your uncle, Mr. *Henry* Gascoigne."

"Uncle Henry? But *he* wasn't married!"

"Oh, yes, he was," said Hercule Poirot, lying unblushingly. "Not a doubt of it. The lady even brought along her marriage certificate."

"It's a lie!" cried George Ramsey. His face was now as purple as a plum. "I don't believe it. You're an impudent liar."

"It is too bad, is it not?" said Poirot. "You have committed murder for nothing."

"Murder?" Ramsey's voice quavered. His pale eyes bulged with terror.

"By the way," said Poirot, "I see you have been eating blackberry tart again. An unwise habit. Blackberries are said to be full of vitamins, but they may be deadly in other ways. On this occasion I rather fancy they have helped to put a rope around a man's neck — your neck, Dr. Ramsey."

"You see, *mon ami*, where you went wrong was over your fundamental assumption." Hercule Poirot, beaming placidly across the table at his friend, waved an expository hand. "A man under severe mental stress doesn't choose that time to do something that he's never done before. His reflexes just follow the track of least resistance. A man who is upset about something *might* conceivably come down to dinner dressed in his pajamas — but they will be his *own* pajamas — not somebody else's.

"A man who dislikes thick soup, suet pudding and blackberries suddenly orders all three one evening. *You* say, because he is thinking of something else. But *I* say *that a man who has got something on his mind will order automatically the dish he has ordered most often before.*

"*Eh bien*, then, what other explanation could there be? I simply could not think of a reasonable explanation. And I was worried! The incident was all wrong.

"Then you told me that the man had disappeared. He had missed a Tuesday and a Thursday the first time for years. I liked that even less. A queer hypothesis sprang up in my mind. If I were right about it *the man was dead*. I made inquiries. The man *was* dead. And he was very neatly and tidily dead. In other words the bad fish was covered up with the sauce!

"He had been seen in the King's Road at seven o'clock. He had had dinner here at 7:30 — two hours before he died. It all fitted in — the evidence of the stomach contents, the evidence of the letter. Much too much sauce! You couldn't see the fish at all!

"Devoted nephew wrote the letter, devoted nephew had beautiful alibi for time of death. Death very simple — a fall down the stairs. Simple accident? Or murder? Everyone says the former.

"Devoted nephew only surviving relative. Devoted nephew will inherit — but is there anything *to* inherit? Uncle notoriously poor.

"But there is a brother. And brother in his time had married a rich wife. And brother lives in a big rich house on Kingston Hill, so it would seem that rich wife must have left him all her money. You see the sequence — rich wife leaves money to Anthony, Anthony leaves money to Henry, Henry's money goes to George — a complete chain."

"All very pretty in theory," said Mr. Bonnington. "But what did you do?"

"Once you *know* — you can usually get hold of what you want. Henry had died two hours after a *meal* — that is all the inquest really bothered about. But supposing that meal was not dinner, but *lunch*. Put yourself in George's place. George wants money — badly. Anthony Gascoigne is dying — but his death is no good to George. His money goes to Henry, and Henry Gascoigne may live for years. So Henry must die too — and the sooner the better — but his death must take place *after* Anthony's, and at the same time George must have an alibi. Henry's habit of dining regularly at a restaurant on two evenings of the week suggests an alibi to George. Being a cautious fellow, he tries his plan out first. *He impersonates his uncle one Monday evening at the restaurant in question.*

"It goes without a hitch. Everyone there accepts him as his uncle. He is satisfied. He has only to wait till Uncle Anthony shows definite signs of pegging out. The time comes. He mails a letter to his uncle on the afternoon of the 2nd November but dates it the 3rd. He comes up to town on the afternoon of the 3rd, calls on his uncle, and carries his scheme into action. A shove and down the stairs goes Uncle Henry.

"George hunts about for the letter he has written, and shoves it in the pocket of his uncle's dressing gown. At 7:30 he is at the Gallant Endeavor, beard, bushy eyebrows, all complete. Undoubtedly Mr. Henry Gascoigne is alive at 7:30. Then a rapid metamorphosis [1] in a lavatory and back full speed in his car to Wimbledon and an evening of bridge. The perfect alibi."

Mr. Bonnington looked at him.

"But the postmark on the letter?"

"Oh, that was very simple. The postmark was smudgy. Why? It had been altered with lampblack from Nov. 2nd to Nov. 3rd. You would not notice it *unless you were looking for it.* And finally there were the blackbirds."

"Blackbirds?"

"Four and twenty blackbirds baked in a pie! Or blackberries if you prefer to be literal! George, you comprehend, was after all not quite a good enough actor. He *looked* like his uncle and *walked* like his uncle and *spoke* like his uncle and had his uncle's beard and eyebrows, but he forgot to *eat* like his uncle. He ordered the dishes that he himself liked.

"Blackberries discolor the teeth — the corpse's teeth were not discolored, and yet Henry Gascoigne ate blackberries at the Gallant Endeavor that night. But there were no blackberries in the stomach. I asked this morning. And George had been fool enough to keep the beard and the rest of the make-up. Oh! plenty of evidence once you look for it. I called on George and rattled him. That finished it! He had been eating blackber-

[1] metamorphosis (mĕt'a·môr'fô·sĭs): change in appearance.

ries again, by the way. A greedy fellow — cared a lot about his food. *Eh bien,* greed will hang him all right unless I am very much mistaken."

A waitress brought them two portions of blackberry-and-apple tart.

"Take it away," said Mr. Bonnington. "One can't be too careful. Bring me a small helping of sago pudding."

NOTING THE PURPOSE OF DETAILS

AT THE GALLANT ENDEAVOR

1. The opening conversation between Poirot and Bonnington appears to be small talk about food, quite unimportant to the plot. Yet in a number of ways, this conversation foreshadows events to come. Can you point out connections between the conversation and the story?

2. In the passage introducing Molly, the waitress, what detail of characterization is important? Why? How does the conversation with her fit into the story?

3. After Molly has departed, do the final deductions and talk foreshadow, in any way, what is to come?

ON THE SUBWAY

4. From the beginning, you may have noted, Poirot is more agitated than Bonnington by what he learns of "Old Father Time." On this occasion, how does this particular distinction between the two friends show itself?

AT DR. MacANDREW'S OFFICE

5. "The plot thickens" — very rapidly at this point. In this scene what clues and suspicions are introduced? Do we learn anything about Henry Gascoigne's youth that could possibly lead one to wonder if he might have known Molly in the past?

AT THE GALLANT ENDEAVOR

6. What has become of Molly? What does she contribute to the author's design for this story?

7. On the evening of his death, which did "Old Father Time" order — his customary meal or the one he chose on his singular Monday appearance?

AN INTERVIEW WITH MRS. AMELIA HILL

8. What light does Poirot's talk with Mrs. Hill shed on the mystery?

AT THE RESIDENCE OF DR. RAMSEY

9. Is it possible Poirot chose the time of his call with any purpose?
10. What device does Poirot use to rattle Dr. Ramsey? Is it successful?

THE FINAL CONVERSATION
AT THE GALLANT ENDEAVOR

11. Mr. Bonnington's earlier reference to a highly flavored sauce concealing the bad fish is revived. What does it now symbolize?

ACHIEVING SUSPENSE IN A DETECTIVE STORY

To achieve suspense, writers often introduce elements of mystery, unusual circumstances for which the reader craves explanation. In "Four and Twenty Blackbirds" one of the most skillful of all writers of mystery and detective tales does exactly this. Go back over the story and locate details that arouse the curiosity of the reader, compelling him to finish the story.

ABOUT THE AUTHOR

Agatha Christie (1891–   ), born in Torquay, England, was educated by her mother whose teaching succeeded in awakening Agatha Christie's interest in a wide variety of subjects. During World War I while working in a hospital dispensary, she planned her first detective story as a means of keeping her mind occupied. *The Mysterious Affair at Styles* started her on the way to becoming one of the few detective writers whose books consistently make the best-seller lists. Her debonair, mustachioed little Belgian, Hercule Poirot, has solved more crimes than Sherlock Holmes, the first renowned story detective. "Four and Twenty Blackbirds"

illustrates Poirot's infallible sharpness of mind. In 1950, Mrs. Christie published her fiftieth mystery novel, *A Murder Is Announced*. She has also written several mystery plays. Her *Witness for the Prosecution* and *The Mousetrap* have been performed before enthusiastic audiences in England and in the United States.

The Author's Plot ➤

In the illustration on the opposite page, artist Lawrence Bjorklund has illustrated four events in "Four and Twenty Blackbirds." These are events of which the reader may not be fully aware until the end of the story when Hercule Poirot discloses them to Henry Bonnington.

In writing a mystery, an author really creates two stories. First, he outlines for himself the events that actually take place. Let us call this the "author's plot." Then, in writing his story, he deliberately conceals certain parts of this plot from the reader. He keeps the reader in suspense until the very end of the story when he has one of his characters — usually a detective — reveal what really took place. The reader matches his skill with the detective in uncovering the missing facts.

In "Four and Twenty Blackbirds" Anthony Gascoigne is a rich old man in poor health. In the event of his death his money will go to his brother Henry. George Ramsey, the nephew of the Gascoigne brothers, is determined to inherit the money himself. To accomplish this, he has to make certain that both Gascoignes die. He begins to proceed with his plan. This is where the pictures start: (1) George Ramsey disguises himself as his Uncle Henry prior to his first masquerade at the Gallant Endeavor in Chelsea. (2) Back in Wimbledon on November 2, as Anthony Gascoigne lies dying, George writes a letter to Henry, dating the letter November 3. (3) Arriving in Chelsea on November 3, George murders Henry, then appears again at the restaurant disguised as his uncle. (4) After dinner, George discards his disguise and dashes back to Wimbledon for an evening of bridge and an alibi that seems indisputable — to everyone except Hercule Poirot. Or did *you* see through the "author's plot"?

The Quiet Man

MAURICE WALSH

Unlike the first two stories in this book, the plot of "The Quiet Man" does not do all, or most of, the work. Of course, what happens is important, but equally important are the characters, the values that determine their actions, and what the author is expressing through characters and action. Like all men and women, the "quiet man" in this story has choices to make, and these choices hinge upon what he values in life. These thoughtful choices make the plot.

Sᴀᴡɴ Kᴇʟᴠɪɴ, a blithe young lad of twenty, went to the States to seek his fortune. And fifteen years thereafter he returned to his native Kerry, his blitheness sobered and his youth dried to the core, and whether he had made his fortune or whether he had not, no one could be knowing for certain. For he was a quiet man, not given to talking about himself and the things he had done. A quiet man, under middle size, with strong shoulders and deep-set blue eyes below brows darker than his dark hair — that was Shawn Kelvin. One shoulder had a trick of hunching slightly higher than the other, and some folks said that came from a habit he had of shielding his eyes in the glare of an open-hearth furnace in a place called Pittsburgh, while others said it used to be a way he had of guarding his chin that time he was a sort of sparring-partner punching bag at a boxing camp.

Shawn Kelvin came home and found that he was the last of the Kelvins, and that the farm of his forefathers had added its few acres to the ranch of Big Liam O'Grady, of Moyvalla. Shawn took no action to recover his land, though O'Grady had got it meanly. He had had enough of fighting, and all he wanted now was peace. He quietly went amongst the old and kindly friends and quietly looked about him for the place and peace he wanted; and when the time came, quietly produced the money for a neat, handy, small farm on the first warm shoulder of Knockanore Hill below the rolling curves of heather. It was not a big place but it was in good heart, and it got all the sun that was going; and, best of all, it suited Shawn to the tiptop notch of contentment; for it held the peace that tuned to his quietness, and it commanded the widest view in all Ireland — vale and mountain and the lifting green plain of the Atlantic Sea.

There, in a four-roomed, lime-washed, thatched cottage, Shawn made his life, and, though his friends hinted his needs and obligations, no thought came to him of bringing a wife into the place. Yet Fate had the thought and the dream in her loom for him. One middling imitation of a man he had to do chores for him, an ex-navy pensioner [1] handy enough about house and byre, but with no relish for the sustained work of the field — and, indeed, as long as he kept house and byre shipshape, he found Shawn an easy master.

Shawn himself was no drudge toiler. He knew all about drudgery and the way it wears out a man's soul. He plowed a little and sowed a little, and at the end of a furrow he would lean on the handles of the cultivator, wipe his brow, if it needed wiping, and lose himself for whole minutes in the great green curve of the sea out there beyond the high black portals of Shannon mouth.[2] And sometimes of an evening he would see, under the glory of the sky, the faint smoke smudge of an American liner. Then he would smile to himself — a pitying smile — thinking of the poor devils, with dreams of fortune luring them, going out to sweat in Ironville, or to stand in a breadline. All

these things were behind Shawn forever.[3]

Market days he would go down and across to Listowel town, seven miles, to do his bartering; and in the long evenings, slowly slipping into the endless summer gloaming, his friends used to climb the winding lane to see him. Only the real friends came that long road, and they were welcome — fighting men who had been out in the "Sixteen"; [4] Matt Tobin the thresher, the schoolmaster, the young curate — men like that. A stone jar of malt whisky would appear on the table, and there would be a haze of smoke and a maze of warm, friendly disagreements.

"Shawn, old son," one of them might hint, "aren't you sometimes terrible lonely?"

"Never!" might retort Shawn derisively. "Why?"

"Nothing but the daylight and the wind and the sun setting with the wrath o' God."

"Just that! Well?"

"But after stirring times beyond in the States —"

"Ay! Tell me, fine man, have you ever seen a furnace in full blast?"

"A great sight."

"Great surely! But if I could jump you into a steel foundry this minute, you would be sure that God had judged you faithfully into the very hob of hell."

And then they would laugh and have another small one from the stone jar.

And on Sundays Shawn used to go to church, three miles down to the gray chapel above the black cliffs of Doon Bay. There Fate laid her lure for him.

Sitting quietly on his wooden bench

---

[1] **pensioner** (pĕn′shŭn-ēr): a man who has retired and who is receiving a pension.

[2] **Shannon** (shăn′ŭn) **mouth**: where the Shannon River empties into the Atlantic Ocean.

[3] From this paragraph we can infer that Shawn was in the United States during the depression of the 1930's.

[4] the "Sixteen": a reference to the army of Irish volunteers who rebelled against English rule in 1916.

or kneeling on the dusty footboard, he would fix his steadfast, deep-set eyes on the vestmented celebrant [1] and say his prayers slowly, or go into that strange trance, beyond dreams and visions, where the soul is almost at one with the unknowable.

But after a time, Shawn's eyes no longer fixed themselves on the celebrant. They went no farther than two seats ahead. A girl sat there, Sunday after Sunday she sat in front of him, and Sunday after Sunday his first casual admiration grew warmer.

She had a white nape to her neck and short red hair above it, and Shawn liked the color and wave of that flame. And he liked the set of her shoulders and the way the white neck had of leaning a little forward and she at her prayers — or her dreams. And the service over, Shawn used to stay in his seat so that he might get one quick but sure look at her face as she passed out. And he liked her face, too — the wide-set gray eyes, cheekbones firmly curved, clean-molded lips, austere yet sensitive. And he smiled pityingly at himself that one of her name should make his pulses stir — for she was an O'Grady.

One person, only, in the crowded chapel noted Shawn's look and the thought behind the look. Not the girl. Her brother, Big Liam O'Grady of Moyvalla, the very man who as good as stole the Kelvin acres. And that man smiled to himself, too — the ugly, contemptuous smile that was his by nature — and, after another habit he had, he tucked away his bit of knowledge in his mind corner against a day when it might come in useful for his own purposes.

The girl's name was Ellen — Ellen O'Grady. But in truth she was no longer a girl. She was past her first youth into that second one that had no definite ending. She might be thirty — she was no less — but there was not a lad in the countryside would say she was past her prime. The poise of her and the firm set of her bones below clean skin saved her from the fading of mere prettiness. Though she had been sought in marriage more than once, she had accepted no one, or rather, had not been allowed to encourage anyone. Her brother saw to that.

Big Liam O'Grady was a great raw-boned, sandy-haired man, with the strength of an ox and a heart no bigger than a sour apple. An overbearing man given to berserk rages. Though he was a churchgoer by habit, the true god of that man was Money — red gold, shining silver, dull copper — the trinity [2] that he worshiped in degree. He and his sister Ellen lived on the big ranch farm of Moyvalla, and Ellen was his housekeeper and maid of all work. She was a careful housekeeper, a good cook, a notable baker, and she demanded no wage. All that suited Big Liam splendidly, and so she remained single — a wasted woman.

Big Liam himself was not a marrying man. There were not many spinsters with a dowry [3] big enough to tempt him, and the few there had acquired expensive tastes — a convent education, the deplorable art of hitting jazz out of a piano, the damnable vice of cigarette smoking, the purse-emptying craze for motor cars — such things.

But in due time, the dowry and the place — with a woman tied to them — came under his nose, and Big Liam was

[1] **vestmented celebrant** (sĕl'ê·brănt): the robed, officiating priest.

[2] **trinity:** "Trinity" usually refers to the Holy Trinity: the Father, the Son, and the Holy Ghost in the Christian religion. O'Grady's *trinity* was of a different sort.

[3] **dowry:** the money or property a woman brings to her husband at the time of marriage.

no longer tardy. His neighbor, James Carey, died in March and left his fine farm and all on it to his widow, a youngish woman without children, a woman with a hard name for saving pennies. Big Liam looked once at Kathy Carey and looked many times at her broad acres. Both pleased him. He took the steps required by tradition. In the very first week of the following Shrovetide,[1] he sent an accredited emissary to open formal negotiations, and that emissary came back within the hour.

"My soul," said he, "but she is the quick one! I hadn't ten words out of me when she was down my throat. 'I am in no hurry,' says she, 'to come wife to a house with another woman at the fire corner. When Ellen is in a place of her own, I will listen to what Liam O'Grady has to say.'"

"She will, I say!" Big Liam stopped him. "She will so."

There, now, was the right time to recall Shawn Kelvin and the look in his eyes. Big Liam's mind corner promptly delivered up its memory. He smiled knowingly and contemptuously. Shawn Kelvin daring to cast sheep's eyes at an O'Grady! The undersized chicken heart, who took the loss of the Kelvin acres lying down! The little Yankee runt hidden away on the shelf of Knockanore! But what of it? The required dowry would be conveniently small, and the girl would never go hungry, anyway. There was Big Liam O'Grady, far descended from many chieftains.

The very next market day at Listowel he sought out Shawn Kelvin and placed a huge, sandy-haired hand on the shoulder that hunched to meet it.

"Shawn Kelvin, a word with you! Come and have a drink."

Shawn hesitated. "Very well," he said then. He did not care for O'Grady, but he would hurt no man's feelings.

They went across to Sullivan's bar and had a drink, and Shawn paid for it. And Big Liam came directly to his subject — almost patronizingly, as if he were conferring a favor.

"I want to see Ellen settled in a place of her own," said he.

Shawn's heart lifted into his throat and stayed there. But that steadfast face with the steadfast eyes gave no sign and, moreover, he could not say a word with his heart where it was.

"Your place is small," went on the big man, "but it is handy, and no load of debt on it, as I hear. Not much of a dowry ever came to Knockanore, and not much of a dowry can I be giving with Ellen. Say two hundred pounds at the end of harvest, if prices improve. What do you say, Shawn Kelvin?"

Shawn swallowed his heart, and his voice came slow and cool: "What does Ellen say?"

"I haven't asked her," said Big Liam. "But what would she say, blast it?"

"Whatever she says, she will say it herself, not you, Big Liam."

But what could Ellen say? She looked within her own heart and found it empty; she looked at the granite crag of her brother's face and contemplated herself a slowly withering spinster at his fire corner; she looked up at the swell of Knockanore Hill and saw the white cottage among the green small fields below the warm brown of the heather. Oh, but the sun would shine up there in the lengthening spring day and pleasant breezes blow in sultry summer; and finally she looked at Shawn Kelvin, that firmly built, small man with the clean face and the lustrous eyes below steadfast brow. She said a prayer to her God and sank head and shoulders in a resignation more pitiful than tears, more proud than the pride of chieftains. Romance? Welladay!

Shawn was far from satisfied with that resigned acceptance, but then was not the time to press for a warmer one. He knew the brother's wizened soul, guessed at the girl's clean one, and saw that she was doomed beyond hope to a fireside sordidly bought for her. Let it be his own fireside then. There were many worse ones — and God was good.

Ellen O'Grady married Shawn Kelvin. One small statement; and it holds the risk of tragedy, the chance of happiness, the probability of mere endurance — choices wide as the world.

But Big Liam O'Grady, for all his resolute promptness, did not win Kathy Carey to wife. She, foolishly enough, took to husband her own cattleman, a gay night rambler, who gave her the devil's own time and a share of happiness in the bygoing. For the first time, Big Liam discovered how mordant[1] the wit of his neighbors could be, and to contempt for Shawn Kelvin he now added an unreasoning dislike.

Shawn Kelvin had got his precious, red-haired woman under his own roof

[1] **mordant** (môr'dănt): sarcastic; biting.

now. He had no illusions about her feelings for him. On himself, and on himself only, lay the task of molding her into a wife and lover. Darkly, deeply, subtly, away out of sight, with gentleness, with restraint, with a consideration beyond kenning,[2] that molding must be done, and she that was being molded must never know. He hardly knew, himself.

First he turned his attention to material things. He hired a small servant maid to help her with the housework. Then he acquired a rubber-tired tub cart and a half-bred gelding[3] with a reaching knee action. And on market days, husband and wife used to bowl down to Listowel, do their selling and their buying, and bowl smoothly home again, their groceries in the well of the cart and a bundle of secondhand American magazines on the seat at Ellen's side. And in the nights, before the year turned, with the wind from the plains of the Atlantic keening[4] above the chimney, they would sit at either side of the flaming peat fire, and he would read aloud strange and almost unbelievable things out of the high-colored magazines. Stories, sometimes, wholly unbelievable.

Ellen would sit and listen and smile, and go on with her knitting or her sewing; and after a time it was sewing she was at mostly — small things. And when the reading was done, they would sit and talk quietly in their own quiet way. For they were both quiet. Woman though she was, she got Shawn to do most of the talking. It could be that she,

[2] **kenning** (kĕn'ĭng): insight; understanding.

[3] **gelding** (gĕld'ĭng): a horse.

[4] **keening** (kēn'ĭng): a lamentation for the dead, usually uttered in a loud, wailing voice; sometimes a wordless cry or wail, sometimes a rhythmic recounting of the life and character of the dead.

too, was probing and seeking, unwrapping the man's soul to feel the texture thereof, surveying the marvel of his life as he spread it diffidently before her. He had a patient, slow, vivid way of picturing for her the things he had seen and felt. He made her see the glare of molten metal, lambent yet searing,[1] made her feel the sucking heat, made her hear the clang; she could see the roped square under the dazzle of the hooded arcs with the curling smoke layer above it, understand the explosive restraint of the game, thrill when he showed her how to stiffen wrist for the final devastating right hook. And often enough the stories were humorous, and Ellen would chuckle, or stare, or throw back her red, lovely curls in laughter. It was grand to make her laugh.

Shawn's friends, in some hesitation at first, came in ones and twos up the slope to see them. But Ellen welcomed them with her smile that was shy and, at the same time, frank, and her table was loaded for them with scones [2] and crumpets [3] and cream cakes and heather honey; and at the right time it was she herself that brought forth the decanter of whisky — no longer the half-empty stone jar — and the polished glasses. Shawn was proud as sin of her. She would sit then and listen to their discussions and be forever surprised at the knowledgeable man her husband was — the way he would discuss war and politics and the making of songs, the turn of speech that summed up a man or a situation. And sometimes she would put in a word or two and he listened too, and they would look to see if her smile commended them, and be a little chastened

by the wisdom of that smile — the age-old smile of the matriarch from whom they were all descended. In no time at all, Matt Tobin the thresher, who used to think, "Poor old Shawn! Lucky she was to get him," would whisper to the schoolmaster: "Herrin's alive! That fellow's luck would astonish nations."

Women, in the outside world, begin by loving their husbands; and then, if Fate is kind, they grow to admire them; and, if Fate is not unkind, may descend no lower than liking and enduring. And there is the end of lawful romance. Look now at Ellen O'Grady. She came up to the shelf of Knockanore and in her heart was only a nucleus [4] of fear in a great emptiness, and that nucleus might grow into horror and disgust. But, glory of God, she, for reason piled on reason, presently found herself admiring Shawn Kelvin; and with or without reason, a quiet liking came to her for this quiet man who was so gentle and considerate; and then, one great heart-stirring dark o'night, she found herself fallen head and heels in love with her own husband. There is the sort of love that endures, but the road to it is a mighty chancy one.

A woman, loving her husband, may or may not be proud of him, but she will fight like a tiger if anyone, barring herself, belittles him. And there was one man that belittled Shawn Kelvin. Her brother, Big Liam O'Grady. At fair or market or chapel that dour [5] giant deigned not to hide his contempt and dislike. Ellen knew why. He had lost a wife and farm; he had lost in herself a frugally cheap housekeeper; he had been made the butt of a sly humor; and for these mishaps, in some twisted way, he blamed Shawn. But — and there

[1] **lambent** (lăm'bĕnt) **yet searing:** softly bright and flickering yet burning.
[2] **scones** (skōnz): round or triangular tea cakes.
[3] **crumpets** (krŭm'pĕtz): thin, flat cakes cooked on a griddle.

[4] **nucleus** (nū'klē-ŭs): a core; the central part.
[5] **dour** (do͞or): sour or sullen in aspect.

came in the contempt — the little Yankee runt, who dared say nothing about the lost Kelvin acres, would not now have the gall or guts to demand the dowry that was due. Lucky the hound to stean [1] an O'Grady to hungry Knockanore! Let him be satisfied with that luck!

One evening before a market day, Ellen spoke to her husband: "Has Big Liam paid you my dowry yet, Shawn?"

"Sure there's no hurry, girl," said Shawn.

"Have you ever asked him?"

"I have not. I am not looking for your dowry, Ellen."

"And Big Liam could never understand that." Her voice firmed. "You will ask him tomorrow."

"Very well so, *agrah*, [2]" agreed Shawn easily.

And the next day, in that quiet diffident way of his, he asked Big Liam. But Big Liam was brusque and blunt. He had no loose money and Kelvin

[1] **stean** (stēn): bring.
[2] *agrah* (à·grŏ'): sweetheart; dear.

would have to wait till he had. "Ask me again, Shawneen," he finished, his face in a mocking smile, and turning on his heel, he plowed his great shoulders through the crowded market.

His voice had been carelessly loud and people had heard. They laughed and talked amongst themselves. "Begogs! The devil's own boy. Big Liam! What a pup to sell! Stealing the land and keeping a grip on the fortune! Ay, and a dangerous fellow, mind you, the same Big Liam! He would smash little Shawn at the wind of a word. And devil the bit his Yankee sparring tricks would help him!"

A friend of Shawn's, Matt Tobin the thresher, heard that and lifted his voice: "I would like to be there the day Shawn Kelvin loses his temper."

"A bad day for poor Shawn!"

"It might then," said Matt Tobin, "but I would come from the other end of Kerry to see the badness that would be in it for someone."

Shawn had moved away with his wife, not heeding or not hearing.

"You see, Ellen?" he said in some discomfort. "The times are hard on the big ranchers, and we don't need the money, anyway."

"Do you think Big Liam does?" Her voice had a cut in it. "He could buy you and all Knockanore and be only on the fringe of his hoard. You will ask him again."

"But, girl dear, I never wanted a dowry with you."

She liked him to say that, but far better would she like to win for him the respect and admiration that was his due. She must do that now at all costs. Shawn, drawing back now, would be the butt of his fellow men.

"You foolish lad! Big Liam would never understand your feelings, with money at stake." She smiled and a pang went through Shawn's breast. For the smile was the smile of an O'Grady, and he could not be sure whether the contempt in it was for himself or for her brother.

Shawn asked Big Liam again, unhappy in his asking, but also dimly comprehending his woman's object. And Shawn asked again a third time. The issue was become a famous one now. Men talked about it, and women too. Bets were made on it. At fair or market, if Shawn was seen approaching Big Liam, men edged closer and women edged away. Some day the big fellow would grow tired of being asked, and in one of his terrible rages half kill the little lad as he had half killed other men. A great shame! Here and there, a man advised Shawn to give up asking and put the matter in a lawyer's hands. "I couldn't do that," was Shawn's only answer. Strangely enough, none of these prudent advisers were amongst Shawn's close friends. His friends frowned and said little, but they were always about, and always amongst them was Matt Tobin.

The day at last came when Big Liam grew tired of being asked. That was the big October cattle fair at Listowel, and he had sold twenty head of fat, Polled Angus beeves at a good price. He was a hard dealer and it was late in the day before he settled at his own figure, so that the banks were closed and he was not able to make a lodgment.[1] He had, then, a great roll of bills in an inner vest pocket when he saw Shawn and Ellen coming across to where he was bargaining with Matt Tobin for a week's threshing. Besides, the day being dank, he had had a drink or two more than was good for him and the whisky had loosened his tongue and whatever he had of discretion. By the powers! — it was time

<hr>

[1] lodgment: deposit.

and past time to deal once and for all with this little gadfly of a fellow, to show him up before the whole market. He strode to meet Shawn, and people got out of his savage way and edged in behind to lose nothing of this dangerous game.

He caught Shawn by the hunched shoulder — a rending grip — and bent down to grin in his face.

"What is it, little fellow? Don't be ashamed to ask!"

Matt Tobin was probably the only one there to notice the ease with which Shawn wrenched his shoulder free, and Matt Tobin's eyes brightened. But Shawn did nothing further and said no word. His deep-set eyes gazed steadily at the big man.

The big man showed his teeth mockingly. "Go on, you whelp! What do you want?"

"You know, O'Grady."

"I do. Listen, Shawneen!" Again he brought his handclap on the little man's shoulder. "Listen, Shawneen! If I had a dowry to give my sister, 'tis not a little shrimp like you would get her!"

His great hand gripped and he flung Shawn backwards as if he were only the image of a man filled with chaff.

Shawn went backwards, but he did not fall. He gathered himself like a spring, feet under him, arms half-raised, head forward into hunched shoulder. But as quickly as the spring coiled, as quickly it slackened, and he turned away to his wife. She was there facing him, tense and keen, her face pale and set, and a gleam of the race in her eyes.

"Woman, woman!" he said in his deep voice. "Why would you and I shame ourselves like this?"

"Shawn!" she cried. "Will you let him shame you now?"

"But your own brother, Ellen — before them all?"

"And he cheating you —"

"Glory of God!" His voice was distressed. "What is his dirty money to me? Are you an O'Grady, after all?"

That stung her and she stung him back in one final effort. She placed a hand below her breast and looked *close* into his face. Her voice was low and bitter, and only he heard: "I am an O'Grady. It is a great pity that the father of this my son is a Kelvin and a coward."

The bosses [1] of Shawn Kelvin's cheekbones were like hard marble, but his voice was as soft as a dove's.

"Is that the way of it? Let us be going home then, in the name of God!"

He took her arm, but she shook his hand off; nevertheless, she walked at his side, head up, through the people that made way for them. Her brother mocked them with his great, laughing bellow.

"That fixes the pair of them!" he cried, brushed a man who laughed with him out of his way, and strode off through the fair.

There was talk then — plenty of it. "Murder, but Shawn had a narrow squeak that time! Did you see the way he flung him? I wager he'll give Big Liam a wide road after this. And he by way of being a boxer! That's a pound you owe me, Matt Tobin."

"I'll pay it," said Matt Tobin, and that is all he said. He stood, wide-legged, looking at the ground, his hand ruefully rubbing the back of his head and dismay and gloom on his face. His friend had failed him in the face of the people.

Shawn and Ellen went home in their tub cart and had not a single word or glance for each other on the road. And all that evening, at table or fireside, a

[1] **bosses** (bŏs′ĕz): the round protuberant part of the cheekbones.

heart-sickening silence held them in its grip. And all that night they lay side by side, still and mute. There was only one subject that possessed them and on that they dared speak no longer. They slept little. Ellen, her heart desolate, lay on her side, staring into the dark, grieving for what she had said and unable to unsay it. Shawn, on his back, contemplated things with a cold clarity. He realized that he was at the fork of life and that a finger pointed unmistakably. He must risk the very shattering of all happiness, he must do a thing so final and decisive that, once done, it could never again be questioned. Before morning, he came to his decision, and it was bitter as gall. He cursed himself. "Oh, you fool! You might have known that you should never have taken an O'Grady without breaking the O'Gradys."

He got up early in the morning at his usual hour and went out, as usual, to his morning chores — rebedding and foddering the cattle, rubbing down the half-bred, helping the servant maid with the milk in the creaming pans — and, as usual, he came in to his breakfast, and ate it unhungrily and silently, which was not usual. But, thereafter he again went out to the stable, harnessed his gelding and hitched him to the tub cart. Then he returned to the kitchen and spoke for the first time.

"Ellen, will you come with me down to see your brother?"

She hesitated, her hands thrown wide in a helpless, hopeless gesture. "Little use you going to see my brother, Shawn. 'Tis I should go and — and not come back."

"Don't blame me now or later, Ellen. It has been put on me and the thing I am going to do is the only thing to be done. Will you come?"

"Very well," she agreed tonelessly. "I will be ready in a minute."

And they went the four miles down into the vale to the big farmhouse of Moyvalla. They drove into the great square of cobbled yard and found it empty.

On one side of the square was the long, low, lime-washed dwelling house; on the other, fifty yards away, the two-stories line of steadings [1] with a wide arch in the middle; and through the arch came the purr and zoom of a threshing machine. Shawn tied the half-bred to the wheel of a farm cart and, with Ellen, approached the house.

A slattern [2] servant girl leaned over the kitchen half-door and pointed through the arch. The master was out beyond in the haggard [3] — the rick-yard [4] — and would she run across for him?

"Never mind, *achara*," [5] said Shawn, "I'll get him. . . . Ellen, will you go in and wait?"

"No," said Ellen, "I'll come with you." She knew her brother.

As they went through the arch, the purr and zoom grew louder and, turning the corner, they walked into the midst of activity. A long double row of cone-pointed cornstacks stretched across the yard and, between them, Matt Tobin's portable threshing machine was busy. The smooth-flying, eight-foot driving wheel made a sleepy purr and the black driving belt ran with a sag and heave to the red-painted thresher. Up there on the platform, bare-armed men were feeding the flying

drum with loosened sheaves, their hands moving in a rhythmic sway. As the toothed drum bit at the corn sheaves it made an angry snarl that changed and slowed into a satisfied zoom. The wide conveying belt was carrying the golden straw up a steep incline to where other men were building a long rick; still more men were attending to the corn shoots, shoulders bending under the weight of the sacks as they ambled across to the granary. Matt Tobin himself bent at the face of his engine, feeding the fire box with sods [6] of hard black peat. There were not less than two score men about the place, for, as was the custom, all Big Liam's friends and neighbors were giv-

[1] **steadings:** farm buildings.
[2] **slattern** (slăt′ērn): an untidy woman.
[3] **haggard** (hăg′ērd): a yard for stacking hay.
[4] **rickyard** (rĭk′yärd): part of a farmyard where the ricks are found. *Ricks* are stacks of hay in the open air usually protected with thatching. (See the picture on this page.)
[5] *achara* (à·kàr′à): a greeting corresponding to "Dear Sir" (or "Dear Madam"), as used in Ireland.

[6] **sods** (sŏdz): pieces of the upper layer of earth and vegetable mold, filled with the roots of grass and other small plants so as to form a kind of mat, called turf; or if semicarbonized, peat.

ing him a hand with the threshing —
"the day in harvest."

Big Liam came round the flank of the
engine and swore. He was in his shirt
sleeves, and his great forearms were
covered with sandy hair.

"Look who's here!"

He was in the worst of tempers this
morning. The stale dregs of yesterday's
whisky were still with him, and he was
in the humor that, as they say, would
make a dog bite its father. He took two
slow strides and halted, feet apart and
head truculently [1] forward.

"What is it this time?" he shouted.
That was the un-Irish welcome he gave
his sister and her husband.

Shawn and Ellen came forward steadily, and, as they came, Matt Tobin
slowly throttled down his engine. Big
Liam heard the change of pitch and
looked angrily over his shoulder.

"What do you mean, Tobin? Get on
with the work!"

"Big Liam, this is my engine, and if
you don't like it, you can leave it!" And
at that he drove the throttle shut and
the purr of the flywheel slowly sank.

"We will see in a minute," threatened
Big Liam, and turned to the two now
near at hand.

"What is it?" he growled.

"A private word with you. I won't
keep you long." Shawn was calm and
cold.

"You will not — on a busy morning,"
sneered the big man. "There is no need
for private words between me and
Shawn Kelvin."

"There is need," urged Shawn. "It
will be best for us all if you hear what
I have to say in your own house."

"Or here on my own land. Out with
it! I don't care who hears!"

Shawn looked round him. Up on the

[1] **truculently** (trŭk′û·lĕnt·lĭ): showing fe-
rocity.

thresher, up on the straw rick, men
leaned idle on fork handles and looked
down at him; from here and there
about the stackyard, men moved in to
see, as it might be, what had caused the
stoppage, but only really interested in
the two brothers-in-law. He was in the
midst of Clan O'Grady, for they were
mostly O'Grady men — big, strong,
blond men, rough, confident, proud of
their breed. Matt Tobin was the only
man he could call a friend. Many of the
others were not unfriendly, but all had
contempt in their eyes, or, what was
worse, pity. Very well! Since he had to
prove himself, it was fitting that he do
it here amongst the O'Grady men.

Shawn brought his eyes back to Big
Liam — deep, steadfast eyes that did not
waver. "O'Grady," said he — and he no
longer hid his contempt — "you set a
great store by money."

"No harm in that. You do it yourself,
Shawneen."

"Take it so! I will play that game
with you, as long as you like. You would
bargain your sister and cheat; I will sell
my soul. Listen, you big brute! You
owe me two hundred pounds. Will you
pay it?" There was an iron quality in
his voice that was somehow awesome.
The big man, about to start forward
overbearingly, restrained himself to a
brutal playfulness.

"I will pay it when I am ready."

"Today."

"No; nor tomorrow."

"Right. If you break your bargain, I
break mine."

"What's that?" shouted Big Liam.

"If you keep your two hundred
pounds, you keep your sister."

"What is it?" shouted Big Liam
again, his voice breaking in astonishment. "What is that you say?"

"You heard me. Here is your sister
Ellen! Keep her!"

He was completely astounded out of his truculence. "You can't do that!"

"It is done," said Shawn.

Ellen O'Grady had been quiet as a statue at Shawn's side, but now, slow like doom, she faced him. She leaned forward and looked into his eyes and saw the pain behind the strength.

"To the mother of your son, Shawn Kelvin?" she whispered that gently to him.

His voice came cold as a stone out of a stone face: "In the face of God. Let Him judge me."

"I know — I know!" That was all she said, and walked quietly across to where Matt Tobin stood at the face of his engine.

Matt Tobin placed a hand on her arm. "Give him time, *acolleen*," [1] he whispered urgently. "Give him his own time. He's slow but he's deadly as a tiger when he moves."

Big Liam was no fool. He knew exactly how far he could go. There was no use, at this juncture, in crushing the runt under a great fist. There was some force in the little fellow that defied dragooning. [2] Whatever people might think of Kelvin, public opinion would be dead against himself. Worse, his inward vision saw eyes leering in derision, mouths open in laughter. The scandal on his name would not be bounded by the four seas of Erin. He must change his stance while he had time. These thoughts passed through his mind while he thudded the ground three times with ironshod heel. Now he threw up his head and bellowed his laugh.

[1] *acolleen* (ä·kŏl'lēn): a term of affection for a girl. In Ireland girls are often called *colleens*.
[2] **dragooning** (drȧ·gōōn'ĭng): being compelled to submit to a course of action by violent measures.

"You fool! I was only making fun of you. What are your dirty few pounds to the likes of me? Stay where you are."

He turned, strode furiously away, and disappeared through the arch.

Shawn Kelvin was left alone in that wide ring of men. The hands had come down off the ricks and thresher to see closer. Now they moved back and aside, looked at one another, lifted eyebrows, looked at Shawn Kelvin, frowned and shook their heads. They knew Big Liam. They knew that, yielding up the money, his savagery would break out into something little short of killing. They waited, most of them, to prevent that savagery going too far.

Shawn Kelvin did not look at anyone. He stood still as a rock, his hands deep in his pockets, one shoulder hunched forward, his eyes on the ground and his face strangely calm. He seemed the least perturbed man there. Matt Tobin held Ellen's arm in a steadying grip and whispered in her ear: "God is good, I tell you."

Big Liam was back in two minutes. He strode straight to Shawn and halted within a pace of him.

"Look, Shawneen!" In his raised hand was a crumpled bundle of greasy bank notes. "Here is your money. Take it, and then see what will happen to you. Take it!" He thrust it into Shawn's hand. "Count it. Make sure you have it all — and then I will kick you out of this haggard — and look" — he thrust forward a hairy fist — "if ever I see your face again, I will drive that through it. Count it, you spawn!" [3]

Shawn did not count it. Instead he crumpled it into a ball in his strong fingers. Then he turned on his heel and walked, with surprising slowness, to the face of the engine. He gestured with one

[3] **spawn** (spôn): the eggs of fishes.

hand to Matt Tobin, but it was Ellen, quick as a flash, who obeyed the gesture. Though the hot bar scorched her hand, she jerked open the door of the fire box and the leaping peat flames whispered out at her. And forthwith, Shawn Kelvin, with one easy sweep, threw the crumpled ball of notes into the heart of the flame. The whisper lifted one tone and one scrap of burned paper floated out of the funnel top. That was all the fuss the fire made of its work.

But there was fuss enough outside.

Big Liam O'Grady gave one mighty shout. No, it was more an anguished scream than a shout:

"My money! My good money!"

He gave two furious bounds forward, his great arms raised to crush and kill. But his hands never touched the small man.

"You dumb ox!" said Shawn Kelvin between his teeth. That strong, hunched shoulder moved a little, but no one there could follow the terrific drive of that hooked right arm. The smack of bone on bone was sharp as whip crack, and Big Liam stopped dead, went back on his heel, swayed a moment and staggered back three paces.

"Now and forever! Man of the Kelvins!" roared Matt Tobin.

But Big Liam was a man of iron. That blow should have laid him out on his back — blows like it had tied men to the ground for the full count. But Big Liam only shook his head, grunted like a boar, and drove in at the little man. And the little man, instead of circling away, drove in at him, compact of power.

The men of the O'Gradys saw then an exhibition that they had not knowledge enough to appreciate fully. Thousands had paid as much as ten dollars each to see the great Tiger Kelvin in

action, his footwork, his timing, his hitting; and never was his action more devastating than now. He was a thunderbolt on two feet and the big man a glutton.

Big Liam never touched Shawn with clenched fist. He did not know how. Shawn, actually forty pounds lighter, drove him by sheer hitting across the yard.

Men for the first time saw a two-hundred-pound man knocked clean off his feet by a body blow. They saw for the first time the deadly restraint and explosion of skill.

Shawn set out to demolish his enemy in the briefest space of time, and it took him five minutes to do it. Five, six, eight times he knocked the big man down, and the big man came again, staggering, slavering, raving, vainly trying to rend and smash. But at last he stood swaying and clawing helplessly, and Shawn finished him with his terrible double hit — left below the breastbone and right under the jaw.

Big Liam lifted on his toes and fell flat on his back. He did not even kick as he lay.

Shawn did not waste a glance at the fallen giant. He swung full circle on the O'Grady men and his voice of iron challenged them:

"I am Shawn Kelvin, of Knockanore Hill. Is there an O'Grady amongst you thinks himself a better man? Come then."

His face was deep-carved stone, his great chest lifted, the air whistled through his nostrils; his deep-set flashing eyes dared them.

No man came.

He swung around then and walked straight to his wife. He halted before her.

His face was still of stone, but his voice quivered and had in it all the dramatic force of the Celt:[1]

"Mother of my son, will you come home with me?"

She lifted to the appeal, voice and eye:

"Is it so you ask me, Shawn Kelvin?"

His face of stone quivered at last, "As my wife only — Ellen Kelvin!"

"Very well, heart's treasure." She caught his arm in both of hers. "Let us be going home."

"In the name of God," he finished for her.

And she went with him, proud as the morning, out of that place. But a woman, she would have the last word.

"Mother of God!" she cried. "The trouble I had to make a man of him!"

"God Almighty did that for him before you were born," said Matt Tobin softly.

[1] **Celt** (sĕlt): an individual of any various Celtic-speaking peoples of whom the ancient Gauls and Britons and the modern Irish, Scots, Welsh, and Bretons are the best known. The name is properly indicative of language, not of race.

TRACING THE INFLUENCE OF VALUES

1. It is obvious early in the story that Shawn Kelvin and Liam O'Grady have different values. What does Shawn seem to value most in life? On what does Big Liam set the highest value?

2. Judging from Ellen's activities in her home, what was her guiding value during the first months of her marriage?

3. Do you think Ellen would have forced Shawn into conflict with Big Liam if she had not fallen in love with him? Explain. Why was it important to her to force the issue of the dowry?

4. Why did Shawn avoid conflict with Big Liam over the dowry? What made him change his mind?

5. Shawn's threat to give Ellen back if her dowry was not paid forced Big Liam to consider a value that he had not given much attention to before. What was it?

6. The incident of Ellen's quickly opening the firebox paved the way for the happy ending. What did this action reveal about Ellen's feeling for Shawn? What did it reveal about her own attitude toward the value of money?

7. Why was the burning of the money an unbearable insult to Big Liam?

8. Will Shawn be respected by the community from now on? Which value probably ranks higher with the group — Shawn's insisting on his rights, or his prowess as a fighter? Explain your answers.

RECOGNIZING PLOT PATTERNS

Almost all stories follow the common pattern of *complications, crises, climax,* and *solution.* Following is a brief, general description of each of these elements:

complications:	circumstances which have to be resolved before the story can be brought to a conclusion.
crises:	critical or decisive moments which affect the events that follow.
climax:	the major turning point in a story; it determines the way the story will end.
solution: (or *resolution*)	the way in which the action is resolved; the final outcome of the story.

Review the plot of "The Quiet Man" and, with specific details from the story, explain what its complications and crises are, where the climax occurs, and what the solution is.

COMPOSITION SUGGESTION

Personal values have a strong influence on human behavior and help to shape the life that goes on around you every day. Write an essay giving your opinions on one of these subjects:

The Guiding Values of My Group
The Values of a Juvenile Delinquent

If you choose the second topic, deal with the values a delinquent lacks as well as the ones he lives by.

In the painting on the opposite page, artist Ray Houlihan has depicted the fight between Shawn and Big Liam. Although the painting emphasizes the action of the scene, the artist has also included details of character and setting. Similarly, short story writers do not rely on action alone. They also must give clear descriptions of character and setting.

ABOUT THE AUTHOR

Maurice Walsh (1879–   ) describes himself as "the son and the grandson and the great-great-grandson of farmers and rebels." He was born in Kerry, the hilly country in the far southwest of Ireland. Until he resigned in 1934 from his job in the Customs Excise Service, which took him around England, Scotland, Wales, and Ireland, Walsh wrote only part time. Thereafter he became known as a spinner of tales, with true romance and high adventure his specialities. He has written about Australian bush-ranging, Klondike gold-digging, and the Boer War. However, the majority of his stories are set in either Ireland or Scotland. His books are usually light, but beneath his irrepressible humor often lies a good deal of wisdom.

Speaking of Plot

Plot may be a story's main feature or it may be only one part of a larger design. In detective stories, the plot events often overshadow all the other elements. This is true of "Four and Twenty Blackbirds" where the plot line, the arrangement of incidents, dominates the story. Did you notice how quickly the characters are sketched in, how economically the settings are indicated? Like most detective stories, "Four and Twenty Blackbirds" impresses us as having been created primarily to quicken a reader's interest, to entertain. The hair-raising events in the untitled story also grip the reader's attention, but unlike "Four and Twenty Blackbirds," this thriller offers more than entertainment. Woven into Tom Benecke's brush with death are comments on how work and fierce ambition lead to a wasted life. These comments — with which you may agree or disagree — do not, however, assume an important position in the story; the actual journey into fear still dominates the story. Once again plot overshadows other elements stirring in the background, and the story must be classified primarily as entertainment.

In "The Quiet Man," however, the author tries to give us more. An idea — that the presence of injustice can force us to choose positive action in preference to quiet withdrawal — dominates this story, and the plot is one means of presenting this idea. You do not have to agree with the idea, but it is an idea worth thinking about. Literature presents such ideas with power and impact, thus granting them a living quality they lack when stated by themselves as straightforward propositions. Literature adds the human touch, makes the idea come alive in human terms.

Thus in our three stories, we see that plot, or the sequence of incidents composing a story, may be employed for various purposes. It may serve merely to entertain the reader with a thrilling yarn or an intriguing mystery. Entertainment is a proper justification of literature, and reading to escape into lands of adventure or excitement is not wrong or harmful as long as the reader knows what he is doing and does not limit his reading to "escape" literature. We have also seen that plot may be a means of presenting significant ideas and human values. Literature which does this offers the reader wisdom as well as pleasure.

Tone

If we read a short story thoughtfully, we enter partially into the author's mind and view the world through his eyes. Thus literature offers us the possibility of extending our own ideas, attitudes, and feelings. To do so, we must be alert, not only to the ideas of the writer but also to his attitude, his feeling toward his material — his *tone*. Is the author serious, amused, or bitter, for example? As you read the three stories in this section, turn your attention particularly to the tone of each author.

The Open Window

SAKI

As his fans never tire of pointing out, every word counts in Saki's stories. The deft and witty sparkle of his prose helps to express his outlook on the follies and absurdities of human behavior.

MY AUNT will be down presently, Mr. Nuttel," said a very self-possessed young lady of fifteen; "in the meantime you must try and put up with me."

Framton Nuttel endeavored to say the correct something which should duly flatter the niece of the moment without unduly discounting the aunt that was to come. Privately he doubted more than ever whether these formal visits on a succession of total strangers would do much toward helping the nerve cure which he was supposed to be undergoing.

"I know how it will be," his sister had said when he was preparing to migrate to this rural retreat; "you will bury yourself down there and not speak to a living soul, and your nerves will be worse than ever from moping. I shall just give you letters of introduction to all the people I know there. Some of them, as far as I can remember, were quite nice."

Framton wondered whether Mrs. Sappleton, the lady to whom he was presenting one of the letters of introduction, came into the nice division.

"Do you know many of the people round here?" asked the niece, when she judged that they had had sufficient silent communion.

"Hardly a soul," said Framton. "My sister was staying here, at the rectory,[1] you know, some four years ago, and she gave me letters of introduction to some of the people here."

He made the last statement in a tone of distinct regret.

"Then you know practically nothing about my aunt?" pursued the self-possessed young lady.

"Only her name and address," admitted the caller. He was wondering whether Mrs. Sappleton was in the married or widowed state. An undefinable something about the room seemed to suggest masculine habitation.

"Her great tragedy happened just three years ago," said the child; "that would be since your sister's time."

"Her tragedy?" asked Framton; somehow in this restful country spot tragedies seemed out of place.

"You may wonder why we keep that window wide open on an October afternoon," said the niece, indicating a large

[1] **rectory:** the house of a clergyman in charge of a parish in the Church of England.

French window that opened on to a lawn.

"It is quite warm for the time of the year," said Framton; "but has that window got anything to do with the tragedy?"

"Out through that window, three years ago to a day, her husband and her two young brothers went off for their day's shooting. They never came back. In crossing the moor to their favorite snipe-shooting[2] ground they were all three engulfed in a treacherous piece of bog. It had been that dreadful wet summer, you know, and places that were safe in other years gave way suddenly without warning. Their bodies were never recovered. That was the dreadful part of it." Here the child's voice lost its self-possessed note and became falteringly human. "Poor aunt always thinks that they will come back some day, they and the little brown spaniel that was lost with them, and walk in at that window just as they used to do. That is why the window is kept open every evening till it is quite dusk. Poor dear aunt, she has often told me how they went out, her husband with his white waterproof coat over his arm, and Ronnie, her youngest brother, singing, 'Bertie, why do you bound?' as he always did to tease her, because she said it got on her nerves. Do you know, sometimes on still, quiet evenings like

[2] **snipe** (snīp) **-shooting:** The *snipe* is a shore bird much sought after by hunters in England.

Getting Full Meaning from Conversation. Like a play, a short story may use conversation to develop its purpose. However, since short stories are for reading rather than for actors' interpretation, readers must develop an "inner ear" to reproduce the shades of meaning and the sound of the characters' words. This story is told almost entirely by conversation, and the most important part of the story — what lies behind the conversation — is never told at all. To appreciate this story fully, try to "hear" the conversation and put together the clues to meaning.

---

this, I almost get a creepy feeling that they will all walk in through that window — "

She broke off with a little shudder. It was a relief to Framton when the aunt bustled into the room with a whirl of apologies for being late in making her appearance.

"I hope Vera has been amusing you?" she said.

"She has been very interesting," said Framton.

"I hope you don't mind the open window," said Mrs. Sappleton briskly; "my husband and brothers will be home directly from shooting, and they always come in this way. They've been out for snipe in the marshes today, so they'll make a fine mess over my poor carpets. So like you menfolk, isn't it?"

She rattled on cheerfully about the shooting and the scarcity of birds, and the prospects for duck in the winter. To Framton it was all purely horrible. He made a desperate but only partially successful effort to turn the talk on to a less ghastly topic; he was conscious that his hostess was giving him only a fragment of her attention, and her eyes were constantly straying past him to the open window and the lawn beyond. It was certainly an unfortunate coincidence that he should have paid his visit on this tragic anniversary.

"The doctors agree in ordering me complete rest, an absence of mental excitement, and avoidance of anything in the nature of violent physical exercise," announced Framton, who labored under the tolerably wide-spread delusion that total strangers and chance acquaintances are hungry for the least detail of one's ailments and infirmities, their cause and cure. "On the matter of diet they are not so much in agreement," he continued.

"No?" said Mrs. Sappleton, in a voice which only replaced a yawn at the last moment. Then she suddenly brightened into alert attention — but not to what Framton was saying.

"Here they are at last!" she cried. "Just in time for tea, and don't they look as if they were muddy up to the eyes!"

Framton shivered slightly and turned towards the niece with a look intended to convey sympathetic comprehension. The child was staring out through the open window with dazed horror in her eyes. In a chill shock of nameless fear Framton swung round in his seat and looked in the same direction.

In the deepening twilight three figures were walking across the lawn toward the window; they all carried guns under their arms, and one of them was additionally burdened with a white coat hung over his shoulders. A tired brown spaniel kept close at their heels. Noiselessly they neared the house, and then a hoarse young voice chanted out of the dusk: "I said, Bertie, why do you bound?"

Framton grabbed wildly at his stick and hat; the hall-door, the gravel-drive, and the front gate were dimly noted stages in his headlong retreat. A cyclist coming along the road had to run into the hedge to avoid imminent collision.

"Here we are, my dear," said the bearer of the white mackintosh, coming in through the window; "fairly muddy, but most of it's dry. Who was that who bolted out as we came up?"

"A most extraordinary man, a Mr. Nuttel," said Mrs. Sappleton; "could only talk about his illnesses, and dashed off without a word of good-by or apology when you arrived. One would think he had seen a ghost."

"I expect it was the spaniel," said the niece calmly; "he told me he had a horror of dogs. He was once hunted into

a cemetery somewhere on the banks of the Ganges [1] by a pack of pariah dogs,[2] and had to spend the night in a newly dug grave with the creatures snarling and grinning and foaming just above him. Enough to make anyone lose their nerve."

Romance [3] at short notice was her specialty.

[1] **Ganges** (găn′jēz): a river in India.

[2] **pariah** (på·rī′å) **dogs**: a mongrel race of half-wild dogs which act as scavengers in India.

[3] **romance**: in this sense, a falsehood or fabrication.

GETTING FULL MEANING FROM CONVERSATION

1. If a reader was not alert, the third paragraph about Framton Nuttel's sister could be confusing. When did this conversation with the sister occur in relation to the events of the story? Can you imagine the way Framton's sister would talk? For the moment, what light do her words seem to throw upon Framton's character or personality?

2. Several students might volunteer to read the conversation between Framton and Vera. At one point, Saki notes that Framton spoke in a "tone of distinct regret" (page 45). Here tone refers to voice, but the total *tone* of the story depends upon hearing all such nuances, or shades of meaning, in conversation. How should this conversation sound when read aloud?

3. Two students might read the parts of Framton and the aunt, with a third student reading the paragraph of exposition on page 46. Does the paragraph of exposition contribute to the tone the author is using in this story?

4. The situation in this story is *apparently* a mournful and depressing encounter between a widow deranged by tragedy and an ailing, infirm man. Yet, long before the last four paragraphs, an astute reader recognizes a tone not in keeping with such a doleful situation. How does the reader detect this? What clues to Saki's tone are present in the story? Begin with

the name Saki has given to his gentleman caller and develop the answer from that point on.

COMPOSITION SUGGESTION

Saki's whimsical stories often show him to be a foe of dull, unimaginative living. Through his tone and the plot in "The Open Window" Saki seems to be commenting on people and, indirectly, to be expressing an outlook on life. What is this comment, this outlook? Try to phrase Saki's attitude toward life in your own words, using as many paragraphs as necessary.

ABOUT THE AUTHOR

Hector Hugh Munro (1870–1916), although born in Burma where his Scottish father was serving in the police force, was raised after his mother's death by two English aunts who strictly regulated his life. Many of his sketches, for example "Shredni Vashtar," present a child's view of life in the company of a stern, unbending aunt. Following a one-year appointment with the Burma police, Saki worked as a foreign correspondent for the conservative London *Morning Post* from 1902 to 1908, after which he lived in England. *Reginald* (1904) established his fame as a writer of whimsical stories. The pen name Saki, taken from "The Rubáiyát" by Omar Khayyám, means "wine-bearer," or "cup-bearer," or "bringer of joy." Saki presents delightfully absurd situations through which his unorthodox characters wander irresponsibly. His children and animals, often left to their own devices, are both charmingly imaginative and shrewdly capable. "The Open Window" demonstrates Saki's mischievous and witty talent.

As the Artist Saw It

On page 47, Jack Ezra Keats has given his interpretation of the return of the hunters. The picture gives you an opportunity to do some interpreting too. Framton Nuttel is the character in the foreground. Describe the expression you imagine on Framton's face as he sees these three figures emerging from the twilight.

Death of Red Peril

WALTER D. EDMONDS

At the heart of many stories you will find a deadly conflict or a struggle. When the struggle is a contest between two caterpillars, however, you may decide that the best course is simply to sit back and relax — and enjoy the story.

Dɪᴅ ʏᴏᴜ ever hear of racing caterpillars? No? Well, it used to be a great thing on the canal. My pa used to have a lot of them insects on hand every fall, and the way he could get them to run would make a man have his eyes examined.

The way we raced caterpillars was to set them in a napkin ring on the table, one facing one way and one the other. Outside the napkin ring was drawed a circle in chalk three feet acrost. Then a man lifted the ring and the handlers was allowed one jab with a darning needle to get their caterpillars started.

The one that got outside the chalk circle the first won the race.

I remember my pa tried out a lot of breeds, and he got hold of some pretty fast steppers. But there wasn't one of them could equal Red Peril.

Pa came acrost Red Peril down in Westernville. Ma's relatives resided there, and it being Sunday, we'd all gone into church. We was riding back in a hired rig when all of a sudden Pa hollers, "Whoa!" and set the horse right down on the breeching.[1] Then he was out on the other side of the road right down in the mud, a-wropping up something in his handkerchief. "What you doing, Pa?" says Ma. "What you got there?" Pa put his handkerchief back into his inside pocket and come back over the wheel. "Leeza," he said, "I got the fastest caterpillar in seven

[1] **breeching:** part of harness that passes around the rear of a horse.

Recognizing a Mock-serious Tone. Sometimes we say an author writes "with his tongue in his cheek." What does this phrase mean? Can you imitate the look of sly innocence that it suggests? In some writing you will find this same tone. Watch for the mock-serious tone in this story.

---

counties. It's an act of Providence I seen him, the way he jumped the ruts." "It's an act of God I ain't laying dead under the back end of that horse," says Ma. "I've gone and spoilt my Sunday hat." "Never mind," says Pa; "Red Peril will earn you a new one." Just like that he named him. He was the fastest caterpillar in seven counties.

When we got back into the boat, while Ma was turning up the supper, Pa set him down to the table and pulled out the handkerchief. "You two imps stand there and there," he says to me and my sister, "and if you let him get by I'll leather the soap out of you."

So we stood there and he undid the handkerchief, and out walked one of them red, long-haired caterpillars. He walked right to the middle of the table, and there he took a short turn and put his nose on his tail and went to sleep.

"Who'd think that insect could make such a break for freedom as I seen him make?" says Pa, and he got out an empty box and filled it up with some towel and put the caterpillar inside. "He needs a rest," says Pa. "He needs to get used to his stall. When he limbers up I'll commence training him. Now, then, don't none of you say a word about him."

He got out a pipe and sat there smoking and figuring, and we could see he was studying out just how he'd make a world-beater out of that bug. Next day we hauled up the Lansing Kill Gorge.[1] Ned Kilbourne, Pa's driver, come aboard in the morning, and he took a look at that caterpillar. He took him out of the box and felt his legs and laid him down on the table and went clean over him. "Well," he says, "he don't look like a great lot, but I've

[1] **Lansing Kill Gorge:** A *kill* is a channel or stream. Here it flows through a *gorge* (gôrj), a narrow passage between steep, rocky walls.

knowed some of that red variety could chug along pretty smart." Then he touched him with a pin. It was a sudden sight.

It looked like the rear end of that caterpillar was racing the front end, but it couldn't never quite get by. Afore either Ned or Pa could get a move, Red Peril had made a turn around the sugar bowl and run solid aground in the butter dish.

Pa let out a loud swear. "Look out he don't pull a tendon," he says. "Butter's a bad thing. A man has to be careful. Jeepers, I'll handle him myself," he says, picking up Red Peril and taking him over to the stove to dry.

There was something extraordinary about that caterpillar. He was intelligent. It seemed he just couldn't abide the feel of sharp iron. It got so that if Pa reached for the lapel of his coat, Red Peril would light out. It must have been he was tender.

We was all terribly proud of that bird. Pa took to timing him on the track. He beat all known time holler. He got to know that as soon as he crossed the chalk he would get back safe in his quarters. Only when we tried sprinting him across the supper table, if he saw a piece of butter, he'd pull up short and bolt back where he come from. He had a mortal fear of butter.

Well, Pa trained him three nights. It was a sight to see him there at the table, a big man with a needle in his hand, moving the lamp around and studying out the identical spot that caterpillar wanted most to get out of the needle's way. Pretty soon he found it, and then he says to Ned, "I'll race him agin all comers at all odds." "Will," says Ned, "I guess it's safe."

Well, Pa raced him a couple of times and he won easy. Pa cleared up close to a hundred dollars in three races. That caterpillar was a mammoth wonder, and word of him got going so it was hard to race him around here.

But about that time the lock-keeper of Number One [1] came across a pretty swift article that the people around Rome [2] thought high of. And as our boat was headed down the gorge, word got ahead about Red Peril, and people began to look out for the race.

We come into Number One about four o'clock, and Pa tied up right there and went on shore with his box in his pocket and Red Peril inside the box. The lock-tender, Henry Buscerck, owned the caterpillar. Him and Pa set their caterpillars on a table for the crowd to see. Buscerck's caterpillar was a handsome brute, bright bay with black points and a short fine coat. But Pa didn't bother to look at him. Red Peril was a natural marvel, and he knew it.

Buscerck was a sly man, and he must've heard about Red Peril—right from the beginning, as it turned out; for he laid out the course in yeller chalk. They used Pa's ring, a big secondhand one he'd bought just for Red Peril. They laid out a lot of money and lifted the ring. The way Red Peril histed himself out from under would raise a man's blood pressure twenty notches. I swear you could see the hair lay down on his back. Why, the black-pointed bay was left nowhere! It didn't seem like he moved.

But Red Peril was just gathering himself for a fast finish over the line when he seen it was yeller. He reared right up; he must've thought it was butter, by jeepers, the way he whirled on his hind legs and went the way he'd

come. Pa began to get scared, and shook his needle behind Red Peril, but that caterpillar was more scared of butter than of cold steel. He passed the other insect before he got halfway to the line. But when he got to that line, danged if that caterpillar didn't shy agin and run around the circle twicet, and then it seemed like his heart had gone in on him, and he crept back to the middle of the circle and lay there hiding his head. It was the pitifullest sight a man ever looked at. You could almost hear him moaning, and he shook all over.

I've never seen a man so riled as Pa was. He picked up Red Peril and he says, "This here's no race." He picked up his money and he says, "The course was illegal with that yeller chalk." Then he squashed the other caterpillar, which was just getting ready to cross the line, and he looks at Buscerck and says, "What're you going to do about it?"

Buscerck says, "I'm going to collect my money. My caterpillar would have beat."

"If you want to call that a finish you can," says Pa, pointing to the squashed bay caterpillar, "but a baby could see he's still got to reach the line. If it was any other man owned him, I'd feel sorry I squashed him."

"You got to pay," Buscerck says. "A man can't get away with no such excuses in the city of Rome."

Pa didn't say nothing.

"I'll have you arrested for this," says Buscerck.

"All right," says Pa, "but if I ever catch you around this lock again I'll let you feel what my fist weighs."

But next morning the sheriff comes aboard and arrests Pa with a warrant and takes him afore a justice of the peace. That was old Oscar Snipe.

[1] **Number One:** the first of a series of locks.
[2] **Rome:** Rome, New York — a city situated on the Erie Canal.

"I hear you've got a good caterpillar," says the judge. "What breed is it?"

Pa says he was a red one.

"That's a good breed," says Oscar, folding his hands. "I kind of fancy the yeller ones myself. You're a connesew-er,"[1] he says to Pa, "and so'm I, and between ourselves I'd like to show you one. He's as neat a stepper as there is in this country." He fetched a box out of his back pocket and shows us a sweet little yeller one.

Pa slung his eyes on the insect which Oscar was holding, and it seemed like he'd just got an idee.

"Fast?" he says, deep down. "That thing run! Why a snail could spit in his eye."

Old Oscar come to a boil quick. "Forty dollars!" he snaps.

And Pa pays and says, "It's worth it!"

Well, we raced Red Peril nine times after that, all along the Big Ditch, and you can hear to this day — yes, sir — that there never was a caterpillar alive could run like Red Peril. Pa got rich onto him. He allowed to buy a new team in the spring. If he could only've started a breed from that bug, his fortune would have been made.

But soon the time come that comes to all caterpillars. And it goes to show that a man ought to be as careful of his enemies as he is lending money to his friends.

We was hauling down the Lansing Kill again and we'd just crossed the aqueduct[2] over Stringer Brook when the lock-keeper that minded it come out and says there was quite a lot of money being put up on a caterpillar they'd collected down in Rome.

Well, Pa went in and got out Red Peril and tried him out. He was fat and his start was a mite slower but he made great speed once he got going.

By what happened after, we might have known that we'd meet up with that caterpillar at Number One Lock; but there wasn't a sign of Buscerck, and Pa was so excited at racing Red Peril again that I doubt if he noticed where he was at all.

"Who owns this-here caterpillar I've been hearing about?" Pa asks. "Where is he? Why don't he bring out his pore contraption?"

A feller says he's in the shanty.

"What's his name?" asks Pa.

"Martin Henry's running him. He's called the Horned Demon of Rome."

"Dinged if I ever thought to see him at my time of life," says Pa, and he goes in. When he entered the shanty the men there let out a great howdy, and when Pa put down Red Peril's box on the table, they give a mammoth shout and crowded around. And well they might when Red Peril climbed out. Yes, sir!

You can tell that caterpillar's a thoroughbred. He's shining right down to the foot of each hair. He's round, but he ain't too fat. He don't look as supple as he used to, but the folks can't tell that.

Pa waited for the admiration to die down, and then he lays out his money, and says to Martin Henry, "Let's see your ring-boned swivel-hocked imitation of a bug."

Martin answers, "Well, he ain't much to look at, maybe, but you'll be surprised to see him push along."

And he lays down the dangest lump of worm you ever set your eyes on. It's the kind of insect a man might expect

---

[1] **connesewer:** he means *connoisseur* (kŏn'-ĭ-sûr'), a person who is competent to judge critically.

[2] **aqueduct** (ăk'wê·dŭkt): a structure for conveying a canal over a river or a hollow. Note the two parts of this word: *aque*, from the Latin *aqua* (water) and *duct*, from *ductus*, a form of the Latin verb *ducere* (to lead).

to see in a furrin' [1] land. It's about two and a half inches long and stands only half a thumbnail at the shoulder. It's green and hairless as an egg, and it crouches down squinting around at Red Peril. It ain't natural nor refined to look at such a bug, let alone race it.

The crowd didn't say much, having more money on the race than ever before: so much money that even Pa commenced to be serious. Well, they put 'em in the ring together, and Red Peril kept over his side with a sort of intelligent dislike. He was the brainiest article in the caterpillar line I ever knowed. The other one just hunkered down with a mean look in his eyes.

The ring come off, and Pa and Martin Henry sunk their needles — at least they almost sunk them — for just then them standing close to the course seen that Horned Demon sink his horns into the back end of Red Peril. If a needle made him start, you can think what them two horns did for him. He cleared twelve inches in one jump, but then he sot right down, trembling.

"Foul," yells Pa, "my 'pillar's fouled."

But it wasn't allowed. The Horned Demon commenced walking to the circle — he couldn't move much faster than a barrel can roll uphill, but he was getting there. We all seen then that Red Peril was dying and we was losing the race. Pa stood there kind of foamy in his beard, and the water running right out of both eyes. It's an awful thing to see a big man cry in public. But Ned saved us. He figured, with the money he had on him, he'd make him win if he could.

He leans over Red Peril's ear, and he shouts:

"My Cripus, you've gone and dropped the butter!"

Something got into that caterpillar's

[1] furrin': foreign.

brain, dying as he was, and he let out the smallest squeak of hollering fright I ever listened to a caterpillar make. There was a convulsion got into him, and he gave a bound. My holy! How that caterpillar did rise up. When he come down again, he was stone dead, but he lay with his chin across the line. He'd won the race. The Horned Demon was only halfway to the line. . . .

Well, we won. But I think Pa's heart was busted by the squeal he heard Red Peril make when he died. He couldn't abide Ned's face after that, though he knowed Ned had saved the day for him. But he put Red Peril's carcase in his pocket with the money and walked out.

And there he seen Buscerck standing at the sluices.[2] Pa looked at him. The sheriff was alongside Buscerck and Oscar Snipe on the other side.

"Who owns the Horned Demon?" says Pa.

"Me," says Buscerck with a sneer. "He may have lost, but he done a good job doing it."

Pa walks right up to him.

"I've got another forty dollars in my pocket," he says, and he hit him hard.

Buscerck's boots showed a minute. Pretty soon they let down the water [3] and pulled him out. The sheriff was worried. He says to Oscar Snipe, "Had I ought to arrest Will?" (Meaning Pa.)

Oscar was a sporting man. He couldn't abide low dealing. He looks at Buscerck there, and says, "Water never hurt a man. It keeps his hide from cracking."

So they let Pa alone. I guess they

[2] sluices (slōōs'ĕz): artificial passages for water, fitted with valves or gates for stopping or regulating the flow (as in canal locks).

[3] let down the water: regulated the locks so as to lower the water.

didn't think it was safe to have a man in jail who would cry about a caterpillar. But then they hadn't lived alongside of Red Peril like us.

RECOGNIZING A MOCK–SERIOUS TONE

1. Have you ever noticed that the training and care of horses is discussed with great seriousness? A veritable folklore has also developed concerning the intelligence, loyalty, and courage of horses. In "Death of Red Peril" can you find a similar outlook applied to caterpillars? How seriously do the canallers take caterpillar racing? Is the author equally serious?

2. What purpose does the speech of the canallers serve? If they spoke standard, conventional English, would the tone of the story be improved or weakened? Try several passages to test your answer.

3. Consider the plot of this story, with its build-up of complications and suspense, as carefully developed as any story about a race in the Olympics. How does this fact contribute to the tone of the story? Explain the discrepancy between the serious deadpan presentation and the author's actual intention.

4. Death scenes in literature are usually intended to be moving and serious. Does the author intend you to be moved by the last moments of Red Peril? Did this scene bring tears to your eyes? Why or why not?

GAINING POWER OVER WORDS

To gain real power from language — power in communicating with others, in thinking, and in enjoying literature — we must learn to exercise power *over* language. We must know specifically what our words stand for; we must learn to use words accurately, and also to detect the different ways in which words are used. This power over words comes largely from experience, and a sizable part of this experience comes from reading. Writers employ larger vocabularies than most of our acquaintances. They also tend to use words more precisely and more colorfully.

Throughout this book you will find special sections, like this one, called "Gaining Power over Words." Each of these brief language studies — whether on Word Building or Figures of Speech or Levels of Usage — is related directly to the story, article, or play that precedes it. In the case of "Death of Red Peril," we will examine the way in which the author used language to achieve humorous effects.

USING WORDS HUMOROUSLY Some of the fun in "Death of Red Peril" rises from the language of the story. Surprising comparisons represent one source of humor. On page 53 we read: "It's green and hairless as an egg, and it crouches down squinting around at Red Peril. It ain't natural nor refined to look at such a bug, let alone race it." Make a list of other comparisons or descriptions, like this one, which add to the humor of the story.

Another source of humor may be found in the colorful and imaginative language of the canallers. For instance, we read that the rival caterpillar "just hunkered down with a mean look in his eyes." Point out other places in the story where the language conveys its meaning with the aptness and humor of *hunkered*?

Unless you are yourself aware of the difference between standard English that is generally acceptable and the strongly flavored rough speech of the canallers, you may miss some of the humor. Point to places in the story where the uneducated speech of the characters made you smile?

ABOUT THE AUTHOR

Walter D. Edmonds (1903–), except for that portion of each year spent in school, lived on a farm in upstate New York. As a student at Harvard, he specialized in English and decided to make writing a career when his first story was accepted for publication. Edmonds' first novel about the Erie Canal country, *Rome Haul* (1929), was later dramatized into the play and motion picture, *The Farmer Takes a Wife*. *Drums Along the Mohawk* (1936) established him as an exceptionally fine writer of historical novels. *The Matchlock Gun* (1941) won the Newbery Medal in 1942 as the outstanding American novel for young people. Edmonds uses New York State as the setting for his stories, and the era of the building of the Erie Canal is his special period.

A Slander

ANTON CHEKHOV

In this, as in many of Chekhov's stories, the characters create their own misfortunes through inept bungling. Here, it is a teacher, Sergei Kapitonich Ahineev (sĕr·gyā′ kȧ·pĭ·tôn′yĭch ȧ·ēn′yĕf), who gets himself into trouble. Notice the detached tone of the author, who writes as if he were a scientist observing life under a microscope.

Sᴇʀɢᴇɪ Kᴀᴘɪᴛᴏɴɪᴄʜ Aʜɪɴᴇᴇᴠ, the writing master, was marrying his daughter to the teacher of history and geography. The wedding festivities were going off most successfully. In the drawing room there was singing, playing, and dancing. Waiters hired from the club were flitting distractedly about the rooms, dressed in black swallowtails and dirty white ties. There was a continual hubbub and din of conversation. Sitting side by side on the sofa, the teacher of mathematics, the French teacher, and the junior assessor of taxes were talking hurriedly and interrupting one another as they described to the guests cases of persons being buried alive, and gave their opinions on spiritualism. None of them believed in spiritualism, but all admitted that there were many things in this world which would always be beyond the mind of man. In the next room the literature master was explaining to the visitors the cases in which a sentry has the right to fire on passersby. The subjects, as you perceive, were alarming, but very agreeable. Persons whose social position precluded them from entering were looking in at the windows from the yard.

Detecting Irony. Irony is a form of expression that involves contrast. It exists in a statement when there is a contrast between what is said and what is really meant. For example, when a person says "You're a fine friend" to someone who has proved himself quite the opposite, he is using irony. In somewhat the same way, there is irony in a situation when what actually happens is the opposite of what appears to be happening or of what was expected. Watch for the enormous gap between appearance and reality in this story — what the main character *thinks* is happening and what really is happening. Afterward you will have a chance to discuss irony.

Just at midnight the master of the house went into the kitchen to see whether everything was ready for supper. The kitchen from floor to ceiling was filled with fumes composed of goose, duck, and many other odors. On two tables the accessories, the drinks and light refreshments, were set out in artistic disorder. The cook, Marfa, a red-faced woman whose figure was like a barrel with a belt around it, was bustling about the tables.

"Show me the sturgeon,[1] Marfa," said Ahineev, rubbing his hands and licking his lips. "What a perfume! I could eat up the whole kitchen. Come, show me the sturgeon."

Marfa went up to one of the benches and cautiously lifted a piece of greasy newspaper. Under the paper on an immense dish there reposed a huge sturgeon, masked in jelly and decorated with capers,[2] olives, and carrots. Ahineev gazed at the sturgeon and gasped. His face beamed, he turned his eyes up. He bent down and with his lips emitted the sound of an ungreased wheel. After standing a moment he snapped his fingers with delight, and once more smacked his lips.

"Ah-ah! the sound of a passionate kiss. . . . Who is it you're kissing out there, little Marfa?" came a voice from the next room, and in the doorway there appeared the cropped head of the assistant usher,[3] Vankin. "Who is it? A-a-h! . . . Delighted to meet you! Sergei Kapitonich! You're a fine grandfather, I must say!"

"I'm not kissing," said Ahineev in confusion. "Who told you so, you fool? I was only . . . I smacked my lips . . . in reference to . . . as an indication of . . . pleasure . . . at the sight of the fish."

"Tell that to the marines!" The intrusive face vanished, wearing a broad grin.

Ahineev flushed.

"Hang it!" he thought, "the beast will go now and talk scandal. He'll disgrace me to all the town, the brute."

Ahineev went timidly into the drawing room and looked stealthily round for Vankin. Vankin was standing by the piano, and, bending down with a jaunty air, was whispering something to the inspector's sister-in-law, who was laughing.

"Talking about me!" thought Ahineev. "About me, blast him! And she believes it . . . believes it! She laughs! Mercy on us! No, I can't let it pass . . . I can't. I must do something to prevent his being believed. . . . I'll speak to them all, and he'll be shown up for a fool and a gossip."

Ahineev scratched his head, and still overcome with embarrassment, went up to the French teacher.

"I've just been in the kitchen to see after the supper," he said to the Frenchman. "I know you are fond of fish, and I've a sturgeon, my dear fellow, beyond everything! A yard and a half long! Ha, ha, ha! And, by the way . . . I was just forgetting. . . . In the kitchen just now, with that sturgeon . . . quite a little story! I went into the kitchen just now and wanted to look at the supper dishes. I looked at the sturgeon and I smacked my lips with relish . . . at the piquancy[4] of it. And at the very moment that fool Vankin came in and

[1] **sturgeon** (stûr'jŭn): a large fish, considered a delicacy.

[2] **capers**: pickled flower buds and young berries of a Mediterranean shrub.

[3] **assistant usher**: in a European school, an usher is an assistant teacher; thus, an assistant usher would occupy a position of very minor importance in scholastic circles.

[4] **piquancy** (pē'kǎn·sĭ): an agreeable sharpness or spiciness. In this case, it is referring to the sight and smell of a favorite food.

said: . . . 'Ha, ha, ha! . . . So you're kissing here!' Kissing Marfa, the cook! What a thing to imagine, silly fool! The woman is a perfect fright, like all the beasts put together, and he talks about kissing! Queer fish!"

"Who's a queer fish?" asked the mathematics teacher, coming up.

"Why he, over there — Vankin! I went into the kitchen . . ."

And he told the story of Vankin. ". . . He amused me, queer fish! I'd rather kiss a dog than Marfa, if you ask me," added Ahineev. He looked round and saw behind him the junior assessor of taxes.

"We were talking of Vankin," he said. "Queer fish, he is! He went into the kitchen, saw me beside Marfa, and began inventing all sorts of silly stories. 'Why are you kissing?' he says. He must have had a drop too much. 'And I'd rather kiss a turkeycock than Marfa,' I said, 'And I've a wife of my own, you fool,' said I. He did amuse me!"

"Who amused you?" asked the priest who taught Scripture in the school, going up to Ahineev.

"Vankin. I was standing in the kitchen, you know, looking at the sturgeon. . . ."

And so on. Within half an hour or so all the guests knew the incident of the sturgeon and Vankin.

"Let him tell away now!" thought Ahineev, rubbing his hands. "Let him! He'll begin telling his story and they'll say to him at once, 'Enough of your improbable nonsense, you fool, we know all about it!'"

And Ahineev was so relieved that in his joy he drank four glasses too many. After escorting the young people to their room, he went to bed and slept like an innocent babe, and next day he thought no more of the incident with the sturgeon. But, alas! man proposes, but God disposes. An evil tongue did its evil work, and Ahineev's strategy was of no avail. Just a week later — to be precise, on Wednesday after the third lesson — when Ahineev was standing in the middle of the teachers' room, holding forth on the vicious propensities [1] of a boy called Visekin, the headmaster went up to him and drew him aside:

"Look here, Sergei Kapitonich," said the headmaster, "you must excuse me. . . . It's not my business; but all the same I must make you realize. . . . It's my duty. You see, there are rumors that you are romancing with that . . . cook. . . . It's nothing to do with me, but . . . flirt with her, kiss her . . . as you please, but don't let it be so public, please. I entreat you! Don't forget that you're a schoolmaster."

Ahineev turned cold and faint. He went home like a man stung by a whole swarm of bees, like a man scalded with boiling water. As he walked home, it seemed to him that the whole town was looking at him as though he were smeared with pitch. At home fresh trouble awaited him.

"Why aren't you gobbling up your food as usual?" his wife asked him at dinner. "What are you so pensive about? Brooding over your amours? [2] Pining for your Marfa? I know all about it, Mohammedan! [3] Kind friends have opened my eyes! O-o-o! . . . you savage!"

And she slapped him in the face. He got up from the table, not feeling the

[1] **propensities** (prŏ·pĕn′sĭ·tĭz): inclinations or tendencies in a person.

[2] **amours** (á·mōōrz′): love affairs.

[3] **Mohammedan** (mŏ·hăm′ĕ·dăn): a follower of the religious leader, Mohammed. According to the laws of the Mohammedans, a man could have more than one wife.

earth under his feet, and without his hat or coat, made his way to Vankin. He found him at home.

"You scoundrel!" he addressed him. "Why have you covered me with mud before all the town? Why did you set this slander going about me?"

"What slander? What are you talking about?"

"Who was it gossiped of my kissing Marfa? Wasn't it you? Tell me that. Wasn't it you, you brigand?"

Vankin blinked and twitched in every fiber of his battered countenance, raised his eyes to the icon [1] and articulated, "God blast me! Strike me blind and lay me out, if I said a single word about you! May I be left without house and home, may I be stricken with worse than cholera!" [2]

Vankin's sincerity did not admit of doubt. It was evidently not he who was the author of the slander.

"But who, then, who?" Ahineev wondered, going over all his acquaintances in his mind and beating himself on the breast. "Who, then?"

[1] icon (ī′kŏn): sacred image or picture.
[2] cholera (kŏl′ẽr·à): a dreaded disease, usually fatal.

DETECTING IRONY

The word *irony* occurs over and over again in people's descriptions of literature. A writer is said to have an "ironical tone," or a story is said to be "heavy with irony." Just what does the word mean? Here is an example of irony: King Midas thought he would be happy if everything he touched should turn to gold — until his wish was granted and he touched his beloved daughter. When we learn that some exceedingly wealthy person has won the lottery prize at a charity bazaar, we say, "Isn't that ironic?" We sense the meaning of irony, too, in the story of the South American Indians who in the old days of conquest turned on their tormentors,

the greedy, gold-hungry Spaniards, and poured molten gold down their throats.

Now look again for irony in "A Slander." Here are some questions to direct your thinking:

1. At the beginning of the story we meet a family on a joyous occasion that should foster only happiness and harmony. Actually the wedding celebration brings about something quite different. What actually does happen? Why is this outcome ironic?
2. What irony is to be found in the final paragraph?
3. Life is full of ironical situations and happenings. Try to recall and describe a personal experience that would be considered ironical.

THINKING IT OVER

1. What were the facts of the case when Vankin came into the kitchen? What do you think was the real intent of his remarks to Ahineev?
2. What confused understanding of Vankin's remarks and later actions made Ahineev think it necessary to tell each of the guests his side of the story?
3. In talking with others to explain Vankin's "story," what explanation does Ahineev suggest for Vankin's telling such a "story"?
4. How does he make matters worse? By what steps does he finally bring about the thing he fears?
5. Why is this story humorous even though it has many of the elements of a tragic situation? What could be done to switch the tone from humorous to tragic?

Chekhov as Dramatist ➤

The photographs on the opposite page show scenes from three Chekhov plays: *The Three Sisters* (top left), *Uncle Vanya* (top right), and *The Cherry Orchard*. Notice the animation in the faces of most of the characters. Though Chekhov's writing contains much sadness, his superior ability as a dramatist enabled him to add touches of humor and gentle irony to the most tragic of subjects.

GAINING POWER OVER WORDS

PREFIXES *Prefixes* are fragments of words, small beginnings which can be added to other words. Prefixes are tremendously useful to us in speaking because they make it possible for us to express our thoughts with fewer words. In "A Slander" we read that the refreshments in the kitchen were spread about in *disorder.* The prefix *dis–* can indicate the "opposite of a quality" or "taking away the quality of." Thus, in a single word we can express the opposite of *order* merely by adding *dis–.* Later in the story Ahineev says of Vankin, "He'll *disgrace* me to all the town." Here, by simply combining the prefix *dis–* with *grace,* Ahineev is saying that grace, or honor, will be taken away from him.

Your dictionary will give several different shades of meaning for the prefix *dis–.* List at least three of these meanings with examples of their use in words.

Other prefixes you will find helpful to know are these:

super– which means "above" or "over" as in *supervise, superimpose, supernatural, superintendent*

trans– which means "across," "beyond," or "through" as in *transfer, transmit, transact, translate, transition*

auto– which means "self" as in *automatic, automobile, autonomous*

per– which means "throughout" or "completely" as in *permeate, permit, persist, persevere, percolate, perforate*

bi– which means "two" or "twice" as in *biennial, bifocal, bilateral, bisect*

ABOUT THE AUTHOR

Anton Chekhov (1860–1904), the son of a liberated serf, was born in Taganrog on the Sea of Azov. He deserted his chosen profession of medicine in favor of writing when his first volume of stories received favorable acclaim. An atmosphere of sadness and futility pervades many of his stories; for he often portrayed poverty, dishonesty, misery, and humility in the lives of his characters. Although his fame rested mainly on his short stories, Chekhov wrote several very famous plays including *The Three Sisters* and *The Cherry Orchard.* "A Slander" is an example of Chekhov's irony and satire; however, few of his stories — of which there are more than 1,000 — are written with so light a touch.

Speaking of Tone

Long before they learn words, babies understand the tone of their parents' voices. They know the inflections which mean love, or anger, or playfulness. Readers, too, learn to detect tone, to understand an author's feeling toward his subject.

What are some of the clues to tone in literature? Consciously or unconsciously, you have been employing such clues in reading Saki, Edmonds, and Chekhov. Can you now identify some of them, listing them in your notebooks or on the chalkboard?

If you read a short story with appreciation you enter partially into the mind of the author and view the world through his eyes. In "The Open Window" you saw

Framton Nuttel as Saki saw him. You learned that he was nervous, inclined to dwell on his own illnesses, and preoccupied mainly with Framton Nuttel. True. But you also saw Framton with that particular brand of witty amusement which was an essential part of Saki's outlook on life. Here was the "feel" of this author's way of thinking, that special tone — contemptuous of sodden, unimaginative living — which belongs to Saki and to no other writer. By reading more of Saki's stories, you can easily check your impression of his personality. Of course, the same is true for other writers. The way to determine the characteristic tone or attitude of any author is to read as many of his stories as possible.

Setting

Have you noticed that, unlike novels, short stories do not include extras? They rarely introduce more than one or two major characters. They never describe a long and complicated series of happenings taking place over a considerable length of time. Because a short story *is* short, the writer must limit the plot to a few incidents. Everything is concentrated on producing a single impression on the reader.

This necessity to avoid anything extra pertains also to the *setting* in which a story is placed. A description of the location of a story or its atmosphere or background *must be necessary* or the author should leave it out. In some stories setting is more important than in others; compare, for instance, the first two stories in this book. A few words quickly indicated the minimum setting needed for "Four and Twenty Blackbirds"; but in the untitled story the plot depended upon the author's ability to create in our minds a vision of a modern city's towering skyscrapers.

A writer tries to create a certain impression on the reader's mind or feelings. In turn, the reader tries to obtain the impression intended by the writer. All the elements of a story are skillfully interwoven by the author to create the desired effect. You must not separate these elements, even though in this book we focus on one at a time for purposes of study and learning. Remember this advice as you read the three stories that follow. Try to see how the setting of each story serves the author's purpose. The South Seas, a hospital, and a corridor of gloomy burial vaults beneath an ancient Italian palace — each of these settings plays a necessary part in the author's plan.

Short stories, with their various settings, can take you anywhere in the world.

The Heathen

JACK LONDON

Each of us has his own destiny, and in its fulfillment a few people will have leading roles. When he boarded the schooner for Tahiti, the pearl trader in this story barely noticed the native sailors on board. Little did he realize that one of the natives was to become the most memorable person he would ever meet.

I MET HIM first in a hurricane; and though we had gone through the hurricane on the same schooner, it was not until the schooner had gone to pieces under us that I first laid eyes on him. Without doubt I had seen him with the rest of the kanaka [1] crew on board, but I had not consciously been aware of his existence, for the *Petite*

[1] **kanaka** (kȧ·năk'ȧ): a South Sea Islander.

Jeanne [2] was rather overcrowded. In addition to her eight or ten kanaka seamen, her white captain, mate, and supercargo, [3] and her six cabin passengers, she sailed from Rangiroa [4] with something like eighty-five deck passengers — Paumotans [5] and Tahitians, [6] men, women, and children each with a trade box,

[2] *Petite Jeanne* (pē·tēt' zhän).

[3] **supercargo:** an officer in a merchant ship whose duty it is to manage the trading matters of the voyage.

[4] **Rangiroa** (räng·ė·rō'ȧ): one of the French Tuamotu (tōō'ä·mō'tōō) Islands located at just about the mid-point in the South Pacific between Australia and the South American coast.

[5] **Paumotans** (pä'ōō·mō'tȧnz): name given to inhabitants of the Tuamotu Islands, which were formerly called Paumotu.

[6] **Tahitians** (tä·hē'tĭ·ȧnz): name given to inhabitants of Tahiti (tä·hē'tė), one of the Society Islands.

Visualizing Setting. Jack London knew the Pacific Ocean and the South Sea Islands. As you read his powerful descriptions, let his words strike your imagination. Visualize each detail in his descriptions so that you, too, can see the sun shining on the ship's deck and the salt spray breaking against the ship. If you use your imagination, your other senses can be brought into play as well. You may find that you can hear the break of the waves, smell and taste the salty spray, and feel the hot tropical sun on your back. Decide for yourself what it is in Jack London's writing that brings so much life and color to the settings of his stories.

to say nothing of sleeping-mats, blankets, and clothes-bundles.

The pearling season in the Paumotus was over, and all hands were returning to Tahiti.

It had been a prosperous season. Not one of us had cause for complaint, nor one of the eighty-five deck passengers either. All had done well, and all were looking forward to a rest-off and a good time in Papeete.[1]

Of course, the *Petite Jeanne* was overloaded. She was only seventy tons, and she had no right to carry a tithe[2] of the mob she had on board. Beneath her hatches she was crammed and jammed with pearl-shell and copra.[3] Even the trade room was packed full with shell. It was a miracle that the sailors could work her. There was no moving about the decks. They simply climbed back and forth along the rails.

In the night-time they walked upon the sleepers, who carpeted the deck, I'll swear, two deep. Oh! and there were pigs and chickens on deck, and sacks of yams, while every conceivable place was festooned with strings of drinking coconuts and bunches of bananas. On both sides, between the fore and main shrouds,[4] guys[5] had been stretched, just low enough for the foreboom to swing clear; and from each of these guys at least fifty bunches of bananas were suspended.

It promised to be a messy passage, even if we did make it in the two or

three days that would have been required if the southeast trades[6] had been blowing fresh. But they weren't blowing fresh. After the first five hours the trade died away in a dozen or so gasping fans. The calm continued all that night and the next day — one of those glaring, glassy calms when the very thought of opening one's eyes to look at it is sufficient to cause a headache.

The second day a man died — an Easter Islander, one of the best divers that season in the lagoon. Smallpox — that is what it was; though how smallpox could come on board, when there had been no known cases ashore when we left Rangiroa, is beyond me. There it was, though — smallpox, a man dead, and three others down on their backs.

That next day there were two deaths; the following day three; then it jumped to eight. It was curious to see how we took it. The natives, for instance, fell into a condition of dumb, stolid fear. The captain — Oudouse,[7] his name was, a Frenchman — became very nervous and voluble. He actually got the twitches. He was a large, fleshy man, weighing at least two hundred pounds, and he quickly became a faithful representation of a quivering jelly-mountain of fat.

It was a pretty time. The sun, going into northern declination, was straight overhead. There was no wind, except for frequent squalls, which blew fiercely for from five minutes to half an hour, and wound up by deluging us with rain. After each squall, the awful sun would come out, drawing clouds of steam from the soaked decks.

At the end of the week, I happened

[1] **Papeete** (pä·pâ·ā′tâ): capital city of French possessions in the South Pacific, located on Tahiti.

[2] **tithe** (tīth): a tenth part, or loosely, a small part.

[3] **copra** (kŏp′rá): dried coconut meat from which coconut oil is taken.

[4] **shrouds** (shroudz): ropes of hemp or wire leading, usually in pairs, from a ship's masthead to give lateral support to the masts.

[5] **guys** (gīz): ropes which hold in place the end of a boom, spar, or yard.

[6] **trades:** trade winds, drying winds blowing almost continually in the same course toward the equator from an easterly direction.

[7] **Oudouse** (ōō·dōōz′).

to glance at the barometer that hung in the cabin companionway. Its normal register in the Paumotus was 29.90, and it was quite customary to see it vacillate between 29.85 and 30.00, or even 30.05; but to see it as I saw it, down to 29.62, was sufficient to sober the most drunken pearl-buyer.

I called Captain Oudouse's attention to it, only to be informed that he had watched it going down for several hours. There was little to do, but that little he did very well, considering the circumstances. He took off the light sails, shortened right down to storm canvas, spread life-lines, and waited for the wind. His mistake lay in what he did after the wind came. He hove to on the port tack,[1] which was the right thing to do south of the Equator, if — and there was the rub — if one were *not* in the direct path of the hurricane.

We were in the direct path. I could see that by the steady increase of the wind and the equally steady fall of the barometer. I wanted him to turn and run with the wind on the port quarter until the barometer ceased falling, and then to heave to. We argued till he was reduced to hysteria, but budge he would not. The worst of it was that I could not get the rest of the pearl-buyers to back me up. Who was I, anyway, to know more about the sea and its ways than a properly qualified captain?

/ Of course the sea rose with the wind frightfully; /and I shall never forget the first three seas[2] the *Petite Jeanne* shipped.[3] She had fallen off, as vessels do at times when hove to, and the first sea made a clean breach. The life-lines were only for the strong and well, and

little good were they even for them when the women and children, the bananas and coconuts, the pigs and trade boxes, the sick and the dying, were swept along in a solid, screeching, groaning mass.

The second sea filled the *Petite Jeanne's* decks flush with the rails; and, as her stern sank down and her bow tossed skyward, all the miserable dunnage[4] of life and luggage poured aft. It was a human torrent. They came head-first, feet-first, sidewise, rolling over and over, twisting, squirming, writhing, and crumpling up. Now and again one caught a grip on a stanchion[5] or a rope; but the weight of the bodies behind tore such grips lose.

The third sea — the biggest of the three — did not do so much damage. By the time it arrived nearly everybody was in the rigging. On deck perhaps a dozen gasping, half-drowned, and half-stunned wretches were rolling about or attempting to crawl into safety. They went by the board, as did the wreckage of the two remaining boats. The other pearl-buyers and myself, between seas, managed to get about fifteen women and children into the cabin, and battened down.[6] Little good it did the poor creatures in the end.

Wind? Out of all my experience I could not have believed it possible for the wind to blow as it did. There is no describing it. How can one describe a nightmare? It was the same way with that wind. It tore the clothes off our bodies. I say *tore them off*, and I mean it. It was a monstrous thing, and the

[1] **hove to on the port tack:** trimmed the ship's sails so that she turned toward the left.
[2] **seas:** in this sense, heavy swells or waves.
[3] **shipped:** took water over the side.

[4] **dunnage** (dŭn′ĭj): baggage or personal effects; so called by sailors. Here it means a general confusion.
[5] **stanchion** (stăn′shŭn): an upright bar for support on a ship's deck.
[6] **battened down:** clamped down the hatch-covers (coverings for the openings in a ship's deck which lead down to the living or storage quarters).

most monstrous thing about it was that it increased and continued to increase.

Imagine countless millions and billions of tons of sand. Imagine this sand tearing along at ninety, a hundred, a hundred and twenty, or any other number of miles per hour. Imagine, further, this sand to be invisible, impalpable,[1] yet to retain all the weight and density of sand. Do all this, and you may get a vague inkling of what that wind was like.

The sea, which had risen at first, was beaten down by that wind. More: it seemed as if the whole ocean had been sucked up in the maw[2] of the hurricane, and hurled on through that portion of space which previously had been occupied by the air.

The situation really would have been favorable had we not been in the path of the storm. True, the wind itself tore our canvas out of the gaskets,[3] jerked out our topmasts, and made a raffle of our running-gear, but still we would have come through nicely had we not been square in front of the advancing storm-center. That was what fixed us. I was in a state of stunned, numbed, paralyzed collapse from enduring the impact of the wind, and I think I was just about ready to give up and die when the center smote us. The blow we received was an absolute lull. The effect on one was sickening.

Remember that for hours we had been at terrific muscular tension, withstanding the awful pressure of that wind. And then, suddenly, the pressure was removed. I know that I felt as though I was about to expand, to fly apart in all directions. It seemed as if

every atom composing my body was repelling every other atom and was on the verge of rushing off irresistibly into space. But that lasted only for a moment. Destruction was upon us.

In the absence of the wind and pressure the sea rose. It jumped, it leaped, it soared straight toward the clouds. Remember, from every point of the compass that inconceivable wind was blowing in toward the center of calm. The result was that the seas sprang up from every point of the compass. There was no wind to check them. They popped up like corks released from the bottom of a pail of water. There was no system to them, no stability. They were hollow, maniacal[4] seas. They were eighty feet high at least. They were not seas at all. They resembled no sea a man had ever seen.

They were splashes, monstrous splashes — that is all. Splashes that were eighty feet high. Eighty! They were more than eighty. They went over our mastheads. They were spouts, explosions. They were drunken. They fell anywhere, anyhow. They jostled one another; they collided. They rushed together and collapsed upon one another, or fell apart like a thousand waterfalls all at once. It was no ocean any man had ever dreamed of, that hurricane center. It was confusion thrice confounded. It was anarchy.[5] It was a hell-pit of sea-water gone mad.

The *Petite Jeanne?* I don't know. The heathen told me afterwards that he did not know. She was literally torn apart, ripped wide open, smashed into kindling wood, annihilated. When I came to I was in the water, swimming automatically, though I was about two-

[1] impalpable (ĭm·păl′pȧ·b'l): extremely fine so that no grit could be felt.
[2] maw (mô): jaws; used especially as a symbol of a devouring appetite.
[3] gaskets: bands or lines used to fasten a furled sail securely.

[4] maniacal (mȧ·nī′ȧ·kăl): characterized by madness.
[5] anarchy (ăn′ȧr·kĭ): complete absence of any regulating power; complete disorder.

thirds drowned. How I got there I had no recollection. I remembered seeing the *Petite Jeanne* fly to pieces at what must have been the instant that my own consciousness was buffeted out of me. But there I was, with nothing to do but make the best of it, and in that best there was little promise. The wind was blowing again, the sea was much smaller and more regular, and I knew that I had passed through the center. Fortunately, there were no sharks about. The hurricane had dissipated the ravenous horde that had surrounded the death ship and fed off the dead.

It was about midday when the *Petite Jeanne* went to pieces, and it must have been two hours afterwards when I picked up with one of her hatch-covers. Thick rain was driving at the time; and it was the merest chance that flung me and the hatch-cover together. A short length of line was trailing from the rope handle; and I knew that I was good for a day, at least, if the sharks did not return. Three hours later, possibly a little longer, sticking close to the cover, and, with closed eyes, concentrating my whole soul upon the task of breathing in enough air to keep me going and at the same time of avoiding breathing in enough water to drown me, it seemed to me that I heard voices. The rain had

ceased, and wind and sea were easing marvelously. Not twenty feet away from me, on another hatch-cover, were Captain Oudouse and the heathen. They were fighting over the possession of the cover — at least, the Frenchman was.

"*Païen noir!*"[1] I heard him scream, and at the same time I saw him kick the kanaka.

Now, Captain Oudouse had lost all his clothes, except his shoes, and they were heavy brogans.[2] It was a cruel blow, for it caught the heathen on the mouth and the point of the chin, half stunning him. I looked for him to retaliate, but he contented himself with swimming about forlornly a safe ten feet away. Whenever a fling of the sea threw him closer, the Frenchman, hanging on with his hands, kicked out at him with both feet. Also, at the moment of delivering each kick, he called the kanaka a black heathen.

"For two centimes[3] I'd come over there and drown you, you white beast!" I yelled.

The only reason I did not go was that I felt too tired. The very thought of the effort to swim over was nauseating. So I called to the kanaka to come to me, and proceeded to share the hatch-cover with him. Otoo, he told me his name was (pronounced ō-tō-ō); also, he told me that he was a native of Bora Bora, the most westerly of the Society Group. As I learned afterward, he had got the hatch-cover first, and, after some time, encountering Captain Oudouse, had offered to share it with him, and had been kicked off for his pains.

[1] *Païen noir* (pä·yĕn′ nwär): French for "Black heathen!"
[2] **brogans** (brō′gănz): coarse, heavy shoes.
[3] **centimes** (sän·tēmz′): A *centime* is a very small unit in French currency, equal to a fraction of a penny in U.S. currency.

And that was how Otoo and I first came together. He was no fighter. He was all sweetness and gentleness, a love-creature, though he stood nearly six feet tall and was muscled like a gladiator. He was no fighter, but he was also no coward. He had the heart of a lion; and in the years that followed I have seen him run risks that I would never dream of taking. What I mean is that while he was no fighter, and while he always avoided precipitating a row, he never ran away from trouble when it started. And it was " 'Ware shoal!" [1] when once Otoo went into action. I shall never forget what he did to Bill King. It occurred in German Somoa. Bill King was hailed the champion heavyweight of the American Navy. He was a big brute of a man, a veritable gorilla, one of those hard-hitting, roughhousing chaps, and clever with his fists as well. He picked the quarrel, and he kicked Otoo twice and struck him once before Otoo felt it necessary to fight. I don't think it lasted four minutes, at the end of which time Bill King was the unhappy possessor of four broken ribs, a broken forearm, and a dislocated shoulder-blade. Otoo knew nothing of scientific boxing. He was merely a manhandler; and Bill King was something like three months in recovering from the bit of manhandling he received that afternoon on Apia beach.

But I am running ahead of my yarn. We shared the hatch-cover between us. We took turn and turn about, one lying flat on the cover and resting, while the other, submerged to the neck, merely held on with his hands. For two days and nights, spell and spell, on the cover and in the water, we drifted over the

ocean. Toward the last I was delirious most of the time; and there were times, too, when I heard Otoo babbling and raving in his native tongue. Our continuous immersion prevented us from dying of thirst, though the sea-water and the sunshine gave us the prettiest imaginable combination of salt pickle and sunburn.

In the end, Otoo saved my life; for I came to lying on the beach twenty feet from the water, sheltered from the sun by a couple of coconut leaves. No one but Otoo could have dragged me there and stuck up the leaves for shade. He was lying beside me. I went off again; and the next time I came round, it was cool and starry night, and Otoo was pressing a drinking coconut to my lips.

We were the sole survivors of the *Petite Jeanne*. Captain Oudouse must have succumbed to exhaustion, for several days later his hatch-cover drifted ashore without him. Otoo and I lived with the natives of the atoll [2] for a week, when we were rescued by the French cruiser and taken to Tahiti. In the meantime, however, we had performed the ceremony of exchanging names. In the South Seas such a ceremony binds two men closer together

---

[1] " 'Ware shoal!": here means "Look out, danger ahead!" A *shoal* is a place where the water is shallow so that a ship is in danger of hitting a sand bar or hidden rocks.

[2] atoll (ăt'ŏl): a coral island or islands consisting of a belt of coral reef surrounding an inner lake.

than blood-brothership. The initiative had been mine; and Otoo was rapturously delighted when I suggested it.

"It is well," he said, in Tahitian. "For we have been mates together for two days on the lips of Death."

"But Death stuttered," I smiled.

"It was a brave deed you did, master," he replied, "and Death was not vile enough to speak."

"Why do you 'master' me?" I demanded, with a show of hurt feelings. "We have exchanged names. To you I am Otoo. To me you are Charley. And between you and me, forever and forever, you shall be Charley, and I shall be Otoo. It is the way of the custom. And when we die, if it does happen that we live again somewhere beyond the stars and the sky, still shall you be Charley to me, and I Otoo to you."

"Yes, master," he answered, his eyes luminous and soft with joy.

"There you go!" I cried indignantly.

"What does it matter what my lips utter?" he argued. "They are only my lips. But I shall think Otoo always. Whenever I think of myself, I shall think of you. Whenever men call me by name, I shall think of you. And beyond the sky and beyond the stars, always and forever, you shall be Otoo to me. Is it well, master?"

I hid my smile, and answered that it was well.

We parted at Papeete. I remained ashore to recuperate; and he went on in a cutter to his own island, Bora Bora. Six weeks later he was back. I was surprised, for he had told me of his wife, and said that he was returning to her, and would give over sailing on far voyages.

"Where do you go, master?" he asked, after our first greetings.

I shrugged my shoulders. It was a hard question.

"All the world," was my answer — "all the world, all the sea, and all the islands that are in the sea."

"I will go with you," he said simply. "My wife is dead."

I never had a brother; but from what I have seen of other men's brothers, I doubt if any man ever had a brother that was to him what Otoo was to me. He was brother and father and mother as well. And this I know: I lived a straighter and better man because of Otoo. I cared little for other men, but I had to live straight in Otoo's eyes. Because of him I dared not tarnish myself. He made me his ideal, compounding me, I fear, chiefly out of his own love and worship; and there were times when I stood close to the steep pitch of hell, and would have taken the plunge had not the thought of Otoo restrained me. His pride in me entered into me, until it became one of the major rules in my personal code to do nothing that would diminish that pride of his.

Naturally, I did not learn right away what his feelings were toward me. He never criticized, never censured; and slowly the exalted place I held in his eyes dawned upon me, and slowly I grew to comprehend the hurt I could inflict upon him by being anything less than my best.

For seventeen years we were together; for seventeen years he was at my shoulder, watching while I slept, nursing me through fever and wounds — ay, and receiving wounds in fighting for me. He signed on the same ships with me; and together we ranged the Pacific from Hawaii to Sydney Head, and from Torres Straits to the Galápagos.[1] We were wrecked three times —

[1] **Galápagos** (gá·lä′pá·gŭs): islands on the equator off the northwest coast of South America and belonging to the nation of Ecuador.

in the Gilberts, in the Santa Cruz group, and in the Fijis. And we traded and salved [1] wherever a dollar promised in the way of pearl and pearl-shell, copra, bêche-de-mer,[2] hawkbill [3] turtle-shell, and stranded wrecks.

It began in Papeete, immediately after his announcement that he was going with me over all the sea, and the islands in the midst thereof. There was a club in those days in Papeete, where the pearlers, traders, captains, and riffraff of South Sea adventurers forgathered. The play ran high, and the drink ran high; and I am very much afraid that I kept later hours than were becoming or proper. No matter what the hour was when I left the club, there was Otoo waiting to see me safely home.

At first I smiled; next I chided him. Then I told him flatly that I stood in need of no wet-nursing. After that I did not see him when I came out of the club. Quite by accident, a week or so later, I discovered that he still saw me home, lurking across the street among the shadows of the mango trees. What could I do? I know what I did do.

Insensibly I began to keep better hours. On wet and stormy nights, in the thick of the folly and the fun, the thought would persist in coming to me of Otoo keeping his dreary vigil under the dripping mangoes. Truly, he made a better man of me.

Otoo had my welfare always at heart. He thought ahead for me, weighed my plans, and took a greater interest in them than I did myself. At first, when I was unaware of this interest of his in my affairs, he had to divine my intentions, as, for instance, at Papeete, when I contemplated going partners with a knavish fellow-countryman on a guano [4] venture. I did not know he was a knave. Nor did any white man in Papeete. Neither did Otoo know, but he saw how thick we were getting, and found out for me, and without my asking him. Native sailors from the ends of the seas knock about on the beach in Tahiti; and Otoo, suspicious merely, went among them till he had gathered sufficient data to justify his suspicions. Oh, it was a nice history, that of Randolph Waters. I couldn't believe it when Otoo first narrated it; but when I sheeted it home to Waters he gave in without a murmur, and got away on the first steamer to Auckland.[5]

At first, I am free to confess, I couldn't help resenting Otoo's poking his nose into my business. But I knew that he was wholly unselfish; and soon I had to acknowledge his wisdom and discretion. He had his eyes open always to my main chance, and he was both keen-sighted and far-sighted. In time he became my counselor, until he knew more of my business than I did myself. He really had my interest at heart more than I did. Mine was the magnificent carelessness of youth, for I preferred romance to dollars, and adventure to a comfortable billet with all night in. So it was well that I had someone to look out for me. I know that if it had not been for Otoo, I should not be here today.

The particular instance I have in mind was on Malaita, the most savage island in the easterly Solomons. The na-

[1] **salved** (sălv'd): salvaged; saved from surplus or from damaged cargo left by ships.
[2] **bêche-de-mer** (băsh'dē-mâr'): a large sea cucumber. It is taken in vast quantities in northern Australia and the East Indies, boiled, dried, and smoked, and then shipped to China for making soup.
[3] **hawkbill**: a sea turtle found in all tropical and subtropical seas, whose shell, about two feet in length, furnishes the best tortoise shell for commercial use.

[4] **guano** (gwä'nŏ): a fertilizer substance.
[5] **Auckland** (ôk'lănd): a city on the northern island of New Zealand.

tives had been remarkably friendly; and how were we to know that the whole village had been taking up a collection for over two years with which to buy a white man's head? The beggars are all head-hunters, and they especially esteem a white man's head. The fellow who captured the head would receive the whole collection. As I say, they appeared very friendly; and on this day I was fully a hundred yards down the beach from the boat. Otoo had cautioned me; and, as usual when I did not heed him, I came to grief.

The first I knew, a cloud of spears sailed out of the mangrove [1] swamp at me. At least a dozen were sticking into me. I started to run, but tripped over one that was fast in my calf, and went down. The natives made a run for me, each with a long-handled, fantail tomahawk with which to hack off my head. They were so eager for the prize that they got in one another's way. In the confusion, I avoided several hacks by throwing myself right and left on the sand.

Then Otoo arrived — Otoo the manhandler. In some way he had got hold of a heavy war club, and at close quarters it was a far more efficient weapon than a rifle. He was right in the thick of them, so that they could not spear him, while their tomahawks seemed worse than useless. He was fighting for me, and he was in a true Berserker [2] rage.

---

[1] **mangrove** (măng'grōv): a tropical tree or shrub growing in swamps and shallow bay waters. There are numerous roots growing from the plant above ground. Ultimately these form a thick mass so that mangrove swamps become active land builders.

[2] **Berserker** (bûr'sûr·kēr): in Norse folklore, one of a class of wild warriors of the heathen age. In battle, a rage or frenzy came upon them; they howled like wolves or growled like bears, bit their shields, foamed at the mouth, and were believed to have enormous strength and to be unconquerable.

The way he handled that club was amazing. It was not until he had driven them back, picked me up in his arms, and started to run, that he received his first wounds. He arrived in the boat with four spear thrusts. Then we pulled aboard the schooner and doctored up.

Seventeen years we were together. He made me. I should today be a supercargo, a recruiter, [3] or a memory, if it had not been for him.

"You spend your money, and you go out and get more," he said one day. "It is easy to get money now. But when you get old, your money will be spent, and you will not be able to go out and get more. I know, master. I have studied the way of white men. On the beaches are many old men who were young once, and who could get money just like you.

"I am a sailor on the schooner. I get fifteen dollars a month. That is because I am a good sailor. I work hard. The captain has a double awning, and drinks beer out of long bottles. I have never seen him haul a rope or pull an oar. He gets one hundred and fifty dollars a month. I am a sailor. He is a navigator. I think it would be very good for you to know navigation."

Otoo spurred me on to it. He sailed with me as second mate on my first schooner, and he was far prouder of my command than I was myself. Later on it was:

"The captain is well paid, but the ship is in his keeping, and he is never free from the burden. It is the owner who is better paid — the owner who sits ashore with many servants and turns his money over."

"True, but a schooner costs five thou-

---

[3] **recruiter**: a sailor who rounds up natives from the small islands to work for the big plantations in the East Indies.

sand dollars — an old schooner at that," I objected. "I should be an old man before I saved five thousand dollars."

"There be short ways for white men to make money," he went on, pointing ashore at the coconut-fringed beach.

We were in the Solomons at the time, picking up a cargo of ivory-nuts along the east coast of Guadalcanal.

"Between this river mouth and the next it is two miles," he said. "The flat land runs far back. It is worth nothing now. Next year — who knows? — or the year after, men will pay much money for that land. The anchorage is good. Big steamers can lie close up. You can buy the land four miles deep from the old chief for ten thousand sticks of to-bacco, ten bottles of square-face,[1] and a Snider,[2] which will cost you, maybe, one hundred dollars. Then you place the deed with the commissioner; and the next year, or the year after, you sell and become the owner of a ship."

I followed his lead, and his words came true, though in three years, in-stead of two. Next came the grasslands deal on Guadalcanal — twenty thou-sand acres, on a governmental nine hundred and ninety-nine years' lease at a nominal [3] sum. I owned the lease for precisely ninety days, when I sold it to a company for half a fortune. Always it was Otoo who looked ahead and saw the opportunity. He was responsible for the salving of the *Doncaster* — bought in at auction for a hundred pounds, and clearing three thousand after every expense was paid. He led me into the

Savai plantation and the cocoa venture on Upolu.

We did not go seafaring so much as in the old days. I was too well off. I married, and my standard of living rose; but Otoo remained the same old-time Otoo, moving about the house or trail-ing through the office, his wooden pipe in his mouth, a shilling [4] undershirt on his back, and a four-shilling lava-lava [5] about his loins. I could not get him to spend money. There was no way of re-paying him except with love, and God knows he got that in full measure from all of us. The children worshiped him; and if he had been spoilable, my wife would surely have been his undoing.

The children! He really was the one who showed them the way of their feet in the world practical. He began by teaching them to walk. He sat up with them when they were sick. One by one, when they were scarcely toddlers, he took them down to the lagoon, and made them into amphibians. He taught them more than I ever knew of the habits of fish and the ways of catching them. In the bush it was the same thing. At seven, Tom knew more woodcraft than I ever dreamed existed. At six,

---

[1] **square-face:** gin used in trade with Afri-can or Polynesian natives — so called because usually shipped in square bottles.

[2] **Snider:** a gun.

[3] **nominal:** implies that the thing named is so small in comparison with what might prop-erly be expected, as scarcely to be entitled to the name.

[4] **shilling** (shĭl'ĭng): a silver coin of Great Britain, approximately equal to fourteen cents in U.S. currency.

[5] **lava-lava** (lä'vä-lä'vä): a printed calico waistcloth or kilt.

Mary went over the Sliding Rock without a quiver, and I have seen strong men balk at that feat. And when Frank had just turned six he could bring up shillings from the bottom in three fathoms.[1]

"My people in Bora Bora do not like heathen — they are all Christians; and I do not like Bora Bora Christians," he said one day, when I, with the idea of getting him to spend some of the money that was rightfully his, had been trying to persuade him to make a visit to his own island in one of our schooners — a special voyage which I had hoped to make a record breaker in the matter of prodigal[2] expense.

I say one of *our* schooners, though legally at the time they belonged to me. I struggled long with him to enter into partnership.

"We have been partners from the day the *Petite Jeanne* went down," he said at last. "But if your heart so wishes, then shall we become partners by the law. I have no work to do, yet are my expenses large. I drink and eat and smoke in plenty — it costs much, I know. I do not pay for the playing of billiards, for I play on your table; but still the money goes. Fishing on the reef is only a rich man's pleasure. It is shocking, the cost of hooks and cotton line. Yes, it is necessary that we be partners by the law. I need the money. I shall get it from the head clerk in the office."

So the papers were made out and recorded. A year later I was compelled to complain.

"Charley," said I, "you are a wicked old fraud, a miserly skinflint, a miserable land-crab. Behold, your share for the year in all our partnership has been thousands of dollars. The head clerk has given me this paper. It says that in the year you have drawn just eighty-seven dollars and twenty cents."

"Is there any owing me?" he asked anxiously.

"I tell you thousands and thousands," I answered.

His face brightened, as with an immense relief.

"It is well," he said. "See that the head clerk keeps good account of it. When I want it, I shall want it, and there must not be a cent missing.

"If there is," he added fiercely, after a pause, "it must come out of the clerk's wages."

And all the time, as I afterwards learned, his will drawn up by Carruthers, and making me sole beneficiary, lay in the American consul's safe.

But the end came, as the end must come to all human associations. It occurred in the Solomons, where our wildest work had been done in the wild young days, and where we were once more — principally on a holiday, incidentally to look after our holdings on Florida Island and to look over the pearling possibilities of the Mboli Pass. We were lying at Savo,[3] having run in to trade for curios.

Now, Savo is alive with sharks. It was my luck to be coming aboard in a tiny, overloaded, native canoe, when the thing capsized. I was peering into the water when I saw a big shark pass directly beneath me. He was fully sixteen feet in length. I abandoned the canoe and started to swim toward the schooner, expecting to be picked up by the boat before I got there.

I swam doggedly on, hoping that that was the last unattached shark. But there

[1] **fathoms** (fă<u>th</u>′ŭmz): A fathom is a measure of length, containing six feet. It is used chiefly in measuring cables, cordage, and the depth of water (by soundings).

[2] **prodigal** (prŏd′ĭ·găl): recklessly extravagant.

[3] **Savo** (sä′vō): one of the Solomon Islands.

was another. I was watching him when he made his first attack. By good luck I got both hands on his nose, and, though his momentum nearly shoved me under, I managed to keep him off. He veered clear, and began circling about again. A second time I escaped him by the same maneuver. The third rush was a miss on both sides. He sheered at the moment my hands should have landed on his nose, but his sandpaper hide (I had on a sleeveless undershirt) scraped the skin off one arm from elbow to shoulder.

By this time I was played out, and gave up hope. The schooner was still two hundred feet away. My face was in the water, and I was watching him maneuver for another attempt, when I saw a brown body pass between us. It was Otoo.

"Swim for the schooner, master!" he said. And he spoke gayly, as though the affair was a mere lark. "I know sharks. The shark is my brother."

I obeyed, swimming slowly on, while Otoo swam about me, keeping always between me and the shark, foiling his rushes and encouraging me.

"The davit tackle [1] carried away, and they are rigging the falls," [2] he explained, a minute or so later, and then went under to head off another attack.

By the time the schooner was thirty feet away I was about done for. I could scarcely move. They were heaving lines at us from on board, but they continually fell short. The shark, finding that it was receiving no hurt, had become bolder. Several times it nearly

[1] davit (dăv'ĭt) tackle: an assemblage of ropes and pulleys attached to the *davit* which is a form of crane, fixed or movable, projecting over the side of a ship for hoisting boats, anchors, etc.
[2] rigging the falls: adjusting the tackle used in lowering and hoisting a ship's boat from or to the davits.

got me, but each time Otoo was there just the moment before it was to late. Of course, Otoo could have saved himself any time. But he stuck by me.

"Good-by, Charley! I'm finished!" I just managed to gasp.

I knew that the end had come, and that the next moment I should throw up my hands and go down.

But Otoo laughed in my face, saying:

"I will show you a new trick. It will make that shark feel sick!"

He dropped in behind me, where the shark was preparing to come at me.

"A little more to the left!" he next called out. "There is a line there on the water. To the left — to the left!"

I changed my course and struck out blindly. I was by that time barely conscious. As my hand closed on the line I heard an exclamation from on board. I turned and looked. There was no sign of Otoo. The next instant he broke surface.

"Otoo!" he called softly. And I could see in his gaze the love that thrilled in his voice.

Then, and then only, at the very last of all our years, he called me by that name.

"Good-by, Otoo!" he called.

Then he was dragged under, and I was hauled aboard, where I fainted in the captain's arms.

And so passed Otoo, who saved me and made me a man, and who saved me in the end. We met in the maw of a hurricane, and parted in the maw of a shark, with seventeen intervening years of comradeship, the like of which I dare to assert has never befallen two men, the one brown and the other white. If Jehovah be from His high place watching every sparrow fall, not least in His kingdom shall be Otoo, the one heathen of Bora Bora.

VISUALIZING SETTING

1. What details does Jack London use to convey the feeling of the hurricane? of the oppressive calm? of the shipwreck?

2. Which scenes in the story might interest a painter, or a movie director proud of the authentic backgrounds he creates?

3. Select four effective words or phrases to illustrate Jack London's skill in description.

4. Jack London knew about ships and the sea. What details testify to this familiarity?

THINKING IT OVER

1. When, presumably, did the white trader actually see Otoo for the first time? Why was he not at that time consciously aware of Otoo's existence?

2. How do hatch-covers figure prominently in this story?

3. Why, in the Bill King episode, does the author depart from the chronological time sequence of his story? What purpose does this flash ahead serve?

4. What is the South Sea "ceremony of exchanging names"? How does it have a significance in this story?

5. What makes possible Otoo's leaving Bora Bora to spend a lifetime looking after Charley?

6. Do Otoo and Charley mean what they say in the following passages? If not, why do they express themselves in the way they do?

Otoo: "Yes, it is necessary that we be partners by the law. I need the money" (page 72).

Charley: ". . . you are a wicked old fraud, a miserly skinflint, a miserable land-crab" (page 72).

7. List five qualities of character which make Otoo a memorable person. For each quality, refer to an incident that supports your judgment.

GAINING POWER OVER WORDS

LEARNING NEW WORDS In "The Heathen" Jack London uses many words which you should add to your working vocabulary. Use the glossary at the back of this book to find the meanings of the following words. Be sure to notice how to pronounce them. Then write one sentence illustrating how each word could be used in every-day conversation.

annihilate	retaliate
chide	stolid
dissipate	vacillate
irresistible	veer
ravenous	voluble

ABOUT THE AUTHOR

Jack London (1876–1916) rose from the extreme poverty of the waterfront in Oakland, California, to the luxury of a yacht and a ranch in the Valley of the Moon, north of San Francisco. Despite his rough life, he had a yearning for knowledge and at ten he was reading his way through the adventure books of the public library. At seventeen he was a longshoreman and a seaman on a sailing vessel which went to Japan and Siberia. The following year he became a tramp, roaming over the United States and Canada. In Niagara he was jailed for vagrancy. Back in Oakland, he completed the entire high school curriculum in three months of intensive study and passed the entrance exams to the University of California. However, he caught the gold fever and left for Alaska in 1896. From this experience he wrote *The Call of the Wild* which became a best seller. By 1913 he was probably the highest paid and best-known writer in the world, but he spent his money lavishly. Jack London considered himself a writer who was in protest against those who looked down on the humble people of the world. Elements of this protest, as well as his sympathy for the common man, can be seen in "The Heathen."

The Setting of the Story →

The photograph on the opposite page shows Korelevu Beach in the Fiji Islands. With its coconut palms, wild plant life, and thatched huts, it is a typical South Sea Island scene. Did you visualize Charley and Otoo in a setting such as this as you read "The Heathen"?

Beware of the Dog

ROALD DAHL

A British Royal Air Force pilot in World War II is lost in the clouds somewhere over France, England, or the English Channel. This would not be too serious if it were not for the fact that France is occupied by the enemy, Hitler's German army. At first the title of this story may appear irrelevant. But you will see that it is a very apt one for this story in which setting is extremely important.

DOWN BELOW there was only a vast white undulating[1] sea of cloud. Above there was the sun, and the sun was white like the clouds, because it is never

[1] **undulating** (ŭn′dŭ·lāt′ĭng): rising and falling as on waves.

yellow when one looks at it from high in the air.

He was still flying the Spitfire. His right hand was on the stick,[2] and he was working the rudder bar with his left leg alone. It was quite easy. The machine was flying well, and he knew what he was doing.

Everything is fine, he thought. I'm doing all right. I'm doing nicely. I know my way home. I'll be there in half an hour. When I land I shall taxi in and switch off my engine and I shall say, help me to get out, will you. I shall make my voice sound ordinary and natural and none of them will take any notice. Then I shall say, someone help

[2] **stick:** the lever by which the controls are operated.

Appreciating Point of View. Point of view in a story is the angle from which the story is told. Sometimes an outside observer narrates the story. At other times the story is told by one or more of the characters within the story; in this case, you usually experience things along with the characters and know how they feel and think. The author may choose to limit the point of view to that of a single character, either the first

person "I" or a named third person; or he may use a multiple point of view where several characters reveal what is going on around them and within their minds.

"Beware of the Dog" is a superb example of the limited point of view. By presenting everything through the eyes of the young pilot, the author forces you into the dramatic present — to feel as if you were living through the pilot's experience.

---

me to get out. I can't do it alone because I've lost one of my legs. They'll all laugh and think that I'm joking, and I shall say, all right, come and have a look. Then Yorky will climb up onto the wing and look inside. He'll probably be sick because of all the blood and the mess. I shall laugh and say, for Heaven's sake, help me out.

He glanced down again at his right leg. There was not much of it left. The cannon shell had taken him on the thigh, just above the knee, and now there was nothing but a great mess and a lot of blood. But there was no pain. When he looked down, he felt as though he were seeing something that did not belong to him. It had nothing to do with him. It was just a mess which happened to be there in the cockpit — something strange and unusual and rather interesting. It was like finding a dead cat on the sofa.

He really felt fine, and because he still felt fine, he felt excited and unafraid.

I won't even bother to call up on the radio for the blood wagon, he thought. It isn't necessary. And when I land I'll sit there quite normally and say, some of you fellows come and help me out, will you, because I've lost one of my legs. That will be funny. I'll laugh a little while I'm saying it, I'll say it calmly and slowly, and they'll think I'm joking. When Yorky comes up onto the wing and gets sick, I'll say, Yorky, have you fixed my car yet? Then when I get out I'll make my report and later I'll go up to London. I won't say much until it's time to go to bed, then I'll say, Bluey, I've got a surprise for you. I lost a leg today. But I don't mind so long as you don't. It doesn't even hurt. We'll go everywhere in cars. I always hated walking, except when I walked down the street of the coppersmiths in Bag-

dad, but I could go in a rickshaw. I could go home and chop wood, but the head always flies off the ax. Hot water, that's what it needs, put it in the bath and make the handle swell. I chopped lots of wood last time I went home, and I put the ax in the bath. . . .

Then he saw the sun shining on the engine cowling [1] of his machine. He saw the rivets in the metal, and he remembered where he was. He realized that he was no longer feeling good; that he was sick and giddy. His head kept falling forward onto his chest because his neck seemed no longer to have any strength. But he knew that he was flying the Spitfire, and he could feel the handle of the stick between the fingers of his right hand.

I'm going to pass out, he thought. Any moment now I'm going to pass out.

He looked at his altimeter. Twenty-one thousand. To test himself he tried to read the hundreds as well as the thousands. Twenty-one thousand and what? As he looked the dial became blurred, and he could not even see the needle. He knew then that he must bail out; that there was not a second to lose, otherwise he would become unconscious. Quickly, frantically, he tried to slide back the hood with his left hand, but he had not the strength. For a second he took his right hand off the stick, and with both hands he managed to push the hood back. The rush of cold air on his face seemed to help. He had a moment of great clearness, and his actions became orderly and precise. That is what happens with a good pilot. He took some quick deep breaths from his oxygen mask, and as he did so, he looked out over the side of the cockpit. Down below there was only a vast white sea of cloud, and he realized that

[1] **engine cowling** (koul'ĭng): a removable metal covering.

he did not know where he was.

It'll be the Channel, he thought. I'm sure to fall in the drink.

He throttled back, pulled off his helmet, undid his straps, and pushed the stick hard over to the left. The Spitfire dipped its port wing, and turned smoothly over onto its back. The pilot fell out.

As he fell he opened his eyes, because he knew that he must not pass out before he had pulled the cord. On one side he saw the sun; on the other he saw the whiteness of the clouds, and as he fell, as he somersaulted in the air, the white clouds chased the sun and the sun chased the clouds. They chased each other in a small circle; they ran faster and faster, and there was the sun and the clouds and the clouds and the sun, and the clouds came nearer until suddenly there was no longer any sun, but only a great whiteness. The whole world was white, and there was nothing in it. It was so white that sometimes it looked black, and after a time it was either white or black, but mostly it was white. He watched it as it turned from white to black, and then back to white again, and the white stayed for a long time, but the black lasted only for a few seconds. He got into the habit of going to sleep during the white periods, and of waking up just in time to see the world when it was black. But the black was very quick. Sometimes it was only a flash, like someone switching off the light, and switching it on again at once, and so whenever it was white, he dozed off.

One day, when it was white, he put out a hand and he touched something. He took it between his fingers and crumpled it. For a time he lay there, idly letting the tips of his fingers play with the thing which they had touched. Then slowly he opened his eyes, looked down at his hand, and saw that he was holding something which was white. It was the edge of a sheet. He knew it was a sheet because he could see the texture of the material and the stitchings on the hem. He screwed up his eyes, and opened them again quickly. This time he saw the room. He saw the bed in which he was lying; he saw the gray walls and the door and the green curtains over the window. There were some roses on the table by his bed.

Then he saw the basin on the table near the roses. It was a white enamel basin, and beside it there was a small medicine glass.

This is a hospital, he thought. I am in a hospital. But he could remember nothing. He lay back on his pillow, looking at the ceiling and wondering what had happened. He was gazing at the smooth grayness of the ceiling which was so clean and gray, and then suddenly he saw a fly walking upon it. The sight of this fly, the suddenness of seeing this small black speck on a sea of gray, brushed the surface of his brain, and quickly, in that second, he remembered everything. He remembered the Spitfire and he remembered the altimeter showing twenty-one thousand feet. He remembered the pushing back of the hood with both hands, and he remembered the bailing out. He remembered his leg.

It seemed all right now. He looked down at the end of the bed, but he could not tell. He put one hand underneath the bedclothes and felt for his knees. He found one of them, but when he felt for the other, his hand touched something which was soft and covered in bandages.

Just then the door opened and a nurse came in.

"Hello," she said. "So you've waked up at last."

She was not good-looking, but she was large and clean. She was between thirty and forty and she had fair hair. More than that he did not notice.

"Where am I?"

"You're a lucky fellow. You landed in a wood near the beach. You're in Brighton.[1] They brought you in two days ago, and now you're all fixed up. You look fine."

"I've lost a leg," he said.

"That's nothing. We'll get you another one. Now you must go to sleep. The doctor will be coming to see you in about an hour." She picked up the basin and the medicine glass and went out.

But he did not sleep. He wanted to keep his eyes open because he was frightened that if he shut them again everything would go away. He lay looking at the ceiling. The fly was still there. It was very energetic. It would run forward very fast for a few inches, then it would stop. Then it would run forward again, stop, run forward, stop, and every now and then it would take off and buzz around viciously in small circles. It always landed back in the same place on the ceiling and started running and stopping all over again. He watched it for so long that after a-while it was no longer a fly, but only a black speck upon a sea of gray, and he was still watching it when the nurse opened the door, and stood aside while the doctor came in. He was an Army doctor, a major, and he had some last war ribbons on his chest. He was bald and small, but he had a cheerful face and kind eyes.

"Well, well," he said. "So you've decided to wake up at last. How are you feeling?"

"I feel all right."

"That's the stuff. You'll be up and about in no time."

The doctor took his wrist to feel his pulse.

"By the way," he said, "some of the lads from your squadron were ringing up and asking about you. They wanted to come along and see you, but I said that they'd better wait a day or two. Told them you were all right, and that they could come and see you a little later on. Just lie quiet and take it easy for a bit. Got something to read?" He glanced at the table with the roses. "No. Well, nurse will look after you. She'll get you anything you want." With that he waved his hand and went out, followed by the large clean nurse.

When they had gone, he lay back and looked at the ceiling again. The fly was still there and as he lay watching it he heard the noise of an airplane in the distance. He lay listening to the sound of its engines. It was a long way away. I wonder what it is, he thought. Let me see if I can place it. Suddenly he jerked his head sharply to one side. Anyone who has been bombed can tell the noise of a Junkers 88. They can tell most other German bombers for that matter, but especially a Junkers 88. The engines seem to sing a duet. There is a deep vibrating bass voice and with it there is a high-pitched tenor. It is the singing of the tenor which makes the sound of a JU-88 something which one cannot mistake.

He lay listening to the noise, and he felt quite certain about what it was. But where were the sirens, and where the guns? That German pilot had a nerve coming near Brighton alone in daylight.

The aircraft was always far away and soon the noise faded away into the distance. Later on there was another. This one, too, was far away but there was the same deep undulating bass and the high singing tenor, and there was no mistaking it. He had heard that noise every day during the battle.

He was puzzled. There was a bell on the table by the bed. He reached out his hand and rang it. He heard the noise of footsteps down the corridor, and the nurse came in.

"Nurse, what were those airplanes?"

"I'm sure I don't know. I didn't hear them. Probably fighters or bombers. I expect they were returning from France. Why, what's the matter?"

"They were JU-88's. I'm sure they were JU-88's. I know the sound of the engines. There were two of them. What were they doing over here?"

The nurse came up to the side of his bed and began to straighten the sheets and tuck them in under the mattress.

"Gracious me, what things you imagine. You mustn't worry about a thing like that. Would you like me to get you something to read?"

"No, thank you."

She patted his pillow and brushed back the hair from his forehead with her hand.

"They never come over in daylight any longer. You know that. They were probably Lancasters or Flying Fortresses."

"Nurse."

"Yes."

"Could I have a cigarette?"

"Why certainly you can."

She went out and came back almost at once with a packet of Players and some matches. She handed one to him and when he had put it in his mouth, she struck a match and lit it.

"If you want me again," she said, "just ring the bell," and she went out.

Once toward evening he heard the noise of another aircraft. It was far away, but even so he knew that it was a single-engined machine. But he could not place it. It was going fast; he could tell that. But it wasn't a Spit, and it wasn't a Hurricane. It did not sound like an American engine either. They make more noise. He did not know what it was, and it worried him greatly. Perhaps I am very ill, he thought. Perhaps I am imagining things. Perhaps I am a little delirious. I simply do not know what to think.

That evening the nurse came in with a basin of hot water and began to wash him.

"Well," she said, "I hope you don't still think that we're being bombed."

She had taken off his pajama top and was soaping his right arm with a flannel. He did not answer.

She rinsed the flannel in the water, rubbed more soap on it, and began to wash his chest.

"You're looking fine this evening," she said. "They operated on you as soon as you came in. They did a marvelous job. You'll be all right. I've got a brother in the RAF,"[1] she added. "Flying bombers."

He said, "I went to school in Brighton."

She looked up quickly. "Well, that's fine," she said. "I expect you'll know some people in the town."

"Yes," he said, "I know quite a few."

She had finished washing his chest and arms, and now she turned back the bedclothes, so that his left leg was uncovered. She did it in such a way that his bandaged stump remained under the sheets. She undid the cord of his pajama trousers and took them off. There was no trouble because they had cut off the right trouser leg, so that it could not interfere with the bandages. She began to wash his left leg and the rest of his body. This was the first time he had had a bed bath, and he was em-

[1] **RAF**: Royal Air Force.

barrassed. She laid a towel under his leg, and she was washing his foot with the flannel. She said, "This wretched soap won't lather at all. It's the water. It's as hard as nails."

He said, "None of the soap is very good now and, of course, with hard water it's hopeless." As he said it he remembered something. He remembered the baths which he used to take at school in Brighton, in the long stone-floored bathroom which had four baths in a room. He remembered how the water was so soft that you had to take a shower afterwards to get all the soap off your body, and he remembered how the foam used to float on the surface of the water, so that you could not see your legs underneath. He remembered that sometimes they were given calcium tablets because the school doctor used to say that soft water was bad for the teeth.

"In Brighton," he said, "the water isn't . . ."

He did not finish the sentence. Something had occurred to him; something so fantastic and absurd that for a moment he felt like telling the nurse about it and having a good laugh.

She looked up. "The water isn't what?" she said.

"Nothing," he answered. "I was dreaming."

She rinsed the flannel in the basin, wiped the soap off his leg, and dried him with a towel.

"It's nice to be washed," he said. "I feel better." He was feeling his face with his hands. "I need a shave."

"We'll do that tomorrow," she said. "Perhaps you can do it yourself then."

That night he could not sleep. He lay awake thinking of the Junkers 88's and of the hardness of the water. He could think of nothing else. They were JU-88's, he said to himself. I know they

were. And yet it is not possible, because they would not be flying so low over here in broad daylight. I know that it is true, and yet I know that it is impossible. Perhaps I am ill. Perhaps I am behaving like a fool and do not know what I am doing or saying. Perhaps I am delirious. For a long time he lay awake thinking these things, and once he sat up in bed and said aloud, "I will prove that I am not crazy. I will make a little speech about something complicated and intellectual. I will talk about what to do with Germany after the war." But before he had time to begin, he was asleep.

He woke just as the first light of day was showing through the slit in the curtains over the window. The room was still dark, but he could tell that it was already beginning to get light outside. He lay looking at the gray light which was showing through the slit in the curtain, and as he lay there he remembered the day before. He remembered the Junkers 88's and the hardness of the water; he remembered the large pleasant nurse and the kind doctor, and now the small grain of doubt took root in his mind and it began to grow.

He looked around the room. The nurse had taken the roses out the night before, and there was nothing except the table with a packet of cigarettes, a box of matches, and an ash tray. Otherwise, it was bare. It was no longer warm or friendly. It was not even comfortable. It was cold and empty and very quiet.

Slowly the grain of doubt grew, and with it came fear, a light, dancing fear that warned but did not frighten; the kind of fear that one gets not because one is afraid, but because one feels that there is something wrong. Quickly the doubt and the fear grew so that he became restless and angry, and when he touched his forehead with his hand, he found that it was damp with sweat. He knew then that he must do something; that he must find some way of proving to himself that he was either right or wrong, and he looked up and saw again the window and the green curtains. From where he lay, that window was right in front of him, but it was fully ten yards away. Somehow he must reach it and look out. The idea became an obsession with him, and soon he could think of nothing except the window. But what about his leg? He put his hand underneath the bedclothes and felt the thick bandaged stump which was all that was left on the right-hand side. It seemed all right. It didn't hurt. But it would not be easy.

He sat up. Then he pushed the bed-clothes aside and put his left leg on the floor. Slowly, carefully, he swung his body over until he had both hands on the floor as well; and then he was out of bed, kneeling on the carpet. He looked at the stump. It was very short and thick, covered with bandages. It was beginning to hurt and he could feel it throbbing. He wanted to collapse, lie down on the carpet and do nothing, but he knew that he must go on.

With two arms and one leg, he crawled over towards the window. He would reach forward as far as he could with his arms, then he would give a lit-tle jump and slide his left leg along after them. Each time he did, it jarred his wound so that he gave a soft grunt of pain, but he continued to crawl across the floor on two hands and one knee. When he got to the window he reached up, and one at a time he placed both hands on the sill. Slowly he raised himself up until he was standing on his left leg. Then quickly he pushed aside the curtains and looked out.

He saw a small house with a gray tiled roof standing alone beside a nar-row lane, and immediately behind it there was a plowed field. In front of the house there was an untidy garden, and there was a green hedge separating the garden from the lane. He was look-ing at the hedge when he saw the sign. It was just a piece of board nailed to the top of a short pole, and because the hedge had not been trimmed for a long time, the branches had grown out around the sign so that it seemed al-most as though it had been placed in the middle of the hedge. There was something written on the board with white paint, and he pressed his head against the glass of the window, trying to read what it said. The first letter was a G, he could see that. The second was an A, and the third was an R. One after another he managed to see what the letters were. There were three words, and slowly he spelled the letters out loud to himself as he managed to read them. G–A–R–D–E A–U C–H–I–E–N. *Garde au chien.*[1] That is what it said.

He stood there balancing on one leg and holding tightly to the edges of the window sill with his hands, staring at the sign and at the whitewashed letter-ing of the words. For a moment he could think of nothing at all. He stood there looking at the sign, repeating the words over and over to himself, and then slowly he began to realize the full meaning of the thing. He looked up at the cottage and at the plowed field. He looked at the small orchard on the left of the cottage and he looked at the countryside beyond. "So this is France," he said. "I am in France."

Now the throbbing in his right thigh was very great. It felt as though some-one was pounding the end of the stump with a hammer, and suddenly the pain

[1] *Garde au chien:* French for "Beware of the dog."

became so intense that it affected his head and for a moment he thought he was going to fall. Quickly he knelt down again, crawled back to the bed and hoisted himself in. He pulled the bedclothes over himself and lay back on the pillow exhausted. He could still think of nothing at all except the small sign by the hedges, and the plowed field and the orchard. It was the words on the sign that he could not forget.

It was some time before the nurse came in. She came carrying a basin of hot water and she said, "Good morning, how are you today?"

He said, "Good morning, nurse."

The pain was still great under the bandages, but he did not wish to tell this woman anything. He looked at her as she busied herself with getting the washing things ready. He looked at her more carefully now. Her hair was very fair. She was tall and big-boned, and her face seemed pleasant. But there was something a little uneasy about her eyes. They were never still. They never looked at anything for more than a moment and they moved too quickly from one place to another in the room. There was something about her movements also. They were too sharp and nervous to go well with the casual manner in which she spoke.

She set down the basin, took off his pajama top and began to wash him.

"Did you sleep well?"

"Yes."

"Good," she said. She was washing his arms and his chest.

"I believe there's someone coming down to see you from the Air Ministry after breakfast," she went on. "They want a report or something. I expect you know all about it. How you got shot down and all that. I won't let him stay long, so don't worry."

He did not answer. She finished washing him, and gave him a tooth-brush and some tooth powder. He brushed his teeth, rinsed his mouth, and spat the water out into the basin.

Later she brought him his breakfast on a tray, but he did not want to eat. He was still feeling weak and sick, and he wished only to lie still and think about what had happened. And there was a sentence running through his head. It was a sentence which Johnny, the Intelligence Officer of his squadron, always repeated to the pilots every day before they went out. He could see Johnny now, leaning against the wall of the dispersal hut with his pipe in his hand, saying, "And if they get you, don't forget, just your name, rank, and number. Nothing else. For God's sake, say nothing else."

"There you are," she said as she put the tray on his lap. "I've got you an egg. Can you manage all right?"

"Yes."

She stood beside the bed. "Are you feeling all right?"

"Yes."

"Good. If you want another egg I might be able to get you one."

"This is all right."

"Well, just ring the bell if you want any more." And she went out.

He had just finished eating, when the nurse came in again.

She said, "Wing Commander Roberts is here. I've told him that he can only stay for a few minutes."

She beckoned with her hand and the Wing Commander came in.

"Sorry to bother you like this," he said.

He was an ordinary RAF officer, dressed in a uniform which was a little shabby, and he wore wings and a DFC.[1] He was fairly tall and thin with plenty of black hair. His teeth, which were ir-

[1] **DFC:** Distinguished Flying Cross.

regular and widely spaced, stuck out a little even when he closed his mouth. As he spoke he took a printed form and a pencil from his pocket, and he pulled up a chair and sat down.

"How are you feeling?"

There was no answer.

"Tough luck about your leg. I know how you feel. I hear you put up a fine show before they got you."

The man in the bed was lying quite still, watching the man in the chair.

The man in the chair said, "Well, let's get this stuff over. I'm afraid you'll have to answer a few questions so that I can fill in this combat report. Let me see now, first of all, what was your squadron?"

The man in the bed did not move. He looked straight at the Wing Commander and he said, "My name is Peter Williamson. My rank is Squadron Leader and my number is nine seven two four five seven."

APPRECIATING POINT OF VIEW

1. This story has only two settings, both seen through the eyes of the aviator. Are the details of both settings appropriate to the kinds of details Peter Williamson might notice? Do they consistently build up a picture of a young man who is trained to be alert and sharply observant of all the details in his environment? What purpose is served by the incident of the fly?

2. How do the aviator's thoughts during his time in the plane foreshadow the kind of character he shows during the last part of the story?

3. What is going on in the mind of the aviator in the following passage (page 81)?

"In Brighton," he said, "the water isn't . . ." He did not finish the sentence. Something had occurred to him; something so fantastic and absurd that for a moment he felt like telling the nurse about it and having a good laugh.

4. How does the title fit the story? Why could the author not use the French phrase *Garde au Chien* without sacrificing interest?

5. What do you finally conclude about where Williamson is and what is happening to him?

6. An author may choose to limit the point of view to a single character in a story, looking at the events through his eyes and through his mind, as Roald Dahl does in this story. In this case, does the controlled or limited point of view improve the story? What would the story lose if the author allowed us, for example, to enter the mind of the nurse? Could a good story be written limiting the point of view solely to that of the nurse? (Don't answer hastily; the question deserves careful thought.)

COMPOSITION SUGGESTION

Tell of a brush with danger that made you more aware than usual of your surroundings and of what was going on around you.

ABOUT THE AUTHOR

Roald Dahl (1916–   ) is an English writer who publishes almost exclusively in the United States because of the small market for the short story in England. Born in Wales of Norwegian parents, he lives in a New York apartment during the winter and in a Georgian-style house on six acres near London during the summer. After being shot down over Libya while a fighter pilot in the Royal Air Force, Dahl came to Washington as an assistant air attaché. The first stories he published were about his war experiences. Malcolm Bradbury of the New York *Times* says, "He builds situations beautifully. . . . Mr. Dahl is the master of the beginning, the middle, and the end. . . . No moralist, no profound seer — but a true craftsman."

Where the Story Began →

This remarkable photograph of a British World War II fighter plane, a spitfire, approaching the English Channel, captures a scene familiar to the hero — and to the author — of this story.

The Cask of Amontillado

EDGAR ALLAN POE

Poe's stories often aim at creating the single effect of horror. "The Cask of Amontillado" has been rated as one of Poe's most successful horror stories. To do Poe justice, you should first read this story through just to see what effect it creates for you. Poe felt strongly that a short story should be read at one sitting with absolutely no interruptions. He wanted the reader to lose himself completely in the mood and power of the story.

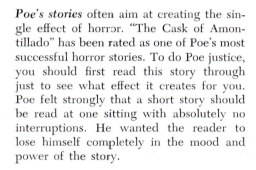

THE THOUSAND injuries of Fortunato I had borne as I best could, but when he ventured upon insult, I vowed revenge. You, who so well know the nature of my soul, will not suppose, however, that I gave utterance to a threat. *At length* I would be avenged; this was a point definitely settled — but the very definitiveness with which it was resolved, precluded the idea of risk. I must not only punish, but punish with impunity. A wrong is unredressed [1] when retribution overtakes its redresser. It is equally unredressed when the avenger fails to make himself felt as such to him who had done the wrong.

It must be understood that neither by word nor deed had I given Fortunato cause to doubt my good will. I continued, as was my wont, to smile in his face, and he did not perceive that my smile *now* was at the thought of his immolation. [2]

He had a weak point — this Fortunato — although in other regards he was a man to be respected and even feared.

[1] **unredressed** (ŭn·rê·drĕst′): not set right or corrected.
[2] **immolation** (ĭm′ô·lā′shŭn): being sacrificed or killed.

Poe's Theory: A Single Effect. Poe once explained his own theory of the short story as follows:

". . . having deliberately conceived of a certain single effect to be wrought, he [the short story writer] then combines such events, and discusses them in such tone as may best serve him in establishing this preconceived effect. If his very first sentence tends not to the outbringing of this effect, then in his very first step he has committed a blunder. In the whole composition there should be no word written of which the tendency, direct or indirect, is not to the one pre-established design."

After you have read this story, you will have a chance to discuss how Poe actually worked out his theory.

He prided himself on his connoisseurship in wine.[1] Few Italians have the true virtuoso[2] spirit. For the most part their enthusiasm is adapted to suit the time and opportunity — to practice imposture upon the British and Austrian millionaires. In painting and gemmary Fortunato, like his countrymen, was a quack — but in the matter of old wines he was sincere. In this respect I did not differ from him materially: I was skillful in the Italian vintages myself, and bought largely whenever I could.

It was about dusk, one evening during the supreme madness of the carnival season, that I encountered my friend. He accosted me with excessive warmth, for he had been drinking much. The man wore motley.[3] He had on a tight-fitting, parti-striped dress, and his head was surmounted by the conical cap and bells. I was so pleased to see him, that I thought I should never have done wringing his hand.

I said to him: "My dear Fortunato, you are luckily met. How remarkably well you are looking today! But I have received a pipe[4] of what passes for Amontillado,[5] and I have my doubts."

"How?" said he. "Amontillado? A pipe? Impossible! And in the middle of the carnival!"

"I have my doubts," I replied; "and I was silly enough to pay the full Amontillado price without consulting you in the matter. You were not to be found, and I was fearful of losing a bargain."

"Amontillado!"

"I have my doubts."

"Amontillado!"

"And I must satisfy them."

"Amontillado!"

"As you are engaged, I am on my way to Luchesi. If anyone has a critical turn, it is he. He will tell me — "

"Luchesi cannot tell Amontillado from Sherry."

"And yet some fools will have it that his taste is a match for your own."

"Come, let us go."

"Whither?"

"To your vaults."

"My friend, no; I will not impose upon your good nature. I perceive you have an engagement. Luchesi — "

"I have no engagement; come."

"My friend, no. It is not the engagement, but the severe cold with which I perceive you are afflicted. The vaults are insufferably damp. They are encrusted with nitre."[6]

"Let us go, nevertheless. The cold is merely nothing. Amontillado! You have been imposed upon. And as for Luchesi, he cannot distinguish Sherry from Amontillado."

Thus speaking, Fortunato possessed himself of my arm. Putting on a mask of black silk, and drawing a *roquelaire*[7] closely about my person, I suffered him to hurry me to my palazzo.[8]

There were no attendants at home; they had absconded to make merry in honor of the time. I had told them that I should not return until the morning, and had given them explicit orders not to stir from the house. These orders were sufficient, I well knew, to insure their immediate disappearance, one and all, as soon as my back was turned.

[1] **connoisseurship** (kŏn'ĭ-sûr'shĭp) **in wine:** knowledge of and competence in judging wine.

[2] **virtuoso** (vûr'tṵ-ō'sō): a skilled collector (in this case, of wines).

[3] **motley** (mŏt'lĭ): a garment of mixed colors; characteristic dress of the professional jester.

[4] **pipe:** a large cask.

[5] **Amontillado** (à·mŏn'tĭ·lä'dō): a sweet variety of Sherry.

[6] **nitre** (nī'tēr): a white, damp salt deposit.

[7] *roquelaire* (rŏk'ĕ·lâr): a knee-length cloak, buttoned in front.

[8] **palazzo** (pä·lät'sō): a palace or town house in Italy.

I took from their sconces [1] two flambeaux, [2] and giving one to Fortunato,
bowed him through several suites of
rooms to the archway that led into the
vaults. I passed down a long and winding staircase, requesting him to be cautious as he followed. We came at length
to the foot of the descent, and stood together on the damp ground of the catacombs of the Montresors.

The gait of my friend was unsteady,
and the bells upon his cap jingled as he
strode.

"The pipe?" said he.

"It is further on," said I; "but observe
the white webwork which gleams from
these cavern walls."

He turned towards me, and looked
into my eyes with two filmy orbs that
distilled the rheum [3] of intoxication.

"Nitre?" he asked, at length.

"Nitre!" I replied. "How long have
you had that cough?"

"Ugh! ugh! ugh! — ugh! ugh! ugh! —
ugh! ugh! ugh! — ugh! ugh! ugh — ugh!
ugh! ugh!"

My poor friend found it impossible
to reply for many minutes.

"It is nothing," he said, at last.

"Come," I said, with decision, "we will
go back; your health is precious. You
are rich, respected, admired, beloved;
you are happy, as once I was. You are
a man to be missed. For me it is no matter. We will go back; you will be ill, and
I cannot be responsible. Besides, there
is Luchesi — "

"Enough," he said; "the cough is a
mere nothing; it will not kill me. I shall
not die of a cough."

"True — true," I replied; "and, indeed, I had no intention of alarming
you unnecessarily — but you should use
all proper precautions. A draught of this
Medoc will defend us from the damps."

Here I knocked off the neck of a bottle which I drew from a long row of its
fellows that lay upon the mold.

"Drink," I said, presenting him the
wine.

He raised it to his lips with a leer. He
paused and nodded to me familiarly,
while his bells jingled.

"I drink," he said, "to the buried that
repose around us."

"And I to your long life."

He again took my arm, and we proceeded.

"These vaults," he said, "are extensive."

"The Montresors," I replied, "were a
great and numerous family."

"I forget your arms." [4]

"A huge human foot d'or, [5] in a field
azure; the foot crushes a serpent rampant [6] whose fangs are imbedded in the
heel."

"And the motto?"

---

[1] **sconces** (skŏns·ĕz): candlesticks secured to
the wall.
[2] **flambeaux** (flăm'bōz): flaming torches.
[3] **rheum** (rōōm): a cold; watering eyes.

[4] **arms:** hereditary symbols of a family.
[5] **d'or** (dōr): of gold.
[6] **rampant** (răm'pănt): rising up threaten-
ingly.

"*Nemo me impune lacessit.*" [1]

"Good!" he said.

The wine sparkled in his eyes and the bells jingled. My own fancy grew warm with the Medoc. We passed through walls of piled bones, with casks and puncheons [2] intermingling, into the inmost recesses of the catacombs. I paused again, and this time I made bold to seize Fortunato by an arm above the elbow.

"The nitre," I said; "see, it increases. It hangs like moss upon the vaults. We are below the river's bed. The drops of moisture trickle among the bones. Come, we will go back ere it is too late. Your cough — "

"It is nothing," he said; "let us go on. But first, another draught of the Medoc."

I broke and reached him a flagon [3] of De Grave. He emptied it at a breath. His eyes flashed with a fierce light. He laughed and threw the bottle upward with a gesticulation I did not understand.

I looked at him in surprise. He repeated the movement — a grotesque one.

"You do not comprehend?" he said.

"Not I," I replied.

"Then you are not of the brotherhood."

"How?"

"You are not of the masons." [4]

"Yes, yes," I said; "yes, yes."

"You? Impossible? A mason?"

"A mason," I replied.

[1] *Nemo me impune lacessit:* No one assails me with impunity (Latin). In other words: "Anyone who attacks me will be punished."

[2] **puncheons** (pŭn′chŭns): short, upright framing timbers.

[3] **flagon** (flăg′ŭn): a vessel, usually with handle and spout, for liquors.

[4] **masons:** referring to the Freemasons, a widespread and celebrated secret fraternal order; also bricklayers.

"A sign," he said.

"It is this," I answered, producing a trowel from beneath the folds of my *roquelaire.*

"You jest," he exclaimed, recoiling a few paces. "But let us proceed to the Amontillado."

"Be it so," I said, replacing the tool beneath the cloak, and again offering him my arm. He leaned upon it heavily. We continued our route in search of the Amontillado. We passed through a range of low arches, descended, passed on, and descending again, arrived at a deep crypt, in which the foulness of the air caused our flambeaux rather to glow than flame.

At the most remote end of the crypt there appeared another less spacious. Its walls had been lined with human remains, piled to the vault overhead, in the fashion of the great catacombs of Paris. Three sides of this interior crypt were still ornamented in this manner. From the fourth the bones had been thrown down, and lay promiscuously upon the earth, forming at one point a mound of some size. Within the wall thus exposed by the displacing of the bones, we perceived a still interior recess, in depth about four feet, in width three, in height six or seven. It seemed to have been constructed for no special use within itself, but formed merely the interval between two of the colossal supports of the roof of the catacombs, and was backed by one of their circumscribing walls of solid granite.

It was in vain that Fortunato, uplifting his dull torch, endeavored to pry into the depth of the recess. Its termination the feeble light did not enable us to see.

"Proceed," I said; "herein is the Amontillado. As for Luchesi — "

"He is an ignoramus," interrupted my friend, as he stepped unsteadily forward, while I followed immediately at his heels. In an instant he had reached the extremity of the niche, and finding his progress arrested by the rock, stood stupidly bewildered. A moment more and I had fettered [1] him to the granite. In its surface were two iron staples,[2] distant from each other about two feet, horizontally. From one of these depended a short chain, from the other a padlock. Throwing the links about his waist, it was but the work of a few seconds to secure it. He was too much astounded to resist. Withdrawing the key I stepped back from the recess.

"Pass your hand," I said, "over the wall; you cannot help feeling the nitre. Indeed it is *very* damp. Once more let me *implore* you to return. No? Then I must positively leave you. But I must first render you all the little attentions in my power."

"The Amontillado!" ejaculated my friend, not yet recovered from his astonishment.

"True," I replied; "the Amontillado."

As I said these words I busied myself among the pile of bones of which I have before spoken. Throwing them aside, I soon uncovered a quantity of building stones and mortar. With these materials and with the aid of my trowel, I began vigorously to wall up the entrance of the niche.

I had scarcely laid the first tier of the masonry when I discovered that the intoxication of Fortunato had in a great measure worn off. The earliest indication I had of this was a low moaning cry from the depth of the recess. It was *not* the cry of a drunken man. There was then a long and obstinate silence. I laid the second tier, and the third, and the fourth; and then I heard the furious vibrations of the chain. The noise lasted for several minutes, during which, that I might hearken to it with the more satisfaction, I ceased my labors and sat down upon the bones. When at last the clanking subsided, I resumed the trowel, and finished without interruption the fifth, the sixth, and the seventh tier. The wall was now nearly upon a level with my breast. I again paused, and holding the flambeaux over the masonwork, threw a few feeble rays upon the figure within.

A succession of loud and shrill screams, bursting suddenly from the throat of the chained form, seemed to thrust me violently back. For a brief moment I hesitated — I trembled. Unsheathing my rapier,[3] I began to grope with it about the recess; but the thought of an instant reassured me. I placed my hand upon the solid fabric of the catacombs, and felt satisfied. I reapproached the wall. I replied to the yells of him who clamored. I re-echoed — I aided — I surpassed them in volume and in strength. I did this, and the clamorer grew still.

It was now midnight, and my task was drawing to a close. I had completed the eighth, the ninth, and the tenth tier. I had finished a portion of the last and the eleventh; there remained but a single stone to be fitted and plastered in. I struggled with its weight; I placed it partially in its destined position. But now there came from out the niche a low laugh that erected the hairs upon my head. It was succeeded by a sad voice, which I had difficulty in recognizing as that of the noble Fortunato. The voice said —

"Ha! ha! ha! — he! he! — a very good joke indeed — an excellent jest. We will

---

[1] **fettered** (fĕt'ẽr'd): shackled or restrained.
[2] **staples**: loops of metal to be driven into wood.

[3] **rapier** (rā'pĭ-ẽr): a straight, two-edged sword with a narrow, pointed blade.

have many a rich laugh about it at the palazzo — he! he! he! — over our wine — he! he! he!"

"The Amontillado!" I said.

"He! he! he! — he! he! he! — yes, the Amontillado. But is it not getting late? Will not they be awaiting us at the palazzo, the Lady Fortunato and the rest? Let us be gone."

"Yes," I said, "let us be gone."

"For the love of God, Montresor!"

"Yes," I said, "for the love of God!"

But to these words I hearkened in vain for a reply. I grew impatient. I called aloud.

"Fortunato!"

No answer. I called again:

"Fortunato!"

No answer still. I thrust a torch through the remaining aperture and let it fall within. There came forth in return only a jingling of the bells. My heart grew sick — on account of the dampness of the catacombs. I hastened to make an end of my labor. I forced the last stone into its position; I plastered it up. Against the new masonry I re-erected the old rampart of bones. For the half of a century no mortal has disturbed them. *In pace requiescat!* [1]

[1] *In pace requiescat:* May he rest in peace (Latin).

SETTING AS PART OF POE'S SINGLE EFFECT

Poe never places all his allusions to setting in a single passage. Rather he inserts them along the way, for by intention he is building toward a single effect of horror. To overdo any emphasis might waste its impact.

1. Note carefully the passages in which the setting is described. Begin with "It was about dusk . . ." (page 87) and conclude with "It was now midnight . . ." (page 90). Do Poe's descriptions help to build an atmosphere of horror? Do these descriptions increase or decrease the effect of the ghastly details? Explain.

2. Have you vivid mental images for *flambeaux, roquelaire,* and *motley* so you can actually *see* the two men passing through the archway down the staircase winding to the damp catacombs? Can you picture their shadows moving on the walls? the white webwork of the nitre? the dampness and the bones? Describe the scenes you visualize most clearly.

3. Poe makes use of contrast in both his setting and his characterization. At the opening of the story, what is the source of the gaiety and fun that contrasts with the dank vaults of Montresor's palazzo? What contrast do you find in the character of Montresor? Explain how he, like many other Poe characters, embodies a contrast between the logical capacities of the human mind and its dark, irrational workings.

4. Poe intends his setting to contribute to the total effect of his story. What other elements, then, does the setting support? For instance, does the setting seem in keeping with the irony of Montresor's words in the conversation following Fortunato's coughing spell (page 88)? (Remember that irony exists when there is a discrepancy between what a man says and what he means.) Does the setting fit with the irony of Montresor's answer when he deliberately misunderstands Fortunato's meaning and claims to be a mason? Can you find other examples of irony in the story? What is ironic about setting this story in carnival time and dressing Fortunato in motley?

TONE OF VOICE IN CONTEXT

The very same words can be said in such a way that they have completely different meanings. By varying your tone of voice in a sentence such as "Isn't he a sweet child?" you can express enthusiasm, sarcasm, desperation, or mild disapproval. In reading aloud, you can determine from the context of a statement the tone of voice in which it should be read. Select for reading aloud several sections of "A Cask of Amontillado" where the author has intended a double meaning.

Read aloud the parts where the reader would know from the context that Mon-

tresor was being sarcastic but where Fortunato does not know. See if you can control the tone of your voice so that a listener would take the words innocently. Discuss any disagreements you may have on interpretation, checking back to the story to improve your sensitivity to the author's intention.

ABOUT THE AUTHOR

Edgar Allan Poe (1809–1849) spent one year at the University of Virginia, where he was a brilliant student, excelling in languages and athletics. However, Poe's talents — as in future years — were not successful in making him popular. His extreme sensitiveness, his moody disposition, and his proud intellect kept others at a distance. Love for his beautiful young wife inspired some of Poe's purest poetry, including "Annabel Lee" and "Lenore," and after her death, "To One in Paradise" and "Ulalume." During a brief period of success while editor of a magazine in Philadelphia, Poe wrote "The Murders in the Rue Morgue," the first short story about a detective who solves a crime by deduction. Poe's stories are mystical and weird, with speculations hovering about the improbable and the horrible. "The Fall of the House of Usher" powerfully portrays the disintegrating effect of fear and horror. "The Cask of Amontillado" illustrates Poe's distinctive style in giving form to the most horrible and fearful aspects of life. Poe was also a distinguished critic of literature. What he wrote *about* the short story as a type of literature — as well as the many stories he wrote — made him an originator of the short story form.

As the Artist Sees It

In the painting on the opposite page, artist Robert Shore attempts to convey the atmosphere and mood of "The Cask of Amontillado." Notice that he uses cool colors to denote the eeriness of the setting. Why do you think he depicts Montresor as a shadow only?

Speaking of Setting

Some stories — "Four and Twenty Blackbirds" is a good example — could really happen anywhere, but most stories require a definite setting. In the best stories, setting helps to reinforce the single effect upon which everything converges — action, characters, and tone. All the elements work together to accomplish the author's purpose.

"The Heathen," for instance, could only have been set in some part of the world where men of different cultures could be shown against the brute forces of nature that are indifferent to all men, regardless of minor differences among them.

The opening and closing paragraphs of "The Heathen" indicate the importance to this story of the forces of nature and of human relations. Furthermore, the opening scene, a ship crowded with men and women, of all kinds and descriptions, moving into an unknown future, is clearly intentional. Jack London wanted to present a view of life in which the differences among mankind are stripped away to show a common humanity and a common destiny. From the first paragraph to the last, he selects his material toward this end, and the setting he provides is by no means accidental.

Can you, in similar fashion, re-examine the settings of stories you have already read and see how they contribute to the author's desired effect? "The Quiet Man," "Death of Red Peril," and "The Slander" will best serve this purpose.

Character

In everyday life you seldom have a chance to examine the inner thoughts and motives of people around you. By guessing, you may shrewdly piece together whatever clues you may have to their true character, but more often than not, your guesses are not right. For many reasons, human beings conceal the reasons for their actions. Indeed, very often they conceal these reasons even from themselves.

In a good short story, however, you are given a "depth-view" of a human being. Authors accomplish this depiction of character, or *characterization*, in various ways. Often the author tells you exactly what a character is thinking. Better yet, he may turn a sharp light on a situation in which a character's behavior is highly significant and let you judge for yourself. In the stories that follow, the authors sometimes tell you about a character's thoughts. At other times they let you draw your own conclusions about a character. Either way, you come to know the character as it is seldom possible to know people in real life.

A Mother in Mannville

MARJORIE KINNAN RAWLINGS

Here is a story told through the thoughts and viewpoints of one person, a woman who rents a cabin in the mountains so that she can find time to write. The story is not about this woman; it is, rather, about a boy named Jerry. Never once are you *told* what goes on in Jerry's mind. Yet when the story closes, you should know a great deal, not only about Jerry's thoughts, but also about his feelings.

THE orphanage is high in the Carolina mountains. Sometimes in winter the snowdrifts are so deep that the institution is cut off from the village below, from all the world. Fog hides the mountain peaks, the snow swirls down the valleys, and a wind blows so bitterly that the orphanage boys who take the milk twice daily to the baby cottage reach the door with fingers stiff in an agony of numbness.

"Or when we carry trays from the cookhouse for the ones that are sick," Jerry said, "we get our faces frostbit, because we can't put our hands over them. I have gloves," he added. "Some of the boys don't have any."

He liked the late spring, he said. The rhododendron was in bloom, a carpet of color, across the mountainsides, soft as the May winds that stirred the hemlocks. He called it laurel.

"It's pretty when the laurel blooms," he said. "Some of it's pink and some of it's white."

I was there in the autumn. I wanted quiet, isolation, to do some troublesome writing. I wanted mountain air to blow out the malaria from too long a time in the subtropics.[1] I was homesick, too, for the flaming maples in October, and for corn shocks and pumpkins and black-walnut trees and the lift of hills. I found them all, living in a cabin that belonged to the orphanage, half a mile beyond the orphanage farm. When I took the cabin, I asked for a boy or man to come and chop wood for the fireplace. The first few days were warm, and I found what wood I needed about the cabin; no one came, and I forgot the order.

I looked up from my typewriter one late afternoon, a little startled. A boy stood at the door, and my pointer dog, my companion, was at his side and had not barked to warn me. The boy was probably twelve years old, but undersized. He wore overalls and a torn shirt, and was barefooted.

He said, "I can chop some wood today."

I said, "But I have a boy coming from the orphanage."

[1] **subtropics:** the region bordering on the tropical zone. The author has evidently been living in some southern country, like Cuba, which is not in the hottest part of the tropics.

"I'm the boy."

"You? But you're small."

"Size don't matter, chopping wood," he said. "Some of the big boys don't chop good. I've been chopping wood at the orphanage a long time."

I visualized mangled and inadequate branches for my fires. I was well into my work and not inclined to conversation. I was a little blunt.

"Very well. There's the ax. Go ahead and see what you can do."

I went back to work, closing the door. At first the sound of the boy dragging brush annoyed me. Then he began to chop. The blows were rhythmic and steady; and shortly I had forgotten him, the sound no more of an interruption than a consistent rain. I suppose an hour and a half passed, for when I stopped and stretched, and heard the boy's steps on the cabin stoop, the sun was drooping behind the farthest mountain and the valleys were purple.

The boy said, "I have to go to supper now. I can come again tomorrow evening."

I said, "I'll pay you now for what you've done," thinking I should probably have to insist on an older boy. "Ten cents an hour?"

"Anything is all right."

We went together back of the cabin. An astonishing amount of solid wood had been cut. There were cherry logs and heavy roots of rhododendron, and blocks from the waste pine and oak left from the building of the cabin.

Putting Together Clues to Character. We can usually learn about a character in four ways: by what the author *tells* us about him; by what a character says about himself; by what other characters say about him; and by what he says or how he acts in important situations. All of these can provide clues to help understand a character. Modern authors do not use the first way as often as writers of the past. In this story, you will need to note and interrelate the other three ways of revealing a character. If you really put together all the clues the author provides, you will find that this story makes a lasting impression.

"But you've done as much as a man," I said. "This is a splendid pile."

I looked at him, actually, for the first time. His hair was the color of the corn shucks, and his eyes, very direct, were like the mountain sky when rain is pending — gray, with a shadowing of that miraculous blue. As I spoke, a light came over him — as though the setting sun had touched him with the same suffused glory with which it touched the mountains. I gave him a quarter.

"You may come tomorrow," I said, "and thank you very much."

He looked at me, and at the coin, and seemed to want to speak, but could not, and turned away.

"I'll split kindling tomorrow," he said over his thin ragged shoulder. "You'll need kindling and medium wood and logs and backlogs."

At daylight I was half awakened by the sound of chopping. Again it was so even in texture that I went back to sleep. When I left my bed in the cool morning, the boy had come and gone; and a stack of kindling was neat against the cabin wall. He came again after school in the afternoon and worked until time to return to the orphanage. His name was Jerry; he was twelve years old, and he had been at the orphanage since he was four. I could picture him at four, with the same grave gray-blue eyes and the same — independence? No, the word that comes to me is "integrity."

The word means something very special to me, and the quality for which I use it is a rare one. My father had it — there is another of whom I am almost sure — but almost no man of my acquaintance possesses it with the clarity, the purity, the simplicity of a mountain stream. But the boy Jerry had it. It is bedded on courage, but it is more than brave. It is honest, but it is more than

honesty. The ax handle broke one day. Jerry said the woodshop at the orphanage would repair it. I brought money to pay for the job and he refused it.

"I'll pay for it," he said. "I broke it. I brought the ax down careless."

"But no one hits accurately every time," I told him. "The fault was in the wood of the handle. I'll see the man from whom I bought it."

It was only then that he would take the money. He was standing back of his own carelessness. He was a free-will agent [1] and he chose to do careful work; and if he failed, he took the responsibility.

And he did for me the unnecessary thing, the gracious thing, that we find done only by the great of heart. Things no training can teach; for they are done on the instant, with no predicated experience. He found a cubbyhole beside the fireplace that I had not noticed. There, of his own accord, he put kindling and "medium" wood, so that I might always have dry fire material ready in case of sudden wet weather. A stone was loose in the rough walk to the cabin. He dug a deeper hole and steadied it, although he came, himself, by a short cut over the bank. I found that when I tried to return his thoughtfulness with such things as candy and apples he was wordless. "Thank you" was, perhaps, an expression for which he had no use, for his courtesy was instinctive. He only looked at the gift and at me, and a curtain lifted so that I saw deep into the clear well of his eyes; and gratitude was there, and affection, soft over the firm granite of his character.

He made simple excuses to come and

[1] **He was a free-will agent:** that is, he had undertaken the work of his own free will and therefore was ready to stand behind it. Jerry was willing to accept responsibility for his acts.

sit with me. I could no more have turned him away than if he had been physically hungry. I suggested once that the best time for us to visit was just before supper, when I left off my writing. After that he waited always until my typewriter had been some time quiet. One day I worked until nearly dark. I went outside the cabin, having forgotten him. I saw him going up over the hill in the twilight toward the orphanage. When I sat down on my stoop, a place was warm from his body where he had been sitting.

He became intimate, of course, with my pointer, Pat. There is a strange communion between a boy and a dog. Perhaps they possess the same singleness of spirit, the same kind of wisdom. It is difficult to explain, but it exists. When I went across the state for a weekend, I left the dog in Jerry's charge. I gave him the dog whistle and the key to the cabin, and left sufficient food. He was to come two or three times a day and let out the dog, and feed and exercise him. I should return Sunday night, and Jerry would take out the dog for the last time Sunday afternoon and then leave the key under an agreed hiding place.

My return was belated, and fog filled the mountain passes so treacherously that I dared not drive at night. The fog held the next morning, and it was Monday noon before I reached the cabin. The dog had been fed and cared for that morning. Jerry came early in the afternoon, anxious.

"The superintendent said nobody would drive in the fog," he said. "I came just before bedtime last night and you hadn't come. So I brought Pat some of my breakfast this morning. I wouldn't have let anything happen to him."

"I was sure of that. I didn't worry."

"When I heard about the fog, I thought you'd know."

He was needed for work at the orphanage, and he had to return at once. I gave him a dollar in payment, and he looked at it and went away. But that night he came in the darkness and knocked at the door.

"Come in, Jerry," I said, "if you're allowed to be away this late."

"I told maybe a story," he said. "I told them I thought you would want to see me."

"That's true," I assured him, and I saw his relief. "I want to hear about how you managed with the dog."

He sat by the fire with me, with no other light, and told me of their two days together. The dog lay close to him, and found a comfort there that I did not have for him. And it seemed to me that being with my dog, and caring for him, had brought the boy and me, too, together, so that he felt that he belonged to me as well as to the animal.

"He stayed right with me," he told, "except when he ran in the laurel. He likes the laurel. I took him up over the hill and we both ran fast. There was a place where the grass was high and I lay down in it and hid. I could hear Pat hunting for me. He found my trail and he barked. When he found me, he acted crazy; and he ran around and around me, in circles."

We watched the flames.

"That's an apple log," he said. "It burns the prettiest of any wood."

We were very close.

He was suddenly impelled to speak of things he had not spoken of before, nor had I cared to ask him.

"You look a little bit like my mother," he said. "Especially in the dark, by the fire."

"But you were only four, Jerry, when you came here. You have remembered how she looked, all these years?"

"My mother lives in Mannville," he said.

For a moment, finding that he had a mother shocked me as greatly as anything in my life has ever done; and I did not know why it disturbed me. Then I understood my distress. I was filled with a passionate resentment that any woman should go away and leave her son. A fresh anger added itself. A son like this one — The orphanage was a wholesome place; the executives were kind, good people; the food was more than adequate; the boys were healthy; a ragged shirt was no hardship, nor the doing of clean labor. Granted, perhaps, that the boy felt no lack, what about the mother? At four he would have looked the same as now. Nothing, I thought, nothing in life could change those eyes. His quality must be apparent to an idiot, a fool. I burned with questions I could not ask.

"Have you seen her, Jerry — lately?"

"I see her every summer. She sends for me."

I wanted to cry out, "Why are you not with her? How can she let you go away again?"

He said, "She comes up here from Mannville whenever she can. She doesn't have a job now."

His face shone in the firelight.

"She wanted to give me a puppy, but they can't let any one boy keep a puppy. You remember the suit I had on last Sunday?" He was plainly proud. "She sent me that for Christmas. The Christmas before that" — he drew a long breath, savoring the memory — "she sent me a pair of skates."

"Roller skates?"

My mind was busy, making pictures of her, trying to understand her. She had not, then, entirely deserted or forgotten him. But why, then — I thought, "I must not condemn her without knowing."

"Roller skates. I let the other boys use them. They're always borrowing them. But they're careful of them."

What circumstances other than poverty —

"I'm going to take the dollar you gave me for taking care of Pat," he said, "and buy her a pair of gloves."

I could only say, "That will be nice. Do you know her size?"

"I think it's eight and a half," he said.

He looked at my hands.

"Do you wear eight and a half?" he asked.

"No. I wear a smaller size, a six."

"Oh! Then I guess her hands are bigger than yours."

I hated her. Poverty or no, there was other food than bread; and the soul could starve as quickly as the body. He was taking his dollar to buy gloves for her big, stupid hands, and she lived away from him, in Mannville, and contented herself with sending him skates.

"She likes white gloves," he said. "Do you think I can get them for a dollar?"

"I think so," I said.

I decided that I should not leave the mountains without seeing her and knowing for myself why she had done this thing.

The human mind scatters its interests as though made of thistledown, and every wind stirs and moves it. I finished my work. It did not please me, and I gave my thoughts to another field. I should need some Mexican material.

I made arrangements to close my Florida place. Mexico immediately, and doing the writing there, if conditions were favorable. Then, Alaska with my brother. After that, heaven knew what or where.

I did not take time to go to Mannville to see Jerry's mother, nor even to talk with the orphanage officials about her. I was a trifle abstracted about the boy, because of my work and plans. And after my first fury at her — we did not speak of her again — his having a mother, any sort at all, not far away, in Mannville, relieved me of the ache I had had about him. He did not question the anomalous [1] relation. He was not lonely. It was none of my concern.

He came every day and cut my wood and did small helpful favors and stayed to talk. The days had become cold, and often I let him come inside the cabin. He would lie on the floor in front of the fire, with one arm across the pointer; and they would both doze and wait quietly for me. Other days they ran with a common ecstasy through the laurel; and since the asters were now gone, he brought me back vermilion maple leaves and chestnut boughs dripping with imperial yellow. [2]

I was ready to go. I said to him, "You have been my good friend, Jerry. I shall often think of you and miss you. Pat will miss you too. I am leaving tomorrow."

He did not answer. When he went away, I remember that a new moon hung over the mountains and I watched him go in silence up the hill. I expected him the next day, but he did not come. The details of packing my personal belongings, loading my car, arranging the bed over the seat — where the dog would ride — occupied me until late in the day. I closed the cabin and started the car, noticing that the sun was in the west and I should do well to be out of the mountains by nightfall. I stopped by the orphanage and left the cabin key and money for my light bill with Miss Clark.

"And will you call Jerry for me to say good-by to him?"

"I don't know where he is," she said. "I'm afraid he's not well. He didn't eat his dinner this noon. One of the other boys saw him going over the hill into the laurel. He was supposed to fire the boiler this afternoon. It's not like him; he's unusually reliable."

I was almost relieved; for I knew I should never see him again, and it would be easier not to say good-by to him.

I said, "I wanted to talk with you about his mother — why he's here — but I'm in more of a hurry than I expected to be. It's out of the question for me to see her now, too. But here's some money I'd like to leave with you to buy things for him at Christmas and on his birthday. It will be better than for me to try to send him things. I could so easily duplicate — skates, for instance."

She blinked her honest eyes.

"There's not much use for skates here," she said.

Her stupidity annoyed me.

---

[1] **anomalous** (à·nŏm′à·lŭs): irregular, exceptional.

[2] **imperial** (ĭm·pēr′ĭ·ál) **yellow**: a bright shade of yellow used officially by the royal families of ancient China.

"What I mean," I said, "is that I don't want to duplicate things his mother sends him. I might have chosen skates if I didn't know she had already given them to him."

She stared at me.

"I don't understand," she said. "He has no mother. He has no skates."

PUTTING TOGETHER CLUES TO CHARACTER

1. In the first part of the story, Jerry is presented as a boy of great honesty. What does he do to give you this impression?

2. At the close of the story, we discover that Jerry has lied about having a mother and receiving presents from her. Does this show another side of his character, or a change in character? Is his total character *consistent*, believable? Explain.

3. Missing the clues to character in this story could lead you to some strange interpretations. What are some of the mistaken judgments a careless reader might make concerning: (a) the woman writer; (b) Jerry; (c) or Miss Clark?

4. Gloves are important in this story. If they represent something more than mere gloves, we can call them *symbols*. At the very beginning and again, toward the end, gloves are given a prominent place in this story. What do you think they might symbolize?

5. What insight into the needs of all human beings does this story offer? Can you point to a sentence in the story that contains the main idea of this story?

6. Here is a story in which almost every word, every incident, and even every omission is important. For instance, the writer presents herself as thoughtless and self-centered. Yet when you have fully understood the story, you realize that these failures in human relations are intended to underscore the meaning of the story. With which of Jerry's actions do these thoughtless actions of the author contrast?

GAINING POWER OVER WORDS

FIGURES OF SPEECH In order to make clear what we mean, all of us use comparisons. When we say, "Sally flew out of the room," we do not mean that she actually flapped her wings, but that her speed was as rapid as a bird's flight. We call such comparisons *figures of speech.* The figure of speech used in this example is a *metaphor,* an implied comparison. If we had said, "Sally flew *like* a bird," we would have been using a *simile,* a direct comparison.

Find several figures of speech in this story and explain how they help to describe a character.

ABOUT THE AUTHOR

Marjorie Kinnan Rawlings (1896–1953) won the Pulitzer prize in 1939 for *The Yearling,* her sensitive story of a Florida backwoods boy and his pet fawn. After graduating from the University of Wisconsin and working as a newspaper woman, Mrs. Rawlings settled in northern Florida where she lived for twenty-five years. She used the swamplands and back country of Florida as settings for her stories of the people she knew from experience.

Studies in Character ➤

A good writer knows that physical appearance is only a small — and often, in itself, misleading — part of developing characterization. Heroes sometimes look like villains, and saints like sinners. These portraits of three historical figures give you a chance to see of how much value physical appearance is as a clue to a person's character. On the basis of physical appearance alone, what would you judge the character of these three men to be? You might even describe each in a brief written composition.

Richard III of England (1452–1485) (No. 1) was thought by many (including Shakespeare) to have murdered two children in order to become king. George Monck (No. 2), a general under Oliver Cromwell, risked his life to help others during the Great Plague in London in 1665. Sir Christopher Wren (1632–1723) (No. 3) is considered England's most honored architect. With a little research in the library, you can "fill out" their characters, by adding to your characterization what they did and what others thought of them — as a writer would do in developing a fictional character.

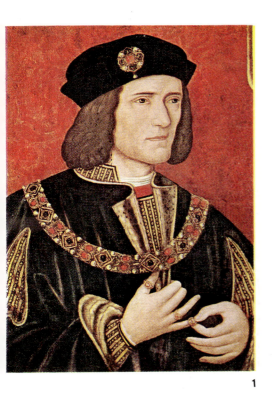

1

2

3

All the Years of Her Life

MORLEY CALLAGHAN

Is it true that people show different sides of their personality in different situations? Does everyone have a single character or many characters? In this story a woman's character surprises even her own son.

THEY WERE CLOSING the drugstore, and Alfred Higgins, who had just taken off his white jacket, was putting on his coat and getting ready to go home. The little gray-haired man, Sam Carr, who owned the drugstore, was bending down behind the cash register, and when Alfred Higgins passed him, he looked up and said softly, "Just a moment, Alfred. One moment before you go."

The soft, confident, quiet way in which Sam Carr spoke made Alfred start to button his coat nervously. He felt sure his face was white. Sam Carr usually said, "Good night," brusquely, without looking up. In the six months he had been working in the drugstore Alfred had never heard his employer speak softly like that. His heart began to beat so loud it was hard for him to get his breath. "What is it, Mr. Carr?" he asked.

"Maybe you'd be good enough to take a few things out of your pocket and leave them here before you go," Sam Carr said.

"What things? What are you talking about?"

"You've got a compact and a lipstick and at least two tubes of toothpaste in your pocket, Alfred."

"What do you mean? Do you think I'm crazy?" Alfred blustered. His face got red and he knew he looked fierce with indignation. But Sam Carr, standing by the door with his blue eyes shining bright behind his glasses and his lips moving underneath his gray mustache, only nodded his head a few times, and then Alfred grew very

Relating the Title to the Story. As the title indicates, time is important in this story. As you read, watch for the ways in which the past throws light on the present. Then ask yourself what the future will hold for this mother and son.

frightened and he didn't know what to say. Slowly he raised his hand and dipped it into his pocket, and with his eyes never meeting Sam Carr's eyes, he took out a blue compact and two tubes of toothpaste and a lipstick, and he laid them one by one on the counter.

"Petty thieving, eh, Alfred?" Sam Carr said. "And maybe you'd be good enough to tell me how long this has been going on."

"This is the first time I ever took anything."

"So now you think you'll tell me a lie, eh? What kind of a sap do I look like, huh? I don't know what goes on in my own store, eh? I tell you you've been doing this pretty steady," Sam Carr said as he went over and stood behind the cash register.

Ever since Alfred had left school he had been getting into trouble wherever he worked. He lived at home with his mother and his father, who was a printer. His two older brothers were married and his sister had got married last year, and it would have been all right for his parents now if Alfred had only been able to keep a job.

While Sam Carr smiled and stroked the side of his face very delicately with the tips of his fingers, Alfred began to feel that familiar terror growing in him that had been in him every time he had got into such trouble.

"I liked you," Sam Carr was saying. "I liked you and would have trusted you, and now look what I got to do." While Alfred watched with his alert, frightened blue eyes, Sam Carr drummed with his fingers on the counter. "I don't like to call a cop in point-blank," he was saying as he looked very worried. "You're a fool, and maybe I should call your father and tell him you're a fool. Maybe I should let them know I'm going to have you locked up."

"My father's not at home. He's a printer. He works nights," Alfred said.

"Who's at home?"

"My mother, I guess."

"Then we'll see what she says." Sam Carr went to the phone and dialed the number. Alfred was not so much ashamed, but there was that deep fright growing in him, and he blurted out arrogantly, like a strong, full-grown man, "Just a minute. You don't need to draw anybody else in. You don't need to tell her." He wanted to sound like a swaggering, big guy who could look after himself, yet the old, childish hope was in him, the longing that someone at home would come and help him. "Yeah, that's right, he's in trouble," Mr. Carr was saying. "Yeah, your boy works for me. You'd better come down in a hurry." And when he was finished Mr. Carr went over to the door and looked out at the street and watched the people passing in the late summer night. "I'll keep my eye out for a cop" was all he said.

Alfred knew how his mother would come rushing in; she would rush in with her eyes blazing, or maybe she would be crying, and she would push him away when he tried to talk to her, and make him feel her dreadful contempt; yet he longed that she might come before Mr. Carr saw the cop on the beat passing the door.

While they waited — and it seemed a long time — they did not speak, and when at last they heard someone tapping on the closed door, Mr. Carr, turning the latch, said crisply, "Come in, Mrs. Higgins." He looked hard-faced and stern.

Mrs. Higgins must have been going to bed when he telephoned, for her hair was tucked in loosely under her hat, and her hand at her throat held her light coat tightly across her chest so her dress would not show. She came in, large and plump, with a little smile on her friendly face. Most of the store lights had been turned out and at first she did not see Alfred, who was standing in the shadow at the end of the counter. Yet as soon as she saw him she did not look as Alfred thought she would look: she smiled, her blue eyes never wavered, and with a calmness and dignity that made them forget that her clothes seemed to have been thrown on her, she put out her hand to Mr. Carr and said politely, "I'm Mrs. Higgins. I'm Alfred's mother."

Mr. Carr was a bit embarrassed by her lack of terror and her simplicity, and he hardly knew what to say to her, so she asked, "Is Alfred in trouble?"

"He is. He's been taking things from the store. I caught him red-handed. Little things like compacts and toothpaste and lipsticks. Stuff he can sell easily," the proprietor said.

As she listened Mrs. Higgins looked at Alfred sometimes and nodded her head sadly, and when Sam Carr had finished she said gravely, "Is it so, Alfred?"

"Yes."

"Why have you been doing it?"

"I been spending money, I guess."

"On what?"

"Going around with the guys, I guess," Alfred said.

Mrs. Higgins put out her hand and touched Sam Carr's arm with an understanding gentleness, and speaking as though afraid of disturbing him, she said, "If you would only listen to me before doing anything." Her simple earnestness made her shy; her humility made her falter and look away, but in a moment she was smiling gravely again, and she said with a kind of patient dignity, "What did you intend to do, Mr. Carr?"

"I was going to get a cop. That's what I ought to do."

"Yes, I suppose so. It's not for me to say, because he's my son. Yet I sometimes think a little good advice is the best thing for a boy when he's at a certain period in his life," she said.

Alfred couldn't understand his mother's quiet composure, for if they had been at home and someone had suggested that he was going to be arrested, he knew she would be in a rage and would cry out against him. Yet now she was standing there with that gentle, pleading smile on her face, saying, "I wonder if you don't think it would be better just to let him come home with me. He looks a big fellow, doesn't he? It takes some of them a long time to get any sense," and they both stared at Alfred, who shifted away with a bit of light shining for a moment on his thin face and the tiny pimples over his cheek-bone.

But even while he was turning away uneasily Alfred was realizing that Mr. Carr had become aware that his mother was really a fine woman; he knew that Sam Carr was puzzled by his mother, as if he had expected her to come in and plead with him tearfully, and instead he was being made to feel a bit ashamed by her vast tolerance. While there was only the sound of the mother's soft, assured voice in the store, Mr. Carr began to nod his head encouragingly at her. Without being alarmed, while being just large and still and simple and hopeful, she was becoming dominant there in the dimly lit store. "Of course, I don't want to be harsh," Mr. Carr was saying, "I'll tell you what I'll do. I'll just fire him and let it go at that. How's that?" and he got up and shook hands with Mrs. Higgins, bowing low to her in deep respect.

There was such warmth and gratitude in the way she said, "I'll never forget your kindness," that Mr. Carr began to feel warm and genial himself.

"Sorry we had to meet this way," he said. "But I'm glad I got in touch with you. Just wanted to do the right thing, that's all," he said.

"It's better to meet like this than never, isn't it?" she said. Suddenly they clasped hands as if they liked each other, as if they had known each other a long time. "Good night, sir," she said.

"Good night, Mrs. Higgins. I'm truly sorry," he said.

The mother and son walked along the street together, and the mother was taking a long, firm stride as she looked ahead with her stern face full of worry. Alfred was afraid to speak to her, he was afraid of the silence that was between them, so he only looked ahead too, for the excitement and relief was still pretty strong in him; but in a little while, going along like that in silence made him terribly aware of the strength and the sternness in her; he began to wonder what she was thinking of as she stared ahead so grimly; she seemed to have forgotten that he walked beside her; so when they were passing under the Sixth Avenue elevated [1] and the rumble of the train seemed to break the silence, he said in his old, blustering way, "Thank God it turned out like that. I certainly won't get in a jam like that again."

"Be quiet. Don't speak to me. You've disgraced me again and again," she said bitterly.

"That's the last time. That's all I'm saying."

"Have the decency to be quiet," she snapped. They kept on their way, looking straight ahead.

When they were at home and his

[1] elevated: a railway running above the streets on elevated tracks.

mother took off her coat, Alfred saw that she was really only half-dressed, and she made him feel afraid again when she said, without even looking at him, "You're a bad lot. God forgive you. It's one thing after another and always has been. Why do you stand there stupidly? Go to bed, why don't you?" When he was going, she said, "I'm going to make myself a cup of tea. Mind, now, not a word about tonight to your father."

While Alfred was undressing in his bedroom, he heard his mother moving around the kitchen. She filled the kettle and put it on the stove. She moved a chair. And as he listened there was no shame in him, just wonder and a kind of admiration of her strength and repose. He could still see Sam Carr nodding his head encouragingly to her; he could hear her talking simply and earnestly, and as he sat on his bed he felt a pride in her strength. "She certainly was smooth," he thought. "Gee, I'd like to tell her she sounded swell."

And at last he got up and went along to the kitchen, and when he was at the door he saw his mother pouring herself a cup of tea. He watched and he didn't move. Her face, as she sat there, was a frightened, broken face utterly unlike the face of the woman who had been so assured a little while ago in the drugstore. When she reached out and lifted the kettle to pour hot water in her cup, her hand trembled and the water splashed on the stove. Leaning back in the chair, she sighed and lifted the cup to her lips, and her lips were groping loosely as if they would never reach the cup. She swallowed the hot tea eagerly, and then she straightened up in relief, though her hand holding the cup still trembled. She looked very old.

It seemed to Alfred that this was the way it had been every time he had been in trouble before, that this trembling had really been in her as she hurried out half-dressed to the drugstore. He understood why she had sat alone in the kitchen the night his young sister had kept repeating doggedly that she was getting married. Now he felt all that his mother had been thinking of as they walked along the street together a little while ago. He watched his mother, and he never spoke, but at that moment his youth seemed to be over; he knew all the years of her life by the way her hand trembled as she raised the cup to her lips. It seemed to him that this was the first time he had ever looked upon his mother.

RELATING THE TITLE TO THE STORY

1. Whose story is this, Alfred's or his mother's? Do you agree with the title in putting the emphasis on Mrs. Higgins?

2. Do you blame anyone for Alfred's thieving? If so, whom?

3. How has Mrs. Higgins previously reacted to such incidents? What is new about her behavior this time?

4. What changes brought about by time might account for Mrs. Higgins' surprising behavior in the drugstore? Do you feel that past experiences have finally taught her how to deal with Alfred and those who catch him misbehaving? Or do you feel that heretofore, when Alfred was younger, the mother had hoped to change him and that now she feels he has reached an age when his character is set and there is nothing further she can do? Perhaps you have still another explanation. Considering all of the various possibilities, how do *you* interpret her behavior?

5. What hints about the home life of the Higgins family occur in the story? Do these throw any light on "all the years" of Mrs. Higgins' life?

6. As they walk home, Alfred sees his mother as stern and strong. As he listens to her in the drugstore, he admires her strength and repose. When he gets up and goes to the kitchen, looking upon her unawares, he sees her in still another way. Which of these is the true picture of Mrs.

Higgins? or are all of them true? Explain.

7. Now that his mother has changed toward him, and he has seen her in a new light, do you think Alfred will behave any differently? Explain your answer.

ABOUT THE AUTHOR

Morley Callaghan (1903–), Irish by descent, was born in Toronto, Canada. Between attending college and law school, he worked in two rather different positions: first, as a reporter on the Toronto *Daily Star*, and later, in charge of a circulating library. He received encouragement in his first writing efforts from Ernest Hemingway, whom Callaghan met while still with the *Daily Star*. In Paris he met through Hemingway many of the so-called "expatriates" from the United States. Callaghan returned to Canada to write while continuing to practice law. He has published more than one hundred short stories. Critics compare his style of writing — with some reservations — with that of Hemingway; for Callaghan's writing is considered spare and intense in style.

Stock Characters ➤

The theatrical posters on the opposite page are from the late nineteenth century. We are not very proud of most of the plays produced in America during this period. Generally, they featured quite predictable characters — villains, heroes, heroines — in equally predictable situations. These *stock characters* were so much the same from play to play that a theater owner could use the same advertising poster over and over. He had merely to add information about the current play.

Unfortunately, stock characters are still around today. There are "good guys" and "bad guys" and "the girl (or boy) next door": you have met them all in second-rate TV shows, movies, books, and magazines. They always show the same traits, and they require no imagination or insight from writer, viewer, or reader.

In dramatic and literary works of merit, however, the characters are more complex, more convincing. They are more like the people we encounter every day. We enjoy meeting them, and we remember them as individuals — not as stock types.

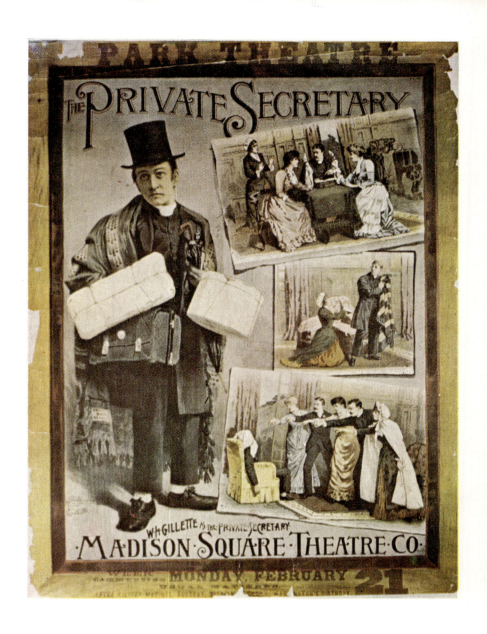

The Duke's Children

FRANK O'CONNOR

To understand a person, it is said, find out what he wants to be like in the future. All of us are pointed in the direction of what we want to become. Everyone is actively, endlessly judging, desiring, adjusting — *becoming.*

In this process of becoming, one important direction given to character is determined by a child's parents or lack of parents. It is interesting that all three of the stories in this group deal with just this relationship. Here is another story in which parents, or a lack of them, affect a young person's judgment of what he would like to *become.*

I COULD NEVER see precisely what was supposed to be exaggerated in the plots of novelists like Dickens. To this day I can still read about some mysterious street-urchin, brought up to poverty and vice by a rag-picker, who turns out to be the missing heir to an earldom, and see nothing peculiar about it. To me, it all seems the most natural thing in the world.

Having always been Mother's pet, I was comparatively grown-up when the truth about my own birth broke on me first. In fact, I was already at work as a messenger boy on the railway. Naturally, I had played with the idea as I had played with scores of other ideas, but suddenly, almost in a day, every other possibility disappeared, and I knew I had nothing whatever in common with the two commonplace creatures with whom my fate had become so strangely linked.

It wasn't only their poverty that repelled me, though that was bad enough, or the tiny terrace house we lived in, with its twelve-foot square of garden in front, its crumbling stumps of gate-posts and low wall that had lost its railing. It was their utter commonness, their squabbles about money, their low friends and fatuous [1] conversations. You could see that no breath of fineness had ever touched them. They seemed like people who had been crippled from birth and never known what it was to walk or run or dance. Though I might be — for the moment, at least — only a messenger, I had those long spells when by some sort of instinct I knew who I really was, could stand aside and watch myself come up the road after my day's work with relaxed and measured steps, turning my head slowly to greet some neighbor and raising my cap with a grace and charm that came of centuries of breeding. Not only could I see myself like that; there were even times when I could hear an interior voice that preceded and dictated each movement as though it were a fragment of a storybook: "He raised his cap gracefully while his face broke into a thoughtful smile."

And then, as I turned the corner, I would see Father at the gate in his house clothes, a ragged trousers and vest, an old cap that came down over his eyes, and boots cut into something that resembled sandals and that he insisted on calling his "slippers." Father was a creature of habit. No sooner was he out of his working clothes than he was peppering for his evening paper, and if the newsboy were five minutes late, Father muttered: "I don't know what's coming over that boy at all!" and drifted down to the main road to listen for him. When the newsboy did at last appear, Father would grab the paper from his hand and almost run home, putting on his spectacles awkwardly as he ran and triumphantly surveying the promised treat of the headlines.

And suddenly everything would go black on me, and I would take the chair by the open back door while Father, sitting at the other end, uttered little exclamations of joy or rage and Mother asked anxiously how I had got on during the day. Most of the time I could reply only in monosyllables. How could I tell her that nothing had happened at work that was not as common as the things that happened at home: nothing but those moments of blinding illumination when I was alone in the station yard on a spring morning with sunlight striking the cliffs above the tunnel, and, picking my way between the rails and the trucks, I realized that it was not for long, that I was a duke or earl, lost, stolen, or strayed from my proper home, and that I had only to be discovered for everything to fall into its place? Illumination came only when I had escaped; most often when I crossed the yard on my way from work and dawdled in the passenger station before the bookstall, or watched a passenger train go out on its way to Queenstown [2] or Dublin [3] and realized that one day some train like that would take me back to my true home and patrimony. [4]

These gloomy silences used to make Father mad. He was a talkative man, and every little incident of his day turned into narrative and drama for him. He seemed forever to be meeting old comrades of his army days whom he had not met for fifteen years, and astounding changes had always taken place in them in the meantime. When one of his old friends called, or even

[1] **fatuous** (făt′ū·ŭs): foolish; without reality.

[2] **Queenstown:** a seaport on the southern coast of Ireland, now known as Cobh.

[3] **Dublin:** a seaport and leading city on the eastern coast of Ireland.

[4] **patrimony** (păt′rĭ·mō′nĭ): an estate inherited from one's father.

when some woman from across the square dropped in for a cup of tea, he would leave everything, even his newspaper, to talk. His corner by the window permitting him no room for drama, he would stamp about the tiny kitchen, pausing at the back door to glance up at the sky or by the other door into the little hallway to see who was passing outside in the Square. It irritated him when I got up in the middle of all this, took my cap, and went quietly out. It irritated him even more if I read while he and the others talked, and, when some question was addressed to me, put down my book and gazed at him blankly. He was so coarse in grain that he regarded it as insolence. He had no experience of dukes, and had never heard that interior voice which dictated my movements and words. "Slowly the lad lowered the book in which he had been immersed and gazed wonderingly at the man who called himself his father."

One evening I was coming home from work when a girl spoke to me. She was a girl called Nancy Harding whose elder brother I knew slightly. I had never spoken to her — indeed, there were not many girls I did speak to. I was too conscious of the fact that, though my jacket was good enough, my trousers were an old blue pair of Father's, cut down and with a big patch in the seat. But Nancy, emerging from a house near the quarry, hailed me as if we were old friends and walked with me up the road. She was slim and dark-haired with an eager and inconsequent manner, and her chatter bewildered and charmed me. My own conversation was of a rather portentous sort.

"I was down with Madge Regan, getting the answers for my homework," she explained. "I don't know what's wrong with me, but I can't do those blooming old sums. Where were you?"

"Oh, I was at work," I answered.

"At work?" she exclaimed in astonishment. "Till this hour?"

"I have to work from eight to seven," I said modestly.

"But aren't they terrible hours?" she said.

"Ah, I'm only filling in time," I explained lightly. "I don't expect to be there long."

This was prophetic, because I was sacked a couple of months later, but at the time I just wanted to make it clear if there was any exploitation being done it was I and not the railway company that was doing it. We walked slowly, and she stood under the gas lamp at the end of the Square with me. Darkness or day, it was funny how people made a rendezvous of gas lamps. They were our playrooms when we were kids and our clubs as we became older. And then, for the first time, I heard the words running through my head as though they were dictating to someone else behind myself. "Pleased with his quiet conversation and well-bred voice, she wondered if he could really be the son of the Delaneys at all." Up to this, the voice had paid no attention to other people; now that it had begun to expand its activities it took on a new reality, and I longed to repeat the experience.

I had several opportunities, because we met like that a couple of times when I was coming home from work. I was not observant, and it wasn't until years after that it struck me that she might have been waiting for me at the same house at the same time. And one evening, when we were standing under our gas lamp, I talked a little too enthusiastically about some storybook, and Nancy asked for the loan of it. I was pleased with her attention but alarmed at the thought of her seeing where I lived.

"I'll bring it with me tomorrow," I said.

"Ah, come on and get it for me now," she said coaxingly, and I glanced over my shoulder and saw Father at the gate, his head cocked, listening for the newsboy. I felt suddenly sick. I knew such a nice girl couldn't possibly want to meet Father, but I didn't see how I was to get the book without introducing them. We went up the little uneven avenue together.

"This is Nancy Harding, Dad," I said in an off-hand tone. "I just want to get a book for her."

"Oh, come in, girl, come in," he said, smiling amiably. "Sit down, can't you, while you're waiting?" Father's sociability almost caused him to forget the newsboy. "Min," he called to Mother, "you keep an eye on the paper," and he set a chair in the middle of the kitchen floor. As I searched in the front room for the book, which in my desperation I could not find, I heard Mother go for the paper and Father talking away like mad to Nancy, and when I went into the kitchen, there he was in his favorite chair, the paper lying unopened on the table beside him while he told an endless, pointless story about old times in the neighborhood. Father had been born in the neighborhood, which he seemed to think a matter for pride, but if there was one of Father's favorite subjects I could not stand, it was the still wilder and more sordid life people had lived there when he was growing up. This story was about a wake [1] — all his juiciest stories were about wakes — and a tired woman getting jealous of the corpse in the bed. He was so pleased with Nancy's attention that he

[1] **wake:** the sitting up of persons to honor someone who has just died.

was dramatizing even more than usual, and I stood silent in the kitchen door for several minutes with a ducal air of scorn before he even noticed me. As I saw Nancy to the road I felt humiliated to the depths of my being. I noticed that the hallway was streaming with damp, that our gate was only a pair of brick stumps from which the cement had fallen away, and that the Square, which had never been adopted by the Council, was full of washing. There were two washerwomen on the terrace, each with a line of her own.

But that wasn't the worst. One evening when I came home, Mother said joyously:

"Oh, your dad ran into that nice little Harding girl on his way home."

"Oh, did he?" I asked indifferently, though feeling I had been kicked hard in the stomach.

"Oh, my goodness!" Father exclaimed, letting down his paper for a moment and crowing. "The way that one talks! Spatter! spatter! spatter! And, by the way," he added, looking at me over his glasses, "her aunt Lil used to be a great friend of your mother's at one time. Her mother was a Clancy. I knew there was something familiar about her face."

"I'd never have recognized it," Mother said gravely. "Such a quiet little woman as Miss Clancy used to be."

"Oh, begor, there's nothing quiet about that niece," chortled Father, but he did not sound disapproving. Father liked young people with something to say for themselves — not like me.

I was mortified. It was bad enough not seeing Nancy myself, but to have her meet Father like that, in his working clothes coming from the manure factory down the Glen, and hear him — as I had no doubt she did hear him — talk in his ignorant way about me was too much. I could not help contrasting Father with Mr. Harding, whom I occasionally met coming from work and whom I looked at with a respect that bordered on reverence. He was a small man with a face like a clenched fist, always very neatly dressed, and he usually carried his newspaper rolled up like a baton and sometimes hit his thigh with it as he strode briskly home.

One evening when I glanced shyly at him, he nodded in his brusque way. Everything about him was brusque, keen, and soldierly, and when I saw that he recognized me I swung into step beside him. He was like a military procession with a brass band, the way he always set the pace for anyone who accompanied him.

"Where are you working now?" he asked sharply with a side glance at me.

"Oh, on the railway still," I said. "Just for a few months, anyway."

"And what are you doing there?"

"Oh, just helping in the office," I replied lightly. I knew this was not exactly true, but I hated to tell anybody that I was only a messenger boy. "Of course, I study in my spare time," I added hastily. It was remarkable how the speeding up of my pace seemed to speed up my romancing as well. There was something breathless about the man that left me breathless, too. "I thought of taking the Indian Civil Service exam [1] or something of the sort. There's no future in railways."

"Isn't there?" he asked with some surprise.

"Not really," I answered indifferently. "Another few years and it will all be trucks. I really do it only as a stop-gap. I wouldn't like to take any permanent job unless I could travel. Outside Ireland, I mean. You see, languages are my major interest."

"Are they?" he asked in the same tone. "How many do you know?"

"Oh, only French and German at the moment — I mean, enough to get round with," I said. The pace was telling on me. I felt I wasn't making the right impression. Maybe to be a proper linguist you needed to know a dozen languages. I mended my hand as best I could. "I'm going to do Italian and Spanish this winter if I get time. You can't get anywhere in the modern world without Spanish. After English it's the most spoken of them all."

"Go on!" he said.

I wasn't altogether pleased with the results of this conversation. The moment I had left him, I slowed down to a gentle stroll, and this made me realize that the quick march had committed me farther than I liked to go. All I really knew of foreign languages was a few odd words and phrases, like echoes

[1] **Indian Civil Service exam:** At the time of this story, Britain was in control of India and required British citizens to pass the civil service examination in order to hold government posts in India. (Southern Ireland, as well as India, is no longer under British rule.)

of some dream of my lost fatherland, which I learned and repeated to myself with a strange, dreamy pleasure. It was not prudent to pretend that I knew the languages thoroughly. After all, Mr. Harding had three daughters, all well-educated. People were always being asked to his house, and I had even been encouraging myself with the prospect of being asked as well. But now, if I were invited, it would be mainly because of my supposed knowledge of foreign languages, and when Nancy or one of her sisters burst into fluent French or German my few poetic phrases would not be much help. I needed something more practical, something to do with railways, for preference. I had an old French phrase-book, which I had borrowed from somebody, and I determined to learn as much as I could of this by heart.

I worked hard, spurred on by an unexpected meeting with Nancy's eldest sister, Rita, who suddenly stopped and spoke to me on the road, though to my astonishment and relief she spoke in English.

Then, one evening when I was on my usual walk, which in those days nearly always brought me somewhere near Nancy's house, I ran into her going in, and we stood at the street corner near her home. I was pleased with this because Rita came out soon afterwards and said in a conspiratorial tone: "Why don't ye grab the sofa before Kitty gets it?" which made Nancy blush, and then her father passed and nodded to us. I waved back to him, but Nancy had turned her back as he appeared so that she did not see him. I drew her attention to him striding down the road, but somehow this only put her in mind of my father.

"I saw him again the other day," she said with a smile that hurt me.

"Did you?" I asked with a sniff. "What was he talking about? His soldiering days?"

"No," she said with interest. "Does he talk about them?"

"Does he ever talk about anything else?" I replied wearily. "I have that last war off by heart. It seems to have been the only thing that ever happened to him."

"He knows a terrible lot, though, doesn't he?" she asked.

"He's concealed it pretty well," I replied. "The man is an out-and-out failure, and he's managed to turn Mother into one as well. I suppose she had whatever brains there were between them — which wasn't much, I'm afraid."

"Go on!" said Nancy with a bewildered air. "Then why did she marry him?"

" 'Echo answers why,' " I said with a laugh at being able to get in a phrase that had delighted me in some storybook. "Oh, I suppose it was the usual thing."

Nancy blushed again and made to leave.

"Well, it's well to be you," she said, "knowing what's wrong with him. God alone knows what's wrong with mine."

I was sorry she had to go in such a hurry, but pleased with the impression of culture and sophistication I had managed to convey, and I looked forward to showing off a bit more when I went to one of their Sunday evening parties. With that, and some really practical French, I could probably get anywhere.

At the same time it struck me that they were very slow about asking me, and my evening walks past their house took on a sort of stubborn defiance. At least, I wouldn't let them ignore me. It wasn't until weeks later that the bitter truth dawned on me — that I was not being invited because nobody wanted

watching it, it even seemed possible that I was what they thought, not the son of a duke but the son of a laborer in the manure factory; but at other times, as I was walking home by myself, tired and dispirited, the truth blazed up angrily in me again, and I knew that when it became known, the Hardings would be the first to regret their blindness. At such times I was always making brilliant loveless matches and then revealing coldly to Nancy that I had never cared for anyone but her.

It was at the lowest depth of my misery that I was introduced to a girl called May Dwyer, and somehow, from the first moment, I found that there was no need for me to indulge in invention. Invention and May would never have gone together. She had a directness of approach I had never met with before in a girl. The very first evening I saw her home she asked me if I could afford the tram fare. That shocked me, but afterwards I was grateful. Then she asked me in to see her parents, which scared me stiff, but I promised to come in another night when it wasn't so late, and at once she told me which evenings she was free. It was not forwardness or lightness in her; it was all part of a directness that made her immediately both a companion and a sweetheart. I owe her a lot, for without her I might still be airing my French and German to any woman who attracted me.

Even when I did go in with her for a cup of tea, I felt at home after the first few minutes. Her father was a long, sad Civil Servant, and her mother a bright, direct little woman not unlike May herself, and whatever he said, the pair of them argued with and jeered him unmercifully. This only made him hang his head lower, but suddenly, after I had been talking for awhile, he began to argue with me about the state

me there. Nancy had seen my home and talked to my parents; her sisters and father had seen me; and all of them had seen my cut-down trousers with the patch on the seat. It mattered nothing to them even if I spoke French and German like an angel, even if I were liable to be sent off to India in the next few months. They did not think I was their class.

Those were the bitterest weeks of my life. With a sort of despair I took my evening walk in the early winter days past their house, but never saw anybody, and as I turned up the muddy lane behind it and heard the wind moaning in the branches, and looked down across the sloping field to their house, nestling in the hollow with the light shining brilliantly in the kitchen, where the girls did their homework, it seemed to be full of all the beauty I would never know. Sometimes, when I was leaning over the lane wall and of the country, which seemed to cause him a lot of concern. In those days I was very optimistic on the subject, and I put my hands deep in my trousers pockets and answered him back politely but firmly. Then he caught me out on a matter of fact, and suddenly he gave a great crow of delight and went out to bring in two bottles of Guinness.[1] By this time I was so much in my element that I accepted the Guinness: I always have loved a good argument.

May said when I was leaving, "Do you ever stop once you start?"

"It's not so often I meet an intelligent talker," I said loftily.

"When you've heard as much of my old fellow as I have, maybe you won't think he's so intelligent," she said, but she did not sound indignant, and I had an impression that she was really quite pleased at having brought home a young fellow who could entertain her father. It gave her the feeling that she was really all the time an intellectual, but had met the wrong sort of boy. In the years I was courting her we quarrelled often, but between her father and me it was a case of love at first sight. After I was fired from the railway, it was he who got me another job and insisted on my looking after it. The poor devil had always been pining for a man in the house.

Then one evening I ran into Nancy Harding, whom I had not seen for months. It was an embarrassing moment because I realized at once that my fantasy had all come true. If I had not actually made a brilliant match, I had as good as done so, and yet she was my first and purest love.

"I hear you and May Dwyer are very great these days," she said, and something in her tone struck me as peculiar.

¹ **Guinness:** a stout; that is, a heavy malt drink.

Afterwards I realized that it was the tone I was supposed to adopt when I broke the news to her.

"I've seen quite a lot of her," I admitted.

"You weren't long getting hooked," she went on with a smile that somehow did not come off.

"I don't know about being 'hooked,' as you call it," I said, getting on my dignity at once. "She asked me to her house and I went, that's all."

"Oh, we know all about it," said Nancy, and this time there was no mistaking the malice in her tone. "You don't have to tell me anything."

"Well, there isn't so much to tell," I replied with a bland smile.

"And I suppose she talks French and German like a native?" asked Nancy.

This reference to the falsehoods I had told did hurt me. I had known they were indiscreet, but it hadn't occurred to me that they would become a joke in the Harding family.

"I don't honestly know what you're talking about, Nancy," I said weakly. "May asked me to her house and I went, just as I'd have gone to yours if you'd asked me. That's all there is to it."

"Oh, is that all?" she asked in her commonest tone, and suddenly, to my astonishment, I saw tears in her eyes. "And if you had a house like mine you wouldn't mind asking people there either, would you? And sisters like mine! And a father like mine! It's all very well for you to grouse ² about your old fellow, but if you had one like mine you'd have something to talk about. Blooming old pig, wouldn't open his mouth to you. 'Tis easy for you to talk, Larry Delaney!"

And then she shot away from me to conceal her tears, and I was left standing there on the pavement, stunned.

² **grouse:** to grumble or complain.

Too stunned really to have done anything about it. It had all happened too suddenly, and been too great an intrusion on my fantasy for me to grasp it at all. I was so astonished and upset that, though I was to have met May that night, I didn't go. Instead I went for a lonely walk by myself, over the hills to the river, to think what I should do about it. In the end, of course, I did nothing at all; I had no experience to indicate to me what I could do; and it was not until years later that I ever realized that the reason I had cared so much for Nancy was that she, like myself, was one of the duke's children, one of those outcasts of a lost fatherland who go through life living above and beyond themselves like some image of man's original aspiration.

THE USE OF IRONY

Irony often gives meaning to a story in such a way that the author does not have to write out every small item. Through irony the reader *sees* with his imagination and therefore does not require pictures drawn in detail or lengthy explanations.

1. Fathers are important in this story. How does Larry look upon his own father? How does he react to Nancy's father?
2. During the time of Larry's interest in her, what do you learn about Nancy's attitude toward Larry's father and her own father? (To answer this question, avoid using the final scene with Nancy Harding. Do not go beyond what is given in the story.)
3. In the final scene, what great irony does the author reveal? What light does this irony throw upon:

(a) Nancy's turning her back on her father (page 113).
(b) Larry's conviction that he was not invited to the Hardings' because he was below their class (pages 113–14).
(c) Larry's assumption that his claims about speaking foreign languages had become a joke in the Harding family (page 115).
(d) Nancy's sarcasm as she begins her last talk with Larry (page 115).
(e) Nancy's tears and her final angry language (page 115).

4. In view of Larry's fantasies, what is ironic about May Dwyer's becoming the first girl he actually courts? Which girl, Nancy or May, is the wiser? Explain.
5. What does Larry's relation to May's father show about his changing character?
6. People often joke about first love, or at least they make light of it. How serious and how important do you consider this feeling between Larry and Nancy to be? Do you find it amusing, or poignant, or would you apply still some other word to it? Does the ironic revelation at the end of the story add anything to your estimate of this first love?

GAINING POWER OVER WORDS

SUFFIXES A *suffix* is a syllable or word particle that follows the main part or root of a word and changes its meaning in a certain way. If you learn the meaning of suffixes found in numerous words, you will have a clue to the basic meanings of these words. A suffix added to the end of a noun may change it to an adjective, as in the case of the suffix *–an* in *Mexican, Republican,* and *partisan.* The suffix *–ous* means "full of" or "possessing the quality of." What then do *wondrous, murderous,* and *vigorous* mean? Suffixes may also change words to verbs, nouns, or adverbs. Some common suffixes are:

–ine, which means "of" or "like" as in *bovine, equine, saline*
–ize, which means "to subject to" as in *vulcanize, hypnotize, satirize*
–ee, which means "one who is" as in *employee, assignee, payee*

Can you explain the meaning of these words and the function of each suffix? On

This photograph shows a typical small village in Ireland. It is in County Kerry, ▶
where the Caha Mountains meet Bantry Bay. (See "The Irish Countryside" on page 118.)

page 112, the boy in this story wonders about being a proper *linguist*. What other words ending in *–ist* do you know? What is the function of *–ist?*

COMPOSITION SUGGESTION

Have you ever had an experience which seemed unhappy at the time but from which you later realized you had learned something valuable? Describe the experience and what you learned.

ABOUT THE AUTHOR

Frank O'Connor (1903–), Irish storyteller and poet, is the pen name of Michael O'Donovan. Most of his early stories appeared in *The Irish Statesman*, a magazine of the literary revival in Ireland, read by intellectuals in most countries as well as by Irish farmers. The magazine introduced poets who — like O'Connor — initiated a second revival in Irish poetry and letters. O'Connor fought in the struggle for political freedom in the early 1920's. Based on his experiences as a rebel, his first book of stories, *Guests of the Nation*, was published in 1931. In addition to several novels, O'Connor has also written plays and several books of verse. "The Duke's Children," like most of his stories, presents the kind of people and life he knew in Cork, the city of his birth. O'Connor has vividly described his first twenty years in his autobiography, *An Only Child.*

The Irish Countryside

The scene in the photograph on page 117 may give you some idea of why Irish writers are proud of their land and love to praise it in beautiful poetry and prose.

Speaking of Character

Older writers used to handle characterization by stopping everything in the story while they told us, straight out, in a solid block of characterization, just what a character was like. Occasionally they allowed another character to do the job. Modern writers, at least the best craftsmen among them, are more likely to avoid such *direct characterization.* As in "A Mother in Mannville" they use *indirect presentation.* Jerry is shown in situations chosen because they let us see his character in action. We *infer* for ourselves the motives and drives compelling Jerry to create "a mother in Mannville" from his deep longing and need. That the woman for whom he works is part of the composite "mother" he imagines is *shown*, but not told, in a number of ways: Jerry says, "You look a little bit like my mother. Especially in the dark, by the fire"; he asks if the writer wears gloves the same size as he imagines for his mother; the day his "home" and dog are to be taken away from him, he is unable to eat and runs away to be alone in the woods. Thus, we infer what Jerry is really like; and this is more convincing, more like the way we judge character in life.

The author's skill lies in putting together scenes and actions in which the characters are *dramatized* — shown speaking or acting, as in a drama. He selects those scenes which will permit us to judge character accurately for ourselves. If you will think back over "All the Years of Her Life" and "The Duke's Children," you will find that the same technique was used in both stories. Some readers do complain; presumably they would prefer the older method in which authors told them what they were to think of a character. Most readers, however, prefer the modern method in which they must infer for themselves. They feel it is more convincing to see for oneself, and they appreciate the skill an author shows in selecting the most significant moments in which to dramatize his characters.

Theme

Reading literature takes place on several levels. The first level, obviously, is the story itself: what it is about and the people who are in it. We can stop with the enjoyment of a story, or we may go on, like archaeologists uncovering hidden cities. When we do dig deeper into a story we come eventually to the base, to the *theme* or the controlling idea.

Not all stories have such controlling ideas. Many adventure and detective stories — "Four and Twenty Blackbirds," for example — merely seek to entertain the reader. But some people try to read *all* short stories as if every one were written purely for entertainment. Unless they grow beyond this level, such readers soon tire of literature and turn back exclusively to firsthand experience in the world beyond books, never realizing their enormous loss.

"What happens next?" is not a satisfactory level of reading for anyone who appreciates literature and the vision of life it offers. Nor is such a reader satisfied with mere analysis of technique. The total effect of the story, poem, or play is always his goal. Realizing the theme, the one idea that underlies and unifies all the elements of the story, is perhaps the most important stage in reaching this goal.

Does recognizing the insight into life that unifies a story mean finding a moral for every story? Not at all. Stories are not sermons designed to preach a moral. They are, instead, a way to make us aware of life and to understand or extend our own vision of life. As a rule an author does not even state a theme; instead he makes us *realize* it through the story itself.

Themes evolve from the common experiences of people in all walks of life.

The Bishop's Candlesticks

VICTOR HUGO

If someone does you harm, should you seek revenge? Is there a difference between being soft-hearted and soft-headed? How far should one go in turning the other cheek? These choices, offered to everyone at some time in his life, confront a French bishop who befriends a criminal in this famous story, an episode from the novel *Les Misérables*.

THERE WAS a rather loud rap at the front door.

"Come in," said the Bishop.

The door was thrown wide open, as if someone were pushing it energetically and resolutely. A man entered and stopped, leaving the door open behind him. He had his knapsack on his shoulder, his stick in his hand, and a rough, bold, wearied, and violent expression in his eyes. The firelight fell on him; he was hideous; it was a sinister[1] apparition.

The Bishop fixed a quiet eye on the man, as he opened his mouth, doubtless to ask the newcomer what he wanted. The man leaned both his hands on his stick, looked in turn at the two aged women and the old man, and, not waiting for the Bishop to speak, said in a loud voice:

"My name is Jean Valjean.[2] I am a galley slave,[3] and have spent nineteen years under confinement. I was liberated four days ago, and started for Pontarlier,[4] which is my destination. I have

[1] **sinister** (sĭn'ĭs·tẽr): giving an impression of lurking evil or harm.
[2] **Jean Valjean:** The French pronunciation of this name is zhäɴ väl'zhäɴ'.
[3] **galley slave:** a slave acting as a rower on a galley; French criminals were once condemned to such work.
[4] **Pontarlier** (pôn'tär'lyā'): a manufacturing town in east France.

Understanding the Theme. What *happens* in this story is easily told; perhaps you have already heard of this story or read it for yourself. But the events of the story do not account for the past reputation of "The Bishop's Candlesticks" or for its impact on each new generation of readers. It is the theme, what the story is *really about*, that radiates with power. An idea can be stronger than atomic energy. When you have finished reading, think back over the story carefully. You should then be able to state the powerful idea that lies back of the events.

---

been walking four days since I left Toulon,[1] and today I have walked twelve leagues. This evening on coming into the town I went to the inn, but was sent away in consequence of my yellow passport,[2] which I had shown at the police office. I went to another inn, and the landlord said to me, 'Be off!' It was the same everywhere, and no one would have any dealings with me. I went to the prison, but the jailer would not take me in. I got into a dog's kennel, but the dog bit me and drove me off, as if it had been a man; it seemed to know who I was. I went into the fields to sleep in the starlight, but there were no stars. I thought it would rain, and as there was no God to prevent it from raining, I came back to the town to sleep in a doorway. I was lying down on a stone in the square, when a good woman pointed to your house, and said, 'Go and knock there.' What sort of a house is this? Do you keep an inn? I have money, 109 francs and 15 sous,[3] which I earned by my nineteen years' toil. I will pay, for what do I care for that, as I have money! I am very tired and frightfully hungry; will you let me stay here?"

"Madame Magloire,"[4] said the Bishop, "you will lay another knife and fork."

The man advanced three paces, and approached the lamp which was on the table. "Wait a minute," he continued, as if he had not comprehended, "that will not do. Did you not hear me say that I was a galley slave, a convict, and have just come from the bagne?"[5] He took from his pocket a large yellow paper, which he unfolded. "Here is my passport, yellow as you see, which turns me out wherever I go. Will you read it? I can read it, for I learned to do so at the bagne, where there is a school for those who like to attend it. This is what is written in my passport: 'Jean Valjean, a liberated convict, native of' — but that does not concern you — 'has been nineteen years at the galleys. Five years for robbery with housebreaking, fourteen years for having tried to escape four times. The man is very dangerous.' All the world has turned me out, and are you willing to receive me? Is this an inn? Will you give me some food and a bed? Have you a stable?"

"Madame Magloire," said the Bishop, "you will put clean sheets on the bed in the alcove." Then to Jean: "Sit down and warm yourself, sir. We shall sup directly, and your bed will be got ready while we are supping."

The man understood this at once. The expression of his face, which had hitherto been gloomy and harsh, was marked with astonishment, joy, and doubt. He began stammering like a lunatic.

"Is it true? You will let me stay, you will not turn me out, a convict? You call me 'sir,' you do not humiliate me. 'Get out, dog!' that is what is always said to me; I really believed you would turn me out, and hence told you at once who I am! Oh, what a worthy woman she was who sent me here! I shall have supper, a bed with mattresses and sheets, like everyone else. For nineteen years I have not slept in a bed! You really mean that I am to stay! You

[1] **Toulon** (too͞'lôn'): a French seaport on the Mediterranean.
[2] The significance of the yellow passport will be explained later on.
[3] *francs* (frăngks) *and sous* (soo͞z): French coins; the franc is the basic French monetary unit.
[4] **Madame Magloire**: The French pronunciation of the housekeeper's name is mä-glwär'.

[5] **bagne** (bȧn'y'), a prison house substituted for the galleys.

are worthy people; besides, I have money and will pay handsomely. By the way, what is your name, Mr. Landlord? I will pay anything you please, for you are a worthy man. You keep an inn, do you not?"

"I am," said the Bishop, "a priest, living in this house."

"A priest?" the man continued. "Oh! what a worthy priest! I suppose you will not ask me for money. The curé,[1] I suppose, the curé of that big church? Oh, yes, what a fool I am, I did not notice your cassock." [2]

While speaking, he deposited his knapsack and stick in a corner, returned his passport to his pocket, and sat down.

"You are humane, sir, and do not feel contempt. A good priest is very good. Then you do not want me to pay?"

"No," said the Bishop, "keep your money. How long did you take in earning your 100 francs?"

"Nineteen years."

"Nineteen years!" The Bishop gave a deep sigh.

The man went on: "I have all my money still; in four days I have spent only 25 sous, which I earned helping to unload carts at Grasse. As you are an abbé [3] I will tell you: We had a chaplain at the galleys, and one day I saw a bishop, Monseigneur,[4] as they call him. He is the curé over the curés; but pardon me, you know that, placed as you are; we convicts know and explain such things badly, and for me in particular it is so far away in the past. He said mass in the middle of the bagne at an altar, and had a pointed gold thing on his

head, which glistened in the bright sunshine; we were drawn up on three sides of a square, with guns, and lighted matches facing us. He spoke, but was too far off, and we did not hear him. That is what a bishop is."

While he was speaking the Bishop had gone to close the door, which had been left open. Madame Magloire came in, bringing a silver spoon and fork, which she placed on the table.

"Madame Magloire," said the Bishop, "lay them as near as you can to the fire"; and turning to his guest, he said, "The night breeze is sharp on the Alps, and you must be cold, sir."

Each time he said the word "sir," with his gentle, grave voice, the man's face was illumined. "Sir" to a convict is the glass of water to the shipwrecked sailor of the *Méduse*.[5] Ignominy [6] thirsts for respect.

"This lamp gives a very bad light," the Bishop continued. Madame Magloire understood, and fetched from the chimney of Monseigneur's bedroom the two silver candlesticks, which she placed on the table already lighted.

"Monsieur le Curé," said the man, "you are good and do not despise me, and yet I have not hidden from you whence I come, and that I am an unfortunate fellow."

The Bishop, who was seated by his side, gently touched his hand. "You need not have told me who you were; this is not my house, but the house of Christ. This door does not ask a man who enters whether he has a name, but if he has sorrow; you are suffering, you are hungry and thirsty, and so be welcome. And do not thank me, or say that

---

[1] **curé** (kŭ·rā′): a French parish priest.
[2] **cassock**: the long close-fitting garment worn by a priest.
[3] **abbé** (ȧ′bā′): a title given in France to a priest.
[4] **Monseigneur** (mŏn′sâ·nyûr′): the title used for church dignitaries in France.

[5] **Méduse:** "The Raft of the *Méduse*" is a famous French painting by Géricault picturing a group of shipwrecked sailors crowded on a small raft.
[6] **ignominy** (ĭg′nô·mĭn·ĭ): disgrace or dishonor.

I am receiving you in my house, for no one is at home here excepting the man who has need of an asylum.[1] I tell you, who are a passer-by, that you are more at home here than I am myself, and all there is here is yours. Why do I want to know your name? Besides, before you told it to me you had one which I knew."

The man opened his eyes in amazement.

"Is that true? You know my name?"

"Yes," the Bishop answered, "you are my brother."

"Monsieur le Curé," the man exclaimed, "I was very hungry when I came in, but you are so kind that I do not know at present what I feel; it has passed."

The Bishop looked at him and said:

"You have suffered greatly?"

"Oh! the red jacket,[2] the cannon ball on your foot, a plank to sleep on, heat, cold, labor, the gang of men, the blows, the double chain for a mere nothing, a dungeon for a word, even when you are ill in bed, and the chain gang. The very dogs are happier. Nineteen years and now I am forty-six; and at present, the yellow passport!"

"Yes," said the Bishop, "you have come from a place of sorrow. Listen to me; there will be more joy in Heaven over the tearful repentance of a repentant sinner than over the white robes of one hundred just men. If you leave that mournful place with thoughts of hatred and anger against your fellow men, you are worthy of pity; if you leave it with thoughts of kindness, gentleness, and peace, you are worth more than any of us."

In the meanwhile Madame Magloire

had served the soup; it was made of water, oil, bread, and salt, and a little bacon, and the rest of the supper consisted of a piece of mutton, figs, a fresh cheese, and a loaf of rye bread. She had herself added a bottle of old Mauves wine. The Bishop's face suddenly assumed the expression of gaiety peculiar to hospitable natures. "To table," he said eagerly, as he was wont to do when any stranger supped with him; and he bade the man sit down on his right hand, while Mlle Baptistine, his sister, perfectly peaceful and natural, took her seat on his left. The Bishop said grace and then served the soup himself, according to his wont. The man began eating greedily. All at once the Bishop said:

"It strikes me that there is something wanting on the table."

Madame Magloire, truth to tell, had only laid the absolutely necessary silver. Now it was the custom in this house, when the Bishop had anyone to supper, to arrange the whole stock of plate [3] on the table, as an innocent display. This graceful semblance of luxury was a species of childishness full of charm in this strict and gentle house which elevated poverty to dignity. Madame Magloire took the hint, went out without a word, and a moment after the remaining spoons and forks glittered on the cloth, symmetrically arranged before each of the guests.

The man paid no attention to anyone; he ate with frightful voracity,[4] but after supper he said:

"Monsieur le Curé, all this is much too good for me, but I am bound to say that the carters [5] who would not let me

[1] asylum: Here, the meaning is "a haven of rest."

[2] red jacket: Galley slaves wore the "red jacket," just as convicts used to wear stripes.

[3] the whole stock of plate: all of the table silver.

[4] voracity: greediness; excessive eagerness.

[5] carters: teamsters, to whom, and to other such working people, Jean Valjean appealed for lodging.

sup with them have better cheer than you."

"They are harder worked than I am."

"No," the man continued, "they have more money. You are poor, as I can plainly see; perhaps you are not even a curé. Ah, if Heaven were just you ought to be a curé."

"Heaven is more than just," said the Bishop.

After bidding his sister good night he took up one of the silver candlesticks, handed the other to his guest, and said: "I will lead you to your room, sir."

The man followed him. In order to reach the oratory [1] where the alcove was it was necessary to pass through the Bishop's bedroom. At the moment when he went through the room Madame Magloire was putting away the plate in the cupboard over the bed head; it was the last thing she did every night before retiring. The Bishop led his guest to the alcove, where a clean bed was prepared for him; the man placed the branched candlestick on a small table.

"I trust you will pass a good night," said the Bishop.

As two o'clock pealed from the cathedral bell Jean Valjean awoke. What aroused him was that the bed was too comfortable; for close on twenty years he had not slept in a bed, and though he had not undressed, the sensation was too novel not to disturb his sleep. He had been asleep for more than four hours and his weariness had worn off. He opened his eyes and looked into the surrounding darkness and then he closed them again to go to sleep once more.

When three o'clock struck he opened his eyes, suddenly sat up, stretched out

his arms, and felt for his knapsack, which he had thrown into a corner of the alcove, then let his legs hang, and felt himself seated on the bedside almost without knowing how. He remained for a while thoughtful in this attitude, which would have had something sinister about it for anyone who had seen him, the only wakeful person in the house. All at once he stooped, took off his shoes, then resumed his thoughtful posture and remained motionless. To work! He rose, hesitated for a moment and listened; all was silent in the house, and he went on tiptoe to the window, through which he peered.

The night was not very dark; there was a full moon, across which heavy clouds were chased by the wind. This produced alternations of light and shade and a species of twilight in the room; this twilight, sufficient to guide him, but intermittent in consequence of the clouds, resembled that livid [2] hue produced by the grating of a cellar over which people are continually passing. On reaching the window Jean Valjean examined it; it was without bars, looked on the garden, and was only closed, according to the fashion of the country, by a small peg. He opened it, but as a cold, sharp breeze suddenly entered the room he closed it again directly. He gazed into the garden with that attentive glance which studies rather than looks and found that it was inclosed by a whitewashed wall, easy to climb over. Beyond it he noticed the tops of trees standing at regular distances, which proved that this wall separated the garden from a public walk.

After taking this glance he walked boldly to the alcove, opened his knapsack, took out something which he laid

---

[1] **oratory:** a small chapel or a place for prayer.

[2] **livid** (lĭv′ĭd): bluish-black in color; discolored.

on the bed, put his shoes in one of the pouches, placed the knapsack on his shoulders, put on his cap, the peak of which he pulled over his eyes, groped for his stick, which he placed in the window nook, and then returned to the bed and took up the object he had laid on it. It resembled a short iron bar, sharpened at one of its ends. It would have been difficult to distinguish in the darkness for what purpose this piece of iron had been fashioned; perhaps it was a lever, perhaps it was a club. By daylight it could have been seen that it was nothing but a miner's candlestick. The convicts at that day were sometimes employed in extracting rock from the lofty hills that surround Toulon and it was not infrequent for them to have mining tools at their disposal. The miners' candlesticks are made of massive steel and have a point at the lower end, by which they are dug into the rock. He took the bar in his right hand and, holding his breath and deadening his footsteps, he walked toward the door of the adjoining room, the Bishop's as we know. On reaching this door he found it ajar — the Bishop had not shut it.

Jean Valjean listened, but there was not a sound; he pushed the door with the tip of his finger lightly and with the furtive, restless gentleness of a cat that wants to get in. The door yielded to the pressure and made an almost imperceptible and silent movement, which slightly widened the opening.

He waited for a moment and then pushed the door again more boldly.

The first danger had passed, but still there was fearful tumult within him. But he did not recoil; he had not done so even when he thought himself lost; he only thought of finishing the job as speedily as possible, and entered the bedroom. The room was in a state of perfect calmness; here and there might be distinguished confused and vague forms, which by day were papers scattered over the table, open folios,[1] books piled on a sofa, an easy-chair covered with clothes, and a prie-dieu,[2] all of which were at this moment only dark nooks and patches of white. Jean Valjean advanced cautiously and carefully and avoided coming into collision with the furniture. He heard from the end of the room the calm and regular breathing of the sleeping Bishop.

Suddenly he stopped, for he was close to the bed; he had reached it sooner than he anticipated.

Nature at times blends her effects and spectacles with our actions with a species of gloomy and intelligent design, as if wishing to make us reflect. For nearly half an hour a heavy cloud had covered the sky, but at the moment when Jean Valjean stopped at the foot of the bed this cloud was rent asunder[3] as if expressly, and a moonbeam passing through the tall window suddenly illumined the Bishop's pale face. He was sleeping peacefully and was wrapped in a long garment of brown wool, which covered his arms down to the wrists. His head was thrown back on the pillow in the easy attitude of repose, and his hand, adorned with the pastoral ring,[4] and which had done so many good deeds, hung out of bed. His entire face was lit up by a vague expression of satisfaction, hope, and beatitude[5] —

[1] folios (fō′lĭ·ōz): books made of sheets, each folded only once; hence, books of the largest kind.
[2] prie-dieu (prē′dyû′): a small desk arranged to support a book, with a foot piece on which to kneel. It is used for private worship.
[3] rent asunder: torn apart.
[4] pastoral ring: the ring a bishop wears (a bishop is a "shepherd").
[5] beatitude (bē·ăt′ĭ·tūd): great happiness; blessedness.

it was more than a smile and almost radiance. He had on his forehead the inexpressible reflection of an invisible light, for the soul of a just man contemplates a mysterious heaven during sleep.

A reflection of this heaven was cast over the Bishop, but it was at the same time a luminous transparency,[1] for the heaven was within him and was conscience.

At the moment when the moonbeam was cast over this internal light the sleeping Bishop seemed to be surrounded by a glory, which was veiled, however, by an ineffable[2] semi-light. The moon in the heavens, the slumbering landscape, the quiet house, the hour, the silence, the moment, added something solemn and indescribable to this man's venerable[3] repose and cast a majestic and serene halo round his white hair and closed eyes, his face, in which all was hope and confidence, his aged head, and his childlike slumber.

There was almost a divinity in this unconsciously august[4] man.

Jean Valjean was standing in the shadow with his crowbar in his hand, motionless and terrified by this luminous old man. He had never seen anything like this before, and such confidence horrified him. The moral world has no greater spectacle than this, a troubled, restless conscience, which is on the point of committing a bad action, contemplating the sleep of a just man.

This sleep in such isolation, and with a neighbor like himself, possessed a species of sublimity which he felt vaguely but imperiously.[5]

No one could have said what was going on within him, not even himself. In order to form any idea of it we must imagine what is the most violent in the presence of what is gentlest. Even in his face nothing could have been distinguished with certainty, for it displayed a sort of haggard astonishment. He looked at the Bishop, that was all, but what his thoughts were it would be impossible to divine; what was evident was that he was moved and shaken, but of what nature was this emotion?

His eye was not once removed from the old man, and the only thing clearly revealed by his attitude and countenance was a strange indecision. It seemed as if he were hesitating between two abysses, the one that saves and the one that destroys; he was ready to dash out the Bishop's brains or kiss his hand.

At the expiration of a few minutes his left arm slowly rose to his cap, which he took off; then his arm fell again with the same slowness and Jean Valjean recommenced his contemplation, with his cap in his left hand, his crowbar in his right, and his hair standing erect on his savage head.

The Bishop continued to sleep peacefully beneath this terrific glance.

A moonbeam rendered the crucifix over the mantelpiece dimly visible, which seemed to open its arms for both, with a blessing for one and a pardon for the other.

All at once Jean Valjean put on his cap again, then he walked rapidly along the bed, without looking at the Bishop, and went straight to the cupboard. He

---

[1] **luminous** (lū′mĭ·nŭs) **transparency** (trăns-pâr′ĕn·sĭ): a state in which light seems to come from within.

[2] **ineffable** (ĭn·ĕf′a·b'l): incapable of being expressed in words.

[3] **venerable** (vĕn′ēr·a·b'l): worthy of honor; awesome. Generally, *venerable* also implies advanced age.

[4] **august** (ô·gŭst′): of majestic dignity; inspiring; worthy of admiration.

[5] **imperiously** (ĭm·pē̯r′ĭ·ŭs·lĭ): commandingly.

raised his crowbar to force the lock, but as the key was in it he opened it, and the first thing he saw was the plate basket, which he seized. He hurried across the room, not caring for the noise he made, re-entered the oratory, opened the window, seized the stick, put the silver into his pocket, threw away the basket, leaped into the garden, bounded over the wall like a tiger, and fled.

The next morning at sunrise the Bishop was walking about the garden when Madame Magloire came running toward him in a state of great alarm.

"Monseigneur! Monseigneur!" she screamed, "does Your Grandeur [1] know where the plate basket is?"

"Yes," said the Bishop.

"The Lord be praised!" she continued. "I did not know what had become of it."

The Bishop had just picked up the basket in a flower bed and now handed it to Madame Magloire. "Here it is," he said.

"Well!" she said, "there is nothing in it; where is the plate?"

"Ah!" the Bishop replied, "it is the plate that troubles your mind. Well, I do not know where that is."

"Good Lord! it is stolen, and that man who came last night is the robber."

In a twinkling Madame Magloire had run to the oratory, entered the alcove, and returned to the Bishop. He was stooping down and looking sorrowfully at a cochlearia,[2] whose stem the basket had broken. He raised himself on hearing Madame Magloire scream.

"Monseigneur, the man has gone! the plate is stolen!"

While uttering this exclamation her eyes fell on a corner of the garden, where there were signs of climbing; the coping [3] of the wall had been torn away.

"That is the way he went! He leaped into Cochefilet lane. Ah, what an abomination; he has stolen our plate!"

The Bishop remained silent for a moment, then raised his earnest eyes and said gently to Madame Magloire:

"By the way, was that plate ours?"

Madame Magloire was speechless; there was another interval of silence, after which the Bishop continued:

"Madame Magloire, I had wrongfully held back this silver, which belonged to the poor. Who was this person? Evidently a poor man."

"Good gracious!" Madame Magloire continued. "I do not care for it, nor does Mademoiselle, but we feel for Monseigneur. With what will Monseigneur eat now?"

The Bishop looked at her in amazement. "Why, are there no pewter forks to be had?"

Madame Magloire shrugged her shoulders. "Pewter smells!"

"Then iron?"

Madame Magloire made an expressive grimace. "Iron tastes."

"Well, then," said the Bishop, "wood!"

A few minutes later he was breakfasting at the same table at which Jean Valjean sat on the previous evening. While breakfasting the Bishop gaily remarked to his sister, who said nothing, and to Madame Magloire, who growled in a low voice, that spoon and fork, even of wood, are not required to dip a piece of bread in a cup of milk.

"What an idea!" Madame Magloire said, as she went back and forth, "to receive a man like that and lodge him by one's side. And what a blessing it is that he only stole! Oh, Lord! the mere thought makes a body shudder."

[1] **Your Grandeur:** a title of respect similar to Your Honor.

[2] **cochlearia** (kŏk·lē·ā′rĭ·à): an herb.

[3] **coping** (kōp′ĭng): wall covering.

As the brother and sister were leaving the table there was a knock at the door.

"Come in," said the Bishop.

The door opened and a strange and violent group appeared on the threshold. Three men were holding a fourth by the collar. The three men were gendarmes;[1] the fourth was Jean Valjean. A corporal, who apparently commanded the party, came in and walked up to the Bishop with a military salute.

"Monseigneur," he said.

At this word Jean Valjean, who was gloomy and crushed, raised his head with a stupefied air.

"Monseigneur," he muttered; "then he is not the curé."

"Silence!" said a gendarme. "This gentleman is Monseigneur the Bishop."

In the meanwhile the Bishop had advanced as rapidly as his great age permitted.

"Ah! there you are," he said, looking at Jean Valjean. "I am glad to see you. Why, I gave you the candlesticks, too, which are also of silver, and will fetch you 200 francs. Why did you not take them away with the rest of the plate?"

Jean Valjean opened his eyes and looked at the Bishop with an expression which no human language could render.

"Monseigneur," the corporal said, "what this man told us was true then? We met him, and as he looked as if he were running away we arrested him. He had this plate —"

"And he told you," the Bishop interrupted with a smile, "that it was given to him by an old priest at whose house he passed the night? I see it all. And you brought him back here? That is a mistake."

"In that case," the corporal continued, "we can let him go?"

"Of course," the Bishop answered.

The gendarmes loosened their hold of Jean Valjean, who tottered backward.

"Is it true that I am at liberty?" he said, in an almost inarticulate voice and as if speaking in his sleep.

"Yes, you are let go; don't you understand?" said a gendarme.

"My friend," the Bishop continued, "before you go take your candlesticks."

He went to the mantelpiece, fetched the two candlesticks, and handed them to Jean Valjean. The two women watched him do so without a word, without a sign, without a look that could disturb the Bishop. Jean Valjean was trembling in all his limbs; he took the candlesticks mechanically and with wandering looks.

"Now," said the Bishop, "go in peace. By the bye, when you return, my friend, it is unnecessary to pass through the front garden, for you can always enter, day and night, by the front door, which is only latched."

Then turning to the gendarmes, he said:

"Gentlemen, you can retire."

They did so. Jean Valjean looked as if he were on the point of fainting; the Bishop walked up to him, and said in a loud voice:

"Never forget that you have promised me to employ this money in becoming an honest man."

Jean Valjean, who had no recollection of having promised anything, stood silent. The Bishop, who had laid a stress on these words, continued solemnly:

"Jean Valjean, my brother, you no longer belong to evil, but to good. I have bought your soul of you. I withdraw it from black thoughts and the spirit of perdition,[2] and give it to God."

---

[1] **gendarmes** (zhän·därmz′): French policemen.

[2] **spirit of perdition** (per·dĭsh′ŭn): mood of damnation.

"The door opened and a strange and violent group appeared on the threshold."

UNDERSTANDING THE THEME

1. Why does the Bishop sigh deeply when he repeats Jean Valjean's, "Nineteen years!" (page 122)?

2. What facts of Jean Valjean's past could have served as a guide to the Bishop in understanding him?

3. What lies back of the Bishop's remark, "You need not have told me who you were"?

4. Why do you think Jean Valjean stole the plate?

5. When people have been wronged, they sometimes think in terms of revenge. Explain how the Bishop and Jean Valjean represent two opposing outlooks on this matter of revenge.

6. Do you think the Bishop was a simple-minded idealist or would you say that he showed wisdom? Explain.

7. What is the author trying to tell you in this story? In other words what seems to be the basic idea? Does it deal with the brotherhood of man? Is it that actually none of us owns anything except by God's grace? Is it that more is accomplished by kindness than by force? Can you agree upon a statement of the theme which covers all these considerations?

GAINING POWER OVER WORDS

WORD DISCRIMINATION *Synonyms* are words with similar meanings, words which can be used more or less interchangeably. But often there are small differences in meaning between synonyms that make one word fit better into a particular context than another. We can see how important it is to choose the right word by examining the use of the word *luminous* in "The Bishop's Candlesticks."

In describing the sleeping Bishop (on pages 125–26), Victor Hugo developed light as a symbol of the Bishop's spiritual goodness. On page 126 he wrote: "A reflection of this heaven was cast over the Bishop, but it was at the same time a *luminous* transparency, for the heaven was within him and was conscience." Then two paragraphs later, he wrote: "Jean Valjean was standing in the shadow with his crowbar in his hand, motionless and terrified by this *luminous* old man."

Brilliant and *enlightened* are two syn-onyms for *luminous*. Why is *luminous* the best of the three words to serve in the two sentences quoted above? Give examples of suitable uses for *brilliant* and *enlightened*. Can they be used interchangeably?

COMPOSITION SUGGESTION

Do you believe a prison should be primarily a place for the punishment of criminals or primarily a place for their education and rehabilitation? What changes, if any, should be made in our treatment of convicted criminals? Explain your point of view and support it with specific suggestions.

ABOUT THE AUTHOR

Victor Hugo (1802–1885) was the greatest poet and leader of the romantic movement in nineteenth-century France and a powerful figure in the political life of his country. Author of beautiful verse and biting satire, Hugo excelled in all forms of literature, including dramas, critical essays, and novels. In exile because of his conflicts with the reigning powers, Hugo wrote his famous and bitter satire on the founder of the Second Empire, "Napoléon le Petit." Later he published one of his best-known novels, *The Hunchback of Notre Dame*. *Les Misérables* (1862), which includes "The Bishop's Candlesticks," is the first in a series of three social novels. After the fall of the empire in 1870, Hugo returned to Paris to spend the final years of his long life adding to his huge list of literary contributions. In honor of his eightieth birthday elaborate celebrations were staged in Paris.

Famous Book Illustrations

The painting on page 129 is a color plate by Mead Schaeffer from the familiar Dodd, Mead edition of *Les Misérables*. Fine illustrations have long been associated with many literary works. You may have your own favorite editions of novels or other books. Beautiful paintings and photographs often contribute much to the lasting enjoyment and personal value of a good book.

The Rat Trap

SELMA LAGERLÖF

Is life an adventure? a joke? Is it a trap that closes in on everyone? In this story a young girl shows herself to be wiser about life than her father or the bitter, cynical thief. Do not be misled by the apparently simple, fairy-tale quality of this story. This Swedish author is noted for the simplicity with which she presents profound ideas.

ONCE UPON a time there was a man who went around selling small rat traps of wire. He made them himself at odd moments, from material he got by begging in the stores or at the big farms. But even so, the business was not especially profitable, so he had to resort to both begging and petty thievery to keep body and soul together. Even so, his clothes were in rags, his cheeks were sunken, and hunger gleamed in his eyes.

No one can imagine how sad and monotonous life can appear to such a vagabond, who plods along the road, left to his own meditations. But one day this man had fallen into a line of thought which really seemed to him entertaining. He had naturally been thinking of his rat traps when suddenly he was struck by the idea that the whole world about him — the whole world with its lands and seas, its cities and villages — was nothing but a big rat trap. It had never existed for any other purpose than to set baits for people. It offered riches and joys, shelter and food, heat and clothing, exactly as the rat trap offered cheese and pork, and as soon as anyone let himself be tempted to touch the bait, it closed in

Relating Story Ideas to Your Own Experience. Relating literature and life is a two-way bridge. One must bring his own experiences to the literature he reads if he is to interpret it. A good reader is just as capable of applying the concepts in a story to the problems of the everyday world. In this story notice the important ideas. After you have finished it, reflect on its application to the world you know. Note, also, the parallel between Selma Lagerlöf's story and "The Bishop's Candlesticks," which is now also part of your own experience.

on him, and then everything came to an end.

The world had, of course, never been very kind to him, so it gave him unwonted joy to think ill of it in this way. It became a cherished pastime of his, during many dreary ploddings, to think of people he knew who had let themselves be caught in the dangerous snare, and of others who were still circling around the bait.

One dark evening as he was trudging along the road he caught sight of a little gray cottage by the roadside, and he knocked on the door to ask shelter for the night. Nor was he refused. Instead of the sour faces which ordinarily met him, the owner, who was an old man without wife or child, was happy to get someone to talk to in his loneliness. Immediately he put the porridge pot on the fire and gave him supper; then he carved off such a big slice from his tobacco roll that it was enough both for the stranger's pipe and his own. Finally he got out an old pack of cards and played "mjölis" with his guest until bedtime.

The old man was just as generous with his confidences as with his porridge and tobacco. The guest was informed at once that in his days of prosperity his host had been a crofter [1] at Ramsjö Ironworks and had worked on the land. Now that he was no longer able to do day labor, it was his cow which supported him. Yes, that bossy was extraordinary. She could give milk for the creamery every day, and last month he had received all of thirty kronor [2] in payment.

The stranger must have seemed incredulous, for the old man got up and went to the window, took down a leather pouch which hung on a nail in

[1] **crofter** (krŏf'tēr): a small tenant farmer.
[2] **kronor** (krō'nôr): plural form of *krona,* the Swedish gold monetary unit.

the very window frame, and picked out three wrinkled ten-kronor bills. These he held up before the eyes of his guest, nodding knowingly, and then stuffed them back into the pouch.

The next day both men got up in good season. The crofter was in a hurry to milk his cow, and the other man probably thought he should not stay in bed when the head of the house had gotten up. They left the cottage at the same time. The crofter locked the door and put the key in his pocket. The man with the rat traps said good-by and thank you, and thereupon each went his own way.

But half an hour later the rat trap peddler stood again before the door. He did not try to get in, however. He only went up to the window, smashed a pane, stuck in his hand, and got hold of the pouch with the thirty kronor. He took the money and thrust it into his own pocket. Then he hung the leather pouch very carefully back in its place and went away.

As he walked along with the money in his pocket he felt quite pleased with his smartness. He realized, of course, that at first he dared not continue on the public highway, but must turn off the road, into the woods. During the first hours this caused him no difficulty. Later in the day it became worse, for it was a big and confusing forest which he had gotten into. He tried, to be sure, to walk in a definite direction, but the paths twisted back and forth so strangely! He walked and walked, without coming to the end of the wood, and finally he realized that he had only been walking around in the same part of the forest. All at once he recalled his thoughts about the world and the rat trap. Now his own turn had come. He had let himself be fooled by a bait and had been caught. The whole forest, with its trunks and branches, its thickets and fallen logs, closed in upon him like an impenetrable prison from which he could never escape.

It was late in December. Darkness was already descending over the forest. This increased the danger, and increased also his gloom and despair. Finally he saw no way out, and he sank down on the ground, tired to death, thinking that his last moment had come. But just as he laid his head on the ground, he heard a sound — a hard regular thumping. There was no doubt as to what that was. He raised himself. "Those are the hammer strokes from an iron mill," he thought. "There must be people near by." He summoned all his strength, got up, and staggered in the direction of the sound.

The Ramsjö Ironworks, which are now closed down, were, not so long ago, a large plant, with smelter,[1] rolling mill,[2] and forge.[3] In the summertime long lines of heavily loaded barges and scows[4] slid down the canal, which led to a large inland lake, and in the wintertime the roads near the mill were black from all the coal dust which sifted down from the big charcoal crates.

During one of the long dark evenings just before Christmas, the master smith and his helper sat in the dark forge near the furnace waiting for the pig iron,[5] which had been put in the fire, to be ready to put on the anvil. Every now and then one of them got up to stir the glowing mass with a long iron

[1] **smelter** (smĕl′tēr): an establishment where metal is refined.
[2] **rolling mill:** an establishment where metal is rolled into plates and bars.
[3] **forge** (fôrj): a furnace where metal is heated and hammered.
[4] **scows** (skouz): flat-bottomed boats or barges used to transport freight short distances.
[5] **pig iron:** a crude casting of iron, of standard size and shape for marketing.

bar, returning in a few moments, dripping with perspiration, though, as was the custom, he wore nothing but a long shirt and a pair of wooden shoes.

All the time there were many sounds to be heard in the forge. The big bellows groaned and the burning charcoal cracked. The fire boy shoveled charcoal into the maw of the furnace with a great deal of clatter. Outside roared the waterfall, and a sharp north wind whipped the rain against the brick-tiled roof.

It was probably on account of all this noise that the blacksmiths did not notice that a man had opened the gate and entered the forge, until he stood close up to the furnace.

Surely it was nothing unusual for poor vagabonds without any better shelter for the night to be attracted to the forge by the glow of light which escaped through the sooty panes, and to come in to warm themselves in front of the fire. The blacksmiths glanced only casually and indifferently at the intruder. He looked the way people of his type usually did, with a long beard, dirty, ragged, and with a bunch of rat traps dangling on his chest.

He asked permission to stay, and the master blacksmith nodded a haughty consent without honoring him with a single word.

The tramp did not say anything, either. He had not come there to talk but only to warm himself and sleep.

In those days the Ramsjö iron mill was owned by a very prominent iron-master, whose greatest ambition was to ship out good iron to the market. He watched both night and day to see that the work was done as well as possible, and at this very moment he came into the forge on one of his nightly rounds of inspection.

Naturally the first thing he saw was

the tall ragamuffin who had eased his way so close to the furnace that steam rose from his wet rags. The ironmaster did not follow the example of the blacksmiths, who had hardly deigned to look at the stranger. He walked close up to him, looked him over very carefully, then tore off his slouch hat to get a better view of his face.

"But of course it is you, Nils Olof!" he said. "How you do look!"

The man with the rat traps had never before seen the ironmaster at Ramsjö and did not even know what his name was. But it occurred to him that if the fine gentleman thought he was an old acquaintance, he might perhaps throw him a couple of kronor. Therefore he did not want to undeceive him all at once.

"Yes, God knows things have gone downhill with me," he said.

"You should not have resigned from the regiment," said the ironmaster. "That was the mistake. If only I had still been in the service at the time, it never would have happened. Well, now of course you will come home with me."

To go along up to the manor house and be received by the owner like an old regimental comrade — that, however did not please the tramp.

"No, I couldn't think of it!" he said, looking quite alarmed.

He thought of the thirty kronor. To go up to the manor house would be like throwing himself voluntarily into the lions' den. He only wanted a chance to sleep here in the forge and then sneak away as inconspicuously as possible.

The ironmaster assumed that he felt embarrassed because of his miserable clothing.

"Please don't think that I have such a fine home that you cannot show yourself there," he said. "Elizabeth is dead, as you may already have heard. My boys are abroad, and there is no one at home except my oldest daughter and myself. We were just saying that it was too bad we didn't have any company for Christmas. Now come along with me and help us make the Christmas food disappear a little faster."

But the stranger said no, and no, and again no, and the ironmaster saw that he must give in.

"It looks as though Captain von Stahle preferred to stay with you tonight, Stjernström," he said to the master blacksmith, and turned on his heel.

But he laughed to himself as he went away, and the blacksmith, who knew him, understood very well that he had not said his last word.

It was not more than half an hour before they heard the sound of carriage wheels outside the forge, and a new guest came in, but this time it was not the ironmaster. He had sent his daughter, apparently hoping that she would have better powers of persuasion than he himself.

She entered, followed by a valet, carrying on his arm a big fur coat. She was not at all pretty, but seemed modest and quite shy. In the forge everything was just as it had been earlier in the evening. The master blacksmith and his apprentice still sat on their bench, and iron and charcoal still glowed in the furnace. The stranger had stretched himself out on the floor and lay with a piece of pig iron under his head and his hat pulled down over his eyes. As soon as the young girl caught sight of him, she went up and lifted his hat. The man was evidently used to sleeping with one eye open. He jumped up abruptly and seemed to be quite frightened.

"My name is Edla Willmansson," said the young girl. "My father came home and said that you wanted to sleep here in the forge tonight, and then I asked permission to come and bring you home to us. I am so sorry, Captain, that you are having such a hard time."

She looked at him compassionately, with her heavy eyes, and then she noticed that the man was afraid. "Either he has stolen something or else he has escaped from jail," she thought, and added quickly, "You may be sure, Captain, that you will be allowed to leave us just as freely as you came. Only please stay with us over Christmas Eve."

She said this in such a friendly manner that the rat trap peddler must have felt confidence in her.

"It would never have occurred to me that you would bother with me yourself, miss," he said. "I will come at once."

He accepted the fur coat, which the valet handed him with a deep bow, threw it over his rags, and followed the young lady out to the carriage, without granting the astonished blacksmiths so much as a glance.

But while he was riding up to the manor house he had evil forebodings.

"Why the devil did I take that fellow's money?" he thought. "Now I am sitting in the trap and will never get out of it."

The next day was Christmas Eve, and when the ironmaster came into the dining room for breakfast he probably thought with satisfaction of his old regimental comrade whom he had run across so unexpectedly.

"First of all we must see to it that he gets a little flesh on his bones," he said to his daughter, who was busy at the table. "And then we must see that he gets something else to do than to run around the country selling rat traps."

"It is queer that things have gone downhill with him as badly as that," said the daughter. "Last night I did not think there was anything about him to show that he had once been an educated man."

"You must have patience, my little girl," said the father. "As soon as he gets clean and dressed up, you will see something different. Last night he was naturally embarrassed. The tramp manners will fall away from him with the tramp clothes."

Just as he said this the door opened and the stranger entered. Yes, now he was truly clean and well dressed. The valet had bathed him, cut his hair, and shaved him. Moreover he was dressed in a good-looking suit of clothes which belonged to the ironmaster. He wore a white shirt and a starched collar and whole shoes.

But although his guest was now so well groomed, the ironmaster did not seem pleased. He looked at him with puckered brow, and it was easy to understand that when he had seen the strange fellow in the uncertain reflection from the furnace he might have made a mistake, but that now, when he stood there in broad daylight, it was impossible to mistake him for an old acquaintance.

"What does this mean?" he thundered.

The stranger made no attempt to dissimulate.[1] He saw at once that the splendor had come to an end.

"It is not my fault, sir," he said. "I never pretended to be anything but a poor trader, and I pleaded and begged to be allowed to stay in the forge. But no harm has been done. At worst I can put on my rags again and go away."

"Well," said the ironmaster, hesitating a little, "it was not quite honest, either. You must admit that, and I should not be surprised if the sheriff would like to have something to say in the matter."

The tramp took a step forward and struck the table with his fist.

"Now I am going to tell you, Mr. Ironmaster, how things are," he said. "This whole world is nothing but a big rat trap. All the good things that are offered you are nothing but cheese rinds and bits of pork, set out to drag a poor fellow into trouble. And if the sheriff comes now and locks me up for this, then you, Mr. Ironmaster, must remember that a day may come when you yourself may want to get a big piece of pork, and then you will get caught in the trap."

The ironmaster began to laugh.

"That was not so badly said, my good fellow. Perhaps we should let the sheriff alone on Christmas Eve. But now get out of here as fast as you can."

But just as the man was opening the door, the daughter said, "I think he ought to stay with us today. I don't want him to go." And with that she went and closed the door.

"What in the world are you doing?" said the father.

The daughter stood there quite embarrassed and hardly knew what to

[1] dissimulate (dĭ·sĭm'ú·lāt): pretend.

answer. That morning she had felt so happy when she thought how homelike and Christmassy she was going to make things for the poor hungry wretch. She could not get away from the idea all at once, and that was why she had interceded for the vagabond.

"I am thinking of this stranger here," said the young girl. "He walks and walks the whole year long, and there is probably not a single place in the whole country where he is welcome and can feel at home. Wherever he turns he is chased away. Always he is afraid of being arrested and cross-examined. I should like to have him enjoy a day of peace with us here — just one in the whole year."

The ironmaster mumbled something in his beard. He could not bring himself to oppose her.

"It was all a mistake, of course," she continued. "But anyway I don't think we ought to chase away a human being whom we have asked to come here, and to whom we have promised Christmas cheer."

"You do preach worse than a parson," said the ironmaster. "I only hope you won't have to regret this."

The young girl took the stranger by the hand and led him up to the table.

"Now sit down and eat," she said, for she could see that her father had given in.

The man with the rat traps said not a word; he only sat down and helped himself to the food. Time after time he looked at the young girl who had interceded for him. Why had she done it? What could the crazy idea be?

After that, Christmas Eve at Ramsjö passed just as it always had. The stranger did not cause any trouble because he did nothing but sleep. The whole forenoon he lay on the sofa in one of the guest rooms and slept at one stretch. At noon they woke him up so that he could have his share of the good Christmas fare, but after that he slept again. It seemed as though for many years he had not been able to sleep as quietly and safely as here at Ramsjö.

In the evening, when the Christmas tree was lighted, they woke him up again, and he stood for a while in the drawing room, blinking as though the candlelight hurt him, but after that he disappeared again. Two hours later he was aroused once more. He then had to go down into the dining room and eat the Christmas fish and porridge.

As soon as they got up from the table, he went around to each one present and said thank you and good night, but when he came to the young girl she gave him to understand that it was her father's intention that the suit which he wore was to be a Christmas present — he did not have to return it; and if he wanted to spend next Christmas Eve in a place where he could rest in peace, and be sure that no evil would befall him, he would be welcomed back again.

The man with the rat traps did not answer anything to this. He only stared at the young girl in boundless amazement.

The next morning the ironmaster and his daughter got up in good season to go to the early Christmas service. Their guest was still asleep, and they did not disturb him.

When, at about ten o'clock, they drove back from church, the young girl sat and hung her head even more dejectedly than usual. At church she had learned that one of the old crofters of the ironworks had been robbed by a man who went around selling rat traps.

"Yes, that was a fine fellow you let into the house," said her father. "I only wonder how many silver spoons are left in the cupboard by this time."

The wagon had hardly stopped at the front steps when the ironmaster asked the valet whether the stranger was still there. He added that he had heard at church that the man was a thief. The valet answered that the fellow had gone and that he had not taken anything with him at all. On the contrary he had left behind a little package which Miss Willmansson was to be kind enough to accept as a Christmas present.

The young girl opened the package, which was so badly done up that the contents came into view at once. She gave a little cry of joy. She found a small rat trap, and in it lay three wrinkled ten-kronor notes. But that was not all. In the rat trap lay also a letter written in large, jagged characters:

"Honored and noble Miss:

"Since you have been so nice to me all day long, as if I was a captain, I want to be nice to you, in return, as if I was a real captain: for I do not want you to be embarrassed at this Christmas season by a thief; but you can give back the money to the old man on the roadside, who has the money pouch hanging on the window frame as a bait for poor wanderers.

"The rat trap is a Christmas present from a rat who would have been caught in this world's rat trap if he had not been raised to captain, because in that way he got power to clear himself.

"Written with friendship
and high regard,
'Captain von Stahle.'"

RELATING STORY IDEAS TO YOUR OWN EXPERIENCE

1. Consider the source of the peddler's belief that the "whole world was nothing but a big rat trap." Such an idea would be quite foreign to Edla Willmansson. Why? What purpose did the idea serve in the peddler's mind? Do you think the comparison represents an accurate observation of life? What conclusion are you led to draw from the peddler's belief about the way a person looks at the world?

2. What was the crofter's motive in showing the peddler his three ten-kronor bills? Why was the peddler "incredulous"? Why wasn't the crofter suspicious of the stranger? Again, what conclusions are you led to draw about how people judge others?

3. To what do you attribute the success of the ironmaster's daughter in getting the peddler to return home with her?

4. At what points in the story does the daughter show herself to be a better judge of character than her father? Where does the ironmaster show that he, like the peddler, believes what he wants to believe? What was it he wanted to believe?

5. What incident do you mark as the turning point in the peddler's life?

6. Was the package containing the rat trap an appropriate Christmas gift for the peddler to leave for the ironmaster's daughter? Why? How do you explain her "little cry of joy" on opening the package?

7. Why did the peddler sign the note he left behind him "Captain von Stahle"? What do you think the name had come to stand for in his life?

8. In what way did the daughter's motives differ from those of the crofter? Why does she have an impact on the peddler whereas the crofter did not? In view of your answers to these questions, what is the theme of this story? Which do you believe more true to life, your statement of the theme or the idea that the world is a rat trap?

GAINING POWER OVER WORDS

CONTEXT We all use dictionaries to find the definitions of words whose meanings are not clear to us. Dictionaries exist for that purpose, but the *context* of a word can also help you to figure out its meaning. The context of a word is its *surroundings* — the other words and phrases that come before and after it in a sentence or paragraph. You can get clues to a word's meaning from its context. In "The Rat Trap," find three unfamiliar words and figure out their meaning from the context.

COMPOSITION SUGGESTION

Jonathan Swift once said that although he detested mankind in the mass, he loved individual men. Discuss this position as part of an attitude toward life. Refer, if you can, to "The Rat Trap" and "The Bishop's Candlesticks."

ABOUT THE AUTHOR

Selma Lagerlöf (1858–1940) won two awards never received previously by a woman: she was honored by the Nobel prize for literature, and she was elected to membership in the exclusive Swedish Academy. The legends and myths of Sweden form the basis for many Lagerlöf stories. The romantic optimism of her first novel, *The Story of Gosta Berling*, offered a change from the period's pessimistic realism. "Romantic," in her writing, meant a concern with the beautiful, joyous, or unusual. A children's classic, *The Wonderful Adventures of Nils*, was written for the Swedish Teacher's Association, who wanted a story presenting the folklore and geographical characteristics of the various Swedish provinces. "The Rat Trap," like many of Selma Lagerlöf's short stories, is typical of her concern with moral questions.

Swedish Peasant Painting →

The painting on the opposite page, by the Swedish artist Snarf Anders Andersson, is typical of the art of Selma Lagerlöf's native land. This type of art is called "peasant painting" since it often appears on walls of farm houses in Sweden. Peasant painting tells a story, though it is often difficult to determine the subject. For example, the inscription at the top of this painting reads, "Would You Like to Buy My Horse?" Did you guess that this was what it meant?

The Dragon

RAY BRADBURY

In this story a noted writer of science fiction tells of a strange meeting, with haunting overtones of mystery and fatality. Beneath the surface events is a theme which is much more general than those you found in the preceding two stories. Here, the author is making a comment on the way change takes place and on how it affects people.

THE NIGHT blew in the short grass on the moor; there was no other motion. It had been years since a single bird had flown by in the great blind shell of sky. Long ago a few small stones had simulated life when they crumbled and fell into dust. Now only the night moved in the souls of the two men bent by their lonely fire in the wilderness; darkness pumped quietly in their veins and ticked silently in their temples and their wrists.

Firelight fled up and down their wild faces and welled in their eyes in orange tatters. They listened to each other's faint, cool breathing and the lizard blink of their eyelids. At last, one man poked the fire with his sword.

"Don't, idiot; you'll give us away!"

"No matter," said the second man. "The dragon can smell us miles off anyway. God's breath, it's cold. I wish I was back at the castle."

"It's death, not sleep, we're after. . . ."

"Why? Why? The dragon never sets foot in the town!"

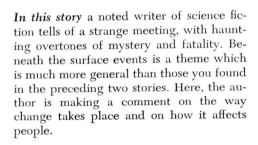

Finding Clues to Meaning. "The Dragon" is a very modern story. Not only is it science fiction, a development of our own time, but it is also a kind of modern writing that bears resemblance to modern painting. Implications, details, and curious conversations are scattered throughout the story. You are never *told* what to make of these seemingly unrelated materials; this you must do for yourself by feeling your way. You must be alert to key words and phrases; you must interpret contrasts and symbols and especially repetitions. Read this story, then, as you might respond to a striking and intriguing painting in some modern art gallery. Let it grow upon you slowly and do not expect to fathom its depth in the same way you get meaning from older stories like "The Bishop's Candlesticks."

"Quiet, fool! He eats men traveling alone from our town to the next!"

"Let them be eaten and let us get home!"

"Wait now; listen!"

The two men froze.

They waited a long time, but there was only the shake of their horses' nervous skin like black velvet tambourines jingling the silver stirrup buckles, softly, softly.

"Ah." The second man sighed. "What a land of nightmares. Everything happens here. Someone blows out the sun; it's night. And then, and *then*, oh, listen! This dragon, they say his eyes are fire. His breath a white gas; you can see him burn across the dark lands. He runs with sulfur and thunder and kindles the grass. Sheep panic and die insane. Women deliver forth monsters. The dragon's fury is such that tower walls shake back to dust. His victims, at sunrise, are strewn hither thither on the hills. How many knights, I ask, have gone for this monster and failed, even as we shall fail?"

"Enough of that!"

"More than enough! Out here in this desolation I cannot tell what year this is!"

"Nine hundred years since the Nativity."

"No, no," whispered the second man, eyes shut. "On this moor is no Time, is only Forever. I feel if I ran back on the road the town would be gone, the people yet unborn, things changed, the castles unquarried from the rocks, the timbers still uncut from the forests; don't ask how I know; the moor knows and tells me. And here we sit alone in the land of the fire dragon, God save us!"

"Be you afraid, then gird on your armor!"

"What use? The dragon runs from nowhere; we cannot guess its home. It vanishes in fog; we know not where it goes. Aye, on with our armor, we'll die well dressed."

Half into his silver corselet,[1] the second man stopped again and turned his head.

Across the dim country, full of night and nothingness from the heart of the moor itself, the wind sprang full of dust from clocks that used dust for telling time. There were black suns burning in the heart of this new wind and a million burnt leaves shaken from some autumn tree beyond the horizon. This wind melted landscapes, lengthened bones like white wax, made the blood roil[2] and thicken to a muddy deposit in the brain. The wind was a thousand souls dying and all time confused and in transit. It was a fog inside of a mist inside of a darkness, and this place was no man's place and there was no year or hour at all, but only these men in a faceless emptiness of sudden frost, storm and white thunder which moved behind the great falling pane of green glass that was the lightning. A squall of rain drenched the turf; all faded away until there was unbreathing hush and the two men waiting alone with their warmth in a cool season.

"There," whispered the first man. "Oh, *there* . . ."

Miles off, rushing with a great chant and a roar — the dragon.

In silence the men buckled on their armor and mounted their horses. The midnight wilderness was split by a monstrous gushing as the dragon roared nearer, nearer; its flashing yellow glare spurted above a hill and then, fold on fold of dark body, distantly seen, therefore indistinct, flowed over

---

[1] **corselet:** armor for the body.
[2] **roil:** to disturb; to stir up.

that hill and plunged vanishing into a valley.

"Quick!"

They spurred their horses forward to a small hollow.

"This is where it passes!"

They seized their lances with mailed fists and blinded their horses by flipping the visors down over their eyes.

"Lord!"

"Yes, let us use His name."

On the instant, the dragon rounded a hill. Its monstrous amber eye fed on them, fired their armor in red glints and glitters. With a terrible wailing cry and a grinding rush it flung itself forward.

"Mercy!"

The lance struck under the unlidded yellow eye, buckled, tossed the man through the air. The dragon hit, spilled him over, down, ground him under. Passing, the black brunt of its shoulder smashing the remaining horse and rider a hundred feet against the side of a boulder, wailing, wailing, the dragon shrieking, the fire all about, around, under it, a pink, yellow, orange sun-fire with great soft plumes of blinding smoke.

"Did you *see* it?" cried a voice. "Just like I told you!"

"The same! The same! A knight in armor, by the Lord Harry! We *hit* him!"

"You goin' to stop?"

"Did once; found nothing. Don't like to stop on this moor. I get the willies. Got a *feel*, it has."

"But we hit *something!*"

"Gave him plenty of whistle; chap wouldn't budge!"

A steaming blast cut the mist aside.

"We'll make Stokely on time. More coal, eh, Fred?"

Another whistle shook dew from the empty sky. The night train, in fire and fury, shot through a gully, up a rise, and vanished away over cold earth toward the north, leaving black smoke and steam to dissolve in the numbed air minutes after it had passed and gone forever.

FINDING CLUES TO MEANING

The student who tries to read "The Dragon" for literal meaning only, as if he were reading a lesson in biology, will soon be lost. How well did you fare? Perhaps the following clues will help you to round out your impressions.

KEY PASSAGES

How did you interpret the following passages?

1. "The dragon never sets foot in the town!" (page 140), and "This is where it passes!" (page 142).

Does the dragon always use one path? Why? If the dragon never enters the town, why have the knights gone out after him?

2. "Its monstrous amber eye fed on them. . . . The lance struck under the unlidded yellow eye . . ." (page 142).

What is this eye of the dragon?

SHIFTS IN PERSPECTIVE

3. At first you view the situation in relation to the two knights. Suddenly the focus shifts and you view things in terms of the trainmen. What effect does this shift have?

4. Another shift occurs in the last paragraph. What purpose does it serve?

REPEATED TIME REFERENCES

5. What references to time occur in the first paragraph? What is strange about the references?

"Church of the Minorites," a painting by Lyonel Feininger (1871–1956). ▶
(See *"Modern Artists"* on page 144).

6. The second knight makes a curious comment when the first man announces that the year is 900 A.D. What effect does this comment have?

7. Reread the paragraph beginning, "Across the dim country . . ." (page 141). It gives an impression of great seriousness, as if the author were particularly interested in saying it just right. What is he telling you about time here?

8. With what impression does the reference to time in the last paragraph leave you?

SYMBOLS

9. What might the dragon, or the train, symbolize?

10. Knowing that knights are associated with the past, and trainmen, with more recent times, what might these two sets of men represent or symbolize?

DETERMINING THE THEME

After tracking down the various clues, you probably have a general idea of what the story is all about. It seems fairly clear that the author is commenting on change — on the manner in which new ideas and inventions replace older ones. The problem now is to go a little farther and determine what the author is saying about change. Perhaps the following questions will be of help. Though there may be no "right" answers, an opinion on these questions should bring you closer to an understanding of the theme.

1. Is the author sympathetic to either set of characters? If so, is it the knights or the trainmen?

2. Do the knights understand the nature of what they are fighting? Are they adequately prepared?

3. Do the trainmen realize what they are doing? How do they feel about it?

4. What does the fact that the knights are destroyed tell you about what happens when the old meets the new?

5. Has this kind of fatal collision occurred before in the course of history? Will it occur over and over again?

If possible, discuss the story, the clues, and the questions above with your classmates. You may be able to agree on a statement of the theme, but do not be concerned if you cannot all agree. It is natural and right for readers to interpret the meaning of a story differently. At least try to find an interpretation that *you* feel is satisfactory.

ABOUT THE AUTHOR

Ray Bradbury (1920–) now writes for many popular magazines, although most of his first stories appeared in fantasy and science-fiction magazines. Born in Waukegan, Illinois, Bradbury graduated from high school in Los Angeles where he continued to live, supporting himself by selling newspapers so that he would have time to write. *The Martian Chronicles* and *The Golden Apples of the Sun* brought the author acclaim from abroad as well as from this country. A master of both types of literature, he feels that science fiction differs from fantasy in that the former is a logical working out of reality, and that fantasy usually depends upon more improbable situations. "The Dragon" is a typical example of Bradbury's inventive skill.

Modern Artists

Perhaps you wonder what Feininger's painting on page 143 has to do with Ray Bradbury's story. Certainly the subject matter of the story and the painting have nothing in common. However, if you stop to think about Bradbury and Feininger *as artists,* you may find some interesting comparisons.

First, you must accept the idea that although the writer and the painter deal in very different mediums — words and paint — they may have a similar purpose. Each may be expressing his own view or idea about a common experience and be attempting to shed new light or understanding on it. Bradbury had an idea about the common experience of change; Feininger saw an ordinary village scene in a new way. Bradbury experimented with time; Feininger, with space.

Think of this story and this painting, then, as artistic experiments. Try to explain what is unique about Bradbury's treatment of time, and Feininger's treatment of space.

The Gift of the Magi

O. HENRY

Sometimes, such is the irony of life, our very mistakes bring us happiness. Of course, this infrequent quirk of fate is not one on which wise men count. If you can find the basic theme in this story, you will also understand what prevents the mistakes of these newlyweds from destroying their happiness.

O<small>NE DOLLAR</small> and eighty-seven cents. That was all. And sixty cents of it was in pennies. Pennies saved one and two at a time by bull-dozing the grocer and the vegetable man and the butcher until one's cheek burned with silent imputation of parsimony [1] that such close dealing implied. Three times Della counted it. One dollar and

[1] **imputation** (ĭm′pû·tā′shŭn) **of parsimony** (pär′sĭ·mō′nĭ): charge of stinginess.

eighty-seven cents. And the next day would be Christmas.

There was clearly nothing to do but flop down on the shabby little couch and howl. So Della did it. Which instigates [2] the moral reflection that life is made up of sobs, sniffles, and smiles, with sniffles predominating.

While the mistress of the home is gradually subsiding from the first stage to the second, [3] take a look at the home. A furnished flat at eight dollars per week. It did not exactly beggar description, [4] but it certainly had that word

[2] **instigates** (ĭn′stĭ·gāts): provokes.
[3] **first stage . . . second:** that is, from sobs to sniffles.
[4] **did not . . . beggar description:** was not beyond description. (The implication is that the condition of the apartment was almost indescribable.)

Relating Theme to Title. This story has an odd title. There are no Magi in the story, no wise men bearing gifts whose journey is told of in the Bible. In fact, the author says that this is the "chronicle of two foolish children." Furthermore, in this story the young married couple give each other

gifts, and the Magi brought gifts to Bethlehem. Why then should O. Henry use the singular *gift* in the title? Once you recognize this story as a form of *parable,* a narrative intended to teach one of life's truths, you will find it not too difficult to explain the title by the theme.

---

on the lookout for the mendicancy squad.[1]

In the vestibule [2] below was a letter box into which no letter would go, and an electric button from which no mortal finger could coax a ring. Also appertaining thereunto [3] was a card bearing the name "Mr. James Dillingham Young."

The "Dillingham" had been flung to the breeze during a former period of prosperity when its possessor was being paid thirty dollars per week. Now, when the income was shrunk to twenty dollars, the letters of "Dillingham" looked blurred, as though they were thinking seriously of contracting to a modest and unassuming D. But whenever Mr. James Dillingham Young came home and reached his flat above he was called "Jim" and greatly hugged by Mrs. James Dillingham Young, already introduced to you as Della. Which is all very good.

Della finished her cry and attended to her cheeks with the powder rag. She stood by the window and looked out dully at a gray cat walking a gray fence in a gray back yard. Tomorrow would be Christmas Day, and she had only one dollar and eighty-seven cents with which to buy Jim a present. She had been saving every penny she could for months, with this result. Twenty dollars a week doesn't go far. Expenses had been greater than she had calculated. They always are. Only one dollar and eighty-seven cents to buy a present for Jim. Her Jim. Many a happy hour

she had spent planning for something nice for him. Something fine and rare and sterling — something just a little bit near to being worthy of the honor of being owned by Jim.

There was a pier glass [4] between the windows of the room. Perhaps you have seen a pier glass in an eight-dollar flat. A very thin and very agile person may, by observing his reflection in a rapid sequence of longitudinal [5] strips, obtain a fairly accurate conception of his looks. Della, being slender, had mastered the art.

Suddenly she whirled from the window and stood before the glass. Her eyes were shining brilliantly, but her face had lost its color within twenty seconds. Rapidly she pulled down her hair and let it fall to its full length.

Now there were two possessions of the James Dillingham Youngs in which they both took a mighty pride. One was Jim's gold watch that had been his father's and his grandfather's. The other was Della's hair. Had the Queen of Sheba [6] lived in the flat across the air shaft, Della would have let her hair hang out the window someday to dry, just to depreciate Her Majesty's jewels and gifts. Had King Solomon been the janitor, with all his treasures piled up in the basement, Jim would have pulled out his watch every time he passed, just to see him pluck at his beard from envy.

So now Della's beautiful hair fell about her, rippling and shining like a cascade of brown waters. It reached below her knee and made itself almost

[1] **mendicancy** (mĕn′dĭ·kăn·sĭ) **squad:** *mendicancy* means "begging"; a *mendicancy squad* would be a police squad that picked up beggars. (This is O. Henry's way of suggesting that the apartment was very shabby.)
[2] **vestibule** (vĕs′tĭ·būl): a hall or small room between the front and the interior of a building.
[3] **appertaining thereunto:** belonging to, or associated with.

[4] **pier glass:** a long mirror intended to fill the space between the two windows.
[5] **longitudinal** (lŏn·jĭ·tū′dĭ·năl): lengthwise.
[6] **Queen of Sheba:** Upon hearing of the wisdom of King Solomon, the Queen of Sheba came "to prove him" with hard questions. When he met her tests, she left him gold, spices, and jewels.

a garment for her. And then she did it up again nervously and quickly. Once she faltered for a minute and stood still while a tear or two splashed on the worn red carpet.

On went her old brown jacket; on went her old brown hat. With a whirl of skirts and with the brilliant sparkle still in her eyes, she fluttered out the door and down the stairs to the street.

Where she stopped the sign read: "Mme. Sofronie. Hair Goods of All Kinds." One flight up Della ran — and collected herself, panting. Madame, large, too white, chilly, hardly looked the "Sofronie."

"Will you buy my hair?" asked Della.

"I buy hair," said Madame. "Take yer hat off and let's have a sight at the looks of it."

Down rippled the brown cascade.

"Twenty dollars," said Madame, lifting the mass with a practiced hand.

"Give it to me quick," said Della.

Oh, and the next two hours tripped by on rosy wings. Forget the hashed metaphor. She was ransacking the stores for Jim's present.

She found it at last. It surely had been made for Jim and no one else. There was no other like it in any of the stores, and she had turned all of them inside out. It was a platinum fob chain simple and chaste in design, properly proclaiming its value by substance alone and not by meretricious [1] ornamentation — as all good things should do. It was even worthy of The Watch. As soon as she saw it she knew that it must be Jim's. It was like him. Quietness and value — the description applied to both. Twenty-one dollars they took from her for it, and she hurried home with the eighty-seven cents. With

[1] **meretricious** (mĕr′ē̇·trĭsh′ŭs): deceitfully showy.

that chain on his watch Jim might be properly anxious about the time in any company. Grand as the watch was, he sometimes looked at it on the sly on account of the old leather strap that he used in place of a chain.

When Della reached home her intoxication gave way a little to prudence and reason. She got out her curling irons and lighted the gas and went to work repairing the ravages made by generosity added to love. Which is always a tremendous task, dear friends — a mammoth task.

Within forty minutes her head was covered with tiny, close-lying curls that made her look wonderfully like a truant schoolboy. She looked at her reflection in the mirror long, carefully, and critically.

"If Jim doesn't kill me," she said to herself, "before he takes a second look at me, he'll say I look like a Coney Island chorus girl. But what could I do — oh! what could I do with a dollar and eighty-seven cents?"

At seven o'clock the coffee was made and the frying pan was on the back of the stove hot and ready to cook the chops.

Jim was never late. Della doubled the fob chain in her hand and sat on the corner of the table near the door that he always entered. Then she heard his step on the stair away down on the first flight, and she turned white for just a moment. She had a habit of saying little silent prayers about the simplest everyday things, and now she whispered, "Please, God, make him think I am still pretty."

The door opened and Jim stepped in and closed it. He looked thin and very serious. Poor fellow, he was only twenty-two — and to be burdened with a family! He needed a new overcoat and he was without gloves.

Jim stopped inside the door, as immovable as a setter at the scent of quail. His eyes were fixed upon Della; and there was an expression in them that she could not read, and it terrified her. It was not anger, nor surprise, nor disapproval, nor horror, nor any of the sentiments that she had been prepared for. He simply stared at her fixedly with that peculiar expression on his face.

Della wriggled off the table and went to him.

"Jim, darling," she cried, "don't look at me that way. I had my hair cut off and sold it because I couldn't have lived through Christmas without giving you a present. It'll grow out again — you won't mind, will you? I just had to do it. My hair grows awfully fast. Say 'Merry Christmas!' Jim, and let's be happy. You don't know what a nice — what a beautiful, nice gift I've got for you."

"You've cut off your hair?" asked Jim laboriously, as if he had not arrived at that patent fact yet even after the hardest mental labor.

"Cut it off and sold it," said Della. "Don't you like me just as well, any-how? I'm me without my hair, ain't I?"

Jim looked about the room curiously.

"You say your hair is gone?" he said, with an air almost of idiocy.

"You needn't look for it," said Della. "It's sold, I tell you — sold and gone, too. It's Christmas Eve, boy. Be good to me, for it went for you. Maybe the hairs of my head were numbered," she went on with a sudden serious sweetness, "but nobody could ever count my love for you. Shall I put the chops on, Jim?"

Out of his trance Jim seemed quickly to wake. He enfolded his Della. For ten seconds let us regard with discreet scrutiny some inconsequential object in the other direction. Eight dollars a week or a million a year — what is the difference? A mathematician or a wit would give you the wrong answer. The Magi [1] brought valuable gifts, but that was not among them. This dark assertion will be illuminated later on.

Jim drew a package from his overcoat pocket and threw it upon the table.

"Don't make any mistake, Dell," he said, "about me. I don't think there's anything in the way of a haircut or a shave or a shampoo that could make me like my girl any less. But if you'll unwrap that package you may see why you had me going awhile at first."

White fingers and nimble tore at the string and paper. And then an ecstatic scream of joy; and then, alas! a quick feminine change to hysterical tears and wails, necessitating the immediate employment of all the comforting powers of the lord of the flat.

For there lay The Combs — the set of combs, side and back, that Della had worshiped for long in a Broadway window. Beautiful combs, pure tortoise shell, with jeweled rims — just the

[1] **Magi** (mā´jī).

shade to wear in the beautiful vanished hair. They were expensive combs, she knew, and her heart had simply craved and yearned over them without the least hope of possession. And now they were hers, but the tresses that should have adorned the coveted adornments were gone.

But she hugged them to her bosom, and at length she was able to look up with dim eyes and a smile and say, "My hair grows so fast, Jim!"

And then Della leaped up like a little singed cat and cried, "Oh, oh!"

Jim had not yet seen his beautiful present. She held it out to him eagerly upon her open palm. The dull precious metal seemed to flash with a reflection of her bright and ardent spirit.

"Isn't it a dandy, Jim? I hunted all over town to find it. You'll have to look at the time a hundred times a day now. Give me your watch. I want to see how it looks on it."

Instead of obeying, Jim tumbled down on the couch and put his hands under the back of his head and smiled.

"Della," said he, "let's put our Christmas presents away and keep 'em awhile. They're too nice to use just at present. I sold the watch to get the money to buy your combs. And now suppose you put the chops on."

The Magi, as you know, were wise men — wonderfully wise men — who brought gifts to the Babe in the manger. They invented the art of giving Christmas presents. Being wise, their gifts were no doubt wise ones, possibly bearing the privilege of exchange in case of duplication. And here I have lamely related to you the uneventful chronicle of two foolish children in a flat who most unwisely sacrificed for each other the greatest treasures of their house. But in a last word to the wise of these days let it be said that of all who give gifts these two were the wisest. Of all who give and receive gifts, such as they are wisest. Everywhere they are wisest. They are the Magi.

RELATING THEME TO TITLE

1. What clues to the concluding surprises does O. Henry give in the beginning of the story?

2. What happens in the story that neither Della nor the reader knows until the end?

3. Irony is often used to indicate the difference between the true nature of a situation and its outward appearance. Can you locate *three* ironies in this story? Two of them are fairly obvious. The third irony is the most important of the three, for it is the important foundation of the theme and the title of the story. Some might call it a *paradox*, a contradictory statement that seems absurd or foolish, yet may be true.

4. What is the theme of this story? Who were the Magi? What connection does the theme have to the title and to O. Henry's use of *gift* rather than *gifts?*

GAINING POWER OVER LANGUAGE

APPROPRIATENESS OF LANGUAGE   Power over language depends upon much more than the mastery of a large vocabulary. Have you noticed that different groups of people do not speak our language in exactly the same way? You would be surprised, wouldn't you, if the President or some member of his cabinet or military staff said, "Us Americans ain't gonna be hog-tied by no gol-durned furriners"? Why would you be surprised?

Is there any danger in the opposite direction, a danger of using overly elegant language when it is not appropriate? Describe a situation to illustrate your point of view on this matter.

In "Gift of the Magi," Della uses *ain't.* We must remember that the way a person speaks is not a sign of his human worth. Does Della's language detract from the goodness of heart she shows in this story?

Just as O. Henry did in his stories, artist John Sloan (1871–1955) in his paintings described scenes of everyday life in New York around the turn of the century. Perhaps it is only coincidence that this painting, "Hairdresser's Window," depicts the same general setting as the O. Henry story and also an event similar to one mentioned in the story. Could this be Della selling her tresses to pay for Jim's Christmas gift?

ABOUT THE AUTHOR

O. Henry (1862–1910) was the pen name of William Sydney Porter, American master of the "surprise ending." Greatly influenced by Edgar Allan Poe, he wrote constantly under the pressure of publishers from whom he had already received advances for his popular stories. For ten years Porter drifted in and out of various positions: as a clerk and bookkeeper, a draftsman, editor of a weekly fiction publication, and reporter for the Houston *Daily Post*. During his early life, he was imprisoned for embezzling money from a bank which closed as a result of bad management. It is now generally believed that Porter was a victim of circumstances. After his release from prison, he spent a brief period in Philadelphia and then moved to New York where he remained until his death. Of his six hundred short stories, his best are set in New York. He described all aspects of city life with an original eye and a keen sense of character.

Speaking of Theme

In the four stories you have just read, your attention has been directed, like an X ray, to that part of the story lying beneath the surface of what happens. In "The Bishop's Candlesticks" and "The Rat Trap" the underlying themes were strikingly similar, even though characters, setting, and incidents differed. Beneath the plots of both stories we found a belief in brotherhood and in the redeeming power of kindness. In "The Gift of the Magi" we found the concept that self-sacrifice, when motivated by love, is not futile but rather a form of wisdom. This idea accounted for all the major incidents in O. Henry's memorable Christmas story.

In "The Dragon" the theme was more elusive. Certainly nothing in the story supported any theme dealing with human relationships. Some idea about the nature of change was suggested as a more likely base for unifying this curious story. Before we can be more certain of his intention, we may need to read a number of stories by Ray Bradbury. Very often, authors work out, in a number of different stories, the ideas which concern them most.

We have noted, also, a danger in studying theme, the danger of expecting every story to have some easily stated moral such as "What can't be cured must be endured." Literature does indeed deal with truth about human values, but it is not a guidance pamphlet to tell us how to get along with brothers and sisters. Nor can we turn to literature for specific advice — on how to behave on a date, for example. Literature is the artistic expression of a writer's experience and his imaginative world. The writer wants to reveal life, not to preach or teach about it. He wants his readers to realize his story through their senses and their emotions as well as their minds. He hopes his story will express its own meaning without any need to point it out. If he makes some part of life come alive for the reader, that is enough. The reader may, if he understands the story theme, extend his own experience and gain wisdom along with pleasure.

Total Effect

Throughout this section, the elements of a short story have been unfolded. You have noticed how plot is handled to create suspense or to reveal character more fully. In stories like "The Open Window" and "The Cask of Amontillado," you have seen how an author's tone or setting contributes to his purpose. You have become familiar with terms that may have been unfamiliar to you, terms like *irony, theme,* and *point of view.* Now we have a question for you. Can you relate all these aspects of a short story in order to appreciate, for yourself, the *total effect* of a short story?

Merely to identify the elements of a short story is a waste of your time. Unless you have learned to relate all such matters of form to the meaning of the stories, you have missed the path to appreciation. What is even worse, you may have come to dislike short stories. There is no value in being able to pick a story to pieces just to analyze its various parts. The study of literature must always lead to an appreciation of the values it offers.

Here, at the close of the short story section, are two stories with much to offer. They provide both wisdom and pleasure. Let your reaction to these stories be your test of how well you have learned to put together all the elements of the short story.

The Jade Goddess

LIN YUTANG

From a collection of stories written during the Sung dynasty in China, this ancient love story, retold after nearly a thousand years, concerns the relation between art and life.

Life is never quite perfect; often it is confusing, the dull and bitter mingled with the sweet. It can never have the order, the pattern, or the harmony of art — of a statue, for example. In some human beings the impulse to achieve this artistic perfection is so intense that to exist without creating it in some way becomes intolerable for them. Such men and women may be born in any place and any time; they may come from the poor as well as from the fortunate of this world.

Here the artist is a country lad of sixteen who goes to the city as a servant. "*Chang Po was one of those original people born to create, not to learn what the world had to teach him.*"

The voyage up the Yangtze Gorges [1] had been exciting and hazardous, but I had finally arrived at the home of the retired governor in a suburban town near Chengtu. The governor was a famous art collector, and it had been said of him that in his days of power, he had used his political position to obtain valuable objects of art. When he wanted a bronze or a painting he had to have it, either by paying for it or by other means. It could not be true that he had practically ruined a family which refused to sell him a piece of Shang bronze,[2] for that was the rumor, but it is known that his love of curios amounted to an obsession. As a result, he had in his collection some of the most priceless treasures.

The governor received me in his parlor on the ground floor of the Western Tower, which was reached by a succession of three courtyards. For a collector of art, the parlor was almost bare of art objects, but was furnished with the usual redwood furniture, covered with red cushions and leopard skins. The décor [3] had that elegance of simplicity, suggestive of a fine, cultivated taste. As I talked with him, I constantly looked at the exquisite silhouette of a sang-de-bœuf [4] vase, and a few sprigs of plum blossoms standing against the landscape window looking out upon his garden.

A painting from the Ming-Ch'ing period by Chien Hung-Shou (1599–1652).

I was surprised that the governor was one of the mildest of men in his appearance. Perhaps old age had softened him, but looking at him, it was difficult to believe the rumors of his cruelty. He treated me as if I was an old friend who had dropped in for a morning chat. I began to wonder whether my friend who had arranged for the visit had told him of my purpose in visiting him, or whether the governor was too old to remember.

I envied this man, for the whole impression he gave me was that he was glad to be alive in this beautiful retreat which he had built for himself.

Politely I mentioned his famous collection.

"Oh," he said, with a mild laugh, "today they belong to me, the next hundred years they will belong to somebody else. You see a family never owns an art treasure for more than a hundred years. Those things have a destiny

---

[1] **Yangtze** (yăng′[t]sē′) **Gorges:** The *Yangtze* is a river flowing into the East China Sea, cutting *gorges*, or narrow ravines, into the mountains.

[2] **Shang** (shäng) **bronze:** "Shang" refers to a Chinese dynasty (about 1500–1050 B.C.) with a high culture, which specialized in bronze work. (See the picture on page 159.)

[3] **décor** (dā′kôr′): that which serves to decorate (French).

[4] *sang-de-bœuf* (sän′dē·bûf′): literally, "ox blood" (French); here, a type of Chinese porcelain vase named for the deep red glaze covering it.

of their own. They see us and laugh at us." His voice had acquired a certain animation as he talked. Now he put a pipe to his lips.

"Do you believe that?"

"Of course," he mumbled without taking his pipe from his mouth.

"What do you mean?" I asked timidly.

"Anything that is really old acquires a personality and a life of its own."

"You mean it becomes a spirit?"

"What is a spirit?" countered the old man. "It is what informs life, gives birth to life. Take an object of art. The artist pours into it his imagination and his life's blood, in just as real a sense as a mother pours her life's blood into the embryo. Why do you wonder that it should have a life of its own, when the soul of the artist enters into it — and in giving birth to it sometimes dies himself, as, for instance, happened with my Jade Goddess of Mercy."

I had intended only to see some of the manuscripts. I had not heard of the Jade Goddess, for very few people had. I was not quite sure what he meant when he referred to his Jade Goddess and the exceptional circumstances of its creation, and during our examination of the manuscripts, I constantly tried to lead the conversation back to that topic.

Pointing to an old manuscript, I said, "Of course, it is true that something of the personality of the artist is left behind and lives after him in his work."

"Yes, anything good and beautiful always lives. It becomes, as it were, an offspring of the artist," the governor replied with conviction.

"But especially when an artist dies in the creation of it," I added. "Like your Jade Goddess."

"That is a particular case. He didn't exactly die on account of it. But he might as well have been dead — might just as well have been dead after that," he added after a pause. "You see the whole circumstances of the life of this artist seem to suggest that he was born to create this piece of work and to be crucified for it. He could not have created it otherwise."

"It must be an extraordinary piece of work. May I see it?"

After more tactful promptings, the governor agreed to show it to me.

While some of his best things were on the first floor of the tower, the Jade Goddess was kept on the top floor.

"Who is the artist?"

"A fellow by the name of Chang Po, practically unknown to the world. I learned about his life from the old prioress [1] of the Cockcrow Convent. I had to donate a large piece of farm property to the nunnery — to that sly, old prioress — before she would part with it. That was after the nun who owned it had died. It certainly is better taken care of here than it would be at the Convent."

The statuette, which was made of an extraordinary white luster with patches of green, stood inside a glass case in the center of the top floor, protected by a latticework of wrought iron so heavy that no one could move it.

"Walk around her a bit," said the governor, "and she will still see you."

I was intrigued by the way he referred to the statuette as if she were truly alive, and, indeed, I had a weird feeling as I circled the jade figure that her eyes followed me.

It was a tragic statue. The expression of the goddess showed her caught in flight at some dramatic moment, with her right arm raised high up, her head turned backward, and her left arm

[1] **prioress** (prī′ĕr-ĕs): a nun in charge of a religious order.

stretching slightly forward. The expression was that of a woman being physically torn apart from somebody she loved. It might have been described as a statuette of the Goddess of Mercy going up to heaven, with her hand outstretched to bless mankind, but nobody who had seen the expression on her face could accept that interpretation. It was incredible how the artist had conveyed, in a figure no higher than eighteen inches, such a living, unforgettable experience. Even the folds of her dress were unconventional. It was an individual and completely personal creation.

"How did the nun come to own it?" I asked.

"Look well at the statue's whole posture, the posture of flight, and the expression of love and terror and agony in her eyes." He paused. "Let's go down," he said suddenly. "I will tell you the whole story."

The nun, whose name was Meilan, had confessed the tale before she died. The prioress may not have told the correct story in all its details and she may even have embellished the story a little to make it more attractive. But the governor had checked some important points and verified them for himself. According to the prioress, the nun was very much confined to herself, but a well-cultivated person. Not until she was on her deathbed did she tell anyone about herself.

It must have been over a hundred years ago. Meilan was then a young happy girl living in a large garden home in Kaifeng.[1] As the only daughter of a high official, Commissioner Chang, she was very much pampered. Her father was a severe judge but upon his daughter he bestowed all his affection. As al-

ways happens, a number of clan relatives had come to live in the mansion, the better educated ones being given jobs in the government and the illiterate ones working as servants in the large household.

One day a distant nephew arrived. His name was Chang Po and he was an intelligent lad of sixteen, vivacious and full of spirit. He was somewhat tall for his age and his hands with beautiful tapering fingers were remarkable for a country lad. He made such a good impression on the family that the mother decided he could be given the job of caring for visitors though he did not know how to read or write.

He was a year older than Meilan and as they were still children they often met and talked and laughed together, for Chang Po could tell Meilan stories of the country and she loved to listen to him.

But after a few weeks the family's first enthusiasm for the boy was somewhat dampened. He was both unusual and difficult. In the first place he was not a good servant; he was often forgetful of his duties and would not, or could not, take a scolding from his elders if he made a mistake. And so the girl's mother asked him to tend the gardens. The boy was finally happy doing this work.

Chang Po was one of those original people born to create, not to learn what the world had to teach him. He was perfectly happy alone with his flowers and trees and he walked about and whistled as if he were lord of the creation. Left alone, he could do amazing things. He had taught himself to paint without a master. In his spare time he made wonderful lanterns and molded the most lifelike clay animals.

At the age of eighteen Chang Po was seemingly good for nothing. What ex-

<hr>

[1] Kaifeng (kī′fŭng′): a city in the Hwang Ho Valley of east central China.

A *jade stag of the Chou dynasty, found in a tomb in Honan, China.*

actly attracted Meilan to him, she herself could not say. He was just different and had grown tall and handsome. He got away with everything and made himself loved by the family with the exception of the father. A natural intimacy grew up between the cousins, although it was clearly understood that as they were of the same clan name marriage between them was out of the question.

One day Chang Po suddenly announced to the mistress of the house that he was leaving to learn a trade. He had found a jade-worker's shop and had offered himself as an apprentice. The mother thought it just as well, since he was too often with Meilan. But Chang continued to live on at the house, returning every night, and he had even more to say to his cousin than before.

"Meilan," the mother said one day, "you are both grown up now and although Brother Po is your cousin, you ought not to see each other too often."

Her mother's words made Meilan think. She had never quite realized that she was in love with the boy Chang.

That night she met Chang Po in the garden. Sitting on a stone bench in the moonlight, she casually mentioned what her mother had said.

"Brother Po," she said, blushing, "Mother says I mustn't see you so much."

"Yes, we are grown up now."

The girl hung her head. "What does that mean?" She spoke half to herself.

Chang Po stole a hand around her waist. "It means that something in you makes you more charming every day to me, something which makes me crave to see you. Something which makes me feel happy when you are near and lonely and sad when I am away."

The girl sighed and asked, "Are you happy now?"

"Yes and everything changes. Meilan, we belong to each other," he said softly.

"You know very well I cannot marry you and that my parents will arrange a match for me before long."

"No, you mustn't say that. You mustn't."

"You must understand."

"I understand only this," Chang said, drawing the girl into his arms. "Since the heaven and earth were created, you were made for me and I was made for you and I will not let you go. It cannot be wrong to love you."

Meilan fled from his embrace and ran to her room.

The awakening of young love was a terrible thing. The more so when with it came the realization of their position, of the sweet poignancy of the unattainable. That night Meilan lay in bed thinking of what her mother had said and then what Chang had said. From that night on she was completely changed. The more they tried to stop the love that had been awakened, the more they felt themselves in its power. They tried not to see each other. After three days, the girl in humiliation came back to him and their excitement was increased by secrecy. Those were the days of young passions and tender regrets, temporary separations and renewed pledges, so sweet and so bitter, and both knew they were in the power of something greater than themselves.

They had no plans. They just loved. According to the customs of the time, Meilan's parents were already suggesting one young man after another for her but she kept putting them off. Sometimes she said she did not want to marry at all, which greatly shocked her mother. As she was yet young the parents did not insist and since she was their only daughter they were half-willing to keep her with them longer.

Meanwhile Chang was working and learning his trade. In jade work, Chang Po had found his natural element. Like a born artist, he had made himself in a short time a master of his trade. He loved it; he worked tirelessly until every detail was perfect. The master of the shop was amazed by him. The rich gentry began to frequent the jade shop with orders.

One day Meilan's father decided to give a present to the empress on her birthday. He wanted to find something special and located an extraordinary large piece of jade of very fine quality. At the mother's suggestion, the commissioner went to the shop where Chang Po worked and explained what he wanted. Examining Chang Po's sculpture, he was quite struck by its individuality.

"Son, here is a very special job for you. This is for the empress, and if you do this job well your fortune is made."

Chang Po examined the jade. His hands traveled slowly over the uncarved stone. He was delighted. It was agreed that he should make it into a Kuan Yin, a goddess of mercy, and Chang Po knew that he would make one of such beauty as no man had set eyes upon before.

Chang Po permitted no one to see the statue until it was completed.

When it was finished, the goddess was in the conventional design and posture but it was a perfect work of art, exquisite in its tender beauty. Chang Po had done what no other craftsman had been able to do before: he had carved a pair of freely revolving earrings on the goddess' ears; and the earlobes themselves were so thin and well modulated that they compelled admiration. The goddess' face was like that of the girl he loved.

Naturally the commissioner was greatly pleased. This piece would be unique even in the palace.

"The face is remarkably like Meilan's," the father remarked.

"Yes," replied Chang Po proudly. "She is the inspiration."

"Good. Young man, from now on your success is assured." He paid Chang generously and added, "You ought to be grateful to me for giving you this opportunity."

Chang Po's name was made. Yet what he wanted most he could not have. The success meant nothing to him without Meilan. He realized that the greatest desire of his heart was beyond him. The young man lost interest in this work. He would not accept lucrative offers. To the chagrin of his master, he just could not work.

Meilan was now approaching the scandalous age of twenty-one and not yet engaged. A match was being arranged with a very influential family. The girl could postpone no longer and her engagement was solemnized by an exchange of gifts.

Reckless with despair, the girl and the boy planned to elope. Assured of Chang's ability to earn a living, Meilan would take away some of her jewels and they could support themselves in some distant province.

The couple prepared to escape one evening through the back of the garden. As it happened an old servant saw them at the dark hour of the night and his suspicion was aroused, for the affair was known inside the household. Thinking it his duty to protect the family from a scandal, the servant held the girl and would not let her go. Chang had no choice. He pushed the servant aside. The old man tottered but would not let go and Chang gave him a blow which felled the poor man at the edge of the rockery. His head struck a jagged rock and he lay limp on the ground. Seeing the servant lifeless, they fled.

The next morning the family discovered the elopement and the dead servant. While they tried to hush the scandal, efforts to trace the couple proved completely fruitless. The commissioner was thrown into a fit of helpless rage. "I shall cover the earth," he vowed, "and bring him back to justice."

After escaping from the capital, the young couple traveled on and on. Finally, avoiding the big towns, they crossed the Yangtze and came down to south China.

"I hear that there is a good jade in Kiangse," [1] Chang said to Meilan.

"Do you think you should work at jade again?" she asked hesitantly. "Your work will be recognized and betray you."

"I thought that was what we planned to do all along," Chang replied.

"That was before old Tai died. They think we murdered him. Can't you change your trade — make lanterns or clay dolls as you used to do?"

"Why? I have made a name for myself with jade."

"You have. That is the whole trouble," Meilan said.

"I don't think we have to worry. Kiangse is almost a thousand miles from the capital. Nobody will know us."

"Then you must change your style. Don't do those extraordinary things. Just do well enough to bring in customers."

Chang Po bit his lips and said nothing. Should he content himself with what a thousand mediocre jade workers were doing to remain safely unknown? Should he destroy his art or allow his art to destroy him? He had not thought of that.

But his wife's instinct was right. She feared it would be against her husband's nature to do cheap, commercial work. She sensed also, after they had crossed the Yangtze, that a mysterious force was dragging her husband toward the jade route in Kiangse, which led from the great mountain pass at Canton into the rich southeast plains. They did not dare stop at Nanchang, the provincial capital, and went on to Kian. The wife again brought up the question of change of profession. Kiangse produced the finest white kaolin [2] and the finest porcelain. Porcelain would satisfy his artistic gift equally well. But Chang Po would not listen.

"Even if I did," said Chang Po, "I would make such porcelain figures that I would be recognized. Or do you want me to do cheap mediocre work? I am sure it is safe here to work in jade."

Against her woman's instinct, the

[1] **Kiangse** (jĭ·äng′sē′): a province in southeastern China.

[2] **kaolin** (kā′ŏ·lĭn): a very pure white clay used to form the paste of porcelain.

wife yielded. "Then please, beloved, for my sake, do not make a name for yourself. We are in trouble, and if you do, we shall be ruined."

She said this because it was her belief, but she knew it was unlikely that her husband would be satisfied with anything but the finest work his hands could produce. With his fine sense of beauty, his love of perfection, his pride in his work, and his passion for jade, what Chang Po really had to escape from was not the police, but himself. He sensed the tragic irony of his situation.

With his wife's jewels Chang Po was able to buy a stock of uncarved stones of various qualities and set up a shop. Meilan watched him at work.

"Good enough, darling," she would say. "Nobody does any better. For my sake, please."

Chang Po looked at her and smiled ruefully. He began to make a number of common round earrings and pendants. But jade is a stone that demands its own expression and its own treatment; it would be wrong to cut up a stone for pendants which could be made into a lovely creation — perhaps a monkey stealing peaches. And so occasionally Chang made — at first stealthily and with a bad conscience — some ingenious and lovely things, strikingly original. These things, the work of his love, were snatched up as fast as he could make them and brought him far greater profits than the cheaper commercial goods.

"Darling, I am worried," Meilan pleaded with him. "You are getting to be too well known. I am expecting a baby. Please be careful."

"A child!" he exclaimed. "Now we are a family!" and Chang Po kissed away what he called her womanish fancies.

A bronze ceremonial vessel of the Shang dynasty.

"But we are doing too well," Meilan murmured.

They were doing well indeed. After a year, the reputation of Paoho jade was established, for that was the name Chang Po had given his shop. All gentry came to buy his ware and the town of Kian itself became known as the city where people on their way to the provincial capital would stop and pick up some delightful jade objects.

One day a man walked into the shop and after looking around casually at the display of goods, asked, "Are you not Chang Po, relative of Commissioner Chang of Kaifeng?"

Chang Po quickly denied it, saying that he had never been to Kaifeng.

The man eyed him suspiciously. "You speak the northern accent well enough. Are you married?"

"That is none of your business."

Meilan peeped from behind the shop. When the man was gone, she told Chang that the stranger was a secretary from her father's office. Perhaps his jade work had really betrayed them.

The next day the man came in again.

"I tell you I don't know what you are talking about," Chang Po said.

"Very well, I will tell you about Chang Po. He is wanted for murder, the abduction of the commissioner's daughter and the theft of his jewels. If you want to convince me that you are not Chang Po, will you ask your wife to serve me a cup of tea? I shall be satisfied when I see that she is not the commissioner's daughter."

"I am running a shop here. If you are trying to create trouble I must ask you to leave."

The man left the shop with a quizzical smile.

Hastily they packed their jadeware and precious belongings, hired a boat and left after dark, fleeing upriver. Their baby was only three months old.

Perhaps it was human perversity or perhaps it was in the divine plan of things. At Kanshien [1] they had to stop, for the baby fell ill and they had run out of money after a month on the voyage. Chang Po had to take out one of his finest creations, a crouching dog with one eye closed, and sell it to a jade merchant named Wang.

"Why, this is Paoho jade," said the merchant. "No other shop makes such things. Absolutely inimitable."

"You are right. I bought it from Paoho," Chang Po said. He was secretly delighted.

Kanshien lay at the foot of a high mountain range. It was winter and Chang Po fell in love with the clear blue sky and mountain air. He and his wife made plans to stay. Their baby was better and Chang decided to open a new shop. Kanshien was a big city,

and they thought it prudent to move farther out and settle in a town some twenty miles away. Chang Po had to sell another of his pieces.

"Why did you do it?" asked Meilan.

"Because we need the money to set up the shop."

"Listen to me this time," Meilan said. "We open a clay shop here."

"Why —" Chang Po stopped short.

"We were nearly caught because you would not listen. Does jade mean so much to you? More than your wife and baby? Later things may change and you can go back to your art again."

Against his wish Chang Po set up a shop making baked black clay figurines. He made hundreds of Buddhas but every week he saw the jade merchants from Canton pass this route and Chang yearned to handle the stone again. He would wander along the streets, stopping at some jadeware shop and anger would roll from his eyes. He came home and seeing the wet clay figures on which he had been working, he crushed them between his fingers.

"Mud! Why should I work with this when I can chisel jade?"

Meilan was frightened by the fire in his eyes. "It will be your ruin."

One day the jade merchant Wang met Chang Po and invited him into his inn, in the hope of getting some more Paoho jade.

"Where have you been?" Chang Po asked.

"I just came back from a trip to Kian," Wang replied. He unwrapped a parcel and said, "You see this is the kind of stuff that Paoho shop is turning out now."

Chang Po was silent. When Wang produced a carnelian [2] monkey, Chang shouted, "Imitation!"

[1] **Kanshien** (gän'shǐ·ĕn'): a city in southeast China, about 200 miles northeast of Canton.

[2] **carnelian** (kär·nēl'yăn): bright red, semiprecious stone.

"You are quite right," the merchant said softly. "There is no expression on the monkey's face. You talk like one who knows."

"I should know," Chang said curtly.

"Yes, I remember you sold me that marvelous crouching dog. I don't mind telling you that I made a hundred percent profit on it. Have you any more pieces of that quality?"

"I will show you what a real Paoho carnelian monkey is like."

At his shop, Chang Po showed him one that he had made in Kian and the merchant was able to persuade Chang to sell it. On his next trip to Nanchang Wang told some of his friends at the jade fair about the remarkable things he had been able to get from the owner of an ordinary clay shop in the south and added, "It seems strange that such a man should possess such lovely jade."

Some six months later three soldiers came with orders to arrest Chang Po and the commissioner's daughter and bring them to the capital. The secretary from the commissioner's office was with them.

"I will come with you if you will let me pack up a few things," Chang said.

"And there are things to bring for the baby," Meilan added.

"Don't forget he is the commissioner's grandson. If he becomes ill on the way you will be responsible."

The men had instructions from the commissioner himself to treat them well on the journey. Chang Po and his wife were allowed to go to the back of the shop while the soldiers waited in front.

It was a hard moment of parting. Chang Po kissed his wife and baby and jumped down from the window, knowing that he would never see them again in this life.

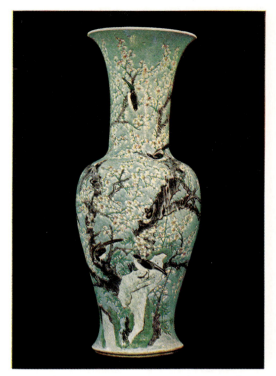

A porcelain vase from the K'ang-hsi period (1662–1722).

"I'll love you always," Meilan whispered softly from the window. "Never touch jade again."

Chang Po took a last look at Meilan as she stood before the window, one arm raised high to bid him good-by forever.

When he had disappeared, she withdrew and calmly entered the front of the shop to put down some of her things in a bag as if she were very busy packing. She told the soldiers to hold her baby and chatted with them as she went about packing. When the soldiers grew suspicious and searched the house, Chang Po was already gone.

Meilan returned to her home to find her mother dead, her father an old man. When she greeted him there was no smile of forgiveness on his face. Only a look at her baby son softened him a

A detail from a painting by Hua Yen (1682–1755), Ch'ing dynasty.

little. In a way the old man was relieved that Chang Po had escaped, for he would not have known what to do with him. Still, he could never forgive the man who had ruined his daughter's life and brought such misery to the whole family.

Years passed and no news had come of Chang Po. Governor Yang from Canton arrived one day at the capital. The commissioner gave a dinner in his honor and in the course of the dinner the governor revealed that he had brought a most precious statue which rivaled the Goddess of Mercy the commissioner had given to the empress and bore a remarkable resemblance to it in style and fineness of workmanship — in fact, it was far more beautiful. He was going to give it to the empress, for the statues would make a pair.

The dinner guests were skeptical and

expressed the opinion that a better piece of workmanship than the empress' goddess was impossible.

"Wait till I show it to you," the governor said triumphantly.

When dinner was over and the table cleared, the governor had a shining wood case brought in. As the white jade Goddess of Mercy was removed from its case and placed on the middle of the table, a hush fell upon them all. Here was the tragic Goddess of Mercy.

A maidservant hurried to inform Meilan. From behind a latticed partition, Meilan looked into the room and paled when she saw the jade figure on the table. "He has done it! I know it is he," she whispered. She pulled herself together to hear whether Chang Po was still alive.

"Who is the artist?" asked a guest.

"That is the most remarkable part of the story," the Canton governor replied. "He is not a regular jade worker. I came to know about him through my wife's niece. She was going to a wedding and had borrowed my wife's antique bracelets to wear for the occasion. They were identical, an intricate design of two intertwining dragons. My niece broke one of them and was horrified. It was really a pity, for the bracelets were unique and very difficult to replace. My niece insisted that she would have the one bracelet duplicated. She went to many shops but none would take the job, saying frankly that it could not be done these days. She advertised in teahouses. Soon after, a shabbily dressed man appeared and said he had come to answer the advertisement. The bracelet was shown to him. He said he could do it and he did. That was how I first heard about this man.

"When I learned that the empress would like another figure to match the Goddess of Mercy, I thought of this man. I ordered the finest piece of jade obtainable at Canton and sent for him. When he was brought in, he looked thoroughly frightened as if he had been caught as a thief. It took me a long time to explain to him that I wanted him to make a Goddess of Mercy to match one in the empress' possession. When I described to him the revolving earrings he winced but he said nothing. Gradually he approached the stone and examined it from every angle. 'What is the matter?' I asked. 'Is it not good enough?' Finally he turned and said proudly, 'This piece will do. It is worth trying. All my life I have been hoping to get white jade of this quality. I will do it, Governor, provided you do not pay me for it — and leave me in complete freedom to execute what I have in mind.'

"I put him in a room with a simple bed and table and installed all the equipment he asked for. He was rather a queer fellow. He talked to no one and was a bit rude to the servant who took things in for him. But he worked like one inspired. I was not allowed to see the statue for five months. Another three months passed before he came with the finished work. I was staggered when I saw it, as you see it before you. As he looked at his own creation, there was a strange expression on his face.

" 'There, Governor,' he said, 'I want to thank you. That statue is my life story.'

"He left before I could answer. I went after him but he was gone. He had completely disappeared."

The guests heard a scream from the next room, a woman's scream so striking and heart-rending that everybody was frozen in his place. Alone, the old commissioner rushed to Meilan, lying on the floor.

A guest who was a close friend of the family whispered to the bewildered governor, "That is the daughter of the commissioner. *She is the goddess.* I am sure your artist is no other than her husband, Chang Po."

When Meilan was revived, she approached the table before all of them. Slowly her hands raised to touch the statuette and then rested tightly on it, as if in seeing and feeling the statue she was in touch with her husband once more. And they all saw that the jade statue and the girl were the same woman.

"Keep the statue, my dear," the governor told her, when he had learned what had happened. "I can find some other present for the empress. I hope it will be some consolation to you. It is yours until you are reunited with your husband."

From that day on Meilan grew weaker, as if some mysterious disease was eating away her body. The commissioner was ready to forgive everything if his son-in-law could be found. By the following spring, word came back from the Canton governor that all efforts to locate Chang Po proved fruitless.

Two years later Chang Po's son died of an epidemic which swept through the city. Meilan then cut off her hair and entered a convent, taking along with her the jade goddess as her only possession. According to the prioress, she seemed to live in a world by herself. She would not permit another nun, not even the prioress, to enter her room.

The prioress told the governor that Meilan had been seen at night writing prayer after prayer and burning it before the statue.

Some twenty years after she joined the convent, Meilan died. And so the perishable Goddess of Mercy passed away and the Jade Goddess remained.

RELATING ALL THE PARTS OF A STORY

1. Throughout this story, the cruelty of life and the beauty of art are interwoven. Show how this is true.

2. The permanence of art and the impermanence of mortal life figure in this story. With what words in the opening part of the story does the old governor allude to these topics? How does the final sentence of the story remind us of his words?

3. Notice that the title of this story is "The Jade Goddess" rather than "The Tragedy of Two Young Lovers." Also look back at the comments on the nature of art made by the old governor at the beginning of the story. How do the title and the governor's comments help to guide the reader to the theme of this story, to its main idea?

4. In this story, does character determine plot? How does *what happens*, in turn, reveal character? For example, what do you learn about Chang Po, Meilan, and her father, as each of them reacts to the events of the story?

5. What do you think art and love have in common? Does "The Jade Goddess" point out this relationship? If so, how?

6. The story suggests that some people are born to be artists. Where is this idea put into words? What is your opinion? Can you support your opinion with any evidence, either from history or your own experience?

7. In "Beware of the Dog" and "The Cask of Amontillado," the authors chose to limit their point of view to one character. This brought you, the reader, into the midst of the stories, for you were forced to live each story as if you were actually a character in it. In "The Jade Goddess" the author has a narrator tell the story. Since the narrator is outside the story, he can describe what happens to all of the characters and make his own comments on events. How does this use of a narrator affect the reader? How does it suit Lin Yutang's purpose in writing the story?

COMPOSITION SUGGESTION

Would a happy ending for Meilan and Chang Po improve this story? Explain your answer in as many paragraphs as you find necessary. If you feel another ending would be better, include some suggestions.

ABOUT THE AUTHOR

Lin Yutang (1895–) was born in Amoy, Fukien Province, China. His extensive education includes a B.A. from St. John's in Shanghai, an M.A. from Harvard, and a Ph.D. from Leipzig University in Germany. In 1923 he became a professor of English philology at the Peking National University. Two of his books were best sellers in the United States: *My Country and My People* has been criticized by some in China who say that to write so frankly of one's country is unpatriotic; the philosophy presented in *The Importance of Living* has been the subject of the author's discussions during several nationwide tours. Dr. Lin (Yutang is really his first name) now lives in New York. Of himself, he states, "I love contradictions. . . . I love China and I criticize her more frankly than any other Chinese." "The Jade Goddess" appears in *Famous Chinese Short Stories* where, in his own style, Dr. Lin presents tales from his country for the English-speaking audience.

Chinese Art ➤

The beautiful porcelain plate on the opposite page was created in the late eighteenth century, during the reign of Ch'ieng-Lung of the Ch'ing dynasty. The Ch'ing dynasty and the one that preceded it — the Ming — spanned a period of more than five centuries, from 1368 to 1912. During this time, the art of ceramics reached new heights in China. Craftsmen experimented with new colors and glazes and achieved excellent effects on delicate pieces of porcelain. The perfection of their work is evident in this plate.

The Chinese have always regarded art as one of the most important forms of self-expression. The examples of Chinese art shown on the preceding pages share with this plate the characteristics of all Chinese artistic expression: delicacy and intricacy of design, perfection of detail, and rhythm of movement.

By the Waters of Babylon

STEPHEN VINCENT
BENÉT

Babylon, mighty city of ancient times, was a proud metropolis of luxury and splendor. Situated between the Tigris and Euphrates Rivers, Babylon the Golden ignored prophets like Jeremiah who warned, "O Babylon . . . Thine end is come." Today Babylon is a ruin where the wind shifts the desert sand among the broken temples. (See the picture above.)

In this story the ruined city of the dead gods is also situated between two rivers, the Ou-dis-sun and another not named in the story. To cross the Ou-dis-sun, to go to the Place of the Gods, is forbidden to the half-savage Hill People, but the son of their priest defies his father, the laws of his tribe, and the legends about the Island of the Dead Gods. Remain alert as you follow this strange boy on his forbidden journey. Eventually you will discover who he is, and where.

THE NORTH and the west and the south are good hunting ground, but it is forbidden to go east. It is forbidden to go to any of the Dead Places [1] except to search for metal, and then he who touches the metal must be a priest or the son of a priest. Afterward, both the man and the metal must be purified. These are the rules and the laws; they are well-made. It is forbidden to cross the great river and look upon the place that was the Place of the Gods — this is most strictly forbidden. We do not even say its name though we know its name. It is there that spirits live, and demons — it is there that there are the ashes of the Great Burning. [2] These things are forbidden — they have been forbidden since the beginning of time.

My father is a priest; I am the son of a priest. I have been in the Dead Places near us, with my father — at first, I was afraid. When my father went into the house to search for the metal, I stood by the door and my heart felt small and weak. It was a dead man's house, a spirit house. It did not have the smell of man, though there were old bones in a corner. But it is not fitting that a priest's

[1] **Dead Places:** places where people from past civilizations once lived.

[2] **the Great Burning:** a reference to how the city was destroyed.

son should show fear. I looked at the bones in the shadow and kept my voice still.

Then my father came out with the metal — a good, strong piece. He looked at me with both eyes but I had not run away. He gave me the metal to hold — I took it and did not die. So he knew that I was truly his son and would be a priest in my time. That was when I was very young — nevertheless my brothers would not have done it, though they are good hunters. After that, they gave me the good piece of meat and the warm corner by the fire. My father watched over me — he was glad that I should be a priest. But when I boasted or wept without a reason, he punished me more strictly than my brothers. That was right.

After a time, I myself was allowed to go into the dead houses and search for metal.[1] So I learned the ways of those houses — and if I saw bones, I was no longer afraid. The bones are light and old — sometimes they will fall into dust if you touch them. But that is a great sin.

I was taught the chants and the spells — I was taught how to stop the running of blood from a wound and many secrets. A priest must know many secrets — that was what my father said. If the hunters think we do all things by chants and spells, they may believe so — it does not hurt them. I was taught how to read in the old books and how to make the old writings — that was hard and took a long time. My knowledge made me happy — it was like a fire in my heart. Most of all, I liked to hear of the Old Days and the stories of the gods. I asked myself many questions that I could not answer, but it was good to ask them. At night, I would lie awake

[1] **metal:** important to a primitive people for tools and weapons.

and listen to the wind — it seemed to me that it was the voice of the gods as they flew through the air.

We are not ignorant like the Forest People — our women spin wool on the wheel, our priests wear a white robe. We do not eat grubs from the tree, we have not forgotten the old writings, although they are hard to understand. Nevertheless, my knowledge and my lack of knowledge burned in me — I wished to know more. When I was a man at last, I came to my father and said, "It is time for me to go on my journey. Give me your leave."

He looked at me for a long time, stroking his beard, then he said at last, "Yes. It is time." That night, in the house of the priesthood, I asked for and received purification. My body hurt but my spirit was a cool stone. It was my father himself who questioned me about my dreams.

He bade me look into the smoke of the fire and see — I saw and told what I saw. It was what I have always seen — a river, and, beyond it, a great Dead Place and in it the gods walking. I have always thought about that. His eyes were stern when I told him — he was no longer my father but a priest. He said, "This is a strong dream."

"It is mine," I said, while the smoke waved and my head felt light. They were singing the Star song in the outer chamber and it was like the buzzing of bees in my head.

He asked me how the gods were dressed and I told him how they were dressed. We know how they were dressed from the book, but I saw them as if they were before me. When I had finished, he threw the sticks three times and studied them as they fell.

"This is a very strong dream," he said. "It may eat you up."

"I am not afraid," I said and looked

at him with both eyes. My voice sounded thin in my ears but that was because of the smoke.

He touched me on the breast and the forehead. He gave me the bow and the three arrows.

"Take them," he said. "It is forbidden to travel east. It is forbidden to cross the river. It is forbidden to go to the Place of the Gods. All these things are forbidden."

"All these things are forbidden," I said, but it was my voice that spoke and not my spirit. He looked at me again.

"My son," he said. "Once I had young dreams. If your dreams do not eat you up, you may be a great priest. If they eat you, you are still my son. Now go on your journey."

I went fasting, as is the law. My body hurt but not my heart. When the dawn came, I was out of sight of the village. I prayed and purified myself, waiting for a sign. The sign was an eagle. It flew east.

Sometimes signs are sent by bad spirits. I waited again on the flat rock, fasting, taking no food. I was very still — I could feel the sky above me and the earth beneath. I waited till the sun was beginning to sink. Then three deer passed in the valley, going east — they did not wind [1] me or see me. There was a white fawn with them — a very great sign.

I followed them, at a distance, waiting for what would happen. My heart was troubled about going east, yet I knew that I must go. My head hummed with my fasting — I did not even see the panther spring upon the white fawn. But, before I knew it, the bow was in my hand. I shouted and the panther lifted his head from the fawn. It is not easy to kill a panther with one arrow but the arrow went through his eye and into his brain. He died as he tried to spring — he rolled over, tearing at the ground. Then I knew I was meant to go east — I knew that was my journey. When the night came, I made my fire and roasted meat.

It is eight suns' journey to the east, and a man passes by many Dead Places. The Forest People are afraid of them but I am not. Once I made my fire on the edge of a Dead Place at night and, next morning, in the dead house, I found a good knife, little rusted. That was small to what came afterward but it made my heart feel big. Always when I looked for game, it was in front of my arrow, and twice I passed hunting parties of the Forest People without their knowing. So I knew my magic was strong and my journey clean, in spite of the law.

Toward the setting of the eighth sun, I came to the banks of the great river. It was half-a-day's journey after I had

[1] **wind:** in this context, smell or get the scent of.

left the god-road — we do not use the god-roads now for they are falling apart into great blocks of stone, and the forest is safer going. A long way off I had seen the water through trees but the trees were thick. At last, I came out upon an open place at the top of a cliff. There was the great river below, like a giant in the sun. It is very long, very wide. It could eat all the streams we know and still be thirsty. Its name is Ou-dis-sun, the Sacred, the Long. No man of my tribe had seen it, not even my father, the priest. It was magic and I prayed.

Then I raised my eyes and looked south. It was there, the Place of the Gods.

How can I tell what it was like — you do not know. It was there, in the red light, and they were too big to be houses. It was there with the red light upon it, mighty and ruined. I knew that in another moment the gods would see me. I covered my eyes with my hands and crept back into the forest.

Surely, that was enough to do, and live. Surely it was enough to spend the night upon the cliff. The Forest People themselves do not come near. Yet, all through the night, I knew that I should have to cross the river and walk in the Place of the Gods, although the gods ate me up. My magic did not help me at all and yet there was a fire in my bowels, a fire in my mind. When the sun rose, I thought, "My journey has been clean. Now I will go home from my journey." But, even as I thought so, I knew I could not. If I went to the Place of the Gods, I would surely die, but, if I did not go, I could never be at peace with my spirit again. It is better to lose one's life than one's spirit, if one is a priest and the son of a priest.

Nevertheless, as I made the raft, the tears ran out of my eyes. The Forest People could have killed me without fight, if they had come upon me then, but they did not come. When the raft was made, I said the sayings for the dead and painted myself for death. My heart was cold as a frog and my knees like water, but the burning in my mind would not let me have peace. As I pushed the raft from the shore, I began my death song — I had the right. It was a fine song.

"I am John, son of John," I sang. "My people are the Hill People. They are the men.

I go into the Dead Places but I am not slain.

I take the metal from the Dead Places but I am not blasted.

I travel upon the god-roads and am not afraid. E-yah! I have killed the panther, I have killed the fawn!

E-yah! I have come to the great river. No man has come there before.

It is forbidden to go east, but I have gone, forbidden to go on the great river, but I am there.

Open your hearts, you spirits, and hear my song.

Now I go to the Place of the Gods, I shall not return.

My body is painted for death and my limbs weak, but my heart is big as I go to the Place of the Gods!"

All the same, when I came to the Place of the Gods, I was afraid, afraid. The current of the great river is very strong — it gripped my raft with its hands. That was magic, for the river itself is wide and calm. I could feel evil spirits about me, in the bright morning; I could feel their breath on my neck as I was swept down the stream. Never have I been so much alone — I tried to think of my knowledge, but it was a squirrel's heap of winter nuts. There was no strength in my knowledge any

more and I felt small and naked as a new-hatched bird — alone upon the great river, the servant of the gods.

Yet, after awhile, my eyes were opened and I saw. I saw both banks of the river — I saw that once there had been god-roads across it, though now they were broken and fallen like broken vines. Very great they were, and wonderful and broken — broken in the time of the Great Burning when the fire fell out of the sky. And always the current took me nearer to the Place of the Gods, and the huge ruins rose before my eyes.

I do not know the customs of rivers — we are the People of the Hills. I tried to guide my raft with the pole but it spun around. I thought the river meant to take me past the Place of the Gods and out into the Bitter Water of the legends. I grew angry then — my heart felt strong. I said aloud, "I am a priest and the son of a priest!" The gods heard me — they showed me how to paddle with the pole on one side of the raft. The current changed itself —

I drew near to the Place of the Gods.

When I was very near, my raft struck and turned over. I can swim in our lakes — I swam to the shore. There was a great spike of rusted metal sticking out into the river — I hauled myself up upon it and sat there, panting. I had saved my bow and two arrows and the knife I found in the Dead Place but that was all. My raft went whirling downstream toward the Bitter Water. I looked after it, and thought if it had trod me under, at least I would be safely dead. Nevertheless, when I had dried my bowstring and re-strung it, I walked forward to the Place of the Gods.

It felt like ground underfoot; it did not burn me. It is not true what some of the tales say, that the ground there burns forever, for I have been there. Here and there were the marks and stains of the Great Burning, on the ruins, that is true. But they were old marks and old stains. It is not true either, what some of our priests say, that it is an island covered with fogs and enchantments. It is not. It is a great Dead Place — greater than any Dead Place we know. Everywhere in it there are god-roads, though most are cracked and broken. Everywhere there are the ruins of the high towers of the gods.

How shall I tell what I saw? I went carefully, my strung bow in my hand, my skin ready for danger. There should have been the wailings of spirits and the shrieks of demons, but there were not. It was very silent and sunny where I had landed — the wind and the rain and the birds that drop seeds had done their work — the grass grew in the cracks of the broken stone. It is a fair island — no wonder the gods built there. If I had come there, a god, I also would have built.

How shall I tell what I saw? The towers are not all broken — here and there one still stands, like a great tree in a forest, and the birds nest high. But the towers themselves look blind, for the gods are gone. I saw a fish hawk, catching fish in the river. I saw a little dance of white butterflies over a great heap of broken stones and columns. I went there and looked about me — there was a carved stone with cut-letters, broken in half. I can read letters but I could not understand these. They said UBTREAS. There was also the shattered image of a man or a god. It had been made of white stone and he wore his hair tied back like a woman's. His name was ASHING, as I read on the cracked half of a stone. I thought it wise to pray to ASHING, though I do not know that god.

How shall I tell what I saw? There was no smell of man left, on stone or metal. Nor were there many trees in that wilderness of stone. There are many pigeons, nesting and dropping in the towers — the gods must have loved them, or, perhaps, they used them for

sacrifices. There are wild cats that roam the god-roads, green-eyed, unafraid of man. At night they wail like demons but they are not demons. The wild dogs are more dangerous, for they hunt in a pack, but them I did not meet till later. Everywhere there are the carved stones, carved with magical numbers or words.

I went north — I did not try to hide myself. When a god or a demon saw me, then I would die, but meanwhile I was no longer afraid. My hunger for knowledge burned in me — there was so much that I could not understand. After awhile, I knew that my belly was hungry. I could have hunted for my meat, but I did not hunt. It is known that the gods did not hunt as we do — they got their food from enchanted boxes and jars. Sometimes these are still found in the Dead Places — once, when I was a child and foolish, I opened such a jar and tasted it and found the food sweet. But my father found out and punished me for it strictly, for, often, that food is death. Now, though, I had long gone past what was forbidden, and I entered the likeliest towers, looking for the food of the gods.

I found it at last in the ruins of a great temple in the mid-city. A mighty temple it must have been, for the roof was painted like the sky at night with its stars — that much I could see, though the colors were faint and dim. It went down into great caves and tunnels — perhaps they kept their slaves there. But when I started to climb down, I heard the squeaking of rats, so I did not go — rats are unclean, and there must have been many tribes of them, from the squeaking. But near there, I found food, in the heart of a ruin, behind a door that still opened. I ate only the fruits from the jars — they had a very sweet taste. There was drink, too, in bottles of glass — the drink of the gods

many of the dead-houses were wrecked, there were some that stood. I went toward this god-road, keeping to heights of the ruins, while the dog followed. When I had reached the god-road, I saw that there were others behind him. If I had slept later, they would have come upon me asleep and torn out my throat. As it was, they were sure enough of me; they did not hurry. When I went into the dead-house, they kept watch at the entrance — doubtless they thought they would have a fine hunt. But a dog cannot open a door and I knew, from the books, that the gods did not like to live on the ground but on high.

I had just found a door I could open when the dogs decided to rush. Ha! They were surprised when I shut the door in their faces — it was a good door, of strong metal. I could hear their foolish baying beyond it but I did not stop to answer them. I was in darkness — I found stairs and climbed. There were many stairs, turning around till my head was dizzy. At the top was another door — I found the knob and opened it. I was in a long small chamber — on one side of it was a bronze door that could not be opened, for it had no handle. Perhaps there was a magic word to open it but I did not have the word. I turned to the door in the opposite side of the wall. The lock of it was broken and I opened it and went in.

Within, there was a place of great riches. The god who lived there must have been a powerful god. The first room was a small anteroom — I waited there for some time, telling the spirits of the place that I came in peace and not as a robber. When it seemed to me that they had had time to hear me, I went on. Ah, what riches! Few, even, of the windows had been broken — it was all as it had been. The great windows that looked over the city had not been

was strong and made my head swim. After I had eaten and drunk, I slept on the top of a stone, my bow at my side.

When I woke, the sun was low. Looking down from where I lay, I saw a dog sitting on his haunches. His tongue was hanging out of his mouth; he looked as if he were laughing. He was a big dog, with a gray-brown coat, as big as a wolf. I sprang up and shouted at him but he did not move — he just sat there as if he were laughing. I did not like that. When I reached for a stone to throw, he moved swiftly out of the way of the stone. He was not afraid of me; he looked at me as if I were meat. No doubt I could have killed him with an arrow, but I did not know if there were others. Moreover, night was falling.

I looked about me — not far away there was a great, broken god-road, leading north. The towers were high enough, but not so high, and while broken at all though they were dusty and streaked with many years. There were coverings on the floors, the colors not greatly faded, and the chairs were soft and deep. There were pictures upon the walls, very strange, very wonderful — I remember one of a bunch of flowers in a jar — if you came close to it, you could see nothing but bits of color, but if you stood away from it, the flowers might have been picked yesterday. It made my heart feel strange to look at this picture — and to look at the figure of a bird, in some hard clay, on a table and see it so like our birds. Everywhere there were books and writings, many in tongues that I could not read. The god who lived there must have been a wise god and full of knowledge. I felt I had right there, as I sought knowledge also.

Nevertheless, it was strange. There was a washing-place but no water — perhaps the gods washed in air. There was a cooking-place but no wood, and though there was a machine to cook food, there was no place to put fire in it. Nor were there candles or lamps — there were things that looked like lamps but they had neither oil nor wick. All these things were magic, but I touched them and lived — the magic had gone out of them. Let me tell one thing to show. In the washing-place, a thing said "Hot" but it was not hot to the touch — another thing said "Cold" but it was not cold. This must have been a strong magic but the magic was gone. I do not understand — they had ways — I wish that I knew.

It was close and dry and dusty in their house of the gods. I have said the magic was gone but that is not true — it had gone from the magic things but it had not gone from the place. I felt the spirits about me, weighing upon me. Nor had I ever slept in a Dead Place before — and yet, tonight, I must sleep there. When I thought of it, my tongue felt dry in my throat, in spite of my wish for knowledge. Almost I would have gone down again and faced the dogs, but I did not.

I had not gone through all the rooms when the darkness fell. When it fell, I went back to the big room looking over the city and made fire. There was a place to make fire and a box with wood in it, though I do not think they cooked there. I wrapped myself in a floor-covering and slept in front of the fire — I was very tired.

Now I tell what is very strong magic. I woke in the midst of the night. When I woke, the fire had gone out and I was cold. It seemed to me that all around me there were whisperings and voices. I closed my eyes to shut them out. Some will say that I slept again, but I do not think that I slept. I could feel the spirits drawing my spirit out of my body as a fish is drawn on a line.

Why should I lie about it? I am a priest and the son of a priest. If there are spirits, as they say, in the small Dead Places near us, what spirits must there not be in that great Place of the Gods? And would not they wish to speak? After such long years? I know that I felt myself drawn as a fish is drawn on a line. I had stepped out of my body — I could see my body asleep in front of the cold fire, but it was not I. I was drawn to look out upon the city of the gods.

It should have been dark, for it was light, but it was not dark. Everywhere there were lights — lines of light — circles and blurs of light — ten thousand torches would not have been the same. The sky itself was alight — you could barely see the stars for the glow in the sky. I thought to myself "This is strong magic" and trembled. There was a roaring in my ears like the rushing of rivers. Then my eyes grew used to the light and my ears to the sound. I knew that I was seeing the city as it had been when the gods were alive.

That was a sight indeed — yes, that was a sight: I could not have seen it in the body — my body would have died. Everywhere went the gods, on foot and in chariots — there were gods beyond number and counting and their chariots blocked the streets. They had turned night to day for their pleasure — they did not sleep with the sun. The noise of their coming and going was the noise of many waters. It was magic what they could do — it was magic what they did.

I looked out of another window — the great vines of their bridges were mended and the god-roads went east and west. Restless, restless, were the gods and always in motion! They burrowed tunnels under rivers — they flew in the air. With unbelievable tools they did giant works — no part of the earth was safe from them, for, if they wished for a thing, they summoned it from the other side of the world. And always, as they labored and rested, as they feasted and made love, there was a drum in their ears — the pulse of the giant city, beating and beating like a man's heart.

Were they happy? What is happiness to the gods? They were great, they were mighty, they were wonderful and terrible. As I looked upon them and their magic, I felt like a child — but a little more, it seemed to me, and they would pull down the moon from the sky. I saw them with wisdom beyond wisdom and knowledge beyond knowledge. And yet not all they did was well done — even I could see that — and yet their wisdom could not but grow until all was peace.

Then I saw their fate come upon them and that was terrible past speech. It came upon them as they walked the streets of their city. I have been in the fights with the Forest People — I have seen men die. But this was not like that. When gods war with gods, they use weapons we do not know. It was fire falling out of the sky and a mist that poisoned. It was the time of the Great Burning and the Destruction. They ran about like ants in the streets of their city — poor gods, poor gods! Then the towers began to fall. A few escaped — yes, a few. The legends tell it. But, even after the city had become a Dead Place, for many years the poison was still in the ground. I saw it happen, I saw the last of them die. It was darkness over the broken city and I wept.

All this, I saw. I saw it as I have told it, though not in the body. When I woke in the morning, I was hungry, but I did not think first of my hunger for my heart was perplexed and confused. I knew the reason for the Dead Places but I did not see why it had happened. It seemed to me it should not have happened, with all the magic they had. I went through the house looking for an answer. There was so much in the house I could not understand — and yet I am a priest and the son of a priest. It was like being on one side of the great river, at night, with no light to show the way.

Then I saw the dead god. He was sitting in his chair, by the window, in a room I had not entered before and, for the first moment, I thought that he was alive. Then I saw the skin on the back of his hand — it was like dry leather. The room was shut, hot and dry — no doubt that had kept him as he was. At first I was afraid to approach him — then the fear left me. He was sitting looking out over the city — he was dressed in the clothes of the gods. His age was neither young nor old — I could not tell his age. But there was wisdom in his face and great sadness. You could see that he would not have run away. He had sat at his window, watching his city die — then he himself had died. But it is better to lose one's life than one's spirit — and you could see from the face that his spirit had not been lost. I knew, that, if I touched him, he would fall into dust — and yet, there was something unconquered in the face.

That is all of my story, for then I knew he was a man — I knew then that they had been men, neither gods nor demons. It is a great knowledge, hard to tell and believe. They were men — they went a dark road, but they were men. I had no fear after that — I had no fear going home, though twice I fought off the dogs and once I was hunted for two days by the Forest People. When I saw my father again, I prayed and was purified. He touched my lips and my breast, he said, "You went away a boy. You come back a man and a priest." I said, "Father, they were men! I have been in the Place of the Gods and seen it! Now slay me, if it is the law — but still I know they were men."

He looked at me out of both eyes. He said, "The law is not always the same shape — you have done what you have done. I could not have done it my time, but you come after me. Tell!"

I told and he listened. After that, I wished to tell all the people but he showed me otherwise. He said, "Truth is a hard deer to hunt. If you eat too much truth at once, you may die of the truth. It was not idly that our fathers forbade the Dead Places." He was right — it is better the truth should come little by little. I have learned that, being a priest. Perhaps, in the old days, they ate knowledge too fast.

Nevertheless, we make a beginning. It is not for the metal alone we go to the Dead Places now — there are the books and the writings. They are hard to learn. And the magic tools are broken — but we can look at them and wonder. At least, we make a beginning. And, when I am chief priest we shall go beyond the great river. We shall go to the Place of the Gods — the place new-york — not one man but a company. We shall look for the images of the gods and find the god ASHING and the others — the gods Lincoln and Biltmore and Moses. But they were men who built the city, not gods or demons. They were men. I remember the dead man's face. They were men who were here before us. We must build again.

RELATING ALL PARTS OF A STORY

If you have read carefully, you know "what happens" — the plain facts. But these facts alone do not account for the power of this story. The total effect is much more than an effect of the plot, setting, character, tone, or theme. All must be fused — in the story and in the mind of the reader — if the full power of the story is to be realized.

PLOT   Perhaps you were aware of the author's deliberate neglect of opportunities to build suspense or excitement in connection with danger to John's life. On his way to the Place of the Gods, John casually mentions hunting parties of the enemy Forest People, and once he kills a panther. In the city of the dead, he encounters a pack of man-eating wild dogs, but this incident — so full of possibilities for thrilling action — is never developed. Whatever the story is about, the adventure element is included only to serve some other purpose the author considers more important. What does the plot accomplish for this story? Does it support the characterization of John? Do the incidents help the theme or setting?

SETTING   As you began to read the story, did you notice that the author does not mention when or where this story takes place? Is this carelessness, or is it part of a plan? Or is it assumed that the reader will say, "Here is a story set in some vague landscape of prehistoric times"? An alert reader notices this curious omission.

Once the boy starts on his journey, a new series of clues is introduced. First we learn that on his journey, John avoids the god-roads, falling apart into great blocks of stone. Next he comes to the great river his people call the Ou-dis-sun, and he sees the high city towers that have not yet fallen into ruins. Once, too, there had been bridges to this fair island. Near one of the ruined buildings is a broken stone with part of a word — UBTREAS — and nearby is the shattered statue of a man who wore his hair in the style of the eighteenth century and part of whose name was ASHING. How are all of these items of setting of use to the story?

CHARACTER   In primitive tribes as in civilized societies, various kinds of personality and temperament make for the leadership required in rulers, warriors, and priests. In primitive tribes, priests possess enormous power, but becoming a priest is not easy. What traits of character in John lead you to believe he will succeed in becoming a chief priest? How do you account for his "stepping out" of his body? ("Now I tell what is very strong magic. I woke in the midst of the night . . ." page 173.) Would such "strong magic" help or hinder him as a priest? Why is John's character significant in this story?

TONE   Contrast the tone of this story with that of "The Open Window" or "Death of Red Peril." How would you describe Benét's attitude toward his material?

THEME   There is a key word in the story: the word *knowledge*. Clearly it has some kind of importance, for it is forced upon our attention over and over again. "My knowledge and my lack of knowledge burned in me — I wished to know more." Another time John says, "I felt I had a right there, as I sought knowledge also." Again, he tells of his fear in spite of his wish for knowledge. At what seems to be the very climax of this story, the dream or vision in the middle of the night, the word *wisdom* is repeated again and again. Whatever may be the main theme of "By the Waters of Babylon," we can be sure that it has some connection with knowledge or wisdom.

Try to formulate a statement that shows clearly what the theme of this story is. Avoid reference to John or to the incidents in the story.

TOTAL EFFECT   Analyzing all of the elements in a story should help you to appreciate it fully. Test yourself: read again the last two paragraphs of "By the Waters of Babylon." Has the entire story helped you to understand what each sentence means? Do these sentences touch your feelings as well as your thoughts? If so, you are experiencing the full impact of the story; you have put all of the parts together and are truly aware of the story's total effect.

Pictured here are three of the world's art treasures. "The Unicorn in Captivity" ▶
is a French or Flemish tapestry; "Head of an Athlete" is a Roman copy of a Greek statue; and the painting is a detail from "Lady with the Lute" by the Dutch artist Jan Vermeer. (See "The Treasures of Civilization" on page 178.)

1. What examples of (a) patriotic spirit and (b) optimism or pessimism can you discover in "By the Waters of Babylon"?

2. What makes this story different from others you have read? Are there any elements in this story that you usually associate with poetry rather than the short story?

ABOUT THE AUTHOR

Stephen Vincent Benét (1898–1943), famous as both a poet and a short-story writer, never wanted any career other than writing and never attempted anything else. By the time he was twenty, he had published two books of poetry. Born in Pennsylvania, he attended schools in California, graduated from Yale, and then accepted a fellowship for additional education at the Sorbonne University in Paris. A Guggenheim fellowship enabled him to work for two years on a long narrative poem about the War Between the States, *John Brown's Body*. This long poem became a best seller and won a Pulitzer prize.

The Treasures of Civilization

The pictures on page 177 show priceless works of art. Every year millions of people visit New York's Metropolitan Museum of Art to see these and thousands of other art treasures. John may even have seen the remains of such masterpieces in the "Place of the Gods."

Art is only one of the treasures of civilization. Literature, music, medicine, law, education, commerce — all belong to and have been developed by man down through the ages. They are all fruits of man's knowledge and skill. As you think about what it would mean to live without these prized possessions, perhaps you will come to a clearer understanding of why Benét wrote "By the Waters of Babylon" — why he was so concerned with man's using knowledge wisely.

Appreciating Short Stories

Now that you have read a number of short stories, you will have a basis for discussing and comparing them. No doubt, there were several stories you particularly enjoyed and several that left a strong effect on your thoughts and feelings. Why did some of the stories bring certain responses from you? How was the writer able to affect your thinking and feeling? By comparing the various stories in this section, you can better discover how the two-way process between the writer and you, the reader, actually works.

Your Responses to the Stories. Which of the stories did you consider most worth reading? To answer this question, of course, you need to have some principles by which to judge stories. We all agree that stories should, first and foremost, give us pleasure; they should offer enter- tainment and enjoyment. But many stories offer us more than entertainment: they give us a view of life that we can apply to our own experience. So we must ask still further questions. Did any of the stories extend your experience by presenting you with a different way of seeing people or life — a way different from your own? Were you introduced to any people who were worth knowing? Did any of the ideas or themes behind the happenings of the stories stir your thinking? Did any of the stories modify or change your attitudes or feelings about anything? Keep these questions in mind as you compare the stories in this section.

1. If your teacher could have only three stories from this book to teach next year, which would you recommend? Why? Which three would you eliminate first?

2. One of the main characters in "The Rat Trap" is a young girl. In "Beware of the Dog" and "The Duke's Children" the main characters are young men, while in "A Slander" an older man is the chief figure. How much difference does the age of a character make to you in your appreciation of a story? Did you find that you were able to understand a character when he or she was of the opposite sex? What have your class discussions of the stories mentioned above revealed about the reactions of boys and girls to the same story? Do they have similar or different reactions?

3. Suppose some junior high school student read the stories and said, "The only good story in the book is 'Four and Twenty Blackbirds'!" What could you say in defense of the stories which do not feature suspense and excitement?

4. In which stories did you feel you were most successful in penetrating beneath the surface of the events to the real meaning of the story? In other words, which stories had deeper meanings expressed through the happenings in the stories?

5. Which stories were concerned with someone's decision? How would you state the theme of each of these stories, the real meaning behind each story?

6. Would you like to try regrouping these stories according to their meaning or subject matter? Try shuffling the stories around so that they will fit under new headings such as "Justice," "The Meaning of Courage," and "The Consequences of Character." You will be able to find headings other than these. Discuss in class the appropriateness of putting individual stories under the headings you and other members of the class suggest.

7. The problems of growing up occur in several of the stories. Can you name three stories which concern these problems? Once the class has agreed on a list of the stories, try to point out for each: (a) what the problems were for the boy or girl, (b) how the problems were met or solved, and (c) how satisfactory — in your own opinion — the solution was.

The Writer's Skill in Storytelling. The foregoing questions have had to do with your responses to the stories. That is one way to judge whether you consider stories "worthwhile." Still another way to judge stories is to evaluate the writer's skill as a storyteller. Every writer uses certain tools in his craft. Some writers use them skillfully and subtly; others do not. The reader should learn to be able to tell how skilled the writer is — how "well written" the story is. The following questions will help you examine and compare the stories on the basis of the various writers' handling of the story elements — plot, character, setting, tone, and theme.

1. On what basis can you justify the ending of "The Jade Goddess"? Why doesn't the story end happily? How does the author prepare the reader for an unhappy ending to this story? Does any other story in the book have an unhappy ending? For such stories, are you able to point out that the ending is the only logical one, given the circumstances and the characters in the story? (A "logical" ending is one that had to turn out as it did because any other ending would have been false to the rest of the story.)

2. What purpose, vital to the story, do the descriptions serve in "By the Waters of Babylon" and "The Heathen"? On what basis can you justify the almost complete absence of description in "Four and Twenty Blackbirds"?

3. The author's tone has a great deal to do with the effect a story has on its readers. Compare O. Henry's tone in "The Gift of the Magi" with that of Saki in "The Open Window." Do you find any points of contrast? Suppose Edgar Allan Poe had written "The Open Window." In what particulars would it have turned out to be a different story altogether? It might be fun to speculate.

4. "Death of Red Peril" is written with many slang or colloquial expressions. On what grounds is such usage justified in writing?

5. In "The Heathen" the author does

not tell in detail the story of Otoo's return to Bora Bora. How does such omission of material help us to know what a writer's purpose is? Point out, in other stories, examples of similar elimination or selection of material. Why does the short story as a form of literature require the writer to be highly selective?

6. Stories, like pieces of music, have a certain movement. Events can develop rapidly or slowly; they can rise quickly to a climax and then recede slowly to the end of the story, or they can build up slowly to the climax and then end suddenly. Which story would you rate as a fast-moving story? Which might be called a slow-moving story?

For Your Bookshelf. You have now read the short story section of this book, but this should be just a beginning for you. You can build your own library of short story collections at very little cost and with very little effort. Each year an annual of the best short stories of that year is published. In addition to these annuals there are many other excellent collections of short stories. These include the works of Anton Chekhov, O. Henry, Edgar Allan Poe, and Jack London. Build your own library of short story collections; you'll discover it is fun.

Suggestions for Further Reading

In your search for good short stories, you will have no trouble finding collections by authors in this book as well as by other important fiction writers of the world. Your school librarian will no doubt recommend appealing books for your enjoyment; you will also find good stories in the best current magazines. The following stories and collections are listed to help you become acquainted with some of the world's master storytellers. *The Short Story Index* in your library will help you find these stories.

Stories by American, English, and Irish Authors

Benét, Stephen Vincent (America), *Selected Poetry and Prose*, edited by Basil Davenport (Holt, Rinehart & Winston, 1959); also *Selected Works* (Holt, Rinehart & Winston, 1942)

All of Benét's stories are imaginative and unusual. Here are tales and poems to stir your thoughts.

Cather, Willa (America), "Neighbor Rosicky," "Paul's Case"

Collier, John (England), "Thus, I Discover Beelzy"

Dahl, Roald (England), "Poison," "Taste"

Doyle, Adrian Conan (England), *Exploits of Sherlock Holmes* (Random House, 1954)

The youngest son of the originator of the Sherlock Holmes stories, Sir Arthur Conan Doyle, has written about some of Holmes's cases that are briefly mentioned in the original stories.

Faulkner, William (America), "Mountain Victory," "Two Soldiers"

Greene, Graham (England), "The Basement Room"

Hawthorne, Nathaniel (America), "The Birthmark," "Feathertop," "The Great Stone Face"

Hemingway, Ernest (America), "In Another Country," "The Undefeated"

Irving, Washington (America), "The Devil and Tom Walker," "The Legend of Sleepy Hollow," "Rip Van Winkle"

Lewis, Sinclair (America), "Land"

London, Jack (America), *Jack London's Tales of Adventure*, edited by Irving Shepard (Doubleday, 1956)

In London's stories nature is often a cruel opponent with whom man must struggle. Boys, especially, like the style and content of his stories.

Marquand, John P. (America), "Good Morning, Major," "You Can't Do That"

Maugham, Somerset (England), "The Lotus-Eater," "Mackintosh"

O'Connor, Frank (Ireland), "The Idealist"

O'Flaherty, Liam (Ireland), "The Sniper"

O. Henry (America), *Best Stories of O. Henry*, selected and with an introduction by Bennett Cerf and Van H. Cartmell (Doubleday, 1945)

O. Henry had a gift for turning incidents into well-told stories. Surprise endings, humor, suspense, and pathos are mixed in these stories which reflect O. Henry's varied life.

Poe, Edgar Allan (America), *Tales* (Dodd, Mead)
These are fascinating tales by a master of short fiction. Poe uses horror, atmosphere, and unusual reasoning to make his stories entertain and excite.

Saki (H. H. Munro) (England), *The Short Stories of Saki* (Viking, 1930)
These tart comments on the weaknesses of the human race will amuse you, but Saki's wit and satire may at times make you uncomfortable.

Steinbeck, John (America), "The Leader of the People," "Red Pony"

Thurber, James (America), "The Dog that Bit People," "The Night the Ghost Got In," "The Secret Life of Walter Mitty"

Twain, Mark (America), "The Man that Corrupted Hadleyburg"

Wells, H. G. (England), "Country of the Blind," "The Man Who Could Work Miracles"

West, Jessamyn (America), "Lead Her Like a Pigeon"

Stories by Authors from Other Countries

Alarcón, Pedro (Spain), "The Stub Book," "The Tall Woman"

Björnson, Björnstjerne (Norway), "The Father," "Fidelity," "The Fisher Maiden"

Chekhov, Anton (Russia), "The Beggar," "The Bet," "Grief," "The Lament," "Vanka"

Daudet, Alphonse (France), "The Death of the Dauphin," "The Last Lesson"

Lagerlöf, Selma (Sweden), "The Outlaws," "The Quoit," "The Seventeen Cats," "The Silver Mine," "A Story from Halstanas"

Lin Yutang (China), "Chienniang," "Lodging for the Night"

Mann, Thomas (Germany), "Mario and the Magician," "The Railway Accident"

De Maupassant, Guy (France), "The Inn," "The Necklace," "A Piece of String," "The Umbrella"

Pirandello, Luigi (Italy), "The Jar," "War"

Pocaterra, José Santos (Venezuela), "La Fajina"

Tagore, Rabindranath (India), "The Hungry Stones," "My Lord, the Baby"

Tolstoy, Leo (Russia), *Tolstoy's Tales of Courage and Conflict,* edited by Charles Nieder (Doubleday, 1958)
This is a collection of thirty-six stories by one of Russia's most famous authors. Especially recommended are "Death of Ivan Ilyitch," "The Long Exile," "What Men Live By," "How Much Land Does a Man Need?"

Collections of Short Stories

Best American Short Stories, edited by Martha Foley and David Burnett (Houghton Mifflin, published annually)

Great Short Stories, edited by Wilbur Schramm (Harcourt, Brace & World, 1950)
This collection is divided into three parts: "The Short Story in America," "The Short Story in Great Britain," and "The Short Story in Other Countries." Particularly valuable are the editor's comments and his account of how he wrote "Windwagon Smith," one of his most popular stories.

Masters of the Modern Short Story, edited by Walter Havighurst (Harcourt, Brace & World, 1955)
This collection of twenty-four short stories represents the best work of foremost American and British writers.

Rinehart Book of Short Stories, edited by C. L. Cline (Holt, Rinehart & Winston, 1952)
Included in this book are the major works of the modern masters.

Short Short Stories, edited by William R. Wood (Harcourt, Brace & World, 1951)

Stories, edited by Frank Jennings and Charles J. Calitri (Harcourt, Brace & World, 1957)

Tales to Be Told in the Dark, edited by Basil Davenport (Dodd, Mead, 1953)
This collection of stories is arranged for reading and telling aloud.

For Listening

Saki's "The Open Window" has been recorded and is available on *Many Voices* 4A.

Nonfiction

Definitions are often handy. From time to time, everyone is glad to be able to turn to a reference book and find the definition of an unfamiliar term. But for many important things in life — including people, ideas, and literature — there are no neat, completely workable definitions. It does not matter, however, that we cannot define the term *short story* as we can define the term *triangle,* for example. What is important with literature is that we understand the meaning and purpose of everything we read and recognize what it is that distinguishes one kind of literature from another.

All of the selections in this part of your book can be labeled *nonfiction.* As you read these selections, you will learn to recognize the distinguishing features of nonfiction. You might begin by recognizing what nonfiction is *not.* Its name already tells you that it is *not* fiction; it is *not* literature with the purely imaginary characters and events of a short story or novel. A glance at the appearance of the selections in this section will show you that nonfiction is not poetry or drama either. It is relatively easy, therefore, to see what types of literature the term *nonfiction* excludes. But what does it include? The answer is: all other types. Prominent among these are true narratives, articles, essays, history, and biography.

A point often made in discussing nonfiction is that it deals with facts — with what is true. To be sure, nonfiction does convey information about real people and real events, but it is important to remember that nonfiction, like fiction, poetry, and drama, also involves imagination. The nonfiction writer selects facts, describes people, records particularly dramatic, humorous, or significant moments, and finds the right words and form within which to present his ideas. Thus, nonfiction can be as artistically demanding on the writer and as satisfying for the reader as any other kind of literature.

◀ Detail from "Aristotle Contemplating the Bust of Homer" by the Dutch artist Rembrandt van Rijn (1606–1669). A true master of technique, Rembrandt ranks among the world's most important artists.

True Narratives

Our word *narrative* comes to us from *narrare*, a Latin word meaning "to relate," to tell of events in the order of their occurrence. Long ago, stories were passed on by word of mouth as bards or minstrels sang songs narrating the events of great battles or the deeds of great heroes. Their audience was usually a small group huddled around a campfire or the hearth of some manor house. Nowadays a narrator may be describing a football game, a political election, or the crowning of a queen, and his audience may be millions of people gathered around their television sets or radios.

As you might guess, a *true narrative* is an account of some actual event. It is a popular type of nonfiction. The three selections that follow tell of courageous men and women at moments of triumph and disaster. Because the narratives are true, and especially because they are forcefully told, they help us to realize something of the spirit and nobility of man. Their meaning lingers in our minds, filling us with something of the same wonder and pride that men felt when bards chanted of the hero who killed a dragon or of the bold men who first sailed upon the seas.

Victory on Everest

JAMES RAMSEY ULLMAN

Gasping for breath, two men pause and lift their eyes upward to a snow-swept summit in the Himalaya Mountains. They can go no farther. One climber begins the descent, but the other stands a moment staring up at the highest peak known to man. His strength is broken, but his will is not. "Just wait, old thing," he promises, "we'll get you yet!"

That was in 1922. More than thirty years passed after young Geoffrey Bruce spoke those words; still the top of Mount Everest remained unconquered. Through these years strong men from ten major expeditions pitted themselves against the glaciers, icefalls, and avalanches of Everest, all in vain. They failed to conquer the mountain.

THEN CAME 1953 . . .

And victory.

As all the world knows, it was the British again: back for the ninth time. And, win or lose, it appeared from the beginning that it might well be their last; for the Swiss had already staked their claim for a new try in 1954, and the French were making plans for '55. What further attempts the Russians might be contemplating was, of course, a mystery. But, with or without them, the competition for the prize had become wide open, and it seemed inconceivable that Everest could continue much longer to withstand attack after attack. For the English, in 1953, it was almost a matter of now or never.

The approach to the heights followed the pattern set by the earlier parties. Up the Khumbu Glacier — the icefall — the Western Cwm.[1] But their schedule allowed them three full weeks for practice climbs and general conditioning, with the result that they became more thoroughly acclimated than any Everesters had ever been before. In general, they used the Swiss routes and camp sites — for which they later made grateful acknowledgment — and by the end of April were established in full strength at their fifth camp, below the great western face of Lhotse.[2] Not only the porters, but the climbers as well, did a great deal of moving back and forth between here and the lower camps, both to carry the loads and to help bring themselves to peak condition. During this stage of the operations, Hillary and Tenzing, working as a team, once climbed from the Khumbu Glacier to the advance base and back in a single day — foreshadowing

their feats of strength and endurance that were still to come.

Above Camp V, the British followed the route up the Lhotse Glacier that the second Swiss party had used after their accident. Working in relays, they hacked steps, strung fixed ropes, and led the porters up for the establishment of the higher camps. All told, there were thirty-four Sherpas [3] with the expedition (as distinguished from the hundreds of nonclimbing coolies who had helped in the approach to the mountain), and, of these, twenty had been chosen for the hardest going beyond the Western Cwm. Almost all were veterans of the earlier expeditions, and their experience paid off in better porterage than any Everest party had enjoyed before.

Originally, only one camp had been planned between No. V and the South Col.[4] But it was soon found that a second was necessary, if the men were to arrive on the col in shape to do anything more than collapse into their tents. Communication between the spread-out groups was maintained by portable radio-telephone, and, in spite of the inevitable storms and minor mishaps, their advance proceeded much according to schedule. The expedition was more plentifully supplied with oxygen than any of its predecessors, and, although they were not yet at an alti-

[1] **Cwm** (ko͞om): the native word for valley.
[2] **Lhotse** (hlŏ'tsĕ): south peak of Mount Everest.

[3] **Sherpas** (shĕr'păz): the short, sturdy hillmen who live in eastern Nepal. Originally of Tibetan stock, Sherpas are known for their mountain-climbing skill.
[4] **Col** (kŏl): a pass between mountains, or low point of a ridge.

Drawing Conclusions. James Ullman calls the conquest of Mount Everest "a shining chapter in the sorry history of our century." This statement is one of the conclusions that can be drawn from Ullman's account of the triumphant Everest expedition. Try to discover for yourself what led the author to draw this conclusion. Also, see what other conclusions you can draw from the facts presented.

tude where it was essential, it was often used experimentally by the climbers who were expected to go highest. There were two types of apparatus: one the so-called "closed-circuit," with which the user breathed oxygen only; the other the "open-circuit," in which the oxygen was mixed with the surrounding air. No one was yet certain which would prove the better; but both had a great advantage over the Swiss apparatus, in that they could be used while the climbers were actually in motion.

On May twenty-first, after three weeks of toil on the Lhotse face, the South Col was attained. The next day no less than twelve porters went up, the day after still more, and soon a new and living Camp VIII had taken shape on the wind-swept plateau. All the labors of the past weeks — grueling though they had been — receded into the background as mere preliminaries. Here, at 25,850 feet, was the base from which the final effort would be launched. And now, at last, all the complex activities and functions of the expedition were drawn together and directed to one single mighty purpose: to get a living human being to the top of Everest.

Following the traditional Himalayan practice, Colonel Hunt selected two summit teams of two men each. One, consisting of Tom Bourdillon and Charles Evans, was to make the first try direct from the South Col, using the closed-circuit oxygen apparatus. But though "first" in point of time, they were not the pair on which the highest hopes were placed, for the thirty-three hundred feet from col to summit seemed too much for mortal men to make in a single day of climbing. Their venture was given the name of reconnaissance-assault. They would go as far

as they could; farther than Lambert,[1] it was hoped; as far, if it was humanly possible, as the so-called south summit of Everest, a promontory on the skyline ridge some five hundred feet below the final crest. This lesser peak shut off from below the approach to the true summit, and it would be the essential job of Bourdillon and Evans to reach the base of this approach and reconnoiter its problems and hazards. If they could go on to the top themselves — all right, so much the better. But it was not expected of them; and if they could not make it they were to descend to the col, and the lead would be taken over by the "second" team of Hillary and Tenzing. For them, a higher camp would be pitched, as far up the summit ridge as men could carry it. And from there, using open-circuit oxygen, they would make their try — *the try* — for the top. If this failed, the expedition might or might not be able to mount still another attack. But as far as current plans went, theirs would be the supreme and ultimate effort.

On the morning of May twenty-sixth, after a day's rest at Camp VIII, Bourdillon and Evans set off for the heights. With them went Colonel Hunt and one Sherpa, Da Namgyal, carrying a tent, food, and fuel for the proposed Camp IX that would — probably — be used later by Hillary and Tenzing. At the very beginning two things went wrong. A second Sherpa who was to have accompanied them was sick and could not go, which of course meant heavier loads for the others; and Evans was having much trouble with the frozen valves of his oxygen set. But in spite of this they made steady, if slow prog-

[1] **Lambert:** Raymond Lambert, a professional guide, member of both of the Swiss expeditions of 1952. He and Tenzing had reached a point only about 1,000 feet from the top in the first attempt of that year.

Mount Everest, 29,002 feet high, looms over the surrounding peaks.

ress across the slopes of the col — up the steep snow-couloir [1] that led to the southeast ridge — finally onto the ridge itself, where they passed the tattered remains of the highest Swiss tent. By this time, Bourdillon and Evans, who were less heavily laden than the others, were well in the lead. Hunt and Da Namgyal struggled on under their burdens and deposited them at a height of about 27,350 feet — not as high as the leader had hoped to go, but to the very limit of their strength. If the two men above them did not make the top, it would remain for the Hillary-Tenzing support party to carry Camp IX still farther.

Meanwhile, Bourdillon and Evans crept up toward the south peak. Following its usual pattern, the weather, fine in the early morning, worsened as the day advanced, and soon they were moving through gray clouds and squalls of snow. Evans was still having trou-

ble with his oxygen, resulting in many stops for adjustment and the consequent loss of precious time. But the going underfoot was not too bad, and at last they came out upon the south summit, at 28,720 feet, and looked beyond it at what no human eyes had ever seen before. What they saw was not encouraging. The last few hundred feet of Everest soared up in a steep and savage pinnacle of rock and ice: climbable, perhaps; but not, they realized bitterly, for them. They might have made it — yes. But their strength would then be gone; their oxygen would be used up; darkness would close in. And death. On that day they had climbed the highest of all men. They had reached the south summit and seen the goal beyond. And that would have to suffice. As it was, they were so close to exhaustion that they suffered several slips on the way down and only narrowly missed disaster.

This had been the first challenge. The second was now to come. . . .

[1] **couloir** (ko͞o'lwar′): a deep gorge or gully on a mountainside.

While Bourdillon and Evans descended to the col, Hillary and Tenzing moved up to it from the lower camps, and with them, as their support team, came Alfred Gregory, George Lowe, and a young porter named Ang Nima. The New Zealander and the head-Sherpa had long since been picked by Hunt as the pair "most likely to succeed." During the weeks of labor on the lower mountain they had been kept largely in reserve: acclimatizing slowly, doing enough work to make them hard and fit, but never so much as might wear them out before the final assault was at hand. And now they were as ready as men could be for the great effort that lay before them. Hillary, at thirty-four, was at the very height of his powers as a mountaineer. Tall, rangy, habitually relaxed both in body and temperament, he had proved himself the best snow-and-ice climber on the expedition, and —even more important — was possessed of a sheer dogged endurance that seemed at times to approach the superhuman. Beside him, the slight wiry Tenzing appeared little more than a boy; but actually, at thirty-nine, he was the older of the two and, in experience, the senior Everester of them all. By birth a simple Oriental peasant, and unable to read or write, he knew little of the technical and scientific aspects of mountaineering. But what he lacked in training he more than made up for in strength and spirit. Alone among the men of his race, he had shown himself not only willing but eager — burningly eager — to climb to the heights; Everest was his dream, no less than of the *sahibs* [1] whom he served; and, as he had pulled himself up from the rank and file of his fellows, so did it seem equally possible that he

---

[1] *sahibs* (sä'ĭbz): a title used by natives in addressing Europeans.

could raise himself, too, to that ultimate eminence. If not by legs and lungs alone, then by the very power of his desire and will.

Their companions knew that in both Edmund Hillary and Tenzing lay the spark of greatness. Now it remained to be seen if it would kindle into flame.

At Camp VIII, on the night of May twenty-sixth, the exhausted Bourdillon and Evans told the second party what they had experienced and seen. It was the plan for the latter to be on their way the following morning, but a great wind blew in, shrieking, across the col and held them pinned in the tents for another twenty-four hours. When the next day dawned, clear and fairly calm, they started off. Hillary and Tenzing for the all-out challenge; Gregory, Lowe (Hillary's fellow-New Zealander) and Ang Nima to pitch Camp IX as high as was humanly possible. All were using the open-circuit oxygen equipment, and each man carried on his back a weight of from forty to fifty pounds.

The route was the same as before: from the col to the snow-couloir; up the couloir to the ridge; up the ridge, past the old Swiss tent, to where Hunt and Da Namgyal had left their share of the Camp IX material. Now this was added to their burdens, making individual loads of up to sixty pounds, and their progress became necessarily slower. Little was left of the tracks made by their predecessors, and for much of the time Lowe and Gregory led the way, to spare the summit team the extra exertion of hacking steps in the snow. Thus hour followed hour. And by early afternoon all were tiring fast. Peering ahead for a possible camp site, they saw only the unrelieved steepness of the ridge; but at last Tenzing, remembering the ground from his climb with Lambert, suggested a traverse [1] off the ridge to the left, and there they found a tiny almost level area in the lee of a cliff. This, at 27,900 feet, was to be the site of Camp IX, the highest habitation that men have ever built.

The support-team, their job well accomplished, dumped their loads and began the descent to the col, while Hillary and Tenzing set about the grueling work of clearing a platform and pitching their tent. At last it was done, and there they spent the long hours of dusk and darkness: checking their equipment, eating sparingly, and drinking huge quantities of soup and lemon juice, sometimes holding for dear life to the sheltering canvas as it trembled and swayed in the gusts of wind. But theirs was not the ordeal that Lambert and Tenzing had suffered the year before. They were better equipped. The wind and cold were less savage. Once in their sleeping bags, they were almost comfortable, and with the aid of oxygen they were even able to doze.

It was well that it was thus, or the story that followed might have been a different one.

At four o'clock on the morning of May twenty-ninth Hillary opened the flap and peered from the tent — and this moment, rather than any that followed, may well have been the crucial one of that epic day. For the weather was clear, windless, perfect. Very slowly, so as not to exhaust themselves before they started, they set about their final preparations. Tenzing brewed up hot drinks, and Hillary adjusted the vital oxygen sets that would comprise almost their entire load from this point on. Thirty pounds each they weighed

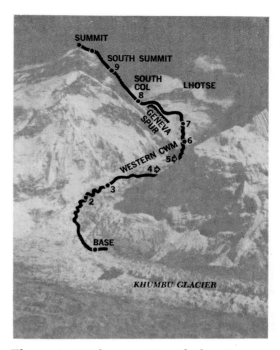

The route to the summit and the nine camps used by the conquerors of Everest.

— a cruel burden at such an altitude; but burden or not, they were life itself. Finally, at six-thirty, Hillary and Tenzing were ready to go. They strapped crampons [2] on to their boots. Over their down clothing went outer windproof jackets, and on to their hands they pulled three pair of gloves: silk, woolen, and windproof. Then they left the tent, roped up, and started off.

For a while Tenzing went first, kicking steps in the soft snow that sloped up from their camp site to the southeast ridge. On the ridge itself, Hillary took over the lead, sometimes following its knife-edged crest, sometimes seeking firmer footing on the snow just below it. The sun was well up now, the sky pure and cloudless, and the mountain gleamed so dazzlingly that without

---

[1] **traverse** (trăv′ērs): a horizontal course. In mountaineering the term is often used to mean climbing horizontally in a zigzag fashion when a slope is steep.

[2] **crampons** (krăm′pŏnz): climbing irons; iron or steel frames with spikes which are attached to the soles of boots for use on snow or ice.

Colonel John Hunt

Thomas Bourdillon

their goggles it would have struck them blind. For an hour they plodded on. And another. Then the ridge dipped into a small hollow, and there they found the last, highest trace of their predecessors: two cylinders of oxygen left for them by Bourdillon and Evans. Scraping the ice from the gauges, Hillary saw that they still contained several liters [1] — enough to get them down from this point to the col and to permit them to use up their own supply on the heights above.

Now, as they moved on again, the ridge steepened into a great snow face, leading up to the south summit. Here, for the first time, the going was definitely dangerous, for the snow was loose and unstable, and a single false step would have plunged them into the abyss on one side or the other. Bourdillon and Evans had already preceded them here. But no vestige of tracks remained in the smooth whiteness, and they had to kick and hack their own steps as they cautiously zigzagged upward. It was nine o'clock when they reached the top and stood on the dome of the south summit, looking up at the final virgin stretch ahead. Their predecessors had described it as formidable, and that it was: a savage thrust of rock and ice clamped like a fang against the

[1] **liters** (lē'tĕrz): units of measure of the metric system; 1 liter equals 1.0567 liquid quarts.

blue-black sky. "It was certainly impressive," reported Hillary, who was no hand for exaggeration — "and even rather frightening."

But it was this way or no way, and slowly the two men attacked the last four hundred feet of the mountaintop. It was still a ridge — the same ridge — on which they were climbing, but far steeper and more precarious than it had been below. On their left — the west — black precipices fell sheer to the distant cwm and icefall; and on the right, projecting out over twelve thousand feet of space, were wind-carved cornices [2] of ice and snow that might crumble and fall at the slightest pressure. Luckily, however, there was a middle route that proved feasible: a slanting, narrow catwalk between precipice and cornice that was composed of firm, hard snow. And it was up this that they now doggedly crept onward.

They moved one at a time: Hillary going first and cutting perhaps forty steps, and then stopping to rest and belay [3] the rope while Tenzing came up after him. Again the maneuver was repeated. And again and again. Sometimes great shoulders of the cornices

[2] **cornices** (kôr'nĭs·ĕz): overhanging formations of snow or rock, usually on a ridge or at the top of a couloir.

[3] **belay** (bē·lā'): to secure a rope by hitching it over a projection or passing it around the body.

Sir Edmund Hillary

Tenzing Norgay

blocked their way, and they had to slant off to the left — so close to the western precipice that their feet rested on its topmost rocks. But always they were able, in the end, to work back to the ridge and the sound snow. At this stage of the climb came a moment they had been eagerly anticipating. Each of them had been carrying two cylinders of oxygen, and now, almost simultaneously, their first cylinders ran out, and they were able to discard them, thus lightening their loads by a half. A bit farther on, both were bothered by the formation of ice in their breathing tubes, but they were able to clear them out and continued their progress.

After an hour of continuous step-cutting they came to the most formidable obstacle on the ridge: a vertical cliff of rock, forty feet high. They had seen this cliff, through binoculars, all the way from the distant Thyangboche [1] Monastery, and there had been much speculation even then as to whether it might prove impassable. Now, seen from close up, it was a thing to chill the blood. The wall of rock itself was smooth and holdless. To the left was space. To the right a cornice — and space. But to the right, too, was the one possible route of ascent: a narrow crack running up the full height of the cliff between the cornice and the rock.

[1] Thyangboche (tē′äng·bŏsh).

For a long time Hillary studied it grimly from below. Then he made the effort of a lifetime. Wedging himself as far into the crack as he could, he strained and clawed upward for the tiniest holds, meanwhile kicking backward with his cramponed boots against the wall of the cornice behind him. At any moment he expected the wall to give, the hard-packed snow to crumble and fall from the mountainside — and himself with it.

But the wall held. His crampons grated upward. Foot by foot, he pushed and pulled and levered himself on, until at last he was able to get a hand over the rim of the cliff and wriggle up to its level summit. For a few moments he lay where he was, too done in to move. Then, his strength returning, he belayed the rope while Tenzing came up after him; and in ten minutes the Sherpa, too, was on top, collapsing on the rocks, as Hillary described it later, "like a giant fish that had just been hauled from the sea after a terrible struggle."

Thus these two indomitable men passed the last barrier of Everest's defenses. Even on an ordinary mountain, the climbing of that vertical pitch [2] would have been no mean achievement. At a height of twenty-nine thou-

[2] **pitch** (pĭch): here, a short, steep section of rock.

sand feet it was all but miraculous.

The struggle behind them had been a thing of the grimmest reality. What followed now had more the form and texture of a dream. From the top of the cliff the ridge continued as before: the cornices on the right the great precipice on the left. They went on cutting steps. They moved up into the steps. The ridge was now curving to the right, rising in a series of white hummocks,[1] and as they worked their way around one, another appeared ahead. Then another and another. Always farther; always higher. The ax rose and fell, and the soft crunch as it struck the snow was the only sound in an immensity of stillness. They were tiring fast now and moving very slowly "As I chipped steps around still another corner," Hillary recounted later, "I wondered, rather dully, just how long we could keep it up. And then I realized that the ridge ahead, instead of still rising, now dropped sharply away, and far below I could see the East Rongbuk Glacier. I looked upwards, to see a narrow snow ridge running up to a sharp summit. . . ."

A few moments later — at eleven-thirty in the morning on May 29, 1953 — two men stood at last on earth's ultimate height.

Foolish people have since asked, "Who was in the lead? Who was first on top?" If they expected an answer, they do not know much about mountaineers — or about the human spirit when it rises to greatness. Edmund Hillary and Tenzing were *together* on top — together in victory — together, grinning through their goggles and masks, clasping hands, thumping each other until forced to stop for lack of breath. "My initial feelings," said Hillary, "were of relief. Relief that there were no more

[1] **hummocks** (hŭm'ŭks): ridges of ice.

steps to cut, no more ridges to traverse, and no more humps to tantalize us with hopes of success." For success was now theirs — success in the richest measure that has ever been given to men upon a mountain. And if relief was quickly followed by joy and pride, these were followed, in turn, by humility and gratitude.

Why climb Everest? . . . "Because it is there," said Mallory.[2] . . . And now *they* were there: in the place of dreams, of hope, of aspiration. The moments passed, as they stood silent and motionless on that crest of snow. Beneath them the world stretched endlessly to the horizon: range upon range of towering mountains, appearing now as no more than foothills; so remote and unreal that the two men seemed to be viewing them not from the same earth at all, but from a fabulous island in the sky. On that island they were alone — as alone as human beings can be on the surface of our planet. And at the same time not alone, for no two men by themselves could have been standing where they now stood. As surely as if they could have reached out and touched them, Bourdillon and Evans were there by their side. Hunt was there too, and all their other companions, far below, who had struggled as hard, and sacrificed more, for the common purpose. Mallory, of the flaming spirit, was there; and young Sandy Irvine. Norton and Somervell, Smythe and Tilman, Shipton and Lambert — the whole company of Everesters, white and brown, alive and dead — all of them were there, joined together at last at the ultimate goal. Geoffrey Bruce was there, mutter-

[2] **Mallory:** George Leigh Mallory, an Englishman, attempted to climb Everest in 1924. When he and a companion (Andrew Irvine) reached a point 800 feet from the summit, clouds closed in on them, and they were never seen again.

ing between cracked and frozen lips: "Just wait, old thing — we'll get you yet."

The ghosts faded. The world returned. Hillary turned off his oxygen, removed the mask, and brought out his camera. From around his ice-ax, where they had been tightly wound, Tenzing unfurled a string of four flags — Nepalese, British, Indian, and United Nations — and held them aloft, while Hillary snapped the picture that was soon to be known throughout the world. Then the New Zealander took more photographs, out and down from all sides of the summit, until presently his hands fumbled and his movements became unsure. Quickly he stowed the camera, replaced his oxygen mask, and turned on the life-giving flow. Meanwhile the Sherpa, in a simple ritual of his Buddhist faith, had made a hollow in the snow and laid in it a few bits of biscuit and chocolate; and Hillary, joining him, placed beside them a small crucifix which Hunt had given him and asked him to take to the top. These they left there: offerings of gratitude to a God — the God of all men — Who had been merciful indeed.

Now fifteen minutes had passed, and it was time to start down. One final thing, however, remained to be done. Slowly, for the last time, their eyes moved over the snowy crest and the slopes below, searching for some sign, some possible hint, of the fate of Mallory and Irvine. But there was only the snow — only height and depth, space and stillness — and, hidden somewhere deep within them, the secret of the years.

Their descent from the summit was a race against time, exhaustion, and their dwindling oxygen supply. But it was a race in slow-motion, for the journey was perilous, and they were resolved to return from their triumph alive.

At the advance base — Camp IV — there were such demonstrations of emotion as to make a good stiff-upper-lipped Englishman blush with embarrassment; and by radio the news was flashed to a waiting world. There followed a brief, ugly interlude when small men tried to make political grist [1] of it — to split white man and brown man in a mean wrangle over honors. But the conquerors of Everest were not small; they would have no part of this sort of thing; and soon the machinations of the troublemakers were forgotten. With happy timing, word of the conquest reached England on the very eve of the Queen's coronation, making that great day an even greater one. Hillary and Hunt were forthwith knighted, and Tenzing received the highest award that could be given a non-British national. From the Thames to the Ganges, from Nepal to New Zealand, there was rejoicing in the common victory.

And in the end, perhaps, it was this, above all else, that gave meaning and greatness to the climbing of Everest: that it *was* a common victory in a common cause. For a few magical minutes on a May morning in 1953 a man of the East and a man of the West stood side by side on the summit of the earth, bound together not only by a nylon rope, but by the bonds of brotherhood and high enterprise. In a world darkened by strife and fear, it was a thing to be remembered and cherished. For the triumph belonged not only to Hillary and Tenzing; not only to the ranks of the Everesters who fought and struggled toward the beckoning goal. It was a triumph for all men, everywhere, and the fitting end to a shining chapter in the sorry history of our century.

[1] **make . . . grist** (grĭst): an expression meaning "turn to one's own advantage."

DRAWING CONCLUSIONS

1. Give reasons why you agree or disagree with this statement: Edmund Hillary and Tenzing climbed to victory on the shoulders of the Everest expeditions that had tried and failed.

2. When Tenzing was asked who reached the top first, his reply was, " . . . If you agree, I like say both got top together almost same time. If you, everybody, write that way, no trouble . . ." What does this statement reveal about Tenzing? Was there any hint in the selection that there were people who tried to make trouble between Tenzing and the other members?

3. Does this mountain-climbing adventure differ in spirit from the adventure of the Western pioneers in our country's history? Explain.

4. What reasons can you give for calling the story of Everest "the greatest story of mountaineering" and "the fitting end to a shining chapter in the sorry history of our century"?

5. Why do you think men climb mountains? Do you agree with James Ramsey Ullman, who has written: "The mountain way is a way of life. An attitude and a response to life. A mountain is there; climb it. An ocean is there; cross it. A disease is there; cure it. A wrong is there; right it. On the surface, perhaps, these are very different things. But in essence they are identically the same thing. The various words, and a hundred more, could be erased, and a single word substituted. The word is challenge. . . . A challenge is there. Meet it. . . . I is the very act of meeting it that makes us more than animals — if somewhat less than gods"? Explain why you agree or disagree with Ullman.

GAINING POWER OVER WORDS

SPECIALIZED VOCABULARIES As you read this account of adventure in high places, you came across words which were strange. Mountain climbers use technical terms just as high school students use a special vocabulary when talking about familiar sports. A member of a basketball team, for example, would not find the following statement confusing: "A charity toss by Jones plus a swisher from the key by Thomas brought victory to the Hunt-ington five." Anyone who is not well acquainted with basketball, however, might fail to grasp the meaning of the sentence because he does not understand the technical vocabulary involved.

A familiarity with at least some of the most frequently used terms in specialized fields will make your own vocabulary more efficient. Which of the mountaineering terms do you remember? In your notebook write down these terms with their meanings and pool your list with ones prepared by other members of the class. The class can then select those terms that everyone agrees are worth remembering. Copy these in your notebook along with their definitions and sentences in which you use the terms correctly. As you continue to read, make similar lists of specialized vocabularies.

ABOUT THE AUTHOR

James Ramsey Ullman (1907–) is a native of New York City and a graduate of Princeton University. He has been a newspaper reporter, playwright-producer, short-story writer, novelist, and explorer. Ullman started mountain climbing in Switzerland during a vacation. In his varied career one daydream has remained unchanged for twenty years — to climb Everest. This ambition is reflected in much of his writing. In 1941 he published a popular history of mountaineering called *High Conquest;* in 1954 it was revised and reissued as *The Age of Mountaineering.* "Victory on Everest" is one chapter in this book.

Climbing Everest ➤

The photographs on the opposite page show highlights of Hillary and Tenzing's historic conquest of Everest. *Upper left,* climbers search for a place to cross the sixty-foot chasm. A snow bridge was finally found near the base of the peak in the background. *Upper right,* Tenzing realizes the full import of the expression "on top of the world." *Lower left,* Hillary and Tenzing toil up the mountain. *Lower right,* a view seen from the ground by only four men: the final ridge before the summit.

R.M.S. Titanic

HANSON W. BALDWIN

Courage in the face of almost certain death is not so rare as is sometimes believed. On the contrary, it is relatively common. Brave men and women have existed in all ages. In every language, among all peoples, courage occurs over and over again as a theme in song and story. It is a deep-lying human trait, peculiar to no single time or place, but characteristic of mankind as a whole.

THE WHITE STAR LINER *Titanic,* largest ship the world had ever known, sailed from Southampton on her maiden voyage to New York on April 10, 1912. The paint on her strakes [1] was fair and bright; she was fresh from Harland and Wolff's Belfast yards, strong in the strength of her forty-six thousand tons

of steel, bent, hammered, shaped, and riveted through the three years of her slow birth.

There was little fuss and fanfare at her sailing; her sister ship, the *Olympic* — slightly smaller than the *Titanic* — had been in service for some months and to her had gone the thunder of the cheers.

But the *Titanic* needed no whistling steamers or shouting crowds to call attention to her superlative qualities. Her bulk dwarfed the ships near her as longshoremen singled up her mooring lines and cast off the turns of heavy rope from the dock bollards. [2] She was not only the largest ship afloat, but was believed to be the safest. Carlisle, her builder, had given her double bottoms and had divided her hull into sixteen watertight compartments, which made

---

[1] **strakes:** breadths of planks or plates forming continuous strips on the bottom or sides of a ship.

[2] **bollards:** upright wooden or iron posts around which ropes are fastened.

Observing the Writer's Selection of Details. Even though the writer is telling the story of an actual occurrence, it is his skill in describing it that enables the reader to feel the drama of the event. It would have

been impossible to record all the incidents of a disaster that involved hundreds of people and lasted several hours. Notice how Hanson Baldwin has selected and emphasized dramatic details.

---

her, men thought, unsinkable. She had been built to be and had been described as a gigantic lifeboat. Her designers' dreams of a triple-screw giant, a luxurious, floating hotel, which could speed to New York at twenty-three knots,[1] had been carefully translated from blueprints and mold loft [2] lines at the Belfast yards into a living reality.

The *Titanic's* sailing from Southampton, though quiet, was not wholly uneventful. As the liner moved slowly toward the end of her dock that April day, the surge of her passing sucked away from the quay [3] the steamer *New York*, moored just to seaward of the *Titanic's* berth. There were sharp cracks as the manila mooring lines of the *New York* parted under the strain. The frayed ropes writhed and whistled through the air and snapped down among the waving crowd on the pier; the *New York* swung toward the *Titanic's* bow, and was checked and dragged back to the dock barely in time to avert a collision. Seamen muttered, thought it an ominous start.

Past Spithead and the Isle of Wight the *Titanic* steamed. She called at Cherbourg at dusk and then laid her course for Queenstown. At 1:30 P.M. on Thursday, April 11, she stood out of Queenstown harbor, screaming gulls soaring in her wake, with 2,201 persons — men, women, and children — aboard.

Occupying the Empire bedrooms and Georgian [4] suites of the first-class accommodations were many well-known men and women — Colonel John Jacob

[1] **knots:** nautical units of speed; each one is equal to 6,080.20 feet an hour.
[2] **mold loft:** a large floor on which the lines of a vessel are laid down and molds made.
[3] **quay** (kē): solid landing place beside a navigable body of water.
[4] **Empire . . . and Georgian:** styles of furniture. *Empire* furniture was developed in France, and *Georgian* furniture originated in England.

Astor and his young bride; Major Archibald Butt, military aide to President Taft, and his friend, Frank D. Millet, the painter; John B. Thayer, vice-president of the Pennsylvania Railroad, and Charles M. Hays, president of the Grand Trunk Railway of Canada; W. T. Stead, the English journalist; Jacques Futrelle, French novelist; H. B. Harris, theatrical manager, and Mrs. Harris; Mr. and Mrs. Isidor Straus; and J. Bruce Ismay, chairman and managing director of the White Star line.

Down in the plain wooden cabins of the steerage class were 706 immigrants to the land of promise, and trimly stowed in the great holds was a cargo valued at $420,000: oak beams, sponges, wine, calabashes, and an odd miscellany of the common and the rare.

The *Titanic* took her departure on Fastnet Light and, heading into the night, laid her course for New York. She was due at Quarantine the following Wednesday morning.

Sunday dawned fair and clear. The *Titanic* steamed smoothly toward the west, faint streamers of brownish smoke trailing from her funnels. The purser held services in the salon in the morning; on the steerage deck aft the immigrants were playing games and a Scotsman was puffing "The Campbells Are Coming" on his bagpipes in the midst of the uproar.

At 9:00 A.M. a message from the steamer *Caronia* sputtered into the wireless shack:

Captain, *Titanic* — Westbound steamers report bergs, growlers, and field ice in 42 degrees N. from 49 degrees to 51 degrees W. 12th April.

Compliments — Barr

It was cold in the afternoon; the sun was brilliant, but the *Titanic*, her screws turning over at seventy-five rev-

The Titanic *leaves Southampton harbor at the start of her maiden voyage.*

olutions per minute, was approaching the Banks.[1]

In the Marconi cabin Second Operator Harold Bride, earphones clamped on his head, was figuring accounts; he did not stop to answer when he heard *MWL*, Continental Morse for the nearby Leyland liner, *Californian*, calling the *Titanic.* The *Californian* had some message about three icebergs; he didn't bother then to take it down. About 1:42 P.M. the rasping spark[2] of those days spoke again across the water. It was the *Baltic*, calling the *Titanic*, warning her of ice on the steamer track. Bride took the message down and sent it up to the bridge. The officer of the deck glanced at it, sent it to the bearded master of the *Titanic*, Captain E. C. Smith, a veteran of the White Star service. It was lunchtime then; the captain, walking along the promenade deck, saw Mr. Ismay, stopped, and handed him the message without comment. Ismay read it, stuffed it in his pocket, told two ladies about the icebergs, and resumed his walk. Later, about 7:15 P.M., the captain requested the return of the message in order to post it in the chart-room for the information of officers.

Dinner that night in the Jacobean[3] dining room was gay. It was bitter on deck, but the night was calm and fine; the sky was moonless but studded with stars twinkling coldly in the clear air.

After dinner some of the second-class passengers gathered in the salon, where the Reverend Mr. Carter conducted a "hymn sing-song." It was almost ten o'clock and the stewards were waiting with biscuits and coffee as the group sang:

> O, hear us when we cry to Thee
> For those in peril on the sea.

On the bridge Second Officer Lightoller — short, stocky, efficient — was relieved at ten o'clock by First Officer Murdoch. Lightoller had talked with other officers about the proximity of ice; at least five wireless ice warnings had reached the ship; lookouts had been cautioned to be alert; captain and officers expected to reach the field at any time after 9:30 P.M. At twenty-two knots, its speed unslackened, the *Titanic* plowed on through the night.

Lightoller left the darkened bridge to his relief and turned in. Captain Smith

[1] **Banks:** the Grand Banks, fishing waters off the coast of Newfoundland.
[2] **rasping spark:** a reference to the crude radio signals of the time.

[3] **Jacobean:** furnished in the style characteristic of the time of James I of England.

went to his cabin. The steerage was long since quiet; in the first and second cabins lights were going out; voices were growing still; people were asleep. Murdoch paced back and forth on the bridge, peering out over the dark water, glancing now and then at the compass in front of Quartermaster Hichens at the wheel.

In the crow's-nest Lookout Frederick Fleet and his partner, Leigh, gazed down at the water, still and unruffled in the dim, starlit darkness. Behind and below them the ship, a white shadow with here and there a last winking light; ahead of them a dark and silent and cold ocean.

There was a sudden clang. "Dong-dong. Dong-dong. Dong-dong. Dong!" the metal clapper of the great ship's bell struck out 11:30. Mindful of the warnings, Fleet strained his eyes, searching the darkness for the dreaded ice. But there were only the stars and the sea.

In the wireless room, where Phillips, first operator, had relieved Bride, the buzz of the *Californian's* set again crackled into the earphones:

Californian: "Say, old man, we are stuck here, surrounded by ice."

Titanic: "Shut up, shut up; keep out. I am talking to Cape Race; you are jamming my signals."

Then, a few minutes later — about 11:40 . . .

Out of the dark she came, a vast, dim, white, monstrous shape, directly in the *Titanic's* path. For a moment Fleet doubted his eyes. But she was a deadly reality, this ghastly *thing.* Frantically Fleet struck three bells — *something dead ahead.* He snatched the telephone and called the bridge:

"Iceberg! Right ahead!"

The first officer heard but did not stop to acknowledge the message.

"Hard-a-starboard!" [1]

Hichens strained at the wheel; the bow swung slowly to port. [2] The monster was almost upon them now.

Murdoch leaped to the engine-room telegraph. Bells clanged. Far below in the engine room those bells struck the first warning. Danger! The indicators on the dial faces swung round to "Stop!" Then "Full speed astern!" Frantically the engineers turned great valve wheels; answered the bridge bells. . . .

There was a slight shock, a brief scraping, a small list to port. Shell ice — slabs and chunks of it — fell on the foredeck. Slowly the *Titanic* stopped.

Captain Smith hurried out of his cabin.

"What has the ship struck?"

Murdoch answered, "An iceberg, sir. I hard-a-starboarded and reversed the engines, and I was going to hard-a-port around it; but she was too close. I could not do any more. I have closed the watertight doors."

Fourth Officer Boxhall, other officers, the carpenter, came to the bridge. The captain sent Boxhall and the carpenter below to ascertain the damage.

A few lights switched on in the first and second cabins; sleepy passengers peered through porthole glass; some casually asked the stewards, "Why have we stopped?"

"I don't know, sir, but I don't suppose it is anything much."

In the smoking room a quorum of gamblers and their prey were still sitting round a poker table; the usual crowd of kibitzers looked on. They had felt the slight jar of the collision and had seen an eighty-foot ice mountain glide by the smoking-room windows;

[1] **starboard:** the right side of a vessel as one faces forward.
[2] **port:** the left side of a vessel as one faces forward.

but the night was calm and clear, the *Titanic* was "unsinkable." They hadn't bothered to go on deck.

But far below, in the warren [1] of passages on the starboard side forward, in the forward holds and boiler rooms, men could see that the *Titanic's* hurt was mortal. In No. 6 boiler room, where the red glow from the furnaces lighted up the naked, sweaty chests of coal-blackened firemen, water was pouring through a great gash about two feet above the floor plates. This was no slow leak; the ship was open to the sea; in ten minutes there were eight feet of water in No. 6. Long before then the stokers had raked the flaming fires out of the furnaces and had scrambled through the watertight doors in No. 5 or had climbed up the long steel ladders to safety. When Boxhall looked at the mailroom in No. 3 hold, twenty-four feet above the keel, the mailbags were already floating about in the slushing water. In No. 5 boiler room a stream of water spurted into an empty bunker. All six compartments forward of No. 4 were open to the sea; in ten seconds the iceberg's jagged claw had ripped a three-hundred-foot slash in the bottom of the great *Titanic*.

Reports came to the bridge; Ismay in dressing gown ran out on deck in the cold, still, starlit night, climbed up the bridge ladder.

"What has happened?"

Captain Smith: "We have struck ice."

"Do you think she is seriously damaged?"

Captain Smith: "I'm afraid she is."

Ismay went below and passed Chief Engineer William Bell, fresh from an inspection of the damaged compartments. Bell corroborated the captain's statement, hurried back down the glistening steel ladders to his duty. Man

[1] **warren**: crowded area.

after man followed him — Thomas Andrews, one of the ship's designers, Archie Frost, the builder's chief engineer, and his twenty assistants — men who had no posts of duty in the engine room but whose traditions called them there.

On deck, in corridor and stateroom, life flowed again. Men, women, and children awoke and questioned; orders were given to uncover the lifeboats; water rose into the firemen's quarters; half-dressed stokers streamed up on deck. But the passengers — most of them — did not know that the *Titanic* was sinking. The shock of the collision had been so slight that some were not awakened by it; the *Titanic* was so huge that she must be unsinkable; the night was too calm, too beautiful, to think of death at sea.

Captain Smith half ran to the door of the radio shack. Bride, partly dressed, eyes dulled with sleep, was standing behind Phillips, waiting.

"Send the call for assistance."

The blue spark danced: "CQD [2] — CQD — CQD — CQ — " Miles away Marconi men heard. Cape Race heard it, and the steamships *La Provence* and *Mt. Temple*.

The sea was surging into the *Titanic's* hold. At 12:20 the water burst into the seamen's quarters through a collapsed fore and aft wooden bulkhead.[3] Pumps strained in the engine rooms — men and machinery making a futile fight against the sea. Steadily the water rose.

The boats were swung out — slowly; for the deck hands were late in reaching their stations, there had been no boat drill, and many of the crew did not know to what boats they were assigned. Orders were shouted; the safety valves

[2] **CQD**: the original code letters of the signal of distress, later changed to SOS.

[3] **bulkhead**: wall separating the compartments of a ship.

had lifted, and steam was blowing off in a great rushing roar. In the charthouse Fourth Officer Boxhall bent above a chart, working rapidly with pencil and dividers.

12:25 A.M. Boxhall's position is sent out to a fleet of vessels: "Come at once; we have struck a berg."

To the Cunarder *Carpathia* (Arthur Henry Rostron, Master, New York to Liverpool, fifty-eight miles away): "It's a CQD, old man. Position 41–46 N.; 50–14 W."

The blue spark dancing: "Sinking; cannot hear for noise of steam."

12:30 A.M. The word is passed: "Women and children in the boats." Stewards finish waking their passengers below; life preservers are tied on; some men smile at the precaution. "The *Titanic* is unsinkable." The *Mt. Temple* starts for the *Titanic;* the *Carpathia,* with a double watch in her stokeholds,[1] radios: "Coming hard." The CQD changes the course of many ships — but not of one; the operator of the *Californian,* near by, has just put down his earphones and turned in.

The CQD flashes over land and sea from Cape Race to New York; newspaper city rooms leap to life and presses whir.

On the *Titanic,* water creeps over the bulkhead between Nos. 5 and 6 firerooms. She is going down by the head;[2] the engineers — fighting a losing battle — are forced back foot by foot by the rising water. Down the promenade deck Happy Jock Hume, the bandsman, runs with his instrument.

12:45 A.M. Murdoch, in charge on the starboard side, eyes tragic but calm and cool, orders boat No. 7 lowered. The women hang back; they want no boat

ride on an ice-strewn sea. "The *Titanic* is unsinkable." The men encourage them, explain that this is just a precautionary measure. "We'll see you again at breakfast." There is little confusion; passengers stream slowly to the boat deck. In the steerage the immigrants chatter excitedly.

A sudden sharp hiss — a streaked flare against the night; Boxhall sends a rocket toward the sky. It explodes, and a parachute of white stars lights up the icy sea. "Rockets!" The band plays ragtime.

No. 8 is lowered, and No. 5. Ismay, still in dressing gown, calls for women and children, handles lines, stumbles in the way of an officer, is told to "get out of here!" Third Officer Pitman takes charge of No. 5; as he swings into the boat, Murdoch grasps his hand. "Goodby and good luck, old man."

No. 6 goes over the side. There are only twenty-eight people in a lifeboat with a capacity of sixty-five.

A light stabs from the bridge; Boxhall is calling in Morse flashes, again and again, to a strange ship stopped in the ice jam five to ten miles away. Another rocket drops its shower of sparks above the ice-strewn sea and the dying ship.

1:00 A.M. Slowly the water creeps higher; the foreports of the *Titanic* are dipping into the sea. Rope squeaks through blocks; lifeboats drop jerkily seaward. Through the shouting on the decks comes the sound of the band playing ragtime.

The "Millionaires' Special"[3] leaves the ship — boat No. 1, with a capacity of forty people, carries only Sir Cosmo and Lady Duff Gordon and ten others. Aft, the frightened immigrants mill and

---

[1] **double watch in her stokeholds:** twice as many men as usual firing the boilers.

[2] **by the head:** bow first.

[3] **"Millionaire's Special":** name that newspapers later gave to the lifeboat that left the ship with only a few rich people in it.

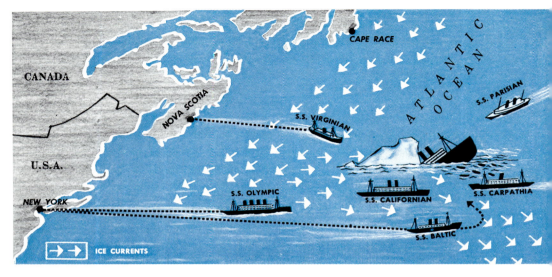

jostle and rush for a boat. An officer's fist flies out; three shots are fired in the air, and the panic is quelled. . . . Four Chinese sneak unseen into a boat and hide in its bottom.

1:20 A.M. Water is coming into No. 4 boiler room. Stokers slice and shovel as water laps about their ankles — steam for the dynamos; steam for the dancing spark! As the water rises, great ash hoes rake the flaming coals from the furnaces. Safety valves pop; the stokers retreat aft, and the watertight doors clang shut behind them.

The rockets fling their splendor toward the stars. The boats are more heavily loaded now, for the passengers know the *Titanic* is sinking. Women cling and sob. The great screws aft are rising clear of the sea. Half-filled boats are ordered to come alongside the cargo ports and take on more passengers, but the ports are never opened — and the boats are never filled. Others pull for the steamer's light miles away but never reach it: the lights disappear; the unknown ship steams off.

The water rises and the band plays ragtime.

1:30 A.M. Lightoller is getting the port boats off; Murdoch, the starboard.

As one boat is lowered into the sea, a boat officer fires his gun along the ship's side to stop a rush from the lower decks. A woman tries to take her Great Dane into a boat with her; she is refused and steps out of the boat to die with her dog. Millet's "little smile which played on his lips all through the voyage" plays no more; his lips are grim, but he waves good-by and brings wraps for the women.

Benjamin Guggenheim, in evening clothes, smiles and says, "We've dressed up in our best and are prepared to go down like gentlemen."

1:40 A.M. Boat 14 is clear, and then 13, 16, 15, and C. The lights still shine, but the *Baltic* hears the blue spark say, "Engine room getting flooded."

The *Olympic* signals: "Am lighting up all possible boilers as fast as can."

Major Butt helps women into the last boats and waves good-by to them. Mrs. Straus puts her foot on the gunwale of a lifeboat, then she draws back and goes to her husband. "We have been together many years; where you go I will go." Colonel John Jacob Astor puts his young wife in a lifeboat, steps back, taps cigarette on fingernail. "Good-by, dearie; I'll join you later."

1:45 A.M. The foredeck is under water, the fo'c'sle head [1] almost awash; the great stern is lifted high toward the bright stars; and still the band plays. Mr. and Mrs. Harris approach a lifeboat arm in arm.

Officer: "Ladies first, please."

Harris bows, smiles, steps back. "Of course, certainly; ladies first."

Boxhall fires the last rocket, then leaves in charge of boat No. 2.

2:00 A.M. She is dying now; her bow goes deeper, her stern higher. But there must be steam. Below in the stokeholds the sweaty firemen keep steam up for the flaring lights and the dancing spark. The glowing coals slide and tumble over the slanted grate bars; the sea pounds behind that yielding bulkhead. But the spark dances on.

The *Asian* hears Phillips try the new signal — SOS.

Boat No. 4 has left now; boat D leaves ten minutes later. Jacques Futrelle clasps his wife. "For God's sake, go! it's your last chance; go!" Madame Futrelle is half forced into the boat. It clears the side.

There are about 660 people in the boats, and 1,500 still on the sinking *Titanic*.

On top of the officers' quarters men work frantically to get the two collapsibles stowed there over the side. Water is over the forward part of A deck now; it surges up the companionways toward the boat deck. In the radio shack Bride has slipped a coat and life jacket about Phillips as the first operator sits hunched over his key, sending — still sending — "41–46 N.; 50–14 W. CQD — CQD — SOS — SOS — "

The captain's tired white face appears at the radio-room door. "Men, you have done your full duty. You can

[1] **fo'c'sle head:** forecastle head, the forward part of the upper deck of a vessel.

do no more. Now, it's every man for himself." The captain disappears — back to his sinking bridge, where Painter, his personal steward, stands quietly waiting for orders. The spark dances on. Bride turns his back and goes into the inner cabin. As he does so, a stoker, grimed with coal, mad with fear, steals into the shack and reaches for the life jacket on Phillips' back. Bride wheels about and brains him with a wrench.

2:10 A.M. Below decks the steam is still holding, though the pressure is falling — rapidly. In the gymnasium on the boat deck the athletic instructor watches quietly as two gentlemen ride the bicycles and another swings casually at the punching bag. Mail clerks stagger up the boat-deck stairways, dragging soaked mail sacks. The spark still dances. The band still plays — but not ragtime:

> Nearer, my God, to Thee
> Nearer to Thee . . .

A few men take up the refrain; others kneel on the slanting decks to pray. Many run and scramble aft, where hundreds are clinging above the silent screws on the great uptilted stern. The spark still dances and the lights still flare; the engineers are on the job. The hymn comes to its close. Bandmaster Hartley, Yorkshireman violinist, taps his bow against a bulkhead, calls for "Autumn" as the water curls about his feet, and the eight musicians brace themselves against the ship's slant. People are leaping from the decks into the near-by water — the icy water. A woman cries, "Oh, save me, save me!" A man answers, "Good lady, save yourself. Only God can save you now." The band plays "Autumn":

> God of Mercy and Compassion!
> Look with pity on my pain . . .

The water creeps over the bridge where the *Titanic's* master stands; heavily he steps out to meet it.

2:17 A.M. "CQ —" The *Virginian* hears a ragged, blurred CQ, then an abrupt stop. The blue spark dances no more. The lights flicker out; the engineers have lost their battle.

2:18 A.M. Men run about blackened decks, leap into the night, are swept into the sea by the curling wave which licks up the *Titanic's* length. Lightoller does not leave the ship; the ship leaves him; there are hundreds like him, but only a few who live to tell of it. The funnels still swim above the water, but the ship is climbing to the perpendicular; [1] the bridge is under and most of the foremast; the great stern rises like a squat leviathan.[2] Men swim away from the sinking ship; others drop from the stern.

The band plays in the darkness, the water lapping upwards:

> Hold me up in mighty waters,
> Keep my eyes on things above,
> Righteousness, divine atonement,
> Peace and everlas . . .

The forward funnel snaps and crashes into the sea; its steel tons hammer out of existence swimmers struggling in the freezing water. Streams of sparks, of smoke and steam, burst from the after funnels. The ship upends to 50 . . . to 60 degrees.

Down in the black abyss of the stokeholds, of the engine rooms, where the dynamos have whirred at long last to a stop, the stokers and the engineers are reeling against hot metal, the rising water clutching at their knees. The boil-

ers, the engine cylinders, rip from their bedplates; crash through bulkheads; rumble — steel against steel.

The *Titanic* stands on end, poised briefly for the plunge. Slowly she slides to her grave — slowly at first, and then more quickly . . . quickly . . . quickly.

2:20 A.M. The greatest ship in the world has sunk. From the calm, dark waters, where the floating lifeboats move, there goes up, in the white wake of her passing, "one long continuous moan."

The boats that the *Titanic* had launched pulled safely away from the slight suction of the sinking ship, pulled away from the screams that came from the lips of the freezing men and women in the water. The boats were poorly manned and badly equipped, and they had been unevenly loaded. Some carried so few seamen that women bent to the oars. Mrs. Astor tugged at an oar handle; the Countess of Rothes took a tiller. Shivering stokers in sweaty, coal-blackened singlets and light trousers steered in some boats; stewards in white coats rowed in others. Ismay was in the last boat that left the ship from the starboard side; with Mr. Carter of Philadelphia and two seamen he tugged at the oars. In one of the lifeboats an Italian with a broken wrist — disguised in a woman's shawl and hat — huddled on the floor boards, ashamed now that fear had left him. In another rode the only baggage saved from the *Titanic* — the carryall of Samuel L. Goldenberg, one of the rescued passengers.

There were only a few boats that were heavily loaded; most of those that were half empty made but perfunctory efforts to pick up the moaning swimmers, their officers and crew fearing they would endanger the living if they pulled back into the midst of the dying.

---

[1] **climbing to the perpendicular:** the bow was pointing straight down; the stern, high in the air.

[2] **leviathan** (le·vī′a·thăn): a huge and fearful object; an aquatic monster in the Bible.

Some boats beat off the freezing victims; fear-crazed men and women struck with oars at the heads of swimmers. One woman drove her fist into the face of a half-dead man as he tried feebly to climb over the gunwale. Two other women helped him in and stanched the flow of blood from the ring cuts on his face.

One of the collapsible boats, which had floated off the top of the officers' quarters when the *Titanic* sank, was an icy haven for thirty or forty men. The boat had capsized as the ship sank; men swam to it, clung to it, climbed upon its slippery bottom, stood knee-deep in water in the freezing air. Chunks of ice swirled about their legs; their soaked clothing clutched their bodies in icy folds. Colonel Archibald Gracie was cast up there. Gracie, who had leaped from the stern as the *Titanic* sank; young Thayer, who had seen his father die; Lightoller, who had twice been sucked down with the ship and twice blown to the surface by a belch of air; Bride, the second operator, and Phillips, the first. There were many stokers, half-naked; it was a shivering company. They stood there in the icy sea, under the far stars, and sang and prayed — the Lord's Prayer. After a while a lifeboat came and picked them off, but Phillips was dead then or died soon afterward in the boat.

Only a few of the boats had lights; only one — No. 2 — had a light that was of any use to the *Carpathia*, twisting through the ice field to the rescue. Other ships were "coming hard" too; one, the *Californian,* was still dead to opportunity.

The blue sparks still danced, but not the *Titanic's*. *La Provence* to *Celtic:* "Nobody has heard the *Titanic* for about two hours."

It was 2:40 when the *Carpathia* first sighted the green light from No. 2 boat; it was 4:10 when she picked up the first boat and learned that the *Titanic* had foundered. The last of the moaning cries had just died away then.

Captain Rostron took the survivors aboard, boatload by boatload. He was ready for them, but only a small minority of them required much medical attention. Bride's feet were twisted and frozen; others were suffering from exposure; one died, and seven were dead when taken from the boats, and were buried at sea.

It was then that the fleet of racing ships learned they were too late; the *Parisian* heard the weak signals of MPA, the *Carpathia*, report of the death of the *Titanic*. It was then — or soon afterward, when her radio operator put on his earphones — that the *Californian,* the ship that had been within sight as the *Titanic* was sinking, first learned of the disaster.

And it was then, in all its white-green majesty, that the *Titanic's* survivors saw the iceberg, tinted with the sunrise, floating idly, pack ice jammed about its base, other bergs heaving slowly near by on the blue breast of the sea.

Thus ended the maiden voyage of the *Titanic*. The lifeboats brought to New York by the *Carpathia,* a few deck chairs and gratings awash in the ice field off the Grand Banks eight hundred miles from shore, were all that was left of the world's greatest ship.

OBSERVING THE WRITER'S SELECTION OF DETAILS

From a vast number of incidents the author selects only those which contribute to his purpose. What he selects and what he leaves out become clues to his purpose in writing. The following questions should help you to appreciate and understand the author's purpose.

1. What are the first twelve words in this story? the last nine? What effect does the author create through the use of these words?

2. Find references to the ship's luxury, wealth, inventions, and improvements, of which people might have said with pride, "Look how far we have advanced since men first ventured out to sea in log canoes!"

3. Why did no one worry greatly about the other ships' messages concerning icebergs? Had there been time for lifeboat drill? Why do you suppose such drill had been neglected?

4. When there is a difference between what seems to be true and what is actually true, we sometimes call such a situation ironic. What was ironic about the Reverend Mr. Carter's choice of a hymn for his evening "sing-song"? Why did the author select the two lines from the hymn that are given on page 198?

5. In the minds of everyone aboard the *Titanic*, what seemed to be true that was actually not true? What attitude did all of the people share? What reassuring statement was repeated several times after the ship struck the iceberg?

6. What effect is produced by the repeated mention of time between 11:40 P.M. and 2:20 A.M.?

7. The name of the ship is significant. What is a titan? What does *titanic* mean? (Note: R.M.S. used before the ship's name means "Royal Mail Steamship.")

8. The author has selected the details that he wished to emphasize, and he has chosen these details with a purpose in mind. Do any of the following phrases come close to expressing the aim of this true narrative? What phrase would you use to describe the author's purpose?

    (a) The importance of ships and travelers being prepared for accidents

    (b) The terror of a disaster at sea

    (c) The insecurity of man's conquests over nature

APPRECIATING HEROISM

The following persons are mentioned in the account of the sinking of the *Titanic*. How was each one brave? What is the common element in their heroism? Which persons belong, in your opinion, on a special roll of honor? Why?

THE SHIP'S CREW

Captain E. C. Smith
Second Officer Lightoller
First Operator Phillips
Second Operator Harold Bride
Bandmaster Hartley
The engineers and stokers

THE PASSENGERS

Benjamin Guggenheim
Mrs. Isidor Straus
Colonel and Mrs. John Jacob Astor
Frank D. Millet, painter

COMPOSITION SUGGESTION

Write the story of a recent disaster that was reported fully in the news. Select a main impression around which to organize your narrative and choose details which contribute to that central impression.

ABOUT THE AUTHOR

Hanson W. Baldwin (1903–) was born in Baltimore, Maryland, where his father was managing editor for the Baltimore *Sun*. He attended Annapolis and worked as a cub reporter on the *Sun* before he joined the New York *Times* as military editor. Known as one of the best military analysts in the United States, Baldwin has a large audience for his sound discussions of complicated military strategy. In 1942 he won the Pulitzer prize in journalism for a series of articles about his visits to military bases in the South Pacific.

Recording a Disaster at Sea →

For understandable reasons, no one photographed the *Titanic* as she went down. The large picture on the opposite page is a scene from the motion picture *A Night to Remember*. The other pictures are actual photographs, taken several hours after the sinking. *Left*, a lifeboat from the *Titanic* is hoisted aboard the *Carpathia*. *Right center*, *Titanic* survivors rest on board the *Carpathia*. *Lower right*, crowds in New York anxiously await news of relatives and friends.

Kon-Tiki

THOR HEYERDAHL

"It can't be done," said the experts. "It will be done," said Thor Heyerdahl. He and his crew promptly launched their replica of a prehistoric raft and set out on a four-thousand-mile journey across the Pacific, risking death to prove an idea.

To the Norsemen of old the sea was the entry-way to unknown worlds. To the modern-day Viking, Thor Heyerdahl (tôr hī'ĕr·däl) the sea was a way to answer a puzzling question: Where had the Polynesians living on the islands in the Pacific come from?

Heyerdahl believed the first people had come to the islands on rafts from Peru. He pointed to the striking likeness between relics found on Easter Island in the South Pacific and the statues that the first Spanish explorers saw in Peru. The Inca Indians of Peru had also told the Spanish explorers tales of a race of white gods who had erected the monuments and then vanished westward across the Pacific. Their leader, reported the Incas, was called Kon-Tiki. Heyerdahl was sure that this chief-god, who had been driven out of Peru, was the same Tiki whom the Polynesians claimed as the founder of their race. Other scientists, however, did not believe that the four-thousand-mile trip could have been made by the little rafts the Peruvian people had used for fishing, and it was known that they had no other boats. Heyerdahl decided to make the voyage himself to show that a raft could ride the Humboldt Current across the Pacific.

Christened Kon-Tiki and bearing the sun-god's likeness upon the sail, an exact copy of the ancient craft of Peru was towed out of Callao Harbor, Peru. Aboard her were a Spanish-speaking parrot and six young Scandinavians. By the next day they were fifty miles from the coast of Peru, riding the Humboldt Current into the Pacific.

1

By the late afternoon the trade wind was already blowing at full strength. It quickly stirred up the ocean into roaring seas which swept against us from astern.[1] For the first time we fully realized that here was the sea itself come to meet us; it was bitter earnest now — our communications were cut. Whether things went well now would depend entirely on the balsa raft's good qualities in the open sea. We knew that, from now onward, we should never get another onshore wind [2] or chance of turning back. We were in the path of the real trade wind, and every day would carry us farther and farther out to sea. The only thing to do was to go ahead under full sail; if we tried to turn homeward, we should only drift farther out to sea stern first. There was only one possible course, to sail before the wind with our bow toward the sunset. And, after all, that was the object of our voyage — to follow the sun in its path as we thought Kon-Tiki and the old sun worshippers must have done when they were driven out to sea from Peru.

We noted with triumph and relief how the wooden raft rose up over the first threatening wave crests that came foaming toward us. But it was impossible for the steersman to hold the oar steady when the roaring seas rolled toward him and lifted the oar out of the tholepins,[3] or swept it to one side so that the steersman was swung round like a helpless acrobat. Not even two men at once could hold the oar steady when the seas rose against us and poured down over the steersmen aft. We hit on the idea of running ropes from the oar blade to each side of the raft; and with other ropes holding the oar in place in the tholepins it obtained a limited freedom of movement and could defy the worst seas if only we ourselves could hold on.

As the troughs of the sea gradually grew deeper, it became clear that we had moved into the swiftest part of the Humboldt Current. This sea [4] was obviously caused by a current and not simply raised by the wind. The water was green and cold and everywhere about us; the jagged mountains of Peru had vanished into the dense cloud banks astern. When darkness crept over the waters, our first duel with the elements began. We were still not sure of the sea; we were still uncertain whether it would show itself a friend or an enemy in the intimate proximity we ourselves had sought. When, swallowed up by the darkness, we heard the general noise from the sea around us suddenly deafened by the hiss of a roller close by and saw a white crest come groping toward us on a level with the cabin roof, we held on tight and waited uneasily to feel the masses of water smash down over us and the raft.

But every time there was the same surprise and relief. The *Kon-Tiki* calmly swung up her stern and rose skyward unperturbed, while the masses of water rolled along her sides. Then we sank down again into the trough of the waves and waited for the next big sea. The biggest seas often came two or three in succession, with a long series of smaller seas in between. It was when two big seas followed each other too closely that the second broke on board aft, because the first was still holding our bow in the air. It became, therefore, an unbreakable law that the steering watch must have ropes round their

[1] **astern:** behind.
[2] **onshore wind:** a wind blowing onto, or toward, the shore.
[3] **tholepins** (thōl'pĭnz'): wooden pegs against which the oar rested.

[4] **sea:** The author uses *sea* in the ordinary sense, as meaning "ocean," and in the nautical sense, as meaning "wave," or "surface motion caused by wind or currents." You can easily see which meaning is intended in each use of the word.

waists, the other ends of which were made fast to the raft, for there were no bulwarks. Their task was to keep the sail filled by holding stern to sea and wind.

We had made an old boat's compass fast to a box aft so that Erik could check our course and calculate our position and speed. For the time being it was uncertain where we were, for the sky was overclouded and the horizon one single chaos of rollers. Two men at a time took turns as steering watch and, side by side, they had to put all their strength into the fight with the leaping oar, while the rest of us tried to snatch a little sleep inside the open bamboo cabin.

When a really big sea came, the men at the helm left the steering to the ropes and, jumping up, hung on to a bamboo pole from the cabin roof, while the masses of water thundered in over them from astern and disappeared between the logs or over the side of the raft. Then they had to fling themselves at the oar again before the raft could turn round and the sail thrash about. For, if the raft took the seas at an angle, the waves could easily pour right into the bamboo cabin. When they came from astern, they disappeared between the projecting logs at once and seldom came so far forward as the cabin wall. The round logs astern let the water pass as if through the prongs of a fork. The advantage of a raft was obviously this: the more leaks the better. Through the gaps in our floor the water ran out but never in.

About midnight a ship's light passed in a northerly direction. At three, another passed on the same course. We waved our little kerosene lamp and hailed them with flashes from an electric torch, but they did not see us and the lights passed slowly northward

into the darkness and disappeared. Little did those on board realize that a real Inca raft lay close to them, tumbling among the waves. And just as little did we on board the raft realize that this was our last ship and the last trace of men we should see till we had reached the other side of the ocean.

We clung like flies, two and two, to the steering oar in the darkness and felt the fresh sea water pouring off our hair while the oar hit us till we were tender both behind and before and our hands grew stiff with the exertion of hanging on. We had a good schooling those first days and nights; it turned landlubbers into seamen. For the first twenty-four hours every man, in unbroken succession, had two hours at the helm and three hours' rest. We arranged that every hour a fresh man should relieve one of the two steersmen who had been at the helm for two hours.

Every single muscle in the body was strained to the uttermost throughout the watch to cope with the steering. When we were tired out with pushing the oar, we went over to the other side and pulled, and when arms and chest were sore with pressing, we turned our backs while the oar kneaded us green and blue in front and behind. When at last the relief came, we crept half-dazed into the bamboo cabin, tied a rope round our legs, and fell asleep with our salty clothes on before we could get into our sleeping bags. Almost at the same moment there came a brutal tug at the rope; three hours had passed, and one had to go out again and relieve one of the two men at the steering oar.

The next night was still worse; the seas grew higher instead of going down. Two hours on end of struggling with the steering oar was too long; a man was not much use in the second half of his watch, and the seas got the better of us and hurled us round and sideways, while the water poured on board. Then we changed over to one hour at the helm and an hour and a half's rest. So the first sixty hours passed, in one continuous struggle against a chaos of waves that rushed upon us, one after another, without cessation. High waves and low waves, pointed waves and round waves, slanting waves and waves on top of other waves.

On the third night the sea went down a bit, although it was still blowing hard. About four o'clock an unexpected deluge came foaming through the darkness and knocked the raft right round before the steersmen realized what was happening. The sail thrashed against the bamboo cabin and threatened to tear both the cabin and itself to pieces. All hands had to go on deck to secure the cargo and haul on sheets and stays in the hope of getting the raft on her right course again, so that the sail might fill and curve forward peacefully. But the raft would not right herself. She would go stern foremost, and that was all. The only result of all our hauling and pushing and rowing was that two men nearly went overboard in a sea when the sail caught them in the dark.

The sea had clearly become calmer. Stiff and sore, with skinned palms and sleepy eyes, we were not worth a row of beans. Better to save our strength in case the weather should call us out to a worse passage of arms. One could never know. So we furled the sail and rolled it round the bamboo yard.[1] The *Kon-Tiki* lay sideways on to the seas and took them like a cork. Everything on board was lashed fast, and all six of us crawled into the little bamboo cabin,

huddled together, and slept like mummies in a sardine can.

We little guessed that we had struggled through the hardest steering of the voyage. Not till we were far out on the ocean did we discover the Incas' simple and ingenious way of steering a raft.[2]

We did not wake till well on in the day, when the parrot began to whistle and halloo and dance to and fro on its perch. Outside the sea was still running high but in long, even ridges and not so wild and confused as the day before. The first thing we saw was that the sun was beating down on the yellow bamboo deck and giving the sea all around us a bright and friendly aspect. What did it matter if the seas foamed and rose high so long as they only left us in peace on the raft? What did it matter if they rose straight up in front of our noses when we knew that in a second the raft would go over the top and flatten out the foaming ridge like a steam roller, while the heavy threatening mountain of water only lifted us up in the air and rolled groaning and gurgling under the floor? The old masters from Peru knew what they were doing when they avoided a hollow hull which could fill with water, or a vessel so long that it would not take the waves one by one. A cork steam roller — that was what the balsa raft amounted to.

2

The cook's first duty, when he got up in the morning, was to go out on deck and collect all the flying fish that had landed on board in the course of the

[1] **yard:** the long pole fastened across the mast to support the sail.

[2] **Incas' . . . raft:** After several weeks at sea, the men discovered by accident that they could steer the raft by raising and lowering the centerboards. These extended underneath the raft about five feet into the water and served the general purpose of a keel.

night. There were usually half a dozen or more, and once we found twenty-six fat flying fish on the raft. Knut was much upset one morning because, when he was standing operating with the frying pan, a flying fish struck him on the hand instead of landing right in the cooking fat.

Our neighborly intimacy with the sea was not fully realized by Torstein till he woke one morning and found a sardine on his pillow. There was so little room in the cabin that Torstein had to lie with his head in the doorway, and, if anyone inadvertently trod on his face when going out at night, he bit him in the leg. He grasped the sardine by the tail and confided to it understandingly that all sardines had his entire sympathy. We conscientiously drew in our legs so that Torstein should have more room the next night, but then something happened which caused Torstein to find himself a sleeping place on top of all the kitchen utensils in the radio corner.

It was a few nights later. It was overcast and pitch dark, and Torstein had placed the kerosene lamp close by his head, so that the night watches could see where they were treading when they crept in and out over his head. About four o'clock Torstein was awakened by the lamp tumbling over and something cold and wet flapping about his ears. "Flying fish," he thought and felt for it in the darkness to throw it away. He caught hold of something long and wet, which wriggled like a snake, and let go as if he had burned himself. The unseen visitor twisted itself away and over to Herman, while Torstein tried to get the lamp lighted again. Herman started up, too, and this made me wake, thinking of the octopus which came up at night in these waters.

When we got the lamp lighted, Herman was sitting in triumph with his hand gripping the neck of a long thin fish which wriggled in his hands like an eel. The fish was over three feet long, as slender as a snake, with dull black eyes and a long snout with a greedy jaw full of long sharp teeth. The teeth were as sharp as knives and could be folded back into the roof of the mouth to make way for what was swallowed. Under Herman's grip a large-eyed white fish, abut eight inches long, was suddenly thrown up from the stomach and out of the mouth of the predatory fish, and soon after up came another like it. These were clearly two deepwater fish, much torn by the snakefish's teeth. The snakefish's thin skin was bluish violet on the back and steel blue underneath, and it came loose in flakes when we took hold of it.

Bengt, too, was awakened at last by all the noise, and we held the lamp and the long fish under his nose. He sat up drowsily in his sleeping bag and said solemnly: "No, fish like that don't exist."

With which he turned over quietly and fell asleep again.

Bengt was not far wrong. It appeared later that we six sitting round the lamp in the bamboo cabin were the first men to have seen this fish alive. Only the skeleton of a fish like this one had been found a few times on the coast of South America and the Galápagos Islands; [1] ichthyologists [2] called it *Gempylus*,[3] or snake mackerel, and thought it lived at the bottom of the sea at a great depth because no one had ever seen it alive. But, if it lived at a great depth, it must have done so by day when the sun

[1] **Galápagos** (gȧ·lä′pȧ·gŭs) **Islands:** a group of Pacific islands located on the equator far off the coast of South America.
[2] **ichthyologists** (ĭk′thĭ·ŏl′ô·jĭsts): scientists who study fish.
[3] *Gempylus* (jĕm·pī′lŭs).

blinded its big eyes. For on dark nights *Gempylus* was abroad high over the surface of the sea; we on the raft had experience of that.

The sea contains many surprises for him who has his floor on a level with the surface and drifts along slowly and noiselessly. A sportsman who breaks his way through the woods may come back and say that no wild life is to be seen. Another may sit down on a stump and wait, and often rustlings and cracklings will begin and curious eyes peer out. So it is on the sea, too. We usually plow across it with roaring engines and piston strokes, with the water foaming round our bow. Then we come back and say that there is nothing to see far out on the ocean.

Not a day passed but we, as we sat floating on the surface of the sea, were visited by inquisitive guests which wriggled and waggled about us, and a few of them, such as dolphins and pilot fish, grew so familiar that they accompanied the raft across the sea and kept round us day and night.

3

We gradually grew accustomed to having these subterranean or submarine creatures under the floor, but nevertheless we were just as surprised every time a new species appeared. About two o'clock on a cloudy night, when the man at the helm had difficulty in distinguishing black water from black sky, he caught sight of a faint illumination down in the water which slowly took the shape of a large animal. It was impossible to say whether it was plankton [1] shining on its body, or whether the animal itself had a phosphorescent

[1] **plankton** (plăngk'tŏn): masses of tiny animals and plants that drift near the ocean surface.

surface, but the glimmer down in the black water gave the ghostly creature obscure, wavering outlines. Sometimes it was roundish, sometimes oval, or triangular, and suddenly it split into two parts which swam to and fro under the raft independently of each other. Finally there were three of these large shining phantoms wandering round in slow circles under us.

They were real monsters, for the visible parts alone were some five fathoms long, and we all quickly collected on deck and followed the ghost dance. It went on for hour after hour, following the course of the raft. Mysterious and noiseless, our shining companions kept a good way beneath the surface, mostly on the starboard side where the light was, but often they were right under the raft or appeared on the port side. The glimmer of light on their backs revealed that the beasts were bigger than elephants; but they were not whales, for they never came up to breathe. Were they giant ray fish which changed shape when they turned over on their sides? They took no notice at all if we held the light right down on the surface to lure them up, so that we might see what kind of creatures they were. And, like all proper goblins and ghosts, they had sunk into the depths when the dawn began to break.

We never got a proper explanation of this nocturnal visit from the three shining monsters, unless the solution was afforded by another visit we received a day and a half later in the full midday sunshine. It was May 24, and we were lying drifting on a leisurely swell in exactly 95° west by 7° south. It was about noon, and we had thrown overboard the guts of two big dolphins we had caught earlier in the morning. I was having a refreshing plunge overboard at the bow, lying in the water but keeping a good lookout and hanging on to a rope end, when I caught sight of a thick brown fish, six feet long, which came swimming inquisitively toward me through the crystal-clear sea water. I hopped quickly up onto the edge of the raft and sat in the hot sun looking at the fish as it passed quietly, when I heard a wild war whoop from Knut, who was sitting aft behind the bamboo cabin. He bellowed "Shark!" till his voice cracked in a falsetto, and, as we had sharks swimming alongside the raft almost daily without creating such excitement, we all realized that this must be something extra special and flocked astern to Knut's assistance.

Knut had been squatting there, washing his pants in the swell, and when he looked up for a moment he was staring straight into the biggest and ugliest face any of us had ever seen in the whole of our lives. It was the head of a veritable sea monster, so huge and so hideous that, if the Old Man of the Sea himself had come up, he could not have made such an impression on us. The head was broad and flat like a frog's, with two small eyes right at the sides, and a toadlike jaw which was four or five feet wide and had long fringes drooping from the corners of the mouth. Behind the head was an enormous body ending in a long thin tail with a pointed tail fin which stood straight up and showed that this sea monster was not any kind of whale. The body looked brownish under the water, but both head and body were thickly covered with small white spots.

The monster came quietly, lazily swimming after us from astern. It grinned like a bulldog and lashed gently with its tail. The large round dorsal fin projected clear of the water and sometimes the tail fin as well, and, when the creature was in the trough of the swell, the water flowed about the broad back as though washing round a submerged reef. In front of the broad jaws swam a whole crowd of zebra-striped pilot fish in fan formation, and large remora fish [1] and other parasites sat firmly attached to the huge body and traveled with it through the water, so that the whole thing looked like a curious zoological collection crowded round something that resembled a floating deepwater reef.

A twenty-five pound dolphin, attached to six of our largest fishhooks, was hanging behind the raft as bait for sharks, and a swarm of the pilot fish shot straight off, nosed the dolphin without touching it, and then hurried back to their lord and master, the sea king. Like a mechanical monster it set its machinery going and came gliding at leisure toward the dolphin which lay, a beggarly trifle, before its jaws. We tried to pull the dolphin in, and the sea monster followed slowly, right up to the side of the raft. It did not open its mouth but just let the dolphin bump against it, as if to throw open the whole door for such an insignificant scrap was not worth while. When the giant came close up to the raft, it rubbed its back against the heavy steering oar, which was just lifted up out of the water, and now we had ample opportunity of studying the monster at the closest quarters — at such close quarters that I thought we had all gone mad, for we roared stupidly with laughter and shouted overexcitedly at the completely fantastic sight we saw. Walt Disney himself, with all his powers of imagination, could not have created a more hair-raising sea monster than that which thus suddenly lay with its terrific jaws along the raft's side.

[1] **remora** (rĕm′ô·rȧ) **fish:** fish that attach themselves by suction to other fish.

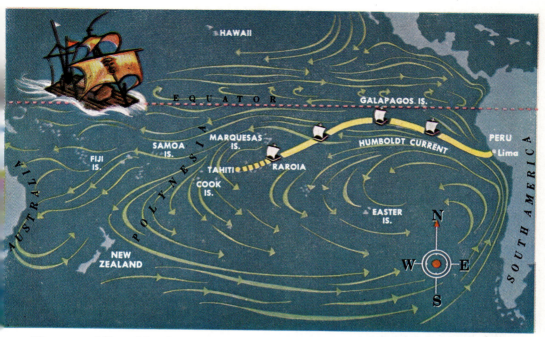

The course followed by the Kon-Tiki *expedition on its four-thousand-mile voyage across the Pacific.*

The monster was a whale shark, the largest shark and the largest fish known in the world today. It is exceedingly rare, but scattered specimens are observed here and there in the tropical oceans. The whale shark has an average length of fifty feet, and according to zoologists it weighs fifteen tons. It is said that large specimens can attain a length of sixty-five feet; one harpooned baby had a liver weighing six hundred pounds and a collection of three thousand teeth in each of its broad jaws.

Our monster was so large that, when it began to swim in circles round us and under the raft, its head was visible on one side while the whole of its tail stuck out on the other. And so incredibly grotesque, inert, and stupid did it appear when seen fullface that we could not help shouting with laughter, although we realized that it had strength enough in its tail to smash both balsa logs and ropes to pieces if it

attacked us. Again and again it described narrower and narrower circles just under the raft, while all we could do was to wait and see what might happen. When it appeared on the other side, it glided amiably under the steering oar and lifted it up in the air, while the oar blade slid along the creature's back.

We stood round the raft with hand harpoons ready for action, but they seemed to us like toothpicks in relation to the mammoth beast we had to deal with. There was no indication that the whale shark ever thought of leaving us again; it circled round us and followed like a faithful dog, close up to the raft. None of us had ever experienced or thought we should experience anything like it; the whole adventure, with the sea monster swimming behind and under the raft, seemed to us so completely unnatural that we could not really take it seriously.

In reality the whale shark went on encircling us for barely an hour, but to us the visit seemed to last a whole day. At last it became too exciting for Erik, who was standing at a corner of the raft with an eight-foot hand harpoon, and, encouraged by ill-considered shouts, he raised the harpoon above his head. As the whale shark came gliding slowly toward him and its broad head moved right under the corner of the raft, Erik thrust the harpoon with all his giant strength down between his legs and deep into the whale shark's grisly head. It was a second or two before the giant understood properly what was happening. Then in a flash the placid half-wit was transformed into a mountain of steel muscles.

We heard a swishing noise as the harpoon line rushed over the edge of the raft and saw a cascade of water as the giant stood on its head and plunged down into the depths. The three men who were standing nearest were flung about the place, head over heels, and two of them were flayed and burned by the line as it rushed through the air. The thick line, strong enough to hold a boat, was caught up on the side of the raft but snapped at once like a piece of twine, and a few seconds later a broken-off harpoon shaft came up to the surface two hundred yards away. A shoal of frightened pilot fish shot off through the water in a desperate attempt to keep up with their old lord and master. We waited a long time for the monster to come racing back like an infuriated submarine, but we never saw anything more of him.

4

[Week after week, across the vast expanse of the Pacific, the Kon-Tiki moved westward toward the Polynesian islands; but the voyagers were destined to have two tantalizing glimpses of land before they actually stepped onto dry earth again. First, after ninety-three days afloat, the mariners sighted an island in the Tuamotu group,[1] but were unable, because of winds and currents, to steer the raft to it. Then, on their ninety-seventh day at sea, the men found their craft near a jagged reef beyond which lay the island of Angatau. With the help of curious and excited natives, who swarmed out in outrigger canoes, the crew tried to maneuver the Kon-Tiki through an opening in the reef; but again wind and current defeated them. After drifting for three more days near dangerous reefs and submerged shoals, the men made plans for possible shipwreck, and decided to stay on the raft at all costs. Finally, on the one-hundred-and-first day at sea, the Kon-Tiki was carried toward a coral reef and inevitable destruction.]

On board the Kon-Tiki all preparations for the end of the voyage were being made. Everything of value was carried into the cabin and lashed fast. Documents and papers were packed into watertight bags, along with films and other things which would not stand a dip in the sea. The whole bamboo cabin was covered with canvas, and especially strong ropes were lashed across it. When we saw that all hope was gone, we opened up the bamboo deck and cut off with machete knives [2] all the ropes which held the centerboards down. It was a hard job to get the centerboards drawn up, because they were all thickly covered with stout barnacles. With the centerboards up the draught [3] of our vessel was no deeper than to the bottom of the timber logs, and we would therefore be more easily washed

[1] **Tuamotu** (tōō′ä·mō′tōō) **group:** a group of about eighty small Polynesian islands.
[2] **machete** (mä·chā′tå) **knives:** large, heavy knives generally used to cut thick stalks.
[3] **draught** (draft): the depth at which a ship rests in the water.

in over the reef. With no centerboards and with the sail down, the raft lay completely sideways on and was entirely at the mercy of wind and sea.

We tied the longest rope we had to the homemade anchor and made it fast to the step of the port mast, so that the *Kon-Tiki* would go into the surf stern first when the anchor was thrown overboard. The anchor itself consisted of empty water cans filled with used radio batteries and heavy scrap, and solid mangrove-wood sticks projected from it, set crosswise.

Order number one, which came first and last, was: Hold on to the raft! Whatever happened, we must hang on tight on board and let the nine great logs take the pressure from the reef. We ourselves had more than enough to do to withstand the weight of the water. If we jumped overboard, we should become helpless victims of the suction which would fling us in and out over the sharp corals. The rubber raft would capsize in the steep seas or, heavily loaded with us in it, it would be torn to ribbons against the reef. But the wooden logs would sooner or later be cast ashore, and we with them, if we only managed to hold fast.

Next, all hands were told to put on their shoes for the first time in a hundred days and to have their life belts ready. The last precaution, however, was not of much value, for if a man fell overboard he would be battered to death, not drowned. We had time, too, to put our passports and such few dollars as we had left into our pockets. But it was not lack of time that was troubling us.

Those were anxious hours in which we lay drifting helplessly sideways, step after step, in toward the reef. It was noticeably quiet on board; we all crept in and out from cabin to bamboo deck, silent or laconic, and carried on with our jobs. Our serious faces showed that no one was in doubt as to what awaited us, and the absence of nervousness showed that we had all gradually acquired an unshakable confidence in the raft. If it had brought us across the sea, it would also manage to bring us ashore alive.

Inside the cabin there was a complete chaos of provision cartons and cargo, lashed fast. Torstein had barely found room for himself in the radio corner, where we had got the short-wave transmitter working. We were now over 4,000 sea miles [1] from our old base at Callao, where the Peruvian Naval War School had maintained regular contact with us, and still farther from Hal and Frank and the other radio amateurs in the United States. But, as chance willed, we had on the previous day got in touch with a capable radio "ham" who had a set on Rarotonga [2] in the Cook Islands, and the operators, quite contrary to our usual practice, had arranged for an extra contact with him early in the morning. All the time we were drifting closer and closer in to the reef, Torstein was sitting tapping his key and calling Rarotonga.

Entries in the *Kon-Tiki's* log ran:

8:15: We are slowly approaching land. We can now make out with the naked eye the separate palm trees inside on the starboard side.

8:45: The wind has veered into a still more unfavorable quarter for us, so we have no hope of getting clear. No nervousness on board, but hectic preparations on deck. There is something lying on the reef ahead of us which looks like the wreck of a sailing vessel, but it may be only a heap of driftwood.

---

[1] **sea miles:** A nautical mile is roughly 6,080 feet; that is, about 800 feet more than our statute mile of 5,280 feet.

[2] **Rarotonga** (răr'ŏ·tŏng'gȧ).

The Kon-Tiki flies all of her flags as the raft nears the island of Angatau. The men tried to land here, but the coral reef and the strong winds made it impossible.

9:45: *The wind is taking us straight toward the last island but one we see behind the reef. We can now see the whole coral reef clearly; here it is built up like a white and red speckled wall which barely sticks up out of the water as a belt in front of all the islands. All along the reef white foaming surf is flung up toward the sky. Bengt is just serving up a good hot meal, the last before the great action!*

It is a wreck lying in there on the reef. We are so close now that we can see right across the shining lagoon behind the reef and see the outlines of other islands on the other side of the lagoon.

As this was written, the dull drone of the surf came near again; it came from the whole reef and filled the air like thrilling rolls of the drum, heralding the exciting last act of the *Kon-Tiki.*

9:50: *Very close now. Drifting along the reef. Only a hundred yards or so away. Torstein is talking to the man on Rarotonga. All clear. Must pack up log now. All in good spirits; it looks bad,* BUT WE SHALL MAKE IT!

A few minutes later the anchor rushed overboard and caught hold of the bottom, so that the *Kon-Tiki* swung around and turned her stern inward toward the breakers. It held us for a few valuable minutes, while Torstein sat hammering like mad on the key. He had got Rarotonga now. The breakers thundered in the air, and the sea rose and fell furiously. All hands were at work on deck, and now Torstein got his message through. He said we were drifting toward the Raroia reef.[1] He asked Rarotonga to listen in on the

[1] **Raroia** (răr-ō′yȧ) **reef:** a coral reef in the South Pacific. It is about twenty-five miles long and encircles a lagoon containing several small, uninhabited islands.

same wave length every hour. If we were silent for more than thirty-six hours, Rarotonga must let the Norwegian Embassy in Washington know. Torstein's last words were:

"O.K. Fifty yards left. Here we go. Good-by."

Then he closed down the station, Knut sealed up the papers, and both crawled out on deck as fast as they could to join the rest of us, for it was clear now that the anchor was giving way.

The swell grew heavier and heavier, with deep troughs between the waves, and we felt the raft being swung up and down, up and down, higher and higher. Again the order was shouted: "Hold on, never mind about the cargo, hold on!"

We were now so near the waterfall inside that we no longer heard the steady continuous roar from all along the reef. We now heard only a separate boom each time the nearest breaker crashed down on the rocks.

All hands stood in readiness, each clinging fast to the rope he thought the most secure. Only Erik crept into the cabin at the last moment; there was one part of the program he had not yet carried out — he had not found his shoes!

No one stood aft, for it was there the shock from the reef would come. Nor were the two firm stays which ran from the masthead down to the stern safe. For if the mast fell they would be left hanging overboard, over the reef. Herman, Bengt, and Torstein had climbed up on some boxes which were lashed fast forward of the cabin wall, and, while Herman clung on to the guy ropes from the ridge of the roof, the other two held on to the ropes from the masthead by which the sail at other times was hauled up. Knut and I chose the stay running from the bow up to the masthead, for, if mast and cabin and everything else went overboard, we thought the rope from the bow would nevertheless remain lying inboard, as we were now head on to the seas.

When we realized that the seas had got hold of us, the anchor rope was cut and we were off. A sea rose straight up under us, and we felt the *Kon-Tiki* being lifted up in the air. The great moment had come; we were riding on the wave back at breathless speed, our ramshackle craft creaking and groaning as she quivered under us. The excitement made one's blood boil. I remember that, having no other inspiration, I waved my arm and bellowed "Hurrah!" at the top of my lungs; it afforded a certain relief and could do no harm anyway. The others certainly thought I had gone mad, but they all beamed and grinned enthusiastically. On we ran with the seas rushing in behind us; this was the *Kon-Tiki's* baptism of fire. All must and would go well.

But our elation was soon dampened. A new sea rose high up astern of us like a glittering, green glass wall. As we sank down, it came rolling after us, and, in the same second in which I saw it high above me, I felt a violent blow and was submerged under floods of water. I felt the suction through my whole body with such great power that I had to strain every single muscle in my frame and think of one thing only — hold on, hold on! I think that in such a desperate situation the arms will be torn off before the brain consents to let go, evident as the outcome is. Then I felt that the mountain of water was passing on and relaxing its devilish grip of my body. When the whole mountain had rushed on, with an ear-splitting roaring and crashing, I saw Knut again hanging on beside me, doubled up into a ball. Seen from behind, the great sea was almost flat and gray. As it rushed on, it swept over the ridge of the cabin roof which projected from the water, and there hung the three others, pressed against the cabin roof as the water passed over them.

We were still afloat.

In an instant I renewed my hold, with arms and legs bent round the strong rope. Knut let himself down and with a tiger's leap joined the others on the boxes, where the cabin took the strain. I heard reassuring exclamations from them, but at the same time I saw a new green wall rise up and come towering toward us. I shouted a warning and made myself as small and hard as I could where I hung. In an instant hell was over us again, and the *Kon-Tiki* disappeared completely under the masses of water. The sea tugged and pulled with all the force it could bring to bear at the poor little bundles of human bodies. The second sea rushed over us, to be followed by a third like it.

Then I heard a triumphant shout from Knut, who was now hanging on to the rope ladder:

"Look at the raft — she's holding!"

After three seas only the double mast and the cabin had been knocked a bit crooked. Again we had a feeling of triumph over the elements, and the elation of victory gave us new strength.

Then I saw the next sea come towering up, higher than all the rest, and again I bellowed a warning aft to the others as I climbed up the stay, as high as I could get in a hurry, and hung on fast. Then I myself disappeared sideways into the midst of the green wall which towered high over us. The others, who were farther aft and saw me disappear first, estimated the height of the wall of water at twenty-five feet, while the foaming crest passed by fifteen feet above the part of the glassy wall into which I had vanished. Then the great wave reached them, and we had all one single thought — hold on, hold on, hold, hold, hold!

We must have hit the reef that time. I myself felt only the strain on the stay, which seemed to bend and slacken jerkily. But whether the bumps came from above or below I could not tell, hanging there. The whole submersion lasted only seconds, but it demanded more endurance than we usually have in our bodies. There is greater strength in the human mechanism than that of the muscles alone. I determined that, if I was to die, I would die in this position, like a knot on the stay. The sea thundered on, over and past, and as it roared by, it revealed a hideous sight. The *Kon-Tiki* was wholly changed, as by the stroke of a magic wand. The vessel we knew from weeks and months at sea was no more; in a few seconds our pleasant world had become a shattered wreck.

5

[From the wrecked *Kon-Tiki*, dashed over the reef and stranded on a great rock, the men salvaged everything they could carry and waded to a small island in the peaceful lagoon within the reef.]

I shall never forget that wade across the reef toward the heavenly palm island that grew larger as it came to meet us. When I reached the sunny sand beach, I slipped off my shoes and thrust my bare toes down into the warm, bone-dry sand. It was as though I enjoyed the sight of every footprint which dug itself into the virgin sand beach that led up to the palm trunks. Soon the palm tops closed over my

Sailing with
the Kon-Tiki

These photographs were taken on the 1947 *Kon-Tiki* expedition. *Above left*, crew members examine a day's catch, which included nine sharks. *Above right*, a hardy sailor lands a shark with his bare hands. *Right*, after being wrecked, the raft washes higher up onto Raroia reef. *Below*, Thor Heyerdahl and other members of the expedition pose informally.

Left to right: *Knut Haugland, Bengt Danielsson, Thor Heyerdahl, Erik Hesselberg, Torstein Raaby, Herman Watzinger.*

head, and I went on, right in toward the center of the tiny island. Green coconuts hung under the palm tufts, and some luxuriant bushes were thickly covered with snow-white blossoms, which smelled so sweet and seductive that I felt quite faint. In the interior of the island two quite tame terns flew about my shoulders. They were as white and light as wisps of cloud. Small lizards shot away from my feet, and the most important inhabitants of the island were large blood-red hermit crabs which lumbered along in every direction with stolen snail shells as large as eggs adhering to their soft hinder parts.

I was completely overwhelmed. I sank down on my knees and thrust my fingers deep down into the dry warm sand.

DRAWING CONCLUSIONS

1. Do you think Heyerdahl proved that the Polynesians came originally from Peru? Why or why not? If you do not accept his theory, what added proof do you feel is necessary?

2. What value did the voyage have beyond supplying evidence to support Heyerdahl's theory of the origin of the Polynesian people?

3. What qualities of the men contributed to making the voyage a successful one? What experience during the first few days of the voyage "turned landlubbers into seamen"?

4. What made Heyerdahl say that the sea has many surprises for anyone who is level with its surface? What were the factors about the raft that encouraged "guests"?

5. Dr. Kenneth Emory, noted anthropologist at the Bishop Museum in Honolulu, does not accept Heyerdahl's theory that the Polynesian people who live in the South Seas came from South America. Emory and his staff excavated throughout the South Sea Islands, finding fishhooks and tools which supported their theory that the peoples of the South Seas came from Asia. How could tools tell Dr. Emory anything about history? Is it *possible* that science might prove both Heyerdahl and Emory correct? What is the likelihood that it might prove both of them wrong?

GAINING POWER OVER WORDS

FIGURES OF SPEECH Heyerdahl uses a great many imaginative comparisons to make the scene vivid to the reader. What does he mean when he calls the raft "a cork steam roller"? What is he emphasizing when he writes that the crew "huddled together, and slept like mummies in a sardine can"? Find other examples of effective comparisons and share them with the class.

VIVID DESCRIPTIONS The author also chooses words which have a definite impact. He speaks of the water "groaning and gurgling under the floor" and of the sea which "tugged and pulled . . . at the poor little bundles of human bodies." Find other passages which seem to you particularly vivid because of the choice of words.

ABOUT THE AUTHOR

Thor Heyerdahl (1914–   ) had a scientific museum and laboratory of his own when he was seven. Even at that age he was leading neighborhood boys on expeditions into the forests and along the beaches near Larvik, Norway, where he was born. Later he attended the University of Oslo, and at twenty-two was sent on his first field expedition to the Marquesas Islands in the South Pacific. During his year on a small isolated island, Heyerdahl noticed prehistoric rock carvings much like those found in South America. He returned to Europe to do research on his theory that the Polynesians might have come to the Pacific islands from South America rather than from Asia, as is commonly believed. His theory later led to the remarkable trip across the Pacific Ocean described in this selection from *Kon-Tiki*. The story of his voyage has been published in more than fifty languages. Heyerdahl's recent book, *Aku-Aku*, relates his adventures during a year-long expedition to Easter Island, where he studied the mysterious stone images found on that island.

Speaking of True Narratives

The term *true narrative* tells only the barest fact about a selection — that it is about real events and actual people. True narratives vary in style, point of view, and purpose.

A narrative may be informal and sprightly, like *"Kon-Tiki,"* which is told in the first person:

"I hopped quickly up onto the edge of the raft and sat in the hot sun looking at the fish as it passed quietly, when I heard a wild war whoop from Knut, who was sitting aft behind the bamboo cabin. He bellowed 'Shark!' till his voice cracked in a falsetto . . ."

A narrative may be more restrained, like "Victory on Everest," which is told in the third person:

"But it was this way or no way, and slowly the two men attacked the last four hundred feet of the mountain-top . . . On their left — the west — black precipices fell sheer to the distant cwm and icefall."

The narrative may shift subtly back and forth from artistic distance to the dramatic present, like a television camera moving in at the right moment for a close-up and then withdrawing again. Note the four stages in "R.M.S. *Titanic*":

(*Opening, like a frame for the picture or drama.*) "The White Star liner *Titanic*, largest ship the world had ever known, sailed from Southampton on her maiden voyage to New York on April 10, 1912."

(*Soon the camera moves closer.*) "Dinner that night in the Jacobean dining room was gay. It was bitter on deck, but the night was calm and fine; the sky was moonless but studded with stars twinkling coldly in the clear air. . . . In the crow's-nest Lookout Frederick Fleet

and his partner, Leigh, gaze down at the water, still and unruffled in the dim starlit darkness."

(*Now the camera moves in for a close-up; the author uses the dramatic present; the reader feels immediately present.*) "Major Butt helps women into the last boats and waves good-by to them. Mrs. Straus puts her foot on the gunwale of a lifeboat, then she draws back and goes to her husband. 'We have been together many years; where you go I will go.' "

(*The narrative returns to the original frame, the artistic distance of the opening.*) "Thus ended the maiden voyage of the *Titanic*. The lifeboats brought to New York by the *Carpathia*, a few deck chairs and gratings awash in the ice field off the Grand Banks eight hundred miles from shore, were all that was left of the world's greatest ship."

As you read a true narrative, think about the author's point of view and style. Determine whether he is writing in the first or third person. Then see whether his treatment of the subject is informal or formal, whether he seems to be close to his subject or to be describing it from a distance. Also notice whether the writer injects his own feelings and interpretations or simply gives a factual account of something that happened.

As you consider these matters of style, you will want to think about the related matter of the author's purpose. Usually a writer has more than one purpose, as in *Kon-Tiki*, where Thor Heyerdahl describes a thrilling personal adventure and, at the same time, tells the world about his theories and his findings. Each time you read a true narrative, try to determine the author's reasons for writing about a particular experience or event.

Articles

Every month in magazines throughout the world, thousands of articles appear in languages ranging from Albanian to Urdu. These brief but complete compositions usually present information, or discuss current problems and ideas. Most articles are written without conscious attempts to evoke the imaginative power of literature that one finds in fiction, drama, and poetry. Nevertheless, they have another kind of power — one that comes from their being rooted in the living puzzles and trends that most affect peoples' minds and lives.

In this section you will find three articles from three separate American magazines. These three have been chosen to represent this type of nonfiction because their lively topics are of more than passing interest. All three articles show man searching for truth in special areas of knowledge. They also show that a modern magazine article can be an example of good, clear, informational writing.

The Riddle of
the Kensington Stone

THOMAS R. HENRY

Found on a Minnesota farm, the Kensington stone tells of forty young Vikings in the middle of North America more than a hundred years before Columbus sailed. Is this stone a devilishly clever hoax or the luckiest find in American history? Here is an intriguing mystery with circumstantial evidence enough to challenge the wisest and most painstaking of detectives.

A CHALLENGING PUZZLE confronts American historians. Did a Norwegian knight named Paul Knutson lead an ill-fated band of forty armored soldier-missionaries to the headwaters of the Red River in West Central Minnesota 130 years before the first voyage of Columbus? Evidence of such an expedition, accumulating through half a century, is now so substantial that some of this country's foremost archaeologists consider the case nearly proved. A few hard facts jut like mountain crags out of the clouds of New World antiquity.

The first of these facts: Late in the autumn of 1354 King Magnus Erikson, first ruler of the combined realms of Norway and Sweden, commissioned Knutson, a "law speaker" — or judge — and one of the most prominent men of his court, to recruit an expedition to rescue the souls of a vanished Norwegian colony on the west coast of Greenland. Presumably the party sailed early the next spring. It was never heard of again.

The second fact: Fifty years ago a stone slab was found clutched in the roots of a tree by a Swedish homesteader near Kensington, Minnesota. It bore what purported to be a message to posterity, carved in runic letters.[1] It recorded an Indian massacre of a group of explorers. Assuming the relic is genuine, these explorers must have been members of Knutson's expedition. The inscription's date was 1362.

The third fact: The slab has been placed in the great hall of the Smithsonian Institution,[2] in Washington. Dr. Matthew W. Stirling, chief of the Government's Bureau of American Ethnology,[3] called it "probably the most important archaeological object yet found in North America."

When it was first discovered, the stone was denounced generally as a naïve fraud. In the half century that has elapsed since its discovery, the major objections have been met with corroborating evidence. For more than ten years, discarded and discredited by

[1] **runic** (rōō′nĭk) **letters:** letters in an early alphabet used by Germanic and Norse peoples.
[2] The real stone was loaned to the Smithsonian. Since the writing of this article, it has been returned to the Chamber of Commerce in Alexandria, Minnesota, and a replica has been placed in the Smithsonian.
[3] **ethnology** (ĕth-nŏl′ō-jĭ): science dealing with the races of man — their origin, distribution, similarities, and differences.

scholars, the relic had been a flagstone in a farmer's muddy barnyard. The very features which once caused experts to denounce it are now cited as bearing witness to its genuineness.

Doubters remain. Possibly they will ultimately be proved right. The Smithsonian authorities will not risk their reputations on an official pronouncement. They only voice their private convictions, subject to change with new evidence. The case for the genuineness of this Kensington stone is entirely circumstantial — but many a murderer has been convicted on less convincing circumstances. There is a high probability, the archaeologists say, that a man whom hardly one American in a million ever heard of before was the first of the white race to make a systematic exploration of North America. It was only by chance that, a few years ago, scholars got a clue to his identity. But now there is a slim possibility that the case for the affirmative may be made overwhelming by the finding of skulls or other remains of Knutson's massacred men.

Nobody wants to rob Columbus of any of his glory. But nobody doubts any more that white men — very likely hundreds of them — preceded him in the New World. Even before the Norse colonies in Greenland at the end of the tenth century, if one is to heed legends which must have grown from some grains of fact, came the Irish, the

---

The Ways of the Scientist. Recognizing the possible significance of the Kensington stone, the Smithsonian Institution in Washington, D. C., has examined it but takes no position on its authenticity. The scientists at the Smithsonian know the importance of testing a theory, of weighing all the available evidence and then asking, "Is the evidence adequate to bear out the

theory?" When there is no clear answer to this question, the true scientist is not at all disturbed at suspending his judgment. He will continue to study and to search for new evidence.

In this article you have an opportunity to test your own ability as a scientific thinker. As you read the article, weigh all the evidence carefully.

Welsh and the Bretons.[1] Centuries before Christ, those far-wandering seafarers, the Phoenicians, may have made landfalls across the Atlantic from the Azores.

But all these are very evanescent [2] specters in the dawn mists of history. They were illiterate sailors and fishermen in a letterless age. It was quite different with Paul Knutson. He was a scholar and a gentleman. He set out on a planned, well-equipped, well-financed voyage of exploration.

The whole case rests, of course, on the authenticity of this blue-gray slab which the highly conservative Smithsonian has just placed among its greatest treasures. It was back in the summer of 1898 that Olaf Ohman, young Swedish immigrant and homesteader near the village of Kensington, in Douglas County, Minnesota, grubbed up the stump of an aspen tree at the edge of a marsh. Clutched in its roots was a flat, gravestone-shaped piece of graywacke, one of the hard glacial sandstone rocks of the region. It was about the size of a headstone in a Swedish country cemetery. Carved on one face and one edge of this slab were strange letters.

All this had no meaning and little interest to Farmer Ohman. He was a stolid, unimaginative man. The character of Ohman is significant in the effort to validate the relic. The circumstances of the stone's discovery are recorded in a sworn affidavit which Ohman made before a local justice of the peace. If Ohman had been a glib talker or student of history — especially if he ever had tried to make any money out of his find — there might be grounds for suspicion. But he was the kind of man who had no inclination — and even less capacity — to perpetrate a fraud.

He told some neighbors about the queer stone. At their suggestion he delivered it to the local bank on his next trip to the county seat for supplies. The banker had a keen interest in local antiquities, and he, in turn, sent the relic to the University of Minnesota, at Minneapolis. There Prof. O. J. Breda, one of the foremost Scandinavian scholars in America, found little difficulty in deciphering most of the inscription. The letters were Norse runes, the curious first alphabet of the Germanic peoples derived in some roundabout way from the letters of the Greeks and Romans. Some of these symbols meant nothing to Breda. In his translation, he left blank spaces where they occurred. It now is known that they represented numbers.

This is the translation, as now accepted: [3]

[We are] 8 Goths [Swedes] and 22 Norwegians on [an] exploration journey from Vinland through [or across] the West. We had camp by [a lake with] two skerries [rocky islands] one day's journey north from this stone. We were [out] and fished one day. After we came home [we] found 10 [of our] men red with blood and dead. AV[e] M[aria], Save [us] from evil. [We] have 10 of [our party] by the sea to look after our ships [or ship] 14 days' journey from this island. Year 1362.

Professor Breda was not at all impressed. It was such an obvious hoax, he said, that it was not worthy of further attention from anybody. The language itself was a dead giveaway. It

---

[1] **Bretons** (brĕt′ŭnz): natives of Brittany, a region in France.

[2] **evanescent** (ĕv′a·nĕs′ĕnt): fleeting.

[3] The material in brackets has evidently been inserted to help clarify the shorthand of the runes.

was a mixture of Norwegian, Swedish and what looked like Old English. In the days of runic writings Swedes and Norwegians had been bitter enemies, and it was incredible that they could have been partners on an expedition. The three letters AVM were Latin, not runic. The Roman alphabet had not been introduced into Scandinavia until early in the Middle Ages.

The learned runologist missed the date — 1362. The figures representing it were not in the early runic alphabet. Breda quite naturally assumed that any Norsemen who could have reached central Minnesota must have come from the Greenland colonies of Eric the Red sometime in the twelfth century. There was no room here for any argument. The Kensington stone could not have been carved by any such Greenlander. It was all a crude and silly fraud perpetrated by somebody with a superficial knowledge of runes together with a gross ignorance of Scandinavian history. The hoaxer, whoever he was, hardly could have expected to be taken seriously. He had said that the stone was carved on an island in a lake. There was no lake within twenty miles of Ohman's homestead.

Nevertheless, the relic was sent to Northwestern University, at Evanston, Illinois, for a further check by runic experts. They agreed with Breda, and the slab was sent back to the county bank, which returned it to Farmer Ohman.

It was rectangular in shape, thirty-one by sixteen by six inches, and weighed about one hundred pounds. The bottom was tapered, as if it had been intended to set the stone upright in the ground. It just about fitted a muddy spot in the farmer's barnyard. He put it there, fortunately leaving the face

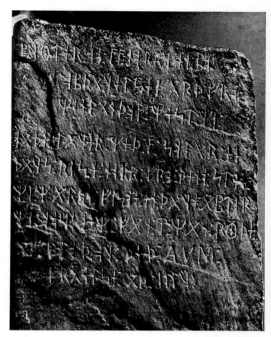

The Kensington stone.

bearing the inscriptions downward so that they were preserved from injury.

What is "probably the most important archaeological object yet found in North America" very likely still would be in that barnyard had it not been for the interest of a Norse-American historian, Hjalmar R. Holand of Ephraim, Wisconsin. For thirty years he has given most of his spare time to its study in every aspect — geological, archaeological, geographic, linguistic and historical. He has taken it to twenty-three European universities for consultation with experts. One after another, the most serious objections to its authenticity have proved the strongest points in its favor. First was the discovery of the meanings of the runic number symbols and the determination of the date. These particular runes were of late origin and local usage in Norway. In the fourteenth century the

Latin alphabet had been introduced, and its letters were intermingled quite often with the ancient Germanic symbols. That disposed of the apparent incongruity of the Roman letters AVM for AV(e) M(aria). This was a well-understood symbol, easy to write. It would have required a lot of space to have produced it in runes.

The biggest break, however, came with the publication in a Danish archaeological journal of a copy, found by chance in the royal library at Copenhagen, of King Magnus' order to Knutson. It was translated as follows:

Magnus, by the grace of God king of Norway, Sweden and Skane,[1] sends to all men who see or hear this letter good health and happiness.

We desire to make known that you, [Paul Knutson], are to take the men who are to go in the Knorr [the royal trading vessel] whether they be named or not named, from my bodyguard and also from among the retainers of other men whom you may wish to take on the voyage, and that Paul Knutson, who shall be the commandant upon the Knorr, shall have full authority to select the men who are best suited either as officers or men. We ask you to accept this, our command, with a right good will for the cause, inasmuch as we do it for the honor of God and for the sake of our soul, and for the sake of our predecessors, who in Greenland established Christianity and have maintained it to this time, and we will not let it perish in our days. Know this for truth, that whoever defies this, our command, shall meet with our serious displeasure and thereupon receive full punishment.

Executed at Bergen, Monday after

Simon and Judah's day in the six and XXX year of our reign (1354). By Orm Ostenson, our regent, sealed.

Thus it was established that a few years before the date found on the Kensington stone a certain Paul Knutson, one of the most prominent citizens of Magnus' kingdom, had been ordered to recruit and lead an expedition across the Atlantic. Certainly, no hoaxer of the nineteenth century could have known this. The date on the stone, eight years after the issuance of the order, would have been a remarkable coincidence with history. Eight years was a reasonable time to have allowed Knutson to have come from Bergen to the headwaters of the Red River.

King Magnus Erikson was a fanatical evangelist. He already had led one crusade to convert Russia, by the sword, to the Church of Rome. At the time the order to Knutson was written he was petitioning the Pope to sanction a second crusade into Muscovy.[2] He had set aside tithes of the churches of Scandinavia to finance such enterprises. He had built up in his court an elite bodyguard of the most promising youths of the Norwegian and Swedish nobilities — "a sort of fourteenth-century SS,"[3] one Smithsonian ethnologist describes it. This elite guard included many from the province of Gottland — hence "Goths." It was from this picked group of knights and esquires that Paul Knutson was ordered to recruit the personnel of his expedition.

Six years before, King Magnus had received distressful tidings — the first word in more than half a century from

---

[1] **Skane** (skô′nĕ): a region in southern Sweden, once a kingdom by itself.

[2] **Muscovy** (mŭs′kô·vĭ): the name for ancient Russia, then a much smaller area.

[3] **SS**: short for *Schutzstaffel* (shōōts′shtä′-fĕl); Adolph Hitler's bodyguard, part of the regular German army during World War II.

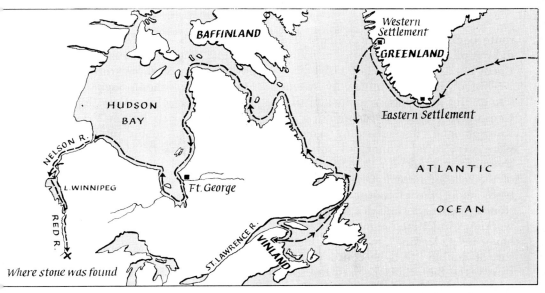

Paul Knutson's expedition may have followed this route in search of the lost colony.

the Norse colony of Vesterbygd, established almost four hundred years before on the west coast of Greenland by Eric the Red. News had come to Iceland that the homes had been abandoned and that the cattle had run wild in the fields. Apparently the whole settlement had left in a body, perhaps because of pressure from hostile Eskimos. There was a high probability that they had moved southwestward to Leif the Lucky's long-abandoned Vinland, the old Viking settlement on the New England coast, near Cape Cod. His lost subjects, the king feared, would be cut off from all religion and their souls doomed.

There can hardly be any question but that the crusade left Norway.[1] Presumably, Knutson, guided by vague descriptions in the Icelandic sagas, proceeded to some point on the New England coast, established a base camp, and made a systematic search for the

lost colony. Failing to find any trace of the Greenlanders, he must have turned northward with a considerable number of his party — perhaps leaving a small rear guard in what is now Massachusetts or Rhode Island — and finally sailed into the iceberg-filled Hudson Bay. Still there was no trace of the men he sought. And very likely his instructions from King Magnus had been quite peremptory:[2] If you don't find them you needn't come back.

He came to the mouth of the great Nelson River, followed it southward to Lake Winnipeg, and thence by a series of lakes and portages to the Red River country, whose waters flow into the Mississippi and the Gulf of Mexico. Even today there is an almost continuous waterway from the ice-filled sea to the Minnesota lakeland where the Kensington stone was found. This, the explorer probably thought, would have been a natural route from Greenland for the lost colonists. He may have thought he was following the easiest

[1] In this paragraph and the next, the author is presenting historian Holand's tentative reconstruction of what happened. The map above is based on Holand's theory.

[2] **peremptory** (pĕr-ĕmp'tô-rĭ): positive.

route back to his base in Vinland. He did not picture North America as a continent but as a group of large islands.

This, of course, is all highly speculative. But one fact remains: If the Kensington stone is genuine, Paul Knutson and his crusading knights were in Central Minnesota in 1362. Evidence increases for the authenticity of the relic. If Farmer Ohman told the truth about the circumstances of the stone's discovery — and this stolid, hardworking, unlettered immigrant must have been leading an extraordinary sort of double life if he concocted the story — the tablet had been in the spot where he found it for at least as long as the aspen tree had been growing. Archaeologists have a reasonably accurate means of dating trees and timbers from the rings in the wood; examination of similar trees in the neighborhood has led to the conservative assumption that the tree in whose roots the rune stone was found was at least forty years old in 1898. This means that, if the relic had been "planted," the attempted deception must have taken place in the 1850's. There were then few white men in that part of Minnesota. It was inhabited by savage and hostile Sioux.

The conglomeration [1] of languages alone was enough to convince Professor Breda that the stone was a fake. But he was thinking in terms of the language of the sagas in which had been related the exploits of Eric the Red and Leif the Lucky. This stone had been inscribed more than three centuries later. Norway then was in contact with all Europe. Some English words had been introduced into the vulgar speech. Both Swedes and Norwegians participated in the expedition. Magnus was

[1] **conglomeration** (kŏn·glŏm′ẽr·ā′shŭn): collection of parts from various sources.

king of both countries. It was natural enough that the "crusaders" should have spoken a slight mixture of tongues. Furthermore, these men were not scribes or scholars. Very likely their priests had been left in Vinland. But they were reasonably intelligent, literate young men. Mr. Holand's researches in the popular literature of fourteenth-century Scandinavia convince him that the words of this despairing note on stone are just about the words to be expected of such a man, especially when he was under emotional stress. Whoever carved these runes may hardly have expected to live to finish the job.

Why did he use runes at all? By that time the Latin alphabet was well known in Norway and was used in most documents. For the simple reason that runic characters had been especially adapted for carving on gravestones. They were used for that purpose in both Iceland and Norway long after they had been abandoned in ordinary writing. It was easier to carve in hard stone the straight-lined runic symbols than the roman letters with curved lines. Whoever inscribed these letters was in a hurry to finish his job. He was working on the edge of eternity.

The message stated that some of the party had been left behind to look after the boats by the sea, "14 days' journey from this island." It has been found that the expression "day's journey" was a conventional term of the time, meaning approximately seventy-five miles, or the distance which a vessel could sail in a day with a fair wind. This would be just about the correct distance to the mouth of the Nelson River. The journey probably had taken Knutson's men at least a year.

The inscription indicates that the party was encamped on an island in a lake, seventy-five miles away from another lake containing two rocky islands, on the shore of which their comrades had been massacred. It is to be assumed that they had come there for temporary security from the Indians. Ohman found the stone at the edge of a marsh. This now is dry land. Geological surveys show that the slightly elevated, rocky land from which the farmer grubbed the aspen stump was almost certainly an island in 1362. The countryside has been getting progressively drier for the past century.

Just about seventy-five miles away is the only lake with two "skerries," or rocky islands. It is Cormorant Lake, in Becker County. On its shore are large glacial boulders with triangular holes drilled in three of them. This was a common device for mooring boats along the fiords of fourteenth-century Norway. Beside one of these rocks a fourteenth-century Norwegian fire steel [1] was recently picked up. Several other such mooring rocks have been found in this section of Minnesota. The implication is that the explorers continued their journey eastward for a time, probably seeking a waterway back to Vinland. Along the course of the Nelson during the past half century various Norwegian implements have been picked up — three battle-axes, a fire steel and a spearhead. This may indicate the route followed by Knutson's men southward from Hudson Bay.

Despite this accumulating mass of authenticating evidence, the Kensington stone remains tarred with the early denunciations. It might long since have been forgotten had it not been for Mr. Holand, to whom Ohman made a gift of the relic, and a continuing local interest. The stone became the property

Head of a Norwegian battle-ax, found near Norway Lake, Minnesota.

of the Alexandria, Minnesota, Chamber of Commerce. For years it was exhibited in a store window facing the main street as an object of interest to tourists. In 1947, Dr. Alexander Wetmore, secretary of the Smithsonian Institution, directed Dr. Waldo R. Wedel, one of the country's foremost experts on Midwest archaeology, to make arrangements for transfer of the relic to Washington if he was satisfied that a strong case could be made out for its authenticity.

In placing what appears to have been the last despairing message of Paul Knutson — inscribed, if genuine, in Central Minnesota 130 years before the arrival of Columbus — among the most precious relics of American history, the Smithsonian remains characteristically conservative.

Nobody, its archaeologists say, could place an official guaranty of genuine-

---

[1] **fire steel:** a piece of steel used with flint to produce the spark for starting a fire.

ness on the stone in the present state of the evidence. Archaeological hoaxes are common, and some of them are diabolically clever. Nobody profits, or really expects to profit, by them. Nobody could possibly have profited by faking the Kensington stone. But there are some distorted minds which get a peculiar pleasure out of deceiving the world. Cheating becomes its own excuse for being, and intricacies of deception are used which are strokes of genius. But if anybody planted this relic, say the Smithsonian authorities, he must have been a supercombination of expert archaeologist, geologist, linguist [1] and historian who had made his way into this wilderness at least a century ago, and of whose existence there is no record.

What became of the survivors on the island? The easiest guess is that they were massacred. There is another possibility. The first white travelers among the Mandans of North Dakota, a Siouan tribe, reported seeing many Indians with blond hair. It has been suggested that Knutson's men may have been absorbed into this tribe and left their imprint in its heredity. Smithsonian physical anthropologists, however, seriously doubt this, for the suggestion hardly fits known laws of genetics. Also there is no certainty that the descriptions of these "blond Mandans" were not greatly exaggerated. They cannot be checked today because the tribe was nearly wiped out in a smallpox epidemic fifty years ago.

There is only a vague suggestion that some of the men left at Vinland, or with the ships at the mouth of the Nelson, returned to Norway: It is said that, in the midst of the great plague, King Magnus received news that his

[1] **linguist** (lĭng'gwĭst): a person skilled in languages.

Greenland colony was lost without trace. Who could have been the bearer of these bad tidings? There still remains a faint possibility that among age-yellowed manuscripts in some European archives there may be found a full account of the expedition by somebody who accompanied Knutson.

THE WAYS OF THE SCIENTIST

1. In your notebook, write at the top of a page this heading: *The Ways of the Scientist*. Then divide the page into two parts with two subheadings: *The Attitudes of the Scientist* and *The Methods of the Scientist*. Place under each subheading appropriate descriptions such as the following:

(a) The scientist carefully states the purpose of any investigation.

(b) The scientist continues to look for evidence until his theory has been satisfactorily proved or disproved.

(c) The scientist checks and rechecks each item of evidence.

(d) The scientist mistrusts wishful thinkers, someone else's word, and unquestioned authority. He is constructively skeptical toward his own work and that of others.

(e) The scientist wants to know when he is wrong and tries to avoid self-deception.

(f) The scientist searches for truth, for correct answers, wherever this search may lead.

2. Now consider each piece of evidence on the Kensington stone listed below. Take each item and consider how a scientist would react to it. After you have finished weighing each item, formulate a statement of what a true scientist's final conclusions might be in a report on the Kensington stone.

GEOLOGICAL EVIDENCE

(a) Surveys showed that the land where the rune stone was found was "almost certainly an island in 1362."

GEOGRAPHICAL EVIDENCE

(b) There are two islands in Cormorant Lake about seventy-five miles away from where the stone was found.

(c) The Kensington stone was found "about 14 days' journey" from the mouth of the Nelson River.

HISTORICAL EVIDENCE

(d) A copy of King Magnus' order to Paul Knutson to form an expedition was found in the Danish Royal Library.

(e) King Magnus' order was dated 1354; the Kensington stone was dated 1362.

(f) The last possible date when a hoaxer could have buried the stone was in the 1850's when there were few settlers in Minnesota.

(g) Mandan Indians with blond hair were reported by the first settlers in North Dakota.

PSYCHOLOGICAL EVIDENCE

(h) Farmer Ohman, who found the stone, did not have the character or personality of a hoaxer.

(i) Historian Holand's enthusiasm, and his belief in the stone's authenticity, made him willing to devote most of his spare time, for thirty years, to studying every aspect of the stone.

ARCHAEOLOGICAL EVIDENCE

(j) Glacial boulders on the shores of Cormorant Lake were found with triangular holes drilled in them; in fourteenth-century Norway boats were often moored in holes like these.

(k) A fourteenth-century Norwegian fire steel was found beside one of these boulders.

(l) Scandinavian artifacts have been found along the Nelson River.

LINGUISTIC EVIDENCE

(m) Runic letters were traditionally used for inscriptions on gravestones.

(n) Latin letters were used to write AVM for Ave Maria.

(o) The language of the stone was a mixture of Norwegian, Swedish, and Old English.

THINKING IT OVER

1. Could a hoaxer have known about Paul Knutson's expedition when — and if — the hoaxer carved the Kensington stone?

2. Here is a question everyone connected with the famous stone has turned over and over in his mind: Why would a hoaxer have decided to say his Viking party was encamped *on an island in a lake?* Could a hoaxer have known that geologists would later find evidence that the slightly elevated, rocky land on which the aspen stump stood *was* once an island?

3. Why didn't Professor Breda's opinion permanently discredit the stone? What can be said, in view of later opinions, about the methods of science?

4. What kinds of evidence might yet be found which would authenticate the Kensington stone? What kinds of evidence might yet be found which would prove it a hoax?

5. Compare the controversy over this stone with the one surrounding the theory that prompted the *Kon-Tiki* voyage. Did the *Kon-Tiki* trip actually prove that the Polynesians came from South America instead of Asia? Does the Kensington stone prove that Vikings came to America long before Columbus? How will science deal with both the *Kon-Tiki* and the Kensington theories?

ABOUT THE AUTHOR

Thomas R. Henry (1893–   ) was born in Sterling, Massachusetts, on St. Patrick's Day. He graduated from Clark University in Worcester, Massachusetts. When he was a newspaper reporter, he spent three years as a war correspondent. Henry is also noted for his articles on scientific developments, and he has journeyed both to the Arctic and Antarctic in his adventurous search for facts about science and exploration. His books include *White Continent*, *Hollow Folks*, *Wilderness Messiah*, and *Strangest Things in the World*. Like his news reports, they are written in a lean, terse style that reflects his journalistic background.

Across the Sea of Stars

ARTHUR C. CLARKE

In the preceding selection, "The Riddle of the Kensington Stone," you saw that scientists are careful to weigh evidence, that the best scientists employ scientific imagination and scientific doubt. In this selection and the one that follows, you will find the same forces of scientific progress at work. In "Across the Sea of Stars," a scientist speculates with imaginative power on man's future. Then, in the next article, a second scientist pours a sobering dash of skepticism on such fanciful speculation. After you have read both articles, try to decide if one way of thinking is more valuable than the other.

AT SOME TIME or other, and not necessarily in moments of depression or illness, most men have known that sudden spasm of unreality which makes them ask, "What am I doing here?" Poets and mystics all down the ages have been acutely aware of this feeling, and have often expressed the belief that we are strangers in a world which is not really ours.

This vague and disturbing premonition is perfectly accurate. We don't belong here, and we're on our way to somewhere else.

We are so accustomed to our terrestrial existence that is it very hard for us to realize the problems that had to be overcome before life emerged from the sea. The shallow, sun-drenched water of the primitive oceans was an almost ideal environment for living creatures. It buffered them from extremes of temperature, and provided them with both food and oxygen. Above all, it sustained them, so that they were untouched by the crippling, crushing influence of gravity. With such advantages, it seems incredible that life ever invaded so hostile an environment as the land.

Hostile? Yes, though that is an adjective few people would apply to it. Certainly I would not have done so before I took up skin diving and discovered — as have so many thousands of men in the past few years — that only when cruising underwater, sightseeing among the myriad strange and lovely creatures of the sea, did I feel completely happy and beyond the cares and worries of everyday life.

No one who has experienced this sensation can ever forget it, or can resist succumbing to its lure once more when the chance arises. Indeed, there are some creatures — the whales and porpoises, for example — who have heeded this call so completely that they have abandoned the land which their remote ancestors conquered long ago.

The sea is far behind us; though its memories have never ceased to stir our minds, and the chemical echo of its waters still flows in our veins, we can never return to our ancient home. We creatures of the land are exiles — displaced organisms on the way from one element to another. We are still in the transit camp, waiting for our visas to come through. Yet there is no need for us to regret our lost home, for we are on the way to one of infinitely greater promise and possibility. We are on our way to space; and there, surprisingly enough, we may regain much that we lost when we left the sea.

The conquest of the land was achieved by blind biological forces; that of space will be the deliberate product of will and intelligence. But otherwise the parallels are striking; each event — the one ages ago, and the other a few decades ahead of us — represents a break with the past, and a massive thrust forward into a new realm of opportunity, of experience and of promise.

Even before the launching of the Earth satellites, no competent expert had any doubts that the conquest of space would be technically feasible within another generation, or that the new science of astronautics now was standing roughly where that of aeronautics was at the close of the last century. The first men to land on the Moon have already been born; today we are much nearer in time to the moment when a man-carrying spaceship descends upon the lunar plains than we are to that day at Kitty Hawk when the Wright brothers gave us the freedom of the sky.

So let us blithely take for granted the greatest technical achievement in human history (one which, by the way, has already cost far more than the project which made the atom bomb) and consider some of its consequences to mankind. Even over short periods they may be impressive; over intervals long enough to produce evolutionary changes they may be staggering.

The most important of these changes will be the result of living in gravitational fields [1] lower than Earth's. On Mars, for example, a 180-pound man would weigh about 70 pounds; on the Moon, less than 30. And on a space station or artificial satellite he would weigh nothing at all. He would have gone full circuit, having gained — and indeed surpassed — the freedom of movement his remote ancestors enjoyed in the weightless ocean.

To see what that may imply, consider what the never-relenting force of gravity does to our bodies here on the surface of the Earth. We spend our entire lives fighting it — and in the end, often enough, it kills us. Remember the energy that has to be exerted pumping the blood round and round the endless circuit of veins and arteries. It is true that some of the heart's work is done against frictional resistance — but how much longer we might live if the weight of the blood, and of our whole bodies, was abolished!

There is certainly a close connection

[1] **gravitational fields:** regions or spaces in which a particle is subject to a gravitational force. For example, the force of gravity from the Earth's center exerts a pull on all objects on or near the Earth.

between weight and the expectation of life, and this is a fact which may be of vast importance before many more decades have passed. The political and social consequences which may follow if it turns out that men can live substantially longer on Mars or the Moon may be revolutionary. Even taking the most conservative viewpoint, the study of living organisms under varying gravitational fields will be a potent new tool of biological and medical science.

Of course, it may be argued that reduced or zero gravity will produce undesirable side effects, but the rapidly growing science of space medicine — not to mention the experience of all the creatures of the sea — suggests that such effects will be temporary and not serious. Perhaps our balance organs and some of our muscles might atrophy [1] after many generations in a weightless environment, but what would that matter since they would no longer be needed? It would be a fair exchange for fallen arches, pendulous paunches, and the other defects and diseases of gravity.

But mere extension of the life span, and even improved health and efficiency, are not important in themselves. We all know people who have done more in forty years than others have done in eighty. What is really significant is richness and diversity of experience, and the use to which that is put by men and the societies they constitute. It is here that the conquest of space will produce an advance in complexity of stimulus even greater than that which occurred when life moved from water to land.

In the sea, every creature exists at the center of a little universe which is seldom more than a hundred feet in radius, and is usually much smaller. This is the limit set by underwater visibility, and though some information comes from greater distances by sound vibrations, the world of the fish is a very tiny place.

That of a land animal is thousands of times larger. It can see out to the horizon, miles away. And at night it can look up to the stars, those piercing points of light whose incredible explanation was discovered by Man himself more recently than the time of Shakespeare.

In space, there will be no horizon this side of infinity. There will be suns and planets without end, no two the same, many of them teeming with strange life forms and perhaps stranger civilizations. The sea which beats against the coasts of Earth, which seems so endless and so eternal, is as the drop of water on the slide of a microscope compared with the shoreless sea of space. And our pause here, between one ocean and the next, may be only a moment in the history of the Universe.

When one contemplates this awe-inspiring fact, one sees how glib, superficial and indeed downright childish are the conceptions of those science-fiction writers who merely transfer their cultures and societies to other planets. Whatever civilizations we may build on distant worlds will differ from ours more widely than mid-twentieth-century America differs from Renaissance Italy or, for that matter, from the Egypt of the Pharaohs. And the differences, as we have seen, will not merely be cultural; in the long run they will be organic [2] as well. In a few thousand years of forced evolution, many of our descendants will be sundered from us

---

[1] atrophy (ăt′rô·fĭ): waste away from lack of use or nourishment.

[2] organic (ôr·găn′ĭk): pertaining to living organisms.

by psychological and biological gulfs far greater than those between the Eskimo and the African pygmy.

The frozen wilderness of Greenland and the steaming forests of the Congo represent the two extremes of the climatic range that Man has been able to master without the use of advanced technology. There are much stranger environments among the stars, and one day we shall pit ourselves against them, employing the tools of future science to change atmospheres, temperatures and perhaps even orbits. Not many worlds can exist upon which an unprotected man could survive, but the men who challenge space will not be unprotected. They will remold other planets as we today bulldoze forests and divert rivers. Yet, in changing worlds, they will also change themselves.

What will be the thoughts of a man who lives on one of the inner moons of Saturn,[1] where the Sun is a fierce but heatless point of light and the great golden orange of the giant planet dominates the sky, passing swiftly through its phases from new to full while it floats within the circle of its incomparable rings? It is hard for us to imagine his outlook on life, his hopes and fears — yet he may be nearer to us than we are to the men who signed the Declaration of Independence.

Go further afield to the worlds of other suns (yes, one day, we shall reach them, though that may not be for ages yet), and picture a planet where the word "night" is meaningless, for with the setting of one sun there rises another — and perhaps a third or fourth — of totally different hue. Try to visualize what must surely be the weirdest sky of all — that of a planet near the center of one of those close-packed star clusters that glow like distant swarms of fireflies in the fields of our telescopes. How strange to stand beneath a sky that is a solid shield of stars, so that there is no darkness between them through which one may look out into the Universe beyond. . . .

Such worlds exist, and one day men will live upon them. But why, it may reasonably be asked, should we worry about such remote and alien places when there is enough work to keep us busy here on Earth for centuries?

Let us face the facts; we do not have centuries ahead of us. We have aeons,[2] barring accidents and the consequences of our own folly. A hundred million years will be but a small fraction of the future history of Earth. This is about the length of time that the dinosaurs reigned as masters of this planet. It we last a tenth as long as the great reptiles which we sometimes speak of disparagingly as one of Nature's failures, we will have time enough to make our mark on countless worlds and suns.

Yet one final question remains. If we have never felt wholly at home here on Earth, which has mothered us for so many ages, what hope is there that we shall find greater happiness or satisfaction on the strange worlds of foreign suns?

The answer lies in the distinction between the race and the individual. For a man, "home" is the place of his birth and childhood — whether that be Siberian steppe,[3] coral island, Alpine valley, Brooklyn tenement, Martian desert, lunar crater, or mile-long interstellar ark.[4] But for Man, home can

[1] **Saturn** (săt′ĕrn): the second largest planet. It is surrounded by three rings.

[2] **aeons** (ē′ŏnz): immeasurably long periods of time.

[3] **steppe** (stĕp): vast, level area without forests.

[4] **interstellar ark**: spaceship.

never be a single country, a single world, a single Solar System, a single star cluster. While the race endures in recognizably human form, it can have no one abiding place short of the Universe itself.

This divine discontent is part of our destiny. It is one more, and perhaps the greatest, of the gifts we inherited from the sea that rolls so restlessly around the world.

It will be driving our descendants on toward a myriad of unimaginable goals when the sea is stilled forever, and Earth itself a fading legend lost among the stars.

THINKING IT OVER

1. The title is more than just a pleasant-sounding sequence of sounds. Can you explain how it ties together the beginning and end of the article?

2. What point is the writer making when he discusses underwater life, skin diving, whales, and porpoises?

3. Why is extending the length of life of human beings not important by itself? What does the author feel *will be* significant about man's future life in space?

4. Do you think the author makes any claims about future events that seem somewhat extravagant or unlikely to come true? If so, which claims?

5. According to the author, how will man's conquest of space differ from his conquest of land?

6. What single idea or "theme" unifies this article? State the main idea in a single carefully thought-out sentence. You might find it helpful to reread:

   (a) the first three paragraphs and the last four paragraphs of this article.

   (b) the paragraph on page 236 beginning, "In space, there will be no horizon this side of infinity."

7. In the third paragraph from the end of this article, the author makes a distinction between *man* and *Man*. What is this distinction, and how is it related to the main idea of the article?

GAINING POWER OVER WORDS

SPECIALIZED WORDS In the present era of rockets and earth satellites, the well-read individual learns new concepts as he adds more and more scientific terms to his vocabulary. He learns, for example, that a *light year* is a measure of distance, not a measure of time.

In "Across the Sea of Stars" the following words appear: *orbit, lunar, satellite,* and *atmosphere.*

1. Have a member of the class report on the definition and origin of each of these words.

2. Which of these words can also be used to describe non-scientific phenomena? Give sentences which show their non-scientific use.

ABOUT THE AUTHOR

Arthur C. Clarke (1917–), born in Somerset, England, spent much time during his youth building gadgets, including telescopes. As a member of the Royal Air Force, he lectured on radar and was a technical officer in charge of the first experimental Ground-Controlled Approach unit. Following the war, Clarke received his degree in physics and mathematics from Kings College, London. In addition to *Interplanetary Flight* and *The Exploration of Space*, he has written thirteen books of science fiction. One of his chief interests is skin diving, and his participation in an expedition to the Great Barrier Reef is described in *The Coast of Coral*. "Across the Sea of Stars" appeared in his first collection of scientific and speculative articles.

Sailing the Sea of Stars ➤

Can you believe that the picture on the opposite page is a photograph, not a painting? Photography has taken its place in the world of art, and skilled cameramen are able to achieve effects as beautiful and inspiring as those in great paintings. Do you agree that here the photographer has captured something of the glory of the heavens, the sense of wonder about the unknown, that is leading modern man to explore the horizons of outer space — to sail the sea of stars?

Sense and Nonsense About Space

LEE A. DuBRIDGE

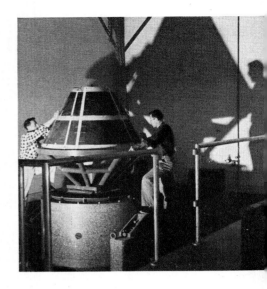

Wait a moment! Before you put on your space suit and stand ready to journey "across the sea of stars" with the author of the preceding selection, you may want to do some realistic thinking about the trip. The thought-provoking comments offered here come from a noted scientist.

Every American citizen of sixty years or more has witnessed in rapid succession the birth of the age of the automobile, the age of the airplane, the age of electronics, of radio, of television, and of nuclear energy — not to mention the age of the movie, of rock 'n' roll, of the supermarket, and a few others. One might indeed expect that most of us would be quite indifferent to the dawn of another age.

But not so.

For no age has had a more shattering impact on the people of the world than the beginning, on October 4, 1957, of the space age. And for good reason. For, although other twentieth-century discoveries have increased the human capacities for speed, for communication, and for destruction, it has been over four hundred years since a wholly new area of geographic exploration has been opened up. Naturally this has been an earth-shaking event. For the first time in world history, men are no longer chained to their tiny planet. Man-made vehicles can now sail the untracked reaches of interplanetary space itself.

It would not be reasonable to expect that such an event would be received calmly. To paraphrase a common Washington quip: "Anyone who is not thoroughly confused just doesn't un-

---

Seeing Structure: Relating the Parts to the Whole. Everything in the world has a structure in which the main purpose dominates the parts and each part contributes to the total structure. This is true of an atom, a political party, a poem, or an article. DuBridge has a vigorous, clear, orderly way of thinking. Watch for his definite line of thought, his examples, and his over-all organization. Try to see how all the parts fit together and how the author has organized his ideas.

"Sense and Nonsense About Space" by Lee A. DuBridge first appeared in *Harper's* Magazine, August 1959; modernized for this book by the author in 1961. Reprinted by permission of the author.

derstand the situation." Exciting things are happening, yet public understanding does not always remain in step with actual events.

The confusion is understandable, for the conditions encountered by an object projected into a space trajectory [1] are so unlike the conditions on Earth as to defy any "common sense" discussion. Common sense is a distillation of human experience. Until 1961 no human being had actually ever had experience in the space environment, where there is no air to breathe or to sustain flight or to prevent liquids from boiling away; where objects have no weight and things that are dropped do not fall. Also, the vast speeds required to project objects into spatial orbits are such as to numb the imagination. How can even the hardened jet-plane traveler who is used to speeds of 600 miles per hour, which is 10 miles per minute, conceive of what it is like to travel at 5 miles *per second?* Yet that is the speed of an Earth satellite. To escape from the Earth's gravitational pull entirely one must travel at 7 miles per second — and to escape from the pull of the Sun takes a speed, with respect to the Sun, of 26 miles per second.

Nevertheless, great as these speeds are, they are overshadowed by the vastness of spatial distances. For example, if one could, in spite of the Sun's pull, maintain in space a speed of 26 miles per second, it would take 23 days to reach Mars, over 3 years to reach Neptune, and *28,000 years* to reach the nearest star (Alpha Centauri). It even takes a beam of light (at a speed of 186,000 miles per second) 4 years to reach that star, 150,000 years to cross the Milky Way, and 6 billion years to travel to the most distant nebula.[2] Clearly the reaches of inter*stellar* [3] space are still far beyond our grasp.

We may have "conquered space" — yet we are still rather like a fly who has reached the outside of the window-pane but who, in a thousand lifetimes, could not begin to explore even the next county. We, too, must be satisfied with nearby interplanetary space for the time being.

Nevertheless, between the Sun and the orbit of tiny Pluto, the most distant planet, there lies a sphere seven billion miles in diameter which is now accessible to human exploration and which may hold a million unimaginable secrets whose discovery, one by one, may keep human beings occupied for a thousand years. Even these relatively near regions of space offer a challenge to human curiosity and human ingenuity unequaled in all history.

Human beings have a right to be excited.

However, just because many of the things about space which are true appear to be fantastic, it does not necessarily follow that everything fantastic is necessarily true.

The laws of physics still apply — science-fiction writers to the contrary notwithstanding. It is *not* possible to propel tangible objects to speeds which exceed or even approach the speed of light. In fact, the problem of obtaining enough energy for space exploration and converting it to a suitable form constitutes the most imposing barrier to many attractive ventures. It takes energy to acquire speed and energy to overcome gravity. And energy always costs money!

[2] **nebula** (nĕb′ú·lă): a celestial structure composed of a cloud of stars plus matter in a gaseous or finely divided state. A nebula is often seen as a luminous patch in the sky.

[3] **interstellar**: located among the stars.

[1] **trajectory** (trȧ·jĕk′tô·rĭ): the curve which a body describes in space.

If we are interested in *human* space travel, it must also be recognized that, as far as we know, there is no place in the solar system other than the Earth where men will find in usable form all four essential things they will need for travel and survival — oxygen, water, food, and fuel. Hence, man must carry with him, as he leaves the Earth, adequate supplies of these things for his entire journey. This will mean a colossal cost in the energy required to get him and his supplies lifted from the Earth into a spatial orbit. It takes roughly 50 to 100 pounds of rocket fuel for each pound placed in an orbit around the Earth or to the vicinity of the Moon. This mounts up to mighty fuel requirements for extended space expeditions.

Let us begin with the problems of orbiting the Earth at distances of only a few hundred to a few thousand miles. As a first step, this is a region well worth thorough exploration. With rocket thrusts of 300,000 to 500,000 pounds (150 to 250 tons), one can place vehicles with a total useful weight of from one-and-a-half to three tons, or so, into orbit (excluding the dead weight of rocket cases and burned-out motors). Such vehicles may carry a large amount of useful instrumentation plus the necessary power supplies for the instruments and the radio to transmit the measurements to Earth, and a man can now go into orbit with enough supplies to sustain him for a short time and return him safely to Earth.

What values may such close-in expeditions have?

First, they will give us valuable experience in what the space environment is like and what it takes to keep men and instruments in operation. Second, they can yield a vast amount of valuable information about the one planet in the universe which will always be of greatest interest to human beings — the Earth itself. The Earth's gravitational, magnetic, and electric fields have very great intrinsic and practical interest, yet they have heretofore been accessible to direct measurement only within a few miles of the Earth's surface. It will take dozens or scores of instrumented satellites in orbits ranging from equatorial to polar, covering distances from 100 miles to 100,000 miles above the Earth, to explore these fields adequately.

What will such explorations reveal? No one knows and no one can predict. Space, it must be emphasized, is a great unknown area. Columbus could not have known what continents he would encounter. He set out to find a western route to India; but America got in the way. So it will be in space. We will set out on one mission and find something else.

The first U.S. satellite, Explorer I, in fact, repeated Columbus' experience. It carried a Geiger counter to make some cosmic-ray [1] measurements. Such radiation — as measured near the Earth's surface — has proved of vast interest to physicists in recent years and has added immeasurably to our understanding of atomic and nuclear structure. But that first Geiger counter in space discovered a new belt of radiation, thousands of times more intense than the known cosmic rays — so intense, in fact, that it paralyzed the counter completely. Later satellite experiments showed that this radiation extends from a few hundred to more than ten thousand miles above the Earth, following the contours of the Earth's magnetic field. The nature and

[1] **cosmic ray:** any of the rays of extremely high penetrating power beyond the Earth's atmosphere.

source of this radiation are still unknown, but it is of great potential theoretical and practical importance and should be thoroughly explored. A dozen large satellites adequately equipped for this one job alone would be a worthwhile investment. Since this radiation is intense enough to kill an unshielded man in a few hours or a few days, it would be wise to know quite a good deal about it before men venture to spend much time within this belt.

Unfortunately, this intense radiation (known as the Van Allen layer) is in just the region in which many of the most valuable observations about the Earth can be taken. The weather patterns, the upper radio-reflection layers, the gravitational irregularities (which may tell something of the shape and structure of the Earth), and many other things should be studied at heights of 200 miles to 10,000 miles. But if men are to be injured and photographic plates fogged and other instruments affected by this radiation, then it poses some difficult problems to be solved.

This is but one example of how a single new discovery may change our preconceived notions and alter many of our plans about space travel and space research. It is, after all, the *unknown* that is the challenge of space. If we were confident we knew all about everything existing out there, it would be useless to spend the money to explore.

As one leaves the Earth behind, the next object of interest is, of course, the Moon, rotating around the Earth about 240,000 miles away. After centuries of speculation it seems almost unbelievable that our generation will at last be able to make contact with the Moon and learn something about it. The Moon's surface has been examined from the Earth with the most

powerful instruments known to science — telescopes, spectroscopes,[1] radiometers.[2] We know a good deal about it — its size, its surface contours (mountains up to 26,000 feet in height), its temperature (250° F. in the middle of the sun-baked day, and down to 220° below zero in the middle of the night). We know that the Moon always presents the same face to the Earth — that is, it rotates about its own axis at exactly the same rate it revolves about the Earth. Hence, the Moon's "day" is about 28 of our days in length — 336 hours of sunshine, followed by 336 hours of darkness, illumined only by reflected light from the Earth.

We know that the Moon has no atmosphere, no free oxygen, no water, no life. But we do not yet know what it is made of — whether the surface is hard rock or soft dust. We do not know what caused the pockmarks — meteor impacts or volcanic eruptions, or both. We do know that the surface is probably unlike anything on Earth, for there has been no erosion by wind or rain or ice or snow, no inundation[3] by oceans or lakes or rivers; hence, there are no sedimentary rocks, no glacier-cut valleys. No corrosion or oxidation or decay has been at work; hence, we shall find no deposits of coal or oil or gas. But otherwise, the same chemical elements that are found on Earth — and throughout the rest of the universe — will surely be present on the Moon in somewhat the same proportions, except for the gases like hydrogen, oxygen, nitrogen, argon, etc., which the Moon's gravitation is too weak to retain. Ordi-

[1] **spectroscopes:** optical instruments that break up beams of light into different wavelengths.
[2] **radiometers:** instruments that measure the intensity of radiant energy.
[3] **inundation** (ĭn'ŭn·dā'shŭn): flooding or overflow.

nary water would also quickly evaporate and escape.

But many things we neither know nor can predict. We must get there first with instruments and, sometime in the future, with human observers to find out.

Our curiosity about the other planets in the solar system is even greater than our curiosity about the Moon, partly because their greater distances make seeing more difficult, and partly because some of them have such cloudy atmospheres that we can never see the surface at all until we get there.

The nearest planets to the Earth are Venus and Mars. The orbit of Venus is closer to the Sun than the Earth's, and when "in conjunction"[1] Venus comes (about once every two years) to within about 26 million miles from the Earth. Mars' orbit is farther away from the Sun than the Earth's, and every 18 months or so Mars comes within 50 million miles of the Earth. The more distant planets are very far away indeed. Probes which will pass in the vicinity of either Venus or Mars, however, are now well within the reach of rocket technology, and the launching of such instrumented probes will no doubt be attempted in the not too distant future.

Vehicles sent out to probe these planets will not return to Earth, of course — until that distant day when extremely large objects can be launched with the huge quantities of fuel and intricate guidance equipment required to achieve a return journey. The first probes will, like the Russian Lunik and the U.S. Pioneer IV, escape from the Earth's gravitational field, will have their orbits disturbed only slightly as they approach their target, and will

[1] in conjunction: when Venus passes directly between the earth and the sun.

then continue on into an orbit around the Sun. A probe fired at Mars will enter a solar orbit somewhat similar to that of Mars itself.

But if the Moon and planets are interesting, we must not forget that space itself will offer some interesting adventures too — either to instruments or to men. We humans have had very little experience in any environment save one in which we can travel in any path at any speed we wish. On land, on sea, or in the air we can, within wide limits, move about as we please, can travel any given path at any speed we select. Imagine our surprise, then, when we find that in any particular orbit around the Earth there is, for any given point, one and only one speed at which we can travel and still stay in that orbit. An automobile on Earth may circle a one-mile track once per hour or once per minute, or anything in between. But a satellite in a circular orbit which is, say, 500 miles above the Earth can only go at a speed of 4½ miles per second, and will thus complete one revolution in about 103 minutes. At 5,000 miles up, the speed will be just under 3 miles per second, or one revolution in 5¼ hours. The Moon, at a distance of 240,000 miles, has revolved for ages at less than two-thirds of a mile per second (about 2,300 miles per *hour*), or one revolution in 28 days.

Thus, two satellites in the same orbit around the Earth (or the Sun) cannot have a "race" — for to have a different speed requires a different orbit. This means, of course, that it is impossible to have a *stationary* space platform near the Earth. Any object in orbit must be rotating about the Earth at the required speed. In the very special case of an object circling west to east above the Earth's equator at 22,000 miles height, the speed of rotation will be once in 24 hours and hence, since the Earth rotates beneath it at the same period, the object will *appear* stationary. It will, nevertheless, actually be traveling at 100 miles per *minute*. Any object which attempts to "catch up" with such a platform can do so only in a lower orbit. Furthermore, only in an orbit over and parallel to the Earth's equator can such an apparently stationary object exist. In any orbit inclined to the equator, the object will appear to drift back and forth each day along a north-south line. Since the continental United States is not crossed by the equator, no "stationary" object will ever appear directly above *us*, though at that height it would still be visible above the southern horizon.

This does not mean that we will have no "space platforms," for vehicles which move in various orbits around the Earth may be very useful for observations, communications, and research. But guiding another vehicle in such a way as to catch up to and land on such a "platform" will offer navigational problems never encountered on Earth.

The weightless condition in free flight also imposes some unfamiliar situations. Imagine, for example, trying to drink a glass of water in the usual way when traveling in a space capsule. If you quickly lower the glass, the water will stay suspended in midair. Of course, this can be solved by taking liquids from a device similar to a baby's bottle.

Can one "drop a bomb" from a satellite? One can certainly *release* a bomb, but it will certainly not fall to Earth. It will, of necessity, continue along with the launching satellite in the same orbit and with the same speed. In order to drop, its speed must be reduced by projecting it forcibly backward from the carrying vehicle by just the right amount to inject it into an orbit which hits the Earth's surface at the desired place. It can be done. But since bombs dropped from 30,000 *feet* do not always hit the target, we must expect additional difficulties when bombing from 300 miles up — especially when traveling at five miles per second, not five miles per minute. At first we would be lucky even to hit the right *hemisphere*.

Even more interesting problems arise if one thinks of establishing a military base on the Moon and shooting weapons at specific targets on the Earth. The Moon is moving about the Earth at 2,300 miles per hour, the Earth is 240,000 miles away and it is spinning so that any target on its surface is moving along at a speed up to 1,000 miles per hour at the equator. A projectile must first escape from the Moon's gravitational field and then get injected into a suitable Earth-bound trajectory. The time of travel to the Earth will probably be a day or two. Any duck hunter can appreciate the problems of hitting a particular spot on a bird when he is shooting from a car going 2,200 miles per hour (and the bird is also spinning!) when the bullet available travels a highly curved path and takes two days to reach the target. It may take quite a lot of practice to attain the desired accuracy under such difficult circumstances. Again we will be lucky at first to hit the Earth at all — still luckier to hit the right *side*.

Even the computation of what the trajectory would be is a major problem. And we haven't even mentioned the problems of getting all the men and materials up to the Moon in the first place. Why not stay home and fire our rockets from *here*? There is, in fact, a serious danger that in concentrating military effort on fanciful space schemes we will neglect the serious and urgent problems of ordinary intercontinental ballistic missiles — one weapon whose future importance is very clear.

The establishment of human colonies on the Moon or Venus or Mars is certainly an irresistible human dream — a dream whose possibilities should be investigated. However, one can hardly suppose that these places will offer very attractive living conditions to the prospective settler. No place on Earth could conceivably be as unattractive as the airless, waterless, lifeless surface of the Moon. The best that can be said is that it is a good place to get away from other people; and it is a fine place — with its low gravity — for ambitious high jumpers, if it is possible to jump at all in a pressurized space suit with oxgyen tank attached.

Furthermore, the difficulties of sending human beings to the Moon are enormous. We might imagine that a man with all the necessary oxygen, space suits, food, water, and instruments could be packed into a vehicle with a total weight of 2,000 pounds. A rocket with a thrust of some 300,000 pounds could project this vehicle into an orbit which would pass near the Moon. But our vehicle must carry along also enough fuel to fire a retrorocket in order to reduce its speed, counter the Moon's gravitational pull, and lower the whole device gently to a suitable spot on the Moon. It seems reasonable to estimate that it would take two or more pounds of fuel for each pound actually landed on the Moon. Thus 4,000 pounds of fuel would have to be lifted from the Earth in addition to the original 2,000-pound load, making a total load of 6,000 pounds. A total thrust of 900,000 pounds would now be needed.

But this would leave our man permanently stranded on the Moon with no fuel to return to Earth. We must then lift from the Earth enough fuel to lift him off the Moon again, and this will multiply our initial thrust requirement by another factor of 3 — to 2,700,000 pounds. And if we want to allow the man and his vehicle to land safely on the Earth again, he will need fuel for that, too — and our initial thrust may climb to 5 million pounds or more.

A single rocket with a thrust of 5 million pounds is far beyond the reach of present technology; large and clumsy (and expensive) *clusters* of rockets would be needed. Furthermore, we can hardly send one man alone on such a journey. Hence, it has been suggested that such journeys be made in installments, using orbiting space platforms to which fuel and equipment may be transported by many rockets, each bearing a smaller load. Or we can land the men on the moon in one capsule and send the fuel and equipment in others. But the total fuel requirement is not reduced by this technique — rather it will be greatly increased, for all the equipment must still be lifted from the Earth and landed gently and accurately on the Moon.

The technical problems to be met are surely not insoluble — but the expense and effort involved will be colossal, and it is unrealistic to expect the "man on the Moon" mission to be achieved immediately. Sending a man to Mars or Venus or other bodies will be even more difficult —and the price of the journey correspondingly higher.

These considerations suggest that it is hardly realistic to expect that we may someday relieve the congestion of the Earth's rapidly rising population

Artist Howard Koslow's conception of a possible "floating platform," designed — as Dr. DuBridge suggests — to relieve overcrowding on Earth.

by establishing colonies on the Moon or on other planets. Since the surface area of the Moon is only one-sixteenth, and of Mars only one-quarter, that of the Earth, it would probably be cheaper to build great floating platforms over the surface of all the Earth's oceans (thus multiplying the available "land" area by four) rather than try to transport a few hundred million people, with all their water, oxygen, and food, to the Moon or Mars.

One hears that there may be valuable minerals on the Moon or Venus or Mars waiting to be mined. There may be. But we are not running out of aluminum or gold or platinum or uranium here on Earth. The chief difficulty is that some of them are found only in rather low-grade ores so that it is very expensive to extract them.

But it would surely be far cheaper to extract gold or other metals from sea water than to haul them in from the Moon. The situation, however, must be investigated. There might, after all, be a vast lunar deposit of diamonds, though it would take a lot of pretty big diamonds to pay for a Moon rocket. And if *that* many diamonds were suddenly thrown on the market the price would promptly collapse!

In other words, research and exploration rather than colonization or militarization or exploitation should be the first goals for the Moon and, indeed, for all other space stations. In spite of the fanciful potentialities, some extraordinarily sober thinking is going to be required to insure a sensible allocation of national resources to space ventures.

Knowledge, after all, can be far more

valuable than any precious materials. And since outer space is a veritable sea of ignorance, the opportunities for new knowledge are enormous. It is pointless to ask at present what the practical value of the new knowledge might be. We cannot even predict *what* the new knowledge will be. But human beings have never yet explored a sea of ignorance or opened up new areas of inquiry without learning things that paid huge — and unforeseeable — rewards. Fortunately, much of the new knowledge we wish to seek can be obtained with unmanned vehicles, and for many purposes we can avoid the great cost of carrying human beings.

One hundred years from now the new knowledge attained in space research will surely have paid untold, unforeseen, and unexpected dividends. Already the dawning of the space age has impelled Americans to seek to improve their schools. That alone may be worth the cost of all our space rockets.

SEEING STRUCTURE: RELATING THE PARTS TO THE WHOLE

1. What is the over-all plan of this article? Do not try to make an outline, but state the major points in the order in which the author presents them. Do you think his order is a good one, or would it be better if the main ideas were re-arranged in some different way?

2. Study carefully these two sentences from page 241. They might be called a pivot or turning point in the structure of this article. Why?

    (a) "Human beings have a right to be excited."

    (b) "However, just because many of the things about space which are true appear to be fantastic, it does not necessarily follow that everything fantastic is necessarily true."

3. How is the title related to the structure of this article?

4. For what purpose does the author introduce Columbus into the discussion?

5. What is the fly outside the windowpane doing in this article? What idea does he illustrate?

6. How does duck-hunting come into the discussion? What is the author driving at?

7. What does the author say about ambitious high jumpers? Where might they go? Why does the author mention them?

8. For what purpose does the author suggest floating platforms to cover the oceans?

GAINING POWER OVER WORDS

SCIENTIFIC TERMS In an age of great technical advances, language becomes ever more specialized. You have already learned the meaning of the scientific terms *orbit*, *lunar*, *satellite*, and *atmosphere*. In "Sense and Nonsense About Space," the scientific terminology is even more complex. For example, you find terms such as the *Van Allen layer*, terms which appear in more scholarly writings but seldom appear in articles written for the novice in scientific matters.

1. Which scientific terms in DuBridge's article do you already know from your previous reading?

2. Make a list in your notebook of the terms in this article which are unfamiliar to you. Define each word, and write a sentence illustrating a proper use of the word.

ABOUT THE AUTHOR

Lee A. DuBridge (1901–) was born in Terre Haute, Indiana. Since 1946 he has been president of the California Institute of Technology. He holds many degrees from several schools and has served on the faculty at the University of Wisconsin, Washington University in St. Louis, and the University of Rochester in New York. During the war Dr. DuBridge was director of the radiation laboratory and radar research at the Massachusetts Institute of Technology. He is the author of *New Theories of the Photoelectric Effect* and co-author of *Photoelectric Phenomena*. Dr. DuBridge has written numerous articles for scientific journals.

Speaking of Articles

Although the great mass of articles have only passing interest, many of, them are important enough to the world to be recorded and indexed so that they can be easily found in libraries by people looking for information on a certain subject. Such articles form a whole storehouse of information on every subject imaginable. In the United States, the *Readers' Guide to Periodical Literature* serves as the key to this storehouse.

The *Readers' Guide* is a reference book that you will often use in high school, and it can be found in any library. It is published in paper binding once a month. Every three months and every six months, cumulative issues for these periods are put together. Each year there is an issue arranging the contents for all twelve months. Bound volumes cover whole periods of years and go back as far as 1890.

The *Readers' Guide* lists the authors and titles of articles, poetry, stories, and plays published in more than one hundred current magazines. It is interesting to look over the list of magazines on the inside of the front cover to see which magazines are considered important enough to be indexed. The names of the authors are arranged alphabetically. The titles of their articles are arranged alphabetically under the authors' names or under subject headings such as:

ARCHITECTURE
AVIATION
MUSIC
POLITICS
SPORTS
YOUTH

Whenever it is necessary, further subdivisions are made under the different subject headings. These, too, are in alphabetical order. For example, under MUSIC there are such subdivisions as MUSIC festivals; MUSIC, Popular; and MUSIC publishing.

Here are the actual author and subject entries for the three articles you have read in this section:

AUTHOR ENTRIES

HENRY, Thomas R.
Riddle of the Kensington stone, Sat Eve Post 221:25 Ag 21 '48; same abr. Read. Digest 53:33–7 N '48

CLARKE, Arthur C.
Man's fate in space;* with biographical sketch. por Coronet 44:5, 88–90 Ag '58

DUBRIDGE, Lee Alvin
Sense and nonsense about space. Harper 219:21–8 Ag '59

SUBJECT ENTRIES:

KENSINGTON rune stone
Riddle of the Kensington stone. T. R. Henry. il Sat Eve Post 221:25 Ag 21 '48; same abr. Read. Digest 53:33–7 N '48

SPACE, Outer
Man's fate in space. A. C. Clarke. il Coronet 44:88–90 Ag '58

SPACE flight
Sense and nonsense about space. L. A. DuBridge. il Harper 219:21–8 Ag '59

Can you interpret each of the numbers and abbreviations in these entries? What do you think is meant by "*il* Sat Eve Post"? By "Harper 219:21–8 Ag '59"? By "*por* Coronet"? You can very likely guess intelligently at these without consulting the key in the *Readers' Guide*, but if you have not already done so, you should familiarize yourself with this helpful publication.

* When Clarke republished this article in his book, *The Challenge of the Spaceship,* he changed the title to "Across the Sea of Stars."

Essays

The very origin of the word *essay* suggests the nature of the writing it describes. The word dates back to a wise and genial sixteenth-century Frenchman named Montaigne who liked to jot down his personal opinions on all manner of things — from the joys of the countryside to the evils of government. He called each of these attempts at self-expression an *essai,* which is the French word for "try" or "attempt." Since Montaigne's time, many writers have tried composing their thoughts, and the essay has become one of the most widely used of all prose forms.

This kind of writing has been put to many different uses. Many essays have a light, informal tone — as if the author were chatting with his friends. Such essays are often called *familiar, informal,* or *personal essays.* Other essays tend to focus on a logical examination of ideas, and the authors do not give familiar or personal glimpses of themselves. These are called *formal essays.*

The essay form, then, can be very flexible. As the writer Carl Van Doren has said, the essay may be "of any length, breadth, depth, weight, density, color, savor, odor, appearance, importance, value, or uselessness which you can or will give it. . . . The essay may be as fastidious as a collector of carved emeralds or as open-minded as a garbage-gatherer."

Irtnog

E. B. WHITE

Have you ever stopped to consider how often wit and humor make you think as well as laugh? The author of this essay is a master at poking fun, but he does his poking with a pen sharpened with wisdom as well as wit. His pen is sharp enough to prod the reader into thought as well as laughter.

ALONG ABOUT 1920 it became apparent that more things were being written than people had time to read. That is to say, even if a man spent his entire time reading stories, articles, and news, as they appeared in books, magazines, and pamphlets, he fell behind. This was no fault of the reading public; on the contrary, readers made a real effort to keep pace with writers, and utilized every spare moment during their waking hours. They read while shaving in the morning and while waiting for trains and while riding on trains. There came to be a kind of tacit agreement among members of the reading public that when one person laid down the baton, someone else must pick it up; and so when a customer entered a barbershop, the barber would lay aside the Boston *Evening Globe* and the customer would pick up *Judge;*[1] or when a customer appeared in a shoeshining parlor, the bootblack would put away the *Racing Form* and the customer would open his briefcase and pull out *The Sheik.* So there was always somebody reading something. Motormen of trolley cars read while they waited on the switch. Errand boys read while walking from the corner of Thirty-ninth and Madison to the corner of Twenty-fifth and Broadway. Subway riders read constantly, even when they were in a crushed, upright position in which nobody could read his own paper but everyone could look over the next man's shoulder. People passing newsstands would pause for a second to read headlines. Men in the back seats of limousines, northbound on Lafayette Street in the evening, switched on tiny dome lights and read the *Wall Street Journal.* Women in semi-detached houses joined circulating libraries and read Vachel Lindsay[2] while the baby was taking his nap.

There was a tremendous volume of stuff that had to be read. Writing began to give off all sorts of by-products. Readers not only had to read the original works of a writer, but they also had to scan what the critics said, and they

had to read the advertisements reprinting the favorable criticisms, and they had to read the book chat giving some rather odd piece of information about the writer — such as that he could write only when he had a gingersnap in his mouth. It all took time. Writers gained steadily, and readers lost.

Then along came the *Reader's Digest.* That was a wonderful idea. It digested everything that was being written in leading magazines, and put new hope in the hearts of readers. Here, everybody thought, was the answer to the problem. Readers, badly discouraged by the rate they had been losing ground, took courage and set out once more to keep abreast of everything that was being written in the world. For a while they seemed to hold their own. But soon other digests and short cuts appeared, like *Time,* and *The Best Short Stories of 1927,* and the new Five-Foot

[1] *Judge:* a humorous magazine, no longer published.
[2] **Vachel Lindsay**: an American poet who became popular in the early 1920's.

Appreciating Satire. Satire is writing in which folly is held up to ridicule. Satire can be biting and sometimes unjust, but it can also be extremely valuable — as it is in this essay where E. B. White points up a common human failing. As you read "Irtnog," look for the sting of truth behind E. B. White's wit.

Shelf,[1] and Wells's *Outline of History*,[2] and *Newsweek*, and *Fiction Parade*. By 1939 there were one hundred and seventy-three digests, or short cuts, in America, and even if a man read nothing but digests of selected material, and read continuously, he couldn't keep up. It was obvious that something more concentrated than digests would have to come along to take up the slack.

It did. Someone conceived the idea of digesting the digests. He brought out a little publication called *Pith*, no bigger than your thumb. It was a digest of *Reader's Digest, Time, Concise Spicy Tales*, and the daily News Summary of the New York *Herald Tribune*. Everything was so extremely condensed that a reader could absorb everything that was being published in the world in about forty-five minutes. It was a tremendous financial success, and of course other publications sprang up, aping it: one called *Core*, another called *Nub*, and a third called *Nutshell*. *Nutshell* folded up, because, an expert said, the name was too long; but half a dozen others sprang up to take its place, and for another short period readers enjoyed a breathing spell and managed to stay abreast of writers. In fact, at one juncture, soon after the appearance of *Nub*, some person of unsound business tendencies felt that the digest rage had been carried too far and that there would be room in the magazine field for a counterdigest — a publication devoted to restoring literary bulk. He raised some money and issued a huge thing called *Amplifo*, undigesting the

digests. In the second issue the name had been changed to *Regurgitans*. The third issue never reached the stands. *Pith* and *Core* continued to gain, and became so extraordinarily profitable that hundreds of other digests of digests came into being. Again readers felt themselves slipping. *Distillate* came along, a superdigest which condensed a Hemingway novel[3] to the single word "Bang!" and reduced a long article about the problem of the unruly child to the words "Hit him."

You would think that with such drastic condensation going on, the situation would have resolved itself and that an adjustment would have been set up between writer and reader. Unfortunately, writers still forged ahead. Digests and superdigests, because of their rich returns, became as numerous as the things digested. It was not until 1960, when a Stevens Tech[4] graduate named Abe Shapiro stepped in with an immense ingenious formula, that a permanent balance was established between writers and readers. Shapiro was a sort of Einstein. He had read prodigiously; and as he thought back over all the things that he had ever read, he became convinced that it would be possible to express them in mathematical quintessence.[5] He was positive that he could take everything that was written and published each day, and reduce it to a six-letter word. He worked out a secret formula and began posting daily bulletins, telling his result. Everything that had been written during the first day of his formula came down to the word "Irtnog." The second day, every-

[1] **Five-Foot Shelf**: the *Harvard Classics*, a collection of over four hundred literary masterpieces, the volumes of which can be placed on five feet of shelf space.

[2] **Wells's *Outline of History***: H. G. Wells (1866–1946) was an English writer whose account of world history is a condensed presentation of a vast subject.

[3] **Hemingway novel**: Ernest Hemingway's novels are noted for their emphasis on violence and strife.

[4] **Stevens Tech**: Stevens Institute of Technology, Hoboken, New Jersey.

[5] **quintessence** (kwĭnt·ĕs'ĕns): here, concentrated form.

thing reduced to "Efsitz." People accepted these mathematical distillations; and strangely enough, or perhaps not strangely at all, people were thoroughly satisfied — which would lead one to believe that what readers really craved was not so much the contents of books, magazines, and papers as the assurance that they were not missing anything. Shapiro found that his bulletin board was inadequate, so he made a deal with a printer and issued a handbill at five o'clock every afternoon, giving the Word of the Day. It caught hold instantly.

The effect on the populace was salutary.[1] Readers, once they felt confident that they had one-hundred-per-cent coverage, were able to discard the unnatural habit of focusing their eyes on words every instant. Freed of the exhausting consequences of their hopeless race against writers, they found their health returning, along with a certain tranquillity and a more poised way of living. There was a marked decrease in stomach ulcers, which, doctors said, had been the result of allowing the eye to jump nervously from one newspaper headline to another after a heavy meal. With the dwindling of reading, writing fell off. Forests, which had been plundered for newsprint, grew tall again; droughts were unheard of; and people dwelt in slow comfort, in a green world.

[1] **salutary** (săl'ū·tĕr'ĭ): beneficial.

APPRECIATING SATIRE

1. Can you find a sentence that sums up the central thought of the essay? Explain how the present popularity of news commentators on radio and television is related to this main idea.

2. Is each stage through which the digests "progressed" more or less absurd

than the previous stage? What is significant about the final stage?

3. What is the effect of mentioning the names of actual magazines such as the *Reader's Digest?* Do you think that underneath the humorous exaggeration in this essay there is some truth in E. B. White's analysis of the reading habits of Americans? Explain.

4. What do you think is the meaning of the last paragraph? Point out some of the drawbacks to a world in which reading and writing are greatly limited. What does the author suggest is the cause of the falling off of reading and writing described in the essay?

5. How are the names of the digests and of the counterdigests suitable? If you are not certain of the meaning of any of the words used for titles, consult a dictionary. What is amusing about the *Nutshell?* Can you think of other suitable titles for the magazines mentioned?

6. Try to state the ideas of this essay in three sentences. Then, tell what is lost in such a condensation.

COMPOSITION SUGGESTIONS

1. "Because they spend all their time watching television and spectator sports, Americans are losing the ability to read, to converse, or to walk." Do you agree or disagree with this statement? Give reasons to support your opinion.

2. Which newspapers and magazines do you read regularly? Which of their features appeal to you most? Why?

3. What seem to you to be the chief differences between your generation's view of life and that of your parents' generation? What do you think caused these differences? What conclusions can you reach about how they might be adjusted for the sake of harmony?

ABOUT THE AUTHOR

E. B. White (1899–) has been a writer ever since his college days on the Cornell University newspaper. Although he writes poetry, light verse, and stories, he is most often thought of as an essayist. He has served for more than twenty-five years on the *New Yorker* Magazine, in which many of his essays have appeared.

Others have appeared in *Harper's* under the column called "One Man's Meat." In the tradition of the great familiar essayists of the past, White builds his essays around his own ideas and experiences. He has the essayist's ability to see meaning in the simplest everyday experience, whether it be a spider building its web in the corner of a barn, a meeting on a crowded city bus, or a headline in a morning newspaper. He writes skillfully and almost always with a warm and understanding sense of humor.

A Cartoonist's Comment

Like E. B. White, and other writers who use the essay form (or light verse) to make witty comments on modern life, some cartoonists use their special skills to make us think as well as smile. James Mulligan's cartoon, below, has much in common with E. B. White's "Irtnog." What points of similarity can you think of? What similarity in purpose, for example? Do you think that James Mulligan and E. B. White would agree at all about some of the trends in modern life and what may happen to us as we try to become more and more efficient?

One point of similarity that may be worth noting is a similarity of method. Notice that both E. B. White and James Mulligan achieve their effects through *exaggeration*. Magazines never really will become as small as E. B. White suggests; nor, we hope, will machines start to turn the tables on man. But, by exaggerating some of the possible effects of our search for efficiency, the writer and cartoonist make their points. Notice how often exaggeration is an important ingredient in humor or wit in any of its forms.

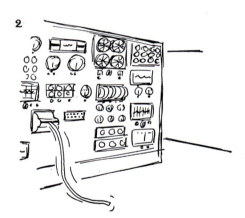

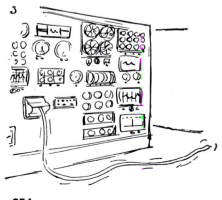

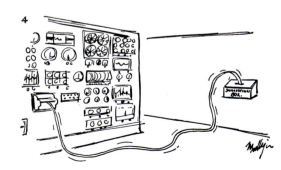

My War with the Ospreys

JOHN STEINBECK

In this informal essay, John Steinbeck, a noted American author, tells about his amusing battle with a family of fish hawks. What would you do if ospreys (ŏs′prĭz) refused your hospitality?

MY WAR with the ospreys, like most wars, was largely accidental and had a tendency to spread in unforeseen directions. It is not over yet. The coming of winter caused an uneasy truce. I had to go into New York while the ospreys migrated to wherever they go in the winter. Spring may open new hostilities, although I can find it in my heart to wish for peace and even friendship. I hope the ospreys, wherever they may be, will read this.

I shall go back to the beginning and set down my side of the affair, trying to be as fair as I possibly can, placing truth above either propaganda or self-justification. I am confident that until near the end of the association, my motives were kind to the point of being sloppy.

Two years and a half ago I bought a little place near Sag Harbor which is quite near to the tip of Long Island. The outer end of Long Island is like the open jaws of an alligator and, deep in the mouth, about where the soft palate would be, is Sag Harbor, a wonderful village inhabited by people who have been here for a long time. It is a fishing town, a local town which has resisted the inroads of tourists by building no motor courts and putting up no hotels.

Sag Harbor was once one of the two great whaling ports of the world and was, according to local accounts, not at all second to Nantucket Island. At that time no fewer than one hundred and fifty whaling bottoms roved the great seas and brought back their riches in oil. Sag Harbor and Nantucket lighted the lamps of the world until kerosene was developed and the whaling industry languished.

With the wealth brought back by the whalers, beautiful houses were built in the village during the early 1800's, houses of neo-Greek architecture with fluted columns, Greek key decorations, with fanlights [1] and Adam [2] doors and mantels. Some of these magnificent old houses have widow's walks, those high balconies on which the women kept watch for the return of their men from their year-long voyages. Some of these old houses are being rediscovered and restored. Many of the streets of Sag Harbor are named after old whaling men. My own place is near Jesse Halsey Lane and he is still locally known as Old Cap'n Jesse. I have a picture of his rough and whiskered face.

The place I bought is not one of the great old houses but a beautiful little point of land on the inland waters, a place called Bluff Point, with its own little bay — incidentally a bay which is considered hurricane-proof. Ordinarily only two boats are moored there, mine and one other, but during hurricane warnings as many as thirty craft come in for anchorage until the all-clear is broadcast.

My point, just under two acres, is shaded by great oak trees of four varieties, and there are many bushes and pines to edge it on the water side. I myself have planted a thousand Japanese black pines, furnished by the State of New York to edge my point, to hold the soil with their roots and eventually to curve beautifully inward, urged by the wind which blows every day of the year — sometimes a zephyr and sometimes a fierce and strident gale.

Greensward [3] grows on my place. On the highest point I have a small, snug cottage and in front of it a pier going out to nine feet at low water so that a fairly large boat can dock. My own boat, the *Lillymaid*, with Astolat as her port of registry, is named for my wife. She, the boat, is a utility craft twenty feet long, a clinker-built [4] Jersey sea skiff. Her eight-foot beam makes her highly dependable and seaworthy. Many of these specifications could also describe my wife. She is not clinker-built, however. The *Lillymaid* has a Navy top to put up when the weather gets too rough and she has a hundred-horsepower engine so we can run for it if a storm approaches. She is a lovely, efficient and sea-worthy craft and all we need for the fishing and coastal exploring which is our pleasure.

Our house, while very small, is double-walled and winterized so that we can drive out during cold weather when the not-so-quiet desperation of New York gets us down.

My young sons, ten and twelve, but eight and ten when the osprey war began, adore the place and spend most of their summers here, exploring about in their skiffs or quarreling happily on the pier or on the lawn under the oak trees. My wife, who I believe was realistically skeptical when I bought the place, has become its stanchest defender.

Our association with the village people of Sag Harbor is, I think, pleasant

---

[1] **fanlights:** semicircular windows with radiating sash bars, like the ribs of a fan, placed over a door or window.

[2] **Adam:** a style of eighteenth-century furniture.

[3] **greensward:** (green'swôrd'): turf green with grass.

[4] **clinker-built:** having the external planks of a ship put on so that one edge of each overlaps the edge of the plank next to it, like clapboards on a house.

to all of us. I come originally from a small town on the West Coast, a fishing town where my people have lived for a long time. And I find that what applies in my home country is equally acceptable in Sag Harbor. If you pay your bills, trade locally as much as possible, mind your own business and are reasonably pleasant, pretty soon they forget that you are an outlander. I feel that I belong in Sag Harbor and I truly believe that the people of the village have accepted us as citizens. I do not sense the resentment from them which is reserved for tourists and summer people.

But I must get back to the ospreys, because with them I have not only failed to make friends but have, on the contrary, been insulted, have thrown down the gauntlet [1] and had it accepted.

On the West Coast, in California's Monterey County where I was born, I learned from childhood the grasses and flowers, the insects and the fishes, the animals from gopher and ground squirrel to bobcat and coyote, deer and mountain lion, and of course the birds, the common ones at least. These are things a child absorbs as he is growing up.

When I first came to Long Island I knew none of these things. Trees, grasses, animals and birds were all strange to me; they had to be learned. And sometimes the natives could not help me much because they knew the things so well and deeply that they could not bring them to the surface.

Thus with books and by asking questions I have begun to learn the names of trees and bushes, of berries and flowers. With a telescope, a birthday present from my wife, I have watched muskrats and a pair of otters swimming in our bay. I have tried to identify the migrating ducks and geese when they sit down in our bay to rest from their journey.

The mallards mate and nest in the reeds along our waterline and bring their ducklings for the bread we throw to them from the pier. I have watched my boys sitting quietly on the lawn with the wild ducks crawling over their legs to get pieces of doughnut from their fingers.

The baby rabbits skitter through my vegetable garden and, since I like the rabbits better than my scrawny vegetables, I permit them not only to live but to pursue happiness on my land.

Our house has a glassed-in sun porch and outside its windows I have built a feeding station for birds. Sitting inside I do my best to identify the different visitors with the help of an Audubon [2] and I have not always, I confess, been successful. There is one common blackish bird which looks to be of the grackle persuasion but his bill is the wrong color and I don't know what he is.

In the upper branches of a half-dead oak tree on the very tip of our point, there was, when I took possession, a tattered lump of trash which looked like an unmade bed in a motor court. In my first early spring a native named Ray Bassenden, our contractor and builder, told me, "That's an osprey's nest. They come back every year. I remember that nest since I was a little boy."

"They build a messy nest," I said.

"Messy, yes," he said professionally, "but I doubt if I could design something the winds wouldn't blow out. It isn't pretty but it's darned good architecture from a staying point of view."

[1] **thrown down the gauntlet**: given a challenge.

[2] **Audubon** (ô'dŏo·bŏn): a comprehensive book on birds, named after John James Audubon (1785–1851), who studied and painted American birds.

Toward the end of May, to my delight, the ospreys came back from wherever they had been, and from the beginning they fascinated me. They are about the best fishermen in the world and I am about the worst. I watched them by the hour. They would coast along hanging on the breeze perhaps fifty feet above the water, then suddenly their wings raised like the fins of a bomb and they arrowed down and nearly always came up with a fish. Then they would turn the fish in their talons so that its head was into the wind and fly to some high dead branch to eat their catch. I became a habitual osprey watcher.

In time, two of my ospreys were nudged by love and began to install new equipment in the great nest on my point. They brought unusual material — pieces of wood, rake handles, strips of cloth, reeds, swatches of seaweed. One of them, so help me, brought a piece of two-by-four pine three feet long to put into the structure. They weren't very careful builders. The ground under the tree was strewn with the excess stuff that fell out.

I mounted my telescope permanently on the sun porch and even trimmed some branches from intervening trees,

and from then on, those love-driven ospreys didn't have a moment of privacy.

Then June came and school was out and my boys trooped happily out to Sag Harbor. I warned them not to go too near the point for fear of offending the nest builders, and they promised they would not.

And then one morning the ospreys were gone and the nest abandoned. When it became apparent that they weren't coming back I walked out to the point and saw, sticking halfway out of the nest, the shaft and feathers of an arrow.

Now Catbird, my youngest son, is the archer of the family. I ran him down and gave him whatfor in spite of his plaintive protests that he had not shot at the nest.

For a week I waited for the birds to come back, but they did not. They were across the bay. I could see them through the telescope building an uneasy nest on top of a transformer on a telephone pole where they were definitely not wanted.

I got a ladder and climbed up to the nest on our point and when I came down I apologized to Catbird for my unjust suspicions. For in the nest I had found not only the arrow, but my bamboo garden rake, three T shirts belonging to my boys and a Plaza Hotel bath towel. Apparently nothing was too unusual for the ospreys to steal for their nest building. But our birds were definitely gone and showed no intention of returning. I went back to my Audubon and it told me the following:

"Osprey (fish hawk) *Pandion haliaëtus*, length 23 inches, wingspread about 6½ feet, weight 3½ pounds.

"Identification — in flight the wings appear long and the outer half has a characteristic backward sweep.

"Habits — (age 21 years) Provided they are not molested, ospreys will nest wherever there is a reasonably extensive body of clear water and some sort of elevated nest sites exist. The birds have little fear of man and are excellent watchdogs, cheeping loudly at intruders and driving off crows and other birds of prey. For this reason platforms on tall poles are often erected to encourage them to nest about homes and farmyards. Their food consists entirely of fish. These they spot from heights of thirty to one hundred feet, then, after hovering for a moment, they half close their wings and plunge into the water. The fish is seized in their talons, the toes of which are used in pairs, two to a side. This and the rough surface of the foot gives them a firm grip on the most slippery prey. After a catch, they rise quickly . . . and arrange the fish head first."

There followed a list of the kinds of fish they eat and their range and habits. Those were our boys, all right.

I must admit I had been pleased and a little proud to have my own osprey nest, apart from being able to watch them fish. I had planned to observe the nestlings when they arrived. The empty nest on the point was a matter of sorrow and perplexity to me. The summer

was a little darkened by the empty nest, and later the winter winds ripped at its half-completed messiness.

It was in February of 1956 that the answer came to me. If people put up platforms on poles, why could I not build a nest so attractive as to be irresistible to any passing osprey with procreation on his mind? Why could I not win back my own birds from the uncomfortable nest which the power company had meanwhile torn off the transformer? I had been to Denmark and had seen what the country people there did for storks. And the storks loved them for it and had their young on the roof tops and year by year brought luck to their benefactors.

In the late winter I went to work. Climbing the oak tree on the point, I cleaned away the old debris of the nest. Then I mounted and firmly wired in place horizontally a large wagon wheel. I cut dry pampas grass stalks and bound them in long faggots. Then with the freezing blasts of winter tearing at my clothes, I reascended the tree and wove the reeds into the spokes of the wheel until I had a nest which, if I had any oviparous [1] impulses, I should have found irresistible.

My wife, dressed in warm clothing, stood dutifully on the ground under the trees and hooked bundles of reeds on the line I threw down to her. She has a highly developed satiric sense which on other occasions I have found charming. She shouted up against the howling wind: "If anybody sees you, a middle-aged man, up a tree in midwinter, building a nest, I will have trouble explaining it to a sanity commission."

Misplaced humor can, under some circumstances, almost amount to bad taste. Silently and doggedly I completed what I believe was the hand-

[1] **oviparous** (ō·vĭp′à·rŭs): egg-laying.

somest nest in the Western Hemisphere. Then I went back to my sun porch to await eventualities.

I did have some difficulty explaining the project to my boys. To my oldest son Thom's question, "Why do you build nests for birds?" I could only jocularly reply, "Well, I can build a better nest than they can, but I can't lay eggs, so you see we have to get together."

The winter was long and cold and there was hardly any spring at all. Summer came without warning about June first. I had trouble with the novel I was writing since I had to rush constantly to the telescope to see whether the ospreys, my prospective tenants, had returned.

Then school was out and my boys moved to Sag Harbor and I put them on watch.

One morning Catbird charged into my study, which is a corner of the garage.

"Ospreys!" he shouted. "Come running — ospreys!"

"Sh!" I shouted back. "Keep your voice down. You'll disturb them."

I rushed for my telescope, bowling Catbird over in my rush and tripping over Thom's feet.

There were the ospreys all right. But they weren't settling into my beautiful nest. They were dismantling it, tearing it to pieces, lifting out the carefully bound reed pads and carrying them across the bay and propping them clumsily on top of the same transformer.

Of course my feelings were hurt. Why should I deny it? And on top of all my work. But on the heels of injury came anger. Those lousy, slipshod, larcenous birds, those ingrates, those — those ospreys. My eyes strayed to the shotgun that hangs over my fireplace, but before I could reach for it a Machi-avellian [1] thought came to me.

I wanted to hurt the ospreys, yes. I wanted revenge on them, but with number four shot? No. I ached to hurt them as they had hurt me — in their feelings, psychologically.

I am an adept at psychological warfare. I know well how to sink the knife into sensibilities. I was coldly quiet, even deadly in my approach and manner, so that my boys walked about under a cloud and Thom asked, "What's the matter, Father, did you lose some money playing poker?"

"You stay out of the garage," I said quietly.

I had made my plan. I declared the garage off limits to everyone. My novel came to a dead stop. Daily I worked in the garage using pieces of chicken wire and a great deal of plaster of Paris.

Then I paid a call on my neighbor, Jack Ramsey, a very good painter, and asked him to come to my work shop and to bring his palette and brushes. At the end of two days we emerged with our product — a lifesize perfect replica of a nesting whooping crane. It is my belief that there are only thirty-seven of these rare and wonderful birds in the world. Well, this was the thirty-eighth.

Chuckling evilly I hoisted the plaster bird up in the tree and wired her firmly in the nest where her blinding white body, black tail and brilliant red mask stood out magnificently against the sky. I had even made her bill a little overlarge to take care of foreshortening.

Finally I went back to the sun porch and turned my telescope on the ospreys who pretended to go about their nest building on the transformer as though nothing had happened. But I knew

[1] **Machiavellian** (măk'ĭ-ȧ·věl'ĭ-ȧn): cunning; this refers to the political theories of the fifteenth-century Italian statesman Machiavelli.

what must be going on over there, although they kept up their façade [1] of listlessness, and I must say they were building an even messier nest than usual.

Mrs. Osprey was saying, "Lord almighty, George! Look who has moved into the apartment *you* didn't want. Why did I listen to you?"

To which he was replying, "*I* didn't want — what do you mean *I* didn't want? It was you who said the neighborhood wasn't good enough. Don't you put words in my mouth, Mildred."

"Everybody knows you have no taste or background," she was replying. "Your Uncle Harry built his nest over a slaughterhouse."

And I laughed to myself. These are the wounds that never heal. This is psychological warfare as it should be fought.

Two days later, Thom came running into my study in the garage.

"The nest," he cried. "Look at the nest."

I bolted for the door. The ospreys in jealous rage were dive-bombing my whooping crane, but all they could accomplish was the breaking of their talons on the hard surface of the plaster. Finally they gave up and flew away, followed by my shouts of derision.

I did hear my oldest boy say to his brother, "Father has been working too hard. He has gone nuts."

Catbird replied, "His id [2] has been ruptured. Sometimes one broods too much on a subject and throws the whole psychic pattern into an uproar."

[1] **façade** (fȧ·säd′): front or appearance.
[2] **id** (ĭd): in psychoanalysis, one of three structures thought to make up a person's mental apparatus; the id is thought to contain all of the biological impulses.

That isn't quite where it rests.

It is true that the ospreys have not attacked any more, but we have had other visitors, human visitors.

One morning I looked out the window to see a rather stout lady in khaki trousers and a turtle-neck sweater creeping across my lawn on her hands and knees. Field glasses dangled from her neck and she held a camera in front of her. When I went out to question her, she angrily waved me away.

"Go back," she whispered hoarsely. "Do you want her to fly away?"

"But you don't understand — " I began.

"*Will* you keep your voice down," she said hoarsely. "Do you know what that is? The club will never believe me. If I don't get a picture of her I'll kill you."

Yes, we have had bird watchers — lots of them. You see, our whooping crane can be sighted from a long way off. After a time they discovered the nature of the thing, but they would not listen to my explanation of the ruse. In fact, they became angry; not at the ospreys, where the blame rests — but at me.

As I write, it is autumn and from the coldness and the growing winds, an early winter and a cold one is indicated. I have taken my whooping crane down and restored the nest to its old beauty. When the spring comes again — we shall see what we shall see. No one can say that I am unforgiving. The nest is ready and waiting. Let us see whether the ospreys are big enough to let bygones be bygones.

My wife says that if she has to go through another year like this she will — no, I won't tell you what she says. Sometimes her sense of humor seems a little strained.

APPRECIATING THE AUTHOR'S PERSONALITY

1. What do we learn about Steinbeck's feeling for nature and animals? Consider, for instance, his attitude toward the rabbits who eat his vegetables, his comments on the wild ducks and birds, and his interest in trees. As for the ospreys, note carefully what Steinbeck says in his very first paragraph and in the next-to-the-last paragraph. How did he feel during the summer the ospreys left the nest empty? In view of these insights, what could you say that would help to characterize Steinbeck?

2. What kind of a neighbor does Steinbeck seem to be? Is there any evidence that he is interested in other people? that his neighbors enjoy him?

3. You probably also have some definite impressions of Steinbeck as a husband and father. How does his family react to him? Do you think he would be fun to have as a father? What does his apology to his son, Catbird, tell us about him?

4. What interests does Steinbeck have other than writing? Does he seem to like learning about other fields? In what ways are his several interests connected?

5. Do you think it is typical of human beings to want revenge and then to feel some remorse over their actions? Is it possible to feel both anger and affection toward the very same person? How does your answer relate to the falling-out Steinbeck has with the two fish hawks?

ABOUT THE AUTHOR

John Steinbeck (1902–   ) was born in Salinas, California. He attended Stanford University off and on for six years but never obtained his degree. His college major, marine biology, led to friendship with Edward F. Ricketts, a marine biologist who operated a laboratory on Cannery Row in Monterey, California. Steinbeck accompanied Ricketts on an expedition in the Gulf of California and later used his friend as the basis for "Doc," a character in the novel *Cannery Row*. The Southwest and the Monterey area furnish the setting for most of his early writing. *Of Mice and Men* brought him attention from literary critics and a wide reading public. The book later became a New York Drama Critics Award prize play and a popular motion picture. In 1940 Steinbeck won the Pulitzer prize for his novel *Grapes of Wrath*, a story of the hardships of a family of Dust Bowl farmers on their way to California. Steinbeck now lives in the eastern United States. He has done a good deal of traveling in the years since World War II and has reported on his trips in various magazine and newspaper articles.

The Steinbeck-Osprey War ➤

The pictures on the opposite page show some of the contenders and two of the battlefields in John Steinbeck's war with the ospreys. At the top, three young osprey warriors eagerly await an opportunity to join their parents in battle with the author (whose picture is at the bottom of this page). At the lower left, a vigilant guard stands ready to defend the ospreys' fortress. The picture in the lower right-hand corner is Steinbeck's castle, his home on Long Island. You can be sure that hidden in those trees are watchful osprey spies keeping a careful check on the enemy's whereabouts and activities.

Insert Flap "A"
and Throw
It Away

S. J. PERELMAN

Have you ever had difficulty following directions in assembling some modern gadget? If you have, you will sympathize with the author of this essay. Noted for his satirical comments on some of the minor annoyances of modern life, S. J. Perelman often exaggerates a situation until it seems ridiculous. Here he is poking fun at the do-it-yourself assembly kits.

O NE STIFLING summer afternoon last August, in the attic of a tiny stone house in Pennsylvania, I made a most interesting discovery: the shortest, cheapest method of inducing a nervous break-

down ever perfected. In this technique, the subject is placed in a sharply sloping attic heated to 340° F. and given a mothproof closet known as the Jiffy-Cloz to assemble. The Jiffy-Cloz, procurable at any department store or neighborhood insane asylum, consists of half a dozen gigantic sheets of red cardboard, two plywood doors, a clothes rack, and a packet of staples. With these is included a set of instructions mimeographed in pale-violet ink, fruity with phrases like "Pass Section F through Slot AA, taking care not to fold tabs behind washers (see Fig. 9)."

The cardboard is so processed that as the subject struggles convulsively to force the staple through, it suddenly buckles, plunging the staple deep into his thumb. He thereupon springs up with a dolorous cry and smites his knob (Section K) on the rafters (RR). As a final demonic touch, the Jiffy-Cloz people cunningly omit four of the staples necessary to finish the job, so that after indescribable purgatory, the best the subject can possibly achieve is a sleazy, capricious structure which would reduce any self-respecting moth to helpless laughter. The cumulative frustration, the tropical heat, and the soft, ghostly chuckling of the moths are calculated to unseat the strongest mentality.

In a period of rapid technological change, however, it was inevitable that a method as cumbersome as the Jiffy-Cloz would be superseded. It was superseded at exactly nine-thirty Christmas morning by a device called the Self-Running 10-Inch Scale-Model Delivery-Truck Kit Powered by Magic Motor, costing twenty-nine cents. About nine on that particular morning, I was spread-eagled on my bed, indulging in my favorite sport of mouth-breathing, when a cork fired from a child's air gun mysteriously lodged in my throat. The pellet proved awkward for a while, but I finally ejected it by flailing the little marksman (and his sister, for good measure) until their welkins rang,[1] and sauntered in to breakfast. Before I could choke down a healing fruit juice, my consort, a tall, regal creature indistinguishable from Cornelia, the Mother of the Gracchi,[2] except that her foot was entangled in a

roller skate, swept in. She extended a large, unmistakable box covered with diagrams.

"Now don't start making excuses," she whined. "It's just a simple cardboard toy. The directions are on the back — "

"Look, dear," I interrupted, rising hurriedly and pulling on my overcoat, "it clean slipped my mind. I'm supposed to take a lesson in crosshatching[3] at Zim's School of Cartooning today."

"On Christmas?" she asked suspiciously.

"Yes, it's the only time they could fit me in," I countered glibly. "This is the big week for crosshatching, you know, between Christmas and New Year's."

"Do you think you ought to go in your pajamas?" she asked.

"Oh, that's O.K.," I smiled. "We often work in our pajamas up at Zim's. Well, good-by now. If I'm not home by Thursday, you'll find a cold snack in the safe-deposit box." My subterfuge, unluckily, went for naught, and in a trice I was sprawled on the nursery floor, surrounded by two lambkins and ninety-eight segments of the Self-Running 10-Inch Scale-Model Delivery-Truck Construction Kit.

The theory of the kit was simplicity itself, easily intelligible to Kettering of General Motors, Professor Millikan, or any first-rate physicist. Taking as my starting point the only sentence I could comprehend, "Fold down on all lines marked 'fold down'; fold up on all lines marked 'fold up,' " I set the children to work. In a few moments, my skin was suffused with a delightful tingling sensation and I was ready for the second phase, lightly referred to in the directions as "Preparing the Spring Motor Unit." As nearly as I could determine

[1] **their welkins** (wĕl′kĭnz) **rang:** the skies rang with their loud cries.
[2] **the Gracchi:** the brothers Gaius and Tiberius Gracchus, famous Roman statesmen.

[3] **crosshatching:** a method of drawing with a series of crossing parallel lines.

after twenty minutes of mumbling, the Magic Motor ("No Electricity — No Batteries — Nothing to Wind — Motor Never Wears Out") was an accordion-pleated affair operating by torsion,[1] attached to the axles. "It is necessary," said the text, "to cut a slight notch in each of the axles with a knife (see Fig. C.). To find the exact place to cut this notch, lay one of the axles over diagram at bottom of page."

"Well, *now* we're getting some place!" I boomed, with a false gusto that deceived nobody. "Here, Buster, run in and get Daddy a knife."

"I dowanna," quavered the boy, backing away. "You always cut yourself at this stage." I gave the wee fellow an indulgent pat on the head that flattened it slightly, to teach him civility, and commandeered a long, serrated bread knife from the kitchen. "Now watch me closely, children," I ordered. "We place the axle on the diagram as in Fig. C, applying a strong downward pressure on the knife handle at all times." The axle must have been a factory second, because an instant later I was in the bathroom grinding my teeth in agony and attempting to stanch the flow of blood. Ultimately, I succeeded in contriving a rough bandage and slipped back into the nursery without awaking the children's suspicions. An agreeable surprise awaited me. Displaying a mechanical aptitude clearly inherited from their sire, the rascals had put together the chassis of the delivery truck.

"Very good indeed," I complimented (naturally, one has to exaggerate praise to develop a child's self-confidence). "Let's see — what's the next step? Ah, yes, 'Lock into box shape by inserting tabs C, D, E, F, G, H, J, K, and L

[1] **torsion** (tôr′shŭn): motion caused by the turning or twisting of a wire or rod.

into slots C, D, E, F, G, H, J, K, and L. Ends of front axle should be pushed through holes A and B.'" While marshalling the indicated parts in their proper order, I emphasized to my rapt listeners the necessity of patience and perseverance. "Haste makes waste, you know," I reminded them. "Rome wasn't built in a day. Remember, your daddy isn't always going to be here to show you."

"Where *are* you going to be?" they demanded.

"In the movies, if I can arrange it," I snarled. Poising tabs C, D, E, F, G, H, J, K, and L in one hand and the corresponding slots in the other, I essayed a union of the two, but in vain. The moment I made one set fast and tackled another, tab and slot would part company, thumbing their noses at me. Although the children were too immature to understand, I saw in a flash where the trouble lay. Some idiotic employee at the factory had punched out the wrong design, probably out of sheer spite. So that was his game, eh? I set my lips in a grim line and, throwing one hundred and fifty-seven pounds of fighting fat into the effort, pounded the component parts into a homogeneous mass.

"There," I said with a gasp, "that's close enough. Now then, who wants candy? One, two, three — everybody off to the candy store!"

"We wanna finish the delivery truck!" they wailed. "Mummy, he won't let us finish the delivery truck!" Threats, cajolery, bribes were of no avail. In their jungle code, a twenty-nine-cent gewgaw bulked larger than a parent's love. Realizing that I was dealing with a pair of monomaniacs, I determined to show them who was master and wildly began locking the cardboard units helter-skelter, without any regard for the directions. When sections refused to fit, I gouged them with my nails and forced them together, cackling shrilly. The side panels collapsed; with a bestial oath, I drove a safety pin through them and lashed them to the roof. I used paper clips, bobby pins, anything I could lay my hands on. My fingers fairly flew and my breath whistled in my throat. "You want a delivery truck, do you?" I panted. "All right, I'll show you!" As merciful blackness closed in, I was on my hands and knees, bunting the infernal thing along with my nose and whinnying, "Roll, confound you, roll!"

"Absolute quiet," a carefully modulated voice was saying, "and fifteen of the white tablets every four hours." I opened my eyes carefully in the darkened room. Dimly I picked out a knife-like character actor in a Vandyke beard [1] and pencil-striped pants folding a stethoscope into his bag. "Yes," he added thoughtfully, "if we play our cards right, this ought to be a long, expensive recovery." From far away, I could hear my wife's voice bravely trying to control her anxiety.

"What if he becomes restless, Doctor?"

"Get him a detective story," returned the leech. "Or better still, a nice, soothing picture puzzle — something he can do with his hands."

[1] **Vandyke beard:** a trim, pointed beard, as in pictures by the Flemish painter Vandyke.

THINKING IT OVER

1. Shakespeare once wrote, "Though this be madness, yet there is method in't." Could Shakespeare's thought be applied to Perelman's essay?

2. Name some of the things you would like to poke fun at in a humorous essay.

ENJOYING THE RIDICULOUS

Perelman has used each of the following devices in his essay:

1. THE EXAGGERATED. Locate several examples of situations Perelman has overstated until they go beyond truth or reason. For example, "The cardboard is so processed that . . . the subject struggles convulsively to force the staple through . . ."

2. THE ABSURD. Locate elements wildly contrary to common sense. ". . . a cork fired from a child's air gun mysteriously lodged in my throat."

3. THE SARCASTIC. Beginning with the very first sentence as an example, find other examples of bitter or scornful irony.

4. THE MOCK-SERIOUS. Find illustrations of mock-serious statements, where Perelman seems to be imitating someone else and doing it with a kind of sly innocence. For example, "In a period of rapid technological change, however, it was inevitable that a method as cumbersome as the Jiffy-Cloz would be superseded."

5. THE UNEXPECTED AND UNUSUAL IN WORDING. Do not miss the humor in Perelman's phrasing: "until their welkins rang," "my rapt listeners," "in their jungle code," "the leech." Find other examples.

ABOUT THE AUTHOR

S. J. Perelman (1904–) worked on the humorous weekly *Judge* after graduation from Brown University. *Dawn Ginsbergh's Revenge* — a wild comedy — brought the author to Hollywood where he wrote jokes for movie comedies. Perelman has also managed a radio show called *Author, Author. Time* Magazine considers him an exponent of "screwball wit" which "calls for an exquisite sense of cliché (over-used words and phrases) and mimicry and . . . delight in knocking over-crystallized words, objects, and other gestures into glassy pieces that cut each other." Most of Perelman's sketches have appeared in the *New Yorker* and *Holiday* magazines before being published in book form. He satirizes everything from advertising and movies to himself as the world-weary traveler. *Westward Ha!* and *The Swiss Family Perelman* report his two trips around the world.

My Financial Career

STEPHEN LEACOCK

A *sense of humor* is the balance wheel of life, giving us enough perspective to avoid taking ourselves too seriously. If Stephen Leacock had merely wanted to explain his uneasiness in banks, he could have done so in a few sentences. His purpose, however, is quite different. Through humor, he sets us to smiling at the painful embarrassments all of us encounter and, in so doing, he offers us a more balanced perspective. We conclude, with him, that for the pains and troubles of life, laughter is a better reaction than despair.

WHEN I GO into a bank I get rattled. The clerks rattle me; the wickets rattle me; the sight of the money rattles me; everything rattles me. The moment I cross the threshold of a bank I am a hesitating jay. If I attempt to transact business there, I become an irresponsible idiot.

I knew this beforehand; but when my salary was raised fifty dollars a month, I felt that the bank was the only place for it. So I shambled in and looked timidly around at the clerks. I had an idea that a person about to open an account needed to consult the manager. I went up to a wicket marked "Accountant." The accountant was a tall, cool devil — the very sight of him rattled me. My voice was sepulchral.[1]

"May I see the manager?" I said, and added solemnly, "Alone?" I don't know why I said "alone."

"Certainly," said the accountant and fetched him. The manager was a grave, calm man. I held my fifty-six dollars clutched in a crumpled ball in my pocket.

[1] sepulchral (sĕ·pŭl′krăl): unnaturally low and grave.

"Are you the manager?" I said. Heaven knows I didn't doubt it.

"Yes," he said.

"May I see you?" I asked. "Alone?" I didn't want to say "alone" again, but without it my question seemed self-evident.

The manager looked at me in some alarm. He felt that I had a terrible secret to reveal.

"Come in here," he said, leading the way to a private room and turning the key.

"We are safe from interruption here," he said. "Sit down."

We both sat down and looked at one another. I found no voice to speak.

"You are a Pinkerton detective, I presume," he said.

He had gathered from my mysterious manner that I was a detective. I knew what he was thinking and felt all the worse.

"No, not from Pinkerton's," I said, seemingly to imply that I came from a rival agency. "To tell the truth," I went on, as if I *had* been prompted to lie about the matter, "I am not a detective at all. I have come to open an account. I intend to keep all my money in this bank."

The manager looked relieved, but still serious; he concluded now that I was a son of Baron Rothschild,[1] or a young Gould.[2]

"A very large account, I suppose," he said.

"Fairly large," I whispered. "I propose to deposit fifty-six dollars now, and fifty dollars a month regularly."

The manager got up and opened the door. He called to the accountant.

"Mr. Montgomery," he said, unkindly loud, "this gentleman is opening an account; he will deposit fifty-six dollars. Good morning."

I rose. A big iron door stood open at the side of the room.

"Good morning," I said and stepped into the safe.

"Come out," said the manager coldly, showing me the other way.

I went up to the accountant's wicket and poked the ball of money at him with a quick, convulsive movement, as if I were doing a trick. My face was ghastly pale.

"Here," I said, "deposit it." The tone of the words seemed to mean, "Let us do this painful business while the fit is on us."

He took the money and gave it to another clerk. He made me write the sum on a slip and sign my name in a book. I no longer knew what I was doing. The bank swam before my eyes.

"Is it deposited?" I asked, in a hollow, vibrating voice.

"It is," said the accountant.

"Then I want to draw a check."

My idea was to draw out six dollars for present use. Someone gave me a checkbook through a wicket, and someone else began telling me how to write the check. The people in the bank had the impression that I was an invalid millionaire. I wrote something on the check and thrust it in at the clerk. He looked at it.

"What! Are you drawing it all out again?" he asked in surprise. Then I realized that I had written fifty-six instead of six. I was too far gone to reason now. I had a feeling that I could not explain my act. All the clerks had stopped writing to look at me.

Reckless with misery, I made a plunge.

"Yes, the whole thing."

"You withdraw your money from the bank!"

---

[1] **Baron Rothschild**: a German financier.
[2] **Gould**: Jay Gould, an American financier.

"Oh." I caught his meaning and answered without even trying to think, "In fifties."

He gave me a fifty-dollar bill.

"And the six?" he asked dryly.

"In sixes," I said.

He gave me the money, and I rushed out. As the big doors swung behind me I caught the echo of a roar of laughter that went up to the ceiling of the bank. Since then I bank no more. I keep my money in cash in my trousers pocket, and my savings in silver dollars in a sock.

APPRECIATING HUMOR

1. What is the effect of Leacock's using the first person "I" in telling about this experience?

2. Locate at least two episodes in which Leacock's words and behavior are exaggerated or absurd.

3. How do you account for the fear many human beings have of acting absurdly? Why do you think people try so hard to fit properly into social situations?

4. Why are we amused rather than saddened by Leacock's mistakes in the bank?

NOTING THE ESSAY'S FLEXIBILITY

Have you noticed that all the essays you have read in this section might with some justification be called fiction rather than nonfiction? Surely you did not take without several grains of salt all the incidents in "Irtnog," "My War with the Ospreys," "Insert Flap 'A' and Throw It Away," and "My Financial Career."

Essays have always been difficult to classify, a fact that is annoying for anyone who likes to have things neatly defined. However, librarians, critics, teachers, and publishers generally do agree on the classification of essays as nonfiction. Why are they justified in making this classification? What justification, particularly, is there with respect to the four essays mentioned above? Might they be placed under short stories? Why or why not?

"Every cent of it."

"Are you not going to deposit any more?" said the clerk, astonished.

"Never!"

An idiot hope struck me that he might think someone had insulted me while I was writing the check and that I had changed my mind. I made a wretched attempt to look like a man with a fearfully quick temper.

The clerk prepared to pay the money.

"How will you have it?" he said.

ABOUT THE AUTHOR

Stephen Leacock (1869–1944) once said that his great-grandfather had made so much money that none of the family had had to work for three generations, but that he, Stephen, had unfortunately slipped into the fourth generation and so had to begin all over again. Although born in England, Leacock lived in Canada from the time he was six years old. After his graduation from the University of Chicago, he returned to Canada to begin his life-long work as a professor at McGill University in the field of political economics. He wrote many serious works, including biographies, books on Canadian history, and material in economics. After publishing his first volume of humorous sketches, *Literary Lapses,* Leacock became a very popular humorist and produced a wealth of humorous books and essays. For the rest of his life he carried on the dual career of humorist and economist.

Speaking of Essays

There is a difference between nonfiction that is primarily informational and non-fiction that is literature. We find, on one hand, a factual report about migratory birds; on the other, we have essays like Steinbeck's, with its observations on the two ospreys. Both pieces reveal accurate information about birds, but we have to agree that Steinbeck's essay is considerably different from the factual report. What is this difference? Why do we classify Steinbeck's essay as literature and the factual report as informational writing?

One brief way to explain the difference might be this: Engineers, scientists, and historians — to choose three examples from among many people who write about facts and ideas — differ in their purpose from writers like Steinbeck. The informational writer deals with truth about facts, and in any civilization his kind of writing is tremendously important. (Consider medical journals, your biology text, or accurate reporting of world news.) The writer of literature has a different purpose. He may also deal with truth about facts, but he has a special way of seeing things, a special way of looking at the world. He may see the same things as the engineer or scientist, but he sees them differently. First of all, he sees them imaginatively; he sees them with his feelings and emotions as well as his mind. They make a different impression on him, and his purpose in writing is to give the reader this impression or feeling as completely as possible. Secondly, the writer of literature is concerned with values — human values. The literary writer views the human situation in relation to the individual and through the individual. For example, Steinbeck did not present us with facts for the sake of facts. He wanted to communicate how he felt, and understanding how people feel is one of the values we gain from reading literature. Thus, we see that literary and informational writing are created for different purposes.

Although essays, like all nonfiction, dwell close to the border of fact, they are not as much concerned with facts and ideas as they are with how facts and ideas affect human beings. Essayists such as Leacock, White, or Perelman have an attitude toward their ideas, and they want their readers to share this attitude. They write to express themselves. Their essays are good talk, clever wit and satire, amusing exaggeration. Like Montaigne's little "attempts," such writing represents an exploring and weighing of ideas. As literature, essays are attempts to communicate imaginatively. They provide insights into individual thought and action — insights into the human meaning of experience. And such insights, like the accurate reporting of information, are indispensable to mankind.

Words and Wisdom

In this unit we are looking at several of the types of writing that are generally classified as nonfiction. These types are presented as one means of helping you to develop a deeper understanding and appreciation of the vast world of literature. It is wise, however, to remember the warning given here and there in the text that classifications and labels are not the most important aspects of literature. The purpose and content, the words, of each selection are what really count.

Though there are many varieties of nonfiction, developed through the ages, they often have a similar aim — to convey wisdom and common sense. The selections that follow have been grouped together because they illustrate this similarity. Here you will find two very different types of nonfiction, both sharing the common purpose of teaching certain truths about life. The first three selections are *fables*, among the oldest of all literary forms; the last is an *interview*, transcribed from the tapes of a television broadcast.

FABLES

Whether you have labeled them as such, you undoubtedly have heard or read fables. These are the brief tales wherein animals talk and act like human beings. A fox and a crow discuss a piece of cheese, or geese offer to carry a turtle on a stick between them. At the end of the story a moral is drawn; in fact, this is the purpose of the fable — to teach some moral truth. Because their essential purpose is to teach, and not just to tell a story, fables are generally classified as nonfiction.

Evidently the fable has long been one of man's favorite forms for preserving and sharing wisdom. It is found in every part of the world and dates far back in history. (Aesop, whose fables are still famous today, lived in Greece more than 2,500 years ago.) The animal-characters often vary from country to country; but regardless of whether the characters are vain peacocks, greedy pigs, or wily foxes, fables reflect the ways of human beings in all ages and on all continents.

THE INTERVIEW

People have always learned by asking questions of one another and particularly of learned men. However, until the development of modern recording techniques, answers and new ideas reached only the ears of the immediate questioner. For these ideas to be made available to large groups of widely separated people, someone had to write them down. This often meant that a writer rephrased things in his own words, with occasional quotes from the speaker. Now, in our time, the human voice can be recorded, and people everywhere can hear ideas as they were originally expressed or can obtain word-for-word transcriptions of the actual talks. Thus we can all derive full value from an interview even though we may be separated from it by considerable distance and time.

The Dog in the Manger

AESOP

"The Dog in the Manger," by the seventeenth-century illustrator Francis Barlow, for an English edition of Aesop's fables.

A DOG lay in a manger, and by his growling and snapping prevented the oxen from eating the hay which had been placed for them. "What a selfish dog!" said one of them to his companions; "he cannot eat the hay himself, and yet refuses to allow those to eat who can."

The Stupid Monkeys

ANONYMOUS

An Ancient Hindu Fable

ONCE UPON a time a tribe of Monkeys made their home in the pleasure-garden of the King of Benares. On a certain holiday, when the drum was beaten to call the people together, the King's head gardener, hearing the drum, said to himself: "Even though it is a holiday, the garden must be watered. Accordingly, I will ask the Monkeys to water the garden for me, so that I can be off to enjoy myself and keep holiday with the rest." So he called to the Monkeys and asked them to water the garden; and when the Monkeys had promised to water all the young trees faithfully, the gardener gave them the waterskins and the wooden watering-pot with which to perform their task.

After the gardener had gone, the Monkeys took up the waterskins and the watering-pot and began to water the young trees. But the leader of the Monkeys stopped them. "Wait," said he, "we must be careful not to waste the water. Before you water them you must first pull up each tree and look at the size of the root. Then, you must give plenty of water to those which have long, deep roots, but only a little water to those that have short roots. For when this water is all gone, we shall have hard work to get any more."

"To be sure," said the other Monkeys, "that is what we must do." So they pulled up all the roots, just as their leader had told them to do. And all the young trees died.

MORAL: With every intention of doing good, the ignorant and foolish succeed only in doing harm.

"The Stupid Monkeys" from *An Argosy of Fables*, edited by Frederic Tabor Cooper. Reprinted by permission of J. B. Lippincott Company.

What Happened to Charles

JAMES THURBER

Here is a fable from our own time by the American humorist, James Thurber. In it you meet a number of animals, including Eva, a duck, who had never heard of the ancient saying: "We have two ears and one mouth that we may listen the more and talk the less." What happened to good old Charley, a farm horse, will make you smile; it will also make you think.

A FARM HORSE named Charles was led to town one day by his owner, to be shod. He would have been shod and brought back home without incident if it hadn't been for Eva, a duck, who was always hanging about the kitchen door of the farmhouse, eavesdropping, and never got anything quite right. Her farm-mates said of her that she had two mouths but only one ear.

On the day that Charles was led away to the smithy, Eva went quacking about the farm, excitedly telling the other animals that Charles had been taken to town to be shot.

"They're executing an innocent horse!" cried Eva. "He's a hero! He's a martyr! He died to make us free!"

"He was the greatest horse in the world," sobbed a sentimental hen.

"He just seemed like Old Charley to me," said a realistic cow. "Let's not get into a moony mood."

"He was wonderful!" cried a gullible goose.

"What did he ever do?" asked a goat.

Eva, who was as inventive as she was inaccurate, turned on her lively imagination. "It was butchers who led him off to be shot!" she shrieked. "They would have cut our throats while we slept if it hadn't been for Charles!"

"I didn't see any butchers, and I can see a burnt-out firefly on a moonless night," said a barn owl. "I didn't hear any butchers, and I can hear a mouse walk across moss."

Applying the Meaning. If a fable is meant to make you wise, you must be able to transfer its meanings from the animals in the story to the weaknesses and follies of mankind (yourself included!). As you read Thurber's modern fable, try to see what qualities of human beings are being satirized.

"We must build a memorial to Charles the Great, who saved our lives," quacked Eva. And all the birds and beasts in the barnyard except the wise owl, the skeptical goat, and the realistic cow set about building a memorial.

Just then the farmer appeared in the lane, leading Charles, whose new shoes glinted in the sunlight.

It was lucky that Charles was not alone, for the memorial-builders might have set upon him with clubs and stones for replacing their hero with just plain old Charley. It was lucky, too, that they could not reach the barn owl, who quickly perched upon the weathervane of the barn, for none is so exasperating as he who is right. The sentimental hen and the gullible goose were the ones who finally called attention to the true culprit — Eva, the one-eared duck with two mouths. The others set upon her and tarred and unfeathered her, for none is more unpopular than the bearer of sad tidings that turn out to be false.

MORAL: Get it right or let it alone. The conclusion you jump to may be your own.

APPLYING THE MEANING

1. In this fable, Thurber aims his criticism at several weaknesses in human behavior. Point out two or three of these.

2. What might explain Eva's wild inventiveness? Why does she ignore the remarks of the barn owl, the realistic cow, and the skeptical goat? Describe any situations — either real or from books or television — in which people have believed rumors instead of the truth? How do you account for such behavior?

3. What comment on human weakness is implied by Thurber's choice of the two animals who fasten the blame on Eva at the end of the story? What kind of human situation might parallel this part of the fable?

4. Do you agree that "none is more unpopular than the bearer of sad tidings that turn out to be false"? If so, why do you think this is true?

COMPOSITION SUGGESTION

Describe an experience with animals which has taught you something valuable. You may even want to try writing a fable of your own.

ABOUT THE AUTHOR

James Thurber (1894–1961) was one of America's best-known humorists in two fields — humorous drawing and writing. After graduating from Ohio State University, Thurber worked for newspapers and then the *New Yorker* Magazine. For this magazine he wrote many humorous short sketches and amusing accounts of his childhood days. His short story "The Secret Life of Walter Mitty" became a successful motion picture. Perhaps his best-known work is the play, *The Male Animal*, written with Elliott Nugent. He wrote *The Thirteen Clocks* as a whimsical fairy tale for adults, and *Many Moons* as a fairy tale for children, but "children," old or young, have made them both very popular. Totally blind at the end of his life, Thurber was no longer able to draw cartoons or illustrations, but he continued to write humorous stories. The fable "What Happened to Charles" is from his book, *Further Fables for Our Time*. The same book includes the Thurber drawings of Charles and Eva which appear on these pages.

Spoken Wisdom

ROBERT FROST

The following transcript is from a tape that was made as Robert Frost, the famous American poet, talked with a group of high school students. It captures those moments of good talk when a creative artist is thinking out loud, when the form is not designed in advance but grows out of the meeting of several minds. Notice how language spoken informally differs from written language.

Frost. We're going to talk to each other about writing, not necessarily poetry. We're going to talk to each other about any kind of writing. And that means chiefly about the matter of having ideas, having thoughts. You've come a long way toward that, I think. I've often said to high school students that, if you're going to college now it's good to be given one more chance to learn to read if you haven't learned to read in the high school. And so it's really a matter of finding out what it means to read — to read with something more than the thought of the piece you're reading, something over and above it. Now that's what you're doing in life, too. You're doing that with books; you're doing that in life. You're having some thoughts, some ideas, over and above what's going on; over and above, like an induced extra current.

IDEAS OF YOUR OWN

You've got to find out, if you are going to do anything I want you to do, what it means to have a thought that's your own. And the best way to do that is to write down in some sort of a notebook or scrapbook or something what you think is a thought. Let it lie for awhile and look at it again to see whether it's absurd or just empty, or whether it is something that *is* something.

Before we came in here, we were talking about having ideas. You see them in the newspapers sometimes; you see them and you're sometimes envious of them. Someone asked the question, "What's grandma reading the Bible so much for lately?" "She's cramming for her finals." I wish I had said that, you know, that's the kind of thing you covet, you wish you'd said. And have you ever had one, have you had little thoughts like that, or big thoughts like that? Have you ever dared to write them down, jot them down, so that you yourself, not your teachers, could try them a year afterwards, see if they have gone empty or gone ridiculous? Many of them will have gone empty; you won't know what you were talking about. You'll say, "What did I write that down for? I don't see what it means." It will be as puzzling to you as some of the writing that you have to read — we won't name any names. You will say, "What did I mean by that? Isn't it funny?" And then something else will look ridiculous to you and you'll be glad you didn't have to show that to anybody.

The time has come for you when you have to begin to do that yourself, not leave it to teachers to mark you for it, to tell you that it's absurd or that it won't do. (They don't say absurd; they can only give you "C" for it or something like that.) But the time has come when you have to decide yourself whether you know how to score, score in thought.

HOW THOUGHTS COME INTO POETRY

This is what I am interested in bringing up with you: the matter of having thoughts you can call your own. You ask me how thoughts come into poetry. Well, they come into poetry the same as they come into words at all. They come into poetry with me metrically because I keep the swing up that's in my head. I'm like a dancer. I'm like Mozart who, they say, could never keep his hands still. He was always making some sort of rhythm or music. His whole body moved with music all the time. I'm not as extremely that way as he was, but I'm somewhat that way. Everything I think about tends to run into meter.

YOUNG PEOPLE TODAY

Student. Mr. Frost, do you think the people today, the teen-agers, think as much as the teen-agers in your time?

Frost. Yes. I make no difference in times that way. I don't think the world's going any faster, either forward or backward. Emerson wrote a poem in which he begins:

> I, Alfonso, live and learn
> Seeing nature go astern.
> Things deteriorate in kind.

He thought things went backward. Some people think they go so fast that you can't see them. But I think it's all about the same. I have not noticed any great change.

MAKING ORDER FROM CONFUSION

I hear commencement addresses in college. I hear the orator of the day say, "In these confused times . . ." as if these were more confused than any other. And let me tell you what I think about that. I think the whole world is a kind of chaos, beginning very far away from us, and confused, where you can't know anything about it. Asia — what do you know about Asia? What do I know about Asia? It's very far away, chaotic in my thoughts, but as it gets nearer to me, I make more and more order to it. I think things about it, think things about the United States. We rise out of disorder into order, and the poems that I make are little bits of order, as if I made baskets or a piece of pottery or a vase or something. If you suffer any sense of confusion in life, the best thing you can do is to make little forms. Form is what saves us from this sense of confusion.

Now I don't think I will stop you from feeling confused. But let me put it this way. There's nothing so composing as composition. That's a poem, putting your thought in order. Call that composition; writing it down on a paper to try it, as I say, a year afterward, and just putting it in order; say, putting in order what I'm saying to you tonight. So the thing I am asking you to do today is to open a little account with yourself. You can throw it away. It's nothing for the future except for a year from now. You open a little account with yourself. Write down something that you've said today, something you thought today, something you thought *was* a thought. So you can see how well it lasts, whether it goes empty, or whether it goes ridiculous.

And then as for meter and rhyme, that is a part of it with me. I don't think I can say what's true and right unless I say it partly for the pleasure of making a poem, making a tune that goes with it, a tune in words.

Student. Mr. Frost, what do you consider your favorite subject? I mean, for example, Edgar Allan Poe used to like to write on death. That seemed to be his favorite subject. Do you have any particular subjects you like to write upon?

Frost. No. I grant, as Poe said, that there are only two subjects, love and death. Death and love and beauty are all in one. That's probably so, but you can't just write on them all the time.

EMOTION IN POETRY

Student. Mr. Frost, do you ever use your poetry as an emotional outlet, a way to let off steam about strong feelings you have?

Frost. That's why it's got to have the tune and the meter and all that, to be an emotional understanding as well as a mental understanding. Not outlet, you're not screaming. If you really wanted an outlet and just that, you would make a noise like a siren whistle, wouldn't you? And some people come near doing that with their verse. They just scream. And you say, an emotional outlet, we have those expressions, "I feel as if I could fly," or, "I feel as if I could scream." That kind of thing has to be harnessed to the wheat mill. You have got to harness it to idea, meaning. Just screaming isn't enough. And some poetry I know is literally screaming. It's come up lately in public. The poet mostly screams.

YOUNG PEOPLE AND CONFUSION

Student. Mr. Frost, do you believe the progress in civilization has helped to make teen-agers more confused? It seems that they are more confused at this time since we've gone through two world wars, and just different things of the times now that weren't present when you were young.

Frost. You know, I have my doubts that you really feel confused. I think you've heard everybody saying you are confused. I bet you aren't confused, are you? What's the sign of your confusion? This is the way to test that. Do you feel more than one loyalty? Have you got a conflict of loyalties?

Student. Of course not.

Frost. Of course not. Then you aren't confused. I don't imagine you feel confused. It's hard for me to think you do. We don't, any of us, know too far ahead what we want, do we? But you know what you want tomorrow. You know what you want of the country tomorrow, too, the United States. You have certain wishes for it. Take it between the two things, liberty and equality. You've gone along saying a lot about liberty and equality. Have you realized that the more liberty you have to succeed and triumph and climb and all that, the more danger there is that you'll forget the idea of equality, staying with people that aren't quite as good as you are at it? The more equality you have, the less liberty you have. We have got a nation where there's a rather nice balance. Every four years, there is the election, balancing that thing about liberty and equality. It is something I've been thinking about lately, and there is no confusion there. Do you think, in school for instance, that everybody should be marked "A"?

Student. Most people feel that they should be marked "A."

Frost. Have you got any confusion about that? Do you know what you think of them for thinking that? I know what I think of them.

A POET AND HIS AUDIENCE

Student. Mr. Frost, when you write your poetry, do you write it for any specific person, for yourself, for your public?

Frost. For the public or myself? I never use the word *public.* I suppose I am writing it to the kind of people I have grown up with, some very nice people. I don't even analyze them, I'm so used to them. And you're just the same. You know to whom you have been talking all these years. You've formed habits of being understood. You know certain things you can't say. You might say — I've never gone into that very much — but often I have decided it is a kind of a cloud of many people that I've lived with that I'm partly talking it to. I'm not talking to the wastebasket. You wouldn't want me to be, would you? I'd rather talk to something or somebody, and I have a growing confidence that I know people that

are in front of me, that I know you pretty well; a growing confidence that I know I am saying what you get. One of the best audiences that anybody can read philosophy or poetry or religion or anything to in America is a mixed town-and-gown audience, a mixture of the people in college, the faculty, and the people that live in the same town, all mixed together in the crowd. That's America.

A POEM'S WISDOM AND DELIGHT

Student. Mr. Frost, you have said a poem should begin in delight and end in wisdom. Could you give us an example?

Frost. Not *should* but *does.* You see, it begins in this emotion of delight and comes through to its own fulfillment in a kind of wisdom or thought that you see. It's more felt to begin with, more felt than thought, and it ends up more thought than felt. That's the only way of saying it. And that's the way with most of our lives, I guess. You're at the delight end, and may you live to see the wisdom end.

A FEW PERSONAL NOTES

Student. Mr. Frost, do you ever write something just for yourself, not intending it for publication?

Frost. No, I never have. There might be something that I might decide, when I got through with it, that it wasn't fit for anybody but myself. I wouldn't leave that around. I wouldn't want it after I was dead and gone.

Even if I botch a poem, I don't like to show a botched poem. If I miss a poem, I throw it away. And, if I went off on a track of thought and things that I felt was unworthy of me, that would be a kind of failure. I don't mean to live that way, and I don't mean to wear my sins on my sleeve.

Student. Well, along with your writing, what else do you enjoy for entertainment or for relaxation?

Frost. Besides writing, you mean. One of them is conversation, another one is farming, scrubbing around in the dirt, and another's been games, baseball and all that — sports. I liked it. I never had anything I could call a hobby, an extra that I'd call a hobby. It's always something that is just off at a tangent, nothing followed. I played baseball and football as long as they let me.

HOW A POEM IS WRITTEN

Student. Mr. Frost, how do you come to write a poem? What inspires you?

Frost. I suppose I would not have written any poetry unless poetry had been written down the ages. I just fell into step with the procession. That yearn, don't you have it, doesn't it get you anywhere, don't you find a certain catchiness in verse? Some of it won't get out of my head. It is so bad I have to say, "I must stop saying that over and over to myself." And then, always, this thing about saying something to what is difficult in the world, clarifying something to myself and then it happens that it is always most happily clarified when I do it in verse.

But anyway, there's all that tone in it, that grows to the rhythm, to the expression, and then underneath it the beat of the meter. And what keeps it from being just jingle is something of rhythm that is brought over, so to speak, from prose. Prose always has the rhythm. But prose is not poetry for me, and I would as soon write free verse as play tennis with the net down. That is to say I want a form, a count, a meter, and something to check it and to fit it into.

Robert Frost in an informal discussion with students.

Student. When you finish your poem, do you have to go over and revise it yourself or do you just leave it stay as it is?

Frost. No — that's a confusing question. "Yes" and "No" is the answer to that. Sometimes when I'm any good, playing a good game of tennis for half an hour or fifteen minutes, when I'm any good, I don't have any regrets. Everything has gone right for me. I knew just where the top of the net was and where the back line was, and the ball behaved just the way I wanted it to and my racket and everything. And it's the same writing a poem. Sometimes I am just right and I have no regrets. I can't go back and correct a tennis game, unfortunately. But I can go back and tinker a poem up, revise it, touch it up, and I do that sometimes. But I never like one as well when I have had to fuss with it afterward. I like the moments I had when I was playing it sure and straight.

"THE GREATEST THING OF ALL"

Student. When you were young and you were thinking about planning your future, did you have any ideas or desires to go into poetry, or did you try a lot of different things?

Frost. Did I think of being poetic? Somewhat, rather secretly, but I didn't dare to say it to myself quite. It was quite a venture. I began writing poems in the high school. I wrote my first poem the second year in the high school, and I've been writing a little ever since. That was many years ago. But the first thing, you know, to me — I discovered that very young — was that the thing I wanted most of all in the world was to understand what was going on in the world and to say things to whatever happened; find something to say for whatever happened, sass it back. And to have what you might call the ready answer, you know, presence of mind in the emergencies of life; to say something that sort of makes my mind up for the day. That was more important to me than the poems. But the poems became that too, my answer to what was happening, my adjustment. The greatest thing of all, of course, is to know what to say to the Sphinx, to sass her back.

THINKING IT OVER

1. What are some of the ways in which speech and writing differ? Begin with the most obvious differences but go on to others. In what ways does this transcript reflect its origin in speech rather than in writing?

2. Select three ideas or definitions expressed by Robert Frost. Do you agree or disagree with any of them? Explain. Which ideas impress you as difficult, perhaps requiring class discussion to make them clear?

3. Find some expressions in this transcript that would make good quotations. For instance, see Frost's definition of a poem at the top of page 278. Find other expressions worth remembering.

4. Reread the passages dealing with order and disorder, confusion and form, free verse and form. Using your own words, state Frost's thoughts on these matters.

5. How do you define wisdom? Does it differ from learning? Would you say that Frost's ideas show his wisdom or learning?

6. According to Frost, what is "the greatest thing of all"? What does the Sphinx represent? What relationship exists between Frost's comments on order and disorder and his statement of "the greatest thing of all"?

GAINING POWER OVER WORDS

APPROPRIATENESS OF WORDS Although a wide and varied vocabulary is something for which students strive, obscure words in themselves have no great merit. A good student achieves balance. In "Spoken Wisdom" Robert Frost uses phrases such as "sass it back" with the same ease and appropriateness with which he quotes Emerson.

Compare Frost's choice of words with those in other selections you have read, such as "The Cask of Amontillado." Would either Frost's or Poe's works be improved by a different choice of words, or is each using the vocabulary best suited to what he intends to communicate?

COMPOSITION SUGGESTIONS

1. Robert Frost has said elsewhere, not in this selection, "Watch the school you are in and under. See if it makes provision for you in the critical stage — the transition from wanting to be told to wanting to tell. It'll bear watching. It's your lookout." Evaluate your own education at the present. In what ways are you making the transition from leaning on your teachers to standing on your own feet? What are some other steps you might begin to take?

2. Frost has said that teen-agers in today's world are not confused. What is your opinion? Give reasons to support your opinion.

3. The following are two of the ideas expressed by Robert Frost in this selection:

"I don't think the world's going any faster, either forward or backward. . . . Some people think they [events] go so fast that you can't see them. But I think it's all about the same. I have not noticed any great change." (page 277)

"If you suffer any sense of confusion in life, the best thing you can do is to make little forms. Form is what saves us from this sense of confusion." (page 277)

Think these ideas through carefully and discuss their meaning in class. You will probably find it helpful to refer back to the context in which Frost expressed these thoughts. Then write down your own understanding of one of the ideas and explain how it applies to your life. In your paper you will undoubtedly want to expand on what Frost has said.

ABOUT THE AUTHOR

For a biography of Robert Frost, see page 394. You will find two of his poems, "Birches" and "A Tuft of Flowers," on pages 391 and 413.

Biographies

Biographies allow us a close look at the actual lives of people the world over — people who lived many centuries ago as well as those living today. They acquaint us with individuals and times that we could not otherwise know. In a good biography we find a complete and honest picture of the life of a particular human being. We discover what he thinks, how he feels, what he does, and how he has affected society as a whole. In the following pages you will meet several people whose lives have been considered worth noting. Some of these people will write about themselves in autobiographies, and some will be described by skillful writers. The three groups of selections will serve as an introduction to the intriguing and informative world of biographical writing.

THREE WORLD FIGURES

The three men that you will read about in this group have achieved greatness — Pasteur, in science; Michelangelo, in art; and Socrates, in philosophy. Like people everywhere, certain incidents, personal characteristics, and influences helped to shape their lives. As you read about the lives of these three men, try to understand the significance of their contributions to Western civilization and to the world.

PERSONAL RECOLLECTIONS

The selections in this group are personal recollections, a special kind of autobiography in which authors recall particular people, places, and experiences that have made a lasting impression on their lives. Typically, this kind of writing reveals outstanding moments in the writer's life rather than a full-scale picture. Here you will find one author depicting her life on an African coffee plantation, another remembering her experiences while teaching English to Japan's Crown Prince, and still another recalling the poignant turning point in her life.

A COMPOSITE VIEW

Reading a single account of a man's life is not the best way to obtain a complete picture of him. Biographers and autobiographers are bound to have some prejudices about their subjects. To really know about a man, you should read all you can that has been written by and about him — biographies, autobiographies, recollections by those who have known him, and, if the man was a writer, various samples of his work. The man you are going to read about here is the famous American author Mark Twain. He wrote many books and articles, and many were written about him — more than enough to give you a very clear picture of the man. To help you start to form your picture, "A Composite View" includes a selection from *The Autobiography of Mark Twain,* an excerpt from *A Tramp Abroad,* one of Twain's humorous travel books; and Rudyard Kipling's recollection of an interview with Twain.

Louis Pasteur

ROGER BURLINGAME

Louis Pasteur was a French chemist who lived from 1822 to 1895. His name and his work should be familiar to you, for — among many other things — he developed a process for keeping milk free from harmful bacteria. We call this process "pasteurization." In all of Pasteur's scientific research, there was a deep concern for improving the human condition. Notice how the author brings out this concern in the story of the boy who was bitten by a mad dog.

NEAR THE TOWN of Meissengott in Alsace [1] a nine-year-old boy used to walk to school by a short cut off the main road. One day as he passed a patch of woods on this path a dog rushed out, attacked him, and threw him on the ground. The boy covered his face with his hands while the dog bit him several times on his body and covered him with foam from its mouth. A bricklayer, working on a nearby house, heard the child's cries and came to the rescue. He beat the dog off and picked up the boy, who ran home to his parents and told them the frightening story.

Joseph Meister's parents made instant inquiries, found that the dog had finally turned up at its master's house obviously mad and that his master had killed him. They then took little Joseph to Doctor Weber, their family physician, and asked his advice. The doctor cauterized [2] the wounds and told them, in effect:

"This is all I can do. It is all that any physician can do. But there is a man in Paris who is not a physician but who knows more about rabies — or 'hydrophobia,' as they call it — than all the physicians in Europe. Take Joseph to him immediately. If anyone can save the boy, this chemist can do it."

But when Madame Meister came with her boy to the laboratory of this chemist, Louis Pasteur shook his head. The culture of virus that he had made from the brains of rabid dogs had, when they had been weakened or "at-

---

[1] **Alsace** (ăl'săs): a province in the northeast of France.

[2] **cauterized** (kô'tēr-īz'd): seared with a hot iron.

"Louis Pasteur" from *Scientists Behind the Inventors*, © 1960 by Roger Burlingame. Reprinted by permission of Harcourt, Brace & World, Inc.

tenuated" as he called it, been used to inoculate dogs that had already been bitten and these dogs had recovered. Again and again they had come back to perfect health. Pasteur was never satisfied with a few experiments; he must make a hundred before he would admit success. Now he was sure that he could prevent the development of rabies in dogs, providing he began his treatment in time and followed an exact procedure in his inoculations. But he had never inoculated a human being. Here, confronted by this desperate mother and her threatened boy, he was forced to the hardest decision of his life.

A less sensitive person would have been less disturbed. Many a physician — especially in those days when the medical profession was relatively in its infancy — would have regarded Joseph as just another patient who must take the consequences of his injury and its treatment. And a doctor who had been successful in so many experiments would hardly have hesitated.

But to Louis Pasteur every human being was an individual and his life was precious. The thought that this woman was putting the destiny of her child in his hands was deeply troubling to him. If Joseph had been his own son, Pasteur could have felt no greater concern for him. The fact that, in this his sixty-fourth year, the name of Pasteur was a byword in every civilized country in the world never entered his mind as he contemplated the boy before him. But the story of Pasteur's fame had been told to Madame Meister and her faith was absolute.

As he stood in the office of his laboratory revolving the great question in his mind, the sound of dogs barking came from outside. More than two hundred dogs, sick and well, mad and sane, were in the laboratory. Whenever a mad dog was caught anywhere in France or even abroad, it was sent to the laboratory of Louis Pasteur. The mad dogs were isolated and closely observed in every phase of their illness. In another section lived the healthy dogs; dogs who had been inoculated again and again with the new serum. The place also swarmed with other animals: rabbits, guinea pigs, hens, and monkeys. Joseph Meister looked out the window at all these creatures in their pens and laughed at what he saw. Pasteur's voice breaking the long silence called him back.

"Yes, Madame Meister, I will do it. This won't hurt you much, Joseph."

"But is that all?" said Joseph as Pasteur withdrew the syringe. "We have come all this way for a little pin prick!"

"No, Joseph, you will stay here for a while. I'll give you a comfortable room to sleep in, and there'll be a pin prick every day."

So Joseph spent his days visiting and talking to the animals and sleeping a long, healthy sleep at night. But Pasteur did not sleep. As the inoculations increased in virulence [1] according to the pattern worked out in hundreds of experiments, he became more and more anxious.

"Pasteur [wrote his biographer who was also his son-in-law] was going through a succession of hopes, fears, anguish, and an ardent yearning to snatch little Meister from death; he could no longer work. At night, feverish visions came to him of this child whom he had seen playing in the garden, suffocating in the mad struggles of hydrophobia. . . . Vainly his experimental genius assured him that the virus of that most terrible of diseases was about to be vanquished, that humanity was about to be delivered from this dread horror

[1] **virulence** (vĭr′ū·lĕns): quality of being deadly or poisonous.

Louis Pasteur at work in his laboratory, painted in 1885 by A. Edelfeldt.

— his human tenderness was stronger than all, his accustomed ready sympathy for the sufferings and anxieties of others was . . . centered in 'the dear lad.' " *

But the end of the treatment came with Joseph still in perfect health; he went home at last to become famous as the first person in the world to be successfully inoculated against rabies after being bitten by a mad dog. From then on, men, women, and children came from all parts of Europe and even from America to take the treatment at the Institut Pasteur in Paris until, in our

* René Vallery-Radot. *The Life of Pasteur*. Translated from the French by Mrs. R. L. Devonshire. New York: Doubleday, Doran and Company, 1923, p. 416.

own day, there are branches of this institute in nearly every city.

The discovery of a vaccine against rabies came as the climax of a long career of usefulness. But can we think of Pasteur as one of the "scientists behind the inventors"? We are inclined to think of an invention as something mechanical or electrical. Yet the devices that have revolutionized medicine, surgery, and agriculture, that have wiped out the diseases that crippled the silk industry, the brewing industry, the manufacture of wine and vinegar, and the raising of sheep, cattle, hogs, and poultry are all true inventions. And the scientific discoveries of Louis Pasteur were behind all of these.

He grew up in the village of Arbois in the Department of Franche-Comté,[1] where his father, a veteran of Napoleon's army, owned a tannery. In his boyhood, his intellectual power seemed dominated by his emotions. In school he was far from the top of his classes; his marks were little better than average.

Perhaps one reason for this was his teacher's annoyance at the boy's constant interruptions. It is said that the science master, driven one day to exasperation, exclaimed, "Who is teaching this class . . . you or I? It is my province to ask questions, not yours!" But his loyalties to his family and, from his earliest consciousness, to France were passionate. Indeed his affection for his parents and sisters and his devotion to his home actually retarded the progress of his education.

He wanted education — in science and mathematics especially — and wanted, early in his adolescence, to become a teacher. The goal of his ambi-

[1] **Franche-Comté** (fränsh' kôn'tä'): a region in eastern France.

tion was the Ecole Normale, the celebrated teacher's college of France. But when at fifteen, he went to Paris to a preparatory school for the great École, his homesickness was so acute that he had to abandon his project and go back to Arbois. This was an early foreshadowing of the conflict that endured in Pasteur as long as he lived, between his affections — his urgent emotional sensibilities — and the hard inexorable [1] work that deep scientific research demanded of him.

It is interesting to the student of the creative mind that in this time of adjustment he worked continuously as an artist, making remarkable portraits of family and friends with pastel crayons.

As he grew older, science won out — at least over his almost pathological [2] attachment to home. When he went again to Paris, he stayed. By this time the intense effort of his study was driving sentimental thoughts from his mind as long as books, chemicals, retorts, [3] and a microscope were before him. Work became almost a part of his religion — work and the resolution that had overcome his nostalgia for home.

"To *will* is a great thing [he wrote to his sister] . . . for Action and Work usually follow Will, and almost always Work is accompanied by success. Those three things, Will, Work, Success, fill human existence." *

[1] **inexorable** (ĭn·ĕk'sô·rà·b'l): relentless.
[2] **pathological** (păth'ô·lŏj'ĭ·kăl): unhealthy.
[3] **retorts** (rê·tôrts'): glass containers used in chemical experiments.
* René Vallery-Radot, *op. cit.*, p. 15.

THINKING IT OVER

1. Why is Louis Pasteur classified as one of the "scientists behind the inventors"? List some of the inventions that were based on Pasteur's work.

2. Why did Pasteur hesitate to treat the boy who had been bitten by a rabid dog? The boy would have died from rabies anyway, so what had he to lose?

3. What problems arose from the "division in his character between the scientist and the humanitarian"?

4. What would you say is the function of the true scientist? Does Pasteur fulfill that function? Does every scientific discovery benefit mankind? Consider, for instance, the splitting of the atom or the invention of high explosives. Does the scientist have any obligation to humanity? How would Pasteur answer this question?

ORAL REPORTS

Five students who are especially interested in science might make oral reports to the class on the accomplishments of Joseph Black, Benjamin Silliman, Michael Pupin, Albert Einstein, and Marie and Pierre Curie—scientists whose work prepared the way for modern miracles of invention. Roger Burlingame's book *Scientists Behind the Inventors* provides information on each of these scientists and on the inventions which resulted from their work.

ABOUT THE AUTHOR

Roger Burlingame (1889–) is an American novelist and nonfiction writer. He attended Morristown School in New Jersey and Harvard College from which he received a B.A. degree in 1913. After World War I, he took some courses at the Sorbonne in Paris, France. In 1919 he began to work as a book editor at Charles Scribner's Sons. He published three novels: *You Too* in 1924, *Susan Shane* in 1926, and *High Thursday* in 1928. In 1936, he bought a farm in West Redding, Connecticut where he raised chickens, tomatoes, and dogs. During World War II, Burlingame was with the Office of War Information from 1942 to 1943. In 1945 he visited the European and Mediterranean theaters of operations as a war correspondent.

His nonfiction writings include magazine and reference work articles as well as books. His work is factual, sound, and interesting to read. Many of his nonfiction works deal with the development of American technology.

Michelangelo

EMIL LUDWIG

One of the outstanding figures of the Italian Renaissance is the sculptor, painter, and architect, Michelangelo Buonarroti (mī'kĕl·ăn'jĕ·lō bwò'när·rô'tĕ). He lived in Italy from 1475 to 1564 creating works of art that are among the greatest ever produced by man. In this selection, Emil Ludwig, a world-famous German biographer, describes the artist as a young man, and the problems that complicated his early career. Notice that the biographer, who lived almost four hundred years after Michelangelo, is not content to write only of bare facts but adds details that make his subject seem human and vital.

W HAT POSSESSED the thirteen-year-old boy, Michelangelo, to declare he wanted to be a painter? There he sat, a quiet lad, gazing with serious eyes at anything standing or lying before him, and scrawling an image of it on a sheet of fine paper. Not only his father, but his brothers too scolded him, for painting was considered a poor, inglorious calling. Michelangelo was so often cuffed and beaten that even in his old age he still would talk of it. He had

no mother to protect him; men ruled the gloomy household. As he seemed to be good for nothing else, however, his father was finally obliged to yield. He took him to Domenico Ghirlandajo,[1] who, surrounded by apprentices [2] and color-grinders,[3] was painting the walls of Santa Maria Novella. The boy was accepted as a pupil for a three year term. His doubting father grumbled, handing over his money and his hopes of making something out of his son. How could anyone expect that Michelangelo would ever do as well as his teacher?

If the boy had had a morsel of tact, he might have found commissions [4] more easily. He had not been at his new craft long, however, before there was trouble with his fellow workers and even with his teacher. When the

[1] **Domenico Ghirlandajo** (dō·mā'nĕ·kō gĕr·län·dä'yō): a Florentine painter (1449–1494).
[2] **apprentices** (ă·prĕn'tĭs·ĕs): students who learn by practical experience under skilled workers.
[3] **color-grinders**: men who ground the coloring matter and mixed the paints.
[4] **commissions**: requests to do paintings for other people.

apprentices were learning to copy draperies from their teacher's sketches, Michelangelo would draw the lines with a powerful stroke. Then he would alter them as his eye told him they ought to be, improving on his teacher. When he had to copy a drawing of the Temptation of Anthony,[1] he went of his own accord to the fish market. There he studied eyes, scales, fins, and then painted the fishes in his copy somewhat differently from those in the original.

The master was startled by Michelangelo's drawing. Ghirlandajo had often shown himself narrow-minded and jealous by nature. Now he displayed this copy as a "studio piece" — which meant that the master had had a hand in it. So it made less of a sensation, and nobody asked any questions about his astonishing pupil. But this action was a terrible blow to the sensitive youth. The harshness and gloom he had known throughout his youth, and the coldness and antagonism of his father had already made the young man doubt himself. Now this first experience with the envy and dislike of his fellow men added to the burden of a heart already oppressed.

But he was still young. Every morning his work made fresh demands on him. He soon had a new idea: to paint his teacher and the other apprentices from below, as he saw them daily on the scaffolding[2] in the Church. He did this with such a sense of perspective that the master began to fear his talent. He withheld his own sketch-book from the boy, though usually it was passed around among the pupils so that they might learn to draw heads, sheep, dogs, ruins. What did Michelangelo do now? Twice snubbed, simply because he had done well, he took his first little revenge. If the master deceived the world with his pupil's work, why should not the pupil deceive the master? He copied an old, yellowed sketch of his teacher's, smoked[3] it, and handed it in, so that Ghirlandajo believed he had got back his own original drawing.

Before a year had gone by, the teacher discovered a way of honorably ridding himself of the troublesome youth. Old Bertoldo, who had ceased to do any carving himself, was looking for capable young men to learn the sculptor's art by studying the recently excavated antiques in the Medici garden.[4] Michelangelo's hands were itching to study this lofty art. He once more prevailed upon his reluctant father, who did not like the idea of his son's becoming a lowly stonemason. It was not long, however, before Michelangelo was standing in the Medici garden, where he had often wandered, learning to carve his first block of marble.

Among his fellow students was a powerfully built youth who was very talkative, and the terror of them all when he frowned. His name was Torrigiano, and he looked like a young warrior. There they stood, side by side, trying their hands at carving and chiseling. Michelangelo had chosen an antique head, the mask of a faun.[5] But

---

[1] **Temptation of Anthony:** a drawing depicting Saint Anthony being carried off by demons, two of which are fishlike.
[2] **scaffolding:** a temporary wooden framework that the painters stood on.
[3] **smoked:** He used smoke to yellow the paper and make it look old.
[4] **Medici** (må′dê·chê) **garden:** garden of the Medici family, famous and wealthy Italians, especially noted for their patronage of art during the Renaissance.
[5] **faun:** in Roman mythology, a field or harvest spirit; a being with a man's body, a goat's legs and tail, a flat nose, pointed ears, and a small horn on his forehead.

standing before it and meaning to copy it, he found his piece of marble transforming itself under his fingers, becoming a grotesque caricature of an old man.

One morning the owner of the garden arrived to look at the young men's work. He stopped when he came to Michelangelo's caricature, glanced alternately from it to the original and then to the boyish copyist. Lorenzo the Magnificent [1] was then forty-one years old; but his face, with its irregular broad nose, was distorted by neuralgic pain so that he looked older than his years. He was not imposing. He affected simplicity, partly because he was ugly, but more because ostentation might have irritated those of whom he always spoke as "my fellow citizens." It was essential that his dictatorship should be carefully disguised. Before him he saw Michelangelo — a boy of fourteen, a slip of an adolescent in blooming health, and at that time undoubtedly handsome. Perhaps he envied the freshness that irradiated the boy's earnest face, his sunburnt olive skin, his straight nose. Or was it the gaze, half awe-struck, half-appealing, of those young eyes? Or was it the audacity of this child who dared to parody the Greek work? "You ought to know that old people don't keep all their teeth," said Lorenzo after a while, and then went on his way.

Lorenzo had spoken to him! The boy was excited, and he set to work chiseling a hole in his mask, so artfully that it looked as if a tooth *had* fallen out. When, soon afterwards, Lorenzo saw the sculpture again, how could he help but laugh? How could he fail to be pleased by such youthful eagerness? He asked about the boy's plans and his parents, and it was not long before Lorenzo took Michelangelo into his house as a guest.

Michelangelo was between fourteen and fifteen when he went to the Palazzo Medici. He must have felt as if it were all fantastic as a dream when for the first time he woke in his beautiful room, high above the loggia [2] and the old garden. He was free as a prince to go where he would, urged daily to his work by his own enthusiasm alone, responsible to none but his own aspiring soul. Where now was the morose father, always reproaching him with the expense of his training, the ingloriousness of his calling? Where was the elder brother who looked down on him? Where was the poverty-stricken house, so dark and narrow, in which they had lived together? One word from Lorenzo had prevailed on the father and a minor post in the customs, given him by the great man, had completely reconciled him. When the father heard that Lorenzo had presented his son with a violet cloak and a seat at his dining table, allowed him to play and study with his own children, and, moreover, gave him five ducats a month, he probably reflected that not only silk and a banking concern, but marble too, could make a man's fortune for him. From then on, he ceased to say that his son was a stonemason; he called him a sculptor. Otherwise he had scarcely an

[1] **Lorenzo the Magnificent:** Lorenzo de' Medici, a brilliant Florentine ruler and statesman. A poet himself, he was the patron of many great Renaissance artists, writers, and scholars.

[2] **loggia** (lŏj'ə): a roofed balcony.

Michelangelo spent four years painting the entire ceiling of the Sistine Chapel ▶ in Rome. Pictured here is one portion of that magnificent ceiling, the Libyan Sibyl.

idea of the amount of knowledge and high culture which for two years was poured into the thirsty young mind of his son. It was literally the sum of all the science, all the art of life, then known to man for all of the best intellects in Italy came to the Medici palace and villas.

Then came an evil day. That Michelangelo could do better than his comrades was acknowledged, and he was still more pride-ridden. This drove him, heedless of danger, to challenge, even to deride, the other artists. That day Torrigiano was among those sketching. He — the Goliath of the students. "We used to go together" (so Torrigiano said afterward) "up to the church and study in the Masaccio [1] chapel. But Michelangelo had a way of quizzing everyone who was sketching there. One day he did this to me. I was more than usually annoyed by it. I clenched my fist and gave him such a whack on his nose that the bones and cartilage felt as soft as a wafer. So he bore my mark as long as he lived!" After that whack Torrigiano fled, was banished from Florence, worked as an artist in foreign towns, and, as a soldier, killed many another man. But the tragedy he was born to inflict lies in that blow on Michelangelo's face.

Michelangelo was carried home for dead. When he recovered, every mirror showed him the disfigurement: a flat, broken nose in the center of that impressive face. He felt that the beauty of male heads, which he had often captured with pencil and chisel, was reft [2] from his own head. Still more profoundly did the sixteen-year-old boy withdraw into himself. More swiftly and more cruelly did mistrust and misan-

thropy [3] consume his spirit. He was marked for life.

Lorenzo, in the meantime, was failing visibly. As soon as his patron was dead, Michelangelo rushed back to his father's house and there spent some days overcome with grief.

Soon Lorenzo's son invited him to return to the Medici palace. Again he had his seat at table, and the young men now enjoyed, at their ease, the inherited luxury. Giulio too was there, Lorenzo's younger son, exactly Michelangelo's age. In time Giulio was to become a mighty Pope, [4] and from this moment he exercised a notable influence on Michelangelo's life. But Piero, the new master of the house, was a sorry heir who regarded the budding artist as an appanage [5] like his Spanish horse. Piero thought it a joke when all of Florence came hurrying to see the marvelous snowman that the sculptor fashioned for him one hard winter.

The people of Florence, meanwhile, more and more unwilling to obey Piero, who was an incompetent ruler, saw in King Charles of France a liberator. The nearer King Charles came with his army, the hotter things grew for the Medici. Gradually their friends fell away from them. What was Michelangelo to do? Disloyalty was foreign to his proud nature, but he felt his loyalty and gratitude were due the dead Lorenzo, not to his son Piero. Politics meant nothing to Michelangelo. He was driven by one desire: to create form. In this dilemma he did what genius in perplexity has ever done: he avoided a decision.

One day a lute-player whom he had

---

[1] **Masaccio** (mä·zät′chō): an Italian painter of the Florentine school.

[2] **reft** (rĕft): taken away.

[3] **misanthropy** (mĭs·ăn′thrō·pĭ): hatred or distrust of mankind.

[4] He became Pope Clement VII.

[5] **appanage** (ăp′*à*·nĭj): a grant of property from a sovereign prince to the younger members of his family.

met at Lorenzo's court came rushing to him, terrified. He told Michelangelo that Lorenzo had appeared to him in dreams, a ghostly figure bidding him tell his son that soon he would be driven out and never would return. But the man had been afraid to tell Piero, and the apparition had come again and soundly boxed his ears for him. Then, urged by his friends, the dreamer *had* ventured to approach the Medici, but Piero had laughed him to scorn and given him another thrashing. Michelangelo, however, with so many current whispers to warn him, could foresee the fall of the Medici. He and two of his friends made ready and fled from Florence two days after the dream was told him. Scarcely had he reached Bologna [1] by way of Venice before everything had come true. Piero Medici was obliged to flee. King Charles entered Florence in triumph, and Florence was again a republic.

At Bologna, Michelangelo's pride and his talent involved him in fresh dilemmas. Every stranger, on entering the town, had to have his thumbnail sealed with red wax. It did not suit the high-spirited youth to bear such a mark of slavery. So he and his companions were confined in the customhouse until a nobleman released him — and him alone — and took him home to his palace. This was astonishing, for he had achieved nothing yet. He was an almost penniless fugitive with a disfigured face, and yet the charm of his youth and his individuality must have been so compelling that a passing stranger came to his rescue and led him home. That evening, he read Dante and Petrarch to his host in his Floren-

Michelangelo's statue of Giuliano de' Medici, in the Medici chapel in Florence.

tine accent, and Boccaccio [2] too, until his host fell asleep.

The youth stayed on with his second wealthy patron. He set to work on a famous monument in the parish church, chiseling an unfinished figure which had been begun by a recently deceased great artist. It was a light-bearing angel. When he had finished, the whole town eagerly praised the stranger's work, but the other artists were soon sulking about the upstart who had dared to surpass them. For the second time he experienced the resentment of comrades.

For the second time he fled from his patron, terrified by human nature, and he returned to Florence a year after his flight. What did he find there? Liberty for the citizens and scorn for art. A father, but no protector. The desolate garden of San Marco, that had once been

[1] **Bologna** (bô·lō′nyä): a province in the north of Italy.

[2] **Dante** (dän′tê) ... **Petrarch** (pē′trärk) ... **Boccaccio** (bôk·kät′chô): great Italian writers. Dante wrote *The Divine Comedy;* Petrarch is famed for his sonnets; and Boccaccio is the author of *The Decameron* tales.

peopled by marble forms. The only man who gave him a commission was a Medici, a cousin of the others. For him Michelangelo made a young St. John with the honey-comb between his hands, frail as though a breeze might shatter him. Amid the dirges, the processions, the requiems that now took the place of the dances and masquerades of pleasure-loving Florence, sat the young sculptor. He hammered a little sleeping Cupid out of stone. It was so heathenish that he was advised to give it a patina [1] and sell it for more money as an antique. A dealer in Rome sent him thirty ducats for it, and later sold the figure to a cardinal for two hundred.

When people began to talk about the Cupid, the Cardinal sent a trusted emissary [2] to Florence. He was to get several young sculptors to bring their work to him as if he wanted them for Rome. Michelangelo brought nothing with him, but on a sheet of paper he drew a masculine hand so realistically that the emissary was astounded. Then, in answer to his questions, Michelangelo enumerated all his works including the Cupid. The man saw that there had been a swindle, and invited the gifted trickster to follow him to Rome. There was nothing to stop Michelangelo. Rome lured him. Moreover, he had hopes of getting more money from the dealer who had sold his Cupid.

Thus, as the result of a forgery, Michelangelo was invited to the abode of the Cardinal, a Prince of the Church. With compliments to dazzle him — but no commission — Michelangelo, at twenty-one, went to Rome for the first time.

---

[1] **patina** (păt'ĭ-à): mellowing or softening of a surface color. This occurs naturally with age and use, but can be induced by treating a surface with certain chemicals.

[2] **emissary** (ĕm'ĭ·sĕrĭ): an agent.

THINKING IT OVER

1. How would you describe Michelangelo as a young man? How did his family life seem to affect his personality? How was he affected by his disfigurement? What evidence is there of Michelangelo's ingenuity?

2. Why was Michelangelo unable to get along with the other artists? Do you think he was too proud of his talent? Point out incidents to support your opinion.

3. How was Michelangelo affected by the political situation in Florence?

4. Before you read this article, did you have any ideas about the personality of artists? Does Michelangelo, as he is described here, fulfill these ideas? Do you think that an artist — any artist — is somehow set apart from the rest of society? Why?

5. Find incidents in this selection that show Emil Ludwig's concern with making his biography reveal Michelangelo as a real person. Look for details that might have been omitted but that bring out Michelangelo's character and personality.

ABOUT THE AUTHOR

Emil Ludwig (ā'mēl loōt'vĭk) (1881–1948) was born in Breslau, Germany, the son of a professor at Breslau University. Emil was educated at Breslau and Heidelberg Universities and received a degree in law. From the age of twenty-five, however, he was a writer. Until he was thirty, he wrote only plays and poems. But in 1914, shortly before World War I, he went to London as a correspondent for a German newspaper. This was his first experience with journalism, and he spent much of his time learning to write factual material. When the war broke out, he returned to Germany.

After the war he moved to Ascona, Switzerland, on Lake Maggiore. From there he set out on his many journeys in search of material for his biographies. He became a Swiss citizen in 1932. During World War II, Ludwig's books were burned in Germany, and he was declared an enemy of the state. When he died at the age of 67, he left behind him a reputation for having added freshness and vitality to the writing of biography.

Socrates

The progress of civilization may, in large part, be attributed to the fact that there have always been some men who ask questions. Such a man was Socrates. Socrates lived more than 2,400 years ago in ancient Greece. His life was dedicated to finding answers and to teaching others, even though this search for knowledge eventually led to his death.

Here are two biographical accounts of Socrates. The first was written by a contemporary American author. The second, a brief portion of a work recognized as one of the great pieces of world literature, was written by Socrates' pupil, the famous philosopher Plato.

His Life

HERMANN HAGEDORN

IF YOUR Greek toga had a buttonhole, Socrates' thumb would be through it, holding you pinned in your place while the goggle-eyed and delightful old gentleman asked you exactly how clever you think you are and what in the world, in the first place, makes you think you are clever anyway.

He is the first and greatest of all buttonholers. It makes no difference where you are, or how busy you are. If Socrates fixes his eyes on you, he will come lumbering across the athletic field or the market place, and, smiling most courteously, he will engage you in conversation. Socrates is a glutton for conversation. Money means nothing to him. Fame, power, influence mean nothing. He never knows exactly where the next meal is coming from; but he must have conversation.

It is not that he wishes to hear himself talk; but he does want to hear what you have to say. He does not seek gossip, tips on the races or the discus throwers, or stories of the dancing girls, or wails on the political situation and the state of the war between Athens and Sparta.[1] But he loves talk of fundamental things, of justice and virtue and wisdom and love and death and im-

[1] **Athens and Sparta:** two rival city-states of ancient Greece.

mortality. He can talk on these matters as no one else in his city — and it is a city of great talkers — and he can make you talk as you have never talked before.

Who is he, this man Socrates? What is his profession, his job? He is the son of a stonemason. For a while he was a stonemason himself. Yes, and he has been a soldier, not from choice, but because Athens needed all her able-bodied men in her wars with Sparta, the physical examination taking no account of height, or of eyes somewhat off center. At thirty-seven he is at the siege of Potidaea,[1] at great risk saving the life of a brilliant young fellow townsman, Alcibiades,[2] who proves, in the end, not to have been worth saving. At forty-five he is in the disastrous defeat at Delium, carrying Xenophon,[3] a young friend of his, who is to make his mark as a historian, off to safety on his broad shoulders. "He stalked along like a pelican," Alcibiades subsequently reports, "glaring around with his projecting crab's eyes, so that none of the enemy dared molest him."

But soldiering is the least important activity of this extraordinary person's life. It is as a conversationalist that Athens knows him — as the man who asks questions. If you enjoy conversation and can answer Socrates' questions with intelligence, you love him and gratefully accept his invitations to walk under the olive trees with him or to spend the night with a few other sympathetic souls, talking about courage or happiness or the ideal republic. But if you don't enjoy high talk, if you think yourself wise and are really dull and Socrates shows you up by a keen question or two, you hate him and talk of him as a public nuisance and go around growling that if the government had any sand in its gizzard it would shut him up.

He is a queer customer, unquestionably. But he has a wise mind, a humble spirit, and a voice within him which he calls his daemon,[4] which lays a check on him, he says, when he is tempted to do wrong or stupid things. His clothes are always shabby. He goes about with bare feet. How he lives no one knows. The truth is that he has a small income, much too small to keep a family on in any style which Athens would approve. But he refuses to increase it, preferring to adjust his needs to his income rather than his income to his supposed needs. His wife, a sharp-tongued lady named Xantippe,[5] rails at him as an irresponsible loafer and gadabout. At home there are arguments in which, it is rumored, all of the questioning and most of the talking is for once done by the other party.

But Socrates is not a philosopher for nothing. When a friend asks him how he happened to marry Xantippe, of all women, he replies, "Those who want to learn to ride well choose restive horses, because, if they can handle these, they can manage any others. I want to learn to associate with all mankind, and I chose Xantippe, knowing that if I could bear her society, I should be able to get along with anyone!" Perhaps he is jok-

---

[1] **Potidaea** (pŏt'ĭ·dē'á): The revolt of this city from the Athenian League was the immediate cause of a war between Athens and Sparta.

[2] **Alcibiades** (ăl'sĭ·bī'à·dēz): a disciple and for many years the devoted friend of Socrates. Political ambition proved his ruination and he became a traitor to Athens.

[3] **Xenophon** (zĕn'ō·fon): another disciple of Socrates. His fame as a historian is based largely on his account of the *March of the Ten Thousand* — an expedition of conquest in which he took part as general.

[4] **daemon** (dē'mŭn): The Greeks had a belief in some indwelling power over the personality. They called it their daemon.

[5] **Xantippe** (zăn·tĭp'ē).

ing; but it would not be safe to be too sure.

He is not what would be called an established citizen, with a pleasant house to live in and taxes to growl about. He is something rarer, an institution. Everybody knows him. He has nothing to do all day except to ask questions and to talk, and as he does these things invariably in public places, he is as familiar a figure as the town constable. Even the comic writers poke fun at him in their plays. His questions always have point; that is one reason why people find them disturbing.

The oracle at Delphi, consulted by all the Greeks, has told Socrates that he is "the wisest of men." Socrates laughs at the idea. He isn't wise, he knows he isn't; that is all, in fact, that he does know. There are countless men wiser than himself, he is certain, in Athens alone. He sets about to prove it, and that is how the questioning begins. He goes to a statesman with a great reputation and asks for light on the nature of wisdom or happiness, and is most astonished to find that the statesman is as much in the dark as he is, though he thinks that he really knows.

"Well," says Socrates to himself, "I am wiser than this fellow anyway. He thinks that he knows, when he doesn't, and at least I know that I don't know."

Thereupon he calls on a great soldier, a great artist, a great philosopher. In every case his experience is the same. They all think they are wise, but when he pins them down, they do not really know anything at all, not even that they are ignorant. Men of vision, whom he thus questions, gratefully accept the light he throws into their darkness. But the men who are vain and self-important are indignant.

Young men crowd about him, however, fascinated and thrilled. It is a pe-riod of change in Athens. Thinking people find it difficult to believe in the old gods as their fathers did. When they look coolly at the stories of Jupiter and his adventures, of Venus and Juno, of Mars and Mercury and the rest, the gods look rather shabby, a little too human in their frailties to be regarded as divine.

The young men are asking, "What is this earth made of; how did it come to be? What are we human beings here for? How can we be happy? What happens when we die?" The old myths give no answers that satisfy these eager questioners.

Socrates says to them, "Do not bother your heads overmuch with problems regarding creation or the substance of things. Here you are, a man, living for awhile in the world with other men. What you must do is to think how you can live and help others to live most nobly and wisely."

They listen, and come day after day to hear his keen questioning and to answer as intelligently as they can. Those are congenial gatherings, for Socrates loves these young men as much as they love him.

"Some men," he has a way of saying, "have a fancy for a fine horse, or a dog, or a bird. What I fancy, and take delight in, is friends of a superior kind. If I know anything, I teach it to them. In common with them I turn over and explore the treasures of the wise men of old which have been left written in books. If we find anything good, we pick it out, and we think it a great gain if we can be beneficial to one another."

Majestic themes are discussed at those gatherings — fundamental questions of right and wrong, of the meaning of justice, the meaning of love. Questions of government are threshed through. Socrates is outspoken and spares no one. The government of Athens, splendid under the great Pericles,[1] has come to troublous times now that the leader is dead. There are wars without and revolutions within; and now the mob rules, and now a small group of powerful and wealthy citizens. The mob and the oligarchy,[2] as this small group is called, are equally unjust and despotic,[3] and in his quiet way Socrates strikes at them both.

When the Thirty Tyrants,[4] who are now ruling, send for Socrates in anger and forbid him to "discourse with the young," he merely asks them most humbly what they mean by "discourse," and whom exactly would they call "the young"? Can't he even ask directions or buy meat of anyone, say, under thirty? The Tyrants rage and threaten him with death. But Socrates pays no attention whatsoever to their orders, teaching as before.

But the old philosopher does not love a stupid mob any more than a stupid committee of tyrants. He says that democracy, if it is stupid and unjust, is as evil as stupid and cruel tyranny. Forms are comparatively unimportant; the essential thing is that government, whatever form it takes, shall be enlightened and just. It is a dangerous doctrine to preach, for it sets the stupid on both sides against him. When the Thirty Tyrants are overthrown and the popular party comes into control, Socrates is a marked man.

Slowly the feeling against him in Athens takes definite form. The men he has shown up to themselves with his straightforward questions, the ruling classes he has made fun of, the blundering mob he has refused to praise and to bow down to, begin to ask themselves why they have borne with this gadfly[5] so long. He is teaching the young men of the city that in government, majorities are not enough. You must have intelligence also. Dangerous doctrine! He is corrupting the youth!

Socrates smiles and goes quietly on, not teaching any philosophy of his own so much as stimulating his pupils to think out an intelligent way of living for themselves. And then one day, a notice is posted in Athens:

'Meletus,[6] son of Meletus, accuses Socrates, son of Sophroniscus,[7] as is underwritten. Socrates is guilty of crime — first, for neglecting the gods whom the city acknowledges, and setting forth other strange gods; next, for corrupting the youth. Penalty — death."

Meletus is a poet (or thinks he is), but there are other accusers, notably a democratic politician named Anytus[8] whose son Socrates has persuaded to give up his father's leather trade and devote himself to learning. Anytus feels strongly that to persuade any young man to give up the leather business for the shadowy rewards of scholarship is clear corruption.

Socrates seems to be the only individual in Athens who is not disturbed

[1] **Pericles** (pĕr'ĭ·klēz): the Greek statesman under whom Athens rose to its greatest height in the fifth century B.C.
[2] **oligarchy** (ŏl'ĭ·gär'kĭ): a small group that rules the government.
[3] **despotic** (dĕs·pŏt'ĭk): tyrannical.
[4] **Thirty Tyrants**: a committee of aristocrats who governed Athens at the close of the war with Sparta. After a reign of terror, they were overthrown and a democratic government was resumed.

[5] **gadfly:** a fly that bites cattle and horses. Socrates believed that a teacher should be a gadfly to the state, criticizing it and bringing about reforms.
[6] **Meletus** (mê·lē'tus).
[7] **Sophroniscus** (sō·frŏ·nĭs'cŭs).
[8] **Anytus** (â·nē'tŭs).

The city of Athens as it looks today. Here, more than 2,300 years ago, the great philosopher Socrates lived and taught.

by the approaching trial. He does not even make any preparations for his speech of defense. All his life has been a preparation for it, he says, having been spent in learning what was right and trying to do it.

The trial is held before a jury of five hundred fifty-seven citizens of Athens. Eloquently, Socrates speaks in his own behalf. He states his case as only he can state it, but his speech is not really a defense, but a lecture. If the jurymen are expecting him to back down in any respect, or to plead for his life, they are doomed to disappointment. On the contrary, he will not accept acquittal if it means that he shall stop his teaching. When he was a soldier and his commander placed him in a post of danger, there he was bound in honor to stay. It is the same now.

"Strange indeed would be my conduct, men of Athens," he insists, "if, now when God orders me, as I believe, to fulfill the philosopher's mission of searching into myself and other men, I were to desert my post through fear of death, or any other fear. Men of Athens, I honor and love you; but I shall obey God rather than you, and while I have life and strength, I shall never cease from the practice and teaching of philosophy."

The court declares him guilty, but only by a majority of five or six. According to ancient custom, he is asked what punishment he would regard as just. Fearlessly he replies that if it is required of him to say how the public in justice ought to treat him, he can only say that he should be recognized as a public benefactor and given a pension for life; but, as an alternative, he proposes a small fine. The court regards his proposal as an insult, and he is condemned to death.

He takes the sentence with perfect calmness. Instead of pleading for mercy or sympathy, in fact, he turns about and encourages the court as though he suspected that their consciences were pricking them for condemning him, and felt sorry for them.

"O Judges, be of good cheer about death," he says, "and know of a certainty that no evil can happen to a good man, either in life or after. I am not angry with my accuser, or with you, my condemners. The hour of departure is at hand, and we go our ways, I to die, and you to live. Which is better, God alone knows."

For a month he is in prison, with fetters on his ankles, surrounded by his friends; talking, questioning as always; refusing to escape, regretting nothing, fearing nothing. Then, one evening as the sun is setting, the young men gather around him for the last time.

One of them, Apollodorus,[1] is loud in his lamentations. "I grieve most for this, Socrates," he cries, "that I see you about to die undeservedly."

But the old gentleman's sense of humor is as active as ever. With a smile he strokes his pupil's hair. "My dearest Apollodorus," he says "would you rather see me die deservedly?"

The last scene has all the sad beauty of autumn, or dying day. Minute by minute the shadows deeper. Xantippe, Socrates' wife, is there, wailing. For all that she abused her philosopher these many years, she loves him, and he has to send her away at last because he will have no lamentations when the end comes.

The jailer, in tears, brings him the hemlock, the poison which he is to drink. Holding the cup to his lips he

drains it and begins to walk about as the jailer has told him to do. His friends try hard to keep back the tears, but when young Apollodorus gives a sudden exclamation of grief, they lose their grip of themselves for a moment.

Socrates alone remains calm. "What is this strange outcry?" he says. "I sent away the women mainly in order that they might not offend in this way, for I have heard that a man should die in peace. Be quiet then, and have patience."

The poison is working. He can no longer walk; he lies down. They all know the end is near. But once more he uncovers his face, remembering a debt he owes to the temple of the god of medicine. "Crito,"[2] he says, turning to one of the young men, "I owe a cock to Aesculapius.[3] Will you remember to pay the debt?"

"The debt shall be paid," Crito answers in low tones. "Is there anything else?"

There is nothing else, no word more. And his friends have, to comfort them, only the words which he spoke in answer to their question what they should do with his body: "You may do with it what you like, provided you do not imagine it to be me."

No, that quiet shape is not Socrates. He is elsewhere, questioning the eternities. And still he halts men in the churches and schools and market places, and on the buzzing highways of the world, asking them what they mean by the words they fling about so lightly; and what do they know — and are they really as wise as they imagine?

Magnificent old questioner that he was! Wisest and noblest of all the Greeks!

---

[1] **Apollodorus** (*á·pŏl'ô·dôr'ŭs*).

[2] **Crito** (krī'tō).

[3] **Aesculapius** (ĕs'kū·lā'pĭ·ŭs): the Greek god of medicine.

His Death

PLATO

". . . Soon I must drink the poison; and I think that I had better repair to the bath first, in order that the women may not have the trouble of washing my body after I am dead."

When he had done speaking, Crito said, "And have you any commands for us, Socrates — anything to say about your children, or any other matter in which we can serve you?"

"Nothing particular," he said. "Only, as I have always told you, I would have you to look to yourselves; that is a service which you may always be doing to me and mine as well as to yourselves. And you need not make professions; for if you take no thought for yourselves, and walk not according to the precepts which I have given you, the warmth of your professions will be of no avail." [1]

"We will do our best," said Crito. "But in what way would you have us bury you?"

"In any way that you like; only you must get hold of me, and take care that I do not walk away from you." Then he turned to us, and added with a smile, "I cannot make Crito believe that I am the same Socrates who has been talking and conducting the arguments. He fancies that I am the other Socrates whom he will soon see — a dead body — and he asks, 'How shall he bury me?' And though I have spoken many words in the endeavor to show that when I have drunk the poison I shall leave you and go to the joys of the blessed — these words of mine with which I comforted you and myself have had, as I perceive, no effect upon Crito. I would not have him sorrow at my hard lot, or say at the burial, 'Thus we lay out Socrates,' or 'Thus we follow him to the grave or bury him'; for false words are not only evil in themselves, but they infect the soul with evil. Be of good cheer then, my dear Crito, and say that you are burying my body only, and do with that as is usual, and as you think best."

When he had spoken these words, he arose and went into the bath chamber with Crito, who bade us wait; and we waited, talking and thinking of death and life after death, and also of the greatness of our sorrow — he was like a father of whom we were being bereaved, and we were about to pass the rest of our lives as orphans. When he had taken the bath, his children were brought to him (he had two young sons and an elder one); and the women of his family also came, and he talked to them and gave them a few directions in the presence of Crito. And he then dismissed them and returned to us.

Now the hour of sunset was near, for a good deal of time had passed while he was within. When he came out, he sat down with us again after his bath, but not much was said. Soon the jailer, who was the servant of the Eleven, [2] entered and stood by him, saying: "To you, Socrates, whom I know to be the noblest and gentlest and best of all who ever came to this place, I will not impute the angry feelings of other men, who rage and swear at me when, in obedience to the authorities, I bid them drink the poison. Indeed I am sure that you will not be angry with me; for others, as you are aware, and not I, are the

[1] Socrates is saying that it will not be necessary for his friends to profess their belief in his teachings. It will be their practice of wisdom that will be the real measure of his influence on them.

[2] **Eleven:** as used here, the Eleven Tyrants, who were ruling Athens at this time.

guilty cause. And so fare you well, and try to bear lightly what must needs be; you know my errand." Then bursting into tears he turned away and went out.

Socrates looked at him and said: "I return your good wishes, and will do as you bid." Then turning to us, he said, "How charming the man is! — Since I have been in prison he has always been coming to see me, and at times he would talk to me, and was as good as could be to me, and now see how generously he sorrows for me. But we must do as he says. Crito. Let the cup be brought, if the poison is prepared. If not, let the attendant prepare some."

"Yet," said Crito, "the sun is still upon the hilltops; and many a one has taken the draught late, and after the announcement has been made to him, he has eaten and drunk, and indulged in sensual delights. Do not hasten then — there is still time."

Socrates said, "Yes, Crito, but I do not think that I should gain anything by drinking the poison a little later. I should be sparing and saving a life which is already gone. I could only laugh at myself for this. Please then to do as I say, and do not refuse me."

Crito, when he heard this, made a sign to the servant; and the servant went in, and remained for some time, and then returned with the jailer carrying the cup of poison. Socrates said, "You, my good friend, who are experienced in these matters, shall give me directions how I am to proceed."

The man answered, "You have only to walk about until your legs are heavy, and then lie down and the poison will act." At the same time he handed the cup to Socrates, who in the easiest and gentlest manner, without the least fear or change of color of feature, looking at the man with all his eyes, as his manner was, took the cup and said, "What do you say about making a libation [1] out of this cup to any god? May I, or not?"

The man answered, "We only prepare, Socrates, just so much as we deem enough."

"I understand," he said, "yet I may and must pray to the gods to prosper my journey from this to that other world. May this, then, which is my prayer, be granted to me." Then holding the cup to his lips, quite readily and cheerfully he drank off the poison.

And hitherto most of us had been able to control our sorrow. But now when we saw him drinking, and saw too that he had finished the draught, we could no longer forbear, and in spite of myself my own tears were flowing fast; so that I covered my face and wept over myself — for certainly I was not weeping over him, but at the thought of my own calamity in having lost such a companion. Nor was I the first. Crito, when he found himself unable to restrain his tears, had got up and moved away, and I followed. And at that moment, Apollodorus, who had been weeping all the time, broke out into a loud cry, which made cowards of us all.

Socrates alone retained his calmness. "What is this strange outcry?" he said. "I sent away the women mainly in order that they might not offend in this way, for I have heard that a man should die in peace. But quiet then, and have patience."

When we heard that, we were ashamed, and refrained our tears. And he walked about until, as he said, his legs began to fail, and then he lay on his back according to the directions. And the man who gave him the poison now and then looked at his feet and

[1] **libation** (lī·bā′shŭn): an ancient ceremony connected with a sacrifice — the pouring of a few drops of liquid on the ground in honor of a deity.

"The Death of Socrates," painted by Jacques Louis David (1748–1825).

legs; and after a while he pressed his foot hard and asked him if he could feel; and he said no; and then his leg, and so upward and upward, and showed us that he was cold and stiff. And he felt them himself, and said, "When the poison reaches the heart, that will be the end."

He was beginning to grow cold about the groin, when he uncovered his face, for he had covered himself up, and said: "Crito, I owe a cock to Aesculapius: will you remember to pay the debt?"

"The debt shall be paid," said Crito. "Is there anything else?"

There was no answer to this question, but in a minute or two a movement was heard, and the attendants uncovered him. His eyes were set, and Crito closed his eyes and mouth.

Such was the end of our friend, who I may truly call the wisest and justest and best of all the men whom I have ever known.

THINKING IT OVER

1. There is a method of teaching called the Socratic method. From your reading of these selections, can you guess what this method might be? (If you are not quite sure, read further dialogues by Socrates' pupil Plato; he uses the same method of instruction.) What would be the advantage to students who are taught by the Socratic method?

2. Do you think that Socrates was right in choosing death instead of giving up his teaching? Why? Could he have accomplished more by living under the conditions required of him? If you had been Socrates, what do you think you would have done? Why?

3. Do you find anything in Socrates' life that you consider of value as an example for your own life? If you had the convictions that Socrates had, how would your own life have to change? Would you be willing to make these changes? Explain your answer.

4. Do you think that Socrates' quest for knowledge was unusual? Why did he always ask questions?

5. Socrates said, "I am wiser than this

fellow anyway. He thinks that he knows, when he doesn't, and at least I know that I don't know." What is the wisdom in this statement? How can you be wise if you don't know? Is there a difference between wisdom and knowledge? What do you think the difference is?

RECOGNIZING CHARACTERIZATION

A good biographer, like a good fiction writer, tries to show what his subject was like as a human being. The biographer uses events from his subject's life and the subject's own actions and words to give you a picture of a distinct person and personality. In addition, he often helps to round out your picture of the subject by showing you how other people have reacted to him and how he has affected different situations.

From your reading of these two selections, list some qualities of Socrates' character and personality. If you had to characterize him from knowing only of his death, what would you be able to say about him?

COMPARING WHAT YOU READ

It is always interesting to compare two persons' ideas on the same subject. Here, you have had a chance to compare two treatments of the same subject. Notice how the authors have used facts in different ways. One biography is written in the present tense; the other is told in the past tense, mostly through conversation.

1. In Hagedorn's biography, what is the effect of the use of the present tense for all of the action? In Plato's biography, what is the effect of the use of conversation to tell the story?
2. Which account of Socrates' death did you find more moving? Why do you think this was so?
3. Authors may write either *objectively* (writer stands apart from his story and reports what happens) or *subjectively* (writer is personally involved in the narration). Which method is used by Hagedorn? by Plato?

ABOUT THE AUTHORS

Hermann Hagedorn (1882–   ), an American poet, novelist, and biographer, was born in New York City. He was educated at the Hill School in Pottstown, Pennsylvania and later at Harvard, where he received his B.A. degree in 1907. From 1909 to 1911 he was an instructor of English at Harvard.

He is a well-known writer in the field of biography. He has edited some of Theodore Roosevelt's letters and has made many biographical studies of him, including the highly praised *Roosevelt Family of Sagamore Hill*. He has also written a biography of Albert Schweitzer, *Prophet in the Wilderness*.

Plato (427?–347 B.C.) was a student of Socrates and himself one of the most influential philosophers of all time. He was born of noble parents in Athens, and, when he was about twenty years old, became a pupil of Socrates. Later he traveled, spent some time in Syracuse, then returned to Athens where he founded a school called the Academy. There he taught mathematics and philosophy for the rest of his life.

Plato's philosophy is expressed in some 25 dialogues, including *Phaedo*, which describes the death of Socrates. In his early writings, Socrates appears as the chief speaker. Because of this, and because Plato worked so closely with his master, it is often difficult to know whether the ideas expressed are those of Socrates or of Plato himself. The Platonic teachings and those of Plato's pupil, Aristotle, form much of the basis for Western thought and belief even in our own day.

As the Artist Sees It

The painting on page 303 shows how one artist imagined the scene in the prison as Socrates accepted the cup of poison. This scene and many others from the world of ancient Greece have captured the imagination of the civilized world for over two thousand years. Perhaps you will want to find other paintings depicting various phases of life in ancient Greece.

Kamante

ISAK DINESEN

Isak Dinesen

Here two distant parts of our world meet in gentle understanding, as an internationally famous Danish writer recalls her life on an African coffee plantation. Notice that in a personal recollection of this kind, writers often include glimpses, or sometimes full-scale pictures, of people who have become part of their lives and memories. Thus biography and autobiography are often interwoven, as in this selection. Notice, also, the author's rare description of the African countryside.

I HAD a farm in Africa, at the foot of the Ngong Hills. The Equator runs across these highlands, a hundred miles to the north, and the farm lay at an altitude of over six thousand feet. In the daytime you felt that you had got high up, near to the sun, but the early mornings and evenings were limpid and restful, and the nights were cold.

The geographical position and the height of the land combined to create a landscape that had not its like in all the world. There was no fat on it and no luxuriance anywhere; it was Africa distilled up through six thousand feet, like the strong and refined essence of a continent. The colors were dry and burnt, like the colors in pottery. The trees had a light delicate foliage, the structure of which was different from that of the trees in Europe. It did not grow in bows or cupolas,[1] but in horizontal layers, and the formation gave to the tall solitary trees a likeness to the palms, or a heroic and romantic air like full-rigged ships with their sails clewed up, and to the edge of a wood a strange appearance as if the whole wood were faintly vibrating. Upon the grass of the great plains, the crooked bare old thorn-trees were scattered, and the grass was spiced like thyme and bog-myrtle; in some places the scent was so strong that it smarted in the nostrils. All the flowers that you found on the plains, or upon the creepers and lianas[2] in the native

[1] cupolas (kū′pṓ·làz): rounded coverings; domes.
[2] lianas (lē·ä′náz): climbing plants that root in the ground.

forest, were diminutive [1] like flowers of the downs — only just in the beginning of the long rains a number of big, massive heavy-scented lilies sprang out on the plains. The views were immensely wide. Everything that you saw made for greatness and freedom, and unequalled nobility.

The chief feature of the landscape, and of your life in it, was the air. Looking back on a sojourn in the African highlands, you are struck by your feeling of having lived for a time up in the air. The sky was rarely more than pale blue or violet, with a profusion of mighty, weightless, ever-changing clouds towering up and sailing on it, but it has a blue vigor in it, and at a short distance it painted the ranges of hills and the woods a fresh deep blue. In the middle of the day the air was alive over the land, like a flame burning; it scintillated, waved and shone like running water, mirrored and doubled all objects, and created great Fata Morgana.[2] Up in this high air you breathed easily, drawing in a vital assurance and lightness of heart. In the highlands you woke up in the morning and thought: Here I am, where I ought to be.

I had six thousand acres of land, and had thus got much spare land besides the coffee plantation. Part of the farm was native forest, and about one thousand acres were squatters' land, what they called their *shambas*. The squatters are natives, who with their families hold a few acres on a white man's farm, and in return have to work for him a certain number of days in the year. My squatters, I think, saw the relationship in a different light, for many of them were born on the farm, and their fathers before them, and they very likely regarded me as a sort of superior squatter on their estates. The squatters' land was more intensely alive than the rest of the farm, and was changing with the seasons the year round. The maize grew up higher than your head as you walked on the narrow hard-trampled footpaths in between the tall green rustling regiments, and then again it was harvested. The beans ripened in the fields, were gathered and thrashed by the women, and the stalks and pods were collected and burned, so that in certain seasons thin blue columns of smoke rose here and there all over the farm. The Kikuyu [3] also grew the sweet potatoes, that have a vine-like leaf and spread over the ground like a dense entangled mat, and many varieties of big yellow and green speckled pumpkins.

It was not easy to get to know the natives. They were quick of hearing, and evanescent; [4] if you frightened them they could withdraw into a world of their own, in a second, like the wild animals which at an abrupt movement from you are gone — simply are not there. Until you knew a native well, it was almost impossible to get a straight answer from him. To a direct question as to how many cows he had, he had an eluding reply — "As many as I told you yesterday." It goes against the feelings of Europeans to be answered in such a manner; it very likely goes against the feelings of the natives to be questioned in this way. If we pressed or pursued them, to get an explanation of their behavior out of them, they receded as long as they possibly could, and then they used a grotesque humorous fan-

---

[1] **diminutive** (dĭ·mĭn′ū·tĭv): very small.
[2] **Fata Morgana**: mirages, so-named because they were once regarded as the work of enchantress Morgan le Fay.

[3] **Kikuyu** (kê·kōō′yōō): a tribe of natives who live in Kenya, on the eastern coast of Africa.
[4] **evanescent** (ĕv·à·nĕs′ĕnt): fleeting.

tasy to lead us on the wrong track. Even small children in this situation had all the quality of old poker players, who do not mind if you overvalue or undervalue their hand, so long as you do not know its real nature. When we really did break into the natives' existence, they behaved like ants when you poke a stick into their ant-hill; they wiped out the damage with unwearied energy, swiftly and silently — as if obliterating an unseemly action.

We could not know, and could not imagine, what the dangers were that they feared from our hands. I myself think that they were afraid of us more in the manner in which you are afraid of a sudden terrific noise, than as you are afraid of suffering and death. And yet it was difficult to tell, for the natives were great at the art of mimicry. In the *shambas* you would sometimes in the early morning come upon a spurfowl [1] which would run in front of your horse as if her wing was broken, and she was terrified of being caught by the dogs. But her wing was not broken, and she was not afraid of the dogs — she could whir up before them the moment she chose — only she had got her brood of young chickens somewhere near by, and she was drawing our attention away from them. Like the spurfowl, the natives might be mimicking a fear of us because of some other deeper dread, the nature of which we could not guess. Or in the end their behavior to us might be some sort of strange joke, and the shy people were not afraid of us at all.

Kamante [2] was a small Kikuyu boy, the son of one of my squatters. I used to know my squatter children well, for they both worked for me on the farm, and used to be up round my house

herding their goats on the lawns, in the faith that here something of interest might always occur. But Kamante must have lived on the farm for some years before I ever met him. I suppose that he had been leading a seclusive existence, like a sick animal.

I came upon him for the first time one day when I was riding across the plain of the farm, and he was herding his people's goats there. He was the most pitiful object that you could set eyes on. His head was big and his body terribly small and thin, the elbows and knees stood out like knots on a stick and both his legs were covered with deep running sores from the thigh to the heel. Here on the plain he looked extraordinarily small, so that it struck you as a strange thing that so much suffering could be condensed into a single point. When I stopped and spoke to him, he did not answer, and hardly appeared to see me. In his flat, angular, harassed, and infinitely patient face, the eyes were without glance, dim like the eyes of a dead person. He looked as if he could not have more than a few weeks to live, and you expected to see the vultures, which are never far away from death on the plain, high up in the pale burning air over his head. I told him to come round to my house the next morning, so that I could try to cure him.

I was a doctor to the people on the farm most mornings from nine to ten, and like all great quacks I had a large circle of patients, and generally between two and a dozen sick people up by my house then.

Kamante to my surprise turned up at my house the morning after our first meeting. He stood there, a little away from the three or four other sick people present, erect, with his half-dead face, as if after all he had some feeling of

---

[1] **spurfowl:** a chicken with a stiff, sharp spine on its legs.

[2] **Kamante** (kä·män'tä).

attachment to life, and had now made up his mind to try this last chance of holding on to it.

He showed himself with time to be an excellent patient. He came when he was ordered to come, without fault, and he could keep account of time when he was told to come back every third or fourth day, which is an unusual thing with the natives. He bore the hard treatment of his sores with a stoicism [1] that I have not known the like of. In all these respects I might have held him up as a model to the others, but I did not do so, for at the same time he caused me much uneasiness of mind.

Rarely, rarely, have I met such a wild creature, a human being who was so utterly isolated from the world, and, by a sort of firm deadly resignation, completely closed to all surrounding life. I could make him answer when I questioned him, but he never volunteered a word and never looked at me. He had no pity whatever in him, and kept a little scornful laughter of contempt and of knowing better, for the tears of the other sick children, when they were washed and bandaged, but he never looked at them either. He had no wish for any sort of contact with the world round him; the contacts that he had known of had been too cruel for that. His fortitude of soul in the face of pain was the fortitude of an old warrior. A thing could never be so bad as to surprise him. He was, by his career and his philosophy, prepared for the worst.

I remember well the first time that he ever looked at me and spoke to me of his own accord. This must have been some time along in our acquaintance, for I had given up my first mode of treatment, and was trying a new thing,

a hot poultice that I had looked up in my books. In my eagerness to do the thing thoroughly, I made it too hot, and as I put it on his leg and clapped the dressing on the top of it Kamante spoke. "*Msabu*," he said, and gave me a great glance. The natives use this Indian word when they address white women, but they pronounce it a little differently, and change it into an African word, with a diverging ring to it. In Kamante's mouth now it was a cry for help, but also a word of warning, such as a loyal friend might give you, to stop you in a proceeding unworthy of you. I thought of it with hope afterwards. I had ambition as a doctor, and I was sorry to have put on the poultice too hot, but I was glad all the same, for this was the first glimpse of an understanding between the wild child and myself. The stark sufferer, who expected nothing but suffering, did not expect it from me.

As far as my doctoring of him went, things did not, however, look hopeful. For a long time I kept on washing and bandaging his legs, but the disease was beyond me. From time to time he would grow a little better, and then the sores would break out in new places. In the end I made up my mind to take him to the hospital of the Scotch Mission.

At the Scotch Mission they kept Kamante for three months. During that time I saw him once. I came riding past the Mission on my way to the Kikuyu railway station, and the road here for awhile runs along the hospital grounds. I caught sight of Kamante in the grounds, he was standing by himself at a little distance from the groups of other convalescents. By this time he was already so much better that he could run. When he saw me, he came up to the fence and ran with me as long as it was following the road. He trotted

[1] **stoicism** (stō′·ĭ·sĭz′m): indifference to pleasure or pain; impassiveness.

along, on his side of the fence, like a foal in a paddock when you pass it on horseback, and kept his eyes on my pony, but he did not say a word. At the corner of the hospital grounds he had to stop, and when as I rode on, I looked back, I saw him standing stock still, with his head up in the air, and staring after me, in the exact manner of a foal when you ride away from it. I waved my hand to him a couple of times, the first time he did not react at all, then suddenly his arm went straight up like a pump-spear, but he did not do it more than once.

Kamante came back to my house on the morning of Easter Sunday, and handed me a letter from the hospital people who declared that he was much better and that they thought him cured for good. He must have known something of its contents for he watched my face attentively while I was reading it, but he did not want to discuss it. He had greater things in his mind. Kamante always carried himself with much collected or restrained dignity, but this time he shone with repressed triumph as well.

All natives have a strong sense for dramatic effects. Kamante had carefully tied old bandages round his legs all the way up to the knee, to arrange a surprise for me. It was clear that he saw the vital importance of the moment, not in his own good luck, but, unselfishly, in the pleasure that he was to give me. He probably remembered the times when he had seen me all upset by the continual failure of my cures with him, and he knew that the result of the hospital's treatment was an astounding thing. As slowly, slowly, he unwound the bandages from his knee to his heel there appeared, underneath them, a pair of whole smooth legs, only slightly marked by gray scars.

Kamante began his life in my house as a dog-toto,[1] later he became a medical assistant to me. There I found out what good hands he had, although you would not have thought so from the look of them, and I sent him into the kitchen to be a cook's boy, a *marmiton,* under my old cook Esa, who was murdered. After Esa's death he succeeded to him, and he was now my chef all the time that he was with me.

Natives have usually very little feeling for animals, but Kamante differed from type here, as in other things. He was an authoritative dog-boy, and he identified himself with the dogs, and would come and communicate to me what they wished, or missed, or generally thought of things. He kept the dogs free of fleas, which are a pest in Africa, and many times in the middle of the night, he and I, called by the howls of the dogs, have, by the light of a hurricane lamp, picked off them, one by one, the murderous big ants, the *Siafu,* which march alone and eat up everything on their way.

He must also have used his eyes at the time when he had been in the Mission hospital — even if it had been as was ever the case with him, without the slightest reverence or prepossession[2] — for he was a thoughtful, inventive doctor's assistant. After he had left this office, he would at times appear from the kitchen to interfere in a case of sickness, and give me very sound advice.

But as a chef he was a different thing, and precluded classification. Nature had here taken a leap and cut away from the order of precedence of faculties and talents; the thing now became mystic and inexplicable, as ever where

---

[1] **dog-toto:** a boy whose job is to take care of the dogs.
[2] **prepossession:** preconceived idea; prejudice.

A Kikuyu village in Kenya.

time made me an offer to come in with him in his business of the restaurant, for the sake of my devotion to the art. Now when I found Kamante at hand, as a familiar spirit to cook with, this devotion again took hold of me.

Kamante, in all cooking matters, had a surprising manual adroitness. The great tricks and tours de force [1] of the kitchen were child's play to his dark crooked hands; they knew on their own everything about omelettes, *vol-au-vents*,[2] sauces, and mayonnaises. He had a special gift for making things light, as in the legend the infant Christ forms birds out of clay and tells them to fly. He scorned all complicated tools, as if impatient of too much independence in them, and when I gave him a machine for beating eggs he set it aside to rust, and beat whites of egg with a weeding knife that I had had to weed the lawn with, and his whites of eggs towered up like light clouds. As a cook he had a penetrating, inspired eye, and would pick out the fattest chicken out of a whole poultry yard, and he gravely weighed an egg in his hand, and knew when it had been laid. He thought out schemes for improvement of my table, and by some means of communication, from a friend who was working for a doctor far away in the country, he got me seed of a really excellent sort of lettuce, such as I had myself for many years looked for in vain.

He had a great memory for recipes. He could not read, and he knew no English so that cookery-books were of no use to him, but he must have held all that he was ever taught stored up in his ungraceful head, according to some systematization of his own, which I

you are dealing with genius. In the kitchen, in the culinary world, Kamante had all the attributes of genius, even to that doom of genius — the individual's powerlessness in the face of his own powers. If Kamante had been born in Europe, and had fallen into the hands of a clever teacher, he might have become famous, and would have cut a droll figure in history. And out here in Africa he made himself a name; his attitude to his art was that of a master.

I was much interested in cookery myself, and on my first visit back to Europe, I took lessons from a French chef at a celebrated restaurant, because I thought it would be an amusing thing to be able to make good food in Africa. The chef, Monsieur Perrochet, at that

[1] **tours de force** (tōōrs′dē·fôrs′): feats of skill.
[2] **vol-au-vents** (vô′-lō′väNz′): puff pastry shells filled with meat, poultry, or fish stew.

should never know. He had named the dishes after some event which had taken place on the day they had been shown to him, and he spoke of the sauce of the lightning that struck the tree, and of the sauce of the gray horse that died. But he did not confound any two of these things. There was only one point that I tried to impress upon him without any success, that was the order of the courses within a meal. It became necessary to me, when I had guests for dinner, to draw up for my chef, as if it were a pictorial menu: first a soup-plate, then a fish, then a partridge, or an artichoke. I did not quite believe this shortcoming in him to be due to a faulty memory. But he did, I think, in his own heart, maintain that there is a limit to everything, and that upon anything so completely immaterial, he would not waste his time.

It is a moving thing to work together with a demon. Nominally the kitchen was mine, but in the course of our co-operations, I felt not only the kitchen, but the whole world in which we were co-operating, pass over into Kamante's hands. For here he understood to perfection what I wished of him, and sometimes he carried out my wishes even before I had told him of them. But as to me I could not make clear to myself how or indeed why he worked as he did. It seemed to me a strange thing that anyone could be so great in an art of which he did not understand the real meaning, and for which he felt nothing but contempt.

Kamante could have no idea as to how a dish of ours ought to taste, and he was, in spite of his conversion, and his connection with civilization, at heart an arrant Kikuyu, rooted in the traditions of his tribe and in his faith in them, as in the only way of living worthy of a human being. He did at times

Zebras and a topi in their native Africa.

taste the food that he cooked, but then with a distrustful face, like a witch who takes a sip out of her cauldron. He stuck to the maizecobs [1] of his fathers. Here even his intelligence sometimes failed him, and he came and offered me a Kikuyu delicacy — a roasted sweet potato or a lump of sheep's fat — as even a civilized dog, that has lived for a long time with people, will place a bone on the floor before you, as a present. In his heart he did, I feel, all the time look upon the trouble that we give ourselves about our food as upon a lunacy. I sometimes tried to extract from him his views upon these things, but although he spoke with great frankness on many subjects, on others he was very close, so that we worked side by side in

[1] **maizecobs:** corncobs.

the kitchen, leaving one another's ideas on the importance of cooking, alone.

I sent Kamante in to the Muthaiga Club to learn, and to the cooks of my friends in Nairobi,[1] when I had had a new good dish in their house, and by the time that he had served his apprenticeship, my own house became famous in the Colony[2] for its table. This was a great pleasure to me. I longed to have an audience for my art, and I was glad when my friends came out to dine with me; but Kamante cared for the praise of no one. All the same he remembered the individual taste of those of my friends who came most often to the farm. "I shall cook the fish in white wine for Bwana[3] Berkeley Cole," he said, gravely, as if he were speaking of a demented person. "He sends you out white wine himself to cook fish in." To get the opinion of an authority, I asked my old friend Mr. Charles Bulpett of Nairobi, out to dine with me. Mr. Bulpett was a great traveler of the former generation, themselves a generation away from Phineas Fogg.[4] He had been all over the world and had tasted everywhere the best it had to offer, and he had not cared to secure his future so long as he could enjoy the present moment. The books about sport and mountaineering, of fifty years ago, tell of his exploits as an athlete, and of his mountain climbings in Switzerland and Mexico. And there is a book of famous bets called *Light Come Light Go*, in which you can read of how for a bet he swam the Thames in evening clothes and a high hat — but later on, and more romantically, he swam the Hellespont like

Leander and Lord Byron.[5] I was happy when he came out to the farm for a tête-à-tête[6] dinner. There is a particular happiness in giving a man whom you like very much, good food that you have cooked yourself. In return he gave me his ideas on food, and on many other things in the world, and told me that he had nowhere dined better.

The Prince of Wales[7] did me the great honor to come and dine at the farm, and to compliment me on a Cumberland Sauce. This is the only time that I have seen Kamante listening with deep interest when I repeated the praise of his cooking to him, for natives have very great ideas of kings and like to talk about them. Many months after, he felt a longing to hear it once more, and suddenly asked me, like a French reading-book, "Did the son of the Sultan like the sauce of the pig? Did he eat it all?"

Since I went away, I have heard from Kamante and from my other houseboys in Africa. It is not more than a month since I had the last letter from him. But these communications from Africa come to me in a strange, unreal way, and are more like shadows, or mirages, than like news of a reality.

For Kamante cannot write, and he does not know English. When he, or my other people, take it into their heads to send me their tidings, they go to one of the professional Indian or native let-

---

[1] **Nairobi** (nī·rō′bĭ): the capital city of Kenya.

[2] **the Colony:** the Kenya colony, a section of British East Africa.

[3] **Bwana** (bwä′nä): Master.

[4] **Phineas Fogg:** the hero of Jules Verne's *Around the World in 80 Days*.

[5] **Hellespont . . . Byron:** Hellespont (hĕl′-ĕs·pŏnt) is the ancient name of the Dardanelles, a mile-wide strait, with strong currents, that unites the Sea of Marmora with the Aegean. **Leander,** a Greek legendary figure, supposedly swam it nightly to visit his beloved Hero. The youthful **Lord Byron,** nineteenth-century English poet, swam the strait and said he was doing so in imitation of Leander.

[6] **tête-à-tête** (tāt′à·tāt′): private; only two persons were present.

[7] **Prince of Wales:** title of the oldest son or heir apparent of the British sovereign.

ter-writers who are sitting with their writing desk, paper, pen and ink, outside the Post Offices, and explain to them what shall be in the letter. The professional writers do not know much English either, and can hardly be said to know how to write, but they themselves believe that they can. To show off their skill they enrich the letters with a number of flourishes, which makes them difficult to decipher. They have also a habit of writing the letters in three or four different kinds of ink and, whatever their motive for this is, it gives the impression that they are short of ink and are squeezing the last drop out of a number of ink bottles. From all these efforts come the sort of messages that people got from the Oracle of Delphi.[1] There is a depth in the letters that I get; you feel that there is some vital communication which has been heavy on the heart of the sender, which had made him walk in a long way from the Kikuyu Reserve to the Post Office. But it is wrapped up in darkness. The cheap and dirty little sheet of paper that, when it comes to you, has traveled many thousand miles seems to speak and speak, even to scream to you, but it tells you nothing at all.

Kamante, however, in this as in most other ways, was different from other people. As a correspondent he has a manner of his own. He puts three or four letters into the same envelope, and has them marked: *1st Letter, 2nd Letter,* and so on. They all contain the same things, repeated over and over. Perhaps he wants to make a deeper impression upon me by repetition. He had

that way in talking when there was anything that he particularly wanted me to understand or remember. Perhaps it is difficult for him to break off when he feels that he has got into contact with a friend at such a great distance.

Kamante writes that he has been out of work for a long time. I was not surprised to hear of it, for he was really "caviar to the general."[2] I had educated a Royal Cook and left him in a new colony. It was with him a case of "Open Sesame." Now the word has been lost, and the stone has closed for good round the mystic treasures that it had in it. Where the great chef walked in deep thought, full of knowledge, nobody sees anything but a little bandy-legged Kikuyu, a dwarf with a flat, still face.

What has Kamante got to say when he walks in to Nairobi, takes up his stand before the greedy supercilious Indian letter-writer, and expounds to him a message that is to go round half the world? The lines are crooked and there is no order in the phrases of the letter. But Kamante had in him a greatness of soul of which the people who knew him will still hear the note in the cracked disordered music, even as an echo of the harp of the herdboy David.[3]

This is a "2nd letter":

"I was not forget you Memsahib. Honored Memsahib. Now all your servants they never glad because you was from the country. If we was bird we fly and see you. Then we turn. Then your old farm it was good place for cow small calf black people. Now they had no anything cows goat sheep they has no anything. Now all bad people they enjoy in their heart because your old servant they come poor people now.

[1] **Oracle of Delphi:** In ancient Greece an oracle was a medium through which a god was supposed to speak. The famous oracle at Delphi issued mysterious messages that only special prophets could understand.

[2] **"caviar to the general":** something not suitable for everyone, but only for a special few; a quotation from Shakespeare's *Hamlet*.
[3] **David:** King David of the Old Testament.

Now God know in his heart all this to help sometime your servant."

And in a "3rd letter" Kamante gives an example of the way in which the native can say a handsome thing to you. He writes:

"Write and tell us if you turn. We think you turn. Because why? We think that you shall never can forget us. Because why? We think that you remembered still all our face and our mother names."

A white man who wanted to say a pretty thing to you would write: "I can never forget you." The African says: "We do not think of you, that you can ever forget us."

THINKING IT OVER

1. What do you think makes the description of the African countryside at the beginning of the selection especially vivid? Point out passages that tell how the author feels about the African countryside.

2. Trace the course of the author's friendship with Kamante. When did she first know him? What was he like as a boy? When did Kamante first show that he thought of the author as a friend? Later, what jobs did Kamante and the author work on together?

3. What characteristics does Kamante have that make him stand out as a person who is worth knowing well? What do the following incidents reveal about Kamante?
   (a) his return from the Scotch mission.
   (b) his work with the dogs.
   (c) his work as a medical assistant.
   (d) his letters to the author.

4. What do the cooking incidents show about Kamante's character and personality? Was it ultimately to his advantage or disadvantage to be trained as a cook?

5. The author was trained as an artist early in her life. What effect might this training have had on her writing? Can you find, for example, particular details in the description of Kamante and the African landscape that might have been overlooked by an untrained eye?

ABOUT THE AUTHOR

Isak Dinesen (ē′säk dē′nĕ·sĕn) (1885–1962) was the pen name of Karen, Baroness Blixen, a Danish author. (Isaac, in Hebrew, and Dinesen in Danish mean "he who laughs.") She studied painting in Copenhagen, Paris, and Rome. During this time she published a few short stories. In 1914 she married Baron Blixen, and they went to live on a large coffee plantation in British East Africa. Later, she took over the management of the farm herself. While in Africa she began to write to amuse herself during the rainy season. She enjoyed her life on the African coffee plantation, but in 1931 the drastic drop in coffee prices forced her to give up the farm and return to Denmark.

Seven Gothic Tales, written in English and published in 1934, brought her recognition as a writer of strangely haunting and eerie stories. In 1943, *Winter's Tales* appeared. *Out of Africa*, published in 1937, tells of her days on the coffee plantation. "Kamante" is from this book. Her last book, *Shadows in the Grass*, also tells of her experiences in Africa.

On an African Plantation ➤

The photograph on the opposite page is of a plantation in Kenya, Africa, very much like Isak Dinesen's farm. Flip back and forth from the picture to the second and third paragraphs of the selection (pages 305–06). See if you do not find that the photograph almost matches Miss Dinesen's descriptions of the "dry and burnt" colors of the landscape, the "light delicate foliage" of the trees, and the "blue vigor" of the sky.

In comparing the photograph with the selection, you will probably notice that there are certain ways in which good descriptive writing surpasses photography in helping you to "see" and have a total feeling for a place. What, for example, does Isak Dinesen tell you about the grass and the air that no photograph could possibly communicate?

Windows for the Crown Prince

ELIZABETH GRAY VINING

Elizabeth Gray Vining

Here is another true story about the meeting of two people from different ends of the earth — an American teacher and a Japanese boy. In this selection, Elizabeth Gray Vining recalls her experiences while teaching English to the Crown Prince of Japan in the years following World War II.

Mrs. matsudaira [1] and Mr. Sumikura [2] both attended my first private lesson with the Crown Prince, sitting at the little table at one side of the room while the Prince and I sat at the big table in the center. The first day I took a

[1] **Mrs. Matsudaira** (mä·tsoō·dī·rä): wife of the former Ambassador to Great Britain and to the United States.

[2] **Mr. Sumikura** (soō·mē·koō·rä): one of the five chamberlains or court attendants.

volume of the *Book of Knowledge* and we looked at the pictures together and talked about them as far as the Prince's limited vocabulary would go, which was not far.

The theory of teaching English entirely in English is that the student, learning or guessing the new words without interpretation, comes to think of them in English, instead of thinking of them in his own language first and then translating. In the second place, if English is the only language used, then he must plunge in and use it as best he can. The trick is the teaching of new words in such a way that the pupil really understands them and the building up of a new vocabulary through explanations in terms of already familiar words.

Noticing Important Details. You have often heard it said, "It's the little things that make the difference." This is just as true in reading as it is in everything else we do. If you pay close attention to details as you read, you will get much more enjoyment and value from your reading. In this selection, be alert for important details which will give you an understanding of the difficulties and accomplishments of Mrs. Vining as she tried to open windows on the Western world for the Crown Prince.

It took time, a great many pictures, and considerable agility. Sometimes I drew pictures on the blackboard, often I made use of the *Golden Dictionary*, a simple picture dictionary, and sometimes I demonstrated a word by getting up and acting it.

One quality of the Crown Prince's that very soon became apparent under the stress of this kind of learning was his intellectual honesty. It would save time and often tiresome repetition to pretend to understand, for instance, the distinction between *bring* and *take* before one actually did, but the Crown Prince never took that short cut. Looking a little worried and puzzled, he would admit frankly that he did not understand, and we would go at the problem again from a different angle. Then suddenly his face would clear and a happy look spread over it, and I would know that he had it. If I labored the point any further, to make sure, he would raise his hand impatiently and say, "Yes, yes, yes," in a way so like my own father that I was flooded with reminiscent amusement.

The presence all that autumn and winter of Mrs. Matsudaira and a chamberlain hampered both of us. It makes one feel a little silly to wave one's arms in the air in a swimming motion or to demonstrate the difference between jumping and hopping before two serious, interested, dignified adult spectators, but I learned in time to forget them. The effect on the Crown Prince, I felt, was more serious. Before answering any question he looked hastily at the chamberlain, whether for reassurance or because he felt self-conscious about making mistakes in front of him I did not know. The fact that he was noticeably more relaxed in the presence of those chamberlains who did not speak English suggests that the latter explanation was the right one. But as I saw him oftener outside of lesson hours, I realized that he was turning in everything to the chamberlains for prompting. The simplest question he seemed unable to answer for himself without seeking their help. This dependence upon them seemed to me undesirable, and I longed for him to have the experience of doing his work entirely on his own, of daring to make mistakes.

At the same time I realized that I was to him a very tall and possibly rather frightening stranger from America and that perhaps he needed the presence of the familiar attendant. I understood also that the chamberlains must wonder uneasily just what I was going to do to their adored Prince, and I was glad to have them see my methods and my subject matter.

After a month we had a lesson with only Mrs. Matsudaira present, no chamberlain, and I find in my diary for that day: "The best lesson yet." As time went on, the chamberlains gradually ceased to attend the lessons and in April, 1947, for the first time, Mrs. Matsudaira was not in the room. After that she attended the lessons only occasionally, in order to report to the Empress about the Prince's progress.

The great problem all the way through was to get reading material that would be simple enough English for the Crown Prince and yet mature enough to engage his interest. I prepared my lessons very carefully, trying to work in each time the words he already knew and to add new words and constructions in a logical way. As he would always answer questions to the best of his ability but never volunteered anything, either question or comment, I spent a good deal of time teaching him how to ask questions in

English, and for a part of each hour he had to ask me questions of his own making.

But my most successful venture during those early weeks was my invention of a tennis match played on paper and in English. I made a chart of a tennis court, and cut balls and rackets out of cardboard, and we played tennis in English, scoring, commenting on the game, and in the end walking to the net and shaking hands over it. The Prince had encountered the simple past tense before, but in the tennis match he was served the perfect tense with: You have won the game. I have lost the game. Who has won the game? Who has lost the game?

After awhile in order to stir up the passivity [1] which tended to leave all decisions, all initiative, to others, I began to say, "What shall we do first, dictation, conversation, reading?" At first he would demur, "You say," but after being prodded, he would generally choose dictation, which he liked least.

Before I went for the first time to meet my classes in the Gakushuin,[2] I was asked if I wouldn't like to have a Japanese teacher sitting in the back of the room throughout my lessons to keep order. There had never been a woman teacher beyond the primary school of Gakushuin before, and furthermore many students were interpreting this new "democracy" to mean that they could do exactly as they liked, and the teachers were afraid that I would have trouble in controlling my classes. Remembering what fierce we were to the French and German conversation teachers when I was in school I thought it quite probable that I might have dif-

ficulty, but I did not think that having a Japanese teacher as a policeman in the room was a satisfactory solution.

One of the most fertile sources of foreign-teacher-torture, I remembered, was derision [3] in all its varied forms of the way in which they mangled our names in pronouncing them. So I thought that I would eliminate that hazard at any rate by giving all the boys English names. There were other reasons also for the decision. One was that in their English textbooks the names of the children were all Japanese — Taro, Jiro, Yoshiko, Fumiko — and I thought they ought to learn to pronounce the English names. Then too I wanted to establish during that one hour as much of the atmosphere of an American classroom as possible. In the third place I thought it would be a good experience for the Crown Prince for once in his life to be on exactly the same level as the other boys, with no title and no special treatment at all.

Accordingly I made out a list of boys' names alphabetically arranged for each section, and I marched into Section A the first morning very calm outwardly but feeling a bit adventurous within.

The boys all stood up. "Good morning, boys," I said. "Good morning, sir," they replied with one voice. I laughed and they laughed. Then I told them that you said "Sir" to a man but you called a woman by her name. The boys sat down and looked very expectant, their black eyes shining.

"My name is Mrs. Vining," I said, and turned to the boy who sat at the first desk on the right-hand side. "What is your name?" He told me.

"That is your real name," I conceded, "but in this class your name is Adam."

---

[1] **passivity** (păs·ĭv′ĭ·tĭ) inactivity; inertness.
[2] **Gakushuin** (gä·ì·kōō·shōō·ḕr): a school for boys, originally intended only for the children of the nobility, now open to all classes.

[3] **derision** (dė·rĭzh′ŭn): ridicule.

Surrounded by court officials, and dressed in his robes of state, the Crown Prince holds a royal audience.

He looked surprised, as well he might.

"Now," I announced, "I am going to give you all English names." I went back to the first boy. "In this class, your name is Adam. Please say Adam. Please say, 'In this class my name is Adam.'"

It took a little while to get the idea over, and in the process we had some practice with pronouns. Your name is Adam. My name is Adam. His name is Adam. I wrote it on the blackboard. Adam wrote it in his notebook. I went on to the next, whose name became Billy.

The second boy caught on more quickly and the third boy jumped up eagerly to get his name. As I worked toward the Prince, who sat in the exact center of the room, I could see the others cutting their eyes around at each other, all agog to see what I was going to do about that situation.

I reached the Prince and said, "In this class your name is Jimmy." There was no particular reason for Jimmy, except that it just happened to be one of my favorite names.

He replied promptly, "No. I am Prince."

"Yes," I agreed cordially. "You are Prince Akihito.[1] That is your real name. But in this class you have an English name. In this class your name is Jimmy." I waited, a little breathless.

He smiled cheerfully, and the whole class beamed. I realized that he probably had thought I hadn't recognized him, seeing him for the first time among the other boys. Also I think that he had always been identified in his own mind with his princeship and was unable at first to think of himself as a boy among other boys.

The other names went off quickly,

[1] **Akihito** (ä·kǐ·hé·tô).

Mrs. Vining and the Crown Prince go over a vocabulary lesson.

and we passed on o the practice of prepositions. Near the end of the hour, Dr. Hozumi,[1] Mr. Kikuchi,[2] and a chamberlain tiptoed in to see how things were going. By that time the boys were answering to their names, and the Crown Prince was raising his hand and responding to "Yes, Jimmy?" just like any other schoolboy.

The observers tiptoed out again. When I joined them in the chamberlains' waiting room for a cup of tea between classes, they all appeared pleased.

Incidentally, I never had any trouble with discipline.

The weather that winter was cold and sunny. We had one five-inch snow that lingered on the ground in patches for about a week, but little rain or sleet. The schools were bitterly cold

and there were many absences among the children. Three boys in the Crown Prince's class dropped out with tuberculosis. Milk that winter was available only from the drugstore and on a doctor's prescription for sick babies, but I was able to get powdered milk for them from LARA.[3] Transportation was hideous. Trains and streetcars were cold, dirty, and often windowless as well as jammed to the roof. People climbed in through the windows after the aisles and steps were filled. Cloth of all kinds was so scarce that even the worn green plush upholstery had been cut off by passengers and taken home to patch clothes. It was not unusual for people to have their ribs broken in the crush, and I myself saw a pencil that had been splintered in a man's breast pocket. One of my pupils wrote, "My foot are stepped on, my hair are drew, my hands are caught. I feel like canned sardine."

As the winter went on, it became obvious to me that the Crown Prince was happiest and most himself when he was with the other boys. I saw him in the classroom between classes, always in a knot of other boys, laughing, alert, and interested. Sometimes I would see him racing down the corridor to the room where they played ping-pong. There were three tables, and he awaited his turn to play, like anybody else, roaming the aisles between tables, picking up the balls that went astray and tossing them back, commenting on the game. The boys called him *Denka* — Highness — and outside the school they bowed to him and kept their distance, but in the school building and on the playground he was one of them, and the difference in his demeanor and his whole expression showed how that

[1] **Dr. Hozumi** (hō·zōō·mė): the Crown Prince's Grand Chamberlain.
[2] **Mr. Kikuchi** (kē·kōō·jē): a teacher at the school.
[3] **LARA**: Licensed Agencies for Relief in Asia.

normal and happy relationship fed and watered his soul.

For this reason and to increase the opportunities for contact outside the schoolroom, I was eager to have two of his classmates join one of his private lessons each week, and when the new term began in April this was done. I chose the boys myself in consultation with the chamberlains and English teacher and, privately, with the Prince, and each term new ones were selected. I was always interested in the Prince's comments on his classmates, for he had a keen sense of character and he sometimes suggested boys whom I would not myself have thought of; in one case it was because he thought it would help the boy. The basis for choice was, first, character and personality, and second, at least a moderate ability in English. I liked to have one whose English was a little better than the Prince's and one whose English was not quite so good. The Prince himself stoutly resisted anyone who could speak very much better than he!

That first winter especially, people outside our immediate circle were interested in what I was teaching the Crown Prince and had large ideas of what I might accomplish. One February afternoon the Women's Committee of the United Christian Church gave a tea for me and presented me with a beautiful piece of hand woven tapestry in a design of mandarin ducks. This was an expression of the hope, which many Christians felt and which others put to me in far more blunt terms, that I should convert the Crown Prince to Christianity.

There were also other misconceptions of the purpose of my work there. A prominent editor, for instance, asked me if there was any resistance to my democratization of the Imperial Family.

This was not what I had been invited for. I had been asked simply to teach the Crown Prince English. But early in my stay in Japan, Grand Steward Matsudaira said to me, "We want you to open windows on to a wider world for our Crown Prince." It seemed to me then that through the medium of English I could present to him the ideals of the western world and help him to understand the essential spirit of that democracy which Japan was embracing with a hasty and bewildered sort of zeal in reaction from her great disillusionment with military dictatorship.

I never tried to indoctrinate him with any specific dogma. I tried only to expose him to the best that I knew. Religion, I have always felt, must be caught before it can be taught, and democracy is learned at least as much through living and doing as through an intellectual understanding of its theory. There were some to whom this point of view was a great disappointment. I reminded them that the Crown Prince's English at that time encompassed no more than a simple discussion of the pictures in the d'Aulaires' *Abraham Lincoln*[1] and a folk story, "The Monkey Wants Its Tail," which appeared in an American first-grade reader, and recommended patience to them.

Much earlier I had realized that I must clarify my own ideas of the essentials of democracy, not only for the sake of the Crown Prince, but for others who asked me. The first essential, I thought, was respect for the worth and dignity of the individual. The second I found best expressed by William Penn when he said, "That government is free to the

[1] d'Aulaires' *Abraham Lincoln:* One of a series of illustrated picture books for children by Edgar and Ingri d'Aulaire.

people under it where the laws rule and the people are a party to those laws."

As a Quaker, I believe in regard to the first, that humanism [1] is not enough, that the individual's worth and dignity derive from the light of the divine within his soul, and that when George Fox, the first Quaker, told his young followers to "walk cheerfully over the earth answering that of God in every man," the kind of *answer* he had in mind was social justice for everyone and a peaceful environment in which each soul can live out its fullest potentialities. So it was natural that my aspirations for the Crown Prince should take the form of a prayer, which I wrote during that first winter and which was a comfort to me when there seemed so little that I could do for him but to pray. It went like this:

"Heavenly Father, bless this child to whom some day will come great responsibility. Grant him free and happy growth to his fullest capacities of mind, body, and spirit. May he learn to know and trust Thy light within his own heart and come to respect its presence in his fellow men. Endow his teachers and chamberlains with wisdom and courage and grant that we may serve singleheartedly his best development, putting aside all selfish interests and desires. For His sake who gathered the children about Him, Amen."

[During the early part of Mrs. Vining's stay in Japan, three years had been mentioned as the probable period of her tutoring. At the end of that time, however, she was urged to stay another year to give the Prince more advanced training in English during the year which would correspond to the sophomore year in an American high school. In addition to her tutoring duties, Mrs. Vining continued to teach classes in English. In the three sections that year there were 110 Japanese boys.]

This term, I told them, we were going to study Great Men and Women of the Twentieth Century. I took a little time to discuss the meaning of the word *century,* and to explain that while our subjects might have been born before 1900, the major part of their lives must have been spent in the twentieth century. A great man I defined somewhat arbitrarily [2] as one who was not merely a figure of power or fame but one who had done something to help the world. We would study ten, of whom they were to choose five and I would choose five.

They made up their lists, and I wrote the names of their candidates on the blackboard and the five most often mentioned were chosen. Gandhi, Einstein, Noguchi,[3] and Madame Curie came out ahead in all three sections. Edison was fifth in two sections, Winston Churchill, surprisingly, in the third. Lenin, Stalin, Hitler, and Tojo were mentioned, probably to get a rise out of me. I wrote their names on the board

[1] **humanism** (hū′măn·ĭz′m): thought or action centering on distinctly human interests or ideals.

[2] **arbitrarily** (är′bĭ·trĕr′ĭ·lĭ): in a manner that is somewhat dictatorial because it is based on one's own will or judgment.
[3] **Noguchi** (nô·gōō·chê): Hideyo Noguchi (1876–1925), a famous Japanese scientist who worked in America. If you are not certain of the other famous people mentioned here, look them up in a biographical dictionary or encyclopedia.

The pictures on the opposite page show a woman working in the fields ▶
near Mt. Fujiyama; the Tusho-Gu Shrine in Nikko; artist Yuki Ogura painting
in her Kamakura studio; and the beautiful Takamatsu Park on Shikoku Island.

TRADITIONAL JAPAN

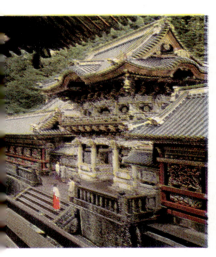

without comment and they got one vote each.

To the five whom the boys chose I added Roald Amundsen,[1] Eleanor Roosevelt, Helen Keller, Albert Schweitzer, and Pierre Ceresole,[2] the last one not because he is universally known but because I wanted to include one whose life had been given wholly to peace and whose *Service Civile Internationale* offered the moral equivalent of war that William James[3] advocated.

I varied the classroom procedure as we studied these great figures. Sometimes I told the story and they asked questions. Sometimes they told the story and I asked questions. Sometimes they carried on prepared conversations about them in pairs. In the examination at the end of the term they were required to say which one of the ten was their favorite and why. Some of the answers were interesting.

"My favorite is H. Noguchi because he is a great man produced by my own country."

"My favorite is the woman whose name is Marie Curie because she gave her life to scientific truth."

"One of my favorites is Miss Helen Keller because she is deaf and dumb and blind and yet she worked hard to learn to speak and to read books by touching the pages with her hand. And she got money for the deaf and dumb and blind and other poor people."

"My favorite is Albert Schweitzer because he found his true happiness by offering all his earthly happiness to helping poor Negroes."

"Gandhi has helped the world in two ways, one he unified India and made it free from English rule, second he showed throughout the world that nonviolent resistance is very strong and peace is very important."

[In still another way Mrs. Vining "opened windows" for the Crown Prince. She invited him to a party in her home to meet two Western boys — Tony Austin, son of Dr. Oliver Austin, who headed the wildlife program of the Natural Resources Section of General Headquarters, and John O'Brien, son of an Australian military general. Also at the party were Masayoshi Shiba (mä·sä·yŏ·shĕ shĕ·bä) and Akira Hashimoto (ä·kĕ·rä hä·shĕ·mŏ·tŏ), who were the two companions of the Prince at the time.]

Tony and John arrived first, in John's jeep, on the afternoon of June eighth, 1949, and I had a chance to brief them a bit before the Prince came. Dr. Koizumi[4] was the next to appear, and he made friends at once with the two Western boys. "Where will the Crown Prince sit?" he whispered to Tané,[5] seeing John and Tony on the sofa, and I realized, not for the first time, how much Americans tend to let things take their natural course, and how carefully the Japanese plan each detail ahead.

The Prince brought Hashimoto San[6] and Shiba San in his car with him when he came, and he was accompanied by Dr. Yumoto, the youngest of the three doctors, and Mr. Kuroki.[7] There were

---

[1] **Roald Amundsen** (rō'äld ä'mōōn·sĕn): (1872–1928) a Norwegian polar explorer; he discovered the South Pole in 1911.

[2] **Pierre Ceresole** (sĕ·rĕ·sòl'): a Swiss, leader of an international pacifist movement and founder of the *Service Civile Internationale*, a voluntary organization working for peace and rehabilitation of war-torn areas.

[3] **William James**: American philosopher and psychologist (1842–1910).

[4] **Dr. Koizumi** (kō·ĕ·zōō·mĕ): director of the Prince's education.

[5] **Tané** (tä·nä'): Mrs. Vining's secretary, Miss Tané Takahashi.

[6] **San** (sän): "San" is the Japanese polite form of address like our "Mr." or "Miss." Note that it is said after the name.

[7] **Dr. Yumoto** (yōō·mŏ·tŏ) . . . **Mr. Kuroki** (kōō·rŏ·kĕ): attendants to the Prince.

introductions and handshakings all around, and then I took all the boys upstairs for the game.

John and Tony were adept at Monopoly; the Japanese boys knew the rudiments of the game. I acted as banker, the boys threw for first turn, and the game was on. The Prince was a little quiet and reserved at first, feeling his way in the new situation, but relaxed after awhile. Tony, the irrepressible, played with zest and loud outcries; the others enjoying themselves more quietly. Presently Dr. Koizumi came in to watch, standing up and looking over their shoulders, laughing at Tony, helping with the translation of a Japanese or an English word when necessary. His natural gift for people and his long association with boys in especial made him always a positive asset in any such group.

They played for about an hour and a half, and then I called a halt for scoring and we went downstairs. Monopoly is an all-day affair, and the game was nowhere near its end. At the halfway point the Crown Prince's score was low, as might be expected. He was not in the least bothered by the fact nor were the Japanese boys; the Western boys were a little uneasy, wondering if they had been rude to defeat him, and they commented afterwards admiringly on his being a good loser.

They were impressed by the Prince's entirely natural manner with the other Japanese boys, and they gave him the accolade [1] of schoolboy praise. "He's a regular feller," they said.

On my last day at the school Prince Akihito was in bed with a cold. As I had asked to continue with his private lessons up to the time of my departure, this was not the final lesson for him,

but nevertheless he sent Mr. Shimizu [2] to the school especially to see me and tell me that he was sorry to miss my last class.

I was to see the other boys again too, singly and collectively, before I left, but this was the final time in the classroom and I felt sad as I faced them. They recited the quotations that they had memorized and then I said to them:

"I have asked you to learn these great words by great men because I hope you will remember them all your lives. When I was in school I had to memorize many poems and most of them I still remember. I have forgotten much that I have learned since then, but what I memorized when I was your age has stayed with me. The parts of two poems that I learned in German are almost all the German I know now, but I often think of them. So I want these great thoughts to be part of the permanent furniture of your minds.

"These are great thoughts of great men, but I want also to give you something from myself." (They sat very still and attentive and there was an electric quality in the silence. They were very different from American students, who begin to squirm and think of something else whenever there is any threat of preaching. The Japanese, on the other hand, like homilies [3] from their teachers; they even ask for them.) "I want you to try always to think for yourselves. Don't believe everything you hear, no matter who says it. Don't believe all you read in the newspapers. Don't take other people's opinions without examining them. Try to find out the truth for yourselves. If you hear a very strong opinion on one side of a ques-

---

[1] accolade (ăk′ō·lād′): high award.

[2] Mr. Shimizu (shĭ·mĭ·zoō): attendant to the Prince.

[3] homilies (hŏm′ĭ·lĭz): sermons.

tion, try to hear also an opinion on the other side, and then decide what you think yourself. In these days there is a great deal of propaganda of all kinds. Some of it is true and some is not. It is very important that young people all over the world should learn to find out the truth for themselves."

Then I wrote "Think for yourselves!" on the blackboard and we spent the last few minutes playing a word game.

NOTICING IMPORTANT DETAILS

Point out incidents which helped Mrs. Vining understand that:
  (a) Prince Akihito was a thoroughly honest student, as the author says, "intellectually honest."
  (b) the presence of the chamberlains hampered the progress of the Prince.
  (c) the Prince lacked initiative.
  (d) the Prince enjoyed the company of Western boys.

THINKING IT OVER

1. Do you think the boys showed good judgment in their choice of Great Men and Women of the Twentieth Century? Would you add or substitute others?

2. How did Mrs. Vining's final thought for the boys sum up everything she had tried to teach the Crown Prince and his companions?

3. What in Mrs. Vining's background especially fitted her for the job she was asked to do? What was her attitude toward her work? What did you learn about her as a person from this selection?

COMPOSITION SUGGESTION

Choose a man (or woman) who has lived most of his life in the twentieth century, and tell why you consider him a great person. Before you begin to write, consult at least three different reference sources so that you have several views of your subject's life and accomplishments. From these sources, select only the facts that are related to your main point — why this particular person is outstanding.

ABOUT THE AUTHOR

Elizabeth Gray Vining (1902–   ) in 1943 was the winner of the Newbery Award, an honor given each year to the author of the most outstanding book in the field of children's literature. Author of a dozen books for children, Mrs. Vining's *Windows for the Crown Prince* was written for adults and became a best seller in 1952. She has written several other books about Japan, including her recent *Return to Japan*. The Quaker woman who achieved fame as the teacher of the Crown Prince of Japan from 1946–1950 was born in Philadelphia. She was graduated from the Germantown Friends School, Bryn Mawr, and Drexel Institute Library School. Her marriage to Morgan Vining, a member of the faculty of the University of North Carolina, was cut short by an automobile accident in which he was killed. Mrs. Vining returned to Philadelphia to write and was engaged in work for the Friends organization when the Emperor of Japan chose her as tutor for his son.

Japan, Traditional and Modern →

The pictures on the opposite page show some of the effects of Westernization and modernization in Tokyo. The bicycle factory, with its assembly line, is quite up-to-date. Western-style dress is worn by people strolling through Asakusa, Tokyo's amusement district. The subway system is similar to that of any large Western city. And the children's reading room in the Hibiya Library provides Japanese youngsters with modern surroundings and facilities.

Compare these pictures with those on page 323. It is hard to believe that the two sets of photographs were taken in the same country — or even in the same century. But they were, and together they show Japan's current blending of the "old" and the "new," of elements from both Eastern and Western culture. Can you give some of the reasons for the changes that have recently taken place in Japan?

MODERN
JAPAN

The Voice of
the Pools

GABRIELLE ROY

Gabrielle Roy

Who can anticipate the time, the place, the incident, or the person that will set you off on the path that you will travel through life? This recollection is more "personal" than either of the others that you have read in this group. In it, a distinguished Canadian writer recalls, not other people or other lands, but herself when she was close to the age you are now.

IN THE POOLS not far from our house, some evening toward April, began a kind of piercing, vibrant music, softly sad withal, which lasted almost all summer, only to cease whenever the water in these pools had been wholly consumed by the sun or by the earth.

The tiny singers — hundreds of frogs — were invisible. Emerging from winter, from their numbness, from the mud, did they recapture this thin, strident voice to talk to each other, to greet each other from one swamp to another? Or else did they live once more, did they free themselves from the viscous [1] bottom only to stir our hearts awhile with a strange music? At first individual, scattered, in the end these voices harmonized and soon made up a single long and continuous cry. I still hear it, drilling through the spring nights around our home; never have I heard a stronger summons toward childhood, toward its somewhat savage joys.

I still often went to my attic, even when I became a hard-working student, even when I was a little older and on the edge of what is called youth. What did I go up there for? I was perhaps

[1] **viscous** (vĭs′kŭs): having a sticky consistency.

Identifying Yourself with the Writer. One of the pleasures of reading a personal recollection of this kind is to try to share the experiences of the writer by putting yourself in her place. As you read this selection, try to identify yourself with the writer. Almost everyone has had times when he was concerned about the future and what he should attempt to do with his life. By recalling your own experiences of this kind you can better understand and share the author's experiences.

---

sixteen on the evening when I climbed there as though in search of myself. What should I be, later on? . . . What should I do with my life? . . . Yes, such were the questions I was beginning to ask myself. Probably I thought the time had come to reach decisions regarding my future, regarding that person all unknown to me who would one day be I.

And it happened that that evening, as I leaned out of the little attic window toward the cry of the pools close by, there appeared to me — if one may say that they appear — those vast, somber lands which time spreads before us. Yes, such was the land that lay stretched in front of me — vast, wholly mine, yet wholly to be discovered.

The frogs, that evening, had swollen their voices to the point of making them a cry of distress, a cry of triumph as well . . . as though they foretold a parting. I then saw, not what I should later become, but that I must set forth on my way to becoming it. It seemed to me that I was at once in the attic and also far away — in the loneliness of the future; and that from yonder, committed at so great a distance, I was showing myself the road, I was calling myself and saying to myself, "Yes, come, this is the way I must travel. . . ."

And so I had the idea of writing. What and why I knew not at all. I would write. It was like a sudden love which, in a moment, binds a heart; it was really a fact as simple, as naïve as love. Having as yet nothing to say . . . I wanted to have something to say.

Did I try my hand at it instantly? Did I at once obey this outlandish command? A gentle wind of spring was blowing my hair, the thousand frog voices filled the night, and I wanted to write as one feels the need to love, to be loved. It was still vague, beneficent,

a bit sad, too. All round me were the books of my childhood, which here I had read and reread, in a dancing beam of dusty light, pouring down like a ray of sun from the gable window. And the happiness the books had given me I wished to repay. I had been the child who reads hidden from everyone, and now I wanted myself to be this beloved book, these living pages held in the hands of some nameless being, woman, child, companion, whom I would keep for myself a few hours. Is there any possession equal to this one? Is there a friendlier silence, a more perfect understanding?

Yet, this other myself, who in the future urged me to attain her, that other myself — oh, the bliss of ignorance! — was clothed as I was that evening in a navy-blue serge blouse, with a broad sailor collar; she had the same slightly thoughtful young face, leaning in the hollow of one hand; she had grown no older.

My mother one evening came to find me in this low-ceilinged chamber, where I so constantly remained, fascinated by the thousand sounds of the night which I was learning to distinguish one from another, fascinated — beyond daring aught else — by the breadth, the mystery of the task I had assigned myself, or else had accepted to undertake. The song of the pools was growing weaker; now, separate one from the other, the little voices sought each other, seemed to reply to one another, or — perchance — to draw apart. . . .

Maman asked me, "Why do you forever shut yourself up here? It doesn't go with your years. You should be playing tennis or having fun with your friends. You've gotten quite pale. And yet these are the best days of your life.

Farm land in Manitoba, Canada, Gabrielle Roy's home province.

Why not put them to better use?"

Thereupon I solemnly announced to Maman what was transpiring; that I was to write. . . . For this, was it not necessary to come to the attic, listen for a long, long while to the intermingling voices . . . and so many things you must untangle?

Maman seemed upset. It was, nevertheless, her fault if I preferred fiction to daily life. She had taught me the power of images, the wonder of a thing revealed by just the right word, and all the love that one simple and beautiful sentence may contain.

"Writing," she told me sadly, "is hard. It must be the most exciting business in the world . . . if it is to be true, you understand! Is it not like cutting yourself in two, as it were — one half trying to live, the other watching, weighing? . . ."

And she went on: "First the gift is needed; if you have not that, it's heartbreak; but if you have it, it's perhaps equally terrible. . . . For we say the gift; but perhaps it would be better to say the command. And here is a very strange gift," Maman continued, "not wholly human. I think other people nev-

er forgive it. This gift is a little like a stroke of ill luck, which withdraws others, which cuts us off from almost everyone. . . ."

How could Maman speak with such exact knowledge? As she talked I felt the truth of what she said, and felt as though I had already suffered it.

Maman's eyes were distant, and she was so concerned to guard me well, to defend me, that they filled with sadness. "To write," she said to me, "is this not, finally, to be far from others . . . to be all alone, poor child?"

After a brief rain, the frogs renewed their song of such fetching wearisomeness. I think one must yearn far in advance for the long road to be traveled, for the ultimate visage which will give us life. Curiosity to know ourselves — perhaps that is what best draws us forward. . . .

"At times words also succeed in being true," said I to Maman. "And without words, would there be a single truth of which you could say: Thus it is; it's true!"

Then Maman made a gesture so desolate, so powerless. She said as she went away, "The future is a terrible thing. It is always something of a defeat."

She left me to the night, to the lonely attic, to the vast sorrow of the land of blackness.

But I still hoped that I could have everything: both a warm and true life, like a shelter — at times, too, unbearable with harsh truth — and also time to capture its reverberation in the depths of the soul; time to walk, and time to halt that I might understand; time to withhold myself a little along the road, and then to catch up with the others, to rejoin them and to cry joyously, "Here I am, and here is what I've found for you along the way! . . . Have you waited for me? . . . Aren't you waiting for me? . . . Oh, do wait for me! . . ."

IDENTIFYING YOURSELF WITH THE AUTHOR

Were you able to identify yourself with the author? Why? Why not? Before you answer — and perhaps reread the selection to be certain of your answer — consider the questions that troubled Gabrielle Roy. How many of these questions have occurred to you at times? Which ones?

THINKING IT OVER

1. What was the "voice of the pools"? What did it mean to the girl?

2. Have you ever had the feeling that you would like to accomplish something great even though you don't know what it is or how to go about it? How does Gabrielle Roy react to this feeling?

3. Do you think the author feels differently about her experience because she is looking back at it after having accomplished what she was determined to do? Do you think her remembrance would have the same quality if she had not become a successful writer? Why?

4. How did the mother react to the girl's decision to become a writer? Do you think the mother gave an accurate description of a writer's life?

GAINING POWER OVER WORDS

USING THE DICTIONARY Although you have been urged to use context in learning the meanings of new words, it is not intended that the value of dictionaries should be discredited. Both context and dictionary are resources to the student who truly wants to increase his control of language.

Select a committee of four or five students to prepare a special group report on the dictionary. The committee should review for you the dictionary skills you have learned in previous years. Probably there are also some new uses of the dictionary that they should teach you. Are all of the members of your class familiar with the special sections at the back of most dictionaries? with diacritical marks? the history of dictionaries? the various meanings of words like *run* or *open* or *pass*? How do the makers of dictionaries determine the meanings or pronunciations of words?

You should avoid the mistake of taking the first dictionary meaning you find for a word. Find the meaning that fits the context surrounding the word. Like chameleons, words change color (meaning) when their surroundings change.

ABOUT THE AUTHOR

Gabrielle Roy (1909–   ) was born in Manitoba, Canada, of a pioneer French-Canadian family. She began writing when she was twelve. While she was working at other jobs, she had several short stories published. She started to work as a country schoolteacher, but gave this up after a short time and began to act with little theater groups. In 1937 she went to England to study drama, and while she was there, she wrote several articles about Canadian life which were published in a Parisian weekly.

When she returned to Canada in 1939, she supported herself by writing for French-Canadian newspapers and magazines. In 1947, her first novel, *The Tin Flute*, was published in America and was greeted with enthusiasm and praise. In 1951, her second book, *Where Nests the Water Hen*, appeared; and in 1956, her third, *The Cashier*. In *Street of Riches*, from which "The Voice of the Pools" was selected, she recalls her own life.

Glimpses of Mark Twain

Mark Twain is the pen name of one of America's great writers and humorists, Samuel Langhorne Clemens. He was born in 1835 in a small town in Missouri, and he grew up in Hannibal, Missouri, on the Mississippi River. As a young man, he was, successively, a printer, a river pilot, a mining prospector in Nevada, a newspaper writer, a traveling correspondent and a lecturer. He took his pen name from his river pilot days. "Mark twain," meaning two fathoms, was the call of the leadsman who sat at the front of a boat and measured the depth of the river waters. The author once said that he chose Mark Twain for his pen name because it made a pilot feel comfortable to know that the water was two fathoms deep.

Twain won his first real popularity with *The Innocents Abroad*, published in 1869. This humorous travelogue was based on his experiences during a trip to Europe, Egypt, and the Near East in 1867. After this trip he returned to America, married, and settled down to write books. He lived in Buffalo, New York, for a while, then moved to Hartford, Connecticut. As the years passed, he became famous and made a great deal of money. Unfortunately, during the 1890's, he lost his money in a poor investment and had to work very hard lecturing and writing in order to pay off his debts. He died in 1910.

In the late nineteenth century, American writers began to free themselves from European literary influences and forms. Mark Twain reflected this independence. His books, *The Adventures of Tom Sawyer*, *The Adventures of Huckleberry Finn*, *Life on the Mississippi*, and *Roughing It*, are written in a distinctively American style and are about truly American experiences.

The selections that follow give you three glimpses of Mark Twain. "Early Days," from *The Autobiography of Mark Twain*, tells about his boyhood in Missouri. The second selection, "The Blue Jay Yarn," provides an example of Mark Twain's particular brand of humorous writing. In the third selection, "An Interview with Mark Twain," he is seen late in life by Rudyard Kipling, a young English author who later became world-famous.

PART ONE

Early Days

MARK TWAIN

Mark Twain's boyhood experiences furnished material for two of his most popular books: *The Adventures of Tom Sawyer,* and *The Adventures of Huckleberry Finn.* How accurately do you think you could remember your childhood, looking back after forty years? In this selection from his autobiography, you find Mark Twain telling about his early days in Missouri in the mock-serious tone and rambling style for which he is famous.

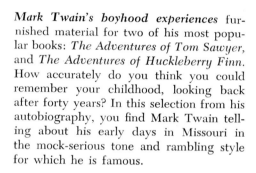

I WAS BORN the 30th of November, 1835, in the almost invisible village of Florida, Monroe County, Missouri. My parents removed to Missouri in the early thirties; I do not remember just when, for I was not born then and cared nothing for such things. It was a long journey in those days and must have been a rough and tiresome one. The village contained a hundred people and I increased the population by one per cent. It is more than many of the best men in history could have done for a town. It may not be modest in me to refer to this but it is true. There is no

record of a person doing as much — not even Shakespeare. But I did it for Florida and it shows that I could have done it for any place — even London, I suppose.

Recently someone in Missouri has sent me a picture of the house I was born in.[1] Heretofore I have always stated that it was a palace, but I shall be more guarded now.

The village had two streets, each a couple of hundred yards long; the rest of the avenues mere lanes, with rail-fences and cornfields on either side. Both the streets and the lanes were paved with the same material — tough black mud in wet times, deep dust in dry.

Most of the houses were of logs — all of them, indeed, except three or four; these latter were frame ones. There were none of brick and none of stone. There was a log church, with a puncheon floor and slab benches. A puncheon floor is made of logs whose upper surfaces have been chipped flat with the

[1] The house in which Mark Twain was born is pictured above.

adz.[1] The cracks between the logs were not filled; there was no carpet; consequently, if you dropped anything smaller than a peach it was likely to go through. The church was perched upon short sections of logs, which elevated it two or three feet from the ground. Hogs slept under there, and whenever the dogs got after them during services the minister had to wait till the disturbance was over. In winter there was always a refreshing breeze up through the puncheon floor; in summer there were fleas enough for all.

A slab bench is made of the outside cut of a saw-log, with the bark side down; it is supported on four sticks driven into auger holes at the ends; it has no back and no cushions. The church was twilighted with yellow tallow candles in tin sconces hung against the walls. Weekdays, the church was a schoolhouse.

There were two stores in the village. My uncle, John A. Quarles, was proprietor of one of them. It was a very small establishment, with a few rolls of "bit" calicoes on half a dozen shelves; a few barrels of salt mackerel, coffee and New Orleans sugar behind the counter; stacks of brooms, shovels, axes, hoes, rakes and such things here and there; a lot of cheap hats, bonnets and tinware strung on strings and suspended from the walls; and at the other end of the room was another counter with bags of shot on it, a cheese or two and a keg of powder; in front of it a row of nail kegs and a few pigs of lead, and behind it a barrel or two of New Orleans molasses and native corn whisky on tap. If a boy bought five or ten cents' worth of anything he was entitled to half a handful of sugar from the barrel; if a woman bought a few yards of calico she was entitled to a spool of thread in addition to the usual gratis "trimmin's"; if a man bought a trifle he was at liberty to draw and swallow as big a drink of whisky as he wanted.

Everything was cheap: apples, peaches, sweet potatoes, Irish potatoes and corn, ten cents a bushel; chickens, ten cents apiece; butter, six cents a pound; eggs, three cents a dozen; coffee and sugar, five cents a pound. I do not know how prices are out there in interior Missouri now, but I know what they are here in Hartford, Connecticut. To wit: apples, three dollars a bushel; peaches, five dollars; Irish potatoes (choice Bermudas), five dollars; chickens, a dollar to a dollar and a half apiece, according to weight; butter, forty-five to sixty cents a pound; eggs, fifty to sixty cents a dozen; coffee, forty-five cents a pound. . . .

My uncle, John A. Quarles, was also a farmer, and his place was in the country four miles from Florida. He had eight children . . . and was also fortunate in other ways, particularly in his character. I have not come across a better man than he was. I was his guest for two or three months every year, from the fourth year after we removed to Hannibal [2] till I was eleven or twelve years old. I have never consciously used him or his wife in a book, but his farm has come very handy to me in literature once or twice. In *Huck Finn* and in *Tom Sawyer, Detective* I moved it down to Arkansas. It was all of six hundred miles, but it was no trouble; it was not a very large farm — five hundred acres, perhaps — but I could have done it if it had been twice as large. And as for the morality of it, I cared nothing for that; I would move a state if the ex-

[1] **adz** (ădz): a cutting tool with an arched blade.

[2] **Hannibal:** When Mark Twain was three years old, the family moved to this small Missouri town.

igencies [1] of literature required it.

It was a heavenly place for a boy, that farm of my uncle John's. The house was a double log one, with a spacious floor (roofed in) connecting it with the kitchen. In the summer the table was set in the middle of that shady and breezy floor, and the sumptuous meals — well, it makes me cry to think of them. Fried chicken, roast pig; wild and tame turkeys, ducks and geese; venison just killed; squirrels, rabbits, pheasants, partridges, prairie-chickens; biscuits, hot batter cakes, hot buckwheat cakes, hot "wheat bread," hot rolls, hot corn pone; fresh corn boiled on the ear, succotash, butter-beans, string-beans, tomatoes, peas, Irish potatoes, sweet potatoes; buttermilk, sweet milk, "clabber," [2] watermelons, muskmelons, cantaloupes — all fresh from the garden; apple pie, peach pie, pumpkin pie, apple dumplings, peach cobbler — I can't remember the rest. The way that the things were cooked was perhaps the main splendor — particularly a certain few of the dishes. For instance, the corn bread, the hot biscuits and wheat bread and the fried chicken. These things have never been properly cooked in the North — in fact, no one there is able to learn the art, so far as my experience goes. The North thinks it knows how to make corn bread, but this is gross superstition. Perhaps no bread in the world is quite so good as Southern corn bread, and perhaps no bread in the world is quite so bad as the Northern imitation of it. The North seldom tries to fry chicken, and this is well; the art cannot be learned north of the line of Mason and Dixon, nor anywhere in Europe. This is not hearsay; it is experience that is speaking. In Europe it is imagined that the custom of serving various kinds of

bread blazing hot is "American," but that is too broad a spread; it is custom in the South but is much less than that in the North. In the North and in Europe hot bread is considered unhealthy. This is probably another fussy superstition, like the European superstition that ice-water is unhealthy. Europe does not need ice-water and does not drink it; and yet, notwithstanding this, its word for it is better than ours, because it describes it, whereas ours doesn't. Europe calls it "iced" water. Our word describes water made from melted ice — a drink which has a characterless taste and which we have but little acquaintance with. . . .

The farmhouse stood in the middle of a very large yard and the yard was fenced on three sides with rails and on the rear side with high palings; against these stood the smoke-house; beyond the palings was the orchard; beyond the orchard were the tobacco fields. The front yard was entered over a stile made of sawed-off logs of graduated heights; I do not remember any gate. In a corner of the front yard were a dozen lofty hickory trees and a dozen black walnuts, and in the nutting season riches were to be gathered there.

Down a piece, abreast the house, stood a little log cabin against the rail fence; and there the woody hill fell sharply away, past the barns, the corn-crib, the stables and the tobacco-curing house, to a limpid brook which sang along over its gravelly bed and curved and frisked in and out and here and there and yonder in the deep shade of overhanging foliage and vines — a divine place for wading, and it had swimming pools, too, which were forbidden to us and therefore much frequented by us. . . .

I can see the farm yet, with perfect clearness. I can see all its belongings,

[1] **exigencies** (ĕk′sĭ·jĕn·sĭz): urgent needs.
[2] **clabber**: curdled milk.

Mark Twain revisits his childhood home in Hannibal, Missouri.

all its details; the family room of the house, with a "trundle" bed [1] in one corner and a spinning wheel in another — a wheel whose rising and falling wail, heard from a distance, was the mournfulest of all sounds to me and made me homesick and low spirited and filled my atmosphere with the wandering spirits of the dead; the vast fireplace, piled high on winter nights with flaming hickory logs from whose ends a sugary sap bubbled out but did not go to waste, for we scraped it off and ate it; the lazy cat spread out on the rough hearthstones; the drowsy dogs braced against the jambs and blinking; my aunt in one chimney corner, knitting; my uncle in the other, smoking his corncob pipe; the slick and carpetless oak floor faintly mirroring the dancing flame tongues and freckled with black indentations where fire coals had popped out and died a leisurely death; half a dozen children romping in the background twilight; "split"-bottomed chairs here and there, some with rock-

ers; a cradle — out of service but waiting with confidence; in the early cold mornings a snuggle of children in shirts and chemises, occupying the hearthstone and procrastinating — they could not bear to leave the comfortable place and go out on the windswept floor space between the house and kitchen where the general tin basin stood, and wash.

Along outside of the front fence ran the country road, dusty in the summertime and a good place for snakes — they liked to lie in it and sun themselves; when they were rattlesnakes or puff adders we killed them; when they were black snakes or racers or belonged to the fabled "hoop" breed we fled without shame; when they were "house snakes" or "garters" we carried them home and put them in Aunt Patsy's work basket for a surprise; [2] for she was prejudiced against snakes, and always when she took the

---

[1] **trundle bed:** a low bed on rollers, that may be pushed under another bed.

[2] **a surprise:** Those of you who have read *The Adventures of Tom Sawyer* may be able to recall an incident or two that may have had their origin in such "surprises."

basket in her lap and they began to climb out of it, it disordered her mind. She never could seem to get used to them; her opportunities went for nothing. And she was always cold toward bats, too, and could not bear them; and yet I think a bat is as friendly a bird as there is. My mother was Aunt Patsy's sister and had the same wild superstitions. A bat is beautifully soft and silky; I do not know any creature that is pleasanter to touch or is more grateful for caressings, if offered in the right spirit. I know all about these coleoptera [1] because our great cave, three miles below Hannibal, was multitudinously stocked with them and often I brought them home to amuse my mother with. It was easy to manage if it was a school day because then I had ostensibly been to school and hadn't any bats. She was not a suspicious person but full of trust and confidence; and when I said, "There's something in my coat pocket for you," she would put her hand in. But she always took it out again, herself; I didn't have to tell her. It was remarkable the way she couldn't learn to like private bats. The more experience she had, the more she could not change her views.

I think she was never in the cave in her life; but everybody else went there. Many excursion parties came from considerable distances up and down the river to visit the cave. It was miles in extent and was a tangled wilderness of narrow and lofty clefts [2] and passages. It was an easy place to get lost in; anybody could do it — including the bats. I got lost myself, along with a lady, and our last candle burned down to almost nothing before we glimpsed the search party's lights winding about in the distance.

"Injun Joe," the half-breed, got lost in there once and would have starved to death if the bats had run short. But there was no chance of that; there were myriads of them. He told me all his story. In the book called *Tom Sawyer* I starved him entirely to death in the cave but that was in the interest of art; it never happened. "General" Gaines, who was our first town drunkard before Jimmy Finn got the place, was lost in there for the space of a week and finally pushed his handkerchief out of a hole in a hilltop near Saverton, several miles down the river from the cave's mouth, and somebody saw it and dug him out. There is nothing the matter with his statistics except the handkerchief. I knew him for years, and he hadn't any. But it could have been his nose. That would attract attention.

Beyond the road where the snakes sunned themselves was a dense young thicket and through it a dim-lighted path led a quarter of a mile; then out of the dimness one emerged abruptly upon a level great prairie which was covered with wild strawberry plants, vividly starred with prairie pinks and walled in on all sides by forests. The strawberries were fragrant and fine, and in the season we were generally there in the crisp freshness of the early morning, while the dew beads still sparkled upon the grass and the woods were ringing with the first songs of the birds.

Down the forest slopes to the left were the swings. They were made of bark stripped from hickory saplings. When they became dry they were dangerous. They usually broke when a child was forty feet in the air, and this was why so many bones had to be mended every year. I had no ill luck

[1] Mark Twain is probably pretending to confuse *chiroptera*, the scientific name for bats, with *coleoptera*, an order of insects.

[2] **clefts** (klĕfts): cracks or openings.

myself but none of my cousins escaped. There were eight of them and at one time and another they broke fourteen arms among them. But it cost next to nothing, for the doctor worked by the year — twenty-five dollars for the whole family. I remember two of the Florida doctors, Chowning and Meredith. They not only tended an entire family for twenty-five dollars a year but furnished the medicines themselves. Good measure, too. Castor oil was the principal beverage. The dose was half a dipperful, with half a dipperful of New Orleans molasses added to help it down and make it taste good, which it never did. The next standby was calomel; the next rhubarb; and the next jalap.[1] Then they bled the patient and put mustard plasters on him. It was a dreadful system, and yet the death rate was not heavy. The calomel was nearly sure to salivate the patient[2] and cost him some of his teeth. There were no dentists. When teeth became touched with decay or were otherwise ailing, the doctor knew of but one thing to do — he fetched his tongs and dragged them out. If the jaw remained, it was not his fault.

Doctor Meredith removed to Hannibal by and by and was our family physician there and saved my life several times. Still, he was a good man and meant well. Let it go.

I was always told that I was a sickly and precarious and tiresome and uncertain child and lived mainly on allopathic medicines[3] during the first seven years of my life. I asked my mother about this, in her old age — she was in her eighty-eighth year — and said:

"I suppose that during all that time you were uneasy about me?"

"Yes, the whole time."

"Afraid I wouldn't live?"

After a reflective pause — ostensibly to think out the facts — "No — afraid you would."

It sounds like plagiarism,[4] but it probably wasn't.

[4] **plagiarism** (plā′jĭ·ȧ·rĭz′m): the act of stealing someone's idea or writing and passing it off as one's own.

THINKING IT OVER

1. Do you think Mark Twain is completely serious as he recalls his early days? Find passages where the author obviously wrote with his tongue in his cheek.

2. Many of the things which Mark Twain says that seem on the surface merely funny, have a grain of truth and an attitude toward life expressed in them. Point out and explain at least one comment of this kind.

3. Perspective or distance is very important in determining your view of anything. How does the distance of years and of his success affect Mark Twain's view of his childhood? Point out experiences that might not have been amusing at the time.

4. Mark Twain speaks of moving his uncle's farm six hundred miles to use in a book and says: "And as for the morality of it, I cared nothing for that; I would move a state if the exigencies of literature required it." What is he talking about here? Do you agree that a writer of fiction has the right to move things about as he pleases? a biographer? Explain.

APPRECIATING DESCRIPTION

1. Reread the description of his uncle's store, and try to discover what method Twain used in picturing it for us. What information about the store is actually given? What kinds of words does he use?

2. How does the description in this selection contribute to your knowledge of Mark Twain's boyhood?

[1] **jalap** (jăl′ăp): a drug prepared from the root of a Mexican plant.
[2] **salivate** (săl′ĭ·vāt) **the patient:** to produce an abnormal flow of saliva in the patient.
[3] **allopathic** (ăl′ṓ·păth′ĭk) **medicines:** remedies that counteract symptoms rather than cure the disease itself.

PART TWO

The Blue Jay Yarn

MARK TWAIN

Part of Mark Twain's full and varied life was spent traveling — both in the United States and abroad. From these journeys came his popular travel books, *Innocents Abroad, Roughing It,* and *A Tramp Abroad.* "The Blue Jay Yarn" is just a brief selection from *A Tramp Abroad,* but it will show you something of the charm and humor of Twain's travelogues. It will also show you Mark Twain the storyteller, the spinner of a good yarn.

ONE AFTERNOON I got lost in the wood [1] about a mile from the hotel and presently fell into a train of dreamy thought about animals which talk, and kobolds,[2] and enchanted folk, and the rest of the pleasant legendary stuff; and so, by stimulating my fancy, I finally got to imagining I glimpsed small flitting shapes here and there down the columned aisles of the forest. It was a place which was peculiarly meet [3] for the occasion. It was a pine wood, with so thick and soft a carpet of brown needles that one's footfall made no more sound than if he were treading on wool; the tree-trunks were as round and straight and smooth as pillars, and stood close together; they were bare of branches to a point about twenty-five feet above ground, and from there upward so thick with boughs that not a ray of sunlight could pierce through. The world was bright with sunshine outside, but a deep and mellow twilight reigned in there, and also a silence so profound that I seemed to hear my own breathings.

When I had stood ten minutes, thinking and imagining, and getting my spirit in tune with the place, and in the right mood to enjoy the supernatural, a raven suddenly uttered a hoarse croak over my head. It made me start; and then I was angry because I started. I looked up, and the creature was sitting on a limb right over me, looking down at me. I felt something of the same sense of humiliation and injury which one feels when he finds that a human stranger has been clandestinely [4] in-

---

[1] **the wood:** the Black Forest in Germany.
[2] **kobolds** (kŏ'bŏldz): gnomes, in German folklore.
[3] **meet:** suitable.

[4] **clandestinely** (klăn-dĕs'tĭn-lĭ): secretly, usually with an evil intent.

specting him in his privacy and mentally commenting upon him. I eyed the raven, and the raven eyed me. Nothing was said during some seconds. Then the bird stepped a little way along his limb to get a better point of observation, lifted his wings, stuck his head far down below his shoulders toward me, and croaked again — a croak with a distinctly insulting expression about it. If he had spoken in English he could not have said any more plainly than he did say in raven, "Well, what do *you* want here?" I felt as foolish as if I had been caught in some mean act by a responsible being, and reproved for it. However, I made no reply; I would not bandy words with a raven. The adversary waited awhile, with his shoulders still lifted, his head thrust down between them, and his keen bright eye fixed on me; then he threw out two or three more insults, which I could not understand, further than that I knew a portion of them consisted of language not used in church.

I still made no reply. Now the adversary raised his head and called. There was an answering croak from a little distance in the wood — evidently a croak of inquiry. The adversary explained with enthusiasm, and the other raven dropped everything and came. The two sat side by side on the limb and discussed me as freely and offensively as two great naturalists might discuss a new kind of bug. The thing became more and more embarrassing. They called in another friend. This was too much. I saw that they had the advantage of me, and so I concluded to get out of the scrape by walking out of it. They enjoyed my defeat as much as any low people could have done. They craned their necks and laughed at me (for a raven *can* laugh, just like a man), they squalled insulting re-

marks after me as long as they could see me. They were nothing but ravens — I knew that — what they thought about me could be a matter of no consequence — and yet when even a raven shouts after you, "What a hat!" "Oh, pull down your vest!" and that sort of thing, it hurts you and humiliates you, and there is no getting around it with fine reasoning and pretty arguments.

Animals talk to each other, of course. There can be no question about that; but I suppose there are very few people who can understand them. I never knew but one man who could. I knew he could, however, because he told me so himself. He was a middle-aged, simple-hearted miner who had lived in a lonely corner of California, among the woods and mountains, a good many years, and had studied the ways of his only neighbors, the beasts and the birds, until he believed he could accurately translate any remark which they made. This was Jim Baker. According to Jim Baker, some animals have only a limited education and use only very simple words, and scarcely ever a comparison or a flowery figure; whereas, certain other animals have a large vocabulary, a fine command of language and a ready and fluent delivery. Consequently, these latter talk a great deal. They like it; they are conscious of their talent, and they enjoy "showing off." Baker said, that after long and careful observation, he had come to the conclusion that the blue jays were the best talkers he had found among birds and beasts. Said he:

"There's more *to* a blue jay than any other creature. He has got more moods, and more different kinds of feelings than other creatures; and, mind you, whatever a blue jay feels, he can put into language. And no mere commonplace language, either, but rattling, out-

and-out book-talk — and bristling with metaphor, too — just bristling! And as for command of language — why *you* never see a blue jay get stuck for a word. No man ever did. They just boil out of him! And another thing: I've noticed a good deal, and there's no bird, or cow, or anything that uses as good grammar as a blue jay. You may say a cat uses good grammar. Well, a cat does — but you let a cat get excited once; you let a cat get to pulling fur with another cat on a shed, nights, and you'll hear grammar that will give you the lockjaw. Ignorant people think it's the *noise* which fighting cats make that is so aggravating, but it ain't so; it's the sickening grammar they use. Now I've never heard a jay use bad grammar but very seldom; and when they do, they are as ashamed as a human; they shut right down and leave.

"You may call a jay a bird. Well, so he is, in a measure — because he's got feathers on him, and don't belong to no church, perhaps; but otherwise he is just as much a human as you be. And I'll tell you for why. A jay's gifts, and instincts, and feelings and interests, cover the whole ground. A jay hasn't got any more principle than a Congressman. A jay will lie, a jay will steal, a jay will deceive, a jay will betray; and four times out of five, a jay will go back on his solemnest promise. The sacredness of an obligation is a thing which you can't cram into no blue jay's head. Now, on top of all this, there's another thing; a jay can outswear any gentleman in the mines. You think a cat can swear. Well, a cat can; but you give a blue jay a subject that calls for his reverse powers, and where is your cat? Don't talk to *me* — I know too much about this thing. And there's yet another thing: in the one little particular of scolding — just good, clean, out-and-

out scolding — a blue jay can lay over anything, human or divine. Yes, sir, a jay can laugh, a jay can feel shame, a jay can reason and plan and discuss, a jay likes gossip and scandal, a jay has got a sense of humor. If a jay ain't human, he better take in his sign, that's all. Now I'm going to tell you a perfectly true fact about some blue jays.

"When I first begun to understand jay language correctly, there was a little incident happened here. Seven years ago, the last man in this region but me moved away. There stands his house — been empty ever since; a log house, with a plank roof — just one big room, and no more; no ceiling — nothing between the rafters and the floor. Well, one Sunday morning I was sitting out here in front of my cabin, with my cat, taking the sun, and looking at the blue hills, and listening to the leaves rustling so lonely in the trees, and thinking of the home away yonder in the states, that I hadn't heard from in thirteen years, when a blue jay lit on that house, with an acorn in his mouth, and says, 'Hello, I reckon I've struck something.' When he spoke, the acorn dropped out of his mouth and rolled down the roof, of course, but he didn't care; his mind was all on the thing he had struck. It was a knothole in the roof. He cocked his head to one side, shut one eye and put the other one to the hole, like a 'possum looking down a jug; then he glanced up with his bright eyes, gave a wink or two with his wings — which signifies gratification, you understand — and says, 'It looks like a hole, it's located like a hole — blamed if I don't believe it *is* a hole!'

"Then he cocked his head down and took another look; he glances up perfectly joyful, this time; winks his wings and his tail both, and says, 'Oh, no, this ain't no fat thing, I reckon! If I ain't in luck! — why it's a perfectly elegant hole!' So he flew down and got that acorn, and fetched it up and dropped it in, and was just tilting his head back, with the heavenliest smile on his face, when all of a sudden he was paralyzed into a listening attitude and that smile faded gradually out of his countenance like breath off'n a razor, and the queerest look of surprise took its place. Then he says, 'Why, I didn't hear it fall!' He cocked his eye at the hole again, and took a long look; raised up and shook his head; stepped around to the other side of the hole and took another look from that side; shook his head again. He studied awhile, then he just went into the *details* — walked round and round the hole and spied into it from every point of the compass. No use. Now he took a thinking attitude on the comb [1] of the roof and scratched the back of his head with his right foot a minute, and finally says, 'Well, it's too many for *me*, that's certain; must be a mighty long hole; however, I ain't got no time to fool around here, I got to 'tend to business; I reckon it's all right — chance it, anyway.'

"So he flew off and fetched another acorn and dropped it in, and tried to flirt his eye to the hole quick enough to see what become of it, but he was too late. He held his eye there as much as a minute; then he raised up and sighed, and says, 'Confound it, I don't seem to understand this thing, no way; however, I'll tackle her again.' He fetched another acorn, and done his level best to see what become of it, but he couldn't. He says, 'Well, I never struck no such a hole as this before; I'm of the opinion it's a totally new kind of a hole.' Then he begun to get mad. He held in for a spell, walking up and down the comb of the roof and shaking

[1] **comb**: ridge.

his head and muttering to himself; but his feelings got the upper hand of him, presently, and he broke loose and cussed himself black in the face. I never see a bird take on so about a little thing. When he got through he walks to the hole and looks in again for half a minute; then he says, 'Well, you're a long hole, and a deep hole, and a mighty singular hole altogether — but I've started in to fill you, and fill you I will, if it takes a hundred years!'

"And with that, away he went. You never see a bird work so since you was born. He laid into his work, and the way he hove acorns into that hole for about two hours and a half was one of the most exciting and astonishing spectacles I ever struck. He never stopped to take a look any more — he just hove 'em in and went for more. Well, at last he could hardly flop his wings, he was so tuckered out. He comes a-drooping down, once more, sweating like an ice-pitcher, drops his acorn in and says, '*Now* I guess I've got the bulge on you by this time!' So he bent down for a look. If you'll believe me, when his head come up again he was just pale with rage. He says, 'I've shoveled acorns enough in there to keep the family thirty years, and if I can see a sign of one of 'em I wish I may land in a museum with a belly full of sawdust in two minutes!'

"He just had strength enough to crawl up on to the comb and lean his back agin the chimbly, and then he collected his impressions and begun to free his mind. I see in a second that what I had mistook for profanity in the mines was only just the rudiments, as you may say.

"Another jay was going by, and heard him doing his devotions, and stops to inquire what was up. The sufferer told him the whole circumstance, and says,

'Now yonder's the hole, and if you don't believe me, go and look for yourself.' So this fellow went and looked, and comes back and says, 'How many did you say you put in there?' 'Not any less than two tons,' says the sufferer. The other jay went and looked again. He couldn't seem to make it out, so he raised a yell, and three more jays come. They all examined the hole, they all made the sufferer tell it over again, then they all discussed it, and got off as many leatherheaded opinions about it as an average crowd of humans could have done.

"They called in more jays; then more and more, till pretty soon this whole region 'peared to have a blue flush about it. There must have been five thousand of them; and such another jawing and disputing and ripping and cussing, you never heard. Every jay in the whole lot put his eye to the hole and delivered a more chuckle-headed opinion about the mystery than the jay that went there before him. They examined the house all over, too. The door was standing half open, and at last one old jay happened to go and light on it and look in. Of course, that knocked the mystery galley-west in a second. There lay the acorns, scattered all over the floor. He flopped his wings and raised a whoop. 'Come here!' he says, 'Come here, everybody; hang'd if this fool hasn't been trying to fill up a house with acorns!' They all came a-swooping down like a blue cloud, and as each fellow lit on the door and took a glance, the whole absurdity of the contract that that first jay had tackled hit him home and he fell over backwards suffocating with laughter, and the next jay took his place and done the same.

"Well, sir, they roosted around here on the housetop and the trees for an hour, and guffawed over that thing like human beings. It ain't any use to tell me a blue jay hasn't got a sense of humor, because I know better. And memory, too. They brought jays here from all over the United States to look down that hole, every summer for three years. Other birds, too. And they could all see the point, except an owl that come from Nova Scotia to visit the Yosemite, and he took this thing in on his way back. He said he couldn't see anything funny in it. But then he was a good deal disappointed about Yosemite, too."

THINKING IT OVER

1. Twain is particularly noted for his ability to reproduce speech. In "The Blue Jay Yarn" Twain uses dialect that would be natural for a man like Jim Baker. What are the peculiarities of Jim Baker's speech? What are some of the colorful expressions he uses? Cite specific examples. How does the dialect add to the humor of the story?

2. Can you find examples of highly serious language used to make absurd statements sound as if they were the solemn truth?

3. In fables and other literature, animals often behave in human ways. Can you give examples of animals you have seen that have acted strangely human?

4. Do you think the story would be as funny if the characters involved were people instead of birds? Why?

5. An English writer, G. K. Chesterton, has said: "Angels can fly because they can take themselves lightly." Can you apply this to Mark Twain? What evidence do you find that very often the person he laughs hardest at is himself?

THE ANECDOTE

The story about Jim Baker and the blue jays is not a short story in the formal sense of the term. It is an *anecdote:* a short, entertaining account of some happening, often personal or biographical. Unlike a short story, an anecdote has no complicated plot nor well-developed characterization, but it can, as you see, make a point. What point is Mark Twain making in this anecdote?

PART THREE

An Interview with Mark Twain

RUDYARD KIPLING

Rudyard Kipling, who later became one of England's most famous authors, left India in search of a publisher for his stories. On his way to London, he stopped in New York City in August of 1890 He was not yet twenty-five, still an unknown English writer, although his poems *Departmental Ditties* and his stories *Plain Tales from the Hills* had appeared in an Indian newspaper. Kipling did not find a publisher for his stories, but he did get one assignment: to interview Mark Twain for a New York City newspaper. So he journeyed to Elmira, New York, to find the fifty-five-year-old humorist in his summer home. His account of the visit appeared in the New York *Herald* on August 17, 1890.

I HAVE SEEN Mark Twain this golden morning, have shaken his hand, and smoked a cigar — no, two cigars — with him, and talked with him for more than two hours! Understand clearly that I do not despise you; indeed, I don't. I am only very sorry for you all. To soothe your envy and to prove that I still regard you as my equals, I will tell you all about it.

They said in Buffalo that he was in Hartford, Connecticut; and again they said perchance he is gone upon a jour-

ney to Portland, Maine; and a big, fat drummer vowed that he knew the great man intimately, and that Mark was spending the summer in Europe — which information so upset me that I embarked upon the wrong train, and was incontinently [1] turned out by the conductor three-quarters of a mile from the station, amid the wilderness of railway tracks. Have you ever, encumbered with great coat and valise, tried to dodge diversely-minded locomotives when the sun was shining in your eyes? But I forgot that you have not seen Mark Twain, you people of no account!

Saved from the jaws of the cowcatcher, [2] I wandered devious, a stranger met.

"Elmira is the place. Elmira in the state of New York — this state, not two hundred miles away"; and he added, perfectly unnecessarily, "Slide, Kelly, slide."

I slid on the West Shore line, I slid till midnight, and they dumped me down at the door of a frowzy hotel in

[1] **incontinently** (ĭn·kŏn'tĭ·nĕnt·lĭ): unrestrainedly.

[2] **cowcatcher:** a strong, metal frame on the front of a locomotive, for throwing obstructions off the tracks.

Elmira. Yes, they knew all about "that man Clemens," but reckoned he was not in town; had gone East somewhere. I had better possess my soul in patience till the morrow, and then dig up the "man Clemens'" brother-in-law, who was interested in coal.

The idea of chasing half-a-dozen relatives in addition to Mark Twain up and down a city of thirty thousand inhabitants kept me awake. Morning revealed Elmira, whose streets were desolated by railway tracks, and whose suburbs were given up to the manufacture of door sashes and window frames. It was surrounded by pleasant, fat, little hills, trimmed with timber and topped with cultivation. The Chemung River flowed generally up and down the town, and had just finished flooding a few of the main streets.

The hotel man and the telephone man assured me that the much-desired brother-in-law was out of town, and no one seemed to know where "the man Clemens" abode. Later on I discovered that he had not summered in that place for more than nineteen seasons, and so was comparatively a new arrival.

A friendly policeman volunteered the news that he had seen Twain or someone very like him driving a buggy on the previous day. This gave me a delightful sense of nearness to the great author. Fancy living in a town where you could see the author of *Tom Sawyer*, or "some one very like him," jolting over the pavements in a buggy!

"He lives out yonder at East Hill," said the policeman; "three miles from here."

Then the chase began — in a hired hack, up an awful hill, where sunflowers blossomed by the roadside, and crops waved, and *Harper's* Magazine cows stood in eligible and commanding attitudes knee-deep in clover, all ready

to be transferred to photogravure. The great man must have been persecuted by outsiders aforetime, and fled up the hill for refuge.

Presently the driver stopped at a miserable, little, white wood shanty, and demanded "Mister Clemens."

"I know he's a big bug and all that," he explained, "but you can never tell what sort of notions those sort of men take it into their heads to live in, anyways."

There rose up a young lady who was sketching thistle tops and golden rod, amid a plentiful supply of both, and set the pilgrimage on the right path.

"It's a pretty Gothic house on the left-hand side a little way farther on."

"Gothic, heck," said the driver. "Very few of the city hacks take this drive, specially if they know they are coming out here," and he glared at me savagely.

It was a very pretty house, anything but Gothic, clothed with ivy, standing in a very big compound, and fronted by a veranda full of all sorts of chairs and hammocks for lying in all sorts of positions. The roof of the veranda was a trellis-work of creepers, and the sun peeped through and moved on the shining boards below.

Decidedly this remote place was an ideal one for working in, if a man could work among these soft airs and the murmur of the long-eared crops just across the stone wall.

Appeared suddenly a lady used to dealing with rampageous outsiders. "Mr. Clemens has just walked downtown. He is at his brother-in-law's house."

Then he was within shouting distance, after all, and the chase had not been in vain. With speed I fled, and the driver, skidding the wheel and swearing audibly, arrived at the bottom of that hill without accidents. It was in the pause that followed between ringing the brother-in-law's bell and getting an answer that it occurred to me for the first time Mark Twain might possibly have other engagements than the entertainment of escaped lunatics from India, be they ever so full of admiration. And in another man's house — anyhow, what had I come to do or say? Suppose the drawing room should be full of people, a levee of crowned heads; suppose a baby were sick anywhere, how was I to explain I only wanted to shake hands with him?

Then things happened somewhat in this order. A big, darkened drawing room; a huge chair; a man with eyes, a mane of grizzled hair, a brown moustache covering a mouth as delicate as a woman's, a strong, square hand shaking mine, and the slowest, calmest, levelest voice in all the world saying:

"Well, you think you owe me something, and you've come to tell me so. That's what I call squaring a debt handsomely."

"Piff!" from a cob pipe (I always said that a Missouri meerschaum [1] was the best smoking in the world), and, behold! Mark Twain had curled himself up in the big armchair, and I was smoking reverently, as befits one in the presence of his superior.

The thing that struck me first was that he was an elderly man. Yet, after a minute's thought, I perceived that it was otherwise, and in five minutes, the eyes looking at me I saw that the gray hair was an accident of the most trivial kind. He was quite young. I was shaking his hand. I was smoking his cigar, and I was hearing him talk — this man I had learned to love and admire fourteen thousand miles away.

[1] meerschaum (mēr'shŭm): a fine pipe made from a white, claylike material.

Reading his books, I had striven to get an idea of his personality, and all my preconceived notions were wrong and beneath the reality. Blessed is the man who finds no disillusion when he is brought face to face with a revered writer. That was a moment to be remembered; the land of a twelve-pound salmon was nothing to it. I had hooked Mark Twain, and he was treating me as though, under certain circumstances, I might be an equal.

Growing bold, and feeling that I had a few hundred thousand folk at my back, I demanded whether Tom Sawyer married Judge Thatcher's daughter and whether we were ever going to hear of Tom Sawyer as a man.

"I haven't decided," quoth Mark Twain, getting up, filling his pipe, and walking up and down the room in his slippers. "I have a notion of writing the sequel to *Tom Sawyer* in two ways. In one I would make him rise to great honor and go to Congress, and in the other I should hang him. Then the friends and enemies of the book could take their choice."

Here I lost my reverence completely, and protested against any theory of the sort, because, to me at least, Tom Sawyer was real.

"Oh, he is real," said Mark Twain. "He's all the boys that I have known or recollect; but that would be a good way of ending the book"; then, turning around, "because, when you come to think of it, neither religion, training, nor education avails anything against the force of circumstances that drive a man. Suppose we took the next four and twenty years of Tom Sawyer's life, and gave a little joggle to the circumstances that controlled him. He would logically and according to the joggle turn out a rip or an angel."

MARK TWAIN'S MISSISSIPPI

Scenes along the Mississippi as it flows through Missouri, and a statue of Huckleberry Finn and Tom Sawyer in Hannibal.

"Do you believe that, then?"

"I think so. Isn't it what you call kismet?" [1]

"Yes; but don't give him two joggles and show the result, because he isn't your property any more. He belongs to us."

Thereat he laughed — a large, wholesome laugh — and this began a dissertation on the rights of a man to do what he liked with his own creations, which being a matter of purely professional interest, I will mercifully omit.

Returning to the big chair, he, speaking of truth and the like in literature, said that an autobiography was the one work in which a man, against his own will and in spite of his utmost striving to the contrary, revealed himself in his true light to the world.

"A good deal of your *Life on the Mississippi* is autobiographical, isn't it?" I asked.

"As near as it can be — when a man is writing to a book and about himself. But in genuine autobiography, I believe it is impossible for a man to tell the truth about himself or to avoid impressing the reader with the truth about himself.

"I made an experiment once. I got a friend of mine — a man painfully given to speak the truth on all occasions — a man who wouldn't dream of telling a lie — and I made him write his autobiography for his own amusement and mine. He did it. The manuscript would have made an octavo volume [2] but — good, honest man that he was — in every single detail of his life that I

knew about he turned out, on paper, a formidable liar. He could not help himself.

"It is not in human nature to write the truth about itself. None the less, the reader gets a general impression from an autobiography whether the man is a fraud or a good man. The reader can't give his reasons any more than a man can explain why a woman struck him as being lovely when he doesn't remember her hair, eyes, teeth, or figure. And the impression that the reader gets is a correct one."

"Do you ever intend writing an autobiography?"

"If I do, it will be as other men have done — with the most earnest desire to make myself out to be the better man in every little business that has been to my discredit; and I shall fail, like the others, to make the readers believe anything except the truth."

Here he told me a little — such things as a man may tell a stranger — of his early life and upbringing, and in what manner he had been influenced for good by the example of his parents. He spoke always through his eyes, a light under the heavy eyebrows; anon crossing the room with a step as light as a girl's, to show me some book or other; then resuming his walk up and down the room, puffing at the cob pipe. I would have given much for nerve enough to demand the gift of that pipe — value, five cents when new. I understood why certain savage tribes ardently desired the liver of brave men slain in combat. That pipe would have given me, perhaps, a hint of his keen insight into the souls of men. But he never laid it aside within stealing reach of my arms.

He recurled himself into the chair and talked of other things.

"I spend nine months of the year at

[1] **kismet** (kĭz′mĕt): destiny or fate, a term that is Turkish in origin but that Twain may be associating with Kipling's India.

[2] **octavo** (ŏk·tä′vō) **volume**: technically, a book of sheets with each one folded into eight leaves. Here, Twain seems to be suggesting that what his friend had to say would have made a complete book.

Hartford. I have long ago satisfied myself that there is no hope of doing much work during those nine months. People come in and call. They call at all hours, about everything in the world. One day I thought I would keep a list of interruptions. It began this way:

"A man came and would see no one but Mr. Clemens. He was an agent for photogravure reproductions of salon pictures. I very seldom use salon pictures in my books.

"After that man, another man, who refused to see anyone but Mr. Clemens, came to make me write to Washington about something. I saw him. I saw a third man, then a fourth. By this time it was noon. I had grown tired of keeping the list. I wished to rest.

"But the fifth man was the only one of the crowd with a card of his own. He sent up his card. 'Ben Koontz, Hannibal, Missouri.' I was raised in Hannibal. Ben was an old schoolmate of mine. Consequently I threw the house wide open and rushed with both hands out at a big, fat, heavy man, who was not the Ben I had ever known nor anything like him.

" 'But is it you, Ben?' I said. 'You've altered in the last thousand years.'

"The fat man said: 'Well, I'm not Koontz exactly, but I met him down in Missouri, and he told me to be sure and call on you, and he gave me his card, and' — here he acted the little scene for my benefit — 'if you can wait a minute till I can get out the circulars — I'm not Koontz exactly, but I'm traveling with the fullest line of rods you ever saw.' "

"And what happened?" I asked breathlessly.

"I shut the door. He was not Ben Koontz — exactly — not my old schoolfellow, but I had shaken him by both hands in love, and . . . I had been bearded by a lightning-rod man in my own house.

"As I was saying, I do very little work in Hartford. I come here for three months every year, and I work four or five hours a day in a study down the garden of that little house on the hill. Of course, I do not object to two or three interruptions. When a man is in the full swing of his work these little things do not affect him. Eight or ten or twenty interruptions retard composition."

I was burning to ask him all manner of impertinent questions, as to which of his works he himself preferred, and so forth; but, standing in awe of his eyes, I dared not. He spoke on, and I listened, groveling.

It was a question of mental equipment that was on the carpet, and I am still wondering whether he meant what he said.

"Personally I never care for fiction or story books. What I like to read about are facts and statistics of any kind. If they are only facts about the raising of radishes, they interest me. Just now, for instance, before you came in" — he pointed to an encyclopedia on the shelves — "I was reading an article about 'Mathematics.' Perfectly pure mathematics.

"My own knowledge of mathematics stops at 'twelve times twelve,' but I enjoyed that article immensely. I didn't understand a word of it; but facts, or what a man believes to be facts, are always delightful. That mathematical fellow believed in his facts. So do I. Get your facts first, and" — the voice dies away to an almost inaudible drone — "then you can distort 'em as much as you please."

Bearing this precious advice in my bosom, I left, the great man assuring me with gentle kindness that I had not interrupted him in the least. Once outside the door, I yearned to go back and ask some questions — it was easy enough to think of them now — but his time was his own, though his books belonged to me.

I should have ample time to look back to that meeting across the graves of the days. But it was sad to think of the things he had not spoken about.

THINKING IT OVER

1. After the first two "glimpses of Mark Twain," you must have formed an impression of the man himself. Did Kipling's visit with Mark Twain change, or support, that impression? In what ways? Were you surprised by anything Mark Twain said or did in this interview? What?

2. In *The Autobiography of Mark Twain* (edited by Charles Neider), Twain gives his version of this interview with Kipling. We learn that Twain had no idea that his visitor was struggling to be a writer and had already written some poems and stories. Do you think Twain would have treated Kipling differently if he had known about Kipling's ambition? Give reasons for your opinion. What did Twain mean when he said at the beginning of the interview (page 346, column 1), "Well, you think you owe me something . . ."?

3. In this interview, what does Mark Twain say about people who write autobiographies (as he would later do)? What does this opinion lead you to look for in reading autobiographies?

4. Explain what Kipling means when he says at the beginning of the selection, "Understand clearly that I do not despise you; indeed I don't. I am only sorry for you all. To soothe your envy and to prove that I still regard you as my equals, I will tell you all about it." What tone is established in this opening?

5. Kipling says: "Blessed is the man who finds no disillusion when he is brought face to face with a revered writer." What is he talking about? Have you ever been disillusioned when you saw or met someone whom you had admired? Do you think

that Kipling's view of Mark Twain is a realistic one, or is it too colored by his admiration? Give reasons for your answer.

RECOGNIZING STYLE

As a poet, short-story writer, and novelist, Rudyard Kipling is noted for his own distinctive style. You may already be familiar with his fiction style from reading some of his novels, *Captains Courageous* and *Kim*, for example. You might, as a special project, want to get one of Kipling's novels and compare its style with the style he uses in this article.

Glance back briefly at this account by Kipling and notice the author's style of writing. Can you find examples that suggest that the style of this article is similar to Mark Twain's?

After you have considered all the evidence, try to decide (1) whether or not Kipling was copying Mark Twain's style in this article and (2) if he was imitating Twain, whether he was doing so consciously and deliberately, and, if so, why.

COMPOSITION SUGGESTION

Suppose that you are a newspaper reporter and are assigned to interview a famous American man or woman. Choose a person to interview, and, using reference books to find out facts about his life, write an imaginary account of your interview.

ABOUT THE AUTHOR

Since Kipling is best known for his fiction and poetry, you may not have known before you read this selection that he began his writing career as a newspaperman. He was editor of his school paper in England and later became one of two editors of a newspaper in Lahore, India.

Kipling loved newspaper work, and had many fascinating experiences as a reporter. Once, long after he had become a famous writer, he visited Lahore and was found one morning sitting at his old desk in the newspaper office. He was busy correcting proofs.

A brief biography of Rudyard Kipling will be found on page 366. "Danny Deever," one of his poems, is on pages 360–61.

Appreciating Nonfiction

All of us are interested in ideas. We are naturally curious, not just inquisitive for the sake of prying into foolish matters but for the sake of seeing things as they really are. What is the truth about the possibilities of space travel? Is it really true that Vikings were in America long before Columbus? Could the Hawaiians and Tahitians have come from South America instead of Asia? Curiosity about such matters and other people's ideas on them is one of the surest signs of a lively intelligence.

Now some literature deals rather directly with ideas and their related facts, and somewhat loosely we classify all such literature as nonfiction. It includes not only the essay, article, true narrative, and biography, but also letters, speeches, diaries, and numerous other types — all those which generally feature ideas and facts rather than the full-scale imaginative and emotional qualities of poetry, fiction, and drama.

The particular type of nonfiction varies, depending upon the writer's purpose, the readers he wants to reach, and his own personality. If he is writing about timely problems and wants to give an analysis of them, the article usually proves to be the best type to use. If he is making amusing comments on life, the informal essay may be the most suitable type. Sometimes the writer wants to express his insight into human relations but fears to appear too preachy. In such a case, he may write a fable, which fuses the reader's love of a story and his need for moral instruction. To appreciate nonfiction, then, it is not so important to analyze all these types as to appreciate how the style and organization of each individual piece helps develop and display the writer's ideas and purpose.

The following questions are intended to help you review your reading of nonfiction and at the same time to increase your own appreciation and understanding of this kind of literature.

1. Since young people need guidance in how to live, and inasmuch as preaching or dictating are ineffective ways to shape values, someone might write some brilliant *Fables for Today's Youth*. With what would such fables deal? What types of young people could be amusingly disguised yet fully recognized in the world of animals and birds? You might find it interesting to speculate . . . or to create.

2. Biography has been called a form of history made literary by the author's selection and interpretation of events. What historical facts did you find in the biographies in this section? Point out examples of the biographers' selection of details and interpretation of events.

3. Which of the authors in this section seemed to communicate sincerity and great interest in their subjects? Which authors revealed that they are people of broad learning? Whose style did you find easiest to follow? Whose style was most difficult to follow?

4. If you had a free evening to read and were given the choice of more selections by the authors included in the nonfiction section, which author would you choose? Why?

5. Which of the selections studied provided ideas that you found applicable in some way to your own life? Which selections were most exciting? entertaining? Which would offer most reward in rereading? Explain your answers.

6. If your teacher found that next year there would be time to teach only three selections from this nonfiction section, which three would you recommend for retention? Why? Which selection would you nominate for exclusion first? Why?

Suggestions for Further Reading

Adamson, Joy, *Born Free* (Pantheon, 1960); *Living Free* (Harcourt, Brace & World, 1961)

The wife of the senior game warden in Kenya tells the true story of her long friendship with the lioness Elsa, who slept on the bed like any house cat but also ate wild game and went on safaris.

Carson, Rachel, *The Sea Around Us* (Oxford Univ. Press, 1951)

This book recounts the origin, history, and dynamic nature of the seas as the original home of life.

Clarke, Arthur C., *The Challenge of the Spaceship* (Harper, 1959)

Clarke has collected twenty articles published during the last fifteen years in British and American magazines. Many of his fantasies have already become realities and others are still being discussed for the future.

Hersey, John, *Hiroshima* (Knopf, 1946)

A top-notch reporter describes what happened when the first atomic bomb fell on a city.

Herzog, Maurice, *Annapurna* (Dutton, 1953)

The leader of the ascent on Annapurna tells the exciting tale of the conquest of the 26,493 foot peak by the French Himalayan Expedition of 1950.

Heyerdahl, Thor, *Aku-Aku, The Secret of Easter Island* (Rand McNally, 1958)

Eight years after his expedition on the *Kon-Tiki* Thor Heyerdahl returned to the South Pacific to study the giant stone statues of Easter Island.

Shippen, Katherine Binney, *The Bright Design* (Viking, 1949)

The history of magnetism and electricity is told, covering the uses of electrical energy from medieval times to the present, through the stories of the people who aided in the discoveries.

Tenzing Norgay and James Ramsey Ullman, *Tiger of the Snows* (Putnam, 1955)

The story of the conquest of Everest as told to James Ullman by Tenzing, one of the two men who reached the top.

Thurber, James, *Fables for Our Time* (Harper, 1940)

A collection of Thurber fables, illustrated with his drawings. In this book, several famous poems are subjected to interpretation by the humorist-artist. Also, *Further Fables for Our Time* (Simon & Schuster, 1957).

Biographies and Autobiographies

Baker, Rachel, *First Woman Doctor; the Story of Elizabeth Blackwell* (Messner, 1944)

The story of the first woman of modern times to graduate as an M.D.

Becker, May, *Introducing Charles Dickens* (Dodd, Mead, 1940)

A biography written especially for young people to introduce them to the popular English novelist.

Brickhill, Paul, *Reach for the Sky* (Norton, 1954)

The uphill fight of an aviator who lost both legs in a plane crash in 1931 but despite his handicap became a hero in the Battle of Britain in World War II.

Chase, Mary Ellen, *The White Gate* (Norton, 1954)

The quiet, sensitive account of a young girl's growing up in a New England background.

Chute, Marchette, *Ben Jonson of Westminster* (Dutton, 1953)

A biography which brings to life one of England's great literary men and a friend of Shakespeare.

* Curie, Eve, *Madame Curie* (Doubleday, 1937)

The life of the famous woman scientist who, with her husband, discovered radium, as told by her daughter.

Daugherty, James Henry, *Marcus and Narcissa Whitman, Pioneers of Oregon* (Viking, 1953)

Missionaries to the Indians in Oregon, the young Whitmans faced hardships and death to further the work of the Christian missions.

Epstein, Beryl and Samuel, *Great Houdini; Magician Extraordinary* (Messner, 1950)

The story of the magician who could

* This biography is included in *Five World Biographies*, edited by Edel, White, and Brown (Harcourt, Brace & World, 1961).

baffle the world with disappearing elephants, escapes from locked vaults, and other spectacular feats.

Gollomb, Joseph, *Albert Schweitzer: Genius in the Jungle* (Vanguard, 1949)
The inspiring life of one of the truly great men of the twentieth century, who is musician, philosopher, and doctor-missionary in Africa.

Holt, Rackham, *George Washington Carver* (Doubleday, 1943)
Biography of the Negro leader who through education and science helped improve the way of life in the South.

James, Will, *Lone Cowboy* (Scribner, 1930)
Autobiography of a wandering cowboy.

Judson, Clara, *Thomas Jefferson; Champion of the People* (Wilcox & Follett, 1952)
A biography of the great believer in democracy, written especially for high school students.

Keller, Helen, *The Story of My Life* (Doubleday, 1954)
In a moving autobiography, Helen Keller who was blind, deaf, and for a long while dumb, records her life in darkness.

Kimbrough, Emily, *Innocents from Indiana* (Harper, 1950)
The upheaval in the life of a teen-age girl who moves from a small town to Chicago.

Ludwig, Emil, *Napoleon*, abridged for *Five World Biographies*, edited by Edel, White, and Brown (Harcourt, Brace & World, 1961)
A dramatic and entertaining story of the rise and fall of the great French conqueror.

Mehdevi, Anne Sinclair, *Persian Adventure* (Knopf, 1953)
An American girl who married a Persian tells of her experiences when they returned to her husband's homeland.

Plutarch, *Life of Caesar*, Dryden-Clough translation, adapted by Frank Jennings for *Five World Biographies*, edited by Edel, White, and Brown (Harcourt, Brace & World, 1961)
Plutarch, the first great biographer of the Western world, depicts the brilliant but often cruel dictator of ancient Rome.

Rama Rau, Santha, *Home to India* (Har-

per, 1945); *East of Home* (Harper, 1950)
The earlier book tells of the author's rediscovery of India after she returned from several years of education in England. The sequel resumes after further schooling in America and concerns her visits in Japan, China, Indochina, Siam, and Indonesia.

Roos, Ann, *Man of Molokai; the Life of Father Damien* (Lippincott, 1943)
Story of the man who brought a new way of life to the leper colony on the island of Molokai.

Sandburg, Carl, *Prairie-Town Boy* (Harcourt, Brace & World, 1954)
Autobiography of the growing years of one of America's greatest poets.

Sheean, Vincent, *Mahatma Gandhi: A Great Life in Brief*, abridged for *Five World Biographies*, edited by Edel, White, and Brown (Harcourt, Brace & World, 1961)
The story of the modern saint of India, who accomplished "miracles" with his spiritually rooted words and actions.

Sperry, Armstrong, *John Paul Jones, Fighting Sailor* (Random House, 1953)
The story of the Scottish-born boy who became the hero of the colonies' navy during the American Revolution.

* Vasari, Giorgio, "Michelangelo Buonarroti" from *Vasari's Lives of the Artists*, edited by Betty Burroughs (Simon & Schuster, 1946)
An intimate picture of the man who created many of the world's most magnificent works of art.

Wong, Jade Snow, *Fifth Chinese Daughter* (Harper, 1950)
A Chinese-American girl's autobiography of her adjustment in two worlds and her struggle for independence.

Wood, Laura, *Raymond L. Ditmars* (Messner, 1944)
Account of how a boy's interest in animals turned into a profession.

* This biography is included in *Five World Biographies*, edited by Edel, White, and Brown (Harcourt, Brace & World, 1961).

For Listening

"Irtnog" by E. B. White has been recorded and is available on *Many Voices*, 4B.

Poetry

Why do people write, read, and study poetry? In fact, why does it exist at all? You might think about these questions before you begin this section. First, read the following statements:

1. *I don't like living in the city, and I want to leave it.*
2. *A wind's in the heart of me, a fire's in my heels,*
   I'm tired of brick and stone and rumbling wagon-wheels.

Now, see if you agree or disagree with the following conclusions:

Each of these statements says approximately the same thing.
It is easy to see that the first is prose and the other poetry.
It is easy to *recognize*, but not to define, poetry.

ABOUT THE PROSE STATEMENT

It can be understood very quickly and easily.
It simply conveys information.
It is dull — unless you happen to care about the writer.

ABOUT THE POETIC STATEMENT

The meaning of this statement is not so easy to grasp as the meaning of the prose statement.
The words themselves are just as easy to understand as those in the prose statement, but they are used in unusual ways.
To understand the meaning you have to guess that *brick* and *stone* and *rumbling wagon-wheels* add up to the word *city*.
Also, you have to doubt that the writer really has *wind* in his *heart* and *fire* in his *heels*. You decide that he simply feels as if these conditions are true.
You find that you care about the writer's feelings.
The writer has used *his* imagination to capture *your* imagination.

If you agree with these conclusions, you understand some important things about poetry — perhaps that poetry requires study and that your study of poetry can be very rewarding. The next step is to read the two poems that follow.

◀ Detail from "Still Life: Apples and Primroses" by the French artist Paul Cézanne (1839–1906). A genius in his ability to capture the essence of his subjects, Cézanne is considered the "father of modern painting."

Jabberwocky

LEWIS CARROLL

Sound is very important in poetry. Many of the words in this poem, a famous one from *Alice's Adventures in Wonderland*, cannot be found in a dictionary. You may decide, though, that the sense of the words does not really matter — that the sound alone is what you have enjoyed and will remember.

'Twas brillig, and the slithy toves
    Did gyre and gimble in the wabe:
All mimsy were the borogoves,
    And the mome raths outgrabe.

"Beware the Jabberwock, my son! 5
    The jaws that bite, the claws that catch!
Beware the Jubjub bird, and shun
    The frumious Bandersnatch!"

He took his vorpal sword in hand;
    Long time the manxome foe he sought — 10
So rested he by the Tumtum tree,
    And stood awhile in thought.

And, as in uffish thought he stood,
    The Jabberwock, with eyes of flame,
Came whiffling through the tulgey wood, 15
    And burbled as it came!

One, two! One, two! And through and through
    The vorpal blade went snicker-snack!
He left it dead, and with its head
    He went galumphing back. 20

"And hast thou slain the Jabberwock?
    Come to my arms, my beamish boy!
O frabjous day! Callooh, Callay!"
    He chortled in his joy.

'Twas brillig, and the slithy toves 25
    Did gyre and gimble in the wabe:
All mimsy were the borogoves,
    And the mome raths outgrabe.

Ars Poetica

ARCHIBALD MacLEISH

The title of this poem is a Latin phrase meaning "the art of poetry."
The poet assumes a definite attitude toward poetry. He considers a
poem a work of art which obeys its own artistic laws. Keep this idea
in mind as you read the other poems in this section. It is an important
point to remember.

A poem should be palpable° and mute
As a globed fruit

Dumb
As old medallions° to the thumb

Silent as the sleeve-worn stone   5
Of casement ledges where the moss has grown —

A poem should be wordless
As the flight of birds

A poem should be motionless in time
As the moon climbs   10

Leaving, as the moon releases
Twig by twig the night-entangled trees,

Leaving, as the moon behind the winter leaves,
Memory by memory the mind —

A poem should be motionless in time   15
As the moon climbs

A poem should be equal to:
Not true

For all the history of grief
An empty doorway and a maple leaf   20

For love
The leaning grasses and two lights above the sea —

A poem should not mean
But be

1. **palpable** (pal'pá·b'l): capable of being touched or felt; tangible. 4. **medallions** (mė·dal'-
yŭnz): large medals.

"Ars Poetica" from *Collected Poems of Archibald MacLeish, 1917–1952*, published by Houghton Mifflin Company
and used with their permission.

THE EXPERIENCE OF POETRY

1. To be appreciated in the fullest sense, poetry should be read aloud. Read "Jabberwocky" aloud as if it were a normal poem with a very clear meaning. What does this experience tell you about the importance of sound in poetry?

2. What is the tone of "Jabberwocky"? Is it serious? light-hearted? How can you tell? Would Archibald MacLeish admire "Jabberwocky"? Why or why not?

3. What do you think the last two lines in "Ars Poetica" mean? Which stanzas in the poem help to make these lines clear? What pictures does MacLeish present in "Ars Poetica" to help us understand his explanation of poetry? What other forms of art "should not mean but be"?

4. If you took these two poems apart word for word and line by line you could probably reproduce in prose a fairly accurate statement of what is being said. Yet both poets would object to this procedure, especially MacLeish. Why?

GAINING POWER OVER WORDS

CLUES TO MEANING Very often, though you may not look up a word in a dictionary, you have a feeling for the meaning of that word, a feeling that is created by the form of the word and by its position in a sentence. Lewis Carroll depends on that feeling in "Jabberwocky." We are told, for example, that "toves" are "slithy" and that the "Bandersnatch" is "frumious." We learn these "facts" because Carroll has paid close attention to the forms of English words and to their customary order in sentences.

Since most plural nouns in English end in *-s* or *-es*, like *leaves* or *dogs*, we feel fairly certain that *toves* is a plural noun. *Slithy* and *frumious* have endings that are like those of real English adjectives (*slimy* and *furious*, for example) so they can be called adjectives. Thus, even in a nonsense word, an *-s* or a *-y* or an *-ous* ending can tell us something about the meaning.

These letter-clues are important, but we can get our best clue to function and meaning from the position of a word in a sentence, its place in a large pattern. For example, the position of *toves* — after *the*, which always signals a noun, and before the verb *did* — makes us certain that it is

a noun. We can also be sure that *slithy* is an adjective by noticing that it occurs in the usual adjective position, between *the* and a noun. In the same way we can learn something about a word like *galumphing*. Since it follows *went*, it probably indicates a certain way to travel.

If we replaced all the nonsense words with real words, we would have to fit the real ones into the same positions in the sentences. Try this kind of substitution, and as you do, try to discover what kind of word best fits into each position, whether noun, verb, adverb, or adjective. Notice that Lewis Carroll does not tamper with certain kinds of words such as *by, in, and, as,* and *the*. Why do you think he has left these unchanged?

About the Poets

Lewis Carroll (1832–1898) is the pen name of Charles Dodgson. Born in Daresbury, England, Carroll was a brilliant student, winning prizes in both mathematics and the classics. He became a deacon of Christ Church College, Oxford, and settled there in a comfortable bachelor's apartment for the rest of his life. He produced mathematical treatises, took endless pictures of his friends and guests in his photographic studio, and wrote *Alice's Adventures in Wonderland* and *Through the Looking-Glass* for a daughter of the college dean. In his apartment Carroll kept an assortment of unusual playthings to entertain child-guests, whom he always welcomed with special delight. After his death, a bed in Children's Hospital in London was endowed in his memory.

Archibald MacLeish (1892–) is an American poet who has often surprised the literary world with new techniques in his poetry. His early poems were highly personal, but his later writing shows an increasing concern with social and political problems. His play in verse, "The Fall of the City," broadcast in 1937, has become a classic among original works for radio. In *J.B.*, a verse drama produced on Broadway in 1958, MacLeish depicted a modern parallel to the situation of the Biblical character, Job.

Types of Poetry

Every poem exists by itself and for itself, a highly individual expression both in content and in form. There are, however, certain types of poetry, broad classifications that you will find useful to know.

There are three major types of poetry. If the chief purpose of a poem is to tell a story, we say that it is a *narrative*. If a poet is primarily concerned with expressing his personal thoughts and feelings, he writes *lyric* poetry. When the poet presents characters speaking and moving before us, we call the result a *dramatic* poem. These three categories sometimes overlap, and within them there are a great many varieties. The poet has a wide choice, and he will write the kind of poem that is best suited to what he wishes to express.

Let's take another step toward appreciation and read some examples of the three major types of poetry mentioned above. In conclusion we will look at a special type of poetry known as *light verse*.

Narrative Poetry

Our literary ancestors found that rhythm, rhyme, and repetition helped them remember stories and tales that they wanted to repeat for enjoyment and information. Something else helped too. They used the words of common speech in new and imaginative ways. For example, they used what we now call figures of speech (metaphor, simile, personification) to create images with words.

For the most part, the earliest narratives were not written down by a specific person. They were passed from generation to generation by word of mouth, with each new generation adding something of its own to the tales. The stories were carried from town to town by wandering minstrels who sang or chanted the poems, accompanying their words with a musical instrument.

When poetry left the word-of-mouth stage and became word-on-paper, it did not lose its earlier form. The accompaniment by an instrument was no longer essential, but the rhythm and picturesque language were still present, and so, very often, was the rhyme.

The Epic Poem

The most ambitious kind of narrative poetry — the *epic poem* — relates the deeds of a great heroic character. The epic uses a strong rhythmic pattern and picturesque language to celebrate the hero's performances through a number of stirring adventures. By its nature and purpose, the epic is quite long. No epic is reproduced in full for you here, but you are probably already familiar with the most famous example of the epic, the *Odyssey* by the Greek poet Homer.

Other nations have their famous epics too, and when you have time you will probably wish to read some of them. Virgil, a Latin poet, wrote the *Aeneid* to celebrate the wanderings of Aeneas and his founding of Rome. The French sing of one of their great national heroes in the *Song of Roland. The Cid,* the tale of the Spanish hero Don Rodrigo, has become the national epic of Spain. The English language boasts a number of great epics, among them *Beowulf* and *Paradise Lost.* Probably the most popular English epic poem is Tennyson's *Idylls of the King,* which tells of King Arthur and his renowned knights. You will read a part of this epic on pages 611 through 619 of this book.

The Ballad

A shorter kind of narrative poetry is the *ballad.* It is one of the most popular ways of telling a story. The ballad was originally sung, and in written form it retains some of its older character through the use of a refrain. A refrain is a group of words that is repeated at regular intervals as the story progresses. Very likely, the entire audience joined in at these points in the tale. The rhythm of the ballad is strong and regular, perfectly suited for singing. The three poems that follow are all slightly different, but they share the characteristics of all ballads: rhythm, picturesque language, and an exciting story.

Danny Deever

RUDYARD KIPLING

In this ballad two soldiers talk about a hanging, and the marching rhythm of the poem gives their words an ominous quality. One of the soldiers is Files-on-Parade, whose duty is to look after various details of military formation. The second soldier, the Color Sergeant, carries the flag. Through their conversation you learn what happened to their fellow soldier, Danny Deever.

"What are the bugles blowin' for?" said Files-on-Parade.
"To turn you out, to turn you out," the Color Sergeant said.
"What makes you look so white, so white?" said Files-on-Parade.
"I'm dreadin' what I've got to watch," the Color Sergeant said.
    For they're hangin' Danny Deever, you can 'ear the dead march play,   5
    The regiment's in 'ollow square — they're hangin' him today;
    They've taken of his buttons off an' cut his stripes away,
    An' they're hangin' Danny Deever in the mornin'.

"Danny Deever" from *Departmental Ditties and Ballads and Barrack-Room Ballads* by Rudyard Kipling, reprinted by permission of Mrs. George Bambridge and Doubleday & Company, Inc.

"What makes the rear-rank breathe so 'ard?" said Files-on-Parade.
"It's bitter cold, it's bitter cold," the Color Sergeant said.   10
"What makes that front-rank man fall down?" says Files-on-Parade.
"A touch o' sun, a touch o' sun," the Color Sergeant said.
   They are hangin' Danny Deever, they are marchin' of 'im round,
   They 'ave 'alted Danny Deever by 'is coffin on the ground;
   An' 'e'll swing in 'arf a minute for a sneakin', shootin' hound —   15
   O they're hangin' Danny Deever in the mornin'!

" 'Is cot was right-'and cot to mine," said Files-on-Parade.
" 'E's sleepin' out an' far tonight," the Color Sergeant said.
"I've drunk 'is beer a score o' times," said Files-on-Parade.
"'E's drinkin' bitter beer alone," the Color Sergeant said.   20
   They are hangin' Danny Deever, you must mark 'im to 'is place,
   For 'e shot a comrade sleepin' — you must look 'im in the face;
   Nine 'undred of 'is county° an' the regiment's disgrace,
   While they're hangin' Danny Deever in the mornin'.

"What's that so black agin the sun?" said Files-on-Parade.   25
"It's Danny fightin' 'ard for life," the Color Sergeant said.
"What's that that whimpers over'ead?" said Files-on-Parade.
"It's Danny's soul that's passin' now," the Color Sergeant said.
   For they're done with Danny Deever, you can 'ear the quickstep play,
   The regiment's in column, an' they're marchin' us away;   30
   Ho! the young recruits are shakin', an' they'll want their beer today,
   After hangin' Danny Deever in the mornin'.

        23. **county:** that is, soldiers from Danny's county.

copy this poem here next.

The Erl-King

JOHANN WOLFGANG VON GOETHE

Though this ballad was written by a famous nineteenth-century German
poet, it captures the flavor of early folk ballads with its air of mystery and
superstition. It is about a German folklore spirit, the Erl-King, who does
mischief and evil, especially to children. Can you imagine a group of people sitting around a fire on a dark and haunted night telling such a tale as
this? The translation is by Sir Walter Scott, Scottish poet and novelist.

    O who rides by night thro' the woodland so wild?
    It is the fond father embracing his child;
    And close the boy nestles within his loved arm.
    To hold himself fast, and to keep himself warm.

"O father, see yonder! see yonder!" he says;   5
"My boy, upon what dost thou fearfully gaze?"
"O, 'tis the Erl-King with his crown and his shroud."
"No, my son, it is but a dark wreath of the cloud."

(The Erl-King speaks)
"O come and go with me, thou loveliest child;
By many a gay sport shall thy time be beguiled;   10
My mother keeps for thee full many a fair toy,
And many a fine flower shall she pluck for my boy."

"O father, my father, and did you not hear
The Erl-King whisper so low in my ear?"
"Be still, my heart's darling — my child, be at ease;   15
It was but the wild blast as it sung thro' the trees."

(Erl-King)
"O wilt thou go with me, thou loveliest boy?
My daughter shall tend thee with care and with joy;
She shall bear thee so lightly thro' wet and thro' wild,
And press thee, and kiss thee, and sing to my child."   20

"O father, my father, and saw you not plain
The Erl-King's pale daughter glide past thro' the rain?"
"O yes, my loved treasure, I knew it full soon;
It was the gray willow that danced to the moon."

(Erl-King)
"O come and go with me, no longer delay,   25
Or else, silly child, I will drag thee away."
"O father! O father! now, now, keep your hold,
The Erl-King has seized me — his grasp is so cold!"

Sore trembled the father; he spurr'd thro' the wild,
Clasping close to his bosom his shuddering child;   30
He reaches his dwelling in doubt and in dread,
But, clasp'd to his bosom, the infant was dead.

La Belle Dame sans Merci

JOHN KEATS

This poem uses an incident that is popular with writers of romantic ballads: a heartless enchantress weaves a spell around a knight and then
deserts him, letting him suffer alone. The title means "the beautiful lady
without mercy"

"O what can ail thee knight-at-arms,
   Alone and palely loitering?
The sedge° has withered from the lake,
   And no birds sing.

"O what can ail thee, knight-at-arms!
   So haggard and so woebegone?   6
The squirrel's granary is full,
   And the harvest's done.

"I see a lily on thy brow
   With anguish moist and fever-dew,
And on thy cheeks a fading rose   11
   Fast withereth, too."

"I met a lady in the meads,
   Full beautiful — a faëry's child;
Her hair was long, her foot was light,
   And her eyes were wild.   16

"I made a garland for her head,
   And bracelets, too, and fragrant
     zone;°
She looked at me as she did love,
   And made sweet moan.   20

"I set her on my pacing steed
   And nothing else saw all day long
For sidelong would she bend, and sing
   A faëry's song.

"She found me roots of relish sweet,
   And honey wild and manna-dew,   26
And sure in language strange she said,
   'I love thee true.'

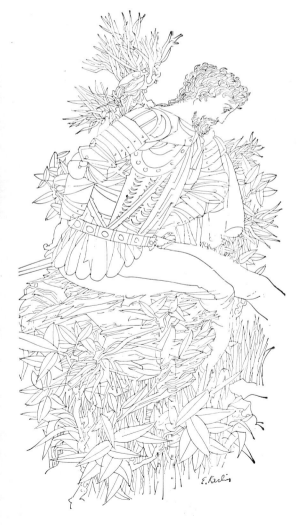

3. **sedge** (sĕj): a coarse, grasslike plant.
18. **zone:** a belt.

"She took me to her elfin grot,°
    And there she wept and sighed full
        sore;   30
And there I shut her wild, wild eyes
    With kisses four.

"And there she lulléd me asleep,
    And there I dreamed — Ah! woe be-
        tide!
The latest dream I ever dreamed   35
    On the cold hill's side.

"I saw pale kings and princes, too,
    Pale warriors, death-pale were they
        all;
They cried — 'La belle dame sans
        merci
    Hath thee in thrall!'°   40

"I saw their starved lips in the gloom°
    With horrid warning gapéd wide,
And I awoke and found me here
    On the cold hill's side.

"And this is why I sojourn here,   45
    Alone and palely loitering,
Though the sedge is withered from the
        lake,
    And no birds sing."

29. **grot** (grŏt): a small cave. 40. **thrall**
(thrôl): bondage. 41. **gloam** (glōm): twilight.

APPRECIATING NARRATIVE POETRY

1. "Danny Deever" is told partly
through the use of dialogue; that is, two
people are speaking to each other about
the incident. Why do you think Kipling
chose these two persons? What is their
relation to the story? How do these two
characters feel about the hanging? Why is
Danny being hanged? Why do the two
men discuss the weather?

2. In "The Erl-King," the boy is aware
of the presence of the spirit, but his father
is not. Why do you think this is so? How
does the father react to the child's fears?
When does the father begin to be upset by
the boy's talk? What does the Erl-King
promise the boy? Why do you have the
feeling that these promises are fearful
things?

3. "La Belle Dame sans Merci," like
"The Erl-King," hints at the mysterious
and supernatural. How much does Keats's
poem really depend on the supernatural
element? How did the woman entice the
knight? What do you know of the duties
of knighthood that would require him to
help the lady? Is it likely that any man
could find himself in such a situation as
this? Could you tell a similar story about
a man of the twentieth century? What
parts of Keats's poem would you have to
change? What parts could you keep?

RHYME

Poetry is a special way of saying things.
It appeals not only to the mind but to the
ear as well. One way in which it appeals
to the ear is through rhythm; another way
is through the repetition of sounds.

If two words are matched in sound we
say they *rhyme*. In poetry, rhyming words
generally occur at the ends of lines. For
example:

O who rides by night thro' the wood-
    land so wild?
It is the fond father embracing his child.

Wild and *child* have partly the same
sound, so we say that these two lines
rhyme. There are definite schemes that a
poet may use in his rhyming, and there is
a definite way we have of marking those
schemes. We call the first line of a stanza
of poetry an *a* line, and every line that
rhymes with it is also called an *a* line. The
first line that does not rhyme with *a* is
called a *b* line, and every line that rhymes
with it is labeled *b*. "Jabberwocky" (page
356) would be marked in this way:

'Twas brillig, and the slithy toves   *a*
    Did gyre and gimble in the wabe: *b*
All mimsy were the borogoves,   *a*
    And the mome raths outgrabe.   *b*

No matter how complex the poem, we
can continue in this fashion, using as
many letters as are required to describe
the rhyme scheme completely. To see how
this works out, finish labeling the lines in
"Jabberwocky."

You can begin to see that a good poem is not a matter of chance, but rather a matter of careful work. A good poet uses both rhythm and rhyme to emphasize the important words in his lines. When we read a poem, though we may be unconscious of the fact, the poet is using our minds, our eyes, and our voices to produce the effect he wants.

GAINING POWER OVER WORDS

FIGURES OF SPEECH In our everyday use of words, we find figures of speech necessary in order to communicate our ideas sharply and vividly. For example, we say that someone has an "iron will" or that someone is "strong as an ox." Even in expressions like "fountain pen" or "sheepish grin," we show our awareness of the resemblance between things. Such comparisons are called *similes* and *metaphors*. In a simile the words *like* or *as* are used to make the comparison. For example:

A poem should be palpable and mute
As a globed fruit
("Ars Poetica," p. 357)

A metaphor avoids the use of *like* or *as,* and makes a direct statement:

I see a lily on thy brow
[meaning that the knight is very pale]
("La Belle Dame sans Merci,"
p. 364)

Look for examples of similes and metaphors in the other poems you read. Can you think of some similes and metaphors that you use in your own speech to clarify ideas for your listeners?

About the Poets

Rudyard Kipling (1865–1936) was born in Bombay, India. On graduating from school in England, he went back to India where he became an editor of the *Civil and Military Gazette.* His name became famous there for his writing, later published as *Departmental Ditties and Other Verses* and *Plain Tales from the Hills.* In 1890 he returned to England, and two years later he married an American girl, with

whom he moved to Brattleboro, Vermont. There they lived until 1897 when, after a trip to Africa, they settled down in England. Kipling's travels were colorful and unusual sources for his many short stories, poems, and novels. Among his books are *Barrack-Room Ballads, Kim, The Light That Failed, The Jungle Book,* and *Captains Courageous.* Kipling achieved international fame and many high honors for the excellence of his writing. Numbered among his awards were the Nobel prize and honorary degrees from eight universities.

Johann Wolfgang von Goethe (1749–1832) was a famous German poet, dramatist, and novelist whose wide interests also extended into science, law, and philosophy. Goethe spent a happy childhood in Frankfort and later studied and practiced law before beginning his writing career. A drama published in 1773 brought him his first recognition, and he became famous the next year with a novel, *The Sorrows of Young Werther.* Goethe was invited to the court of Charles Augustus, Duke of Saxe-Weimar, in 1775. He remained there for the rest of his life, at one time serving as the Duke's chief minister. His travels in Italy, and his friendship with Schiller, another German writer and philosopher, did much to influence his writings. His finest work, the one on which his fame rests, is his long poetic drama, *Faust.*

John Keats (1795–1821), one of the English Romantic poets, was educated to be a surgeon, but gave up his studies to concentrate on poetry. Though a few fellow poets recognized the value of his work, much of his poetry was severely attacked by the critics of his day. Keats was particularly discouraged by the criticism of his now greatly admired poem *Endymion,* which was published in 1818. He considered abandoning poetry, but changed his mind and published a volume of poems in 1820. Keats had shown symptoms of tuberculosis since 1817, and he journeyed to Italy in 1821 in the hope of improving his health. He died in Rome shortly after he arrived. Despite a comparatively small output of poetry, Keats is now recognized as one of the greatest of English poets.

Lyric Poetry

When a poet writes chiefly to express his own thoughts and feelings, he is writing what is called *lyric poetry*. Like much of narrative poetry, lyric poems were originally accompanied by a musical instrument, usually the lyre, a small harp. The term "lyric" grew from this source.

In lyric poetry, as in narrative poetry and in music, certain emotions and ideas are best expressed by certain rhythm and rhyme patterns. There are many varieties of lyric poetry. The poems that follow will introduce you to four that occur frequently.

The Song

Sometimes a poet, like all of us, simply wants to sing. His song may be one of joy or love. It may be religious or patriotic. Or, as in the case of the song that follows, it may be a lullaby.

Sweet and Low

ALFRED, LORD TENNYSON

Sweet and low, sweet and low,
  Wind of the western sea,
Low, low, breathe and blow,
  Wind of the western sea!
  Over the rolling waters go,   5
  Come from the dying moon, and blow,
  Blow him again to me;
While my little one, while my pretty one sleeps.

Sleep and rest, sleep and rest,
  Father will come to thee soon;   10
Rest, rest, on mother's breast,
  Father will come to thee soon;
  Father will come to his babe in the nest,
  Silver sails all out of the west
  Under the silver moon;   15
Sleep, my little one, sleep, my pretty one, sleep.

The Sonnet

Of all the kinds of lyric poems, the sonnet is probably the most difficult to write. It is generally restricted to fourteen lines, with a definite rhythm and rhyme pattern.

Sonnet on Chillon

GEORGE GORDON, LORD BYRON

The famous British poet, Lord Byron, was throughout his life committed to the idea of freedom. In this sonnet he celebrates the spirit of liberation. The incident on which the poem is based occurred in the sixteenth century. François de Bonnivard sought to liberate the city of Geneva, Switzerland, from the Duke of Savoy, but was captured and imprisoned for six years in the castle of Chillon on the banks of Lake Geneva.

> Eternal Spirit of the chainless Mind!
> Brightest in dungeons, Liberty! thou art,
> For there thy habitation is the heart —
> The heart which love of thee alone can bind;
> And when thy sons to fetters° are consigned —   5
> To fetters, and the damp vault's dayless gloom,
> Their country conquers with their martyrdom,
> And Freedom's fame finds wings on every wind.
> Chillon! thy prison is a holy place,
> And thy sad floor an altar — for 'twas trod,   10
> Until his very steps have left a trace
> Worn, as if thy cold pavement were a sod,
> By Bonnivard! May none those marks efface!
> For they appeal from tyranny to God.

5. **fetters** (fĕt'ẽrz): shackles or chains for the feet.

The Ode

An ode is a lyric poem which generally is characterized by dignified style and lofty thought and emotion. Many odes are very long and complex in structure—the length and the complexity enabling the poet to develop fully his thoughts on a serious subject. They are often addressed in a grand, formal manner to some person or thing. Other odes state their thought directly, are relatively short, and have a simpler structure. The following poem is an example of this simpler, more direct ode. Written by the master eighteenth-century poet, Alexander Pope, it is based on an ode by the Roman poet Horace. In turning back to the classics, Pope was following a common practice of his time. As you read this poem, notice the attitude that Pope assumes toward solitude.

Ode on Solitude

ALEXANDER POPE

Happy the man whose wish and care
  A few paternal acres bound,
Content to breathe his native air
    In his own ground.

Whose herds with milk, whose fields with bread,   5
  Whose flocks supply him with attire,
Whose trees in summer yield him shade,
    In winter fire.

Bless'd who can unconcern'dly find
  Hours, days, and years slide soft away,   10
In health of body, peace of mind,
    Quiet by day,

Sound sleep by night; study and ease
  Together mix'd; sweet recreation;
And innocence, which most does please   15
    With meditation.

Thus let me live, unseen, unknown,
  Thus unlamented let me die;
Steal from the world, and not a stone
    Tell where I lie.   20

The Elegy

The elegy is another variety of lyric poetry. Elegies vary greatly in form, but they usually have a common theme, the theme of death or mourning. The following poem by Edna St. Vincent Millay was written in memory of a college friend who had died. In it, the poet expresses her sadness and also her thoughts on death.

Elegy

EDNA ST. VINCENT MILLAY

Let them bury your big eyes
In the secret earth securely,
Your thin fingers, and your fair,
Soft, indefinite-colored hair —
All of these in some way, surely,   5
From the secret earth shall rise.
Not for these I sit and stare,
Broken and bereft° completely;
Your young flesh that sat so neatly
On your little bones will sweetly   10
Blossom in the air.

But your voice — never the rushing
Of a river underground,
Not the rising of the wind
In the trees before the rain,   15
Not the woodcock's watery call,
Not the note the white-throat utters,
Not the feet of children pushing
Yellow leaves along the gutters
In the blue and bitter fall,   20
Shall content my musing mind
For the beauty of that sound
That in no new way at all
Ever will be heard again.

Sweetly through the sappy stalk   25
Of the vigorous weed,
Holding all it held before,

8. **bereft** (bê·rĕft′): left sad and lonely by the loss of someone dear.

"Elegy" from "Memorial to D. C." in *Collected Poems* by Edna St. Vincent Millay, Harper & Brothers. Copyright 1921–1948 by Edna St. Vincent Millay. Reprinted by permission of Norma Millay Ellis.

Cherished by the faithful sun,
On and on eternally
Shall your altered fluid run,   30
Bud and bloom and go to seed;
But your singing days are done;
But the music of your talk
Never shall the chemistry
Of the secret earth restore.   35
All your lovely words are spoken.
Once the ivory box is broken,
Beats the golden bird no more.

APPRECIATING LYRIC POETRY

1. "Sweet and Low" is a lullaby. What is a lullaby? How do you learn that a woman is singing this song? As she quiets her child you find out something about her too. Why is she lonely?

2. A sonnet has a regular rhyme scheme. What is the rhyme scheme of "Sonnet on Chillon"? How does Byron feel about the prisoner of Chillon? How does he feel about the reason for Bonnivard's imprisonment? Does he think it will do any good? Why? Why not?

3. In his ode, Pope asks for solitude. Where does he think it can best be found? Does he feel it would be possible to achieve solitude in a crowded city? What does the poet mean when he asks to be unlamented?

4. What do you discover of the poet's attitude toward death in "Elegy"? Do you think that the poet is sad only because of the loss of her friend? What does she regret most about her friend's death?

MOOD AND MUSIC

How do the rhythm and rhyme of each of these poems help the poet to express his mood and meaning? "Sweet and Low" has been set to music. If you do not already know its tune perhaps you can find it for the class. Could this song be sung to a tune with a gay, rapid rhythm? Why, or why not? It might be interesting for you to do a program of poetry readings with musical backgrounds. What kinds of music would you choose for each of the poems in this section?

GAINING POWER OVER WORDS

FIGURES OF SPEECH In the poem "Sonnet on Chillon," Byron addresses an abstract idea, Liberty, as if it were present and capable of hearing him. This figure of speech, that of addressing an abstract idea or inanimate object directly, is known as *apostrophe*. Byron uses another important poetic device in the poem, *personification*. This figure of speech occurs when a poet gives the attributes of human beings to things that are not themselves human. Thus Byron speaks of *Liberty* having *sons*. Look for other examples of apostrophe and personification in the things you read, the things you say, and the things you hear. These and the other figures of speech are all methods by which men communicate with each other.

The ancient Greeks said that Apollo drove his fiery chariot up out of the ocean, across the sky, then down again, at the end of day, into the water. We still say "the sun rises and the sun sets," though we know that this is not the scientific explanation of what happens. Why do you think we say it?

About the Poets

George Gordon, Lord Byron (1788–1824), had a difficult childhood in Aberdeen, Scotland. The child of a cruel-tempered mother and a wastrel father, he was further handicapped with a crippled foot. From a grand-uncle he inherited a title and an estate which made possible his education at Harrow and Cambridge, and gave him, at twenty-one, a seat in the House of Lords. He traveled widely in Europe, keeping detailed notes, which were later used in *Childe Harold's Pilgrimage,* a long narrative poem which made him famous overnight. Handsome and proud, his brilliance and charm won friends, and his undisciplined ways lost them. Socially exiled from England, he moved restlessly about southern Europe for several years. In 1824 he joined the Greek fight for independence against Turkey and died of a fever while in service.

Alexander Pope (1688–1744) was the son of a clothmaker. He decided early in life to make literature his career and began an intensive study of poetry and literary criticism. Pope published his first poems before he was twenty, and he gained general recognition at twenty-three when his *Essay on Criticism,* a long poem on the techniques of literature, was published. In addition to his poetry and criticism, Pope made successful translations of the *Iliad* and the *Odyssey* by Homer. In his later years he edited the plays of Shakespeare. Pope was famous for his biting wit and many of his critics found themselves the victims of his sharp pen.

Many a poor versifier of Pope's day is remembered now solely because Pope chose to make fun of him and his poetry.

Edna St. Vincent Millay (1892–1950) was born in Rockland, Maine. She began writing poetry early, and first gained recognition while still a student at Vassar College, with her poem "Renascence." Her first volume of poetry was published the year of her graduation. She spent the next few years in New York, writing plays and acting with a little theater group in Greenwich Village. In 1923 her volume of poetry, *The Harp-Weaver,* won the Pulitzer prize. The same year she married a successful importer who decided to give up his business in order to travel with his wife and encourage her writing career. In later years, the two spent more and more time on their isolated farm in New York State. During her lifetime, Millay was recognized as probably the most important woman poet of her time. Her poems, whether haunting lyrics or attacks on social injustice, clearly indicate the extent of her perception and feeling.

Alfred, Lord Tennyson's biography appears on pages 620–21, following the selection from his *Idylls of the King.*

Dramatic Poetry

When a playwright presents characters speaking and moving on a stage, and uses a regular rhythm and figurative language in the speeches of the characters, we say that what he writes is *dramatic poetry.* This type of poetry is often written in blank verse — verse that has a strong rhythmic pattern but is not rhymed. Although the pattern is flexible, each line generally contains ten syllables, with accents falling on the even-numbered syllables. You will read a good example of this form of poetry in the play *Julius Caesar* on pages 510 through 576.

A special type of dramatic poetry is the *dramatic monologue.* As the prefix *mono–* suggests, this type of poetry presents a single speaker. In reading *Julius Caesar,* you will find a scene in which Brutus is the only person speaking. He is alone on the stage uttering his thoughts. This is called a *soliloquy* and is a device which dramatists use to permit the audience to know what a character is thinking or feeling. A dramatic monologue differs from a soliloquy in that though only one person is speaking, you are aware that he is speaking to *someone else* who is present. He is not, as in a soliloquy, speaking to himself. In the dramatic monologue an entire story is unfolded through a single person's speech. As you read the dramatic monologue that follows, ask yourself these questions: Who is speaking? To whom is he or she speaking? What story is unfolded as he or she speaks?

The Laboratory

Ancien Regime

ROBERT BROWNING

The subtitle of this poem, *Ancien Regime*, means "the old order." It refers to the time before the French Revolution when the government of France was a monarchy. During this period of European history men known as alchemists acquired skill in developing chemicals, especially poisons. Through experiments they were able to control the speed and effectiveness with which a poison would work. Naturally, alchemists were regarded with suspicion by the majority of people. In this poem the English poet Robert Browning does not tell the story in a conventional way. You will have to read carefully to know what is happening, what is about to happen, and why.

Now that I, tying thy glass mask° tightly,
May gaze through these faint smokes curling whitely,
As thou pliest thy trade in this devil's smithy —
Which is the poison to poison her, prithee?

He is with her; and they know that I know   5
Where they are, what they do. They believe my tears flow
While they laugh, laugh at me, at me fled to the drear
Empty church, to pray God in, for them! — I am here.

Grind away, moisten and mash up thy paste,
Pound at thy powder — I am not in haste!   10
Better sit thus, and observe thy strange things,
Than go where men wait me and dance at the King's.

That in the mortar° — you call it a gum?
Ah, the brave tree whence such gold oozings come!
And yonder soft phial,° the exquisite blue,   15
Sure to taste sweetly — is that poison too?

1. **glass mask:** evidently a protection against poisonous gases or particles. 13. **mortar** (môr′tĕr): a very hard bowl in which softer substances are ground or pounded to a powder. 15. **phial** (fī′*al*): a small glass bottle.

Had I but all of them, thee and thy treasures,
What a wild crowd of invisible pleasures!
To carry pure death in an earring, a casket,
A signet, a fan-mount, a filigree-basket!°   20

Soon, at the King's, a mere lozenge° to give,
And Pauline should have just thirty minutes to live!
But to light a pastille,° and Elise, with her head,
And her breast, and her arms, and her hands, should drop dead!

Quick — is it finished? The color's too grim!   25
Why not soft like the phial's, enticing and dim?
Let it brighten her drink, let her turn it and stir,
And try it and taste, ere she fix and prefer!

What, a drop? She's not little, no minion° like me!
That's why she ensnared him; this never will free   30
The soul from those masculine eyes — say, "no!"
To that pulse's magnificent come-and-go.

For only last night, as they whispered, I brought
My own eyes to bear on her so, that I thought
Could I keep them one-half-minute fixed, she would fall,   35
Shriveled; she fell not; yet this does it all!

Not that I bid you spare her the pain!
Let death be felt and the proof remain;
Brand, burn up, bite into its grace —
He is sure to remember her dying face!   40

Is it done? Take my mask off! Nay, be not morose;
It kills her, and this prevents seeing it close:
The delicate droplet, my whole fortune's fee —
If it hurts her, beside, can it ever hurt me?

Now, take all my jewels, gorge gold to your fill,   45
You may kiss me, old man, on my mouth if you will!
But brush this dust off me, lest horror it brings
Ere I know it — next moment I dance at the King's!

19–20: These lines refer to the practice of concealing poisons in a piece of jewelry or wearing apparel. 21. **lozenge** (lŏz'ĕnj): a cough drop or piece of candy. 23. **pastille** (păs·tēl'): a pellet of aromatic paste, burned for fumigating or deodorizing. 29. **minion** (mĭn'yŭn): here, a small, delicate person.

APPRECIATING DRAMATIC POETRY

1. What is the effect of having a story told to you through someone's speech? Is there a directness in dramatic poetry that might not be present in a narrative poem?

2. What story is Browning telling? If you learn nothing else from the monologue, you should be aware that someone is going to be poisoned. Why? What are the motives of the poisoner? What does she hope to gain? What is the role of the alchemist? What is the attitude of the speaker toward him?

3. The most interesting person in the poem is the speaker. How would you describe her character? What does she reveal about herself? Do you think she realizes that she is revealing so much of her own personality?

4. You might be interested in finding other dramatic monologues and presenting them to the class. If you listen carefully to the words of our popular songs, you will find that many of them are dramatic monologues.

POINT OF VIEW

In "The Laboratory" Browning has adopted *a point of view;* that is, the story is seen through the eyes of one person, the speaker, and we learn everything from her alone. This is called the *first person* point of view. It has the advantage of involving you immediately in a situation, but it places certain restrictions on an author. When one person is telling what he sees, thinks, and feels, he is obviously limited. For example, he may guess what other people are thinking or feeling, but he cannot know for certain. He also cannot know what is going on some distance from him, or what will happen in the future. The author who writes in the first person must restrict himself accordingly.

If an author wants to allow himself more freedom, he may adopt a *third person* point of view. Then he talks not as "I," but about "him," "her," and "it." Most narration is in the third person. It allows the author to explain what all the characters are thinking and feeling, what they are doing even though they are in widely separated places, and, sometimes, what will happen to them in the future.

About the Poet

Robert Browning (1812–1889) was an English poet famous for his dramatic monologues and his long narrative poems. His ability to create vivid and realistic characters distinguished him from many of the other poets of his time. The story of his marriage to Elizabeth Barrett, despite her family's objections, is probably one of the best known and most appealing love stories of the age. Elizabeth, a famous poet in her own right, was an invalid, and after the marriage, the Brownings went to Italy in an attempt to restore her health. They both loved Italy and a number of Robert Browning's poems have Italian settings or Italian characters. Browning's famous narrative poem, *The Ring and the Book,* is based on an account of a murder trial in seventeenth-century Rome. Many of his dramatic monologues concern similar historical incidents or characters. Browning achieved an extraordinary success in his lifetime, enjoying great popularity in America as well as in England. He continued writing poetry until the end of his life. When he died in Venice, Italy, he was given a public funeral there and then was buried in the Poet's Corner of Westminster Abbey.

Light Verse

No discussion of poetry is complete without *light verse*. It is intended to amuse, but you will find that it almost always asks you to sharpen your wits. It takes thought to be amusing, and it takes thought to enjoy light verse. See how well you fare with the poems that follow.

The Rhinoceros

OGDEN NASH

Ogden Nash is one of the best modern light-verse writers. He has particular fun with distortions. The distortion may be in rhythm, in ideas, or, in the case of this poem, in words.

The rhino is a homely beast,
For human eyes he's not a feast,
But you and I will never know
Why nature chose to make him so.
Farewell, farewell, you old rhinoceros,
I'll stare at something less prepoceros!

FOUR POEMS BY MARTIAL

Wit, at least in some of its best and most appealing forms, is not limited by time and place. The following four poems were written by the Latin poet Martial, who lived in the first century A.D. We call Martial a satirist because he poked fun at the weaknesses and follies of human beings.

Bought Locks

The golden hair that Gulla wears
  Is hers: who would have thought it?
She swears 'tis hers, and true she
    swears,
  For I know where she bought it.
    Translated by Sir John Harington

A Hinted Wish

You told me, Maro, whilst you live
You'd not a single penny give,
But that, whene'er you chanct to die,
You'd leave a handsome legacy:
You must be mad beyond redress,
If my next wish you cannot guess!
    Translated by Francis Lewis

Critics

The readers and the hearers like my
books,
And yet some writers cannot them digest;
But what care I? for when I make a
feast,
I would my guests should praise it, not
the cooks.

Translated by Sir John Harington

Post-Obits* and the Poets

He unto whom thou art so partial,
Oh, reader! is the well-known Martial,
The Epigrammatist: while living,
Give him the fame thou wouldst be
giving;
So shall he hear, and feel, and know
it —
Post-obits rarely reach a poet.

Translated by Lord Byron

* **Post-Obits:** here, things said about a
person after he is dead. 5. **Epigrammatist**
(ĕp′ĭ·grăm′ă·tĭst): a writer of epigrams. An epigram is a short poem with a witty or satirical
point.

APPRECIATING LIGHT VERSE

1. Besides the final word, can you point
out some other sources of humor in Ogden
Nash's "The Rhinoceros"? One of the
things that can make us laugh is understatement; that is, treating important
things in a casual way. Does Nash use
understatement in this poem?
2. "Bought Locks" might well have
been written today. How does Martial
achieve humor here? Do you feel that
Martial is unkind? Why or why not?
3. What is the "hinted wish"? Do you
think that Martial has a real understanding of human nature? Why?
4. What does Martial think of other
writers? With what does he compare them
in "Critics"? Is this comparison apt?

5. Martial is a satirist. He observes with
pointed humor the things he sees around
him. What point does he make in his poem
"Post-Obits and the Poets"? Do you think
that all of us would like some recognition
while we are alive?

About the Poets

Ogden Nash (1902–   ), one of America's most popular writers of humorous
verse, is descended from a distinguished
family. His great-great-grandfather was an
early governor of North Carolina and his
great-great-uncle gave Nashville, Tennessee, its name. Nash attended Harvard
for one year, worked as a bond salesman,
wrote advertising copy for a publishing
company for six years, was on the staff of
the *New Yorker,* and wrote scenarios in
Hollywood. *The Face Is Familiar* is one
of Nash's most popular volumes of humorous poetry. His poems, full of oddities of
spelling, rhyme, and rhythm, manage to
disguise as nonsense some very shrewd
and witty observations on modern society.
His clever lines are quoted frequently, and
every year his already vast audience grows
larger.

Martial (40?–104 A.D.) is the Latin poet
who brought the epigram to its perfection.
He has provided a remarkably accurate
and witty picture of society in the early
years of the Roman Empire. Martial was
born in Spain, but in 64 A.D. he came to
Rome where he was to spend the greater
part of his life. What we know of him, we
learn chiefly through his writings. He
lived at first in poor circumstances, but
later, obviously successful, he had a house
in town and a small place in the country
as well. He was evidently popular at court
since he received from the emperor the
privilege to hold public office before he
was twenty-five. In 84 or 85 A.D., two
books of his epigrams appeared and he
continued to publish volumes at almost
yearly intervals. He returned to Spain in
his later years and died there shortly after
the publication of his twelfth collection
of poems.

The Eyes of the Poet

You have been introduced to the three major types of poetry — narrative, lyric, and dramatic — and to some of the most popular varieties of these types. You now recognize the ballad as narrative poetry, the song and the elegy as lyric poetry, and the dramatic monologue as dramatic poetry.

You have also become familiar with some of the forms, or patterns, of poetry, including the sonnet, the most famous short lyric form. You have examined the poet's way with words and have seen how he uses their sounds to create patterns of rhythm and rhyme, their suggestive power to brighten his comparisons. This introduction to the poet's materials and techniques, along with further study of the structure of poetry, should help you to understand *how* the poet communicates. In the following pages we will widen our view to look at *what* the poet communicates. Or, to put it another way, we will study the content of poems, the poet's ideas and feelings about the many things he sees and experiences.

As the first step in studying content, let's look closely at what the poet sees. Naturally, he sees many of the same things we all see. But he sees them in a different way. He sees more clearly, and he knows how to reproduce in words his own clear vision. The poet sees people and nature and life, and he describes what he sees in such a way that we say to ourselves, "Yes, he's right. That's exactly how it is." The poet forces us to recognize suddenly the things we had always been looking at but had never really seen. That sudden recognition teaches us what our own eyes can do if we use them properly. The poet's vision widens and sharpens our own vision of people, nature, and life.

Looking at People

Poets seem to possess a special ability to see people: to see what it is about them that sets each apart as an individual and what it is that binds each one to all humanity. In the following poems, five persons are masterfully portrayed. Two famous light-verse poets, W. S. Gilbert and Ogden Nash, take a shrewd and witty look at special kinds of people. A famous American poet, Stephen Vincent Benét, looks back at one of our national heroes. And finally, an Irish poet, Anthony Raftery, looks at a poet (perhaps himself). If we look carefully through the eyes of the poet, we will learn something about each of these people, and we may learn something about ourselves as well.

The Duke of Plaza-Toro

W. S. GILBERT

Poking fun at pompous figures has been the delight of poets through the ages. This poem is from the operetta "The Gondoliers," which was written by Gilbert and Sullivan in 1889; but lampooning people is as much a part of light verse today as it was then. Does the Duke remind you of anyone you know today?

In enterprise of martial° kind,
  When there was any fighting,
He led his regiment from behind
  (He found it less exciting).
But when away his regiment ran,   5
  His place was at the fore, O!
    That celebrated
    Cultivated,
    Underrated
    Nobleman,   10
  The Duke of Plaza-Toro!

When, to evade destruction's hand,
  To hide they all proceeded,
No soldier in that gallant band
  Hid half as well as he did.   15
He lay concealed throughout the war,
  And so preserved his gore, O!
    That unaffected,
    Undetected,
    Well-connected   20
    Warrior,
  The Duke of Plaza-Toro!

In every doughty° deed, ha, ha!
He always took the lead, ha, ha!
    That unaffected,   25
    Undetected,
    Well-connected
    Warrior,
  The Duke of Plaza-Toro!

When told that they would all be shot
  Unless they left the service,   31
That hero hesitated not,
  So marvelous his nerve is.
He sent his resignation in,
  The first of all his corps, O!   35
    That very knowing,
    Overflowing,
    Easygoing
    Paladin,°
  The Duke of Plaza-Toro!   40

To men of grosser clay, ha, ha!
He always showed the way, ha, ha!
    That very knowing,
    Overflowing,
    Easygoing   45
    Paladin,
  The Duke of Plaza-Toro!

39. **paladin** (păl′á·dĭn): knight or champion; from *paladins,* the name given to the twelve brave knights who acted as a guard of honor for Charlemagne.

The Purist

OGDEN NASH

Now here is a character you should recognize quite easily. He is the one who is very much concerned with being correct. If a bomb fell at tea-time, he would, quite likely, go on pouring tea.

I give you now Professor Twist,
A conscientious scientist.
Trustees exclaimed, "He never bungles!"
And sent him off to distant jungles.
Camped on a tropic riverside,   5
One day he missed his loving bride.
She had, the guide informed him later,
Been eaten by an alligator.
Professor Twist could not but smile.
"You mean," he said, "a crocodile."   10

1. **martial** (mär′shǎl): warlike. 23. **doughty** (dou′tǐ): brave, with a touch of boastfulness.

Lee

from *John Brown's Body*

STEPHEN VINCENT BENÉT

In the quest for freedom, heroism has not always been limited to the side
that eventually triumphed. General Robert E. Lee led the Confederate
Army to the last bitter moment of surrender. Considerate of others to the
last, the proud General's only request was that his men might keep their
horses for spring plowing. Today he is recognized as an American hero
whose courage is a part of our proud history.

In this poem, one of his aides waits to enter General Lee's tent. The
aide is on night duty during the last bitter weeks when it is certain that
the end of the South's resistance is near.

The night had fallen on the narrow tent.
— Deep night of Virginia summer when the stars
Are burning wax in the near, languid sky
And the soft flowers hardly close all night
But bathe in darkness, as a woman bathes   5
In a warm, fragrant water, and distill
Their perfume still, without the fire of the sun.

The army was asleep as armies sleep.
War lying on a casual sheaf of peace
For a brief moment, and yet with armor on,   10
And yet in the child's deep sleep, and yet so still.
Even the sentries seemed to walk their posts
With a ghost footfall that could match that night.
The aide-de-camp knew certain lines of Greek
And other such unnecessary things   15
As birds and music, that are good for peace
But are not deemed so serviceable for war.
He was a youth with an inquisitive mind
And doubtless had a failing for romance,
But then he was not twenty, and such faults   20
May sometimes be excused in younger men
Even when such creatures die, as they have done
At one time or another, for some cause
Which we are careful to point out to them
Much later, was no cause worth dying for,   25
But cannot reach them with our arguments
Because they are uneconomic dust.

So, when the aide-de-camp came toward the tent,
He knew that he was sleepy as a dog,
And yet the starlight and the gathered scents   30
Moved in his heart — like the unnecessary
Themes of a music fallen from a cloud
In light, upon a dark water.
                                   And though he had
Some bitterness of mind to chew upon,   35
As well as messages that he must give
Before he slept, he halted in his tracks.
He saw, imprinted on the yellow light,
That made the tent a hollow jack-o'-lantern,
The sharp, black shadow of a seated man,   40
The profile like the profile on a bust.
Lee in his tent, alone.
He had some shadow papers in his hand,
But you could see he was not reading them,
And, if he thought, you could not read his thoughts,   45
Even as shadows, by any light that shines.

"You'd know that face among a million faces,"
Thought the still watcher, "and yet, his hair and beard
Have quite turned white, white as the dogwood bloom
That blossomed on the way to Chancellorsville°   50
When Jackson° was alive and we were young
And we were winning and the end was near.
And now, I guess, the end is near enough
In spite of everything that we can do,
And he's alone tonight and Jackson's dead.   55
I saw him in the Wilderness° that day
When he began to lead the charge himself
And the men wouldn't let him.

50. **Chancellorsville:** The Battle of Chancellorsville, a Confederate victory, was fought May 1, 2, and 3, 1863. Chancellorsville is south of the Rappahannock River in Virginia. 51. **Jackson:** Thomas J. Jackson, one of the greatest Confederate generals, generally known as "Stonewall" Jackson. He died in the Battle of Chancellorsville. 56. **Wilderness:** A furious battle, favorable to the Confederates, was fought May 5 and 6, 1864, in the Wilderness, a section south of the Rapidan River in Virginia.

Detail from the mural "Scenes from the Civil War" by Charles Hoffbauer. ▶

                                        Gordon° spoke
And then the men themselves began to yell   60
'Lee to the rear — General Lee to the rear!'
I'll hear that all my life. I'll see those paws
Grabbing at Traveller° and the bridle rein
And forcing the calm image back from death.
Reckon that's what we think of you, Marse Robert,°   65
Reckon that's what we think, what's left of us,
The poor old devils that are left of us.
I wonder what he thinks about it all.
He isn't staring, he's just sitting there.
I never knew a man could look so still   70
And yet look so alive in his repose.

"It doesn't seem as if a cause could lose
When it's believed in by a man like that.
And yet we're losing.
                        And he knows it all.   75
No, he won't ever say it. But he knows.

"I'd feel more comfortable if he'd move.
We had a chance at Spotsylvania,°
We had some chances in the Wilderness.
We always hurt them more than we were hurt   80
And yet we're here — and they keep coming on.
What keeps us going on? I wish I knew.
Perhaps you see a man like that go on
And then you have to follow.
                                There can't be   85
So many men that men have followed so.

"And yet, what is it for? What is it for?
What does he think?
                        His hands are lying there
Quiet as stones or shadows in his lap.   90
His beard is whiter than the dogwood bloom,
But there is nothing ruined in his face,
And nothing beaten in those steady eyes.
If he's grown old, it isn't like a man,

---

59. **Gordon:** General John B. Gordon of the Confederate Army. 63. **Traveller:** the name of General Lee's horse. 65. **Marse Robert:** the name by which Lee was affectionately known to his men. 78. **Spotsylvania:** At Spotsylvania Court House in Virginia, May 10, 12, and 18, 1864, the Confederates foiled General Grant's efforts to break through their lines.

It's more the way a river might grow old.   95
My mother knew him at old dances once.
She said he liked to joke and he was dark then,
Dark and as straight as he can stand today.
If he would only move, I could go forward.

"You see the faces of spear-handling kings   100
In the old books they taught us from at school;
Big Agamemnon° with his curly beard,
Achilles° in the cruelty of his youth,
And Oedipus° before he tore his eyes.
I'd like to see him in that chariot-rank,   105
With Traveller pulling at the leader pole.
I don't think when the winged claws° come down
They'll get a groan from him.
                                        So we go on.
Under the claws. And he goes on ahead."   110

The sharp-cut profile moved a fraction now.
The aide-de-camp went forward on his errand.

---

102. **Agamemnon** (ăg'à·mĕm'nŏn): commander in chief of the Greeks at the siege of Troy.
103. **Achilles** (à·kĭl'ēz): a Greek hero of the Trojan War. 104. **Oedipus** (ĕd'ĭ·pŭs): the Greek
hero who solved the riddle of the Sphinx, but who came to a tragic end, blinded by his own
hands. 107. **winged claws:** a reference to the mythological female flying figures, the Harpies,
who attacked dying men with their claws and carried them off to devour.

I Am Raftery

ANTHONY RAFTERY

Symbols are one way of expressing ideas
powerfully and dramatically. For instance,
Raftery, in the poem that follows, can be
understood as a symbol of human courage
in meeting the adversities of life. He is
also a symbol of the true artist who creates
beauty for its own sake.

"I Am Raftery" by Anthony Raftery, translated by
James Stephens in *Reincarnations*, copyright 1918, by
The Macmillan Company, and used with their per-
mission.

I am Raftery the poet,
Full of hope and love,
My eyes without sight,
My mind without torment,

Going west on my journey   5
By the light of my heart,
Tired and weary
To the end of the road.

Behold me now
With my back to a wall,   10
Playing music
To empty pockets.

Translated from Gaelic by James Stephens

LOOKING AT PEOPLE

1. What sort of soldier is the Duke of Plaza-Toro? Do you feel that his cowardice is something to be despised? Why is this man a humorous figure?

2. Is there something wrong with being a purist? What does the word mean? What is unrealistic about the purist's attitude toward life?

3. In the portrait of Lee from *John Brown's Body*, Benét describes a great hero of the War Between the States. What touches does Benét use to show the kind of man, and leader, Lee was?

4. Somehow identity is important to each of us. Notice how Anthony Raftery identifies himself. What does he consider important about himself? From this apparently simple statement, can you tell what he feels is important in life? What do you think the last stanza means? What associations do you have with the phrase "my back to the wall"? Why does Raftery play music "to empty pockets"?

READING POETRY ALOUD

For full appreciation, poetry should always be read aloud. But reading poetry intelligibly is not an easy matter. For instance, you should never assume that the poet, having established a rhythm pattern for the poem, will follow that rhythm rigidly throughout every line. He may alter the basic rhythm for variety or emphasis. The reader who follows the basic rhythm blindly will miss both the pleasure and the sense of the poem.

The best procedure is to concentrate first on the sense of the poem rather than the rhythm pattern. Let the rhythm remain subdued. Meaningful phrases should be read together, without giving full emphasis to every accented syllable. What about meaning that carries over from one line of the poem to the next? By all means, follow the meaning. There is nothing more foolish than the notion some people have that a reader should pause firmly at the end of every line of a poem.

On the other hand, William Butler Yeats, an Irish poet, stated once before reading his own poetry, "It took me a devil of a time to get this into verse, and I'm not going to read it as if it were prose." All poetry is rhythmic, even though this

may not be obvious at the first reading. The rhythm of a poem is gained by the repetition of accents at regular intervals. Rhythm is one means used by the poet to attract and hold the reader's attention. It is effective because it appeals to the ear and to the emotions of the reader.

But rhythm is more than just a device in a poem. Rhythm helps convey the feeling or attitude the poet wishes to express. With different rhythms the poet may suggest speed and excitement, or peace and tranquillity, or even monotony. The rhythm of the best poetry helps express emotion and thought as much as the words themselves do.

About the Poets

Sir William Schwenck Gilbert (1836–1911) was kidnapped in Naples, Italy, at the age of two and held for ransom. Perhaps this event stimulated Gilbert's famous temper which gained him so many enemies and finally broke the Gilbert and Sullivan partnership in light opera. Yet by the time he was twenty-four he had written fifteen plays successful enough to make him a noted playwright and he was regularly contributing his famous *Bab Ballads* to a popular magazine. In 1877 he met the composer Sir Arthur Sullivan, and they launched their famous light operas. Among the best known of these merry productions are *H.M.S. Pinafore*, *The Mikado*, and *The Pirates of Penzance*.

Anthony Raftery (1784?–1835) was a blind poet who wandered about the western coast of Ireland, playing his fiddle and reciting his poetry. In recent years his poetry has been collected from the oral versions handed down by the common people who treasured them. Donn Byrne has memorialized him in a novel, *Blind Raftery*, and many of his poems have been translated into English from Gaelic.

Ogden Nash's biography is on page 378.

Stephen Vincent Benét's biography follows his short story, "By the Waters of Babylon," on page 178.

Looking at Nature

Poets have always been concerned with the world that surrounds them, with the abrupt changes of the seasons, with the subtle changes that occur from day to day. Sometimes it seems as though we are too close to nature to understand and observe it clearly, but if we look through the eyes of the poet, we may catch a better glimpse of the significant events of nature. The poems that follow describe things we all have seen or experienced — spring, summer, rain, wind, a snowflake — but these commonplace things renew their importance as they are observed and recorded by the poet.

in Just-

E. E. CUMMINGS

Your first reaction to E. E. Cummings' unusual spacing and punctuation may be one of dislike, especially if you are suspicious of anything that departs from the way things have always been done before. But Cummings had reasons for the way his poetry appeared on a page. From the words and spirit of this poem, perhaps you can tell why he used his unusual devices.

in Just-
spring   when the world is mud-
luscious the little
lame balloonman

whistles   far   and wee   5

and eddieandbill come
running from marbles and
piracies and it's
spring

when the world is puddle-wonderful

the queer   11
old balloonman whistles
far   and   wee
and bettyandisbel come dancing

from hop-scotch and jump-rope and   15

it's
spring
and
     the

          goat-footed°   20

balloonMan   whistles
far
and
wee

20. **goat-footed:** In Greek mythology one of the symbols of spring was Pan, a creature who had the upper body of a man and the legs and feet of a goat.

To a Snowflake

FRANCIS THOMPSON

Although this is a winter poem, note that it is more than a poem of the seasons. The first ten lines are a question and the last twelve lines are an answer. Together they represent a deep awareness of beauty and reverence before it. Once you discover that the poet uses familiar words in perhaps unfamiliar forms (for example, *devisal*, in line 2, is simply a noun formed from the verb *devise*), you will have no difficulty enjoying this poem.

What heart could have thought you?
Past our devisal
(O filigree petal!)
Fashioned so purely,
Fragilely, surely,   5
From what Paradisal
Imagineless metal,
Too costly for cost?
Who hammered you, wrought you,
From argentine° vapor? —   10
   "God was my shaper.
Passing surmisal,
He hammered, He wrought me,
From curled silver vapor,
To lust° of his mind; —   15
Thou could'st not have thought me!
So purely, so palely,
Tinily, surely,
Mightily, frailly,
Insculped and embossed,   20
With His hammer of wind,
And His graver° of frost."

Spring Thunder

MARK VAN DOREN

There is something exciting about the first spring storm. Often it is difficult to understand exactly what this excitement is. In the question he asks at the end of this poem, Mark Van Doren may have hit upon the explanation.

Listen. The wind is still,
And far away in the night —
See! The uplands fill
With a running light.°

Open the doors. It is warm;   5
And where the sky was clear —
Look! The head of a storm
That marches here!

Come under the trembling hedge —
Fast, although you fumble.   10
There! Did you hear the edge
Of winter crumble?

4. **running light:** in other words, lightning.

10. **argentine:** silvery. 15. **lust:** desire. 22. **graver:** any cutting tool, such as a chisel, used by engravers and sculptors.

What Is So Rare as a Day in June?

from *The Vision of Sir Launfal*

JAMES RUSSELL LOWELL

This poet sings in praise of summer. He is not interested in spring, the period of the year when nature only *begins* to cover the earth with growing things. His song of joy is to the "high tide of the year."

And what is so rare as a day in June?
  Then, if ever, come perfect days;
Then Heaven tries earth if it be in tune,
  And over it softly her warm ear lays;
Whether we look, or whether we listen   5
We hear life murmur, or see it glisten;
Every clod feels a stir of might,
  An instinct within it that reaches and towers,
And groping blindly above it for light,
  Climbs to a soul in grass and flowers.   10
The flush of life may well be seen
  Thrilling back over hills and valleys;
The cowslip startles in meadows green,
  The buttercup catches the sun in its chalice,
And there's never a leaf or a blade too mean   15
  To be some happy creature's palace;
The little bird sits at his door in the sun,
  Atilt like a blossom among the leaves,
And lets his illumined being o'errun
  With the deluge of summer it receives;   20
His mate feels the eggs beneath her wings,
And the heart in her dumb breast flutters and sings;
He sings to the wide world, and she to her nest —
In the nice° ear of Nature which song is the best?

Now is the high tide of the year,   25
  And whatever of life hath ebbed away
Comes flooding back with a ripply cheer
  Into every bare inlet and creek and bay;
Now the heart is so full that a drop overfills it;
We are happy now because God wills it;   30
No matter how barren the past may have been,
'Tis enough for us now that the leaves are green;
We sit in the warm shade and feel right well
How the sap creeps up and the blossoms swell;
We may shut our eyes, but we cannot help knowing   35
That skies are clear and grass is growing.

24. **nice:** here, refined; able to detect slight differences.

LOOKING AT NATURE

1. In Cummings' poem "in Just-" he uses visual images as well as sounds to create a view of spring. What are these images? Why is the balloon man an effective image for a poem about spring? What does it bring to mind? Why is the sound of the balloon man's whistle important in this poem? What do the unusual spacing and punctuation contribute to the over-all impression this poem creates?

2. "Spring Thunder" describes a violent side of this season. Compare "Spring Thunder" to "in Just-." How do the different images in each poem create different impressions of spring?

3. Reread "To a Snowflake," looking only for the ways the snowflake is described. Which words or descriptions seem especially effective? This poem expresses a philosophy as well as a description. What is this philosophy?

4. Lowell's verses about June form one of the most famous descriptions in American literature. In these lines he not only describes a time of year but also expresses a philosophy, or view of life. What is his philosophy?

About the Poets

E. E. Cummings (1894–1962) grew up and received his education in Cambridge, Massachusetts. His father was a professor of English at Harvard and Cummings took his B.A. and M.A. there. He served as an ambulance driver in World War I and was kept in a detention camp for three months for a minor military offense. Cummings used this experience in writing *The Enormous Room,* which gained him his first real popularity. In Paris, in 1920, he was known as a painter, draftsman, and writer. On his return to the United States, he devoted most of his time to writing. Cummings was always opposed to rigid systems and regimentation. His individualism is reflected in the typography, the punctuation, and the language of his poems. The form of his poetry resulted from his constant efforts to represent direct experience and his belief that "poetry . . . is and forever will be strictly and distinctly a question of individuality."

Mark Van Doren (1894–   ) was awarded the 1939 Pulitzer prize for his *Collected Poems* (1922–1938). Besides his verses he has produced four volumes of criticism and a scholarly but imaginative work called *Shakespeare.* Van Doren has been judged a disciple of Robert Frost, following the latter's restrained treatment of everyday affairs with a serious or universal inner meaning. He was born in Illinois and attended the University of Illinois and Columbia University, where he later taught English from 1920 to 1959.

Francis Joseph Thompson's life (1859–1907) seemed permanently damaged by his failure to be accepted into the priesthood. He then tried to follow his father's profession of medicine but failed the exams three times. He deserted his studies for London, where he spent a half-starved existence and began writing poetry while sitting on curbs or leaning against walls. An influential family of culture finally "discovered" him, but he was now heavily dependent on opium to relieve his tubercular pain. He did, however, write his most famous poem, "The Hound of Heaven," during a convalescence in a peaceful monastery.

James Russell Lowell (1819–1891), in his senior year at Harvard, met Ralph Waldo Emerson, whose friendship he cultivated and kept for the rest of his life. Maria White, Lowell's wife and also a poet, encouraged his antislavery writing between 1846–1848, which appeared as the first series of the *Biglow Papers.* These stimulated a tremendous moral indignation during the critical days before The War Between the States. During the war itself, Lowell wrote a second series of the *Papers.* Besides his antislavery activities, he later took Longfellow's place at Harvard, teaching modern languages and literature. He also became known as an eminent interpreter of Dante and old French poetry and a connoisseur of Italian art. Following his teaching career, he was appointed minister to Spain and later transferred as minister to England.

Looking at Life

Poets are not satisfied merely to describe someone or something accurately; they wish to discover the meaning and significance of everything they observe. People behave and act in a variety of ways, and their behavior falls into a series of patterns. With the poet, we look at these patterns and try to discover their importance, and perhaps we can say with the poet, "This is where it all leads. This is what it's all about." The following poems provide their own answers to some of the questions we ask of life.

Birches

ROBERT FROST

In his poems Robert Frost sharpens our powers of observation by sharing with us the scenes that have captured his imagination. He also leads us to reflect on these scenes. In "Birches," climbing and swinging on trees becomes a symbol of an attitude toward life.

When I see birches bend to left and right
Across the line of straighter darker trees,
I like to think some boy's been swinging them.
But swinging doesn't bend them down to stay.
Ice storms do that. Often you must have seen them   5
Loaded with ice a sunny winter morning
After a rain. They click upon themselves
As the breeze rises, and turn many-colored
As the stir cracks and crazes° their enamel.
Soon the sun's warmth makes them shed crystal shells   10
Shattering and avalanching on the snow crust —
Such heaps of broken glass to sweep away
You'd think the inner dome of heaven had fallen.
They are dragged to the withered bracken° by the load,
And they seem not to break; though, once they are bowed   15
So low for long, they never right themselves:
You may see their trunks arching in the woods
Years afterward, trailing their leaves on the ground
Like girls on hands and knees that throw their hair
Before them over their heads to dry in the sun.   20
But I was going to say when Truth broke in
With all her matter of fact about the ice storm

9. **crazes:** makes tiny cracks on the surface. 14. **bracken:** large ferns.

I should prefer to have some boy bend them
As he went out and in to fetch the cows —
Some boy too far from town to learn baseball,   25
Whose only play was what he found himself,
Summer or winter, and could play alone.
One by one he subdued his father's trees
By riding them down over and over again
Until he took the stiffness out of them,   30
And not one but hung limp, not one was left
For him to conquer. He learned all there was
To learn about not launching out too soon
And so not carrying the tree away
Clear to the ground. He always kept his poise   35
To the top branches, climbing carefully
With the same pains you use to fill a cup
Up to the brim, and even above the brim.
Then he flung outward, feet first, with a swish,
Kicking his way down through the air to the ground.   40
So was I once myself a swinger of birches;
And so I dream of going back to be.
It's when I'm weary of considerations,
And life is too much like a pathless wood
Where your face burns and tickles with the cobwebs   45
Broken across it, and one eye is weeping
From a twig's having lashed across it open.
I'd like to get away from earth awhile
And then come back to it and begin over.
May no fate willfully misunderstand me   50
And half grant what I wish and snatch me away
Not to return. Earth's the right place for love:
I don't know where it's likely to go better.
I'd like to go by climbing a birch tree,
And climb black branches up a snow-white trunk   55
Toward heaven, till the tree could bear no more,
But dipped its top and set me down again.
That would be good both going and coming back.
One could do worse than be a swinger of birches.

The Sword

WILLIAM BLAKE

In just four lines William Blake discusses
building and destroying, peace and war,
and at the same time draws a strong conclusion about life.

The sword sung on the barren heath,
The sickle in the fruitful field:
The sword he sung a song of death,
But could not make the sickle yield.

Requiem

ROBERT LOUIS STEVENSON

What a man feels about death can tell us a great deal about his thoughts
on life. Robert Louis Stevenson has expressed a philosophy of life in the
eight concise lines of the poem which follows. His title, "Requiem," comes
from the Latin word for *rest*, and means a poem or song for the dead.

Under the wide and starry sky
   Dig the grave and let me lie:
Glad did I live and gladly die,
   And I laid me down with a will.

This be the verse you 'grave for me:
   Here he lies where he long'd to be;
Home is the sailor, home from the sea,
   And the hunter home from the hill.

"Requiem" by Robert Louis Stevenson, published by Charles Scribner's Sons.

About the Poets

Robert Frost (1874–   ) decided while in high school that he wanted to be a poet, but he was forty before he gained the recognition that has since won him four Pulitzer prizes. Born in San Francisco, he lived after his tenth year in Lawrence, Massachusetts, the home of eight generations of his family. He left college to take on a variety of jobs, many of them manual labor. Marrying at twenty he lived for eleven years as a farmer in New Hampshire. From 1912 to 1915, he lived in England where his first volumes of poetry, *A Boy's Will* and *North of Boston*, were published. The New England poet returned to America with a reputation that continued to grow with each succeeding volume of poetry. In 1961, Frost read one of his poems at the ceremony following the presidential inauguration.

William Blake (1757–1827) was an English poet, painter, and engraver who earned a reputation as a mystic. As a child, he claimed to have visions of saints, and he once said that he had spoken to the prophet Ezekiel. Blake's childhood was remarkable in other ways as well. At ten he entered a drawing school and four years later he became an apprentice engraver. He had begun writing during this time and several poems in his first book, *Poetical Sketches*, were written when he was only twelve. He continued to publish poetry, but throughout his life he was known primarily as an artist, even after the publication of his most famous collections of poetry, *Songs of Innocence* and *Songs of Experience*. His engravings for *The Book of Job* made Blake one of the most respected artists in England. Since his death, however, his poetry has received more and more serious attention. In our century especially, the symbolism of his later poetry has become an important subject of study.

Robert Louis Stevenson (1850–1894) studied law only to abandon it for a writing career. Born in Edinburgh, Scotland, he was chronically ill all his life, but remained cheerful and courageous. He wrote travel books until the publication of *Treasure Island* made him famous. *A Child's Garden of Verses* (almost as popular with children as *Mother Goose*) and *The Strange Case of Dr. Jekyll and Mr. Hyde* followed. After a dangerous physical breakdown, Stevenson left England in a search for health that took him first to the United States and then to Samoa. Having fought injustice all his life, he interested himself in the problems of the Samoan natives. In his honor they built "The Road of the Loving Heart," and when he died of tuberculosis they cut a way to the top of a mountain so that "Tusitala" (the teller of tales) might be buried there as he wished. The last three lines of "Requiem" are carved on his tomb, in English toward the east and in Samoan toward the west.

FIVE POEMS OF THE EAST

The poetry of the Middle East and the Orient gains its effects with delicate strokes, much like Oriental landscape painting. Each stroke has to be exactly right in order to make the observer see what the artist is portraying.

The Rubáiyát of Omar Khayyám

TRANSLATED BY EDWARD FITZGERALD

Rubáiyát (roō·bī′yät′) is the Arabic word for quatrains, or four-lined stanzas. In the eleventh century, Omar Khayyám (ō′mär kī·äm′), a Persian astronomer, mathematician, and scientist, used quatrains as the verse form in which he expressed his observations on life. In the late nineteenth century, the Englishman Edward FitzGerald made a superb translation of these stanzas, and now, more than eight hundred years after Omar Khayyám's death, *The Rubáiyát of Omar Khayyám* is famous throughout the world.

Each *rubáiyáh* (the singular of *rubáiyát*) is more or less independent, but the same thoughts tie some of the *rubáiyát* into sequences. Here twenty of them have been arranged into three groups, stressing the brevity of life, the mystery of existence, and a wry discontent with fate.

1

Whether at Naishápúr or Babylon,°
Whether the Cup with sweet or bitter run,
  The Wine of Life keeps oozing drop by drop,
The Leaves of Life keep falling one by one.

Some for the Glories of This World; and some   5
Sigh for the Prophet's Paradise to come;
  Ah, take the Cash, and let the Credit go,
Nor heed the rumble of a distant Drum!

The Worldly Hope men set their Hearts upon
Turns Ashes — or it prospers; and anon,   10
  Like Snow upon the Desert's dusty Face,
Lighting a little hour or two — is gone.

Think, in this batter'd Caravanserai°
Whose Portals are alternate Night and Day,
  How Sultán after Sultán with his Pomp   15
Abode his destined Hour, and went his way.

1. **Naishápúr** (nā′ĭ·sha·poōr′) **or Babylon:** Naishápúr was Omar Khayyám's birthplace; **Babylon** was an ancient city, fallen to ruin before Khayyám's time. 13. **Caravanserai** (kăr′·á·văn′sĕ·rā): an inn where caravans rest at night. Here it is used as a symbol for the world.

2

Myself when young did eagerly frequent°
Doctor and Saint,° and heard great argument
   About it and about: but evermore
Came out by the same door where in I went.   20

With them the seed of Wisdom did I sow,
And with mine own hand wrought to make it grow;
   And this was all the Harvest that I reap'd —
"I came like Water, and like Wind I go."

Into this Universe, and *Why* not knowing   25
Nor *Whence*, like Water willy-nilly flowing;
   And out of it, as Wind along the Waste,
I know not *Whither*, willy-nilly blowing.

Up from Earth's Center through the Seventh Gate°
I rose, and on the Throne of Saturn sate,°   30
   And many a Knot unravel'd by the Road;
But not the Master-knot of Human Fate.

There was the Door to which I found no Key;
There was the Veil through which I might not see:
   Some little talk awhile of Mᴇ and Tʜᴇᴇ   35
There was — and then no more of Tʜᴇᴇ and Mᴇ.

Earth could not answer; nor the Seas that mourn
In flowing Purple, of their Lord forlorn;
   Nor rolling Heaven, with all his Signs° reveal'd
And hidden by the sleeve of Night and Morn.   40

A Moment's Halt — a momentary taste
Of Bᴇɪɴɢ from the Well amid the Waste —
   And Lo! — the phantom Caravan has reach'd
The Nᴏᴛʜɪɴɢ it set out from — Oh, make haste!

Oh threats of Hell and Hopes of Paradise!   45
One thing at least is certain — *This* Life flies;
   One thing is certain and the rest is Lies;
The Flower that once has blown forever dies.

---

    17. **frequent** (frē·kwĕnt´): visit often. 18. **Doctor and Saint:** In Omar Khayyám's time, these were the names given to men of great wisdom who might be thought to know the answer to the riddle of existence. 29. **Seventh Gate:** Saturn was regarded as the Lord of the Seventh Heaven. According to the old astronomy, there were nine concentric spheres surrounding the earth. 30. **sate:** archaic form of *sat.* 39. **Signs:** signs of the zodiac; the patterns of stars in the heavens. Note how Omar Khayyám's profession as astronomer appears in his poetry.

Strange, is it not? that of the myriads° who
Before us pass'd the door of Darkness through,   50
    Not one returns to tell us of the Road,
Which to discover we must travel too.

The Moving Finger writes; and, having writ,
Moves on: nor all your Piety nor Wit
    Shall lure it back to cancel half a Line,   55
Nor all your Tears wash out a Word of it.

And that inverted Bowl they call the Sky,
Whereunder crawling coop'd we live and die,
    Lift not your hands to *It* for help — for It
As impotently moves as you or I.   60

3

And fear not lest Existence closing your
Account, and mine, should know the like no more;
    The Eternal Sákí° from that Bowl has pour'd
Millions of Bubbles like us, and will pour.

When You and I behind the Veil are past,   65
Oh, but the long, long while the World shall last,
    Which of our Coming and Departure heeds
As the Sea's self should heed a pebble-cast.

Yet Ah, that Spring should vanish with the Rose!
That Youth's sweet-scented manuscript should close!   70
    The Nightingale that in the branches sang,
Ah whence, and whither flown again, who knows!

Would but some wingéd Angel ere too late
Arrest the yet unfolded Roll of Fate,
    And make the stern Recorder otherwise   75
Enregister, or quite obliterate!

Ah Love! could you and I with Him conspire
To grasp this sorry Scheme of Things entire,
    Would not we shatter it to bits — and then
Re-mold it nearer to the Heart's Desire!   80

49. **myriads** (mĭr'ĭ-ădz): great numbers. 63. **Sákí**: the wine-bearer.

Two Modern Haiku

NAKAMURA KUSADAO (*Japanese*)

Haiku (hi'koo) are special verse forms used most effectively by the Japanese. The poems use three lines, seventeen syllables in all, to express an idea. These ideas are expressed in terms of simple things: spring, a baby, an apple. The thought is subtle and delicate. This poetry requires careful reading. Though it points toward a conclusion, it invariably leaves that conclusion to you. Generally, the poems are untitled. In the following examples, the poems are given first in English and then in Japanese.

I

In the midst of
All things verdant, my baby
Has begun to teethe.

Banryoku no
Uchi ya ako no ha
Haesomuru

II

The sky is the blue
Of the world's beginning — from my wife
I accept an apple.

Sora wa taisho no
Aosa tsuma yori
Ringo uku

Japanese Poetry and Art

Haiku poetry is characterized by its use of simple words and images and brief phrases to convey profound thoughts and emotions. In much the same way, Japanese art utilizes simplicity of line, color, and subject in depicting beautiful scenes. Pictured on the opposite page is the print "The Cliffs of Yui" by the famous Japanese artist Hiroshige (1797–1858). Can you detect a relationship between this picture and the images in the haiku poems? How would you describe this relationship?

Detail from a fifteenth-century Chinese hand scroll.

The Harp

PO CHÜ-I (*Chinese*)

The Orient is noted for meditation and a calm acceptance of fate. The following poem captures those attitudes well. Could the poet be using the harp as a symbol for something else?

> I lay my harp on the curved table,
> Sitting there idly, filled only with emotions.
> Why should I trouble to play?
> A breeze will come and sweep the strings.

The Soul

from *The Meditations*

ABU-AL-ALA AL-MAARRI (*Arabic*)

The thought of this poem might seem simple at first glance, but there are richer meanings implied here, and deeper emotions. Be sure to look carefully through the eyes of the poet.

> The body, which gives thee during life a form,
> Is but thy vase: be not deceived, my soul!
> Cheap is the bowl thou storest honey in,
> But precious for the contents of the bowl.

1. Robert Frost uses specific details in "Birches" to express an idea. Point out some of these details. How closely has Frost observed the trees? What does climbing the birches represent to the poet? What does swinging back down to earth mean to him?

2. What is the theme of "The Sword"? How is William Blake able to communicate a rather complicated idea in just four lines?

3. What do you think is the meaning of *home* in "Requiem"? How do you think Stevenson feels about death? about life?

4. Omar Khayyám uses many symbols in his *Rubáiyát*. What associations did he expect you to have for the "Cup," the "distant Drum," the "Caravansarai," and the "Veil"? The "Moving Finger" is one of the most admired of his symbols. What do you think it represents?

5. Do you feel that the "poems of the East" are greatly different from the other poetry you have read? Do you find beauty in these poems? Why, or why not? What comment about life is made in each of the poems?

About the Poets

Omar Khayyám (ō′mär kī·äm′) (died approximately 1123). Khayyám means "tent-maker," designating the trade of this famous Persian poet's father. Khayyám's works on algebra rank him as one of the noted mathematicians of his time. His real fame, however, lies in a collection of some five hundred epigrams, translated into a collection, the *Rubáiyát*, by an English poet named Edward FitzGerald. There is some controversy over the extent of Khayyám's work and the extent of FitzGerald's contribution. Khayyám has sometimes been criticized for feeling that life has no direction and that man should concentrate on pleasure alone.

Edward FitzGerald (1809–1883) was a poet himself, but it is not for his poetry that he is known today; it is for his translation of the *Rubáiyát*. He was one of the few people fortunate enough financially to live as he pleased. Pleasure meant the enjoyment of literature, and FitzGerald indulged his love of books as few others have ever been able to do. Many of his friends were famous — Tennyson and Carlyle, for instance — and they have described him as quiet, amiable, and humorous. One of his friends, an Oriental scholar, introduced FitzGerald to the verses of Omar Khayyám. When he published his translation of these verses, FitzGerald suddenly became famous. A modest man who heartily shunned publicity, FitzGerald experienced the irony of undesired fame.

Po Chü-i (bô′jōō-ē′) was a Chinese poet who lived from 772 to 846 A.D. He was born in the Honan province of eastern China. During his lifetime he held a number of important government posts, reaching his highest position in the last five years of his life when he served as president of the council of justice. Po Chü-i published over 3,000 poems in more than seventy books, and was perhaps the most influential poet of his time. He is especially noted for his tender and sensitive lyrics.

Nakamura Kusadao (1901–) studied haiku poetry at Tokyo University and became a member of a group of young poets who were interested in reviving some of the older forms of Japanese poetry. Following World War II, he became an editor of a poetry magazine for young people, and he is now a professor at Seikei College in Tokyo. His poems generally display a deep interest in human nature. Although he has published a number of books in Japanese, very few of his poems have been translated into English.

Abu-al-Ala al-Maarri (à·bōōl′à·lä′ äl′mà·är′rī) (973–1057) was an Arabian poet with interests in many subjects. He gained his extensive culture and broad education even though he became blind early in life. As a young man he spent a few years with a group of writers in Baghdad, but he later returned to his birthplace and spent the last years of his life teaching and writing. He is famous as a letter-writer as well as a poet. His writings reveal an interest in reason and conscience rather than in authority and tradition, and much of his work is colored by a pessimistic outlook. He is best known for his *Meditations*.

The Heart of the Poet

We have learned that the poet sees the same things we all see, and that his particular skill lies in his ability to observe clearly and accurately and to record his vision in poetic form. The poet also feels the emotions we all feel. He feels joy, grief, anger, and all the rest of human emotions, and, because he is a poet, he is able to express these emotions in precise poetic form.

Two of the emotions we feel most deeply are love and fear. The poems that follow are all concerned with these emotions. As you read, you may find that the poets have been able to capture in words the emotions that you have experienced yourself.

When I Was One-and-Twenty

A. E. HOUSMAN

This is one of A. E. Housman's best-loved poems, and after you have read it you will understand why. As you read, notice the contrast between the last two lines of the two stanzas.

> When I was one-and-twenty
>   I heard a wise man say,
> "Give crowns and pounds and guineas
>   But not your heart away;
> Give pearls away and rubies   5
>   But keep your fancy free."
> But I was one-and-twenty.
>   No use to talk to me.
>
> When I was one-and-twenty
>   I heard him say again,   10
> "The heart out of the bosom
>   Was never given in vain;
> 'Tis paid with sighs a-plenty
>   And sold for endless rue."°
> And I am two-and-twenty,   15
>   And oh, 'tis true, 'tis true.

14. **rue:** grief, regret; also an herb with bitter leaves, the emblem of bitter grief.

O, My Luve's like a Red, Red Rose

ROBERT BURNS

In this poem Robert Burns has caught the youthful spirit of a lad in love. Compare the mood and the wild promises of this poem with the idea expressed in "When I Was One-and-Twenty."

O, my luve's like a red, red rose,
  That's newly sprung in June;
O, my luve's like the melodie
  That's sweetly played in tune.

As fair art thou, my bonnie lass,   5
  So deep in luve am I;
And I will luve thee still, my dear,
  Till a' the seas gang dry.

Till a' the seas gang dry, my dear,
  And the rocks melt wi' the sun: 10
And I will luve thee still, my dear,
  While the sands o' life shall run.

And fare thee well, my only luve!
  And fare thee well a while!
And I will come again, my luve,   15
  Though it were ten thousand mile.

Love Is Not All: It Is Not Meat nor Drink

EDNA ST. VINCENT MILLAY

In this sonnet, Edna St. Vincent Millay seems to take a realistic look at love in terms of other necessities and pressures of life. Her conclusion is stated indirectly, but it leaves little doubt in your mind about her feelings.

Love is not all: it is not meat nor drink
Nor slumber nor a roof against the rain;
Nor yet a floating spar to men that sink
And rise and sink and rise and sink again;
Love can not fill the thickened lung with breath,   5
Nor clean the blood, nor set the fractured bone;
Yet many a man is making friends with death
Even as I speak, for lack of love alone.
It well may be that in a difficult hour,
Pinned down by pain and moaning for release,   10
Or nagged by want past resolution's power,
I might be driven to sell your love for peace,
Or trade the memory of this night for food.
It well may be. I do not think I would.

Boy at the Window

RICHARD WILBUR

The boy in the poem is surrounded by warmth, light, and love, but also
by "so much fear." Can you guess what the child fears?

Seeing the snowman standing all alone
In dusk and cold is more than he can bear.
The small boy weeps to hear the wind prepare
A night of gnashings and enormous moan.
His tearful sight can hardly reach to where   5
The pale-faced figure with bitumen° eyes
Returns him such a god-forsaken stare
As outcast Adam gave to Paradise.

The man of snow is, nonetheless, content,
Having no wish to go inside and die.   10
Still, he is moved to see the youngster cry.
Though frozen water is his element,
He melts enough to drop from one soft eye
A trickle of the purest rain, a tear
For the child at the bright pane surrounded by   15
Such warmth, such light, such love, and so much fear.

6. bitumen (bĭ·tū′mĕn): soft coal.

Fear

HART CRANE

The unknown has always frightened man, probably because it is something he cannot control. Do you ever feel a shiver of apprehension and yearn for the security of companionship only to find that it does not warm the chill inside you?

> The host, he says that all is well
> And the fire-wood glow is bright;
> The food has a warm and tempting smell, —
> But on the window licks the night.
>
> Pile on the logs. . . . Give me your hands,
> Friends! No, — it is not fright. . . .
> But hold me . . . somewhere I heard demands. . . .
> And on the window licks the night.

THE HEART OF THE POET

1. What is the poet saying in "When I Was One-and-Twenty"? What is his attitude toward love?

2. Why do you think Robert Burns compares his love to a rose and a tune? Are the comparisons effective? Do you think the tone of the final stanza differs from that of the earlier ones? If so, how?

3. What is Edna St. Vincent Millay's attitude toward love in her sonnet? Do you think her attitude is realistic or unrealistic? Why? Do you think the poet would ever exchange love for food or warmth?

4. The word *fear* in the last stanza of "Boy at the Window" comes as a surprise. Your first reaction is probably "What does he fear"? Can you answer that question?

5. Try to recapture in your own words what Hart Crane is saying in "Fear." Have you ever felt this particular emotion — perhaps alone in your own house at night where you know you are safe, but the sounds of the house unsettle you? The emotion is not an unusual one, but it is often difficult to put the feeling into words so that you can re-create the emotion in someone else. Why do you think this difficulty exists? How does Crane make you aware of fear?

TYPES OF LANGUAGE

There are two major types of language. One kind of language, the language of information, seeks to communicate facts as accurately as possible. Here is a typical sample of the language of information:

"The kingdom which is made up of Sweden and Finland is, according to our measurement, about 200 leagues broad and 300 long, and stretches from south to north as far as the 55th degree or thereabouts."

(*The History of Charles XII* by Voltaire)

The other kind of language, the language of imagination, seeks to present images which will awaken certain responses and attitudes in the reader. Here is an example of the language of imagination:

"And here were gardens bright with sinu-
ous rills,
Where blossomed many an incense-bear-
ing tree."

("Kubla Khan"
by Samuel Taylor Coleridge)

In the language of imagination, the very choice and arrangement of words influence the reader; any change would disturb the image they present and the response they awaken. Symbols, comparisons, rhythms, and sounds combine to evoke a particular mood in the reader, and if the reader is imaginative, he will respond to the language of imagination and appreciate it.

Both kinds of language are valuable to us. Through the language of information, people can learn important facts about the world in which they live. Through the language of imagination, human beings can enrich their lives by gaining new insights into themselves and the people and places of the past and present.

About the Poets

Alfred Edward Housman (1859–1936), born in Worcestershire, England, was educated at Oxford where his failure in the honors examination was a deep shock to him. Working in the government patent office for ten years, he studied at night in the British Museum doing research which finally gained for him the reputation of a noted classical scholar. He subsequently held professorships in Latin at University College and at Cambridge. He is widely known for his translations of the Latin poets and is equally famous for his own poetry. *A Shropshire Lad*, his first volume of poetry, is known to readers everywhere.

Robert Burns (1759–1796) was born into a poor peasant family near Ayr, Scotland. His father's opposition to his sweetheart, Jean Armour, influenced him to consider going to Jamaica. To finance this venture, he published a volume called *Poems: Chiefly in the Scottish Dialect*. The great success of this book led Burns to remain in Scotland. He became a social favorite in Edinburgh where he was regarded as a curiosity because of his unpolished manners and boisterous conduct. He returned to farm life, married Jean Armour, and in the next few years produced some of the world's best-loved songs and poems.

Richard Wilbur (1921–) was born in New York City and was raised on a farm in New Jersey. After receiving his B.A. from Amherst College in 1942, he enlisted with the 36th Infantry Division and served overseas for two years. After the war, he entered Harvard for graduate work. He has taught English at Harvard, Wellesley, and at Wesleyan University in Connecticut. His first collection of poetry was *The Beautiful Changes*. It was followed by *Ceremony* and *Things of This World*. The latter book won the 1957 Pulitzer prize for poetry. In 1956 he wrote the lyrics for the musical comedy, *Candide*, and he has made a translation of *The Misanthrope*, a famous play by the French dramatist, Molière.

Hart Crane (1899–1932) was a potentially great American poet who, unable to balance a number of personal conflicts, committed suicide before his talent had matured. Victim of an unhappy childhood, Crane left home at sixteen, and wandered about the country, writing poetry as he drifted from place to place. After turning down an opportunity to enter college, he continued to roam for a number of years, supporting himself by taking any job that was offered. At various times he worked in a bookstore, a shipyard, a munitions plant, a publishing house, and an advertising agency. Crane was able to devote his full time to poetry when, in 1925, he was given funds by a wealthy friend. His first volume, *White Buildings*, showed Crane clearly to be a poet of the city. His most important work, *The Bridge*, brought him a fellowship which allowed him to spend a year in Mexico.

Edna St. Vincent Millay's biography appears on page 372.

The Imagination of the Poet

All writing requires imagination of one sort or another, but one of the most difficult feats of the imagination is to enter the world of the fantastic and make it convincing. In using his imagination to picture a world which he has not personally experienced, the poet depends on you to leave the world you know and go with him to another time or place which he has created or re-created for your observation.

The three poems that follow require that you "suspend" this moment and live another. If you do this effectively, your imagination, too, will become poetic.

Thirteen O'Clock

KENNETH FEARING

Have you ever walked past a graveyard late at night? If you have, the odds are that you whistled a little tune, walked a little faster, and had your heart in your mouth some of the way. But what about the other "people" involved? In this poem, Kenneth Fearing does some imaginative speculating on what they may be "thinking."

Why do they whistle so loud, when they walk past the graveyard late
     at night?
Why do they look behind them when they reach the gates?
     Why do they have any gates? Why don't they go through
     the wall?
But why, O why do they make that horrible whistling sound?

Go away, live people, stop haunting the dead.

If they catch you, it is said, they make you rap, rap, rap on a
    table all night,
And blow through a trumpet and float around the room in long white   10
    veils,
While they ask you, and ask you: Can you hear us, Uncle Ted?
Are you happy, Uncle Ted? Should we buy or should we sell? Should
    we marry, Uncle Ted?
What became of Uncle Ned, Uncle Ted, and is he happy, and ask him   15
    if he knows what became of Uncle Fred?

Keep away, live people, keep far away,
Stay in the world's other world where you really be-
    long, you will probably be much happier there.

And who knows what they are hunting for, always looking,   20
    looking, looking with sharp bright eyes where they
    ought to have sockets?
Whoever saw them really grin with their teeth?
Who knows why they worry, or what they scheme, with a brain
    where there should be nothing but good, damp air?   25

Stay away, live people, stay away, stay away,
You mean no harm, and we aren't afraid of you, and we
    don't believe such people exist,
But what are you looking for? Who do you want?
Who? Who? Who? O who?   30

Old Christmas Morning

ROY HELTON

This next poem is based on an old folk legend that grew up among the
hill people in Kentucky. The strange story captured the imagination of
the poet Roy Helton, and he recorded it in ballad form. Like many ballads
this one is told mostly in dialogue. Watch for the change of speaker.
Lomey Carter's words are in italics; Sally Anne Barton's are in regular
type.

    "Where you coming from, Lomey Carter,
        So early over the snow?
    And what's them pretties you got in your hand,
        And where you aiming to go?

"Step in, honey! Old Christmas° morning   5
    I ain't got nothing much;
Maybe a bite of sweetness and corn bread,
    A little ham meat and such.

"But come in, honey! Sally Anne Barton's
    Hungering after your face.   10
Wait till I light my candle up:
    Set down! There's your old place.

"Now where you been so airly this morning?"
    "Graveyard, Sally Anne.
Up by the trace° in the salt-lick meadows   15
    Where Taulbe kilt my man."

"Taulbe ain't to home this morning. . . .
    I can't scratch up a light:
Dampness gets on the heads of the matches;
    But I'll blow up the embers bright."   20

"Needn't trouble. I won't be stopping:
    Going a long ways still."
"You didn't see nothing, Lomey Carter,
    Up on the graveyard hill?"

"What should I see there, Sally Anne Barton?"   25
    "Well, sperits do walk last night."
"There were an elderbush a-blooming
    While the moon still give some light."

"Yes, elderbushes, they bloom, Old Christmas,
    And critters kneel down in their straw.   30
Anything else up in the graveyard?"

    "One thing more I saw:
I saw my man with his head all bleeding
    Where Taulbe's shot went through."

"What did he say?"   35
                "He stooped and kissed me."
        "What did he say to you?"

5. **Old Christmas:** January 5, the date on which Christmas was celebrated until about 1750, when it was changed to December 25. In some places in the South, particularly in the mountains, people maintain the tradition of celebrating on January 5 and call it "Old Christmas" to distinguish it from December 25. 15. **trace:** path.

"Said, Lord Jesus forguv your Taulbe;
    But he told me another word;
He said it soft when he stooped and kissed me.   40
    That were the last I heard."

"Taulbe ain't to home this morning."

    "I know that, Sally Anne,
For I kilt him coming down through the meadow
    Where Taulbe kilt my man.   45

"I met him upon the meadow trace
    When the moon were fainting fast,
And I had my dead man's rifle gun
    And kilt him as he come past."

"But I heard two shots."   50
                    " 'Twas his was second:
    He shot me 'fore he died:
You'll find us at daybreak, Sally Anne Barton:
    I'm laying there dead at his side."

The Eve of Waterloo

from *Childe Harold's Pilgrimage*

GEORGE GORDON, LORD BYRON

Here, the poet's imagination brings to life an historic event. The following
poem transports you to the scene of the brilliant military ball which was
interrupted by Napoleon's opening gunfire on the eve of the famous Battle
of Waterloo. You will feel, as you read, something of the urgency and
panic which swept through the halls of Belgium's nearby capital on the
night of June 17, 1815.

There was a sound of revelry by night,
And Belgium's capital had gathered then
Her Beauty and her Chivalry, and bright
The lamps shone o'er fair women and brave men;
A thousand hearts beat happily; and when   5
Music arose with its voluptuous swell,
Soft eyes looked love to eyes which spake again,
And all went merry as a marriage bell;
But hush! hark! a deep sound strikes like a rising knell!

"On the Evening of the Battle of Waterloo," detail from the painting by Ernest Crofts.

Did ye not hear it? — No, 'twas but the wind,°   10
Or the car° rattling o'er the stony street;
On with the dance! let joy be unconfined;
No sleep till morn, when Youth and Pleasure meet
To chase the glowing Hours with flying feet —
But, hark! — that heavy sound breaks in once more   15
As if the clouds its echo would repeat;
And nearer, clearer, deadlier than before!
Arm! Arm! it is — it is — the cannon's opening roar! . . .

Ah! then and there was hurrying to and fro,
And gathering tears, and tremblings of distress,   20

10. Pronounce *wind* with a long "i" to rhyme with *unconfined* in line 12.   11. **car:** a cart; obviously not the modern use of the word.

And cheeks all pale, which but an hour ago
Blushed at the praise of their own loveliness;
And there were sudden partings, such as press
The life from out young hearts, and choking sighs
Which ne'er might be repeated; who could guess   25
If ever more should meet those mutual eyes,
Since upon night so sweet such awful morn could rise!

And there was mounting in hot haste: the steed,
The mustering squadron, and the clattering car,
Went pouring forward with impetuous speed,   30
And swiftly forming in the ranks of war;
And the deep thunder peal on peal afar;
And near, the beat of the alarming drum
Roused up the soldier ere the Morning Star;
While thronged the citizens with terror dumb,   35
Or whispering, with white lips — "The foe! they come! they come!"

THE IMAGINATION OF THE POET

1. Poets create moods as well as meanings. In responding to the mood of a poem, we experience something richer and more valuable than just a simple understanding of the meaning. What is the mood of "Thirteen O'Clock"? How do the sounds of the words contribute to a feeling of eeriness? Which sounds are most effective?

2. What is the story of "Old Christmas Morning"? How did you react to the knowledge that one of the speakers was dead? When do you first learn this?

3. Lord Byron does not describe the situation on the evening before the Battle of Waterloo as a historian might. How does his account differ? What are some of the details he includes? What effect do they have on you?

About the Poets

Kenneth Fearing (1902–1961) was a poet of the big city and he wrote about the city — its speeded-up, nervous activity, its mechanical wonders, even its tawdriness — with as much ease as poets centuries ago wrote about the beauties of nature. The poems in Fearing's chief books, *Afternoon of a Pawnbroker* and *Stranger at Coney Island*, deal with a variety of city characters: business executives, longshoremen, women's club presidents, charwomen, gangsters, and dime-store clerks. He was born in Chicago and educated at the University of Wisconsin, but spent the later years of his life in New York.

Roy Helton (1886–) is a native of Washington, D.C., and a graduate of the University of Pennsylvania. He has studied art, made a hobby of inventions, taught as a schoolmaster in Pennsylvania, and earned a living as a radio commentator and free-lance writer. Mr. Helton makes his home in Harrisburg, Pennsylvania, where he has served as a state official in various capacities. He learned the primitive origins of folk poetry by spending long periods in the mountains of South Carolina and Kentucky. *Lonesome Water* (1930) shows his use of this primitive structure of poetry.

George Gordon, Lord Byron's biography appears on pages 371–72.

The Mind of the Poet

What does a poet think about? He thinks of the same things we all consider at one time or another. He faces the same situations we all face. He faces the same problems, the same difficulties, the same questions. You may discover that the poet's insight will help your own thinking about some questions and problems.

The Tuft of Flowers

ROBERT FROST

In this poem, Robert Frost discovers something important about human nature and the bonds that unite one man with another.

> I went to turn the grass once after one
> Who mowed it in the dew before the sun.
>
> The dew was gone that made his blade so keen
> Before I came to view the levelled scene.
>
> I looked for him behind an isle of trees;   5
> I listened for his whetstone° on the breeze.
>
> But he had gone his way, the grass all mown,
> And I must be, as he had been, — alone,
>
> "As all must be," I said within my heart,
> "Whether they work together or apart."   10
>
> But as I said it, swift there passed me by
> On noiseless wing a bewildered butterfly,
>
> Seeking with memories grown dim o'er night
> Some resting flower of yesterday's delight.
>
> And once I marked his flight go round and round,   15
> As where some flower lay withering on the ground.
>
> And then he flew as far as eye could see,
> And then on tremulous wing came back to me.
>
> I thought of questions that have no reply,
> And would have turned to toss the grass to dry;   20

6. **whetstone** (wet'stōn): an abrasive stone for sharpening knives or other edged tools.

"The Tuft of Flowers" from *You Come Too* by Robert Frost. Copyright, © 1959 by Henry Holt and Company, Inc. By permission of Holt, Rinehart and Winston, Inc.

But he turned first, and led my eye to look
At a tall tuft of flowers beside a brook,

A leaping tongue of bloom the scythe had spared
Beside a reedy brook the scythe had bared.

I left my place to know them by their name,   25
Finding them butterfly weed when I came.

The mower in the dew had loved them thus,
Leaving them to flourish, not for us,

Nor yet to draw one thought of ours to him,
But from sheer morning gladness at the brim.   30

The butterfly and I had lit upon,
Nevertheless, a message from the dawn,

That made me hear the wakening birds around,
And hear his long scythe whispering to the ground,

And feel a spirit kindred to my own;   35
So that henceforth I worked no more alone;

But glad with him, I worked as with his aid,
And weary, sought at noon with him the shade;

And dreaming, as it were, held brotherly speech
With one whose thought I had not hoped to reach.   40

"Men work together," I told him from the heart,
"Whether they work together or apart."

Four Preludes on Playthings of the Wind

CARL SANDBURG

The following poem employs a technique that we have not discussed previously. Here, Carl Sandburg writes what is called *free verse*. The name acts as a good description. The verse is "free": free from rigid rhyme and rhythm schemes. It is difficult to use this type of verse, however, and not have it sound like prose. Good free verse still retains a strong rhythm, though the pattern is not as regular as that of ordinary verse. As you read "Four Preludes on Playthings of the Wind," try to be aware of the rhythms generated by Sandburg's handling of free verse.

1

The woman named Tomorrow
sits with a hairpin in her teeth
and takes her time
and does her hair the way she wants it
and fastens at last the last braid and coil   5
and puts the hairpin where it belongs
and turns and drawls: "Well, what of it?
My grandmother, Yesterday, is gone.
What of it? Let the dead be dead."

2

The doors were cedar   10
and the panels strips of gold
and the girls were golden girls
and the panels read and the girls chanted:
    We are the greatest city,
    the greatest nation: 15
    nothing like us ever was.

The doors are twisted on broken hinges.
Sheets of rain swish through on the wind
    where the golden girls ran and the panels read:
    We are the greatest city,   20
    the greatest nation,
    nothing like us ever was.

"Four Preludes on Playthings of the Wind" from *Smoke and Steel* by Carl Sandburg, copyright, 1920, by Harcourt, Brace & World, Inc.; renewed by Carl Sandburg. Reprinted by permission of Harcourt, Brace & World, Inc.

It has happened before.
Strong men put up a city and got a
    nation together,   25
And paid singers to sing and women
    to warble: We are the greatest city,
        the greatest nation,
        nothing like us ever was.

And while the singers sang   30
and the strong men listened
and paid the singers well,
and felt good about it all,
    there were rats and lizards who listened
    . . . and the only listeners left now   35
    . . . are . . . the rats . . . and the lizards.

And there are black crows
crying, "Caw, caw,"
bringing mud and sticks
building a nest   40
    over the words carved
    on the doors where the panels were cedar
    and the strips on the panels were gold
    and the golden girls came singing:
        We are the greatest city,   45
        the greatest nation:
        nothing like us ever was.

The only singers now are crows crying, "Caw, caw,"
And the sheets of rain whine in the wind and doorways.
And the only listeners now are . . . the rats . . . and the lizards.   50

The feet of the rats
scribble on the doorsills;
the hieroglyphs° of the rat footprints
chatter the pedigrees of the rats
and the babble of the blood   55
and gabble of the breed
of the grandfathers and the great-grandfathers
of the rats.

---

53. **hieroglyphs** (hī′ĕr·ô·glĭfs′): characters in ancient picture-writing; used in a general sense to mean any sign or symbol.

And the wind shifts
and the dust on a doorsill shifts 60
and even the writing of the rat footprints
tells us nothing, nothing at all
about the greatest city, the greatest nation
where the strong men listened
and the women warbled: Nothing like us ever was. 65

Spring and Fall: To a Young Child

GERARD MANLEY HOPKINS

Here a young child seems to weep over the falling leaves of autumn, but
her grief may have a deeper cause, a cause that all men share. In this
poem Hopkins uses a technique called "sprung rhythm." It involves a
shifting of accents to gain greater flexibility and variety in the verse. The
shifted accents will sometimes fall on syllables that are ordinarily unac-
cented, and in such cases you will find that Hopkins helps you by placing
a mark over the syllable to be accented.

Márgarét, are you gríeving
Over Goldengrove unleaving?°
Leáves, líke the things of man, you
With your fresh thoughts care for, can you?
Ah! ás the heart grows older 5
It will come to such sights colder
By and by, nor spare a sigh
Though worlds of wanwood leafmeal° lie;
And yet you wíll weep and know way.°
Now no matter, child, the name: 10
Sórrow's spríngs° áre the same.
Nor mouth had, no nor mind, expressed
What heart heard of, ghost° guessed:
It ís the blight man was born for,
It is Margaret you mourn for. 15

2. Hopkins often uses unusual words or word-combinations, **Goldengrove unleaving** refers to a grove in autumn whose golden leaves are beginning to fall. 8. **wanwood leafmeal:**
two combined forms: **wanwood** means "dark wood" or "bare wood"; **leafmeal** means "leaf by
leaf." 9. The accent in this line gives a clue to the meaning *Will* is used here in the sense
of "insist on" and the meaning is approximately, "and yet you will insist on weeping and being told why you weep." 11. **springs:** sources. 13. **ghost:** soul (archaic).

"Spring and Fall: To a Young Child" from *Poems of Gerard Manley Hopkins* published by Oxford University
Press, Inc. and used with their permission.

Hi-Yo, Hi-Yo, Discernible Today

A Song After Reading Toynbee

MAXWELL ANDERSON

Arnold J. Toynbee is a British historian who has written *A Study of History* in six volumes. Mr. Toynbee is concerned with the way nations continually decay and slide downhill, but not everyone who reads Mr. Toynbee agrees with him. One such dissenter is Maxwell Anderson. As you will see in the following poem, Mr. Anderson does not feel that the decline of civilization is just around the corner.

Has it come to your attention how the race of man
Has been climbing upward since time began,
How it's been climbing steady, and it's climbing there still,
But every time you notice it, it's going down hill?

Chorus

Going down hill is the natural way, 5
For the old folks work and the young folks play,
And the pioneer morals universally decay —
Yet a definite improvement is discernible today!
Hi-yo, hi-yo, discernible today!

Now there's been a quite demonstrable and healthy gain 10
In higher mathematics and the size of the brain,
Between us and the oyster there were great strides made —
But every time you look at us, we're slipping down grade.

Chorus

Going down hill is the natural trend,
For the old folks gather and the young folks spend, 15
Yet line up all our forebears on the path that we descend
And a definite improvement is apparent at this end!
Hi-yo, hi-yo, apparent at this end!

A monument from the past — the Parthenon, built in Athens in the fifth century B.C.

The Egyptians, the Assyrians, the Greeks and Romans, too,
Hung up some fancy records when their world was new,   20
And some they hung so high the boys are shooting at them still —
But they saw themselves continually going down hill.

Chorus

Going down hill is the way things run,
For the old have illusions and the young have fun,
And our manners and religions everlastingly decay,   25
Yet astonishing improvement is discernible today!
Hi-yo, hi-yo, discernible today!

THE MIND OF THE POET

1. The poet changes his mind during the poem "A Tuft of Flowers." What is the change? What causes it? What reason does Frost give for the action of the first worker?

2. What attitude does Sandburg express in "Four Preludes on Playthings of the Wind"? Would you call this a pessimistic poem? Why, or why not?

"Four Preludes on Playthings of the Wind" is written in free verse, a form that is free in its use of both rhyme and rhythm. Free verse, however, is not prose.

Can you point out some of the things that make free verse different from prose? What does free verse have in common with the other poems you have studied?

3. According to Gerard Manley Hopkins, why does Margaret really weep? Is it possible to feel sorrow without knowing the cause? What does Hopkins say about the real cause of all sorrow?

4. Would you say that "Hi-Yo, Hi-Yo, Discernible Today" is pessimistic about man's future? The poem is written "after reading Toynbee." Which point of view — Toynbee's or Anderson's — seems more common today?

RELATING FORM AND MEANING

You have noted how rhythm helped Maxwell Anderson communicate his jaunty impudence toward Toynbee's six volumes of history. You have responded to the sound of ghosts, a Jabberwocky, and spring thunder. You have noticed how visual patterns on the page have been planned by some poets, and you have studied the language of poetry — its images, symbols, and figures of speech. Now here is a question for you. Can you relate all of the methods poets use to the meaning of their poems?

Merely to identify a symbol or to define a quatrain is the most pitiful waste of your time. Unless you relate such matters of form to the meaning of the poems, you have missed the path to the appreciation of poetry. What is worse, you may even have learned to dislike poetry. Before you close this section of the book, turn back to one poem which "reached" you. Read it again, first just for the feeling of pleasure it gives you. Then read it a second time, alert to everything the poet has done to grip your imagination and compel you to share his vision.

About the Poets

Carl Sandburg (1878–   ) often writes in the colorful language found on streets, in factories, and on the farms. Born of Swedish immigrants, he tried working at many jobs in many places — as a farm hand, railroad laborer, and mill worker — and found little time for formal schooling. After serving in the Spanish-American War, he entered Lombard College, Illinois, where he published a book of poems he printed himself. He won national notice when, in 1916, he published *Chicago Poems,* which includes the now famous "Skyscraper" and "Fog." He is a singer of folk songs and a collector of America's old ballads, as well as a biographer of Abraham Lincoln and a novelist. His *Complete Poems* won the 1950 Pulitzer prize for poetry.

Gerard Manley Hopkins (1844–1889) was born in England and educated at Oxford University. At Oxford he was converted to Catholicism, and after leaving the university he entered the priesthood. He had been writing poetry since he was fifteen, but he destroyed all his work when he became a priest, feeling that poetry would conflict with the life he had chosen. Later, however, he asked and was granted permission to resume writing, and he completed his longest poem, "The Wreck of the Deutschland," about 1875. From that time on his output grew steadily, but with a few exceptions, Hopkins refused to publish any of his work. While at Oxford, Hopkins had met Robert Bridges, who later became poet laureate of England. The two kept up an extensive correspondence for much of Hopkins' life, and in the letters, Bridges was sent most of Hopkins' poems as well as some brilliant criticism of other poets. Bridges finally published the poetry in 1919, thirty years after Hopkins' death. When his work appeared Hopkins was immediately recognized as one of the most distinctive and original poets in the English language. He has had great influence on the poetry of this century.

Maxwell Anderson's (1888–   ) play *Winterset,* written in verse, won the first annual New York Drama Critics award in 1934. Anderson is a foremost American playwright, turning out a great amount of work. You have probably heard of his plays *What Price Glory?* and *Knickerbocker Holiday.* After graduating from the University of North Dakota, he was a high school principal for two years before he went on to earn his graduate degrees and to teach English at Stanford University and Whittier College in California. He did some journalistic work on the West Coast and later edited and wrote for the New York papers. In 1928 he stopped his journalistic career to devote full time to playwriting. Anderson's works have helped to keep the tradition of serious drama alive in the contemporary theater.

Robert Frost's biography appears on page 394.

Three Poets and Their Worlds

There is another important thing to be said about the poet and his work. A poet does not exist and write in a vacuum. He exists in time and space. He lives in a certain place, and in a certain era; and he is influenced by his surroundings, by the society he knows, and by his daily activities. For example, Robert Frost has spent most of his life in New England, and his poetry quite naturally is filled with the events and objects of that environment. A poet is first of all an individual, with his own interests, feelings, and ideas; but a poet is also a man who has lived and worked like everyone else. Often his imagination is captured by the people, the region, and the activities around him; and we find his poetry reflecting, to some extent, the physical world in which he lives.

The poems that follow were written by three poets whose worlds are greatly different. John Masefield's outer world is that of the English countryside; it is a world in which he is free to express his love for the sea and for his fellow human beings. Phyllis McGinley's world is geographically limited — the outwardly quite commonplace world of the modern American housewife. The world of Kahlil Gibran, born in Lebanon and a resident of the United States for twenty-one years, is quite different; it is a world in which the mysticism and simplicity of the East play an important part. As you read the work of these three poets, try to be aware of the particular world that each writer expresses.

John Masefield

In his early years, John Masefield's world was the world of the traveler — specifically, the world of the sailor. His poems are filled with images of the sea, of ships, of the adventure and romance of sailing. The title of his first successful book was *Salt Water Ballads,* and all of his best work has continued to reveal his interest in the sea.

Born in England in 1878, Masefield attended school for a few years, but after his father's death, he was sent to a training ship in preparation for a career in the British Merchant Service. He did well in his studies, and at fifteen he was apprenticed aboard a sailing vessel. Masefield rounded Cape Horn in this windjammer, and later was appointed sixth officer on a passenger liner. He went to New York to join his new ship, but when he arrived he decided to abandon his sailing career. Masefield stayed in New York for three years, supporting himself with odd jobs, and reading extensively in the English classics. Toward the end of his stay in this country, he began writing poems and essays, and in 1897 he returned to London determined to be a professional writer.

In the years preceding World War I, Masefield established his reputation as an original and striking poet of the sea. His early work was characterized by vigorous language and realistic, sometimes brutal, subject matter. Some of his most popular poems are imaginative retellings of old, traditional sea-tales.

John Masefield is not only a poet, but a novelist, playwright, critic, and military and naval historian. His volume of work has been tremendous in almost all phases of writing. He has received a number of honorary degrees and high awards from his own nation, and was granted the highest honor an English poet can receive when he was appointed poet laureate in 1930. In recent years, John Masefield has lived quietly in a region of England near Oxford University. He is described as gentle, courteous, understanding, and sensitive to criticism.

Many of John Masefield's best poems reflect the world of the mysterious, dangerous, restless sea. In the following poems we will enter this world briefly.

Biography

John Masefield introduces himself and his world in this excerpt from "Biography." Notice that the things he considers important about his life have little to do with dates.

When I am buried, all my thoughts and acts
Will be reduced to lists of dates and facts,
And long before this wandering flesh is rotten
The dates which made me will be all forgotten;
And none will know the gleam there used to be   5
About the feast days freshly kept by me,
But men will call the golden hour of bliss
"About this time," or "shortly after this."

Men do not heed the rungs by which men climb
Those glittering steps, those milestones upon Time,   10
Those tombstones of dead selves, those hours of birth,
Those moments of the soul in years of earth
They mark the height achieved, the main result
The power of freedom in the perished cult,
The power of boredom in the dead man's deeds,   15
Not the bright moments of the sprinkled seeds.

By many waters and on many ways
I have known golden instants and bright days;
The day on which, beneath an arching sail,
I saw the Cordilleras° and gave hail;   20
The summer day on which in heart's delight
I saw the Swansea Mumbles° bursting white,
The glittering day when all the waves wore flags
And the ship *Wanderer* came with sails in rags;
That curlew°-calling time in Irish dusk   25
When life became more splendid than its husk,

When the rent chapel on the brae° at Slains
Shone with a doorway opening beyond brains;
The dawn when, with a brace-block's° creaking cry,
Out of the mist a little barque° slipped by,   30
Spilling the mist with changing gleams of red,
Then gone, with one raised hand and one turned head;
The howling evening when the spindrift's° mists
Broke to display the four Evangelists,°
Snow-capped, divinely granite, lashed by breakers,   35
Wind-beaten bones of long since buried acres;
The night alone near water when I heard
All the sea's spirit spoken by a bird;
The English dusk when I beheld once more
(With eyes so changed) the ship, the citied shore,   40
The lines of masts, the streets so cheerly trod
(In happier seasons) and gave thanks to God.
All had their beauty, their bright moments' gift,
Their something caught from Time, the ever-swift.

All of those gleams were golden; but life's hands   45
Have given more constant gifts in changing lands,
And when I count those gifts, I think them such
As no man's bounty could have bettered much:
The gift of country life, near hills and woods
Where happy waters sing in solitudes,   50
The gift of being near ships, of seeing each day
A city of ships with great ships under weigh,°
The great street paved with water, filled with shipping,
And all the world's flags flying and seagulls dipping.

---

20. **Cordilleras** (kôr′thē·yä′räs): the Andes Mountains in South America. 22. **Mumbles:** a district of the town of Swansea (swŏn′zē) in Wales. 25. **curlew** (kŭr′lōō): a large, long-legged bird. 27. **brae** (brā): a sloping bank. 29. **brace-block:** a pulley used in rigging sails. 30. **barque** (bark): a three-masted sailing vessel. 33. **spindrift:** sea spray. 34. **the four Evangelists:** rock formations at the Pacific end of the Straits of Magellan. 52. **weigh:** nautical for "way."

Yet when I am dust my penman° may not know   55
Those water-trampling ships which made me glow,
But think my wonder mad and fail to find
Their glory, even dimly, from my mind,
And yet they made me . . .

Best trust the happy moments. What they gave   60
Makes man less fearful of the certain grave,
And gives his work compassion and new eyes.
The days that make us happy make us wise.

55. penman: biographer.

The Yarn of the Loch Achray

The sea, while fascinating, is also something to fear, because its moods
can change so quickly. Men tell tales like these and then go to sea again.
Have you ever wondered why?

The *Loch Achray* was a clipper tall
With seven-and-twenty hands in all.
Twenty to hand and reef and haul,
A skipper to sail and mates to bawl
"Tally on to the tackle-fall,   5
Heave now 'n' start her, heave 'n' pawl!"°
     Hear the yarn of a sailor,
     An old yarn learned at sea.

Her crew were shipped and they said "Farewell,
So-long, my Tottie, my lovely gell;   10
We sail to-day if we fetch to hell,
It's time we tackled the wheel a spell."
     Hear the yarn of a sailor,
     An old yarn learned at sea.

The dockside loafers talked on the quay°   15
The day that she towed down to sea:
"Lord, what a handsome ship she be!
Cheer her, sonny boys, three times three!"
And the dockside loafers gave her a shout
As the red-funnelled tug-boat towed her out;   20

6. heave 'n' pawl: pull and make fast the tackle. 15. quay (kē): wharf.

They gave her a cheer as the custom is,
And the crew yelled "Take our loves to Liz —
Three cheers, bullies, for old Pier Head
'N' the bloody stay-at-homes!" they said.
      Hear the yarn of a sailor,   25
      An old yarn learned at sea.

In the grey of the coming on of night
She dropped the tug at the Tuskar Light,
'N' the topsails went to the topmast head
To a chorus that fairly awoke the dead.   30
She trimmed her yards° and slanted South
With her royals° set and a bone in her mouth.°
      Hear the yarn of a sailor,
      An old yarn learned at sea.

She crossed the Line° and all went well,   35
They ate, they slept, and they struck the bell
And I give you a gospel truth when I state
The crowd didn't find any fault with the Mate,
But one night off the River Plate.°
      Hear the yarn of a sailor,   40
      An old yarn learned at sea.

It freshened up till it blew like thunder
And burrowed her deep lee-scuppers° under.
The old man said, "I mean to hang on
Till her canvas busts or her sticks are gone" —   45
Which the blushing looney did, till at last
Overboard went her mizzen-mast.°
      Hear the yarn of a sailor,
      An old yarn learned at sea.

Then a fierce squall struck the *Loch Achray*   50
And bowed her down to her water-way;
Her main-shrouds° gave and her forestay,°
And a green sea carried her wheel away;
Ere the watch below had time to dress
She was cluttered up in a blushing mess.   55
      Hear the yarn of a sailor,
      An old yarn learned at sea.

---

31. **yards:** a long spar used to support a square sail. 32. **royals:** small sails near the top of
the mast; **a bone in her mouth:** the line refers to the appearance of the foam at the prow of a
fast-moving ship. 35. **Line:** the Equator. 39. **River Plate:** a large river between Uruguay and
Argentina. 43. **lee-scuppers:** the *lee* side of a ship is the side facing away from the wind, the
protected side. *Scuppers* are openings in a ship's side that allow water to run off the deck.
47. **mizzen-mast:** the mast closest to the stern of the ship. 52. **main-shrouds:** ropes supporting
the mainmast; **forestay:** a large rope which supports the foremast.

"Northeaster," a painting by Winslow Homer.

She couldn't lay-to° nor yet pay-off,°
And she got swept clean in the bloody trough;
Her masts were gone, and afore you knowed   60
She filled by the head and down she goed.
Her crew made seven-and-twenty dishes
For the big jack-sharks and the little fishes,
And over their bones the water swishes.
    Hear the yarn of a sailor,   65
    An old yarn learned at sea.

The wives and girls they watch in the rain
For a ship as won't come home again.
"I reckon it's them head-winds," they say,
"She'll be home to-morrow, if not to-day.   70
I'll just nip home 'n' I'll air the sheets
'N' buy the fixins 'n' cook the meats
As my man likes 'n' as my man eats."

So home they goes by the windy streets,
Thinking their men are homeward bound   75
With anchors hungry for English ground,
And the bloody fun of it is, they're drowned!
    Hear the yarn of a sailor,
    An old yarn learned at sea.

58. **lay-to**: turn toward the wind; **pay-off**: turn away from the wind.

Roadways

In John Masefield's poetry, it is difficult to stay long from the sea. Even roadways lead him there, and in the following poem he takes us with him.

One road leads to London,
  One road runs to Wales,
My road leads me seawards
  To the white dipping sails.

One road leads to the river,   5
  As it goes singing slow;
My road leads to shipping,
  Where the bronzed sailors go.

Leads me, lures me, calls me
  To salt green tossing sea;   10
A road without earth's road-dust
  Is the right road for me.

A wet road heaving, shining,
  And wild with seagulls' cries,
A mad salt sea-wind blowing   15
  The salt spray in my eyes.

My road calls me, lures me
  West, east, south, and north;
Most roads lead men homewards,
  My road leads me forth   20

To add more miles to the tally
  Of grey miles left behind,
In quest of that one beauty
  God put me here to find.

Being Her Friend

Though Masefield often sought and found beauty on the sea, it would be wrong to think of him as responding only to the sea. In this poem he reveals his sensitivity to people — his deep appreciation of the "beauty" of another human being.

Being her friend, I do not care, not I,
  How gods or men may wrong me, beat me down;
Her word's sufficient star to travel by,
  I count her quiet praise sufficient crown.

Being her friend, I do not covet gold,   5
  Save for a royal gift to give her pleasure;
To sit with her, and have her hand to hold,
  Is wealth, I think, surpassing minted treasure.

Being her friend, I only covet art,
  A white pure flame to search me as I trace   10
In crooked letters from a throbbing heart
  The hymn to beauty written on her face.

A Wanderer's Song

This poem is Masefield's answer to the question of why men keep returning to face the dangers of the sea. Do you sometimes feel this yearning
for adventure and romance?

A wind's in the heart of me, a fire's in my heels,
I am tired of brick and stone and rumbling wagon-wheels;
I hunger for the sea's edge, the limits of the land.
Where the wild old Atlantic is shouting on the sand.

Oh I'll be going, leaving the noises of the street,   5
To where a lifting foresail-foot is yanking at the sheet;°
To a windy, tossing anchorage where yawls° and ketches° ride,
Oh I'll be going, going, until I meet the tide.

And first I'll hear the sea-wind, the mewing of the gulls,
The clucking, sucking of the sea about the rusty hulls,   10
The songs at the capstan° in the hooker° warping out,
And then the heart of me'll know I'm there or thereabout.

Oh I am tired of brick and stone, the heart of me is sick,
For windy green, unquiet sea, the realm of Moby Dick;°
And I'll be going, going, from the roaring of the wheels,   15
For a wind's in the heart of me, a fire's in my heels.

6. **sheet:** a rope or chain attached to the foot of a sail. 7. **yawls** (yôlz): small, two-masted
ships; **ketches** (kĕch'ĕz): ships similar to yawls. 11. **capstan:** an upright cylinder on which a
rope is wound and used to lift heavy weights; **hooker:** slang for an old ship. 14. **Moby Dick:**
the huge, white whale in Herman Melville's novel of the same name.

THE WORLD OF JOHN MASEFIELD

1. According to "Biography," what are
the important things in Masefield's life?
Why are they important?
2. What is the story of "The Yarn of
the Loch Achray"? The tale itself is about
a tragic accident, yet the poem ends with
a remark about "the bloody fun of it." Why
does it end this way? Much traditional sea
lore is contained in ballads like this. They
are known as "sea chanteys." You might
be interested in looking up some more of
these chanteys and comparing them to
Masefield's poem.

3. Why do you think Masefield is so
concerned with wandering? What does the
last stanza of "Roadways" tell you about
Masefield's search? What new dimension
does the poem, "Being Her Friend," add
to your understanding of this search?
4. How did Masefield's particular background affect his poetry? The poet spent
only a short time as a sailor, yet his poetry
is constantly concerned with the sea. How
would you explain this fact?
5. The sea is often used as a symbol in
literature. What examples of this can you
find in Masefield's poetry? What does the
sea symbolize in these examples?

Phyllis McGinley

Phyllis McGinley was born in 1905. Today she is married, has two daughters, and lives in a suburb of New York City. Her major occupation is being a housewife. To many, this may seem a life of dull routine, a small, insignificant world quite unlike the wide, romantic world of John Masefield. But through the perceptive eyes of this poet, the small things of life assume large proportions. Through her heart pours a warmth for the daily routine, and from her we learn that nothing is merely routine. She shares with us her knowledge of the importance of what to some may seem insignificant. If she does not express a yearning for great adventure, it is because her own small world turns out to be remarkably large and meaningful. A poet's world is never small, no matter how limited it may seem.

Though she is best known as a writer of light verse, Phyllis McGinley's poetry contains elements of truth that make it command serious attention. One of the many tributes paid to the art of this housewife-poet was the award of the Pulitzer prize for poetry in 1961. Now let Phyllis McGinley share her world and her art with you.

A Garland of Precepts

In the following poem, Phyllis McGinley recalls some of the many different "truths" and bits of advice she's heard. Her final piece of advice is one that seems to fit all occasions.

Though a seeker since my birth,
Here is all I've learned on earth,
This the gist° of what I know:
Give advice and buy a foe.
Random truths are all I find   5
Stuck like burs about my mind.
Salve a blister. Burn a letter.
Do not wash a cashmere sweater.
Tell a tale but seldom twice.
Give a stone before advice.   10

Pressed for rules and verities,°
All I recollect are these:
Feed a cold to starve a fever.
Argue with no true believer.
Think-too-long is never-act.   15
Scratch a myth and find a fact.
Stitch in time saves twenty stitches.
Give the rich, to please them, riches.
Give to love your hearth and hall.
But do not give advice at all.   20

3. **gist** (jĭst): the main point. 11. **verities** (vĕr′ĭ·tĭz): truths.

"A Garland of Precepts" from *The Love Letters of Phyllis McGinley* by Phyllis McGinley. Copyright 1954 by Phyllis McGinley. Originally printed in the *New Yorker*. Reprinted by permission of The Viking Press, Inc.

The News

Watching television can be informative, entertaining, and relaxing. But you will probably agree with Phyllis McGinley that there are times when one wonders . . .

Now that the crisp or thunderous word
Has been made flesh upon the screen,
The day's events a little blurred
Come to my ear. Ah, could it mean
Newscasters should be only heard,
Not seen?

Saturday Storm

A storm can bring the opportunity to do things inside that you've been meaning to do for weeks. It can also give you a chance to be lazy if you are inside and warm and dry. But what of those who must be out, even during a Saturday storm?

This flooded morning is no time to be
Abroad on any business of mankind.
The rain has lost its casual charity;
It falls and falls and falls and would not mind
Were all the world washed blind.   5

No creature out of doors goes weatherproof.
Birds cower in their nests. The beast that can
Has found himself a roof.
This hour's for man
To waken late in, putter by his fire,   10
Leaf through old books or tear old letters up,
Mend household things with bits of thrifty wire,
Refill his coffee cup,
And, thus enclosed in comfort like a shell,
Give thought to, wish them well   15
Who must this day
On customary errands take their way:

The glistening policemen in the street,
For instance, blowing their whistles through the welter
And stamping their wet feet;   20
And grocery boys flung in and out of shelter
But faithful to their loads;
And people changing tires beside the roads;
Doormen with colds and doctors in damp suits;
And milkmen on their routes,   25
Scuttling like squirrels; and men with cleated boots
Aloft on telephone poles in the rough gale;
But chiefly trudging men with sacks of mail
Slung over shoulder,
Who slog from door to door and cannot rest   30
Till they've delivered the last government folder,
The final scribbled postcard, misaddressed.

Oh, all at ease
Should say a prayer for these —
That they come, healthy, homeward before night,   35
Safer than beasts or birds,
To no dark welcome but an earned delight
Of pleasant words,
Known walls, accustomed love, fires burning steady,
And a good dinner ready.   40

A GIRL'S–EYE VIEW OF RELATIVES

In the following poems Phyllis McGinley writes about relatives from a young girl's point of view. As you read, watch to see whether you recognize members of your own family in her clever verse portraits. Also, see whether you share her feelings about particular relatives.

First Lesson

The thing to remember about fathers is, they're men.
A girl has to keep it in mind.
They are dragon-seekers, bent on improbable rescues.
Scratch any father, you find
Someone chock-full of qualms and romantic terrors,   5
Believing change is a threat —
Like your first shoes with heels on, like your first bicycle
It took such months to get.

Walk in strange woods, he warns you about the snakes there.
Climb, and he fears you'll fall.   10
Books, angular boys, or swimming in deep water —
Fathers mistrust them all.
Men are the worriers. It is difficult for them
To learn what they must learn:
How you have a journey to take, and very likely,   15
For a while, will not return.

Triolet * Against Sisters

Sisters are always drying their hair,
Locked into rooms, alone.
They pose at the mirror, shoulders bare,
Trying this way and that their hair,
Or fly importunate down the stair
  To answer a telephone.
Sisters are always drying their hair,
  Locked into rooms, alone.

Turn of the Screw

Girl cousins condescend. They wear
Earrings, and dress like fashion's sam-
  ple,
Have speaking eyes and curly hair,
And parents point to their example.

But the boy cousins one's allotted
Are years too young for one. And spotted.

* **Triolet** (trī'ō-lĕt): a stanza of eight lines, with lines 1, 3, 4, 5, and 7 having one rhyme, and lines 2, 6, and 8 having another. Usually lines 4 and 7 repeat the first line in its entirety, and line 8 repeats line 2.

432   POETRY

In Defense of Brothers

Big brothers mock you
   About your braces.
Little ones shock you,
   Have dirty faces,
And fill their closets with snips and
     snails   5
And what are possibly
   Puppy-dog tails.

Their shoes are undone.
   Their exploits bore you.
But small brothers run   10
   On errands for you,
While others bring home with them,
     now and then,
Shambling, beautiful,
   Gruff young men.

The Adversary

A mother's hardest to forgive.
Life is the fruit she longs to hand you,
Ripe on a plate. And while you live,
Relentlessly she understands you.

In Praise of Aunts

Of all that tribe the young must do
Familial obedience to,
Whom we salute on anniversaries,
Whose names we learn while new in nurseries
Or borrow at baptismal fonts,   5
The soothingest are aunts.

Aunts are discreet, a little shy
By instinct. They forbear to pry
Into recesses of the spirit
Where apprehensions lie.   10
Yet, given a tale to hear, they *hear it*

"In Defense of Brothers," "The Adversary" and "In Praise of Aunts" from *Times Three* by Phyllis McGinley.
Copyright © 1959 by Phyllis McGinley. Originally printed in the *New Yorker*. Reprinted by permission of The
Viking Press, Inc.

Aunts spinster pamper us with praise,
And seats for worldly matinées
With coffee, after. Married aunts,
Attentive to material wants,   15
Run rather to the shared comestible,°
Taboo or indigestible;
Are lenient but cool;
And let us, if we must, play fool.

Aunts carry no duty in their faces.   20
Their letters, mailed from far-off places,
Are merely letters meant to read
(Answerable at a moderate speed),
Not cries of need
Or vessels heavy with their hopes.   25
Aunts also send,
Tucked into casual envelopes,
Money entirely ours to spend.

At night they do not lie awake
Shuddering for our sorrow's sake.   30
Beneath our flesh we seldom wear
Their skeletons, nor need we stare
Into a looking glass and see
Their images begin to be.
Aunts care, but only mildly care,   35
About our winter moods,
Postures, or social attitudes,
And whether we've made a friend or dropped one.
All should have aunts, or else adopt one.

16. **comestible** (kŏ·měs′tĭ·b'l): food.

THE WORLD OF PHYLLIS McGINLEY

1. How true are the "truths" which Phyllis McGinley lists in the poem "A Garland of Precepts"?

2. Television offers many opportunities for the critic and the satirist. What other things besides the news might Phyllis McGinley have criticized in "The News"? What would you point out if you were going to criticize television programs?

3. Why should Phyllis McGinley be any more concerned for those who are out in a Saturday storm than for those out in a storm on some other day of the week?

4. In what particular ways do the portraits of relatives seem accurate to you? Point to specific examples. Point out some lines that indicate that the poems are written from the viewpoint of a teen-age girl. Are there any relatives in whom the poet fails to find some good?

COMPOSITION SUGGESTION

Perhaps you would like to write some light verse of your own. You might begin by following Phyllis McGinley's example and depicting some of the people you know. Or, you might try expressing in verse your impressions of movies, parties, sports events, and various school activities.

Kahlil Gibran

Kahlil Gibran (kă·lēl' jŏob·rän'), a Syrian-American poet and artist, was born in Lebanon in 1883. His family was well-to-do and highly cultured, and as a boy Gibran showed unusual talent in drawing and modeling. He received his early education in Lebanon, then studied art and sculpture in Paris In 1910 he came to the United States, where he remained until his death in 1931.

Gibran's early works were written in Arabic, and gained wide circulation and great popularity within the Arabic world. A new term, *Gibranism*, was coined to describe his unusual ideas and methods of writing, and Gibranism spread quickly throughout a large portion of the Eastern world. As his poetry was translated into more than twenty different languages, his fame and influence spread throughout the Western world. Later he adopted the English language for many of his writings.

Gibran's writings are often spoken of as mystical. Although he spent much of his life in America, Gibran retained the eyes, the mind, and the heart of a man of another culture. His works speak to us out of the wisdom and simplicity of the mystical East. He contradicts our mad pace and impatience, but we understand very clearly what he has to say. In his writings, he attempts to express some workable way of thinking, feeling, and acting that will lead to a purposeful life.

Most of Gibran's writings were in the form of "prose poems." Prose poems abandon conventional poetic rhythms but retain the vivid language and elevated thought found in much poetry. As you read these prose poems you will find that they create a special rhythm of their own through the repetition of certain key words, and the use of parallel clauses and sentences.

Gibran's most popular book is a collection of prose poems called *The Prophet*. In this book, a prophet bids farewell to the people of his adopted country as he prepares to return to his native land. He speaks to the people on the nature of life, expressing his ideas on such things as love, work, and friendship. Undoubtedly the prophet's poetic statements are expressions of Gibran's own philosophy of life. The following selections from *The Prophet* will give you a glimpse of the view of life Gibran found in his own special world. Perhaps some of the ideas have meaning for all of us — in whatever world we find ourselves.

On Work

In this poem, Kahlil Gibran expresses his ideas about work. His belief
that love is an essential part of any man's work causes us to re-examine
our own attitude toward what we do.

Then a ploughman said, Speak to us of Work.
And he answered, saying:
You work that you may keep pace with the earth and the soul of the earth.
For to be idle is to become a stranger unto the seasons, and to step out of life's
procession, that marches in majesty and proud submission towards the infinite.

When you work you are a flute through whose heart the whispering of the
hours turns to music.   5
Which of you would be a reed, dumb and silent, when all else sings together
in unison?

Always you have been told that work is a curse and labor a misfortune.
But I say to you that when you work you fulfil a part of earth's furthest dream,
assigned to you when that dream was born,
And in keeping yourself with labor you are in truth loving life,
And to love life through labor is to be intimate with life's inmost secret.   10

But if you in your pain call birth an affliction and the support of the flesh a
curse written upon your brow, then I answer that naught but the sweat of your
brow shall wash away that which is written.

You have been told also that life is darkness, and in your weariness you echo
what was said by the weary.
And I say that life is indeed darkness save when there is urge,
And all urge is blind save when there is knowledge,
And all knowledge is vain save when there is work,   15
And all work is empty save when there is love;
And when you work with love you bind yourself to yourself, and to one another,
and to God.

And what is it to work with love?
It is to weave the cloth with threads drawn from your heart, even as if your
beloved were to wear that cloth.
It is to build a house with affection, even as if your beloved were to dwell in
that house.   20
It is to sow seeds with tenderness and reap the harvest with joy, even as if your
beloved were to eat the fruit.
It is to charge all things you fashion with a breath of your own spirit,
And to know that all the blessed dead are standing about you and watching.

"On Work." Reprinted from *The Prophet* by Kahlil Gibran, by permission of Alfred A. Knopf, Inc., copyright
1951 by Administrators of C. T. A. of Kahlil Gibran Estate, and Mary G. Gibran.

Often have I heard you say, as if speaking in sleep, "He who works in marble, and finds the shape of his own soul in the stone, is nobler than he who ploughs the soil.

And he who seizes the rainbow to lay it on a cloth in the likeness of man, is more than he who makes the sandals for our feet."   25

But I say, not in sleep but in the overwakefulness of noontide, that the wind speaks not more sweetly to the giant oaks than to the least of all the blades of grass;

And he alone is great who turns the voice of the wind into a song made sweeter by his own loving.

Work is love made visible.

And if you cannot work with love but only with distaste, it is better that you should leave your work and sit at the gate of the temple and take alms of those who work with joy.

For if you bake bread with indifference, you bake a bitter bread that feeds but half man's hunger.   30

And if you grudge the crushing of the grapes, your grudge distils a poison in the wine.

And if you sing though as angels, and love not the singing, you muffle man's ears to the voices of the day and the voices of the night.

On Friendship

Friendship is a word used loosely to include relationships which range from casual acquaintance to complete sharing. Here Gibran gives new meaning to the word.

And a youth said, Speak to us of Friendship.
And he answered, saying:
Your friend is your needs answered.
He is your field which you sow with love and reap with thanksgiving.
And he is your board and your fireside.   5
For you come to him with your hunger, and you seek him for peace.

When your friend speaks his mind you fear not the "nay" in your own mind, nor do you withhold the "ay."
And when he is silent your heart ceases not to listen to his heart;
For without words, in friendship, all thoughts, all desires, all expectations are born and shared, with joy that is unacclaimed.
When you part from your friend, you grieve not;   10
For that which you love most in him may be clearer in his absence, as the mountain to the climber is clearer from the plain.
And let there be no purpose in friendship save the deepening of the spirit.

"On Friendship." Reprinted from *The Prophet* by Kahlil Gibran, by permission of Alfred A. Knopf, Inc., copyright 1951 by Administrators C. T. A. of Kahlil Gibran Estate, and Mary G. Gibran.

For love that seeks aught but the disclosure of its own mystery is not love but a net cast forth: and only the unprofitable is caught.

And let your best be for your friend.
If he must know the ebb of your tide, let him know its flood also.   15
For what is your friend that you should seek him with hours to kill?
Seek him always with hours to live.
For it is his to fill your need, but not your emptiness.
And in the sweetness of friendship let there be laughter, and sharing of pleasures.
For in the dew of little things the heart finds its morning and is refreshed.   20

On Joy and Sorrow

If you look for comfort in your sorrow, you may find it in philosophy. Gibran expresses a philosophy that gives each experience significance when it is placed in proper perspective.

Then a woman said, Speak to us of Joy and Sorrow.
And he answered:
Your joy is your sorrow unmasked.
And the selfsame well from which your laughter rises was oftentimes filled with your tears.
And how else can it be?   5
The deeper that sorrow carves into your being, the more joy you can contain.
Is not the cup that holds your wine the very cup that was burned in the potter's oven?
And is not the lute° that soothes your spirit, the very wood that was hollowed with knives?
When you are joyous, look deep into your heart and you shall find it is only that which has given you sorrow that is giving you joy.
When you are sorrowful look again in your heart, and you shall see that in truth you are weeping for that which has been your delight.   10

Some of you say, "Joy is greater than sorrow," and others say, "Nay, sorrow is the greater."
But I say unto you, they are inseparable.
Together they come, and when one sits lone with you at your board, remember that the other is asleep upon your bed.

Verily you are suspended like scales between your sorrow and your joy.
Only when you are empty are you at standstill and balanced.   15
When the treasure-keeper lifts you to weigh his gold and his silver, needs must your joy or your sorrow rise or fall.

8. **lute** (lo͞ot): a stringed instrument similar to a guitar.

THE WORLD OF KAHLIL GIBRAN

1. "On Work" is often quoted. What do you think Gibran means in this poem? What do you think the poet means by "Work is love made visible"?

2. What are some of the things Gibran believes are essential to a true friendship?

3. According to Gibran, you can know joy only in the degree you have known sorrow. Do you agree with this idea?

4. What do these poems tell you about Gibran's beliefs and ideas? Do you think many people would be willing to follow the way of life expressed here? Why, or why not? Does what the poet says seem impractical in our world? Explain.

5. Can you point out some of the similarities between Gibran's prose poems and the other poems you have read? What distinguishes prose poetry from ordinary prose? Do these prose poems have any kind of rhythm at all? If they do, how is the rhythm achieved?

6. What are the most striking features of Kahlil Gibran's world? How does Gibran's world differ from John Masefield's or Phyllis McGinley's? Can you point out any similarities among these three worlds?

COMPOSITION SUGGESTION

In flowing lines like Gibran's, try to express some of your own deeply held beliefs about life and how to live it. Let thought guide the rhythm, but be sure to keep the rhythm smooth. Hold to a solemn, elevated tone.

THE POET BEHIND THE POEM

As a reader, your first concern should always be with the particular piece of literature you are reading. What does it say? How does it say it? What is its effect? But it is difficult to ignore the fact that any piece of literature is written by a specific person. When a writer writes, he is attempting to communicate with you, to converse with you. In all conversations something of the speakers themselves enters into the talk, and the same thing is true of the poet's conversation with you. Even if he is not writing about himself directly — if he writes, for example, dramatic poetry — the incidents he selects and the characters he creates tell you a great deal about him.

Part of reading poetry, then, is allowing the poet to converse with you. Through his poetry, discover how the poet thinks and feels, what he has to say and the way he says it. Get to know him better. Engage him in further conversations by reading more of his work. You might find that you have made a friend for life.

Suggestions for Further Reading

As with all other reading, you will find in poetry that some authors appeal to your taste more than others. If a poem in this book particularly took your fancy or excited your interest, look for other poems by its author. Check your school or public library for titles of books under the poet's name, or look in the index of authors in a large anthology of poetry to find which of his poems are included there. (A list of general anthologies is given below.) Here are some poets and poems which high school students have especially enjoyed.

Benét, Stephen Vincent, *John Brown's Body* (Holt, Rinehart & Winston, 1928)
The story, in verse, of the War Between the States and its great men and women.

Burns, Robert: "Tam O'Shanter," "To a Louse," "To a Mouse," "Sweet Afton"
The poetry of Burns is a treasure-trove of melodious verse — tender love lyrics, humorous verse, narratives — written in a softly musical Scottish dialect.

Byron, Lord, George Gordon: "The Prisoner of Chillon," "The Destruction of Sennacherib," "She Walks in Beauty"
Lord Byron was a dashing, romantic hero in real life, and his poetry is a reflection of his vivid, colorful personality.

Cummings, E. E., *Poems: 1923–1954* (Harcourt, Brace & World, 1954)
Behind the unexpected appearance of these poems, readers with an energetic mentality and curiosity will find witty comment and satire.

Dickinson, Emily, *The Poems of Emily Dickinson* (Little, Brown, 1930)
The insight into life that characterizes

Emily Dickinson's poetry is often like a flash of lightning or the sun breaking through clouds on a dark day. Intense personal experiences are expressed in a manner that stirs the imagination. Emerson called poetry "the enormous force of a few words," and Emily Dickinson's poems illustrate his definition.

Frost, Robert, *Complete Poems of Robert Frost* (Holt, Rinehart & Winston, 1949)

Frost's poems, written in the everyday speech of his native New England, reveal a deeply sympathetic attitude toward people and their problems.

Masefield, John, *Collected Poems* (Macmillan, 1953)

This collection includes Masefield's *Salt Water Ballads* as well as most of the longer famous poems.

McGinley, Phyllis, *The Love Letters of Phyllis McGinley* (Viking, 1954) and *Times Three: Selected Verses from Three Decades* (Viking, 1960)

Two collections of Phyllis McGinley's humorous poems about urban and suburban life.

Millay, Edna St. Vincent, *Collected Poems* (Harper, 1956)

All of Miss Millay's poems except those of her childhood are collected in this definitive edition.

Nash, Ogden, *Versus* (Little, Brown, 1949)

Humorous comments on taxes, marriage, and other aspects of modern living.

Sandburg, Carl, *Smoke and Steel* (Harcourt, Brace & World, 1920); *The People Yes* (Harcourt, Brace & World, 1936)

Themes for many of Sandburg's poems are the harsh life of American industrial cities, the unexpected beauty in the everyday world, and the common people.

Teasdale, Sara, *Collected Poems* (Macmillan, 1937)

Sara Teasdale's poems are brief but always memorable for their exceptional musical beauty and haunting sadness.

Wilbur, Richard, *Advice to a Prophet and Other Poems* (Harcourt, Brace & World, 1961)

A collection of poems by a distinguished contemporary American poet.

General Anthologies

Auslander, Joseph, and Frank Ernest Hill, eds., *The Winged Horse Anthology* (Doubleday, 1929)

A selection of outstanding poems from the time of the Greeks through the first part of the twentieth century.

Creekmore, Hubert, ed., *A Little Treasury of World Poetry* (Scribner, 1952)

Translations of the great poetry in other languages, covering the years from 2600 B.C. to A.D. 1950.

Untermeyer, Louis, ed., *Doorways to Poetry* (Harcourt, Brace & World, 1938)

This is a fine introduction to poetry if you are just beginning to like it.

Untermeyer, Louis, ed., *The New Modern American and British Poetry* (Harcourt, Brace & World, 1950)

A good way to become acquainted with the whole field of modern poetry is to leaf through this anthology.

Williams, Oscar, ed., *A Little Treasury of Modern Poetry* (Scribner, 1952)

A collection of many of the best English and American modern poems.

Williams, Oscar, ed., *A Little Treasury of British Poetry* (Scribner, 1951)

An anthology of more than 700 poems written by England's chief poets from 1500 to 1950.

For Listening

The following poems have been recorded and are available on *Many Voices* 4A: "Birches;" "Boy at the Window;" "Danny Deever;" "The Duke of Plaza-Toro;" "The Eve of Waterloo;" "Four Preludes on Playthings of the Wind;" "Hi-Yo, Hi-Yo, Discernible Today;" "I Am Raftery;" "in Just–;" "Jabberwocky;" "Lee;" "Old Christmas Morning;" "The Purist;" "Requiem;" "The Rhinoceros;" "Spring Thunder;" "Thirteen O'Clock;" "To a Snowflake;" and "What Is So Rare as a Day in June?"

Available on *Many Voices* 10A are: "Ars Poetica;" "The Erl-King;" "The Harp;" "The Laboratory;" "La Belle Dame sans Merci;" "O, My Luve's like a Red, Red Rose;" "On Friendship;" "Saturday Storm;" "The Soul;" "Spring and Fall: To a Young Child;" "Two Modern Haiku;" and "A Wanderer's Song."

Drama

Drama is one of the oldest types of literature, dating back to the days of ancient Greece when plays were performed in amphitheaters before large, enthusiastic audiences. Those ancient Greek plays are still being performed today, before audiences that are equally enthusiastic. Drama — good drama — is timeless; it is also immensely rewarding and entertaining.

Plays, of course, are written to be performed; the playwright's words are meant to be spoken by actors before an audience. It is necessary, therefore, to approach the reading of a play in a special way. You, as the reader, must take yourself out of your armchair and imagine that you are a member of the audience. As you read a play, your imagination must supply all the elements that would be present in a stage performance. You must try to hear the dialogue. You must visualize the settings and also try to visualize the actors' movements, attitudes, appearances, and facial expressions.

Here are two plays which should provide exciting reading experiences for you. Both plays are biographical — they use actual persons for their subjects — but otherwise they are very different. *The Miracle Worker* was written by William Gibson, a modern American playwright. Its language is the prose of the twentieth century. The other play, *Julius Caesar,* was written more than three hundred years ago by the master English dramatist, William Shakespeare. The characters in *Julius Caesar* belong to history, and they speak the soaring, poetic language for which Shakespeare is famous. Other differences between the two plays will become apparent to you as you read the texts. But you will find that the two selections have this quality in common: they both tell exciting stories in vivid, theatrical terms. They are two plays capable of holding an audience spellbound.

You are now invited to become a reading member of that audience.

◀ Detail from "View of Toledo" by El Greco (1548?–?1614). El Greco lived most of his life in Spain and was a dominant figure in the art world of sixteenth-century western Europe. Notice the dramatic, brooding mood of this world-famous painting.

The Miracle Worker

WILLIAM GIBSON

Words are usually taken for granted. We forget that they are a primary means of understanding and communicating with other human beings, that they put us in touch with the world. Suppose, though, that words had no meaning for you, that you did not know how to refer to the things around you. If you were blind and deaf and could not speak, how could you learn anything? How could you express yourself? What key could unlock your mind?

In 1887, a young woman named Annie Sullivan went to Alabama to try to help a family whose seven-year-old daughter had been blind and deaf since infancy. The daughter's name was Helen Keller. When Annie Sullivan entered her life, the child was like a caged and frantic young animal. Everyone was close to giving up all hope of ever helping the pathetic youngster. Annie Sullivan, however, achieved what no one believed possible. She brought words into Helen Keller's dark world and thereby started her on the path to becoming one of the most brilliant and accomplished women of the twentieth century.

How did Annie Sullivan accomplish this miracle? Her story is one of the greatest true stories of our time. It is the story that William Gibson has dramatized in *The Miracle Worker.*

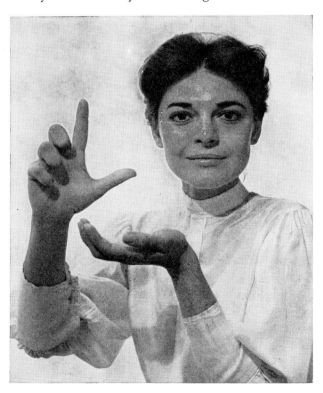

Anne Bancroft as Annie Sullivan. This picture and the others with the play are from the Broadway production of The Miracle Worker.

Characters

A DOCTOR	PERCY	VINEY
KATE	AUNT EV	BLIND GIRLS
ARTHUR KELLER	JAMES	A SERVANT
HELEN	ANAGNOS	OFFSTAGE VOICES
MARTHA	ANNIE SULLIVAN	

The stage is divided into two areas by a more or less diagonal line, which runs from downstage right to upstage left.

The area behind this diagonal is on platforms and represents the Keller house; inside we see a family room, and upstairs a bedroom. On stage level near center, outside a porch, there is a water pump.

The other area, in front of the diagonal, is neutral ground; it accommodates various places as designated at various times — the yard before the Keller home, the Perkins Institution for the Blind, the garden house, and so forth.

[See page 466 of this book for illustrations of the set used in the Broadway production of The Miracle Worker.]

TIME. The 1880's.

PLACE. In and around the Keller homestead in Tuscumbia, Alabama; also, briefly, the Perkins Institute for the Blind, in Boston.

ACT I

SCENE 1

It is night over the Keller homestead. Inside, three adults in the bedroom are grouped around a crib, in lamplight. They have been through a long vigil, and it shows in their tired bearing and disarranged clothing. One is a young gentlewoman with a sweet girlish face, KATE KELLER; the second is an elderly DOCTOR, stethoscope at neck, thermometer in fingers; the third is a hearty gentleman in his forties with chin whiskers, CAPTAIN ARTHUR KELLER.

DOCTOR. She'll live.

KATE. Thank God.

[The DOCTOR leaves them together over the crib, packs his bag.]

DOCTOR. You're a pair of lucky parents. I can tell you now, I thought she wouldn't.

KELLER. Nonsense, the child's a Keller, she has the constitution of a goat. She'll outlive us all.

DOCTOR (amiably). Yes, especially if some of you Kellers don't get a night's sleep. I mean you, Mrs. Keller.

KELLER. You hear, Katie?

KATE. I hear.

KELLER (indulgent). I've brought up

Visualizing the Setting and Action. A person who reads a play has to do more work than someone who sees the play being acted on a stage. The reader must try to visualize the setting and the action, for these are essential parts of a drama. Remember that much of the meaning of a play is shown by action instead of dialogue. In this play, be sure to read the author's careful descriptions of setting and action, and notice how smoothly one scene changes into the next. As you read, try to visualize where the characters are on the stage and what they are doing.

---

two of them, but this is my wife's first, she isn't battle-scarred yet.

KATE. Doctor, don't be merely considerate, will my girl be all right?

DOCTOR. Oh, by morning she'll be knocking down Captain Keller's fences again.

KATE. And isn't there anything we should do?

KELLER (*jovial*). Put up stronger fencing, ha?

DOCTOR. Just let her get well, she knows how to do it better than we do. (*He is packed, ready to leave.*) Main thing is the fever's gone, these things come and go in infants, never know why. Call it acute congestion of the stomach and brain.

KELLER. I'll see you to your buggy, Doctor.

DOCTOR. I've never seen a baby with more vitality, that's the truth.

[*He beams a good night at the baby and* KATE, *and* KELLER *leads him downstairs with a lamp. They go down the porch steps, and across the yard, where the* DOCTOR *goes off left;* KELLER *stands with the lamp aloft.* KATE *meanwhile is bent lovingly over the crib, which omits a bleat; her finger is playful with the baby's face.*]

KATE. Hush. Don't you cry now, you've been trouble enough. Call it acute congestion, indeed, I don't see what's so cute about a congestion, just because it's yours? We'll have your father run an editorial in his paper — the wonders of modern medicine — they don't know what they're curing even when they cure it. Men, men and their battle scars, we women will have to — (*But she breaks off, puzzled, moves her finger before the baby's eyes.*) Will have to — Helen? (*Now she moves her hand, quickly.*) Helen. (*She snaps her fingers at the baby's eyes twice, and her*

hand falters; after a moment she calls out, loudly.*) Captain. Captain, will you come — (*But she stares at the baby, and her next call is directly at her ears.*) Captain!

[*And now, still staring,* KATE *screams.* KELLER *in the yard hears it, and runs with the lamp back to the house.* KATE *screams again, her look intent on the baby and terrible.* KELLER *hurries in and up.*]

KELLER. Katie? What's wrong?

KATE. Look.

[*She makes a pass with her hand in the crib, at the baby's eyes.*]

KELLER. What, Katie? She's well, she needs only time to —

KATE. She can't see. Look at her eyes. (*She takes the lamp from him, moves it before the child's face.*) She can't *see!*

KELLER (*hoarsely*). Helen.

KATE. Or hear. When I screamed she didn't blink. Not an eyelash —

KELLER. Helen. Helen!

KATE. She can't *hear* you!

KELLER. *Helen!*

[*His face has something like fury in it, crying the child's name;* KATE *almost fainting presses her knuckles to her mouth, to stop her own cry.*]

[*The room dims out quickly.*]

SCENE 2

The Keller yard and house.

Time, in the form of a slow tune of distant belfry chimes which approaches in a crescendo and then fades, passes; the light comes up again on a day five years later, on three kneeling children and an old dog outside around the pump.

The dog is a setter named BELLE, *and she is sleeping. Two of the children are*

Negroes, MARTHA *and* PERCY. *The third child is* HELEN, *six and a half years old, quite unkempt, in body a vivacious little person with a fine head, attractive, but noticeably blind, one eye larger and protruding; her gestures are abrupt, insistent, lacking in human restraint, and her face never smiles. She is flanked by the other two, in a litter of paper-doll cutouts, and while they speak* HELEN's *hands thrust at their faces in turn, feeling baffledly at the movements of their lips.*

MARTHA (*snipping*). First I'm gonna cut off this doctor's legs, one, two, now then —

PERCY. Why you cuttin' off that doctor's legs?

MARTHA. I'm gonna give him a operation. Now I'm gonna cut off his arms, one, two. Now I'm gonna fix up — (*She pushes* HELEN's *hand away from her mouth.*) You stop that.

PERCY. Cut off his stomach, that's a good operation.

MARTHA. No, I'm gonna cut off his head first. He got a bad cold.

PERCY. Ain't gonna be much of that doctor left to fix up, time you finish all them opera —

[*But* HELEN *is poking her fingers inside his mouth, to feel his tongue; he bites at them, annoyed, and she jerks them away.* HELEN *now fingers her own lips, moving them in imitation, but soundlessly.*]

MARTHA. What you do, bite her hand?

PERCY. That's how I do, she keep pokin' her fingers in my mouth, I just bite 'em off.

MARTHA. What she tryin' do now?

PERCY. She tryin' *talk.* She gonna get mad. Looka her tryin' talk.

[HELEN *is scowling, the lips under her fingertips moving in ghostly silence,*

growing more and more frantic, until in a bizarre rage she bites at her own fingers. This sends PERCY *off into laughter, but alarms* MARTHA.]

MARTHA. Hey, you stop now. (*She pulls* HELEN's *hand down.*) You just sit quiet and —

[*But at once* HELEN *topples* MARTHA *on her back, knees pinning her shoulders down, and grabs the scissors.* MARTHA *screams.* PERCY *darts to the bell string on the porch, yanks it, and the bell rings.*

Inside, the lights have been gradually coming up on the main room, where we see the family informally gathered, talking, but in pantomime: KATE *sits darning socks near a cradle, occasionally rocking it;* CAPTAIN KELLER *in spectacles is working over newspaper pages at a table; a benign visitor in a hat,* AUNT EV, *is sharing the sewing basket, putting the finishing touches on a big shapeless doll made out of towels; an indolent [1] young man,* JAMES KELLER, *is at the window watching the children.*

With the ring of the bell, KATE *is instantly on her feet and out the door onto the porch, to take in the scene; now we see what these five years have done to her, the girlish playfulness is gone, she is a woman steeled in grief.*]

KATE (*for the thousandth time*). Helen. (*She is down the steps at once to them, seizing* HELEN's *wrists and lifting her off* MARTHA; MARTHA *runs off in tears and screams for momma, with* PERCY *after her.*) Let me have those scissors.

[*Meanwhile the family inside is alerted,* AUNT EV *joining* JAMES *at the window;* CAPTAIN KELLER *resumes work.*]

[1] indolent (ĭn′dō·lĕnt): lazy.

JAMES (*blandly*). She only dug Martha's eyes out. Almost dug. It's always almost, no point worrying till it happens, is there?

[*They gaze out, while* KATE *reaches for the scissors in* HELEN'S *hand. But* HELEN *pulls the scissors back, they struggle for them a moment, then* KATE *gives up, lets* HELEN *keep them. She tries to draw* HELEN *into the house.* HELEN *jerks away.* KATE *next goes down on her knees, takes* HELEN'S *hands gently, and using the scissors like a doll, makes* HELEN *caress and cradle them; she points* HELEN'S *finger housewards.* HELEN'S *whole body now becomes eager; she surrenders the scissors,* KATE *turns her toward the door and gives her a little push.* HELEN *scrambles up and toward the house, and* KATE *rising follows her.*]

AUNT EV. How does she stand it? Why haven't you seen this Baltimore man? It's not a thing you can let go on and on, like the weather.

JAMES. The weather here doesn't ask permission of me, Aunt Ev. Speak to my father.

AUNT EV. Arthur. Something ought to be done for that child.

KELLER. A refreshing suggestion. What?

[KATE *entering turns* HELEN *to* AUNT EV, *who gives her the towel doll.*]

AUNT EV. Why, this very famous oculist in Baltimore I wrote you about, what was his name?

KATE. Dr. Chisholm.

AUNT EV. Yes, I heard lots of cases of blindness people thought couldn't be cured he's cured. He just does wonders. Why don't you write to him?

KELLER. I've stopped believing in wonders.

KATE (*rocks the cradle*). I think the Captain will write to him soon. Won't you, Captain?

KELLER. No.

JAMES (*lightly*). Good money after bad, or bad after good. Or bad after bad —

AUNT EV. Well, if it's just a question of money, Arthur, now you're marshal you have this Yankee money. Might as well —

KELLER. Not money. The child's been to specialists all over Alabama and Tennessee, if I thought it would do good I'd have her to every fool doctor in the country.

KATE. I think the Captain will write to him soon.

KELLER. Katie. How many times can you let them break your heart?

KATE. Any number of times.

[HELEN *meanwhile sits on the floor to explore the doll with her fingers, and her hand pauses over the face: There is no face, only a blank area of towel, and it troubles her. Her hand searches for features, and taps questioningly for eyes, but no one notices. She then yanks at her* AUNT'S *dress, and taps again vigorously for eyes.*]

AUNT EV. What, child?

[*Obviously not hearing,* HELEN *commences to go around, from person to person, tapping for eyes, but no one attends or understands.*]

KATE (*no break*). As long as there's the least chance. For her to see. Or hear, or —

KELLER. There isn't. Now I must finish here.

KATE. I think, with your permission, Captain, I'd like to write.

KELLER. I said no, Katie.

AUNT EV. Why, writing does no harm, Arthur, only a little bitty letter. To see if he can help her.

KELLER. He can't.

KATE. We won't know that to be a fact, Captain, until after you write.

KELLER (*rising, emphatic*). Katie, he can't.

[*He collects his papers.*]

JAMES (*facetiously*). Father stands up, that makes it a fact.

KELLER. You be quiet! I'm badgered enough here by females without your impudence. (JAMES *shuts up, makes himself scarce.* HELEN *now is groping among things on* KELLER's *desk, and paws his papers to the floor.* KELLER *is exasperated.*) Katie. (KATE *quickly turns* HELEN *away, and retrieves the papers.*) I might as well try to work in a henyard as in this house —

JAMES (*placating*). You really ought to put her away, Father.

KATE (*starting up*). What?

JAMES. Some asylum. It's the kindest thing.

AUNT EV. Why, she's your sister, James, not a nobody —

JAMES. Half sister, and half — mentally defective, she can't even keep herself clean. It's not pleasant to see her about all the time.

KATE. Do you dare? Complain of what you *can* see?

KELLER (*very annoyed*). This discussion is at an end! I'll thank you not to broach it again, Ev. (*Silence descends at once.* HELEN *gropes her way with the doll, and* KELLER *turns back for a final word, explosive.*) I've done as much as I can bear, I can't give my whole life to it! The house is at sixes and sevens from morning till night over the child. It's time some attention was paid to Mildred here instead!

KATE (*gently dry*). You'll wake her up, Captain.

KELLER. I want some peace in the house, I don't care how, but one way we won't have it is by rushing up and down the country every time someone hears of a new quack. I'm as sensible to this affliction as anyone else. It hurts me to look at the girl.

KATE. It was not our affliction I meant you to write about, Captain.

[HELEN *is back at* AUNT EV, *fingering her dress, and yanks two buttons from it.*]

AUNT EV. Helen! My buttons.

[HELEN *pushes the buttons into the doll's face.* KATE *now sees, comes swiftly to kneel, lifts* HELEN's *hand to her own eyes in question.*]

KATE. Eyes? (HELEN *nods energetically.*) She wants the doll to have eyes.

[*Another kind of silence now, while* KATE *takes pins and buttons from the sewing basket and attaches them to the doll as eyes.* KELLER *stands, caught, and watches morosely.* AUNT EV *blinks, and conceals her emotion by inspecting her dress.*]

AUNT EV. My goodness me, I'm not decent.

KATE. She doesn't know better, Aunt Ev. I'll sew them on again.

JAMES. Never learn with everyone letting her do anything she takes it into her mind to —

KELLER. You be quiet!

JAMES. What did I say now?

KELLER. You talk too much.

JAMES. I was agreeing with you!

KELLER. Whatever it was. Deprived child, the least she can have are the little things she wants.

[JAMES, *very wounded, stalks out of the room onto the porch; he remains here, sulking.*]

AUNT EV (*indulgently*). It's worth a couple of buttons, Kate. Look. (HELEN *now has the doll with eyes, and cannot contain herself for joy; she rocks the doll, pats it vigorously, kisses it.*) This child has more sense than all these men Kellers, if there's ever any way to reach that mind of hers.

[*But* HELEN *suddenly has come upon the cradle, and unhesitatingly overturns it; the swaddled baby tumbles out, and* CAPTAIN KELLER *barely manages to dive and catch it in time.*]

KELLER. *Helen!*

[*All are in commotion, the baby screams, but* HELEN *unperturbed is laying her doll in its place.* KATE *on her knees pulls her hands off the cradle, wringing them;* HELEN *is bewildered.*]

KATE. Helen, Helen, you're not to do such things, how can I make you understand —

KELLER (*hoarsely*). Katie.

KATE. How can I get it into your head, my darling, my poor —

KELLER. Katie, some way of teaching her an iota of discipline has to be —

KATE (*flaring*). How can you discipline an afflicted child? Is it her fault?

[HELEN's *fingers have fluttered to her* MOTHER's *lips, vainly trying to comprehend their movements.*]

KELLER. I didn't say it was her fault.

KATE. Then whose? I don't know what to do! How can I teach her? Beat her — until she's black and blue?

KELLER. It's not safe to let her run around loose. Now there must be a way of confining her, somehow, so she can't —

KATE. Where, in a cage? She's a growing child, she has to use her limbs!

KELLER. Answer me one thing, is it fair to Mildred here?

KATE (*inexorably*). Are you willing to put her away?

[*Now* HELEN's *face darkens in the same rage as at herself earlier, and her hand strikes at* KATE's *lips.* KATE *catches her hand again, and* HELEN *begins to kick, struggle, twist.*]

KELLER. Now what?

KATE. She wants to talk, like — be like you and me. (*She holds* HELEN *struggling until we hear from the child her first sound so far, an inarticulate weird noise in her throat such as an animal in a trap might make; and* KATE *releases her. The second she is free* HELEN *blunders away, collides violently with a chair, falls, and sits weeping.* KATE *comes to her, embraces, caresses, soothes her, and buries her own face in her hair, until she can control her voice.*) Every day she slips further away. And I don't know how to call her back.

AUNT EV. Oh, I've a mind to take her up to Baltimore myself. If that doctor can't help her, maybe he'll know who can.

KELLER (*presently, heavily*). I'll write the man, Katie.

[*He stands with the baby in his clasp, staring at* HELEN's *head, hanging down on* KATE's *arm.*

The lights dim out, except the one on KATE *and* HELEN. *In the twilight,* JAMES, AUNT EV, *and* KELLER *move off slowly, formally, in separate directions;* KATE *with* HELEN *in her arms remains, motionless, in an image which overlaps into the next scene and fades only when it is well under way.*]

SCENE 3

Boston. The Perkins Institution for the Blind.

Without pause, from the dark down left we hear a man's voice with a Greek accent speaking.

ANAGNOS. — who could do nothing for the girl, of course. It was Dr. Bell who thought she might somehow be taught. I have written the family only that a suitable governess, Miss Annie Sullivan, has been found here in Boston —

[*The lights begin to come up, down left, on a long table and chair. The table contains equipment for teaching the blind by touch — a small replica of the human skeleton, stuffed animals, models of flowers and plants, piles of books. The chair contains a girl of 20,* ANNIE SULLIVAN, *with a face which in repose is grave and rather obstinate, and when active is impudent, combative, twinkling with all the life that is lacking in* HELEN'S, *and handsome; there is a crude vitality to her. Her suitcase is at her knee.* ANAGNOS, *a stocky bearded man, comes into the light only towards the end of his speech.*]

ANAGNOS. — and will come. It will no doubt be difficult for you there, Annie. But it has been difficult for you at our school too, hm? Gratifying, yes, when you came to us and could not spell your name, to accomplish so much here in a few years — but always an Irish battle. For independence. (*He studies* ANNIE, *humorously; she does not open her eyes.*) This is my last time to counsel you, Annie, and you do lack some — by some I mean *all* — what? — tact or talent to bend. To others. And what has saved you on more than one occasion here at Perkins is that there was nowhere to expel you to. Your eyes hurt?

ANNIE. My ears, Mr. Anagnos.

[*And now she has opened her eyes; they are inflamed, vague, slightly crossed, clouded by the granular growth of trachoma, and she often*

keeps them closed to shut out the pain of light.]

ANAGNOS (*severely*). Nowhere but back to Tewksbury, where children learn to be saucy. Annie, I know how dreadful it was there, but that battle is dead and done with. Why not let it stay buried?

ANNIE (*cheerily*). I think God must owe me a resurrection.

ANAGNOS (*a bit shocked*). What?

ANNIE (*taps her brow*). Well, He keeps digging up that battle!

ANAGNOS. That is not a proper thing to say, Annie. It is what I mean.

ANNIE (*meekly*). Yes. But I know what I'm like, what's this child like?

ANAGNOS. Like?

ANNIE. Well — bright or dull, to start off.

ANAGNOS. No one knows. And if she is dull, you have no patience with this?

ANNIE. Oh, in grownups you have to, Mr. Anagnos. I mean in children it just seems a little — precocious,[1] can I use that word?

ANAGNOS. Only if you can spell it.

ANNIE. Premature. So I hope at least she's a bright one.

ANAGNOS. Deaf, blind, mute — who knows? She is like a little safe, locked, that no one can open. Perhaps there is a treasure inside.

ANNIE. Maybe it's empty, too?

ANAGNOS. Possible. I should warn you, she is much given to tantrums.

ANNIE. Means something is inside. Well, so am I, if I believe all I hear. Maybe you should warn *them*.

ANAGNOS (*frowns*). Annie. I wrote them no word of your history. You will find yourself among strangers now, who know nothing of it.

ANNIE. Well, we'll keep them in a

---

[1] **precocious** (prê·kō'shŭs): unusually early in development.

state of blessed ignorance.

ANAGNOS. Perhaps *you* should tell it?

ANNIE (*bristling*). Why? I have enough trouble with people who don't know.

ANAGNOS. So they will understand. When you have trouble.

ANNIE. The only time I have trouble is when I'm right. (*But she is amused at herself, as is* ANAGNOS.) Is it my fault it's so often? I won't give them trouble, Mr. Anagnos. I'll be so ladylike they won't notice I've come.

ANAGNOS. Annie, be — humble. It is not as if you have so many offers to pick and choose. You will need their affection, working with this child.

ANNIE (*humorously*). I hope I won't need their pity.

ANAGNOS. Oh, we can all use some pity. (*Crisply.*) So. You are no longer our pupil, we throw you into the world, a teacher. If the child can be taught. No one expects you to work miracles, even for twenty-five dollars a month. Now, in this envelope a loan, for the railroad, which you will repay me when you have a bank account. But in this box, a gift. With our love. (ANNIE *opens the small box he extends, and sees a garnet ring. She looks up, blinking, and down.*) I think other friends are ready to say good-by. (*He moves as though to open doors.*)

ANNIE. Mr. Anagnos. (*Her voice is trembling.*) Dear Mr. Anagnos, I — (*But she swallows over getting the ring on her finger, and cannot continue until she finds a woe-begone joke.*) Well, what should I say, I'm an ignorant opinionated girl, and everything I am I owe to you?

ANAGNOS (*smiles*). That is only half true, Annie.

ANNIE. Which half? I crawled in here like a drowned rat. I thought I died when Jimmie died, that I'd never again

— come alive. Well, you say with love so easy, and I haven't *loved* a soul since and I never will, I suppose, but this place gave me more than my eyes back. Or taught me how to spell, which I'll never learn anyway, but with all the fights and the trouble I've been here it taught me what help is, and how to live again, and I don't want to say good-by. Don't open the door, I'm crying.

ANAGNOS (*gently*). They will not see.

[*He moves again as though opening doors, and in comes a group of girls, 8-year-olds to 17-year-olds; as they walk we see they are blind.* ANAGNOS *shepherds them in with a hand.*]

A CHILD. Annie?

ANNIE (*her voice cheerful*). Here, Beatrice.

[*As soon as they locate her voice they throng joyfully to her, speaking all at once;* ANNIE *is down on her knees to the smallest, and the following are the more intelligible fragments in the general hubbub.*]

CHILDREN. There's a present. We brought you a going-away present, Annie!

ANNIE. Oh, now you shouldn't have —

CHILDREN. We did, we did, where's the present?

SMALLEST CHILD (*mournfully*). Don't go, Annie, away.

CHILDREN. Alice has it. Alice! Where's Alice? Here I am! Where? Here!

[*An arm is aloft out of the group, waving a present;* ANNIE *reaches for it.*]

ANNIE. I have it. I have it, everybody, should I open it?

CHILDREN. Open it! Everyone be quiet! Do, Annie! She's opening it. Ssh! (*A settling of silence while* ANNIE *unwraps it. The present is a pair of smoked*

glasses, and she stands still.) Is it open, Annie?

ANNIE. It's open.

CHILDREN. It's for your eyes, Annie. Put them on, Annie! 'Cause Mrs. Hopkins said your eyes hurt since the operation. And she said you're going where the sun is *fierce.*

ANNIE. I'm putting them on now.

SMALLEST CHILD (*mournfully*). Don't go, Annie, where the sun is fierce.

CHILDREN. Do they fit all right?

ANNIE. Oh, they fit just fine.

CHILDREN. Did you put them on? Are they pretty, Annie?

ANNIE. Oh, my eyes feel hundreds of per cent better already, and pretty — why, do you know how I look in them? Splendiloquent. Like a race horse!

CHILDREN (*delighted*). There's another present! Beatrice! We have a present for Helen, too! Give it to her, Beatrice. Here, Annie! (*This present is an elegant doll, with movable eyelids and a momma sound.*) It's for Helen.

And we took up a collection to buy it. And Laura dressed it.

ANNIE. It's beautiful!

CHILDREN. So don't forget, you be sure to give it to Helen from us, Annie!

ANNIE. I promise it will be the first thing I give her. If I don't keep it for myself, that is. You know I can't be trusted with dolls!

SMALLEST CHILD (*mournfully*). Don't go, Annie, to her.

ANNIE (*her arm around her*). Sarah, dear. I don't *want* to go.

SMALLEST CHILD. Then why are you going?

ANNIE (*gently*). Because I'm a big girl now, and big girls have to earn a living. It's the only way I can. But if you don't smile for me first, what I'll just have to do is — (*She pauses, inviting it.*)

SMALLEST CHILD. What?

ANNIE. Put *you* in my suitcase, instead of this doll. And take *you* to Helen in Alabama!

[*This strikes the children as very funny, and they begin to laugh and tease the smallest child, who after a moment does smile for* ANNIE.]

ANAGNOS (*then*). Come, children. We must get the trunk into the carriage and Annie into her train, or no one will go to Alabama. Come, come.

[*He shepherds them out and* ANNIE *is left alone on her knees with the doll in her lap. She reaches for her suitcase, and by a subtle change in the color of the light, we go with her thoughts into another time. We hear a boy's voice whispering; perhaps we see shadowy intimations of these speakers in the background.*]

BOY'S VOICE.[1] Where we goin', Annie?
ANNIE (*in dread*). Jimmie.
BOY'S VOICE. Where we goin'?
ANNIE. I said — I'm takin' care of you —
BOY'S VOICE. Forever and ever?
MAN'S VOICE (*impersonal*). Annie Sullivan, aged nine, virtually blind. James Sullivan, aged seven — What's the matter with your leg, Sonny?
ANNIE. Forever and ever.
MAN'S VOICE. Can't he walk without that crutch? (ANNIE *shakes her head, and doesn't stop shaking it.*) Girl goes to the women's ward. Boy to the men's.
BOY'S VOICE (*in terror*). Annie! Annie, don't let them take me — Annie!
ANAGNOS (*offstage*). Annie! Annie?

[*But this voice is real, in the present, and* ANNIE *comes up out of her horror, clearing her head with a final shake; the lights begin to pick out*

---

[1] Here, as will happen again in the play, Annie is remembering experiences from her childhood. In each instance, the audience knows what she is thinking, for it can hear the voices of the people who were involved in these experiences.

KATE *in the* KELLER *house, as* ANNIE *in a bright tone calls back.*]

ANNIE. Coming!

[*This word catches* KATE, *who stands half-turned and attentive to it, almost as though hearing it. Meanwhile* ANNIE *turns and hurries out, lugging the suitcase.*]

SCENE 4

The Keller home.
The room dims out; the sound of railroad wheels begins from off left, and maintains itself in a constant rhythm underneath the following scene; the remaining lights have come up on the KELLER *homestead.* JAMES *is lounging on the porch, waiting. In the upper bedroom which is to be* ANNIE'S, HELEN *is alone, puzzledly exploring, fingering and smelling things, the curtains, empty drawers in the bureau, water in the pitcher by the washbasin, fresh towels on the bedstead. Downstairs in the family room* KATE *turning to a mirror hastily adjusts her bonnet, watched by a Negro servant in an apron,* VINEY.

VINEY. Let Mr. Jimmy go by hisself. You been pokin' that garden all day. You ought to rest your feet.
KATE. I can't wait to see her, Viney.
VINEY. Maybe she ain't gone be on this train neither.
KATE. Maybe she is.
VINEY. And maybe she ain't.
KATE. And maybe she is. Where's Helen?
VINEY. She upstairs, smellin' around. She know somethin' funny goin' on.
KATE. Let her have her supper as soon as Mildred's in bed, and tell Captain Keller when he comes that we'll be delayed tonight.

VINEY. Again.

KATE. I don't think we need say *again*. Simply delayed will do.

[*She runs upstairs to* ANNIE's *room,* VINEY *speaking after her.*]

VINEY. I mean that's what he gone say. "What, again?"

[VINEY *works at setting the table. Upstairs* KATE *stands in the doorway, watching* HELEN's *groping explorations.*]

KATE. Yes, we're expecting someone. Someone for my Helen. (HELEN *happens upon her skirt, clutches her leg;* KATE *in a tired dismay kneels to tidy her hair and soiled pinafore.*) Oh, dear, this was clean not an hour ago. (HELEN *feels her bonnet, shakes her head darkly, and tugs to get it off.* KATE *retains it with one hand, diverts* HELEN *by opening her other hand under her nose.*) Here. For while I'm gone. (HELEN *sniffs, reaches, and pops something into her mouth, while* KATE *speaks a bit guiltily.*) I don't think one peppermint drop will spoil your supper. (*She gives* HELEN *a quick kiss, evades her hands, and hurries downstairs again. Meanwhile* CAPTAIN KELLER *has entered the yard from around the rear of the house, newspaper under arm, cleaning off and munching on some radishes; he sees* JAMES *lounging at the porch post.*)

KELLER. Jimmie?

JAMES (*unmoving*). Sir?

KELLER (*eyes him*). You don't look dressed for anything useful, boy.

JAMES. I'm not. It's for Miss Sullivan.

KELLER. Needn't keep holding up that porch, we have wooden posts for that. I asked you to see that those strawberry plants were moved this evening.

JAMES. I'm moving your — Mrs. Keller, instead. To the station.

KELLER (*heavily*). Mrs. Keller. Must you always speak of her as though you haven't met the lady?

[KATE *comes out on the porch, and* JAMES *inclines his head.*]

JAMES (*ironic*). Mother. (*He starts off the porch, but sidesteps* KELLER's *glare like a blow.*) I said mother!

KATE. Captain.

KELLER. Evening, my dear.

KATE. We're off to meet the train, Captain. Supper will be a trifle delayed tonight.

KELLER. What, again?

KATE (*backing out*). With your permission, Captain?

[*And they are gone.* KELLER *watches them offstage, morosely. Upstairs,* HELEN *meanwhile has groped for her mother, touched her cheek in a meaningful gesture, waited, touched her cheek, waited, then found the open door, and made her way down. Now she comes into the family room, touches her cheek again;* VINEY *regards her.*]

VINEY. What you want, honey — your momma? (HELEN *touches her cheek again.* VINEY *goes to the sideboard, gets a tea-cake, gives it into* HELEN's *hand;* HELEN *pops it into her mouth.*) Guess one little tea-cake ain't gone ruin your appetite. (*She turns* HELEN *toward the door.* HELEN *wanders out onto the porch, as* KELLER *comes up the steps. Her hands encounter him, and she touches her cheek again, waits.*)

KELLER. She's gone. (*He is awkward with her; when he puts his hand on her head, she pulls away.* KELLER *stands regarding her, heavily.*) She's gone, my son and I don't get along, you don't know I'm your father, no one likes me, and supper's delayed. (HELEN *touches* her cheek, waits. KELLER *fishes in his pocket.*) Here. I brought you some stick candy, one nibble of sweets can't do any harm. (*He gives her a large stick candy;* HELEN *falls to it.* VINEY *peers out the window.*)

VINEY (*reproachfully*). Cap'n Keller, now how'm I gone get her to eat her supper you fill her up with that trash?

KELLER (*roars*). Tend to your work!

[VINEY *beats a rapid retreat.* KELLER *thinks better of it, and tries to get the candy away from* HELEN, *but* HELEN *hangs on to it; and when* KELLER *pulls, she gives his leg a kick.* KELLER *hops about,* HELEN *takes refuge with the candy down behind the pump, and* KELLER *then irately flings his newspaper on the porch floor, stamps into the house past* VINEY *and disappears.*

SCENE 5

The railroad station.

The lights half dim on the homestead, where VINEY *and* HELEN *going about their business soon find their way off. Meanwhile, the railroad sounds off left have mounted in a crescendo to a climax typical of a depot at arrival time, the lights come up on stage left, and we see a suggestion of a station. Here* ANNIE *in her smoked glasses and disarrayed by travel is waiting with her suitcase, while* JAMES *walks to meet her. She has a battered paper-bound book, which is a Perkins report, under her arm.*

JAMES (*coolly*). Miss Sullivan?

ANNIE (*cheerily*). Here! At last, I've been on trains so many days I thought they must be backing up every time I dozed off —

JAMES. I'm James Keller.

ANNIE. James? (*The name stops her.*)

I had a brother Jimmie. Are you Helen's?

JAMES. I'm only half a brother. You're to be her governess?

ANNIE (*lightly*). Well. Try!

JAMES (*eying her*). You look like half a governess. (KATE *enters.* ANNIE *stands motionless, while* JAMES *takes her suitcase.* KATE's *gaze on her is doubtful, troubled.*) Mrs. Keller, Miss Sullivan. (KATE *takes her hand.*)

KATE (*simply*). We've met every train for two days.

[ANNIE *looks at* KATE's *face, and her good humor comes back.*]

ANNIE. I changed trains every time they stopped, the man who sold me that ticket ought to be tied to the tracks —

JAMES. You have a trunk, Miss Sullivan?

ANNIE. Yes. (*She passes* JAMES *a claim check, and he bears the suitcase out behind them.* ANNIE *holds the battered book.* KATE *is studying her face, and* ANNIE *returns the gaze; this is a mutual appraisal, southern gentlewoman and working-class Irish girl, and* ANNIE *is not quite comfortable under it.*) You didn't bring Helen, I was hoping you would.

KATE. No, she's home.

[*A pause.* ANNIE *tries to make ladylike small talk, though her energy now and then erupts; she catches herself up whenever she hears it.*]

ANNIE. You — live far from town, Mrs. Keller?

KATE. Only a mile.

ANNIE. Well. I suppose I can wait one more mile. But don't be surprised if I get out to push the horse!

KATE. Helen's waiting for you, too. There's been such a bustle in the house, she expects something — heaven knows what. (*Now she voices part of her doubt, not as such, but* ANNIE *under-*

stands it.) I expected — a desiccated [1] spinster. You're very young.

ANNIE (*resolutely*). Oh, you should have seen me when I left Boston. I got much older on this trip.

KATE. I mean, to teach anyone as difficult as Helen.

ANNIE. *I* mean to try. They can't put you in jail for trying!

KATE. Is it possible, even? To teach a deaf-blind child *half* of what an ordinary child learns — has that ever been done?

ANNIE. Half?

KATE. A tenth.

ANNIE (*reluctantly*). No. (KATE's *face loses its remaining hope, still appraising her youth.*) Dr. Howe did wonders, but — an ordinary child? No, never. But then I thought when I was going over his reports — (*She indicates the one in her hand.*) — he never treated them like ordinary children. More like — eggs everyone was afraid would break.

KATE (*a pause*). May I ask how old you are?

ANNIE. Well, I'm not in my teens, you know! I'm twenty.

KATE. All of twenty.

[ANNIE *takes the bull by the horns, valiantly.*]

ANNIE. Mrs. Keller, don't lose heart just because I'm not on my last legs. I have three big advantages over Dr. Howe that money couldn't buy for you. One is his work behind me, I've read every word he wrote about it and he wasn't exactly what you'd call a man of few words. Another is to *be* young, why, I've got energy to do anything. The third is, I've been blind. (*But it costs her something to say this.*)

KATE (*quietly*). Advantages.

ANNIE (*wry*). Well, some have the luck of the Irish, some do not.

[1] desiccated (dĕs′ĭ-kāt'd): dried-up.

[KATE *smiles; she likes her.*]

KATE. What will you try to teach her first?

ANNIE. First, last, and — in between, language.

KATE. Language.

ANNIE. Language is to the mind more than light is to the eye. Dr. Howe said that.

KATE. Language. (*She shakes her head.*) We can't get through to teach her to sit still. You *are* young, despite your years, to have such — confidence. Do you, inside? (ANNIE *studies her face; she likes her, too.*)

ANNIE. No, to tell you the truth I'm as shaky inside as a baby's rattle!

[*They smile at each other, and* KATE *pats her hand.*]

KATE. Don't be. (JAMES *returns to usher them off.*) We'll do all we can to help, and to make you feel at home. Don't think of us as strangers, Miss Annie.

ANNIE (*cheerily*). Oh, strangers aren't so strange to me. I've known them all my life!

[KATE *smiles again,* ANNIE *smiles back, and they precede* JAMES *offstage.*]

SCENE 6

The Keller home.
The lights dim on them, having simultaneously risen full on the house; VINEY *has already entered the family room, taken a water pitcher, and come out and down to the pump. She pumps real water. As she looks offstage, we hear the clop of hoofs, a carriage stopping, and voices.*

VINEY. Cap'n Keller! Cap'n Keller, they comin'! (*She goes back into the house, as* KELLER *comes out on the porch to gaze.*) She sure 'nuff came, Cap'n.

[KELLER *descends, and crosses toward the carriage; this conversation begins offstage and moves on.*]

KELLER (*very courtly*). Welcome to Ivy Green, Miss Sullivan. I take it you are Miss Sullivan —

KATE. My husband, Miss Annie, Captain Keller.

ANNIE (*her best behavior*). Captain, how do you do.

KELLER. A pleasure to see you, at last. I trust you had an agreeable journey?

ANNIE. Oh, I had several! When did this country get so big?

JAMES. Where would you like the trunk, father?

KELLER. Where Miss Sullivan can get at it, I imagine.

ANNIE. Yes, please. Where's Helen?

KELLER. In the hall, Jimmie —

KATE. We've put you in the upstairs corner room, Miss Annie, if there's any breeze at all this summer, you'll feel it —

[*In the house the setter* BELLE *flees into the family room, pursued by* HELEN *with groping hands; the dog doubles back out the same door, and* HELEN *still groping for her makes her way out to the porch; she is messy, her hair tumbled, her pinafore now ripped, her shoelaces untied.* KELLER *acquires the suitcase, and* ANNIE *gets her hands on it too, though still endeavoring to live up to the general air of propertied manners.*]

KELLER. *And* the suitcase —

ANNIE (*pleasantly*). I'll take the suitcase, thanks.

KELLER. Not at all, I have it, Miss Sullivan.

ANNIE. I'd like it.

KELLER (*gallantly*). I couldn't think of it, Miss Sullivan. You'll find in the South we —

ANNIE. Let me.

KELLER. — view women as the flowers of civiliza —

ANNIE (*impatiently*). I've got something in it for Helen! (*She tugs it free;* KELLER *stares.*) Thank you. When do I see her?

KATE. There. There is Helen.

[ANNIE *turns, and sees* HELEN *on the porch. A moment of silence. Then* ANNIE *begins across the yard to her, lugging her suitcase.*]

KELLER (*sotto voce* [1]). Katie —

[KATE *silences him with a hand on his arm. When* ANNIE *finally reaches the porch steps she stops, contemplating* HELEN *for a last moment before entering her world. Then she drops the suitcase on the porch with intentional heaviness,* HELEN *starts with the jar, and comes to grope over it.* ANNIE *puts forth her hand, and touches* HELEN'S. HELEN *at once grasps it, and commences to explore it, like reading a face. She moves her hand on to* ANNIE'S *forearm, and dress; and* ANNIE *brings her face within reach of* HELEN'S *fingers, which travel over it, quite without timidity, until they encounter and push aside the smoked glasses.* ANNIE'S *gaze is grave, unpitying, very attentive. She puts her hands on* HELEN'S *arms, but* HELEN *at once pulls away, and they confront each other with a distance between. Then* HELEN *returns to the suitcase, tries to open it, cannot.* ANNIE *points* HELEN'S *hand overhead.* HELEN *pulls away, tries to open the suitcase again;*

---

[1] **sotto voce** (sŏt′tō vō′chä): in an undertone.

ANNIE *points her hand overhead again.* HELEN *points overhead, a question, and* ANNIE, *drawing* HELEN's *hand to her own face, nods.* HELEN *now begins tugging the suitcase toward the door; when* ANNIE *tries to take it from her, she fights her off and backs through the doorway with it.* ANNIE *stands a moment, then follows her in, and together they get the suitcase up the steps into* ANNIE's *room.*]

KATE. Well?

KELLER. She's very rough, Katie.

KATE. I like her, Captain.

KELLER. Certainly rear a peculiar kind of young woman in the North. How old is she?

KATE (*vaguely*). Ohh — Well, she's not in her teens, you know.

KELLER. She's only a child. What's her family like, shipping her off alone this far?

KATE. I couldn't learn. She's very closemouthed about some things.

KELLER. Why does she wear those glasses? I like to see a person's eyes when I talk to —

KATE. For the sun. She was blind.

KELLER. Blind.

KATE. She's had nine operations on her eyes. One just before she left.

KELLER. Blind, good heavens, do they expect one blind child to teach another? Has she experience at least, how long did she teach there?

KATE. She was a pupil.

KELLER (*heavily*). Katie, Katie. This is her first position?

KATE (*in a bright voice*). She was valedictorian —

KELLER. Here's a houseful of grownups can't cope with the child, how can an inexperienced half-blind Yankee schoolgirl manage her?

[JAMES *moves in with the trunk on his shoulder.*]

JAMES (*easily*). Great improvement. Now we have two of them to look after.

KELLER. You look after those strawberry plants!

[JAMES *stops with the trunk.* KELLER *turns from him without another word, and marches off.*]

JAMES. Nothing I say is right.

KATE. Why say anything? (*She calls.*) Don't be long, Captain, we'll have supper right away —

[*She goes into the house, and through the rear door of the family room.* JAMES *trudges in with the trunk, takes it up the steps to* ANNIE's *room, and sets it down outside the door. The lights elsewhere dim somewhat.*]

SCENE 7

Annie's room.

Meanwhile, inside, ANNIE *has given* HELEN *a key; while* ANNIE *removes her bonnet,* HELEN *unlocks and opens the suitcase. The first thing she pulls out is a voluminous shawl. She fingers it until she perceives what it is; then she wraps it around her, and acquiring* AN-NIE's *bonnet and smoked glasses as well, dons the lot: the shawl swamps her, and the bonnet settles down upon the glasses, but she stands before a mirror cocking her head to one side, then to the other, in a mockery of adult action.* AN-NIE *is amused, and talks to her as one might to a kitten, with no trace of company manners.*

ANNIE. All the trouble I went to and that's how I look? (HELEN *then comes back to the suitcase, gropes for more, lifts out a pair of female drawers.*) Oh, no. Not the drawers! (*But* HELEN *dis-*

carding them comes to the elegant doll. Her fingers explore its features, and when she raises it and finds its eyes open and close, she is at first startled, then delighted. She picks it up, taps its head vigorously, taps her own chest, and nods questioningly. ANNIE takes her finger, points it to the doll, points it to HELEN, and touching it to her own face, also nods. HELEN sits back on her heels, clasps the doll to herself, and rocks it. ANNIE studies her, still in bonnet and smoked glasses like a caricature [1] of herself, and addresses her humorously.) All right, Miss O'Sullivan. Let's begin with doll. (She takes HELEN's hand; in her palm ANNIE's forefinger points, thumb holding her other fingers clenched.) D. (Her thumb next holds all her fingers clenched, touching HELEN's palm.) O. (Her thumb and forefinger extend.) L. (Same contact repeated.) L. (She puts HELEN's hand to the doll.) Doll.

JAMES. You spell pretty well. (ANNIE in one hurried move gets the drawers swiftly back into the suitcase, the lid banged shut, and her head turned, to see JAMES leaning in the doorway.) Finding out if she's ticklish? She is.

[ANNIE regards him stonily, but HELEN after a scowling moment tugs at her hand again, imperious. ANNIE repeats the letters, and HELEN interrupts her fingers in the middle, feeling each of them, puzzled. ANNIE touches HELEN's hand to the doll, and begins spelling into it again.]

JAMES. What is it, a game?
ANNIE (curtly). An alphabet.
JAMES. Alphabet?
ANNIE. For the deaf. (HELEN now repeats the finger movements in air, ex-

actly, her head cocked to her own hand, and ANNIE's eyes suddenly gleam.) Ho. How bright she is!

JAMES. You think she knows what she's doing? (He takes HELEN's hand, to throw a meaningless gesture into it; she repeats this one too.) She imitates everything, she's a monkey.

ANNIE (very pleased). Yes, she's a bright little monkey, all right.

[She takes the doll from HELEN, and reaches for her hand; HELEN instantly grabs the doll back. ANNIE takes it again, and HELEN's hand next, but HELEN is incensed now. When ANNIE draws her hand to her face to shake her head no, then tries to spell to her, HELEN slaps at ANNIE's face. ANNIE grasps HELEN by both arms, and swings her into a chair, holding her pinned there, kicking, while glasses, doll, bonnet fly in various directions. JAMES laughs.]

JAMES. She wants her doll back.
ANNIE. When she spells it.
JAMES. Spell, she doesn't know the thing has a name, even.
ANNIE. Of course not, who expects her to, now? All I want is her fingers to learn the letters.
JAMES. Won't mean anything to her. (ANNIE gives him a look. She then tries to form HELEN's fingers into the letters, but HELEN swings a haymaker instead, which ANNIE barely ducks, at once pinning her down again.) Doesn't like that alphabet, Miss Sullivan. You invent it yourself?

[HELEN is now in a rage, fighting tooth and nail to get out of the chair, and ANNIE answers while struggling and dodging her kicks.]

ANNIE. Spanish monks under a — vow of silence. Which I wish you'd take! (And suddenly releasing HELEN's hands,

---

[1] **caricature** (kăr′ĭ·ká·tūr): humorous picture or imitation.

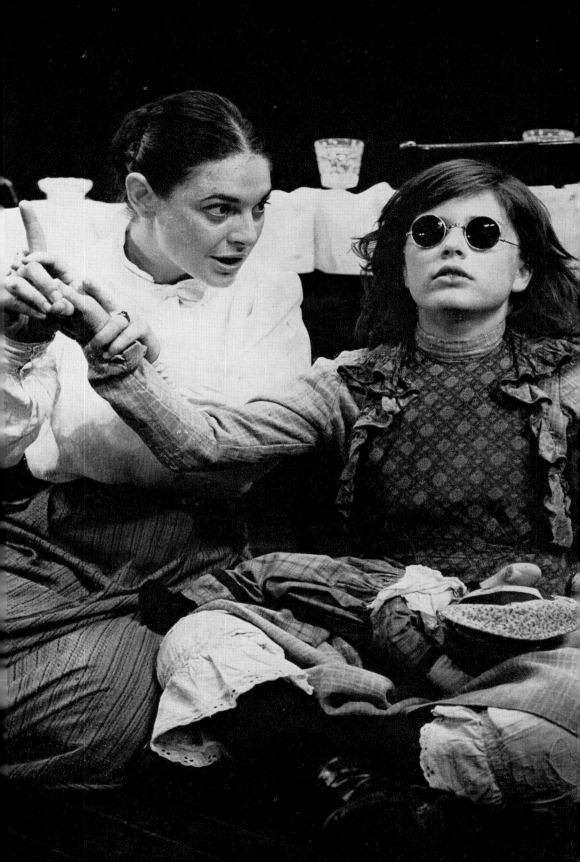

she comes and shuts the door in JAMES's face. HELEN *drops to the floor, groping around for the doll.* ANNIE *looks around desperately, sees her purse on the bed, rummages in it, and comes up with a battered piece of cake wrapped in newspaper. With her foot she moves the doll deftly out of the way of* HELEN's *groping, and going on her knee she lets* HELEN *smell the cake. When* HELEN *grabs for it,* ANNIE *removes the cake and spells quickly into the reaching hand.*) Cake. From Washington up north, it's the best I can do. (HELEN's *hand waits, baffled.* ANNIE *repeats it.*) C, a, k, e. Do what my fingers do, never mind what it means. (*She touches the cake briefly to* HELEN's *nose, pats her hand, presents her own hand.* HELEN *spells the letters rapidly back.* ANNIE *pats her hand enthusiastically, and gives her the cake;* HELEN *crams it into her mouth with both hands.* ANNIE *watches her, with humor.*) Get it down fast, maybe I'll steal that back too. Now. (*She takes the doll, touches it to* HELEN's *nose, and spells again into her hand.*) D, o, l, l. Think it over. (HELEN *thinks it over, while* ANNIE *presents her own hand. Then* HELEN *spells three letters.* ANNIE *waits a second, then completes the word for* HELEN *in her palm.*) L. (*She hands over the doll, and* HELEN *gets a good grip on its leg.*) Imitate now, understand later. End of the first les — (*She never finishes, because* HELEN *swings the doll with a furious energy. It hits* ANNIE *squarely in the face, and she falls back with a cry of pain, her knuckles up to her mouth.* HELEN *waits, tensed for further combat. When* ANNIE *lowers her knuckles she looks at blood on them; she works her lips, gets to her feet, finds the mirror, and bares her teeth at herself. Now she is furious herself.*) You little wretch, no one's taught you *any* manners? I'll — (*But rounding*

from the mirror she sees the door slam, HELEN *and the doll are on the outside, and* HELEN *is turning the key in the lock.* ANNIE *darts over, to pull the knob; the door is locked fast. She yanks it again.*) Helen! Helen, let me out of — (*She bats her brow at the folly of speaking, but* JAMES, *now downstairs, hears her and turns to see* HELEN *with the key and doll groping her way down the steps.* JAMES *takes in the whole situation, makes a move to intercept* HELEN, *but then changes his mind, lets her pass, and amusedly follows her out onto the porch. Upstairs* ANNIE *meanwhile rattles the knob, kneels, peers through the keyhole, gets up. She goes to the window, looks down, frowns.* JAMES *from the yard sings gaily up to her.*)

JAMES. "Buffalo girl, are you coming out tonight,
Coming out tonight,
Coming out — "

[*He drifts back into the house.* ANNIE *takes a handkerchief, nurses her mouth, stands in the middle of the room, staring at door and window in turn, and so catches sight of herself in the mirror, her cheek scratched, her hair dishevelled, her handkerchief bloody, her face disgusted with herself. She addresses the mirror, with some irony.*]

ANNIE. Don't worry. They'll find you, you're not lost. Only out of place. (*But she coughs, spits something into her palm, and stares at it, outraged.*) And toothless. (*She winces.*) Oo! It hurts.

[*She pours some water into the basin, dips the handkerchief, and presses it to her mouth. Standing there, bent over the basin in pain — with the rest of the set dim and unreal, and the lights upon her taking on the subtle color of the past — she hears again, as do we, the faraway voices, and slowly she lifts her head to them; the boy's voice is the same, the others are cracked old crones in a nightmare, and perhaps we see their shadows.*]

BOY'S VOICE. It hurts. Annie, it hurts.

FIRST CRONE'S VOICE. Keep that brat shut up, can't you, girlie, how's a body to get any sleep in this damn ward?

BOY'S VOICE. It hurts. It hurts.

SECOND CRONE'S VOICE. Shut up, you!

BOY'S VOICE. Annie, when are we goin' home? You promised!

ANNIE. Jimmie —

BOY'S VOICE. Forever and ever, you said forever — (ANNIE *drops the handkerchief, averts to the window, and is arrested there by the next cry.*) Annie? Annie, you there? Annie! It *hurts!*

THIRD CRONE'S VOICE. Grab him, he's fallin'!

BOY'S VOICE. *Annie!*

DOCTOR'S VOICE (*a pause, slowly*). Little girl. Little girl, I must tell you your brother will be going on a —

[*But* ANNIE *claps her hands to her ears, to shut this out; there is instant silence.*

As the lights bring the other areas in again JAMES *goes to the steps to listen for any sound from upstairs.* KELLER *re-entering from left crosses toward the house; he passes* HELEN *en route to her retreat under the pump.* KATE *re-enters the rear door of the family room, with flowers for the table.*]

KATE. Supper is ready, Jimmie, will you call your father?

JAMES. Certainly. (*But he calls up the stairs, for* ANNIE's *benefit:*) Father! Supper!

KELLER (*at the door*). No need to shout, I've been cooling my heels for an hour. Sit down.

JAMES. Certainly.

KELLER. Viney!

[VINEY *backs in with a roast, while they get settled around the table.*]

VINEY. Yes, Cap'n, right here.

KATE. Mildred went directly to sleep, Viney?

VINEY. Oh yes, that babe's a angel.

KATE. And Helen had a good supper?

VINEY (*vaguely*). I dunno, Miss Kate, somehow she didn't have much of a appetite tonight —

KATE (*a bit guilty*). Oh. Dear.

KELLER (*hastily*). Well, now. Couldn't say the same for my part. I'm famished. Katie, your plate.

KATE (*looking*). But where is Miss Annie?

[*A silence.*]

JAMES (*pleasantly*). In her room.

KELLER. In her room? Doesn't she know hot food must be eaten hot? Go bring her down at once, Jimmie.

JAMES (*rises*). Certainly. I'll get a ladder.

KELLER (*stares*). What?

JAMES. I'll need a ladder. Shouldn't take me long.

KATE (*stares*). What shouldn't take you —

KELLER. Jimmie, do as I say! Go upstairs at once and tell Miss Sullivan supper is getting cold —

JAMES. She's locked in her room.

KELLER. Locked in her —

KATE. What on earth are you —

JAMES. Helen locked her in and made off with the key.

KATE (*rising*). And you sit here and say nothing?

JAMES. Well, everyone's been telling me not to say anything.

[*He goes serenely out and across the yard, whistling.* KELLER *thrusting up from his chair makes for the stairs.*]

KATE. Viney, look out in back for Helen. See if she has that key.

VINEY. Yes, Miss Kate.

[VINEY *goes out the rear door.*]

KELLER (*calling down*). She's out by the pump! (KATE *goes out on the porch after* HELEN, *while* KELLER *knocks on* ANNIE's *door, then rattles the knob, imperiously.*) Miss Sullivan! Are you in there?

ANNIE. Oh, I'm in here, all right.

KELLER. Is there no key on your side?

ANNIE (*with some asperity*[1]). Well, if there was a key in here, *I* wouldn't be in here. Helen took it. The only thing on my side is me.

KELLER. Miss Sullivan. I — (*He tries, but cannot hold it back.*) Not in the house ten minutes, I don't see *how* you managed it! (*He stomps downstairs again, while* ANNIE *mutters to herself.*)

ANNIE. And even I'm not on my side.

KELLER (*roaring*). Viney!

VINEY (*reappearing*). Yes, Cap'n?

KELLER. Put that meat back in the oven!

[VINEY *bears the roast off again, while* KELLER *strides out onto the porch.* KATE *is with* HELEN *at the pump, opening her hands.*]

KATE. She has no key.

KELLER. Nonsense, she must have the key. Have you searched in her pockets?

KATE. Yes. She doesn't have it.

KELLER. Katie, she must have the key.

KATE. Would you prefer to search her yourself, Captain?

KELLER. No, I would not prefer to search her! She almost took my knee-

cap off this evening, when I tried merely to — (JAMES *reappears carrying a long ladder, with* PERCY *running after him to be in on things.*) Take that ladder back!

JAMES. Certainly.

[*He turns around with it.* MARTHA *comes skipping around the upstage corner of the house to be in on things, accompanied by the setter* BELLE.]

KATE. She could have hidden the key.

KELLER. Where?

KATE. Anywhere. Under a stone. In the flower beds. In the grass —

KELLER. Well, I can't plow up the entire grounds to find a missing key! Jimmie!

JAMES. Sir?

KELLER. Bring me a ladder!

JAMES. Certainly.

[VINEY *comes around the downstage side of the house to be in on things; she has* MILDRED *over her shoulder, bleating.* KELLER *places the ladder against* ANNIE's *window and mounts.* ANNIE *meanwhile is running about making herself presentable, washing the blood off her mouth, straightening her clothes, tidying her hair. Another Negro servant enters to gaze in wonder, increasing the gathering ring of spectators.*]

KATE (*sharply*). What is Mildred doing up?

VINEY. Cap'n woke her, ma'am, all that hollerin'.

KELLER. Miss Sullivan!

[ANNIE *comes to the window, with as much air of gracious normality as she can manage;* KELLER *is at the window.*]

ANNIE (*brightly*). Yes, Captain Keller?

KELLER. Come out!

---

[1] **asperity** (ăs·pĕr′ĭ·tĭ): harshness.

ANNIE. I don't see how I can. There isn't room.

KELLER. I intend to carry you. Climb onto my shoulder and hold tight.

ANNIE. Oh, no. It's — very chivalrous of you, but I'd really prefer to —

KELLER. Miss Sullivan, follow instructions! I will not have you also tumbling out of our windows.

[ANNIE *obeys, with some misgivings.*]

I hope this is not a sample of what we may expect from you. In the way of simplifying the work of looking after Helen.

ANNIE. Captain Keller, I'm perfectly able to go down a ladder under my own —

KELLER. I doubt it, Miss Sullivan. Simply hold onto my neck. (*He begins down with her, while the spectators stand in a wide and somewhat awe-stricken circle, watching.* KELLER *half-misses a rung, and* ANNIE *grabs at his whiskers.*) My *neck*, Miss Sullivan!

ANNIE. I'm sorry to inconvenience you this way —

KELLER. No inconvenience, other than having that door taken down and the lock replaced, if we fail to find that key.

ANNIE. Oh, I'll look everywhere for it.

KELLER. Thank you. Do not look in any rooms that can be locked. There.

[*He stands her on the ground.* JAMES *applauds.*]

ANNIE. Thank you very much.

[*She smooths her skirt, looking as composed and ladylike as possible.* KELLER *stares around at the spectators.*)

KELLER. Go, go, back to your work. What are you looking at here? There's nothing here to look at. (*They break up, move off.*) Now would it be possible for us to have supper, like other people? (*He marches into the house.*)

KATE. Viney, serve supper. I'll put Mildred to sleep.

[*They all go in.* JAMES *is the last to leave, murmuring to* ANNIE *with a gesture.*]

JAMES. Might as well leave the l, a, d, d, e, r, hm?

[ANNIE *ignores him, looking at* HELEN; JAMES *goes in too. Imperceptibly the lights commence to narrow down.* ANNIE *and* HELEN *are now alone in the yard,* HELEN *seated at the pump, where she has been oblivious to it all, a battered little savage, playing with the doll in a picture of innocent contentment.* ANNIE *comes near, leans against the house, and taking off her smoked glasses, studies her, not without awe. Presently* HELEN *rises, gropes around to see if anyone is present;* ANNIE *evades her hand, and when* HELEN *is satisfied she is alone, the key suddenly protrudes out of her mouth. She takes it in her fingers, stands thinking, gropes to the pump, lifts a loose board, drops the key into the well, and hugs herself gleefully.* AN-NIE *stares. But after a moment she shakes her head to herself, she cannot keep the smile from her lips.*]

ANNIE. You *devil.* (*Her tone is one of great respect, humor, and acceptance of challenge.*) You think I'm easily gotten rid of? You have a thing or two to learn, first. I have nothing else to do. (*She goes up the steps to the porch, but turns for a final word, almost of warning.*) And nowhere to go.

[*And presently she moves into the house to the others, as the lights dim down and out, except for the small circle upon* HELEN *solitary at the pump, which ends the act.*]

Stage setting performs a vital function in bringing a play to life. It draws the audience into the world of the play itself and also meets the exacting physical requirements of the various scenes. Shown opposite are scenic designer George Jenkins' drawings for the set of the Broadway production of *The Miracle Worker*.

The main area of action in *The Miracle Worker* is the Keller home. In the drawing of the house at the top of the page you see the family room at the right, and a bedroom, upstairs, to the left. This bedroom was designed to serve as the nursery at the beginning of Act I and later as Annie's room.

For action that occurs away from the Keller home, the area at the lower left of the house was used. The wall was removed and, with flats and props, this space was converted for the various scenes. The center drawing shows this area as the railroad station, and the bottom drawing shows it as the garden house. As the drawings illustrate, lighting was used to focus attention on the area where the action was taking place.

ACT II

SCENE 1

Annie's room. It is evening.

The only room visible in the KELLER *house is* ANNIE's, *where by lamplight* ANNIE *in a shawl is at a desk writing a letter; at her bureau* HELEN *in her customary unkempt state is tucking her doll in the bottom drawer as a cradle, the contents of which she has dumped out, creating as usual a fine disorder.* ANNIE *mutters each word as she writes her letter, slowly, her eyes close to and almost touching the page, to follow with difficulty her penwork.*

ANNIE. ". . . and, nobody, here, has, attempted, to, control, her. The, greatest, problem, I, have, is, how, to, discipline, her, without, breaking, her, spirit." (*In a resolute voice.*) "But, I, shall, insist, on, reasonable, obedience, from, the, start —"* (*At which point* HELEN, *groping about on the desk, knocks over the inkwell.* ANNIE *jumps up, rescues her letter, rights the inkwell, grabs a towel to stem the spillage, and then wipes at* HELEN's *hands;* HELEN *as always pulls free, but not until* ANNIE *first gets three letters into her palm.*) Ink. (HELEN *is enough interested in and puzzled by this spelling that she proffers her hand again; so* ANNIE *spells and impassively dunks it back in the spillage.*) Ink. It has a name. (*She wipes the hand clean, and leads* HELEN *to her bureau, where she looks for something to engage her. She finds a sewing card, with needle and thread, and going to her knees, shows* HELEN's *hand how to connect one row of holes.*) Down. Under. Up. And be careful of the needle —* (HELEN *gets it, and* ANNIE *rises.*) Fine. You keep out of the ink and perhaps I can keep out of — the soup. (*She returns to the desk, tidies it, and resumes writing her letter, bent close to the page.*) "These, blots, are, her, handiwork. I —"* (*She is interrupted by a gasp:* HELEN *has stuck her finger, and sits sucking at it, darkly. Then with vengeful resolve she seizes her doll, and is about to dash its brains out on the floor when* ANNIE *diving catches it in one hand, which she at once shakes with hopping pain, but otherwise ignores, patiently.*) All right, let's try temperance. (*Taking the doll, she kneels, goes through the motion of knocking its head on the floor, spells into* HELEN's *hand:*)

Bad, girl. (*She lets* HELEN *feel the grieved expression on her face.* HELEN *imitates it. Next she makes* HELEN *caress the doll and kiss the hurt spot and hold it gently in her arms, then spells into her hand:*) Good, girl. (*She lets* HELEN *feel the smile on her face.* HELEN *sits with a scowl, which suddenly clears; she pats the doll, kisses it, wreathes her face in a large artificial smile, and bears the doll to the washstand, where she carefully sits it.* ANNIE *watches, pleased.*) Very good girl — (*Whereupon* HELEN *elevates the pitcher and dashes it on the floor instead.* ANNIE *leaps to her feet, and stands inarticulate;* HELEN *calmly gropes back to sit to the sewing card and needle.* ANNIE *manages to achieve self-control. She picks up a fragment or two of the pitcher, sees* HELEN *is puzzling over the card, and resolutely kneels to demonstrate it again. She spells into* HELEN'S *hand.* KATE *meanwhile coming around the corner with folded sheets on her arm, halts at the doorway and watches them for a moment in silence; she is moved, but level.*)

KATE (*presently*). What are you saying to her?

[ANNIE *glancing up is a bit embarrassed, and rises from the spelling, to find her company manners.*]

ANNIE. Oh, I was just making conversation. Saying it was a sewing card.

KATE. But does that — (*she imitates with her fingers*) — mean that to her?

ANNIE. No. No, she won't know what spelling is till she knows what a word is.

KATE. Yet you keep spelling to her. Why?

ANNIE (*cheerily*). I like to hear myself talk!

KATE. The Captain says it's like spelling to the fence post.

ANNIE (*a pause*). Does he, now.

KATE. Is it?

ANNIE. No, it's how I watch you talk to Mildred.

KATE. Mildred.

ANNIE. Any baby. Gibberish, grown-up gibberish, baby-talk gibberish, do they understand one word of it to start? Somehow they begin to. If they hear it, I'm letting Helen hear it.

KATE. Other children are not — impaired.

ANNIE. Ho, there's nothing impaired in that head, it works like a mousetrap!

KATE (*smiles*). But after a child hears how many words, Miss Annie, a million?

ANNIE. I guess no mother's ever minded enough to count.

[*She drops her eyes to spell into* HELEN'S *hand, again indicating the card;* HELEN *spells back, and* ANNIE *is amused.*]

KATE (*too quickly*). What did she spell?

ANNIE. I spelt card. She spelt cake! (*She takes in* KATE'S *quickness, and shakes her head, gently.*) No, it's only a finger-game to her, Mrs. Keller. What she has to learn first is that things have names.

KATE. And when will she learn?

ANNIE. Maybe after a million and one words.

[*They hold each other's gaze;* KATE *then speaks quietly.*]

KATE. I should like to learn those letters, Miss Annie.

ANNIE (*pleased*). I'll teach you tomorrow morning. That makes only half a million each!

KATE (*then*). It's her bedtime. (AN-NIE *reaches for the sewing card,* HELEN *objects,* ANNIE *insists, and* HELEN *gets rid of* ANNIE's *hand by jabbing it with the needle.* ANNIE *gasps, and moves to grip* HELEN's *wrist; but* KATE *intervenes with a proffered sweet, and* HELEN *drops the card, crams the sweet into her mouth, and scrambles up to search her mother's hands for more.* ANNIE *nurses her wound, staring after the sweet.*) I'm sorry, Miss Annie.

ANNIE (*indignantly*). Why does she get a reward? For stabbing me?

KATE. Well — (*Then, tiredly*) We catch our flies with honey, I'm afraid. We haven't the heart for much else, and so many times she simply cannot be compelled.

ANNIE (*ominous*). Yes. I'm the same way myself. (KATE *smiles, and leads* HELEN *off around the corner.* ANNIE *alone in her room picks up things and in the act of removing* HELEN's *doll gives way to unmannerly temptation: she throttles it. She drops it on her bed, and stands pondering. Then she turns back, sits decisively, and writes again, as the lights dim on her.*) (*Grimly.*) "The, more, I, think, the, more, certain, I, am, that, obedience, is, the, gateway, through, which, knowledge, enters, the, mind, of, the, child — "

[*On the word "obedience" a shaft of sunlight hits the water pump outside, while* ANNIE's *voice ends in the dark, followed by a distant cockcrow; daylight comes up over another corner of the sky, with* VINEY's *voice heard at once.*]

SCENE 2

The Keller home. It is the following morning.

VINEY. Breakfast ready!

[VINEY *comes down into the sunlight beam, and pumps a pitcherful of wa-*

ter. While the pitcher is brimming we hear conversation from the dark; the light grows to the family room of the house where all are either entering or already seated at breakfast, with KELLER *and* JAMES *arguing the war.* HELEN *is wandering around the table to explore the contents of the other plates. When* ANNIE *is in her chair, she watches* HELEN. VINEY *re-enters, sets the pitcher on the table;* KATE *lifts the almost empty biscuit plate with an inquiring look,* VINEY *nods and bears it off back, neither of them interrupting the men.* ANNIE *meanwhile sits with fork quiet, watching* HELEN, *who at her mother's plate pokes her hand among some scrambled eggs.* KATE *catches* ANNIE's *eyes on her, smiles with a wry gesture.* HELEN *moves on to* JAMES's *plate, the male talk continuing,* JAMES *deferential*[1] *and* KELLER *overriding.*]

JAMES. — no, but shouldn't we give the devil his due, father? The fact is we lost the South two years earlier when he out-thought us behind Vicksburg.

KELLER. Out-thought is a peculiar word for a butcher.

JAMES. Harness maker, wasn't he?

KELLER. I said butcher. His only virtue as a soldier was numbers and he led them to slaughter with no more regard than for so many sheep.

JAMES. But even if in that sense he was a butcher, the fact is he —

KELLER. And a drunken one, half the war.

JAMES. Agreed, father. If his own people said he was, I can't argue he —

KELLER. Well, what is it you find to admire in such a man, Jimmie — the butchery or the drunkenness?

JAMES. Neither, father, only the fact that he beat us.

[1] **deferential** (dĕf'ẽr·ĕn'shăl): respectful.

KELLER. He didn't.

JAMES. Is it your contention we won the war, sir?

KELLER. He didn't beat us at Vicksburg. We lost Vicksburg because Pemberton gave Bragg five thousand of his cavalry and Loring, whom I knew personally for a nincompoop before you were born, marched away from Champion's Hill with enough men to have held them. We lost Vicksburg by stupidity verging on treason.

JAMES. I would have said we lost Vicksburg because Grant was one thing no Yankee general was before him —

KELLER. Drunk? I doubt it.

JAMES. Obstinate.

KELLER. Obstinate. Could any of them compare even in that with old Stonewall? If he'd been there we would still have Vicksburg.

JAMES. Well, the butcher simply wouldn't give up, he tried four ways of getting around Vicksburg and on the fifth try he got around. Anyone else would have pulled north and —

KELLER. He wouldn't have got around if we'd had a Southerner in command, instead of a half-breed Yankee traitor like Pemberton —

[*While this background talk is in progress*, HELEN *is working around the table, ultimately toward* ANNIE'*s plate. She messes with her hands in* JAMES'*s plate, then in* KELLER'*s, both men taking it so for granted they hardly notice. Then* HELEN *comes groping with soiled hands past her own plate, to* ANNIE'*s; her hand goes to it, and* ANNIE, *who has been waiting, deliberately lifts and removes her hand.* HELEN *gropes again,* ANNIE *firmly pins her by the wrist, and removes her hand from the table.* HELEN *thrusts her hands again,* ANNIE *catches them, and* HELEN *begins to flail and make noises.*

The interruption brings KELLER'*s gaze upon them.*]

What's the matter there?

KATE. Miss Annie. You see, she's accustomed to helping herself from our plates to anything she —

ANNIE (*evenly*). Yes, but I'm not accustomed to it.

KELLER. No, of course not. Viney!

KATE. Give her something, Jimmie, to quiet her.

JAMES (*blandly*). But her table manners are the best she has. Well.

[*He pokes across with a chunk of bacon at* HELEN'*s hand, which* ANNIE *releases; but* HELEN *knocks the bacon away and stubbornly thrusts at* ANNIE'*s plate,* ANNIE *grips her wrists again, the struggle mounts.*]

KELLER. Let her this time, Miss Sullivan. It's the only way we get any adult conversation. If my son's half merits that description. (*He rises.*) I'll get you another plate.

ANNIE (*gripping* HELEN). I have a plate, thank you.

KATE (*calling*). Viney! I'm afraid what Captain Keller says is only too true, she'll persist in this until she gets her own way.

KELLER (*at the door*). Viney, bring Miss Sullivan another plate —

ANNIE (*stonily*). I have a plate, nothing's wrong with the *plate*, I intend to keep it.

[*Silence for a moment, except for* HELEN'*s noises as she struggles to get loose. The* KELLERS *are a bit nonplussed,*[1] *and* ANNIE *is too darkly intent on* HELEN'*s manners to have any thoughts now of her own.*]

[1] **nonplussed** (nŏn'plŭst): baffled; perplexed.

JAMES. Ha. You see why they took Vicksburg?

KELLER (*uncertainly*). Miss Sullivan. One plate or another is hardly a matter to struggle with a deprived child about.

ANNIE. Oh, I'd sooner have a more — (HELEN *begins to kick,* ANNIE *moves her ankles to the opposite side of the chair.*) — heroic issue myself, I —

KELLER. No, I really must insist you — (HELEN *bangs her toe on the chair and sinks to the floor, crying with rage and feigned* [1] *injury;* ANNIE *keeps hold of her wrists, gazing down, while* KATE *rises.*) Now she's hurt herself.

ANNIE (*grimly*). No, she hasn't.

KELLER. Will you please let her hands go?

KATE. Miss Annie, you don't know the child well enough yet, she'll keep —

ANNIE. I know an ordinary tantrum well enough, when I see one, and a badly spoiled child —

JAMES. Hear, hear.

KELLER (*very annoyed*). Miss Sullivan! You would have more understanding of your pupil if you had some pity in you. Now kindly do as I —

ANNIE. Pity? (*She releases* HELEN *to turn equally annoyed on* KELLER *across the table. Instantly* HELEN *scrambles up and dives at* ANNIE's *plate. This time* ANNIE *intercepts her by pouncing on her wrists like a hawk, and her temper boils.*) For this *tyrant?* The whole house turns on her whims, is there anything she wants she doesn't get? I'll tell you what I pity, that the sun won't rise and set for her all her life, and every day you're telling her it will. What good will your pity do her when you're under the strawberries, Captain Keller?

KELLER (*outraged*). Kate, for the love of heaven will you —

KATE. Miss Annie, please, I don't think it serves to lose our —

[1] **feigned** (fānd): pretended.

ANNIE. It does you good, that's all. It's less trouble to feel sorry for her than to teach her anything better, isn't it?

KELLER. I fail to see where you have taught her anything yet, Miss Sullivan!

ANNIE. I'll begin this minute, if you'll leave the room, Captain Keller!

KELLER (*astonished*). Leave the —

ANNIE. Everyone, please.

[*She struggles with* HELEN, *while* KELLER *endeavors to control his voice.*]

KELLER. Miss Sullivan, you are here only as a paid teacher. Nothing more, and not to lecture —

ANNIE. I can't *unteach* her six years of pity if you can't stand up to one tantrum! Old Stonewall, indeed. Mrs. Keller, you promised me help.

KATE. Indeed I did, we truly want to —

ANNIE. Then leave me alone with her. Now!

KELLER (*in a wrath*). Katie, will you come outside with me? At once, please.

[*He marches to the front door.* KATE *and* JAMES *follow him. Simultaneously* ANNIE *releases* HELEN's *wrists, and the child again sinks to the floor, kicking and crying her weird noises.* ANNIE *steps over her to meet* VINEY *coming in the rear doorway with biscuits and a clean plate, surprised at the general commotion.*]

VINEY. Heaven sakes —

ANNIE. Out, please.

[*She backs* VINEY *out with one hand, closes the door on her astonished mouth, locks it, and removes the key.* KELLER *meanwhile snatches his hat from a rack, and* KATE *follows him down the porch steps.* JAMES *lingers in the doorway to address* ANNIE *across the room with a bow.*]

JAMES. If it takes all summer, general.

[ANNIE *comes over to his door in turn, removing her glasses grimly; as* KELLER *outside begins speaking,* ANNIE *closes the door on* JAMES, *locks it, removes the key, and turns with her back against the door to stare ominously at* HELEN, *who is kicking on the floor.* JAMES *takes his hat from the rack, and going down the porch steps joins* KATE *and* KELLER *talking in the yard,* KELLER *in a sputter of ire.*]

KELLER. This girl, this — cub of a girl — *presumes!* I tell you, I'm of half a mind to ship her back to Boston before the week is out. You can inform her so from me!

KATE (*eyebrows up*). I, Captain?

KELLER. She's a *hireling!* Now I want it clear, unless there's an apology and complete change of manner she goes back on the next train! Will you make that quite clear?

KATE. Where will you be, Captain, while I am making it quite —

KELLER. At the office!

[*He begins off left, finds his napkin still in his irate hand, is uncertain with it, dabs his lips with dignity, gets rid of it in a toss to* JAMES, *and marches off.* JAMES *turns to eye* KATE.]

JAMES. Will you? (KATE'S *mouth is set, and* JAMES *studies it lightly.*) I thought what she said was exceptionally intelligent. I've been saying it for years.

KATE (*not without scorn*). To his face? (*She comes to relieve him of the white napkin, but reverts again to it.*) Or will you take it, Jimmie? As a flag?

[JAMES *stalks out, much offended, and* KATE *turning stares across the yard at the house; the lights narrowing down to the following pantomime in the family room leave her motionless in the dark.*]

ANNIE[1] *meanwhile has begun by slapping both keys down on a shelf out of* HELEN'S *reach; she returns to the table, upstage.* HELEN'S *kicking has subsided, and when from the floor her hand finds* ANNIE'S *chair empty she pauses.* ANNIE *clears the table of* KATE'S, JAMES'S, *and* KELLER'S *plates; she gets back to her own across the table just in time to slide it deftly away from* HELEN'S *pouncing hand. She lifts the hand and moves it to* HELEN'S *plate, and after an instant's exploration,* HELEN *sits again on the floor and drums her heels.* ANNIE *comes around the table and resumes her chair. When* HELEN *feels her skirt again, she ceases kicking, waits for whatever is to come, renews some kicking, waits again.* ANNIE *retrieving her plate takes up a forkful of food, stops it halfway to her mouth, gazes at it devoid of appetite, and half-lowers it; but after a look at* HELEN *she sighs, dips the forkful toward* HELEN *in a for-your-sake toast, and puts it in her own mouth to chew, not without an effort.*

HELEN *now gets hold of the chair leg, and half-succeeds in pulling the chair out from under her.* ANNIE *bangs it down with her rear, heavily, and sits with all her weight.* HELEN'S *next attempt to topple it is unavailing, so her fingers dive in a pinch at* ANNIE'S *flank.* ANNIE *in the middle of her mouthful almost loses it with startle, and she slaps down her fork to round*

[1] Read this scene carefully, for it is one of the high points in the play. Follow the action, step by step, as Annie and Helen begin their battle. As you read, try to visualize the action on a stage. During the Broadway production, both actresses wore padding under their clothing to protect themselves from each other's blows. Dishes and glasses were broken every night, and chairs had to be replaced frequently.

on HELEN. *The child comes up with curiosity to feel what* ANNIE *is doing, so* ANNIE *resumes eating, letting* HEL- EN's *hand follow the movement of her fork to her mouth; whereupon* HELEN *at once reaches into* ANNIE's *plate.* AN- NIE *firmly removes her hand to her own plate.* HELEN *in reply pinches* ANNIE's *thigh, a good mean pinchful that makes* ANNIE *jump.* ANNIE *sets the fork down, and sits with her mouth tight.* HELEN *digs another pinch into her thigh, and this time* ANNIE *slaps her hand smartly away;* HELEN *retaliates with a roundhouse fist that catches* ANNIE *on the ear, and* ANNIE's *hand leaps at once in a force- ful slap across* HELEN's *cheek;* HELEN *is the startled one now.* ANNIE's *hand in compunction falters to her own face, but when* HELEN *hits at her again,* ANNIE *deliberately slaps her again.* HELEN *lifts her fist irresolute for another slap, and they freeze in this posture, while* HELEN *mulls it over. She thinks better of it, drops her fist, and giving* ANNIE *a wide berth, gropes around to her* MOTHER's *chair, to find it empty; she blunders her way along the table, upstage, and encoun- tering the empty chairs and missing plates, she looks bewildered; she gropes back to her* MOTHER's *chair, again touches her cheek and indicates the chair, and waits for the world to answer.*

ANNIE *now reaches over to spell into her hand, but* HELEN *yanks it away; she gropes to the front door, tries the knob, and finds the door locked, with no key. She gropes to the rear door, and finds it locked, with no key. She commences to bang on it.* ANNIE *rises, crosses, takes her wrists, draws her resisting back to the table, seats her, and releases her hands upon her*

plate; as ANNIE *herself begins to sit,* HELEN *writhes out of her chair, runs to the front door, and tugs and kicks at it.* ANNIE *rises again, crosses, draws her by one wrist back to the table, seats her, and sits;* HELEN *escapes back to the door, knocking over her* MOTHER's *chair en route.* ANNIE *rises again in pursuit, and this time lifts* HELEN *bodily from behind and bears her kicking to her chair. She deposits her, and once more turns to sit.* HELEN *scrambles out, but as she passes* AN- NIE *catches her up again from behind and deposits her in the chair;* HELEN *scrambles out on the other side for the rear door, but* ANNIE *at her heels catches her up and deposits her again in the chair. She stands behind it.* HELEN *scrambles out to her right, and the instant her feet hit the floor* ANNIE *lifts and deposits her back; she scram- bles out to her left, and is at once lift- ed and deposited back. She tries right again and is deposited back, and tries left again and is deposited back, and now feints* ANNIE *to the right but is off to her left, and is promptly depos- ited back. She sits a moment, and then starts straight over the tabletop, dish- ware notwithstanding;* ANNIE *hauls her in and deposits her back, with her plate spilling in her lap, and she melts to the floor and crawls under the ta- ble, laborious among its legs and chairs; but* ANNIE *is swift around the table and waiting on the other side when she surfaces, immediately bear- ing her aloft.* HELEN *clutches at* JAMES's *chair for anchorage, but it comes with her, and halfway back she abandons it to the floor.* ANNIE *deposits her in her chair, and waits.* HELEN *sits tensed, motionless. Then she tentatively puts out her left foot and hand,* ANNIE *interposes her own hand, and at the contact* HELEN *jerks hers in. She tries her right foot,* ANNIE *blocks it with her own, and* HELEN *jerks hers in. Finally, leaning back, she slumps down in her chair, in a sullen biding.*

ANNIE *backs off a step, and watches;* HELEN *offers no move.* ANNIE *takes a deep breath. Both of them and the room are in considerable disorder, two chairs down and the table a mess, but* ANNIE *makes no effort to tidy it; she only sits on her own chair, and lets her energy refill. Then she takes up knife and fork, and resolutely addresses her food.* HELEN's *hand comes out to explore, and seeing it* ANNIE *sits without moving; the child's hand goes over her hand and fork, pauses — * ANNIE *still does not move — and withdraws. Presently it moves for her own plate, slaps about for it, and stops, thwarted. At this,* ANNIE *again rises, recovers* HELEN's *plate from the floor and a handful of scattered food from the deranged tablecloth, drops it on the plate, and pushes the plate into contact with* HELEN's *fist. Neither of them now moves for a pregnant moment — until* HELEN *suddenly takes a grab of food and wolfs it down.* ANNIE *permits herself the humor of a minor bow and warming of her hands together; she wanders off a step or two, watching.* HELEN *cleans up the plate.*

After a glower of indecision, she holds the empty plate out for more. ANNIE *accepts it, and crossing to the removed plates, spoons food from them onto it; she stands debating the spoon, tapping it a few times on* HELEN's *plate; and when she returns with the plate she brings the spoon, too. She puts the spoon first into* HELEN's *hand, then sets the plate down.* HELEN, *discarding the spoon, reaches*

with her hand, and ANNIE *stops it by the wrist; she replaces the spoon in it.* HELEN *impatiently discards it again, and again* ANNIE *stops her hand, to replace the spoon in it. This time* HELEN *throws the spoon on the floor.* ANNIE *after considering it lifts* HELEN *bodily out of the chair, and in a wrestling match on the floor closes her fingers upon the spoon, and returns her with it to the chair.* HELEN *again throws the spoon on the floor.* ANNIE *lifts her out of the chair again; but in the struggle over the spoon* HELEN *with* ANNIE *on her back sends her sliding over her head;* HELEN *flees back to her chair and scrambles into it. When* ANNIE *comes after her she clutches it for dear life;* ANNIE *pries one hand loose, then the other, then the first again, then the other again, and then lifts* HELEN *by the waist, chair and all, and shakes the chair loose.* HELEN *wrestles to get free, but* ANNIE *pins her to the floor, closes her fingers upon the spoon, and lifts her kicking under one arm; with her other hand she gets the chair in place again, and plunks* HELEN *back on it. When she releases her hand,* HELEN *throws the spoon at her.*

ANNIE *now removes the plate of food.* HELEN, *grabbing, finds it missing, and commences to bang with her fists on the table.* ANNIE *collects a fistful of spoons and descends with them and the plate on* HELEN; *she lets her smell the plate, at which* HELEN *ceases banging, and* ANNIE *puts the plate down and a spoon in* HELEN's *hand.* HELEN *throws it on the floor.* ANNIE *puts another spoon in her hand,* HELEN *throws it on the floor.* ANNIE *puts another spoon in her hand.* HELEN *throws it on the floor. When* ANNIE *comes to her last spoon she sits next to* HELEN, *and gripping the spoon in*

HELEN's *hand compels her to take food in it up to her mouth.* HELEN *sits with lips shut.* ANNIE *waits a stolid moment, then lowers* HELEN's *hand. She tries again;* HELEN's *lips remain shut.* ANNIE *waits, lowers* HELEN's *hand. She tries again; this time* HELEN *suddenly opens her mouth and accepts the food.* ANNIE *lowers the spoon with a sigh of relief, and* HELEN *spews the mouthful out at her face.* ANNIE *sits a moment with eyes closed, then takes the pitcher and dashes its water into* HELEN's *face, who gasps astonished.* ANNIE *with* HELEN's *hand takes up another spoonful, and shoves it into her open mouth.* HELEN *swallows involuntarily, and while she is catching her breath* ANNIE *forces her palm open, throws four swift letters into it, then another four, and bows toward her with devastating pleasantness.*]

ANNIE. Good girl.

[ANNIE *lifts* HELEN's *hand to feel her face nodding;* HELEN *grabs a fistful of her hair, and yanks. The pain brings* ANNIE *to her knees, and* HELEN *pummels her; they roll under the table, and the lights commence to dim out on them.*

Simultaneously the light at left has been rising, slowly, so slowly that it seems at first we only imagine what is intimated in the yard: a few ghost-like figures, in silence, motionless, waiting. Now the distant belfry chimes commence to toll the hour, also very slowly, almost — it is twelve — interminably; the sense is that of a long time passing. We can identify the figures before the twelfth stroke, all facing the house in a kind of watch: KATE *is standing exactly as before, but now with the baby* MIL-DRED *sleeping in her arms, and placed here and there, unmoving, are* AUNT EV *in her hat with a hanky to her nose, and the two Negro children,* PERCY *and* MARTHA, *with necks outstretched eagerly, and* VINEY *with a knotted kerchief on her head and a feather duster in her hand.*

The chimes cease, and there is silence. For a long moment none of the group moves.]

VINEY (*presently*). What am I gone do, Miss Kate? It's noontime, dinner's comin', I didn't get them breakfast dishes out of there yet.

[KATE *says nothing, stares at the house,* MARTHA *shifts* HELEN's *doll in her clutch, and it plaintively says momma.*]

KATE (*presently*). You run along, Martha.

[AUNT EV *blows her nose.*]

AUNT EV (*wretchedly*). I can't wait out here a minute longer, Kate, why, this could go on all afternoon, too.

KATE. I'll tell the Captain you called.

VINEY (*to the children*). You hear what Miss Kate say? Never you mind what's going on here. (*Still no one moves.*) You run along tend you own bizness. (*Finally* VINEY *turns on the children with the feather duster.*) Shoo!

[*The two children divide before her. She chases them off.* AUNT EV *comes to* KATE, *on her dignity.*]

AUNT EV. Say what you like, Kate, but that child is a *Keller*. (*She opens her parasol, preparatory to leaving.*) I needn't remind you that all the Kellers are cousins to General Robert E. Lee. I don't know *who* that girl is. (*She waits; but* KATE *staring at the house is without response.*) The only Sullivan I've heard of — from Boston too, and I'd think twice before locking her up with that kind — is that man John L.[1]

[*And* AUNT EV *departs, with head high. Presently* VINEY *comes to* KATE, *her arms out for the baby.*]

VINEY. You give me her, Miss Kate, I'll sneak her in back, to her crib.

[*But* KATE *is motionless, until* VINEY *starts to take the baby;* KATE *looks down at her before relinquishing her.*]

KATE (*slowly*). This child never gives me a minute's worry.

VINEY. Oh yes, this one's the angel of the family, no question 'bout *that.*

[*She begins off rear with the baby, heading around the house; and* KATE *now turns her back on it, her hand to her eyes. At this moment there is the slamming of a door, and when* KATE *wheels,* HELEN *is blundering down the porch steps into the light, like a ruined bat.* VINEY *halts, and* KATE *runs in;* HELEN *collides with her mother's knees, and reels off and back to clutch them as her savior.* ANNIE *with smoked glasses in hand stands on the porch, also much undone, looking as though she had indeed just taken Vicksburg.* KATE *taking in* HELEN'S *ravaged[2] state becomes steely in her gaze up at* ANNIE.]

KATE. What happened?

[ANNIE *meets* KATE'S *gaze, and gives a factual report, too exhausted for anything but a flat voice.*]

ANNIE. She ate from her own plate.

---

[1] **John L.:** John L. Sullivan, a famous boxer in the 1880's.
[2] **ravaged** (răv'ĭjd): damaged.

(*She thinks a moment.*) She ate with a spoon. Herself. (KATE *frowns, uncertain with thought, and glances down at* HELEN.) And she folded her napkin. (KATE'S *gaze now wavers, from* HELEN *to* ANNIE, *and back.*)

KATE (*softly*). Folded — her napkin?

ANNIE. The room's a wreck, but her napkin is folded. (*She pauses — then:*) I'll be in my room, Mrs. Keller.

[*She moves to re-enter the house; but she stops at* VINEY'S *voice.*]

VINEY (*cheery*). Don't be long, Miss Annie. Dinner be ready right away!

[VINEY *carries* MILDRED *around the back of the house.* ANNIE *stands unmoving, takes a deep breath, stares over her shoulder at* KATE *and* HELEN, *then inclines her head graciously, and goes with a slight stagger into the house. The lights in her room above steal up in readiness for her.* KATE *remains alone with* HELEN *in the yard, standing protectively over her, in a kind of wonder.*]

KATE (*slowly*). Folded her napkin. (*She contemplates the wild head in her thighs, and moves her fingertips over it, with such a tenderness, and something like a fear of its strangeness, that her own eyes close; she whispers, bending to it:*) My Helen — folded her napkin —

[*And still erect, with only her head in surrender,* KATE *for the first time that we see loses her protracted war with grief; but she will not let a sound escape her, only the grimace of tears comes, and sobs that shake her in a grip of silence. But* HELEN *feels them, and her hand comes up in its own wondering, to interrogate her mother's face, until* KATE *buries her lips in the child's palm.*]

SCENE 3

Annie's room.

Upstairs, ANNIE *enters her room, closes the door, and stands back against it; the lights, growing on her with their special color, commence to fade on* KATE *and* HELEN. *Then* ANNIE *goes wearily to her suitcase, and lifts it to take it toward the bed. But it knocks an object to the floor, and she turns back to regard it. A new voice comes in a cultured murmur, hesitant as with the effort of remembering a text:*

MAN'S VOICE. This — soul — (ANNIE *puts the suitcase down, and kneels to the object: it is the battered Perkins report, and she stands with it in her hand, letting memory try to speak:*) This — blind, deaf, mute — woman — (ANNIE *sits on her bed, opens the book, and finding the passage, brings it up an inch from her eyes to read, her face and lips following the overheard words, the voice quite factual now:*) Can nothing be done to disinter this human soul? The whole neighborhood would rush to save this woman if she were buried alive by the caving in of a pit, and labor with zeal until she were dug out. Now if there were one who had as much patience as zeal, he might awaken her to a consciousness of her immortal —

[*When the boy's voice comes,* ANNIE *closes her eyes, in pain.*]

BOY'S VOICE. Annie? Annie, you there?
ANNIE. Hush.
BOY'S VOICE. Annie, what's that noise?

[ANNIE *tries not to answer; her own voice is drawn out of her, unwilling.*]

ANNIE. Just a cot, Jimmie.
BOY'S VOICE. Where they pushin' it?

ANNIE. To the deadhouse.
BOY'S VOICE. Annie. Does it hurt, to be dead?

[ANNIE *escapes by opening her eyes, her hand works restlessly over her cheek; she retreats into the book again, but the cracked old crones interrupt, whispering.* ANNIE *slowly lowers the book.*]

FIRST CRONE'S VOICE. There is schools.
SECOND CRONE'S VOICE. There is schools outside —
THIRD CRONE'S VOICE. — schools where they teach blind ones, worse'n you —
FIRST CRONE'S VOICE. To read —
SECOND CRONE'S VOICE. To read and write —
THIRD CRONE'S VOICE. There is schools outside where they —
FIRST CRONE'S VOICE. There is schools —

[*Silence.* ANNIE *sits with her eyes shining, her hand almost in a caress over the book. Then:*]

BOY'S VOICE. You ain't goin' to school, are you, Annie?
ANNIE (*whispering*). When I grow up.
BOY'S VOICE. You ain't either, Annie. You're goin' to stay here take care of me.
ANNIE. I'm goin' to school when I grow up.
BOY'S VOICE. You said we'll be together, forever and ever and ever —
ANNIE (*fierce*). I'm goin' to school when I grow up!
DOCTOR'S VOICE (*slowly*). Little girl. Little girl, I must tell you. Your brother will be going on a journey, soon.

[ANNIE *sits rigid, in silence. Then the boy's voice pierces it, a shriek of terror.*]

BOY'S VOICE. *Annie!*

[*It goes into* ANNIE *like a sword, she doubles over; the book falls to the floor. It takes her a racked moment to find herself and what she was engaged in here; when she sees the suitcase she remembers, and lifts it once again toward the bed. But the voices are with her, as she halts with suitcase in hand.*]

FIRST CRONE'S VOICE. Good-by, Annie.

DOCTOR'S VOICE. Write me when you learn how.

SECOND CRONE'S VOICE. Don't tell anyone you came from here. Don't tell anyone —

THIRD CRONE'S VOICE. Yeah, don't tell anyone you came from —

FIRST CRONE'S VOICE. Yeah, don't tell anyone —

SECOND CRONE'S VOICE. Don't tell any —

[*The echoing voices fade. After a moment* ANNIE *lays the suitcase on the bed; and the last voice comes faintly, from far away.*]

BOY'S VOICE. Annie. It hurts, to be dead. Forever.

[ANNIE *falls to her knees by the bed, stifling her mouth in it. When at last she rolls blindly away from it, her palm comes down on the open report; she opens her eyes, regards it dully, and then, still on her knees, takes in the print.*]

MAN'S VOICE (*in a factual tone*). — might awaken her to a consciousness of her immortal nature. The chance is small indeed; but with a smaller chance they would have dug desperately for her in the pit; and is the life of the soul of less import than that of the body?

[ANNIE *gets to her feet. She drops the book on the bed, and pauses over her suitcase; after a moment she unclasps and opens it. Standing before it, she comes to her decision; she at once turns to the bureau, and taking her things out of its drawers, commences to throw them into the open suitcase.*]

SCENE 4

The garden house. It is evening.

In the darkness down left a hand strikes a match, and lights a hanging oil lamp. It is KELLER'S *hand, and his voice accompanies it, very angry; the lights rising here before they fade on* ANNIE *show* KELLER *and* KATE *inside a suggestion of a garden house, with a bay-window seat towards center and a door at back.*

KELLER. Katie, I will not *have* it! Now you did not see when that girl after supper tonight went to look for Helen in her room —

KATE. No.

KELLER. The child practically climbed out of her window to escape from her! What kind of teacher *is* she? I thought I had seen her at her worst this morning, shouting at me, but I come home to find the entire house disorganized by her — Helen won't stay one second in the same room, won't come to the table with her, won't let herself be bathed or undressed or put to bed by her, or even by Viney now, and the end result is that *you* have to do more for the child than before we hired this girl's services! From the moment she stepped off the train she's been nothing but a burden, incompetent, impertinent, ineffectual, immodest —

KATE. She folded her napkin, Captain.

KELLER. What?

KATE. Not ineffectual. Helen did fold her napkin.

KELLER. What in heaven's name is so extraordinary about folding a napkin?

KATE (*with some humor*). Well. It's more than you did, Captain.

KELLER. Katie. I did not bring you all the way out here to the garden house to be frivolous. Now, how does Miss Sullivan propose to teach a deaf-blind pupil who won't let her even touch her?

KATE (*a pause*). I don't know.

KELLER. The fact is, today she scuttled any chance she ever had of getting along with the child. If you can see any point or purpose to her staying on here longer, it's more than —

KATE. What do you wish me to do?

KELLER. I want you to give her notice.

KATE. I can't.

KELLER. Then if you won't, I must. I simply will not — (*He is interrupted by a knock at the back door.* KELLER *after a glance at* KATE *moves to open the door;* ANNIE *in her smoked glasses is standing outside.* KELLER *contemplates her, heavily.*) Miss Sullivan.

ANNIE. Captain Keller. (*She is nervous, keyed up to seizing the bull by the horns again, and she assumes a cheeriness which is not unshaky.*) Viney said I'd find you both over here in the garden house. I thought we should — have a talk?

KELLER (*reluctantly*). Yes, I — Well, come in. (ANNIE *enters, and is interested in this room; she rounds on her heel, anxiously, studying it.* KELLER *turns the matter over to* KATE, *sotto voce.*) Katie.

KATE (*turning it back, courteously*). Captain.

[KELLER *clears his throat, makes ready.*]

KELLER. I, ah — wanted first to make my position clear to Mrs. Keller, in private. I have decided I — am not satisfied — in fact, am deeply dissatisfied — with the manner in which —

ANNIE (*intent*). Excuse me, is this little house ever in use?

KELLER (*with patience*). In the hunting season. If you will give me your attention, Miss Sullivan. (ANNIE *turns her smoked glasses upon him; they hold his unwilling stare.*) I have tried to make allowances for you because you come from a part of the country where people are — women, I should say — come from who — well, for whom — (*It begins to elude him.*) — allowances must — be made. I have decided, nevertheless, to — that is, decided I — (*vexedly*) Miss Sullivan, I find it difficult to talk through those glasses.

ANNIE (*eagerly, removing them*). Oh, of course.

KELLER (*dourly*). Why do you wear them, the sun has been down for an hour.

ANNIE (*pleasantly, at the lamp*). Any kind of light hurts my eyes.

[*A silence;* KELLER *ponders her, heavily.*]

KELLER. Put them on. Miss Sullivan, I have decided to — give you another chance.

ANNIE (*cheerfully*). To do what?

KELLER. To — remain in our employ. (ANNIE'*s eyes widen.*) But on two conditions. I am not accustomed to rudeness in servants or women, and that is the first. If you are to stay, there must be a radical change of manner.

ANNIE (*a pause*). Whose?

KELLER (*exploding*). Yours, young lady, isn't it obvious? And the second is that you persuade me there's the slightest hope of your teaching a child who flees from you now like the plague, to anyone else she can find in this house.

ANNIE (*a pause*). There isn't.

[KATE *stops sewing, and fixes her eyes upon* ANNIE.]

KATE. What, Miss Annie?

ANNIE. It's hopeless here. I can't teach a child who runs away.

KELLER (*nonplussed*). Then — do I understand you — propose —

ANNIE. Well, if we all agree it's hopeless, the next question is what —

KATE. Miss Annie. (*She is leaning toward* ANNIE, *in deadly earnest; it commands both* ANNIE *and* KELLER.) I am not agreed. I think perhaps you — underestimate Helen.

ANNIE. I think everybody else here does.

KATE. She did fold her napkin. She learns, she learns, do you know she began talking when she was six months old? She could say "water." Not really — "wahwah." "Wahwah," but she meant water, she knew what it meant, and only six months old, I never saw a child so — bright, or outgoing — (*Her voice is unsteady, but she gets it level.*) It's still in her, somewhere, isn't it? You should have seen her before her illness, such a good-tempered child —

ANNIE (*agreeably*). She's changed.

[*A pause,* KATE *not letting her eyes go; her appeal at last is unconditional, and very quiet.*]

KATE. Miss Annie, put up with it. And with us.

KELLER. Us!

KATE. Please? Like the lost lamb in the parable, I love her all the more.

ANNIE. Mrs. Keller, I don't think Helen's worst handicap is deafness or blindness. I think it's your love. And pity.

KELLER. Now what does that mean?

ANNIE. All of you here are so sorry for her you've kept her — like a pet, why, even a dog you housebreak. No wonder she won't let me come near her. It's useless for me to try to teach her language or anything else here. I might as well —

KATE (*cuts in*). Miss Annie, before you came we spoke of putting her in an asylum.

[ANNIE *turns back to regard her. A pause.*]

ANNIE. What kind of asylum?

KELLER. For mental defectives.

KATE. I visited there. I can't tell you what I saw, people like — animals, with — rats, in the halls, and — (*She shakes her head on her vision.*) What else are we to do, if you give up?

ANNIE. Give up?

KATE. You said it was hopeless.

ANNIE. Here. Give up, why, I only today saw what has to be done, to begin! (*She glances from* KATE *to* KELLER, *who stare, waiting; and she makes it as plain and simple as her nervousness permits.*) I — want complete charge of her.

KELLER. You already have that. It has resulted in —

ANNIE. No, I mean day and night. She has to be dependent on me.

KATE. For what?

ANNIE. Everything. The food she eats, the clothes she wears, fresh — (*She is amused at herself, though very serious*) — air, yes, the air she breathes, whatever her body needs is a — primer, to teach her out of. It's the only way, the one who lets her have it should be her teacher. (*She considers them in turn; they digest it,* KELLER *frowning,* KATE *perplexed.*) Not anyone who *loves* her. You have so many feelings they fall over each other like feet. You won't use your chances and you won't let me.

KATE. But if she runs from you — *to* us —

ANNIE. Yes, that's the point. I'll have to live with her somewhere else.

KELLER. What!

ANNIE. Till she learns to depend on and listen to me.

KATE (*not without alarm*). For how long?

ANNIE. As long as it takes. (*A pause. She takes a breath.*) I packed half my things already

KELLER. Miss — Sullivan!

[*But when* ANNIE *attends upon him he is speechless, and she is merely earnest.*]

ANNIE. Captain Keller, it meets both your conditions. It's the one way I can get back in touch with Helen, and I don't see how I can be rude to you again if you're not around to interfere with me.

KELLER (*red-faced*). And what is your intention if I say no? Pack the other half, for home, and abandon your charge to — to —

ANNIE. The asylum? (*She waits, appraises* KELLER's *glare and* KATE's *uncertainty, and decides to use her weapons.*) I grew up in such an asylum. The state almshouse. (KATE's *head comes up on this, and* KELLER *stares hard;* ANNIE's *tone is cheerful enough, albeit level as gunfire.*) Rats — why, my brother Jimmie and I used to play with the rats because we didn't have toys. Maybe you'd like to know what Helen will find there, not on visiting days? One ward was full of the — old women, crippled, blind, most of them dying, but even if what they had was catching there was nowhere else to move them, and that's where they put us. There were younger ones across the hall, with T.B., and epileptic fits, and some insane. Some just had the D.T.'s. In another ward, there were the foundlings, and we played with them too, but not many of them lived. The first year we had eighty, seventy died. The room Jimmie and I played in was the deadhouse, where they kept the bodies till they could dig —

KATE (*closes her eyes*). Oh, my dear —

ANNIE. — the graves. (*She is immune to* KATE's *compassion.*) No, it made me strong. But I don't think you need send Helen there. She's strong enough. (*She waits again; but when neither offers her a word, she simply concludes.*) No, I have no conditions, Captain Keller.

KATE (*not looking up*). Miss Annie.

ANNIE. Yes.

KATE (*a pause*). Where would you — take Helen?

ANNIE. Ohh — (*Brightly*) Italy?

KELLER (*wheeling*). What?

ANNIE. Can't have everything. How would this garden house do? Furnish it, bring Helen here after a long ride so she won't recognize it, and you can see her every day. If she doesn't know. Well?

KATE (*a sigh of relief*). Is that all?

ANNIE. That's all.

KATE. Captain. (KELLER *turns his head; and* KATE's *request is quiet but firm.*) With your permission?

KELLER (*teeth in cigar*). Why must she depend on you for the food she eats?

ANNIE (*a pause*). I want control of it.

KELLER. Why?

ANNIE. It's a way to reach her.

KELLER (*stares*). You intend to *starve* her into letting you touch her?

ANNIE. She won't starve, she'll learn. All's fair in love and war, Captain Keller, you never cut supplies?

KELLER. This is hardly a war!

ANNIE. Well, it's not love. A siege is a siege.

KELLER (*heavily*). Miss Sullivan. Do you *like* the child?

ANNIE (*straight in his eyes*). Do you?

[*A long pause.*]

KATE. You could have a servant here —

ANNIE (*amused*). I'll have enough work without looking after a servant!

But that boy Percy could sleep here, run errands —

KATE (*also amused*). We can let Percy sleep here, I think, Captain?

ANNIE (*eagerly*). And some old furniture, all our own —

KATE (*also eager*). Captain? Do you think that walnut bedstead in the barn would be too —

KELLER. I have not yet consented to Percy! Or to the house, or to the proposal! Or to Miss Sullivan's — staying on when I — (*But he erupts in an irate surrender.*) Very well, I consent to everything! (*He shakes the cigar at ANNIE.*) For two weeks. I'll give you two weeks in this place, and it will be a miracle if you get the child to tolerate you.

KATE. Two weeks? Miss Annie, can you accomplish anything in two weeks?

KELLER. Anything or not, two weeks, then the child comes back to us. Make up your mind, Miss Sullivan, yes or no?

ANNIE. Two weeks. For only one miracle? (*She nods at him, nervously.*) I'll get her to tolerate me.

[KELLER *marches out, and slams the door.* KATE *on her feet regards* ANNIE, *who is facing the door.*]

KATE (*then*). You can't think as little of love as you said. (ANNIE *glances questioning.*) Or you wouldn't stay.

ANNIE (*a pause*). I didn't come here for love. I came for money!

[KATE *shakes her head to this, with a smile; after a moment she extends her open hand.* ANNIE *looks at it, but when she puts hers out it is not to shake hands, it is to set her fist in* KATE's *palm.*]

KATE (*puzzled*). Hm?

ANNIE. A. It's the first of many. Twenty-six!

[KATE *squeezes her fist, squeezes it hard, and hastens out after* KELLER.

ANNIE *stands as the door closes behind her, her manner so apprehensive that finally she slaps her brow, holds it, sighs, and, with her eyes closed, crosses herself for luck.*]

SCENE 5

The garden house. Later.

The lights dim into a cool silhouette scene around her, the lamp paling out, and now, in formal entrances, persons appear around ANNIE *with furniture for the room:* PERCY *crosses the stage with a rocking chair and waits;* MARTHA *from another direction bears in a stool,* VINEY *bears in a small table, and the other Negro servant rolls in a bed partway from left; and* ANNIE, *opening her eyes to put her glasses back on, sees them. She turns around in the room once, and goes into action, pointing out locations for each article. The servants place them and leave, and* ANNIE *then darts around, interchanging them. In the midst of this — while* PERCY *and* MARTHA *reappear with a tray of food and a chair, respectively —* JAMES *comes down from the house with* ANNIE's *suitcase, and stands viewing the room and her quizzically.* ANNIE *halts abruptly under his eye, embarrassed, then seizes the suitcase from his hand, explaining herself brightly.*

ANNIE. I always wanted to live in a doll's house!

[*She sets the suitcase out of the way, and continues;* VINEY *at left appears to position a rod with drapes for a doorway, and the other servant at center pushes in a wheelbarrow loaded with a couple of boxes of* HELEN's *toys and clothes.* ANNIE *helps lift them into the room, and the servant pushes the wheelbarrow off. In none of this is any heed taken of the imaginary walls of the garden house, the furniture is moved in from every side and itself defines the walls.*

ANNIE *now drags the box of toys into center, props up the doll conspicuously on top; with the people melted away, except for* JAMES, *all is again still. The lights turn again without pause, rising warmer.*]

JAMES. You don't let go of things easily, do you? How will you — win her hand now, in this place?

ANNIE (*curtly*). Do I know? I lost my temper, and here we are!

JAMES (*lightly*). No touching, no teaching. Of course, you *are* bigger —

ANNIE. I'm not counting on force, I'm counting on her. That little imp is dying to know.

JAMES. Know what?

ANNIE. Anything. Any and every crumb in God's creation. I'll have to use that appetite too.

[*She gives the room a final survey, straightens the bed, arranges the curtains.*]

JAMES (*a pause*). Maybe she'll teach you.

ANNIE. Of course.

JAMES. That she isn't. That there's such a thing as — dullness of heart. Acceptance. And letting go. Sooner or later we all give up, don't we?

ANNIE. Maybe you all do. It's my idea of the original sin.

JAMES. What is?

ANNIE (*witheringly*). Giving up.

JAMES (*nettled*). You won't open her. Why can't you let her be? Have some — pity on her, for being what she is —

ANNIE. If I'd ever once thought like that, I'd be dead!

JAMES (*pleasantly*). You will be. Why trouble? (ANNIE *turns to glare at him;*

he is mocking.*) Or will you teach me? (*And with a bow, he drifts off.*)

[*Now in the distance there comes the clopping of hoofs, drawing near, and nearer, up to the door; and they halt.* ANNIE *wheels to face the door. When it opens this time, the* KELLERS — KATE *in traveling bonnet,* KELLER *also hatted — are standing there with* HELEN *between them; she is in a cloak.* KATE *gently cues her into the room.* HELEN *comes in groping, baffled, but interested in the new surroundings;* ANNIE *evades her exploring hand, her gaze not leaving the child.*]

ANNIE. Does she know where she is?

KATE (*shakes her head*). We rode her out in the country for two hours.

KELLER. For all she knows, she could be in another town —

[HELEN *stumbles over the box on the floor and in it discovers her doll and other battered toys, is pleased, sits to them, then becomes puzzled and suddenly very wary. She scrambles up and back to her mother's thighs, but* ANNIE *steps in, and it is hers that* HELEN *embraces.* HELEN *recoils, gropes, and touches her cheek instantly.*]

KATE. That's her sign for me.

ANNIE. I know. (HELEN *waits, then recommences her groping, more urgently.* KATE *stands indecisive, and takes an abrupt step toward her, but* ANNIE'S *hand is a barrier.*) In two weeks.

KATE. Miss Annie, I — Please be good to her. These two weeks, try to be very good to her —

ANNIE. I will. (KATE, *turning then, hurries out. The* KELLERS *cross back of the main house.* ANNIE *closes the door.* HELEN *starts at the door jar, and rushes it.* ANNE *holds her off.* HELEN *kicks her, breaks free, and careens around the*

room like an imprisoned bird, colliding
with furniture, groping wildly, repeatedly touching her cheek in a growing
panic. When she has covered the room,
she commences her weird screaming.
ANNIE moves to comfort her, but her
touch sends HELEN into a paroxysm of
rage: she tears away, falls over her box
of toys, flings its contents in handfuls in
ANNIE's direction, flings the box too,
reels to her feet, rips curtains from the
window, bangs and kicks at the door,
sweeps objects off the mantelpiece and
shelf, a little tornado incarnate, all destruction, until she comes upon her doll
and, in the act of hurling it, freezes.
Then clutches it to herself, and in exhaustion sinks sobbing to the floor. AN-
NIE stands contemplating her, in some
awe.) Two weeks. (She shakes her
head, not without a touch of disgusted
bewilderment.) What did I get into
now?

[The lights have been dimming
throughout, and the garden house is
lit only by moonlight now, with AN-
NIE lost in the patches of dark.]

SCENE 6

The Keller house.

KATE, *now hatless and coatless, enters the family room by the rear door,
carrying a lamp.* KELLER, *also hatless,
wanders simultaneously around the
back of the main house to where* JAMES
*has been waiting, in the rising moon-
light, on the porch.*

KELLER. I can't understand it. I had
every intention of dismissing that girl,
not setting her up like an empress.

JAMES. Yes, what's her secret, sir?

KELLER. Secret?

JAMES (*pleasantly*). That enables her
to get anything she wants out of you?
When I can't.

[JAMES *turns to go into the house, but*
KELLER *grasps his wrist, twisting him
half to his knees.* KATE *comes from
the porch.*]

KELLER (*angrily*). She does *not* get
anything she —

JAMES (*in pain*). Don't — don't —

KATE. Captain.

KELLER. He's afraid. (*He throws*
JAMES *away from him, with contempt.*)
What *does* he want out of me?

JAMES (*with an outcry.*) My God,
don't you know? (*He gazes from* KELLER
to KATE.) Everything you forgot, when
you forgot my mother.

KELLER. What! (JAMES *wheels into
the house.* KELLER *takes a stride to the
porch, to roar after him.*) One thing
that girl's secret is not, she doesn't fire
one shot and disappear! (KATE *stands
rigid, and* KELLER *comes back to her.*)
Katie. Don't mind what he —

KATE. Captain, *I* am proud of you.

KELLER. For what?

KATE. For letting this girl have what
she needs.

KELLER. Why can't my son be? He
can't bear me, you'd think I treat him
as hard as this girl does Helen — (*He
breaks off, as it dawns on him.*)

KATE (*gently*). Perhaps you do.

KELLER. But he has to learn some respect!

KATE (*a pause, wryly*). Do you like
the child? (*She turns again to the porch,
but pauses, reluctant.*) How empty the
house is, tonight.

[*After a moment she continues on in.*
KELLER *stands moveless, as the moonlight dies on him.*]

SCENE 7

*The garden house.
The distant belfry chimes toll, two*

o'clock, and with them, a moment later, comes the boy's voice on the wind, in a whisper:

BOY'S VOICE. Annie. Annie.

[*In her patch of dark* ANNIE, *now in her nightgown, hurls a cup into a corner as though it were her grief, getting rid of its taste through her teeth.*]

ANNIE. No! No pity, I won't have it. (*She comes to* HELEN, *prone on the floor.*) On either of us. (*She goes to her knees, but when she touches* HELEN's *hand the child starts up awake, recoils, and scrambles away from her under the bed.* ANNIE *stares after her. She strikes her palm on the floor, with passion.*) I *will* touch you! (*She gets to her feet, and paces in a kind of anger around the bed, her hand in her hair, and confronting* HELEN *at each turn.*) How, how? How do I — (ANNIE *stops. Then she calls out urgently, loudly.*) Percy! Percy! (*She moves swiftly to the drapes, at left.*) Percy, wake up! (PERCY'S *voice comes in a thick sleepy mumble, unintelligible.*) Get out of bed and come in here, I need you. (ANNIE *darts away, finds and strikes a match, and touches it to the hanging lamp; the lights come up dimly in the room, and* PERCY *stands bare to the waist in torn overalls between the drapes with eyes closed, swaying.* ANNIE *goes to him, pats his cheeks vigorously.*) Percy. You awake?

PERCY. No'm.

ANNIE. How would you like to play a nice game?

PERCY. Whah?

ANNIE. With Helen. She's under the bed. Touch her hand.

[*She kneels* PERCY *down at the bed, thrusting his hand under it to contact* HELEN's; HELEN *emits an animal sound and crawls to the opposite side,*

but commences sniffing. ANNIE *rounds the bed with* PERCY *and thrusts his hand again at* HELEN; *this time* HELEN *clutches it, sniffs in recognition, and comes scrambling out after* PERCY, *to hug him with delight.* PERCY *alarmed, struggles, and* HELEN's *fingers go to his mouth.*]

PERCY. Lemme go. Lemme go — (HELEN *fingers her own lips, as before, moving them in dumb imitation.*) She tryin' talk. She gonna hit me —

ANNIE (*grimly*). She *can* talk. If she only knew, I'll show you how. She makes letters. (*She opens* PERCY's *other hand, and spells into it:*) This one is C. C. (*She hits his palm with it a couple of times, her eyes upon* HELEN *across him;* HELEN *gropes to feel what* PERCY's *hand is doing, and when she encounters* ANNIE's *she falls back from them.*) She's mad at me now, though, she won't play. But she knows lots of letters. Here's another, A. C, a. C, a. (*But she is watching* HELEN, *who comes groping, consumed with curiosity;* ANNIE *makes the letters in* PERCY's *hand, and* HELEN *pokes to question what they are up to. Then* HELEN *snatches* PERCY's *other hand, and quickly spells four letters into it.* ANNIE *follows them aloud.*) C, a, k, e! She spells cake, she gets cake. (*She is swiftly over to the tray of food, to fetch cake and a jug of milk.*) She doesn't know yet it means this. Isn't it funny she knows how to spell it and doesn't *know* she knows? (*She breaks the cake in two pieces, and extends one to each;* HELEN *rolls away from her offer.*) Well, if she won't play it with me, I'll play it with you. Would you like to learn one she doesn't know?

PERCY. No'm.

[*But* ANNIE *seizes his wrist, and spells to him.*]

ANNIE. M, i, l, k. M is this. I, that's an easy one, just the little finger. L is this — (*And* HELEN *comes back with her hand, to feel the new word.* ANNIE *brushes her away, and continues spelling aloud to* PERCY. HELEN's *hand comes back again, and tries to get in;* ANNIE *brushes it away again.* HELEN's *hand insists, and* ANNIE *puts it away rudely.*) No, why should I talk to you? I'm teaching Percy a new word. L. K is this — (HELEN *now yanks their hands apart; she butts* PERCY *away, and thrusts her palm out insistently.* ANNIE's *eyes are bright, with glee.*) Ho, you're jealous, are you! (HELEN's *hand waits, intractably* [1] *waits.*) All *right*. (ANNIE *spells into it, milk; and* HELEN *after a moment spells it back to* ANNIE. ANNIE *takes her hand, with her whole face shining. She gives a great sigh.*) Good! So I'm finally back to where I can touch you, hm? Touch and go! No love lost, but here we go. (*She puts the jug of milk into* HELEN's *hand and squeezes* PERCY's *shoulder.*) You can go to bed now, you've earned your sleep. Thank you. (PERCY *stumbling up weaves his way out through the drapes.* HELEN *finishes drinking, and holds the jug out, for* ANNIE; *when* ANNIE *takes it,* HELEN *crawls onto the bed, and makes for sleep.* ANNIE *stands, looks down at her.*) Now all I have to teach you is — one word. Everything. (*She sets the jug down. On the floor now* ANNIE *spies the doll, stoops to pick it up, and with it dangling in her hand, turns off the lamp. A shaft of moonlight is left on* HELEN *in the bed, and a second shaft on the rocking chair; and* ANNIE, *after putting off her smoked glasses, sits in the rocker with the doll. She is rather happy, and dangles the doll on her knee, and it makes its momma sound.* ANNIE *whispers to it in mock solicitude.*) Hush, lit-

tle baby. Don't — say a word — (*She lays it against her shoulder, and begins rocking with it, patting its diminutive behind; she talks the lullaby to it, humorously at first.*)

"Momma's gonna buy you — a mockingbird:
If that — mockingbird don't sing —

(*The rhythm of the rocking takes her into the tune, softly, and more tenderly.*)

Momma's gonna buy you a diamond ring:
If that diamond ring turns to brass —

(*A third shaft of moonlight outside now rises to pick out* JAMES *at the main house, with one foot on the porch step; he turns his body, as if hearing the song:*)

Momma's gonna buy you a looking-glass:
If that looking-glass gets broke —

(*In the family room a fourth shaft picks out* KELLER, *seated at the table, in thought; and he, too, lifts his head, as if hearing.*)

Momma's gonna buy you a billy goat:
If that billy goat won't pull —

(*The fifth shaft is upstairs in* ANNIE's *room, and picks out* KATE, *pacing there; and she halts, turning her head, too, as if hearing.*)

Momma's gonna buy you a cart and bull:
If that cart and bull turns over,
Momma's gonna buy you a dog named Rover;
If that dog named Rover won't bark — "

[*With the shafts of moonlight on* HELEN, *and* JAMES, *and* KELLER, *and* KATE, *all motionless, and* ANNIE *rocking the doll, the curtain ends the act.*]

[1] **intractably** (ĭn·trăk′tá·b′lĭ): stubbornly.

ACT III

SCENE 1

The garden house and the Keller home. Two weeks have passed.

The stage is totally dark, until we see ANNIE *and* HELEN *silhouetted on the bed in the garden house.* ANNIE'S *voice is audible, very patient, and worn; it has been saying this for a long time.*

ANNIE. Water, Helen. This is water. W, a, t, e, r. It has a *name.* (*A silence. Then*) Egg, e, g, g. It has a *name,* the name stands for a thing. Oh, it's so simple, simple as birth, to explain. (*The lights have commenced to rise, not on the garden house but on the homestead. Then*) Helen, Helen, the chick *has* to come out of its shell, sometime. You come out, too. (*In the bedroom upstairs, we see* VINEY *unhurriedly washing the window, dusting, turning the mattress, readying the room for use again; then in the family room a diminished group at one end of the table —* KATE, KELLER, JAMES — *finishing up a quiet breakfast; then outside, down right, the other Negro servant on his knees, assisted by* MARTHA, *working with a trowel around a new trellis and wheelbarrow. The scene is one of everyday calm, and all are oblivious to* ANNIE'S *voice.*) There's only one way out, for you, and it's language. To learn that your fingers can talk. And say anything, anything you can name. This is mug. Mug, m, u, g. Helen, it has a *name.* It — has — a — *name —*

[KATE *rises from the table.*]

KELLER (*gently*). You haven't eaten, Katie.

KATE (*smiles, shakes her head*). I haven't the appetite. I'm too — restless, I can't sit to it.

KELLER. You should eat, my dear. It will be a long day, waiting.

JAMES (*lightly*) But it's been a short two weeks. I never thought life could be so — noiseless, went much too quickly for me.

[KATE *and* KELLER *gaze at him, in silence.* JAMES *becomes uncomfortable.*]

ANNIE. C, a, r, d. Card. C, a —
JAMES. Well, the house has been practically normal, hasn't it?
KELLER (*harshly*). Jimmie.
JAMES. Is it wrong to enjoy a quiet breakfast, after five years? And you two even seem to enjoy each other —
KELLER. It could be even more noiseless, Jimmie, without your tongue running every minute. Haven't you enough feeling to imagine what Katie has been undergoing, ever since —

[KATE *stops him, with her hand on his arm.*]

KATE. Captain. (*To* JAMES.) It's true. The two weeks have been normal, quiet, all you say. But not short. Interminable. (*She rises, and wanders out; she pauses on the porch steps, gazing toward the garden house.*)
ANNIE (*fading*). W, a, t, e, r. But it means *this.* W, a, t, e, r. This. W, a, t —
JAMES. I only meant that Miss Sullivan is a boon. Of contention, though, it seems.
KELLER (*heavily*). If and when you're a parent, Jimmie, you will understand what separation means. A mother loses a — protector.
JAMES (*baffled*). Hm?
KELLER. You'll learn, we don't just keep our children safe. They keep us safe. (*He rises, with his empty coffee*

cup and saucer.) There are of course all kinds of separation, Katie has lived with one kind for five years. And another is disappointment. In a child.

[*He goes with the cup out the rear door. JAMES sits for a long moment of stillness. In the garden house the lights commence to come up; ANNIE, haggard at the table, is writing a letter, her face again almost in contact with the stationery; HELEN, apart on the stool, and for the first time as clean and neat as a button, is quietly crocheting an endless chain of wool, which snakes all around the room.*]

ANNIE. "I feel, every, day, more, and, more, in — " (*She pauses, and turns the pages of a dictionary open before her; her finger descends the words to a full stop. She elevates her eyebrows, then copies the word.*) "— adequate." (*In the main house JAMES pushes up, and goes to the front doorway, after KATE.*)

JAMES. Kate? (*KATE turns her glance. JAMES is rather weary.*) I'm sorry. Open my mouth, like that fairy tale, frogs jump out.

KATE. No. It has been better. For everyone. (*She starts away, up center.*)

ANNIE (*writing*). "If, only, there, were, someone, to, help, me, I, need, a, teacher, as, much, as, Helen — "

JAMES. Kate. (*KATE halts, waits.*) What does he want from me?

KATE. That's not the question. Stand up to the world. Jimmie. That comes first.

JAMES (*a pause, wryly*). But the world is him.

KATE. Yes. And no one can do it for you.

JAMES. Kate. (*His voice is humble.*) At least we — Could you — be my friend?

KATE. I am.

[*KATE turns to wander, up back of the garden house. ANNIE's murmur comes at once; the lights begin to die on the main house.*]

SCENE 2

The garden house.

ANNIE. " — my, mind, is, undisciplined, full, of, skips, and, jumps, and — " (*She halts, rereads, frowns.*) Hm. (*ANNIE puts her nose again in the dictionary, flips back to an earlier page, and fingers down the words; KATE presently comes down toward the bay window with a trayful of food.*) Disinter — disinterested — disjoin — dis — (*She backtracks, indignant.*) Disinterested, disjoin — Where's disipline? (*She goes a page or two back, searching with her finger, muttering.*) What a dictionary! Have to know how to spell it before you can look up how to spell it, disciple, *discipline!* Diskipline. (*She corrects the word in her letter.*) Undisciplined. (*But her eyes are bothering her, she closes them in exhaustion and gently fingers the eyelids. KATE watches her through the window.*)

KATE. What are you doing to your eyes?

[*ANNIE glances around; she puts her smoked glasses on, and gets up to come over, assuming a cheerful energy.*]

ANNIE. It's worse on my vanity! I'm learning to spell. It's like a surprise party, the most unexpected characters turn up.

KATE. You're not to overwork your eyes, Miss Annie.

ANNIE. Well. (*She takes the tray, sets it on her chair, and carries chair and tray to HELEN.*) Whatever I spell to Helen I'd better spell right.

KATE (*almost wistful*). How — serene she is.

ANNIE. She learned this stitch yesterday. Now I can't get her to stop! (*She disentangles one foot from the wool chain, and sets the chair before* HELEN. HELEN *at its contact with her knee feels the plate, promptly sets her crocheting down, and tucks the napkin in at her neck, but* ANNIE *withholds the spoon; when* HELEN *finds it missing, she folds her hands in her lap, and quietly waits.* ANNIE *twinkles at* KATE *with mock devoutness.*) Such a little lady, she'd sooner starve than eat with her fingers. (*She gives* HELEN *the spoon, and* HELEN *begins to eat, neatly.*)

KATE. You've taught her so much, these two weeks. I would never have —

ANNIE. Not enough. (*She is suddenly gloomy, shakes her head.*) Obedience isn't enough. Well, she learned two nouns this morning, key and water, brings her up to eighteen nouns and three verbs.

KATE (*hesitant*). But — not —

ANNIE. No. Not that they mean things. It's still a finger-game, no meaning. (*She turns to* KATE, *abruptly.*) Mrs. Keller — (*But she defers it; she comes back, to sit in the bay and lift her hand.*) Shall we play our finger-game?

KATE. How will she learn it?

ANNIE. It will come.

[*She spells a word;* KATE *does not respond.*]

KATE. How?

ANNIE (*a pause*). How does a bird learn to fly? (*She spells again.*) We're born to use words, like wings, it has to come.

KATE. How?

ANNIE (*another pause, wearily*). All right. I don't know how. (*She pushes up her glasses, to rub her eyes.*) I've done everything I could think of. What-

ever she's learned here — keeping herself clean, knitting, stringing beads, meals, setting-up exercises each morning, we climb trees, hunt eggs, yesterday a chick was born in her hands — all of it I spell, everything we do, we never stop spelling. I go to bed with — writer's cramp from talking so much!

KATE. I worry about you, Miss Annie. You must rest.

ANNIE. Now? She spells back in her *sleep*, her fingers make letters when she doesn't know! In her bones those five fingers know, that hand aches to — speak out, and something in her mind is asleep, how do I — nudge that awake? That's the one question.

KATE. With no answer.

ANNIE (*long pause*). Except keep at it. Like this.

[*She again begins spelling — "I, need" — and* KATE's *brows gather, following the words.*]

KATE. More — time? (*She glances at* ANNIE, *who looks her in the eyes, silent.*) Here?

ANNIE. Spell it.

[KATE *spells a word — "no" — shaking her head;* ANNIE *spells two words — "why, not" — back, with an impatient question in her eyes; and* KATE *moves her head in pain to answer it.*]

KATE. Because I can't —

ANNIE. Spell it! If she ever learns, you'll have a lot to tell each other, start now.

[KATE *painstakingly spells in air. In the midst of this the rear door opens, and* KELLER *enters with the setter* BELLE *in tow.*]

KELLER. Miss Sullivan? On my way to the office, I brought Helen a playmate —

ANNIE. Outside please, Captain Keller.

KELLER. My dear child, the two weeks are up today, surely you don't object to —

ANNIE (*rising*). They're not up till six o'clock.

KELLER (*indulgent*). Oh, now. What difference can a fraction of one day —

ANNIE. An agreement is an agreement. Now you've been very good, I'm sure you can keep it up for a few more hours.

[*She escorts* KELLER *by the arm over the threshold; he obeys, leaving* BELLE.]

KELLER. Miss Sullivan, you are a tyrant.

ANNIE. Likewise, I'm sure. You can stand there, and close the door if she comes.

KATE. I don't think you know how eager we are to have her back in our arms —

ANNIE. I do know, it's my main worry.

KELLER. It's like expecting a new child in the house. Well, she *is*, so — composed, so — (*Gently*) Attractive. You've done wonders for her, Miss Sullivan.

ANNIE (*not a question*). Have I.

KELLER. If there's anything you want from us in repayment tell us, it will be a privilege to —

ANNIE. I just told Mrs. Keller. I want more time.

KATE. Miss Annie —

ANNIE. Another week.

[HELEN *lifts her head, and begins to sniff.*]

KELLER. We miss the child. *I* miss her, I'm glad to say, that's a different debt I owe you —

ANNIE. Pay it to Helen. Give *her* another week.

KATE (*gently*). Doesn't she miss us?

KELLER. Of course she does. What a wrench this unexplainable — exile must be to her, can you say it's not?

ANNIE. No. But I —

[HELEN *is off the stool, to grope about the room; when she encounters* BELLE, *she throws her arms around the dog's neck in delight.*]

KATE. Doesn't she need affection too, Miss Annie?

ANNIE (*wavering*). She — never shows me she needs it, she won't have any — caressing or —

KATE. But you're not her mother.

KELLER. And what would another week accomplish? We are more than satisfied, you've done more than we ever thought possible, taught her constructive —

ANNIE. I can't promise anything. All I can —

KELLER (*no break*). — things to do, to behave like — even look like — a human child, so manageable, contented, cleaner, more —

ANNIE (*withering*). Cleaner.

KELLER. Well. We say cleanliness is next to godliness, Miss —

ANNIE. Cleanliness is next to nothing, she has to learn that everything has its name! That words can be her *eyes*, to everything in the world outside her, and inside too, what is she without words? With them she can think, have ideas, be reached, there's not a thought or fact in the world that can't be hers. You publish a newspaper, Captain Keller, do I have to tell you what words are? And she has them already —

KELLER. Miss Sullivan.

ANNIE. — eighteen nouns and three verbs, they're in her fingers now, I need only time to push *one* of them into her mind! One, and everything under the sun will follow. Don't you see what she's learned here is only clearing the way for that? I can't risk her unlearning it, give me more time alone with her, another week to —

KELLER. Look. (*He points, and* ANNIE

turns. HELEN *is playing with* BELLE's *claws; she makes letters with her fingers, shows them to* BELLE, *waits with her palm, then manipulates the dog's claws.*) What is she spelling? (*A silence.*)

KATE. Water?

[ANNIE *nods.*]

KELLER. Teaching a dog to spell. (*A pause*) The dog doesn't know what she means, any more than she knows what you mean, Miss Sullivan. I think you ask too much, of her and yourself. God may not have meant Helen to have the — eyes you speak of.

ANNIE (*toneless*). I mean her to.

KELLER (*curiously*). What is it to you? (ANNIE's *head comes slowly up.*) You make us see how we indulge her for our sake. Is the opposite true, for you?

ANNIE (*then*). Half a week?

KELLER. An agreement *is* an agreement.

ANNIE. Mrs. Keller?

KATE (*simply*). I want her back.

[*A wait;* ANNIE *then lets her hands drop in surrender, and nods.*]

KELLER. I'll send Viney over to help you pack.

ANNIE. Not until six o'clock. I have her till six o'clock.

KELLER (*consenting*). Six o'clock. Come, Katie.

[KATE *leaving the window joins him around back, while* KELLER *closes the door; they are shut out. Only the garden house is daylit now, and the light on it is narrowing down.* ANNIE *stands watching* HELEN *work* BELLE's *claws. Then she settles beside them on her knees, and stops* HELEN's *hand.*]

ANNIE (*gently*). No. (*She shakes her head, with* HELEN's *hand to her face, then spells.*) Dog, D, o, g. Dog. (*She*

touches HELEN's *hand to* BELLE. HELEN *dutifully pats the dog's head, and resumes spelling to its paw.*) Not water. (ANNIE *rolls to her feet, brings a tumbler of water back from the tray, and kneels with it, to seize* HELEN's *hand and spell.*) Here. Water. *Water.* (*She thrusts* HELEN's *hand into the tumbler.* HELEN *lifts her hand out dripping, wipes it daintily on* BELLE's *hide, and taking the tumbler from* ANNIE, *endeavors to thrust* BELLE's *paw into it.* ANNIE *sits watching, wearily.*) I don't know how to tell you. Not a soul in the world knows how to tell you. Helen, Helen. (*She bends in compassion to touch her lips to* HELEN's *temple, and instantly* HELEN *pauses, her hands off the dog, her head slightly averted. The lights are still narrowing, and* BELLE *slinks off. After a moment* ANNIE *sits back.*) Yes, what's it to me? They're satisfied. Give them back their child and dog, both housebroken, everyone's satisfied. But me, and you. (HELEN's *hand comes out into the light, groping.*) Reach. *Reach!* (ANNIE *extending her own hand grips* HELEN's; *the two hands are clasped, tense in the light, the rest of the room changing in shadow.*) I wanted to teach you — oh, every-thing the earth is full of, Helen — everything on it that's ours for a wink and it's gone, and what we are on it; the — light we bring to it and leave behind in — words. Why, you can see five thousand years back in a light of words, everything we feel, think, know — and share, in words, so not a soul is in darkness, or done with, even in the grave. And I know, I *know*, one word and I can — put the world in your hand — and whatever it is to me, I won't take less! How, how, how do I tell you that this — (*She spells.*) — means a *word*, and the word means this *thing*, wool? (*She thrusts the wool at* HELEN's *hand;* HELEN *sits, puzzled.* ANNIE *puts the crocheting aside.*) Or this — s, t, o, o, l — means this *thing*, stool? (*She claps* HELEN's *palm to the stool.* HELEN *waits, uncomprehending.* ANNIE *snatches up her napkin, spells:*) Napkin! (*She forces it on* HELEN's *hand, waits, discards it, lifts a fold of the child's dress, spells:*) Dress! (*She lets it drop spells:*) F, a, c, e, face! (*She draws* HELEN's *hand to her cheek, and pressing it there, staring into the child's responseless eyes, hears the distant belfry begin to toll, slowly: one, two, three, four, five, six.*)

[*On the third stroke the lights stealing in around the garden house show us figures waiting:* VINEY, *the other servant,* MARTHA, PERCY *at the drapes, and* JAMES *on the dim porch.* ANNIE *and* HELEN *remain, frozen. The chimes die away. Silently* PERCY *moves the draperod back out of sight;* VINEY *steps into the room — not using the door — and unmakes the bed; the other servant brings the wheelbarrow over, leaves it hardy, rolls the bed off;* VINEY *puts the bed linens on top of a waiting boxful of* HELEN's *toys, and loads the box on the wheelbarrow;* MARTHA *and* PERCY *take out the chairs, with the trayful, then the table; and* JAMES, *coming down and into the room, lifts* ANNIE's *suitcase from its corner.* VINEY *and the other servant load the remaining odds and ends on the wheelbarrow, and the servant wheels it off.* VINEY *and the children departing leave only* JAMES *in the room with* ANNIE *and* HELEN. JAMES *studies the two of them, without mockery, and then, quietly going to the door and opening it, bears the suitcase out, and housewards. He leaves the door open.*]

(KATE *steps into the doorway, and stands.* ANNIE *lifting her gaze from* HELEN *sees her; she takes* HELEN's *hand from her cheek, and returns it to the child's own, stroking it there twice, in her mother-sign, before spelling slowly into it:*) M, o, t, h, e, r. Mother. (HELEN *with her hand free strokes her cheek, suddenly forlorn.* ANNIE *takes her hand again.*) M, o, t, h — (*But* KATE *is trembling with such impatience that her voice breaks from her, harsh.*)

KATE. Let her *come!*

[ANNIE *lifts* HELEN *to her feet, with a turn, and gives her a little push. Now* HELEN *begins groping, sensing something, trembling herself; and* KATE *falling one step in onto her knees clasps her, kissing her.* HELEN *clutches her, tight as she can.* KATE *is inarticulate, choked, repeating* HELEN's *name again and again. She wheels with her in her arms, to stumble away out the doorway;* ANNIE *stands unmoving, while* KATE *in a blind walk carries* HELEN *like a baby behind the main house, out of view.* ANNIE *is now alone on the stage. She turns, gazing around at the stripped room, bidding it silently farewell, impassively, like a defeated general on the deserted battlefield. All that remains is a stand with a basin of water; and here* ANNIE *takes up an eyecup, bathes each of her eyes, empties the eyecup, drops it in her purse, and tiredly locates her smoked glasses on the floor. The lights alter subtly; in the act of putting on her glasses* ANNIE *hears something that stops her, with head lifted. We hear it too, the voices out of the past, including her own now, in a whisper:*]

BOY'S VOICE. You said we'd be together, forever — You promised, forever and — Annie!

ANAGNOS' VOICE. But that battle is dead and done with, why not let it stay buried?

ANNIE'S VOICE (*whispering*). I think God must owe me a resurrection.

ANAGNOS' VOICE. What?

[*A pause; and* ANNIE *answers it herself, heavily.*]

ANNIE. And I owe God one.

BOY'S VOICE. Forever and ever — (AN-NIE *shakes her head.*) — forever, and ever, and — (ANNIE *covers her ears.*) — forever, and ever, and ever — (*It pursues* ANNIE; *she flees to snatch up her purse, wheels to the doorway, and* KEL-LER *is standing in it. The lights have lost their special color.*)

KELLER. Miss — Annie. (*He has an envelope in his fingers.*) I've been waiting to give you this.

ANNIE (*after a breath*). What?

KELLER. Your first month's salary. (*He puts it in her hand.*) With many more to come, I trust. It doesn't express what we feel, it doesn't pay our debt. For what you've done.

ANNIE. What have I done?

KELLER. Taken a wild thing, and given us back a child.

ANNIE (*presently*). I taught her one thing, no. Don't do this, don't do that —

KELLER. It's more than all of us could, in all the years we —

ANNIE. I wanted to teach her what language is. I wanted to teach her *yes*.

KELLER. You will have time.

ANNIE. I don't know how. I know without it to do nothing but obey is — no gift, obedience without understanding is a — blindness, too. Is that all I've wished on her?

KELLER (*gently*). No, no —

ANNIE. Maybe. I don't know what else to do. Simply go on, keep doing what I've done, and have — faith that inside she's — That inside it's waiting. Like water, underground. All I can do is keep on.

KELLER. It's enough. For us.

ANNIE. You can help, Captain Keller.

KELLER. How?

ANNIE. Even learning *no* has been at a cost. Of much trouble and pain. Don't undo it.

KELLER. Why should we wish to —

ANNIE (*abruptly*). The world isn't an easy place for anyone. I don't want her just to obey — but to let her have her way in everything is a lie, to *her*, I can't — (*Her eyes fill, it takes her by surprise, and she laughs through it.*) And I don't even love her, she's not my child! Well. You've got to stand between that lie and her.

KELLER. We'll try.

ANNIE. Because *I* will. As long as you let me stay, that's one promise I'll keep.

KELLER. Agreed. We've learned something too, I hope. (*A pause*) Won't you come now, to supper?

ANNIE. Yes. (*She wags the envelope, ruefully.*) Why doesn't God pay His debts each month?

KELLER. I beg your pardon?

ANNIE. Nothing. I used to wonder how I could — (*The lights are fading on them, simultaneously rising on the family room of the main house, where* VINEY *is polishing glassware at the table set for dinner.*) — earn a living.

KELLER. Oh, you do.

ANNIE. I really do. Now the question is, can I survive it! (KELLER *smiles, offers his arm.*)

KELLER. May I?

[ANNIE *takes it, and the lights lose them as he escorts her out.*]

SCENE 3

The Keller house and yard.

Now in the family room the rear door opens, and HELEN *steps in. She stands a moment, then sniffs in one deep grateful*

*breath, and her hands go out vigorously
to familiar things, over the door panels,
and to the chairs around the table, and
over the silverware on the table, until
she meets* VINEY; *she pats her flank approvingly.*

VINEY. Oh, we glad to have you back
too, prob'ly.

[HELEN *hurries groping to the front
door, opens and closes it, removes its
key, opens and closes it again to be
sure it is unlocked, gropes back to
the rear door and repeats the procedure, removing its key and hugging
herself gleefully.*

AUNT EV *is next in by the rear door,
with a relish tray; she bends to kiss*
HELEN's *cheek.* HELEN *finds* KATE *behind her, and thrusts the keys at her.*]

KATE. What? Oh. (*To* EV) Keys. (*She
pockets them, lets* HELEN *feel them.*)
Yes, *I'll* keep the keys. I think we've
had enough of locked doors, too.

[JAMES, *having earlier put* ANNIE's *suitcase inside her door upstairs and taken himself out of view around the
corner, now reappears and comes
down the stairs as* ANNIE *and* KELLER
*mount the porch steps. Following
them into the family room, he pats*
ANNIE's *hair in passing, rather to her
surprise.*]

JAMES. Evening, general. (*He takes
his own chair opposite.*)

[VINEY *bears the empty water pitcher
out to the porch. The remaining suggestion of garden house is gone now,
and the water pump is unobstructed;*
VINEY *pumps water into the pitcher.*
KATE *surveying the table breaks the
silence.*]

KATE. Will you say the grace, Jimmie?

[*They bow their heads, except for* HELEN, *who palms her empty plate and
then reaches to be sure her mother is
there.* JAMES *considers a moment,
glances across at* ANNIE, *lowers his
head again, and obliges.*]

JAMES (*lightly*). And Jacob was left
alone, and wrestled with an angel until the breaking of the day; and the hollow of Jacob's thigh was out of joint,
as he wrestled with him; and the angel
said, Let me go, for the day breaketh.
And Jacob said, I will not let thee go,
except thou bless me. Amen. (ANNIE *has
lifted her eyes suspiciously at* JAMES,
*who winks expressionlessly and inclines
his head to* HELEN.) Oh, you angel.
(*The others lift their faces;* VINEY *returns with the pitcher, setting it down
near* KATE, *then goes out the rear door;
and* ANNIE *puts a napkin around* HELEN.)

AUNT EV. That's a very strange grace,
James.

KELLER. Will you start the muffins,
Ev?

JAMES. It's from the Good Book, isn't
it?

AUNT EV (*passing a plate*). Well, of
course it is. Didn't you know?

JAMES. Yes. I knew.

KELLER (*serving*). Ham, Miss Annie?

ANNIE. Please.

AUNT EV. Then why ask?

JAMES. I meant it *is* from the Good
Book, and therefore a fitting grace.

AUNT EV. Well. I don't know about
that.

KATE (*with the pitcher*). Miss Annie?

ANNIE. Thank you.

AUNT EV. There's an awful *lot* of
things in the Good Book that I wouldn't
care to hear just before eating.

[*When* ANNIE *reaches for the pitcher,*
HELEN *removes her napkin and drops
it to the floor.* ANNIE *is filling* HELEN's

glass when she notices it; she considers HELEN's *bland expression a moment, then bends, retrieves it, and tucks it around* HELEN's *neck again.*]

JAMES. Well, fitting in the sense that Jacob's thigh was out of joint, and so is this piggie's.

AUNT EV. I declare, James —

KATE. Pickles, Aunt Ev?

AUNT EV. Oh, I should say so, you know my opinion of your pickles —

KATE. This is the end of them, I'm afraid. I didn't put up nearly enough last summer, this year I intend to —

[*She interrupts herself, seeing* HELEN *deliberately lift off her napkin and drop it again to the floor. She bends to retrieve it, but* ANNIE *stops her arm.*]

KELLER (*not noticing*). Reverend looked in at the office today to complain his hens have stopped laying. Poor fellow, *he* was out of joint, all he could —

[*He stops too, to frown down the table at* KATE, HELEN, *and* ANNIE *in turn, all suspended in mid-motion.*]

JAMES (*not noticing*). I've always suspected those hens.

AUNT EV. Of what?

JAMES. I think they're Papists. Has he tried —

[*He stops, too, following* KELLER's *eyes.* ANNIE *now stoops to pick the napkin up.*]

AUNT EV. James, now you're pulling my — lower extremity, the first thing you know we'll be —

[*She stops, too, hearing herself in the silence.* ANNIE, *with everyone now watching, for the third time puts the napkin on* HELEN. HELEN *yanks it off, and throws it down.* ANNIE *rises, lifts* HELEN's *plate, and bears it away.* HEL-

EN, *feeling it gone, slides down and commences to kick up under the table; the dishes jump.* ANNIE *contemplates this for a moment, then coming back takes* HELEN's *wrists firmly and swings her off the chair.* HELEN *struggling gets one hand free, and catches at her mother's skirt; when* KATE *takes her by the shoulders,* HELEN *hangs quiet.*]

KATE. Miss Annie.

ANNIE. No.

KATE (*a pause*). It's a very special day.

ANNIE (*grimly*). It will be, when I give in to that.

[*She tries to disengage* HELEN's *hand;* KATE *lays hers on* ANNIE's.]

KATE. Please. I've hardly had a chance to welcome her home —

ANNIE. Captain Keller.

KELLER (*embarrassed*). Oh. Katie, we — had a little talk, Miss Annie feels that if we indulge Helen in these —

AUNT EV. But what's the child done?

ANNIE. She's learned not to throw things on the floor and kick. It took us the best part of two weeks and —

AUNT EV. But only a napkin, it's not as if it were breakable!

ANNIE. And everything she's learned is? Mrs. Keller, I don't think we should — play tug-of-war for her. Either give her to me or you keep her from kicking.

KATE. What do you wish to do?

ANNIE. Let me take her from the table.

AUNT EV. Oh, let her stay, my goodness, she's only a child. She doesn't have to wear a napkin if she doesn't want to her first evening —

ANNIE (*in a level voice*). And ask outsiders not to interfere.

AUNT EV (*astonished*). Out — outsi — I'm the child's *aunt!*

KATE (*distressed*). Will once hurt so much, Miss Annie? I've — made all Helen's favorite foods, tonight.

[*A pause*]

KELLER (*gently*). It's a homecoming party, Miss Annie.

[ANNIE *after a moment releases* HELEN. *But she cannot accept it, at her own chair she shakes her head and turns back, intent on* KATE.]

ANNIE. She's testing you. You realize?

JAMES (*to Annie*). She's testing you.

KELLER. Jimmie, be quiet. (JAMES *sits, tense.*) Now she's home, naturally she —

ANNIE. And wants to see what will happen. At your hands. I said it was my main worry, is this what you promised me not half an hour ago?

KELLER (*reasonably*). But she's *not* kicking, now —

ANNIE. And not learning not to. Mrs. Keller, teaching her is bound to be painful, to everyone. I know it hurts to watch, but she'll live up to just what you demand of her, and no more.

JAMES (*palely*). She's testing *you*.

KELLER (*testily*). Jimmie.

JAMES. I have an opinion, I think I should —

KELLER. No one's interested in hearing your opinion.

ANNIE. *I'm* interested. Of course she's testing me. Let me keep her to what she's learned and she'll go on learning from me. Take her out of my hands and it all comes apart. (KATE *closes her eyes, digesting it;* ANNIE *sits again, with a brief comment for her.*) Be bountiful, it's at her expense. (*She turns to* JAMES, *flatly.*) Please pass me more of — her favorite foods. (*Then* KATE *lifts* HELEN's *hand, and turning her toward* ANNIE, *surrenders her;* HELEN *makes for her own chair.*)

KATE (*low*). Take her, Miss Annie.

ANNIE (*then*). Thank you.

[*But the moment* ANNIE *rising reaches for her hand,* HELEN *begins to fight and kick, clutching to the tablecloth, and uttering laments.* ANNIE *again tries to loosen her hand, and* KELLER *rises.*]

KELLER (*tolerant*). I'm afraid you're the difficulty, Miss Annie. Now I'll keep her to what she's learned, you're quite right there — (*He takes* HELEN's *hands from* ANNIE, *pats them;* HELEN *quiets down.*) — but I don't see that we need send her from the table, after all, she's the guest of honor. Bring her plate back.

ANNIE. If she was a seeing child, none of you would tolerate one —

KELLER. Well, she's not, I think some compromise is called for. Bring her plate, please. (ANNIE's *jaw sets, but she restores the plate, while* KELLER *fastens the napkin around* HELEN's *neck; she permits it.*) There. It's not unnatural, most of us take some aversion to our teachers, and occasionally another hand can smooth things out. (*He puts a fork in* HELEN's *hand;* HELEN *takes it. Genially:*) Now. Shall we start all over? (*He goes back around the table, and sits.* ANNIE *stands watching.* HELEN *is motionless, thinking things through, until with a wicked glee she deliberately flings the fork on the floor. After another moment she plunges her hand into her food, and crams a fistful into her mouth.*)

JAMES (*wearily*). I think we've started all over —

[KELLER *shoots a glare at him, as* HELEN *plunges her other hand into* ANNIE's *plate.* ANNIE *at once moves in, to grasp her wrist, and* HELEN *flinging out a hand encounters the pitcher; she swings with it at* ANNIE; ANNIE *falling back blocks it with an elbow,*

but the water flies over her dress. AN-
NIE *gets her breath, then snatches the
pitcher away in one hand, hoists* HEL-
EN *up bodily under the other arm,
and starts to carry her out, kicking.*
KELLER *stands.*]

ANNIE (*savagely polite*). Don't get
up!
KELLER. Where are you going?
ANNIE. Don't smooth anything else
out for me, don't interfere in any way!
I treat her like a seeing child because I
ask her to see, I *expect* her to see, don't
undo what I do!
KELLER. Where are you taking her?
ANNIE. To make her fill this pitcher
again!

[*She thrusts out with* HELEN *under her
arm, but* HELEN *escapes up the stairs
and* ANNIE *runs after her.* KELLER
stands rigid. AUNT EV *is astounded.*]

AUNT EV. You let her speak to you like
that, Arthur? A creature who *works* for
you?
KELLER (*angrily*). No, I don't.

[*He is starting after* ANNIE *when* JAMES,
*on his feet with shaky resolve, inter-
poses his chair between them in* KEL-
LER's *path.*]

JAMES. Let her go.
KELLER. What!
JAMES (*a swallow*). I said — let her
go. She's right. (KELLER *glares at the
chair and him.* JAMES *takes a deep
breath, then headlong:*) She's right,
Kate's right, I'm right, and you're
wrong. If you drive her away from here
it will be over my dead — chair, has it
never occurred to you that on one occasion you might be consummately
wrong? (KELLER's *stare is unbelieving,
even a little fascinated.* KATE *rises in
trepidation,*[1] *to mediate.*)

[1] **trepidation** (trĕp'ĭ·dā'shŭn): alarm.

KATE. Captain.

[KELLER *stops her with his raised hand;
his eyes stay on* JAMES's *pale face, for
a long hold. When he finally finds his
voice, it is gruff.*]

KELLER. Sit down, everyone. (*He sits.*
KATE *sits.* JAMES *holds onto his chair.*
KELLER *speaks mildly.*) Please sit down,
Jimmie. (JAMES *sits, and moveless silence prevails;* KELLER's *eyes do not
leave him.* ANNIE *has pulled* HELEN
*downstairs again by one hand, the
pitcher in her other hand, down the
porch steps, and across the yard to the
pump. She puts* HELEN's *hand on the
pump handle, grimly.*)
ANNIE. All right. Pump. (HELEN
touches her cheek, waits uncertainly.)
No, she's not here. Pump! (*She forces*
HELEN's *hand to work the handle, then
lets go. And* HELEN *obeys. She pumps
till the water comes, then* ANNIE *puts
the pitcher in her other hand and guides
it under the spout, and the water tumbling half into and half around the
pitcher douses* HELEN's *hand.* ANNIE
*takes over the handle to keep water
coming, and does automatically what
she has done so many times before,
spells into* HELEN's *free palm:*) Water.
W, a, t, e, r. *Water.* It has a — *name* —

[*And now the miracle happens.* HELEN
*drops the pitcher on the slab under
the spout, it shatters. She stands trans-
fixed.* ANNIE *freezes on the pump handle: there is a change in the sundown
light, and with it a change in* HELEN's
*face, some light coming into it we
have never seen there, some struggle
in the depths behind it; and her lips
tremble, trying to remember something the muscles around them once
knew, till at last it finds its way out,
painfully, a baby sound buried under
the debris of years of dumbness.*]

HELEN. Wah. Wah. (*And again, with great effort*) Wah. Wah. (HELEN *plunges her hand into the dwindling water, spells into her own palm. Then she gropes frantically,* ANNIE *reaches for her hand, and* HELEN *spells into* ANNIE'S *hand.*)

ANNIE (*whispering*). Yes. (HELEN *spells into it again.*) Yes! (HELEN *grabs at the handle, pumps for more water, plunges her hand into its spurt and grabs* ANNIE'S *to spell it again.*) Yes! Oh, my dear — (*She falls to her knees to clasp* HELEN'S *hand, but* HELEN *pulls it free, stands almost bewildered, then drops to the ground, pats it swiftly, holds up her palm, imperiously.*[1] ANNIE *spells into it:*) Ground. (HELEN *spells it back.*) Yes! (HELEN *whirls to the pump, pats it, holds up her palm, and* ANNIE *spells into it.*) Pump. (HELEN *spells it back.*) Yes! Yes! (*Now* HELEN *is in such an excitement she is possessed, wild, trembling, cannot be still, turns, runs, falls on the porch step, claps it, reaches out her palm, and* ANNIE *is at it instantly to spell:*) Step. (HELEN *has no time to spell back now, she whirls groping, to touch anything, encounters the trellis, shakes it, thrusts out her palm, and* ANNIE *while spelling to her cries wildly at the house.*) Trellis. Mrs. Keller! *Mrs. Keller!* (*Inside,* KATE *starts to her feet.* HELEN *scrambles back onto the porch, groping, and finds the bell string, tugs it; the bell rings, the distant chimes begin tolling the hour, all the bells in town seem to break into speech while* HELEN *reaches out and* ANNIE *spells feverishly into her hand.* KATE *hurries out, with* KELLER *after her.* AUNT EV *is on her feet, to peer out the window. Only* JAMES *remains at the table, and with a napkin wipes his damp brow. From up right and left the servants —* VINEY, *the two Negro children, the other servant — run*

---

[1] imperiously (ĭm·pēr′ĭ·ŭs·lĭ): urgently.

in, and stand watching from a distance as HELEN, *ringing the bell, with her other hand encounters her mother's skirt; when she throws a hand out,* ANNIE *spells into it:*) Mother. (KELLER *now seizes* HELEN'S *hand, she touches him, gestures a hand, and* ANNIE *again spells:*) Papa — She *knows!* (KATE *and* KELLER *go to their knees, stammering, clutching* HELEN *to them, and* ANNIE *steps unsteadily back to watch the threesome,* HELEN *spelling wildly into* KATE'S *hand, then into* KELLER'S, KATE *spelling back into* HELEN'S; *they cannot keep their hands off her, and rock her in their clasp. Then* HELEN *gropes, feels nothing, turns all around, pulls free, and comes with both hands groping, to find* ANNIE. *She encounters* ANNIE'S *thighs,* ANNIE *kneels to her,* HELEN'S *hand pats* ANNIE'S *cheek impatiently, points a finger, and waits; and* ANNIE *spells into it:*) Teacher. (HELEN *spells it back, slowly;* ANNIE *nods.*) Teacher. (*She holds* HELEN'S *hand to her cheek. Presently* HELEN *withdraws it, not jerkily, only with reserve, and retreats a step. She stands thinking it over, then turns again and stumbles back to her parents. They try to embrace her, but she has something else in mind, it is to get the keys, and she hits* KATE'S *pocket until* KATE *digs them out for her.* ANNIE, *with her own load of emotion, has retreated, her back turned, toward the pump, to sit.* KATE *moves to* HELEN, *touches her hand questioningly, and* HELEN *spells a word to her.* KATE *comprehends it, their first act of verbal communication, and she can hardly utter the word aloud, in wonder, gratitude, and deprivation; it is a moment in which she simultaneously finds and loses a child.*)

KATE. Teacher?

[ANNIE *turns; and* KATE, *facing* HELEN *in her direction by the shoulders, holds*

her back, folds her back, and then relinquishes her. HELEN feels her way across the yard, rather shyly, and when her moving hands touch ANNIE's skirt she stops. Then she holds out the keys and places them in ANNIE's hand. For a moment neither of them moves. Then HELEN slides into ANNIE's arms, and lifting away her smoked glasses, kisses her on the cheek. ANNIE gathers her in.

KATE, torn both ways, turns from this, gestures the servants off, and makes her way into the house, on KELLER's arm. The servants go, in separate directions.

The lights are half down now, except over the pump. ANNIE and HELEN are here, alone in the yard. ANNIE has found HELEN's hand, almost without knowing it, and she spells slowly into it, her voice unsteady, whispering:]

ANNIE. I, love, Helen. (She clutches the child to her, tight this time, not spelling, whispering into her hair.) Forever, and — (She stops. The lights over the pump are taking on the color of the past, and it brings ANNIE's head up, her eyes opening in fear; and as slowly as though drawn she rises, to listen, with her hands on HELEN's shoulders. She waits, waits, listening with ears and eyes both, slowly here, slowly there — and hears only silence. There are no voices. The color passes on, and when her eyes come back to HELEN she can breathe the end of her phrase without fear:) — ever.

[In the family room KATE has stood over the table, staring at HELEN's plate, with KELLER at her shoulder; now JAMES takes a step to move her chair in, and KATE sits, with head erect, and KELLER inclines his head to JAMES; so

it is AUNT EV, hesitant, and rather humble, who moves to the door.

Outside HELEN tugs at ANNIE's hand, and ANNIE comes with it. HELEN pulls her toward the house; and hand in hand, they cross the yard, and ascend the porch steps, in the rising lights, to where AUNT EV is holding the door open for them.

The curtain ends the play.]

THINKING IT OVER

ACT I

1. What happens in the first scene of the play? What two main facts do you learn about the baby, Helen?

2. In the second scene, how does Helen show her intelligence, temper, and strong will? What indications are there that she is spoiled?

3. Explain what the second scene shows about the attitude of the following characters toward Helen. How does each character feel about Helen's future?
(a) Kate Keller
(b) Captain Keller
(c) James Keller
(d) Aunt Ev

4. What is happening as the third scene of the play begins? In this scene, what do you learn about Annie Sullivan's past? What do you think she means when she says, "I think God must owe me a resurrection"?

5. Describe Annie's character and personality, as shown in the third scene. What comment does Annie make about her ability to love?

6. At the end of the third scene, Annie is alone, remembering a scene from the past. Explain what the voices she hears in her mind tell you about her past. Whose voices are these?

7. What is Kate Keller's attitude toward Annie when she meets her in the railroad station? What is the first reaction of the other Kellers to Annie?

ACT II

8. How does Annie Sullivan treat Helen in the first scene of Act II? What does she attempt to do for Helen that no one else has ever done?

9. What is Kate's attitude toward Annie and her work with Helen? Do Kate's feelings about Annie change, or do they always stay the same?

10. Scene 2, showing the Kellers at breakfast, begins quietly. What does Helen do while the others are eating and talking? What action does Annie take? Explain the reactions of Kate, Captain Keller, and James.

11. The climactic action in Scene 2 starts when Annie is alone with Helen in the family room. What is the importance of this scene? Do you think Annie Sullivan's treatment of Helen is cruel? What is she trying to teach Helen?

12. Why did Captain Keller change his mind about dismissing Annie?

13. In the scene in the garden house, what does Annie tell the Kellers about her past life? Why does she tell them this? How does this information help the audience to understand the voices that Annie hears?

14. Find the lines in which Annie tells James what she considers "the original sin." What does this conversation reveal about Annie? about James?

15. In Scene 6, find lines that show the conflict between James and his father. What has caused this conflict? Is James also in conflict with Kate? How?

16. Describe Helen's change in feelings toward Annie. How does Helen show her feelings?

17. Why does Helen let Annie touch her again? Why is it so important for Annie to be able to touch Helen?

ACT III

18. What does Kate mean when she tells James, "Stand up to the world, Jimmie. That comes first"? Explain James's reply, "But the world is him." Why could this scene be called a turning point in James's conflict with his father?

19. Describe Helen as she appears in the second scene. How has she changed since Act II?

20. What has Annie been unable to teach Helen? How does she plan to do this? What does Annie mean when she tells Kate, "We're born to use words. Like wings, it has to come"?

21. When the two weeks are up, what does Annie want to do? Who opposes her in this? Why?

22. What happens during Helen's homecoming meal? Why does Helen change? How do each of the Kellers react to this?

23. What happens to Helen when she is pumping water? What does Annie mean when she says, "She *knows*"? The dramatist has carefully built up to this scene. Look back over the play and find lines in which water is mentioned and the pump is highlighted.

24. What is the importance of Annie's last line in the play? How has Annie changed? Why does she stop hearing the voices?

25. Tell how Helen, Kate, Captain Keller, and James have changed during the play. How has Annie influenced them?

LINES TO TALK ABOUT

1. Annie: "The more I think, the more certain I am that obedience is the gateway through which knowledge enters the mind of the child." Explain what she means. Do you agree?

2. Annie: "She has to be dependent on me . . . not anyone who *loves* her. You have so many feelings they fall over each other like feet. You won't use your chances and you won't let me." What does Annie mean by this statement? Do you think she is right?

3. Annie: ". . . she'll live up to just what you demand of her and no more." Do you think that most people live up to only what is demanded of them? Explain.

4. James Keller to Annie: "Sooner or later, we all give up, don't we?" What do you think of James's attitude toward life? What do you think might make some people feel this way? What do you think might cause them to change?

5. Annie: ". . . words. Why, you can see five thousand years back in a light of words, everything we feel, think, know — and share, in words, so not a soul is in darkness, or done with, even in the grave."

What does Annie mean in this line? What have you learned from this play about words and language?

6. Annie says that ". . . obedience without understanding is a — blindness, too." Can you give an example of such obedience without understanding? Do you think that this idea is true? Why?

ANALYZING THE AUTHOR'S INTERPRETATION

In *The Miracle Worker*, William Gibson has written about real people and a real situation. Like any artist, however, he has *interpreted* this reality in creating his play. He has an attitude and feelings toward the characters in his play. He reveals this attitude by the incidents he chooses from among all those that happened, and by the way in which he portrays his characters.

1. What is William Gibson's attitude in the play toward the Keller family? How can you tell? How does he make you feel about each of the Kellers?

2. What do you think the author feels toward Helen? Is his attitude toward Helen most like Kate's attitude toward her? Or does it resemble that of Captain Keller? Annie? Aunt Ev?

3. What is the author's attitude toward Annie Sullivan?

VISUALIZING THE SETTING AND ACTION

ACT I

1. Try to visualize the setting and physical action of the first scene. Where does it take place? What is the Doctor doing? Captain Keller? Mrs. Keller? Describe what happens after Mrs. Keller screams.

2. How is the fact that time has passed between the first and second scenes indicated to the audience? If you were seeing the play, how would you know approximately how many years had gone by?

ACT II

3. Reread the scene in which Annie teaches Helen to eat with a spoon from her own plate. Discuss what this scene would be like when played onstage.

4. Try to visualize the end of the last scene in Act II. Where is Annie? Helen? the rest of the Keller family? What is each person doing? Why is this an effective ending for Act II?

ACT III

5. Describe the action onstage in the first scene in Act III. Where are Annie and Helen? Where are the Kellers?

6. Reread the ending of the play where Helen finally realizes what words are. The characters say very little, but there is a world of meaning in each of their actions. Discuss what this scene would be like onstage and how it would make you feel.

ABOUT THE AUTHOR

William Gibson (1914–   ) was born and educated in New York City, and he has written about the city in much of his work. His first short story was published in the mid-thirties, and his first Broadway play, *Two for the Seesaw*, was produced more than twenty years later. Gibson has lived in the Midwest, with interludes in the Rocky Mountains, and these sections of the country are the settings for the poems in *Winter Crook* and a novel, *The Cobweb*. *The Miracle Worker* was first written as a television play and then expanded into a drama for Broadway production. It has also been made into a movie.

Helen Keller ➤

Biographies of Helen Keller reveal the miraculous achievement of Annie Sullivan as a teacher. Photographs offer further testimony. The photograph shown here records an instant in the remarkable life that began with that triumphant cry of recognition in the final scene of *The Miracle Worker*.

Explain why, in your opinion, this photograph is a fitting epilogue to the play.

As you examine this picture, you might also consider the following quotation from a conversation between Annie Sullivan and Helen Keller. It shows Annie Sullivan's view of life and the spirit behind her accomplishments.

"At another time she [Helen Keller] asked, 'What is a soul?' 'No one knows,' I replied; 'but we know it is not the body, and it is that part of us which thinks and loves and hopes.'"

JULIUS CAESAR

WILLIAM SHAKESPEARE

The time is an autumn afternoon in 1599. The place is the newly constructed Globe Theatre in Bankside, a suburb of London. Though the performance will not begin until two o'clock, spectators have been coming in since noon. Attendants are dashing about with apples and nuts to sell to those who ate a hasty meal in order to come early for choice seats. Members of the audience shout to one another, eat, drink, and even play cards to amuse themselves until the time when the play will begin.

Suddenly there is a trumpet blast. The crowd becomes quiet. A new play, *The Tragedy of Julius Caesar,* is about to begin. The author is William Shakespeare, who just a few years ago was an unknown lad from the small town of Stratford. Now he is both a leading actor and the main playwright for a company whose reputation is growing in Merrie England.

The galleries are full. Wealthy gentlemen in their laces and satins, law students from nearby schools, merchants taking the day off, all lean forward in the balcony with eager anticipation. Down in the yard, level with the stage, stand the "groundlings" who can afford but a penny admission. Here are the apprentices with a free afternoon, soldiers, sailors, and roustabouts. What is there about the plays of this young dramatist that draws such a diverse crowd?

What appeals to such a varied audience? Is it the rollicking humor of the comedies? Is it the fast action of the patriotic plays? Is it the characters who in each play seem so new and yet so real and true? Perhaps it is the skillfulness of the language, as natural in poetry as it is in prose.

There are many reasons why William Shakespeare was a popular playwright in England. Probably the most important was that in his hands the tools of the dramatist — characters, language, and plot — ceased to be fragments of fancy and became a living world. Into the world which he created, Shakespeare took his audience. They loved that world, and they loved him for creating it.

No one has ever found the secret of Shakespeare's creative powers, but by examining some of the ways in which he worked, we can discover why he became a popular playwright in his day and why, almost four hundred years later, his dramas still play to full houses all over the world.

The elements which make a football or baseball game thrilling to present-day fans are the same ones which interested the crowd at the Globe Theatre. In the action of Shakespeare's plays there is a struggle between two powerful forces with exciting incidents, growing anticipation, and tense moments mounting to a climax.

The *theme,* or purpose, of his plays is often presented very clearly. Sometimes, however, interpretations of the theme vary widely, and over the years many different opinions have been put forth about the meaning of some of the plays.

You are about to begin reading *Julius Caesar*. From the title you might assume that Caesar himself is the hero of the play, but you will discover when you have read a few scenes that the theme is not that simple. Is Brutus, the friend who became a conspirator, the real hero of the play? Is Shakespeare's primary aim to reveal what happens to a republic when men of politics and of military might begin to maneuver against each other? Is the killing of Caesar justice, or is it murder? These are questions you will think about as you read.

Shakespeare's *characters* are as real and believable as the people we meet everyday. We learn to know these characters much as we have learned to know our friends — by what they say and do and by what others say about them. In reading *Julius Caesar*, you will come to know such men as Mark Antony, Brutus, and Cassius. Just as in real life we do not always agree with others in their judgment of people, so you may disagree with your classmates about the characters in this play. Try to analyze them on the basis of what they say and do and what other characters reveal about them. Even then, you may not be positive in your judgment. Just as friends whom we think we all know well sometimes puzzle us with actions which seem unlike them, so the characters in *Julius Caesar* evade classification into "black" or "white" types. They seem, instead, to be real people — people with feelings and ambitions like our own.

The stage of the Globe Theatre.

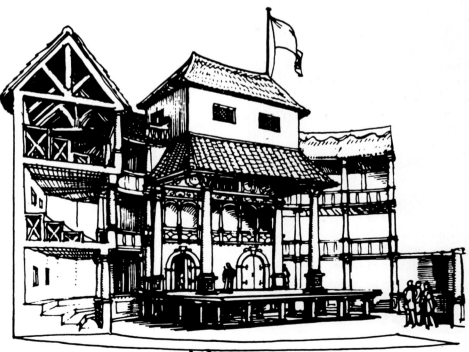

Watch for the parts played by minor characters. In *Julius Caesar* there will be several minor characters whose purpose may not be obvious at first glance. Lucius, for example, is a servant with very few lines, but Shakespeare uses him for a definite purpose, and the few lines he does speak deepen the meaning of the play.

The characters and the lines they speak are important in another way. Since almost no scenery was used on the Elizabethan stage, Shakespeare had to let his audience know the *setting*, or time and place, through the words of the players. Each area of the stage represented a different setting, but that setting had to come alive for the audience through the descriptive lines spoken by each actor.

We have talked about Shakespeare's ability to use theme, characters, and setting to get the lasting effect of true literature into his drama. All of these would be of little value were it not for Shakespeare's extraordinary ability with *language*. In his use of language lies his real genius. You will notice as you read *Julius Caesar* that Shakespeare gets across many effects through his use of comparisons. His similes and metaphors are like well-drawn pictures which impress us with their beauty and truth. The glory of Shakespeare's language is such that it stirs the emotions at the same time that it challenges the mind. It takes us out of our everyday world into a world in which we feel a deeper sense of the mysteries of life.

ROME IN THE DAYS OF CAESAR

Statue of Julius Caesar.

As you listen to a discussion today concerning politics, you hear questions such as these being asked: What are we going to do about the national debt? Is our national defense adequate? Will the Republicans or the Democrats control the next Congress? If a person two thousand years from now could hear a recording of one of our twentieth-century discussions, he might be very puzzled by ideas and terms and wonder what we were talking about.

The action of the play you are about to read took place some fifty years before the birth of Christ. You will enjoy the play more if you understand how the people of that time lived and thought. Imagine, for a moment, that you are a young citizen living in Rome in the year 44 B.C. What are the political questions you hear being discussed? Who are the prominent people? Just what is life like in Rome?

The Roman Forum.

Much depends upon the kind of family of which you are a part. If you are fortunate, you may be the son of a Roman Senator. Born into a noble household, you have been taught to respect the splendid traditions of the Roman Republic. You have often heard the story about the patriots who, five hundred years before, drove out the last of the Tarquin kings. Their leader was Lucius Junius Brutus; and, according to many people, he was the ancestor of Marcus Brutus, who has often been in your home to discuss the affairs of Rome with your father. You have heard them speak of the glorious growth of the Republic under which Rome absorbed all of Italy and eventually became mistress of the whole Mediterranean world.

You have learned that the greatness of the Republic is not just the greatness of force, for with the extension of Rome's might has gone also the heritage of respect for law and government. You realize that you are indeed fortunate. To be a member of a family active in the rule of the Roman Republic is the greatest privilege in the world, and you hope to grow up to take your place in the Senate, the main governing body of the Republic.

But what if you have not been born into a noble family? What if you are a member of a family of common people, or plebeians, as they are called? You are, perhaps, not very happy. Times are hard, and you hear your parents complain that slaves brought in from conquered provinces make it difficult for plebeians to earn a living.

They complain, too, that the government is no longer democratic. They sigh for the old days when the assembly of common people elected ten men called tribunes who could veto legislation passed by the Senate. In those days the Senate, made up predominantly of

Bust of Brutus by Michelangelo.

You perhaps dream of growing up to be an important official in the government, such as a consul, and in that way earning the right to become a Senator. But you know that very rarely can a man of unknown ancestry rise to such an important position. The Senate is dominated by men whose families have been important for generations.

You might become a soldier and help win new glories for Rome. If only you had been born a little earlier! Perhaps you could have helped Pompey clear the Mediterranean Sea of dangerous pirates; but Pompey is dead now, enemy of Caesar who had at one time been his friend. Pompey and Caesar once united forces with Crassus, an exceptionally wealthy businessman, to form "The Triumvirate." With the powerful combination of Pompey's military power, Caesar's popularity with the people, and Crassus' money, they were able to make the Senate do as they wished. Caesar secured the consulship, highest office in the Senate, and later went to Gaul as proconsular governor of the province.

Soon word came back to Rome of Caesar's great victories — victories which earned him the reputation of being a military genius. He practically doubled the size of the empire and at the same time won the intense admiration of his legions. He served for nearly ten years and then asked for a second renewal of his proconsulship.

You are not quite sure what was back of all the events that happened then. Was the Senate afraid of Caesar's might and popularity? Instead of granting the renewal, they ordered him home to run for the consulship. By that action the

noblemen, was not all-powerful; but now membership in the assembly has been widened to include nobles also, and elaborate systems of voting have made it possible for politicians of wealth to control the elections.

Sometimes, in a despairing mood, your father shrugs his shoulders and says he might as well do what so many plebeians are doing. He can sell his vote. Very little work is available for a free man since slave labor is used to perform most of the tasks in the city. Many discouraged plebeians sell their votes and then spend their time at the great circus entertainments provided by the government.

You hear friends of your father's speaking bitterly about the politicians who control not only the lawmaking but also the decisions in the court. Judges and juries are selected by officials who often owe allegiances to Senators or wealthy businessmen.

You wonder what is in store for you.

Senate would deprive Caesar of much of his power, for no consul in Rome could legally maintain an army. Caesar, however, did not obey. He took his troops with him, crossed the little Rubicon River, and marched on Rome.

The events that happened then are still fresh in your mind. Pompey, once Caesar's friend, had joined the Senate against him. The effort by Pompey to raise an army proved futile, and he fled the country along with many of the ruling class. As there was no government, Caesar had himself appointed dictator for eleven days until he could be nominated for the consulship. Then he went off in search of Pompey, who was eventually killed in Egypt.

When Caesar returned, he was made dictator for a year. He did not punish his political opponents, and many of the Senators hoped he would remain an absolute ruler only long enough to establish order and then restore the Republic. No one was terribly anxious, for, after all, Rome had used dictatorship before as a temporary measure during troubled times.

Just this year, however, something has happened which has been a subject for great talk. Caesar has had himself elected dictator for life. His statue has been added to those of the seven kings of Rome on top of the Capitol, and rumors fly about that he intends to become king and emperor.

Yesterday you overheard your father say, "In the forces that are organizing against Caesar, there is no one class and no one motive. There are Senators to whom the Republic stands for a life of liberty and honor for free men. There are selfish Senators to whom the Republic means the right to govern and exploit the empire to their own advantage. There are the former supporters of Pompey, and there are disgruntled, ambitious men within Caesar's own party. I fear that trouble lies ahead for Rome."

Yes, there was trouble ahead. If you had been living in Rome in 44 B.C., you would have found it a dangerous time, an exciting time. It is at this point in history that William Shakespeare begins *Julius Caesar*.

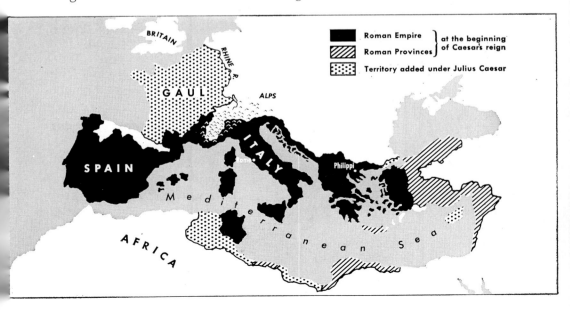

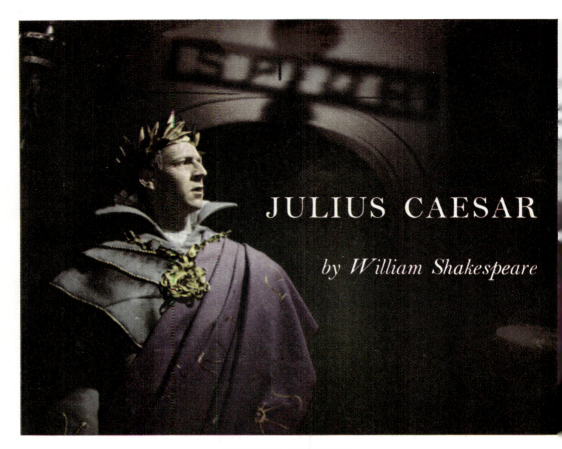

JULIUS CAESAR

by *William Shakespeare*

DRAMATIS PERSONAE

JULIUS CAESAR

OCTAVIUS CAESAR } *triumvirs*
MARCUS ANTONIUS } *after the death*
M. AEMILIUS LEPIDUS } *of Julius Caesar*

CICERO }
PUBLIUS } *Senators*
POPILIUS LENA }

MARCUS BRUTUS }
CASSIUS }
CASCA }
TREBONIUS }
LIGARIUS } *conspirators*
DECIUS BRUTUS }
METELLUS CIMBER }
CINNA }

FLAVIUS }
MARULLUS } *tribunes*

ARTEMIDORUS
A SOOTHSAYER
CINNA, *a poet*

LUCILIUS }
TITINIUS }
MESSALA } *friends of Brutus*
YOUNG CATO } *and Cassius*
VOLUMNIUS }

VARRO }
CLITUS }
CLAUDIUS }
STRATO } *servants of Brutus*
LUCIUS }
DARDANIUS }

CALPURNIA, *wife of Caesar*
PORTIA, *wife of Brutus*
PINDARUS, *servant of Cassius*

SENATORS, CITIZENS, GUARDS, ATTENDANTS, ETC.

NOTE: The pictures of *Julius Caesar* are from a production by the Oregon Shakespearean Festival Association. The costumes and the stage design in this production are basically Elizabethan.

SCENE. *During a great part of the play, at Rome; afterward at Sardis, in Asia Minor, and near Philippi, in Macedonia.*

[*Some stage directions used in the play:* **Exit** (*plural,* **exeunt**): *character(s) leave the stage;* **flourish:** *a blare of music announcing the entrance of royalty or a person of high rank;* **train:** *a group of followers, as in a procession;* **alarum:** *trumpet calls and cries signifying battle action or the approach of soldiers.*]

ACT I

SCENE 1. *Rome.*

It is early afternoon on February 15, 44 B.C., and beneath the clear Italian sky the lemon-colored buildings glint in the warm sunshine. An expectant mob of people have crowded the narrow streets and archways to celebrate two important events. The first is a grand military parade being held to commemorate Caesar's victory over the sons of Pompey in Spain, and the second is the annual feast of the Lupercal, an old Roman festival.

While waiting for the parade, many of the crowd are putting wreaths on the statues of Roman heroes nearby. Suddenly, dramatically, two tribunes enter — Marullus and Flavius.° When they see the common people putting garlands on a statue of Caesar, they scowl and begin to heckle the crowd.

FLAVIUS. Hence! Home, you idle creatures! get you home!
    Is this a holiday? What! Know you not,
    Being mechanical,° you ought not walk
    Upon a laboring day without the sign
    Of your profession?° Speak, what trade art thou?   5
CARPENTER. Why sir, a carpenter.
MARULLUS. Where is thy leather apron and thy rule?
    What dost thou with thy best apparel on?
    You, sir, what trade are you?
COBBLER. Truly, sir, in respect of a fine workman, I am but, as you would   10
    say, a cobbler.°
MARULLUS. But what trade art thou? Answer me directly.
COBBLER. A trade, sir, that, I hope, I may use with a safe conscience; which is, in-
    deed, sir, a mender of bad soles.°
MARULLUS. What trade, thou knave? Thou naughty knave, what trade?   15
COBBLER. Nay, I beseech you, sir, be not out with me.° Yet if you be out, sir, I can
    mend you.

° Before starting to read, pronounce the characters' names to yourself: **Marullus** (mȧ-rŭl′-ŭs) and **Flavius** (flā′vĭ-ŭs). 3. **mechanical:** mechanics, workmen. 4–5. **sign of your profession:** that is, tools and working clothes. 11. **cobbler** has a double meaning here: (1) a mender of shoes; (2) a bungler. Using words like this in a double sense is *punning*. Such plays on words were very popular in Shakespeare's day. 14. Do you see the double meaning of **soles?** 16. What is the pun in **out with me?**

MARULLUS. What mean'st thou by that? Mend me, thou saucy fellow!

COBBLER. Why, sir, cobble you.

FLAVIUS. Thou art a cobbler, art thou? 20

COBBLER. Truly, sir, all that I live by is with the awl. I meddle with no tradesman's
matters, nor women's matters, but with awl.° I am, indeed, sir, a surgeon to
old shoes. When they are in great danger, I recover them. As proper men as
ever trod upon neat's leather° have gone upon my handiwork.

FLAVIUS. But wherefore art not in thy shop today? 25
Why dost thou lead these men about the streets?

COBBLER. Truly, sir, to wear out their shoes, to get myself into more work. But, indeed, sir, we make holiday, to see Caesar and to rejoice in his triumph.

MARULLUS. Wherefore rejoice? What conquest brings he home?
What tributaries° follow him to Rome, 30
To grace in captive bonds his chariot wheels?
You blocks, you stones, you worse than senseless things!
O you hard hearts, you cruel men of Rome,
Knew you no Pompey? Many a time and oft
Have you climbed up to walls and battlements, 35
To towers and windows, yea, to chimney tops,
Your infants in your arms, and there have sat
The livelong day, with patient expectation,
To see great Pompey pass the streets of Rome.
And when you saw his chariot but appear, 40
Have you not made a universal shout,
That Tiber trembled underneath her banks?
And do you now put on your best attire?
And do you now cull out° a holiday?
And do you now strew flowers in his way 45
That comes in triumph over Pompey's blood?
Be gone!
Run to your houses, fall upon your knees,
Pray to the gods to intermit° the plague
That needs must light on this ingratitude. 50

[*Exeunt all the* COMMONERS.]

FLAVIUS. See, whether their basest metal be not moved;
They vanish tongue-tied in their guiltiness.
Go you down that way toward the Capitol;
This way will I. Disrobe the images,°
If you do find them decked with ceremonies. 55

MARULLUS. May we do so?
You know it is the feast of Lupercal.

FLAVIUS. It is no matter. Let no images
Be hung with Caesar's trophies. I'll about,

21–22. **awl:** instrument for piercing holes in leather. The cobbler is still punning. Do you
follow him? 24. **neat's leather:** oxhide. 30. **tributaries:** slaves. 44. **cull out:** choose to take.
49. **intermit:** withold. 54. **Disrobe the images:** that is, strip the statues of Caesar of their
decorations (**ceremonies**).

And drive away the vulgar from the streets: 60
So do you too, where you perceive them thick.
These growing feathers plucked from Caesar's wing
Will make him fly an ordinary pitch,
Who else would soar above the view of men°
And keep us all in servile fearfulness.   65

[*Exeunt.*]

SCENE 2. *A public place.*

The scene has changed to a large public square. Pillared buildings, statues of heroes, wreathed in garlands, and a fountain in the center present a scene of splendor and dignity.

More crowds are milling about waiting for the athletic games to begin. In celebration of the Lupercalia, young men of the nobility, anointed with oil of olives, are preparing to run up and down the city striking those they meet with a whip of goat's hide.

It was considered a good omen for women to be struck by the whips, for it was believed that such women could thus "shake off their curse" of childlessness. Antony is anointed in readiness for this custom.

[*Flourish. Enter* CAESAR; ANTONY, *for the course;* CALPURNIA, PORTIA, DECIUS, BRUTUS, CASSIUS,* *and* CASCA; *a great crowd following, among them a* SOOTHSAYER.]

CAESAR. Calpurnia!
CASCA.   Peace, ho! Caesar speaks.
CAESAR.   Calpurnia!
CALPURNIA. Here, my lord.
CAESAR. Stand you directly in Antonius' way,   5
          When he doth run his course. Antonius!
ANTONY. Caesar, my lord?
CAESAR. Forget not, in your speed, Antonius,
          To touch Calpurnia; for our elders say,
          The barren, touched in this holy chase,   10
          Shake off their sterile curse.°
ANTONY.   I shall remember:
          When Caesar says "Do this," it is performed.
CAESAR. Set on; and leave no ceremony out.

[*Flourish. They start out, with music playing.*]

SOOTHSAYER. Caesar!   15
CAESAR (*halting*). Ha! Who calls?
CASCA. Bid every noise be still; peace yet again!

62–64. pitch: a word used in falconry to mean height. The tribunes are saying that if they take care to pluck Caesar's power at the beginning, he will never be able to soar beyond control (above the view of men). * Pronounce these characters' names before you start to read: Calpurnia (kăl·pŭr′nĭ·à), Decius (dē′shĭ·ŭs). Cassius (kăsh′ĭ·ŭs). 8–11. So far Caesar's wife has remained childless.

[*Music ceases. The whole procession comes to a halt.*]

CAESAR. Who is it in the press° that calls on me?
    I hear a tongue, shriller than all the music,
    Cry "Caesar!" Speak. Caesar is turned to hear.   20
SOOTHSAYER. Beware the ides of March.°
CAESAR.   What man is that?
BRUTUS. A soothsayer bids you beware the ides of March.
CAESAR. Set him before me. Let me see his face.
CASSIUS. Fellow, come from the throng.

[SOOTHSAYER *advances;* CASCA *sets him before* CAESAR.]

                             Look upon Caesar.   25
CAESAR. What say'st thou to me now? Speak once again.
SOOTHSAYER. Beware the ides of March.
CAESAR. He is a dreamer. Let us leave him. Pass.

[*Caesar covers his momentary uneasiness by brusquely turning away. The hush which has swept over the crowd is broken as the music starts up again. The last stragglers depart down the street, leaving Brutus standing alone, serious and thoughtful. Cassius, who has purposely waited for such an opportunity, approaches him.*]

CASSIUS. Will you go see the order of the course?°
BRUTUS. Not I.   30
CASSIUS. I pray you, do.
BRUTUS. I am not gamesome.° I do lack some part
    Of that quick spirit that is in Antony.
    Let me not hinder, Cassius, your desires.
    I'll leave you.   35
CASSIUS. Brutus, I do observe you now of late;
    I have not from your eyes that gentleness
    And show of love as I was wont to have.
    You bear too stubborn and too strange a hand
    Over your friend that loves you.   40
BRUTUS.   Cassius,
    Be not deceived. If I have veiled my look,
    I turn the trouble of my countenance
    Merely upon myself. Vexèd I am
    Of late with passions of some difference,   45
    Conceptions only proper to myself,
    Which give some soil perhaps to my behaviors.
    But let not therefore my good friends be grieved —
    Among which number, Cassius, be you one —
    Nor construe any further my neglect,   50
    Than that poor Brutus, with himself at war,°
    Forgets the shows of love to other men.

18. **press:** in other words, crowd. 21. **the ides of March:** March 15. 29. **see . . . course:** that is, watch the running. 32. **gamesome:** in a playful mood. 51. Keep in mind that Brutus is **with himself at war.** Before you have finished the scene, you will find out why.

"Beware the ides of March."

CASSIUS. Then, Brutus, I have much mistook your passion;
  By means whereof this breast of mine hath buried
  Thoughts of great value, worthy cogitations.°   55
  Tell me, good Brutus, can you see your face?
BRUTUS. No, Cassius; for the eye sees not itself
  But by reflection, by some other things.
CASSIUS. 'Tis just.
  And it is very much lamented, Brutus,   60
  That you have no such mirrors as will turn
  Your hidden worthiness into your eye,
  That you might see your shadow. I have heard,
  Where many of the best respect in Rome —
  Except immortal Caesar° — speaking of Brutus   65
  And groaning underneath this age's yoke,
  Have wished that noble Brutus had his eyes.
BRUTUS. Into what dangers would you lead me, Cassius,
  That you would have me seek into myself
  For that which is not in me?   70
CASSIUS. Therefore, good Brutus, be prepared to hear.
  And since you know you cannot see yourself
  So well as by reflection, I, your glass,
  Will modestly discover to yourself

53–55. Cassius is saying that because he was mistaken about Brutus' troubled appearance, he has not revealed his plans and thoughts (**cogitations**) to him. The last line of this speech is said after a pause. **65. immortal Caesar:** This is spoken with a bitter tone. Cassius is not meaning to praise Caesar when he calls him *immortal*.

That of yourself which you yet know not of. 75
And be not jealous on me,° gentle Brutus.
Were I a common laugher,° or did use
To stale with ordinary oaths my love
To every new protester;° if you know
That I do fawn on men and hug them hard 80
And after scandal them, or if you know
That I profess myself in banqueting
To all the rout,° then hold me dangerous.

[*Flourish and shout.*]

BRUTUS. What means this shouting? I do fear the people
    Choose Caesar for their king. 85
CASSIUS.   Ay, do you fear it?°
    Then must I think you would not have it so.
BRUTUS. I would not, Cassius; yet I love him well.
    But wherefore do you hold me here so long?
    What is it that you would impart to me? 90
    If it be aught toward the general good,
    Set honor in one eye and death i' th' other,
    And I will look on both indifferently;
    For let the gods so speed me as I love
    The name of honor more than I fear death. 95
CASSIUS. I know that virtue to be in you, Brutus,
    As well as I do know your outward favor.°
    Well, honor is the subject of my story.
    I cannot tell what you and other men
    Think of this life; but, for my single self, 100
    I had as lief not be, as live to be
    In awe of such a thing as I myself.
    I was born free as Caesar; so were you;
    We both have fed as well, and we can both
    Endure the winter's cold as well as he. 105
    For once,° upon a raw and gusty day,
    The troubled Tiber chafing with her shores,
    Caesar said to me, "Dar'st thou, Cassius, now
    Leap in with me into this angry flood,
    And swim to yonder point?" Upon the word, 110
    Accoutered as I was, I plungèd in
    And bade him follow. So indeed he did.
    The torrent roared, and we did buffet it
    With lusty sinews, throwing it aside

---

76. **jealous on me:** suspicious of me. 77. **laugher:** jester. 79. **protester:** a person who professes friendship. 82–83. **profess . . . rout:** publicize myself and seek the favor of all the rabble. 86. **Ay . . . fear it:** Notice how Cassius has caught Brutus up on his use of the word *fear*. It gives him the opening he has been seeking. 97. **outward favor:** face. 106. Cassius here tells of a time when Caesar and he were young men togther.

And stemming it with hearts of controversy.°   115
But ere we could arrive the point proposed,
Caesar cried, "Help me, Cassius, or I sink!"
I, as Aeneas, our great ancestor,
Did from the flames of Troy upon his shoulder
The old Anchises bear, so from the waves of Tiber   120
Did I the tired Caesar. And this man
Is now become a god, and Cassius is
A wretched creature and must bend his body,
If Caesar carelessly but nod on him.
He had a fever when he was in Spain,   125
And when the fit was on him, I did mark
How he did shake. — 'Tis true, this god did shake.
His coward lips did from their color fly,
And that same eye whose bend doth awe the world
Did lose his luster. I did hear him groan.   130
Ay, and that tongue of his that bade the Romans
Mark him and write his speeches in their books,
Alas, it cried, "Give me some drink, Titinius,"
As a sick girl. Ye gods, it doth amaze me
A man of such a feeble temper should   135
So get the start° of the majestic world
And bear the palm° alone.

[Shout. Flourish.]

BRUTUS. Another general shout!
   I do believe that these applauses are
   For some new honors that are heaped on Caesar.   140
CASSIUS. Why, man, he doth bestride the narrow world
   Like a Colossus,° and we petty men
   Walk under his huge legs and peep about
   To find ourselves dishonorable graves.
   Men at some time are masters of their fates.   145
   The fault, dear Brutus, is not in our stars,°
   But in ourselves, that we are underlings.
   "Brutus" and "Caesar": what should be in that "Caesar"?
   Why should that name be sounded more than yours?
   Write them together, yours is as fair a name;   150
   Sound them, it doth become the mouth as well;
   Weigh them, it is as heavy. Conjure with 'em,°

---

115. You are familiar with the word **controversy** in the sense of an argument. Here it means rivalry. 136. **get the start:** become the leader. 137. The **palm** is a symbol of victory. It was given by Romans as a prize in athletic contests. 142. The **Colossus** was an immense bronze statue that, according to legend, stood astride the entrance to the harbor at Rhodes (an island in the Aegean Sea), and was regarded as one of the seven wonders of the ancient world. It was broken by an earthquake. 146. **stars:** Men believed that their destinies were governed by the stars. 152. **conjure with 'em:** Cassius is referring to the old art of black magic in which conjurers used big and important names to raise evil spirts from the lower world.

"Brutus" will start a spirit as soon as "Caesar."
Now, in the names of all the gods at once,
Upon what meat doth this our Caesar feed,   155
That he is grown so great? Age, thou art shamed!
Rome, thou hast lost the breed of noble bloods!
When went there by an age, since the great flood,
But it was famed with more than with one man?
When could they say till now, that talked of Rome,   160
That her wide walls encompassed but one man?
Now is it Rome indeed and room° enough,
When there is in it but one only man.
O, you and I have heard our fathers say,
There was a Brutus,° once, that would have brooked   165
The eternal devil to keep his state in Rome
As easily as a king.
BRUTUS. That you do love me, I am nothing jealous.°
        What you would work me to, I have some aim.°
        How I have thought of this and of these times,   170
        I shall recount hereafter; for this present,
        I would not, so with love I might entreat you,
        Be any further moved. What you have said
        I will consider. What you have to say
        I will with patience hear, and find a time   175
        Both meet° to hear and answer such high things.
        Till then, my noble friend, chew upon this:
        Brutus had rather be a villager
        Than to repute himself a son of Rome°
        Under these hard conditions as this time   180
        Is like to lay upon us.
CASSIUS. I am glad that my weak words
        Have struck but thus much show of fire from Brutus.
BRUTUS. The games are done and Caesar is returning.
CASSIUS. As they pass by, pluck Casca by the sleeve;   185
        And he will, after his sour fashion, tell you
        What hath proceeded worthy note today.

        [A march playing. Re-enter CAESAR and his train.]

BRUTUS. I will do so. But, look you, Cassius,
        The angry spot doth glow on Caesar's brow,

---

162. Cassius is punning here on the sound of **Rome** and **room**. In Shakespeare's day the two words were pronounced very nearly alike. 165. Brutus believed himself a descendant of an ancient Roman patriot, Lucius Junius Brutus, who led the revolt that expelled Tarquin, the last king of Rome, and established the Roman Republic. 168. **nothing jealous:** not doubtful. 169. **aim:** Brutus is saying he has an idea of his own similar to what Cassius is urging on him. 176. **meet:** fit. 178–79. Brutus fears the humiliations likely in the future. Better to be a villager from the provinces who had never known the proud traditions of liberty in Rome than to have known and lost them.

And all the rest look like a chidden° train.   190
Calpurnia's cheek is pale; and Cicero°
Looks with such ferret and such fiery eyes
As we have seen him in the Capitol,
Being crossed in conference° by some senators.
CASSIUS. Casca will tell us what the matter is.   195
CAESAR. Antonius!
ANTONY. Caesar?
CAESAR. Let me have men about me that are fat:
Sleek-headed men and such as sleep o' nights.
Yond Cassius has a lean and hungry look;   200
He thinks too much; such men are dangerous.
ANTONY. Fear him not, Caesar. He's not dangerous;
He is a noble Roman and well given.
CAESAR. Would he were fatter! But I fear him not.
Yet, if my name were liable to fear,   205
I do not know the man I should avoid
So soon as that spare Cassius. He reads much;
He is a great observer, and he looks
Quite through the deeds of men; he loves no plays,
As thou dost, Antony; he hears no music.   210
Seldom he smiles, and smiles in such a sort
As if he mocked himself and scorned his spirit
That could be moved to smile at anything.
Such men as he be never at heart's ease
Whiles they behold a greater than themselves,   215
And therefore are they very dangerous.
I rather tell thee what is to be feared
Than what I fear; for always I am Caesar.
Come on my right hand, for this ear is deaf,
And tell me truly what thou think'st of him.   220

[A march. Exeunt CAESAR and all his train but CASCA.]

CASCA. You pulled me by the cloak; would you speak with me?
BRUTUS. Ay, Casca; tell us what hath chanced today,
That Caesar looks so sad.
CASCA. Why, there was a crown offered him: and being offered him, he put it by
with the back of his hand, thus. And then the people fell a-shouting.   225
BRUTUS. What was the second noise for?
CASCA. Why, for that too.
CASSIUS. They shouted thrice. What was the last cry for?
CASCA. Why, for that too.
BRUTUS. Was the crown offered him thrice?   230

---

190. **chidden** comes from the word *chide*, which means "scold." Brutus says Caesar's companions look like a scolded band. 191. **Cicero**, a famous and powerful orator, was one of the most powerful men in the Senate. 194. **crossed in conference:** opposed in debate.

CASCA. Ay, marry,° was 't, and he put it by thrice, every time gentler than other; and at every putting-by mine honest neighbors shouted.

CASSIUS. Who offered him the crown?

CASCA. Why, Antony.

BRUTUS. Tell us the manner of it, gentle Casca.   235

CASCA. I can as well be hanged as tell the manner of it. It was mere foolery; I did not mark it. I saw Mark Antony offer him a crown — yet 'twas not a crown neither, 'twas one of these coronets — and, as I told you, he put it by once. But, for all that, to my thinking, he would fain have had it. Then he offered it to him again; then he put it by again. But, to my thinking,   240 he was very loath to lay fingers off it. And then he offered it the third time; he put it the third time by. And still as he refused it, the rabblement shouted and clapped their chapped hands and threw up their sweaty nightcaps and uttered such a deal of stinking breath because Caesar refused the crown that it had almost choked Caesar; for he swooned and fell   245 down at it. And for mine own part, I durst not laugh, for fear of opening my lips and receiving the bad air.

CASSIUS. But, soft, I pray you. What! did Caesar swoon?

CASCA. He fell down in the market place, and foamed at mouth, and was speechless.   250

BRUTUS. 'Tis very like — he hath the falling sickness.°

CASSIUS. No, Caesar hath it not. But you and I
And honest Casca, we have the falling sickness.°

CASCA. I know not what you mean by that; but I am sure Caesar fell down. If the tag-rag people did not clap him and hiss him, according as he   255 pleased and displeased them, as they use to do the players in the theater, I am no true man.

BRUTUS. What said he when he came unto himself?

CASCA. Marry, before he fell down, when he perceived the common herd was glad he refused the crown, he plucked me ope his doublet and offered   260 them his throat to cut.° And so he fell. When he came to himself again, he said if he had done or said anything amiss, he desired their worships to think it was his infirmity. Three or four wenches, where I stood, cried, "Alas, good soul!" and forgave him with all their hearts. But there's no heed to be taken of them. If Caesar had stabbed their mothers, they   265 would have done no less.

BRUTUS. And after that, he came, thus sad, away?

CASCA. Ay.

CASSIUS. Did Cicero say anything?

CASCA. Ay, he spoke Greek.   270

CASSIUS. To what effect?

---

231. **marry:** an oath meaning "I swear." 251. **falling sickness:** According to Plutarch, Caesar was subject to epilepsy, but later historians have disputed the idea. 253. What double meaning do you see in the use of **falling sickness** here? 259–61. Caesar, far from insisting on the crown, appears to offer to allow the people to cut his throat if that is their wish.

CASCA. Nay, an I tell you that, I'll ne'er look you i' th' face again. But those that understood him smiled at one another and shook their heads; but, for mine own part, it was Greek to me. I could tell you more news too. Marullus and Flavius, for pulling scarfs off Caesar's images, are put to silence.° Fare you well. There was more foolery yet, if I could remember it. 275

CASSIUS. Will you sup with me tonight, Casca?

CASCA. No, I am promised forth.

CASSIUS. Will you dine with me tomorrow?

CASCA. Ay, if I be alive and your mind hold, and your dinner worth the eating. 280

CASSIUS. Good; I will expect you.

CASCA. Do so. Farewell, both. (*Exit.*)

BRUTUS. What a blunt fellow is this grown to be!
He was quick mettle when he went to school.

CASSIUS. So is he now in execution 285
Of any bold or noble enterprise,
However he puts on this tardy form.°
This rudeness is a sauce to his good wit,
Which gives men stomach to digest his words
With better appetite. 290

BRUTUS. And so it is. For this time I will leave you.
Tomorrow, if you please to speak with me,
I will come home to you; or, if you will,
Come home to me, and I will wait for you.

CASSIUS. I will do so. Till then, think of the world. 295

[*Exit* BRUTUS.]

Well, Brutus, thou art noble. Yet, I see,
Thy honorable metal may be wrought
From that it is disposed.° Therefore it is meet
That noble minds keep ever with their likes;
For who so firm that cannot be seduced? 300
Caesar doth bear me hard; but he loves Brutus.
If I were Brutus now and he were Cassius,
He should not humor° me. I will this night,
In several hands,° in at his windows throw,
As if they came from several citizens, 305
Writings all tending to the great opinion
That Rome holds of his name; wherein obscurely
Caesar's ambition shall be glanced at.°
And after this let Caesar seat him sure,°
For we will shake him, or worse days endure. 310

274–76. What has happened to Flavius and Marullus is indicative of the temper of the times. 287. **However:** even though; **tardy form:** sluggish manner. 298. **From . . . disposed:** from its usual or natural quality. 302–03. Cassius seems to mean that he would not let Brutus influence (**humor**) him as he does Brutus. 304. **several hands:** different handwritings. 308. **glanced at:** examined. 309. **seat him(self) sure:** make himself secure.

SCENE 3. *Late evening on the fourteenth of March. A street in Rome.*

*It is thundering and lightning and the street is seen only in intermittent flashes.
The earth "shakes like a thing unfirm," and those men who are about "go through
a tempest dropping fire." Such "strife in heaven" was regarded as an ill omen.*

[*Enter* CASCA *and* CICERO *from opposite sides.*]

CICERO. Good even, Casca. Brought you Caesar home?
 Why are you breathless, and why stare you so?
CASCA. Are you not moved, when all the sway of earth
 Shakes, like a thing unfirm? O Cicero,
 I have seen tempests, when the scolding winds   5
 Have rived the knotty oaks, and I have seen
 Th' ambitious ocean swell, and rage, and foam,
 To be exalted with the threat'ning clouds.
 But never till tonight, never till now,
 Did I go through a tempest dropping fire.   10
 Either there is a civil strife in Heaven,
 Or else the world, too saucy with the gods,
 Incenses them to send destruction.
CICERO. Good night then, Casca; this disturbed sky
 Is not to walk in.   15
CASCA. Farewell, Cicero.

[*Exit* CICERO. *Enter* CASSIUS.]

CASSIUS. Who's there?
CASCA.   A Roman.
CASSIUS.   Casca, by your voice.
CASCA. Your ear is good. Cassius, what night is this!   20
CASSIUS. A very pleasing night to honest men.
CASCA. Who ever knew the heavens menace so?
CASSIUS. Those that have known the earth so full of faults.
 Now could I, Casca, name to thee a man
 Most like this dreadful night,   25
 A man no mightier than thyself or me
 In personal action, yet prodigious grown
 And fearful, as these strange eruptions are.
CASCA. 'Tis Caesar that you mean; is it not, Cassius?
CASSIUS. Let it be who it is: for Romans now   30
 Have thews and limbs like to their ancestors;
 But, woe the while!° our fathers' minds are dead,
 And we are governed with our mothers' spirits;
 Our yoke and sufferance° show us womanish.
CASCA. Indeed, they say the Senators tomorrow   35
 Mean to establish Caesar as a king;

32. **woe the while:** alas for these times. 34. **sufferance:** weak acceptance.

And he shall wear his crown by sea and land,
In every place, save here in Italy.

CASSIUS. I know where I will wear this dagger then;
Cassius from bondage will deliver Cassius.° 40
If I know this, know all the world besides,
That part of tyranny that I do bear
I can shake off at pleasure.

[*Thunder still.*]

CASCA.   So can I:
So every bondman in his own hand bears 45
The power to cancel his captivity.

CASSIUS. And why should Caesar be a tyrant then?
Poor man! I know he would not be a wolf,
But that he sees the Romans are but sheep.
He were no lion, were not Romans hinds.° 50
Those that with haste will make a mighty fire
Begin it with weak straws. What trash is Rome,
What rubbish and what offal, when it serves
For the base matter to illuminate°
So vile a thing as Caesar! But, O Grief, 55
Where hast thou led me? I perhaps speak this
Before a willing bondman;° then I know
My answer must be made. But I am armed,
And dangers are to me indifferent.

CASCA. You speak to Casca, and to such a man 60
That is no fleering° telltale. Hold — my hand.
Be factious° for redress of all these griefs,
And I will set this foot of mine as far
As who goes farthest.

CASSIUS.   There's a bargain made. 65
Now know you, Casca, I have moved already
Some certain of the noblest-minded Romans
To undergo with me an enterprise
Of honorable-dangerous consequence.
And I do know, by this, they stay for me 70
In Pompey's porch;° for now, this fearful night,
There is no stir or walking in the streets;
And the complexion of the element
In favor's like the work we have in hand,°

---

40. **Cassius . . . will deliver Cassius:** in other words, Cassius will take his own life.
50. **hinds:** female deer, i.e., gentle, timid creatures. 52–54. **What trash . . . illuminate:** Cassius is comparing Romans who let Caesar assume power to twigs (**trash**), rubbish, and garbage (**offal**), which serve as kindling for a fire. Here Caesar is the fire that cannot be lit without the assistance of the citizens who give up their rights. 57. **willing bondman:** a person submissive to Caesar, who might inform on him. 61. **fleering:** mocking. 62. **Be factious:** form a party. 71. **Pompey's porch:** the portico of Pompey's theater. 73–74. **complexion . . . hand:** The color of the sky is in appearance (**favor**) like our work.

Most bloody, fiery, and most terrible.   75
CASCA. Stand close awhile, for here comes one in haste.
CASSIUS. 'Tis Cinna;° I do know him by his gait;
    He is a friend.

                 [Enter CINNA.]

            Cinna, where haste you so?
CINNA. To find out you. Who's that? Metellus Cimber?°   80
CASSIUS. No, it is Casca; one incorporate
    To our attempts.° Am I not stayed for, Cinna?
CINNA. I am glad on't. What a fearful night is this!
CASSIUS. Am I not stayed for? tell me.
CINNA.   Yes, you are.   85
    O Cassius, if you could
    But win the noble Brutus to our party —
CASSIUS. Be you content. Good Cinna, take this paper,
    And look you lay it in the praetor's chair,
    Where Brutus may but find it; and throw this   90
    In at his window; set this up with wax
    Upon old Brutus' statue.° All this done,
    Repair to Pompey's porch, where you shall find us.
    Is Decius Brutus and Trebonius° there?
CINNA. All but Metellus Cimber; and he's gone   95
    To seek you at your house. Well, I will hie,
    And so bestow these papers as you bade me.
CASSIUS. That done, repair to Pompey's theater.

               [Exit CINNA.]

    Come, Casca, you and I will yet ere day
    See Brutus at his house. Three parts of him   100
    Is ours already, and the man entire
    Upon the next encounter yields him ours.
CASCA. O, he sits high in all the people's hearts;
    And that which would appear offense° in us,
    His countenance, like richest alchemy,   105
    Will change to virtue and to worthiness.
CASSIUS. Him and his worth and our great need of him
    You have right well conceited.° Let us go,
    For it is after midnight; and ere day
    We will awake him and be sure of him.

               [Exeunt.]

    77. Cinna (sĭn′à). **80. Metellus Cimber** (mė·tĕl′lŭs sĭm′bēr). **81–82. one incorporate to our
attempts:** partner to our plots. **88–92.** Do you remember what Cassius told himself he was
going to do at the end of the last scene to wake Brutus up? He is now putting his plans into
action. **Praetor** refers to the Roman official next in rank to the consul, the highest official in
the state; **old Brutus** refers to Lucius Junius Brutus (see Scene 2, lines 165–67). **94. Trebonius**
(trė·bō′nĭ·ŭs): a trusted officer of Caesar. **104. that which . . . offense:** that is, Caesar's murder. **108. conceited:** thought out or grasped.

ACT II

SCENE 1. *Rome.* BRUTUS' *orchard. It is now the early morning hours.*

A garden with fountains and flowers. Beneath tall dark cypress trees are statues carved from white marble. At the opening of the scene Brutus is wandering out into the night, restless and wakeful, during a lull in the storm referred to in the last scene. The lightning still flashes, and the stars are hidden from view so that Brutus cannot guess "how near to day" it is.

[*Enter* BRUTUS.]

BRUTUS. What, Lucius,° ho!
    I cannot by the progress of the stars,
    Give guess how near to day. Lucius, I say!
    I would it were my fault to sleep so soundly.°

[*Enter* LUCIUS.]

LUCIUS. Called you, my lord?   5
BRUTUS. Get me a taper in my study, Lucius.
    When it is lighted, come and call me here.
LUCIUS. I will, my lord. (*Exit.*)
BRUTUS. It must be by his° death; and for my part,
    I know no personal cause to spurn at him,   10
    But for the general.° He would be crowned.
    How that might change his nature, there's the question.
    It is the bright day that brings forth the adder;
    And that craves° wary walking. Crown him? — That! —
    And then, I grant, we put a sting in him,   15
    That at his will he may do danger with.
    The abuse of greatness is, when it disjoins
    Remorse from power; and, to speak truth of **Caesar,**
    I have not known when his affections swayed
    More than his reason. But 'tis a common proof,   20
    That lowliness is young ambition's ladder,
    Whereto the climber upward turns his face;
    But when he once attains the upmost round,
    He then unto the ladder turns his back,
    Looks in the clouds, scorning the base degrees   25
    By which he did ascend. So Caesar may.
    Then, lest he may, prevent.° And, since the quarrel
    Will bear no color for the thing he is,

1. Pronounce **Lucius** (lū'shĭ·ŭs) before you start to read. 4. Brutus is wishing he could sleep as soundly as Lucius does. Apparently Brutus has been deeply worried about Caesar's rising power. 9. **his:** Caesar's. 11. **general:** general good. 14. **craves:** demands. 27. **prevent:** forestall him.

Fashion it thus:° that what he is, augmented,
Would run to these and these extremities.   30
And therefore think him as a serpent's egg
Which, hatched, would, as his kind, grow mischievous,
And kill him in the shell.

[Re-enter LUCIUS.]

LUCIUS. The taper burneth in your closet, sir.
Searching the window for a flint, I found   35
This paper,° thus sealed up; and I am sure
It did not lie there when I went to bed.

[Gives him the letter.]

BRUTUS. Get you to bed again. It is not day.
Is not tomorrow, boy, the ides of March?
LUCIUS. I know not, sir.   40
BRUTUS. Look in the calendar, and bring me word.
LUCIUS. I will, sir. (*Exit.*)
BRUTUS. The exhalations whizzing° in the air
Give so much light that I may read by them.

[Opens the letter and reads.]

Brutus, thou sleep'st. Awake! and see thyself.   45
Shall Rome, etc. Speak! Strike! Redress!

"Brutus, thou sleep'st. Awake!"°
Such instigations have been often dropped
Where I have took them up.°
"Shall Rome, etc." Thus must I piece it out: 50
Shall Rome stand under one man's awe? What, Rome?
My ancestors did from the streets of Rome
The Tarquin drive, when he was called a king.
"Speak! Strike! Redress!" Am I entreated
To speak and strike? O Rome, I make thee promise;   55
If the redress will follow, thou receivest
Thy full petition at the hand of Brutus!

[Re-enter LUCIUS.]

LUCIUS. Sir, March is wasted fifteen days.

[Knocking within.]

27–29. **And, since . . . thus:** Since Caesar's present conduct cannot be said to justify his re-
moval, look at the matter this way. 36. **paper:** Cinna has apparently obeyed Cassius' orders in
Act I, Scene 3. 43. **exhalations whizzing:** After the storm in which Cassius and Casca meet on
the street, extraordinary displays resembling meteors continue to flash. 47. From here on, notice carefully the quotation marks, so that you can distinguish Brutus' comments from those
in the note. 48–49. **Such instigations . . . up:** Evidently, in the weeks since he first seized
upon the plan, Cassius has had many notes placed where Brutus would find them.

BRUTUS. 'Tis good. Go to the gate. Somebody knocks.

[*Exit* LUCIUS.]

Since Cassius first did whet me against Caesar,   60
I have not slept.
Between the acting of a dreadful thing
And the first motion, all the interim is
Like a phantasma, or a hideous dream.°
The Genius and the mortal instruments   65
Are then in council; and the state of man,
Like to a little kingdom, suffers then
The nature of an insurrection.°

[*Re-enter* LUCIUS.]

LUCIUS. Sir, 'tis your brother° Cassius at the door,
Who doth desire to see you.   70
BRUTUS.   Is he alone?
LUCIUS. No sir, there are more with him.
BRUTUS.   Do you know them?
LUCIUS. No, sir. Their hats are plucked about their ears,
And half their faces buried in their cloaks,°   75
That by no means I may discover them
By any mark of favor.
BRUTUS.   Let 'em enter.

[*Exit* LUCIUS.]

They are the faction. O Conspiracy!
Sham'st thou to show thy dang'rous brow by night,   80
When evils are most free? O, then by day
Where wilt thou find a cavern dark enough
To mask thy monstrous visage? Seek none, Conspiracy;
Hide it in smiles and affability.
For if thou put thy native semblance on,   85
Not Erebus itself were dim enough
To hide thee from prevention.°

[*Enter the conspirators,* CASSIUS, CASCA, DECIUS, CINNA, METELLUS CIMBER, *and*
TREBONIUS.]

CASSIUS. I think we are too bold upon your rest.

62–64. **Between . . . dream:** The interval between the first inkling, or idea, and the deed
itself is like a nightmare or hideous dream. 65–68. **Genius . . . insurrection:** The ideals
which a man wishes to follow (**Genius**) and the emotions which he feels (**mortal instruments**)
are in conflict over what course to follow, and the turmoil within the man is like that suffered
by a kingdom torn by civil war. 69. **brother:** brother-in-law, actually. 74–75. **Their hats . . .
cloaks:** In this play Shakespeare often, as here, describes Elizabethan rather than Roman
scenes and costumes. 83–87. **Seek . . . prevention:** Brutus means that the safe way to hide
a conspiracy is behind smiles and pleasant manners. If the conspirators show their true colors
(**thy native semblance on**), nothing, not even darkness itself — **Erebus** (ĕr'ĕ·bŭs), the gloomy
passage to Hell — can keep their purpose concealed (**hide thee from prevention**).

Good morrow, Brutus. Do we trouble you?

BRUTUS. I have been up this hour — awake all night.   90
    Know I these men that come along with you?

CASSIUS. Yes, every man of them; and no man here
    But honors you; and every one doth wish
    You had but that opinion of yourself
    Which every noble Roman bears of you.   95
    This is Trebonius.

BRUTUS.   He is welcome hither.

CASSIUS. This, Decius Brutus.

BRUTUS.   He is welcome too.

CASSIUS. This, Casca; this, Cinna; and this, Metellus Cimber.   100

BRUTUS. They are all welcome.
    What watchful cares do interpose themselves
    Betwixt your eyes and night?

CASSIUS. Shall I entreat a word?

               [BRUTUS *and* CASSIUS *whisper.*]

DECIUS. Here lies the east. Doth not the day break here?   105

CASCA. No.

CINNA. O, pardon, sir, it doth; and yon gray lines
    That fret the clouds are messengers of day.

CASCA. You shall confess that you are both deceived.
    Here, as I point my sword, the sun arises,   110
    Which is a great way growing on the south,
    Weighing the youthful season of the year.°
    Some two months hence up higher toward the north
    He first presents his fire; and the high east
    Stands, as the Capitol, directly here.   115

BRUTUS. Give me your hands all over, one by one.

CASSIUS. And let us swear our resolution.

BRUTUS. No, not an oath! If not the face of men,
    The sufferance of our souls, the time's abuse —
    If these be motives weak, break off betimes,°   120
    And every man hence to his idle bed.
    So let high-sighted tyranny range on,
    Till each man drop by lottery. But if these,
    As I am sure they do, bear fire enough
    To kindle cowards and to steel with valor   125
    The melting spirits of women, then, countrymen,
    What need we any spur but our own cause,
    To prick us to redress? what other bond
    Than secret Romans, that have spoke the word,

111–12. **great . . . year:** In the first quarter of the year the sun rises south of true east. 118–20. **If not the face of men . . . betimes:** That is, if honor (**face**), the suffering of our souls, and the abuses of this time are not sufficient motives and bonds for conspiracy, it will end in good time (**betimes**).

And will not palter?° And what other oath 130
Than honesty to honesty engaged,
That this shall be, or we will fall for it?
CASSIUS. But what of Cicero? Shall we sound him?
I think he will stand very strong with us.
CASCA. Let us not leave him out! 135
CINNA.   No, by no means!
METELLUS. O, let us have him! for his silver hairs
Will purchase us a good opinion
And buy men's voices to commend our deeds.
It shall be said, his judgment ruled our hands; 140
Our youths and wildness shall no whit appear,
But all be buried in his gravity.
BRUTUS. O, name him not. Let us not break with him;°
For he will never follow anything
That other men begin. 145
CASSIUS.   Then leave him out.
CASCA. Indeed he is not fit.
DECIUS. Shall no man else be touched but only Caesar?
CASSIUS. Decius, well urged. I think it is not meet
Mark Antony, so well beloved of Caesar, 150
Should outlive Caesar. We shall find of him
A shrewd contriver; and you know his means,
If he improve them, may well stretch so far
As to annoy us all. Which to prevent,
Let Antony and Caesar fall together. 155
BRUTUS. Our course shall seem too bloody, Caius° Cassius,
To cut the head off and then hack the limbs,
Like wrath in death and envy afterward.
For Antony is but a limb of Caesar.
Let us be sacrificers, but not butchers, Caius. 160
We all stand up against the spirit of Caesar;
And in the spirit of men there is no blood.
O, that we then could come by Caesar's spirit,
And not dismember Caesar! But, alas,
Caesar must bleed for it! And, gentle friends, 165
Let's kill him boldly, but not wrathfully.
Let's carve him as a dish fit for the gods,
Not hew him as a carcass fit for hounds.
And let our hearts, as subtle masters do,
Stir up their servants to an act of rage, 170
And after seem to chide 'em. This shall make
Our purpose necessary and not envious;
Which so appearing to the common eyes,

130. **palter:** play false. 143. **break with him:** disclose our plot to him. 156. **Caius** (kā′yŭs).

We shall be called purgers,° not murderers.
And for Mark Antony, think not of him;   175
For he can do no more than Caesar's arm
When Caesar's head is off.

CASSIUS.   Yet I fear him;°
For in the ingrafted love he bears to Caesar —

BRUTUS. Alas, good Cassius, do not think of him.   180
If he love Caesar, all that he can do
Is to himself, take thought and die for Caesar.
And that were much he should; for he is given
To sports, to wildness and much company.°

TREBONIUS. There is no fear° in him; let him not die;   185
For he will live, and laugh at this hereafter.

[*Clock strikes.*]

BRUTUS. Peace! Count the clock.

CASSIUS. The clock hath stricken three.

TREBONIUS. 'Tis time to part.

CASSIUS.   But it is doubtful yet,   190
Whether Caesar will come forth today, or no;
For he is superstitious grown of late,
Quite from the main opinion he held once
Of fantasy, of dreams and ceremonies.
It may be, these apparent prodigies,   195
The unaccustomed terror of this night,
And the persuasion of his augurers,°
May hold him from the Capitol today.

DECIUS. Never fear that. If he be so resolved,
I can o'ersway him. For he loves to hear   200
That unicorns may be betrayed with trees,
And bears with glasses,° elephants with holes,
Lions with toils° and men with flatterers;
But when I tell him he hates flatterers,
He says he does, being then most flattered.   205
Let me work;
For I can give his humor the true bent,
And I will bring him to the Capitol.

174. **purgers:** those who clean out dirt or evil. In some present-day dictatorships there have been "purges" whereby officials were murdered "for the good of the State." 178. **Yet . . . him:** Notice that Cassius and Brutus disagree on Antony's fate. 181–84. Brutus thinks that the only violence Antony can do is to himself, that is, become despondent (**take thought**) and commit suicide; but since he is a man who loves fast living — something of a waster — he probably wouldn't commit suicide. Keep in mind this estimate of Antony by Brutus as you read further. 185. **fear:** cause for fear. 197. **augurers:** religious officials whose duty it was to foretell the future by interpreting omens. 201–02. **unicorns . . . glasses:** It was believed that unicorns could be tricked into capture by having them charge into trees, thus becoming impaled on their horns; similarly bears could be lured into traps by the use of mirrors (**glasses**). 203. **toils:** traps.

CASSIUS. Nay, we will all of us be there to fetch him.
BRUTUS. By the eighth hour. Is that the uttermost? 210
CINNA. Be that the uttermost, and fail not then.
METELLUS. Caius Ligarius° doth bear Caesar hard,
      Who rated° him for speaking well of Pompey.
      I wonder none of you have thought of him.
BRUTUS. Now, good Metellus, go along by him. 215
      He loves me well, and I have given him reasons.
      Send him but hither, and I'll fashion him.°
CASSIUS. The morning comes upon 's. We'll leave you, Brutus.
      And, friends, disperse yourselves; but all remember
      What you have said, and show yourselves true Romans. 220
BRUTUS. Good gentlemen, look fresh and merrily;
      Let not our looks put on our purposes,
      But bear it as our Roman actors do,
      With untired spirits and formal constancy.°
      And so good morrow to you every one. 225

           [*Exeunt all but* BRUTUS.]

      Boy! Lucius! Fast asleep? It is no matter;
      Enjoy the honey-heavy dew of slumber.
      Thou hast no figures° nor no fantasies,
      Which busy care draws in the brains of men;
      Therefore thou sleep'st so sound. 230

           [*Enter* PORTIA.]

PORTIA.   Brutus, my lord!
BRUTUS. Portia, what mean you? Wherefore rise you now?
      It is not for your health thus to commit
      Your weak condition to the raw cold morning.
PORTIA. Nor for yours neither. You've ungently, Brutus, 235
      Stole from my bed. And yesternight, at supper,
      You suddenly arose, and walked about,
      Musing and sighing, with your arms across,
      And when I asked you what the matter was,
      You stared upon me with ungentle looks. 240
      I urged you further; then you scratched your head,
      And too impatiently stamped with your foot;
      Yet I insisted; yet you answered not,
      But, with an angry wafture of your hand.
      Gave sign for me to leave you. 245
                      Dear my lord,
      Make me acquainted with your cause of grief.
BRUTUS. I am not well in health, and that is all.

---

   212. **Ligarius** (lĭ·gâr′ĭ·ŭs). 213. **rated:** rebuked. 217. **fashion him:** mold his opinions. 224. **formal constancy:** outward appearance of steadfastness. 228. **figures:** visions, as in a dream.

PORTIA. Brutus is wise, and, were he not in health,
　　He would embrace the means to come by it.　　　　　250
BRUTUS. Why, so I do.° Good Portia, go to bed.
PORTIA. Is Brutus sick? And is it physical
　　To walk unbraced and suck up the humors
　　Of the dank morning?° What, is Brutus sick,
　　And will he steal out of his wholesome bed,　　　　255
　　To dare the vile contagion of the night
　　And tempt the rheumy and unpurgèd air
　　To add unto his sickness? No, my Brutus;
　　You have some sick offense within your mind,
　　Which, by the right and virtue of my place,　　　　260
　　I ought to know of. And, upon my knees,
　　I charm you, by my once commended beauty,
　　By all your vows of love and that great vow
　　Which did incorporate and make us one,
　　That you unfold to me, yourself, your half,　　　　265
　　Why you are heavy, and what men tonight
　　Have had resort to you; for here have been
　　Some six or seven, who did hide their faces
　　Even from darkness.
BRUTUS.　　　　　　　　Kneel not, gentle Portia.　　　270
PORTIA. I should not need, if you were gentle Brutus.
　　Within the bond of marriage, tell me, Brutus,
　　Is it excepted I should know no secrets
　　That appertain to you?
　　　　　　　　　　　　Am I your self,　　　　　　275
　　But, as it were, in sort or limitation?
　　I grant I am a woman; but withal,
　　A woman that Lord Brutus took to wife.
　　I grant I am a woman; but withal,
　　A woman well reputed — Cato's daughter.　　　　280
　　Think you I am no stronger than my sex,
　　Being so fathered, and so husbanded?
　　Tell me your counsels, I will not disclose 'em.
BRUTUS.　　　　　　　　　　　　O ye gods!
　　Render me worthy of this noble wife!　　　　　　285

　　　　　　　[Knocking within.]

　　Hark, hark! One knocks. Portia, go in awhile;
　　And by and by thy bosom shall partake
　　The secrets of my heart.
　　All my engagements I will construe° to thee,

---

251. Brutus means that he *is* setting about to restore his health (**embrace the means to come by it**), but he does not here tell Portia that it is by removing Caesar that he will do so. 252–54. **physical . . . morning:** good for your health to go uncovered and expose yourself to moistures or vapors (**humors**) of the cold, damp morning. 289. **construe:** explain.

All the charactery of my sad brows.   290
Leave me with haste.

[*Exit* PORTIA.]

Lucius, who's that knocks?

[*Re-enter* LUCIUS *with* LIGARIUS, *who has a handkerchief tied about his head.*]

LUCIUS. Here is a sick man that would speak with you.
BRUTUS. Caius Ligarius, that Metellus spake of.
     Boy, stand aside. Caius Ligarius! How?   295
LIGARIUS. Vouchsafe good morrow from a feeble tongue.
BRUTUS. O, what a time have you chose out, brave Caius,
     To wear a kerchief!° Would you were not sick!
LIGARIUS. I am not sick, if Brutus have in hand
     Any exploit worthy the name of honor.   300
BRUTUS. Such an exploit have I in hand, Ligarius,
     Had you a healthful ear to hear of it.
LIGARIUS. By all the gods that Romans bow before,
     I here discard my sickness!°
                              What's to do?   305
BRUTUS. A piece of work that will make sick men whole.
LIGARIUS. But are not some whole that we must make sick?
BRUTUS. That must we also. What it is, my Caius,
     I shall unfold to thee, as we are going
     To whom it must be done.   310
LIGARIUS.   Set on your foot,
     And with a heart new-fired I follow you,
     To do I know not what; but it sufficeth
     That Brutus leads me on.
BRUTUS.   Follow me, then.   315

[*Exeunt.*]

SCENE 2. CAESAR'S *house.*

*It is early morning after the stormy night on which the conspirators met at
Brutus' house. The heavens are still troubled, and Caesar's night, like Brutus',
has been robbed of its rest.*

*Caesar's house is on the Palatine Hill overlooking the Forum. Heavy draperies,
patterned floors of marble, statues on pedestals, and draped couches convey an
atmosphere of magnificence. Tall candelabra shed a soft light.*

[*Thunder and lightning. Enter* CAESAR *in his dressing gown.*]

CAESAR. Nor heaven nor earth have been at peace tonight.

298. **To wear a kerchief:** It was the custom in Shakespeare's day for a sick person to tie a
handkerchief or scarf on his head in the hope that it would "mend him." An old English
custom is thus assigned to the Romans. 304. **discard my sickness:** he takes off his handkerchief.

Thrice hath Calpurnia in her sleep cried out,
"Help, ho! They murder Caesar!" Who's within?

[*Enter a* SERVANT.]

SERVANT. My lord?
CAESAR. Go bid the priests do present° sacrifice,   5
   And bring me their opinions of success.
SERVANT. I will, my lord. (*Exit.*)

[*Enter* CALPURNIA.]

CALPURNIA. What mean you, Caesar? Think you to walk forth?
   You shall not stir out of your house today!
CAESAR. Caesar shall forth. The things that threatened me   10
   Ne'er looked but on my back. When they shall see
   The face of Caesar, they are vanishèd.
CALPURNIA. Caesar, I never stood on ceremonies,°
   Yet now they fright me. There is one within,
   Besides the things that we have heard and seen,   15
   Recounts most horrid sights seen by the watch.°
   A lioness hath whelpèd° in the streets;
   And graves have yawned, and yielded up their dead;
   Fierce fiery warriors fight upon the clouds,
   In ranks and squadrons and right form of war,   20
   Which drizzled blood upon the Capitol.
   The noise of battle hurtled in the air,
   Horses did neigh and dying men did groan,
   And ghosts did shriek and squeal about the streets.
   O Caesar! these things are beyond all use,°   25
   And I do fear them.
CAESAR.   What can be avoided
   Whose end is purposed by the mighty gods?
   Yet Caesar shall go forth; for these predictions
   Are to the world in general as to Caesar.°   30
CALPURNIA. When beggars die, there are no comets seen;
   The heavens themselves blaze forth the death of princes.
CAESAR. Cowards die many times before their deaths;°
   The valiant never taste of death but once.
   Of all the wonders that I yet have heard,   35
   It seems to me most strange that men should fear,
   Seeing that death, a necessary end,
   Will come when it will come.

---

   5. **present:** immediate. 13. **stood on ceremonies:** believed much in omens or auguries. 16. **watch:** These things are reported by a guard who was on watch during the night. 17. **whelpèd:** given birth to its young. 25. **use:** custom, usualness. 29–30. Caesar means that there is nothing about the signs just mentioned by his wife that shows them aimed particularly at him. Rather, they seem to apply **to the world in general.** 33. Do you understand why **Cowards die many times before their deaths?**

[Re-enter SERVANT.]

What say the augurers?

SERVANT. They would not have you stir forth today.   40
    Plucking the entrails of an offering forth,
    They could not find a heart within the beast.°
CAESAR. The gods do this in shame of cowardice;
    Caesar should be a beast without a heart°
    If he should stay at home today for fear.   45
CALPURNIA.   Alas, my lord,
    Your wisdom is consumed in confidence.
    Do not go forth today. Call it my fear
    That keeps you in the house, and not your own.
    We'll send Mark Antony to the Senate House;   50
    And he shall say you are not well today. (*She kneels.*)
    Let me, upon my knee, prevail in this.
CAESAR. Mark Antony shall say I am not well;
    And for thy humor,° I will stay at home.

[Enter DECIUS.]

    Here's Decius Brutus, he shall tell them so.   55
DECIUS. Caesar, all hail! Good morrow, worthy Caesar;
    I come to fetch you to the Senate House.
CAESAR. And you are come in very happy time
    To bear my greetings to the Senators
    And tell them that I will not come today.   60
    Cannot, is false, and that I dare not, falser;
    I will not come today. Tell them so, Decius.
CALPURNIA. Say he is sick.
CAESAR.   Shall Caesar send a lie?
    Have I in conquest stretched mine arm so far   65
    To be afeared to tell graybeards the truth?
    Decius, go tell them Caesar will not come.
DECIUS. Most mighty Caesar, let me know some cause,
    Lest I be laughed at when I tell them so.
CAESAR. The cause is in my will; I will not come.   70
    That is enough to satisfy the Senate,
    But for your private satisfaction,
    Because I love you, I will let you know,
    Calpurnia here, my wife, stays me at home.
    She dreamt tonight she saw my statuë,   75
    Which, like a fountain with a hundred spouts,
    Did run pure blood; and many lusty Romans
    Came smiling, and did bathe their hands in it;

    41–42. Plucking . . . beast: The augurers have killed an animal as a sacrifice (**offering**) to the gods; the absence of the animal's heart (or any other abnormality in the body) was a bad omen. **44. should** (would) **be a beast without a heart:** would be a coward. **54. thy humor:** your whim.

And these does she apply for warnings, and portents,
And evils imminent;° and on her knee   80
Hath begged that I will stay at home today.
DECIUS. This dream is all amiss interpreted!
    It was a vision fair and fortunate!
    Your statue spouting blood in many pipes,
    In which so many smiling Romans bathed,   85
    Signifies that from you great Rome shall suck
    Reviving blood, and that great men shall press
    For tinctures, stains, relics, and cognizance.°
    This by Calpurnia's dream is signified.°
CAESAR. And this way have you well expounded it.   90
DECIUS. I have, when you have heard what I can say.
    And know it now. The Senate have concluded
    To give this day a crown to mighty Caesar.
    If you shall send them word you will not come,
    Their minds may change. Besides, it were a mock   95
    Apt to be rendered, for someone to say,
    "Break up the Senate till another time,
    When Caesar's wife shall meet with better dreams!"
    If Caesar hide himself, shall they not whisper,
    "Lo, Caesar is afraid"?   100
CAESAR. How foolish do your fears seem now, Calpurnia!
    I am ashamèd I did yield to them.
    Give me my robe, for I will go.

[*Enter* PUBLIUS, BRUTUS, LIGARIUS, METELLUS, CASCA, TREBONIUS *and* CINNA.]

    And look where Publius° is come to fetch me.
PUBLIUS. Good morrow, Caesar.   105
CAESAR.   Welcome, Publius.
    What, Brutus, are you stirred so early too?
    Good morrow, Casca. Caius Ligarius,
    Caesar was ne'er so much your enemy
    As that same ague which hath made you lean.°   110

[*Enter* ANTONY.]

    See! Antony, that revels long o' nights,
    Is notwithstanding up. Good morrow, Antony.
ANTONY. So to most noble Caesar.
CAESAR.   Bid them prepare within.
    I am to blame to be thus waited for.   115

---

80. **imminent:** threatening to occur immediately. 87–88. **men . . . cognizance:** That is, men will want signs, such as coats of arms (**tinctures**) and badges (**cognizance**) to indicate that they are Caesar's servants. 89. Do you remember how in the last scene Decius promised the conspirators that he could "o'ersway" Caesar if "the persuasion of his augurers" should "hold him from the Capitol"? Notice how skillfully he is doing it. 104. **Publius** (pŭb′lĭ-ŭs). 110. Think back to Act II, Scene 1, where Ligarius first appears.

Now, Cinna; now, Metellus; what, Trebonius!°
I have an hour's talk in store for you.
Remember that you call on me today.
Be near me, that I may remember you.
TREBONIUS. Caesar, I will. (*Aside*) and so near will I be,   120
    That your best friends shall wish I had been further.
CAESAR. Good friends, go in, and taste some wine with me;
    And we, like friends, will straightway go together.
BRUTUS (*aside*). That every like is not the same, O Caesar,
    The heart of Brutus yearns to think upon!°   125

                            [*Exeunt.*]

SCENE 3.   *A street near the Capitol.*

*The Capitol is on the southern summit of the Capitoline Hill. One hundred
steps lead up to it from the Forum. In this scene its white columns are visible in
the distance.*
    *It is still early morning of the day on which Caesar expects to go to the Senate.
Soon the crowds will gather to watch him pass by with his train. Artemidorus
(är'tĕ·mĭ·dō'rŭs), a teacher of rhetoric, who is familiar with some of Brutus' confederates and knows something of the plot against Caesar, is astir while yet the
streets are empty. He has an important "schedule" — or document — to present to
Caesar.*

            [*Enter* ARTEMIDORUS, *with a paper.*]

ARTEMIDORUS (*reads*). "Caesar, beware of Brutus; take heed of Cassius; come not
    near Casca; have an eye to Cinna; trust not Trebonius; mark well Metellus
    Cimber; Decius Brutus loves thee not; thou hast wronged Caius Ligarius.
    There is but one mind in all these men, and it is bent against Caesar. If
    thou beest not immortal, look about you. Security gives away to con-   5
    spiracy. The mighty gods defend thee!
                                        Thy lover, ARTEMIDORUS."

Here will I stand till Caesar pass along,
And as a suitor will I give him this.
My heart laments that virtue cannot live   10
Out of the teeth of emulation.°
If thou read this, O Caesar, thou mayest live;
If not, the Fates with traitors do contrive.

                            [*Exit.*]

116. Caesar was interrupted in his greetings to these men by the entrance of Antony. He
now resumes his greetings. 123–25. Brutus winces at the phrase **like friends**. He grieves (**yearns**)
to think that not all things are as they appear (**every like is not the same**). 11. **emulation:** envy.

SCENE 4. *Rome. Before Brutus' house.*

[*Enter* PORTIA *and* LUCIUS.]

PORTIA. I prithee,° boy, run to the Senate House.
    Stay not to answer me, but get thee gone.
    Why dost thou stay?
LUCIUS. To know my errand, madam.
    Run to the Capitol, and nothing else?   5
    And so return to you, and nothing else?
PORTIA. Yes, bring me word, boy, if thy lord look well,
    For he went sickly forth. And take good note
    What Caesar doth, what suitors press to him.
    Hark boy! What noise is that?   10
LUCIUS. I hear none, madam.
PORTIA.   Prithee, listen well.
    I heard a bustling rumor like a fray,
    And the wind brings it from the Capitol.
LUCIUS. Sooth, madam, I hear nothing.   15

[*Enter the* SOOTHSAYER.]

PORTIA. Come hither, fellow. Which way hast thou been?
    Is Caesar yet gone to the Capitol?
SOOTHSAYER. Madam, not yet. I go to take my stand,
    To see him pass on to the Capitol.
PORTIA. Thou hast some suit to Caesar, hast thou not?   20
SOOTHSAYER. That I have, lady, if it will please Caesar
    To be so good to Caesar as to hear me,
    I shall beseech him to befriend himself.
PORTIA. Why, know'st thou any harm's intended toward him?
SOOTHSAYER. None that I know will be, much that I fear may chance.   25
    Good morrow to you.

[*Exit.*]

PORTIA.   Ay me! How weak a thing
    The heart of woman is! Oh Brutus,
    The heavens speed thee in thine enterprise.
    Run Lucius, and commend me to my lord.   30
    Say I am merry. Come to me again,
    And bring me word what he doth say to thee.

[*Exeunt severally.*]

1. **prithee:** I pray thee.

ACT III

SCENE 1. *Rome. Before the Capitol.*

Caesar and his followers have paused just outside the Capitol. Several people advance and present him with petitions as he ascends the stairs. Artemidorus is one. When the scene shifts, the crowd moves inside. An arc of stiff-backed wooden seats for the Senators, set in tiers, faces the great statue of Pompey. After he makes his entrance, Caesar sits on a raised platform in a chair of state, while around him press his petitioners, some on bended knees, all eager for his attention. Beside him on a bench are many scrolls, petitions set aside temporarily. He is holding before him the unwound scroll of Cimber's suit. Casca stands to one side and behind Caesar. The other conspirators are close by.

[*A crowd of people; among them* ARTEMIDORUS *and the* SOOTHSAYER. *Flourish. Enter* CAESAR, BRUTUS, CASSIUS, CASCA, DECIUS, METELLUS, TREBONIUS, CINNA, ANTONY, LEPIDUS, POPILIUS, PUBLIUS, *and others.*]

CAESAR (*to the* SOOTHSAYER). The ides of March are come.
SOOTHSAYER. Ay, Caesar; but not gone.
ARTEMIDORUS. Hail, Caesar! (*Gives him a paper.*) Read this schedule.
DECIUS (*giving him a paper*). Trebonius doth desire you to o'erread,
    At your best leisure, this humble suit.   5
ARTEMIDORUS. O Caesar, read mine first; for mine's a suit
    That touches Caesar nearer. Read it, great Caesar!
CAESAR. What touches us ourself shall be last served.
ARTEMIDORUS. Delay not, Caesar. Read it instantly!
CAESAR. What, is the fellow mad?   10
PUBLIUS (*thrusting him back*). Sirrah, give place.
CASSIUS. What, urge you your petitions in the street?
    Come to the Capitol.

[CAESAR *goes up to the Senate House, the rest following.*]

POPILIUS. I wish your enterprise today may thrive.
CASSIUS. What enterprise, Popilius?   15
POPILIUS.   Fare you well.

[*Advances to* CAESAR.]

BRUTUS. What said Popilius Lena?°
CASSIUS. He wished today our enterprise might thrive.
    I fear our purpose is discovered.
BRUTUS. Look, how he makes to Caesar. Mark him.   20
CASSIUS. Casca, be sudden, for we fear prevention.
    Brutus, what shall be done? If this be known,

17. **Popilius Lena** (pṓ·pǐl'ǐ·ŭs lē'nȧ).

Cassius or Caesar never shall turn back,
For I will slay myself.
BRUTUS.   Cassius, be constant.   25
    Popilius Lena speaks not of our purposes,
    For, look, he smiles, and Caesar doth not change.
CASSIUS. Trebonius knows his time; for, look you, Brutus,
    He draws Mark Antony out of the way °

        [*Exeunt* ANTONY *and* TREBONIUS.]

DECIUS. Where is Metellus Cimber? Let him go,   30
    And presently prefer his suit to Caesar.
BRUTUS. He is addressed. Press near and second him.
CINNA. Casca, you are the first that rears your hand.
CAESAR. Are we all ready? What is now amiss
    That Caesar and his Senate must redress?   35
METELLUS. Most high, most mighty, and most puissant° Caesar,
    Metellus Cimber throws before thy seat
    A humble heart — (*Kneeling*)
CAESAR.   I must prevent thee, Cimber.
    Thy brother by decree is banished.   40
    Know, Caesar doth not wrong; nor without cause
    Will he be satisfied.
METELLUS. Is there no voice more worthy than my own,
    To sound more sweetly in great Caesar's ear
    For the repealing° of my banished brother?   45
BRUTUS. I kiss thy hand, but not in flattery, Caesar,
    Desiring thee that Publius Cimber may
    Have an immediate freedom of repeal.
CAESAR. What, Brutus!
CASSIUS.   Pardon, Caesar; Caesar, pardon!   50
    As low as to thy foot doth Cassius fall,
    To beg enfranchisement for Publius Cimber.
CAESAR. I could be well moved, if I were as you:
    If I could pray to move, prayers would move me:°
    But I am constant as the northern star,   55
    Of whose true-fixed and resting quality
    There is no fellow° in the firmament.
    The skies are painted with unnumbered sparks,
    They are all fire and every one doth shine;
    But there's but one in all doth hold his place.   60
    So in the world. 'Tis furnished well with men,
    And men are flesh and blood, and apprehensive;°

---

29. Trebonius' part in the plot seems to be to draw Antony away from Caesar. 36. **puissant** (pū'ĭ-sănt): powerful. 45. **repealing**: recalling from exile. 53–54. **if I . . . move me**: People who plead for others are likely to be themselves moved by pleading. Caesar is above pleading and is not moved by it. Cassius is not so constant. 57. **fellow**: equal. 62. **apprehensive**: quick-witted.

Yet in the number I do know but one
That unassailable holds on his rank,
Unshaked of motion. And that I am he,   65
Let me a little show it, even in this;
That I was constant Cimber should be banished,
And constant do remain to keep him so.
CINNA. O Caesar —
CAESAR.   Hence! wilt thou lift up Olympus?   70
DECIUS. Great Caesar —
CAESAR.   Doth not Brutus bootless kneel?°
CASCA. Speak, hands, for me!

[*The conspirators have been edging closer and closer toward Caesar who, seeing that they still press forward, violently thrusts them from him. Then Cimber
with both his hands wrenches Caesar's mantle, or robe, from his shoulders, and
Casca draws his dagger first and strikes Caesar on the shoulder, but gives him no
great wound. Caesar seizes Casca's hand and cries out, but, as the others set upon
him, he sees Brutus with a sword drawn in his hand ready to strike. Then he lets
go Casca's hand, and casting his robe over his face, suffers every man to strike at
him that will.*]

CAESAR. *Et tu, Brute!* Then fall, Caesar! (*Dies.*)
CINNA. Liberty! Freedom! Tyranny is dead!   75
      Run hence, proclaim, cry it about the streets!
CASSIUS. Some to the common pulpits, and cry out,
      "Liberty, freedom, and enfranchisement!"
BRUTUS. People and Senators, be not affrighted;
      Fly not; stand still. Ambition's debt is paid.   80
CASCA. Go to the pulpit, Brutus.
DECIUS.   And Cassius too.
BRUTUS. Where's Publius?°
CINNA. Here, quite confounded with this mutiny.
METELLUS. Stand fast together, lest some friend of Caesar's   85
      Should chance —
BRUTUS. Talk not of standing. Publius, good cheer;
      There is no harm intended to your person,
      Nor to no Roman else. So tell them, Publius.
CASSIUS. And leave us, Publius, lest that the people,   90
      Rushing on us, should do your age some mischief.
BRUTUS. Do so; and let no man abide° this deed,
      But we the doers.

                [*Re-enter* TREBONIUS.]

CASSIUS.   Where is Antony?
TREBONIUS. Fled to his house amazed.   95

72. Caesar means it is useless for Decius to plead when Brutus, Caesar's best friend, kneels
in vain (**bootless**). 83. Publius is a Senator, evidently an elderly man. 92. **abide**: pay the
penalty for.

[ACT III, SCENE 1]   JULIUS CAESAR   **541**

Men, wives, and children stare, cry out, and run
As it were doomsday.
BRUTUS.   Fates, we will know your pleasures!
    That we shall die, we know; 'tis but the time
    And drawing days out, that men stand upon.°   100
CASSIUS. Why, he that cuts off twenty years of life
    Cuts off so many years of fearing death.
BRUTUS. Grant that, and then is death a benefit.
    So are we Caesar's friends, that have abridged
    His time of fearing death. Stoop, Romans, stoop,   105
    And let us bathe our hands in Caesar's blood
    Up to the elbows, and besmear our swords.
    Then walk we forth, even to the market place,
    And, waving our red weapons o'er our heads,
    Let's all cry, "Peace, freedom, and liberty!"   110
CASSIUS. Stoop, then, and wash. How many ages hence
    Shall this our lofty scene be acted over
    In states unborn and accents yet unknown!
BRUTUS. How many times shall Caesar bleed in sport,
    That now on Pompey's basis lies along   115
    No worthier than the dust!°
CASSIUS.   So oft as that shall be,
    So often shall the knot of us be called
    The men that gave their country liberty.
DECIUS. What, shall we forth?   120
CASSIUS.   Ay, every man away.
    Brutus shall lead; and we will grace his heels
    With the most boldest and best hearts of Rome.

                    [Enter a SERVANT.]

BRUTUS. Soft! Who comes here? A friend of Antony's.
SERVANT. Thus, Brutus, did my master bid me kneel;   125
    Thus did Mark Antony bid me fall down;
    And, being prostrate, thus he bade me say:
    Brutus is noble, wise, valiant, and honest;
    Caesar was mighty, bold, royal, and loving;
    Say I love Brutus, and I honor him;   130
    Say I feared Caesar, honored him, and loved him.
    If Brutus will vouchsafe that Antony
    May safely come to him and be resolved°
    How Caesar hath deserved to lie in death,

99–100. That is, since the only uncertain thing about death is the actual time when it will
occur, men are concerned with (**stand upon**) how long they will live (**drawing days out**)
rather than that they will die. Notice that Brutus and Cassius begin to minimize the horror
of their deed in the lines that follow. 111–16. **How many ages . . . than the dust**: Caesar lies
at the foot (**basis**) of Pompey's statue, no better than dust now that he is dead. Cassius and
Brutus believe that the assassination of Caesar will be re-enacted in plays (**sport**) in times to
come. 133. **resolved**: freed from doubts.

Mark Antony shall not love Caesar dead   135
So well as Brutus living, but will follow
The fortunes and affairs of noble Brutus
Thorough the hazards of this untrod state°
With all true faith. So says my master Antony.
BRUTUS. Thy master is a wise and valiant Roman;   140
  I never thought him worse.
  Tell him, so please him come unto this place,
  He shall be satisfied, and, by my honor,
  Depart untouched.
SERVANT.   I'll fetch him presently.   145

                        [*Exit.*]

BRUTUS. I know that we shall have him well to friend.
CASSIUS. I wish we may: but yet have I a mind
    That fears him much.
BRUTUS. But here comes Antony.

                   [*Re-enter* ANTONY.]

                    Welcome, Mark Antony.   150
ANTONY (*looking at the body of* CAESAR). O mighty Caesar! dost thou lie so low?
  Are all thy conquests, glories, triumphs, spoils,
  Shrunk to this little measure? Fare thee well.
  I know not, gentlemen, what you intend,°
  Who else must be let blood, who else is rank.°   155
  If I myself, there is no hour so fit
  As Caesar's death hour, nor no instrument
  Of half that worth as those your swords, made rich
  With the most noble blood of all this world.
  I do beseech ye, if you bear me hard,   160
  Now, whilst your purpled hands do reek and smoke,
  Fulfill your pleasure. Live a thousand years,
  I shall not find myself so apt to die.
  No place will please me so, no mean° of death,
  As here by Caesar, and by you cut off,   165
  The choice and master spirits of this age.
BRUTUS. O Antony, beg not your death of us!
  Though now we must appear bloody and cruel,
  As, by our hands and this our present act,
  You see we do, yet see you but our hands   170
  And this the bleeding business they have done.
  Our hearts you see not; they are pitiful;
  And pity to the general wrong of Rome —
  To you, our swords have leaden° points, Mark Antony.

138. **Thorough . . . untrod state:** through the dangers of the uncertain future. 154. Antony's
voice and manner change with this line as he now addresses the conspirators. 155. **rank:** here,
to be killed. 164. **mean:** means, way. 174. **leaden:** blunt.

CASSIUS. Your voice shall be as strong as any man's   175
    In the disposing of new dignities.°
BRUTUS. Only be patient till we have appeased
    The multitude, beside themselves with fear,
    And then we will deliver you the cause,
    Why I, that did love Caesar when I struck him,   180
    Have thus proceeded.
ANTONY.   I doubt not of your wisdom.
    Let each man render me his bloody hand.
    First, Marcus Brutus, will I shake with you.
    Next, Caius Cassius, do I take your hand.   185
    Now, Decius Brutus, yours; now yours, Metellus;
    Yours, Cinna; and, my valiant Casca, yours;
    Though last, not least in love, yours, good Trebonius.
    Gentlemen all — alas, what shall I say?
    My credit now stands on such slippery ground,   190
    That one of two bad ways you must conceit° me,
    Either a coward or a flatterer. (*Looks down at* CAESAR's *body*.)
    That I did love thee, Caesar, O, 'tis true.
    If then thy spirit look upon us now,
    Shall it not grieve thee dearer than thy death   195
    To see thy Antony making his peace,
    Shaking the bloody fingers of thy foes,
    Most noble! in the presence of thy corse?°
    Had I as many eyes as thou hast wounds,
    Weeping as fast as they stream forth thy blood,   200
    It would become me better than to close
    In terms of friendship with thine enemies.
CASSIUS. Mark Antony —
ANTONY.   Pardon me, Caius Cassius!
    The enemies of Caesar shall say this;   205
    Then, in a friend, it is cold modesty.°
CASSIUS. I blame you not for praising Caesar so;
    But what compact mean you to have with us?
    Will you be pricked in number° of our friends;
    Or shall we on, and not depend on you?   210
ANTONY. Therefore I took your hands, but was, indeed,
    Swayed from the point, by looking down on Caesar.
    Friends am I with you all and love you all,
    Upon this hope, that you shall give me reasons
    Why and wherein Caesar was dangerous.   215

---

176. **dignities:** offices or titles in the government. Notice that Cassius, knowing Antony better perhaps than Brutus, offers him rewards rather than noble sentiments. 191. **conceit:** that is, judge. 198. **corse:** corpse. 204–06. **Pardon . . . modesty:** Antony fears that Cassius is taking alarm over his grief at Caesar's death. He reminds Cassius that even Caesar's enemies would lament the fall of so great a man and therefore the grief that Antony, Caesar's friend, has shown is really quite moderate (**cold modesty**). 209. **pricked in number:** marked in the list.

BRUTUS. Or else were this a savage spectacle.
  Our reasons are so full of good regard°
  That were you, Antony, the son of Caesar,
  You should be satisfied.
ANTONY.   That's all I seek;   220
  And am moreover suitor that I may
  Produce his body to the market place,
  And in the pulpit, as becomes a friend,
  Speak in the order of his funeral.
BRUTUS. You shall, Mark Antony.   225
CASSIUS.   Brutus, a word with you.
  (*Aside to* BRUTUS) You know not what you do. Do not consent
  That Antony speak in his funeral!
  Know you how much the people may be moved
  By that which he will utter?   230
BRUTUS.   By your pardon.
  I will myself into the pulpit first,
  And show the reason of our Caesar's death.
  What Antony shall speak, I will protest
  He speaks by leave and by permission,   235
  And that we are contented Caesar shall
  Have all true rites and lawful ceremonies.
  It shall advantage more than do us wrong.°
CASSIUS. I know not what may fall. I like it not.
BRUTUS. Mark Antony, here take you Caesar's body.   240
  You shall not in your funeral speech blame us,
  But speak all good you can devise of Caesar,
  And say you do 't by our permission.
  Else shall you not have any hand at all
  About his funeral. And you shall speak   245
  In the same pulpit whereto I am going,
  After my speech is ended.
ANTONY.   Be it so;
  I do desire no more.
BRUTUS. Prepare the body then, and follow us.   250

                [*Exeunt all but* ANTONY.]

ANTONY. O, pardon me, thou bleeding piece of earth,
  That I am meek and gentle with these butchers!
  Thou art the ruins of the noblest man
  That ever lived in the tide of times.
  Woe to the hand that shed this costly blood!   255
  Over thy wounds now do I prophesy —
  Which, like dumb mouths, do ope their ruby lips

---

217. **full of good regard:** deserving of approval. 238. What are the advantages that Brutus
sees in according Caesar **all true rites?**

To beg the voice and utterance of my tongue —
A curse shall light upon the limbs of men.
Domestic fury and fierce civil strife   260
Shall cumber all the parts of Italy.
Blood and destruction shall be so in use
And dreadful objects so familiar
That mothers shall but smile when they behold
Their infants quartered with the hands of war;   265
All pity choked with custom of fell deeds.°
And Caesar's spirit, ranging° for revenge,
With Ate° by his side come hot from Hell,
Shall in these confines with a monarch's voice
Cry "Havoc,"° and let slip the dogs of war,   270
That this foul deed shall smell above the earth
With carrion men, groaning for burial.

[*Enter a* SERVANT.]

You serve Octavius Caesar,° do you not?
SERVANT. I do, Mark Antony.
ANTONY. Caesar did write for him to come to Rome.   275
SERVANT. He did receive his letters, and is coming;
    And bid me say to you by word of mouth —
    O Caesar! — (*Seeing the body*)
ANTONY. Thy heart is big. Get thee apart and weep.
    Passion, I see, is catching; for mine eyes,   280
    Seeing those beads of sorrow stand in thine,
    Began to water. Is thy master coming?
SERVANT. He lies tonight within seven leagues of Rome.
ANTONY. Post back with speed and tell him what hath chanced.
    Here is a mourning Rome, a dangerous Rome,   285
    No Rome of safety for Octavius yet;
    Hie hence, and tell him so. Yet, stay awhile;
    Thou shalt not back till I have borne this corse
    Into the market place. There shall I try,
    In my oration, how the people take   290
    The cruel issue of these bloody men;°
    According to the which, thou shalt discourse
    To young Octavius of the state of things.
    Lend me your hand.

[*Exeunt with* CAESAR's *body.*]

265–66. **infants . . . deeds**: Infants will be cut to pieces (**quartered**), and cruel (**fell**) deeds
will be so common men will no longer have pity. 267. **ranging**: roaming like a beast of prey.
268. **Ate** (ā′tē): a goddess of revenge. 270. **Cry "Havoc"**: a signal in battle to kill without
quarter, taking no prisoners. 273. **Octavius** (ŏk·tā′vĭ·ŭs) **Caesar**: grand-nephew of Caesar,
adopted as his heir. 287–291. Antony wishes the messenger to wait till he sees if the people
will accept Caesar's murderers as their new rulers.

"Speak, hands, for me!" ▶

SCENE 2. *The Forum.*

In the Forum, Rome's great public square, are the speaker's stands, the "pulpits" referred to in the last scene, from which the eloquent voices of Roman orators move the people. It is to one of these pulpits that Brutus and Cassius are proceeding, followed by the noisy citizens. At some distance back Mark Antony solemnly follows the body of Caesar carried on a bier.

[*Enter* BRUTUS *and* CASSIUS, *and a throng of* CITIZENS.]

CITIZENS. We will be satisfied! Let us be satisfied!
BRUTUS. Then follow me and give me audience, friends.
    Cassius, go you into the other street,
    And part the numbers.
    Those that will hear me speak, let 'em stay here;   5
    Those that will follow Cassius, go with him;
    And public reasons shall be rendered
    Of Caesar's death.
FIRST CITIZEN. I will hear Brutus speak.
SECOND CITIZEN. I will hear Cassius; and compare their reasons,   10
    When severally we hear them rendered.

[*Exit* CASSIUS, *with some of the* CITIZENS. BRUTUS *goes into the pulpit.*]

THIRD CITIZEN. The noble Brutus is ascended. Silence!
BRUTUS. Be patient till the last.
    Romans, countrymen, and lovers! Hear me for my cause, and be silent, that
    you may hear. Believe me for mine honor, and have respect to mine   15
    honor, that you may believe. Censure° me in your wisdom, and awake your
    senses, that you may the better judge. If there be any in this assembly, any
    dear friend of Caesar's, to him I say, that Brutus' love to Caesar was no
    less than his. If then that friend demand why Brutus rose against Caesar,
    this is my answer: Not that I loved Caesar less, but that I loved   20
    Rome more.° Had you rather Caesar were living and die all slaves, than
    that Caesar were dead, to live all free men? As Caesar loved me, I weep for
    him; as he was fortunate, I rejoice at it; as he was valiant, I honor him; but,
    as he was ambitious, I slew him. There is tears for his love; joy for his for-
    tune; honor for his valor; and death for his ambition. Who is here so   25
    base that would be a bondman? If any, speak; for him have I offended.
    Who is here so rude° that would not be a Roman? If any, speak; for him
    have I offended. Who is here so vile that will not love his country? If any,
    speak; for him have I offended. I pause for a reply.
ALL. None, Brutus, none!   30
BRUTUS. Then none have I offended. I have done no more to Caesar than you shall
    do to Brutus. The question of his death is enrolled in the Capitol; his glory

---

16. **censure:** judge. 20–21. In these famous lines you have Brutus' justification for killing a friend. 27. **so rude:** such a barbarian.

not extenuated, wherein he was worthy, nor his offenses enforced,° for which he suffered death.

[*Enter* ANTONY *and others, with* CAESAR'S *body.*]

Here comes his body, mourned by Mark Antony; who, though he   35
had no hand in his death, shall receive the benefit of his dying, a place in
the commonwealth; as which of you shall not? With this I depart — that, as
I slew my best lover for the good of Rome, I have the same dagger for
myself, when it shall please my country to need my death.

ALL. Live, Brutus! live! live!   40

FIRST CITIZEN. Bring him with triumph home unto his house!

SECOND CITIZEN. Give him a statue with his ancestors!

THIRD CITIZEN. Let him be Caesar!°

FOURTH CITIZEN.   Caesar's better parts
   Shall be crowned in Brutus!   45

FIRST CITIZEN.   We'll bring him to his house
   With shouts and clamors!

BRUTUS.   My countrymen —

SECOND CITIZEN. Peace! silence! Brutus speaks.

FIRST CITIZEN.   Peace, ho!   50

BRUTUS. Good countrymen, let me depart alone,
   And, for my sake, stay here with Antony.
   Do grace to Caesar's corpse, and grace his speech
   Tending to Caesar's glories, which Mark Antony,
   By our permission, is allowed to make.   55
   I do entreat you, not a man depart
   Save I alone, till Antony have spoke.

[*Descends from the pulpit, and goes out.*]

FIRST CITIZEN. Stay, ho! and let us hear Mark Antony.

THIRD CITIZEN. Let him go up into the public chair;
   We'll hear him. Noble Antony, go up.   60

ANTONY. For Brutus' sake, I am beholding° to you.

[*Goes into the pulpit.*]

FOURTH CITIZEN. What does he say of Brutus?

THIRD CITIZEN. °   He says, for Brutus' sake,
   He finds himself beholding to us all.

FOURTH CITIZEN. 'Twere best he speak no harm of Brutus here!   65

FIRST CITIZEN. This Caesar was a tyrant!

                Nay, that's certain.
   We are blest that Rome is rid of him.

32–33. **question . . . enforced:** The reason for his death is recorded; his glory is not belittled, nor his offenses exaggerated. 43. **Caesar:** ruler. The Roman populace seem already eager to have another Caesar, though they had a few minutes before approved his murder. 61. **beholding:** We say "beholden" or "indebted."

SECOND CITIZEN. Peace! let us hear what Antony can say.
ANTONY. You gentle Romans —   70
CITIZENS.   Peace, ho! let us hear him.
ANTONY. Friends, Romans, countrymen, lend me your ears.
    I come to bury Caesar, not to praise him.
    The evil that men do lives after them,
    The good is oft interred with their bones.   75
    So let it be with Caesar. The noble Brutus
    Hath told you Caesar was ambitious.
    If it were so, it was a grievous fault;
    And grievously hath Caesar answered it.
    Here, under leave of Brutus and the rest —   80
    For Brutus is an honorable man;
    So are they all, all honorable men —
    Come I to speak in Caesar's funeral.
    He was my friend, faithful and just to me.
    But Brutus says he was ambitious;   85
    And Brutus is an honorable° man.
    He hath brought many captives home to Rome,
    Whose ransoms did the general coffers° fill;
    Did this in Caesar seem ambitious?
    When that the poor have cried, Caesar hath wept;   90
    Ambition should be made of sterner stuff.
    Yet Brutus says he was ambitious;
    And Brutus is an honorable man.
    You all did see that on the Lupercal
    I thrice presented him a kingly crown,   95
    Which he did thrice refuse. Was this ambition?
    Yet Brutus says he was ambitious;
    And, sure, he is an honorable man.
    I speak not to disprove what Brutus spoke,°
    But here I am to speak what I do know.   100
    You all did love him once, not without cause.
    What cause withholds you, then, to mourn for him?
    O judgment! Thou art fled to brutish beasts,
    And men have lost their reason! Bear with me;
    My heart is in the coffin there with Caesar,   105
    And I must pause till it come back to me.
FIRST CITIZEN. Methinks there is much reason in his sayings.

86. From this point on in his speech, notice how often and with what growing force Antony
uses the word *honorable*. 88. **general coffers:** public treasury. 99. Is Antony speaking his true
mind here?

"Friends, Romans, countrymen, lend me your ears." ▶

SECOND CITIZEN. If thou consider rightly of the matter,
    Caesar has had great wrong.
THIRD CITIZEN.   Has he, masters?   110
    I fear there will a worse come in his place.
FOURTH CITIZEN. Marked ye his words? He would not take the crown,
    Therefore 'tis certain he was not ambitious.
FIRST CITIZEN. If it be found so, some will dear abide it!°
SECOND CITIZEN. Poor soul! His eyes are red as fire with weeping.   115
THIRD CITIZEN. There's not a nobler man in Rome than Antony.
FOURTH CITIZEN. Now mark him, he begins again to speak.
ANTONY. But yesterday the word of Caesar might
    Have stood against the world. Now lies he there,
    And none so poor to do him reverence.   120
    O masters, if I were disposed to stir
    Your hearts and minds to mutiny and rage,°
    I should do Brutus wrong, and Cassius wrong,
    Who, you all know, are honorable men.
    I will not do them wrong; I rather choose   125
    To wrong the dead, to wrong myself and you,
    Than I will wrong such honorable men.

                [ANTONY *holds up a rolled paper.*]

    But here's a parchment with the seal of Caesar.
    I found it in his closet; 'tis his will.
    Let but the commons° hear this testament —   130
    Which, pardon me, I do not mean to read —
    And they would go and kiss dead Caesar's wounds
    And dip their napkins° in his sacred blood,
    Yea, beg a hair of him for memory,
    And, dying, mention it within their wills,   135
    Bequeathing it as a rich legacy
    Unto their issue.
FOURTH CITIZEN. We'll hear the will! Read it, Mark Antony.
ALL. The will! the will! We will hear Caesar's will!
ANTONY. Have patience, gentle friends, I must not read it.   140
    It is not meet you know how Caesar loved you.
    You are not wood, you are not stones, but men;
    And, being men, hearing the will of Caesar,
    It will inflame you, it will make you mad.
    'Tis good you know not that you are his heirs;   145
    For, if you should, O, what would come of it!
FOURTH CITIZEN. Read the will! We'll hear it, Antony!
    You shall read us the will! Caesar's will!

---

114. **dear abide it:** pay a severe penalty for it. 121–25. Antony is again speaking ironically.
He is really trying to do exactly what he says would be wrong to do. 130. **commons:** common
people. 133. **napkins:** handkerchiefs.

ANTONY. Will you be patient? Will you stay awhile?
    I have o'ershot myself to tell you of it.   150
    I fear I wrong the honorable men
    Whose daggers have stabbed Caesar; I do fear it.
FOURTH CITIZEN. They were traitors! Honorable men!
ALL. The will! the testament!
SECOND CITIZEN. They were villains, murderers. The will! read the will!   155
ANTONY. You will compel me, then, to read the will?
    Then make a ring about the corpse of Caesar,
    And let me show you him that made the will.
    Shall I descend? and will you give me leave?
SEVERAL CITIZENS. Come down.   160
SECOND CITIZEN. Descend.
THIRD CITIZEN. You shall have leave.

        [ANTONY *comes down from the pulpit.*]

FOURTH CITIZEN. A ring. Stand round.
FIRST CITIZEN. Stand from the hearse; stand from the body.
SECOND CITIZEN. Room for Antony, most noble Antony!   165
ANTONY. Nay, press not so upon me. Stand far off.
SEVERAL CITIZENS. Stand back! Room! Bear back!
ANTONY. If you have tears, prepare to shed them now.
    You all do know this mantle. I remember
    The first time ever Caesar put it on.   170
    'Twas on a summer's evening, in his tent,
    That day he overcame the Nervii.°
    Look, in this place ran Cassius' dagger through.
    See what a rent the envious Casca made!
    Through this the well-belovèd Brutus stabbed,   175
    And as he plucked his cursèd steel away,
    Mark how the blood of Caesar followed it,
    As rushing out of doors, to be resolved
    If Brutus so unkindly knocked, or no.
    For Brutus, as you know, was Caesar's angel.   180
    Judge, O you gods, how dearly Caesar loved him!
    This was the most unkindest cut of all;
    For when the noble Caesar saw him stab,
    Ingratitude, more strong than traitors' arms,
    Quite vanquished him. Then burst his mighty heart;   185
    And, in his mantle muffling up his face,
    Even at the base of Pompey's statue,
    Which all the while ran blood, great Caesar fell.
    O, what a fall was there, my countrymen!

---

172. **Nervii** (nûr'vĭ·ī): one of the barbarian tribes that Caesar conquered during the course of the Gallic Wars.

Then I, and you, and all of us fell down,   190
Whilst bloody treason flourished over us.
O, now you weep; and, I perceive, you feel
The dint° of pity. These are gracious drops.
Kind souls, what! weep you when you but behold
Our Caesar's vesture° wounded? Look at you here,   195
Here is himself, marred, as you see, with traitors.

[*Lifting the mantle from* CAESAR'*s body.*]

FIRST CITIZEN. O piteous spectacle!
SECOND CITIZEN. O noble Caesar!
THIRD CITIZEN. O woeful day!
FOURTH CITIZEN. O traitors, villains!   200
FIRST CITIZEN. O most bloody sight!
SECOND CITIZEN. We will be revenged!
ALL. Revenge! About! Seek! Burn! Fire! Kill! Slay!
        Let not a traitor live!
ANTONY.   Stay, countrymen.   205
FIRST CITIZEN. Peace there! Hear the noble Antony.
SECOND CITIZEN. We'll hear him, we'll follow him, we'll die with him!
ANTONY. Good friends, sweet friends, let me not stir you up
        To such a sudden flood of mutiny.
        They that have done this deed are honorable.   210
        What private griefs they have, alas, I know not,
        That made them do it. They are wise and honorable,
        And will, no doubt, with reasons answer you.
        I come not, friends, to steal away your hearts.
        I am no orator, as Brutus is;   215
        But, as you know me all, a plain blunt man
        That love my friend; and that they know full well
        Who gave me public leave to speak of him.
        For I have neither wit, nor words, nor worth,
        Action, nor utterance, nor the power of speech,   220
        To stir men's blood. I only speak right on.
        I tell you that which you yourselves do know;
        Show you sweet Caesar's wounds — poor, poor, dumb mouths! —
        And bid them speak for me. But were I Brutus,
        And Brutus Antony, there were an Antony   225
        Would ruffle up your spirits and put a tongue
        In every wound of Caesar that should move
        The stones of Rome to rise and mutiny!
ALL. We'll mutiny!
FIRST CITIZEN. We'll burn the house of Brutus.   230
THIRD CITIZEN. Away, then! Come, seek the conspirators!
ANTONY. Yet hear me, countrymen. Yet hear me speak.

193. **dint:** stroke. 195. **vesture:** clothing.

ALL. Peace, ho! Hear Antony. Most noble Antony
ANTONY. Why, friends, you go to do you know not what.
    Wherein hath Caesar thus deserved your loves?   235
    Alas, you know not. I must tell you, then.
    You have forgot the will I told you of.
ALL. Most true. The will! Let's stay and hear the will.
ANTONY. Here is the will, and under Caesar's seal.
    To every Roman citizen he gives,   240
    To every several° man, seventy-five drachmas.°
SECOND CITIZEN. Most noble Caesar! We'll revenge his death!
THIRD CITIZEN. O royal Caesar!
ANTONY. Hear me with patience.
ALL. Peace, ho!   245
ANTONY. Moreover, he hath left you all his walks,
    His private arbors and new-planted orchards,
    On this side Tiber. He hath left them you,
    And to your heirs forever, common pleasures,
    To walk abroad, and recreate yourselves.   250
    Here was a Caesar! When comes such another?
FIRST CITIZEN. Never, never! Come, away, away!
    We'll burn his body in the holy place,
    And with the brands fire the traitors' houses.
    Take up the body.   255
SECOND CITIZEN. Go fetch fire.
THIRD CITIZEN. Pluck down benches.
FOURTH CITIZEN. Pluck down forms,° windows, anything!

        [*Exeunt* CITIZENS *with the body.*]

ANTONY. Now let it work. Mischief, thou art afoot,
    Take thou what course thou wilt!   260

        [*Enter a* SERVANT.]

            How now, fellow!
SERVANT. Sir, Octavius is already come to Rome.
ANTONY. Where is he?
SERVANT. He and Lepidus are at Caesar's house.
ANTONY. And thither will I straight to visit him.   265
    He comes upon a wish. Fortune is merry,
    And in this mood will give us anything.
SERVANT. I heard him say, Brutus and Cassius
    Are rid like madmen through the gates of Rome.
ANTONY. Belike they had some notice of the people,   270
    How I had moved them. Bring me to Octavius.

        [*Exeunt.*]

    241. **several:** individual; **drachmas:** Greek coins. 258. **forms:** benches.

SCENE 3. *A street in Rome.*

[*Enter* CINNA THE POET, *and after him* CITIZENS.]

CINNA. I dreamt to-night that I did feast with Caesar,
   And things unluckily charge my fantasy.
   I have no will to wander forth of doors,
   Yet something leads me forth.
FIRST CITIZEN. What is your name?   5
SECOND CITIZEN. Whither are you going?
THIRD CITIZEN. Where do you dwell?
FOURTH CITIZEN. Are you a married man, or a bachelor?
SECOND CITIZEN. Answer every man directly.
FIRST CITIZEN. Ay, and briefly.   10
FOURTH CITIZEN. Ay, and wisely.
THIRD CITIZEN. Ay, and truly, you were best.
CINNA. What is my name? Whither am I going? Where do I dwell? Am I a married
   man, or a bachelor? Then to answer every man, directly and briefly, wisely
   and truly — wisely I say, I am a bachelor.   15
SECOND CITIZEN. That's as much as to say, they are fools that marry. You'll bear
   me a bang for that I fear. Proceed directly.
CINNA. Directly I am going to Caesar's funeral.
FIRST CITIZEN. As a friend, or an enemy?
CINNA. As a friend.   20
SECOND CITIZEN. That matter is answered directly.
FOURTH CITIZEN. For your dwelling — briefly.
CINNA. Briefly, I dwell by the Capitol.
THIRD CITIZEN. Your name sir, truly.
CINNA. Truly, my name is Cinna.   25
FIRST CITIZEN. Tear him to pieces! He's a conspirator.
CINNA. I am Cinna the poet, I am Cinna the poet!
FOURTH CITIZEN. Tear him for his bad verses, tear him for his bad verses!
CINNA. I am not Cinna the conspirator.
FOURTH CITIZEN. It is no matter, his name's Cinna! Pluck but his name out of   30
   his heart, and turn him going.
THIRD CITIZEN. Tear him, tear him! Come, brands, ho! Firebrands! To Brutus', to
   Cassius', burn all. Some to Decius' house and some to Casca's; some to
   Ligarius'. Away, go!

[*Exeunt.*]

ACT IV

Months have elapsed since the assassination of Julius Caesar. A triumvirate, or ruling council of three, composed of Antony, Octavius, and Lepidus, has been proclaimed in Rome. Brutus and Cassius have fled from Rome to gather an army in Asia Minor and Greece.

Sitting around a table with a list of the chief citizens before them, Antony, Octavius, and Lepidus are picking out the names of those whom they suspect to be unfriendly to their cause. Before leaving Rome to combat the forces of Brutus and Cassius in Asia Minor, the triumvirs decide to leave no enemies in their rear. They are so ruthless as to add to the list of those who must die the names of their own kinsmen. You will see that the triumvirs do not trust one another.

[ANTONY, OCTAVIUS, *and* LEPIDUS, *seated at a table.*]

ANTONY. These many, then, shall die;° their names are pricked.
OCTAVIUS. Your brother too must die. Consent you, Lepidus?°
LEPIDUS. I do consent —
OCTAVIUS.   Prick him down, Antony.
LEPIDUS. Upon condition Publius shall not live,   5
    Who is your sister's son, Mark Antony.
ANTONY. He shall not live. Look, with a spot I damn him.
    But, Lepidus, go you to Caesar's house.
    Fetch the will° hither, and we shall determine
    How to cut off some charge in legacies.   10
LEPIDUS. What, shall I find you here?
OCTAVIUS. Or here, or at the Capitol.

[*Exit* LEPIDUS.]

ANTONY. This is a slight unmeritable man,
    Meet to be sent on errands. Is it fit,
    The threefold world divided, he should stand   15
    One of the three to share it?
OCTAVIUS.   So you thought him;°
    And took his voice who should be pricked to die
    In our black sentence and proscription.°
ANTONY. Octavius, I have seen more days than you;   20
    And though we lay these honors on this man
    To ease ourselves of divers sland'rous loads,
    He shall but bear them as the ass bears gold,

---

1. Antony is condemning to death those who now oppose his own will. 2. **Lepidus** (lĕp′ĭ-dŭs). 9. **the will:** Caesar's will, which Antony had used to inflame the mob and now wants to study so as to avoid paying some of (**cut off some charge in**) the legacies. 17. That is, you thought him fit when you chose him as our partner. 19. **proscription:** death list.

To groan and sweat under the business,
Either led or driven, as we point the way.   25
And having brought our treasure where we will,
Then take we down his load, and turn him off,
Like to the empty ass, to shake his ears,
And graze in commons.
OCTAVIUS.   You may do your will;   30
But he's a tried and valiant soldier.
ANTONY. So is my horse, Octavius; and for that
I do appoint him store of provender.
It is a creature that I teach to fight,
To wind, to stop, to run directly on,   35
His corporal motion governed by my spirit.
And, in some taste, is Lepidus but so.
He must be taught and trained and bid go forth;
A barren-spirited fellow; one that feeds
On abjects, orts,° and imitations,   40
Which, out of use and staled by other men,
Begin his fashion.° Do not talk of him,
But as a property. And now, Octavius,
Listen great things — Brutus and Cassius
Are levying powers. We must straight make head.   45
Therefore let our alliance be combined,
Our best friends made, our means stretched;
And let us presently go sit in council
How covert matters° may be best disclosed,
And open perils surest answered.   50
OCTAVIUS. Let us do so, for we are at the stake,°
And bayed about with many enemies;
And some that smile have in their hearts, I fear,
Millions of mischiefs.

[Exeunt.]

SCENE 2. *Camp near Sardis. Before* BRUTUS' *tent.*

*About a year has elapsed since the last scene. Brutus and Cassius are encamped
near Sardis, an ancient city in Asia Minor, famous once as the city whose burning
started the war between the Greeks and the Persians. Since fleeing from Rome
after Mark Antony had aroused the people, the conspirators have been raising a
large army in northern Greece (Macedonia) and Asia Minor.*

*The scene is that of a military encampment. The only light is in Brutus' tent.
He is in armor, awaiting the arrival of Cassius.*

40. **abjects, orts:** things thrown away, fragments. 41–42. **Which . . . fashion:** When other
men have discarded such things, he begins to use them. 49. **covert matters:** secret plans (of the
enemy). 51. **at the stake** a comparison that comes from the sport of bearbaiting popular in
Shakespeare's time, in which a bear was tied to a stake and tormented by dogs.

[*Drum. Enter* BRUTUS *and the boy* LUCIUS. *Meeting them is* LUCILIUS (lù·sĭl'ĭ·ŭs), *one of* BRUTUS' *officers, who has just returned from seeing* CASSIUS. *With him are* CASSIUS' *friend,* TITINIUS (tĭ·tĭn'ĭ·ŭs), *and* PINDARUS (pĭn'dá·rŭs), *servant sent from* CASSIUS.]

BRUTUS. Stand, ho!

LUCILIUS. Give the word, ho, and stand!

BRUTUS. What now, Lucilius! Is Cassius near?

LUCILIUS. He is at hand; and Pindarus is come
        To do you salutation from his master.   5

BRUTUS. He greets me well. Your master, Pindarus,
        In his own change, or by ill officers°
        Hath given me some worthy cause to wish
        Things done, undone. But, if he be at hand,
        I shall be satisfied.   10

PINDARUS.   I do not doubt
        But that my noble master will appear
        Such as he is, full of regard and honor.°

BRUTUS. He is not doubted. A word, Lucilius:
        How he received you let me be resolved.   15

LUCILIUS. With courtesy and with respect enough;
        But not with such familiar instances,
        Nor with such free and friendly conference,
        As he hath used of old.

BRUTUS.   Thou hast described   20
        A hot friend cooling. Ever note, Lucilius,
        When love begins to sicken and decay,
        It useth an enforcèd ceremony.
        There are no tricks in plain and simple faith.
        But hollow men, like horses hot at hand,°   25
        Make gallant show and promise of their mettle;
        But when they should endure the bloody spur,
        They fall their crests, and, like deceitful jades,
        Sink in the trial.° Comes his army on?

LUCILIUS. They mean this night in Sardis to be quartered.   30
        The greater part, the horse in general,
        Are come with Cassius.

BRUTUS.   Hark! He is arrived.

[*Low march within.*]

    March gently on to meet him.

[*Enter* CASSIUS *and his powers.*]

---

    7. **In . . . officers**: because of some change in himself, or because of mistakes made by his subordinates. 13. **full . . . honor**: worthy of respect. Notice that some issue has arisen between Brutus and Cassius. 25. **hot at hand**: that are spirited when checked. 29. **Sink in the trial**: fail in the final test.

CASSIUS. Stand, ho! 35

BRUTUS. Stand, ho! Speak the word along.

FIRST SOLDIER. Stand!

SECOND SOLDIER. Stand!

THIRD SOLDIER. Stand!

CASSIUS. Most noble brother, you have done me wrong. 40

BRUTUS. Judge me, you gods! Wrong I mine enemies?
    And, if not so, how should I wrong a brother?

CASSIUS. Brutus, this sober form of yours hides wrongs;
    And when you do them —

BRUTUS.   Cassius, be content; 45
    Speak your grief softly. I do know you well.
    Before the eyes of both our armies here,
    Which should perceive nothing but love from us,
    Let us not wrangle. Bid them move away;
    Then in my tent, Cassius, enlarge your griefs, 50
    And I will give you audience.

CASSIUS.   Pindarus.
    Bid our commanders lead their charges off
    A little from this ground.

BRUTUS. Lucilius, do you the like; and let no man 55
    Come to our tent till we have done our conference.

[Exeunt.]

SCENE 3.   *The interior of* BRUTUS' *tent.*

[Enter BRUTUS *and* CASSIUS.]

CASSIUS. That you have wronged me doth appear in this:
    You have condemned and noted° Lucius Pella
    For taking bribes here of the Sardians;
    Wherein my letters, praying on his side
    Because I knew the man, were slighted off. 5

BRUTUS. You wronged yourself to write in such a case.

CASSIUS. In such a time as this it is not meet
    That every nice offense should bear his comment.°

BRUTUS. Let me tell you, Cassius, you yourself
    Are much condemned to have an itching palm; 10
    To sell and mart your offices for gold
    To underservers.

CASSIUS.   I an itching palm!
    You know that you are Brutus that speaks this,
    Or, by the gods, this speech were else your last! 15

2. **noted:** marked for disgrace. 7–8. **it . . . comment:** It is not fitting that every trivial (**nice**) offense should be noticed.

BRUTUS. The name of Cassius honors this corruption,
        And chastisement doth therefore hide his head.°
CASSIUS. Chastisement!
BRUTUS. Remember March, the ides of March remember.
        Did not great Julius bleed for justice's sake?   20
        What villain touched his body, that did stab,
        And not for justice? What, shall one of us,
        That struck the foremost man of all this world
        But for supporting robbers,° shall we now
        Contaminate our fingers with base bribes?   25
        I had rather be a dog, and bay the moon,
        Than such a Roman.
CASSIUS.   Brutus, bait not me!
        I'll not endure it. You forget yourself,
        To hedge me in. I am a soldier, I,   30
        Older in practice, abler than yourself
        To make conditions.°
BRUTUS.   Go to. You are not, Cassius.
CASSIUS. I am.
BRUTUS. I say you are not.   35
CASSIUS. Urge me no more, I shall forget myself.
        Have mind upon your health! Tempt me no further.
BRUTUS. Away, slight man!
CASSIUS. Is 't possible?
BRUTUS.   Hear me, for I will speak.   40
        Must I give way and room to your rash choler?°
        Shall I be frightened when a madman stares?
CASSIUS. O ye gods, ye gods! Must I endure all this?
BRUTUS. All this! Ay, more. Fret till your proud heart break.
        Go show your slaves how choleric you are,   45
        And make your bondmen tremble. Must I budge?
        Must I observe you? Must I stand and crouch
        Under your testy humor? By the gods,
        You shall digest the venom of your spleen,°
        Though it do split you! For, from this day forth,   50
        I'll use you for my mirth, yea, for my laughter,
        When you are waspish.
CASSIUS.   Is it come to this?
BRUTUS. You say you are a better soldier:
        Let it appear so; make your vaunting true,   55
        And it shall please me well. For mine own part,
        I shall be glad to learn of noble men.

16–17. Brutus is saying that when a person as great as Cassius is corrupt he goes unpunished.
24. **But for supporting robbers:** One reason for killing Caesar, so Brutus believes, is that Caesar himself protected those who robbed and plundered under his authority. 32. **make conditions:**
make decisions. 41. **choler:** wrath. 49. The **spleen** was considered that part of the human body
which was the source of anger and jealousy.

CASSIUS. You wrong me every way; you wrong me, Brutus;
        I said, an elder soldier, not a better.
        Did I say "better"?   60
BRUTUS.   If you did, I care not.
CASSIUS. When Caesar lived, he durst not thus have moved me.
BRUTUS. Peace, peace! you durst not so have tempted him.
CASSIUS. I durst not!
BRUTUS. No.   65
CASSIUS. What! durst not tempt him!
BRUTUS.   For your life you durst not.°
CASSIUS. Do not presume too much upon my love.
        I may do that I shall be sorry for.
BRUTUS. You have done that you should be sorry for.   70
        There is no terror, Cassius, in your threats,
        For I am armed so strong in honesty
        That they pass by me as the idle wind,
        Which I respect not. I did send to you
        For certain sums of gold, which you denied me.   75
        For I can raise no money by vile means.
        By heaven, I had rather coin my heart,
        And drop my blood for drachmas, than to wring
        From the hard hands of peasants their vile trash
        By any indirection.° I did send   80
        To you for gold to pay my legions,
        Which you denied me. Was that done like Cassius?
        Should I have answered Caius Cassius so?
        When Marcus Brutus grows so covetous,
        To lock such rascal counters° from his friends,   85
        Be ready, gods, with all your thunderbolts;
        Dash him to pieces!
CASSIUS.   I denied you not.
BRUTUS. You did.
CASSIUS. I did not. He was but a fool that brought   90
        My answer back. Brutus hath rived my heart.
        A friend should bear his friend's infirmities,
        But Brutus makes mine greater than they are.°
BRUTUS. I do not, till you practice them on me.
CASSIUS. You love me not.   95
BRUTUS.   I do not like your faults.
CASSIUS. A friendly eye could never see such faults.
BRUTUS. A flatterer's would not, though they do appear
        As huge as high Olympus.
CASSIUS. Come, Antony, and young Octavius, come!   100
        Revenge yourselves alone on Cassius,

67. Here Brutus looks straight at Cassius and says each word very slowly. **80. indirection:** dishonest means. **85. rascal counters:** base coins. **92–93.** Notice that Cassius is changing his attitude. He half admits, now, he has been guilty.

For Cassius is aweary of the world;
Hated by one he loves; braved by his brother;
Checked like a bondman;° all his faults observed,
Set in a notebook, learned, and conned by rote, 105
To cast into my teeth. O, I could weep
My spirit from mine eyes! There is my dagger,
And here my naked breast; within, a heart
Dearer than Plutus' mine,° richer than gold.
If that thou be'st a Roman, take it forth; 110
I, that denied thee gold, will give my heart.
Strike, as thou didst at Caesar; for, I know,
When thou didst hate him worst, thou lovedst him better
Than ever thou lovedst Cassius!

BRUTUS.   Sheath your dagger. 115
Be angry when you will, it shall have scope;
Do what you will, dishonor shall be humor.°
O Cassius, you are yokèd with a lamb
That carries anger as the flint bears fire;
Who, much enforcèd, shows a hasty spark, 120
And straight is cold again.

CASSIUS.   Hath Cassius lived
To be but mirth and laughter to his Brutus,
When grief and blood ill-tempered, vexeth him?

BRUTUS. When I spoke that, I was ill-tempered too. 125

CASSIUS. Do you confess so much? Give me your hand.

BRUTUS. And my heart too.

CASSIUS. I did not think you could have been so angry.

BRUTUS. O Cassius, I am sick of many griefs.

                                      Portia is dead. 130

CASSIUS. Ha! Portia!

BRUTUS. She is dead.

CASSIUS. How 'scaped I killing when I crossed you so?
O insupportable and touching loss!
Upon what sickness? 135

BRUTUS.   Impatient of my absence,
And grief that young Octavius with Mark Antony
Have made themselves so strong — for with her death
That tidings came — with this she fell distract,
And, her attendants absent, swallowed fire.° 140

CASSIUS. And died so?

BRUTUS.   Even so.

CASSIUS.   O ye immortal gods!

104. **Checked . . . bondman:** rebuked like a slave. 109. **Plutus' mine:** all the riches belonging to Plutus, the god of wealth. 117. **dishonor . . . honor:** I will call your dishonorable conduct merely a whim or caprice. Brutus is changing his attitude, too. 140. **fire:** According to the ancient biographer, Plutarch, Portia swallowed burning coals. Such an act appears rather improbable and may be a rumor fashioned from the swallowing of poison.

[Enter LUCIUS *with wine and taper.]*

BRUTUS. Speak no more of her. Give me a bowl of wine.
    In this I bury all unkindness, Cassius. *(Drinks.)*   145
    Come in, Titinius!

[Exit LUCIUS. *Enter* TITINIUS, *with* MESSALA.]

            Welcome, good Messala.°
    Now sit we close about this taper here,
    And call in question our necessities.
CASSIUS. Portia, art thou gone?   150
BRUTUS.   No more, I pray you.
    Messala, I have here received letters,
    That young Octavius and Mark Antony
    Come down upon us with a mighty power,
    Bending their expedition toward Philippi.°   155
MESSALA. Myself have letters of the selfsame tenor.
BRUTUS. With what addition?
MESSALA. That by proscription of bills of outlawry,
    Octavius, Antony, and Lepidus
    Have put to death an hundred Senators.   160
BRUTUS. Therein our letters do not well agree.
    Mine speak of seventy Senators that died
    By their proscriptions, Cicero being one.
CASSIUS. Cicero one!
MESSALA.   Cicero is dead,   165
    And by that order of proscription.
BRUTUS. Well, to our work alive. What do you think
    Of marching to Philippi presently?
CASSIUS. I do not think it good.
BRUTUS.   Your reason?   170
CASSIUS.   This it is:
    'Tis better that the enemy seek us.
    So shall he waste his means, weary his soldiers,
    Doing himself offense; whilst we, lying still,
    Are full of rest, defense, and nimbleness.   175
BRUTUS. Good reasons must, of force, give place to better.
    The people 'twixt Philippi and this ground
    Do stand but in a forced affection;
    For they have grudged us contribution.
    The enemy, marching along by them,   180
    By them shall make a fuller number up,°

---

147. **Messala** (mĕ·sä′lå). 155. **Philippi** (fĭ·lĭp′pī): a city in Macedonia, now part of northern Greece. Keep in mind that Brutus and Cassius are now at Sardis, in what is today the country of Turkey. 181. Brutus fears that the people between Philippi and Sardis might be won over to Antony's cause, and thus swell his numbers.

Come on refreshed, new-added, and encouraged.
From which advantage shall we cut him off,
If at Philippi we do face him there,
These people at our back.   185
CASSIUS.   Hear me, good brother.
BRUTUS. Under your pardon. You must note beside,
     That we have tried the utmost of our friends,
     Our legions are brimful, our cause is ripe.
     The enemy increaseth every day;   190
     We, at the height, are ready to decline.
     There is a tide in the affairs of men,
     Which, taken at the flood, leads on to fortune;
     Omitted, all the voyage of their life
     Is bound in shallows and in miseries.   195
     On such a full sea are we now afloat;
     And we must take the current when it serves,
     Or lose our ventures.
CASSIUS.   Then, with your will, go on.
     We'll along ourselves, and meet them at Philippi.°   200
BRUTUS. The deep of night is crept upon our talk,
     And nature must obey necessity;
     Which we will niggard with a little rest.
     There is no more to say?
CASSIUS.   No more. Good night.   205
     Early tomorrow will we rise and hence.
BRUTUS. Lucius!

                        [*Enter* LUCIUS.]

     My gown.

                        [*Exit* LUCIUS.]

                     Farewell, good Messala.
Good night, Titinius. Noble, noble Cassius,   210
Good night, and good repose.
CASSIUS.   O my dear brother!
     This was an ill beginning of the night.
     Never come such division 'tween our souls!
     Let it not, Brutus.   215
BRUTUS.   Everything is well.
CASSIUS. Good night, my lord.
BRUTUS.   Good night, good brother.
TITINIUS. MESSALA. Good night, Lord Brutus.
BRUTUS.   Farewell, everyone.   220

199–200. Twice before Brutus' opinion has prevailed — once, in not killing Antony and then
in allowing him to make the funeral speech. It would seem that Brutus often makes the wrong
decision, yet Cassius complies with him.

[Exeunt all but BRUTUS. *Re-enter* LUCIUS, *with the gown.*]

Give me the gown. Where is thy instrument?°
LUCIUS. Here in the tent.
BRUTUS.   What, thou speak'st drowsily?
    Poor knave, I blame thee not; thou art o'erwatched.°
    Call Claudius° and some other of my men.   225
    I'll have them sleep on cushions in my tent.
LUCIUS. Varro° and Claudius!

[Enter VARRO *and* CLAUDIUS.]

VARRO. Calls my lord?
BRUTUS. I pray you, sirs, lie in my tent and sleep.
    Look, Lucius, here's the book I sought for so;   230
    I put it in the pocket of my gown.

*[*VARRO *and* CLAUDIUS *lie down.*]

LUCIUS. I was sure your lordship did not give it me.
BRUTUS. Bear with me, good boy, I am much forgetful.
    Canst thou hold up thy heavy eyes awhile,
    And touch thy instrument a strain or two?   235
LUCIUS. Ay, my lord, an 't please you.
BRUTUS.   It does, my boy.
    I trouble thee too much, but thou art willing.
LUCIUS. It is my duty, sir.
BRUTUS. I should not urge thy duty past thy might;   240
    I know young bloods look for a time of rest.
LUCIUS. I have slept, my lord, already.
BRUTUS. It was well done; and thou shalt sleep again;
    I will not hold thee long. If I do live,°
    I will be good to thee.   245

[Music, and a song.]

    This is a sleepy tune. O murd'rous slumber,
    Lay'st thou thy leaden mace upon my boy,
    That plays the music? Gentle knave, good night;
    I will not do thee so much wrong to wake thee.
    If thou dost nod, thou break'st thy instrument;   250
    I'll take it from thee. And, good boy, good night.
    Let me see, let me see; is not the leaf turned down
    Where I left reading? Here it is, I think.

[Enter the Ghost of CAESAR.]

---

221. The **instrument** was a kind of lute. 224. **o'erwatched:** weary from too much watching.
225. **Claudius** (klô'dĭ·ŭs) 227. **Varro** (văr'ō). 244. Note that Brutus seems doubtful about the
outcome of tomorrow.

How ill this taper burns!° Ha! Who comes here?
I think it is the weakness of mine eyes
That shapes this monstrous apparition. 255
It comes upon me. Art thou anything?
Art thou some god, some angel, or some devil,
That mak'st my blood cold and my hair to stare?°
Speak to me what thou art. 260
GHOST. Thy evil spirit, Brutus.
BRUTUS.   Why com'st thou?
GHOST. To tell thee thou shalt see me at Philippi.
BRUTUS. Well; then I shall see thee again?
GHOST. Ay, at Philippi. 265
BRUTUS. Why, I will see thee at Philippi, then.

                     [*Exit Ghost.*]

Now I have taken heart, thou vanishest:
Ill spirit, I would hold more talk with thee.
Boy, Lucius! Varro! Claudius! Sirs, awake!
Claudius! 270
LUCIUS. The strings, my lord, are false.
BRUTUS. He thinks he is still at his instrument.
        Lucius, awake!
LUCIUS. My lord?
BRUTUS. Didst thou dream, Lucius, that thou so criedst out? 275
LUCIUS. My lord, I do not know that I did cry.
BRUTUS. Yes, that thou didst. Didst thou see anything?
LUCIUS. Nothing, my lord.
BRUTUS. Sleep again, Lucius. Sirrah Claudius! (*To* VARRO)
        Fellow thou, awake! 280
VARRO. My lord?
CLAUDIUS. My lord?
BRUTUS. Why did you so cry out, sirs, in your sleep?
VARRO. CLAUDIUS. Did we, my lord?
BRUTUS.   Ay. Saw you anything? 285
VARRO. No, my lord, I saw nothing.
CLAUDIUS.   Nor I, my lord.
BRUTUS. Go and commend me to my brother Cassius:
        Bid him set on his powers betimes before,°
        And we will follow. 290
VARRO. CLAUDIUS. It shall be done, my lord.

                   [*Exeunt.*]

---

254. The presence of a ghost was supposed to cause candles to flicker and burn blue.
259. **stare:** stand on end. 289. **Bid . . . before:** Tell Cassius to lead on his army in good time ahead of Brutus.

ACT V

SCENE 1. *The plains of Philippi.*

Philippi was a city in northern Greece founded by Philip of Macedon, the father of Alexander the Great. Cassius' and Brutus' armies are here to meet the armies of Antony and Octavius coming from Rome. The scene is a desolate plain edged with low hills and jutting rocks.

[*Enter* OCTAVIUS, ANTONY, *and* SOLDIERS.]

OCTAVIUS. Now Antony, our hopes are answerèd.
    You said the enemy would not come down,
    But keep the hills and upper regions.
    It proves not so; their battles are at hand;
    They mean to warn us at Philippi here,   5
    Answering before we do demand of them.
ANTONY. Tut, I am in their bosoms, and I know
    Wherefore they do it. They could be content
    To visit other places, and come down
    With fearful bravery, thinking by this face   10
    To fasten in our thoughts that they have courage.
    But 'tis not so.

[*Enter a* MESSENGER.]

MESSENGER.   Prepare you generals;
    The enemy comes on in gallant show.
    Their bloody sign of battle° is hung out,   15
    And something to be done immediately.
ANTONY. Octavius, lead your battle softly on,
    Upon the left hand of the even field.
OCTAVIUS. Upon the right hand I. Keep thou the left.
ANTONY. Why do you cross me in this exigent?°   20
OCTAVIUS. I do not cross you; but I will do so.

[*March. Drum. Enter* BRUTUS, CASSIUS, *and* SOLDIERS; LUCILIUS,
TITINIUS, MESSALA, *and others.*]

BRUTUS. They stand, and would have parley.
CASSIUS. Stand fast Titinius. We must out and talk.
OCTAVIUS. Mark Antony, shall we give sign of battle?
ANTONY. No, Caesar, we will answer on their charge.   25
    Make forth; the generals would have some words.

---

15. **bloody . . . battle:** red flag of defiance. 20. **exigent:** critical moment.

OCTAVIUS. Stir not until the signal.
BRUTUS. Words before blows. Is it so, countrymen?
OCTAVIUS. Not that we love words better, as you do.
BRUTUS. Good words are better than bad strokes, Octavius.   30
ANTONY. In your bad strokes, Brutus, you give good words;
    Witness the hole you made in Caesar's heart,
    Crying, "Long live! Hail, Caesar!"
CASSIUS.   Antony,
    The posture of your blows are yet unknown;   35
    But for your words, they rob the Hybla° bees,
    And leave them honeyless.
ANTONY.   Not stingless too.
BRUTUS. O yes, and soundless too.
    For you have stolen their buzzing, Antony,   40
    And very wisely threat before you sting.
ANTONY. Villains, you did not so, when your vile daggers
    Hacked one another in the sides of Caesar.
    You showed your teeth like apes, and fawned like hounds,
    And bowed like bondmen, kissing Caesar's feet;   45
    Whilst damnèd Casca, like a cur, behind
    Struck Caesar on the neck.
OCTAVIUS. Look,
    I draw a sword against conspirators.
    When think you that the sword goes up° again?   50
    Never, till Caesar's three and thirty wounds
    Be well avenged.
BRUTUS. Caesar, thou canst not die by traitors' hands,
    Unless thou bring'st them with thee.
OCTAVIUS.   Come Antony; away!   55
    Defiance, traitors, hurl we in your teeth.
    If you dare fight today, come to the field;
    If not, when you have stomachs.

          [*Exeunt* OCTAVIUS, ANTONY, *and* SOLDIERS.]

CASSIUS.   Now, most noble Brutus,
    The gods today stand friendly, that we may,   60
    Lovers in peace, lead on our days to age!
    But since the affairs of men rest still° incertain,
    Let's reason with the worst that may befall.
    If we do lose this battle, then is this
    The very last time we shall speak together.   65
    What are you then determined to do?
    You are contented to be led in triumph
    Through the streets of Rome?

---

36. **Hybla:** a mountain in Sicily famous for the honey produced there. 50. **goes up:** returns to the scabbard. 62. **still:** always.

BRUTUS. No, Cassius, no. Think not, thou noble Roman,
    That ever Brutus will go bound to Rome.   70
    He bears too great a mind. But this same day
    Must end that work the ides of March begun;
    And whether we shall meet again I know not.
    Therefore our everlasting farewell take.
    For ever, and for ever, farewell, Cassius!   75
    If we do meet again, why, we shall smile;
    If not, why then, this parting was well made.
CASSIUS. For ever, and for ever, farewell, Brutus!
    If we do meet again, we'll smile indeed;
    If not, 'tis true this parting was well made.   80
BRUTUS. Why, then, lead on. O, that a man might know
    The end of this day's business ere it come!
    But it sufficeth that the day will end,
    And then the end is known. Come, ho! Away!

[Exeunt.]

SCENE 2.   *The field of battle.*

A part of Cassius' army, obeying Brutus' orders to attack the flank of Octavius' army, fail to watch the enemy's other flank and are soon surrounded by the troops of Mark Antony. Whereupon some of Cassius' horsemen and footmen break rank and flee for their lives toward the sea.

[Alarums. Enter CASSIUS *and* TITINIUS.]

CASSIUS. O, look, Titinius, look, the villains fly!
    Myself have to mine own turned enemy.°
    This ensign here of mine was turning back.
    I slew the coward, and did take it from him.°
TITINIUS. O Cassius, Brutus gave the word too early;   5
    Who, having some advantage on Octavius,
    Took it too eagerly. His soldiers fell to spoil,
    Whilst we by Antony are all enclosed.

[Enter PINDARUS.]

PINDARUS. Fly further off, my lord, fly further off!
    Mark Antony is in your tents, my lord.   10
    Fly, therefore, noble Cassius, fly far off!
CASSIUS. The hill is far enough. Look, look, Titinius;
    Are those my tents where I perceive the fire?
TITINIUS. They are, my lord.

2. **Myself . . . enemy:** I am now the enemy of my own men because they are cowards. 3–4. Perceiving his soldiers losing ground, Cassius did his best to keep them from fleeing. He took a flag (**ensign**) from one of the bearers and held it above his head, but he failed to check the retreat.

Battle Scene from Act V.

CASSIUS.   Titinius, if thou lovest me,   15
    Mount thou my horse, and hide thy spurs in him
    Till he have brought thee up to yonder troops,°
    And here again; that I may rest assured
    Whether yond troops are friend or enemy.
TITINIUS. I will be here again, even with a thought.   20

                   [*Exit.*]

CASSIUS. Go, Pindarus, get higher on that hill;
    My sight was ever thick. Regard Titinius,
    And tell me what thou not'st about the field.

          [PINDARUS *ascends the hill.*]

    This day° I breathed first: time is come round,
    And where I did begin, there shall I end;   25
    My life is run his compass. Sirrah, what news?
PINDARUS (*above*). O my lord!

  17. **yonder troops:** These are troops that Brutus has sent to aid Cassius. **24. This day:** It happens to be Cassius' birthday.

CASSIUS. What news?

PINDARUS (*above*). Titinius is enclosed round about
    With horsemen, that make to him on the spur!   30
    Yet he spurs on! Now they are almost on him!
    Now, Titinius! Now some light. O, he lights too.
    He's ta'en! (*Shout*) And, hark! They shout for joy.°

CASSIUS. Come down; behold no more.
    O, coward that I am, to live so long   35
    To see my best friend ta'en before my face!

[PINDARUS *descends*.]

    Come hither, sirrah:
    In Parthia did I take thee prisoner;
    And then I swore thee, saving of thy life,
    That whatsoever I did bid thee do,   40
    Thou shouldst attempt it. Come now, keep thine oath.
    Now be a freeman: and with this good sword,
    That ran through Caesar's bowels, search this bosom.°
    Stand not to answer. Here, take thou the hilts;
    And, when my face is covered, as 't is now,   45
    Guide thou the sword.

[PINDARUS *stabs him*.]

              Caesar, thou art revenged,
    Even with the sword that killed thee. (*Dies.*)

PINDARUS. So, I am free; yet would not so have been,
    Durst I have done my will, O Cassius,   50
    Far from this country Pindarus shall run,
    Where never Roman shall take note of him.

[*Exit.*]

[*Re-enter* TITINIUS *with* MESSALA.]

MESSALA. It is but change, Titinius; for Octavius
    Is overthrown by noble Brutus' power,
    As Cassius' legions are by Antony.   55

TITINIUS. These tidings will well comfort Cassius.

MESSALA. Where did you leave him?

TITINIUS.   All disconsolate,
    With Pindarus, his bondman, on this hill.

MESSALA. Is not that he that lies upon the ground?   60

TITINIUS. He lies not like the living. O my heart!

MESSALA. Is not that he?

29–33. Pindarus, the servant of Cassius, does not interpret the scene correctly. Titinius is enclosed by friends who shout for joy at Brutus' victory over Octavius. **Light** means alight from a horse. 43. Cassius here directs Pindarus to kill him with his sword, the very one with which he stabbed Caesar.

TITINIUS.   No, this was he, Messala,
        But Cassius is no more. O setting sun,
        As in thy red rays thou dost sink to night,   65
        So in his red blood Cassius' day is set;
        The sun of Rome is set! Our day is gone;
        Clouds, dews, and dangers come. Our deeds are done!
        Mistrust of my success hath done this deed.
MESSALA. Mistrust of good success hath done this deed.   70
        O hateful error, melancholy's child,
        Why dost thou show to the apt thoughts of men
        The things that are not? O error, soon conceived,
        Thou never comest unto a happy birth,
        But kill'st the mother that engendered thee!   75
TITINIUS. What, Pindarus! Where art thou, Pindarus?
MESSALA. Seek him, Titinius, whilst I go meet
        The noble Brutus, thrusting this report
        Into his ears; I may say, thrusting it;
        For piercing steel and darts envenomed°   80
        Shall be as welcome to the ears of Brutus
        As tidings of this sight.
TITINIUS.   Hie you, Messala,
        And I will seek for Pindarus the while.

                    [*Exit* MESSALA.]

        Why didst thou send me forth, brave Cassius?   85
        Did I not meet thy friends? And did not they
        Put on my brows this wreath of victory,
        And bid me give it thee? Didst thou not hear their shouts?
        Alas, thou hast misconstrued everything!
        But, hold thee, take this garland on thy brow.   90
        Thy Brutus bid me give it thee, and I
        Will do his bidding. Brutus, come apace,
        And see how I regard Caius Cassius.
        By your leave, gods, — this is a Roman's part.
        Come, Cassius' sword, and find Titinius' heart.   95

                    [*Kills himself.*]

[*Re-enter* MESSALA *with* BRUTUS, *young* CATO, STRATO (strā'tō), VOLUMNIUS (vȯ-
lŭm'nĭ·ŭs), *and* LUCILIUS.]

BRUTUS. Where, where, Messala, doth his body lie?
MESSALA. Lo, yonder.
CATO.   He is slain.
BRUTUS. O Julius Caesar, thou art mighty yet!
        Thy spirit walks abroad, and turns our swords   100
        In our own proper entrails.

                    80. envenomed: poisoned.

[*Low alarums.*]

The last of all the Romans, fare thee well!
It is impossible that ever Rome
Should breed thy fellow. Friends, I owe more tears
To this dead man than you shall see me pay.   105
I shall find time, Cassius, I shall find time.
Come, therefore, and to Thasos send his body:
His funerals shall not be in our camp,
Lest it discomfort us. Lucilius, come;
'Tis three o'clock; and, Romans, yet ere night   110
We shall try fortune in a second fight.

[*Exeunt.*]

SCENE 3.   *Another part of the field.*

The battle continues and as the tide of victory turns for Antony's armies, Brutus
withdraws, barely escaping capture. It is night and therefore difficult to recognize
faces.

[*Enter* BRUTUS, DARDANIUS (där·dā'nĭ·ŭs), CLITUS (clī'tŭs), STRATO, *and* VOLUM-
    NIUS.]

BRUTUS. Come, poor remains of friends, rest on this rock.
CLITUS. Statilius° showed the torchlight, but my lord,
    He came not back. He is or ta'en or slain.
BRUTUS. Sit thee down, Clitus. Slaying is the word;
    It is a deed in fashion. Hark thee, Clitus. (*Whispers.*)   5
CLITUS. What, I, my lord? No, not for all the world.
BRUTUS. Peace then! no words.
CLITUS.   I'll rather kill myself.
BRUTUS. Hark thee, Dardanius. (*Whispers.*)
DARDANIUS.   Shall I do such a deed?   10
CLITUS. What ill request did Brutus make to thee?
DARDANIUS. To kill him, Clitus. Look, he meditates.
CLITUS. Now is that noble vessel full of grief,
    That it runs over even at his eyes.
BRUTUS. Come hither, good Volumnius; list a word.   15
VOLUMNIUS. What says my lord?
BRUTUS.   Why, this, Volumnius:
    The ghost of Caesar hath appeared to me
    Two several times by night; at Sardis once,
    And, this last night, here in Philippi fields: 20
    I know my hour is come.

2. **Statilius** (stá·tĭ'lĭ·ŭs) is a scout sent out by Brutus to check up on the results of the battle.
If all went well with him he was to signal with a torchlight once.

VOLUMNIUS.   Not so, my lord.
BRUTUS. Nay, I am sure it is, Volumnius.
    Thou seest the world, Volumnius, how it goes;
    Our enemies have beat us to the pit.   25

              [*Low alarums.*]

    It is more worthy to leap in ourselves,
    Than to tarry till they push us. Good Volumnius,
    Thou know'st that we two went to school together.
    Even for that our love of old, I prithee,
    Hold thou my sword hilts, whilst I run on it.   30
VOLUMNIUS. That's not an office for a friend, my lord.

              [*Alarum still.*]

CLITUS. Fly, fly, my lord; there is no tarrying here.
BRUTUS. Farewell to you, and you, and you, Volumnius.
    Strato, thou hast been all this while asleep;
    Farewell to thee too, Strato. Countrymen,   35
    My heart doth joy that yet in all my life
    I found no man but he was true to me.
    I shall have glory by this losing day
    More than Octavius and Mark Antony
    By this vile conquest shall attain unto.   40
    So fare you well at once; for Brutus' tongue
    Hath almost ended his life's history.
    Night hangs upon mine eyes; my bones would rest,
    That have but labored to attain this hour.

        [*Alarum. Cry within, "Fly, fly, fly!"*]

CLITUS. Fly, my lord, fly.   45
BRUTUS.   Hence! I will follow.

        [*Exeunt* CLITUS, DARDANIUS, *and* VOLUMNIUS.]

    I prithee, Strato, stay thou by thy lord.
    Thou art a fellow of a good respect;
    Thy life hath had some smatch° of honor in it.
    Hold then my sword, and turn away thy face,   50
    While I do run upon it. Wilt thou, Strato?
STRATO. Give me your hand first. Fare you well, my lord.
BRUTUS. Farewell, good Strato. (*Runs on his sword.*)
    Caesar, now be still.
    I killed not thee with half so good a will. (*Dies.*)   55

    [*Alarum. Retreat. Enter* OCTAVIUS, ANTONY, *and the* ARMY.]

[*Octavius halts his men while Antony walks forward and kneels by the body of
    Brutus. He regards the face of Brutus intently; then he speaks as if to himself.*]

                49. smatch: taste.

ANTONY. This was the noblest Roman of them all.
    All the conspirators, save only he,
    Did that they did in envy of great Caesar.
    He only, in a general honest thought
    And common good to all, made one of them.   60
    His life was gentle, and the elements
    So mixed in him that Nature might stand up
    And say to all the world "This was a man!"
OCTAVIUS. According to his virtue let us use him,
    With all respect, and rites of burial.   65
    Within my tent his bones to-night shall lie,
    Most like a soldier, ordered honourably.
    So call the field to rest, and let's away,
    To part the glories of this happy day.

                          [*Exeunt.*]

FOLLOWING THE ACTION

ACT I, SCENE 1

1. Find the lines which show that:
    (a) The cobbler is saucy to Marullus.
    (b) Marullus thinks Pompey did more for Rome than Caesar has done.
    (c) The two tribunes have other plans to carry out after leaving the scene.
    (d) Marullus and Flavius fear the power of Caesar.

ACT I, SCENE 2

2. Find the lines which show that:
    (a) Casca is very respectful to Caesar while in his presence.
    (b) Antony respects and fulfills Caesar's commands.
    (c) Caesar does not pay attention to the soothsayer.
    (d) Brutus was worried about the power of Caesar even before Cassius spoke to him about it.
    (e) Cassius finds fault with Caesar on the basis of physical weakness.
    (f) Cassius is clever at arguing that in all ways Brutus is on a par with Caesar.
    (g) Caesar distrusts Cassius.
    (h) Casca believes Caesar wanted to accept the crown.
    (i) Caesar desires the approval of the people.
    (j) Casca has not lived up to the promise of his youth, according to Brutus.

    (k) Cassius intends to use Brutus for his own purposes.

ACT I, SCENE 3

3. Find the lines which show that:
    (a) Casca hints the "strife in Heaven" may be a sign the gods are displeased with affairs in the world.
    (b) Casca thinks the Senators intend to offer Caesar a crown.
    (c) Cassius has the Roman's hatred of bondage.
    (d) Cassius is not sure at first of Casca's support.
    (e) In the month which has elapsed, Cassius has organized a party opposing Caesar.
    (f) Others besides Cassius are eager to have Brutus join the conspiracy.

ACT II, SCENE 1

4. Find the lines which show that:
    (a) Brutus does not hate Caesar.
    (b) Brutus fears the future action of Caesar.
    (c) Cinna has done the task assigned to him by Cassius earlier in the evening.
    (d) Brutus takes pride in what his ancestors did for Rome.
    (e) Brutus, while apparently accepting the necessity of killing Caesar, finds the actual plotting hideous.
    (f) Casca reverses his opinions easily.

(g) Brutus insists the killing must be done on the level of justice and sacrifice to country, and with no impure motives.

(h) The conspirators differ in opinion as to what Antony will do following the assassination.

(i) Cassius accuses Caesar of becoming superstitious.

(j) Portia has been watching and has seen the conspirators.

ACT II, SCENE 2

5. Find the lines which show that:

(a) Caesar intends to disregard the omens described by his wife.

(b) Decius persuades Caesar to go to the Senate House by appealing to his desire for power and implying that he will be thought cowardly if he does not go.

(c) Brutus continues to be at war with himself.

ACT II, SCENE 3

6. How does this scene show that all Romans do not wish Caesar's death? How would the scene affect both the thinking and the emotions of the audience?

ACT III, SCENE 1

7. Find the lines that:

(a) Would anger the members of the Senate because to the Senators Caesar would seem arrogant and insulting.

(b) Indicate Mark Antony will support the party if given reasons for Caesar's death.

(c) Show Cassius and Brutus disagreeing over Antony again.

(d) Reveal how Antony truly feels about Caesar's death.

(e) Disclose what message the servant is to take back to Octavius.

ACT III, SCENE 2

8. Find the lines which show that:

(a) The citizens are critical of the conspirators before Brutus gives his speech.

(b) The speech of Brutus is addressed to the patriotism of his audience.

(c) In spite of Brutus' words about freedom from tyranny, the crowd is eager to have another Caesar.

(d) Antony stirs up the crowd by various appeals.

(e) Brutus and Cassius hear of the effects of Antony's speech upon the mob.

ACT III, SCENE 3

9. How does this scene reveal the extent to which Antony's speech has aroused the mob?

ACT IV, SCENE 1

10. Find the lines which show that:

(a) Antony is merely making use of Lepidus for his own purposes.

(b) The triumvirs are surrounded by enemies.

ACT IV, SCENE 2

11. Find the lines which show that:

(a) Brutus is disappointed in his friend Cassius.

(b) Cassius feels that Brutus is in the wrong.

ACT IV, SCENE 3

12. Find the lines which show that:

(a) Cassius feels that Brutus should not have condemned Lucius Pella.

(b) Brutus feels that his friend is sinking to actions which are not worthy.

(c) Brutus loses his temper.

(d) Cassius seems to be overcome by Brutus' treatment of him.

(e) Cassius is genuinely sorrowful over Portia's death.

(f) Octavius, Antony, and Lepidus have tried to destroy all opposition to them in Rome.

(g) Brutus and Cassius do not agree about military strategy.

ACT V, SCENES 1 and 2

13. Find the lines which show that:

(a) Cassius and Brutus are doubtful about the result of the coming battle.

(b) Brutus makes an error in the battle which leads to serious consequences.

(c) Both Cassius and Brutus feel that the spirit of Caesar is still a vital force in the world.

(d) Brutus is planning to continue the battle.

14. Find the lines which show that:

(a) Brutus' friends love him too much to kill him.

(b) Antony feels that Brutus had pure motives though the other conspirators did not.

IN SUMMARY

15. Which marks the climax of the play: the death of Caesar or Antony's funeral oration? Before you answer, consider these questions: (a) Which event marks a turning point in the story and starts a chain of events which can only end in tragedy? (b) Which event seems to highlight all the conflicts of the play and makes us feel the tragedy of their interaction?

16. Why do you think Shakespeare made Brutus speak in prose rather than poetry in his speech to the people?

17. Why would it be less effective to have the Forum scene follow the assassination, leaving out the conversation between Antony, Brutus, and Cassius?

18. What effect on the audience is gained from having a variety of conflicts — conflicts between groups, conflicts between individuals, conflicts within the minds of characters?

THEME

In following the action of *Julius Caesar*, you have considered one level of the play. Now you are ready to plunge deeper to consider the theme or central idea which the author had in mind when he wrote the play. You will need to consider all the elements thoughtfully, for Shakespeare wove many themes into his dramas, just as in real existence many purposes intermingle in the lives of human beings. No one has ever been able to give a simple answer to the question, "What is life all about?" and you will find that you need to think carefully before deciding, "What is this play all about?"

Consider the following ideas to see which one you think Shakespeare might have intended as the *main* theme of the play. Be prepared to back up your decision with good reasoning and quotations in case other students do not agree with you.

1. The result of effective oratory and propaganda upon the masses.

2. The evils of dictatorship in ignoring the right of the people to freedom of thought, freedom of speech, and freedom of action.

3. The decay of a great republic, with its leaders and statesmen engaged in intrigues and conspiracies to gain power; and the tragedy of a great man caught between the various factions struggling for power.

4. The error of thinking that if your goal is virtuous, any means used to achieve it are justifiable.

5. The lonely world of a man of honor surrounded by men of selfish motives.

CREATION OF CHARACTER

In real life people very often do not feel the same way about an individual. The pampered, selfish boy may be an object of disgust to his schoolmates, but to his misguided mother he is still "my darling boy."

Shakespeare, in creating characters, tried to present them in many dimensions, so that we see his people just as we do those in real life, not from one viewpoint, but from many. This ability to present all sides of a character is, no doubt, one reason why the people in Shakespeare's plays are unforgettable and why we find it interesting and challenging to go back again and again to his plays to see if we can discover new truths about the characters he created.

1. A list of qualities is given below. Which ones are characteristic of Caesar according to his own statements and actions? Which ones are attributed to him by others? Are some opinions contradictory? In the total picture which you formed of Caesar from the play, which are truly his qualities? Which are not? Be prepared to give reasons for believing as you do. It would be wise to jot down quotations from the play which support your opinion.

(a) ambitious for power
(b) masterful
(c) superstitious
(d) weak in body
(e) emotional
(f) easily flattered

(g) faithful
(h) considerate of others
(i) shrewd in judging others
(j) constant

2. How are Brutus and Cassius alike or different in:
(a) their motives in entering the conspiracy
(b) their opinions of themselves
(c) their attitudes toward truth
(d) their control of emotion
(e) their ability to judge Antony
(f) their ability to hold the loyalty of their supporters
(g) their skill in battle

3. Mark Antony seems to be a man with a many-sided nature. Which characters see him as each of the following:
(a) a lover of fun and sports, a reveler, a man who does not have the qualities of leadership
(b) a dangerous man who is shrewd, clever, and capable of moving the masses
(c) a beloved friend who enjoys life and is without envy
(d) a noble friend of Caesar, loyal to him and to the people
(e) a man of much experience but one who makes mistakes after taking over the government of Rome

4. Do Casca and Decius Brutus deserve the name of hypocrite more than the other conspirators? Why or why not?

PAINTING THE SETTING: PLACE, TIME, MOOD

In the Elizabethan theater in which Shakespeare worked, little scenery was used; thus he could not depend, as modern dramatists often can, upon an elaborate setting to establish time, place, and mood. Instead, Shakespeare had to let the audience know the setting through lines in the play. In determining how successfully he accomplished that purpose in *Julius Caesar*, consider the following questions about the play:

1. What lines in Act II, Scene 1, make the audience conscious that time is passing? Why is this awareness important?

2. Where are the time and place revealed in the opening lines of Act III, Scene 1? Why is the time important to the reaction of the audience?

3. How are the following important in creating moods which add to the suspense or the impact of ideas?
(a) Flavius and Marullus begin the action of the play by driving the citizens from the street.
(b) The conspirators meet at night.
(c) Caesar invites the conspirators into his home to "taste some wine" with him before going to the Senate.
(d) We hear Brutus speak to the people instead of hearing Cassius.
(e) Antony reveals the provisions of the will at the end of his speech.
(f) Cassius and Brutus have a last meeting to say farewell before the battle.

SYMBOLS

As you think back over your reading of *Julius Caesar*, can you identify events and ideas which are used as symbols to reinforce and deepen the meanings in the play? Consider the following:

1. What do the strange disturbances in nature seem to signify?

2. How are the following used as symbols of deeper meanings?
(a) sleeplessness
(b) the ghost of Caesar
(c) darkness
(d) unhealthiness and infirmities

COMPOSITION SUGGESTION

Select one of the important themes in *Julius Caesar* and explain how happenings in the play and the words of the characters give this theme special force. Or, select one of the major characters in the play for a study. Use references to his actions, remarks of other characters about him, and his own words to show different aspects of his character and different opinions of him held by his associates.

ABOUT THE AUTHOR

William Shakespeare (1564–1616) was born into the family of a merchant in Stratford, a little town on the Avon River north of London.

Little is known of the early life of the man who was to become the leading playwright of England, but it is generally believed that he attended grammar school in the village. In Stratford he grew to young manhood, married Anne Hathaway, and became the father of three children.

In the 1580's the story shifts to London, where William Shakespeare began his work in the theater and in eight years became the chief writer for the important company of actors known as the Lord Chamberlain's Men. Friend of earls and performer at the royal court, Shakespeare was one of the first actors to win a coat of arms and the title of gentleman.

In 1597 he bought New Place, second largest house in Stratford, and there his wife and children lived while he continued his work in London. By 1612 he had retired and had joined his family at New Place, where he lived the life of a country gentleman until his death at the age of fifty-two.

No writer in the English language before Shakespeare or after has been able to rival his genius as a dramatist and poet. His most important works are thirty-seven plays, including comedies, historical dramas, and tragedies.

Suggestions for Further Reading

Long Plays

Barrie, Sir James M., *What Every Woman Knows* (Samuel French)
Maggie, a plain, young Scotswoman, is the unappreciated spark and spirit behind her husband's political success.

Benét, Stephen Vincent, *The Devil and Daniel Webster* (Dramatists Play Service)
Jabez Stone sells his soul to the devil. When the time comes for delivery, Daniel Webster tries to save him.

Besier, Rudolph, *The Barretts of Wimpole Street* (Little, Brown, 1930)
Elizabeth Barrett is afflicted with poor health and a tyrannical father but is freed from both when she falls in love with and eventually marries poet Robert Browning.

Chodorov, Jerome, and Joseph Fields, *Junior Miss* (Dramatists Play Service)

A thirteen-year-old girl, with ideas culled from the movies, attempts to make her family conform to those ideas.

Christie, Agatha, *The Mousetrap* (Samuel French)
Several people are stranded in a boarding house during a snow storm and a murder takes place in their midst. The murderer has to be one of them, but who is it?

Goodrich, Frances, and Albert Hackett, *The Diary of Anne Frank* (Random House, 1956)
This is the moving, true story of a young Jewish girl's experiences when she and her family are forced to hide from the Nazis.

Hart, Moss, and George S. Kaufman, *You Can't Take It with You* (Dramatists Play Service, 1937)
This delightful comedy deals with the antics of the Sycamores, a slightly mad family whose members live very much as they please.

Lindsay, Howard, and Russel Crouse, *Life with Father* (Knopf, 1940)
This play, adapted from the book *Life with Father* by Clarence Day, has all the charm and humor of the original. The "hero" is Father — lovable, quick-tempered, fiercely kind.

Mantle, Burns, ed., *The Best Plays of 19—* (an annual publication since 1894, Dodd, Mead)

Rattigan, Terence, *The Winslow Boy* (Dramatists Play Service)
An innocent boy is accused of stealing and is expelled from an English school. His father fights to save his reputation, and the ensuing case raises the issue of an individual's basic rights.

Rodgers, Richard, and Oscar Hammerstein, *Six Plays by Rodgers and Hammerstein* (Modern Library, 1959)
Included are *Oklahoma!, Carousel, Allegro, South Pacific, The King and I*, and *Me and Juliet*.

Rostand, Edmond, *Cyrano de Bergerac* (Holt, Rinehart & Winston, trans. by Brian Hooker, 1923)
Cyrano, the hero of this play, is ready to fight at any mention of his enormous nose. He is a swordsman, a wit, a poet — and a lover.

Shaw, George Bernard, *Pygmalion* (Penguin and Samuel French)

A language professor undertakes to transform a flower girl with a cockney accent into a cultivated young woman. This is the play upon which the musical *My Fair Lady* was based.

Sherwood, Robert E., *Abe Lincoln in Illinois* (Scribner, 1940)
This play deals with the life of Lincoln from his meeting with Ann Rutledge to his election to the Presidency.

One-Act Plays

Cerf, Bennett, and Van H. Cartmell, eds., Twenty-four Favorite One-Act Plays (Doubleday, 1958)

Cohen, Helen, ed., *One-Act Plays by Modern Authors* (Harcourt, Brace & World, 1934)
Especially recommended in this collection are Oliphant Down's "The Maker of Dreams," Lord Dunsany's "A Night at an Inn," and A. A. Milne's "Wurzel Flummery."

Griffith, Francis, and Joseph Mersand, eds., *Modern One-Act Plays* (Harcourt, Brace & World, 1950)
An up-to-date collection of short plays, edited for classroom use.

Mayorga, Margaret, ed., *The Best One-Act Plays of 19–* (an annual publication since 1938, Dodd, Mead)

Milne, A. A., "The Ugly Duckling" (Samuel French, 1941)
An amusing satire on the plots and plans of royalty to marry off their children.

Wilder, Thornton, "Happy Journey to Camden and Trenton" (Samuel French, 1934)
The American family goes on a trip.

Life of Shakespeare

Chute, Marchette, *Shakespeare of London* (Dutton, 1949)
This book reads like a novel but is prepared from documentary sources to show Will Shakespeare as his contemporaries saw him in his work in London theaters.

Norman, Charles, *Playmaker of Avon* (McKay, 1949)
A short, very readable biography with descriptions of the theaters, Shakespeare's writing and acting, and his friends.

Interpretation and Staging of Shakespeare's Plays

Chute, Marchette, *Introduction to Shakespeare* (Dutton, 1951)
This book brings the London theater days of Shakespeare to life with emphasis on the staging, costuming, and acting of Shakespeare's plays.

Webster, Margaret, *Shakespeare Without Tears* (World Publishing, rev. ed., 1955)
A famous director tells about staging the dramas of Shakespeare.

Biographies of Actors and Actresses Who Have Played in Shakespeare

Le Gallienne, Eva, *With a Quiet Heart* (Viking, 1953)
This autobiography of an actress who has been devoted to the best in theater continues from where her earlier book, *At 33*, stopped.

Malvern, Gladys, *Curtain Going Up!* (Messner, 1943)
Description of Katharine Cornell's climb up from small parts to stardom.

Skinner, Cornelia Otis, *Family Circle* (Houghton Mifflin, 1948)
The story of the Skinner family's early struggle for success in the theater.

Stewart, Anna B., *Enter David Garrick* (Lippincott, 1951)
A biography of the eighteenth-century actor who has been called by many the greatest interpreter of Shakespeare.

Fiction Based on Elizabethan Times

Irwin, Margaret, *Young Bess* (Harcourt, Brace & World, 1945), and *Elizabeth, Captive Princess* (Harcourt, Brace & World, 1948)
Two novels about the early life of Elizabeth I.

Scott, Walter, *Kenilworth*
The story of Queen Elizabeth and the Earl of Leicester.

For Listening

A 45-minute recording of the five acts of *Julius Caesar* by the Dublin Gate Theatre is available on *Many Voices* 10B. Available on *Many Voices* 4B are the funeral orations by Brutus and Mark Antony.

The King Arthur Legend

From: T. H. WHITE'S *The Once and Future King*

SIR THOMAS MALORY'S *Morte d'Arthur*

ALFRED, LORD TENNYSON'S *Idylls of the King*

A song is heard just before the curtain goes down on the musical play *Camelot*, which opened on Broadway more than one thousand years after men first began to tell stories about King Arthur, who founded the court called Camelot. Listen to it now:

> Each evening from December to December
> Before you drift to sleep upon your cot
> Think back on all the tales that you remember
> Of Camelot.
>
> Ask every person if he's heard the story
> And tell it strong and clear if he has not
> That once there was a fleeting wisp of glory
> Called Camelot.

This section of your book includes some of those tales of Camelot. It is about the "fleeting wisp of glory" that some unknown poet and storyteller recognized on a hillside in Britain sometime back in the fifth or sixth century and that for over a thousand years has remained at the heart of the King Arthur legend.

The King Arthur legend is the great legend of the English-speaking people. It is our great legend. "Think back on all the tales that you re-member of Camelot" — of King Arthur and his Knights of the Round Table, of Sir Lancelot (lăn'cĕ·lŏt), of Sir Galahad (găl'a·hăd) and the Holy Grail. There are a great many of these tales, and all of them have something to do with the legend of King Arthur. For there is something about the King Arthur legend that, generation after generation, cap-tures the imagination of the greatest poets and storytellers of our language. Over the centuries this great legend, like a magnet, has

◄ King Arthur, as depicted in the central part of a large tapestry hanging in the Metropolitan Museum of Art. Woven in France in the late fourteenth century, this tapestry of Arthur is the oldest in existence, and it is the only one in which he is shown life size.

drawn to itself many stories that were originally unrelated. What is its strange power of attraction? What exactly is a legend, anyway?

First of all, a legend is a story, but no ordinary kind of story. The story must be so good, so powerful, that people are unable to forget it: century after century it lives on and grows. The story must be so good that no single person, however great a storyteller he may be, can tell it completely. It is better than the best of the storytellers, although many try to tell it.

The great legends usually begin with historical fact — a certain person lived, or a certain war was fought — but soon bare fact is left behind. The story develops its own kind of truth, a truth about what people want and dream of, or fear. The story grows because people — children, adults, novelists, poets — will not let the man or the event rest with history. The hearts and voices of the people take over where history leaves off. Most legends concern a hero. Most legends contain magic or the supernatural. Most legends reveal hopes or fears. The great legends reveal great hopes and fears, and also great ideas.

So it is with the legend of Arthur.

For over one thousand years this story has been growing. Was there a real King Arthur? Some historians writing in the ninth century suggest that there was in Britain in the fifth or sixth century a king, or at least a chieftain, by that name. But even by the ninth century it seems his story had begun to outgrow history, for one account is as follows:

"The twelfth battle was on the mount of Badon, wherein fell nine hundred and sixty men in one day at a single onset of Arthur; and no one overthrew them but he alone, and in all the battles he came out victorious."

Thus the King Arthur legend began. It had its hero, and in the ninth century, the storytellers wanted a hero who was all-powerful in battle.

It was another three hundred years before the story began to take shape as the legend we know today, with its exciting cast of heroes. Arthur was part of it, of course, and so were the magician Merlin, the Knights of the Round Table, and the lovely and mysterious ladies — Arthur's queen, Guinevere (gwĭn′ĕ·vēr), the enchantress Morgan le Fay, and others. By the twelfth century, the story had become a series of stories with a host of great deeds and adventures played out before a tapestry of courtly life. The spires of Camelot towered in medieval splendor over all of the Arthur legends.

French artist Gustave Doré's conception of the castle of Camelot and the countryside surrounding it, done for a nineteenth-century edition of Idylls of the King.

A twelfth-century writer, Geoffrey of Monmouth, brought together most of these stories. He was the first to describe the fifteen-year-old boy king, his magician-tutor, Merlin, and the famous court. He also told of Arthur's marriage to Guinevere and of the final betrayal of Arthur by Modred (mō′drĕd) that led to Arthur's death. Still other writers of this period added ideas of courtly romance and chivalry. By the twelfth century, you see, the medieval storytellers wanted a new kind of hero. They brought to the growing story of Arthur their own love of romance and knightly adventure and their own dream of chivalry.

In 1470, as the Middle Ages drew to a close, Sir Thomas Malory gathered together all the different tales of King Arthur in a single, unified story. The result was the book he called *Morte d'Arthur* (literally, "Arthur's Death"), told in simple, dignified prose and as enjoyable today as it was five hundred years ago. Since Malory, the Arthurian

A fourteenth-century artist's depiction of Sir Lancelot performing a chivalrous deed. Lancelot is helping the outnumbered forces of King Bagdemagus in a battle with the King of Wales.

story has intrigued many famous writers, but the most famous and popular retelling was by the nineteenth-century British poet Alfred, Lord Tennyson, in his *Idylls of the King*. Tennyson brought his own high idealism to the story, and Arthur became a high-minded hero whose best knights shared with him a lofty and religious mission — to create a noble, just, and ordered society based on love. In Tennyson's *Idylls*, it is Sir Galahad — not the bravest or most skillful warrior of the Round Table, but the *purest* — who is finally permitted to see the holy vision of the Grail, the cup used in the Last Supper, symbolic of the most sacred rite of the Christian religion. Thus, the legend had changed from the story of Arthur the bloody all-conquering hero-chieftain whom ninth-century England had idolized to the story of Arthur the king who marshalled force for justice and dreamed of peace. Arthur, you see, had changed with the changing dreams of the English-speaking people.

In our own day, the English-speaking people have discovered a delightful new retelling of the Arthur story in *The Once and Future King*, by the British novelist T. H. White. To Malory's version of the legend, T. H. White brought, of course, his own understanding of that "fleeting wisp of glory." Yet his lighthearted, modern telling of the story still emphasizes the theme that to us seems most important: Arthur's great idea of using the valor and skill of the warrior for good, of using might in the cause of right; and of working for the high ideal of a peaceful, ordered, and just world.

Why does this great legend continue to live and grow? Is it because of the dream it embodies, or because of the sheer excitement and joy of high adventure it contains? Whatever the reason, there is no doubt that Arthur and his court are alive today in literature.

Legends grow from the hearts and dreams of a whole people, but in each generation it is the individual storytellers who shape our legends. Many men have had a hand in the legend of King Arthur, some of them as famous as Tennyson, some of them long since forgotten. As you read this section, remember that it was a now-unknown storyteller who first recognized in Arthur the beginnings of a glorious legend and began to make Arthur larger-than-fact. Remember that Malory, Tennyson, T. H. White, and all the other molders of this legend recognized something in this story that most people could not see. It was their skill as artists that made *us* see it too.

But above all, as you read, remember that this is *your* legend. What you find in it will depend in part on your own hopes and fears, your own dreams of glory — for yourself, your friends, your country, and all mankind. For in the hearts and minds of all who love justice, honor, and courage, Camelot's glory is as alive today as it was centuries ago.

King Arthur and Queen Guinevere bestow knighthood upon Lancelot and several others in this scene from the Broadway play Camelot.

A Preview

Here is the way the three selections in this section tell the story of King Arthur:

The Beginning: **A Boy Becomes King**

THE STORYTELLER: T. H. White (1906–   ) in *The Once and Future King.*

THE STORY: There is magic in the way Arthur acquires his kingdom and a glimpse of future glory in the idea he presents at his first council meeting.

Chivalry at Its Height: **Sir Lancelot**

THE STORYTELLER: Sir Thomas Malory (1394?–1471) in *Morte d'Arthur;* retold in modern English in 1858 by Thomas Bulfinch.

THE STORY: At the height of Arthur's glory, he had at Camelot the famous Knights of the Round Table, a Code of Chivalry, his beautiful Queen Guinevere — and Sir Lancelot.

The Ending: **The Passing of Arthur**

THE STORYTELLER: Alfred, Lord Tennyson (1809–1892), in his epic poem *Idylls of the King.*

THE STORY: Arthur, wounded in combat, prepares to die. He gives up Excalibur and sails toward the sea on a dusky barge. But before he goes, he utters a mysterious prophecy: "I pass but shall not die."

THE BEGINNING

A Boy Becomes King

from *The Once and Future King*

by T. H. WHITE

In T. H. White's lighthearted retelling of the great legend, there is little in his description of the boy Arthur to suggest that he will ever be a king. As White tells the story, Arthur was an orphan, and he grew up near London in the castle of his guardian, a fine old knight named Sir Ector. He spent his days with Kay, Sir Ector's son, practicing such manly medieval sports as jousting, falconry, and boar hunting. When Kay himself became a knight, Arthur was to be his personal servant — his squire. Kay nicknamed Arthur the "Wart."

There was nothing kingly about the boy. And yet his aged tutor and friend, the magician Merlin, saw something in him that others could not see. From Merlin, the boy had learned much. Above all, he had learned to love and understand the world around him and to appreciate the instinctive wisdom of the wild animals he encountered in the English countryside.

Then, when Arthur was fifteen, something happened. England's king was dead, and there was no one to succeed him. All of England's knights and barons were going to London to show their prowess in a great jousting tournament, each hoping to be acclaimed king. And there was something else in London: a sword stuck hilt-

deep in an anvil on a slab of stone. The sword was called Excalibur (ĕks·kăl′ĭbĕr). A message, written in golden letters on the stone, said that whoever could pull it out would become king.

Naturally, Kay, who had just been knighted and was now Sir Kay, insisted on going to the tournament, the first in which he would have a chance to joust. So he, Sir Ector, and the Wart (now Kay's squire), set out for London, accompanied by an old friend, Sir Grummore (grü·mōr′). What happened next is the story T. H. White tells here.

Lᴏɴᴅᴏɴ was full to the brim. If Sir Ector had not been lucky enough to own a little land in Pie Street, on which there stood a respectable inn, they would have been hard put to it to find a lodging. But he did own it, and as a matter of fact drew most of his dividends[1] from that source, so they were able to get three beds between the four

[1] **dividends:** here, T. H. White is having fun with history. A *dividend* is paid to stockholders in a corporation. Sir Ector received feudal tithes.

of them. They thought themselves fortunate.

On the first day of the tournament, Sir Kay managed to get them on the way to the lists [1] at least an hour before the jousts could possibly begin. He had lain awake all night, imagining how he was going to beat the best barons in England, and he had not been able to eat his breakfast. Now he rode at the front of the cavalcade, with pale cheeks, and Wart wished there was something he could do to calm him down.

For country people, who only knew the dismantled tilting ground of Sir Ector's castle, the scene which met their eyes was ravishing. It was a huge green pit in the earth, about as big as the arena at a football match. It lay ten feet lower than the surrounding country, with sloping banks, and the snow had been swept off it. It had been kept warm with straw, which had been cleared off that morning, and now the close-worn grass sparkled green in the white landscape. Round the arena there was a world of color so dazzling and moving and twinkling as to make one blink one's eyes. The wooden grandstands were painted in scarlet and white. The silk pavilions [2] of famous people, pitched on every side, were azure and green and saffron [3] and checkered. The pennons and pennoncels [4] which floated everywhere in the sharp wind were flapping with every color of the rainbow, as they strained and slapped at their flagpoles, and the barrier down the middle of the arena [5] itself was done in chessboard squares of black and white. Most of the combatants and their friends had not yet arrived, but one could see from those few who had come how the very people would turn the scene into a bank of flowers, and how the armor would flash, and the scalloped sleeves of the heralds jig in the wind, as they raised their brazen trumpets to their lips to shake the fleecy clouds of winter with joyances [6] and fanfares.

"Good heavens!" cried Sir Kay. "I have left my sword at home."

"Can't joust without a sword," said Sir Grummore. "Quite irregular."

"Better go and fetch it," said Sir Ector. "You have time."

[1] **lists:** the wooden barriers enclosing a playing field; or as used here, the field itself.

[2] **pavilions** (pá·vǐl′yŭnz): tents.

[3] **saffron:** orange-yellow.

[4] **pennons and pennoncels:** narrow, pointed flags, each with the emblem of its knightly owner on it. A pennoncel is smaller than a pennon.

[5] **barrier . . . arena:** a stout wooden fence divided the jousting field. The knights rode at each other with the barrier between them to prevent serious injury.

[6] **joyances:** gaieties; delights.

"My squire will do," said Sir Kay. "What a mistake to make! Here, squire, ride hard back to the inn and fetch my sword. You shall have a shilling if you fetch it in time."

The Wart went as pale as Sir Kay was, and looked as if he were going to strike him. Then he said, "It shall be done, master," and turned his ambling palfrey [1] against the stream of newcomers. He began to push his way toward their hostelry as best he might.

"To offer me money!" cried the Wart to himself. "To look down at this beastly little donkey-affair off his great charger and call me Squire! Oh, Merlin, give me patience with the brute, and stop me from throwing his filthy shilling in his face."

When he got to the inn it was closed. Everybody had thronged to see the famous tournament, and the entire household had followed after the mob. Those were lawless days, and it was not safe to leave your house — or even to go to sleep in it — unless you were certain that it was impregnable. The wooden shutters bolted over the downstairs windows were two inches thick, and the doors were double-barred.

"Now what do I do," asked the Wart, "to earn my shilling?"

He looked ruefully at the blind little inn, and began to laugh.

"Poor Kay," he said. "All that shilling stuff was only because he was scared and miserable, and now he has good cause to be. Well, he shall have a sword of some sort if I have to break into the Tower of London." [2]

"How does one get hold of a sword?"

he continued. "Where can I steal one? Could I waylay some knight, even if I am mounted on an ambling pad, [3] and take his weapons by force? There must be some swordsmith or armorer in a great town like this, whose shop would still be open."

He turned his mount and cantered off along the street. There was a quiet churchyard at the end of it, with a kind of square in front of the church door. In the middle of the square there was a heavy stone with an anvil on it, and a fine new sword was stuck through the anvil.

"Well," said the Wart, "I suppose it is some sort of war memorial, but it will have to do. I am sure nobody would grudge Kay a war memorial, if

[1] **palfrey:** a saddle horse, usually one small and gentle enough for a woman.

[2] **Tower of London:** a fortress on the bank of the River Thames (tĕmz) in London, formerly a royal residence, a prison, and an arsenal, now a museum of medieval armor; completed in 1100.

[3] **pad:** a nag; a horse ridden with a pad because it is not worth saddling is usually called a "pad-horse."

they knew his desperate straits."

He tied his reins round a post of the lich gate,[1] strode up the gravel path, and took hold of the sword.

"Come sword," he said. "I must cry your mercy and take you for a better cause."

"This is extraordinary," said the Wart. "I feel strange when I have hold of this sword, and I notice everything much more clearly. Look at the beautiful gargoyles of the church, and of the monastery which it belongs to. See how splendidly all the famous banners in the aisle are waving. How nobly that yew[2] holds up the red flakes of its timbers to worship God. How clean the snow is. I can smell something like feverfew[3] and sweet briar[4] — and is it music that I hear?"

It was music, whether of pan-pipes[5] or of recorders,[6] and the light in the churchyard was so clear, without being dazzling, that one could have picked a pin out twenty yards away.

"There is something in this place," said the Wart. "There are people. Oh, people, what do you want?"

Nobody answered him, but the music was loud and the light beautiful.

"People," cried the Wart, "I must take this sword. It is not for me, but for Kay. I will bring it back."

There was still no answer, and Wart turned back to the anvil. He saw the golden letters, which he did not read, and the jewels on the pommel,[7] flashing in the lovely light.

"Come sword," said the Wart.

He took hold of the handles with both hands, and strained against the stone. There was a melodious consort[8] on the recorders, but nothing moved.

The Wart let go of the handles when they were beginning to bite into the palms of his hands and stepped back, seeing stars.

"It is well fixed," he said.

He took hold of it again and pulled with all his might. The music played more strongly, and the light all about the churchyard glowed like amethysts;[9] but the sword still stuck.

"Oh, Merlin," cried the Wart, "help me to get this weapon."

There was a kind of rushing noise, and a long chord played along with it. All around the churchyard there were hundreds of old friends. They rose over the church wall all together, like the Punch and Judy ghosts of remembered days, and there were badgers and nightingales and vulgar crows and hares and wild geese and falcons and fishes and dogs and dainty unicorns[10] and solitary wasps and corkindrills[11] and hedgehogs and griffins[12] and the thousand other animals he had met. They loomed round the churchyard wall, the lovers and helpers of the Wart, and they all

[1] **lich** (lĭch) **gate:** a roofed gate leading into a churchyard.

[2] **yew:** an evergreen with wide-spreading limbs.

[3] **feverfew** (fē'vēr-fū): an herb supposed to reduce fever.

[4] **sweet briar:** a kind of rose with sweet-smelling leaves.

[5] **pan-pipes:** musical instruments made by binding a series of pipes together in a row, each pipe making a different note (usually plural); so called from *Pan*, the mischievous Greek god of the woods and hills.

[6] **recorders:** musical instruments something like a clarinet in shape, with a sound like that of a flute.

[7] **pommel** (pŭm'ĕl): the rounded, ornamental knob on the handle of the sword.

[8] **consort:** harmony.

[9] **amethysts** (ăm'ē-thĭsts): semi-precious purple stones.

[10] **unicorns:** imaginary, horse-like animals with a single horn on their foreheads; symbolic of purity in the Middle Ages and now part of the British coat of arms.

[11] **corkindrills:** beasts feared in medieval times, now identified as *crocodiles*.

[12] **griffins:** huge, mythical animals, half-lion and half-eagle.

spoke solemnly in turn. Some of them had come from the banners in the church, where they were painted in heraldry, some from the waters and sky and fields about — but all, down to the smallest shrew mouse, had come to help on account of love. Wart felt his power grow.

The Wart walked up to the great sword for the third time. He put out his right hand softly and drew it out as gently as from a scabbard.

There was a lot of cheering, a noise like a hurdy-gurdy which went on and on. In the middle of this noise after a long time, he saw Kay and gave him the sword. The people at the tournament were making a frightful row.

"But this is not my sword," said Sir Kay.

"It was the only one I could get," said the Wart. "The inn was locked."

"It is a nice-looking sword. Where did you get it?"

"I found it in a stone, outside a church."

Sir Kay had been watching the tilting nervously, waiting for his turn. He had not paid much attention to his squire.

"That is a funny place to find one," he said.

"Yes, it was stuck through an anvil."

"What!" cried Sir Kay, suddenly rounding upon him. "Did you just say this sword was stuck in a stone?"

"It was," said the Wart. "It was sort of a war memorial."

Sir Kay stared at him for several seconds in amazement, opened his mouth, shut it again, licked his lips, then turned his back and plunged through the crowd. He was looking for Sir Ector, and the Wart followed after him.

"Father," cried Sir Kay, "come here a moment."

"Yes, my boy," said Sir Ector. "Splendid falls these professional chaps manage. Why, what's the matter, Kay? You look as white as a sheet."

"Do you remember that sword which the King of England would pull out?"

"Yes."

"Well, here it is. I have it. It is in my hand. I pulled it out."

Sir Ector did not say anything silly. He looked at Kay and he looked at the Wart. Then he stared at Kay again, long and lovingly, and said, "We will go back to the church."

"Now then, Kay," he said, when they were at the church door. He looked at his first-born kindly, but straight between the eyes. "Here is the stone, and you have the sword. It will make you the King of England. You are my son that I am proud of, and always will be, whatever you do. Will you promise me that you took it out by your own might?"

Kay looked at his father. He also looked at the Wart and at the sword.

Then he handed the sword to the Wart quite quietly.

He said, "I am a liar. Wart pulled it out."

As far as the Wart was concerned, there was a time after this in which Sir Ector kept telling him to put the sword back into the stone — which he did — and in which Sir Ector and Kay then vainly tried to take it out. The Wart took it out for them, and then stuck it back again once or twice. After this, there was another time which was more painful.

He saw that his dear guardian was looking quite old and powerless, and that he was kneeling down with difficulty on a gouty [1] knee.

"Sir," said Sir Ector, without looking up, although he was speaking to his own boy.

---

[1] **gouty:** afflicted with gout, a disease that causes a painful swelling of the joints.

"Please do not do this, father," said the Wart, kneeling down also. "Let me help you up, Sir Ector, because you are making me unhappy."

"Nay, nay, my lord," said Sir Ector, with some very feeble old tears. "I was never your father nor of your blood, but I wot [1] well ye are of an higher blood than I wend [2] ye were."

"Plenty of people have told me you are not my father," said the Wart, "but it does not matter a bit."

"Sir," said Sir Ector humbly, "will ye be my good and gracious lord when ye are King?"

"Don't!" said the Wart.

"Sir," said Sir Ector, "I will ask no more of you but that you will make my son, your foster-brother, Sir Kay, seneschal [3] of all your lands."

---

[1] **wot:** learn, discover; first-person singular, present tense, of the old verb *to wit*.
[2] **wend:** past tense of an obsolete verb meaning *to imagine*.
[3] **seneschal** (sĕn′ė·shȧl): chief administrator of a medieval noble's estate.

Kay was kneeling down too, and it was more than the Wart could bear.

"Oh, do stop," he cried. "Of course he can be seneschal, if I have got to be this King, and oh, father don't kneel down like that, because it breaks my heart. Please get up, Sir Ector, and don't make everything so horrible. Oh dear, oh dear, I wish I had never seen that filthy sword at all."

And the Wart also burst into tears.

[After Arthur became king, he was plunged into war with a number of local rulers of England and Scotland who did not accept his right to rule them. In the Middle Ages, the King of England did not rule the whole land directly. He ruled it through local leaders, each of whom was all-powerful in his own territory but was also bound to the king above him by an oath of obedience. Lot, mentioned in this selection, was the leader of those who fought against Arthur. The medieval tellers of the Arthurian legend called Lot and others like him kings, following an old tradition from the early time when Great Britain was in fact divided up into many small, independent kingdoms.

In the following selection we see Arthur as the King of England. He is preparing to unite his kingdom and establish a new order — one that will emphasize peace and good deeds.]

The King of England painfully climbed the two hundred and eight steps which led to Merlin's tower room. The magician was inside. He closed his book with a bang, leaped to his feet, seized his wand of lignum vitae, [4] and rushed at Arthur as if he were trying to shoo away a stray chicken.

"Go away!" he shouted. "What are you doing here? What do you mean by

---

[4] **lignum vitae** (lĭg′nŭm vī′tē): a tree having a greenish-brown, hard, heavy wood; from Latin, meaning *wood of life*.

it? Aren't you the King of England? Go away and send for me! Get out of my room! I never heard of such a thing! Go away at once and send for me!"

"But I am here."

"No, you're not," retorted the old man resourcefully. And he pushed the King out of the door, slamming it in his face.

"Well!" said Arthur, and he went off sadly down the two hundred and eight stairs.

An hour later, Merlin presented himself in the Royal Chamber, in answer to a summons which had been delivered by a page.

"That's better," he said, and sat down comfortably on a carpet chest.

"Stand up," said Arthur, and he clapped his hands for a page to take away the seat.

Merlin stood up, boiling with indignation. The whites of his knuckles blanched as he clenched them.

"About our conversation on the subject of chivalry," began the King in an airy tone . . .

"I don't recollect such a conversation."

"No?"

"I have never been so insulted in my life!"

"But I am the King," said Arthur. "You can't sit down in front of the King."

"Rubbish!"

Arthur began to laugh more than was seemly, and his foster-brother, Sir Kay, and his old guardian, Sir Ector, came out from behind the throne, where they had been hiding. Kay took off Merlin's hat and put it on Sir Ector, and Sir Ector said, "Well, bless my soul, now I am a necromancer.[1] Hocus-pocus."

Then everybody began laughing, including Merlin eventually, and seats

[1] necromancer (něk′rŏ·măn′sẽr): magician.

were sent for so that they could sit down, and bottles of wine were opened so that it should not be a dry meeting.

"You see," Arthur said proudly, "I have summoned a council."

There was a pause, for it was the first time that Arthur had made a speech, and he wanted to collect his wits for it.

"Well," said the King. "It is about chivalry. I want to talk about that."

Merlin was immediately watching him with a sharp eye. His knobbed fingers fluttered among the stars and secret signs of his gown, but he would not help the speaker. You might say that this moment was the critical one in his career — the moment towards which he had been living for heaven knows how many centuries, and now he was to see for certain whether he had lived in vain.

"I have been thinking," said Arthur, "about Might and Right. I don't think things ought to be done because you are *able* to do them. I think they should be done because you *ought* to do them.

After all, a penny is a penny in any case, however much Might is exerted on either side, to prove that it is or is not. Is that plain?"

Nobody answered.

"Well, I was talking to Merlin on the battlements one day, and he mentioned that the last battle we had — in which seven hundred kerns [1] were killed — was not so much fun as I had thought it was. Of course, battles are not fun when you come to think about them. I mean, people ought not to be killed, ought they? It is better to be alive.

"Very well. But the funny thing is that Merlin was helping me to win battles. He is still helping me, for that matter, and we hope to win the battle of Bedegraine, when it comes off."

"We will," said Sir Ector, who was in on the secret.

"That seems to me to be inconsistent.

[1] kerns: low-born foot soldiers.

Why does he help me to fight wars, if they are bad things?"

There was no answer from anybody, and the King began to speak with agitation.

"I could only think," he said, beginning to blush, "I could only think that I — that we — that he — that he wanted me to win them for a reason."

He paused and looked at Merlin, who turned his head away.

"The reason was — was it? — the reason was that if I could be the master of my kingdom by winning these two battles, I could stop them afterwards and then do something about the business of Might. Have I guessed? Was I right?"

The magician did not turn his head, and his hands lay still in his lap.

"I was!" exclaimed Arthur.

And he began talking so quickly that he could hardly keep up with himself.

"You see," he said, "Might is not Right. But there is a lot of Might knocking about in this world, and something has to be done about it. It is as if people were half horrible and half nice. Perhaps they are even more than half horrible, and when they are left to themselves they run wild. You get the average baron that we see nowadays, people like Sir Bruce Sans Pitié,[2] who simply go clod-hopping round the country dressed in steel, and doing exactly what they please, for sport. It is our Norman [3] idea about the upper classes having a monopoly of power, without reference to justice. Then the horrible side gets uppermost, and there is thieving and plunder and torture. The people become beasts.

[2] **Sans Pitié** (sănz pē·tyā): here, used as a man's name, but in French meaning without pity; pitiless.
[3] **Norman:** The **Normans** — invaders from the French province of Normandy — conquered England in 1066 and became the ruling class of England.

"But, you see, Merlin is helping me to win my two battles so that I can stop this. He wants me to put things right.

"Lot and Uriens and Anguish [1] and those — they are the old world, the old-fashioned order who want to have their private will. I have got to vanquish them with their own weapons — they force it upon me, because they live by force — and then the real work will begin. This battle at Bedegraine is the preliminary, you see. It is *after* the battle that Merlin is wanting me to think about."

Arthur paused again for comment or encouragement, but the magician's face was turned away. It was only Sir Ector, sitting next to him, who could see his eyes.

"Now what I have thought," said Arthur, "is this. Why can't you harness Might so that it works for Right? I know it sounds nonsense, but, I mean, you can't just say there is no such thing. The Might is there, in the bad half of people, and you can't neglect it. You can't cut it out, but you might be able to direct it, if you see what I mean, so that it was useful instead of bad."

The audience was interested. They leaned forward to listen, except Merlin.

"My idea is that if we can win this battle in front of us, and get a firm hold of the country, then I will institute a sort of order [2] of chivalry. I will not punish the bad knights, or hang Lot, but I will try to get them into our Order. We shall have to make it a great honor, you see, and make it fashionable and all that. Everybody must want to be in. And then I shall make the oath of the order that Might is only to be used for Right. Do you follow? The knights in my order will ride all over the world, still dressed in steel and whacking away with their swords — that will give an outlet for wanting to whack, you understand, an outlet for what Merlin calls the foxhunting spirit — but they will be bound to strike only on behalf of what is good, to restore what has been done wrong in the past and to help the oppressed and so forth. Do you see the idea? It will be using the Might instead of fighting against it, and turning a bad thing into a good. There, Merlin, that is all I can think of. I have thought as hard as I could, and I suppose I am wrong, as usual. But I did think. I can't do any better. Please say something!"

The magician stood up as straight as a pillar, stretched out his arms in both directions, looked at the ceiling, and said the first few words of the Nunc Dimittis.[3]

[3] **Nunc Dimittis** (nŭngk dĭ-mĭt′ĭs): The usual title of the Song of Simeon (Luke 2: 29–32), from its first words in Latin. The Nunc Dimittis begins, "Lord, now lettest thou thy servant depart in peace . . . for mine eyes have seen thy salvation." According to the Biblical account, Simeon, an old man, had prayed God to let him live just long enough to see the infant Jesus. When the infant Jesus was brought to him, he uttered these words and was ready to die.

[1] **Lot and Uriens** (ū′rĭ-ĕnz) **and Anguish:** local rulers in Britain before Arthur.

[2] **order:** here, a group of persons living together under a common rule of conduct (from the Latin *ordo*). In the Middle Ages there were many orders of knights organized on the lines of the religious orders of monks and nuns.

THINKING IT OVER

1. In what ways does Arthur show himself to be still very boyish? Does he reveal any qualities that you admire? What are these qualities and how are they revealed?

2. Throughout his boyhood Sir Kay had probably been worried about Arthur as a rival and tried to prove that, as Sir Ector's real son and heir, he would make a

worthy knight. Even so, can you defend Sir Kay's conduct when Arthur tells him where he got the sword? Explain your opinion.

3. Do you think Sir Ector acted as a wise parent in dealing with Sir Kay? Explain.

4. Explain the role that Merlin plays in this story. What do you think Merlin represents to T. H. White?

5. Explain Merlin's reactions to the "idea" that Arthur tells about in his first council meeting.

6. What do you think of Arthur's idea? What do you suppose T. H. White thinks of Arthur's idea? What applications do you think it has for us today?

THE STORYTELLER'S METHODS

Explain, with examples from the selection, how T. H. White uses each of the following in retelling this famous story:

(a) descriptions of color
(b) descriptions of music
(c) historical details
(d) humor
(e) modern ideas

ANACHRONISMS

An *anachronism* is a reference that places an object, event, or person in a period of history in which it did not exist. For example, if an author wrote a story about ancient Rome and had one of his characters take a trip on a jet plane, the author would be creating an anachronism. Authors do sometimes create anachronisms by mistake; often careful research is needed in order to avoid them.

In this selection by T. H. White you may have thought that you spotted a few anachronisms. There was a reference to football, for example. You can be certain, however, that such references were not made through carelessness. T. H. White is an excellent historian, as you may have guessed from the number of interesting historical facts he has included in this selection. He uses such apparent anachronisms deliberately in order to provide comparisons that help you understand the way things were in medieval Britain. It is

a small but effective way of modernizing this ancient story.

See if you can find other *apparent* anachronisms in this selection. How do they help you to understand and appreciate the story?

ABOUT THE AUTHOR

T. H. White now lives on one of Great Britain's Channel Islands, nine miles off the coast of France. He was born in Bombay, India, in 1906, but returned to England to attend school and later Cambridge University. His first book, a collection of poems, was published when he was only nineteen. Later he wrote a number of detective stories. He is a man who becomes tremendously interested in a wide variety of subjects and works hard at each interest before he goes on to a new one. Among his past interests have been flying and movie-making and the sports of sailing and falconry (a medieval sport that is still practiced by a few people today). His book *The Once and Future King* took almost twenty years to prepare, and he is not through writing about the King Arthur legend yet. He visited America for the first time in 1960 when *Camelot*, based on *The Once and Future King*, opened on Broadway. He loved America and the play.

Depicting the Medieval Spirit ➤

The painting on the opposite page (Plate I: "The Tournament," and those on pages 606 and 618 [Plates II and III]) exemplify the spirit and art of medieval times. Contemporary artist Isador Seltzer has painted them in the style of manuscript illuminations — the pictures that were painted as decorations on medieval handwritten manuscripts.

The pictures at the beginning of each of the three selections (pages 589, 600, and 611) are photographs of actual manuscript illuminations. They are from fourteenth-century French manuscripts that dealt with the Arthurian legend. What similarities do you see between these illuminations and artist Seltzer's paintings?

CHIVALRY AT ITS HEIGHT

Sir Lancelot

from *Morte d'Arthur*

by SIR THOMAS MALORY

As modernized by Thomas Bulfinch

Young King Arthur's great idea won out. After many adventures, the Round Table ("round," Arthur insisted, "so that no man would sit at its head or foot") of valiant knights dedicated to the use of "Might for Right" was established at Camelot. Arthur's beautiful young queen, Guinevere, and her ladies now gave Camelot an air of courtly romance. Also Arthur now had a friend. His name was Lancelot, often known as Lancelot of the Lake.

Lancelot is the best known of all King Arthur's knights. He was the bravest and the most skillful, and for this reason alone his exploits have been told and retold by the storytellers of the Arthurian legend. More than that, no knight was more truly dedicated to Arthur's idea or tried more earnestly to live up to the ideals that Arthur had now established at his court. In Lancelot, therefore, we find the model knight that Sir Kay as a boy had wanted so desperately to become. Sir Lancelot came from France (as chivalry itself had come to England from France), and he represents chivalry at its height.

But there is another reason why Lancelot is so well known: he was King Arthur's friend. Arthur, as you can judge from T. H. White's account, was the kind of person who was a good friend and the kind of person who needed a good friend, especially after Merlin was forced by the mysterious laws of magic to leave him.

The friendship of Arthur and Lancelot would never have become such an important part of the legend, however, had it not been for Guinevere. For Lancelot and Guinevere fell in love. Lancelot has been remembered all these years with pity, for he was a man torn between an undying friendship for Arthur and an undying love for Arthur's queen. This was the scar on Lancelot's soul — a wound that led at last to the downfall of Camelot and the end of Arthur's great experiment.

Here you will read about Lancelot at the height of his career, at a time when all was well at Camelot. The account is by Sir Thomas Malory, one of the first great compilers of the King Arthur legend. As you read this selection, ask yourself in what ways chivalry, as practiced by Lancelot, fulfilled Arthur's great idea.

A FTER KING ARTHUR was crowned, all the Knights of the Table Round resorted unto him and made him many jousts and tournaments. And in especial Sir Lancelot of the Lake, in all tournaments and jousts and deeds of arms, both for life and death, passed[1] all

[1] **passed:** here, surpassed.

other knights and was never overcome, except it were by treason [1] or enchantment; and he increased marvelously in worship,[2] wherefore Queen Guinevere had him in great favor, above all other knights. And for certain he loved the queen again above all other ladies; and for her he did many deeds of arms and saved her from peril through his noble chivalry.

LIONEL DISAPPEARS

Thus Sir Lancelot rested him long with play and game, and then he thought to prove himself in strange adventures; so he bade his nephew, Sir Lionel, to make him ready — "for we two will seek adventures." So they mounted on their horses, armed at all sights,[3] and rode into a forest, and so into a deep plain. And the weather was hot about noon, and Sir Lancelot had great desire to sleep. Then Sir Lionel espied a great apple tree that stood by a hedge, and he said, "Brother,[4] yonder is a fair shadow. There may we rest us and our horses."

"It is well said," replied Sir Lancelot. So they there alighted, and Sir Lancelot laid him down, his helm under his head, and soon was asleep passing fast. And Sir Lionel waked [5] while he slept. And presently there came three knights riding as fast as ever they might ride, and there followed them but one knight. And Sir Lionel thought he never saw so great a knight before. So within a while this great knight overtook one of those knights and smote him so that he fell to the earth. Then he rode to the second knight and smote him; and so he did to the third knight. Then he alighted down and bound all the three knights fast with their own bridles. When Sir Lionel saw him do thus he thought to assay [6] him, and made him ready, silently, not to awake Sir Lancelot, and rode after the strong knight, and bade him turn. And the other smote Sir Lionel so hard that horse and man fell to the earth; and then he alighted down, and bound Sir Lionel, and threw him across his own horse; and so he served them all four, and rode with them away to his own castle. And when he came there, he put them in a deep prison, in which were many more knights in great distress.

LANCELOT IS IMPRISONED

Now while Sir Lancelot lay under the apple tree sleeping there came by him four queens [7] of great estate.[8] And that the heat should not grieve them, there rode four knights about them, and bare a cloth of green silk, on four spears, betwixt them and the sun. And the queens rode on four white mules.

Thus as they rode they heard by them a great horse grimly neigh. Then they were aware of a sleeping knight that lay all armed under an apple tree; and as the queens looked on his face they knew it was Sir Lancelot. Then they began to strive for that knight, and each one said she would have him for her love.

"We will not strive," said Morgan

---

[1] **treason:** here, betrayal of trust.

[2] **worship:** here, honor, respect.

[3] **at all sights:** to the eyeholes (**sights**) of a helmet; in other words, from head to foot.

[4] **Brother:** although Sir Lionel was actually Sir Lancelot's nephew, they call each other "brother" in the sense of close friend.

[5] **waked:** here, stayed awake, kept watch.

[6] **assay** (ă·sā'): here, try or test (in combat).

[7] **queens:** Malory looks back to a time when by tradition England was divided into many small kingdoms, each with its own sovereign.

[8] **of great estate:** making a great display of wealth; a traditional Medieval phrase.

le Fay,[1] "for I will put an enchantment upon him, that he shall not wake for six hours, and we will take him away to my castle; and then when he is surely within my hold I will take the enchantment from him, and then let him choose which of us he will have for his love."

So the enchantment was cast upon Sir Lancelot. And then they laid him upon his shield, and bare him so on horseback between two knights, and brought him unto the castle and laid him in a chamber, and at night they sent him his supper.

And on the morning came early those four queens, richly dight,[2] and bade him good morning, and he them.

"Sir knight," they said, "thou must understand that thou art our prisoner; and we know thee well, that thou art Sir Lancelot of the Lake, and that thou art the noblest knight living. And we know well that there can no lady have thy love but one, and that is Queen Guinevere; and now thou shalt lose her forever, and she thee; and therefore it behooveth thee now to choose one of us. I am the Queen Morgan le Fay, and here is the Queen of North Wales, and the Queen of Eastland, and the Queen of the Isles. Now choose one of us which thou wilt have, for if thou choose not, in this prison thou shalt die."

"This is a hard case," said Sir Lancelot, "that either I must die or else choose one of you; yet had I liever to [3] die in this prison with worship than have to have one of you for my paramour, for ye be false enchantresses."

"Well," said the queens, "is this your answer, that ye will refuse us?"

"Yea, on my life it is," said Sir Lancelot. Then they departed, making great sorrow.

Then at noon came a damsel unto him with his dinner, and asked him, "What cheer?"

"Truly, fair damsel," said Sir Lancelot, "never so ill."

"Sir," said she, "if you will be ruled by me, I will help you out of this distress — If you will promise me to help my father on Tuesday next, who hath made a tournament betwixt him and the king of North Wales; for the last Tuesday my father lost the field." [4]

"Fair maiden," said Sir Lancelot, "tell me what is your father's name, and then will I give you an answer."

"Sir knight," she said, "my father is King Bagdemagus."

"I know him well," said Sir Lancelot, "for a noble king and a good knight, and, by the faith of my body, I will be ready to do your father and you service at that day."

So she departed, and came on the next morning early and found him ready, and brought him out of twelve locks,[5] and brought him to his own horse, and lightly he saddled him, and so rode forth.

LANCELOT HELPS KING BAGDEMAGUS

And on the Tuesday next he came to a little wood where the tournament should be. And there were scaffolds and holds,[6] that lords and ladies might look on, and give the prize. Then came into the field the king of North Wales, with

---

[1] **Morgan le Fay:** King Arthur's wicked half-sister, an enchantress.

[2] **dight** (dīt): adorned.

[3] **had I liever** (lēv'ẽr): I would more willingly (liever is the comparative form of lief).

[4] **lost the field:** was defeated in the tournament.

[5] **brought him out of twelve locks:** unlocked twelve locks in order to let him out of the castle.

[6] **holds:** shelters; refuges.

eightscore helms,[1] and King Bagdemagus came with fourscore helms. And
then they couched [2] their spears and
came together with a great dash, and
there were overthrown at the first encounter twelve of King Bagdemagus'
party and six of the king of North
Wales's party, and King Bagdemagus'
party had the worse.

With that came Sir Lancelot of the
Lake, and thrust in with his spear in
the thickest of the press; and he smote
down five knights ere he held his hand;
and he smote down the king of North
Wales, and he brake his thigh in that
fall. And then the knights of the king
of North Wales would joust no more;
and so the gree was given [3] to King
Bagdemagus.

And Sir Lancelot rode forth with
King Bagdemagus unto his castle; and
there he had passing good cheer, both
with the king and with his daughter.
And on the morn he took his leave, and
told the king he would go and seek his
brother, Sir Lionel, that went from him
when he slept.

LANCELOT FACES A DANGEROUS ENEMY

So he departed, and by adventure [4]
he came to the same forest where he
was taken sleeping. And in the highway
he met a damsel riding on a white palfrey, and they saluted each other.

"Fair damsel," said Sir Lancelot,
"know ye in this country any adventures?"

"Sir knight," said the damsel, "here

are adventures near at hand, if thou
durst pursue them."

"Why should I not prove [5] adventures," said Sir Lancelot, "since for that
came I hither?"

"Sir," said she, "hereby dwelleth a
knight that will not be overmatched for
any man I know, except thou outmatch
him. His name is Sir Turquine, and, as
I understand, he is a deadly enemy of
King Arthur, and he has in his prison
good knights of Arthur's court three-
score and more, that he hath won with
his own hands."

"Damsel," said Lancelot, "I pray you
bring me unto this knight." So she told
him:

"Hereby, within this mile, is his castle, and by it on the left hand is a ford

---

[1] **helms:** helmets; here, used figuratively for
the knights who wore the helmets.
[2] **couched:** here, lowered to an attacking
position, pointed at the opponent; when not
using it, the knight carried his spear or lance
upright.
[3] **gree was given:** victory was officially conceded.
[4] **adventure:** here, chance.

[5] **prove:** here, try, attempt, or test; an older
meaning found in modern English only in
phrases like *proving grounds* (a place where
new cars are tested).

for horses to drink of, and over that ford there groweth a fair tree, and on that tree hang many shields that good knights wielded aforetime, that are now prisoners; and on the tree hangeth a basin of copper and latten,[1] and if thou strike upon that basin thou shalt hear tidings."

And Sir Lancelot departed and rode as the damsel had shown him, and shortly he came to the ford and the tree where hung the shields and basin. And among the shields he saw Sir Lionel's shield, besides many others of knights that he knew.

Then Sir Lancelot struck on the basin with the butt of his spear; and long he did so, but he saw no man. And at length he was ware[2] of a great knight that drove a horse before him, and across the horse there lay an armed knight bounden. And as they came near, Sir Lancelot thought he should know the captive knight. Then Sir Lancelot saw that it was Sir Gaheris, a knight of the Table Round.

"Now, fair knight," said Sir Lancelot, "put that wounded knight off the horse, and let him rest awhile, and let us two prove our strength. For, as it is told me,

thou hast done great despite and shame unto knights of the Round Table; therefore, now defend thee."

"If thou be of the Table Round," said Sir Turquine, "I defy thee and all thy fellowship."

"That is overmuch said," said Sir Lancelot.

Then they put their spears in the rests, and came together with their horses as fast as they might run. And each smote the other in the middle of their shields, so that their horses fell under them, and the knights were both staggered; and as soon as they could clear their horses, they drew out their swords and came together eagerly, and each gave the other many strong strokes, for neither shield nor harness might withstand their strokes. So within a while both had grimly[3] wounds and bled grievously. Then at the last they were breathless both, and stood leaning upon their swords.

"Now, fellow," said Sir Turquine, "thou art the stoutest man that ever I met with, and best breathed; and so be it thou be not the knight that I hate above all other knights, the knight that slew my brother, Sir Caradoc, I will gladly accord with thee; and for thy love I will deliver all the prisoners that I have."

"What knight is he that thou hatest so above others?"

"Truly," said Sir Turquine, "his name is Sir Lancelot of the Lake."

"I am Sir Lancelot of the Lake, and very knight of the Table Round; and now I defy thee do thy best."

"Ah," said Sir Turquine, "Lancelot, thou art to me the most welcome that ever was knight; for we shall never part till the one of us be dead."

And then they hurtled together like

[1] **latten:** brass hammered into thin sheets.
[2] **ware:** aware.

[3] **grimly:** hideous (an old adjective form).

two wild bulls, rashing [1] and lashing with their swords and shields, so that sometimes they fell, as it were, headlong. Thus they fought two hours and more, till the ground where they fought was all bepurpled with blood.

Then at the last Sir Turquine waxed sore faint, and gave somewhat aback, and bare his shield full low for weariness. That spied Sir Lancelot, and leapt then upon him fiercely as a lion, and took him by the beaver [2] of his helmet, and drew him down on his knees. And he rased off [3] his helm, and smote his neck in sunder.

And Sir Gaheris, when he saw Sir Turquine slain, said, "Fair lord, I pray you tell me your name, for this day I say ye are the best knight in the world, for ye have slain this day in my sight the mightiest man and the best knight except you that ever I saw."

"Sir, my name is Sir Lancelot of the Lake, that ought to help you of right for King Arthur's sake. Now I pray you, that ye go into yonder castle, and set free all the prisoners ye find there, for I am sure ye shall find there many knights of the Table Round, and especially my brother Sir Lionel. I pray you greet them all from me, and tell them I bid them take there such stuff as they find; and tell my brother to go unto the court and abide me there, for by the feast of Pentecost [4] I think to be there; but at this time I may not stop, for I have adventures on hand."

So he departed, and Sir Gaheris rode into the castle and took the keys from the porter, and hastily opened the prison door and let out all the prisoners. There was Sir Lionel, and many more. And when they saw Sir Gaheris, they all thanked him, for they thought, because he was wounded, that he had slain Sir Turquine.

"Not so," said Sir Gaheris. "It was Sir Lancelot that slew him, right worshipfully; I saw it with mine eyes."

LANCELOT PERFORMS THREE GOOD DEEDS

Sir Lancelot rode till at nightfall he came to a fair castle, and therein he found an old gentlewoman, who lodged him with goodwill, and there he had good cheer for him and his horse. And when time was, his host brought him to a fair chamber over the gate, [5] to his bed. Then Sir Lancelot unarmed him, and set his harness by him, and went to bed, and anon he fell asleep. And soon after, there came one on horseback and knocked at the gate in great haste; and when Sir Lancelot heard this, he arose and looked out of the window, and saw by the moonlight three knights riding after that one man, and all three lashed on him with their swords, and that one knight turned on them knightly again and defended himself.

"Truly," said Sir Lancelot, "yonder one knight will I help, for it is shame to see three knights on one."

Then he took his harness and went out at the window by a sheet down to the four knights; and he said aloud, "Turn you knights unto me, and leave your fighting with that knight."

Then the knights left Sir Kay, for it was he they were upon, and turned unto Sir Lancelot, and struck many great strokes at Sir Lancelot, and assailed him on every side.

---

[1] **rashing:** cutting.
[2] **beaver:** a visor; the hinged part of the helmet protecting the mouth, chin, and eyes.
[3] **rased off:** tore off by smashing completely; similar in meaning to *raze.*
[4] **feast of Pentecost:** a church holiday which falls on the seventh Sunday after Easter and may occur any time from May 10 to June 13; often called *Whitsunday.*
[5] **over the gate:** the main gate into the castle; built into a tower, usually with one large room on each floor above the gate.

Then Sir Kay addressed him [1] to help Sir Lancelot, but he said, "Nay, sir, I will none of your help; let me alone with them."

So Sir Kay suffered him to do his will, and stood one side. And within six strokes, Sir Lancelot had stricken them down.

Then they all cried, "Sir knight, we yield [2] us unto you."

"As to that," said Sir Lancelot, "I will not take your yielding unto me. If so be ye will yield you unto Sir Kay the seneschal, I will save your lives, but else not."

"Fair knight," then they said, "we will do as thou commandest us."

"Then shall ye," said Sir Lancelot, "on Whitsunday next, go unto the court of King Arthur, and there shall ye yield you unto Queen Guinevere, and say that Sir Kay sent you thither to be her prisoners."

"Sir," they said, "it shall be done, by the faith of our bodies"; and then they swore, every knight upon his sword. And so Sir Lancelot suffered them to depart.

On the morn Sir Lancelot rose early and left Sir Kay sleeping; and Sir Lancelot took Sir Kay's armor and his shield, and armed him, and went to the stable and took his horse, and so he departed. Then soon after arose Sir Kay and missed Sir Lancelot. And then he espied that he had taken his armor and his horse.

"Now, by my faith, I know well," said Sir Kay, "that by cause of his armor

I shall ride in peace." Then Sir Kay thanked his host and departed.

LANCELOT IS DECEIVED

And Sir Lancelot rode through many strange countries, till, by fortune, he came to a fair castle; and as he passed beyond the castle, he thought he heard two bells ring. And then he perceived how a falcon came flying over his head toward a high elm; and she had long lunes [3] about her feet, and she flew unto the elm to take her perch, and the lunes got entangled in a bough; and when she would have taken her flight, she hung by the legs fast, and Sir Lancelot saw how she hung and beheld the fair falcon entangled, and he was sorry for her. Then came a lady out of the castle and cried aloud, "O Lancelot, Lancelot, as thou art the flower of all knights, help me to get my hawk; for if my hawk be lost, my lord will slay me, he is so hasty."

"What is your lord's name?" said Sir Lancelot.

"His name is Sir Phelot, a knight that belongeth to the king of North Wales."

"Well, fair lady, since ye know my name, and require me of knighthood to help you, I will do what I may to get your hawk; and yet, in truth, I am an ill climber and the tree is passing high and few boughs to help me."

And therewith Sir Lancelot alighted and tied his horse to a tree, and prayed the lady to unarm him. And when he was unarmed, he put off his jerkin, and with might and force he clomb up to the falcon, and tied the lunes to a rotten bough, and threw the hawk down

---

[1] **addressed him:** prepared himself; here, the sense is that Sir Kay moved to a position where he could join the fight and got his weapons ready to do so.
[2] **yield:** here, surrender; allow oneself to be made prisoner.

[3] **lunes:** the strings with which the falcon is held.

◀ *Plate II: "The Round Table."*

with it; and the lady got the hawk in her hand. Then suddenly there came out of the castle her husband all armed, and with his naked sword in his hand, and said, "O Knight Lancelot, now have I got thee as I would"; and stood at the boll [1] of the tree to slay him.

"Ah, lady!" said Sir Lancelot, "Why have ye betrayed me?"

"She hath done," said Sir Phelot, "but as I commanded her; and therefore there is none other way but thine hour is come, and thou must die."

"That were shame unto thee," said Sir Lancelot, "thou an armed knight to slay an unarmed man by treason."

"Thou gettest none other grace," [2] said Sir Phelot, "and therefore help thyself if thou canst."

"Alas!" said Sir Lancelot, "that ever a knight should die weaponless!"

And therewith he turned his eyes upward and downward; and over his head he saw a big bough leafless, and he brake it off from the trunk. And then he came lower, and watched how his own horse stood; and suddenly he leapt on the further side of his horse from the knight. Then Sir Phelot lashed at him eagerly, meaning to have slain him. But Sir Lancelot put away the stroke with the big bough, and smote Sir Phelot therewith on the side of the head, so that he fell down in a swoon to the ground. Then Sir Lancelot took his sword out of his hand and struck his head from the body. Then said the lady, "Alas! why hast thou slain my husband?"

"I am not the cause," said Sir Lancelot, "for with falsehood ye would have slain me, and now it is fallen on yourselves."

Thereupon Sir Lancelot got all his armor and put it upon him hastily for

---

[1] **boll** (bōl): trunk.
[2] **grace:** here, mercy.

---

fear of more resort, [3] for the knight's castle was nigh. And as soon as he might, he took his horse and departed, and thanked God he had escaped that adventure.

LANCELOT RETURNS TO CAMELOT

And two days before the feast of Pentecost, Sir Lancelot came home; and the king and all the court were passing glad of his coming. Then there was laughing and merriment among them; and from time to time came all the knights that Sir Turquine had prisoners, and they all honored and worshipped Sir Lancelot. Then Sir Gaheris said, "I saw all the battle from the beginning to the end," and he told King Arthur all how it was.

Then Sir Kay told the king how Sir Lancelot had rescued him, and how he "made the knights yield to me, and not to him." And there they were, all three, and confirmed it all.

"And by my faith," said Sir Kay, "because Sir Lancelot took my harness and left me his, I rode in peace, and no man would have to do with me."

And so at that time Sir Lancelot had the greatest name of any knight of the world, and most was he honored of high and low.

---

[3] **resort:** help, assistance; meaning here, the coming forth of knights from Sir Phelot's castle.

THINKING IT OVER

1. This selection from Malory's *Morte d'Arthur* is an exciting story in its own right. It also tells you a good deal about the character of one of the most famous of the Knights of the Round Table, Sir Lancelot. He is more than just an individual knight, however, acting according to his own ideas of right and wrong.

Lancelot represents the ideal of knighthood, and his actions are governed by that Code of Chivalry which all of Arthur's knights were sworn to obey. Therefore, as you review the selection in your mind, try to work out for yourself what it tells you both about Sir Lancelot as an individual and about chivalry or knighthood in general. Be ready to have a class discussion on both Sir Lancelot and chivalry, pointing to incidents and actions that illustrate:

LANCELOT'S
(a) bravery
(b) skill as a warrior
(c) quick-wittedness
(d) sense of justice
(e) devotion to Arthur
(f) devotion to Guinevere
(g) treatment of other knights of the Round Table
(h) regard for women
(i) consideration of others

CHIVALRY IN GENERAL
(a) its guiding spirit
(b) its function in the society of the Middle Ages
(c) its duties
(d) its weaknesses

2. Relate briefly the adventures of (a) Sir Lionel and (b) Sir Kay. Is Sir Kay much the same in this selection as he was in the T. H. White selection? In what ways is he the same? In what ways is he different? What single action of Sir Lancelot's seems to have meant the most to Sir Kay?

3. The ideals of chivalry have had an influence on our own history and conduct. Point out all the influences that you can think of that it has had on our society today. Point out also aspects of our conduct today that quite definitely are *not* in the tradition of chivalry.

4. Did Lancelot, in this selection, represent perfectly all that Arthur included in his idea for a better society, as expressed at the end of the White selection? Explain your opinion.

5. Do you think that Malory's interest in the Arthur legend is the same as White's? Do both authors feel strongly about the same things? Is the tone of their writing similar? Explain your answers.

ABOUT THE AUTHORS

Sir Thomas Malory has been the subject of considerable research. For a long time little was known about him, but modern scholars have been able to piece together a number of the facts of his life. They have found, for example, that he probably lived from 1394 to 1471, that he was a knight who fought in the Hundred Years' War in France, and that he was a member of the British Parliament in 1445.

The great fact of Malory's life, however, was the series of disastrous civil wars fought from 1455 to 1485 between the supporters of the two great families that claimed the right to rule all of England, the House of Lancaster and the House of York. We call these wars the Wars of the Roses, from the emblems of the two families — the red rose for Lancaster, the white rose for York. The old order of the Middle Ages was dying out. A new kind of national government, from which modern England is descended, was struggling to be born. A nation founded on a loose federation of local barons could no longer survive, and with the power of the barons' knights was also dying the ideal of knighthood — chivalry — on which that power was based.

Malory's own life was caught up in this great conflict. In 1451 he was imprisoned for a long list of offenses, twice escaped, and finally received a royal pardon. He spent the last years of his life in prison again, however, and there, in 1469 and 1470, he compiled his great work, the *Morte d'Arthur*. (He based his book on French sources, French having been the language of the English upper classes for centuries after the Norman conquest in 1066.) William Caxton, the first English printer, published Malory's book in 1485, and it was immediately popular. It has remained so to this day.

Thomas Bulfinch lived from 1796 to 1867. He was a native of Boston and a professor at Harvard University. *The Age of Chivalry*, the book which includes this selection, was published in 1858. It is one of three parts of Bulfinch's *Mythology*, which has become one of the most famous books ever to come out of America, certainly the most famous and distinguished source book of myths and legends.

THE ENDING

The Passing of Arthur

from *Idylls of the King*
by
ALFRED, LORD TENNYSON

As a boy the nineteenth-century English poet Tennyson read Malory's tales of Camelot. As he grew older and in time became poet laureate — England's official poet — Tennyson never lost his interest in the excitement, romance, and medieval pageantry that he found in the legend. And he became more and more interested in the moral struggle which the legend revealed. Nineteenth-century England during Queen Victoria's reign was deeply concerned with two things: *morality* and *progress*. So was Tennyson. It is not surprising, therefore, that Tennyson saw in Arthur a hero who represented *moral progress*.

When Tennyson came to write about Arthur in *Idylls of the King*, one of the great epic poems of English literature, he told the story as the rise and fall of a great moral hero and of a great moral idea. As a poet-storyteller, he made his own changes in the details of the story. But in this long poem, divided into twelve separate parts, Tennyson re-told many of the tales that Malory had told. The main outline of the story is the same: Arthur becomes king, his court and his queen are established, and there are days of youth and spring and beauty, filled with high ideals and high adventure. Then, in Tennyson's version, the Knights of the Round Table begin to quarrel about Guinevere

and Lancelot. Like ripples widening from a pebble thrown into a pond, the disloyal love of Lancelot and Guinevere gradually spreads until it destroys the moral virtue and the high ideals of all the Knights of the Round Table. How can others keep faith, Tennyson suggests, if the noblest man and woman of the court do not?

The knights, forgetting their vows, fall to quarreling among themselves. Arthur's nephew, Sir Modred, plots to overthrow him. Finally, their disloyal love discovered, Lancelot and Guinevere part forever and flee the court. Lancelot, having lost the two people he prizes most dearly, departs in exile to his castle in France. Guinevere enters a convent where she ends her days in peace and repentance. Arthur, betrayed by the two people dearest to him, goes forth to his last great battle with the rebel Modred. All of the remaining Knights of the Round Table are killed except the faithful Sir Bedivere (bĕd'ĭ·vẽr'). Arthur himself is mortally wounded in combat with Modred, whom he kills. Close to death, he is moved from the battlefield to a chapel near an inlet of the sea.

Now as he prepares to die, King Arthur laments "the goodliest fellowship of famous knights whereof this world holds record — the men I loved." Then he commands Sir Bedivere to take his great sword Excalibur and throw it into the lake. This is the point at which Tennyson takes up the legend in this selection. It is the end of Arthur and all his noble dreams.

But is it the end? Long ago, at the beginning of Arthur's reign, Merlin, a prophet as well as a magician, had foretold Arthur's fate in a strange verse: "From the great deep to the great deep he goes." Merlin had then sworn that after death Arthur would return to rule again. Arthur himself recalls the prophecy. As he is dying he says, "I pass but shall not die." And here Bedivere, as he watches the dark spirits bear his king away, comforts himself with the hope that Arthur will indeed come again. This is Tennyson's theme: that, once brought to life, noble ideas like Arthur's can never die.

To him replied° the bold Sir Bedivere:
"It is not meet, Sir King, to leave thee thus,
Aidless, alone, and smitten through the helm —
A little thing may harm a wounded man;
Yet I thy hest ° will all perform at full,   5
Watch what I see, and lightly bring thee word."

So saying, from the ruined shrine he stept,
And in the moon athwart° the place of tombs,
Where lay the mighty bones of ancient men,
Old knights, and over them the sea-wind sang   10
Shrill, chill, with flakes of foam. He, stepping down
By zigzag paths, and juts of pointed rock,
Came on the shining levels of the lake.

There drew he forth the brand° Excalibur,
And o'er him, drawing it, the winter moon,   15
Brightening the skirts of a long cloud, ran forth
And sparkled keen with frost against the hilt;
For all the haft° twinkled with diamond sparks,
Myriads of topaz-lights, and jacinth°-work
Of subtlest jewelry. He gazed so long   20
That both his eyes were dazzled as he stood,
This way and that dividing the swift mind,
In act to throw: but at the last it seemed
Better to leave Excalibur concealed

1. **replied:** Arthur has just commanded Bedivere to throw his sword into the lake. 5. **hest:** command. 8. **athwart:** across. 14. **brand:** sword. 18. **haft:** handle. 19. **jacinth** (jă′sĭnth): a semi-precious stone, orange in color.

There in the many-knotted waterflags,° 25
That whistled stiff and dry about the marge.°
So strode he back slow to the wounded King.

Then spake King Arthur to Sir Bedivere:
"Hast thou performed my mission which I gave?
What is it thou hast seen? or what hast heard?" 30

And answer made the bold Sir Bedivere:
"I heard the ripple washing in the reeds,
And the wild water lapping on the crag."

To whom replied King Arthur, faint and pale:
"Thou hast betrayed thy nature and thy name, 35
Not rendering true answer, as beseemed
Thy fealty,° nor like a noble knight;
For surer sign had followed, either hand,
Or voice, or else a motion of the mere.°
This is a shameful thing for men to lie. 40
Yet now, I charge thee, quickly go again,
As thou art lief° and dear, and do the thing
I bade thee, watch, and lightly bring me word."

Then went Sir Bedivere the second time
Across the ridge, and paced beside the mere, 45
Counting the dewy pebbles, fixed in thought;
But when he saw the wonder of the hilt,
How curiously and strangely chased,° he smote
His palms together, and he cried aloud:

"And if indeed I cast the brand away, 50
Surely a precious thing, one worthy note,
Should thus be lost for ever from the earth,
Which might have pleased the eyes of many men.
What good should follow this, if this were done?
What harm, undone? Deep harm to disobey, 55
Seeing obedience is the bond of rule.
Were it well to obey then, if a king demand
An act unprofitable, against himself?
The King is sick, and knows not what he does.
What record, or what relic of my lord 60
Should be to aftertime, but empty breath
And rumors of a doubt? But were this kept,

---

25. **waterflags:** a waterflag is a kind of iris, with a flower usually yellow but sometimes blue.
26. **marge:** edge (of the lake); poetic for *margin*. 37. **fealty:** duty sworn to one's ruler. 39. **mere:**
an enclosed body of water, usually a pond or lake but here, opening out to the sea at one end
like the long, narrow, high-walled fiords of Scotland and Norway. The battle with Modred had
taken place on a narrow point of land with the ocean on one side and the mere on the other.
42. **lief** (lēf): loved. 48. **chased:** decorated with a raised design.

Stored in some treasure-house of mighty kings,
Some one might show it at a joust of arms,
Saying: 'King Arthur's sword, Excalibur,   65
Wrought by the lonely maiden of the Lake.°
Nine years she wrought it, sitting in the deeps
Upon the hidden bases of the hills.'
So might some old man speak in the aftertime
To all the people, winning reverence.   70
But now much honor and much fame were lost."

So spake he, clouded with his own conceit,°
And hid Excalibur the second time,
And so strode back slow to the wounded King.

Then spoke King Arthur, breathing heavily: 75
"What is it thou hast seen? or what hast heard?"

And answer made the bold Sir Bedivere:
"I heard the water lapping on the crag,
And the long ripple washing in the reeds."

To whom replied King Arthur, much in wrath: 80
"Ah miserable and unkind, untrue,
Unknightly, traitor-hearted! Woe is me!
Authority forgets a dying king,
Laid widowed of the power in his eye
That bowed the will. I see thee what thou art,   85
For thou, the latest-left of all my knights,
In whom should meet the offices of all,
Thou wouldst betray me for the precious hilt;
Either from lust of gold, or like a girl
Valuing the giddy pleasure of the eyes.   90
Yet, for a man may fail in duty twice,
And the third time may prosper, get thee hence;
But, if thou spare to fling Excalibur,
I will arise and slay thee with my hands."

Then quickly rose Sir Bedivere, and ran,   95
And, leaping down the ridges lightly, plunged
Among the bulrush beds, and clutched the sword,
And strongly wheeled and threw it. The great brand
Made lightnings in the splendor of the moon,
And flashing round and round, and whirled in an arch,   100
Shot like a streamer of the northern morn,°

66. **maiden of the Lake:** Tennyson tells a different story about Arthur and Excalibur than does T. H. White, although White's version is equally well-known. In the *Idylls*, Excalibur is given to Arthur by a magic Lady of the Lake to help him drive the heathens out of England. 72. **conceit:** fancy. 101. **streamer of the northern morn:** the aurora borealis.

KING ARTHUR   LANCELOT   URIEN

Coats of arms of knights and companions of the Round Table, from a fifteenth-century French manuscript.

Seen where the moving isles° of the winter shock
By night, with noises of the Northern Sea.
So flashed and fell the brand Excalibur:
But ere he dipped the surface, rose an arm   105
Clothed in white samite,° mystic, wonderful,
And caught him° by the hilt, and brandished him
Three times, and drew him under in the mere.
And lightly went the other to the King.

    Then spoke King Arthur, drawing thicker breath: 110
"Now see I by thine eyes that this is done.
Speak out: what is it thou hast heard, or seen?"

    And answer made the bold Sir Bedivere:
"Sir King, I closed mine eyelids, lest the gems
Should blind my purpose, for I never saw,   115
Nor shall see, here or elsewhere, till I die,
Not though I live three lives of mortal men,
So great a miracle as yonder hilt.
Then with both hands I flung him, wheeling him;
But when I looked again, behold an arm,   120
Clothed in white samite, mystic, wonderful,
That caught him by the hilt, and brandished him
Three times, and drew him under in the mere."

    And answer made King Arthur, breathing hard:
"My end draws nigh; 'tis time that I were gone.   125

102. **moving isles:** icebergs. 106. **samite** (săm′ĭt): a heavy silk cloth with threads of gold and silver woven into it. 107. **him:** Excalibur. The poet speaks of the sword as if it were a living person.

GEOFFREY DE LA TOUR   GAWAIN   BRANDELIS

Make broad thy shoulders to receive my weight,
And bear me to the margin; yet I fear
My wound hath taken cold, and I shall die."

    So saying, from the pavement he half rose,
Slowly, with pain, reclining on his arm,   130
And looking wistfully with wide blue eyes
As in a picture. Him Sir Bedivere
Remorsefully regarded through his tears,
And would have spoken, but he found not words;
Then took with care, and kneeling on one knee,   135
O'er both his shoulders drew the languid hands,
And rising bore him through the place of tombs.

    But, as he walked, King Arthur panted hard,
Like one that feels a nightmare on his bed
When all the house is mute. So sighed the King,   140
Muttering and murmuring at his ear, "Quick, quick!
I fear it is too late, and I shall die."
But the other swiftly strode from ridge to ridge,
Clothed with his breath, and looking, as he walked,
Larger than human on the frozen hills.   145
He heard the deep° behind him, and a cry
Before. His own thought drove him like a goad.
Dry clashed his harness° in the icy caves
And barren chasms, and all to left and right
The bare black cliff clanged round him, as he based   150

146. **deep:** the open sea. 148. **harness:** armor and other equipment.

His feet on juts of slippery crag that rang
Sharp-smitten with the dint° of armèd° heels —
And on a sudden, lo, the level lake,
And the long glories of the winter moon!

Then saw they how there hove a dusky barge,   155
Dark as a funeral scarf from stem to stern,
Beneath them; and descending they were ware
That all the decks were dense with stately forms,
Black-stoled,° black-hooded, like a dream — by° these
Three Queens with crowns of gold — and from them° rose   160
A cry that shivered to the tingling stars,
And, as it were one voice, an agony
Of lamentation, like a wind that shrills
All night in a waste land, where no one comes,
Or hath come, since the making of the world.   165

Then murmured Arthur, "Place me in the barge."
So to the barge they came. There those three Queens
Put forth their hands, and took the King, and wept.
But she that rose the tallest of them all
And fairest, laid his head upon her lap,   170
And loosed the shattered casque,° and chafed his hands,
And called him by his name, complaining loud,
And dropping bitter tears against a brow
Striped with dark blood: for all his face was white
And colorless, and like the withered moon   175
Smote by the fresh beam of the springing east;
And all his greaves° and cuisses° dashed with drops
Of onset;° and the light and lustrous curls —
That made his forehead like a rising sun
High from the dais-throne — were parched with dust;   180
Or, clotted into points and hanging loose,
Mixed with the knightly growth that fringed his lips.
So like a shattered column lay the King;
Not like that Arthur who, with lance in rest,
From spur to plume a star of tournament,   185
Shot through the lists° at Camelot, and charged
Before the eyes of ladies and of kings.

152. **dint:** blow. **armèd:** the knight wore steel boots as part of his armor. 159. **black-stoled:** wearing a black stole, a long, loose robe reaching to the feet. **by:** beside. 160. **them:** the "stately forms," *not* the "Three Queens." 171. **casque** (căsk): helmet. 177. **greaves:** the parts of a knight's armor that cover the shins (usually plural). **cuisses** (kwĭs'ēz): the parts of a suit of armor that cover the thighs (usually plural). 178. **onset:** symptoms of the beginning of disease or death; here, Arthur's blood. 186. **lists:** here, the jousting field.

Then loudly cried the bold Sir Bedivere:
"Ah! my Lord Arthur, whither shall I go?
Where shall I hide my forehead and my eyes?   190
For now I see the true old times are dead,
When every morning brought a noble chance,
And every chance brought out a noble knight.
Such times have been not since the light that led
The holy Elders° with the gift of myrrh.   195
But now the whole Round Table is dissolved
Which was an image of the mighty world;
And I, the last, go forth companionless,
And the days darken round me, and the years,
Among new men, strange faces, other minds."   200

And slowly answered Arthur from the barge:
"The old order changeth, yielding place to new,
And God fulfils himself in many ways,
Lest one good custom should corrupt the world.
Comfort thyself; what comfort is in me?   205
I have lived my life, and that which I have done
May He within himself make pure! but thou,
If thou shouldst never see my face again,
Pray for my soul. More things are wrought by prayer
Than this world dreams of. Wherefore, let thy voice   210
Rise like a fountain for me night and day.
For what are men better than sheep or goats
That nourish a blind life within the brain,
If, knowing God, they lift not hands of prayer
Both for themselves and those who call them friend?   215
For so the whole round earth is every way
Bound by gold chains about the feet of God.
But now farewell. I am going a long way
With these thou seest — if indeed I go
(For all my mind is clouded with a doubt) —   220
To the island-valley of Avilion;°
Where falls not hail, or rain, or any snow,
Nor ever wind blows loudly; but it lies
Deep-meadowed, happy, fair with orchard lawns°
And bowery hollows crowned with summer sea,   225
Where I will heal me of my grievous wound."

195. **The holy Elders:** the Magi, who brought gold and frankincense and myrrh to the infant Jesus (see Matthew 2:1–12). 221. **Avilion** (å·vĭl′yŭn) or Avalon; the name is used in the same connection by Malory; in Celtic mythology it was Paradise. 224. **orchard lawns:** like the grass sod often planted between the trees in fruit orchards.

So said he, and the barge with oar and sail
Moved from the brink, like some full-breasted swan
That, fluting a wild carol° ere her death,
Ruffles her pure cold plume, and takes the flood°   230
With swarthy webs.° Long stood Sir Bedivere
Revolving many memories, till the hull
Looked one black dot against the verge of dawn,
And on the mere the wailing died away.

But when that moan had passed for evermore,   235
The stillness of the dead world's winter dawn
Amazed him, and he groaned, "The King is gone."
And therewithal came on him the weird rhyme,
"From the great deep to the great deep he goes."

Whereat he slowly turned and slowly clomb   240
The last hard footstep of that iron crag;
Thence marked the black hull moving yet, and cried,
"He passes to be King among the dead,
And after healing of his grievous wound
He comes again; but — if he come no more —   245
O me, be yon dark Queens in yon black boat,
Who shrieked and wailed, the three whereat we gazed
On that high day, when, clothed with living light,
They stood before his throne in silence, friends
Of Arthur, who should help him at his need?"   250

Then from the dawn it seemed there came, but faint
As from beyond the limit of the world,
Like the last echo born of a great cry,
Sounds, as if some fair city were one voice
Around a king returning from his wars.   255

Thereat once more he moved about, and clomb
Ev'n to the highest he could climb, and saw,
Straining his eyes beneath an arch of hand,
Or thought he saw, the speck that bare the King,
Down that long water opening on the deep   260
Somewhere far off, pass on and on, and go
From less to less and vanish into light.
And the new sun rose bringing the new year.

229. **wild carol:** a reference to the old belief that the swan sings just before her death.
230. **flood:** deep water, as opposed to the shallows at the **brink** (line 228). 231. **swarthy webs:** the dark, webbed feet of the swan.

◀ *Plate III: "The Passing of Arthur."*

THINKING IT OVER

1. Tennyson's nineteenth-century idea of heroism, with its moral emphasis, is somewhat different from Malory's fifteenth-century idea of the hero. However, in this Tennyson selection, Arthur displays heroic qualities that Malory would certainly have recognized. What are these qualities?

2. Although stories differ as to just how Arthur acquired his sword Excalibur, all agree that it plays an important role at the beginning and now at the end of the Arthur legend. Why do you suppose Arthur was so concerned about his sword?

3. Do you think less of Sir Bedivere for hesitating to throw the sword into the lake? Why, or why not? What qualities of knighthood did Bedivere finally display?

4. "Every morning brought a noble chance" (line 192): Does this line in any way express the great idea that Arthur first had for Camelot? Explain. Does it in any way express your understanding of Arthur's idea?

5. Find one or two lines or brief passages that, in your opinion, express Tennyson's own understanding of Arthur's great idea. Give reasons for your selections.

6. The season of the year is usually important in legends. Did you notice that the three storytellers in this section made clear what season of the year it was during their part of the story? In what season did each story take place? Why is each season significant and appropriate? What is especially significant, to Tennyson, about the day of Arthur's passing? Explain its relation to the line "The old order changeth, yielding place to new" (line 202).

7. When Sir Bedivere (lines 244 and 245) says of Arthur, "After healing of his grievous wound he comes again," he expresses his own understanding of Merlin's mysterious prophecy. What statements in the next few lines suggest that Bedivere merely hopes that Arthur will come again but is not sure? What happens before the end of the poem to strengthen his hope? Do you think that the prophecy refers simply to Arthur's return to earth as a flesh-and-blood king, or may it have another, less literal meaning? Explain.

8. Try to show in what ways Arthur's great idea lives on in the hearts and minds of men today and how it may be kept alive in the future. As you review the different aspects of this idea, as seen in this section, decide how you think Arthur's idea has changed since it first came into human history. How is it the same?

9. Of the three storytellers in this section, only Tennyson chose to tell his tale in poetry. Are there advantages to telling the stories in poetry — especially this one about the passing of Arthur? Select lines of the poem that you think are particularly effective. Then turn back to T. H. White's description of the day of Sir Kay's tournament and compare it with Tennyson's descriptions. Which do you prefer? Why? Did you notice the figure of speech that Tennyson used in line 183, comparing the dying Arthur to "a shattered column." Why is this figure of speech especially effective? Find other figures of speech in "The Passing of Arthur" that struck you as particularly forceful.

10. Of the three selections in this section, which did you like best? Why?

ALLUSIONS

An *allusion* is a reference to a famous event in history or in another work of literature. Tennyson's reference to the holy Elders (wise men or Magi) in line 195, for example, is an allusion to the Bible story of the birth of Jesus (Matthew 2:1–12). Do you recall a short story in this book that used the same allusion — in its title?

COMPOSITION SUGGESTIONS

As ideas for your next composition, you may want to consider: (1) "A Tale of Modern Chivalry," basing your story on a situation involving sportsmanship or courtesy (at a party, for example); or (2) if you prefer to write an essay rather than a story, "Chivalry Is (or Is Not) Dead" or "King Arthur's Great Idea — Today and Tomorrow."

ABOUT THE AUTHOR

Alfred, Lord Tennyson (1809–1892) was brought up, with his seven brothers and four sisters, in the comfortable rectory of the English country town where his father was rector. The children were encouraged to draw on the family's extensive library, and often they re-enacted the legends they had read. They grew up knowing far more about knights, giants, and princesses than about the busy world a few miles distant.

At seven young Alfred was sent to a grammar school where a cruel teacher cracked the pupils' heads together as part of the daily routine. He hated the school and later returned home, where his father prepared him for college. At Cambridge, the famous old English university, he was not an exceptional student, and in fact never took a degree, but he read widely and soon established himself as a masterful poet.

All his life Tennyson tended to withdraw from society. He devoted himself to reading, to enjoying nature, but above all, to writing poetry. Eight years before his death he was made a lord, a title he valued highly. He was a shy man who, above all things, sought serenity. He was unwilling and perhaps unable to enter the bustling, busy world of his own time, yet in his poetry he created for others a timeless world.

Suggestions for Further Reading

Before leaving the study of King Arthur, you may wish to know more about the great heroes of Arthurian legend. From the following books you may learn more about any of the characters who have aroused your curiosity.

Lanier, Sidney, *The Boy's King Arthur* (Scribner, 1917)
A simplified version of the original stories by Sir Thomas Malory.
Picard, Barbara L., *Stories of King Arthur and His Knights* (Walck, 1955)
Pyle, Howard, *The Story of the Champions of the Round Table* (Scribner, 1933); *The Story of the Grail and the Passing of Arthur* (Scribner, 1933); *The Story of King Arthur and His Knights*

(Scribner, 1903); *The Story of Sir Launcelot and His Companions* (Scribner, 1907)
Robinson, Mabel L., *King Arthur and His Knights* (Random House, 1953)
Sterling, M. B., *The Story of Sir Galahad* (Dutton, 1908)
Tennyson, Alfred, Lord, *Idylls of the King*

Some writers have not approached the legend of King Arthur with either Malory's or Tennyson's tone of seriousness. A humorous treatment of chivalry in Arthur's realm is found in both of the novels mentioned below. You will find it interesting to compare them with Malory's *Morte d'Arthur* and Tennyson's *Idylls of the King.*

Twain, Mark, *A Connecticut Yankee in King Arthur's Court*
White, T. H., *The Once and Future King* (Putnam, 1958)

Books About the Middle Ages

Kingsley, Charles, *Hereward the Wake* (Everymans Library, Dutton, 1909)
Muntz, Hope, *The Golden Warrior* (Scribner, 1949)
Scott, Sir Walter, *Ivanhoe*

Pictures

Abbey, Edwin, "The Quest of the Holy Grail" (a series of paintings)
Burne-Jones, Edward, a series of tapestries depicting the search for the Holy Grail
Doré, Gustave, illustrations for Tennyson's *Idylls of the King*
Rossetti, Dante Gabriel, illustrations for Malory's *Morte d'Arthur*

Music

Lerner, Alan J. and Frederick Loewe, *Camelot* (musical drama)
Purcell, Henry, *King Arthur* (opera)
Wagner, Richard, *Parsifal; Tristan and Isolde* (operas)

For Listening

An excerpt from Tennyson's "The Passing of Arthur" (lines 95–263) is available on *Many Voices* 10A.

The Novel

Down through the ages people have always loved a good story and honored a skillful storyteller. The ancient Greeks gloried in recitations of Homer's great epic poems about the Trojan War and the adventures of Ulysses. The company in a medieval lord's castle was entertained by minstrels chanting romances about heroes like King Arthur and Sir Lancelot. Meanwhile the peasants built up their own store of ballads about heroes more to their liking, notably Robin Hood, the champion of the poor. The most popular stories always reflected the life and ideals of the audiences for whom they were told.

As towns grew and larger audiences could be assembled, the drama became the popular form of storytelling, with happenings acted out on the stage for the eye as well as the ear to follow. Shakespeare's plays flourished at a time when printing was still young and crude and only a handful of the population could read.

In eighteenth-century England conditions were favorable for a new kind of storytelling. Printing had been vastly improved, so that books could be made rapidly and inexpensively. Education had spread, and many people could read. A middle class had developed with money to buy books and leisure to enjoy them. Members of this new audience were interested in their own world. They enjoyed stories about heroes and tales of fantasy and adventure, but they also wanted to read about the lives of people like themselves, people with whom they could identify in some way. At this time, writers began to develop long prose stories with characters and happenings drawn from real life. The stories were fictional, but there was a definite sense of reality about the characters and their experiences. These works were received with enthusiasm, and the English novel was born. Since its beginnings over two hundred years ago, the novel has continued to picture real life. It has mirrored the people, ideals, customs, problems, and developments of each of the ages through which it has passed.

Novels, of course, vary with the interests and the writing styles of

◀ Detail from "The Hay Wain" by the English artist John Constable (1776–1837). Constable delighted in nature and brought new charm and vitality to landscape painting.

different authors. Some writers excel in historical fiction; some, in adventure stories; some, in novels of character; and still others, in philosophical or social novels. However, variations in content and style do not alter the fact that all novels are made up of the basic elements of fiction — the elements that you have already examined in your study of the short story.

Unlike the short story, the novel can and often does have more than one plot. Of course, the various plots are carefully interwoven; they meet at several points in the novel and are drawn together at the end. Novels also often have more than one theme. The scope of the novel enables the writer, and reader, to examine these themes in depth, exploring the many different sides of a particular question or idea.

The characters in a novel are carefully drawn. Novelists have plenty of room within which to develop and interpret their major characters — presenting a character's ideas, feelings, impressions, and judgments as he or she encounters various experiences. The reader comes to know a character in all of his human dimensions. Novelists also are free to introduce as many minor characters as are necessary. These minor characters serve a number of purposes; they provoke situations for the major characters to face, set off an action or reaction in the major characters' lives, contribute to the solution of the plot, or implement the setting by providing background or demonstrating the characteristics and habits of people during a certain period in history.

Setting is much more important and is given more emphasis in a novel than in a short story. The conditions and atmosphere of the time and place in which the action occurs have a direct bearing on the plot and the characterization. The novelist sets his stage in detail, whether the setting be a certain region of the world, a particular historical period, or a commonplace scene. Often the settings are so well defined and described that the reader can see and understand a world that is removed from his own experience. *Moby Dick,* for example, gives a very complete picture of the world of whalers on the open sea, and *A Tale of Two Cities* shows what Paris was like during the French Revolution.

GEORGE ELIOT, AND *Silas Marner*

George Eliot's *Silas Marner* offers a fine example of a well-constructed novel — a novel in which all the elements of fiction are skillfully combined. For the more than one hundred years since its publication, *Silas Marner* has appealed to readers everywhere. The reasons for its appeal you will soon discover for yourselves, but first you might like to know something about the person who wrote this famous novel. We know her as "George Eliot," but her real name was Mary Ann Evans. She was born on a farm in Warwickshire, England, in 1819, and after a full life, died in London at the age of sixty-one.

The youngest of three children, she was fortunate in her family, for both father and mother were strong and affectionate parents. Her days were filled with typical childhood experiences — fishing with her brother, keeping pets, learning about dairying from her father and household management from her mother. Mary Ann liked to read, and in school she learned to write so well that one teacher saved her letters.

Mary Ann Evans became more and more interested in writing and finally in 1858 published her first novel. Because there was prejudice against women writers in the nineteenth century, Mary Ann used the masculine pen name of George Eliot for the first and then for all the rest of her works. By the time *Silas Marner* was published in 1861, George Eliot was considered one of England's finest novelists.

Silas Marner is set in England in the early nineteenth century. At that time English society was sharply divided into classes. The country squires, or landowners, maintained large manor houses and enjoyed many pleasures. They oversaw their lands, raised horses, and went fox-hunting. Their tenants lived in small thatched cottages, and while they did not have the comforts of the wealthy classes, they managed a hearty and independent existence. In villages near the country estates lived the tradesmen — weavers, cobblers, and tavernkeepers, among others — who provided the goods and services needed.

During those years great social and industrial changes were under-way. Machines were being invented and were used for a variety of purposes. Railroads were preparing to thrust their steel tracks and smoking engines into the quiet farming and sheep lands. A working class was soon to develop. However, all of these overwhelming changes were but distant echoes in Raveloe, a small village in central England, whose inhabitants lived isolated and peaceful lives. It is near this village, at the beginning of the novel, that we first see the linen weaver named Silas Marner. Silas has chosen a life of solitude after an experience that caused him to lose faith in his fellow men and in God.

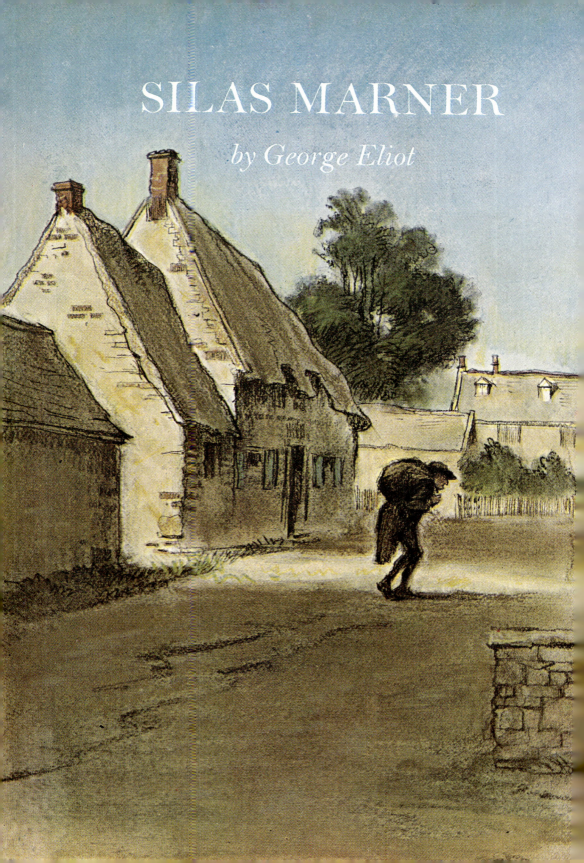

SILAS MARNER

by George Eliot

Because this is a novel, you must expect a form different from the drama, poetry, or short story. The novelist takes time to lay the scene and does not hasten to introduce all the main characters at the start. Slowly and carefully George Eliot prepares the ground on which events are to take place; and the reader is thus given a chance to accustom himself to the setting and to observe the characters carefully as they appear.

As you read the chapters that follow, allow your imagination to assist you. Try to see in your mind's eye the village of Raveloe. Also try to see the people of Raveloe, noting that although their lives differ from ours, their actions nevertheless show that human beings have not changed very much during the last one hundred and fifty years. Keep in mind also that Raveloe is in a parish of the Church of England at a time when some Dissenters had broken away from that church to set up their own chapels.

Part One

CHAPTER I

Silas Marner, Past and Present

In the days when the spinning wheels hummed busily in the farmhouses there might be seen, in districts far away among the lanes, or deep in the bosom of the hills, certain pallid, undersized men, who, by the side of the brawny countryfolk, looked like the remnants of a disinherited race. The shepherd's dog barked fiercely when one of these alien-looking men appeared on the upland, dark against the early winter sunset; for what dog likes a figure bent under a heavy bag? — and these pale men rarely stirred abroad without that mysterious burden.

The shepherd himself, though he had good reason to believe that the bag held nothing but flaxen thread, or else the long rolls of strong linen spun from that thread, was not quite sure that this trade of weaving, indispensable though it was, could be carried on entirely without the help of the Evil One.

In that far-off time superstition clung easily round every person or thing that was at all unwonted,[1] like the visits of the peddler or the knife grinder. No one knew where wandering men had their homes or their origin; and how was a man to be explained unless you at least knew somebody who knew his father and mother?

To the peasants of old times, the world outside their own direct experience was a region of vagueness and mystery; to their untraveled thought a state of wandering was a conception as

[1] **unwonted** (ŭn·wŭn′tĕd): unfamiliar.

dim as the winter life of the swallows that came back with the spring; and even a settler, if he came from distant parts, hardly ever ceased to be viewed with a remnant of distrust, especially if he had any reputation for knowledge, or showed any skill in handicraft.

All cleverness, whether in the rapid use of that difficult instrument the tongue, or in some other art unfamiliar to villages, was in itself suspicious; honest folk, born and bred in a visible manner, were mostly not overwise or clever — at least, not beyond such a matter as knowing the signs of the weather.

In this way it came to pass that those scattered linen weavers — emigrants from the town into the country — were to the last regarded as aliens by their rustic neighbors, and usually contracted [1] the eccentric habits which belong to a state of loneliness.

In the early years of this century, such a linen weaver, named Silas Marner, worked at his vocation in a stone cottage that stood near the village of Raveloe, and not far from the edge of a deserted stone pit. The questionable sound of Silas's loom had a half-fearful fascination for the Raveloe boys, who would often leave off their nutting or bird's-nesting to peep in at the window of the stone cottage.

But sometimes it happened that Marner, pausing to adjust an irregularity in his thread, became aware of the small scoundrels, and, though chary of his time,[2] he liked their intrusion so ill that he would descend from his loom, and, opening the door, would fix on them a gaze that was always enough to make them take to their legs in terror. For how was it possible to believe that those large brown protuberant [3] eyes in Silas Marner's pale face really saw nothing very distinctly that was not close to them, and not rather that their dreadful stare could dart cramp, or rickets, or a wry mouth at any boy who happened to be in the rear? They had, perhaps, heard their fathers and mothers hint that Silas Marner could cure folks' rheumatism if he had a mind, and add, still more darkly, that if you could only speak the devil fair enough he might save you the cost of the doctor.

Raveloe was a village where many old echoes lingered, undrowned by new voices. Not that it was one of those barren parishes lying on the outskirts of civilization; on the contrary, it lay in the rich central plain of what we are pleased to call Merry England, and held farms which paid highly desirable tithes.[4] But it was nestled in a snug well-wooded hollow, quite an hour's journey on horseback from any turnpike,[5] where it was never reached by the vibrations of the coach horn or of public opinion.

It was an important-looking village, with a fine old church and large churchyard in the heart of it, and two or three large brick-and-stone homesteads, with well-walled orchards and ornamental weathercocks, standing close upon the road, and lifting more imposing fronts than the rectory, which peeped from among the trees on the other side of the churchyard — a village which showed that there were several chiefs in Raveloe who could farm badly quite at their ease, drawing enough money from their bad farming, in those wartimes,[6] to live in a rollicking fashion.

[1] **contracted:** acquired.
[2] **chary** (châr′ĭ) **of his time:** not liking to waste his time.
[3] **protuberant** (prō·tū′bēr·ănt): bulging.
[4] **tithes** (tīŧħz): taxes, amounting to one tenth of one's income, paid to the church.
[5] **turnpike:** a main highway with toll gates.
[6] **in those wartimes:** Between the years 1789 and 1815 England warred with France.

It was fifteen years since Silas Marner had first come to Raveloe; he was then simply a pallid young man, with prominent, shortsighted brown eyes whose appearance would have had nothing strange for people of average culture and experience, but for the villagers near whom he had come to settle it had mysterious peculiarities which corresponded with the exceptional nature of his occupation and his advent from an unknown region called "north-'ard." So had his way of life; he invited no comer to step across his doorsill, and he never strolled into the village to drink a pint at the Rainbow, or to gossip at the wheelwright's; he sought no man or woman, save for the purposes of his calling, or in order to supply himself with necessaries; and it was soon clear to the Raveloe lasses that he would never urge one of them to accept him against her will — quite as if he had heard them declare that they would never marry a dead man come to life again.

This view of Marner's personality was not without another ground than his pale face and unexampled [1] eyes; for Jem Rodney, the mole catcher, averred that, one evening as he was returning homeward, he saw Silas Marner leaning against a stile with a heavy bag on his back; and that, on coming up to him, he saw that Marner's eyes were set like a dead man's, and he spoke to him, and shook him, and his limbs were stiff, and his hands clutched the bag as if they'd been made of iron; but just as he had made up his mind that the weaver was dead, he came all right again, like, as you might say, in the winking of an eye, and said "Good night," and walked off.

All this Jem swore he had seen. Some said Marner must have been in a "fit,"

[1] **unexampled:** unique, very unusual.

a word which seemed to explain things otherwise incredible; but the argumentative Mr. Macey, clerk of the parish, shook his head, and asked if anybody was ever known to go off in a fit and not fall down. A fit was a stroke, wasn't it? and it was in the nature of a stroke to partly take away the use of a man's limbs. No, no; it was no stroke that would let a man stand on his legs, like a horse between the shafts, and then walk off as soon as you can say "Gee!"

But there might be such a thing as a man's soul being loose from his body, and going out and in, like a bird out of its nest and back; and that was how folks got overwise, [2] for they went to school in this shell-less [3] state to those who could teach them more than their neighbors could learn with their five senses and the parson. And where did Master Marner get his knowledge of herbs from — and charms, too, if he liked to give them away? Jem Rodney's story was no more than what might have been expected by anybody who had seen how Marner had cured Sally Oates, and made her sleep like a baby, when her heart had been beating enough to burst her body for two months and more, while she had been under the doctor's care. He might cure more folks if he would; but he was worth speaking fair, if it was only to keep him from doing you a mischief.

It was partly to this vague fear that Marner was indebted for protecting him from persecution, but still more to the fact that, the old linen weaver in the neighboring parish of Tarley being dead, his handicraft made him a highly welcome settler to the richer housewives of the district, and even to the more provident cottagers, who had their little stock of yarn at the year's end.

[2] **got overwise:** got supernatural power.
[3] **shell-less:** bodiless.

And the years had rolled on without producing any change in the impressions of the neighbors concerning Marner, except the change from novelty to habit.

At the end of fifteen years the Raveloe men said just the same things about Silas Marner as at the beginning; they did not say them quite so often, but they believed them much more strongly when they did say them. There was only one important addition which the years had brought; it was that Master Marner had lain by a fine sight of money somewhere, and that he could buy up "bigger men" than himself.

But while opinion concerning him had remained nearly stationary, and his daily habits had presented scarcely any visible change, Marner's inward life had been a history and a metamorphosis,[1] as that of every nature must be when it has fled, or been condemned, to solitude. His life, before he came to Raveloe, had been filled with the mental activity, and the close fellowship which marked the life of an artisan early incorporated in a narrow religious sect. Marner was highly thought of in that little hidden world, known to itself as the church assembling in Lantern Yard:[2] he was believed to be a young man of exemplary life and ardent faith; and a peculiar interest had been centered in him ever since he had fallen, at a prayer meeting, into a mysterious rigidity and suspension of consciousness, which, lasting for an hour or more, had been mistaken for death. To have sought a medical explanation for this phenomenon would have been held by

Silas himself, as well as by his minister and fellow members, a willful self-exclusion from the spiritual significance that might lie therein. Silas was evidently a brother selected for a peculiar discipline; though the effort to interpret this discipline was discouraged by the absence, on his part, of any spiritual vision during his outward trance. A less truthful man than he might have been tempted into the subsequent creation of a vision; a less sane man might have believed in such a creation; but Silas was both sane and honest.

He had inherited from his mother some acquaintance with medicinal herbs and their preparation — a little store of wisdom which she had imparted to him as a solemn bequest — but of late years he had had doubts about the lawfulness of applying this knowledge, believing that herbs could have no efficacy without prayer, and that prayer might suffice without herbs; so that his inherited delight to wander through the fields in search of foxglove and dandelion and coltsfoot[3] began to wear to him the character of a temptation.

Among the members of his church there was one young man, a little older than himself, with whom he had long lived in such close friendship that it was the custom of their Lantern Yard brethren to call them David and Jonathan.[4] The real name of the friend was William Dane, and he, too, was regarded as a shining instance of youthful piety, though somewhat given to overseverity toward weaker brethren, and to be so dazzled by his own light as to hold himself wiser than his teachers. But whatever blemishes others might discern

[1] **metamorphosis** (mĕt′á·môr′fô·sĭs): a complete change.
[2] **the church assembling in Lantern Yard:** presumably, a group of religious dissenters who had broken away from the Church of England.

[3] **foxglove and dandelion and coltsfoot:** medicinal plants.
[4] **David and Jonathan:** two friends in the Bible.

in William, to his friend's mind he was faultless; for Marner had one of those impressible, self-doubting natures which, at an inexperienced age, admire imperativeness.

The expression of trusting simplicity in Marner's face, that defenseless, deer-like gaze which belongs to large, prominent eyes, was strongly contrasted by the self-complacent suppression of inward triumph that lurked in the narrow slanting eyes and compressed lips of William Dane.

One of the most frequent topics of conversation between the two friends was assurance of salvation; Silas confessed that he could never arrive at anything higher than hope mingled with fear, and listened with longing wonder when William declared that he had possessed unshaken assurance ever since, in the period of his conversion, he had dreamed that he saw the words "calling and election sure" standing by themselves on a white page in the open Bible.

It had seemed to the unsuspecting Silas that the friendship had suffered no chill even from his formation of another attachment of a closer kind. For some months he had been engaged to a young servant woman, waiting only for a little increase to their mutual savings in order to set their marriage; and it was a great delight to him that Sarah did not object to William's occasional presence in their Sunday interviews. It was at this point in their history that Silas's cataleptic fit [1] occurred during the prayer meeting; and amidst the various queries and expressions of interest addressed to him by his fellow members, William's suggestion alone jarred with the general sympathy toward a brother thus

Lantern Yard

singled out for special dealing.[2] He observed that, to him, this trance looked more like a visitation of Satan than a proof of divine favor, and exhorted his friend to see that he hid no accursed thing within his soul.

Silas felt no resentment, but only pain, at his friend's doubts concerning him; and to this was soon added some anxiety at the perception that Sarah's manner toward him began to exhibit involuntary signs of shrinking and dislike. He asked her if she wished to break off their engagement; but she denied this: their engagement was known to the church, and had been recognized in the prayer meetings; it could not be broken off without strict

[1] **cataleptic** (kăt′a·lĕp′tĭk) **fit**: a motionless, unfeeling, trancelike state, accompanied by stiffening of the muscles.

[2] **special dealing**: special attention, supposedly from heaven.

investigation, and Sarah could render no reason that would be sanctioned by the feeling of the community.

At this time the senior deacon was taken dangerously ill, and, being a childless widower, he was tended night and day by some of the younger brethren or sisters. Silas frequently took his turn in the night watching with William, the one relieving the other at two in the morning. The old man, contrary to expectation, seemed to be on the way to recovery, when one night Silas, sitting up by his bedside, observed that his usual audible breathing had ceased. The candle was burning low, and he had to lift it to see the patient's face distinctly. Examination convinced him that the deacon was dead — had been dead some time, for the limbs were rigid.

Silas asked himself if he had been asleep, and looked at the clock: it was already four in the morning. How was it that William had not come? In much anxiety he went to seek for help, and soon there were several friends assembled in the house, the minister among them, while Silas went away to his work, wishing he could have met William to know the reason for his non-appearance.

But at six o'clock, as he was thinking of going to seek his friend, William came, and with him the minister. They came to summon him to Lantern Yard, to meet the church members there; and to his inquiry concerning the cause of the summons the only reply was, "You will hear." Nothing further was said until Silas was seated in the vestry, in front of the minister, with the eyes of those who to him represented God's people fixed solemnly upon him. Then the minister, taking out a pocketknife, showed it to Silas, and asked him if he knew where he had left that knife?

Silas said he did not know that he had left it anywhere out of his own pocket — but he was trembling at this strange interrogation. He was then exhorted not to hide his sin, but to confess and repent. The knife had been found in the bureau by the departed deacon's bedside — found in the place where the little bag of church money had lain, which the minister himself had seen the day before. Some hand had removed that bag; and whose hand could it be, if not that of the man to whom the knife belonged?

For some time Silas was mute with astonishment; then he said, "God will clear me; I know nothing about the knife being there, or the money being gone. Search me and my dwelling; you will find nothing but three pounds five of my own savings, which William Dane knows I have had these six months."

At this William groaned, but the minister said, "The proof is heavy against you, Brother Marner. The money was taken in the night last past, and no man was with our departed brother but you, for William Dane declares to us that he was hindered by sudden sickness from going to take his place as usual, and you yourself said that he had not come; and moreover, you neglected the dead body."

"I must have slept," said Silas. Then, after a pause, he added, "Or I must have had another visitation like that which you have all seen me under, so that the thief must have come and gone while I was not in the body, but out of the body.[1] But, I say again, search me and my dwelling, for I have been nowhere else."

The search was made, and it ended — in William Dane's finding the well-known bag, empty, tucked behind the

[1] out of the body: in a trance.

chest of drawers in Silas's chamber! On this William exhorted his friend to confess, and not to hide his sin any longer. Silas turned a look of keen reproach on him, and said, "William, for nine years that we have gone in and out together, have you ever known me to tell a lie? But God will clear me."

"Brother, said William, "how do I know what you may have done in the secret chambers of your heart, to give Satan an advantage over you?"

Silas was still looking at his friend. Suddenly a deep flush came over his face, and he was about to speak impetuously, when he seemed checked again by some inward shock that sent the flush back and made him tremble. But at last he spoke feebly, looking at William.

"I remember now — the knife wasn't in my pocket."

William said, "I know nothing of what you mean." The other persons present, however, began to inquire where Silas meant to say that the knife was, but he would give no further explanation; he only said, "I am sore stricken; I can say nothing. God will clear me."

On their return to the vestry there was further deliberation. Any resort to legal measures for ascertaining the culprit was contrary to the principles of the church in Lantern Yard. But the members were bound to take other measures for finding out the truth, and they resolved on praying and drawing lots.[1] Silas knelt with his brethren, relying on his own innocence being certified by immediate divine interference, but feeling that his trust in man had been cruelly bruised.

The lots declared that Silas Marner

---

[1] **drawing lots**: probably, taking one piece of paper from a box in which an equal number were marked "guilty" and "not guilty."

was guilty. He was solemnly suspended from church membership, and called upon to render up the stolen money; only on confession, as the sign of repentance, could he be received once more within the folds of the church. Marner listened in silence. At last, when everyone rose to depart, he went toward William Dane, and said, in a voice shaken by agitation:

"The last time I remember using my knife was when I took it out to cut a strap for you. I don't remember putting it in my pocket again. *You* stole the money, and you have woven the plot to lay the sin at my door. But you may prosper, for all that; there is no just God that governs the earth righteously, but a God of lies, that bears witness against the innocent."

There was a general shudder at this blasphemy.

William said meekly, "I leave our brethren to judge whether this is the voice of Satan or not. I can do nothing but pray for you, Silas."

Poor Marner went out with that despair in his soul, that shaken trust in God and man, which is little short of madness to a loving nature. In the bitterness of his wounded spirit, he said to himself, "*She* will cast me off, too." And he reflected that, if she did not believe the testimony against him, her whole faith must be upset, as his was.

Marner went home, and for a whole day sat alone, stunned by despair, without any impulse to go to Sarah and attempt to win her belief in his innocence. The second day he took refuge from benumbing unbelief by getting into his loom and working away as usual; and before many hours were past, the minister and one of the deacons came to him with the message from Sarah that she held her engagement to him at an end. Silas received the message mutely, and then turned away from the messengers to work at his loom again. In little more than a month from that time Sarah was married to William Dane; and not long afterward it was known to the brethren in Lantern Yard that Silas Marner had departed from the town.

CHAPTER II

The Making of a Miser

Even people whose lives have been made various [1] by learning sometimes find it hard to keep a fast hold on their habitual views of life, on their faith in the invisible, when they are suddenly transported to a new land, where the beings around them know nothing of their history, and share none of their ideas. But even *their* experience may hardly enable them thoroughly to imagine what was the effect on a simple weaver like Silas Marner, when he left his own country and people and came to settle in Raveloe.

Nothing could be more unlike his native town, set within sight of the widespread hillsides, than this low, wooded region where he felt hidden even from the heavens by the screening trees and hedgerows. There was nothing here, when he rose in the deep morning quiet and looked out on the dewy brambles and rank, tufted grass, that seemed to have any relation with that life centering in Lantern Yard. The whitewashed walls; the little pews where well-known figures entered with a subdued rustling, and the recurrent swell of voices in song; these things had been the channel of divine influences to Marner — they were the fostering home of his

religious emotions — they were Christianity and God's kingdom upon earth. A weaver who finds hard words in his hymnbook knows nothing of abstractions; as the little child knows nothing of parental love, but only knows one face and one lap toward which it stretches its arms for refuge and nurture.

And what could be more unlike that Lantern Yard world than the world in Raveloe — orchards looking lazy with neglected plenty; the large church in the wide churchyard, which men gazed at lounging at their own doors in service-time; the purple-faced farmers jogging along the lanes or turning in at the Rainbow; homesteads, where men supped heavily and slept in the light of the evening hearth, and where women seemed to be laying up a stock of linen for the life to come. There were no lips in Raveloe from which a word could fall that would stir Silas Marner's benumbed faith to a sense of pain. It seemed to him that the Power he had vainly trusted in among the streets and at the prayer meetings was very far away from this land in which he had taken refuge, where men lived in careless abundance, knowing and needing nothing of that trust which, for him, had been turned to bitterness.

His first movement after the shock had been to work in his loom; and he went on with this unremittingly, never asking himself why, now he was come to Raveloe, he worked far on into the night to finish the tale [2] of Mrs. Osgood's table linen sooner than she expected — without contemplating beforehand the money she would put into his hand for the work. He seemed to weave, like the spider, from pure impulse, without reflection. Every man's

[1] **made various:** broadened.

[2] **tale:** an uncommon use of the word, here, meaning sum or amount.

He seemed to weave, like the spider, from pure impulse, without reflection.

work, pursued steadily, tends in this way to become an end in itself, and so to bridge over the loveless chasms of his life. Silas's hand satisfied itself with throwing the shuttle, and his eye with seeing the little squares in the cloth complete themselves under his effort. Then there were the calls of hunger; and Silas had to provide his own breakfast, dinner, and supper, to fetch his own water from the well, and put his own kettle on the fire; and all these immediate promptings helped to reduce his life to the unquestioning activity of a spinning insect. He hated the thought of the past; there was nothing that called out his love and fellowship toward the strangers he had come amongst; and the future was all dark.

But at last Mrs. Osgood's table linen was finished, and Silas was paid in gold. His earnings in his native town, where he worked for a wholesale dealer, had been after a lower rate; he had been paid weekly, and of his weekly earnings a large proportion had gone to objects of piety and charity.[1] Now, for the first time in his life, he had five bright guineas [2] put into his hand; no man expected a share of them, and he loved no man that he should offer him a share. But what were the guineas to him who saw no vista beyond countless days of weaving? It was needless for him to ask that, for it was pleasant to him to feel them in his palm, and look at their bright faces, which were all his own; it was another element of life, like the weaving and the satisfaction of hunger, subsisting quite aloof from the life of belief and love from which he had been cut off.

The weaver's hand had known the touch of hard-won money even before the palm had grown to its full breadth; for twenty years, mysterious money had stood to him as the symbol of earthly good, and the immediate object of toil. He had seemed to love it little in the years when every penny had its purpose for him; for he loved the *purpose* then. But now, when all purpose was gone, that habit of looking toward the money and grasping it with a sense of fulfilled effort made a loam that was deep enough for the seeds of desire; and as Silas walked homeward across the fields in the twilight, he drew out the money, and thought it was brighter in the gathering gloom.

About this time an incident happened which seemed to open a possibility of some fellowship with his neighbors. One day, taking a pair of shoes to be mended, he saw the cobbler's wife seated by the fire, suffering from the terrible symptoms of heart disease and dropsy,[3] which he had witnessed as the precursors [4] of his mother's death. He felt a rush of pity at the mingled sight and remembrance, and, recalling the relief his mother had found from a simple preparation of foxglove, he promised Sally Oates to bring her something that would ease her, since the doctor did her no good.

In this office of charity, Silas felt, for the first time since he had come to Raveloe, a sense of unity between his past and present life, which might have been the beginning of his rescue from the insect-like existence into which his

---

[1] **objects of piety and charity:** contributions to his religious group.
[2] **guineas** (gĭn´ĭz): English gold coins issued from 1663 to 1813, said to be made of gold from Guinea. In 1717 the guinea's value was fixed at 21 shillings. Today the guinea is no longer in circulation, but the sum of 21 shillings (almost three dollars in our currency) is still referred to as a guinea.

[3] **dropsy:** an unusual accumulation of watery fluid in some part of the body.
[4] **precursors** (prė·kûr´sẽrz): forerunners.

nature had shrunk. But Sally Oates's disease had raised her into a personage of much interest and importance among the neighbors, and the fact of her having found relief from drinking Silas Marner's "stuff" became a matter of general discourse.

When Dr. Kimble gave physic, it was natural that it should have an effect; but when a weaver, who came from nobody knew where, worked wonders with a bottle of brown waters, the occult [1] character of the process was evident. Such a sort of thing had not been known since the wisewoman [2] at Tarley died; and she had charms as well as "stuff"; everybody went to her when their children had fits. Silas Marner must be a person of the same sort, for how did he know what would bring back Sally Oates's breath, if he didn't know a fine sight more than that? The wisewoman had words that she muttered to herself, so that you couldn't hear what they were, and if she tied a bit of red thread round the child's toe the while, it would keep off the water in the head. Silas Marner could very likely do as much, and more; and now it was all clear how he should have come from unknown parts, and be so "comical-looking." But Sally Oates must mind and not tell the doctor, for he would be sure to set his face against Marner; he was always angry about the wisewoman, and used to threaten those who went to her that they should have none of his help any more.

Silas now found himself and his cottage suddenly beset by mothers who wanted him to charm away the whooping cough, and by men who wanted stuff against the rheumatics or the knots in the hands; and, to secure themselves against a refusal, the applicants brought silver in their palms.

Silas might have driven a profitable trade in charms as well as in his small list of drugs; but money on this condition was no temptation to him; and he drove one after another away with growing irritation. The hope in his wisdom was at length changed into dread, for no one believed him when he said he knew no charms and could work no cures, and every man and woman who had an accident or a new attack after applying to him set the misfortune down to Master Marner's ill will and irritated glances. Thus it came to pass that his movement of pity toward Sally Oates, which had given him a transient sense of brotherhood, heightened the repulsion between him and his neighbors, and made his isolation more complete.

Gradually the guineas, the crowns, [3] and the half crowns grew to a heap, and Marner drew less and less for his own wants, trying to solve the problem of keeping himself strong enough to work sixteen hours a day on as small an outlay as possible. Have not men, shut up in solitary imprisonment, found an interest in marking the moments by straight strokes of a certain length on the wall, until the growth of the sum of straight strokes, arranged in triangles, has become a mastering purpose? That will help us to understand how the love of accumulating money grows an absorbing passion in men whose imaginations, even in the very beginning of their hoard, showed them no purpose beyond it.

Marner wanted the heaps of ten to grow into a square, and then into a larger square; and every added guinea, while it was itself a satisfaction, bred a new desire. The money not only grew,

[1] **occult** (ŏ·kŭlt′): mysterious, supernatural.
[2] **wisewoman:** a person who "healed" the sick with superstition and magic.

[3] **crowns:** British silver coins.

. . . every added guinea . . . bred a new desire.

but it remained with him. He began to think it was conscious of him, as his loom was, and he would on no account have exchanged those coins, which had become his familiars, for other coins with unknown faces. He handled them, he counted them, till their form and color were like the satisfaction of a thirst to him; but it was only in the night, when his work was done, that he drew them out to enjoy their companionship. He had taken up some bricks in his floor underneath his loom, and here he had made a hole in which he set the iron pot that contained his guineas and silver coins, covering the bricks with sand whenever he replaced them.

Not that the idea of being robbed presented itself often or strongly to his mind; hoarding was common in coun-try districts in those days; there were old laborers in the parish of Raveloe who were known to have their savings by them, probably inside their flock beds;[1] but their rustic neighbors had not imaginations bold enough to lay a plan of burglary. How could they have spent the money in their own village without betraying themselves? They would be obliged to "run away" — a course as dark and dubious as a balloon journey.

So, year after year, Silas Marner had lived in this solitude, his guineas rising in the iron pot, and his life narrowing and hardening itself more and more. His life had reduced itself to the functions of weaving and hoarding, without any contemplation of an end toward which the functions tended. Strangely Marner's face and figure shrank and bent themselves into a constant mechanical relation to the objects of his life,[2] so that he produced the same sort of impression as a handle or a crooked tube, which has no meaning standing apart. The prominent eyes that used to look trusting and dreamy now looked as if they had been made to see only one kind of thing that was very small, like tiny grain, for which they hunted everywhere; and he was so withered and yellow that, though he was not yet forty, the children always called him "Old Master Marner."

Yet even in this stage of withering a little incident happened which showed that the sap of affection was not all gone. It was one of his daily tasks to fetch his water from a well a couple of fields off, and for this purpose, ever since he came to Raveloe, he had had a brown earthenware pot, which he held

[1] **flock beds:** mattresses filled with wool.
[2] **a constant . . . life:** He became bent over in the position he adopted for weaving at his loom and counting his gold.

as his most precious utensil, among the very few conveniences he had granted himself. It had been his companion for twelve years, always standing on the same spot, always lending its handle to him in the early morning, so that its form had an expression for him of willing helpfulness, and the impress of its handle on his palm gave a satisfaction mingled with that of having the fresh clear water.

One day as he was returning from the well he stumbled against the step of the stile, and his brown pot, falling with force against the stones that overarched the ditch below him, was broken in three pieces. Silas picked up the pieces and carried them home with grief in his heart. The brown pot could never be of use to him any more, but he stuck the bits together and propped the ruin in its old place for a memorial.

This is the history of Silas Marner until the fifteenth year after he came to Raveloe. The livelong day he sat in his loom, his ear filled with its monotony, his eyes bent close down on the slow growth of sameness in the brownish web. But at night came his revelry; at night he closed his shutters, and made fast his doors, and drew forth his gold.

Long ago the heap of coins had become too large for the iron pot to hold them, and he had made for them two thick leather bags, which wasted no room in their resting place, but lent themselves flexibly to every corner. How the guineas shone as they came pouring out of the dark leather mouths! The silver bore no large proportion in amount to the gold,[1] because the long pieces of linen which formed his chief work were always partly paid for in gold, and out of the silver he supplied his own bodily wants.

[1] silver . . . gold: There was much less silver than gold.

He loved the guineas best, but he would not change the silver — the crowns and half crowns that were his own earnings, begotten by his labor; he loved them all. He spread them out in heaps and bathed his hands in them; then he counted them and set them up in regular piles, and felt their rounded outline between his thumb and fingers, and thought fondly of the guineas that were only half-earned by the work in his loom — thought of the guineas that were coming slowly through the coming years, through all his life, which spread far away before him, the end quite hidden by countless days of weaving.

But about the Christmas of that fifteenth year a second great change came over Marner's life, and his history became blended in a singular manner with the life of his neighbors.

CHAPTER III

The Cass Brothers Quarrel

[Not infrequently when brothers fall out they become bitter enemies. It is so with the Cass brothers, whom you are to meet in this chapter. Their quarrel at the Red House sows the first seeds of the story's dramatic situation. As you read, pay special attention to the contrast in their characters. What differences do you notice? What hints of future difficulty does their hostility give?]

The greatest man in Raveloe was Squire Cass, who lived in the large red house, with the handsome flights of stone steps in front and the high stables behind it, nearly opposite the church. He was only one among several landed parishioners, but he alone was honored with the title of Squire; for though Mr. Osgood's family was also understood to be of timeless origin — still he merely owned the farm he occupied; whereas Squire Cass had a tenant or two, who complained of the game to him quite as if he had been a lord.

It was still that glorious wartime which was felt to be a peculiar favor of Providence toward the landed interest.[1] Raveloe lay low among the bushy trees and the rutted lanes, aloof from the currents of industrial energy and Puritan earnestness; the rich ate and drank freely, accepting gout[2] and apoplexy[3] as things that ran mysteriously in respectable families, and the poor thought that the rich were entirely in the right of it to lead a jolly life. For the Raveloe feasts were like the rounds of beef and the barrels of ale — they were on a large scale, and lasted a good while, especially in the wintertime.

After ladies had packed up their best gowns and topknots[4] in bandboxes, and had incurred the risk of fording streams on pillions[5] with the precious burden in rainy or snowy weather, it was not to be supposed that they looked forward to a brief pleasure. On this ground it was always contrived in the dark seasons, when there was little work to be done, that several neighbors should keep open house in succession.

So soon as Squire Cass's standing dishes diminished in plenty and freshness, his guests had nothing to do but to walk a little higher up the village to Mr. Osgood's, at the Orchards, and they found hams and chines[6] uncut, pork pies with the scent of the fire in them, spun butter in all its freshness — everything, in fact, that appetites at leisure could desire, in perhaps greater perfection, though not in greater abundance, than at Squire Cass's.

For the Squire's wife had died long ago, and the Red House was without that presence of the wife and mother which is the fountain of wholesome love and fear in parlor and kitchen; and this helped to account not only for there being more profusion than finished excellence in the holiday provisions, but also for the frequency with which the proud Squire condescended to preside in the parlor of the Rainbow rather than under the shadow of his own dark wainscot;[7] perhaps, also, for the fact that his sons had turned out rather ill.

Raveloe was not a place where moral censure was severe, but it was thought a weakness in the Squire that he had kept all his sons at home in idleness; and though some license[8] was to be allowed to young men whose fathers could afford it, people shook their heads at the courses of the second son, Dunstan, commonly called Dunsey Cass, whose taste for swapping and betting might turn out to be a sowing of something worse than wild oats. To be sure, the neighbors said, it was no matter what became of Dunsey — a spiteful, jeering fellow — always provided that his doings did not bring trouble on a

---

[1] **wartime . . . interest:** In time of war, food prices go up. Therefore, land becomes more valuable.

[2] **gout:** a disease in which there is inflammation of the joints, very often of the big toe. Overeating and drinking increase the irritation.

[3] **apoplexy** (ăp'ô·plĕk'sĭ): a disease of the blood vessels, now commonly called a "stroke." It occurs more often to people who are overweight.

[4] **topknots:** arrangements of ribbons, flowers, and feathers for decorating the hair.

[5] **pillions** (pĭl'yŭnz): cushions put behind a man's saddle for a woman to ride on.

[6] **chines** (chīnz): cuts of meat including the backbone.

[7] **wainscot** (wān'skŭt): wooden paneling on an interior wall.

[8] **license:** greater freedom of action than is usually considered proper.

family like Squire Cass's, with a monument in the church, and tankards older than King George. But it would be a thousand pities if Mr. Godfrey, the eldest, a fine, open-faced, good-natured young man, who was to come into the land someday, should take to going along the same road with his brother, as he had seemed to do of late. If he went on in that way, he would lose Miss Nancy Lammeter; for it was well known that she had looked very shyly on him ever since last Whitsuntide [1] twelvemonth, when there was so much talk about his being away from home days and days together. There was something wrong, more than common — that was quite clear; for Mr. Godfrey didn't look half so fresh-colored and open as he used to do.

At one time everybody was saying, What a handsome couple he and Miss Nancy Lammeter would make! and if she could come to be mistress at the Red House there would be a fine change, for the Lammeters had been brought up in that way, that they never suffered a pinch of salt to be wasted, and yet everybody in their household had of the best, according to his place. Such a daughter-in-law would be a saving to the old Squire, if she never brought a penny to her fortune; for it was to be feared that, notwithstanding his incomings, there were more holes in his pocket than the one where he put his own hand in. But if Mr. Godfrey didn't turn over a new leaf, he might say "Good-by" to Miss Nancy Lammeter.

It was the once hopeful Godfrey who was standing, with his hands in his side pockets and his back to the fire, in the dark wainscoted parlor, one late November afternoon, in that fifteenth year of Silas Marner's life at Raveloe. The fading gray light fell dimly on the walls decorated with guns, whips, and foxes' brushes, on coats and hats flung on the chairs, on tankards sending forth a scent of flat ale, and on a half-choked fire, signs of a domestic life destitute of any hallowing charm, with which the look of gloomy vexation on Godfrey's blond face was in sad accordance. He seemed to be waiting and listening for someone's approach, and presently the sound of a heavy step, with an accompanying whistle, was heard across the large, empty entrance hall.

The door opened, and a thickset, heavy-looking young man entered, with the flushed face and the elated bearing which mark the first stage of intoxication. It was Dunsey, and at the sight of him Godfrey's face parted with some of its gloom to take on the more active expression of hatred. The handsome brown spaniel that lay on the hearth retreated under the chair in the chimney corner.

"Well, Master Godfrey, what do you want with me?" said Dunsey, in a mocking tone. "You're my elders and betters, you know; I was obliged to come when you sent for me."

"Why, this is what I want — and just shake yourself sober and listen, will you?" said Godfrey savagely. He had himself been drinking more than was good for him, trying to turn his gloom into uncalculating anger. "I want to tell you, I must hand over that rent of Fowler's to the Squire, or else tell him I gave it you; for he's threatening to distrain [2] for it, and it'll all be out soon, whether I tell him or not. He said, just now, before he went out, he should send word to Cox to distrain, if Fowler didn't come and pay up his arrears this week.

---

[1] **Whitsuntide** (hwĭt'sŭn-tīd'): the seventh week after Easter.

[2] **distrain** (dĭs-trān'): a legal word meaning to seize property in payment of debt.

The Squire's short o' cash, and in no humor to stand any nonsense; and you know what he threatened, if ever he found you making away with his money again. So, see and get the money, and pretty quickly, will you?"

"Oh!" said Dunsey sneeringly, coming nearer to his brother and looking in his face. "Suppose, now, you get the money yourself, and save me the trouble, eh? Since you was so kind as to hand it over to me, you'll not refuse me the kindness to pay it back for me; it was your brotherly love made you do it, you know."

Godfrey bit his lips and clenched his fist. "Don't come near me with that look, else I'll knock you down."

"Oh, no, you won't," said Dunsey, turning away on his heel, however. "Because I'm such a good-natured brother, you know. I might get you turned out of house and home, and cut off with a shilling any day. I might tell the Squire how his handsome son was married to that nice young woman, Molly Farren, and was very unhappy because he couldn't live with his drunken wife, and I should slip into your place as comfortable as could be. But, you see, I don't do it — I'm so easy and good-natured. You'll take any trouble for me. You'll get the hundred pounds for me — I know you will."

"How can I get the money?" said Godfrey, quivering. "I haven't a shilling to bless myself with. And it's a lie that you'd slip into my place; you'd get yourself turned out, too, that's all. For if you begin telling tales, I'll follow. Bob's my father's favorite — you know that very well. He'd only think himself well rid of you."

"Never mind," said Dunsey, nodding his head sideways as he looked out of the window. "It 'ud be very pleasant to me to go in your company — you're such a handsome brother, and we've always been so fond of quarreling with one another I shouldn't know what to do without you. But you'd like better for us both to stay at home together; I know you would. So you'll manage to get that little sum o' money, and I'll bid you good-by, though I'm sorry to part."

Dunstan was moving off, but Godfrey rushed after him and seized him by the arm, saying, with an oath —

"I tell you, I have no money; I can get no money."

"Borrow of old Kimble."

"I tell you, he won't lend me any more, and I shan't ask him."

"Well, then, sell Wildfire."

"Yes, that's easy talking. I must have the money directly."

"Well, you've only got to ride him to the hunt tomorrow. There'll be Bryce and Keating there, for sure. You'll get more bids than one."

"I dare say, and get back home at eight o'clock, splashed up to the chin. I'm going to Mrs. Osgood's birthday dance."

"Oho!" said Dunsey, turning his head on one side, and trying to speak in a small mincing treble. "And there's sweet Miss Nancy coming; and we shall dance with her, and promise never to be naughty again, and be taken into favor, and —"

"Hold your tongue about Miss Nancy, you fool," said Godfrey, turning red, "else I'll throttle you."

"What for?" said Dunsey, still in an artificial tone, but taking a whip from the table and beating the butt end of it on his palm. "You've a very good chance. I'd advise you to creep up her sleeve again; it 'ud be saving time if Molly should happen to take a drop too much laudanum [1] some day, and make

[1] laudanum (lô'dȧ·nŭm): a narcotic made from opium.

a widower of you. Miss Nancy wouldn't mind being a second, if she didn't know it. And you've got a good-natured brother, who'll keep your secret well, because you'll be so very obliging to him."

"I'll tell you what it is," said Godfrey, quivering, and pale again. "My patience is pretty near at an end. If you'd a little more sharpness in you, you might know that you may urge a man a bit too far, and make one leap as easy as another. I don't know but what it is so now; I may as well tell the Squire everything myself — I should get you off my back, if I got nothing else. And, after all, he'll know sometime. She's been threatening to come herself and tell him. So, don't flatter yourself that your secrecy's worth any price you choose to ask. You drain me of money till I have got nothing to pacify *her* with, and she'll do as she threatens some day. It's all one. I'll tell my father everything myself, and you may go to the devil."

Dunsey perceived that he had overshot his mark, and that there was a point at which even the hesitating Godfrey might be driven into decision. But he said, with an air of unconcern:

"As you please; but I'll have a draught of ale first." And ringing the bell, he threw himself across two chairs, and began to rap the window seat with the handle of his whip.

Godfrey stood, still with his back to the fire, uneasily moving his fingers among the contents of his side pockets, and looking at the floor. That big muscular frame of his held plenty of animal courage, but helped him to no decision when the dangers to be braved were such as could neither be knocked down nor throttled. His natural irresolution and moral cowardice were exaggerated by a position in which dreaded

". . . you've got a good-natured brother, who'll keep your secret well . . ."

consequences seemed to press equally on all sides, and his irritation had no sooner provoked him to defy Dunstan and anticipate all possible betrayals, than the miseries he must bring on himself by such a step seemed more unendurable to him than the present evil. The utmost concession to Dunstan about the horse began to seem easy, compared with the fulfillment of his own threat. But his pride would not let him recommence the conversation otherwise than by continuing the quarrel. Dunstan was waiting for this, and took his ale in shorter draughts than usual.

"It's just like you," Godfrey burst out, in a bitter tone, "to talk about my selling Wildfire in that cool way — the last thing I've got to call my own, and the best bit of horseflesh I ever had in my life. And if you'd got a spark of pride in you, you'd be ashamed to see the stables emptied, and everybody's sneering about it. But it's my belief you'd sell yourself, if it was only for the pleasure of making somebody feel he'd got a bad bargain."

"Ay, ay," said Dunstan, very placably,[1] "you do me justice, I see. You know I'm a jewel for 'ticing people into bargains. For which reason I advise you to let *me* sell Wildfire. I'd ride him to the hunt tomorrow for you with pleasure. I shouldn't look so handsome as you in the saddle, but it's the horse they'll bid for, and not the rider."

"Yes, I dare say — trust my horse to you!"

"As you please," said Dunstan, rapping the window seat again with an air of great unconcern. "It's *you* have got to pay Fowler's money; it's none of my business. You received the money from him when you went to Bramcote, and *you* told the Squire it wasn't paid. If you don't want to pay the money, let it alone; it's all one to me. But I was willing to accommodate you by undertaking to sell the horse, seeing it's not convenient to you to go so far tomorrow."

Godfrey was silent for some moments. He would have liked to spring on Dunstan, wrench the whip from his hand, and flog him to within an inch of his life; and no bodily fear could have deterred him; but he was mastered by another sort of fear, which was fed by feelings stronger even than his resentment. When he spoke again, it was in a half-conciliatory tone.

"Well, you mean no nonsense about the horse, eh? You'll sell him all fair, and hand over the money? If you don't, you know, everything 'ull go to smash, for I've got nothing else to trust to. And

you'll have less pleasure in pulling the house over my head, when your own skull's to be broken, too."

"Ay, ay," said Dunstan, rising; "all right. I thought you'd come round. I'm the fellow to bring old Bryce up to the scratch. I'll get you a hundred and twenty for him, if I get you a penny."

"But it'll perhaps rain cats and dogs tomorrow, as it did yesterday, and then you can't go," said Godfrey, hardly knowing whether he wished for that obstacle or not.

"Not *it*," said Dunstan. "I'm always lucky in my weather. It might rain if you wanted to go yourself. You never hold trumps, you know — I always do. You've got the beauty, you see, and I've got the luck, so you must keep me by you for your crooked sixpence;[2] you'll nev-er get along without me."

"Confound you, hold your tongue!" said Godfrey impetuously. "And take care to keep sober tomorrow, else you'll get pitched on your head coming home, and Wildfire might be the worse for it."

"Make your tender heart easy," said Dunstan, opening the door. "You never knew me see double when I'd got a bargain to make; it 'ud spoil the fun. Besides, whenever I fall, I'm warranted to fall on my legs."

With that, Dunstan slammed the door behind him, and left Godfrey to that bitter rumination on his personal circumstances which was now unbroken from day to day save by the excitement of sporting, drinking, cardplaying, or the rarer pleasure of seeing Miss Nancy Lammeter.

That was the condition of Godfrey Cass in this six and twentieth year of his life. A movement of compunction[3] had urged him into a secret marriage, which was a blight on his life. It was an ugly story of low passion, delusion, and waking from delusion, which needs not to be dragged from the privacy of Godfrey's bitter memory. He had long known that the delusion was partly due to a trap laid for him by Dunstan, who saw in his brother's degrading marriage the means of gratifying at once his jealous hate and his cupidity. But he had something else to curse — his own vicious folly, which now seemed as mad and unaccountable to him as almost all our follies and vices do when their promptings have long passed away.

For four years he had thought of Nancy Lammeter, and wooed her with patient worship, as the woman who made him think of the future with joy; she would be his wife, and would make home lovely to him, as his father's home had never been; and it would be easy, when she was always near, to shake off those foolish habits that were no pleasures, but only a feverish way of annulling vacancy.

Godfrey's was an essentially domestic nature; the need of some tender permanent affection, the longing for some influence that would make the good he preferred easy to pursue, caused the neatness, purity, and liberal orderliness of the Lammeter household, sunned by the smile of Nancy, to seem like those fresh bright hours of the morning, inviting to industry, sobriety, and peace.

And yet the hope of this paradise had not been enough to save him from a course which shut him out of it forever. Instead of keeping fast hold of the strong silken rope by which Nancy would have drawn him safe to the green banks, where it was easy to step firmly, he had let himself be dragged back into mud and slime, in which it was useless to struggle. He had made ties for himself which robbed him of all wholesome motive, and were a constant exasperation.

Still, there was one position worse than the present; it was the position he would be in when the ugly secret was disclosed; and the desire that continually triumphed over every other was that of warding off the evil day when he would have to bear the consequences of his father's violent resentment for the wound inflicted on his family pride — would have, perhaps, to turn his back on their hereditary ease and dignity which, after all, was a sort of reason for living, and would carry with him the certainty that he was banished forever from the sight and esteem of Nancy Lammeter.

The longer the interval, the more chance there was of deliverance from some, at least, of the hateful consequences to which he had sold himself; the more opportunities remained for him to snatch the strange gratification of seeing Nancy, and gathering some faint indications of her lingering regard. Toward this gratification he was impelled, fitfully, every now and then, after having passed weeks in which he had avoided her as the far-off, bright-winged prize that only made him spring forward and find his chain all the more galling.

One of those fits of yearning was on him now, and it would have been strong enough to have persuaded him to trust Wildfire to Dunstan rather than disappoint the yearning, even if he had not had another reason for his disinclination toward the morrow's hunt. That other reason was the fact that the morning's meet was near Batherley, the market town where the unhappy woman lived whose image became more odious to him every day; and to his thought the whole vicinage [1] was haunted by her.

The yoke a man creates for himself by wrongdoing will breed hate in the kindliest nature; and the good-humored, affectionate-hearted Godfrey Cass was fast becoming a bitter man.

What was he to do this evening to pass the time? He might as well go to the Rainbow, and hear the talk about the cockfighting; everybody was there, and what else was there to be done? Though, for his own part, he did not care a button for cockfighting. Snuff, the brown spaniel, who had placed herself in front of him, and had been watching him for some time, now jumped up in impatience for the expected caress. But Godfrey thrust her away without looking at her, and left the room, followed humbly by the unresenting Snuff — perhaps because she saw no other career open to her.

CHAPTER IV

The Theft

Dunstan Cass, setting off in the raw morning, had to take his way along the lane which, at its farther extremity, passed by the piece of unenclosed ground called the stone pit, where stood the cottage, once a stonecutter's shed, now for fifteen years inhabited by Silas Marner. The spot looked very dreary at this season, with the moist, trodden clay about it, and the red, muddy water high up in the deserted quarry. That was Dunstan's first thought as he approached it; the second was that the old fool of a weaver, whose loom he heard rattling already, had a great deal of money hidden somewhere.

[1] **vicinage** (vĭs'ĭ·nĭj): neighborhood, vicinity.

How was it that he, Dunstan Cass, who had often heard talk of Marner's miserliness, had never thought of suggesting to Godfrey that he should frighten or persuade the old fellow into lending the money on the excellent security of the young Squire's prospects? The resource occurred to him now as so easy and agreeable, that he had almost turned the horse's head toward home again.

Godfrey would be ready enough to accept the suggestion; he would snatch eagerly at a plan that might save him from parting with Wildfire. But when Dunstan's meditation reached this point, the inclination to go on grew strong and prevailed. He didn't want to give Godfrey that pleasure; he preferred that Master Godfrey should be vexed. Moreover, Dunstan enjoyed the self-important consciousness of having a horse to sell, and the opportunity of driving a bargain, swaggering, and, possibly, taking somebody in. He might have all the satisfaction attendant on selling his brother's horse, and not the less have the further satisfaction of setting Godfrey to borrow Marner's money. So he rode on.

Bryce and Keating were there, as Dunstan was quite sure they would be — he was such a lucky fellow.

"Heyday," said Bryce, who had long had his eye on Wildfire, "you're on your brother's horse today; how's that?"

"Oh, I've swapped with him," said Dunstan, whose delight in lying was not to be diminished by the likelihood that his hearer would not believe him. "Wildfire's mine now."

"What! has he swapped with you for that big-boned hack of yours?" said Bryce, quite aware that he should get another lie in answer.

"Oh, there was a little account between us," said Dunsey carelessly, "and

Wildfire made it even. I accommodated him by taking the horse, though it was against my will. But I shall keep Wildfire, now I've got him, though I'd a bid of a hundred and fifty for him the other day. But I mean to stick to Wildfire; I shan't get a better at a fence in a hurry."

Bryce, of course, divined that Dunstan wanted to sell the horse, and Dunstan knew that he divined it (horse dealing is only one of many human transactions carried on in this manner); and they both considered that the bargain was in its first stage, when Bryce replied ironically:

"I wonder at that now; I wonder you mean to keep him; for I never heard of a man who didn't want to sell his horse getting a bid of half as much again as the horse was worth. You'll be lucky if you get a hundred."

Keating rode up now, and the transaction became more complicated. It ended in the purchase of the horse by Bryce for a hundred and twenty, to be paid on the delivery of Wildfire, safe and sound, at the Batherley stables. It did occur to Dunsey that it might be wise for him to give up the day's hunting, proceed at once to Batherley, and, having waited for Bryce's return, hire a horse to carry him home with the money in his pocket. But the inclination for a run, encouraged by confidence in his luck, and by a draught of brandy from his pocket-pistol[1] at the conclusion of the bargain, was not easy to overcome, especially with a horse under him that would take the fences to the admiration of the field.

Dunstan, however, took one fence too many, and got his horse pierced with a hedge stake. His own ill-favored person escaped without injury; but poor Wildfire, unconscious of his price, turned on his flank, and painfully panted his last.

[1] **pocket-pistol:** pocket flask.

Dunstan . . . took one fence too many, and got his horse pierced with a hedge stake.

It happened that Dunstan, a short time before, having had to get down to arrange his stirrup, had muttered a good many curses at this interruption, which had thrown him in the rear of the hunt near the moment of glory, and under this exasperation had taken the fences more blindly. He would soon have been up with the hounds again, when the fatal accident happened; and hence he was between eager riders in advance, and far-off stragglers, who were as likely as not to pass quite aloof from the line of road in which Wildfire had fallen.

Dustan, whose nature it was to care more for immediate annoyances than for remote consequences, no sooner recovered his legs, and saw that it was all over with Wildfire, than he felt a satisfaction at the absence of witnesses to a position which no swaggering could make enviable. Reinforcing himself, after his shake, with a little brandy and much swearing, it occurred to him that he could make his way to Batherley without danger of encountering any member of the hunt.

His first intention was to hire a horse there and ride home forthwith. He did not much mind about taking the bad news to Godfrey, for he had to offer him at the same time the resource of Marner's money; and if Godfrey kicked, as he always did, at the notion of making a fresh debt, from which he himself got the smallest share of advantage, why, he wouldn't kick long; Dunstan felt sure he could worry Godfrey into anything.

The idea of Marner's money kept growing in vividness, now the want of it had become immediate; the prospect of having to make his appearance with the muddy boots of a pedestrian at Batherley, and to encounter the grinning queries of stablemen, stood unpleasantly in the way of his impatience to be back at Raveloe and carry out his felicitous [1] plan; and a casual visitation of his waistcoat pocket, as he was ruminating, awakened his memory to the fact that the two or three small coins his forefinger encountered there were of too pale a color to cover that small debt without payment of which the stablekeeper had declared he would never do any more business with Dunsey Cass.

After all, according to the direction in which the run had brought him, he was not so very much farther from home than he was from Batherley; but Dunsey, not being remarkable for clearness of head, was only led to this conclusion by the gradual perception that

there were other reasons for choosing the unprecedented course of walking home.

It was now nearly four o'clock, and a mist was gathering; the sooner he got into the road the better. He remembered having crossed the road and seen the finger post [2] only a little while before Wildfire broke down; so, buttoning his coat, twisting the lash of his hunting whip compactly round the handle, and rapping the tops of his boots with a self-possessed air, he set off.

It was Godfrey's whip, which he had chosen to take without leave because it had a gold handle; of course no one could see, when Dunstan held it, that the name *Godfrey Cass* was cut in deep letters on that gold handle — they could only see that it was a very handsome whip. Dunsey was not without fear that he might meet some acquaintance in whose eyes he would cut a pitiable figure, for mist is no screen when people get close to each other; but when he at last found himself in the well-known Raveloe lanes without having met a soul, he silently remarked that that was part of his usual good luck. But now the mist, helped by the evening darkness, was more of a screen than he desired, for it hid the ruts into which his feet were liable to slip — hid everything, so that he had to guide his steps by dragging his whip along the low bushes in advance of the hedgerow. He must soon, he thought, be getting near the opening at the stone pit; he should find it out by the break in the hedgerow. He found it out, however, by another circumstance which he had not expected — namely, by certain gleams of light, which he presently guessed to proceed from Silas Marner's cottage.

That cottage and the money hidden

---

[1] **felicitous** (fê·lĭs′ĭ·tŭs): fortunately made.

[2] **finger post:** guidepost with a finger pointing the direction.

within it had been in his mind continually during his walk, and he had been imagining ways of cajoling [1] and tempting the weaver to part with the immediate possession of his money for the sake of receiving interest. By the time he saw the light gleaming through the chinks of Marner's shutters, the idea of a dialogue with the weaver had become so familiar to him that it occurred to him as quite a natural thing to make the acquaintance forthwith.

There might be several conveniences attending this course; the weaver had possibly got a lantern, and Dunstan was tired of feeling his way. He was still nearly three-quarters of a mile from home, and the lane was becoming unpleasantly slippery, for the mist was passing into rain. He turned up the bank, not without some fear lest he might miss the right way, since he was not certain whether the light was in front or on the side of the cottage. But he felt the ground before him cautiously with his whip handle, and at last arrived safely at the door. He knocked loudly, rather enjoying the idea that the old fellow would be frightened at the sudden noise. He heard no movement in reply; all was silence in the cottage. Was the weaver gone to bed, then? If so, why had he left a light? That was a strange forgetfulness in a miser.

Dunstan knocked still more loudly, and, without pausing for a reply, pushed his fingers through the latch hole, intending to shake the door and pull the latch-string up and down, not doubting that the door was fastened. But, to his surprise, at this double motion the door opened, and he found himself in front of a bright fire, which lit up every corner of the cottage — the bed, the loom, the three chairs, and the table — and showed him that Marner was not there.

Nothing at that moment could be much more inviting to Dunsey than the bright fire on the brick hearth; he walked in and seated himself by it at once. There was something in front of the fire, too, that would have been inviting to a hungry man, if it had been in a different stage of cooking. It was a small bit of pork suspended from the kettle hanger by a string passed through a large door key, in a way known to primitive housekeepers unpossessed of jacks.[2] But the pork had been hung at the farthest extremity of the hanger, apparently to prevent the roasting from proceeding too rapidly during the owner's absence. The old staring simpleton had hot meat for his supper, then? thought Dunstan. People had always said he lived on moldy bread, on purpose to check his appetite. But where could he be at this time, and on such an evening, leaving his supper in this stage of preparation, and his door unfastened?

Dunstan's own recent difficulty in making his way suggested to him that the weaver had perhaps gone outside his cottage to fetch in fuel, or for some such brief purpose, and had slipped into the stone pit. That was an interesting idea to Dunstan, carrying consequences of entire novelty. If the weaver was dead, who had a right to his money? Who would know where his money was hidden? *Who would know that anybody had come to take it away?* He went no farther into the subtleties of evidence; the pressing question, "Where *is* the money?" now took such entire possession of him as to make him quite forget that the weaver's death was not a certainty.

---

[1] **cajoling** (kȧ·jōl′ĭng): persuading, especially by deceit or flattery.

[2] **jacks:** A jack is an instrument for turning the rod that holds roasting meat.

Dunstan . . . hastily replaced the bricks, and spread the sand over them.

There were only three hiding places where he had ever heard of cottagers' hoards being found: the thatch, the bed, and a hole in the floor. Marner's cottage had no thatch; and Dunstan's first act was to go up to the bed; but while he did so, his eyes traveled eagerly over the floor, where the bricks, distinct in the firelight, were discernible under the sprinkling of sand. But not everywhere; for there was one spot, and one only, which was quite covered with sand, and sand showing the marks of fingers which had apparently been careful to spread it over a given space. It was near the treadles of the loom.

In an instant Dunstan darted to that spot, swept away the sand with his whip, and, inserting the thin end of the hook between the bricks, found that they were loose. In haste he lifted up two bricks, and saw what he had no doubt was the object of his search; for what could there be but money in those two leathern bags? And, from their weight, they must be filled with guineas. Dunstan felt round the hole, to be certain that it held no more; then hastily replaced the bricks, and spread the sand over them.

Hardly more than five minutes had passed since he entered the cottage, but it seemed to Dunstan like a long while; he felt an undefinable dread laying hold on him as he rose to his feet with the bags in his hand. He would hasten out into the darkness, and then consider what he should do with the bags. He closed the door behind him immediately, that he might shut in the stream of light; a few steps would be enough to carry him beyond betrayal by the gleams from the shutter chinks and the latch hole. The rain and darkness had got thicker, and he was glad of it; though it was awkward walking with both hands filled, so that it was as much as he could do to grasp his whip along with one of the bags. But when he had gone a yard or two, he might take his time. So he stepped forward into the darkness.

CHAPTER V

The Theft Discovered

When Dunstan Cass turned his back on the cottage, Silas Marner was not more than a hundred yards away from it, plodding along from the village with a sack thrown round his shoulders as an overcoat, and with a horn lantern [1] in his hand. His legs were weary, but his mind was at ease, free from the pre-

---

[1] **horn lantern:** one made from an animal's horn, scraped thin enough for the light to shine through.

sentiment [1] of change. Silas was thinking with double complacency of his supper, first, because it would be hot and savory; and, secondly, because it would cost him nothing. For the little bit of pork was a present from that excellent housewife, Miss Priscilla Lammeter, to whom he had this day carried home a handsome piece of linen; and it was only on occasion of a present like this that Silas indulged himself with roast meat. Supper was his favorite meal, because it came at his time of revelry, when his heart warmed over his gold; whenever he had roast meat, he always chose to have it for supper. But this evening, he had no sooner knotted his string fast round his bit of pork, twisted the string according to rule over his door key, passed it through the handle, and made it fast on the hanger, than he remembered that a piece of very fine twine was indispensable to his "setting up" a new piece of work in his loom early in the morning. It had slipped his memory, because, in coming from Mr. Lammeter's, he had not had to pass through the village; but to lose time by going on errands in the morning was out of the question.

It was a nasty fog to turn out into, but there were things Silas loved better than his own comfort; so, drawing his pork to the extremity of the hanger, and arming himself with his lantern and his old sack, he set out on what, in ordinary weather, would have been a twenty minutes' errand. He could not have locked his door without undoing his well-knotted string and retarding his supper; it was not worth his while to make that sacrifice. What thief would find his way to the stone pit on such a night as this? and why should he come on this particular night, when he had

never come through all the fifteen years before?

He reached his door in much satisfaction that his errand was done; he opened it, and to his shortsighted eyes everything remained as he had left it, except that the fire sent out a welcome increase of heat. He trod about the floor while putting by his lantern and throwing aside his hat and sack, so as to merge the marks of Dunstan's feet on the sand in the marks of his own nailed boots. Then he moved his pork nearer to the fire, and sat down to the agreeable business of tending the meat and warming himself at the same time.

As soon as he was warm he began to think it would be a long while to wait till after supper before he drew out his guineas, and it would be pleasant to see them on the table before him as he ate his unwonted feast, for joy is the best wine, and Silas's guineas were the golden wine of that sort.

He rose and placed his candle unsuspectingly on the floor near his loom, swept away the sand without noticing any change, and removed the bricks. The sight of the empty hole made his heart leap violently, but the belief that his gold was gone could not come at once — only terror, and the eager effort to put an end to the terror. He passed his trembling hand all about the hole trying to think it possible that his eyes had deceived him; then he held the candle in the hole and examined it curiously, trembling more and more. At last he shook so violently that he let fall the candle and lifted his hands to his head, trying to steady himself, that he might think. Had he put his gold somewhere else, by a sudden resolution last night, and then forgotten it? He searched in every corner, he turned his bed over, and shook it, and kneaded it; he looked in his brick oven where he

[1] **presentiment** (pre·zĕn'tĭ·mĕnt): a feeling that something will happen.

laid his sticks. When there was no other place to be searched, he kneeled down again, and felt once more all round the hole. There was no unsearched refuge left for a moment's shelter from the terrible truth.

Silas got up from his knees trembling, and looked round at the table; didn't the gold lie there after all? The table was bare. Then he turned and looked behind him — looked all round his dwelling, seeming to strain his brown eyes after some possible appearance of the bags, where he had already sought them in vain. He could see every object in his cottage — and his gold was not there.

Again he put his trembling hands to his head, and gave a wild ringing scream, the cry of desolation. For a few moments after, he stood motionless; but the cry had relieved him from the first maddening pressure of the truth. He turned, and tottered toward his loom, and got into the seat where he worked, instinctively seeking this as the strongest assurance of reality.

And now that all the false hopes had vanished, and the first shock of certainty was past, the idea of a thief began to present itself, and he entertained it eagerly, because a thief might be caught and made to restore the gold. The thought brought some new strength with it, and he started from his loom to the door. As he opened it, the rain beat in upon him, for it was falling more and more heavily.

There were no footsteps to be tracked on such a night — footsteps? When had the thief come? During Silas's absence in the daytime the door had been locked, and there had been no marks of any inroad on his return by daylight. And in the evening, too, he said to himself, everything was the same as when he had left it. The sand and bricks

looked as if they had not been moved. *Was* it a thief who had taken the bags? or was it a cruel power that no hands could reach, which had delighted in making him a second time desolate?

He shrank from this vaguer dread, and fixed his mind with struggling effort on the robber with hands, who could be reached by hands. His thoughts glanced at all the neighbors who had made any remarks, or asked any questions which he might now regard as a ground of suspicion. There was Jem Rodney, a known poacher,[1] and otherwise disreputable; he had often met Marner in his journeys across the fields, and had said something jestingly about the weaver's money; nay, he had once irritated Marner by lingering at the fire when he called to light his pipe, instead of going about his business.

Jem Rodney was the man — there was ease in the thought. Jem could be found and made to restore the money. Marner did not want to punish him, but only to get back his gold. The robber must be laid hold of. Marner's ideas of legal authority were confused, but he felt that he must go and proclaim his loss; and the great people in the village — the clergyman, the constable, and Squire Cass — would make Jem Rodney, or somebody else, deliver up the stolen money. He rushed out in the rain, under the stimulus of this hope, forgetting to cover his head, not caring to fasten his door; for he felt as if he had nothing left to lose. He ran swiftly till want of breath compelled him to slacken his pace as he was entering the village at the turning close to the Rainbow.

The Rainbow, in Marner's view, was the place where he was likely to find the powers and dignities of Raveloe,

[1] **poacher:** one who steals game or fish from private preserves.

and where he could most speedily make his loss public. He lifted the latch, and turned into the bright bar or kitchen on the right hand, where the less lofty customers of the house were in the habit of assembling, the parlor on the left being reserved for the more select society in which Squire Cass frequently enjoyed the double pleasure of conviviality and condescension. But the parlor was dark tonight, the chief personages who ornamented its circle being all at Mrs. Osgood's birthday dance, as Godfrey Cass was. And in consequence of this, the party on the high-screened seats in the kitchen was more numerous than usual; several personages, who would otherwise have been admitted into the parlor, being content this evening to vary their enjoyment by taking their spirits and water in company that called for beer.

CHAPTER VI

Town Talk

[The following scene at the Rainbow Inn gives a faithful picture of English village life in the early nineteenth century. The speakers at the inn and the subjects they talk about may seem unfamiliar to you and unrelated to your modern world. But do not miss the complete naturalness of this conversation. Like people in all times, these characters meet in their little informal social groups; they partake of refreshments and while away time talking of whatever happens to interest them at the moment. As you read, consider in what respects the group at the Rainbow is like some present-day gathering within your own experience — a group of American businessmen at a coffee counter, or a group of high school students at a soda fountain after school. As you listen in on the conversation in Mr. Snell's tavern, what impression do you form of Raveloe folks? What village gossip can you pick up? What "village characters" do you recognize?]

The conversation, which was at a high pitch of animation when Silas approached the door of the Rainbow, had, as usual, been slow and intermittent when the company first assembled. The pipes began to be puffed in a silence which had an air of severity; the more important customers, who drank spirits and sat nearest the fire, staring at each other as if a bet were depending on the first man who winked; while the beer drinkers kept their eyelids down and rubbed their hands across their mouths, as if their draughts of beer were a funereal duty attended with embarrassing sadness.

At last, Mr. Snell, the landlord, a man of a neutral disposition, broke silence by saying in a doubtful tone to his cousin the butcher:

"Some folks 'ud say that was a fine beast you druv in yesterday, Bob?"

The butcher, a jolly, smiling, red-haired man, was not disposed to answer rashly. He gave a few puffs before he spat and replied, "And they wouldn't be fur wrong, John."

After this feeble delusive thaw, a silence set in as severely as before.

"Was it a red Durham?" said the farrier,[1] taking up the thread of discourse after the lapse of a few minutes.

"Red it was," said the butcher, in his good-humored husky treble, "and a Durham it was."

"Then you needn't tell *me* who you bought it of," said the farrier, looking round with some triumph; "I know who it is has got the red Durhams o' this countryside. And she'd a white star on

---

[1] **farrier** (făr′ĭ-ẽr): blacksmith and animal doctor.

her brow, I'll bet a penny?" The farrier leaned forward and his eyes twinkled knowingly.

"Well; yes — she might," said the butcher slowly, considering that he was giving a decided affirmative. "I don't say contrary."

"I knew that very well," said the farrier, throwing himself backward again, and speaking defiantly; "if *I* don't know Mr. Lammeter's cows, I should like to know who does — that's all."

The farrier looked fierce, and the mild butcher's conversational spirit was roused a little.

"I'm not for contradicking no man," he said; "I'm for peace and quietness. Some are for cutting long ribs — I'm for cutting 'em short, myself; but *I* don't quarrel with 'em. All I say is, it's a lovely carkiss — and anybody as was reasonable, it 'ud bring tears into their eyes to look at it."

"Well," pursued the farrier angrily, "it was Mr. Lammeter's cow, else you told a lie when you said it was a red Durham."

"I tell no lies," said the butcher, with the same mild huskiness as before, "and I contradick none — not if a man was to swear himself black; he's no meat o' mine, nor none o' my bargains. All I say is, it's a lovely carkiss. And what I say, I'll stick to; but I'll quarrel wi' no man."

"No," said the farrier, with bitter sarcasm, looking at the company generally; "and p'rhaps you aren't pigheaded; and p'rhaps you didn't say the cow was a red Durham; and p'rhaps you didn't say she'd got a star on her brow — stick to that, now you're at it."

"Come, come," said the landlord, "let the cow alone. The truth lies atween you; you're both right and both wrong, as I allays say. And for the matter o' that, if the talk is to be o' the Lamme-

ters, *you* know the most upo' that head, eh, Mr. Macey? You remember when first Mr. Lammeter's father come into these parts, and took the Warrens?"

"I should think I did," said the old man, "and a fine old gentleman he was — as fine, and finer nor the Mr. Lammeter as now is. He came from a bit north'ard, so far as I could ever make out. We heared tell as he'd sold his own land to come and take the Warrens, and that seemed odd for a man as had land of his own, to come and rent a farm in a strange place. But they said it was along of his wife's dying; though there's reasons in things as nobody knows on — that's pretty much what I've made out. Howsomever, it was soon seen as we'd got a new parish'ner as know'd the rights and customs o' things, and kep' a good house, and was well looked on by everybody. And the young man — that's the Mr. Lammeter as now is, for he'd niver a sister — soon begun to court Miss Osgood, that's the sister o' the Mr. Osgood as now is, and a fine handsome lass she was — they pretend this young lass is like her, but that's the way wi' people as don't know what come before 'em. *I* should know, for I helped the old rector, Mr. Drumlow as was — I helped him marry 'em."

Here Mr. Macey paused; he always gave his narrative in installments, expecting to be questioned according to precedent.[1]

"Ay, and a partic'lar thing happened, didn't it, Mr. Macey, so as you were likely to remember that marriage?" said the landlord, in a congratulatory tone.

"I should think there did — a *very* partic'lar thing," said Mr. Macey, nodding sideways. "For Mr. Drumlow — poor old gentleman, I was fond on him, though he'd got a bit confused in his

[1] **precedent** (prĕs′ė·dĕnt): customary procedure.

head. And young Mr. Lammeter, he'd have no way but he must be married in Janiwary, which, to be sure, 's a unreasonable time to be married in; and so Mr. Drumlow — poor old gentleman, I was fond on him — but when he come to put the questions, he put 'em by the rule o' contrairy, like, and he says, 'Wilt thou have this man to thy wedded wife?' says he, and then he says, 'Wilt thou have this woman to thy wedded husband?' says he. But the partic'larest thing of all is, as nobody took any notice on it but me, and they answered straight off 'Yes,' like as if it had been me saying 'Amen' i' the right place, without listening to what went before."

"But *you* knew what was going on well enough, didn't you, Mr. Macey? You were live enough, eh?" said the butcher.

"Lor' bless you!" said Mr. Macey, pausing, and smiling in pity at the impotence of his hearer's imagination; "why, I was all of a tremble; it was as if I'd been a coat pulled by the two tails, like; for I couldn't stop the parson, I couldn't take upon me to do that; and yet I said to myself, I says, 'Suppose they shouldn't be fast married, 'cause the words are contrairy?' and my head went working like a mill, and I says to myself, 'Is't the meanin' or the words as makes folks fast i' wedlock?' For the parson meant right, and the bride and bridegroom meant right. But then, when I come to think on it, meanin' goes but a little way i' most things, for you may mean to stick things together and your glue may be bad, and then where are you? And so I says to mysen, 'It isn't the meanin', it's the glue.' "

"But you held in for all that, didn't you, Mr. Macey?" said the landlord.

"Ay, I held in tight till I was by mysen wi' Mr. Drumlow. And he made light on it, and he says, 'Pooh, pooh, Macey, make yourself easy,' he says; 'it's neither the meaning nor the words — it's the re*ges*ter does it — that's the glue.' So you see he settled it easy. And sure enough the wedding turned out all right, on'y poor Mrs. Lammeter — that's Miss Osgood as was — died afore the lasses was growed up; but for prosperity and everything respectable, there's no family more looked on."

Every one of Mr. Macey's audience had heard this story many times, but it was listened to as if it had been a favorite tune, and at certain points the puffing of the pipes was momentarily suspended, that the listeners might give their whole minds to the expected words. But there was more to come; and Mr. Snell, the landlord, duly put the leading question.

"Why, old Mr. Lammeter had a pretty fortin,[1] didn't they say, when he come into these parts?"

"Well, yes," said Mr. Macey; "but I dare say it's as much as this Mr. Lammeter's done to keep it whole. For there was allays a talk as nobody could get rich on the Warrens, though he holds it cheap, for it's what they call Charity Land."

"Ay, and there's few folks know so well as you how it come to be Charity Land, eh, Mr. Macey?" said the butcher.

"How should they?" said the old clerk, with some contempt. "Why, my grandfather made the grooms' livery for that Mr. Cliff as came and built the big stables at the Warrens. Why, they're stables four times as big as Squire Cass's, for he thought o' nothing but hosses and hunting, Cliff didn't — a Lunnon tailor, some folks said, as had gone mad wi' cheating. For he couldn't ride; my grandfather heared old Squire Cass say so many and many a time. But

1 **fortin:** fortune.

ride he would, as if Old Harry [1] had been a-driving him; and he'd a son, a lad o' sixteen; and nothing would his father have him do, but he must ride and ride — though the lad was frighted, they said. And it was a common saying as the father wanted to ride the tailor out o' the lad, and make a gentleman on him — not but what I'm a tailor myself, but in respect as God made me such, I'm proud on it, for 'Macey, Taylor,' 's been wrote up over our door since afore the queen's heads went out on the shillings.[2] But Cliff, he was ashamed o' being called a tailor. Howsomever, the poor lad got sickly and died, and the father didn't live long after him, for he got queerer nor ever, and they said he used to go out i' the dead o' the night, wi' a lantern in his hand, to the stables, and set a lot o' lights burning, and there he'd stand, cracking his whip and looking at his hosses. But at last he died raving, and they found as he'd left all his property, Warrens and all, to a Lunnon Charity, and that's how the Warrens come to be Charity Land."

"Ay, but there's more going on in the stables than what folks see by daylight, eh, Mr. Macey?" said the landlord.

"Ay, ay; go that way of a dark night, that's all," said Mr. Macey, winking mysteriously, "and then make believe, if you like, as you didn't see lights i' the stables, nor hear the stamping o' the hosses, nor the cracking o' the whips, and howling, too, if it's tow'rt daybreak. 'Cliff's holiday' has been the name of it ever sin' I was a boy; that's to say, some said as it was the holiday Old Harry gev him from roasting, like."

"What do you say to that, eh, Dow-

las?" said the landlord, turning to the farrier, who was swelling with impatience for his cue. "There's a nut for *you* to crack."

Mr. Dowlas was the negative spirit in the company, and proud of his position.

"Say? I say what a man *should* say as doesn't shut his eyes to look at a finger post. I say, as I'm ready to wager any man ten pound, if he'll stand out wi' me any dry night in the pasture before the Warren stables, as we shall neither see lights nor hear noises. That's what I say, and I've said it many a time; but there's nobody 'ull ventur a ten pun' note on their ghos'es [3] as they make so sure of."

"Why, Dowlas, that's easy betting, that is," said Ben Winthrop. "You might as well bet a man as he wouldn't catch the rheumatise if he stood up to 's neck in the pool of a frosty night. Folks as believe in Cliff's Holiday aren't a-going to ventur near it for a matter o' ten pound."

"If Master Dowlas wants to know the truth on it," said Mr. Macey, with a sarcastic smile, tapping his thumbs together, "he's no call to lay any bet — let him go and stan' by himself — there's nobody 'ull hinder him."

"Thank you! I'm obliged to you," said the farrier, with a snort of scorn. "If folk are fools, its no business o' mine. *I* don't want to make out the truth about ghos'es; I know it a'ready. But I'm not against a bet — everything fair and open. Let any man bet me ten pound as I shall see Cliff's Holiday, and I'll go and stand by myself. I want no company. I'd as lief do it as I'd fill this pipe."

"Ah, but who's to watch you, Dowlas, and see you do it? That's no fair bet," said the butcher.

"No fair bet?" replied Mr. Dowlas angrily. "I should like to hear any man

---

[1] **Old Harry:** another name for the devil.
[2] **afore . . . shillings:** In Queen Anne's time, that is, early in the eighteenth century, several issues of shillings bearing her likeness were made.

[3] **ghos'es:** ghosts.

stand up and say I want to bet unfair. Come now, Master Lundy, I should like to hear you say it."

"Very like you would," said the butcher. "But it's no business o' mine. If anybody'll bid for you at your own vallying, let him. I'm for peace and quietness, I am."

"Yes, that's what every yapping cur is, when you hold a stick up at him," said the farrier. "But I'm afraid o' neither man nor ghost, and I'm ready to lay a fair bet. *I* aren't a turntail cur."

"Ay, but there's this in it, Dowlas," said the landlord, speaking in a tone of much candor and tolerance. "There's folks, i' my opinion, they can't see ghos'-es, not if they stood as plain as a pike-staff [1] before 'em. And there's reason i' that. For there's my wife, now, can't smell, not if she'd the strongest o' cheese under her nose. I never see'd a ghost myself, but then I says to myself, 'Very like I haven't got the smell for 'em.' I mean, putting a ghost for a smell, or else contrairiways. And so, I'm for holding with both sides; for, as I say, the truth lies between 'em. And if Dowlas was to go and stand, and say he'd never seen a wink o' Cliff's Holiday all the night through, I'd back him; and if anybody said as Cliff's Holiday was certain sure, for all that, I'd back *him* too. For the smell's what I go by."

The landlord's analogical argument [2] was not well received by the farrier — a man intensely opposed to compromise.

"Tut, tut," he said, setting down his glass with refreshed irritation; "what's the smell got to do with it? Did ever a ghost give a man a black eye? That's what I should like to know. If ghos'es

<hr>

[1] **plain as a pikestaff:** as unmistakable as anything can be. The original expression was "plain as a packstaff."
[2] **analogical** (ăn′a·lŏj′ĭ·kăl) **argument:** argument showing the likeness between two things or situations.

want me to believe in 'em, let 'em leave off sulkin' i' the dark and i' lone places — let 'em come where there's company and candles."

"As if ghos'es 'ud want to be believed in by anybody so ignirant!" said Mr. Macey, in deep disgust.

CHAPTER VII

Apparition at the Rainbow

Yet the next moment there seemed to be some evidence that ghosts had a more condescending disposition than Mr. Macey attributed to them, for the pale thin figure of Silas Marner was suddenly seen standing in the warm light, uttering no word, but looking round at the company with his strange, unearthly eyes. The long pipes gave a simultaneous movement, like the antennae of startled insects, and every man present, not excepting even the skeptical farrier, had an impression that he saw, not Silas Marner in the flesh, but an apparition; for the door by which Silas had entered was hidden by the high-screened seats, and no one had noticed his approach. Mr. Macey, sitting a long way off from the ghost, might be supposed to have felt an argumentative triumph, which would tend to neutralize his share of the general alarm. Had he not always said that when Silas Marner was in that strange trance of his, his soul went loose from his body? Here was the demonstration; nevertheless, on the whole, he would have been as well contented without it.

For a few moments there was a dead silence, Marner's want of breath and agitation not allowing him to speak. The landlord, under the habitual sense that he was bound to keep his house

For a few moments there was a dead silence, Marner's want of breath
and agitation not allowing him to speak.

open to all company, and confident in the protection of his unbroken neutrality, at last took on himself the task of adjuring the ghost.

"Master Marner," he said, in a conciliatory tone, "what's lacking to you? What's your business here?"

"Robbed!" said Silas gaspingly. "I've been robbed! I want the constable — and the Justice — and Squire Cass — and Mr. Crackenthorp."

"Lay hold on him, Jem Rodney," said the landlord, the idea of a ghost subsiding; "he's off his head, I doubt.[1] He's wet through."

Jem Rodney was the outermost man, and sat conveniently near Marner's standing place; but he declined to give his services.

"Come and lay hold on him yourself, Mr. Snell, if you've a mind," said Jem rather sullenly. "He's been robbed, and murdered, too, for what I know," he added, in a muttering tone.

"Jem Rodney!" said Silas, turning and fixing his strange eyes on the suspected man.

"Ay, Master Marner, what do ye want wi' me?" said Jem, trembling a little, and seizing his drinking can as a defensive weapon.

"If it was you stole my money," said Silas, clasping his hands entreatingly, and raising his voice to a cry, "give it me back — and I won't meddle with you. I won't set the constable on you. Give it me back, and I'll let you — I'll let you have a guinea."

"Me stole your money!" said Jem angrily. "I'll pitch this can at your eye if you talk o' *my* stealing your money."

"Come, come, Master Marner," said the landlord, now rising resolutely, and seizing Marner by the shoulder, "if you've got any information to lay, speak it out sensible, and show as you're in

[1] **I doubt:** I suppose.

your right mind, if you expect anybody to listen to you. You're as wet as a drowned rat. Sit down and dry yourself, and speak straightforrard."

"Ah, to be sure, man," said the farrier, who began to feel that he had not been quite on a par with himself and the occasion. "Let's have no more staring and screaming, else we'll have you strapped for a madman.[2] That was why I didn't speak at the first — thinks I, the man's run mad."

"Ay, ay, make him sit down," said several voices at once, well pleased that the reality of ghosts remained still an open question.

The landlord forced Marner to take off his coat, and then to sit down on a chair aloof from everyone else, in the center of the circle, and in the direct rays of the fire. The weaver, too feeble to have any distinct purpose beyond that of getting help to recover his money, submitted unresistingly. The transient fears of the company were now forgotten in their strong curiosity, and all faces were turned toward Silas, when the landlord, having seated himself again, said:

"Now, then, Master Marner, what's this you've got to say — as you've been robbed? Speak out."

"He'd better not say again as it was me robbed him," cried Jem Rodney hastily. "What could I ha' done with his money? I could as easy steal the parson's surplice,[3] and wear it."

"Hold your tongue, Jem, and let's hear what he's got to say," said the landlord. "Now, then, Master Marner."

Silas now told his story under frequent questioning, as the mysterious

[2] **strapped for a madman:** at this time, insane persons were usually kept tied up.

[3] **surplice** (sûr′plĭs): an outer garment of white linen which is worn over a longer, close-fitting garment.

character of the robbery became evident.

This strangely novel situation of opening his trouble to his Raveloe neighbors, of sitting in the warmth of a hearth not his own, and feeling the presence of faces and voices which were his nearest promise of help, had doubtless its influence on Marner, in spite of his passionate preoccupation and his loss. Our consciousness rarely registers the beginning of a growth within us any more than without us; there have been many circulations of the sap before we detect the smallest sign of the bud.

The slight suspicion with which his hearers at first listened to him gradually melted away before the convincing simplicity of his distress: it was impossible for the neighbors to doubt that Marner was telling the truth, not because they were capable of arguing at once from the nature of his statements to the absence of any motive for making them falsely, but because, as Mr. Macey observed, "Folks as had the devil to back 'em were not likely to be so mushed" as poor Silas was. Rather, from the strange fact that the robber had left no traces, and had happened to know the nick of time, utterly incalculable by mortal agents, when Silas would go away from home without locking his door, the more probable conclusion seemed to be, that his disreputable intimacy in that quarter,[1] if it ever existed, had been broken up, and that, in consequence, this ill turn had been done to Marner by somebody it was quite in vain to set the constable after. Why this preternatural felon[2] should be obliged to wait till the door was left unlocked was a question which did not present itself.

"It isn't Jem Rodney as has done this work, Master Marner," said the landlord. "You mustn't be a-casting your eye at poor Jem. There may be a bit of a reckoning against Jem for the matter of a hare or so, if anybody was bound to keep their eyes staring open, and niver to wink; but Jem's been a-sitting here drinking his can, like the decentest man i' the parish, since before you left your house, Master Marner, by your own account."

"Ay, ay," said Mr. Macey, "let's have no accusing o' the innicent. That isn't the law. There must be folks to swear again' a man before he can be ta'en up. Let's have no accusing o' the innicent, Master Marner."

Memory was not so utterly torpid in Silas that it could not be wakened by these words. With a movement of compunction, as new and strange to him as everything else within the last hour, he started from his chair and went close up to Jem, looking at him as if he wanted to assure himself of the expression in his face.

"I was wrong," he said; "yes, yes — I ought to have thought. There's nothing to witness against you, Jem. Only you'd been into my house oftener than anybody else, and so you came into my head. I don't accuse you — I won't accuse anybody — only," he added, lifting up his hands to his head, and turning away with bewildered misery, "I try — I try to think where my guineas can be."

"Ay, ay, they're gone where it's hot enough to melt 'em, I doubt," said Mr. Macey.

"Tchuh!" said the farrier. And then he asked, with a cross-examining air, "How much money might there be in the bags, Master Marner?"

---

[1] **his disreputable . . . quarter:** Silas's supposed association with the Devil.

[2] **preternatural** (prē'tĕr·năt'û·răl) **felon:** strange, unexplainable criminal; that is, the Devil.

"Two hundred and seventy-two pounds, twelve and sixpence, last night when I counted it," said Silas, seating himself again, with a groan.

"Pooh! why, they'd be none so heavy to carry. Some tramp's been in, that's all; and as for the no footmarks, and the bricks and the sand being all right — why — your eyes are pretty much like a insect's, Master Marner; they're obliged to look so close, you can't see much at a time. It's my opinion as, if I'd been you, or you'd been me — for it comes to the same thing — you wouldn't have thought you'd found everything as you left it. But what I vote is, as two of the sensiblest o' the company should go with you to Master Kench, the constable's — he's ill i' bed, I know that much — and get him to appoint one of us his deppity; for that's the law, and I don't think anybody 'ull take upon him to contradick me there. It isn't much of a walk to Kench's; and then, if it's me as is deppity, I'll go back with you, Master Marner, and examine your premises; and if anybody's got any fault to find with that, I'll thank him to stand up and say it out like a man."

By this pregnant speech the farrier had re-established his self-complacency, and waited with confidence to hear himself named as one of the superlatively sensible men.

"Let us see how the night is, though," said the landlord, who also considered himself personally concerned in this proposition. "Why, it rains heavy still," he said, returning from the door.

"Well, I'm not the man to be afraid o' the rain," said the farrier. "For it'll look bad when Justice Malam hears as respectable men like us had a information laid before 'em and took no steps."

The landlord agreed with this view, and after taking the sense of the company, and duly rehearsing a small cere-

mony known in high ecclesiastical life as the *nolo episcopari,*[1] he consented to take on himself the chill dignity of going to Kench's. But to the farrier's strong disgust, Mr. Macey now started an objection to his proposing himself as a deputy constable; for that oracular old gentleman, claiming to know the law, stated, as a fact delivered to him by his father, that no doctor could be a constable.

"And you're a doctor, I reckon, though you're only a cow doctor — for a fly's a fly, though it may be a hossfly," concluded Mr. Macey, wondering a little at his own "'cuteness."

There was a hot debate upon this, the farrier being of course indisposed to renounce the quality of doctor, but contending that a doctor could be a constable if he liked — the law meant, he needn't be one if he didn't like. Mr. Macey thought this was nonsense, since the law was not likely to be fonder of doctors than of other folks. Moreover, if it was in the nature of doctors more than of other men not to like being constables, how came Mr. Dowlas to be so eager to act in that capacity?

"*I* don't want to act the constable," said the farrier, driven into a corner by this merciless reasoning; "and there's no man can say it of me, if he'd tell the truth. But if there's to be any jealousy and envying about going to Kench's in the rain, let them go as like it — you won't get me to go, I can tell you."

By the landlord's intervention, however, the dispute was accommodated.[2] Mr. Dowlas consented to go as a second person disinclined to act officially; and so poor Silas, furnished with some old

[1] *nolo episcopari* (nō'lō ē·pĭs'kō·pä'rī): Latin for "I do not wish to be made a bishop." The landlord politely said that he did not want to head the group going to the constable.
[2] **accommodated:** here, settled.

coverings, turned out with his two companions into the rain again, thinking of the long night hours before him, not as those do who long to rest, but as those who expect to "watch for the morning."

CHAPTER VIII

Clues

[To appreciate this chapter fully, you must feel the stir of excitement caused by the robbery. Note that superstition plays a large part in the lives of these simple village people. What made the villagers eager to follow up any clue — even the wrong one? And can you understand the sense of uneasiness that soon directed Godfrey's attention back to his own worrisome problems?]

When Godfrey Cass returned from Mrs. Osgood's party at midnight, he was not much surprised to learn that Dunsey had not come home. Perhaps he had not sold Wildfire, and was waiting for another chance — perhaps, on that foggy afternoon, he had preferred housing himself at the Red Lion at Batherley for the night; for he was not likely to feel much concern about leaving his brother in suspense. Godfrey's mind was too full of Nancy Lammeter's looks and behavior, too full of the exasperation against himself and his lot, which the sight of her always produced in him, for him to give much thought to Wildfire or to the probabilities of Dunstan's conduct.

The next morning the whole village was excited by the story of the robbery, and Godfrey, like everyone else, was occupied in gathering and discussing news about it, and in visiting the stone pit. The rain had washed away all possibility of distinguishing footmarks, but a close investigation of the spot had disclosed, in the direction opposite to the village, a tinderbox,[1] with a flint and steel, half sunk in the mud. It was not Silas's tinderbox, for the only one he had ever had was still standing on his shelf; and the inference generally accepted was that the tinderbox in the ditch was somehow connected with the robbery.

A small minority shook their heads, and intimated their opinion that it was not a robbery to have much light thrown on it by tinderboxes, that Master Marner's tale had a queer look with it, and that such things had been known as a man's doing himself a mischief, and then setting the justice to look for the doer. But when questioned closely as to their grounds for this opinion, and what Master Marner had to gain by such false pretenses, they only shook their heads.

While these discussions were going on amongst the group outside the Rainbow, a higher consultation was being carried on within, under the presidency of Mr. Crackenthorp, the rector,[2] assisted by Squire Cass and other substantial parishioners. It had just occurred to Mr. Snell, the landlord — he being, as he observed, a man accustomed to put two and two together — to connect with the tinderbox which, as deputy constable, he himself had had the honorable distinction of finding, certain recollections of a peddler who had called to drink at the house about a month before, and had actually stated that he carried a tinderbox about with him to light his pipe. Here, surely, was a clue to be followed out. Mr. Snell

[1] **tinderbox:** a small box, usually metal, used to carry objects for lighting a fire — some bit of inflammable material, and flint and steel for striking a spark. Matches did not come into general use till the 1830's.

[2] **rector** (rĕk′tēr): a clergyman.

The next morning the whole village was excited by the story of the robbery . . .

gradually recovered a vivid impression of the effect produced on him by the peddler's countenance and conversation. He had a "look with his eye." He didn't say anything particular — no, except that about the tinderbox — but it isn't what a man says, it's the way he says it. Moreover, he had a swarthy foreignness of complexion which boded little honesty.

"Did he wear earrings?" Mr. Crackenthorp wished to know, having some acquaintance with foreign customs.

"Well — stay — let me see," said Mr. Snell. "Well, he'd got earrings in his box to sell, so it's nat'ral to suppose he might wear 'em. But he called at every house, a'most, in the village; there's somebody else, mayhap, saw 'em in his ears, though I can't take upon me rightly to say."

Mr. Snell was correct in his surmise that somebody else would remember the peddler's earrings. For, on the spread of inquiry among the villagers, it was stated with gathering emphasis that the parson had wanted to know whether the peddler wore earrings in his ears, and an impression was created that a great deal depended on this fact. Of course everyone who heard the question, not having any distinct image of the peddler as *without* earrings, immediately had an image of him *with* earrings, larger or smaller, as the case might be; and the image was presently taken for a vivid recollection, so that the glazier's [1] wife, a well-intentioned woman, not given to lying, and whose house was among the cleanest in the village, was ready to declare, as sure as ever she meant to take the sacrament [2]

---

[1] **glazier** (glā′zhẽr): a person who sets glass in window frames.

[2] **sacrament**: Holy Communion, the Lord's Supper.

the very next Christmas that was ever coming, that she had seen big earrings, in the shape of the young moon, in the peddler's two ears; while Jinny Oates, the cobbler's daughter, being a more imaginative person, stated not only that she had seen them, too, but that they had made her blood creep, as it did at that very moment while there she stood.

Also, by way of throwing further light on this clue of the tinderbox, a collection was made of all the articles purchased from the peddler at various houses, and carried to the Rainbow to be exhibited there. In fact, there was a general feeling in the village that for the clearing-up of this robbery there must be a great deal done at the Rainbow, and that no man need offer his wife an excuse for going there while it was the scene of severe public duties.

Some disappointment was felt, and perhaps a little indignation also, when it became known that Silas Marner, on being questioned by the Squire and the parson, had retained no other recollection of the peddler than that he had called at his door, but had not entered his house, having turned away at once when Silas, holding the door ajar, had said that he wanted nothing. This had been Silas's testimony, though he clutched strongly at the idea of the peddler's being the culprit, if only because it gave him a definite image of a whereabout for his gold, after it had been taken away from its hiding place; he could see it now in the peddler's box. But it was observed with some irritation in the village that anybody but a "blind creatur" like Marner would have seen the man prowling about, for how came he to leave his tinderbox in the ditch close by if he hadn't been lingering there? It was a wonder the peddler hadn't murdered him; men of that sort, with rings in their ears, had been known for murderers often and often.

Godfrey Cass, indeed, entering the Rainbow during one of Mr. Snell's frequently repeated recitals of his testimony, had treated it lightly, stating that he himself had bought a penknife of the peddler, and thought him a merry grinning fellow enough; it was all nonsense, he said, about the man's evil looks. But this was spoken of in the village as the talk of youth, "as if it was only Mr. Snell who had seen something odd about the peddler!" On the contrary, there were at least half a dozen who were ready to go before Justice Malam, and give in much more striking testimony than any the landlord could furnish. It was to be hoped Mr. Godfrey would not go to Tarley and throw cold water on what Mr. Snell said there, and so prevent the justice from drawing up a warrant. He was suspected of intending this, when, after midday, he was seen setting off on horseback in the direction of Tarley.

But by this time Godfrey's interest in the robbery had faded before his growing anxiety about Dunstan and Wildfire, and he was going, not to Tarley, but to Batherley, unable to rest in uncertainty about them any longer. The possibility that Dunstan had played him the ugly trick of riding away with Wildfire, to return at the end of a month, when he had gambled away or otherwise squandered the price of the horse, was a fear that urged itself upon him more, even, than the thought of an accidental injury; and now that the dance at Mrs. Osgood's was past, he was irritated with himself that he had trusted his horse to Dunstan. He heard a horse approaching at a trot, but no sooner did the horse come within sight than his heart sank again. It was not Wildfire; and in a few moments more he discerned that the rider was not

Dunstan, but Bryce, who pulled up to speak, with a face that implied something disagreeable.

"Well, Mr. Godfrey, that's a lucky brother of yours, that Master Dunsey, isn't he?"

"What do you mean?" said Godfrey hastily.

"Why, hasn't he been home yet?" said Bryce.

"Home? — no. What has happened? Be quick. What has he done with my horse?"

"Ah, I thought it was yours, though he pretended you had parted with it to him."

"Has he thrown him down and broken his knees?" said Godfrey, flushed with exasperation.

"Worse than that," said Bryce. "You see, I'd made a bargain with him to buy the horse for a hundred and twenty — a swinging price, but I always liked the horse. And what does he do but go and stake him — fly at a hedge with stakes in it, atop of a bank with a ditch before it. The horse had been dead a pretty good while when he was found. So he hasn't been home since, has he?"

"Home? — no," said Godfrey, "and he'd better keep away. Confound me for a fool! I might have known this would be the end of it."

"Well, to tell you the truth," said Bryce, "after I'd bargained for the horse, it did come into my head that he might be riding and selling the horse without your knowledge, for I didn't believe it was his own. I knew Master Dunsey was up to his tricks sometimes. But where can he be gone? He's never been seen at Batherley. He couldn't have been hurt, for he must have walked off."

"Hurt?" said Godfrey bitterly. "He'll never be hurt — he's made to hurt other people."

"And so you *did* give him leave to sell the horse, eh?" said Bryce.

"Yes; I wanted to part with the horse — he was always a little too hard in the mouth for me," said Godfrey, his pride making him wince under the idea that Bryce guessed the sale to be a matter of necessity. "I was going to see after him — I thought some mischief had happened. I'll go back now," he added, turning the horse's head, and wishing he could get rid of Bryce; for he felt that the long-dreaded crisis in his life was close upon him. "You're coming on to Raveloe, aren't you?"

"Well, no, not now," said Bryce. "I *was* coming round there, and just let you know all I knew myself about the horse. I suppose Master Dunsey didn't like to show himself till the ill news had blown over a bit. He's perhaps gone to pay a visit at the Three Crowns, by Whitbridge — I know he's fond of the house." [1]

"Perhaps he is," said Godfrey, rather absently. Then rousing himself, he said, with an effort at carelessness, "We shall hear of him soon enough, I'll be bound."

"Well, here's my turning," said Bryce, not surprised to perceive that Godfrey was rather "down"; "so I'll bid you good day, and wish I may bring you better news another time."

Godfrey rode along slowly, representing to himself the scene of confession to his father from which he felt that there was now no longer any escape. The revelation about the money must be made the very next morning; and if he withheld the rest, Dunstan would be sure to come back shortly, and, finding that he must bear the brunt of his father's anger, would tell the whole story out of spite, even though he had nothing to gain by it. There was one step, perhaps, by which he might still win

---

[1] **house:** public house, inn.

Dunstan's silence and put off the evil day; he might tell his father that he had himself spent the money paid to him by Fowler; and as he had never been guilty of such an offense before, the affair would blow over after a little storming. But Godfrey could not bend himself to this. He felt that in letting Dunstan have the money he had already been guilty of breach of trust hardly less culpable than that of spending the money directly for his own behoof; and yet there was a distinction between the two acts which made him feel that the one was so much more blackening than the other as to be intolerable to him.

"I don't pretend to be a good fellow," he said to himself, "but I'm not a scoundrel — at least, I'll stop short somewhere. I'll bear the consequences of what I *have* done sooner than make believe I've done what I never would have done. I'd never have spent the money for my own pleasure — I was tortured into it."

Through the remainder of this day Godfrey, with only occasional fluctuations, kept his will bent in the direction of a complete avowal to his father, and he withheld the story of Wildfire's loss till the next morning, that it might serve him as an introduction to heavier matter. The old Squire was accustomed to his son's frequent absence from home, and thought neither Dunstan's nor Wildfire's nonappearance a matter calling for remark. Godfrey said to himself again and again that if he let slip this one opportunity of confession he might never have another; the revelation might be made even in a more odious way than by Dunstan's malignity [1] — *she* might come, as she had threatened to do. And then he tried to make the scene easier to himself by rehearsal; he

[1] malignity (má·lĭg′nĭ·tĭ): evilness.

made up his mind how he would pass from the admission of his weakness in letting Dunstan have the money to the fact that Dunstan had a hold on him which he had been unable to shake off, and how he would work up his father to expect something very bad before he told him the fact.

The old Squire was an implacable man; he made resolutions in violent anger, and he was not to be moved from them after his anger had subsided — as fiery volcanic matters cool and harden into rock. This was his system with his tenants; he allowed them to get into arrears, neglect their fences, reduce their stock, sell their straw, and otherwise go the wrong way — and then, when he became short of money in consequence of this indulgence, he took the hardest measures and would listen to no appeal.

Godfrey knew all this, and felt it with the greater force because he had constantly suffered annoyance from witnessing his father's sudden fits of unrelentingness. Still there was just the chance, Godfrey thought, that his father's pride might see this marriage in a light that would induce him to hush it up, rather than turn his son out and make the family the talk of the country for ten miles around.

This was the view of the case that Godfrey managed to keep before him pretty closely till midnight, and he went to sleep thinking that he had done with inward debating. But when he awoke in the still morning darkness, instead of arguments for confession, he could now feel the presence of nothing but its evil consequences; the old dread of disgrace came back — the old shrinking from the thought of raising a hopeless barrier between himself and Nancy — the old disposition to rely on chances which might be favorable to him, and save him from betrayal. Why, after all, should he cut off the hope of them by his own act? He had seen the matter in a wrong light yesterday. He had been in a rage with Dunstan, and had thought of nothing but a thorough breakup of their mutual understanding; but what it would be really wisest for him to do was to try and soften his father's anger against Dunsey, and keep things as nearly as possible in their old condition. If Dunsey did not come back for a few days (and Godfrey did not know but that the rascal had enough money in his pocket to enable him to keep away still longer) everything might blow over.

CHAPTER IX

The Squire Loses His Temper

Godfrey rose and took his own breakfast earlier than usual, but lingered in the wainscoted parlor till his younger brothers had finished their meal and gone out, awaiting his father, who always took a walk with his managing man before breakfast. Everyone breakfasted at a different hour in the Red House, and the Squire was always the latest. The table had been spread with substantial eatables nearly two hours before he presented himself — a tall, stout man of sixty, with a face in which the knit brow and rather hard glance seemed contradicted by the slack and feeble mouth. His person showed marks of habitual neglect; his dress was slovenly;[1] and yet there was something in the presence of the old Squire distinguishable from that of the ordinary farmers in the parish. The Squire had been used to parish homage all his life,

used to the presupposition[2] that his family, his tankards, and everything that was his were the oldest and best; and as he never associated with any gentry higher than himself, his opinion was not disturbed by comparison.

He glanced at his son as he entered the room, and said, "What, sir! haven't *you* had your breakfast yet?" but there was no pleasant morning greeting between them; not because of any unfriendliness, but because the sweet flower of courtesy is not a growth of such homes as the Red House.

"Yes, sir," said Godfrey, "I've had my breakfast, but I was waiting to speak to you."

"Ah! well," said the Squire, throwing himself indifferently into his chair, and speaking in a ponderous, coughing fashion, while he cut a piece of beef, and held it up before the deerhound that had come in with him. "Ring the bell for my ale, will you? You youngsters' business is your own pleasure mostly. There's no hurry about it for anybody but yourselves."

Godfrey waited, before he spoke again, until the ale had been brought and the door closed — an interval during which Fleet, the deerhound, had consumed enough bits of beef to make a poor man's holiday dinner.

"There's been a cursed piece of ill luck with Wildfire," he began; "happened the day before yesterday."

"What! broke his knees?" said the Squire, after taking a draught of ale. "I thought you knew how to ride better than that, sir. I never threw a horse down in my life. If I had, I might ha' whistled for another, for *my* father wasn't quite so ready to unstring as some other fathers I know of. But they

[1] **slovenly** (slŭv'ĕn·lĭ): untidy; careless-looking.

[2] **presupposition** (prē'sŭp·ô·zĭsh'ŭn): something assumed beforehand, or taken for granted.

must turn over a new leaf — *they* must. What with mortgages and arrears I'm as short o' cash as a roadside pauper. And that fool Kimble says the newspaper's talking about peace. Why, the country wouldn't have a leg to stand on. Prices 'ud run down like a jack, and I should never get my arrears, not if I sold all the fellows up. And there's that damned Fowler, I won't put up with him any longer; I've told Winthrop to go to Cox this very day. The lying scoundrel told me he'd be sure to pay me a hundred last month. He takes advantage because he's on that outlying farm and thinks I shall forget him."

The Squire had delivered this speech in a coughing and interrupted manner, but with no pause long enough for Godfrey to make it a pretext for taking up the word again. He felt that his father meant to ward off any request for money on the ground of the misfortune with Wildfire, and that the emphasis he had thus been led to lay on his shortness of cash and his arrears was likely to produce an attitude of mind the most unfavorable for his own disclosure. But he must go on now he had begun.

"It's worse than breaking the horse's knees — he's been staked and killed," he said, as soon as his father was silent, and had begun to cut his meat. "But I wasn't thinking of asking you to buy me another horse; I was only thinking I'd lost the means of paying you with the price of Wildfire as I'd meant to do. Dunsey took him to the hunt to sell him for me the other day, and after he'd made a bargain for a hundred and twenty with Bryce he went after the hounds, and took some fool's leap or other that did for the horse at once. If it hadn't been for that, I should have paid you a hundred pounds this morning."

The Squire had laid down his knife and fork and was staring at his son in amazement.

"The truth is, sir — I'm very sorry — I was quite to blame," said Godfrey. "Fowler did pay that hundred pounds. He paid it to me when I was over there one day last month. And Dunsey bothered me for the money, and I let him have it, because I hoped I should be able to pay it you before this."

The Squire was purple with anger before his son had done speaking, and found utterance difficult.

"You let Dunsey have it, sir? And how long have you been so thick with Dunsey that you must plot with him to embezzle my money? Are you turning out a scamp? I tell you I won't have it. I'll turn the whole pack of you out of the house together, and marry again. I'd have you to remember, sir, my property's got no entail on it;[1] since my grandfather's time the Casses can do as they like with their land. Remember that, sir. Let Dunsey have the money! Why should you let Dunsey have the money? There's some lie at the bottom of it."

"There's no lie, sir," said Godfrey. "I wouldn't have spent the money myself, but Dunsey bothered me, and I was a fool and let him have it. But I meant to pay it whether he did or not. That's the whole story. I never meant to embezzle money, and I'm not the man to do it. You never knew me do a dishonest trick, sir."

"Where's Dunsey, then? What do you stand talking there for? Go and fetch Dunsey, as I tell you, and let him give account of what he wanted the money for, and what he's done with it. He shall

[1] **got no entail on it:** An *entail* was a provision made in willing property that it should be kept intact and should be handed on to one heir only; usually this would be the eldest son.

repent it. I'll turn him out. I said I would, and I'll do it. He shan't brave me. Go and fetch him."

"Dunsey isn't come back, sir."

"What! did he break his own neck, then?" said the Squire with some disgust at the idea that, in that case, he could not fulfill his threat.

"No, he wasn't hurt, I believe, for the horse was found dead, and Dunsey must have walked off. I dare say we shall see him again by and by. I don't know where he is."

"And what must you be letting him have my money for? Answer me that," said the Squire, attacking Godfrey again, since Dunsey was not within reach.

"Well, sir, I don't know," said Godfrey hesitatingly. That was a feeble evasion, but Godfrey was not fond of lying, and he was quite unprepared with invented motives.

"You don't know? I tell you what it is, sir. You've been up to some trick, and you've been bribing him not to tell," said the Squire with a sudden acuteness which startled Godfrey, who felt his heart beat violently at the nearness of his father's guess. The sudden alarm pushed him on to take the next step — a very slight impulse suffices for that on a downward road.

"Why, sir," he said, trying to speak with careless ease, "it was a little affair between me and Dunsey; it's no matter to anybody else. It's hardly worthwhile to pry into young men's fooleries; it wouldn't have made any difference to you, sir, if I'd not had the bad luck to lose Wildfire, I should have paid you the money."

"Fooleries! Pshaw! it's time you'd done with fooleries. And I'd have you know, sir, you *must* ha' done with 'em," said the Squire, frowning and casting an angry glance at his son. "Your go-ings on are not what I shall find money for any longer. There's my grandfather had his stables full o' horses, and kept a good house, too, and in worse times, by what I can make out; and so might I, if I hadn't four good-for-nothing fellows to hang on me like horseleeches. I've been too good a father to you all — that's what it is. But I shall pull up, sir."

Godfrey was silent. He was not likely to be very penetrating in his judgments, but he had always had a sense that his father's indulgence had not been kindness, and had had a vague longing for some discipline that would have checked his own errant weakness and helped his better will. The Squire ate his bread and meat hastily, took a deep draught of ale, then turned his chair from the table, and began to speak again.

"It'll be all the worse for you, you know — you'd need try and help me keep things together."

"Well, sir, I've often offered to take the management of things, but you know you've taken it ill always, and seemed to think I wanted to push you out of your place."

"I know nothing o' your offering or o' my taking it ill," said the Squire, whose memory consisted in certain strong impressions unmodified by detail; "but I know one while you seemed to be thinking o' marrying, and I didn't offer to put any obstacles in your way, as some fathers would. I'd as lieve you married Lammeter's daughter as anybody. I suppose if I'd said you nay, you'd ha' kept on with it; but for want o' contradiction you've changed your mind. You're a shilly-shally fellow; you take after your poor mother. She never had a will of her own; a woman has no call for one, if she's got a proper man for her husband. But *your* wife had need have one, for you hardly know

"Think! why haven't you the courage to ask her?"

your own mind enough to make both your legs walk one way. The lass hasn't said downright she won't have you, has she?"

"No," said Godfrey, feeling very hot and uncomfortable; "but I don't think she will."

"Think! why haven't you the courage to ask her? Do you stick to it, you want to have *her* — that's the thing?"

"There's no other woman I want to marry," said Godfrey evasively.

"Well, then, let me make the offer for you, that's all, if you haven't the pluck to do it yourself. Lammeter isn't likely to be loath for his daughter to marry into *my* family, I should think. And as for the pretty lass, she wouldn't have her cousin — and there's nobody else, as I see, could ha' stood in your way."

"I'd rather let it be, please, sir, at present," said Godfrey, in alarm. "I think she's a little offended with me just now, and I should like to speak for

myself. A man must manage these things for himself."

"Well, speak then and manage it, and see if you can't turn over a new leaf. That's what a man must do when he thinks o' marrying."

"I don't see how I can think of it at present, sir. You wouldn't like to settle me on one of the farms, I suppose, and I don't think she'd come to live in this house with all my brothers. It's a different sort of life to what she's been used to."

"Not come to live in this house? Don't tell me. You ask her, that's all," said the Squire, with a short, scornful laugh.

"I'd rather let the thing be at present, sir," said Godfrey. "I hope you won't try to hurry it on by saying anything."

"I shall do what I choose," said the Squire, "and I shall let you know I'm master; else you may turn out and find an estate to drop into somewhere else. Go out and tell Winthrop not to go to Cox's, but wait for me. And tell 'em to get my horse saddled. And, stop; look out and get that hack [1] o' Dunsey's sold, and hand me the money, will you? He'll keep no more hacks at my expense. And if you know where he's sneaking — I dare say you do — you may tell him to spare himself the journey o' coming back home. Let him turn ostler [2] and keep himself. He shan't hang on me any more."

"I don't know where he is; and if I did, it isn't my place to tell him to keep away," said Godfrey, moving toward the door.

"Confound it, sir, don't stay arguing, but go and order my horse," said the Squire, taking up a pipe.

Godfrey left the room, hardly knowing whether he were more relieved by

[1] **hack:** a saddle horse.
[2] **ostler** (ŏs′lẽr): stableboy, or groom.

the sense that the interview was ended without having made any change in his position, or more uneasy that he had entangled himself still further in deceit. What had passed about his proposing to Nancy had raised a new alarm, lest by some after-dinner words of his father's to Mr. Lammeter he should be thrown into the embarrassment of being obliged absolutely to decline her when she seemed to be within his reach. He fled to his usual refuge, that of hoping for some unforeseen turn of fortune, some favorable chance which would save him from unpleasant consequences.

CHAPTER X

Christmas Draws Near

[In this chapter you will notice that a change takes place in the attitude of the villagers toward Silas Marner. What caused the change? How does their changed attitude affect Silas Marner? To appreciate the chapter, you must follow closely the implied meaning of events. Notice particularly that it is Christmas. How does Silas Marner's Christmas compare with that of the others in Raveloe?]

Justice Malam was naturally regarded in Tarley and Raveloe as a man of capacious [1] mind, seeing that he could draw much wider conclusions without evidence than could be expected of his neighbors who were not on the commission of the peace. Such a man was not likely to neglect the clue of the tinderbox, and an inquiry was set on foot concerning a peddler, name unknown, with curly black hair and a foreign complexion, carrying a box of cutlery and jewelry, and wearing large rings in his ears. But weeks passed

[1] **capacious** (kȧ·pā′shŭs): vast, roomy.

away, and there was no other result concerning the robbery than a gradual cessation of the excitement it had caused in Raveloe.

Dunstan Cass's absence was hardly a subject of remark; he had once before had a quarrel with his father, and had gone off, nobody knew whither, to return at the end of six weeks, take up his old quarters unforbidden, and swagger as usual. His own family, who equally expected this issue, with the sole difference that the Squire was determined this time to forbid him the old quarters, never mentioned his absence.

To connect the fact of Dunsey's disappearance with that of the robbery occurring on the same day lay quite away from the track of everyone's thought — even Godfrey's, who had better reason than anyone else to know what his brother was capable of. He remembered no mention of the weaver between them since the time, twelve years ago, when it was their boyish sport to tease him; and, besides, his imagination constantly created an alibi for Dunstan; he saw him continually in some congenial haunt, to which he had walked off on leaving Wildfire — saw him sponging on chance acquaintances, and meditating a return home to the old amusement of tormenting his elder brother.

When the robbery was talked of at the Rainbow and elsewhere, in good company, the balance continued to waver between the explanation founded on the tinderbox and the theory of a mystery that mocked investigation. The advocates of the tinderbox-and-peddler view considered the other side a muddleheaded set, and the adherents of the inexplicable more than hinted that their antagonists were animals inclined to crow before they had found any corn.

But while poor Silas's loss served thus

to brush the slow current of Raveloe conversation, Silas himself was feeling the withering desolation of that bereavement about which his neighbors were arguing at their ease. To anyone who had observed him before he lost his gold it might have seemed that so withered and shrunken a life as his could hardly be susceptible of a bruise. But in reality it had been an eager life, filled with immediate purpose, which fenced him in from the wide, cheerless unknown. It had been a clinging life; and though the object round which its fibers had clung was a dead, disrupted thing, it satisfied the need for clinging. But now the fence was broken down — the support was snatched away.

Marner's thoughts were baffled by a blank like that which meets a plodding ant when the earth has broken away on its homeward path. The loom was there, and the weaving, and the growing pattern in the cloth; but the bright treasure in the hole under his feet was gone; the prospect of handling and counting it was gone; the evening had no delight to still the poor soul's craving. The thought of the money he would get by his actual work could bring no joy, for its meager image was only a fresh reminder of his loss; and hope was too heavily crushed by the sudden blow for his imagination to dwell on the growth of a new hoard from that small beginning.

He filled up the blank with grief. As he sat weaving, he every now and then moaned low, like one in pain; it was the sign that his thoughts had come round again to the sudden chasm — to the empty evening time. And all the evening, as he sat in his loneliness by his dull fire, he leaned his elbows on his knees, and clasped his head with his hands, and moaned very low — not as one who seeks to be heard.

And yet he was not utterly forsaken in his trouble. The repulsion Marner had always created in his neighbors was partly dissipated [1] by the new light in which this misfortune had shown him. Instead of a man who had more cunning than honest folks could come by, and, what was worse, had not the inclination to use that cunning in a neighborly way, it was now apparent that Silas had not cunning enough to keep his own. He was generally spoken of as a "poor mushed creatur"; and that avoidance of his neighbors, which had before been referred to his ill will, and to a probable addiction to worse company, was now considered mere craziness.

This change to a kindlier feeling was shown in various ways. The odor of Christmas cooking being on the wind, it was the season when superfluous pork and black puddings are suggestive of charity in well-to-do families; and Silas's misfortune had brought him uppermost in the memory of housekeepers like Mrs. Osgood. Mr. Crackenthorp, too, while he admonished Silas that his money had probably been taken from him because he thought too much of it and never came to church, enforced the doctrine by a present of pigs' pettitoes. [2] Neighbors who had nothing but verbal consolation to give showed a disposition not only to greet Silas, and discuss his misfortune at some length when they encountered him in the village, but also to take the trouble of calling at his cottage, and getting him to repeat all the details on the very spot; and then they would try to cheer him by saying, "Well, Master Marner, you're no worse off nor other poor folks, after all; and if you was to be crippled, the parish 'ud give you a 'lowance."

Mr. Macey, coming one evening ex-

[1] **dissipated** (dĭs′ĭ·pāt′ĕd): scattered, wasted.
[2] **pettitoes** (pĕt′ĭ·tōz): feet.

pressly to let Silas know that recent events had given him the advantage of standing more favorably in the opinion of a man whose judgment was not formed lightly, opened the conversation by saying, as soon as he had seated himself and adjusted his thumbs:

"Come, Master Marner, why, you've no call to sit a-moaning. You're a deal better off to ha' lost your money, nor to ha' kep' it by foul means. I used to think, when you first come into these parts, as you were no better nor you should be; you were younger a deal than what you are now; but you were allays a staring, white-faced creatur, partly like a bald-faced calf, as I may say. But there's no knowing; it isn't every queer-looksed thing as Old Harry's had the making of — I mean, speaking o' toads and such; for they're often harmless, and useful against varmin. And it's pretty much the same wi' you, as fur as I can see. Though as to the yarbs [1] and stuff to cure the breathing, if you brought that sort o' knowledge from distant parts, you might ha' been a bit freer of it. And if the knowledge wasn't well come by, why, you might ha' made up for it by coming to church reg'lar; for, as for the children as the wisewoman charmed, I've been at the christening of 'em again and again, and they took the water just as well. I've been clerk o' this parish forty year, and I know, when the parson and me does the cussing [2] of a Ash Wednesday, there's no cussing o' folks as have a mind to be cured without a doctor, let Kimble say what he will. And so, Master Marner, as I was saying, my advice is, as you keep up your sperrits; for as for

[1] yarbs: herbs.

[2] cussing: Mr. Macey is referring to that part of the service used on Ash Wednesday in the Church of England which begins "Cursed is he."

thinking you're a deep un, and ha' got more inside you nor 'ull bear daylight, I'm not o' that opinion at all, and so I tell the neighbors. For, says I, you talk o' Master Marner making out a tale — why, it's nonsense, that is; it 'ud take a 'cute man to make a tale like that; and, says I, he looked as scared as a rabbit."

Another of Silas's comforters, besides Mr. Macey, came to him with a mind highly charged on the same topic. This was Mrs. Winthrop, the wheelwright's wife. The inhabitants of Raveloe were not severely regular in their churchgoing, and perhaps there was hardly a person in the parish who would not have held that to go to church every Sunday in the calendar would have shown a greedy desire to stand well with Heaven, and get an undue advantage over their neighbors. At the same time it was understood to be requisite for all who were not household servants, or young men, to take the sacrament at one of the great festivals; Squire Cass himself took it on Christmas Day; while those who were held to be "good livers" went to church with greater, though still with moderate, frequency.

Mrs. Winthrop was one of these. She was in all respects a woman of scrupulous conscience, so eager for duties that life seemed to offer them too scantily unless she rose at half-past four. She was a very mild, patient woman, the person always first thought of in Raveloe when there was illness or death in a family, when leeches were to be applied, [3] or there was a sudden disappointment in a monthly nurse. She was a "comfortable woman" — good-looking, fresh-complexioned, having her lips al-

[3] leeches . . . applied: This was a method of drawing blood from a sick person — a common remedy for many illnesses as late as the nineteenth century.

ways slightly screwed, as if she felt herself in a sickroom with the doctor or the clergyman present. But she was never whimpering; no one had seen her shed tears; she was simply grave and inclined to shake her head and sigh. It seemed surprising that Ben Winthrop, who loved his quart pot and his joke, got along so well with Dolly; but she took her husband's jokes and joviality as patiently as everything else, considering that "men *would* be so."

This good, wholesome woman could hardly fail to have her mind drawn strongly toward Silas Marner now that he appeared in the light of a sufferer, and one Sunday afternoon she took her little boy Aaron with her, and went to call on Silas, carrying in her hand some small lard cakes, flat pastelike articles, much esteemed in Raveloe. Aaron, an apple-cheeked youngster of seven, with a clean, starched frill, needed all his adventurous curiosity to embolden him against the possibility that the big-eyed weaver might do him some bodily injury.

They had to knock loudly before Silas heard them, but when he did come to the door he showed no impatience, as he would once have done, at a visit that had been unasked for and unexpected. Silas had inevitably a sense, though a dull and half-despairing one, that if any help came to him it must come from without; and there was a slight stirring of expectation at the sight of his fellow men, a faint consciousness of dependence on their good will. He opened the door wide to admit Dolly, but without otherwise returning her greeting than by moving the chair a few inches as a sign that she was to sit down in it. Dolly, as soon as she was seated, removed the white cloth that covered her lard cakes, and said in her gravest way:

"I'd a baking yisterday, Master Marner, and the lard cakes turned out better nor common."

Dolly sighed gently as she held out the cakes to Silas, who thanked her kindly, and looked very close at them, absently, being accustomed to look so at everything he took into his hand — eyed all the while by the wondering bright orbs of the small Aaron, who had made an outwork of his mother's chair, and was peeping round from behind it.

"There's letters pricked on 'em," said Dolly. "I can't read 'em myself, and there's nobody, not Mr. Macey himself, rightly knows what they mean; but they've a good meaning, for they're the same as is on the pulpit cloth at church. What are they, Aaron, my dear?"

Aaron retreated completely behind his outwork.

"Oh, go, that's naughty," said his mother mildly. "Well, whativer the letters are, they've a good meaning; and it's a stamp as has been in our house, Ben says, ever since he was a little un, and his mother used to put it on the cakes, and I've allays put it on, too; for if there's any good, we've need of it i' this world."

"It's I.H.S.,"[1] said Silas, at which proof of learning Aaron peeped round the chair again.

"Well, to be sure, you can read 'em off," said Dolly. "Ben's read 'em to me many and many a time, but they slip out o' my mind again; the more's the pity, for they're good letters, else they wouldn't be in the church; and so I prick 'em on all the loaves and all the cakes, though sometimes they won't hold because o' the rising — for, as I said, if there's any good to be got we've need of it i' this world — that we have;

[1] **I.H.S.:** an ancient symbol of Christianity, a Latin version of the Greek letters spelling "Jesus."

and I hope they'll bring good to you, Master Marner, for it's wi' that will I brought you the cakes, and you see the letters have held better nor common."

Silas was as unable to interpret the letters as Dolly, but there was no possibility of misunderstanding the desire to give comfort that made itself heard in her quiet tones. He said, with more feeling than before, "Thank you — thank you kindly." But he laid down the cakes and seated himself absently — drearily unconscious of any distinct benefit toward which the cakes and the letters, or even Dolly's kindness, could tend for him.

"Ah, if there's good anywhere, we've need of it," repeated Dolly, who did not lightly forsake a serviceable phrase. She looked at Silas pityingly as she went on. "But you didn't hear the church bells this morning, Master Marner? I doubt you didn't know it was Sunday. Living so alone here, you lose your count, I dare say; and then, when your loom makes a noise, you can't hear the bells, more partic'lar now the frost kills the sound."

"Yes, I did; I heard 'em," said Silas, to whom Sunday bells were a mere accident of the day, and not part of its sacredness. There had been no bells in Lantern Yard.

"Dear heart!" said Dolly, pausing before she spoke again. "But what a pity it is you should work of a Sunday, and not clean yourself — if you *didn't* go to church; for if you'd a roasting bit,[1] it might be as you couldn't leave it, being a lone man. But there's the bakehus, if you could make up your mind to spend a twopence on the oven now and then — not every week, in course — I shouldn't like to do that myself — you might carry your bit o' dinner there, for it's nothing but right to have a bit o'

[1] **bit**: piece of meat.

summat hot of a Sunday, and not to make it as you can't know your dinner from Saturday. But now, upo' Christmas Day, this blessed Christmas as is ever coming, if you was to take your dinner to the bakehus, and go to church, and see the holly and the yew, and hear the anthim, and then take the sacremen', you'd be a deal the better, and you'd know which end you stood on, and you could put your trust i' Them as knows better nor we do, seein' you'd ha' done what it lies on us all to do."

Dolly's exhortation, which was an unusually long effort of speech for her, was uttered in the soothing persuasive tone with which she would have tried to prevail on a sick man to take his medicine or a basin of gruel. Silas had never before been closely urged on the point of his absence from church, and he was too direct and simple to evade Dolly's appeal.

"Nay, nay," he said, "I know nothing o' church. I've never been to church."

"No!" said Dolly in a low tone of wonderment. Then bethinking herself of Silas's advent from an unknown country, she said, "Could it ha' been as they'd no church where you were born?"

"Oh, yes," said Silas meditatively, sitting in his usual posture of leaning on his knees and supporting his head. "There was churches — a many — it was a big town. But I knew nothing of 'em — I went to chapel." [2]

Dolly was much puzzled at this new word, but she was rather afraid of inquiring further, lest "chapel" might mean some haunt of wickedness. After a little thought she said:

[2] **went to chapel:** Silas Marner was formerly a religious dissenter; that is, he belonged to a sect which had broken away from the Church of England. Evidently dissenters worshipped in "chapels" rather than in "churches."

"Well, Master Marner, it's niver too late to turn over a new leaf, and if you've niver had no church, there's no telling the good it'll do you. For I feel so set up and comfortable as niver was when I've been and heard the prayers, and the singing; and if a bit o' trouble comes, I feel as I can put up wi' it, for I've looked for help i' the right quarter, and gev myself up to Them as we must all give ourselves up to at the last; and if we'n done our part, it isn't to be believed as Them as are above us 'ull be worse nor we are, and come short o' Their'n."

Poor Dolly's exposition of her simple Raveloe theology [1] fell rather unmeaningly on Silas's ears, for there was no word in it that could rouse a memory of what he had known as religion. He remained silent, not feeling inclined to assent to the part of Dolly's speech which he fully understood — her recommendation that he should go to church. Indeed, Silas was so unaccustomed to talk that words did not easily come to him without the urgency of a distinct purpose.

But now, little Aaron, having become used to the weaver's awful presence, had advanced to his mother's side, and Silas, seeming to notice him for the first time, tried to return Dolly's signs of good will by offering the lad a bit of lard cake. Aaron shrank back a little, but still thought the piece of cake worth the risk of putting his hand out for it.

"Oh, for shame, Aaron," said his mother, taking him on her lap, however; "why, you don't want cake again yet awhile. He's wonderful hearty," she went on, with a little sigh; "that he is, God knows. He's my youngest, and we spoil him sadly, for either me or the father must allays hev him in our sight — that we must."

[1] **theology** (thē·ŏl'ō·jĭ): religious belief.

She stroked Aaron's brown head, and thought it must do Master Marner good to see such a "pictur of a child." But Marner, on the other side of the hearth, saw the neat-featured rosy face as a mere dim round, with two dark spots in it.

"And he's got a voice like a bird — you wouldn't think," Dolly went on; "he can sing a Christmas carril as his father's taught him; and I take it for a token as he'll come to good, as he can learn the good tunes so quick. Come, Aaron, stan' up and sing the carril to Master Marner, come."

Aaron replied by rubbing his forehead against his mother's shoulder.

"Oh, that's naughty," said Dolly gently. "Stan' up, when mother tells you, and let me hold the cake till you've done."

Aaron was not indisposed to display his talents, even to an ogre under protecting circumstances, and after a few more signs of coyness, consisting chiefly in rubbing the backs of his hands over his eyes, and then peeping between them at Master Marner to see if he looked anxious for the "carril," he at length allowed his head to be duly adjusted, and standing behind the table, which let him appear above it only as far as his broad frill, so that he looked like a cherubic head untroubled with a body, he began with a clear chirp and in a melody that had the rhythm of an industrious hammer:

> God rest you merry, gentlemen,
>   Let nothing you dismay,
> For Jesus Christ our Savior
>   Was born on Christmas Day.

Dolly listened with a devout look, glancing at Marner in some confidence that this strain would help to allure him to church.

"That's Christmas music," she said,

when Aaron had ended and had secured his piece of cake again. "There's no other music equil to the Christmas music — 'Hark, the 'erol angels sing.' And you may judge what it is at church, Master Marner, with the bassoon and the voices, as you can't help thinking you've got to a better place a'ready — for I wouldn't speak ill o' this world, seeing as Them put us in it as knows best. The boy sings pretty, don't he, Master Marner?"

"Yes," said Silas absently, "very pretty."

The Christmas carol, with its hammerlike rhythm, had fallen on his ears as strange music, quite unlike a hymn. But he wanted to show her that he was grateful, and the only mode that occurred to him was to offer Aaron a bit more cake.

"Oh, no, thank you, Master Marner," said Dolly, holding down Aaron's willing hands. "We must be going home now. And so I wish you good-by, Master Marner; and if you ever feel anyways bad in your inside, as you can't fend for yourself, I'll come and clean up for you, and get you a bit o' victual, and willing. But I beg and pray of you to leave off weaving of a Sunday, for it's bad for soul and body — and the money as comes i' that way 'ull be a bad bed to lie down on at the last, if it doesn't fly away, nobody knows where, like the white frost. And you'll excuse me being that free with you, Master Marner, for I wish you well — I do. Make your bow, Aaron."

Silas said "Good-by, and thank you kindly," as he opened the door for Dolly, but he couldn't help feeling relieved when she was gone — relieved that he might weave again and moan at his ease. Her simple view of life and its comforts, by which she had tried to cheer him, was only like a report of unknown objects, which his imagination could not fashion.

And so, notwithstanding the honest persuasions of Mr. Macey and Dolly Winthrop, Silas spent his Christmas Day in loneliness, eating his meat in sadness of heart, though the meat had come to him as a neighborly present. In the morning he looked out on the black frost that seemed to press cruelly on every blade of grass, while the half-icy red pool shivered under the bitter wind; but toward evening the snow began to fall and curtained from him even that dreary outlook, shutting him close up with his narrow grief. And he sat in his robbed home through the livelong evening, not caring to close his shutters or lock his door, pressing his head between his hands and moaning, till the cold grasped him and told him that his fire was gray.

Nobody in this world but himself knew that he was the same Silas Marner who had once loved his fellow with tender love, and trusted in an unseen goodness. Even to himself that past experience had become dim.

But in Raveloe village the bells rang merrily, and the church was fuller than all through the rest of the year, with red faces among the abundant dark green boughs — faces prepared for a longer service than usual by an odorous breakfast of toast and ale. And then the red faces made their way through the black, biting frost to their own homes, feeling themselves free for the rest of the day to eat, drink, and be merry.

At Squire Cass's family party that day nobody mentioned Dunstan — nobody was sorry for his absence, or feared it would be too long. The doctor and his wife, Uncle and Aunt Kimble, were there, and the annual Christmas talk was carried through without any omissions. Cards followed, with

Aunt Kimble's annual failure to follow suit and Uncle Kimble's irascibility [1] concerning the odd trick which was rarely explicable to him, when it was not on his side.

But the party on Christmas Day, being a strictly family party, was not the pre-eminently brilliant celebration of the season at the Red House. It was the great dance on New Year's Eve that made the glory of Squire Cass's hospitality, as of his forefathers', time out of mind. This was the occasion when all the society of Raveloe and Tarley counted on meeting and on comporting themselves with mutual appropriateness. This was the occasion on which fair dames who came on pillions sent their bandboxes before them, supplied with more than their evening costume; for the feast was not to end with a single evening. The Red House was provisioned as if for a siege; and as for the spare featherbeds ready to be laid on floors, they were as plentiful as might naturally be expected in a family that had killed its own geese for many generations.

Godfrey Cass was looking forward to this New Year's Eve with a foolish, reckless longing that made him half deaf to his importunate [2] companion, Anxiety.

"Dunsey will be coming home soon; there will be a great blowup, and how will you bribe his spite to silence?" said Anxiety.

"Oh, he won't come home before New Year's Eve, perhaps," said Godfrey; "and I shall sit by Nancy then and dance with her, and get a kind look from her in spite of herself."

"But money is wanted in another quarter," said Anxiety, in a louder voice,

"and how will you get it without selling your mother's diamond pin? And if you don't get it . . . ?"

"Well, but something may happen to make things easier. At any rate, there's one pleasure for me close at hand — Nancy is coming."

"Yes, and suppose your father should bring matters to a pass that will oblige you to decline marrying her — and to give your reasons?"

"Hold your tongue, and don't worry me. I can see Nancy's eyes, just as they will look at me, and feel her hand in mine already."

But Anxiety went on, though in noisy Christmas company, refusing to be utterly quieted even by much drinking.

CHAPTER XI

A New Year's Eve Party

[In this chapter you are to catch another typical glimpse of the times. Notice especially all the little details which make everyday life of the early nineteenth century seem so strangely unlike that of today. Notice, too, the words new to you which stand for things of long ago and give a quaint, old-fashioned touch to the picture.]

Some women, I grant, would not appear to advantage seated on a pillion, attired in a drab joseph [3] and a drab beaver bonnet, with a crown resembling a small stewpan. It was all the greater triumph to Miss Nancy Lammeter's beauty that she looked thoroughly bewitching in that costume, as, seated on the pillion behind her tall, erect father, she held one arm around him, and looked down, with open-eyed anxiety, at the treacherous snow-cov-

[1] **irascibility** (ĭ-răs′ĭ-bĭl′ĭ-tĭ): hot temper.
[2] **importunate** (ĭm-pôr′tū-nĭt): troublesomely urgent.

[3] **drab joseph**: yellowish-brown riding cloak.

ered pools and puddles, which sent up formidable [1] splashings of mud under the stamp of Dobbin's foot.

Certainly the bloom on her cheeks was at its highest point of contrast with the surrounding drab when she arrived at the door of the Red House, and saw Mr. Godfrey Cass ready to lift her from the pillion. She wished her sister Priscilla had come up at the same time, behind the servant, for then she would have contrived that Mr. Godfrey should have lifted off Priscilla first, and, in the meantime, she would have persuaded her father to go round to the horse block instead of alighting at the doorstep.

It was very painful when you had made it quite clear to a young man that you were determined not to marry him, however much he might wish it, that he would still continue to pay you marked attentions; besides, why didn't he always show the same attentions if he meant them sincerely, instead of being so strange as Mr. Godfrey Cass was, sometimes behaving as if he didn't want to speak to her, and taking no notice of her for weeks and weeks, and then, all of a sudden, almost making love again? Moreover, it was quite plain he had no real love for her, else he would not let people have *that* to say of him which they did say. Did he suppose that Miss Nancy Lammeter was to be won by any man, squire or no squire, who led a bad life? That was not what she had been used to see in her own father, who was the soberest and best man in that countryside, only a little hot and hasty now and then if things were not done to the minute.

All these thoughts rushed through Miss Nancy's mind, in their habitual

succession, in the moments between her first sight of Mr. Godfrey Cass standing at the door and her own arrival there. Happily, the Squire came out, too, and gave a loud greeting to her father, so that, somehow, under cover of this noise, she seemed to find concealment of her confusion and neglect of any suitably formal behavior while she was being lifted from the pillion by strong arms which seemed to find her ridiculously small and light. And there was the best reason for hastening into the house at once, since the snow was beginning to fall again.

The Lammeters were guests whose arrival had evidently been thought of so much that it had been watched for from the windows, for Mrs. Kimble, who did the honors at the Red House on these great occasions, came forward to meet Miss Nancy in the hall, and conduct her upstairs. Mrs. Kimble was the Squire's sister, as well as the doctor's wife — a double dignity, with which her diameter was in direct proportion; so that a journey upstairs being rather fatiguing to her, she did not oppose Miss Nancy's request to be allowed to find her way alone to the Blue Room, where the Miss Lammeters' bandboxes had been deposited on their arrival in the morning.

There was hardly a bedroom in the house where feminine compliments were not passing and feminine toilettes going forward, in various stages, in space made scanty by extra beds spread upon the floor; and Miss Nancy, as she entered the Blue Room, had to make her little formal curtsy to a group of six. On the one hand, there were ladies no less important than the two Miss Gunns, the wine merchant's daughters from Lytherly, dressed in the height of fashion, with the tightest skirts and the shortest waists.

[1] **formidable** (fôr′mĭ-dá-b'l): exciting fear or apprehension; evidently Dobbin is splashing quite high.

But Miss Nancy had no sooner made her curtsy than an elderly lady came forward, whose full white muslin kerchief and mobcap round her curls of smooth gray hair were in daring contrast with the puffed yellow satins and topknotted caps of her neighbors.

"Niece, I hope I see you well in health."

Miss Nancy kissed her aunt's cheek dutifully, and answered, "Quite well, I thank you, aunt, and I hope I see you the same."

"Thank you, niece, I keep my health for the present. And how is my brother-in-law?"

These dutiful questions and answers were continued until it was ascertained in detail that the Lammeters were all as well as usual, and the Osgoods likewise; also that niece Priscilla must certainly arrive shortly. Then Nancy was formally introduced to her aunt's visitors, the Miss Gunns, and these ladies were so taken by surprise at finding such a lovely face and figure in an out-of-the-way country place that they began to feel some curiosity about the dress she would put on when she took off her joseph.

Miss Nancy, whose thoughts were always conducted with the propriety and moderation conspicuous in her manners, remarked to herself that the Miss Gunns were rather hard-featured than otherwise, and that such very low dresses as they wore might have been attributed to vanity if their shoulders had been pretty, but that, being as they were, it was not reasonable to suppose that they showed their necks from a love of display, but rather from some obligation not inconsistent with sense and modesty. She felt convinced, as she opened her box, that this must be her Aunt Osgood's opinion, for Miss Nancy's mind resembled her aunt's to a degree that

everybody said was surprising, considering the kinship was on Mr. Osgood's side; and there was a devoted attachment and mutual admiration between aunt and niece. Even Miss Nancy's refusal of her cousin Gilbert Osgood (on the ground solely that he was her cousin), though it had grieved her aunt greatly, had not in the least cooled the preference which had determined her to leave Nancy several of her hereditary ornaments,[1] let Gilbert's future wife be whom she might.

Three of the ladies quickly retired, but the Miss Gunns were quite content that Mrs. Osgood's inclination to remain with her niece gave them also a reason for staying to see the rustic beauty's toilette. And it was really a pleasure — from the first opening of the bandbox, where everything smelt of lavender and rose leaves, to the clasping of a small coral necklace that fitted closely round her little white neck.

Everything belonging to Miss Nancy was of delicate purity and, as for her own person, it gave the same idea of perfect unvarying neatness as the body of a little bird. It is true that her light brown hair was cropped behind like a boy's, and was dressed in front in a number of flat rings, that lay quite away from her face; but there was no sort of coiffure that could make Miss Nancy's cheek and neck look otherwise than pretty; and when at last she stood complete in her silvery twilled silk, her lace tucker,[2] her coral necklace, and coral eardrops, the Miss Gunns could see nothing to criticize except her hands, which bore the traces of buttermaking, cheese crushing, and even still coarser work. But Miss Nancy was not ashamed

[1] **hereditary ornaments:** family jewels that are handed down from generation to generation.

[2] **tucker:** scarf for the neck.

of that, for while she was dressing she narrated to her aunt how she and Priscilla had packed their boxes yesterday, because this morning was baking morning, and as she concluded this judicious remark, she turned to the Miss Gunns that she might not commit the rudeness of not including them in the conversation.

The Miss Gunns smiled stiffly, and thought what a pity it was that these rich country people, who could afford to buy such good clothes (really Miss Nancy's lace and silk were very costly), should be brought up in utter ignorance and vulgarity. She actually said "mate" for "meat," " 'appen" for "perhaps," and " 'oss" for "horse."

Miss Nancy, indeed, had never been to any school higher than Dame Tedman's. There is hardly a servant maid in these days who is not better informed than Miss Nancy; yet she had the essential attributes of a lady — high veracity,[1] delicate honor in her dealings, deference to others, and refined personal habits.

The anxiety about sister Priscilla, which had grown rather active by the time the coral necklace was clasped, was happily ended by the entrance of that cheerful-looking lady herself, with a face made blowsy by cold and damp. After the first questions and greetings, she turned to Nancy and surveyed her from head to foot — then wheeled her round to ascertain that the back view was equally faultless.

"What do you think o' these gowns, Aunt Osgood?" said Priscilla, while Nancy helped her to unrobe.

"Very handsome indeed, niece," said Mrs. Osgood, with a slight increase of formality. She always thought niece Priscilla too rough.

[1] **veracity** (vĕ·răs′ĭ·tĭ): truthfulness and accuracy.

"I'm obliged to have the same as Nancy, you know, for all I'm five years older, and it makes me look yellow; for she never *will* have anything without I have mine just like it, because she wants us to look like sisters. And I tell her folks 'ull think it's my weakness makes me fancy as I shall look pretty in what she looks pretty in. For I *am* ugly — there's no denying that; I feature my father's family. But, law! I don't mind, do you?" Priscilla here turned to the Miss Gunns, rattling on in too much preoccupation with the delight of talking to notice that her candor was not appreciated. "The pretty uns do for flycatchers — they keep the men off us. I've no opinion o' the men, Miss Gunn. And as for fretting and stewing about what *they'll* think of you from morning till night, and making your life uneasy about what they're doing when they're out o' your sight — as I tell Nancy, it's a folly no woman need be guilty of, if she's got a good father and a good home; let her leave it to them as have got no fortin, and can't help themselves. As I say, Mr. Have-your-own-way is the best husband, and the only one I'd ever promise to obey."

The delicate process of getting her narrow gown over her head without injury to her smooth curls obliged Miss Priscilla to pause in this rapid survey of life, and Mrs. Osgood seized the opportunity of rising and saying:

"Well, niece, you'll follow us. The Miss Gunns will like to go down."

"Sister," said Nancy, when they were alone, "you've offended the Miss Gunns, I'm sure."

"What have I done, child?" said Priscilla, in some alarm.

"Why, you asked them if they minded about being ugly — you're so very blunt."

"Law, did I? Well, it popped out; it's

a mercy I said no more, for I'm a bad un to live with folks when they don't like the truth. But as for being ugly, look at me, child, in this silver-colored silk — I told you how it 'ud be — I look as yellow as a daffodil. Anybody'd say you wanted to make a mawkin [1] of me."

"No, Priscy, don' say so. I begged and prayed of you not to let us have this silk if you'd like another better. I was willing to have *your* choice, you know I was," said Nancy, in anxious self-vindication.

"Nonsense, child! you know you'd set your heart on this; and reason good, for you're the color o' cream. It 'ud be fine doings for you to dress yourself to suit *my* skin. What I find fault with is that notion o' yours as I must dress myself just like you. But you do as you like with me — you always did from when first you begun to walk."

"Priscy," said Nancy gently, as she fastened a coral necklace, exactly like her own, round Priscilla's neck, which was very far from being like her own, "I'm sure I'm willing to give way as far as is right, but who shouldn't dress alike if it isn't sisters? Would you have us go about looking as f we were no kin to one another — us that have got no mother and not another sister in the world? I'd do what was right, if I dressed in a gown dyed with cheese coloring; and I'd rather you'd choose, and let me wear what pleases you."

"There you go again! You'd come round to the same thing if one talked to you from Saturday night till Saturday morning. It'll be fine fun to see how you'll master your husband and never raise your voice above the singing o' the kettle all the while. I like to see the men mastered!"

"Don't talk *so*, Priscy," said Nancy, blushing. "You know I don't mean ever to be married."

"Oh, you never mean a fiddlestick's end!" said Priscilla, as she arranged her discarded dress, and closed her band-box. "Who shall *I* have to work for when father's gone, if you are to go and take notions in your head and be an old maid, because some folks are no better than they should be? I haven't a bit o' patience with you. One old maid's enough out o' two sisters; and I shall do credit to a single life, for God A'mighty meant me for it. Come, we can go down now. I'm as ready as a mawkin *can* be —there's nothing a-wanting to frighten the crows, now I've got my eardroppers in."

Places of honor had been kept for the Miss Lammeters near the head of the principal tea table in the wainscoted parlor, now looking fresh and pleasant with handsome branches of holly, yew, and laurel, from the abundant growths of the old garden; and Nancy felt an inward flutter, that no firmness of purpose could prevent, when she saw Mr. Godfrey Cass advancing to lead her to a seat between himself and Mr. Crackenthorp, while Priscilla was called to the opposite side between her father and the Squire.

It certainly did make some difference to Nancy that the lover she had given up was the young man of quite the highest consequence in the parish — at home in a venerable [3] and unique parlor, which was the extremity of grandeur in her experience, a parlor where *she* might one day have been mistress, with the consciousness that she was spoken of as "Madam Cass," the Squire's wife. Nothing but a becoming blush be-

---

[1] **mawkin:** scarecrow.
[2] **self-vindication** (sĕlf'-vĭn'dĭ-kā'shŭn): defense or justification of oneself.

[3] **venerable** (vĕn'ẽr-à-b'l): worthy of honor and respect; the word generally implies advanced age.

Godfrey made no reply, and avoided looking at Nancy . . .

trayed the moving thoughts that urged themselves upon her as she accepted the seat next to Mr. Crackenthorp; for she was so instinctively neat and adroit in all her actions, and her pretty lips met each other with such quiet firmness, that it would have been difficult for her to appear agitated.

It was not the rector's practice to let a charming blush pass without an appropriate compliment. He was not in the least lofty or aristocratic, but simply a merry-eyed, small-featured, gray-haired man, with his chin propped by an ample, many-creased white neckcloth.

"Ha, Miss Nancy,' he said, turning his head within his cravat, and smiling down pleasantly upon her, "when anybody pretends this has been a severe winter, I shall tell them I saw the roses blooming on New Year's Eve — eh, Godfrey, what do *you* say?"

Godfrey made no reply, and avoided looking at Nancy very markedly; for though these complimentary personalities were held to be in excellent taste in old-fashioned Raveloe society, reverent love has a politeness of its own which it teaches to men otherwise of small schooling. But the Squire was rather impatient at Godfrey's showing himself a dull spark in this way. By this advanced hour of the day, the Squire was always in higher spirits than we have seen him in at the breakfast table, and felt it quite pleasant to fulfill the hereditary duty of being noisily jovial and patronizing; the large silver snuffbox was in active service, and was offered without fail to all neighbors from time to time, however often they might have declined the favor.

At present, the Squire had only given an express welcome to the heads of families as they appeared; but always as the evening deepened, his hospitality rayed out more widely, till he had tapped the youngest guests on the back and shown a peculiar fondness for their presence, in the full belief that they must feel their lives more happy by their belonging to a parish where there was such a hearty man as Squire Cass to invite them and wish them well. Even in this early stage of his jovial mood, it was natural that he should wish to supply his son's deficiencies by looking and speaking for him.

"Ay, ay," he began, offering his snuffbox to Mr. Lammeter, who for the second time bowed his head and waved his hand in stiff rejection of the offer, "us old fellows may wish ourselves young tonight, when we see the mistletoe bough in the White Parlor. It's true, most things are gone back'ard in these last thirty years — the country's going down since the old king [1] fell ill. But when I look at Miss Nancy here, I begin to think the lasses keep up their quality; ding me if I remember a sample to match her. No offense to you madam," he added, bending to Mrs. Crackenthorp, who sat by him, "I didn't know *you* when you were as young as Miss Nancy here."

Mrs. Crackenthorp — a small blinking woman, who fidgeted incessantly with her lace, ribbons, and gold chain — now blinked and fidgeted toward the Squire, and said, "Oh, no — no offense."

"Miss Nancy's wonderful like what her mother was, though; isn't she, Kimble?" said the stout lady of that name, looking round for her husband.

But Dr. Kimble, being a thin and agile man, was flitting about the room with his hands in his pockets, making himself agreeable to his feminine patients, with medical impartiality, and being welcomed everywhere. Time out of mind the Raveloe doctor had been a Kimble; Kimble was inherently a doc-

[1] **old king:** George III, who fell ill in 1810.

tor's name; and it was difficult to contemplate firmly the melancholy fact that the actual Kimble had no son, so that his practice might one day be handed over to a successor with the incongruous name of Taylor or Johnson.

"Did you speak to me, my dear?" said the doctor, coming quickly to his wife's side; but, as if foreseeing that she would be too much out of breath to repeat her remark, he went on immediately — "Ha, Miss Priscilla, the sight of you revives the taste of that superexcellent pork pie. I hope the batch isn't near an end."

"Yes, indeed, it is, doctor," said Priscilla; "but I'll answer for it the next shall be as good. My pork pies don't turn out well by chance."

"Not as your doctoring does, eh, Kimble? — because folks forget to take your physic, eh?" said the Squire, who regarded physic and doctors as many loyal churchmen regard the church and the clergy — tasting a joke against them when he was in health, but impatiently eager for their aid when anything was the matter with him. He tapped his box, and looked round with a triumphant laugh.

"Ah, she has a quick wit, my friend Priscilla has," said the doctor. "She saves a little pepper to sprinkle over her talk — that's the reason why she never puts too much into her pies. There's my wife now, she never has an answer at her tongue's end; but if I offend her, she's sure to scarify [1] my throat with black pepper the next day. That's an awful tit for tat." The vivacious doctor made a pathetic grimace.

"Did you ever hear the like?" said Mrs. Kimble, laughing above her double chin with much good humor, aside to Mrs. Crackenthorp, who blinked and nodded, and amiably intended to smile,

[1] **scarify** (skăr'ĭ-fī): to mark with scars.

but the intention lost itself in small twitchings and noises.

"I suppose that's the sort of tit for tat adopted in your profession, Kimble, if you've a grudge against a patient," said the rector.

"Never do have a grudge against our patients," said Dr. Kimble, "except when they leave us; and then, you see, we haven't the chance of prescribing for 'em. Ha, Miss Nancy," he continued, suddenly skipping to Nancy's side, "you won't forget your promise? You're to save a dance for me, you know."

"Come, come, Kimble, don't you be too for'ard," said the Squire. "Give the young uns fair play. There's my son Godfrey'll be wanting to have a round with you if you run off with Miss Nancy. He's bespoke her for the first dance, I'll be bound. Eh, sir! what do you say?" he continued, throwing himself backward, and looking at Godfrey. "Haven't you asked Miss Nancy to open the dance with you?"

Godfrey, sorely uncomfortable under this significant insistence about Nancy, and afraid to think where it would end by the time his father had set his usual hospitable example of drinking before and after supper, saw no course open but to turn to Nancy and say, with as little awkwardness as possible:

"No, I've not asked her yet, but I hope she'll consent — if somebody else hasn't been before me."

"No, I've not engaged myself," said Nancy quietly, though blushingly. (If Mr. Godfrey founded any hopes on her consenting to dance with him he would soon be undeceived, but there was no need for her to be uncivil.)

"Then I hope you've no objections to dancing with me," said Godfrey, beginning to lose the sense that there was anything uncomfortable in this arrangement.

Solomon . . . fell into the tune which he knew would be taken as a special compliment . . .

"No, no objections," said Nancy, in a cold tone.

"Ah, well, you're a lucky fellow, Godfrey," said Uncle Kimble; "but you're my godson, so I won't stand in your way. Else I'm not so very old, eh, my dear?" he went on, skipping to his wife's side again. "You wouldn't mind my having a second after you were gone — not if I cried a good deal first?"

"Come, come, take a cup o' tea and stop your tongue, do," said good-humored Mrs. Kimble, feeling some pride in a husband who must be regarded as so clever and amusing by the company generally. If he had only not been irritable at cards!

While safe, well-tested personalities were enlivening the tea in this way, the sound of the fiddle approaching made the young people look at each other with sympathetic impatience for the end of the meal.

"Why, there's Solomon in the hall," said the Squire, "and playing my fav'rite tune, I believe — 'The Flaxenheaded Plowboy.' Bob," he called out to his third long-legged son, who was at the other end of the room, "open the door, and tell Solomon to come in. He shall give us a tune here."

Bob obeyed, and Solomon walked in, fiddling as he walked, for he would on no account break off in the middle of a tune.

"Here, Solomon," said the Squire, with loud patronage. "Round here, my man. Ah, I knew it was 'The Flaxenheaded Plowboy'; there's no finer tune."

Solomon Macey, a small, hale old man with an abundant crop of long white hair reaching nearly to his shoulders, advanced to the indicated spot, bowing reverently while he fiddled. As soon as he had repeated the tune and lowered his fiddle, he bowed again to the Squire and the rector, and said, "I hope I see your honor and your reverence well, and wishing you health and long life and a happy New Year. And wishing the same to you, Mr. Lammeter, sir; and to the other gentlemen, and the madams, and the young lasses."

As Solomon uttered the last words, he bowed in all directions; thereupon he fell into the tune which he knew would be taken as a special compliment by Mr. Lammeter.

"Thank ye, Solomon, thank ye," said Mr. Lammeter, when the fiddle paused again. "That's 'Over the Hills and Far Away,' that is. My father used to say to me whenever we heard that tune, 'Ah, lad, *I* come from over the hills and far away.' There's a many tunes I don't make head or tail of; but that speaks to me like the blackbird's whistle. I suppose it's the name; there's a deal in the name of a tune."

But Solomon was already impatient to prelude again, and presently broke with much spirit into "Sir Roger de Coverley," at which there was a sound of chairs pushed back, and laughing voices.

"Ay, ay, Solomon, we know what that means," said the Squire, rising. "It's time to begin the dance, eh? Lead the way, then, and we'll all follow you."

So Solomon, holding his white head on one side and playing vigorously, marched forward at the head of the gay procession into the White Parlor, where the mistletoe bough was hung, and multitudinous tallow candles made rather a brilliant effect, gleaming from among the berried holly boughs, and reflected in the old-fashioned oval mirrors fastened in the panels of the white wainscot.

Already, Mr. Macey and a few other privileged villagers, who were allowed to be spectators on these great occasions, were seated on benches placed for them near the door; and great was the admiration and satisfaction in that quarter when the couples had formed themselves for the dance, and the Squire led off with Mrs. Crackenthorp, joining hands with the rector and Mrs. Osgood. That was as it should be — that was what everybody had been used to — and the charter of Raveloe seemed to be renewed by the ceremony.

It was not thought of as unbecoming for the old and middle-aged people to dance a little before sitting down to cards, but rather as part of their social duties.

"The Squire's pretty springy, considering his weight," said Mr. Macey, "and he stamps uncommon well. But Mr. Lammeter beats 'em all for shapes; you see, he holds his head like a codger, and he isn't so cushiony as most o' the oldish gentlefolks — they run fat in gen-

eral; and he's got a fine leg. The parson's nimble enough, but he hasn't got much of a leg; it's a bit too thick down'ard, and his knees might be a bit nearer wi'out damage; but he might do worse, he might do worse. Though he hasn't that grand way o' waving his hand as the Squire has."

"Talk o' nimbleness, look at Mrs. Osgood," said Ben Winthrop, who was holding his son Aaron between his knees. "She trips along with her little steps, so as nobody can see how she goes -- it's like as if she had little wheels to her feet."

"Fayder," said Aaron, whose feet were busy beating out the tune, "how does that big cock's feather stick in Mrs. Crackenthorp's yead? Is there a little hole for it, like in my shuttle-cock?"

"Hush, lad, hush; that's the way the ladies dress theirselves, that is," said the father; adding, however, in an undertone to Mr. Macey, "It does make her look funny, though — partly like a short-necked bottle wi' a long quill in it. Hey, by jingo, there's the young Squire leading off now, wi' Miss Nancy for partners. There's a lass for you! — like a pink-and-white posy — there's nobody 'ud think as anybody could be so pritty. I shouldn't wonder if she's Madam Cass some day, arter all — and nobody more rightfuller, for they'd make a fine match. You can find nothing against Master Godfrey's shapes, Macey, I'll bet a penny."

"Tchuh!" said Mr. Macey, provoked to increased severity, "he isn't come to his right color yet; he's partly like a slack-baked [1] pie. And I doubt he's got a soft place in his head, else why should he be turned round the finger by that offal Dunsey as nobody's seen o' late, and let him kill that fine hunting hoss as

[1] slack-baked: underdone.

was the talk o' the country? And one while he was allays after Miss Nancy, and then it all went off again, like a smell o' hot porridge, as I may say. That wasn't my way when *I* went a-coorting."

"Ah, but mayhap Miss Nancy hung off, like, and your lass didn't," said Ben.

"I should say she didn't," said Mr. Macey, significantly. "Before I said 'sniff,' I took care to know as she'd say 'snaff,' and pretty quick, too. I wasn't a-going to open *my* mouth, like a dog at a fly, and snap it to again, wi' nothing to swaller."

"Well, I think Miss Nancy's a-coming round again," said Ben, "for Master Godfrey doesn't look so downhearted tonight. And I see he's for taking her away to sit down, now they're at the end o' the dance: that looks like sweethearting, that does."

The reason why Godfrey and Nancy had left the dance was not so tender as Ben imagined. In the close press of couples a slight accident had happened to Nancy's dress, which, while it was short enough to show her neat ankle in front, was long enough behind to be caught under the stately stamp of the Squire's foot, so as to rend certain stitches at the waist, and cause much sisterly agitation in Priscilla's mind, as well as serious concern in Nancy's.

Nancy had no sooner completed her duty in the figure they were dancing than she said to Godfrey, with a deep blush, that she must go and sit down till Priscilla could come to her. No reason less urgent than this could have prevailed on Nancy to give Godfrey this opportunity of sitting apart with her. As for Godfrey, he was feeling so happy and oblivious under the long charm of the country-dance [1] with Nancy, that he got rather bold on the strength of her

[1] **country-dance:** a dance in which partners are arranged in two lines facing each other.

confusion, and was capable of leading her straight away, without leave asked, into the adjoining small parlor, where the card tables were set.

"Oh, no, thank you," said Nancy coldly, as soon as she perceived where he was going, "not in there. I'll wait here till Priscilla's ready to come to me. I'm sorry to bring you out of the dance and make myself troublesome."

"Why, you'll be more comfortable here by yourself," said the artful Godfrey; "I'll leave you here till your sister can come." He spoke in an indifferent tone.

That was an agreeable proposition, and just what Nancy desired; why, then, was she a little hurt that Mr. Godfrey should make it? They entered, and she seated herself on a chair against one of the card tables, as the stiffest and most unapproachable position she could choose.

"Thank you, sir," she said immediately. "I needn't give you any more trouble. I'm sorry you've had such an unlucky partner."

"That's very ill-natured of you," said Godfrey, standing by her without any sign of intended departure, "to be sorry you've danced with me."

"Oh, no, sir, I don't mean to say what's ill-natured at all," said Nancy, looking distractingly prim and pretty. "When gentlemen have so many pleasures, one dance can matter but very little."

"You know that isn't true. You know one dance with you matters more to me than all the other pleasures in the world."

It was a long, long while since Godfrey had said anything so direct as that, and Nancy was startled. But her instinctive dignity made her sit perfectly still, and only throw a little more decision into her voice as she said:

"No, indeed, Mr. Godfrey, that's not known to me, and I have very good reasons for thinking different. But if it's true, I don't wish to hear it."

"Would you never forgive me, then, Nancy — never think well of me, let what would happen — would you never think the present made amends for the past? Not if I turned a good fellow, and gave up everything you didn't like?"

Godfrey was half conscious that this sudden opportunity of speaking to Nancy alone had driven him beside himself; but blind feeling had got the mastery of his tongue. Nancy really felt much agitated by the possibility Godfrey's words suggested, but this very pressure of emotion roused all her power of self-command.

"I should be glad to see a good change in anybody, Mr. Godfrey," she answered, with the slightest discernible difference of tone, "but it 'ud be better if no change was wanted."

"You're very hardhearted, Nancy," said Godfrey pettishly. "You might encourage me to be a better fellow. I'm very miserable — but you've no feeling."

"I think those have the least feeling that act wrong to begin with," said Nancy, sending out a flash in spite of herself. Godfrey was delighted with that little flash, and would have liked to go on and make her quarrel with him; Nancy was so exasperatingly quiet and firm. But she was not indifferent to him yet.

The entrance of Priscilla, bustling forward and saying, "Dear heart alive, child, let us look at this gown," cut off Godfrey's hopes of a quarrel.

"I suppose I must go now," he said to Priscilla.

"It's no matter to me whether you go or stay," said that frank lady, searching for something in her pocket, with a preoccupied brow.

"Do *you* want me to go?" said Godfrey, looking at Nancy, who was now standing up by Priscilla's order.

"As you like," said Nancy, trying to recover all her former coldness, and looking down carefully at the hem of her gown.

"Then I like to stay," said Godfrey, with a reckless determination to get as much of this joy as he could tonight, and think nothing of the morrow.

CHAPTER XII

Gold on Silas's Hearth

While Godfrey Cass was taking draughts of forgetfulness from the sweet presence of Nancy, willingly losing all sense of that hidden bond which at other moments galled and fretted him, Godfrey's wife was walking with slow, uncertain steps through the snow-covered Raveloe lanes, carrying her child in her arms.

This journey on New Year's Eve was a premeditated act of vengeance which she had kept in her heart ever since Godfrey, in a fit of passion, had told her he would sooner die than acknowledge her as his wife. There would be a great party at the Red House on New Year's Eve, she knew; her husband would be smiling and smiled upon, hiding *her* existence in the darkest corner of his heart. But she would mar his pleasure; she would go in her dingy rags, with her faded face, once as handsome as the best, with her little child that had its father's hair and eyes, and disclose herself to the Squire as his eldest son's wife.

It is seldom that the miserable can help regarding their misery as a wrong inflicted by those who are less miserable. Molly knew that the cause of her dingy rags was not her husband's neglect, but the demon Opium to whom she was enslaved, body and soul, except in the lingering mother's tenderness that refused to give him her hungry child. She knew this well; and yet, the sense of her want and degradation transformed itself continually into bitterness toward Godfrey. *He* was well off; and if she had her rights she would be well off, too. The belief that he repented his marriage, and suffered from it, only aggravated her vindictiveness.

She had set out at an early hour, but had lingered on the road, inclined by her indolence to believe that if she waited under a warm shed the snow would cease to fall. She had waited longer than she knew, and, now that she found herself belated in the snow-hidden ruggedness of the long lanes, even the animation of a vindictive purpose could not keep her spirit from failing. It was seven o'clock, and by this time she was not very far from Raveloe, but she was not familiar enough with those monotonous lanes to know how near she was to her journey's end. She needed comfort, and she knew but one comforter — the familiar demon in her bosom; but she hesitated a moment, after drawing out the black remnant, before she raised it to her lips.

In that moment the mother's love pleaded for painful consciousness rather than oblivion — pleaded to be left in aching weariness, rather than to have the encircling arms benumbed so that they could not feel the dear burden. In another moment Molly had flung something away, but it was not the black remnant — it was an empty phial. And she walked on again under the breaking cloud, from which there came now and then the light of a quickly veiled

star, for a freezing wind had sprung up since the snowing had ceased. But she walked always more and more drowsily, and clutched more and more automatically the sleeping child at her bosom.

Slowly the demon was working his will, and cold and weariness were his helpers. Soon she felt nothing but a supreme immediate longing — the longing to lie down and sleep. She sank down against a straggling furze [1] bush, an easy pillow enough; and the bed of snow, too, was soft. She did not feel that the bed was cold, and did not heed whether the child would wake and cry for her. But her arms had not yet relaxed their instinctive clutch; and the little one slumbered on as gently as if it had been rocked in a lace-trimmed cradle.

But complete torpor [2] came at last: the fingers lost their tension, the arms unbent; then the little head fell away from the bosom, and the blue eyes opened wide on the cold starlight. At first there was a little peevish cry of "mammy," and an effort to regain the pillowing arm and bosom; but mammy's ear was deaf, and the pillow seemed to be slipping away backward.

Suddenly, as the child rolled downward on its mother's knees, all wet with snow, its eyes were caught by a bright glancing light on the white ground, and, with the ready transition of infancy, [3] it was immediately absorbed in watching the bright living thing running toward it, yet never arriving. That bright living thing must be caught; and in an instant the child had slipped on all

[1] **furze** (fûrz): a spiny evergreen shrub with yellow flowers.
[2] **torpor** (tôr′pẽr): suspended motion; insensibility.
[3] **ready transition of infancy:** a child's quick shifts of interest and attention.

fours, and held out one little hand to catch the gleam. But the gleam would not be caught in that way, and now the head was held up to see where the cunning gleam came from. It came from a very bright place; and the little one, rising on its legs, toddled through the snow, the old grimy shawl in which it was wrapped trailing behind it, and the queer little bonnet dangling at its back — toddled on to the open door of Silas Marner's cottage, and right up to the warm hearth, where there was a bright fire of logs and sticks, which had thoroughly warmed the old sack (Silas's greatcoat) spread out on the bricks to dry.

The little one, accustomed to be left to itself for long hours without notice from its mother, squatted down on the sack, and spread its tiny hands toward the blaze, in perfect contentment, gurgling and making many inarticulate communications to the cheerful fire, like a new-hatched gosling beginning to find itself comfortable. But presently the warmth had a lulling effect, and the little golden head sank down on the old sack, and the blue eyes were veiled by their delicate, half-transparent lids.

But where was Silas Marner while this strange visitor had come to his hearth? He was in the cottage, but he did not see the child. During the last few weeks, since he had lost his money, he had contracted the habit of opening his door and looking out from time to time, as if he thought that his money might be somehow coming back to him, or that some trace, some news of it, might be mysteriously on the road, and be caught by the listening ear or the straining eye. It was chiefly in the evening twilight, and later whenever the night was not dark, that Silas looked out on that narrow prospect round the stone pit, listening and gazing, not with

. . . the warmth had a lulling effect . . .

hope, but with mere yearning and unrest.

This morning he had been told by some of his neighbors that it was New Year's Eve, and that he must sit up and hear the old year rung out and the new rung in, because that was good luck, and might bring his money back again. This was only a friendly Raveloe way of jesting with the half-crazy oddities of a miser, but it had perhaps helped to throw Silas into a more than usually excited state. Since the oncoming of twilight he had opened his door again and again, though only to shut it immediately at seeing all distance veiled by the falling snow. But the last time he opened it the snow had ceased, and the clouds were parting here and there. He stood and listened, and gazed for a long while — there was really something on the road coming toward him then, but he caught no sign of it; and the stillness and the wide trackless snow seemed to narrow his solitude, and touched his yearning with the chill of despair. He went in again, and put his right hand on the latch of the door to close it — but he did not close it; he was arrested by the invisible wand of catalepsy [1] and stood like a graven image, with wide but sightless eyes, holding open his door, powerless to resist either the good or evil that might enter there.

When Marner's sensibility returned, he continued the action which had been arrested, and closed his door, unaware of the chasm in his consciousness, unaware of any intermediate change, except that the light had grown dim, and that he was chilled and faint. Turning toward the hearth, where the two logs had fallen apart and sent forth only a red uncertain glimmer, he seated himself on his fireside chair, and was stooping to push his logs together, when, to his blurred vision, it seemed as if there were gold on the floor in front of the hearth. Gold! — his own gold — brought back to him as mysteriously as it had been taken away! He felt his heart begin to beat violently, and for a few moments he was unable to stretch out his hand and grasp the restored treasure. The heap of gold seemed to glow and get larger beneath his agitated gaze.

He leaned forward at last, and stretched forth his hand; but instead of the hard coin with the familiar resisting outline, his fingers encountered soft warm curls. In utter amazement, Silas fell on his knees and bent his head low to examine the marvel; it was a sleeping child — a round, fair thing, with soft yellow rings all over its head. Could this be his little sister come back to him in a dream — his little sister whom he had carried about in his arms for a year be-fore she died, when he was a small boy without shoes or stockings? That was the first thought that darted across Silas's blank wonderment. *Was it a dream?* He rose to his feet again, pushed his logs together, and, throwing on some dried leaves and sticks, raised a flame; but the flame did not disperse the vision — it only lit up more distinctly the little round form of the child and its shabby clothing. It was very much like his little sister.

Silas sank into his chair powerless, under the double presence of an inexplicable surprise and a hurrying influx of memories. How and when had the child come in without his knowledge? He had never been beyond the door. But along with that question, and almost thrusting it away, there was a vision of the old home and the old streets leading to the Lantern Yard — and within that vision another, of the thoughts which had been present with him in those far-off scenes. The thoughts were strange to him now, like old friendships impossible to revive; and yet he had a dreamy feeling that this child was somehow a message come to him from that far-off life; it stirred fibers that had never been moved in Raveloe — old quiverings of tenderness — old impressions of awe at the presentiment of some Power presiding over his life; for his imagination had not yet extricated [2] itself from the sense of mystery in the child's sudden presence.

But there was a cry on the hearth; the child had awaked, and Marner stooped to lift it on his knee. It clung round his neck, and burst louder and louder into that mingling of inarticulate cries with "mammy" by which little children express the bewilderment of waking. Silas pressed it to him, and al-

---

[1] **catalepsy** (kăt′ɑ·lĕp·sĭ): the trancelike state to which Silas Marner was subject.

[2] **extricated** (ĕks′trĭ·kāt′ĕd): freed, disentangled.

most unconsciously uttered sounds of hushing tenderness, while he bethought himself that some of his porridge, which had got cold by the dying fire, would do to feed the child with if it were only warmed up a little.

He had plenty to do through the next hour. The porridge, sweetened with some dry brown sugar from an old store which he had refrained from using for himself, stopped the cries of the little one, and made her lift her blue eyes with a wide, quiet gaze at Silas, as he put the spoon into her mouth. Presently she slipped from his knee and began to toddle about, but with a pretty stagger that made Silas jump up and follow her lest she should fall against anything that would hurt her. But she only fell in a sitting posture on the ground, and began to pull at her boots, looking up at him with a crying face as if the boots hurt her.

He took her on his knee again, but it was some time before it occurred to Silas's dull bachelor mind that the wet boots were the grievance, pressing on her warm ankles. He got them off with difficulty, and baby was at once happily occupied with the primary mystery of her own toes, inviting Silas, with much chuckling, to consider the mystery, too. But the wet boots had at last suggested to Silas that the child had been walking on the snow.

Under the prompting of this new idea and without waiting to form conjectures, he raised the child in his arms, and went to the door. As soon as he had opened it, there was the cry of "mammy" again, which Silas had not heard since the child's first hungry waking. Bending forward, he could just discern the marks made by the little feet on the virgin snow, and he followed their track to the furze bushes. "Mammy!" the little one cried again and again, stretching itself forward, before he himself was aware that there was something more than the bush before him — that there was a human body, with the head sunk low in the furze, and half-covered with the shaken snow.

CHAPTER XIII

A Crisis

It was after the early suppertime at the Red House, and the entertainment was in that stage when bashfulness itself had passed into easy jollity, when gentlemen, conscious of unusual accomplishments, could at length be prevailed on to dance a hornpipe,[1] and when the Squire preferred talking loudly, scattering snuff, and patting his visitors' backs, to sitting longer at the whist table. When the evening had advanced to this pitch of freedom and enjoyment, it was usual for the servants, the heavy duties of supper being well over, to get their share of amusement by coming to look on at the dancing; so that the back regions of the house were left in solitude.

There were two doors by which the White Parlor was entered from the hall, and they were both standing open for the sake of air; but the lower one was crowded with the servants and villagers, and only the upper doorway was left free. Bob Cass was figuring in a hornpipe, and his father, very proud of his lithe son, whom he repeatedly declared to be just like himself in his younger days, was the center of a group

[1] **hornpipe** (hôrn'pīp'): a lively, energetic dance. When sailors performed this dance aboard ship, they were accompanied by a hornpipe, a musical instrument made of a long wooden pipe with a horn opening at the bottom.

who had placed themselves opposite the performer, not far from the upper door. Godfrey was standing a little way off, not to admire his brother's dancing, but to keep sight of Nancy, who was seated in the group, near her father. He stood aloof, because he wished to avoid suggesting himself as a subject for the Squire's fatherly jokes in connection with matrimony and Miss Nancy Lammeter's beauty. But he had the prospect of dancing with her again when the hornpipe was concluded, and in the meanwhile it was very pleasant to get long glances at her quite unobserved.

But when Godfrey was lifting his eyes from one of those long glances they encountered an object as startling to him at that moment as if it had been an apparition from the dead. It *was* an apparition from that hidden life which lies, like a dark by-street, behind the goodly ornamented façade [1] that meets the sunlight and the gaze of respectable admirers. It was his own child, carried in Silas Marner's arms. That was his instantaneous impression, unaccompanied by doubt, though he had not seen the child for months past; and when the hope was rising that he might possibly be mistaken, Mr. Crackenthorp and Mr. Lammeter had already advanced to Silas in astonishment at this strange advent. Godfrey joined them immediately, unable to rest without hearing every word — trying to control himself, but conscious that if anyone noticed him they must see that he was white-lipped and trembling.

But now all eyes at the end of the room were bent on Silas Marner; the Squire himself had risen, and asked angrily, "How's this? — what's this? —

---

[1] **façade** (fȧ·säd′) the exterior or front of something, often quite different from its true nature.

what do you do coming in here in this way?"

"I'm come for the doctor — I want the doctor," Silas had said, in the first moment, to Mr. Crackenthorp.

"Why, what's the matter, Marner?" said the rector. "The doctor's here; but say quietly what you want him for."

"It's a woman," said Silas, speaking low, and half breathlessly, just as Godfrey came up. "She's dead, I think — dead in the snow at the stone pit — not far from my door."

Godfrey felt a great throb; there was one terror in his mind at that moment; it was, that the woman might *not* be dead. That was an evil terror — an ugly inmate to have found a nestling place in Godfrey's kindly disposition; but no disposition is a security from evil wishes to a man whose happiness hangs on duplicity.

"Hush, hush!" said Mr. Crackenthorp. "Go out into the hall there. I'll fetch the doctor to you. Found a woman in the snow — and thinks she's dead," he added, speaking low to the Squire. "Better say as little about it as possible; it will shock the ladies. Just tell them a poor woman is ill from cold and hunger. I'll go and fetch Kimble."

By this time, however, the ladies had pressed forward, curious to know what could have brought the solitary linen weaver there under such strange circumstances, and interested in the pretty child, who, half alarmed and half attracted by the brightness and the numerous company, now frowned and hid her face, now lifted up her head again and looked round.

"What child is it?" said several ladies at once, and, among the rest, Nancy Lammeter, addressing Godfrey.

"I don't know — some poor woman's who has been found in the snow, I believe," was the answer Godfrey wrung from himself with a terrible effort. ("After all, *am* I certain?" he hastened to add, in anticipation of his own conscience.)

"Why, you'd better leave the child here, then, Master Marner," said good-natured Mrs. Kimble, hesitating, however, to take those dingy clothes into contact with her own ornamented satin bodice. "I'll tell one o' the girls to fetch it."

"No — no — I can't part with it, I can't let it go," said Silas abruptly. "It's come to me — I've a right to keep it."

The proposition to take the child from him had come to Silas quite unexpectedly, and his speech, uttered under a strong sudden impulse, was almost like a revelation to himself; a minute before he had no distinct intention about the child.

"Did you ever hear the like?" said Mrs. Kimble, in mild surprise, to her neighbor.

"Now, ladies, I must trouble you to stand aside," said Mr. Kimble, coming from the cardroom, in some bitterness at the interruption, but drilled by the long habit of his profession into obedience to unpleasant calls, even when he was hardly sober.

"It's a nasty business turning out now, eh, Kimble?" said the Squire. "He might ha' gone for your young fellow — the 'prentice, there — what's his name?"

"Might? ay — what's the use of talking about might?" growled Uncle Kimble, hastening out with Marner, and followed by Mr. Crackenthorp and Godfrey. "Get me a pair of thick boots, Godfrey, will you? And stay, let somebody run to Winthrop's and fetch Dolly — she's the best woman to get. Ben was here himself before supper; is he gone?"

"Yes, sir, I met him," said Marner; "but I couldn't stop to tell him anything, only I said I was going for the doctor,

and he said the doctor was at the Squire's. And I made haste and ran, and there was nobody at the back o' the house, and so I went in to where the company was."

The child, no longer distracted by the bright light and the smiling women's faces, began to cry and call for "mammy," though always clinging to Marner, who had apparently won her thorough confidence. Godfrey had come back with the boots, and felt the cry as if some fiber were drawn tight within him.

"I'll go," he said hastily, eager for some movement; "I'll go and fetch the woman — Mrs. Winthrop."

"Oh, pooh, — send somebody else," said Uncle Kimble, hurrying away with Marner.

"You'll let me know if I can be of any use, Kimble," said Mr. Crackenthorp. But the doctor was out of hearing.

Godfrey, too, had disappeared; he was gone to snatch his hat and coat, having just reflection enough to remember that he must not look like a madman; but he rushed out of the house into the snow without heeding his thin shoes.

In a few minutes he was on his rapid way to the stone pit by the side of Dolly, who, though feeling that she was entirely in her place in encountering cold and snow on an errand of mercy, was much concerned at a young gentleman's getting his feet wet under a like impulse.

"You'd a deal better go back, sir," said Dolly, with respectful compassion. "You've no call to catch cold."

"No, I'll stay, now I'm once out — I'll stay outside here," said Godfrey, when they came opposite Marner's cottage. "You can come and tell me if I can do anything."

"Well, sir, you're very good; you've

a tender heart," said Dolly, going to the door.

Godfrey was too painfully preoccupied to feel a twinge of self-reproach at this undeserved praise. He walked up and down, unconscious that he was plunging ankle-deep in snow, unconscious of everything but trembling suspense about what was going on in the cottage, and the effect of each alternative on his future lot. No, not quite unconscious of everything else. Deeper down, and half smothered by passionate desire and dread, there was the sense that he ought not to be waiting on these alternatives; that he ought to accept the consquences of his deeds, own the miserable wife, and fulfill the claims of the helpless child. But he had not moral courage enough to contemplate that active renunciation of Nancy as possible for him; he had only conscience and heart enough to make him forever uneasy under the weakness that forbade the renunciation And at this moment his mind leaped away from all restraint toward the sudden prospect of deliverance from his long bondage.

"Is she dead?" said the voice that predominated over every other within him. "If she is, I may marry Nancy; and then I shall be a good fellow in future, and have no secrets, and the child — shall be taken care of somehow." But across that vision came the other possibility — "She may live, and then it's all up with me."

Godfrey never knew how long it was before the door of the cottage opened and Mr. Kimble came out. He went forward to meet his uncle, prepared to suppress the agitation he must feel, whatever news he was to hear.

"I waited for you, as I'd come so far," he said, speaking first.

"Pooh, it was nonsense for you to come out. Why didn't you send one of the men? There's nothing to be done. She's dead — has been dead for hours, I should say."

"What sort of woman is she?" said Godfrey, feeling the blood rush to his face.

"A young woman, but emaciated, with long black hair. Some vagrant — quite in rags. She's got a wedding ring on, however. They must fetch her away to the workhouse tomorrow. Come, come along."

"I want to look at her," said Godfrey. "I think I saw such a woman yesterday. I'll overtake you in a minute or two."

Mr. Kimble went on, and Godfrey turned back to the cottage. He cast only one glance at the dead face on the pillow, which Dolly had smoothed with decent care; but he remembered that last look at his unhappy, hated wife so well that at the end of sixteen years every line in the worn face was present to him when he told the full story of this night.

He turned immediately toward the hearth where Silas Marner sat lulling the child. She was perfectly quiet now, but not asleep — only soothed by sweet porridge and warmth into that wide-gazing calm which makes older beings feel a certain awe in the presence of a little child. The wide-open blue eyes looked up at Godfrey's without any uneasiness or sign of recognition; the child could make no visible, audible claim on its father; and the father felt a strange mixture of feelings, a conflict of regret and joy, that the pulse of that little heart had no response for the half-jealous yearning in his own, when the blue eyes turned away from him slowly, while the small hand began to pull Marner's withered cheek with loving disfiguration.

"You'll take the child to the parish tomorrow?" asked Godfrey, speaking as indifferently as he could.

"Who says so?" said Marner sharply. "Will they make me take her?"

"Why, you wouldn't like to keep her, should you — an old bachelor like you?"

"Till anybody shows they've a right to take her away from me," said Marner. "The mother's dead, and I reckon it's got no father; it's a lone thing — and I'm a lone thing. My money's gone, I don't know where — and this is come from I don't know where. I know nothing — I'm partly mazed."

"Poor little thing!" said Godfrey. "Let me give something toward finding it clothes."

He had put his hand in his pocket and found half a guinea, and, thrusting it into Silas's hand, he hurried out of the cottage to overtake Mr. Kimble.

"Ah, I see it's not the same woman I saw," he said, as he came up. "It's a pretty little child; the old fellow seems to want to keep it; that's strange for a miser like him. But I gave him a trifle to help him out; the parish isn't likely to quarrel with him for the right to keep the child."

"No; but I've seen the time when I might have quarreled with him for it myself. It's too late now, though. If the child ran into the fire, your aunt's too fat to overtake it; she could only sit and grunt like an alarmed sow. But what a fool you are, Godfrey, to come out in your dancing shoes and stockings in this way — and you one of the beaux of the evening, and at your own house! What do you mean by such freaks, young fellow? Has Miss Nancy been cruel, and do you want to spite her by spoiling your pumps?"

"Oh, everything has been disagreeable tonight. I was tired to death of jigging and gallanting,[1] and that bother about the hornpipes. And I'd got to dance with the other Miss Gunn," said Godfrey, glad of the subterfuge [2] his uncle had suggested to him.

Godfrey reappeared in the White Parlor with dry feet, and, since the truth must be told, with a sense of relief and gladness that was too strong for painful thoughts to struggle with. For could he not venture now, whenever opportunity offered, to say the tenderest things to Nancy Lammeter — to promise her and himself that he would always be just what she would desire to see him? There was no danger that his dead wife would be recognized; those were not days of active inquiry and wide report; and as for the registry of their marriage, that was a long way off, buried in unturned pages, away from everyone's interest but his own. Dunsey might betray him if he came back; but Dunsey might be won to silence.

And when events turn out so much better for a man than he has had reason to dread, is it not a proof that his conduct has been less foolish and blameworthy than it might otherwise have appeared? Where, after all, would be the use of his confessing the past to Nancy Lammeter, and throwing away his happiness? — nay, hers? for he felt some confidence that she loved him. As for the child, he would see that it was cared for; he would never forsake it; he would do everything but own it. Perhaps it would be just as happy in life without being owned by its father, seeing that nobody could tell how things would turn out, and that — is there any other reason wanted? — well, then, that the father would be much happier without owning the child.

---

[1] **gallanting** (gǎl·ǎnt'ing): being courteously attentive to the wishes and requests of the ladies.

[2] **subterfuge** (sŭb'tẽr·fūj): a device or plan to evade or conceal something.

CHAPTER XIV

Eppie

There was a pauper's burial that week in Raveloe, and up Kench Yard at Batherley it was known that the dark-haired woman with the fair child, who had lately come to lodge there, was gone away again. That was all the express note taken that Molly had disappeared from the eyes of men. But the unwept death, which, to the general lot, seemed as trivial as the summer-shed leaf, was charged with the force of destiny to certain human lives that we know of, shaping their joys and sorrows even to the end.

Silas Marner's determination to keep the "tramp's child" was matter of hardly less surprise in the village than the robbery of his money. That softening of feeling toward him which dated from his misfortune was now accompanied with a more active sympathy, especially amongst the women. Notable mothers, who knew what it was to keep children "whole and sweet"; lazy mothers, who knew what it was to be interrupted in folding their arms and scratching their elbows by mischievous children just firm on their legs, were equally interested in conjecturing how a lone man would manage with a two-year-old child on his hands, and were equally ready with their suggestions.

Among the mothers, Dolly Winthrop was the one whose neighborly offices were the most acceptable to Marner, for they were rendered without any show of bustling instruction. Silas had shown her the half guinea given to him by Godfrey, and had asked her what he should do about getting some clothes for the child.

"Eh, Master Marner," said Dolly, "there's no call to buy, no more nor a pair o' shoes; for I've got the little petticoats as Aaron wore five years ago, and it's ill spending the money on them baby clothes, for the child 'ull grow like grass i' May, bless it — that it will."

And the same day Dolly brought her bundle, and displayed to Marner, one by one, the tiny garments in their due order of succession, most of them patched and darned, but clean and neat as fresh-sprung herbs. This was the introduction to a great ceremony with soap and water, from which Baby came out in new beauty, and sat on Dolly's knee, handling her toes and chuckling and patting her palms together with alternate sounds of "gug-gug-gug," and "mammy." The "mammy" was not a cry of need or uneasiness; Baby had been used to utter it without expecting either tender sound or touch to follow.

"Anybody 'ud think the angils in heaven couldn't be prettier," said Dolly, rubbing the golden curls and kissing them. "And to think of its being covered wi' them dirty rags — and the poor mother — froze to death; but there's Them as took care of it, and brought it to your door, Master Marner. The door was open, and it walked in over the snow, like as if it had been a little starved robin. Didn't you say the door was open?"

"Yes," said Silas meditatively. "Yes — the door was open. The money's gone I don't know where, and this is come from I don't know where."

He had not mentioned to anyone his unconsciousness of the child's entrance, shrinking from questions which might lead to the fact he himself suspected — namely, that he had been in one of his trances.

"Ah," said Dolly, with soothing gravity, "it's like the night and the morning,

*Among the mothers, Dolly Winthrop was the one whose neighborly offices
were the most acceptable to Marner . . .*

and the sleeping and the waking, and the rain and the harvest — one goes and the other comes, and we know nothing how nor where. We may strive and scrat and fend, but it's little we can do arter all — the big things come and go wi' no striving o' our'n — they do, that they do; and I think you're in the right on it to keep the little un, Master Marner, seeing as it's been sent to you, though there's folks as thinks different. You'll happen [1] be a bit moithered [2] with it while it's so little; but I'll come, and welcome, and see to it for you; I've a bit o' time to spare most days, for when one gets up betimes i' the morning, the clock seems to stan' still tow'rt ten, afore it's time to go about the victual. So, as I say, I'll come and see to the child for you, and welcome."

"Thank you . . . kindly," said Silas, hesitating a little. "I'll be glad if you'll tell me things. But," he added uneasily, leaning forward to look at Baby with some jealousy, as she was resting her head backward against Dolly's arm, and eying him contentedly from a distance, "but I want to do things for it myself, else it may get fond o' somebody else, and not fond o' me. I've been used to fending for myself in the house — I can learn, I can learn."

"Eh, to be sure," said Dolly gently. "I've seen men as are wonderful handy wi' children. The men are awk'ard and contrary mostly, God help 'em — but when the drink's out of 'em, they aren't unsensible. You see this goes first, next the skin," proceeded Dolly, taking up the little shirt and putting it on.

"Yes," said Marner docilely, bringing his eyes very close, that they might be initiated in the mysteries; whereupon Baby seized his head with both her small arms, and put her lips against his face with purring noises.

"See there," said Dolly, with a woman's tender tact, "she's fondest o' you. She want's to go o' your lap, I'll be bound. Go, then; take her, Master Marner; you can put the things on, and then you can say as you've done for her from the first of her coming to you."

Marner took her on his lap, trembling, with an emotion mysterious to himself, at something unknown dawning on his life. Thought and feeling were so confused within him that if he had tried to give them utterance he could only have said the child was come instead of the gold — the gold had turned into the child. He took the garments from Dolly, and put them on under her teaching, interrupted, of course, by Baby's gymnastics.

"There, then! why, you take to it quite easy, Master Marner," said Dolly; "but what shall you do when you're forced to sit in your loom? For she'll get busier and mischievouser every day — she will, bless her. It's lucky as you've got that high hearth, for that keeps the fire more out of her reach; but if you've got anything as can be split or broke, or as is fit to cut her fingers off, she'll be at it — and it is but right you should know."

Silas meditated a little while in some perplexity. "I'll tie her to the leg o' the loom," he said at last — "tie her with a good long strip o' something."

"Well, mayhap that'll do, as it's a little gell, for they're easier persuaded to sit i' one place nor the lads. I know what the lads are, for I've had four — four I've had, God knows — and if you was to take and tie 'em up, they'd make a fighting and a crying as if you was ringing the pigs.[3] But I'll bring you my lit-

---

[1] **happen:** probably.

[2] **moithered** (moi'thĕrd): bothered or worried.

[3] **ringing the pigs:** putting rings in their noses.

tle chair, and some bits o' red rags and things for her to play wi' an' she'll sit and chatter to 'em as if they was alive. Eh, if it wasn't a sin to the lads to wish 'em made different, bless 'em, I should ha' been glad for one of 'em to be a little gell; I could ha' taught her to scour, and mend, and the knitting, and everything. But I can teach this little un, Master Marner, when she gets old enough."

"But she'll be *my* little un," said Marner hastily. "She'll be nobody else's."

"No, to be sure; you'll have a right to her if you're a father to her, and bring her up. But," added Dolly, coming to a point which she had determined beforehand to touch upon, "you must bring her up like christened folk's children, and take her to church, and let her learn her catechise,[1] as my little Aaron can say — the 'I believe,' and everything, and 'hurt nobody by word or deed' — as well as if he was the clerk. That's what you must do, Master Marner, if you'd do the right thing by the orphin child."

Marner's pale face flushed suddenly under a new anxiety. His mind was too busy trying to give some definite bearing to Dolly's words for him to think of answering her.

"And it's my belief," she went on, "as the poor little creature has never been christened, and it's nothing but right as the parson should be spoke to; and if you was noways unwilling, I'd talk to Mr. Macey about it this very day. For if the child ever went anyways wrong, and you hadn't done your part by it, Master Marner — 'noculation, and everything to save it from harm — it 'ud be a thorn i' your bed forever o' this side the grave; and I can't think as it

'ud be easy lying down for anybody when they'd got to another world, if they hadn't done their part by the helpless children as come wi'out their own asking."

Dolly herself was disposed to be silent for some time now, for she had spoken from the depths of her own simple belief, and was much concerned to know whether her words would produce the desired effect on Silas. He was puzzled and anxious, for Dolly's word "christened" conveyed no distinct meaning to him. He had only heard of baptism, and had only seen the baptism of grown-up men and women.

"What is it as you mean by 'christened'?" he said at last timidly. "Won't folks be good to her without it?"

"Dear, dear! Master Marner," said Dolly, with gentle distress and compassion. "Had you never no father nor mother as taught you to say your prayers, and as there's good words and good things to keep us from harm?"

"Yes," said Silas, in a low voice; "I know a deal about that — used to, used to. But your ways are different; my country was a good way off." He paused a few moments, and then added, more decidedly, "But I want to do everything as can be done for the child. And whatever's right for it i' this country, and you think 'ull do it good, I'll act according, if you'll tell me."

"Well, then, Master Marner," said Dolly, inwardly rejoiced, "I'll ask Mr. Macey to speak to the parson about it; and you must fix on a name for it, because it must have a name giv' it when it's christened."

"My mother's name was Hephzibah," said Silas, "and my little sister was named after her."

"Eh, that's a hard name," said Dolly. "I partly think it isn't a christened name."

---

[1] **catechise** (kăt′ė·kīz): Dolly means *cate-chism* (kăt′ė·kĭz′m), a set of questions and answers used for religious instruction.

"It's a Bible name," said Silas, old ideas recurring.

"Then I've no call to speak again' it," said Dolly, rather startled by Silas's knowledge on this head; "but it was awk'ard calling your little sister by such a hard name, when you'd got nothing big to say, like — wasn't it, Master Marner?"

"We called her Eppie," said Silas.

"Well, if it was noways wrong to shorten the name, it 'ud be a deal handier. And so I'll go now, Master Marner, and I'll speak about the christening afore dark; and I wish you the best o' luck, and it's my belief as it'll come to you, if you do what's right by the orphin child; — and there's the 'noculation to be seen to; and as to washing its bits o' things, you need look to nobody but me, for I can do 'em wi' one hand when I've got my suds about. Eh, the blessed angil! you'll let me bring my Aaron one o' these days, and he'll show her his little cart as his father's made for him, and the black and white pup as he's got a-rearing."

Baby *was* christened, the rector deciding that a double baptism was the lesser risk to incur; and on this occasion Silas, making himself as clean and tidy as he could, appeared for the first time within the church, and shared in the observances held sacred by his neighbors. He was quite unable, by means of anything he heard or saw, to identify the Raveloe religion with his old faith. He had no distinct idea about the baptism and the churchgoing, except that Dolly had said it was for the good of the child; and in this way, as the weeks grew to months, the child created fresh and fresh links between his life and the lives from which he had hitherto shrunk continually into narrower isolation.

Unlike the gold which needed noth-ing, and must be worshiped in close-locked solitude, Eppie was a creature of endless claims and ever-growing desires, seeking and loving sunshine, and living sounds, and living movements; making trial of everything, with trust in new joy, and stirring the human kindness in all eyes that looked on her. The gold had kept his thoughts in an ever-repeated circle, leading to nothing beyond itself; but Eppie was an object compacted [1] of changes and hopes that forced his thoughts onward, and carried them away to the new things that would come with the coming years, when Eppie would have learned to understand how her Father Silas cared for her; and made him look for images of that time in the ties and charities that bound together the families of his neighbors.[2] The gold had asked that he should sit weaving longer and longer, deafened and blinded more and more to all things except the monotony of his loom and the repetition of his web; but Eppie called him away from his weaving, and made him think all its pauses a holiday, reawakening his senses with her fresh life, and warming him into joy because *she* had joy.

And when the sunshine grew strong and lasting, so that the buttercups were thick in the meadows, Silas might be seen in the sunny midday, or in the late afternoon when the shadows were lengthening under the hedgerows, strolling out with uncovered head to carry Eppie beyond the stone pit to where the flowers grew, till they reached some favorite bank where he could sit down, while Eppie toddled to pluck the flowers. Then she would turn her ear to some sudden bird note, and

[1] **compacted:** composed, made up.
[2] **images . . . neighbors:** Silas imagined what his own future would be like by observing his neighbors and their children.

Silas learned to please her by making signs of hushed stillness, that they might listen for the note to come again; so that when it came she laughed with gurgling triumph. Sitting on the banks in this way, Silas began to look for the once familiar herbs again; and as the leaves, with their unchanged outline and markings, lay on his palm, there was a sense of crowding remembrances from which he turned away timidly, taking refuge in Eppie's little world, that lay lightly on his enfeebled spirit.

As the child's mind was growing into knowledge, his mind was growing into memory; as her life unfolded, his soul, long stupefied in a cold, narrow prison, was unfolding too, and trembling gradually into full consciousness.

It was an influence which must gather force with every new year; the tones that stirred Silas's heart grew articulate, and called for more distinct answers; shapes and sounds grew clearer for Eppie's eyes and ears, and there was more that "Dad-dad" was required to notice and account for. Also, by the time Eppie was three years old, she developed a fine capacity for mischief. Sorely was poor Silas puzzled on such occasions by the incompatible demands of love. Dolly Winthrop told him that punishment was good for Eppie, and that as for rearing a child without making it tingle a little in soft and safe places now and then it was not to be done.

"To be sure, there's another thing you might do, Master Marner," added Dolly meditatively; "you might shut her up once i' the coalhole. That was what I did wi' Aaron; for I was that silly wi' the youngest lad as I could never bear to smack him. Not as I could find i' my heart to let him stay i' the coalhole more nor a minute, but it was enough to colly [1] him all over, so as he must be

new washed and dressed, and it was as good as a rod to him — that was. But I put it upo' your conscience, Master Marner, as there's one of 'em you must choose — ayther smacking or the coalhole — else she'll get so masterful, there'll be no holding her."

Silas was impressed with the melancholy truth of this last remark; but his force of mind failed before the only two penal methods open to him, not only because it was painful to him to hurt Eppie, but because he trembled at a moment's contention with her, lest she should love him the less for it. It was clear that Eppie, with her short toddling steps, must lead Father Silas a pretty dance on any fine morning when circumstances favored mischief.

He had wisely chosen a broad strip of linen as a means of fastening her to his loom when he was busy; it made a broad belt round her waist, and was long enough to allow of her reaching the truckle bed [2] and sitting down on it, but not long enough for her to attempt any dangerous climbing. One bright summer's morning Silas had been more engrossed than usual in "setting up" a new piece of work, an occasion on which his scissors were in requisition. These scissors, owing to an especial warning of Dolly's, had been kept carefully out of Eppie's reach; but the click of them had had a peculiar attraction for her ear.

Silas had seated himself in his loom, and the noise of weaving had begun; but he had left his scissors on a ledge which Eppie's arm was long enough to reach; and now, like a small mouse, watching her opportunity, she stole quietly from her corner, secured the scissors, and toddled to the bed again, setting up her back as a mode of con-

[1] colly: dirty with coal dust.

[2] truckle bed: a low bed that was slid under a big one when not in use.

cealing the fact. She had a distinct intention as to the use of the scissors; and having cut the linen strip in a jagged but effectual manner, in two moments she had run out at the open door where the sunshine was inviting her, while poor Silas believed her to be a better child than usual. It was not until he happened to need his scissors that the terrible fact burst upon him; Eppie had run out by herself — had perhaps fallen into the stone pit.

Silas, shaken by the worst fear that could have befallen him, rushed out, calling "Eppie!" and ran eagerly about the unenclosed space, exploring the dry cavities into which she might have fallen, and then gazing with questioning dread at the smooth red surface of the water. The cold drops stood on his brow. How long had she been out? There was one hope — that she had crept through the stile and got into the fields where he habitually took her to stroll. Poor Silas, after peering all round the hedgerows, traversed the grass, beginning with perturbed vision to see Eppie behind every group of red sorrel.

The meadow was searched in vain; and he got over the stile into the next field, looking with dying hope toward a small pond which was now reduced to its summer shallowness, so as to leave a wide margin of mud. Here, however, sat Eppie, discoursing cheerfully to her own small boot, which she was using as a bucket to convey the water into a deep hoofmark, while her little naked foot was planted comfortably on a cushion of olive-green mud. A red-headed calf was observing her with alarmed doubt through the opposite hedge.

Here was clearly a case which demanded severe treatment; but Silas, overcome with convulsive joy at finding his treasure again, could do nothing

but snatch her up, and cover her with half-sobbing kisses. It was not until he had carried her home, and had begun to think of the necessary washing, that he recollected the need that he should punish Eppie, and "make her remember." The idea that she might run away again and come to harm gave him unusual resolution, and for the first time he determined to try the coalhole — a small closet near the hearth.

"Naughty, naughty Eppie," he suddenly began, holding her on his knee, and pointing to her muddy feet and clothes; "naughty to cut with the scissors, and run away. Eppie must go into the coalhole for being naughty. Daddy must put her in the coalhole."

He had expected that this would be shock enough, and that Eppie would begin to cry. But instead of that, she began to shake herself on his knee, as if the proposition opened a pleasing novelty. Seeing that he must proceed to extremities, he put her into the coalhole, and held the door closed, with a trembling sense that he was using a strong measure. For a moment there was silence, but then came a little cry, "Opy, opy!" and Silas let her out again, saying, "Now Eppie 'ull never be naughty again, else she must go in the coalhole — a black, naughty place."

The weaving must stand still a long while this morning, for now Eppie must be washed and have clean clothes on; but it was to be hoped that this punishment would have a lasting effect, and save time in the future; though, perhaps, it would have been better if Eppie had cried more.

In half an hour she was clean again, and Silas, having turned his back to see what he could do with the linen band, threw it down again, with the reflection that Eppie would be good without fastening for the rest of the morning. He turned round again, and was going to place her in her little chair near the loom, when she peeped out at him with black face and hands again, and said, "Eppie in de toalhole!"

This total failure of the coalhole discipline shook Silas's belief in punishment. "She'd take it all for fun," he observed to Dolly, "if I didn't hurt her, and that I can't do, Mrs. Winthrop. If she makes me a bit o' trouble I can bear it. And she's got no tricks but what she'll grow out of."

"Well, that's partly true, Master Marner," said Dolly sympathetically; "and if you can't bring your mind to frighten her off touching things, you must do what you can to keep 'em out of her way. That's what I do wi' the pups as the lads are allays a-rearing. They *will* worry and gnaw — worry and gnaw they will. They know no difference, God help 'em; it's the pushing o' the teeth as sets 'em on, that's what it is."

So Eppie was reared without punishment, the burden of her misdeeds being borne vicariously by Father Silas. The stone hut was made a soft nest for her, lined with downy patience; and also in the world that lay beyond the stone hut she knew nothing of frowns and denials.

Notwithstanding the difficulty of carrying her and his yarn or linen at the same time, Silas took her with him in most of his journeys to the farmhouses, unwilling to leave her behind at Dolly Winthrop's, who was always ready to take care of her; and little curly-headed Eppie, the weaver's child, became an object of interest.

Hitherto he had been treated very much as if he had been a useful gnome or brownie, with whom one would be glad to make all greetings and bargains as brief as possible, but who must be dealt with and occasionally have a present of pork or garden stuff to carry home with him, seeing that without him there was no getting the yarn woven. But now Silas was met with open, smiling faces and cheerful questioning, as a person whose satisfactions and difficulties could be understood. Everywhere he must sit a little and talk about the child, and words of interest were always ready for him: "Ah, Master Marner, you'll be lucky if she takes the measles soon and easy!" — or "Why, there isn't many lone men 'ud ha' been wishing to take up with a little un like that."

Elderly masters and mistresses, seated observantly in large kitchen armchairs, shook their heads over the difficulties attendant on rearing children, felt Eppie's round arms and legs, and pronounced them remarkably firm, and told Silas that if she turned out well (which however, there was no telling), it would be a fine thing for him to have a steady lass to do for him when he got helpless. Servant maidens were fond of carrying her out to look at the hens and chickens, or to see if any cherries could be shaken down in the orchard; and the small boys and girls approached her slowly, with cautious movement and steady gaze, like little dogs face to face with one of their own kind, till attraction had reached the point at which the soft lips were put out for a kiss.

No child was afraid of approaching Silas when Eppie was near him; there was no repulsion around him now, either for young or old; for the little child had come to link him once more with the whole world. There was love between him and the child that blended them into one, and there was love between the child and the world — from men and women with parental looks and tones to the red ladybirds and the round pebbles.

Silas began now to think of Raveloe life entirely in relation to Eppie; she must have everything that was good in Raveloe; and he listened docilely, that he might come to understand better what this life was, from which, for fifteen years, he had stood aloof.

The disposition to hoard had been utterly crushed at the very first by the loss of his long-stored gold; the coins he earned afterward seemed as irrelevant as stones brought to complete a house suddenly buried by an earthquake. And now something had come to replace his hoard which gave a growing purpose to the earnings, drawing his hope and joy continually onward beyond the money.

In old days there were angels who came and took men by the hand and led them away from the city of destruction. We see no white-winged angels now. But yet men are led away from threatening destruction; a hand is put into theirs which leads them forth gently toward a calm and bright land, so that they look no more backward; and the hand may be a little child's.

CHAPTER XV

Brighter Days

There was one person, as you will believe, who watched, with keener though more hidden interest than any other, the prosperous growth of Eppie under the weaver's care. He dared not do anything that would imply a stronger interest in a poor man's adopted child than could be expected from the kindliness of the young Squire, when a chance meeting suggested a little present to a simple old fellow whom others noticed with good will; but he told himself that the time would come when he might do something toward furthering the welfare of his daughter without incurring suspicion. Was he very uneasy in the meantime at his inability to give his daughter her birthright? I cannot say that he was. The child was being taken care of, and would very likely be happy, as people in humble stations often were — happier, perhaps, than those brought up in luxury.

Godfrey Cass's cheek and eye were brighter than ever now. He was so undivided in his aims that he seemed like a man of firmness. No Dunsey had come back; people had made up their minds that he was gone for a soldier, or gone "out of the country," and no one cared to be specific in their inquiries on a subject delicate to a respectable family. Godfrey had ceased to see the shadow of Dunsey across his path; and the path now lay straight forward to the accomplishment of his best, longest-cherished wishes.

Everybody said Mr. Godfrey had taken the right turn; and it was pretty clear what would be the end of things, for there were not many days in the week that he was not seen riding to the Warrens. Godfrey himself, when he was asked jocosely [1] if the day had been fixed, smiled with the pleasant consciousness of a lover who could say "yes," if he liked. He felt a reformed man, delivered from temptation; and the vision of his future life seemed to him as a promised land. He saw himself with all his happiness centered on his own hearth, while Nancy would smile on him as he played with the children.

And that other child — not on the hearth — he would not forget it; he would see that it was well provided for. That was a father's duty.

[1] **jocosely** (jō·kōs′lĭ): jokingly.

Part Two

CHAPTER XVI

A Sunday Afternoon

[Why do people act the way they do? Why, for example, was Silas Marner a hermit and a miser? Was it because he was bewitched, as some of the simple folk in Raveloe thought? Or was there some natural explanation for his strange behavior?

George Eliot thought that there was. She believed that people were what they were largely because the conditions under which they lived made them so. During the period in which she was at work on *Silas Marner*, she wrote to her publisher, "It is intended to set in a strong light the remedial influences of pure, natural relations." This is the underlying idea of the story, and it is illustrated particularly in this chapter and the one following.

As you read, notice the changes that have taken place in the character of Silas Marner in the sixteen years that elapsed between Parts One and Two. Can you recognize the "remedial influences" that have been at work? What stunted ways of life have been remedied? What "pure, natural relations" have caused the remedy?]

It was a bright autumn Sunday, sixteen years after Silas Marner had found his new treasure on the hearth. The bells of the old Raveloe church were ringing the cheerful peal which told that the morning service was ended; and out of the arched doorway in the tower came slowly, retarded by friendly greetings and questions, the richer parishioners who had chosen this bright Sunday morning as eligible for churchgoing. It was the rural fashion of that time for the more important members of the congregation to depart first, while their humbler neighbors waited and looked on, stroking their bent heads or dropping their curtsies to any large ratepayer who turned to notice them.

Foremost among these advancing groups of well-clad people there are some whom we shall recognize. The tall blond man of forty is not much changed in feature from the Godfrey Cass of six and twenty; he is only fuller in flesh, and has only lost the indefinable look of youth — a loss which is marked even when the eye is undulled and the wrinkles are not yet come. Perhaps the pretty woman, not much younger than he, who is leaning on his arm, is more changed than her husband; the lovely bloom that used to be always on her cheek now comes but fitfully; yet to all who love human faces best for what they tell of human experience, Nancy's beauty has a heightened interest. The firm yet placid mouth, the clear veracious glance of the brown eyes, speak now of a nature that has been tested and has kept its highest qualities; and even the costume, with its dainty neatness and purity, has more significance now the coquetries of youth can have nothing to do with it.

Mr. and Mrs. Godfrey Cass (any higher title has died away from Raveloe lips since the old Squire was gathered to his fathers and his inheritance was divided) have turned round to look for the tall, aged man and the plainly dressed woman who are a little behind — Nancy having observed that they must wait for "father and Priscilla."

May there not be some others in this departing congregation whom we should like to see again — some of those who are not likely to be handsomely clad, and whom we may not recognize so easily as the master and mistress of the Red House?

But it is impossible to mistake Silas Marner. His large brown eyes seem to have gathered a longer vision, but in everything else one sees signs of a frame much enfeebled by the lapse of the sixteen years. The weaver's bent shoulders and white hair give him almost the look of advanced age, though he is not more than five and fifty; but

there is the freshest blossom of youth close by his side — a blonde, dimpled girl of eighteen, who has vainly tried to chastise her curly auburn hair into smoothness under her brown bonnet. Eppie cannot help being rather vexed about her hair, for there is no other girl in Raveloe who has hair at all like it, and she thinks hair ought to be smooth. She does not like to be blameworthy even in small things; you see how neatly her prayer book is folded in her spotted handkerchief.

That good-looking young fellow, in a new fustian [1] suit, who walks behind her, is not quite sure upon the question of hair in the abstract, but he doesn't want Eppie's hair to be different. She surely divines that there is someone behind her who is thinking about her very particularly, and mustering courage to come to her side as soon as they are out in the lane, else why should she look rather shy, and take care not to turn away her head from her Father Silas.

"I wish *we* had a little garden, father, with double daisies in, like Mrs. Winthrop's," said Eppie, when they were out in the lane; "only they say it 'ud take a deal of digging and bringing fresh soil — and you couldn't do that, could you, father? Anyhow, I shouldn't like you to do it, for it 'ud be too hard work for you."

"Yes, I could do it, child, if you want a bit o' garden; these long evenings I could work at taking in a little bit o' the waste, just enough for a root or two o' flowers for you; and again, i' the morning, I could have a turn wi' the spade before I sat down to the loom. Why didn't you tell me before as you wanted a bit o' garden?"

"*I* can dig it for you, Master Marner,"

[1] **fustian** (fŭs'chăn): coarse cloth, probably cotton.

said the young man in fustian, who was now by Eppie's side, entering into the conversation without the trouble of formalities. "It'll be play to me after I've done my day's work, or any odd bits o' time when the work's slack. And I'll bring you some soil from Mr. Cass's garden — he'll let me, and willing."

"Eh, Aaron, my lad, are you there?" said Silas. "I wasn't aware of you; for when Eppie's talking o' things, I see nothing but what she's a-saying. Well, if you could help me with the digging, we might get her a bit o' garden all the sooner."

"Then, if you think well and good," said Aaron, "I'll come to the stone pit this afternoon, and we'll settle what land's to be taken in, and I'll get up an hour earlier i' the morning, and begin on it."

"But not if you don't promise me not to work at the hard digging, father," said Eppie. "For I shouldn't ha' said anything about it," she added, half bashfully, half roguishly, "only Mrs. Winthrop said as Aaron 'ud be so good, and —"

"And you might ha' known it without mother telling you," said Aaron. "And Master Marner knows too, I hope, as I'm able and willing to do a turn o' work for him, and he won't do me the unkindness to anyways take it out o' my hands."

"There, now, father, you won't work in it till it's all easy," said Eppie; "and you and me can mark out the beds and make holes and plant the roots. It'll be a deal livelier at the stone pit when we've got some flowers. I'll have a bit o' rosemary, and bergamot, and thyme, because they're so sweet-smelling; but there's no lavender only in the gentlefolks' gardens, I think."

"That's no reason why you shouldn't have some," said Aaron, "for I can bring you slips of anything; I'm forced to cut no end of 'em when I'm gardening, and throw 'em away mostly. There's a big bed o' lavender at the Red House; the missis is very fond of it."

"Well," said Silas gravely, "so as you don't make free for us, or ask for anything as is worth much at the Red House; for Mr. Cass's been so good to us, and built us up the new end o' the cottage, and given us beds and things, as I couldn't abide to be imposin' for garden stuff or anything else."

"No, no, there's no imposin'," said Aaron; "there's never a garden in all the parish but what there's endless waste in it for want o' somebody as could use everything up. It's what I think to myself sometimes, as there need nobody run short o' victuals if the land was made the most on,[1] and there was never a morsel but what could find its way to a mouth. It sets one thinking o' that — gardening does. But I must go back now, else mother 'ull be in trouble as I aren't there."

"Bring her with you this afternoon, Aaron," said Eppie; "I shouldn't like to fix about the garden, and her not know everything from the first — should *you*, father?"

"Ay, bring her if you can, Aaron," said Silas; "she's sure to have a word to say as 'll help us to set things on their right end."

Aaron turned back up the village, while Silas and Eppie went on up the lonely sheltered lane.

"O Daddy!" she began, when they were in privacy, clasping and squeezing Silas's arm, and skipping round to give him an energetic kiss. "My little old Daddy! I'm so glad. I don't think I shall want anything else when we've got a little garden; and I knew Aaron would dig it for us," she went on with roguish

[1] **most on:** most of.

triumph; "I knew that very well."

"You're a deep little puss, you are," said Silas, with the mild passive happiness of love-crowned age in his face; "but you'll make yourself fine and beholden to Aaron."

"Oh, no, I shan't,' said Eppie, laughing and frisking; "he likes it."

"Come, come, let me carry your prayer book, else you'll be dropping it, jumping i' that way."

Eppie was now aware that her behavior was under observation, but it was only the observation of a friendly donkey, browsing with a log fastened to his foot—a meek donkey, not scornfully critical of human trivialities, but thankful to share in them, if possible, by getting his nose scratched; and Eppie did not fail to gratify him with her usual notice, though it was attended with the inconvenience of his following them, painfully, up to the very door of their home.

But the sound of a sharp bark inside, as Eppie put the key in the door, modified the donkey's views, and he limped away again without bidding. The sharp bark was the sign of an excited welcome that was awaiting them from a knowing brown terrier, who, after dancing at their legs in a hysterical manner, rushed with a worrying noise at a tortoise-shell kitten under the loom, and then rushed back with a sharp bark again, as much as to say, "I have done my duty by this feeble creature, you perceive"; while the lady mother of the kitten sat sunning her white bosom in the window, and looked round with a sleepy air of expecting caresses, though she was not going to take any trouble for them.

The presence of this happy animal life was not the only change which had come over the interior of the stone cottage. There was no bed now in the living room, and the small space was well filled with decent furniture, all bright and clean. The oaken table and three-cornered oaken chair were hardly what was likely to be seen in so poor a cottage; they had come, with the beds and other things, from the Red House; for Mr. Godfrey Cass, as everyone said in the village, did very kindly by the weaver; and it was nothing but right a man should be looked on and helped by those who could afford it, when he had brought up an orphan child, and been father and mother to her—and had lost his money, too, so as he had nothing but what he worked for week by week, and when the weaving was going down, too—for there was less and less flax spun—and Master Marner was none so young.

Nobody was jealous of the weaver, for he was regarded as an exceptional person, whose claims on neighborly help were not to be matched in Raveloe. Any superstition that remained concerning him had taken an entirely new color; and Mr. Macey, now a very feeble old man of fourscore and six, never seen except in his chimney corner or sitting in the sunshine at his doorsill, was of opinion that when a man had done what Silas had done by an orphan child it was a sign that his money would come to light again, or leastwise that the robber would be made to answer for it.

Silas sat down now and watched Eppie with a satisfied gaze as she spread the clean cloth, and set on it the potato pie, warmed up slowly in a safe Sunday fashion, by being put into a dry pot over a slowly dying fire, as the best substitute for an oven. For Silas would not consent to have a grate and oven added to his conveniences; he loved the old brick hearth as he had loved his brown pot—and was it not there when he had found Eppie?

Silas ate his dinner more silently than usual, soon laying down his knife and fork, and watching Eppie's play with Snap and the cat. It was a sight that might well arrest wandering thoughts; Eppie, with the rippling radiance of her hair and the whiteness of her rounded chin and throat set off by the dark blue cotton gown, laughing merrily as the kitten held on with her four claws to one shoulder, like a design for a jug handle, while Snap on the right hand and Puss on the other put up their paws toward a morsel which she held out of the reach of both — till Eppie relented, caressed them both, and divided the morsel between them.

But at last Eppie, glancing at the clock, checked the play and said, "O Daddy, you're wanting to go into the sunshine to smoke your pipe. But I must clear away first, so as the house may be tidy when godmother comes. I'll make haste — I won't be long."

Silas had taken to smoking a pipe daily during the last two years, having been strongly urged to it by the sages of Raveloe, as a practice "good for the fits"; and this advice was sanctioned by Dr. Kimble, on the ground that it was as well to try what could do no harm — a principle which was made to answer for a great deal of work in that gentleman's medical practice.

Silas did not highly enjoy smoking, and often wondered how his neighbors could be so fond of it; but a humble sort of acquiescence in what was held to be good had become a strong habit; it had been the only clue his bewildered mind could hold by in cherishing this young life that had been sent to him out of the darkness into which his gold had departed. By seeking what was needful for Eppie, by sharing the effect that everything produced on her, he had himself come to appropriate [1] the forms of custom and belief which were the mold of Raveloe life; and as, with reawakening sensibilities, memory also reawakened, he had begun to ponder over the elements of his old faith, and blend them with his new impressions, till he recovered a consciousness of unity between his past and present.

The sense of presiding goodness and human trust had given him a dim impression that there had been some error, some mistake, which had thrown that dark shadow over the days of his best years; and as it grew more and more easy to him to open his mind to Dolly Winthrop, he gradually communicated to her all he could describe of his early life. The communication was necessarily a slow and difficult process, for Silas's meager power of explanation was not aided by any readiness of interpretation in Dolly, whose narrow outward experience gave her no key to strange customs, and made every novelty a source of wonder that arrested them at every step of the narrative.

It was only by fragments, and at intervals which left Dolly time to revolve what she had heard till it acquired some familiarity for her, that Silas at last arrived at the climax of the sad story — the drawing of lots, and its false testimony concerning him; and this had to be repeated in several interviews, under new questions on her part as to the nature of this plan for detecting the guilty and clearing the innocent.

"And yourn's the same Bible, you're sure o' that, Master Marner — the Bible as you brought wi' you from that country — it's the same as what they've got at church, and what Eppie's a-learning to read in?"

"Yes," said Silas, "every bit the same; and there's drawing o' lots in the Bible,

[1] **appropriate** (ă-prō′prĭ-āt): adopt.

mind you," he added in a lower tone.

"Oh, dear, dear," said Dolly, in a grieved voice, as if she were hearing an unfavorable report of a sick man's case. She was silent for some minutes; at last she said:

"There's wise folks, happen, as know how it all is; the parson knows, I'll be bound; but it takes big words to tell them things, and such as poor folks can't make much out on. But what lies upo' your mind — it's this, Master Marner: as, if Them above had done the right thing by you, They'd never ha' let you be turned out for a wicked thief when you was innicent."

"Ah!" said Silas, who had now come to understand Dolly's phraseology, "that was what fell on me like as if it had been red-hot iron; because, you see, there was nobody as cared for me or clave [1] to me above nor below. And him as I'd gone out and in wi' for ten year and more, since when we was lads and went halves — my own familiar friend, in whom I trusted, had lifted up his heel again' me, and worked to ruin me."

"Eh, but he was a bad un — I can't think as there's another such," said Dolly. "But I'm o'ercome, Master Marner; I'm like as if I'd waked and didn't know whether it was night or morning. I feel somehow as sure as I do when I've laid something up though I can't justly put my hand on it, as there was a rights in what happened to you, if one could but make it out; and you'd no call to lose heart as you did. But we'll talk on it again; for sometimes things come into my head when I'm leeching or poulticing,[2] or such, as I could never think on when I was sitting still."

Dolly was too useful a woman not to

have many opportunities of illumination of the kind she alluded to, and she was not long before she recurred to the subject.

"Master Marner," she said, one day that she came to bring home Eppie's washing, "I've been sore puzzled for a good bit wi' that trouble o' yourn and the drawing o' lots. But it come to me all clear like, that night when I was sitting up wi' poor Bessy Fawkes. It come to me as clear as daylight; but whether I've got hold on it now, or can anyways bring it to my tongue's end, that I don't know. For I've often a deal inside me as 'll never come out; and for what you talk o' your folks in your old country niver saying prayers by heart nor saying 'em out of a book, they must be wonderful cliver; for if I didn't know 'Our Father,' and little bits o' good words as I can carry out o' church wi' me, I might down o' my knees every night, but nothing could I say."

"But you can mostly say something as I can make sense on, Mrs. Winthrop," said Silas.

"Well, then, Master Marner, it come to me summat like this: I can make nothing o' the drawing o' lots and the answer coming wrong; it 'ud mayhap take the parson to tell that, and he could only tell us i' big words. But what come to me as clear as the daylight — it comes into my head as Them above has got a deal tenderer heart nor what I've got — for I can't be anyways better nor Them as made me; and if anything looks hard to me, it's because there's things I don't know on; and for the matter o' that, there may be plenty o' things I don't know on, for it's little as I know — that it is. And so, while I was thinking o' that, you come into my mind, Master Marner, and it all came pouring in; if *I* felt i' my inside what was the right and just thing by you, and them as prayed

---

[1] **clave** (klāv): an old form of the word *cleaved*, meaning "held fast."

[2] **poulticing** (pōl'tĭs·ĭng): applying medication to relieve inflammation.

and drawed the lots, all but that wicked un, if *they*'d ha' done the right thing by you if they could, isn't there Them as was at the making on us, and knows better and has a better will? And that's all as ever I can be sure on, and everything else is a big puzzle to me when I think on it. Eh, there's trouble i' this world, and there's things as we can niver make out the rights on. And all as we've got to do is to trusten, Master Marner — to do the right thing as fur as we know, and to trusten. For if us as knows so little can see a bit o' good and rights, we may be sure as there's a good and a rights bigger nor what we can know — I feel it i' my own inside as it must be so. And if you could but ha' gone on trustening, Master Marner, you wouldn't ha' run away from your fellow creaturs and been so lone."

"Ah, but that 'ud ha' been hard," said Silas, in an undertone; "it 'ud ha' been hard to trusten then."

"And so it would," said Dolly; "them things are easier said nor done; and I'm partly ashamed o' talking."

"Nay, nay," said Silas, "you're i' the right, Mrs. Winthrop — you're i' the right. There's good i' this world — I've a feeling o' that now; and it makes a man feel as there's a good more nor he can see, i' spite o' the trouble and the wickedness. That drawing o' the lots is dark; but the child was sent to me; there's dealings with us — there's dealings."

This dialogue took place in Eppie's earlier years, when Silas had to part with her for two hours every day, that she might learn to read at the dame school.[1] Now that she was grown up, Silas had often been led, in those moments of quiet outpouring which come to people who live together in perfect

[1] **dame school:** local primary school where children were taught reading and writing by a woman, usually in her own house.

love, to talk with *her*, too, of the past, and how and why he had lived a lonely man until she had been sent to him. For it would have been impossible for him to hide from Eppie that she was not his own child.

So Eppie had long known how her mother had died on the snowy ground, and how she herself had been found on the hearth by Father Silas, who had taken her golden curls for his lost guineas brought back to him. The tender and peculiar love with which Silas had reared her in almost inseparable companionship with himself, aided by the seclusion of their dwelling, had preserved her from the lowering influences of the village talk and habits. Perfect love has a breath of poetry which can exalt the relations of the least instructed human beings; and this breath of poetry had surrounded Eppie from the time when she had followed the bright gleam that beckoned her to Silas's hearth; so that it is not surprising if, in other things besides her delicate prettiness, she was not quite a common village maiden, but had a touch of refinement. She was too childish and simple for her imagination to rove into questions about her unknown father; and the first time that the idea of her mother having had a husband presented itself to her was when Silas showed her the wedding ring which had been taken from the wasted finger, and had been carefully preserved by him in a little lacquered box shaped like a shoe.

He delivered this box into Eppie's charge when she had grown up, and she often opened it to look at the ring; but still she thought hardly at all about the father of whom it was the symbol. Had she not a father very close to her, who loved her better than any real fathers in the village seemed to love their daughters? On the contrary, who her mother was and how she came to die in that forlornness were questions that often pressed on Eppie's mind. Her knowledge of Mrs. Winthrop, who was her nearest friend next to Silas, made her feel that a mother must be very precious: and she had again and again asked Silas to tell her how her mother looked, whom she was like, and how he had found her against the furze bush, led toward it by the little footsteps and the outstretched arms. The furze bush was there still; and this afternoon, when Eppie came out with Silas into the sunshine, it was the first object that arrested her eyes and thoughts.

"Father," she said, in a tone of gentle gravity, which sometimes came like a sadder, slower cadence across her playfulness, "we shall take the furze bush into the garden; it'll come into the corner, and just against it I'll put snowdrops and crocuses, 'cause Aaron says they won't die out, but 'll always get more and more."

"Ah, child," said Silas, always ready to talk when he had his pipe in his hand, apparently enjoying the pauses more than the puffs, "it wouldn't do to leave out the furze bush; and there's nothing prettier, to my thinking, when it's yellow with flowers. But it's just come into my head what we're to do for a fence — mayhap Aaron can help us to a thought; but a fence we must have, else the donkeys and things 'ull come and trample everything.'

"Oh, I'll tell you, Daddy," said Eppie, clasping her hands suddenly, after a minute's thought. "There's lots o' loose stones about, some of 'em not big, and we might lay 'em atop o' one another, and make a wall. You and me could carry the smallest, and Aaron 'ud carry the rest — I know he would.'

"Eh, my precious un," said Silas, "there isn't enough stones to go all round; and as for your carrying, why, wi' your little arms you couldn't carry a stone no bigger than a turnip. You're dillicate made, my dear," he added, with a tender intonation — "that's what Mrs. Winthrop says."

"Oh, I'm stronger than you think, Daddy," said Eppie; "and if there wasn't stones enough to go all round, why they'll go part o' the way, and then it'll be easier to get sticks and things for the rest. See here, round the big pit, what a many stones!"

She skipped forward to the pit, meaning to lift one of the stones and exhibit her strength, but she started back in surprise.

"Oh, father, just come and look here," she exclaimed — "come and see how the water's gone down since yesterday! Why, yesterday the pit was ever so full!"

"Well, to be sure," said Silas, coming to her side. "Why, that's the draining they're begun on, since harvest, i' Mr. Osgood's fields, I reckon. The foreman said to me the other day, when I passed by 'em, 'Master Marner,' he said, 'I shouldn't wonder if we lay your bit o' waste as dry as a bone.' It was Mr. Godfrey Cass, he said, had gone into the draining; he'd been taking these fields o' Mr. Osgood."

"How odd it'll seem to have the old pit dried up!" said Eppie, turning away, and stooping to lift rather a large stone." See, Daddy, I can carry this quite well," she said, going along with much energy for a few steps, but presently letting it fall.

"Ah, you're fine and strong, aren't you?" said Silas, while Eppie shook her aching arms and laughed. "Come, come, let us go and sit down on the bank against the stile there, and have no more lifting. You might hurt yourself, child. You'd need have somebody to work for you — and my arm isn't over-strong."

Silas uttered the last sentence slowly, as if it implied more than met the ear; and Eppie, when they sat down on the bank, nestled close to his side, and, taking hold caressingly of the arm that was not overstrong, held it on her lap.

"Father," said Eppie, very gently, after they had been sitting in silence a little while, "if I was to be married, ought I to be married with my mother's ring?"

Silas gave an almost imperceptible start, though the question fell in with the undercurrent of thought in his own mind, and then said, in a subdued tone, "Why, Eppie, have you been a-thinking on it?"

"Only this last week, father," said Eppie, "since Aaron talked to me about it."

"And what did he say?" said Silas, still in the same subdued way, as if he were anxious lest he should fall into the slightest tone that was not for Eppie's good.

"He said he should like to be married, because he was a-going on four and twenty, and had got a deal of gardening work, now Mr. Mott's given up; and he goes twice a week regular to Mr. Cass's and once to Mr. Osgood's, and they're going to take him on at the rectory."

"And who is it as he's wanting to marry?" said Silas, with rather a sad smile.

"Why, me, to be sure, Daddy," said Eppie, with dimpling laughter, kissing her father's cheek; "as if he'd want to marry anybody else!"

"And you mean to have him, do you?" said Silas.

"Yes, sometime," said Eppie. "I don't know when. Everybody's married sometime, Aaron says. But I told him that wasn't true; for, I said, look at father — he's never been married."

". . . you'll never be lone again . . ."

"No, child," said Silas, "your father was a lone man till you was sent to him."

"But you'll never be lone again, father," said Eppie tenderly. "That was what Aaron said — 'I could never think o' taking you away from Master Marner, Eppie.' And I said, 'It 'ud be no use if you did, Aaron.' And he wants us all to live together, so as you needn't work a bit, father, only what's for your own pleasure; and he'd be as good as a son to you — that was what he said."

"And should you like that, Eppie?" said Silas, looking at her.

"I shouldn't mind it, father," said Eppie, quite simply. "And I should like things to be so as you needn't work much. But if it wasn't for that, I'd sooner things didn't change. I'm very happy. I like Aaron to be fond of me, and come and see us often, and behave pretty to you — he always *does* behave pretty to you, doesn't he, father?"

"Yes, child, nobody could behave better," said Silas emphatically. "He's his mother's lad."

"But I don't want any change," said Eppie. "I should like to go on a long, long while, just as we are. Only Aaron does want a change; and he made me cry a bit — only a bit — because he said I didn't care for him, for if I cared for him I should want us to be married, as he did."

"Eh, my blessed child," said Silas, laying down his pipe as if it were useless to pretend to smoke any longer, "you're o'er-young to be married. We'll ask Mrs. Winthrop — we'll ask Aaron's mother what *she* thinks; if there's a right thing to do, she'll come at it. But there's this to be thought on, Eppie: things *will* change, whether we like it or not; things won't go on for a long while just as they are and no difference. I shall get older and helplesser, and be a burden on you, belike, if I don't go away from you altogether. Not as I mean you'd think me a burden — I know you wouldn't — but it 'ud be hard upon you; and when I look for'ard to that, I like to think as you'd have somebody else besides me — somebody young and strong, as 'll outlast your own life, and take care on you to the end." Silas paused, and, resting his wrists on his knees, lifted his hands up and down meditatively as he looked on the ground.

"Then, would you like me to be married, father?" said Eppie, with a little trembling in her voice.

"I'll not be the man to say no, Eppie," said Silas emphatically; "but we'll ask your godmother. She'll wish the right thing by you and her son, too."

"There they come, then," said Eppie. "Let us go and meet 'em. Oh, the pipe! won't you have it lit again, father?"

"Nay, child," said Silas, "I've done enough for today. I think a little of it does me more good than so much at once."

CHAPTER XVII

The Childless Home

[The next four chapters show the changes in Godfrey and Nancy Cass in the sixteen years between Parts One and Two. You should be able to account for these changes by your knowledge of what has happened earlier in the story.]

While Silas and Eppie were seated on the bank discoursing in the fleckered shade of the ash tree, Miss Priscilla Lammeter was resisting her sister's arguments that it would be better to take tea at the Red House, and let her father have a long nap, than drive home to the Warrens so soon after dinner. The family party (of four only) were seated round the table with the Sunday dessert before them, of fresh filberts, apples, and pears, duly ornamented with leaves by Nancy's own hand before the bells had rung for church.

A great change has come over the dark wainscoted parlor since we saw it in Godfrey's bachelor days, and under the wifeless reign of the old Squire. Now all is polish, on which no yesterday's dust is ever allowed to rest, from the yard's width of oaken boards round the carpet to the old Squire's gun and whips and walking sticks, ranged on the stag's antlers above the mantelpiece. All other signs of sporting and outdoor occupation Nancy has removed to another room; but she has brought into the Red House the habit of filial reverence, and preserves sacredly in a place of honor these relics of her husband's departed father. All is purity and order in this once dreary room, for, fifteen years ago, it was entered by a new presiding spirit.

"Now, father," said Nancy, "*is* there any call for you to go home to tea? Mayn't you just as well stay with us? — such a beautiful evening as it's likely to be."

The old gentleman had been talking with Godfrey about the increasing poor rate [1] and the ruinous times, and had not heard the dialogue between his daughters.

"My dear, you must ask Priscilla," he said, in the once firm voice, now become rather broken. "She manages me and the farm, too."

"And reason good as I should manage you, father," said Priscilla, "else you'd be giving yourself your death with rheumatism. And as for the farm, if anything turns out wrong, as it can't but do in these times, there's nothing kills a man so soon as having nobody to find fault with but himself."

"Well, well, my dear," said her father, with a quiet laugh, "I didn't say you don't manage for everybody's good."

"Then manage so as you may stay for tea, Priscilla," said Nancy, putting her hand on her sister's arm affectionately. "Come now; and we'll go round the garden while father has his nap."

"My dear child, he'll have a beautiful nap in the gig,[2] for I shall drive. And as for staying for tea, I can't hear of it; for there's this dairymaid, now she knows she's to be married, she'd as lief pour the new milk in the pig trough as into the pans. So come and let me put my bonnet on, and there'll be time for us to walk round the garden while the horse is being put in."

When the sisters were treading the neatly swept garden walks, Priscilla said: "I'm glad as anything at your husband's making that exchange o' land with Cousin Osgood, and beginning the dairying. It's a thousand pities you didn't do it before; for it'll give you something to fill your mind. There's nothing like a dairy if folks want a bit o' worrit [3] to make the days pass. For as for rubbing furniture, when you can once see your face in a table there's nothing else to look for; but there's always something fresh with the dairy. My dear," added Priscilla, pressing her sister's hand affectionately as they walked side by side, "you'll never be low when you've got a dairy."

"Ah, Priscilla," said Nancy, returning the pressure with a grateful glance of her clear eyes, "but it won't make up to Godfrey; a dairy's not so much to a man. And it's only what he cares for that ever makes me low. I'm contented with the blessings we have, if he could be contented."

"It drives me past patience," said Priscilla impetuously, "that way o' the men — always wanting and wanting, and never easy with what they've got; they can't sit comfortable in their chairs when they've neither ache nor pain, but either they must stick a pipe in their mouths, to make 'em better than well, or else they must be swallowing something strong, though they're forced to make haste before the next meal comes in. But joyful be it spoken, our father was never that sort o' man. And if it had pleased God to make you ugly, like me, so as the men wouldn't ha' run after you, we might have kept to our own family, and had nothing to do with folks as have got uneasy blood in their veins."

"Oh, don't say so, Priscilla," said Nancy, repenting that she had called forth this outburst, "nobody has any occasion

---

[1] **poor rate:** a tax levied by the church wardens in a parish for relief of the poor.

[2] **gig:** two-wheeled carriage.

[3] **worrit** (wûr′ĭt): worry or trouble.

to find fault with Godfrey. It's natural he should be disappointed at not having any children; every man likes to have somebody to work for and lay by for, and he always counted so on making a fuss with 'em when they were little. There's many another man 'ud hanker more than he does He' the best of husbands."

"Oh, I know," said Priscilla, smiling sarcastically, "I know the way o' wives; they set one on to abuse their husbands, and then they turn round on one and praise 'em as if they wanted to sell 'em. But father 'll be waiting for me; we must turn now."

The large gig with the steady old gray was at the front door, and Mr. Lammeter was already on the stone steps, passing the time in recalling to Godfrey what very fine points Speckle had when his master used to ride him.

"Mind you bring Nancy to the Warrens before the week's out, Mr. Cass," was Priscilla's parting injunction, as she took the reins, and shook them gently.

"I shall just take a turn to the fields against the stone pit, Nancy, and look at the draining," said Godfrey.

"You'll be in again by teatime, dear?"

"Oh, yes, I shall be back in an hour."

It was Godfrey's custom on a Sunday afternoon to do a little contemplative farming in a leisurely walk. Nancy seldom accompanied him; for the women of her generation were not given to much walking beyond their own house and garden, finding sufficient exercise in domestic duties. So when Priscilla was not with her, she usually sat with Mant's Bible [1] before her, and after following the text with her eyes for a little while, she would gradually permit them to wander as her thought had already insisted on wandering.

[1] **Mant's Bible:** an edition of the Bible published by Richard Mant in 1817.

But Nancy's Sunday thoughts were rarely quite out of keeping with the devout and reverential intention implied by the book spread open before her. She filled the vacant moments by living inwardly, again and again, through all her remembered experience, especially through the fifteen years of her married time, in which her life and its significance had been doubled. She recalled the small details, the words, tones, and looks, in the critical scenes which had opened a new epoch for her by giving her a deeper insight into the relations and trials of life, or which had called on her for some little effort of forbearance, or of painful adherence to an imagined or real duty — asking herself continually whether she had been in any respect blamable.

There was one main thread of painful experience in Nancy's married life, and on it hung certain deeply felt scenes, which were the oftenest revived in retrospect. The short dialogue with Priscilla in the garden had determined the current of retrospect in that frequent direction this particular Sunday afternoon. The first wandering of her thought from the text was into an imaginary enlargement of the defense she had set up for her husband against Priscilla's implied blame. Nancy's deepest wounds had all come from the perception that the absence of children from their hearth was dwelt on in her husband's mind as a privation to which he could not reconcile himself.

Yet sweet Nancy might have been expected to feel still more keenly the denial of a blessing to which she had looked forward with all the varied expectations and preparations, solemn and prettily trivial, which fill the mind of a loving woman when she expects to become a mother. Was there not a drawer filled with the neat work of her hands, all unworn and untouched, just as she had arranged it there fourteen years ago — just, but for one little dress, which had been made the burial dress? But under this immediate personal trial Nancy was so firmly unmurmuring that years ago she had suddenly renounced the habit of visiting this drawer, lest she should in this way be cherishing a longing for what was not given.

Perhaps it was this very severity toward any indulgence of what she held to be sinful regret in herself that made her shrink from applying her own standard to her husband. "It is very different — it is much worse for a man to be disappointed in that way; a woman can always be satisfied with devoting herself to her husband, but a man wants something that will make him look forward more — and sitting by the fire is so much duller to him than to a woman." And always, when Nancy reached this point in her meditations — trying to see everything as Godfrey saw it — there came a renewal of self-questioning. *Had* she done everything in her power to lighten Godfrey's privation? Had she really been right in the resistance which had cost her so much pain six years ago, and again four years ago — the resistance to her husband's wish that they should adopt a child?

Adoption was more remote from the ideas and habits of that time than of our own; still Nancy had her opinion on it. And her opinions were always principles to be unwaveringly acted on. Pretty Nancy Lammeter, by the time she was three and twenty, had her unalterable little code, and had formed every one of her habits in strict accordance with that code. She carried these decided judgments within her in the most unobtrusive way; they rooted themselves in her mind, and grew there as quietly as grass.

It was one of those rigid principles which had been the ground of Nancy's difficult resistance to her husband's wish. To adopt a child, because children of your own had been denied you, was to try and choose your lot in spite of Providence; the adopted child, she was convinced, would never turn out well, and would be a curse to those who had willfully and rebelliously sought what it was clear that, for some high reason, they were better without. When you saw a thing was not meant to be, said Nancy, it was a bounden duty to leave off so much as wishing for it.

"But why should you think the child would turn out ill?" said Godfrey. "She has thriven as well as a child can do with the weaver; and *he* adopted her. There isn't such a pretty little girl anywhere else in the parish, or one fitter for the station we could give her. Where can be the likelihood of her being a curse to anybody?"

"Yes, my dear Godfrey," said Nancy, who was sitting with her hands tightly clasped together, and with yearning, regretful affection in her eyes. "The child may not turn out ill with the weaver. But, then, he didn't go to seek her, as we should be doing. It will be wrong; I feel sure it will. Don't you remember what that lady we met at the Royston Baths told us about the child her sister adopted? That was the only adopting I ever heard of; and the child was transported [1] when it was twenty-three. Dear Godfrey, don't ask me to do what I know is wrong; I should never be happy again. I know it's very hard for *you* — it's easier for me — but it's the will of Providence."

Godfrey had from the first specified Eppie, then about twelve years old, as

[1] **transported:** as used here, sent to a penal colony in Australia.

a child suitable for them to adopt. It had never occurred to him that Silas would rather part with his life than with Eppie. Surely the weaver would wish the best to the child he had taken so much trouble with, and would be glad that such good fortune should happen to her; she would always be very grateful to him, and he would be well provided for to the end of his life — provided for as the excellent part he had done by the child deserved.

Was it not an appropriate thing for people in a higher station to take a charge off the hands of a man in a lower? It seemed an appropriate thing to Godfrey, for reasons that were known only to himself; and by a common fallacy, he imagined the measure would be easy because he had private motives for desiring it.

"I was right," Nancy said to herself, when she had recalled all their scenes of discussion — "I feel I was right to say him nay, though it hurt me more than anything; but how good Godfrey has been about it! Many men would have been very angry with me for standing out against their wishes; and they might have thrown out that they'd had ill luck in marrying me; but Godfrey has never been the man to say me an unkind word. It's only what he can't hide; everything seems so blank to him, I know; and the land — what a difference it 'ud make to him, when he goes to see after things, if he'd children growing up that he was doing it all for! But I won't murmur; and perhaps if he'd married a woman who'd have had children, she'd have vexed him in other ways."

This possibility was Nancy's chief comfort; and to give it greater strength, she labored to make it impossible that any other wife should have had more perfect tenderness. She had been *forced* to vex him by that one denial. Godfrey was not insensible to her loving effort, and did Nancy no injustice as to the motives of her obstinacy. It was impossible to have lived with her fifteen years and not be aware that an unselfish clinging to the right and a sincerity clear as the flower-born dew were her main characteristics; indeed, Godfrey felt this so strongly that he was kept in a certain awe of this gentle wife who watched his looks with a yearning to obey them. It seemed to him impossible that he should ever confess to her the truth about Eppie; she would never recover from the repulsion the story of his earlier marriage would create, told to her now, after that long concealment. And the child, too, he thought, must become an object of repulsion; the very sight of her would be painful. The shock to Nancy's mingled pride and ignorance of the world's evil might even be too much for her delicate frame. Since he had married her with that secret on his heart he must keep it there to the last. Whatever else he did, he could not make an irreparable breach between himself and his long-loved wife.

On this Sunday afternoon it was already four years since there had been any allusion to the subject between them, and Nancy supposed it was forever buried.

"I wonder if he'll mind it less or more as he gets older," she thought; "I'm afraid more. Aged people feel the miss of children; what would father do without Priscilla? And if I die, Godfrey will be very lonely — not holding together with his brothers much. But I won't be overanxious, and trying to make things out beforehand; I must do my best for the present."

With that last thought Nancy roused herself from her reverie, and turned her eyes again toward the forsaken page. It had been forsaken longer than she imagined, for she was presently surprised by the appearance of the servant with the tea things. It was, in fact, a little before the usual time for tea; but Jane had her reasons.

"Is your master come into the yard, Jane?"

"No'm, he isn't," said Jane, with a slight emphasis, of which, however, her mistress took no notice.

"I don't know whether you've seen 'em, 'm," continued Jane, after a pause, "but there's folks making haste all one way, afore the front window. I doubt something's happened. There's niver a man to be seen i' the yard, else I'd send and see. I've been up into the top attic, but there's no seeing anything for trees. I hope nobody's hurt, that's all."

"Oh, no, I dare say there's nothing much the matter," said Nancy. "It's perhaps Mr. Snell's bull got out again, as he did before."

"I wish he mayn't gore anybody, then, that's all," said Jane.

"The girl is always terrifying me," thought Nancy; "I wish Godfrey would come in."

She went to the front window and looked as far as she could see along the road, with an uneasiness which she felt to be childish, for there were now no such signs of excitement as Jane had spoken of, and Godfrey would not be likely to return by the village road, but by the fields. She continued to stand, however, looking at the placid churchyard with the long shadows of the gravestones across the bright green hillocks, and at the glowing autumn colors of the rectory trees beyond. Before such calm external beauty the presence of a vague fear is more distinctly felt — like a raven flapping its slow wings across the sunny air. Nancy wished more and more that Godfrey would come in.

CHAPTER XVIII

Revelations

[It was a favorite theme of George Eliot's that wrongdoing carried with it the germ of its own punishment, and that somehow righteous living would be rewarded. Notice how *justly* the problems of the story are solved in the next three chapters.]

Someone opened the door at the other end of the room, and Nancy felt that it was her husband. She turned from the window with gladness in her eyes, for the wife's chief dread was stilled.

"Dear, I'm so thankful you're come," she said, going toward him. "I began to get — "

She paused abruptly, for Godfrey was laying down his hat with trembling hands, and turned toward her with a pale face and a strange unanswering glance, as if he saw her indeed, but saw her as part of a scene invisible to herself. She laid her hand on his arm, not daring to speak again; but he left the touch unnoticed, and threw himself into his chair.

Jane was already at the door with the hissing urn.

"Tell her to keep away, will you?" said Godfrey; and when the door was closed again he exerted himself to speak more distinctly.

"Sit down, Nancy — there," he said, pointing to a chair opposite him. "I came back as soon as I could, to hinder anybody's telling you but me. I've had a great shock — but I care most about the shock it'll be to you."

"It isn't father and Priscilla?" said Nancy, with quivering lips, clasping her hands together tightly on her lap.

"No, it's nobody living," said Godfrey, unequal to the considerate skill with which he would have wished to make his revelation. "It's Dunstan — my brother Dunstan, that we lost sight of sixteen years ago. We've found him — found his body — his skeleton."

The deep dread Godfrey's look had created in Nancy made her feel these words a relief. She sat in comparative calmness to hear what else he had to tell. He went on:

"The stone pit has gone dry suddenly — from the draining, I suppose; and there he lies — has lain for sixteen years, wedged between two great stones. There's his watch and seals, and there's my goldhandled hunting whip, with my name on; he took it away, without my knowing, the day he went hunting on Wildfire, the last time he was seen."

Godfrey paused; it was not so easy to say what came next. "Do you think he drowned himself?" said Nancy, almost wondering that her husband should be so deeply shaken by what had happened all those years ago to an unloved brother.

"No, he fell in," said Godfrey, in a low but distinct voice, as if he felt some deep meaning in the fact. Presently he added, "Dunstan was the man that robbed Silas Marner."

The blood rushed to Nancy's face and neck at this surprise and shame, for she had been bred up to regard even a distant kinship with crime as a dishonor.

"O Godfrey!" she said, with compassion in her tone, for she had immediately reflected that the dishonor must be felt still more keenly by her husband.

"There was the money in the pit," he continued — "all the weaver's money. Everything's been gathered up, and they're taking the skeleton to the Rainbow. But I came back to tell you; there was no hindering it; you must know."

He was silent, looking on the ground for two long minutes. Nancy would have said some words of comfort under this disgrace, but she refrained, from an instinctive sense that there was something behind — that Godfrey had something else to tell her. Presently he lifted his eyes to her face, and kept them fixed on her, as he said:

"Everything comes to light, Nancy, sooner or later. When God Almighty wills it, our secrets are found out. I've lived with a secret on my mind, but I'll keep it from you no longer. I wouldn't have you know it by somebody else, and not by me — I wouldn't have you find it out after I'm dead. I'll tell you now. It's been 'I will' and 'I won't' with me all my life — I'll make sure of myself now."

Nancy's utmost dread had returned. The eyes of the husband and wife met with awe in them, as at a crisis which suspended affection.

"Nancy," said Godfrey slowly, "when I married you, I hid something from you — something I ought to have told you. That woman Marner found dead in the snow — Eppie's mother — that wretched woman — was my wife; Eppie is my child."

He paused, dreading the effect of his confession. But Nancy sat quite still, only that her eyes dropped and ceased to meet his. She was pale and quiet as a meditative statue, clasping her hands on her lap.

"You'll never think the same of me again," said Godfrey, after a little while, with some tremor in his voice.

She was silent.

"I oughtn't to have left the child unowned; I oughtn't to have kept it from you. But I couldn't bear to give you up, Nancy. I was led away into marrying her — I suffered for it."

Still Nancy was silent, looking down; and he almost expected that she would presently get up and say she would go to her father's. How could she have any mercy for faults that must seem so black to her, with her simple, severe notions?

But at last she lifted up her eyes to his again and spoke. There was no indignation in her voice — only deep regret.

"Godfrey, if you had but told me this six years ago, we could have done some of our duty by the child. Do you think I'd have refused to take her in, if I'd known she was yours?"

At that moment Godfrey felt all the bitterness of an error that was not simply futile, but had defeated its own end. He had not measured this wife with whom he had lived so long. But she spoke again, with more agitation.

"And — O Godfrey — if we'd had her from the first, if you'd taken to her as you ought, she'd have loved me for her mother — and you'd have been happier with me; I could better have bore my little baby dying, and our life might have been more like what we used to think it 'ud be."

The tears fell, and Nancy ceased to speak.

"But you wouldn't have married me then, Nancy, if I'd told you," said Godfrey, urged, in the bitterness of his self-reproach, to prove to himself that his conduct had not been utter folly. "You may think you would now, but you wouldn't then. With your pride and your father's, you'd have hated having anything to do with me after the talk there'd have been."

"I can't say what I should have done about that, Godfrey. I should never have married anybody else. But I wasn't worth doing wrong for — nothing is in this world. Nothing is so good as it seems beforehand — not even our marrying wasn't, you see." There was a faint sad smile on Nancy's face as she said the last words.

"I'm a worse man than you thought I was, Nancy," said Godfrey, rather tremulously. "Can you forgive me ever?"

"The wrong to me is but little, Godfrey; you've made it up to me — you've been good to me for fifteen years. It's another you did the wrong to; and I doubt it can never be all made up for."

"But we can take Eppie now," said Godfrey. "I won't mind the world knowing at last. I'll be plain and open for the rest o' my life."

"It'll be different coming to us, now she's grown up," said Nancy, shaking her head sadly. "But it's your duty to acknowledge her and provide for her; and I'll do my part by her, and pray to God Almighty to make her love me."

"Then we'll go together to Silas Marner's this very night, as soon as everything's quiet at the stone pit."

CHAPTER XIX

Conflicting Claims

Between eight and nine o'clock that evening Eppie and Silas were seated alone in the cottage. After the great excitement the weaver had undergone from the events of the afternoon, he had felt a longing for this quietude, and had even begged Mrs. Winthrop and Aaron, who had naturally lingered behind everyone else, to leave him alone with his child. The excitement had not passed away; it had only reached that intensity of inward life, under which sleep is an impossibility.

Silas's face showed a sort of transfiguration,[1] as he sat in his armchair and looked at Eppie. She had drawn her own chair toward his knees, and leaned

---

[1] **transfiguration:** a change in appearance. Silas's face reflected the brightness and warmth of his inner feelings.

forward, holding both his hands, while she looked up at him. On the table near them, lit by a candle, lay the recovered gold — the old long-loved gold, ranged in orderly heaps, as Silas used to range it in the days when it was his only joy. He had been telling her how he used to count it every night, and how his soul was utterly desolate till she was sent to him.

"At first, I'd a sort o' feeling come across me now and then," he was saying in a subdued tone, "as if you might be changed into the gold again; for sometimes, turn my head which way I would, I seemed to see the gold; and I thought I should be glad if I could feel it, and find it was come back. But that didn't last long. After a bit, I should have thought it was a curse come again if it had drove you from me, for I'd got to feel the need o' your looks and your voice and the touch o' your little fingers. You didn't know then, Eppie, when you were such a little un — you didn't know what your old Father Silas felt for you."

"But I know now, father," said Eppie. "If it hadn't been for you, they'd have taken me to the workhouse, and there'd have been nobody to love me."

"Eh, my precious child, the blessing was mine. If you hadn't been sent to save me, I should ha' gone to the grave in my misery. The money was taken away from me in time; and you see it's been kept — kept till it was wanted for you. It's wonderful — our life is wonderful."

Silas sat in silence a few minutes, looking at the money.

"It takes no hold of me now," he said, ponderingly — "the money doesn't. I wonder if it ever could again — I doubt it might if I lost you, Eppie. I might come to think I was forsaken again, and lose the feeling that God was good to me."

At that moment there was a knocking at the door, and Eppie was obliged to rise without answering Silas. Beautiful she looked, with the tenderness of gathering tears in her eyes and a slight flush on her cheeks, as she stepped to open the door. The flush deepened when she saw Mr. and Mrs. Godfrey Cass. She made her little rustic curtsy, and held the door wide for them to enter.

"We're disturbing you late, my dear," said Mrs. Cass, taking Eppie's hand, and looking in her face with an expression of anxious interest and admiration. Nancy herself was pale and tremulous.

Eppie, after placing chairs for Mr. and Mrs. Cass, went to stand against Silas, opposite to them.

"Well, Marner," said Godfrey, trying to speak with perfect firmness, "it's a great comfort to me to see you with your money again, that you've been deprived of so many years. It was one of my family did you the wrong — the more grief to me — and I feel bound to make up to you for it in every way. Whatever I can do for you will be nothing but paying a debt, even if I looked no further than the robbery. But there are other things I'm beholden — shall be beholden to you for, Marner."

Godfrey checked himself. It had been agreed between him and his wife that the subject of his fatherhood should be approached very carefully, and that, if possible, the disclosure should be reserved for the future, so that it might be made to Eppie gradually. Nancy had urged this, because she felt strongly the painful light in which Eppie must inevitably see the relation between her father and mother.

Silas, always ill at ease when he was being spoken to by "betters," such as Mr. Cass — tall, powerful men, seen chiefly on horseback — answered with some constraint:

"Sir, I've a deal to thank you for a'ready. As for the robbery, I count it no loss to me. And if I did, you couldn't help it; you aren't answerable for it."

"You may look at it in that way, Marner, but I never can; and I hope you'll let me act according to my own feeling of what's just. I know you're easily contented; you've been a hard-working man all your life."

"Yes, sir, yes," said Marner meditatively. "I should ha' been bad off without my work; it was what I held by when everything else was gone from me."

"Ah," said Godfrey, applying Marner's words simply to his bodily wants, "it was a good trade for you in this country, because there's been a great deal of linen weaving to be done. But you're getting rather past such close work, Marner; it's time you laid by and had some rest. You look a good deal pulled down, though you're not an old man, *are* you?"

"Fifty-five, as near as I can say, sir," said Silas.

"Oh, why, you may live thirty years longer — look at old Macey! And that money on the table, after all, is but little. It won't go far either way — whether it's put out to interest, or you were to live on it as long as it would last; it wouldn't go far if you'd nobody to keep but yourself, and you've had two to keep for a good many years now."

"Eh, sir," said Silas, unaffected by anything Godfrey was saying, "I'm in no fear o' want. We shall do very well — Eppie and me 'ull do well enough. There's few workingfolks have got so much laid by as that. I don't know what it is to gentlefolks, but I look upon it as a deal — almost too much. And as for us, it's little we want."

"Only the garden, father," said Eppie, blushing up to the ears the moment after.

"You love a garden, do you, my dear?" said Nancy, thinking that this turn in the point of view might help her husband. "We should agree in that; I give a deal of time to the garden."

"Ah, there's plenty of gardening at the Red House," said Godfrey, surprised at the difficulty he found in approaching a proposition which had seemed so easy to him in the distance. "You've done a good part by Eppie, Marner, for sixteen years. It 'ud be a great comfort to you to see her well provided for, wouldn't it? She looks blooming and healthy, but not fit for any hardships; she doesn't look like a strapping girl come of working parents. You'd like to see her taken care of by those who can leave her well off, and make a lady of her; she's more fit for it than for a rough life, such as she might come to have in a few years' time."

A slight flush came over Marner's face, and disappeared, like a passing gleam. Eppie was simply wondering Mr. Cass should talk so about things that seemed to have nothing to do with reality; but Silas was hurt and uneasy.

"I don't take your meaning, sir," he answered, not having words at command to express the mingled feelings with which he had heard Mr. Cass's words.

"Well, my meaning is this, Marner," said Godfrey, determined to come to the point. "Mrs. Cass and I, you know, have no children — nobody to be the better for our good home and everything else we have — more than enough for ourselves. And we should like to have somebody in the place of a daughter to us — we should like to have Eppie, and treat her in every way as our own child. It 'ud be a great comfort to you in your old age, I hope, to see her fortune made in that way, after you've been at the trouble of bringing her up so well. And it's right you should have every reward for that. And Eppie, I'm sure, will always love you and be grateful to you; she'd come and see you very often, and we should all be on the lookout to do everything we could toward making you comfortable."

A plain man like Godfrey Cass, speaking under some embarrassment, necessarily blunders on words that are coarser than his intentions, and that are likely to fall gratingly on susceptible feelings. While he had been speaking, Eppie had quietly passed her arm behind Silas's head, and let her hand rest against it caressingly; she felt him trembling violently. He was silent for some moments when Mr. Cass had ended — powerless under the conflict of emotions, all alike painful. Eppie's heart was swelling at the sense that her father was in distress; and she was just going to lean down and speak to him, when one struggling dread at last gained the mastery over every other in Silas, and he said faintly:

"Eppie, my child, speak. I won't stand in your way. Thank Mr. and Mrs. Cass."

Eppie took her hand from her father's head, and came forward a step. Her cheeks were flushed, but not with shyness this time: the sense that her father was in doubt and suffering banished that sort of self-consciousness. She dropped a low curtsy, first to Mrs. Cass and then to Mr. Cass, and said:

"Thank you, ma'am — thank you, sir. But I can't leave my father, nor own anybody nearer than him. And I don't want to be a lady — thank you all the same" (here Eppie dropped another curtsy). "I couldn't give up the folks I've been used to."

Eppie's lip began to tremble a little at the last words. She retreated to her father's chair again, and held him round the neck; while Silas, with a subdued sob, put up his hands to grasp hers.

The tears were in Nancy's eyes, but her sympathy with Eppie was, naturally, divided with distress on her husband's account. She dared not speak, wondering what was going on in her husband's mind.

Godfrey felt an irritation inevitable to almost all of us when we encounter an unexpected obstacle. He had been full of his own penitence and resolution to retrieve his error as far as the time was left to him; he was possessed with all-important feelings, that were to lead to a predetermined course of action which he had fixed on as the right, and he was not prepared to enter with lively appreciation into other people's feelings counteracting his virtuous resolves. The agitation with which he spoke again was not quite unmixed with anger.

"But I've a claim on you, Eppie — the strongest of all claims. It's my duty, Marner, to own Eppie as my child, and provide for her. She's my own child; her mother was my wife. I've a natural claim on her that must stand before every other."

Eppie had given a violent start, and turned quite pale. Silas, on the contrary, who had been relieved, by Eppie's answer, from the dread lest his mind should be in opposition to hers, felt the spirit of resistance in him set free, not without a touch of parental fierceness. "Then, sir," he answered, with an accent of bitterness that had been silent in him since the memorable day when his youthful hope had perished — "then, sir, why didn't you say so sixteen year ago, and claim her before I'd come to love her, i'stead o' coming to take her from me now, when you

". . . I'll cleave to him as long as he lives, and nobody shall ever come between him and me."

might as well take the heart out o' my body? God gave her to me because you turned your back upon her, and He looks upon her as mine; you've no right to her! When a man turns a blessing from his door, it falls to them as take it in."

"I know that, Marner. I was wrong. I've repented of my conduct in that matter," said Godfrey, who could not help feeling the edge of Silas's words.

"I'm glad to hear it, sir," said Marner, with gathering excitement; "but repentance doesn't alter what's been going on for sixteen year. Your coming now and saying 'I'm her father,' doesn't alter the feelings inside us. It's me she's been calling her father ever since she could say the word."

"But I think you might look at the thing more reasonably, Marner," said Godfrey, unexpectedly awed by the weaver's direct truth-speaking. "It isn't as if she was to be taken quite away from you, so that you'd never see her again. She'll be very near you, and come to see you very often. She'll feel just the same toward you."

"Just the same?" said Marner, more bitterly than ever. "How'll she feel just the same for me as she does now, when we eat o' the same bit, and drink o' the same cup, and think o' the same things from one day's end to another? Just the same? That's idle talk. You'd cut us i' two."

Godfrey felt rather angry again. It seemed to him that the weaver was very selfish (a judgment readily passed by those who have never tested their own power of sacrifice) to oppose what was undoubtedly for Eppie's welfare; and he felt himself called upon, for her sake, to assert his authority.

"I should have thought, Marner," he said severely, "I should have thought your affection for Eppie would make you rejoice in what was for her good, even if it did call upon you to give up something. You ought to remember your own life's uncertain, and she's at an age now when her lot may soon be fixed in a way very different from what it would be in her father's home; she may marry some low workingman, and then, whatever I might do for her, I couldn't make her well off. You're putting yourself in the way of her welfare; and though I'm sorry to hurt you after what you've done, and what I've left undone, I feel now it's my duty to insist on taking care of my own daughter. I want to do my duty."

It would be difficult to say whether

it were Silas or Eppie that was most deeply stirred by this last speech of Godfrey's. Thought had been very busy in Eppie as she listened to the contest between her old, long-loved father and this new unfamiliar father who had suddenly come to fill the place of that black featureless shadow which had held the ring and placed it on her mother's finger. Her imagination had darted backward in conjectures, and forward in previsions, of what this revealed fatherhood implied; and there were words in Godfrey's last speech which helped to make the previsions especially definite. Not that these thoughts, either of past or future, determined her resolution — that was determined by the feelings which vibrated to every word Silas had uttered; but they raised, even apart from these feelings, a repulsion toward the offered lot and the newly revealed father.

Silas, on the other hand, was again stricken in conscience, and alarmed lest Godfrey's accusation should be true — lest he should be raising his own will as an obstacle to Eppie's good. For many moments he was mute, struggling for the self-conquest necessary to the uttering of the difficult words. They came out tremulously.

"I'll say no more. Let it be as you will. Speak to the child. I'll hinder nothing."

Even Nancy, with all the acute sensibility of her own affections, shared her husband's view, that Marner was not justifiable in his wish to retain Eppie, after her real father had avowed himself. She felt that it was a very hard trial for the poor weaver, but her code allowed no question that a father by blood must have a claim above that of any foster father. Besides, Nancy, used all her life to plenteous circumstances and privileges of "respectability," could not enter into the pleasures of the poor who are born poor; to her mind, Eppie, in being restored to her birthright, was entering on a too-long-withheld but unquestionable good. Hence she heard Silas's last words with relief, and thought, as Godfrey did, that their wish was achieved.

"Eppie, my dear," said Godfrey, looking at his daughter, not without some embarrassment, under the sense that she was old enough to judge him, "it'll always be our wish that you should show your love and gratitude to one who's been a father to you so many years, and we shall want to help you to make him comfortable in every way. But we hope you'll come to love us as well; and though I haven't been what a father should ha' been to you all these years, I wish to do the utmost in my power for you for the rest of my life, and provide for you as my only child. And you'll have the best of mothers in my wife — that'll be a blessing you haven't known since you were old enough to know it."

"My dear, you'll be a treasure to me," said Nancy, in her gentle voice. "We shall want for nothing when we have our daughter."

Eppie did not come forward and curtsy, as she had done before. She held Silas's hand in hers, and grasped it firmly, while she spoke with colder decision than before.

"Thank you, ma'am — thank you, sir, for your offers — they're very great, and far above my wish. For I should have no delight i' life any more if I was forced to go away from my father, and knew he was sitting at home a-thinking of me and feeling lone. We've been used to be happy together every day, and I can't think o' no happiness without him. And he says he'd nobody i' the world till I was sent to him, and he'd have nothing when I was gone. And he's took care of me and loved me from the first, and I'll cleave to him as long as he lives, and nobody shall ever come between him and me."

"But you must make sure, Eppie," said Silas, in a low voice — "you must make sure as you won't ever be sorry, because you've made your choice to stay among poor folks, and with poor clothes and things, when you might ha' had everything o' the best."

His sensitiveness on this point had increased as he listened to Eppie's words of faithful affection.

"I can never be sorry, father," said Eppie. "I shouldn't know what to think on or to wish for with fine things about me, as I haven't been used to. And it 'ud be poor work for me to put on things, and ride in a gig, and sit in a place at church, as 'ud make them as I'm fond of think me unfitting company for 'em. What could I care for then?"

Nancy looked at Godfrey with a pained, questioning glance. But his eyes were fixed on the floor, where he was moving the end of his stick, as if he were pondering on something absently. She thought there was a word which might perhaps come better from her lips than from his.

"What you say is natural, my dear child — it's natural you should cling to those who've brought you up," she said mildly; "but there's a duty you owe to your lawful father. There's perhaps something to be given up on more sides than one. When your father opens his home to you, I think it's right you shouldn't turn your back on it."

"I can't feel as I've got any father but one," said Eppie impetuously, while the tears gathered. "I've always thought of a little home where he'd sit i' the corner and I should fend and do everything for him; I can't think o' no other home. I wasn't brought up to be a lady, and I can't turn my mind to it. I like the workingfolks, and their victuals, and their ways. And," she ended passionately, while the tears fell, "I'm promised to marry a workingman, as 'll live with father, and help me to take care of him."

Godfrey looked up at Nancy with a flushed face and smarting, dilated eyes. This frustration of a purpose toward which he had set out under the exalted consciousness that he was about to compensate in some degree for the greatest demerit of his life, made him feel the air of the room stifling.

"Let us go," he said, in an undertone.

"We won't talk of this any longer now," said Nancy, rising. "We're your well-wishers, my dear — and yours, too, Marner. We shall come and see you again. It's getting late now."

In this way she covered her husband's abrupt departure, for Godfrey had gone straight to the door, unable to say more.

CHAPTER XX

The Dead Past

Nancy and Godfrey walked home under the starlight in silence. When they entered the oaken parlor, Godfrey threw himself into his chair, while Nancy laid down her bonnet and shawl, and stood on the hearth near her husband, unwilling to leave him even for a few minutes, and yet fearing to utter any word lest it might jar on his feeling. At last Godfrey turned his head toward her, and their eyes met, dwelling in that meeting without any movement on either side. That quiet mutual gaze of a trusting husband and wife is like the first moment of rest or refuge from a great weariness or a great danger.

But presently he put out his hand, and as Nancy placed hers within it, he drew her toward him, and said:

"That's ended!"

She bent to kiss him, and then said, as she stood by his side, "Yes, I'm afraid we must give up the hope of having her for a daughter. It wouldn't be right to want to force her to come to us against her will. We can't alter her bringing up and what's come of it."

"No," said Godfrey, with a keen decisiveness of tone, in contrast with his usually careless and unemphatic speech — "there's debts we can't pay like money debts, by paying extra for the years that have slipped by. While I've been putting off and putting off, the trees have been growing — it's too late now. Marner was in the right in what he said about a man's turning away a blessing from his door; it falls to somebody else. I wanted to pass for childless once, Nancy — I shall pass for childless now against my wish."

Nancy did not speak immediately, but after a little while she asked, "You won't make it known, then, about Eppie's being your daughter?"

"No — where would be the good to anybody? — only harm. I must do what I can for her in the state of life she chooses. I must see who it is she's thinking of marrying."

"If it won't do any good to make the thing known," said Nancy, "I should be very thankful for father and Priscilla never to be troubled with knowing what was done in the past, more than about Dunsey; it can't be helped, their knowing that."

"I shall put it in my will — I think I shall put it in my will. I shouldn't like to leave anything to be found out, like this about Dunsey," said Godfrey meditatively. "But I can't see anything but difficulties that 'ud come from telling it now. I must do what I can to make her happy in her own way. I've a notion," he added, after a moment's pause, "it's Aaron Winthrop she meant she was engaged to. I remember seeing him with her and Marner going away from church."

"Well, he's very sober and industrious," said Nancy, trying to view the matter as cheerfully as possible.

Godfrey fell into thoughtfulness again. Presently he looked up at Nancy sorrowfully, and said: "She's a very pretty, nice girl, isn't she, Nancy?"

"Yes, dear; and with just your hair and eyes. I wonder it had never struck me before."

"I think she took a dislike to me at the thought of my being her father. I could see a change in her manner after that."

"She couldn't bear to think of not looking on Marner as her father," said Nancy, not wishing to confirm her husband's painful impression.

"She thinks I did wrong by her mother as well as by her. She thinks me worse than I am. But she *must* think it; she can never know all. It's part of my punishment, Nancy, for my daughter to dislike me. I should never have got into that trouble if I'd been true to you — if I hadn't been a fool. I'd no right to expect anything but evil could come of that marriage — and when I shirked doing a father's part too."

Nancy was silent; her spirit of rectitude [1] would not let her try to soften the edge of what she felt to be a just compunction. He spoke again after a little while, but the tone was rather changed; there was tenderness mingled with the previous self-reproach.

"And I got *you*, Nancy, in spite of

[1] **rectitude** (rĕk'tĭ·tūd): strict observance of standards of integrity and honesty.

all; and yet I've been grumbling and uneasy because I hadn't something else — as if I deserved it."

"You've never been wanting to me, Godfrey," said Nancy, with quiet sincerity. "My only trouble would be gone if you resigned yourself to the lot that's been given us."

"Well, perhaps it isn't too late to mend a bit there. Though it *is* too late to mend some things, say what they will."

CHAPTER XXI

Return to Lantern Yard

[For many years, you remember, Silas Marner had brooded over the grave wrong done him by his old friend William Dane, and he had confided to Dolly Winthrop his secret misgivings about the drawing of lots. At the opening of this chapter he has an old question to settle before he can be completely happy. Notice how skillfully the author sets the old man's heart at rest — and the reader's mind — without starting up again the story that has already been told. On what note does the story end? Is it in harmony with the note on which it began?]

The next morning, when Silas and Eppie were seated at their breakfast, he said to her:

"Eppie, there's a thing I've had on my mind to do this two year, and now the money's been brought back to us, we can do it. I've been turning it over and over in the night, and I think we'll set out tomorrow, while the fine days last. We'll leave the house and everything for your godmother to take care on, and we'll make a little bundle o' things and set out."

"Where to go, Daddy?" said Eppie, in much surprise.

"To my old country — to the town where I was born — up Lantern Yard. I want to see Mr. Paston, the minister; something may ha' come out to make 'em know I was innicent o' the robbery. And Mr. Paston was a man with a deal o' light — I want to speak to him about the drawing o' the lots. And I should like to talk to him about the religion o' this countryside, for I partly think he doesn't know on it."

Eppie was very joyful, for there was the prospect not only of wonder and delight at seeing a strange country, but also of coming back to tell Aaron all about it. Aaron was so much wiser than she was about most things — it would be rather pleasant to have this little advantage over him. Mrs. Winthrop, though possessed with a dim fear of dangers attendant on so long a journey, and requiring many assurances that it would not take them out of the region of carriers' carts and slow wagons, was nevertheless well pleased that Silas should revisit his own country, and find out if he had been cleared from that false accusation.

"You'd be easier in your mind for the rest o' your life, Master Marner," said Dolly — "that you would. And if there's any light to be got up the Yard as you talk on, we've need of it i' this world, and I'd be glad on it myself, if you could bring it back."

So, on the fourth day from that time, Silas and Eppie, in their Sunday clothes, with a small bundle tied in a blue linen handkerchief, were making their way through the streets of a great manufacturing town. Silas, bewildered by the changes thirty years had brought over his native place, had stopped several persons in succession to ask them the name of this town, that he might be sure he was not under a mistake about it.

"Ask for Lantern Yard, father — ask this gentleman with the tassels on his shoulders a-standing at the shop door; he isn't in a hurry like the rest," said Eppie, in some distress at her father's bewilderment, and ill at ease, besides, amidst the noise, the movement, and the multitude of strange, indifferent faces.

"Eh, my child, he won't know anything about it," said Silas; "gentlefolks didn't ever go up the Yard. But happen somebody can tell me which is the way to Prison Street, where the jail is. I know the way out o' that as if I'd seen it yesterday."

With some difficulty, after many turnings and new inquiries, they reached Prison Street; and the grim walls of the jail, the first object that answered to any image in Silas's memory, cheered him with the certitude that he was in his native place.

"Ah," he said, drawing a long breath, "there's the jail, Eppie; that's just the same; I aren't afraid now. It's the third turning on the left hand from the jail doors — that's the way we must go."

"Oh, what a dark ugly place!" said Eppie. "How it hides the sky! It's worse than the workhouse. I'm glad you don't live in this town now, father. Is Lantern Yard like this street?"

"My precious child," said Silas, smiling, "it isn't a big street like this. I never was easy i' this street myself, but I was fond o' Lantern Yard. The shops here are all altered, I think — I can't make 'em out; but I shall know the turning, because it's the third."

"Here it is," he said, in a tone of satisfaction, as they came to a narrow alley. "And then we must go to the left again, and then straight for'ard for a bit, up Shoe Lane; and then we shall be at the entry next to the o'erhanging window, where there's the nick in the road for the water to run. Eh, I can see it all."

"O father, I'm like as if I was stifled," said Eppie. "I couldn't ha' thought as any folks lived i' this way, so close together. How pretty the stone pit 'ull look when we get back!"

"It looks comical to *me*, child, now — and smells bad. I can't think as it usened to smell so."

Here and there a sallow, begrimed face looked out from a gloomy doorway at the strangers, and increased Eppie's uneasiness, so that it was a longed-for relief when they issued from the alleys into Shoe Lane, where there was a broader strip of sky.

"Dear heart!" said Silas; "why, there's people coming out o' the Yard as if they'd been to chapel at this time o' day — a weekday noon!"

Suddenly he started and stood still, with a look of distressed amazement that alarmed Eppie. They were before an opening in front of a large factory, from which men and women were streaming for their midday meal.

"Father," said Eppie, clasping his arm, "what's the matter?"

But she had to speak again and again before Silas could answer her.

"It's gone, child," he said, at last, in strong agitation — "Lantern Yard's gone. It must ha' been here, because here's the house with the o'erhanging window — I know that — it's just the same; but they've made this new opening; and see that big factory! It's all gone — chapel and all."

"Come into that little brush shop and sit down, father — they'll let you sit down," said Eppie, always on the watch lest one of her father's strange attacks should come on. "Perhaps the people can tell you all about it."

But neither from the brushmaker, who had come to Shoe Lane only ten years ago, when the factory was already built, nor from any other source within his reach, could Silas learn anything of the old Lantern Yard friends, or of Mr. Paston, the minister.

"The old place is all swep' away," Silas said to Dolly Winthrop on the night of his return — "the little graveyard and everything. The old home's gone; I've no home but this now. I shall never know whether they got at the truth o' the robbery, nor whether Mr. Paston could ha' given me any light about the drawing o' the lots. It's dark to me, Mrs. Winthrop, that is; I doubt it'll be dark to the last."

"Well, yes, Master Marner," said Dolly, who sat with a placid listening face, now bordered by gray hairs; "I doubt it may. It's the will o' Them above as a many things should be dark to us; but there's some things as I've never felt i' the dark about, and they're mostly what comes i' the day's work. You were hard done by that once, Master Marner, and it seems as you'll never know the rights of it; but that doesn't hinder there *being* a rights, Master Marner, for all it's dark to you and me."

"No," said Silas, "no; that doesn't hinder. Since the time the child was sent to me and I've come to love her as myself, I've had light enough to trusten by; and, now she says she'll never leave me, I think I shall trusten till I die."

CONCLUSION

The Wedding

There was one time of the year which was held in Raveloe to be especially suitable for a wedding. It was when the great lilacs and laburnums [1] in the old-fashioned gardens showed their golden and purple wealth. People were not so busy then as they must become when the full cheese-making and the mowing had set in; and, besides, it was a time when a light bridal dress could be worn with comfort and seen to advantage.

Happily the sunshine fell more warmly than usual on the lilac tufts the morning that Eppie was married, for her dress was a very light one. She had often thought that the perfection of a wedding dress would be a white cotton, with the tiniest pink sprig at wide intervals; so that when Mrs. Godfrey Cass begged to provide one, and asked Eppie to choose what it should be, previous meditation had enabled her to give a decided answer at once.

Seen at a little distance as she walked across the churchyard and down the village, she seemed to be attired in pure white, and her hair looked like a dash of gold on a lily. One hand was on her husband's arm, and with the other she clasped the hand of her Father Silas.

"You won't be giving me away, father," she had said before they went to church; "you'll only be taking Aaron to be a son to you."

Dolly Winthrop walked behind with her husband; and there ended the little bridal procession.

There were many eyes to look at it, and Miss Priscilla Lammeter was glad that she and her father had happened to drive up to the door of the Red House just in time to see this pretty sight. They had come to keep Nancy company today, because Mr. Cass had to go away to Lytherly, for special rea-

[1] **laburnums** (là·bûr′nŭmz): a small shrub or tree with bright yellow flowers.

sons. That seemed to be a pity, for otherwise he might have gone, as Mr. Crackenthorp and Mr. Osgood certainly would, to look on at the wedding feast which he had ordered at the Rainbow, naturally feeling a great interest in the weaver who had been wronged by one of his own family.

"I could ha' wished Nancy had had the luck to find a child like that and bring her up," said Priscilla to her father, as they sat in the gig; "I should ha' had something young to think of then, besides the lambs and the calves."

"Yes, my dear, yes," said Mr. Lammeter; "one feels that as one gets older. Things look dim to old folks; they'd need have some young eyes about 'em, to let 'em know the world's the same as it used to be."

Nancy came out now to welcome her father and sister; and the wedding group had passed on beyond the Red House to the humbler part of the village.

Dolly Winthrop was the first to divine that old Mr. Macey, who had been set in his armchair outside his own door, would expect some special notice as they passed.

"Mr. Macey's looking for a word from us," said Dolly; "he'll be hurt if we pass him and say nothing — and him so racked with rheumatiz."

So they turned aside to shake hands with the old man. He had looked forward to the occasion, and had his premeditated speech.

"Well, Master Marner," he said, in a voice that quavered a good deal, "I've lived to see my words come true. I was the first to say there was no harm in you, though your looks might be again' you; and I was the first to say you'd get your money back. And it's nothing but rightful as you should. And I'd ha' said

the 'Amens,' and willing, at the holy matrimony; but Tookey's done it a good while now, and I hope you'll have none the worse luck."

In the open yard before the Rainbow the party of guests were already assembled, though it was still nearly an hour before the appointed feast time. But by this means they could not only enjoy the slow advent of their pleasure; they had also ample leisure to talk of Silas Marner's strange history, and arrive by due degrees at the conclusion that he had brought a blessing on himself by acting like a father to a lone, motherless child. Even the farrier did not negative this sentiment; on the contrary, he took it up as peculiarly his own, and invited any hardy person present to contradict him. But the company were merged in a general agreement with Mr. Snell's sentiment, that when a man had deserved his good luck it was the part of his neighbors to wish him joy.

As the bridal group approached, a hearty cheer was raised in the Rainbow yard; and Ben Winthrop found it agreeable to turn in there and receive congratulations, not requiring the proposed interval of quiet at the stone pit before joining the company.

Eppie had a larger garden than she had ever expected there now; and in other ways there had been alterations at the expense of Mr. Cass, the landlord, to suit Silas's larger family. For he and Eppie had declared that they would rather stay at the stone pit than go to any new home. The garden was fenced with stones on two sides, but in front there was an open fence, through which the flowers shone with answering gladness, as the four united people came within sight of them.

"O father," said Eppie, "what a pretty home ours is! I think nobody could be happier than we are."

"I think nobody could be happier than we are."

THE EVENTS IN THE NOVEL: PLOT

All novels depend on a dramatic situation to give interest and significance to the stories they tell. A dramatic situation can be explained this way: something happens to the characters that will have consequences for them; or, something happens that forces the characters to act and in some way to work out certain problems they face. A plot is the sequence of happenings by which the characters resolve the dramatic situation or problem that confronts them: it is *how* they work their way out. If you are interested in the characters — if you care what happens to them — then you will want to follow the sequence of events that lead them from one problem to another, until they finally reach a solution.

FOLLOWING THE SEQUENCE OF EVENTS

1. Two plots combine to make the story of *Silas Marner.* How would you define each? By what circumstance are they first connected? How are they drawn together at the end?

2. Without mentioning all the events in detail, can you tell generally what main events of the story are told in Part One? in Part Two? in the Conclusion? How much time elapses between Part One and Part Two? between Part Two and the Conclusion?

3. Where does the climax occur in *Silas Marner?* In answering, consider the things that happen to Silas and the resulting changes in his personality and philosophy. Try to determine the final turning point in his life.

4. One aspect of the story is left unconcluded, or to put it another way, one conflict in the story is never resolved. That is the false accusation of young Silas Marner. Why does George Eliot avoid trying to settle this matter? In your opinion, would the novel by a better or worse story had Marner discovered the people he once knew at Lantern Yard when he returned there as an old man? Explain.

5. Does the story end at the right time? What other endings might it have?

6. One good way to review the events of the novel is to suggest chapter titles for it. The titles that occur in this text were not written by George Eliot; they were supplied by the editors of this book. Together with the class, draw up a list of titles that differ from these. Perhaps you can find better ones.

FORESHADOWING IN THE PLOT

A careful writer manages to put into a story many hints which suggest or actually foretell what later events will take place. Such hints are called *foreshadowing.* Try to find the foreshadowing of events in the novel, now that you have read the book through.

1. At the end of Chapter II, page 639, find the sentence that foretells a great change in Marner's life, and a new relationship with his neighbors.

2. In Chapter I, page 628, find the first mention of the stone pit. Note that it is in the story, from the beginning, as a commonplace feature of the setting. In Chapter IV, page 649, find the suggestion that someone could slip into the stone pit and drown. In Chapter XIV, page 704, how does the author re-echo the idea that the pit is dangerous? There are other intentional references to the pit. Can you locate any of them?

3. Find in Chapters III and IV at least five references that prepare for the kind of weather that prevails when Dunstan leaves Marner's cottage, and steps "forward into the darkness."

4. In Chapter XIII, page 696, find the sentence that states positively that Godfrey will one day tell the full story of his secret marriage.

5. Find in Chapter XVI, page 713, some explanation for Eppie's lack of interest in knowing anything of her real father; in this, and in Chapter XIX, page 724, find a foreshadowing of her refusal to leave Silas for Godfrey.

THE PEOPLE IN THE NOVEL: CHARACTERIZATION

One important aspect of all novels, though not necessarily of short stories, is that the characters usually *change* during the course of the story. Events and the influence of other persons cause in a character some change of attitude, of habit, or of feeling. In a good novel, the plot and characterization are closely connected. Apply these ideas about characterization to the people you have met in *Silas Marner.*

SILAS MARNER

1. Cite details from Chapters I and II which show that Silas was the victim of injustice. What was the effect of William Dane's treachery? Did Silas feel and act as you might expect a person to under such circumstances?

2. What kind of satisfaction did gold bring Silas? What does his feeling toward the little brown pot tell us about him?

3. What passage can you quote from Chapter XII to show a connection, in Silas's mind, between the child and the lost gold? What has gold stood for in Silas Marner's warped life? What satisfaction has it brought? How does the child represent for him a return of his gold?

4. What are the changes wrought in Silas Marner by his love for Eppie? What details in Chapters XIV and XVI describe her influence? What were the first signs of change to be noticed in Chapter XIV? What change came over the villagers' regard for him? How do you account for the change?

5. What kind of old man is Silas in Chapters XVI to XXI? What qualities endear him to Eppie? To what qualities of his are Godfrey and Nancy Cass blind?

DOLLY WINTHROP

1. How does the purpose of Dolly Winthrop's first visit to Silas differ from Mr. Macey's visit in Chapter X? How is Dolly's purpose in this visit related to the title of the chapter?

2. Aside from her connection with Silas and Eppie, Dolly's life in Raveloe is mentioned from time to time. What activities and interests did she have? Did these activities give her pleasure?

3. What instances of Dolly's consideration for Silas's feelings can you point to in Chapter XIV? How does Silas respond to this tactfulness?

4. Contrast Dolly with William Dane, Squire Cass, Molly Farren, and Godfrey Cass. Why is she necessary to this novel?

5. In Chapter XVI and in Chapter XXI, Dolly states her philosophy of life. What are the essential elements of this philosophy? What is your own opinion of the values by which she lives? How would you state the philosophies of Godfrey? Dunstan? Molly Farren? Squire Cass?

GODFREY CASS

1. What instances can you cite from Chapters III, VIII, and XIII to show that Godfrey Cass is at the mercy of his conscience? How sincerely does he regret his misdeeds? Or is he just regretful of the consequences? How can you tell?

2. What is your impression of Godfrey when he is the victim of his father's wrath in Chapter IX? Do you feel sorry for him? Do you respect him? How do you account for the lack of any socially useful ambition on the part of Squire Cass's sons?

3. In what way does Godfrey appear in a better light as the gallant wooer of Nancy? What qualities does Nancy see in him? Is her love for him a tribute to his character or to hers? On what reasoning do you base your answer?

4. What are your feelings about Godfrey in connection with the events of Chapter XIX? Do you think he deserves to have his way? How does he take this last disappointment? Has he gained in manliness since his younger days? Do you like him better or less? Why?

NANCY LAMMETER

1. What do you think of Nancy as the coy maiden resisting Godfrey's advances? Would a modern girl, uncertain of the status of a love affair, be as hurt and embarrassed as Nancy was at the New Year's Eve party?

2. What illustrations can you cite from Chapters XVII through XX to show Nancy as the dutiful and understanding wife? How does she reconcile herself to the loss of her only child?

3. Is Nancy Lammeter a believable character as far as you are concerned? Consider Nancy the girl and Nancy the mature woman. How has she changed with the years? Are the changes logical ones? Give specific reasons for your answers.

EPPIE

1. If Eppie had accepted Godfrey's and Nancy's proposal that she live with them as their daughter, would you have liked her as well? To what lack in her character would such a decision have testified? Is she just or heartless in her decision?

2. In what way has Eppie's character been influenced by her life with Silas?

MINOR CHARACTERS

1. What amusing pictures does your imagination supply of the lesser lights of Raveloe? What details can you quote from Chapter VI to show the tendency of the farrier to argue? the peace-making traits of Mr. Snell? the talkativeness of Mr. Macey? What picture do you get in Chapter XI of the merry-eyed rector? the jesting doctor? old Solomon, the fiddler? Priscilla Lammeter, the self-appointed spinster?

2. What is wrong with the Squire as a father, judging from a modern point of view? What excuses can you make for him? What details can you quote from Chapter XI to show Squire Cass in a more attractive light? What do you think his guests think of him?

3. What factors in his home life do you think turned Dunstan into a reckless, dissipated idler?

4. What more would you like to know about Molly Farren before deciding how much she is to be blamed for her actions? What indication do you have that she was not completely lacking in pride?

5. The various characters in *Silas Marner* help to create a picture of society in early nineteenth-century England. What social classes are represented by characters in the novel? What are some of the characteristics of the different classes?

THE TIME AND PLACE OF THE NOVEL: SETTING

Silas Marner, as you immediately discovered, is a novel that was written in and describes a time and place quite different from our own. If an author makes the setting real to us, we are more likely to believe in the reality of the characters and to see the effect on them of their environment.

1. Make sure you know the historical setting of the novel. In what period of time did the story occur? What references in the text tell you the time? Look at a map of England to find the general area of the Midlands, where *Silas Marner* takes place.

2. What clothes were in fashion in the early nineteenth century? What quaint customs are revealed in Chapter XI? What contrasts or comparisons with life today

occurred to you as you watched the festivities at the Red House on New Year's Eve?

3. How important was the horse both for work and sport in those days? What pictures of the "horse age" caught your eye in Chapters III and IV?

4. What were the typical amusements of the day? Review Chapters VI and XI in particular and see how many details of pleasurable activities you can find.

5. What did you notice in Chapter XI about the hospitality of the rich? What kind of host did Squire Cass make? How far did his hospitality extend? Is there anything to suggest that his annual entertainment was a typical custom of squires?

6. What occupations are referred to in Chapter VI? To what kind of life could an ordinary village boy like Aaron look forward? To what occupations would he turn? As the son of a squire, what were Godfrey Cass's prospects? What differences in social station among the village people are suggested in Chapter XI?

7. What incidents can you quote from Chapter IX to show the rights of a father over his son in Silas Marner's day? What deference did a son show to his father's judgment? In what respects has the relationship of father and son changed since that time?

8. How does the whole story of *Silas Marner* illustrate the fact that in small, isolated communities people who are different are regarded with suspicion?

THE NOVEL'S CENTRAL IDEA: THEME

The idea back of a story, the point of the story, is its *theme.* If the theme is important to human beings and if the story is artistically written, it will last through the years. *Silas Marner* has a central idea, or theme, which expresses its author's general view of life and her basic values. The importance of George Eliot's theme is testified to by the fact that *Silas Marner* lives on while many other novels of its time have long since been forgotten.

1. In your own words, discuss the underlying theme of *Silas Marner.* Illustrate your ideas with specific references to the story. For help in identifying the theme, turn to the last paragraph of Chapter XIV, page

706, and the last paragraph of Chapter XXI, page 733, and especially the introduction to Part II, page 707. Try to express the theme in your own words.

2. Another idea worth exploring in *Silas Marner* is that wrongdoing carries its own punishment, just as doing good brings its own reward. In Chapter XX, for example, Godfrey felt his childlessness a punishment for not acknowledging Eppie as his daughter. Is there evidence that in Silas's life good deeds brought their own repayment? The idea is worth thinking about. After you have come to some conclusion, try illustrating your ideas by reference to your own experience or to your other reading. A good talk or a written composition might be based on this theme.

THE NOVEL'S ATMOSPHERE AND MOOD

Each dramatic situation in a novel casts its own mood on the reader. A scene like the ball in the Red House casts a mood of gaiety, while the scene of Dunstan approaching Silas's cottage creates a sense of foreboding and danger. Review some of the more important scenes of the novel and see how well you responded to their atmosphere or mood.

1. What details suggest to you the loneliness of the stone pit in Chapter IV? What phrases communicate the dreariness of the fog?

2. What details suggest the sociability of the Rainbow kitchen in Chapters VI and VII?

3. What picture do you get of the dance at the Red House through the eyes of the village spectators? What details attracted the villagers' attention?

4. On two occasions in the novel, both related to very important events, the weather has an influence on the story. What are the occasions? How are you made aware of the weather at the time? How is the weather a part of the atmosphere of each scene?

5. At the close of Chapter XVII the reader's mood is transformed from that of a peaceful Sunday afternoon to one of tense crisis. How does Jane, the servant girl, contribute to this shift in mood? Read carefully the very last paragraph of this chapter. Does it assist the change?

Suggestions
for Further Reading

The republic of literature is a commonwealth to which all readers may belong. It is a republic that stretches over political boundaries and bridges the lines of color, race, and religion.

As the advances of science shrink the globe in time and space, readers want to understand the customs and lives of people in foreign countries and to see, beneath these customs, the ways in which all mankind is alike. Here are some suggestions of famous novels from our own and other countries which may give you a start toward the republic of literature.

Novels by American Authors

Annixter, Paul, *Swiftwater* (Hill & Wang, 1950)
   This novel is about the Calloway family, which lives by hunting and trapping. Bucky and his father, Cam Calloway, plan a sanctuary for wild geese, keep a pet bear cub, experience disappointments and hardships. Bucky's loyalty to his father, conflicting with conformity to the patterns of society, deepens the story's interest and value.

Carroll, Gladys Hasty, *As the Earth Turns* (Macmillan, 1933)
   Polish immigrants and New England farmers discover love of the land, which they share, can make them good neighbors. Particularly interesting are the various children in the New England farm family and the lives they lead.

Hemingway, Ernest, *The Old Man and the Sea* (Scribner, 1952)
   A heartbreaking struggle with a giant marlin follows eighty-four days of bad luck for a poor Cuban fisherman.

Jackson, Helen Hunt, *Ramona* (Little, Brown, 1939)
   This romantic novel of Spanish and Indian life in the early days of southern California has long been a favorite.

London, Jack, *Call of the Wild* (Macmillan, 1923)
   Buck, the magnificent wolf-dog, living in the rough days of the Klondike gold

rush, begins life as a beloved pet in a sunny California valley. Stolen from his master's home and taken to Alaska, he grows closer to his primitive ancestry.

Michener, James A., *The Bridges of Toko-ri* (Random House, 1953)

This stirring short novel concerns a few days in the life of Harry Brubaker, who must fly a jet plane and destroy four bridges. His story of courage raises questions about the nature of war.

Pease, Howard, *Thunderbolt House* (Doubleday, 1944)

A San Francisco family receives sudden wealth. The San Francisco earthquake and fire of 1906 take it away again, but the family finds answers to life beyond the accidents of fate.

Rawlings, Marjorie Kinnan, *The Yearling* (Scribner, 1938)

Jody Baxter, his understanding father, his practical mother, and a pet fawn live on a backwoods Florida farm.

*Steinbeck, John, *The Pearl* (Viking, 1947)

A poor Mexican fisherman finds a great pearl. Instead of good fortune the pearl brings evil and unhappiness into his world.

Stewart, George R., *Storm* (Modern Library, 1947)

The main character, a storm, brings drama and tragedy to a variety of people.

Twain, Mark, *Huckleberry Finn* (Dutton, 1955)

Huck, who has run away from civilization, and Jim, a Negro slave, float down the Mississippi on a raft. Their days, and nights, are filled with adventure.

West, Jessamyn, *Cress Delahanty* (Harcourt, Brace & World, 1954)

Cress Delahanty is a lively teen-age girl with understanding, likeable parents. Her experiences are hilarious and poignant by turns.

Novels by Authors from Other Countries

Bagnold, Enid (British), *National Velvet* (Morrow, 1949)

Horses fill the life of Velvet Brown, who disguises herself as a jockey to ride in the Grand National Steeplechase.

Balzac, Honoré de (French), *Père Goriot* (Dodd, Mead, 1954)

Father Goriot's heartless daughters drive him into poverty while they seek pleasure in the fashionable Parisian world.

*Brontë, Charlotte (British), *Jane Eyre* (Modern Library)

We follow the heroine, an orphan, through school days to life as a governess in the home of a man whose love for her is troubled by something he cannot explain. Jane knows only that a demoniac laugh and a forbidden third floor are involved in the mystery.

Dickens, Charles (British), *David Copperfield* (Modern Library)

The story of David's sad experiences as a child, his struggles to earn a living, and his eventual success.

Dumas, Alexandre (French), *The Three Musketeers* (Dodd, Mead)

When they become involved in a court intrigue, D'Artagnan and his three companions find enemies in high places.

Gulbranssen, Trygve (Norwegian), *Beyond Sing the Woods* (Putnam, 1954) and its sequel, *The Wind from the Mountains* (Putnam, 1954)

Three generations of the Björndals, a Norwegian family of heroic character, appear in these two novels.

Hugo, Victor (French), *Les Misérables* (Dodd, Mead, 1925)

The story of an escaped convict who struggles to overcome his background.

*Kipling, Rudyard (British), *Kim* (Doubleday)

This exciting adventure story deals with the orphan Kim, who is brought up and educated in British India.

*Saint-Exupéry, Antoine de (French), *Night Flight* (Harcourt, Brace & World, 1932)

Saint-Exupéry, a pilot himself, tells the thrilling story of men who flew and organized night mail routes when flying was still in its infancy.

* This novel is included in *Four Novels for Appreciation*, edited by Fuller and Thompson. *Jane Eyre*, abridged. (Harcourt, Brace & World, 1961)

For Listening

Chapter VI, "Town Talk," from *Silas Marner* is available on *Many Voices* 10A. Chapter VII, "Apparition at the Rainbow," is available on *Many Voices* 4B.

ACKNOWLEDGMENTS

ART WORK DONE SPECIFICALLY FOR THIS BOOK

Lawrence Bjorklund: pp. 16, 18, 23, 27, 49, 119, 131, 135; Donald Bolognese: pp. 251, 264, 268, 270, 377; Harvey Dinnerstein: pp. 626, 631, 635, 638, 643, 647, 650, 658, 663, 670, 683, 686, 691, 699, 707, 715, 727, 734; William Hofman: pp. 362, 363, 375; Raymond Houlihan: pp. 2, 6, 11, 28, 31, 34, 37, 42, 61, 62, 66, 67, 71, 145, 148, 168, 170, 172, 173; Eugene Karlin: pp. 365, 392, 393; Jack Ezra Keats: pp. 44, 47, 102; Howard Koslow: pp. 234, 247; Marilyn Miller: pp. 55, 97, 108, 111, 114, 119, 120; Isadore Seltzer from Pushpin Studios: pp. 591, 592, 594, 595, 596, 599, 603, 607, 619; Robert Shore: pp. 86, 88, 92. MAPS: Raphael Palacios: p. 229; Viet-Martin: pp. 202, 214, 509.

PHOTO CREDITS

P. ii, Musée National du Louvre, Foto Girau-don; p. xiv, Kunsthist, Museum of Vienna; p. 15, Susan McCartney; p. 59, Roy Schatt; p. 61, United Press International; p. 75, Fred Lyon from Rapho-Guillumette; p. 76, United Press International; p. 85, Air Ministry, London; p. 101, National Portrait Gallery, London; p. 107, Museum of the City of New York; p. 117, F. L. Stage from Photo Researchers; p. 129, reprinted by permission of Dodd, Mead & Co. from *Les Misérables*, illustrated by Mead Schaeffer, copyright 1925; p. 139, Nordiska Museet, Stockholm; p. 140, Museum of Fine Arts, Boston; p. 143, Walker Art Center, Min-neapolis; p. 150, Wadsworth Atheneum, The Ella Gallup Sumner & Mary Catlin Sumner Coll., Hartford; p. 153, Freer Gallery of Art; p. 156, Metropolitan Museum of Art; p. 159, Freer Gallery of Art; p. 161, Metropolitan Museum of Art, B. Altman Collection; p. 162, Freer Gallery of Art; p. 165, Paris Musée Guimet, Foto Giraudon; p. 166, Eva Besseney; p. 177, Metropolitan Museum of Art (top left: The Cloisters Collection, Gift of John D. Rockefeller, Jr., 1937; top right: Rogers Fund, 1911; bottom: Bequest of Collis P. Huntington, 1925); p. 182, Metro-politan Museum of Art; (Photo: Parke-Benet Galleries, Inc.); p. 187, 189, Swiss Founda-tion for Alpine Research; pp. 190, 191, 195, Mount Everest Foundation; p. 196, Culver Service; p. 199, Radio Times Hulton; p. 207, bottom three: Brown Brothers, top: Culver Service; pp. 208, 218, 221, from *Kon-Tiki* by Thor Heyerdahl, copyright 1950 by Thor Hey-erdahl, published in the U.S. by Rand Mc-Nally & Company; p. 227, Smithsonian Institu-tion; p. 231, Milwaukee Public Museum Photo; p. 239, California Institute of Tech-nology; p. 240, E. Erwitt from Magnum; p. 254, drawing by Mulligan, copyright 1961 The New Yorker Magazine, Inc.; p. 255, Roy Wilcox from National Audubon Society; p. 258, Russ Kinne from Photo Researchers; p. 262, Hans Namuth; p. 263, National Audu-bon Society (top: H. Cruickshanks, bottom left: H. Harrison, bottom right: M. McMil-len); p. 273, New York Public Library; p. 274, copyright © 1937, The New Yorker Magazine, Inc.; p. 275, copyright © 1940 James Thurber; p. 276, Tom Hollyman from Photo Research-ers; p. 279, Clyde Hare; p. 284, Brown Broth-ers; p. 286, Bettmann Archive; pp. 288, 291, 293, 295, Alinari Photo; p. 299, Ray Manley from Shostal; p. 303, Metropolitan Museum of Art, Wolfe Fund, 1931; p. 305, from *Shad-ows on the Grass* by Isak Dinesen, copyright 1960, by Isak Dinesen, reprinted by permis-sion of Random House, Inc.; p. 310, 315, Lawrence Lawry from Rapho-Guillumette; p. 311, Grzimek from Opika Foto; p. 316, Clara E. Sipprell; p. 320, Japanese Imperial House-hold Agency; p. 323, Shostal (right: Ace Williams, top left: Paul Hufner, bottom left (2): Joe Barnell); p. 327, Shostal (top left, bottom right: Dave Forbert, top right: Ray Halin, bottom left: Max Tatch); p. 330, R. Leahey from Shostal; p. 332, Library of Con-gress; p. 333, Brown Brothers; p. 336, Library of Congress, p. 339, J. J. Audubon from Na-tional Audubon Society; p. 344, Yale Univer-sity Library, Morse Collection of Mark Twain; p. 347, Shostal (top left: A. M. Wettach, bot-tom: J. Zehrt), Photo Researchers (top right: R. Jacques, middle right: T. Hollyman); p. 354, Metropolitan Museum of Art; p. 368, Silberstein from Monkmeyer; p. 376, Bett-mann Archive; p. 383, Virginia Historical So-ciety, Richmond (Colonial Studio); p. 388, W. Stewart from A. J. Dollar Assoc., Inc.; p. 394, Bettmann Archive; p. 399, Comerford Gallery; p. 400, Freer Gallery of Art; p. 404, E. Hartmann from Magnum; p. 407, Susan McCartney; p. 411, Walker Art Gallery, Liver-pool; p. 414, J. Barnell from Shostal; p. 419, Brandt from Photo Researchers; p. 426, Met-ropolitan Museum of Art; p. 431, Susan Mc-Cartney; p. 435, A. Knopf; p. 437, Arthur La-vine; p. 442, Metropolitan Museum of Art; pp. 444, 453, 461, 499, Sheldon from Secunda; p. 503, George Hamill; p. 505, drawing by C. Walter Hodges from *The Globe Restored*, courtesy Ernest Benn, Ltd.; p. 506, Alinari Photo; p. 507, New York Public Library; p. 508, Alinari Photo; pp. 510, 515, 547, 555, 575, Classic Studio, Ashland, Oregon; p. 582, Metropolitan Museum of Art, The Cloisters Collection, Munsey Fund; p. 585, New York Public Library; p. 586, Pierpont Morgan Li-brary; p. 587, Friedman-Abeles; p. 588, The British Museum; pp. 589, 600, 604, 611, 614, 615, The Pierpont Morgan Library; p. 622, The National Gallery, London.

Special Indexes

READING SKILLS AND SPECIAL STUDY AIDS. Some exercises are introduced on the opening page of a selection by a separate pre-reading hint and are followed up by questions at the end of the selection. Page references for both portions of these exercises are indicated below as continuous pages, for example, 16–25.

GENERAL SKILLS
Action, following the, 576
Author's personality, appreciating the, 255–62
Character, recognizing clues to, 95–100, 304
Comparing what you read, 304
Conclusions, drawing, 185–94, 222
Description, appreciating, 222, 338
Details, recognizing, 16–25, 196–205, 316–26
Identifying yourself with the writer, 328–31
Interpretation, analyzing the author's, 502
Language, recognizing types of, 405
Meaning: finding clues to, 140–42; from conversation, 45–48; in fables, 274–75; relating form and, 420
Relating all parts of a story, 164, 175
Relating reading to your own experience, 131–38
Relating the title to the selection, 102–06
Structure, recognizing, 248
Style, recognizing, 350
Tone, recognizing, 49–54, 91
Visualizing: in short stories, 62–74; in drama, 445–502

LITERARY TYPES, TERMS, AND TECHNIQUES
Allusions, 620
Anachronisms, 598
Anecdote, the, 343
Apostrophe, 371
Atmosphere and mood in the novel, 739
Characterization: in drama, 578; in the novel, 736
Essays, noting flexibility in, 270
Humor, appreciating, 267, 270
Irony, 55–58, 108–16
Language: appropriateness of, 149, 282; humorous, 54

Metaphor, 100, 222, 366
Mood, in the novel. See Atmosphere and mood in the novel.
Mood and music in poetry, 371
Nonfiction, appreciating, 351
Personification, 371
Plot: recognizing patterns, 41; in the novel, 736
Poetry: the experience of, 358; appreciating narrative poetry, 365; appreciating lyric poetry, 371; appreciating dramatic poetry, 376; appreciating light verse, 378; reading aloud, 386; the poet behind the poem, 440
Point of view, 76–84, 376
Rhyme, 365
Satire, 251–53
Setting: in drama, 579; in the novel, 738
Short stories, appreciating, 179
Simile, 100, 222, 366
Single effect, Poe's theory of, 86–91
Storyteller's methods, 598
Symbols, 579
Theme: understanding, 120–30, 144; in the novel, 738; relating to title, 145–49

General Discussions
Short Stories: introduction, 1; plot, 2, 43; tone, 44, 60; setting, 61, 93; character, 94, 118; theme, 119, 151; total effect, 152
Nonfiction: introduction, 183; true narratives, 184, 223; articles, 224, 249; essays, 250, 271; fables, 272; biographies, 283
Poetry: introduction, 355; narrative, 359; epic, 359; the ballad, 360; lyric, 367; dramatic, 372; light verse, 377
Drama, 443
The King Arthur Legend, 583
The Novel, 623

VOCABULARY DEVELOPMENT. The following vocabulary exercises appear under the heading "Gaining Power over Words" in the study material at the end of the selections.

Clues to function and meaning of words, 358
Context (clues to meaning), 138
Descriptive words, 222
Figures of speech. *See specific figures of speech under* "Literary Types, Terms, and Techniques."

Learning new words, 74
Prefixes, 60
Specialized vocabularies, 194, 238, 248
Suffixes, 116
Using the dictionary, 331
Word discrimination (synonyms), 130

COMPOSITION SUGGESTIONS. Listed below are the pages on which the composition exercises appear, together with the selections they accompany.

Page:
41 ("The Quiet Man")
48 ("The Open Window")
84 ("Beware of the Dog")

118 ("The Duke's Children")
130 ("The Bishop's Candlesticks")
138 ("The Rat Trap")

ILLUSTRATIONS. Reproductions of famous paintings, prints, sculpture, and art objects (in detail or in full) appear as follows.

COMMENTARY AND STUDY MATERIAL relating to illustrations and to the selections that they accompany appear on the following pages.

Glossary

Listed below are words from the selections in the book that you will find useful to add to your vocabulary. The words are defined according to the context in which they appear in the selections. Proper names and words that are specialized, archaic, or not generally useful are not included in this glossary but have been footnoted, when appropriate, in the text.

A

abide (à·bīd′). **1.** To remain or stay. **2.** To bear.

abolish (à·bŏl′ĭsh). To put an end to; to do away with.

abscond (ăb·skŏnd′). To depart secretly.

abstracted (ăb·străk′tĕd). Absent-minded.

abstraction (ăb·străk′shŭn). A theory; a generality.

abyss (à·bĭs′). Any deep immeasurable space or chasm; a vast depth.

accessory (ăk·sĕs′ō·rĭ). Something not absolutely necessary that adds to the convenience, usefulness, or enjoyment of something else.

acclimate (ăk′lĭ·māt). To become accustomed to an unfamiliar climate.

accost (à·kŏst′). **1.** To approach, make up to. **2.** To address, greet.

acute (à·kūt′). **1.** Keen or quick of mind. **2.** Severe and sharp, as *acute* pain or jealousy.

adjure (à·jŏŏr′). To appeal to solemnly; to entreat earnestly.

adroit (à·droit′). Skillful; clever. *Noun,* **adroitness.**

advocate (ăd′vō·kāt). A person who declares himself in favor of some policy, cause, idea, etc.

affect (à·fĕkt′). **1.** To assume the character or appearance of; to pretend. **2.** To influence.

agility (à·jĭl′ĭ·tĭ). Lively activeness.

agog (à·gŏg′). Eager; excited.

alien (āl′yĕn). A foreigner.

allocation (ăl′ō·kā′shŭn). Distribution or apportionment.

alternate (ŏl′tēr·nāt). To happen in succession, first one event and then another. *Noun,* **alternation.**

amble (ăm′b'l). To move with an easy gait.

amiable (ā′mĭ·à·b'l). Good-natured.

amphibian (ăm·fĭb′ĭ·ăn). An animal or plant able to live both on land and in water.

animation (ăn′ĭ·mā′shŭn). Liveliness; vigor.

annihilate (à·nī′ĭ·lāt′). To reduce to nothing; to destroy completely.

antagonism (ăn·tăg′ō·nĭz′m). Active opposition; hostility.

aperture (ăp′ēr·tûr). An opening or hole.

archaeologist (är′kē·ŏl′ō·jĭst). A specialist in studying remains of past human life and activities.

archives (är′kīvz). **1.** A place for keeping public records. **2.** Public records.

arrears (à·rērs′). Something due but not yet paid; a debt.

artisan (är′tĭ·zăn). One trained in an art or trade involving manual skill.

ascertain (ăs′ēr·tān′). To find out or learn for a certainty, by inspection or test.

aspire (ăs·pīr′). To desire earnestly; to seek to obtain something high, noble, or great.

assertion (à·sûr′shŭn). A positive statement or declaration.

assessor (à·sĕs′ēr). One appointed to set a value on property for purposes of taxation.

audacity (ô·dăs′ĭ·tĭ). **1.** Bold courage; daring. **2.** Insolence; impudence.

auger (ô′gēr). A carpenter's tool used for boring holes.

austere (ôs·tēr′). Stern; severe.

authenticity (ô′thĕn·tĭs′ĭ·tĭ). Genuineness.

aver (à·vûr′). To declare positively.

avowal (à·vou′ăl). A frank acknowledgment; an open declaration.

azure (ăzh′ēr). Blue; strictly, the blue of a clear sky.

B

bay (bā). *Noun,* a dark reddish-brown horse. *Verb,* to bark with deep, prolonged tones, as a dog in hunting.

beggarly (bĕg′ēr·lĭ). Of little value; humble.

beneficent (bē·nĕf′ĭ·sĕnt). Kind; generous.

beneficial (bĕn′ē·fĭsh′ăl). Producing good results; helpful.

bestial (bĕst′yăl). Having animal qualities; brutish.

billet (bĭl′ĕt). Assigned living quarters.

bland (blănd). Smooth and soothing; gentle.

bode (bōd). To foretell by signs.

āpe, chăotic, bâre, ăt, ăttend, ärt, flăsk, àtop; ēke, mẹrely, ĕlect, ĕcho, prudĕnt, doēr; ītem, ĭnn, rarĭty; ōde, ŏpaque, fôr, dŏt, lôft, cŏnfide; sōōn, tŏŏk; sour, toil; tūbe, ūnique, tûrn, sŭp, ŭntil.

bolt (bōlt). **1.** To dart away; to flee. **2.** To swallow without chewing.

brazen (brā'z'n). **1.** Made of brass. **2.** Impudent; shameless.

brigand (brĭg'ănd). A lawless fellow; a bandit.

brood (brŏŏd). To think long and seriously about something.

brunt (brŭnt). The force of a blow or shock of an attack.

brusque (brŭsk). Blunt; rough and short in manner.

C

cajolery (kå·jōl'ēr·ĭ). The practice of persuading by artful flattery or deceit; coaxing.

calamity (kå·lăm'ĭ·tĭ). Deep misfortune or distress.

calcium (kăl'sĭ·ŭm). A mineral element necessary in the body for the building of bones and teeth and for proper functioning of cells.

capricious (kå·prĭsh'ŭs). Apt to change suddenly.

caricature (kăr'ĭ·kå·tûr). A picture or description in which characteristic features are exaggerated for humorous effect; a deliberately distorted picture.

cascade (kăs·kād'). **1.** A waterfall. **2.** A fall of something in a zigzag or wavy line.

casing (kās'ĭng). **1.** Something that encloses. **2.** The enclosing framework of a window.

catacomb (kăt'å·kōm). An underground burial place, usually having recesses for tombs.

censure (sĕn'shēr). **1.** Hostile criticism. **2.** The act of blaming or condemning as wrong.

cessation (sĕ·să'shŭn). A pausing or stopping in the course of action.

chagrin (shå·grĭn'). Mental distress caused by disappointment or humiliation.

chamberlain (chām'bēr·lĭn). An officer in charge of the private rooms of a ruler or other royal person.

chant (chånt). A statement or phrase uttered monotonously.

chaos (kā'ŏs). A confused state; complete disorder.

cherish (chĕr'ĭsh). To hold dear; to cling to.

chide (chīd). To scold or find fault with.

chronicle (krŏn'ĭ·k'l). An account of events told in the order in which they happened.

circumscribe (sûr'kŭm·skrīb'). **1.** To encircle or surround. **2.** To limit, especially narrowly.

coax (kōks). To urge; to succeed by soft words or flattery.

commit (kŏ·mĭt'). To pledge or bind.

communion (kŏ·mūn'yŭn). Coming into understanding; participating or sharing together.

compassionate (kŏm·păsh'ŭn·ĭt). Sympathetic; disposed to pity.

complacent (kŏm·plā'sĕnt). Satisfied, especially self-satisfied; smug.

composure (kŏm·pō'zhēr). Calmness; self-control.

compunction (kŏm·pŭngk'shŭn). Uneasiness of the conscience; remorse; regret.

computation (kŏm'pū·tā'shŭn). Counting; reckoning; determining by calculation.

conception (kŏn·sĕp'shŭn). An idea; a notion.

concoct (kŏn·kŏkt'). **1.** To compose, devise, or make up. **2.** To prepare by combining different ingredients.

confirmation (kŏn'fēr·mā'shŭn). Proof.

congenial (kŏn·jēn'yăl). Agreeable; suitable.

congestion (kŏn·jĕs'chŭn). Overcrowding.

consort (kŏn'sôrt). A mate; a wife or husband.

contempt (kŏn·tĕmpt'). Scorn, disdain. *Adj.*, **contemptuous** (kŏn·tĕmp'tû·ŭs).

contention (kŏn·tĕn'shŭn). Disagreement; strife; controversy.

convalescent (kŏn'vå·lĕs'ĕnt). A person recovering from an illness.

convulsion (kŏn·vŭl'shŭn). A violent, uncontrolled spasm or drawing together of muscles. *Adj.*, **convulsive.**

coquetry (kō'kē·trĭ). Flirtatious behavior.

coronation (kŏr'ō·nā'shŭn). The ceremonies attending the crowning of a ruler.

corroborate (kŏ·rŏb'ō·rāt). To confirm; to establish.

corrosion (kŏ·rō'zhŭn). The eating away or being eaten away by acid, rust, etc.

countenance (koun'tē·nåns). The face; or the expression on one's face.

covet (kŭv'ĕt). To desire, especially something belonging to someone else.

coyness (koi'nĕs). Pretended bashfulness or shyness.

credentials (krē·dĕn'shǎlz). Documents such as letters that verify who a person is or entitle him to certain privileges.

crypt (krĭpt). A vault partly or wholly underground.

culpable (kŭl'på·b'l). Blameworthy.

cumbersome (kŭm'bēr·sŭm). Clumsy; burdensome.

cumulative (kū'mů·lā'tĭv). Becoming larger by successive additions; increasing in force or strength.

cupidity (kū·pĭd'ĭ·tĭ). Greed; a desire for wealth.

---

bar; church; dog; ardŭous; fat; go; hear; jail; key; lame; meat; not; ring; pay; ran; see; shell; ten; there, thick; pastŭre; vast; wind; yes; zoo, zh = z in azure.

curate (kū′rāt). An assistant to a rector or vicar.

D

dank (dăngk). Wet; damp.

decanter (dḗ·kăn′tēr). A kind of glass bottle for serving wine or other liquids.

deft (dĕft). Quick and neat in action; skillful. *Noun*, **deftness.**

degradation (dĕg′rȧ·dā′hŭn). **1.** Disgrace; lowering of self-respect. **2.** Reduction in rank.

deign (dān). To condescend to give.

dejected (dḗ·jĕk′tĕd). Depressed; despairing.

delirious (dḗ·lĭr′ĭ·ŭs). Mentally upset or disordered.

delusion (dḗ·lū′zhŭn). **1.** A misleading of the mind. **2.** A persistent and unreasonable belief in something that has no existence in fact. *Similar to* **illusion** in meaning something which one accepts as true but is actually untrue. **Delusion,** however, is a much stronger word than **illusion.** It generally implies self-deception and often a disordered state of mind.

demented (dḗ·mĕn′tĕd). Mentally ill; insane.

demonic (dḗ·mŏn′ĭk). Devilish.

denounce (dḗ·nouns′). **1.** To condemn something as blameworthy or evil. **2.** To accuse. *Noun*, **denunciation** (dḗ·nŭn′sĭ·ā′shŭn).

depreciate (dḗ·prē′shĭ·āt). To belittle; to lessen in price or value.

derelict (dĕr′ĕ·lĭkt). Given up; abandoned.

deride (dḗ·rīd′). To ridicule; to mock or scorn. *Noun*, **derision** (dḗ·rĭzh′ŭn).

derisive (dḗ·rī′sĭv). Scornful; mocking.

desolate (dĕs′ō·lĭt). Deserted and lonely; forsaken.

devious (dē′vĭ·ŭs). Roundabout; out of the usual path, line, or course.

diffident (dĭf′ĭ·dĕnt). Reserved; shy.

dilemma (dĭ·lĕm′ȧ). A situation in which one must choose between two unsatisfactory alternatives; a predicament.

dirge (dûrj). A song, poem, or musical composition of grief or mourning; a lament.

discreet (dĭs·krēt′). Showing good judgment in conduct and especially in things said.

disparage (dĭs·păr′ĭj). To speak slightingly of; to belittle. *Adv.*, **disparagingly.**

dissimulate (dĭ·sĭm′ū·lāt). To feign; to pretend.

dissipate (dĭs′ĭ·pāt). **1.** To scatter; to drive away. **2.** To waste or squander.

distillation (dĭs′tĭ·lā′shŭn). The extraction of the fundamental nature of something.

distract (dĭs·trăkt′). **1.** To divert; to draw one's attention to something else. **2.** To confuse. *Adv.*, **distractedly.**

diversity (dī·vûr′sĭ·tĭ). Variety.

dividend (dĭv′ĭ·dĕnd). The share of a sum or quantity to be divided and distributed, especially profits or benefits.

docile (dŏs′ĭl). Easily taught, led, or managed. *Adv.*, **docilely.**

dogged (dŏg′ĕd). Stubbornly determined. *Adv.*, **doggedly.**

dogma (dŏg′mȧ). A doctrine; an opinion held to be true by a school of philosophy, a church, or some similar organization.

dolorous (dŏl′ēr·ŭs). **1.** Painful; grievous. **2.** Sorrowful.

dominate (dŏm′ĭ·nāt). To rule; to control.

draught (drȧft). A drink.

droll (drōl). Amusing in a quaint way; humorously odd.

E

eccentric (ĕk·sĕn′trĭk). Odd; deviating from accepted standards.

efficacy (ĕf′ĭ·kȧ·sĭ). The power to produce desired results.

ejaculate (ḗ·jăk′ū·lāt). To utter suddenly, as an exclamation.

elation (ḗ·lā′shŭn). A feeling of well-being; joy.

embellish (ĕm·bĕl′ĭsh). **1.** To decorate; to adorn. **2.** To enrich.

eminence (ĕm′ĭ·nĕns). **1.** High rank. **2.** A high ground or place. *Adj.*, **eminent,** distinguished as being above others.

engross (ĕn·grōs′). To occupy; to absorb fully.

entreat (ĕn·trēt′). To ask earnestly; to beg.

esquire (ĕs·kwīr′). In the age of chivalry, a candidate for knighthood who served as a knight's attendant.

essay (ĕ·sā′). To attempt; to try.

evangelist (ḗ·văn′jĕ·lĭst). A person interested in spreading religion.

evolutionary (ĕv′ō·lū′s hŭn·ĕr′ĭ). **1.** Pertaining to an unfolding or development. **2.** In biology, pertaining to the process of development of a living thing.

exemplary (ĕg·zĕm′plȧ·rĭ). Serving as an example or model; deserving imitation.

exhalation (ĕks′hȧ·lā′shŭn). Breathing out.

exodus (ĕk′sō·dŭs). A departure from some specific area.

expiration (ĕk′spĭ·rā′shŭn). **1.** The emitting of air from the lungs. **2.** The coming to a close; the end.

exploitation (ĕks′ploi·tā′shŭn). Using unfairly for one's own advantage or profit.

āpe, chȧotic, bâre, ăt, ȧttend, ärt, flásk, ȧtop; ēke, mẹrely, ḗlect, ĕcho, prudĕnt, doēr; ītem, ĭnn, rarĭty; ōde, ŏpaque, fôr, dŏt, lôft, cŏnfide; sōon, took; sour, toil; tūbe, ūnique, tûrn, sŭp, ŭntil.

expository (ĕks·pŏz′ĭ·tō′rĭ). Explanatory; serving to explain or set forth a meaning or purpose.

exquisite (ĕks′kwĭ·zĭt). **1.** Pleasing by its beauty or excellence. **2.** Keen; intense.

F

falter (fôl′tẽr). To hesitate in speech; to stammer. *Adv.*, **falteringly.**

fanatical (fȧ·năt′ĭ·kȧl). Overly enthusiastic, especially on religious subjects.

fanfare (făn′fâr). A blowing of trumpets; hence, a showy display.

feasible (fē′zĭ·b′l). Possible; reasonable.

festoon (fĕs·tōōn′). To decorate, especially with a garland of leaves or flowers falling in curves.

filet (fē·lĕ′). A piece of lean meat or fish without a bone.

filial (fĭl′ĭ·ȧl). Relating to or befitting a son or daughter.

flagstone (flăg′stōn′). A flat stone used in paving walks.

fluent (flōō′ĕnt). Ready in the use of words; smooth and flowing.

foliage (fō′lĭ·ĭj). The leaves of a plant.

formidable (fôr′mĭ·dȧ·b′l). **1.** Threatening; exciting fear or dread. **2.** Difficult to deal with.

fortitude (fôr′tĭ·tūd). Courage in facing trouble.

frailty (frāl′tĭ). Weakness.

fray (frā). To wear into shreds by rubbing; to ravel.

frictional (frĭk′shŭn·ȧl). Produced by the rubbing of one object against another.

frivolous (frĭv′ō·lŭs). **1.** Of little value or importance; trivial. **2.** Not properly serious or sensible.

frowzy (frouz′ĭ). Disordered and unclean.

furtive (fûr′tĭv). Sly; secretive.

futile (fū′tĭl). Useless; having no result.

G

genetics (jē·nĕt′ĭks). The science dealing with the handing down of traits from parents to offspring.

geniality (jē′nĭ·ăl′ĭ·tĭ). Pleasant cheerfulness.

gesticulation (jĕs·tĭk′ū·lā′shŭn). The making of gestures, especially when speaking; a gesture.

glib (glĭb). Spoken with careless ease.

glutton (glŭt′′n). A person who overeats; hence, one who overdoes something.

gorge (gôrj). A narrow passage between two mountains, often containing a river.

gratis (grā′tĭs). Free of charge.

grimace (grĭ·mās′). A distortion of the face to show contempt or disapproval.

grotesque (grō·tĕsk′). Distorted in appearance, shape, or manner; bizarre.

grub (grŭb). A soft, thick wormlike form in which most insects, especially beetles, hatch from the egg.

gullible (gŭl′ĭ·b′l). Easily fooled or deceived. *Noun*, **gullibility** (gŭl′ĭ·bĭl′ĭ·tĭ).

gunwale (gŭn′ĕl). The upper edge of the side of a vessel or boat.

H

habitual (hȧ·bĭt′û·ȧl). Customary; according to habit. *Adv.*, **habitually.**

harass (hăr′ȧs). To torment; to annoy.

hideous (hĭd′ē·ŭs). Horribly shocking and disgusting.

homogeneous (hō′mō·jē′nē·ŭs). Of the same kind or nature; made up of similar elements. Opposed to **heterogeneous** (hĕt′ẽr·ō·jē′nē·ŭs), having unlike qualities.

hypothesis (hī·pŏth′ē·sĭs). **1.** A theory or supposition that explains certain facts and helps in the discovery of others. **2.** An assumption for the purpose of argument or action.

I

illiterate (ĭl·lĭt′ẽr·ĭt). Unable to read and write.

illumine (ĭ·lū′mĭn). To light up; enlighten. *Noun*, **illumination.**

illusion (ĭ·lū′zhŭn). **1.** An unreal or misleading image; a deceptive appearance. **2.** A false impression; a misconception. *See also* **delusion.**

immensity (ĭ·mĕn′sĭ·tĭ). Hugeness; infinite space.

immerse (ĭ·mûrs′). **1.** To plunge into liquid. **2.** To absorb one's attention.

imminent (ĭm′ĭ·nĕnt). Dangerous and close at hand; likely to happen immediately.

impartiality (ĭm′pär·shĭ·ăl′ĭ·tĭ). Freedom from bias or favoritism; fairness. *Adj.*, **impartial.**

impel (ĭm·pĕl′). To drive or urge on; to arouse to action.

impenetrable (ĭm·pĕn′ē·trȧ·b′l). **1.** Incapable of being entered. **2.** Incapable of being understood. **3.** Unimpressible, not moved by arguments or motives.

imperative (ĭm·pĕr′ȧ·tĭv). **1.** Commanding; authoritative. **2.** Not to be avoided; compulsory. *Noun*, **imperativeness.**

---

bar; **ch**ur**ch**; dog; ard̯u̯ous; fat; **g**o; **h**ear; jail; key; lame; meat; not; ring; pay; ran; see; **sh**ell; ten; **th**ere, **th**ick; pas**t**u̯re; vast; wind; yes; zoo, **zh** = z in azure.

imperceptible (ĭm·pēr·sĕp′tĭ·b'l). Not noticeable to the senses or mind; very slight.

impetuous (ĭm·pĕt′ū·ŭs). Hastily or rashly energetic; impulsive in action or feeling.

implacable (ĭm·plā′kà·b'l). Not of a nature to be pacified or appeased.

implication (ĭm′plĭ·kā′shŭn). Something suggested or implied but not stated directly.

imposing (ĭm·pōz′ĭng). Impressive because of size, appearance, dignity.

imposture (ĭm·pŏs′tûr). Fraud; deception.

impregnable (ĭm·prĕg′nà·b'l). Able to resist attack; unconquerable.

improvise (ĭm′prō·vīz). To make or do without previous preparation.

impunity (ĭm·pū′nĭ·tĭ). Exemption or freedom from penalty of any kind.

inadvertent (ĭn′ăd·vû′tĕnt). 1. Unintentional; accidental. 2. Heedless; inattentive.

inarticulate (ĭn·är·tĭk′ū·lât). 1. Not intelligible; incomprehensible. 2. Unable to express oneself.

inaudible (ĭn·ô′dĭ·b'l). Not able to be heard.

incompatible (ĭn·kŏm·păt′ĭ·b'l). Unable to exist together; opposing or contradictory.

inconsequent (ĭn·kŏn′sē·kwĕnt). Not logically related to or connected with a subject.

inconsequential (ĭn·kŏn′sē·kwĕn′shăl). Unimportant.

incongruity (ĭn′kŏng·grōō′ĭ·tĭ). Lack of harmony with surrounding or associated objects; unsuitableness; inconsistency.

inconspicuous (ĭn′kŏn·spĭk′ū·ŭs). Not easily noticeable.

incredible (ĭn·krĕd′ĭ·b'l). Beyond belief.

incredulous (ĭn·krĕd′ū·lŭs). Unbelieving; skeptical.

indifferent (ĭn·dĭf′ēr·ĕnt). Unconcerned.

indignation (ĭn′dĭg·nā′shŭn). Righteous anger at something disgraceful or unworthy.

indispensable (ĭn′dĭs·pĕn′sà·b'l). Absolutely necessary.

indistinguishable (ĭn′dĭs·tĭng′gwĭsh·à·b'l). Not capable of being clearly recognized as different from something else.

indoctrinate (ĭn·dŏk′trĭ·nāt). To instruct in doctrines, principles, or beliefs.

indomitable (ĭn·dŏm′ĭ·tà·b'l). Not to be subdued; unconquerable.

induce (ĭn·dūs′). 1. To bring on or cause. 2. To lead on or move by persuasion.

indulge (ĭn·dŭlj′). To yield to; to gratify.

inert (ĭn·ûrt′). Lacking power to move itself; inactive or lifeless.

inexorable (ĭn·ĕk′sō·rà·b'l). Not to be influenced; relentless.

inexplicable (ĭn·ĕks′plĭ·kà·b'l). Not capable of being explained.

infernal (ĭn·fûr′năl). Detestable.

infinite (ĭn′fĭ·nĭt). Endless; boundless; limitless.

inflict (ĭn·flĭkt′). To cause to suffer; to give as by striking.

inglorious (ĭn·glō′rĭ·ŭs). Shameful.

inherent (ĭn·hēr′ĕnt). Belonging by nature or settled habit.

inimitable (ĭn·ĭm′ĭ·tà·b'l). Beyond imitation; matchless.

initiative (ĭ·nĭsh′ĭ·ā′tĭv). 1. The ability to take the first step; self-reliant enterprise. 2. Responsibility for beginning or originating something.

inquisitive (ĭn·kwĭz′ĭ·tĭv). 1. Given to seeking truth or knowledge. 2. Improperly curious and questioning.

inroad (ĭn′rōd′). An invasion; an intrusion.

insolence (ĭn′sō·lĕns). Rudeness; disrespect.

instantaneous (ĭn′stăn·tā′nē·ŭs). 1. Occurring in an instant; sudden. 2. Done without any delay.

intercede (ĭn′tēr·sēd′). To act between parties with a view to reconciling differences; to intervene.

interlude (ĭn′tēr·lūd). An intervening feature, event, or period of time.

interminable (ĭn·tûr′mĭ·nà·b'l). Endless.

intermittent (ĭn′tēr·mĭt′ĕnt). Coming and going at intervals; periodic.

intimacy (ĭn′tĭ·mà·sĭ). Close friendship; familiarity.

intricate (ĭn′trĭ·kĭt). Entangled; involved; difficult to understand or follow. *Noun,* **intricacy** (ĭn′trĭ·kà·sĭ).

intrinsic (ĭn·trĭn′sĭk). Belonging to the essence of a thing; inherent.

involuntary (ĭn·vŏl′ŭn·tēr′ĭ). Not under the control of the will. *Adv.,* **involuntarily.**

irradiate (ĭ·rā′dĭ·āt). To shine or shine upon.

irrelevant (ĭr·rĕl′ē·vănt). Unrelated to the matter at hand; extraneous.

irreparable (ĭ·rĕp′à·rà·b'l). Not capable of being repaired.

irresistible (ĭr′rē·zĭs′tĭ·b'l). Not to be successfully resisted or opposed.

J

jaunty (jôn′tĭ). Cheerful; sprightly.

jocular (jŏk′ū·lēr). 1. In the nature of a joke. 2. Mirthful; merry. *Adv.,* **jocularly.**

K

keen (kēn). 1. Eager or enthusiastic. 2. Sharp, with a fine point or edge. 3. Mentally acute.

āpe, chăotic, bâre, ăt, ăttend, ärt, flåsk, àtop; ēke, mẽrely, ĕlect, ĕcho, prudĕnt, doẽr; ītem, ĭnn, rarĭty; ōde, ȯpaque, fôr, dŏt, lŏft, cǒnfide; sōōn, tŏŏk; sour, toil; tūbe, ûnique, tûrn, sŭp, ŭntil.

L

laconic (lȧ·kŏn′ĭk). Sparing of words; concise.

lagoon (lȧ·gōōn′). A shallow pond or lake, especially one near or flowing into the sea.

lamentation (lăm′ĕn·tā′shŭn). An expression of grief; wailing.

languish (lăng′gwĭsh). To fade away; to lose force.

larcenous (lär′sĕ·nŭs). Thievish.

leer (lēr). To give a sly or sinister look.

limpid (lĭm′pĭd). Perfectly clear; transparent.

linguist (lĭng′gwĭst). A person skilled in languages.

lucrative (lū′krȧ·tĭv). Profitable.

luminous (lū′mĭ·nŭs). Shining; giving forth light.

lunar (lū′nēr). Of, or having to do with, the moon.

lustrous (lŭs′trŭs). Shining; radiant.

luxuriance (lŭks·ū′rĭ·ăns). The quality or condition of being abundant in growth, as vegetation.

M

mailed (māld). Protected by a suit of armor made of a fabric of interlinked metal rings.

massive (măs′ĭv). Bulky; large; solid.

meditative (mĕd′ĭ·tā′tĭv). Given to close or continued thought.

militant (mĭl′ĭ·tănt). Inclined to fight; aggressive.

miscellany (mĭs′ĕ·lā′nĭ). A collection of many things of different sorts.

modulate (mŏd′ū·lāt). **1.** To vary the tone in speaking or singing. **2.** To form or adjust to a certain proportion; to soften.

monomaniac (mŏn′ō·mā′nĭ·ăk). A person who is so absorbed in a single subject or idea as to seem mentally deranged.

monstrous (mŏn′strŭs). **1.** Enormous. **2.** Deviating greatly from the natural.

morose (mō·rōs′). Gloomy; sullen.

myriad (mĭr′ĭ·ăd). An indefinitely large number.

N

naïve (nä·ēv′). Having unaffected simplicity; artless; unsophisticated. *Noun,* **naïveté** (nä·ēv′tā′), the quality of being *naïve.*

neuralgic (nū·răl′jĭk). Pertaining to **neuralgia** (nū·răl′jȧ), a sharp pain that follows the course of a nerve to its branches.

nominal (nŏm′ĭ·năl). Existing in name only; not real or actual. *Adv.,* **nominally.**

nostalgia (nŏs·tăl′jĭ·ȧ). Homesickness; longing for something far away or long ago.

O

obliterate (ŏb·lĭt′ēr·āt). To blot out leaving no traces; to erase.

oblivious (ŏb·lĭv′ĭ·ŭs). Unmindful.

obsession (ŏb·sĕsh′ŭn). A constant, persistent, inescapable feeling.

odious (ō′dĭ·ŭs). Deserving of or provoking hatred; hateful.

ominous (ōm′ĭ·nŭs). Threatening; pertaining to an evil omen.

orbit (ôr′bĭt). The path described by one celestial body in its revolution about another.

ornate (ôr·nāt′). Elaborately adorned or decorated.

ostentation (ŏs′tĕn·tā′shŭn). Showiness; boastful display.

oxidation (ŏk′sĭ·dā′shŭn). Combining with oxygen.

P

palette (păl′ĕt). A thin oval board on which a painter mixes his colors.

pallid (păl′ĭd). Pale.

parody (păr′ō·dĭ). A literary or musical composition in which the style of an author or composer is imitated, usually for comic effect. *Verb,* **parody,** to write a parody; to imitate or mimic.

patent (pā′tĕnt). Plain; evident; obvious.

patronizing (pā′trŭn·īz′ĭng). Condescending.

pendant (pĕn′dănt). Something that hangs down, especially a hanging ornament.

pendulous (pĕn′dū·lŭs). Hanging so as to swing loosely and freely.

penetrating (pĕn′ē·trāt′ĭng). **1.** Sharp; piercing. **2.** Discriminating.

pensive (pĕn′sĭv). Musingly thoughtful.

perceive (pēr·sēv′). To understand or see clearly; to recognize.

perfunctory (pēr·fŭngk′tō·rĭ). **1.** Indifferent; without interest or zeal. **2.** Done automatically without thought.

perilous (pĕr′ĭ·lŭs). Full of danger; hazardous.

perpetrate (pûr′pē·trāt). **1.** To commit, as an offense. **2.** To do or perform.

perplex (pēr·plĕks′). To puzzle; to confuse.

pertinacity (pûr′tĭ·năs′ĭ·tĭ). Persistence; unyielding perseverance.

perturb (pēr·tûrb′). To disturb or trouble greatly.

---

bar; church; dog; ardŭous; fat; go; hear; jail; key; lame; meat; not; ring; pay; ran; see; shell; ten; there, thick; pastŭre; vast; wind; yes; zoo, zh = z in azure.

perverse (pẽr·vûrs′). **1.** Obstinate. **2.** Wrong; wayward. *Noun*, **perverseness** or **perversity.**

phial (fī′ăl). A vial; a small glass bottle.

phosphorescent (fŏs′fō·rĕs′ĕnt). Gleaming in the dark; emitting light without heat.

placid (plăs′ĭd). Calm; peaceful.

plague (plāg). **1.** Anything that afflicts or troubles. **2.** A contagious disease threatening to kill.

plaintive (plān′tĭv). Expressing sorrow; mournful.

poignant (poin′yănᵗ). **1.** Piercing; keen. **2.** Affecting the emotions; touching; painfully moving. *Noun* **poignancy.**

ponderous (pŏn′dẽr·ŭs). Heavy; dull.

portentous (pōr·tĕn′tŭs). Forewarning of evil; ominous; significant.

porterage (pōr′tẽr·ĭj). The work of carrying burdens for hire.

potentiality (pō·tĕn′shĭ·ăl′ĭ·tĭ). A possibility; capability of becoming real or actual.

precarious (prē·kâr′ĭ·ŭs). Dependent upon circumstances; insecure; uncertain.

precedence (prē·sēd′ĕns). Being before others in importance.

precept (prē′sĕpt). A order, commandment, or rule meant to guide one's conduct.

precipice (prĕs′ĭ·pĭs). A very steep or overhanging place, as the face of a cliff.

precipitate (prē·sĭp′ĭ·tāt). To cause to happen suddenly; to set off.

precise (prē·sīs′). Carefully exact.

preclude (prē·klōōd′). To prevent; to make impossible.

predatory (prĕd′à·tō′rĭ). **1.** Related to or characterized by plundering. **2.** Living by preying on other animals.

predecessor (prĕd′ē·sĕs′ẽr). **1.** A person or thing that goes before. **2.** An ancestor.

predominate (prē·dŏm′ĭ·nāt). **1.** To be superior in strength, number, or authority. **2.** To rule.

premeditate (prē·mĕd′ĭ·tāt). To think out or plan beforehand.

premonition (prē′mō·nĭsh′ŭn). A forewarning.

presentiment (prē·zĕn′tĭ·mĕnt). A feeling that evil is about to occur; a premonition.

procrastinate (prō·krăs′tĭ·nāt). To delay; to postpone.

procreation (prō′krē·ā′shŭn). Reproduction; bringing offspring into the world.

procurable (prō·kūr′à·b′l). Obtainable.

prodigious (prō·dĭj′ŭs). Extraordinary in quantity or degree; huge; vast.

profanity (prō·făn′ĭ·tĭ). Abusive language or acts; irreverence

promenade (prŏm′ē·nād′). *Noun*, a place for walking. *Verb*, to take a walk:

promiscuous (prō·mĭs′kū·ŭs). **1.** Distributed, applied, or granted at random. **2.** Haphazard; irregular. *Adv.*, **promiscuously.**

promontory (prŏm′ŭn·tō′rĭ). A high point of land or rock projecting into the sea; a headland.

propaganda (prŏp′à·găn′dà). A doctrine or ideas spread by an organized group to win others to its point of view.

prophetic (prō·fĕt′ĭk). Foretelling future events.

prospective (prō·spĕk′tĭv). Expected; likely to become.

provident (prŏv′ĭ·dĕnt). Saving; providing for the future.

proximity (prŏks·ĭm′ĭ·tĭ). Nearness.

prudence (prōō′dĕns). **1.** Ability to discipline oneself by means of reason. **2.** Skill in managing practical affairs. *Adj.*, **prudent**

psychic (sī′kĭk). **1.** Of or relating to the mind. **2.** Sensitive to nonphysical forces.

purgatory (pûr′gà·tō′rĭ). A state of temporary punishment.

purport (pûr·pōrt′). To have the appearance of being; to imply or profess outwardly.

Q

quail (kwāl). A small game bird that nests on the ground; a bobwhite.

quarry (kwŏr′ĭ). An open excavation, usually for obtaining building stone, slate, or limestone.

quell (kwĕl). **1.** To overpower, subdue, or suppress. **2.** To quiet; to pacify.

quizzical (kwĭz′ĭ·kăl). **1.** Odd; amusing. **2.** Bantering; teasing.

quorum (kwô′rŭm). The number of members (usually more than half) of a group that must be present at a meeting in order to transact business legally.

R

rabid (răb′ĭd). Afflicted with **rabies** (rā′bēz), a severe, often fatal, disease of the central nervous system, occurring chiefly among dogs but capable of being passed on to man. **2.** Eager; fanatical.

radiance (rā′dĭ·ăns). Vivid brightness; brilliancy.

rampageous (răm·pā′jŭs). Rushing about wildly or excitedly.

rapt (răpt). **1.** Carried away in thoughts or spirit to another place. **2.** Wholly absorbed.

ravage (răv′ĭj). *Noun*, ruin; devastation. *Verb*, to lay waste; to plunder.

āpe, chăotic, bâre, ăt, ăttend, ärt, flăsk, átop; ēke, mẽrely, ĕlect, ĕcho, prudĕnt, doẽr; ītem, ĭnn, rarĭty; ōde, ōpaque, fôr, dŏt, lŏft, cŏnfide; sōōn, tŏŏk; sour, toil; tūbe, ūnique, tûrn, sŭp, ŭntil.

ravenous (răv′ĕn·ŭs). Greedy; eager for food or satisfaction.

ravishing (răv′ĭsh·ĭng). Inspiring great feeling, especially joy or delight.

recluse (rė·kloos′). A person who lives in seclusion; a hermit.

reconcile (rĕk′ŏn·sīl). 1. To bring to acceptance. 2. To adjust; to settle.

reconnoiter (rĕk′ŏ·noi′tēr). To inspect; to survey, especially for military or engineering purposes.

regimental (rĕj′ĭ·mĕn′tăl). Pertaining to a **regiment,** a body of soldiers commanded by a colonel and consisting of several companies or troops.

relic (rĕl′ĭk). An object surviving from the past.

reluctant (rė·lŭk′tănt). Unwilling; disinclined.

reminiscent (rĕm′ĭ·nĭs′ĕnt). Bringing to mind something else; suggestive of.

remnant (rĕm′nănt). Something left over.

rendezvous (rän′dė·voo). 1. A place appointed for a meeting. 2. A meeting by appointment.

repentance (rė·pĕn′tăns). Regret for sins or wrongdoing, with a desire to correct one's ways.

resentment (rė·zĕnt′mĕnt). A feeling of angry displeasure because of a wrong, insult, or slight.

resignation (rĕz′ĭg·nā′shŭn). 1. Surrender to circumstances. 2. The act of giving up, as one's job.

resolute (rĕz′ō·lūt). Determined; purposeful; hence, bold or steady.

restive (rĕs′tĭv). Restless.

retaliate (rė·tăl′ĭ·āt). To return like for like, especially to return evil for evil.

retreat (rė·trēt′). A place where one may go for safety and quiet; a refuge.

retribution (rĕt′rĭ·bū′shŭn). That which is given or exacted in return; specifically, punishment.

retrieve (rė·trēv′). To bring back.

retrospect (rĕt′rō·spĕkt). A looking back; reflection upon things past.

revel (rĕv′ĕl). 1. To take great delight in. 2. To be festive in a noisy manner.

revelation (rĕv′ė·lā′shŭn). 1. The revealing to others of something previously unknown to them. 2. That which is revealed; a disclosure.

reverberation (rė·vûr′bēr·ā′shŭn). An echo; a reflection.

rudiment (roo′dĭ·mĕnt). 1. A first step or beginning. 2. A first principle of any art or science.

rueful (roo′fool). Mournful; regretful.

ruminate (roo′mĭ·nāt). To consider again and again; to ponder. *Noun,* **rumination.**

ruse (rooz). A trick.

rustic (rŭs′tĭk). 1. Rural; of or pertaining to the country. 2. Plain; simple.

S

satiric (să·tĭr′ĭk). Pertaining to the use of wit or sarcasm to ridicule or poke fun at.

savor (sā′vēr). To taste or smell with pleasure; to delight in.

scintillate (sĭn′tĭ·lāt). To sparkle.

sconce (skŏns). A candle holder fastened to a wall.

scrupulous (skroo′pū·lŭs). Careful or strict in doing what is right or proper.

scrutiny (skroo′tĭ·nĭ). Critical observation.

scud (skŭd). To move swiftly.

semblance (sĕm′blăns). Outward appearance.

serrated (sĕr′āt·ĕd). Notched or toothed on the edge, like a saw.

shoal (shōl). 1. A large number; a crowd, especially of fish. 2. A shallow place in a sea or river.

simulate (sĭm′û·lāt). To assume the appearance of, without the reality; to feign.

sire (sīr). A father.

solemnize (sŏl′ĕm·nīz). To perform with solemn ceremony.

solicitor (sō·lĭs′ĭ·tēr). 1. One who requests funds or contributions. 2. In England, a person authorized to practice law.

somber (sŏm′bēr). 1. So shaded as to be dark and gloomy. 2. Melancholy; depressing.

sordid (sôr′dĭd). 1. Mean; greedy. 2. Vile; despicable.

spasmodic (spăz·mŏd′ĭk). With sudden, brief spurts of energy.

spatial (spā′shăl). Of or pertaining to space.

spiritualism (spĭr′ĭt·û·ăl·ĭz′m). The belief that dead people's spirits communicate with the living by means of sounds, such as rappings on tables, and through a person called a "medium."

stability (stå·bĭl′ĭ·tĭ). Firmness; steadiness.

stanch (stänch). *Verb,* to check the flow of, as blood. *Adj.,* loyal; true.

steerage (stēr′ĭj). In a passenger ship, a section occupied by passengers paying the lowest fare and receiving inferior accommodations.

sterling (stûr′lĭng). Genuine; of full value.

stolid (stŏl′ĭd). Not easily excited; unfeeling; inexpressive.

---

bar; church; dog; ardǔous; fat; go; hear; jail; key; lame; meat; not; ring; pay; ran; see; shell; ten; there, thick; pastǔre; vast; wind; yes; zoo, zh = z in azure.

strait (strāt). **1.** A situation of perplexity or distress (often used in plural). **2.** A comparatively narrow channel connecting two large bodies of water.

strident (strī'dĕnt). Harsh-sounding; shrill.

sublimity (sŭb·lĭm'ĭ·tĭ). Exalted character or quality.

subterfuge (sŭb'tẽr·fūj). A plan or device for evading an issue or concealing something.

succession (sŭk·sĕsh'ŭn). A series of things that follow in sequence.

succumb (sŭ·kŭm'). To yield.

suffice (sŭ·fīs'). To meet or satisfy a need.

suffuse (sŭ·fūz'). To overspread, as with a fluid or color.

sumptuous (sŭmp'tụ·ŭs). Luxurious; lavish.

sunder (sŭn'dẽr). To force apart or separate by rending, cutting, breaking; to sever.

supercilious (sū'pẽr·sĭl'ĭ·ŭs). Haughty; proud.

superfluous (sŭ·pûr'flo͞o·ŭs). In excess of what is enough; surplus.

symmetrical (sĭ·mĕt'rĭ·kăl). Balanced; regular.

T

tacit (tăs'ĭt). Unspoken; silent.

tangent (tăn'jĕnt). An abrupt change of course.

tangible (tăn'jĭ·b'l). **1.** Capable of being touched; concrete. **2.** Capable of being realized by the mind; perceptible.

tidings (tī'dĭngz). Information; news.

tolerance (tŏl'ẽr·ăns). The quality of allowing, by not preventing, the existence of beliefs, practices, or habits different from one's own. **2.** Endurance.

torpid (tôr'pĭd). **1.** Having lost the power of motion and feeling; numb. **2.** Lacking energy; dull.

tranquillity (trăn·kwĭl'ĭ·tĭ). Calmness; quietness.

transient (trăn'shĕnt). **1.** Of short duration; fleeting. **2.** Not settled or permanent.

transpire (trăn·spīr'). To come to pass; to happen.

tremulous (trĕm'ụ·lŭs). **1.** Trembling; shaking. **2.** Timid.

trice (trīs). A single pull or effort; hence, an instant; a moment.

truant (tro͞o'ănt). One who shirks his duty, as a child who stays out of school without permission.

twinkling (twĭng'klĭng). A moment; an instant.

U

ultimate (ŭl'tĭ·mĭt). **1.** Last; final. **2.** Fundamental; absolute.

unassuming (ŭn·ȧ·sūm'ĭng). Modest; reserved.

undulate (ŭn'dụ·lāt). To rise and fall in pitch or volume.

unimpeded (ŭn'ĭm·pēd'ĕd). Unobstructed; unhindered.

unperturbed (ŭn'pẽr·tûrbd'). Undisturbed; unworried.

unquarried (ŭn·kwŏr'ĭd). Not dug from rocks or earth.

unremitting (ŭn'rē·mĭt'ĭng). Incessant; continual.

V

vacillate (văs'ĭ·lāt). **1.** To fluctuate. **2.** To incline first to one opinion and then to another in making up one's mind.

validate (văl'ĭ·dāt). **1.** To confirm. **2.** To make valid; to give legal force to.

veer (vēr). To change position or direction; to swerve.

veracious (vē·rā'shŭs). Truthful; honest.

verify (vĕr'ĭ·fī). To prove the truth or authenticity of.

veritable (vĕr'ĭ·tȧ·b'l). Genuine; true.

vermilion (vẽr·mĭl'yŭn). Bright yellowish-red.

vibrant (vī'brănt). **1.** Vibrating; pulsing with life and energy. **2.** Sounding as a result of vibration; hence, *resonant.*

vicarious (vī·kâr'ĭ·ŭs). **1.** By substitution. **2.** Performed or suffered on behalf of another person.

victuals (vĭt''ls). Food (now used chiefly in dialect).

vindictive (vĭn·dĭk'tĭv). Revengeful.

visage (vĭz'ĭj). The face of a person or animal; appearance.

vivacious (vī·vā'shŭs). Lively; active.

voluble (vŏl'ụ·b'l). Talkative; glib.

W

wince (wĭns). To shrink, as from a blow.

wizened (wĭz''nd). Withered; shriveled.

Z

zeal (zēl). Great earnestness; fervor.

zephyr (zĕf'ẽr). **1.** Any soft, gentle breeze. **2.** The west wind.

āpe, chȧotic, bâre, ăt, ȧttend, ärt, flásk, ȧtop; ēke, mẹrely, ĕlect, ĕcho, prudĕnt, doẽr; ītem, ĭnn, rarĭty; ōde, ȯpaque, fôr, dŏt, lŏft, cȯnfide; so͞on, to͝ok; sour, toil; tūbe, ūnique, tûrn, sŭp, ŭntil. bar; church; dog; ardụous; fat; go; hear; jail; key; lame; meat; not; ring; pay; ran; see; shell; ten; there, thick; pastụre; vast; wind; yes; zoo, zh = z in azure.

Index of Authors and Titles

The letter *b* preceding a page number after an author's name
indicates the page on which his biography can be found.